Senate Court
Southernhay Gardens
Exeter
Devon
EX1 1NT

www.footanstey.com

Clinical Negligence

Clinical Negligence

Fifth edition

Editors

Dr Michael J Powers QC BSc MB BS DA FFFLM LLD (Hons)
Master of the Bench of Lincoln's Inn

Dr Anthony Barton
Solicitor and Medical Practitioner

Assistant editor
Sir Barry Jackson

Bloomsbury Professional

Bloomsbury Professional Ltd, Maxwelton House, 41–43 Boltro Road, Haywards Heath, West Sussex, RH16 1BJ

© Powers and Barton

Bloomsbury Professional, an imprint of Bloomsbury Publishing plc

A CIP Catalogue record for this book is available from the British Library.

ISBN: 978 1 78043 485 8

Typeset by Phoenix Photosetting, Chatham, Kent
Printed in the United Kingdom by CPI Group (UK) Ltd, Croydon, CR0 4YY

Foreword

Since the last edition of this text, the main changes in clinical negligence have concerned the economics of litigation rather than the substantive law. I am informed by the editors that the major developments and challenges have taken place in the Houses of Parliament rather than in the courts. The principles of law remains mostly familiar but its practice provides opportunities and challenges.

In my Foreword to the previous edition I expressed my concerns about the NHS Redress Act 2006 which I opposed in Parliament when Shadow Health Minister. Thankfully, very little has become of this enabling legislation – Anthony Barton's chapter describes it as 'fundamentally misconceived'. So it may be a good thing that so far it has proved to be merely useless, rather than worse than useless.

There has been wide-ranging legislation revising the ancient coronial system: the Coroners and Justice Act 2009.

Politics, society and natural justice demand that we develop a justice system that is accessible to all, fair and economically viable. The Legal Aid, Sentencing and Punishment of Offenders Act 2012 has effectively privatised access to justice for clinical negligence – legal aid is preserved for brain-damaged baby cases. Access to justice is available to anyone according to the merits of the case. The indications are that the funding regime is working, as judged by the number of cases funded by conditional fees. Nothing is ever static. A concern now is that the fees claimed by claimant lawyers may be disproportionate in respect of lower value claims. The Department of Health proposes a consultation in respect of cost capping and fixed fees.

The common law is flexible, pragmatic, and robust. This is particularly so in how it addresses novel clinical situations and medical innovation. It nearly always finds the right answer. The best thing legislators can do is, by and large, to leave well enough alone. This is why it is important Parliament properly scrutinises two forthcoming Bills which address medical innovation and so raise issues of patient safety: the Medical Innovation Bill in the House of Lords, and the Access to Medical Treatment (Innovation) Bill in the House of Commons, which is unpublished at present. I am aware of no evidence that doctors are deterred from innovation by threat of litigation. Doctors are sued for poor practice, not innovative practice.

My concern in Parliament has always been to promote the interests of the individual, whether patient or medical litigant, whilst safeguarding the interests of the wider community. It is a delicate balancing exercise which requires informed debate. This competition between individual rights and community interests is especially prominent in clinical negligence. I share the editors' hope that this text can in any small way inform such debate.

John Baron MP
House of Commons
August 2015

Preface

Litigation for damages for clinical professional negligence has the objective of providing financial compensation for patients who suffer injuries as a result of incompetent treatment. The objective is an award of damages which places claimants as nearly as possible in the position, in so far as money can achieve, as they would have been in had they not been injured, although no money can compensate for bodily injury and the experience of pain. Those damages come from the public funds allocated to provide care through the NHS. For the fair and proper resolution of disputes over breaches of the standard of care and causation of injury, specialist lawyers, medical experts and an effective judicial system are required. It is a regular cause of concern that so much money is spent on legal costs when they are borne by the public purse. Prompt recognition of culpable error, a genuine apology, and an early offer of appropriate compensation would minimise these costs. Such remedies lie in the hands of the NHS and action in these areas will result in improved standards of care for all.

The new 'Duty of Candour' ('Robbie's Law') will help to achieve the accountability which patients seek when things go wrong and reduce the number of those motivated to find it through litigation. Sir Robert Francis QC and James Berry have written an important new chapter on NHS complaints procedures reflecting the changes since Mid Staffordshire Inquiry.

Twenty-five years have passed since the first edition (then *Medical Negligence*) was published and seven years since the fourth edition. We have sought to reflect the changes in clinical negligence practice since 2008. The substantive law of clinical negligence remains comfortingly familiar. The major changes concern legal practice and the economics of litigation. As John Baron MP wrote in the Foreword to the previous edition 'get the finances right, and the rest follows'. It seems that privatisation of funding litigation has successfully replaced legal aid, as judged by the increased number of cases, and it has not been a disincentive to lawyers.

We take no position on the government's present proposals to cap costs, save to emphasise that there must equality of parties. The true costs of defending cases may be a reasonable measure of claimants' lawyers' costs. The purpose of defending cases is presumably only to stop *unmeritorious* claims. The NHS

Litigation Authority should not be taking money from the public purse for defending meritorious claims when claimants' lawyers can no longer recover costs from the public purse for advancing those cases which are unmeritorious.

There is enormous concern about the proposal to bring back, for another time, legislation which is intended to allow doctors wishing to use innovative treatments to avoid being sued in negligence. Worse still, there are private members' bills in both Houses of Parliament with this aim. This is a matter of such importance that it justifies mention of it in this Preface. Concern is not limited to those lawyers who practise in this field as it extends to oncologists, medical research scientists and the whole medical profession as represented by the medical royal colleges.

Many patients with terminal illnesses are desperate to try anything which might offer hope of treatment or prolongation of life but a statutory defence which undermines the long established *Bolam* principle will not help them. On the contrary, it would inevitably encourage irresponsible use of therapies of no proven value. The essentials of efficacy and safety would be side-stepped. The proposed legislation would only provide a charter for quacks who, finding no responsible body of specialist professional opinion to support their treatments, would find easy prey amongst the sick and vulnerable.

No evidence has been produced to show that medical innovation is inhibited by fear of litigation. Legislation would only provide false hope and the real risk of injury and further suffering from untested treatments not supported by responsible practitioners. Moreover, the Supreme Court case of *Montgomery v Lanarkshire Health Board* demonstrates a judicial retreat from *Bolam*, based on societal rejection of medical paternalism. Surely the common law is sufficiently pragmatic, robust, and flexible to deal with the challenges of novel clinical situations without clumsy and misconceived legislation.

For those who cannot obtain redress without litigating, the guidance given on procedure by Marek Bednarczyk and Master David Cook (who replaces Master John Ungley) is the starting point. As in earlier editions, we have sought to avoid a series of monographs on every legal and medical topic. Rather we focused on the major areas of litigation and the emerging ones such as vascular surgery (Cliff Shearman), pain management (Tim Johnson), plastic surgery (Tim Goodacre) and sports medicine (Simon Paul). The distinguished contributors of the medical chapters have been encouraged to be forthright in their opinions on the standards now to be expected in their specialties. Thirty-six of the fifty-five contributors are new to this edition, providing a significant injection of new style and insight. Integrating all the chapters, excluding overlap (save where it has been considered important enough to have different view points), chasing contributors, resolving differences of view between them and the editors has required an enormous effort by all concerned.

There are many who have provided essential help and guidance but to mention a few, Melissa Coutinho on professional regulation and the General Medical Council, Ricardo Williams on the requirements of practitioners in common law jurisdictions where medical negligence is a developing speciality and John Newton who, besides contributing a new chapter on epidemiology, has played a major role in identifying those willing and able to contribute to many of the medical chapters.

Two are most deserving of our gratitude. First, Sir Barry Jackson who bravely accepted the role of assistant editor and has helped to maintain the focus of the contributors on the purpose of this text so as to achieve the right balance between law and medicine. Second, Kiran Goss, our publisher, who has been a tower of strength, demonstrating infinite patience with us during the three years between conception and publication of this edition. Over 5,000 e-mails have jammed our inboxes and Kiran has helped resolve numerous issues. Even we editors have had our differences. The value of this publication to the two professions and to lay readers comes from the diversity of its contributors and the efforts which have gone in to their contributions. To all those who have given their time and effort to the success of this project, we are enormously grateful.

The law is stated as at 1 June 2015.

Michael J Powers QC
Dr Anthony Barton
July 2015

Contents

Contents

Contributors

Dr Anthony Barton
Solicitor and Medical Practitioner

Kate Beattie
Barrister, 1 Crown Office Row, Temple, London

Marek Bednarczyk
Partner, Hart Brown Solicitors, Guildford

James Berry MP
Barrister, Serjeants' Inn Chambers, London

David Black
Partner, Bower and Bailey Solicitors, Oxford

Professor Martin M Brown MA MD FRCP
Professor of Stroke Medicine, UCL Institute of Neurology, University College London; Consultant Neurologist, the National Hospital for Neurology and Neurosurgery, Queen Square, London

Dr Adrian T H Casey MB BS FRCS FRCS SN
Consultant Spinal Surgeon; The National Hospital for Neurology and Neurosurgery, Queen Square, London; The Royal National Orthopaedic Hospital, Brockley Hill, Stanmore

Professor Tony Cheesman BSc, MBBS,FRCS, FRCSLT
Late Professor of Otolaryngology and Skull Base Surgery, Barts Health NHS Trust

Dr Michael J Clancy MSc, FCEM,FRCS
Consultant Emergency Physician, University Hospitals of Southampton Foundation Trust

David Cook
Master of the High Court, Queen's Bench Division, Royal Courts of Justice, Strand, London

Contributors

Dr David Corless-Smith BDS LLM
Solicitor & Dental Surgeon, Director, Dental Law Partnership

Dr Michael Davidson MBBS BSc MRCP
Specialist Registrar in Medical Oncology, Department of Medicine, Royal
Marsden NHS Foundation Trust

Dr Christopher Dean BDS LLB MA
Solicitor & Dental Surgeon, Director, Dental Law Partnership

Christopher P Dorries OBE
HM Senior Coroner, South Yorkshire (West)

Leroy Edozien LLB, BSc, MSc, PhD, MRCPI, FWACS, FRCOG
Consultant Obstetrician and Gynaecologist, Manchester Academic Health
Science Centre, St Mary's Hospital, Manchester

Michael Fertleman FRCP FHEA FFFLM Barrister (NP)
Consultant Physician, St Mary's Hospital, London;
Honorary Senior Lecturer, Imperial College, London

Dr Alan Fletcher B Med Sci, MB ChB, FRCP, FRCEM
Lead Medical Examiner (of the documents and cause of death), Consultant
Emergency Physician, Sheffield

Sir Robert Francis QC LLB (Exeter)
Master of the Bench of the Inner Temple, Serjeants' Inn Chambers, London

Charles Gibson QC
Henderson Chambers, 2 Harcourt Buildings, Temple, London

Mr Martin Gillies PhD MRCP, SpR Neurosurgery

Professor Fergus Gleeson FRCP FRCR FCCP
Professor of Radiology, Consultant Radiologist, Oxford University
Hospitals NHS Trust

Timothy E E Goodacre BSc MB BS FRCS
Lecturer in Clinical Medicine, The Queen's College, Oxford; Consultant
Plastic & Reconstructive Surgeon, Oxford University Hospitals NHS Trust

Professor Martin Gore PhD FRCP
Consultant Medical Oncologist, Department of Medicine, Royal Marsden
NHS Foundation Trust

Caroline Harrison QC MA (Oxon) MA (Lon)
2 Temple Gardens, Temple, London, Master of the Bench of Lincoln's Inn

Philip Havers QC
1 Crown Office Row, Temple, London

Andrew Hockton
Barrister, Serjeants' Inn Chambers, London

Dr Keiran Hogarth
Consultant Radiologist, Royal Berkshire NHS Foundation Trust

Dr John S F Holden MB BS MPhil DCH DRCOG MRCGP MFFLM
Joint Head of Medical Division, Medical and Dental Defence Union of
Scotland

Dr Tim W Johnson MB, BS, FRCA
Consultant in Anaesthesia and Pain Management, Salford Royal Hospital

Mr Richard S C Kerr BSc MS FRCS
Consultant Neurosurgeon

Dr Abdul Ghaaliq Lalkhen MB ChB FRCA FFPMRCA DPMCAI PGDip
Med Ed
Consultant in Anaesthesia and Pain Medicine; Honorary Senior Lecturer,
University of Manchester; Honorary Senior Lecturer, University of Salford

Brent McDonald
Barrister, Old Square Chambers, 10–11 Bedford Row, London

Rachel Marcus
Barrister, 1 Crown Office Row, Temple, London

John Mead BA FCII
Technical Claims Director, NHS Litigation Authority

Dr Aisha Miah BMedSci MBBS MRCP FRCR PhD
Consultant Clinical Oncologist, Sarcoma Unit, The Royal Marsden NHS
Foundation Trust

Dr Laurence Mynors-Wallis MA, DM MRCP FRCPsych
Consultant Psychiatrist, Dorset Healthcare NHS Foundation Trust;
Chair of South West Clinical Network for Mental Health;
Visiting Professor, Bournemouth University

Professor John N Newton FRCP FFPH
Professor of Public Health and Epidemiology, University of Manchester

Dr Simon Paul MBBS BSc Dip AvMed Dip SEM MFSEM MRAeS FRCP
Pg Dip Law Pg Cert Dis Res
Consultant Rheumatologist

Mr Ian A Pearce MB ChB BSc FRCOPHTH
Consultant Ophthalmologist, Director of Clinical Eye Research Centre,
St Paul's Eye Unit, Royal Liverpool University Hospital

Dr Evelyn M M Pollock BSc MD FFARCS,
Barrister, Inner Temple, London

James Purnell
Barrister, Henderson Chambers, 2 Harcourt Buildings, Temple, London

Contributors

Peter Reilly MS FRCS (Orth)
Consultant Orthopaedic Surgeon, St Marys Hospital; Honorary Senior
Lecturer, Imperial College London

Mr John Reynard DM, MA, LLM, FRCS Urol
Consultant Urological Surgeon, Oxford University Hospitals NHS Trust
and the National Spinal Injuries Centre, Stoke Mandeville Hospital

Mr James R H Scurr BSc, MB BS, MD, FRCS
Consultant Surgeon, Royal Liverpool University Hospital

Professor Cliff Shearman BSc MS FRCS
Professor of Vascular Surgery, University of Southampton; Department of
Vascular Surgery, University Hospital of Southampton NHS Foundation
Trust

Jennifer Stone
Director, Nestor Financial Group Ltd, Independent Financial Advisors

Dr Howard Thompson MB ChB D Obst RCOG
Former NHS General Practitioner, GP Expert Witness and Medical Advisor
to three Primary Care Trusts in the North West of England

Justin Turner MB ChB, FRCA, FFPMRCA
Consultant in Anaesthetics and Pain Management, Salford Royal NHS
Foundation Trust; Honorary Senior Lecturer, University of Manchester

Dr Mark Vanderpump
Consultant Physician and Honorary Senior Lecturer in Diabetes and
Endocrinology, Royal Free London NHS Foundation Trust

Professor Graham Venables DM FRCP
Consultant Neurologist and Clinical Director Neurosciences, Sheffield
Teaching Hospitals; Honorary Professor of Vascular Neurology UoS

Geraint Webb QC BA (Oxon)
Barrister, Henderson Chambers, 2 Harcourt Buildings, Temple, London

Professor A Michael Weindling BSc, MA, MD, FRCP, FRCPCH, HonFRCA
Emeritus Professor of Perinatal Medicine, University of Liverpool;
Honorary Consultant Neonatologist, Liverpool Women's Hospital

Mr Robert A Wheeler FRCS MS LLB LLM
Consultant Neonatal & Paediatric Surgeon; Director, Department of
Clinical Law, Southampton Children's Hospital, University Hospital of
Southampton

Professor John S Wyatt BSc, MBBS, FRCP, FRCPCH
Emeritus Professor of Neonatal Paediatrics, University College London;
Honorary Consultant Neonatologist, University College London Hospitals
Trust

Table of Statutes

Table of Statutory Instruments

[References are to paragraph number]

Table of Cases

[References are to paragraph number]

C

D

H

K

M

N

O

U

V

X

Y

Z

CHAPTER 1

The law

Brent McDonald

1

THE LEGAL CONTEXT OF PROFESSIONAL LIABILITY

1.1   Clinical negligence is, as a matter of analysis, but one part and example of the tort of negligence at common law. The law relating to it is in principle, therefore, consistent with the general rules and precedents which have evolved under the common law relating to negligence.

1.2   Yet, for reasons which are discussed in this book, legal actions for alleged clinical negligence differ from those arising out of 'ordinary' accidents such as those on the road or in the workplace. In particular, clinical practice requires a degree of professional judgment.

1.3   Thus in a medical case the factual circumstances to which the law must be applied are somewhat different from other types of accident or mishap, and tend to require some degree of specialist understanding or explanation. Further, a finding against a clinician will involve criticism of his (or her) professional competence, so that the courts are alert to ensure that such a finding is not lightly made.

1.4   In his book *The Discipline of Law*[1] Lord Denning wrote:

'… an action for negligence against a doctor is for him unto a dagger. His professional reputation is as dear to him as his body, perhaps more so, and an action for negligence can wound his reputation as severely as a dagger can his body'.

He was quoting from his own direction to the jury in the case of *Hatcher v Black*[2], in which he went on to guide the jury's consideration of the professional conduct of the doctor in question, in terms of his possible breach of duty to his patient, thus:

'You must not, therefore, find him negligent simply because something happens to go wrong; if, for instance, one of the risks inherent in an operation actually takes away the benefits that were hoped for, or if in a matter of opinion he makes an error of judgment. You should only find him guilty of negligence when he falls short of the standard of a reasonably skilful medical man, in short, when he is deserving of censure – for negligence in a medical man is deserving of censure'.

1 1979.
2 (1954) Times, 2 July.

1.5   Lord Woolf, at his inaugural Provost's lecture at University College London in January 2001, said that in the past English courts were 'excessively deferential' to doctors in their reluctance to find them guilty of negligence[1]. The last half-century has seen a gradual change and doctors have become more readily accountable for injuries and deaths caused through negligence. This chapter gives an overview of the three elements of the tort of negligence: duty of care; breach of that duty by failure to display an acceptable level of professional conduct; and damage or injury in consequence of that breach of duty.

1 Cf Lord Woolf: Daily Telegraph (24 April 2014) in support of the contentious Medical Innovation Bill: '…but what I do know about, from sitting as a judge, are the cases where doctors are sued for negligence because they have innovated in the treatment they offer, rather than following generally-accepted medical standards…'

1.6   These are essential elements of the tort of negligence which may be in issue in any case of alleged accident or mishap: on the road, in the workplace, or wherever. In the context of alleged clinical negligence, or 'medical malpractice' as it is sometimes called, each one of these essential elements of negligence may present parties to litigation with particular obstacles to surmount and particular medico-legal research to pursue.

THE DUTY OF CARE

The physician

1.7   The issue of whether a physician owes the claimant a duty of care rarely (if ever) presents a difficulty in the context of a clinical negligence claim. That duty arises, not solely by reason of the concepts of foreseeability and proximity, but by virtue of the doctor-patient relationship itself. Accordingly, a doctor may incur liability in respect of an omission once that relationship has come into being, or put another way he has accepted a responsibility towards the patient.

'If a person holds himself out as possessing special skill and knowledge and he is consulted, as possessing such skill and knowledge, by or on behalf of a patient, he owes a duty to the patient to use due caution in undertaking the treatment. If he accepts the responsibility and undertakes the treatment and the patient submits to his direction and treatment accordingly, he owes a duty to the patient to use diligence, care, knowledge, skill and caution in administering the treatment. No contractual relation is necessary, nor is it necessary that the service be rendered for reward[1]'.

In the case of a child who is being treated, the normal situation is that the child will be the patient so that there is no doctor-patient relationship between the medical practitioner and the parents; it follows that there is, for example, no duty of care to the parents of a dead child patient to tell the truth about the circumstances of the child's treatment[2]. Likewise in *ABC v St George's Healthcare NHS Trust*[3] Nicol J held that it was not fair, just or reasonable to impose a duty of care on a clinician requiring him to inform his patient's pregnant daughter of her father's diagnosis of Huntingdon's Disease (a condition which has a 50 per cent chance of being passed on to children). This was so even though the daughter, who was in due course also found to have Huntingdon's Disease, would have terminated her pregnancy had she known of the diagnosis. On the other hand, distinguishing *Powell*, Gage J in the *Organ Group Litigation*[4] found that a duty of care could be and was owed by doctors to the parents of a child who had died, on the basis that there was (on the expert and factual evidence he heard in that case) a doctor-patient relationship.

1 Per Hewitt CJ, in *R v Bateman* (1925) 94 LJKB 791 at 794. Equally that acceptance of responsibility may (arguably) arise by virtue of the physician's contract with the NHS.
2 *Powell and Boldaz* [1997] 39 BMLR 35, CA; overruled on different grounds in *Revenue and Customs Commissioners v Total Network SL* [2008] 1 AC 1174.
3 [2015] EWHC 1394 (QB).
4 *AB v Leeds Teaching Hospitals NHS Trust* [2004] All ER (D) 5–6 (Mar).

General practitioners and similar healthcare providers

1.8   General practitioners (GPs) owe a duty of care to their patients in the same way as any other physician. However, many GPs work in partnerships.

Therefore, in a clinical negligence action against a GP the normal rules of actions against partnerships may apply. A GP may be sued in his own name or that of the partnership. Where a GP partner commits a negligent act in the normal course of business of the partnership (ie in the diagnosis and/or treatment of and/or failure to attend a patient) the partnership is liable to the same extent as the individual practitioner[1]. Further, every partner is jointly and severally liable in that situation[2].

1 Partnership Act 1890, s 10.
2 Partnership Act 1890, s 12.

1.9 The situation of dentists or other health professionals who form partnerships is the same as that of GPs. Absent partnership, issues of vicarious liability will need to be considered given recent developments in this area[1].

1 *Whetstone (trading as Welby House Dental Practice) v Medical Protection Society Ltd* [2014] EWHC 1024 (QB). Permission to appeal was refused by Underhill LJ: see [2015] EWCA Civ 127.

Institutional health care providers: a brief introduction

1.10 The structure of the National Health Service (NHS) in England underwent radical change in April 2013 following implementation of the Health and Social Care Act 2012 and has become significantly more complex. A graphic of the new structure can found on the NHS website[1]. Strategic Health Authorities and Primary Care Trusts have been abolished and new forms of trust to manage services have been created. A full description of the new structure and its many organisations defies a brief exposition, but the following sets out the main providers of health services only.

(1) *NHS England.* NHS England took over statutory responsibility from the Department of Health (DoH) with the stated aim of improving health outcomes for people in England, although it is still subject to overview by the Secretary of State for Health. Many of the functions performed by the old Primary Care Trusts (PCTs) in commissioning primary care and specialist services are now undertaken by NHS England. It also allocates resources to Clinical Commissioning Groups (CCGs). The organisation is divided into nine different Directorates covering matters such as Nursing, Policy, Medical, Patients and Information, Commissioning Development and Finance.

(2) *Health Trusts.* Health Trusts have responsibility for the management of many of the services provided by the NHS. For example Acute Trusts now manage hospitals in England, as well as some services in the community through clinics, health centres or by way of home visits. Trusts that have gained Foundation status are overseen by a regulator called Monitor. Monitor works alongside the Care Quality Commission (CQC) in addition to a number of specialist regulatory bodies to maintain standards across the sector. These regulators are now joined by a 'consumer champion' called Healthwatch England.

(3) *Clinical Commissioning Groups* (CCGs). CCGs have taken on much of the functions of PCTs, but also some of the functions previously carried out by the DoH. All GPs must now belong to CCGs. CCGs have responsibility for commissioning services provided by the NHS, including emergency and out-of-hours care, hospital care, mental health

and disability services and community health services. Services can be commissioned from any provider able to meet NHS standards and costs (Health Trusts but also those in the private sector, charities etc). In commissioning services CCGs are obliged to take into account The National Institute for Health and Care Excellence (NICE) guidelines and data from the CQC.

(4) *Public Health England* (PHE). PHE has responsibility to provide public health services such as protection against infectious diseases (such as Legionnaires' disease). It performs all of the functions previously provided by the Health Protection Agency. It works with local authorities and with the NHS.

1 See www.nhs.uk/NHSEngland/thenhs/about/Documents/nhs-system-overview.pdf.

Institutional health care providers: vicarious duty and direct duty

1.11   Healthcare providers such as GPs, health authorities and NHS Trust hospitals clearly owe a vicarious duty of care to patients in respect of the acts and omissions of their staff committed in the course of their employment[1].

It is equally well established that institutional health care providers owe to patients a direct duty of care identical to that of their clinicians.

The classic statement of this principle was made, again by Denning LJ (as he then was), in the case of *Cassidy v Ministry of Health*[2]:

'In my opinion authorities who run a hospital, be they local authorities, government boards, or any other corporation, are in law under the self same duty as the humblest doctor; whenever they accept a patient for treatment, they must use reasonable care and skill to cure him of his ailment. The hospital authorities cannot, of course, do it by themselves: they have no ears to listen through the stethoscope, and no hands to hold the surgeon's knife. They must do it by the staff which they employ; and if their staff are negligent in giving the treatment, they are just as liable for that negligence as is anyone else who employs others to do his duties for him ... I take it to be clear law, as well as good sense, that, where a person is himself under a duty to use care, he cannot get rid of his responsibility by delegating the performance of it to someone else, no matter whether the delegation be to a servant under a contract of service or to an independent contractor under a contract for services'[3].

1 *Gold v Essex County Council* [1942] 2 All ER 237, CA; *Razzel v Snowball* [1954] 3 All ER 429, CA.
2 [1951] 2 KB 343, CA.
3 [1951] 2 KB 343 at 356, CA.

1.12   In *M v Calderdale and Kirklees Health Authority*[1], purporting to apply *Gold* and *Cassidy*, where a health authority whose doctor arranged (by contract with a private hospital) for the claimant to have her pregnancy terminated at the hospital, it was held to owe a non-delegable duty to her as its patient to provide an effective termination. When therefore, owing to the negligence of the clinic and the operator (neither of whom were insured or able to satisfy a judgment), the claimant was found still to be pregnant, the health authority was found liable to her for her pain, suffering and loss. It was further found to be in breach of its duty under s 1 of the National Health Service Act 1977 in failing to provide or secure the effective provision of services.

1 [1998] Lloyd's Rep Med 157.

1.13   In *A v Ministry of Defence*[1] the claimant, a child who was born to the wife of a British solider serving in Germany, sought a declaration that he was entitled to sue the Ministry of Defence. He was suffering from cerebral palsy due to the negligence of an obstetrician at a German hospital. His mother had been taken to that hospital, when she went into premature labour, pursuant to arrangements made by the Ministry of Defence to replace military hospitals in Germany with designated local hospitals that service personnel and their families could attend. The claimant argued, by analogy with *Cassidy* and *M* that the Ministry of Defence owed him a non-delegable duty of care to provide obstetric treatment of reasonable skill and care.

1 [2005] QB 183.

1.14   The Court of Appeal rejected this contention and in doing so Lord Phillips MR expressly disapproved the decision in *M*[1]. He recognised (at [43]–[45]) that two Australian cases had imposed a non-delegable duty of care on hospitals towards patients that they accepted for treatment[2]. He further noted the statements of Lord Greene MR in *Gold* and Denning LJ in *Cassidy* (quoted above), albeit that these were obiter (at [51]). Nevertheless, Lord Phillips reasoned (at [52]) that an important element in establishing a non-delegable duty of care was that the person on whom the duty was imposed should have control of the environment in which the claimant suffered injury:

'In each of these cases the court was concerned with the duty of the hospital that was actually carrying out the treatment of the patient. The Australian cases postulated the non-delegable duty of a hospital on the basis that the hospital had accepted the patient for treatment. Judge Garner [in *M*] extended the principle beyond this'.

1 *M v Calderdale and Kirklees Health Authority* [1998] Lloyd's Rep Med 157.
2 *Ellis v Wallsend District Hospital* (1989) 17 NSWLR 553; *Kondis v State Transport Authority* (1984) 154 CLR 672.

1.15   It followed that the claimant, A, was trying to extend the law of negligence beyond the bounds of *Cassidy* etc since the Ministry of Defence had no control over the German hospital. Lord Phillips held that there were no sound policy reasons for permitting such an extension of the law and so the claim failed.

Similarly in *Farraj v King's Healthcare NHS Trust*[1] the Court of Appeal dismissed a claim against a hospital which had employed an independent laboratory to analyse a tissue sample for a patient who was not being treated by the hospital and was therefore not in its custody or care. The hospital had not assumed any responsibility for the well-being or safety of the patient.

Likewise in *Morgan v Ministry of Defence*[2] it was held that the defendant, who ran a Young Offender Institution, could not be liable for the negligence of the doctors who worked at the Institution. The claimant alleged that they had failed to recognise the deceased's mental health problems, which led to the deceased hanging himself. Supperstone J held that a non-delegable duty was not owed to the deceased, as the doctors were not the defendant's employees.

1 [2009] EWCA Civ 1203, [2010] 1 WLR 2139.
2 [2010] EWHC 2248 (QB).

1.16   In *Woodland v Swimming Teachers Association*[1], the Supreme Court reviewed in detail the rationale for the existence of non-delegable duties.

Woodland concerned a severe brain injury suffered by a pupil at a local authority school during a swimming lesson. The lesson was supervised by a swimming teacher and a lifeguard who were employed by an independent contractor which had contracted with the local authority to organise and provide the lesson. A separate local authority ran the pool.

The claimant claimed *inter alia* that the local authority owed her a non-delegable duty of care to secure that reasonable care was taken during the school day, including those periods when she was off school premises. Langstaff J struck out this part of the claim at first instance. The Court of Appeal subsequently upheld his decision[2].

In allowing the claimant's appeal Lord Sumption JSC, with whom all the other Justices agreed, identified five factors which characterised cases where a non-delegable duty had been found:

'(1) The claimant is a patient or a child, or for some other reason is especially vulnerable or dependent on the protection of the defendant against the risk of injury. Other examples are likely to be prisoners and residents in care homes.

(2) There is an antecedent relationship between the claimant and the defendant, independent of the negligent act or omission itself, (i) which places the claimant in the actual custody, charge or care of the defendant, and (ii) from which it is possible to impute to the defendant the assumption of a positive duty to protect the claimant from harm, and not just a duty to refrain from conduct which will foreseeably damage the claimant. It is characteristic of such relationships that they involve an element of control over the claimant, which varies in intensity from one situation to another, but is clearly very substantial in the case of schoolchildren.

(3) The claimant has no control over how the defendant chooses to perform those obligations, ie whether personally or through employees or through third parties.

(4) The defendant has delegated to a third party some function which is an integral part of the positive duty which he has assumed towards the claimant; and the third party is exercising, for the purpose of the function thus delegated to him, the defendant's custody or care of the claimant and the element of control that goes with it.

(5) The third party has been negligent not in some collateral respect but in the performance of the very function assumed by the defendant and delegated by the defendant to him'[3].

1 [2014] AC 537.
2 [2013] 3 WLR 853.
3 [2014] AC 537 at [23].

1.17   The essential element in finding a non-delegable duty was not control of the environment, Lord Sumption held, but the control over the claimant for the purpose of performing a function for which the defendant had assumed responsibility. In the case of *Woodland* there was an assumption of responsibility for the claimant's safety during the school day when she was under the defendant's control, giving rise to a non-delegable duty. In the clinical context Dyson LJ had been correct to state in *Farraj* that the rationale of any non-delegable duty owed by a hospital was that:

'the hospital undertakes the care, supervision and control of its patients who are in special need of care. Patients are a vulnerable class of persons who place themselves in the care and under the control of a hospital and, as a result, the hospital assumes a particular responsibility for their well-being and safety'.

Absent such an undertaking no duty would exist. Therefore in Lord Sumption's view, the outcome of both *A v Ministry of Defence* and *Farraj* was correct. In *A v Ministry of Defence* for example the defendant had merely arranged for treatment to be carried out by its contractor; it had not delegated any function to the hospital nor had the claimant been placed in its custody or care.

1.18   The approval of *A v Ministry of Defence* and *Farraj* by the Supreme Court makes it unlikely that a non-delegable duty will be held to exist where a body does not have control of the claimant for the purposes of performing a function for which it had assumed responsibility. It will therefore be difficult to make out claims against organisations where, for example, they merely arrange for patients to visit private medical facilities and the patients suffer injury there.

1.19   However, where such control does exist it seems the courts are now willing to find the existence of a non-delegable duty.

In *GB v Home Office*[1] the claimant sued the Home Office for breach of its non-delegable duty due to medical staff prescribing her an anti-malarial drug which caused her to suffer a severe psychotic reaction whilst she was detailed at Yarl's Wood Immigration Removal Centre. The detention centre was run on the Home Office's behalf by a company named Serco. Serco had contracted with a GP employed by a local surgery to provide care to detainees. Applying Lord Sumption's judgment in *Woodland*, Coulson J concluded (at [38]) that the five ingredients identified in *Woodland* were present, and that it was fair, just and reasonable to impose a non-delegable duty of care on the Home Office. Coulson J observed (at [44]–[52]) that the law had moved on from *Morgan*, which could no longer be regarded as good law[2].

1 [2015] EWHC 819 (QB).
2 See also *Amadou Nyang v G4S Care and Justice Services Ltd* [2013] EWHC 3946 (QB) per Lewis J.

1.20   The NHS indemnity, introduced in 1990, might arguably mean that the importance of the *Cassidy* principle (as delimited by the case of *A*[1]) has lessened in the context of some claims against the NHS. Under the indemnity, NHS bodies are to accept liability where clinical negligence is committed by a healthcare professional who is working under a contract with the NHS body to provide services to persons to whom the body owed a duty of care (as opposed to working under a contract of employment). It should be noted, however, that the indemnity does not extend to, amongst others, GPs or dentists who are working under contracts for services, employees of such general practices, employees of private hospitals (even when they are treating NHS patients) and self-employed healthcare professionals such as independent midwives[2].

1 *A v Ministry of Defence* [2005] QB 183.
2 See the *NHS Indemnity: Arrangements for Clinical Negligence Claims in the NHS*, HSG 96/48 helpfully summarised at http://www.nhsla.com/claims/Documents/NHS%20Indemnity. pdf.

1.21 The effect of this is that where an NHS body contracts for a healthcare professional to provide services to a patient and that patient suffers injury through negligence, the patient's advisers should examine whether or not the healthcare professional may be included within the terms of the NHS indemnity; but also against this background whether proceedings should additionally be brought against other parties so as not to prejudice the patient's position.

1.22 Finally in this section, it must be stressed that the liability of the health authority or trust hospital, whether vicarious or *Cassidy* direct, depends upon whether the act or omission complained of is such as to constitute a breach of duty of the relevant individual healthcare professional.

Institutional health care providers' own duty to make provision

1.23 It is additionally possible that a provider unit, be it an Acute Trust hospital or private sector health care provider may be primarily, and even exclusively, liable for its failure to institute and maintain a safe system of health care provision without there being fault on the part of any health care professional.

1.24 In *Wilsher v Essex Area Health Authority*[1], one of the allegations made was that the authority had failed to provide sufficient or properly qualified and competent medical staff. An inexperienced house officer working in an intensive care neonatal unit in which the infant claimant was being cared for inserted a catheter into the claimant's vein rather than an artery. He did, however, ask the senior registrar to check what he had done: the registrar failed to see the mistake, and later himself repeated it. The mistake in each case caused a misleading blood/oxygen reading to be given with the result that the child was over-oxygenated; when subsequently he suffered from near blindness which was capable of being attributed to the over-oxygenation, he contended that this want of care had caused his injury.

1 [1987] QB 730, CA: the decision was reversed by the House of Lords on another point [1988] 1 All ER 871, HL (the claimant was held to have failed to discharge the burden of proof on causation) but the Court of Appeal decision remains good authority on this.

1.25 An allegation was therefore made against the authority, directed to the alleged lack of competence of the staff it had provided. It is now established that, whilst no health care practitioner is able in law to shift the burden of liability entirely to another if personal professional conduct or judgment was at fault, the managers of any provider unit may be directly liable for failure to provide sufficient or properly qualified and competent medical staff for the unit. As Sir Nicholas Browne-Wilkinson (as he then was), observed in the Court of Appeal:

'In my judgment, a health authority which so conducts its hospital that it fails to provide doctors of sufficient skill and experience to give the treatment offered at the hospital may be directly liable in negligence to the patient. Although we were told in argument that no case has ever been decided on this ground and that it is not the practice to formulate claims in this way, I can see no reason why, in principle, the health authority should not be so liable if its organisation is at fault'[1].

1 [1986] 3 All ER 801 at 833h–j.

1.26   By way of pointing to some of the organisational and legal difficulties which may beset provider units, which are inevitably cash-limited and must act within their budget, Sir Nicholas Browne-Wilkinson continued:

'Claims against a health authority that it has itself been directly negligent, as opposed to vicariously liable for the negligence of its doctors, will, of course, raise awkward questions. To what extent should the authority be liable if (eg in the use of a junior houseman) it is only adopting a practice hallowed by tradition? Should the authority be liable if it demonstrates that, due to the financial stringency under which it operates, it cannot afford to fill the posts with those possessing the necessary experience? But, in my judgment, the law should not be distorted by making findings of personal fault against individual doctors who are, in truth, not at fault in order to avoid such questions. To do so would be to cloud the real issues which arise. In the modern world with its technological refinements is it sensible to persist in making compensation for those who suffer from shortcomings in technologically advanced treatment depend on proof of fault, a process which the present case illustrates can consume years in time and huge sums of money in costs? Given limited resources, what balance is to be struck in the allocation of such resources between compensating those whose treatment is not wholly successful and the provision of required treatment for the world at large? These are questions for Parliament, not the courts. But I do not think the courts would do society a favour by distorting the existing law so as to conceal the real social questions which arise'[1].

In *Woodland* Lord Sumption cautioned that:

'The courts should be sensitive about imposing unreasonable financial burdens on those providing critical public services'[2].

1 [1986] 3 All ER 801 at 833j–834c.
2 [2014] AC 537 at [25].

Institutional health care providers' own duty: public and private law

1.27   Given the increasing attention being paid in recent years to economic aspects of health care provision, with cash-limited budgets, restrictive pressures on prescribing and the like, the question is what remedy an individual patient may have who feels that he has been affected by such decisions adverse to his own healthcare provision.

1.28   For this purpose a distinction needs to be drawn between cases where remedies are available in public law by way of judicial review, and cases where private law remedies will be available by action at common law. It is, strictly speaking, possible to combine a claim for judicial review with one for damages, although a successful judicial review claim does not in itself give rise to financial compensation: see the Senior Courts Act 1981, s 31(4) and CPR 54.3(2). In practice, though, this is seldom done in the field of clinical negligence. The tight time limits imposed on judicial review claims are likely to mean that there will be insufficient time properly to formulate a claim in negligence for damages. Moreover, even if that were done, the damages claim would probably be stayed pending resolution of the public law issues.

1.29   The Human Rights Act 1998 (HRA 1998) created a free-standing remedy in damages against public authorities whose acts are incompatible with rights under the European Convention on Human Rights. For a detailed analysis of the impact of HRA 1998 on clinical negligence claims see **Chapter 4**.

In *Savage v South Essex Partnership NHS Foundation Trust*[1] it was held that Article 2 imposed an 'operational' obligation on health providers and their staff to do all that was practical to safeguard a patient's life, if they knew, or ought to have known, that a particular patient was under a real and immediate risk of death. In *Rabone v Pennine Care NHS Foundation Trust*[2] it was held that the operational duty under Article 2 applied to patients who were voluntarily detained as well as those committed under the Mental Health Act 1983.

The HRA 1998 has also had an impact on wrongful birth cases. It was (unsuccessfully) contended, for example, that the fact that childcare costs were awardable as damages only for the difference in cost between raising a disabled and a healthy child is incompatible with Articles 6 and 8 of the Convention[3]. The courts have also rejected an argument that the HRA 1998 requires them to provide a remedy where a healthy child is born following a failure to diagnose a pregnancy[4].

1 [2009] 1 AC 681.
2 [2012] 2 AC 72.
3 *Groom v Selby* [2001] Lloyd's Rep Med 39, QBD at 45–46. HHJ Peter Clark rejected the argument.
4 *Greenfield v Flather* [2001] EWCA Civ 113, [2001] 1 WLR 1279.

1.30   Returning to our initial distinction, the first (public law) type of case will tend to arise out of alleged *failure in provision, or non-provision,* of facilities, drugs, treatment or care. The remedy sought will be a public law remedy, and this type of case has only limited and indirect relevance to this work: nevertheless the administrative court may make qualitative comment about clinical, medical or administrative practice, in assessing whether considerations were improperly taken into account, or left out of account, in a decision by an institutional health provider.

1.31   The second (private law) type of case, whilst it may also involve allegations of *failure in provision, or non-provision,* will more frequently deal with issues of *inadequate provision*. The case will take the form of an action for negligence, and the remedy sought will be damages, it being alleged that the negligent failure to provide appropriate treatment and care has given rise to injury and loss.

1.32   An example of the first type of case is provided by *R v Secretary of State for Social Services, ex p Hincks*[1]. The applicants were orthopaedic patients at a hospital in Birmingham who had waited for treatment for periods longer than was medically advisable, because of a shortage of facilities, arising, in part, from a decision not to build a new block at the hospital on grounds of cost. The applicants sought declarations that the Secretary of State, the Regional Health Authority and Area Health Authority were in breach of their obligations under the National Health Service Act 1977, s 1 to continue to promote a comprehensive health service designed to secure improvement in health and the prevention of illness, and under s 3 to provide accommodation, facilities and services for those purposes (see now Part 1 of the Health and Social Care Act 2012).

1 (1979) 123 Sol Jo 436; affd (1980) 1 BMLR 93, CA.

1.33 It was held by Wien J (and affirmed by the Court of Appeal) that it was not the court's function to direct Parliament as to what funds to make available to the health service and how to allocate them. The Secretary of State's duty under s 3 to provide services 'to such extent as he considers necessary' gave him a broad discretion as to the disposition of financial resources. The court could only interfere if the Secretary of State had acted so as to frustrate the policy of the Act or had acted as no reasonable Minister could have acted. No such breach had been established and accordingly the applications failed. Given the continued imposition of public duties for the provision of care (see for example the Care Act 2014, s 18) combined with increased pressure on resources in government, challenges in the Administrative Court are likely to continue.

1.34 Other examples of this type of public law case are:

(1)   *R v Central Birmingham Health Authority, ex p Walker*[1]: decision not to expand intensive care unit, held 'not justiciable';

(2)   *R v Cambridge Health Authority, ex p B*[2]: extra-contractual referral by Health Authority of child with leukaemia refused: decision of Laws J at first instance to intervene overturned. Sir Thomas Bingham MR said that the application was:

'an attempt, wholly understandable but nonetheless misguided, to involve the court in a field of activity where it is not fitted to make any decision favourable to the patient';

(3)   *R v North Derbyshire Health Authority, ex p Fisher*[3]: decision not to allocate resources for prescription of beta-interferon held unlawful, *but* upon the basis that no proper policy had been formulated to take account of national policy (as per Circular) that beta-interferon be introduced;

(4)   *R (on the application of Rose) v Thanet*[4]: high-profile recent challenge to a decision of the PCT not to fund treatment with a breast cancer drug, Herceptin. That decision was held unlawful by the Court of Appeal. The PCT's policy to refuse funding for Herceptin save in cases of exceptional personal or clinical circumstances was irrational: it appeared that the policy did not envisage what such circumstances might be so that it amounted to a policy of exceptionality.

1 (1987) 3 BMLR 32, CA.
2 [1995] 2 All ER 129, CA.
3 [1997] 8 Med LR 327; see also *R v Secretary of State for Health, ex p Pfizer Ltd* [1999] Lloyd's Med Rep 289 (Collins J): the Department of Health Circular 1998/158 advising doctors not to prescribe Viagra and health authorities not to support its NHS provision (save in exceptional circumstances) was held to be unlawful as (inter alia) overriding doctors' professional judgment and placing them in breach of their terms of service. The sequel to this case followed after the Secretary of State then made a further decision to the effect that the circumstances in which Viagra could be prescribed should be restricted. In *R v Secretary of State for Health, ex p Pfizer Ltd* [2002] EWHC 791 (Admin): at first instance Turner J upheld the Secretary of State's decision, and his decision was upheld by the Court of Appeal: [2002] EWCA Civ 1566.
4 [2014] EWHC 1182 (Admin), (2014) 138 BMLR 101.

1.35   In the second type of case, ie in the context of a private law negligence action, there are indications that the courts may not always adhere to the view[1] that certain questions are for Parliament and not for the courts, but will be prepared in an appropriate case to arrive at a determinative view of the standard of provision.

1 Cf *Wilsher v Essex Area Health Authority* [1987] QB 730, CA.

Private law duty: resource issues

1.36   In *Bull v Devon AHA*[1] the first of twins was born without disability, but the second (the infant second claimant), born 68 minutes after the first, suffered brain damage. In fact the health authority's relevant maternity services operated between two sites, a mile distant from each other. Tucker J held that there was unacceptable delay between the deliveries of the twins, and that the defendant health authority was in breach of its duty to the damaged infant and the mother. The health authority contended, inter alia, that the hospital staff could not be expected to do more than their best, operating on a total of three sites and allocating their limited resources as favourably as possible.

1 [1993] 4 Med LR 117 (case decided February 1989).

1.37   In dismissing the health authority's appeal on the issues of delay, breach of duty and causation, on other grounds (so that observations as to system strictly did not fall for decision) Mustill LJ (as he then was) said[1]:

'Is there not a contradiction in asserting at the same time that the system put the foetus at risk and that it was good enough? … I have some reservations about [the defendant's contention], which are not allayed by the submission that hospital medicine is a public service. So it is, but there are other public services in respect of which it is not necessarily an answer to allegations of unsafety that there were insufficient resources to enable the administrators to do everything which they would like to do … It is however unnecessary to go further into these matters, which raise important issues of social policy, which the courts may one day have to address'.

1 (1993) 4 Med LR 117 at 141.

1.38   A similar point was made in *Knight v Home Office*[1], in which the personal representatives of the deceased, who was detained in a remand prison pending admission to hospital, sued on account of his suicide by hanging. It was held that the standard of care in a remand prison was not as high as that in a psychiatric hospital, so that the patient/staff ratio applicable to such a hospital did not apply. On the facts of that case it was held that the prison medical staff were not negligent in deciding that the deceased be observed at 15-minute intervals, and for this reason the claimants failed in their action. Nevertheless Pill J (as he then was) said (again obiter):

'I cannot accept what was at one time submitted by counsel for the defendants that the claimants' only remedy would be a political one. To take an extreme example, if the evidence was that no funds were available to provide any medical facilities in a large prison there would be a failure to achieve the standard of care appropriate for prisoners. In a different context, lack of funds would not excuse a public body which operated its vehicles on the public roads without any system of maintenance for the vehicles if an accident occurred because of lack of maintenance. The law would require a higher standard of care towards other road users'[2].

1 [1990] 3 All ER 237.
2 [1990] 3 All ER 237 at 243b.

1.39   Following the decision in *Knight*, in *Brooks v Home Office*[1] Garland J held that a pregnant woman prisoner in a prison hospital who lost her baby following delay in seeking specialist obstetric advice was entitled to the same standard of obstetric care, as she would have received if she were at liberty. The claim, however, failed because the loss of the baby was not caused by the breach of duty; and there has been judicial resistance to the proposition that the decision and dicta in *Knight* should be followed so widely as to allow intervention by the courts into all circumstances involving resource allocation[2].

1 (1999) 48 BMLR 109.
2 See the observations of Roderick Evans J In *R v Secretary of State for the Home Department, ex p McFadyen* [2002] EWHC 790 (Admin) and [32] of the judgment of Simon J in *Ball v Wirral HA* [2003] Lloyd's Rep. Med. 165.

1.40   Reference to the general law of negligence is appropriate here. In general, when the courts come to assess whether a particular act or omission constitutes a breach of duty, the standard normally set is by reference to the conduct of the notional reasonable and prudent person, and the yardstick of 'reasonableness' is sufficiently flexible to be applied to the circumstances of any given case. Thus, generally speaking, the standard required relates to the activity, rather than the personal circumstances of the actor[1]. In this context there is limited room for an individual or corporate defendant to plead that his actual resources were insufficient for reasonable care to be taken.

1 *Wilsher v Essex Area Health Authority* [1987] QB 730, CA; *Nettleship v Weston* [1971] 2 QB 691 (learner driver liable although doing her best, because standard required is that of skilled driver on roads).

1.41   The analogy with the general law needs, however, to be applied with care. The basis of fixing liability on a defendant in this way is that it is assumed that that individual or entity has a choice: if the resources are inadequate, the defendant should not be undertaking the activity, and could decline to do so. This assumption is one whose application to a particular public authority may not be appropriate: it will depend on the facts and the activity being undertaken. See for example the judgment of Colman J in *Walker v Northumberland CC*[1], which expressly recognised that consideration of the steps which public authorities take needs to take into account the resources and facilities which are at their disposal.

1 [1995] ICR 702.

1.42   The negligence liability of public authorities is a complex area of the law and one whose boundaries are constantly being redrawn. A full survey is beyond the scope of this chapter. Nevertheless the following summary of the law is suggestive of the approach that courts are likely to take to negligence claims against such authorities:

(1)   the decision of *X v Bedfordshire County Council*[1] established a threshold question in the field of public authority liability, namely whether or not the negligence relied on by a claimant was negligence in the exercise of a statutory discretion involving policy considerations. Lord Browne-

Wilkinson stated that if the alleged negligent act did involve such considerations of policy the claim would fail as being non-justiciable;

(2)   in subsequent cases this threshold test of justiciability has been adopted. Thereafter the court will apply the classic three-stage *Caparo*[2] test (foreseeability; proximity; and fairness, justice and reasonableness) to determine the existence or otherwise of a duty of care[3];

(3)   in the field of clinical negligence the courts have on occasion been alert to dismiss claims for negligence which centre on whether an NHS health care provider has allocated its resources appropriately. *Hardaker v Newcastle Health Authority*[4] was a claim brought by a diver who suffered decompression illness ('the bends') after surfacing from a dive. He sued the first defendant, which operated a nearby hospital that had a decompression chamber. When he was taken by the emergency services to the first defendant's hospital the chamber was not operational, as it was not staffed due to insufficient resources. On this point Burnton J held that the claimant could not hope to succeed in establishing negligence. His allegation would require the court to undertake an assessment of the priorities of allocating resources, which it could not perform[5]. It would appear that in essence the claim on this point failed on the threshold test of justiciability[6].

1 [1995] 2 AC 633.
2 *Caparo Industries v Dickman* [1990] 2 AC 605, HL.
3 See the decision in *Carty v London Borough of Croydon* [2005] EWCA Civ 19, [2005] 1 WLR 2312 at [28], per Dyson LJ.
4 [2001] Lloyd's Rep Med 512, QBD.
5 See [54]. Burnton J's comments echo the judgment of Lord Woolf MR in *Kent v Griffiths* [2001] QB 36, CA (a case against an ambulance service) in which he commented that where a claimant attacked a public authority's allocation of resources via a negligence claim there might be issues which were not suitable for resolution by the courts.
6 As to the reluctance of the courts to assess allocation of resources by health authorities see *Jain v Trent Strategic Health Authority* [2007] EWCA Civ 1186, [2008] QB 246.

Private law duty: general observations

1.43   The potential availability of a direct claim against an institutional provider is important in three respects.

First, in a given case it may not be possible to identify and establish negligence on the part of an individual physician who may, for example, be faced with more patients who demand attention than he can reasonably be expected to cope with at any one time, or be lacking in the equipment he requires.

1.44   Second, once conduct has been classified as operational, the courts may be more willing to find negligence on the part of the institutional provider than they would on the part of the individual physician. Compliance with any recognised and properly accepted procedure would in practice be fatal to a claim against an individual physician. It is less likely to be so where the claim is being brought against an institution.

1.45   Third, the standard of proof required to establish negligence on the part of the professional man is an onerous one. Again, the courts may be prepared to accept a lower standard of proof where the allegation is being made against an institution.

1.46 Claims continue to be brought against institutional health care providers for breach of their direct duties to patients. Courts have been willing to find for claimants without the need to show any personal negligence of any employee:

(1)   in *Robertson v Nottingham Health Authority*[1] the claimant was a brain-damaged child. The Court of Appeal held that there had been significant breakdowns in the defendant's systems of communication around the claimant's birth which placed it in breach of duty. However, the claim failed on causation;

(2)   in *Loraine v Wirral University Teaching Hospital NHS Foundation Trust*[2] the claimant successfully sued the Trust for failing to supply his mother's medical team with access to her medical records which would have shown a history of a fibroid and a footling breach in her third and fourth pregnancies. Plender J held that if the records had been available the claimant would have been admitted to hospital earlier, thereby avoiding the injury which led to the claimant developing cerebral palsy. It was held that the failure to provide an adequate system amounted to a breach of the Trust's duty to provide the claimant with reasonable care whilst at hospital, applying *Robertson v Nottingham Health Authority*;

(3)   in *Steele v Home Office*[3] a prisoner recovered damages for delays in receiving dental treatment whilst serving a sentence of life imprisonment. Smith LJ held that the defendant had breached its duty to provide adequate access to health services by imposing a 'one dentist take it or leave it approach'. The duty to provide services also included a duty to provide access to an alternate dentist when resident dentists refused to treat the claimant;

(4)   in *Richards v Swansea NHS Trust*[4] the claimant suffered from cerebral palsy. At his birth, it had taken 55 minutes from the decision to perform a Caesarean section being made until his delivery. It was agreed that the national standard for decision-to-delivery time was 30 minutes. The defendant submitted that 55 minutes was not too long because it fell into the bracket being achieved by most hospitals at the time. Field J held that the failure to achieve the 30-minute target time had to be due to some exculpatory external constraint, such as competing demands on the attentions of doctors, or a failure to exercise reasonable care. The onus was on the defendant to adduce evidence of exculpatory reasons. It had failed to provide evidence of such logistical constraints. Therefore the claimant's claim succeeded.

1   [1997] 8 Med LR 1.
2   [2008] EWHC 1565 (QB), [2008] LS Law Medical 573.
3   [2010] EWCA Civ 724, (2010) 115 BMLR 218.
4   [2007] EWHC 487 (QB), (2007) 96 BMLR 180, Field J. Note that the question of the appropriate decision-to-delivery time itself will depend upon a number of factors in a given case, eg local conditions, local protocols etc; the 'national standard' and its relevance seem to have been agreed in this case. Issues as to decision-to-delivery times are dealt with in detail at paras [20]–[27] of the judgment.

Liability in contract: NHS bodies

1.47   The accepted state of the law at present appears to be that there is no contract between a patient and his treating clinicians who are providing services under the NHS[1].

1 See the 1978 *Report of the Royal Commission on Civil Liability and Compensation for Personal Injuries* (Cmd 7054), para 1313.

Liability in contract: non-NHS health care

1.48   The freedom of CCGs to commission NHS services from the private sector makes it increasingly important for practitioners to consider the possibility of framing a claim both in tort and contract providing some consideration can be found.

1.49   The courts will readily find an implied term that the physician will use reasonable skill and care in his examination, diagnosis and treatment of the patient. However, it is clear that the courts will be very slow to find that the representations of the physician constitute a warranty or guarantee of a certain result, as opposed to mere 'therapeutic reassurance'[1].

1 *Eyre v Measday* [1986] 1 All ER 488; *Thake v Maurice* [1986] 1 All ER 497, CA; see *Dow v Tayside University Hospitals NHS Trust* (2006) SCLR 865 in which the Scottish courts adopted a similar position.

1.50   Nevertheless, it is possible for a doctor to give a contractual warranty that he will achieve a certain result.

'I accept that there may be cases where, because of the claims made by a surgeon or physician for his method of treatment, the court is driven to the conclusion that the result of the treatment is guaranteed or warranted'[1].

1 Per Neill LJ, *Thake v Maurice* [1986] 1 All ER 497, CA at 510e–f.

1.51   Whilst each case will, of course, turn on its own facts, it is likely that the courts will more readily accept the existence of a contractual warranty, the more removed the contract is from therapeutic treatment. An example of this is provided by the Canadian authority of *La Fleur v Cornelis*[1].

1 (1979) 28 NBR (2d) 569 (NBSC).

1.52   The claimant entered into a contract with the defendant, a plastic surgeon, for the reduction of her nose. He drew her a sketch to illustrate the changes he would make and told her that there would be 'no problem' and that she would be 'very happy'. However, the claimant was left with scarring and deformity. Barry J, whilst accepting that the courts should be slow to find any representations to constitute contractual terms, was, on the facts of the case, prepared to find that there had been a collateral warranty as to the success of the operation. It is quite clear from his judgment that in doing so he had particular regard to the nature of the service, equating the surgeon more with the businessman providing a product than the physician providing treatment.

1.53   If a contractual claim is to be made, some analysis may be required as to exactly when the contract to effect any particular treatment or procedure was entered into, what its terms were at that stage, and whether they were subsequently varied or a subsequent contract was entered into and if so on what terms.

1.54 Unless it is to be contended that some warranty or guarantee was given, framing a claim in contract may not in practice materially assist the claimant in his claim, the extent of the duty being identical in practical content to that imposed by the law of torts.

1.55 The situation where a parallel claim in contract is likely to be most advantageous is where the contract also involves the supply of goods such as drugs, prosthetics etc. If it can be established that the product is either of unsatisfactory quality or not reasonably fit for its purpose, a claim framed in contract in principle obviates the need to establish fault on the part of the supplier[1].

For example, in the high-profile litigation arising out of PIP breast implants (*XYZ v Various Companies*[2]) it is alleged that the implants used were of unsatisfactory quality in breach of the Supply of Goods and Services Act 1982, s 4(2).

1 The position as to claims arising out of the supply of allegedly defective goods, their potential limitations, and defences available to the supplier of the goods, is discussed elsewhere.
2 Currently proceeding to trial at the time of writing, although interim proceedings concerning funding have been reported at [2014] Lloyd's Rep IR 431.

BREACH OF DUTY

1.56 The classic statement of negligence is that laid down by Alderson B in *Blyth v Birmingham Waterworks Co*:

'Negligence is the omission to do something which a reasonable man, guided upon those considerations which ordinarily regulate the conduct of human affairs, would do, or doing something which a prudent and reasonable man would not do'[1].

1 (1856) 11 Ex Ch 781 at 784.

1.57 Within this test are two requirements. First, the appropriate standard of care must be determined; second, the claimant must establish that the conduct in question fell below that ascertained standard. Because of the particular characteristics of a clinical negligence claim,[1] each of these elements merits separate consideration.

1 See paras **1.2–1.5** above.

ASCERTAINING THE STANDARD OF CARE

1.58 Evidently the requisite standard of care must be determined by a legal standard framed by the courts, rather than by the medical profession. It is prescriptive. Considerable respect is, however, paid to the practices of the profession, and judicial notice taken of them.

The *Bolam* test

1.59 This was recognised in the classic direction of McNair J to a jury in *Bolam v Friern Hospital Management Committee*:

'A doctor is not guilty of negligence if he has acted in accordance with a practice accepted as proper by a responsible body of medical men skilled in that particular art ... Putting it the other way round, a doctor is not negligent, if he is acting in accordance with such a practice, merely because there is a body of opinion which takes a contrary view'[1].

1 [1957] 2 All ER 118 at 122.

1.60 This form of words has now been applied as the correct formulation of the relevant law for 50 years. It is frequently referred to as the *Bolam* test or principle. It is now uniformly applied to all aspects of the doctor-patient relationship. Notwithstanding continuing reappraisal of this principle by the courts, the only gloss that has effectively been added to the test has been that the practice accepted as proper by a responsible body of medical men must be 'rightly' so accepted[1].

1 *Sidaway v Board of Governors of the Bethlem Royal and Maudsley Hospital* [1984] 2 WLR 778 at 792, CA endorsed by Lord Bridge in the House of Lords [1985] 2 WLR 480 at 505.

1.61 The *Bolam* test is a rule of practice or of evidence, or perhaps even a rule of thumb. It is descriptive. It is not a rule of law: doctors do not determine their own legal liability. In *Sidaway* Lord Bridge observed about the application of the *Bolam* test:

'... But I do not see that this approach involves the necessity 'to hand over to the medical profession the entire question of the scope of the duty of disclosure, including the question whether there has been a breach of that duty.' Of course, if there is a conflict of evidence as to whether a responsible body of medical opinion approves of non-disclosure in a particular case, the judge will have to resolve that conflict. But even in a case where, as here, no expert witness in the relevant medical field condemns the non-disclosure as being in conflict with accepted and responsible medical practice, I am of opinion that the judge might in certain circumstances come to the conclusion that disclosure of a particular risk was so obviously necessary to an informed choice on the part of the patient that no reasonably prudent medical man would fail to make it ...'[1].

These dicta anticipated *Bolitho* by many years.

1 *Sidaway v Board of Governors of the Bethlem Royal and Maudsley Hospital* [1984] 2 WLR 778.

1.62 It is important to set the context here: the *Bolam* approach to the standard of care here is of general application to all skilled occupations, not just doctors and surgeons. In *Whitehouse v Jordan* Lord Edmund-Davies said:

'But doctors and surgeons fall into no special legal category, and, to avoid any future disputation of a similar kind, I would have it accepted that the true doctrine was enunciated – and by no means for the first time – by McNair J in *Bolam v Friern Hospital Management Committee* [1957] 1 WLR 582, at 586 in the following words, which were applied by the Privy Council in *Chin Keow v Government of Malaysia* [1967] 1 WLR 813:

"Where you get a situation which involves the use of some special skill or competence, then the test as to whether there has been negligence or not is not the test of the man on the top of a Clapham omnibus, because he has not got this special skill. The test is the standard of the ordinary skilled man exercising and professing to have that special skill".

If a surgeon fails to measure up to that standard in any respect (clinical "judgment" or otherwise), he has been negligent and should be so adjudged ...'[1].

1 [1981] 1 WLR 246 at 258A–D.

1.63   The basis of liability in clinical negligence cases, as well as issues on causation, was reviewed in the House of Lords in *Bolitho v City and Hackney Health Authority*[1]. The authority of *Bolam* was confirmed as 'the locus classicus for the standard of care required of a doctor or any other person professing some skill or competence' (per Lord Browne-Wilkinson)[2].

1 [1997] 4 All ER 771.
2 [1997] 4 All ER 771 at 776a.

The development of the *Bolam* test: *Bolitho*

1.64   The facts of *Bolitho* were as follows. In January 1984 a two-year-old boy was admitted to the defendant's hospital suffering from respiratory problems. The following day he suffered two short episodes of further respiratory problems: on each occasion a doctor was called but did not attend. On the first occasion the child recovered. On the second the child appeared to recover, but half an hour later collapsed, owing to failure of his respiratory system, and suffered a cardiac arrest: as a result he suffered severe brain damage (and subsequently, after issue of proceedings, died). It was agreed that the cardiac arrest would have been prevented if after the respiratory problem the child had been intubated.

1.65   The defendant admitted breach of duty in the failure to attend the child, but contended (and the judge at first instance found) that even if the doctor had attended she would not have arranged for the child to be intubated anyway, so that the breach of duty gave rise to no injury or damage. The claimant contended in turn that such hypothetical failure to intubate would have been negligent. The judge heard expert evidence on behalf of the defendant to the effect that intubation would not have been appropriate, and held that a decision not to intubate would have been (in terms of the *Bolam* test) in accordance with a body of responsible professional opinion, and that accordingly causation had not been proved. Appeals to the Court of Appeal and the House of Lords were unsuccessful, and the claimants' action failed.

1.66   In the House of Lords, however, Lord Browne-Wilkinson (with whose speech the other Law Lords agreed), whilst confirming the authority of *Bolam*, and its applicability to the issue of causation as well as liability, approved what is likely to be an important development of it. This results from the emphasis he gave to the original words of McNair J in *Bolam* as follows:

'McNair J stated that the defendant had to have acted in accordance with a practice accepted as proper by a "*responsible* body of medical men". Later he referred to "a standard of practice recognised as proper by a competent *reasonable* body of opinion". Again, [in *Maynard*] Lord Scarman refers to a "respectable" body of professional opinion. The use of these adjectives – responsible, reasonable and respectable – all show that the court has to be satisfied that the exponents of the body of opinion relied on can demonstrate that such opinion has a logical basis. In particular, in cases involving, as they so often do, the weighing of risks against benefits, the judge before accepting a body of opinion as being responsible, reasonable or respectable, will need to be satisfied that, in forming their views, the experts have directed their minds to the question of comparative risks and benefits and have reached a defensible conclusion on the matter'[1].

1 [1997] 4 All ER 771 at 778d–g applied in *Penney v East Kent* (16 November 1999, unreported), CA.

1.67   It was, the H   , to be expected that in most cases, in the light of the evidence of a professional body of opinion in support of the defendant's conduct, such conduct would be demonstrably reasonable. If, however, the professional opinion called in support of the defence case was not capable of withstanding logical analysis, then the court would be entitled to hold that the body of opinion was not reasonable or responsible.

The decision in *Bolitho* raises also issues of causation; this topic is dealt with elsewhere.

1 [1997] 4 All ER 771 at 779e–h.

1.68   Thus where appropriate (albeit rarely) the courts will be prepared to reject an established practice shown to be manifestly wrong. One such case of some antiquity is *Clarke v Adams*[1]. The claimant was severely burned during a course of heat treatment administered by a physiotherapist. The defendant warned him of the danger in the manner approved by the Chartered Society of Physiotherapists. Nevertheless, the court was prepared to find the warning to be inadequate properly to safeguard the patient.

1 (1950) 94 Sol Jo 599.

1.69   Following the decision in *Bolitho*, the Court of Appeal considered a case which involved a qualitative analysis of the evidence of the expert practitioner called in support of the defendant's conduct. In *Marriott v West Midlands HA*[1] a GP left a patient at home despite (as was found) the fact that he knew of a history of head injury and increasing symptoms of drowsiness and headache. After subjecting the expert evidence in support of the defendant's conduct to analysis, HHJ Alton concluded that the defendant's conduct fell below the appropriate standard of care.

1 [1999] Lloyd's Rep Med 23.

1.70   The members of the Court of Appeal who heard *Marriott* disagreed as to whether *Bolitho* applied (the majority applied it), or did not arise (per Pill LJ, on the basis that on the facts the judge had found against the defendant's personal recollection upon which the expert evidence brought on his behalf was based). In *Birch v University College London Hospital NHS Foundation Trust*[1] Cranston J emphasised that a judge without medical training should be cautious before concluding that a professional opinion could not withstand logical analysis.

'By suggesting that the court can depart from professional opinion in rare cases, Lord Browne-Wilkinson was indicating that such an opinion is not to be lightly set aside. The body of medical opinion must be incapable of withstanding logical analysis, in other words, cannot be logically supported at all …

Not only am I bound by this view but I conceive it to be eminently sensible: it would be folly for a judge with no training in medicine to conclude that one body of medical opinion should be preferred over another, when both are professionally sanctioned and both withstand logical attack'[2].

1 (2008) 104 BMLR 168.
2 (2008) 104 BMLR 168 at [55].

1.71   *Marriott* highlights the court's duty to weigh up and evaluate the evidence. This is a truism of court procedure, but its application to clinical negligence cases is of particular importance. In *Smith v Southampton University Hospital NHST* it was said that:

'Where there is a clear conflict of medical opinion, the court's duty is not merely to say which view it prefers, but to explain why it prefers one to the other'[1].

In *Smith*'s case the claimant had sustained injury in the course of a procedure ancillary to a radical hysterectomy. The defence expert was eminent and he supported the action taken by the practitioner whose conduct of the procedure was criticised. It was emphasised by the Court of Appeal in allowing the appeal that a judge at first instance should not merely refer to the *Bolam* principle and then in effect find that the claimant has failed to prove to that standard because the defence expert's evidence is preferred. The judge must give reasons, which will of course entail consideration of the qualifications, experience and credibility of the experts who have given evidence, but also must include consideration of the procedure involved, the problem it posed for the practitioner at the time, and how each of the experts has dealt with the evidence about whether or not the practitioner fell short of the appropriate standard.

1 [2007] EWCA Civ 387, (2007) 96 BMLR 79, per Wall LJ at [44].

1.72 Subject to the appropriate analysis of the acts or omissions complained of, however, compliance by a healthcare practitioner with an accepted practice is likely to be fatal to a claim of clinical negligence. The evidential and practical consequences of this are discussed below.

Particular aspects of the standard of care

The specialist

1.73 It is inherent within the *Bolam* test itself that the specialist is expected to achieve the standard of care of the reasonably competent specialist practising in that field. This was recognised by Lord Bridge in *Sidaway v Governors of the Bethlem Royal Hospital*:

'The language of the *Bolam* test clearly requires a different degree of skill from a specialist in his own special field than from a general practitioner. In the field of neuro-surgery it would be necessary to substitute for the ... phrase "no doctor of ordinary skill", the phrase "no neuro-surgeon of ordinary skill". All this is elementary, and ... firmly established law'[1].

1 [1985] 1 All ER 643 at 660f–g.

1.74 The more skills a person in a specialist field possesses, the higher the standard of skill expected of him. However, he is not required to attain the highest degree of skill and competence, merely a reasonable level of skill within that field. The *Bolam* test will therefore be applied simply by substituting surgeon, dermatologist etc in the place of doctor without gloss either way[1].

1 Kilner Brown J, in *Ashcroft v Mersey Regional Health Authority* [1983] 2 All ER 245; affd [1985] 2 All ER 96, CA.

The alternative medical practitioner

1.75   The alternative medical practitioner is expected to achieve the standard of care of the reasonably competent practitioner in the relevant type or class of alternative medicine. Additionally, however, it will in an appropriate case be necessary for the court to have regard to the appropriate standard of care of the orthodox practitioners alongside whom he practises. In particular, he may owe his patient a duty not to administer remedies which are actually or potentially harmful to the knowledge of such practitioners. In *Shakoor v Situ*[1] the claimant's husband died from acute liver failure after taking traditional Chinese herbal medicine prescribed by the defendant. It was held that the appropriate equivalent orthodox speciality to be borne in mind was that of an ordinary careful GP, and that the alternative practitioner had, as against this standard, not been negligent.

1   Bernard Livesey QC sitting as Dep HCJ, [2000] 1 WLR 410.

Inexperience

1.76   The standard of care expected of the reasonable man is objective, paying no regard to the frailties, idiosyncrasies or weaknesses of the defendant[1]. Accordingly, inexperience will afford no defence to an allegation of negligence, as was confirmed by the Court of Appeal in *Wilsher v Essex Area Health Authority*[2]. An example of this can be seen in *Djemal v Bexley HA*[3], where the inexperience of a casualty officer afforded no defence where an inadequate history had been taken.

1   *Glasgow Corpn v Muir* [1943] AC 448.
2   [1987] QB 730; see also *Nettleship v Weston* [1971] 2 QB 691.
3   [1995] 6 Med LR 269.

1.77   It will be recalled that in *Wilsher* a junior doctor acquiring training and experience in an intensive care neonatal unit inserted a catheter into a vein rather than an artery, so (allegedly) causing – together with the registrar, who failed to check and then made the same error – serious injury to the infant patient's sight.

The Court of Appeal held by a majority[1], on the issue of the appropriate standard of care, that the law requires the trainee or learner to be judged by the same standards as his more experienced colleagues. The majority view on this issue was expressed by Mustill LJ thus:

'To my mind, this notion of a duty tailored to the actor, rather than to the act which he elects to perform, has no place in the law of tort. Indeed, the defendants did not contend that it could be justified by any reported authority on the general law of tort. Instead, it was suggested that the medical profession is a special case. Public hospital medicine has always been organised so that young doctors and nurses learn on the job. If the hospitals abstained from using inexperienced people, they could not staff their wards and theatres, and the junior staff could never learn. The longer-term interests of patients as a whole are best served by maintaining the present system, even though this may diminish the legal rights of the individual patient for, after all, medicine is about curing, not litigation.

I acknowledge the appeal of this argument ... Nevertheless, I cannot accept that there should be a special rule for doctors in public hospitals ... To my mind, it would be a false step to subordinate the legitimate expectation of the patient that he will receive from each person concerned with his care a degree of skill appropriate to the task which he undertakes to an understandable wish to minimise the psychological and financial pressures on hard-pressed young doctors'[2].

1 On this issue Browne-Wilkinson LJ dissented, but as we have already seen, he would have found in favour of *direct* liability of the health authority.
2 [1986] 3 All ER 801, per Mustill LJ at 813 d–g.

Prevention of the self-infliction of harm

1.78   A case of liability for self-harm by a patient is *Selfe v Ilford and District Hospital Management Committee*[1]. A 17-year-old patient was admitted to what was in fact a general ward after having taken an overdose of sleeping pills. He was put on the ground floor with an open window at the back of his bed, which was grouped with the beds of three other patients who had demonstrated suicidal tendencies. He absconded through the window and climbed some steps onto a roof from which he threw himself, sustaining serious injuries. The health authority was held negligent, and the judge observed that the duty of those in charge of such a patient included the duty to avoid actions by the patient himself which could foreseeably occur and cause self-inflicted harm.

1 (1970) 114 Sol Jo 935.

1.79   The decision in *Selfe* involved, inter alia, consideration of staffing levels: insofar as this issue has resource implications these are discussed in this chapter. In *Selfe* there had been three nurses on duty in the ward to which Mr Selfe was admitted, and each of them knew that he presented a risk of suicide and had to be kept under constant observation. In addition to the charge nurse there was another nurse who, just before the occurrence which gave rise to this action, had gone to the lavatory without informing the charge nurse. The third on duty, a nursing auxiliary, went into the ward kitchen and was out of vision of the patient. The charge nurse answered a call for assistance by another patient, with the result that none of the staff were observing Mr Selfe. The judge was highly critical of the ward organisation, saying that the incident should never have been allowed to happen, and would not have happened if three or even two nurses had been in the ward keeping Mr Selfe under observation.

1.80   The decision in *Selfe* demonstrates the legal duty owed by the provider unit to a patient who is a known suicide risk to institute and maintain a safe environment for the patient. In considering such cases practitioners must now also have regard to the positive obligations imposed to protect life by Article 2 of the European Convention of Human Rights following the decisions in *Savage v South Essex Partnership NHS Foundation Trust*[1] and *Rabone v Pennine Care NHS Foundation Trust*[2]. A full discussion of the application of human rights law is to be found at **Chapter 4**.

1 [2009] 1 AC 681.
2 [2012] 2 AC 72.

1.81   As to the standard of care, decisions will depend on their own facts. Thus a different result was reached in *Thorne v Northern Group Hospital Management Committee*[1]. In that case the deceased was being nursed in a medical ward of a general hospital, whose ward sister knew that she had threatened suicide. Arrangements were instituted to transfer her to a psychiatric unit, but the deceased somehow managed to leave the hospital unobserved, went home and committed suicide. An allegation of negligence against the hospital and its staff, in particular the nurses, failed.

1 (1964) 108 Sol Jo 484.

1.82   Edmund Davies J, as he then was, held that the degree of care and supervision required of hospital staff in relation to a patient with known or suspected suicidal tendencies was clearly greater than that called for in relation to patients generally. But, as to the standard of care applicable, he asked:

'Could it be said that a member of the hospital staff should have remained constantly in sight of the patient until she had departed for the neurosis unit, and ought they to have reasonably foreseen that she might make an unannounced departure from the ward or hospital, or, in some other way, do something harmful to herself?'

He concluded that the deceased:

'... was set upon making her escape for the purpose of self-destruction, and it was highly conceivable that she kept a wary eye on the nurses and seized her opportunity immediately their backs were turned and they had absented themselves temporarily'.

That did not, he held, connote negligence on the part of the nurses. The defendant health authority was therefore not liable in negligence.

1.83   In *Drake v Pontefract HA*[1] a claim by a claimant who attempted suicide by jumping from a footbridge, but survived, seriously disabled, succeeded against the defendant health authority. One finding was (by contrast with *Thorne*'s case) that the claimant *should* have been observed on a one-to-one basis: that should, however, be taken in context and together with the extensive findings made against the defendant's doctors, who were found to have failed in their duty to give her an adequate psychiatric examination, to arrive at the appropriate diagnosis, and thereafter to treat her by appropriate medication; further the defendant's staff after her admission were held to have failed properly to evaluate her high risk of suicide.

1 [1999] Lloyd's Med Rep 425.

1.84   Whilst suicide could be a *novus actus* if a person took his own life as a conscious decision in the absence of any disabling mental illness[1], where a person is not fully responsible for their actions by reason of mental illness such as depression the defence will not apply. See *Corr v IBC Vehicles Ltd*[2].

1 *Corr v IBC Vehicles Ltd* [2008] 1 AC 884 at 904B, applying *Wright v Davidson* (1992) 88 DLR (4th) 698.
2 [2008] 1 AC 884.

Disclosure of risks

1.85   The tendency of English courts had been to apply the *Bolam*[1] approach to all aspects of the practitioner-patient relationship, from initial information, through diagnosis and advice, to treatment and aftercare. In addition to the well-known passage in his direction to the jury which has become the encapsulation of the law referred to as 'the *Bolam* test', McNair J directed the jury thus:

'You have to make up your minds whether it has been proved to your satisfaction that when the defendants adopted the practice they did (namely, the practice of saying very little and waiting for questions from the patient), they were falling below a proper standard of competent professional opinion on the question of whether or not it is right to warn'[2].

The *Bolam* test was, however, firmly rejected as the test to be applied to decide whether a doctor's omission to advise a patient of risks involved in treatment amounted to a breach of duty of care, following a decision of the Supreme Court's decision in *Montgomery v Lanarkshire Health Board*[3].

1 [1957] 2 All ER 118.
2 [1957] 2 All ER 118 at 126.
3 [2015] UKSC 11.

1.86 While, as is pointed out elsewhere[1], the law had moved on in respect of the question of enquiring or non-enquiring patients, prior to *Montgomery* it had been accepted that a practitioner's duty of care to a patient was an indivisible whole.

Lord Diplock observed in the case of *Sidaway v Bethlem Royal Hospital Governors*[2]:

'In English Jurisprudence the doctor's relationship with his patient which gives rise to the normal duty of care to exercise his skill and judgment to improve that patient's health in any particular respect in which the patient has sought aid has hitherto been treated as a single comprehensive duty covering all the ways in which a doctor is called on to exercise his skill and judgment in the improvement of the physical or mental condition of the patient for which his services as a general practitioner or as a specialist have been engaged'[3].

As such, the majority's view was that the *Bolam* test should be used to determine whether a doctor has satisfied his duty to warn a patient of the risks of treatment. Lord Diplock stated:

'To decide what risks the existence of which a patient should be voluntarily warned and the terms in which such warning, if any, should be given, having regard to the effect that the warning may have, is as much an exercise of professional skill and judgment as any other part of the doctor's comprehensive duty of care to the individual patient, and expert medical evidence on this matter should be treated in just the same way. The *Bolam* test should be applied'[4].

Lord Diplock formed the view that judges would nonetheless ensure that a medical practitioner would be required to answer questions from the inquisitive patient determined to make his own mind up[5]. The majority held there was no duty to provide unsolicited information when dealing with those who were less forthcoming with their concerns:

'The only effect that mention of risks can have on the patient's mind, if it has any at all, can be in the direction of deterring the patient from undergoing the treatment which in the expert opinion of the doctor it is in the patient's interest to undergo'[6].

1 See **Chapter 11**.
2 [1985] 1 All ER 643 at 667h–668b.
3 [1985] 1 All ER 643 at 668b–d.

4 [1985] 1 All ER 643 at 657g and 659d–e.
5 [1985] 1 All ER 643 at 659b–c.
6 [1985] 1 All ER 643 at 659c–d.

1.87 In his dissenting speech Lord Scarman warned of the implications of the majority decision to allow the medical profession to determine the extent of the duty to warn by applying the *Bolam* test. He said:

'The implications of this view of the law are disturbing. It leaves the determination of a legal duty to the judgment of doctors. Responsible medical judgment may, indeed, provide the law with an acceptable standard in determining whether a doctor in diagnosis or treatment has complied with his duty. But is it right that medical judgment should determine whether there exists a duty to warn of risk and its scope? It would be a strange conclusion if the courts should be led to conclude that our law, which undoubtedly recognises a right in the patient to decide whether he will accept or reject the treatment proposed, should permit the doctors to determine whether and in what circumstances a duty arises requiring the doctor to warn his patient of the risks inherent in the treatment which he proposes'[1].

Lord Scarman instead took a different starting point, one which was far ahead of its time. He emphasised the importance of 'the patient's right to make his own decision, which may be seen as a basic human right protected by the common law'[2]. As such, the law should provide a remedy where there had been a failure to respect the patient's rights:

'If, therefore, the failure to warn a patient of the risks inherent in the operation which is recommended does constitute a failure to respect the patient's right to make his own decision, I can see no reason in principle why, if the risk materialises and injury or damage is caused, the law should not recognise and enforce a right in the patient to compensation by way of damages'[3].

1 [1985] 1 All ER 643 at 649e–g.
2 [1985] 1 All ER 643 at 649g–h.
3 [1985] 1 All ER 643 at 651f–g.

1.88 Commonwealth jurisdictions were first to move away from the approach in *Sidaway*, echoing the concerns of Lord Scarman. In Canada, the Supreme Court of Canada held in *Reibl v Hughes* that:

'Merely because medical evidence establishes the reasonableness of a recommended operation does not mean that a reasonable person in the patient's position would necessarily agree to it, if proper disclosure had been made of the risks attendant upon it, balanced by those against it'[1].

Laskin CJ famously observed:

'To allow expert medical evidence to determine what risks are material and, hence, should be disclosed and, correlatively, what risks are not material is to hand over to the medical profession the entire question of the scope of the duty of disclosure, including the question whether there has been a breach of that duty'.

1 (1980) 114 DLR (3d) 1. See also the decision of the Supreme Court of New South Wales in *Rogers v Whittaker* [1992] 3 Med LR 331 (upheld by the High Court of Australia): (1992) 109 ALR 625 (High Ct Aus).

1.89 In *Pearce v United Bristol Healthcare NHS Trust*[1] Lord Woolf MR signalled that an approach which did not depend on the *Bolam* test could be taken where a significant risk existed.

'In a case where it is being alleged that a plaintiff has been deprived of the opportunity to make a proper decision as to what course he or she should take in relation to treatment, it seems to me to be the law, as indicated in the cases to which I have just referred, that if there is a significant risk which would affect the judgment of a reasonable patient, then in the normal course it is the responsibility of a doctor to inform the patient of that significant risk, if the information is needed so that the patient can determine for him or herself as to what course he or she should adopt'[2].

1 [1999] PIQR P 53.
2 [1999] PIQR P 53 at [21].

1.90 This approach was then adopted in *Wyatt v Curtis*[1] by Sedley LJ. Again departing from *Bolam*, he held that a medical practitioner could be expected to warn of substantial and grave risks having regard to how seriously the risks would be viewed as such by the patient:

'...what is substantial and what is grave are questions on which the doctor's and the patient's perception may differ, and in relation to which the doctor must therefore have regard to what may be the patient's perception. To the doctor, a chance in a hundred that the patient's chickenpox may produce an abnormality in the foetus may well be an insubstantial chance, and an abnormality may in any case not be grave. To the patient, a new risk which (as I read the judge's appraisal of the expert evidence) doubles, or at least enhances, the background risk of a potentially catastrophic abnormality may well be both substantial and grave, or at least sufficiently real for her to want to make an informed decision about it'[2].

1 [2003] EWCA Civ 1779.
2 [2003] EWCA Civ 1779 at [16].

1.91 Lord Woolf's formulation of the duty to warn was applied in *Chester v Afshar*. Lord Steyn said that:

'A surgeon owes a legal duty to a patient to warn him or her in general terms of possible serious risks involved in the procedure. The only qualification is that there may be wholly exceptional cases where objectively in the best interests of the patient the surgeon may be excused from giving a warning. This is, however, irrelevant in the present case. In modern law medical paternalism no longer rules and a patient has a prima facie right to be informed by a surgeon of a small, but well established, risk of serious injury as a result of surgery'[1].

As such, the surgeon was in breach of his duty to warn the claimant of the 0.9 per cent risk of cauda equina damage which eventuated, leading to paralysis. Lord Walker observed that in the 20 years since *Sidaway* the importance of personal autonomy had been more widely recognised. Patients were, he said, entitled to information and advice about possible alternative or variant treatments where a decision might have a profound effect on health and wellbeing. Even though the risk was not increased by the failure to warn and the patient had not shown that she would never have had an operation carrying the same risk, the test for causation would be modified to allow recovery to avoid the duty being hollow. However, their Lordships stopped short of finding that the *Bolam* test should no longer be used or that *Sidaway* was wrongly decided.

1 [2004] UKHL 41 at [20].

1.92 All questions of failure to warn of risks must now be viewed in light of the Supreme Court's decision in *Montgomery v Lanarkshire Health Board*[1].

Mrs Montgomery was a lady of small stature who was also diabetic. As diabetics are more likely to give birth to larger babies, during her pregnancy Mrs Montgomery was seen by a consultant obstetrician. At her 36-week appointment it was noted that Mrs Montgomery was worried about the size of her baby. The consultant chose not to inform Mrs Montgomery of the 9–10 per cent risk of shoulder dystocia, because the risk of serious injury was, in her estimation, very slight. The consultant's evidence was that had she informed Mrs Montgomery of the risk she would no doubt have requested a Caesarean section.

1 [2015] UKSC 11.

1.93   During an induced delivery, shoulder dystocia occurred. The umbilical cord was completely or partially occluded for twelve minutes, depriving the baby of oxygen. The baby was born with cerebral palsy in addition to a brachial plexus injury leading to paralysis of one arm.

During the trial, the expert called by the claimant conceded that an explanation that warned the patient that there were risks due to the size of the baby and that if things went wrong there would be a need for a Caesarean section would be acceptable, subject to the proviso that the mother was then asked, 'Are you happy with that decision?' This was accepted, even though the suggested warning did not specifically mention shoulder dystocia or the risk of cord occlusion.

The Court of Session[1] accordingly rejected the claimant's argument that she should have been told of the risk of shoulder dystocia. Following the approach of the majority in *Sidaway*, and based on the expert evidence, it was held that the *Bolam* test had not been satisfied. The Court of Session said that it was only if the claimant had asked specifically about the risks of shoulder dystocia that a duty to warn would have arisen. For good measure the Court of Session also concluded that even if the claimant had been advised about the risk of serious harm to her baby as a consequence of shoulder dystocia, she would not have opted for a Caesarean. The claimant appealed.

1 [2013] CSIH 3.

1.94   A panel of seven Supreme Court Justices unanimously allowed the claimant's appeal. Their Lordships noted that in England and Wales, lower courts had tacitly ceased to apply the *Bolam* test in relation to the advice given by doctors to their patients, and had effectively adopted Lord Scarman's approach. That was reflected in the guidance issued by the Department of Health and the General Medical Council, which treated *Chester* as the leading authority. The law had moved on from *Sidaway* to recognise the importance of a patient's right to make their own decision as to the risks they were prepared to run, rather than viewing patients as passive recipients of care. Further, patients were now generally better informed. A default assumption of ignorance, with the exception of highly educated men of experience, was no longer tenable.

1.95   The correct approach was set out in a joint judgment between Lord Kerr and Lord Reed (with whom Lord Neuberger, Lord Clarke, Lord Wilson and Lord Hodge agreed):

'48…The determination of the scope of the doctor's duty, and the question whether she had acted in breach of her duty, were however ultimately legal rather than medical in character'.

And:

'84…because the extent to which a doctor may be inclined to discuss risks with a patient is not determined by medical learning or experience, the application of the *Bolam* test to this question is liable to result in the sanctioning of differences in practice which are attributable not to divergent schools of thought in medical science, but merely to divergent attitudes among doctors as to the degree of respect owed to their patients'.

The duty of care is thus a legal issue which is informed by medical practice but not determined by it. The court continued:

'87 An adult person of sound mind is entitled to decide which, if any, of the available forms of treatment to undergo, and her consent must be obtained before treatment interfering with her bodily integrity is undertaken. The doctor is therefore under a duty to take reasonable care to ensure that the patient is aware of any material risks involved in any recommended treatment, and of any reasonable alternative or variant treatments. The test of materiality is whether, in the circumstances of the particular case, a reasonable person in the patient's position would be likely to attach significance to the risk, or the doctor is or should reasonably be aware that the particular patient would be likely to attach significance to it.

88 The doctor is however entitled to withhold from the patient information as to a risk if he reasonably considers that its disclosure would be seriously detrimental to the patient's health. The doctor is also excused from conferring with the patient in circumstances of necessity, as for example where the patient requires treatment urgently but is unconscious or otherwise unable to make a decision. It is unnecessary for the purposes of this case to consider in detail the scope of those exceptions'.

Their Lordships also advised that: (1) the assessment of whether a risk is material cannot be reduced to percentages. Such an assessment would always be fact-sensitive, and sensitive also to the characteristics of the patient; (2) information provided as part of the doctor's advisory capacity must be comprehensible. Bombarding the patient with technical information would not fulfil the doctor's duty; (3) the therapeutic exception should not be used to enable the doctor to prevent the patient from making an informed choice where she is liable to make a choice which the doctor considers to be contrary to her best interests[1].

The Supreme Court went on to find that, as the consultant had acknowledged, had the risks and potential consequences of shoulder dystocia been discussed dispassionately with the claimant, she would probably have opted for a Caesarean. As such the claim succeeded. It was not necessary to consider whether in the light of *Chester v Afshar*[2] causation could be established on some other basis[3].

1 [2015] UKSC 11 at [89]–[91].
2 [2004] UKHL 41.
3 A useful discussion on how *Montgomery* is to be applied to cases involving disclosure of risk and the legal effects of a failure to provide information on a patient's consent is contained in *Connolly v Croydon Health Services NHS Trust* [2015] EWHC 1376 (QB).

Negligence and malcommunication

1.96   Probably as many medical accidents are caused by deficiencies in communication as are caused by failure to exercise ordinary skill and competence in diagnosis and treatment. Typical is the discharge from an accident and emergency department of an elderly person who has just received treatment, without making adequate arrangements for safe discharge and return to home or another place of safety.

1.97   Deficiencies in communication may occur as between members of the same, or different, professions involved in an individual patient's treatment and care. Examples include unclear instructions by a surgeon to an anaesthetist or theatre nurse; unclear care plans on the ward; and unclear or illegible prescriptions for medication. Legal liability for injury to a patient resulting from deficiencies in communication may fall on both or all parties concerned, and not just on the shoulders of the person whose instruction is initially unclear. In *Prendergast v Sam and Dee Ltd*[1] a dispensing pharmacist was held 75 per cent to blame for the harmful consequences of an erroneous prescription, the balance of the blame resting with the GP who wrote it.

1 [1989] 1 Med LR 36, CA.

1.98   Deficiencies in communication may amount to 'maladministration' susceptible to investigation by the Parliamentary and Health Service Ombudsman[1].

1 See www.ombudsman.org.uk. For further consideration of the jurisdiction of the Commissioner to investigate, see **Chapter 3**.

ESTABLISHING BREACH

Proof of negligence

1.99   The legal burden of proof in all clinical negligence cases lies on the claimant. The standard of proof required to discharge that burden is on the balance of probabilities.

1.100   Where the claim involves an allegation of clinical negligence and an attack on the competence of the professional man, the standard of proof required to discharge the legal burden of establishing negligence on the balance of probabilities is commensurate with the perceived gravity of the allegation[1]:

'A charge of professional negligence against a medical man was a serious charge, on a different footing to a charge of negligence against a motorist or an employer. The reason is because the consequences for the professional man are far more grave. A finding of negligence affects his standing and reputation. It impairs the confidence which his clients have in him. The burden of proof is correspondingly greater. The principle applies that: "In proportion as the charge is grave, so ought the proof to be clear": see *Hornal v Neuberger Products Ltd* [1957] 1 QB 247.

Another difference lies in the fact that, with the best will in the world, things do sometimes go amiss in surgical operations or medical treatment. A striking illustration was *Roe v Minister of Health* [1954] 2 QB 66. So a doctor is not to be held negligent simply because something goes wrong. It is not right to invoke against him the maxim *res ipsa loquitur* save in an extreme case. He is not liable for mischance or misadventure. Nor is he liable for an error of judgment. He is not liable for choosing one course out of two which may be open to him, or for following one school of thought rather than another. He is liable only if he falls below the standard of a reasonably competent practitioner in his field – so much so that his conduct may fairly be held to be – I will not say deserving of censure, but, at any rate, inexcusable'[2].

1 Per Lord Denning MR in *Hucks v Cole* (1993) 4 Med LR 393 at 396; adopted in *Bolitho*.
2 (1993) 4 Med LR 393 at 484.

Role of the expert

1.101   If compliance with a properly accepted practice will defeat any claim of negligence, it follows that the claimant must establish either that the accepted practice was improperly so accepted or that no reasonable doctor could have behaved in the way the defendant did. A graphic example of the evidential consequences of *Bolam* is provided by *Maynard v West Midlands Regional Health Authority*[1].

1 [1984] 1 WLR 634, [1985] 1 All ER 635.

1.102   Mrs Maynard consulted a surgeon and a consultant physician with symptoms indicative of tuberculosis. However, in the opinion of both the physician and the surgeon, Hodgkin's Disease, carcinoma and sarcoidosis were also possibilities. Because Hodgkin's Disease was fatal unless remedial steps were taken in its early stages, they decided that, rather than await the result of a sputum test, which would involve some weeks' delay, a mediastinoscopy should be performed to provide them with a biopsy. Such a procedure, even when carefully performed, carries a known risk of damage to the left recurrent laryngeal nerve. Although the operation was carried out properly, that injury in fact ensued. The biopsy subsequently proved negative and the claimant was subsequently confirmed to be suffering from tuberculosis. The claimant brought an action against the defendant health authority contending, inter alia, that the decision to carry out the mediastinoscopy rather than await the result of the sputum test had been negligent. At trial a distinguished body of expert medical opinion was called, approving of the operation. However, the judge preferred the evidence of an expert witness called for the claimant who had stated that the case had almost certainly been one of tuberculosis from the outset and should have been so diagnosed. To undertake the mediastinoscopy was unnecessary, dangerous and accordingly negligent, he said.

1.103   The Court of Appeal had no hesitation in upholding the judge on causation but reversed him on negligence. The decision of the Court of Appeal was upheld by the House of Lords.

'I have to say that a judge's "preference" for one body of distinguished professional opinion to another also professionally distinguished is not sufficient to establish negligence in a practitioner whose actions have received the seal of approval if those opinions, truthfully expressed, honestly held, were not preferred. If this was the real reason for the judge's finding, he erred in law even though elsewhere in his judgment he stated the law correctly. For in the realm of diagnosis and treatment negligence is not established by preferring one respectable body of professional opinion to another.

Failure to exercise the ordinary skill of a doctor (in the appropriate speciality, if he be a specialist) is necessary'[1].

1 [1984] 1 WLR 634, [1985] 1 All ER 635 at 639d, per Lord Scarman.

1.104 Compliance with an accepted practice will in all probability satisfy the *Bolam* test and thereby defeat an allegation of negligence. This raises the obvious question: will departure from accepted practice constitute prima facie evidence of negligence? This question arose in *Clark v MacLennan*[1].

1 [1983] 1 All ER 416.

1.105 In that case the claimant suffered from stress incontinence after the delivery of her first child. Early attempts at conservative treatment failed to bring about any improvement in her condition. An anterior colporrhaphy operation was carried out one month and eleven days after the birth. It was normal practice amongst gynaecologists not to perform such an operation until at least three months after birth so as to ensure its success and to prevent the risk of haemorrhage. The operation was not successful and after it was performed haemorrhage occurred causing the repair to break down. Two further operations were unsuccessful, with the result that the stress incontinence from which the claimant suffered became a permanent disability.

1.106 Peter Pain J held that while it was for the claimant to prove negligence, once she had established that the defendants had departed from an accepted practice designed to guard her from the very sort of harm she suffered, the burden shifted to the defendants to justify their departure, which they failed to do.

In doing so his Lordship sought to rely on *McGhee v National Coal Board*[1]. In that case the claimant, who worked at the defendants' brick kilns, contracted dermatitis as the result of exposure to brick dust. The defendants were not at fault in allowing the exposure during working hours, but were at fault for failing to provide adequate washing facilities, thereby increasing the period of time the claimant was exposed to the dust before he could return home and wash. It was accepted that the dust had caused the claimant's dermatitis. However, such was the state of current medical knowledge that it could not be established whether or not the claimant would have contracted dermatitis had he been able to take a shower at work. The claimant could not therefore establish that 'but for' the 'guilty' exposure he would not have suffered dermatitis. A majority of the House of Lords, however, were prepared to equate (in the absence of other evidence) a 'material increase in the risk' with a 'material contribution' to the damage. Purporting to apply this, Peter Pain J said:

'It is very difficult to draw a distinction between the damage and the duty where the duty arises only because of a need to guard against the damage. In *McGhee's* case it was accepted that there was a breach of duty. In the present case the question of whether there was a breach remains in issue. It seems to me that it follows from *McGhee* that where there is a situation in which a general duty of care arises and there is a failure to take a precaution, and that very damage occurs against which the precaution is designed to be a protection, then the burden lies on the defendant to show that he was not in breach of duty as well as to show that the damage did not result from his breach of duty'[2].

1 [1972] 3 All ER 1008.
2 *Clark v MacLennan* [1983] 1 All ER 416 at 427f–g.

1.107   However, the Court of Appeal in *Wilsher v Essex Area Health Authority*[1] was critical of such an approach:

'None the less, I would find it impossible, unless impelled by binding authority, to hold that proof of primary facts constituting negligence is in some way dispensed with merely by showing that some step, which is designed to minimise or avert a risk, has not in the particular circumstances been taken'[2].

Mustill LJ then went on to state:

'If I may say so, the summary of the evidence contained in the judgment in *Clark v MacLennan* has certainly persuaded me that, as a decision on the facts, the case is unimpeachable. Moreover, although the judge indicated that he proposed to decide the case on the burden of proof, this could be understood as an example of the forensic commonplace that, where one party has, in the course of a trial, hit the ball into the other's court, it is for that other to return it. But the prominence given in the judgment to *McGhee* and the citation from *Clark* in the present case suggest that the judge may have set out to assert a wider proposition, to the effect that in certain kinds of case of which *Clark* and the present form examples, there is a general burden of proof on the defendant. If this is so, then I must respectfully say that I find nothing in *McGhee* or in general principle to support it'[3].

This latter passage is reminiscent of the approach encapsulated in the maxim *res ipsa loquitur*.

1 [1986] 3 All ER 801.
2 [1986] 3 All ER 801, per Mustill LJ at 814g.
3 [1986] 3 All ER 801 at 815e–g.

Res ipsa loquitur

1.108   If successful, the application of *res ipsa loquitur* has the practical effect of shifting the argument on negligence to the defendant's shoulders. Thus, while it is for the claimant to prove his case in negligence on the balance of probabilities (ie that it is more likely than not that there was negligence), circumstances can arise in which the defendant is put to an explanation of how the matter in hand (the *res*, or event) could have occurred in the absence of negligence. The nature of this contention was most memorably explained by Denning LJ in *Cassidy v Ministry of Health*[1] in which a patient entered hospital for treatment of Dupuytren's contracture of the hand and left in a worse state. Denning LJ said:

'If the claimant had to prove that some particular doctor or nurse is negligent, he would not be able to do it. But he was not put to that impossible task: he says, "I went into the hospital to be cured of two stiff fingers. I have come out with four stiff fingers, and my hand is useless". That should not have happened if due care had been used. Explain it, if you can'.

1 [1951] 2 KB 343.

1.109   An issue which arises from time to time is the extent to which this maxim is now, in the context of clinical negligence cases, of practical application as a means for a claimant to discharge the burden of proof. The main authority on this evidential issue is now the judgment of the Court of Appeal in *Ratcliffe v Plymouth and Torbay HA*[1], which is discussed below.

1 (1998) Lloyd's Med Rep 162.

1.110 The former law on the requirements for the application of the maxim was set out in the judgment of Scott LJ in *Mahon v Osborne*[1], a case which involved an allegation that a swab had been negligently left post-operatively in the patient's body. It was held that for the defendant to be required to (in Denning LJ's later words) 'explain it if you can', the court must be satisfied that control over the relevant situation, environment or events rested solely with the defendant, and furthermore, that 'in the ordinary experience of mankind such an event does not happen unless the person in control has failed to exercise due care'.

1 [1939] 2 KB 14.

1.111 That judges could differ over the applicability, and therefore availability to the claimant, of the plea of *res ipsa loquitur* in any given case was demonstrated by the result in *Mahon v Osborne* itself, where Scott LJ dissented from his two brethren in the Court of Appeal which held by a majority that the plea was available on the particular facts of that case.

1.112 In practice the maxim is less likely to be of use to a claimant than might at first sight appear. In the first place, in a contested clinical negligence case the factual evidence of the claimant will almost invariably be supported by expert medical opinion, if not directly to the effect that there was negligence in specified respects, then at least to the effect that the result which occurred does not ordinarily occur in the absence of negligence. Second, the defendants will themselves expect to call both factual and expert evidence about the circumstances surrounding the procedure the subject of the proceedings.

1.113 This was noted by Brooke LJ in *Ratcliffe v Plymouth & Torbay HA*[1]. Having reviewed the authorities, he went on to set out an explanation of the effect of the maxim in practice[2]:

'... although in very simple situations the *res* may speak for itself at the end of the lay evidence adduced on behalf of the claimant, in practice the inference is then buttressed by expert evidence adduced on his behalf, and if the defendant were to call no evidence, the judge would be deciding the case on inferences he was entitled to draw from the whole of the evidence (including the expert evidence), and not on the application of the maxim in its purest form'.

Hobhouse LJ (as he then was) agreeing, pointed out that by the time of any final hearing full disclosure would have taken place, details of all parties' cases given, witness statements exchanged and experts' reports lodged. Trenchantly, he went on[3]:

'... if I were to say anything further it would be confined to suggesting that the expression *res ipsa loquitur* should be dropped from the litigator's vocabulary and replaced by the phrase a *prima facie* case. *Res ipsa loquitur* is not a principle of law: it does not relate to or raise any presumption. It is merely a guide to help to identify when a *prima facie* case is being made out. Where expert and factual evidence has been called on both sides at a trial its usefulness will normally have long since been exhausted'.

Accordingly in *Hussain v King Edward VII Hospital* Eady J said:

'There is no mystique about the doctrine of *res ipsa loquitur*. It does not represent a principle of law: nor can it be invoked as giving rise to a presumption of any kind. It is simply a conventional way of saying that the facts, as known to the claimant at the time he pleads his case, give rise in themselves to a *prima facie* case of negligence. This may or may not be upheld at trial, but at the pleading stage it has the effect of compelling the defendant to respond. Once the defendant has done so, the question will be whether the court has been satisfied in the light of *all* the evidence at trial that negligence and causation have been proved. Each case will depend upon its own facts. In the course of reaching a conclusion, the judge may or may not be prepared to draw the inference originally invited by the claimant'[4].

1 [1998] Lloyd's Rep Med 162 at 172 at [48]. See also *Delaney v Southmead Health Authority* [1995] 6 Med LR 355 per Stuart Smith J at 359.
2 [1998] Lloyd's Rep Med 162 at 172–173.
3 [1998] Lloyd's Rep Med 162 at 177.
4 [2012] EWHC 3441 (QB) at [11].

1.114   The usefulness of the maxim *res ipsa loquitur*, as such, may now be regarded as limited, but the principle behind it lives on. In the first place it would appear still to apply for example to simple situations (swab left in operation site, wrong limb removed, patient awake despite general anaesthetic)[1]. Second, an analogous principle has in effect continued to be applied, most notably in two cases[2] concerning the requirement for and carrying out of specialised scanning of infants in utero. In the second of these, *Lillywhite v University College London Hospitals NHS Trust*[3], the Court of Appeal considered *Ratcliffe* in detail, and (by a majority) noted that:

'… in some cases the evidence produced by a claimant may be such as to require the court to focus with some care on the explanation given by a defendant to displace that which would otherwise be the inevitable inference from the claimant's case that negligence has been established'[4].

It held that it was relevant to the application of this principle that the circumstances giving rise to the case before it had been a focused referral to a specialist based on the concerns of a non-specialist first radiographer; and, whilst the expert in question asserted that he had in fact visualised structures which subsequently turned out to be absent, there was no plausible explanation for how he could have done so in the exercise of reasonable care and skill so that the claimant succeeded in her claim of negligence.

1 Per Brooke LJ in *Ratcliffe v Plymouth and Torbay Health Authority* [1998] Lloyd's Rep Med 162 at 172. For an example of such situations see NHS England's list of 'Never Events' at https://www.england.nhs.uk/ourwork/patientsafety/never-events/. Never events are 'serious incidents that are wholly preventable as guidance or safety recommendations that provide strong systemic protective barriers are available at a national level and should have been implemented by all healthcare providers'.
2 *Lillywhite v University College London Hospitals NHS Trust* [2005] EWCA Civ 1466, [2006] Lloyd's Rep Med 268; and before that *Pithers v Leeds Teaching Hospitals NHS Trust* [2004] EWHC 1392 (QB), Holland J. For another case with a different result, in which an ultrasound scan which failed to detect an abnormality in the fetus was held to have been carried out competently, see *B v South Tyneside Healthcare NHS Trust* [2004] EWHC 1169 (QB), Simon J.
3 [2006] Lloyd's Rep Med 268.
4 [2006] Lloyd's Rep Med 268 at [30] per Latham LJ, adopted by Buxton LJ.

Precedent, practice and the use of literature in court

1.115   Considerable attention is paid, as a contested case nears trial and the expert evidence is prepared, to identifying all the medical or technical literature or administrative records which will assist the court in determining what was the accepted practice at the time of the alleged negligence, any relevant hospital protocols which prescribed local standards, and any other contemporaneous indications as to what appropriate practice was.

1.116   By contrast, the usefulness, when considering the issue of breach of duty, of decided cases as factual precedents for given fact-situations is limited. Similarly, consideration of 'best practice', though possibly useful as an indication of evolving knowledge and practice, is not in itself relevant to ascertainment of the appropriate standard of care.

DAMAGE

General requirement to prove: strictness of requirement

1.117   The burden of establishing that the conduct complained of caused harm or loss rests squarely on the shoulders of the claimant, the test most generally accepted by the courts being the 'but for' test: but for the negligence would the harm to the claimant have occurred in any event?

1.118   The application of the test is neatly demonstrated by the old case of *Barnett v Chelsea and Kensington Hospital Management Committee*[1]. Three night watchmen, one of whom was the claimant's husband, presented themselves at the defendant's hospital complaining of vomiting after drinking tea, which unknown at the time had been laced with arsenic. The nurse consulted the duty doctor by telephone who advised that the men should go home and see their own doctors in the morning. Later that day the claimant's husband died of arsenical poisoning. It was held that in failing to examine the watchmen, the doctor was in breach of his duty. However, even had the deceased been examined and treated, the probability was that he would have died in any event and the claim therefore failed.

1 [1969] 1 QB 428.

Breach must be causative and relevant

1.119   In the context of clinical negligence, issues of causation pose particular difficulties. The claimant will usually ex hypothesi have been suffering from illness in the first place. Further, though breach of duty may be held to have occurred, that particular breach of duty may be held in the particular time-sensitive circumstances of the case not to have been causative of the damage suffered.[1] *Anderson v Milton Keynes General NHS Trust and Oxford Radcliffe Hospital NHS Trust*[2] concerned a claimant who had suffered injury to his accident at work, and who after contracting MRSA was left with significant disability in, and pain and shortening of, the left leg. It was held that although there was an admitted breach of duty in that the presence of MRSA had not been notified in time to the plastic surgeons, on the balance of probabilities the bacteria would by the relevant time have been immune to attack, and further reconstructive surgery to the claimant's leg would have been required in any event, so that the hospital was not liable in damages.

1 See eg *Brooks v Home Office* (1999) 48 BMLR 109.
2 [2006] EWCA Civ 632, (2006) 150 SJLB 707, HHJ Macduff QC.

1.120   A number of points may be briefly noted:

(1)   the situation with claims of MRSA is for this reason particularly problematic (there are many problems here: frequently it is difficult to identify or in any event to prove to the requisite standard the source of an infection which is believed to have been hospital-originated). A current avenue of investigation in a number of ongoing cases is the potential for claims making joint use of allegations of common law breach of duty and breach of statutory duty involving allegations under the health and safety regime governing hospitals and healthcare premises[1];

(2)   the difficulties in proving damage as arising from relevant breach of duty as found by the court not infrequently leads to proliferation of the contested issues of breach of duty. In a single case a number of allegations of breach of duty may each need severally to be fought to a contested hearing and adjudicated upon, because the court's finding as to *which* breach of duty is or is not established will be material to whether the claimant recovers material (or any) damages;

(3)   consideration of the prospects of proof of causation will in many cases be an essential step in considering whether it is practical or economic to pursue any claim at all; in others it will be crucial in determining whether the claim is a substantial claim which will encompass all or most of a claimant's injury, pain and loss, or a relatively slight claim which needs to be pursued as economically as possible with an eye to settlement;

(4)   the decision of the court on the causation aspect of any case is in practice highly dependent upon the quality of the medical expert evidence adduced by either party (particularly the claimant).

1 See Medical Law Monitor (December 2006) Vol 13/12, at p 8.

Causation and proof in the field of clinical negligence: difficult issues

1.121   It is not the function of this chapter to explore in detail the logical problems posed by issues of causation, or the practical problems of proving it. For further consideration of legal arguments on causation, and of the logistics and requirements of evidence gathering, reference should be made to the full text in the relevant chapters of this book. However a useful summary of the law was provided by Otton LJ in *Tahir v Haringey Health Authority*[1]:

'(1) The burden of proving causation was upon the plaintiff.

(2) Causation is a question of past fact, to be decided on a balance of probabilities: see *Mallett v McMonagle* [1970] AC 166.

(3) If he proves that the negligence was the sole cause, or a substantial cause, or that it materially contributed to the damage, he will succeed in full: see *Bonnington Castings v Wardlaw* [1956] AC 613 and *McGhee v National Coal Board* [1973] 1 WLR 1.

(4) If he fails to cross this threshold then he fails to recover any damages: see *Barnett v Chelsea & Kensington Hospital Management Committee* [1969] 1 QB 428.

(5) A plaintiff cannot recover damages for the loss of a chance of a complete or better recovery: see *Hotson v East Berkshire District Health Authority* [1987] AC 750'.

1 [1998] Lloyds Rep (Med) 104.

1.122 It is, however, important at this stage to note the difficulty of some of the issues which arise, and the resulting necessity for careful analysis of the nature of the injury allegedly sustained, of the circumstances in which it occurred, and of the precise mechanism by which it came about. Particular difficulties have been encountered by the courts in dealing with the two following issues.

(1) Inability of the claimant to prove causation: proof of material contribution to the risk of the damage which occurred:

  (a) reference has already been made to the case of *McGhee v National Coal Board*, in which (because of the state of the then current medical knowledge) there was an evidential gap: the claimant could not establish 'but for' causation arising out of the defendants' admitted breach of duty in failing to provide showers. He could not prove that he would not have contracted dermatitis had he been able to take a shower at work. But he could show that the dermatitis was caused by repeated abrasion to the skin, and that the longer the delay between exposure and washing the worse was the abrasion problem; and the evidence was that washing would have materially reduced the risk of him developing dermatitis. A majority of the House of Lords were prepared to equate (in the absence of other evidence) a 'material increase in the risk' with a 'material contribution to the damage'[1];

  (b) in *Wilsher*[2] whilst it was admitted that a mistake had occurred when the child was over-oxygenated, and that he suffered from a serious eye condition which made him nearly blind, it was further agreed that premature babies could suffer the same form of injury from a number of causes which did not involve over-oxygenation. The House of Lords was not prepared to apply *McGhee*, on the basis that no-one could tell whether excess oxygen had in fact caused the injury.

  Wilsher and *McGhee* remain good law[3]. Nevertheless these authorities are not easy to reconcile; and it is suggested that the 'but for' test of causation may in appropriate cases be less strictly insisted on where the 'evidential gap' is caused by a deficit in the state of medical knowledge.

(2) No recovery for loss of a chance: In *Gregg v Scott*[4] the claimant suffered from a lump under his arm which was negligently misdiagnosed by the defendant as being benign but was in fact cancerous. Diagnosis was therefore delayed for a year after which the claimant attended another doctor who appropriately referred him. He contended that his prospects of cure and survival would have been better had be been diagnosed earlier, but it was held that because, at the time of his misdiagnosis, he had less than a 50 per cent chance of surviving more than 10 years anyway he was unable to recover. Since, it was said, his prospects of

survival had never been 50 per cent, he had lost only the chance of a better outcome, which did not sound in damages so that there was no claim.

The case may be thought to be a hard one, but it is highest authority for the proposition that there can be no claim in clinical negligence cases for loss of a chance. A claimant suing for alleged clinical negligence must prove that on the balance of probabilities the practitioner's breach of duty caused the damage of which he complains: nothing less will do.

1 [1972] 3 All ER 1008.
2 [1988] AC 1074, HL.
3 See *Barker v Corus (UK) Ltd* [2006] 2 AC 572, see especially the speech of Lord Hoffmann on *McGhee*; and see also *Fairchild v Glenhaven Funeral Services Ltd* [2002] UKHL 22, [2003] 1 AC 32, especially per Lord Nicholls on *McGhee*.
4 [2005] 2 AC 176.

Recovery for 'wrongful birth'

1.123   Such claims can be conveniently divided into three categories:

(1)   a claim by either parent for damages in respect of the costs of caring for or maintaining a child born as a result of an unwanted pregnancy or birth, or the losses resulting from having to bring up the child;
(2)   a claim by the mother for damages in respect of personal injury she has suffered as a result of pregnancy and labour, and such incidental consequential losses and expenses as arise; and
(3)   a claim by a disabled child for damages in respect of the child's disabilities, referred to as 'wrongful life' claims.

Limited damages may be awarded for categories (1) and (2); the law does not allow recovery of damages for claims in category (3) at present[1].

A successful claim for caring for a child as a result of an unwanted pregnancy in tort gives rise to a conventional award (currently £15,000[2]) for the loss of the freedom to limit the size of their family[3]. Claims for the ordinary costs of raising a child are not allowed on the basis that this is pure economic loss for which it is not fair, just and reasonable to award damages and/or on policy grounds[4]. However the additional costs of bringing up a disabled child which results from an unwanted pregnancy can be recovered[5]. The position of claims for the costs of raising a child in contract has yet to be clarified[6].

Whilst an award for personal injury as a result of a mother's pregnancy and labour and incidental consequential losses and expenses can be made, loss of earnings incurred due to caring for the child are not recoverable[7].

1 *McKay v Essex Area Health Authority* [1982] 2 QB 1166.
2 See Kemp and Kemp, Vol 1 at para [15-014].
3 *McFarlane v Tayside Health Board* [2000] 2 AC 59.
4 *McFarlane v Tayside Health Board.*
5 *Parkinson v St James and Seacroft University Hospital NHS Trust* [2001] EWCA Civ 530, [2002] QB 266 as approved in *Rees v Darlington Memorial Hospital NHS Trust* [2003] UKHL 52, [2003] 3 WLR 1091.
6 See the speech of Lord Clyde in *McFarlane* at 99F. In *Thomson v Sheffield Fertility Clinic* (24 November 2000, unreported) Hooper J (as he then was) held that the defendant had breached its contractual duty owed to a claimant who gave birth to triplets as a result of IVF treatment

in a private fertility clinic. Three embryos were implanted in the claimant's womb contrary to an agreement that only two embryos should be implanted. Quantum was compromised before the court could rule on the question of whether damages for the costs of raising a third child could be recovered in contract.
7 See the speech of Lord Hope in *McFarlane* at 89D–98E.

FURTHER CONTEXT OF CLINICAL NEGLIGENCE CASES: THE HUMAN RIGHTS ACT 1998

1.124   The HRA 1998 came into force on 2 October 2000. The Act provides that the rights[1] set out in the European Convention on Human Rights will have effect in domestic law, and that:

'so far as it is possible to do so, primary legislation and subordinate legislation must be read and given effect in a way which is compatible with the Convention rights'[2].

1 As defined at HRA 1998, s 1(1), and subject to specified derogation or reservation as per s 1(2).
2 HRA 1998, s 2(1).

1.125   Some provisions of the HRA 1998 are aimed at ensuring the compatibility of UK legislation with the Convention: thus, the courts may make a declaration that a provision of primary legislation is incompatible with a Convention right (s 4), and a Minister of the Crown in charge of a Bill in either House of Parliament must, before its second reading, make a statement about the compatibility of the Bill with Convention rights (s 19).

1.126   Of more direct relevance to the enforcement of the Convention in terms of private remedies is the provision by HRA 1998, s 6 that it is unlawful for a public authority to act in a way which is incompatible with a Convention right, and the provision by s 7 of a new cause of action where a public authority has acted in such a way. Moreover, since 'public authority' is expressly stated to include a court or tribunal[1] this in effect means that the courts in their decision making will be required to conform to the Convention, even in cases which do not involve a public authority, and this, it is thought by some, may result in the Convention applying to purely private litigation as well as litigation involving a public authority.

1 HRA 1998, s 6(3)(a).

The rights themselves: the Convention

1.127   The rights and freedoms guaranteed by the Convention and incorporated into domestic law are set out in the HRA 1998, Sch 1. These include the following:

(1)   right to life (Article 2);
(2)   right not to be subjected to torture or to inhuman or degrading treatment or punishment (Article 3);
(3)   right to liberty and security of person (Article 5);
(4)   right to a fair trial (Article 6);
(5)   right to respect for private and family life (Article 8);
(6)   freedom of expression (Article 10).

1.128 For present purposes it should be noted that each Article should be read and analysed carefully, as appears from the pre-2000 Strasbourg jurisprudence (and relevant decisions on the Convention in other jurisdictions). The European Court and Commission and the courts of other contracting states have been prepared to give a wide construction to the wording of the individual provisions.

1.129 Articles 1 and 13 of the Convention are not, as such, incorporated in Schedule 1 to the Act. These are the articles which respectively oblige contracting states to 'secure' Convention rights to everyone within their jurisdiction, and provide that anyone whose Convention rights are violated shall have an effective remedy before a national authority. The scheme of the HRA 1998, however, is that the courts in the UK will provide a forum for people here to raise rights issues and apply for remedies. In particular:

(1) by HRA 1998, s 2, a court determining a question which has arisen in connection with a Convention right must take into account (inter alia) judgments, decisions, declarations and advisory opinions of the European Court of Human Rights, and Commission opinions;

(2) by HRA 1998, s 8, a court may grant such relief or remedies within its powers as it considers just and appropriate, including (where a court has power to make an award of damages, or order compensation, in civil proceedings) such monetary award or order.

A full treatment of this topic appears at **Chapter 8**.

Development of the law since 2000

1.130 Although there was an initial reluctance to use the HRA 1998 in consideration of clinical negligence claims, it is submitted that it is becoming of greater significance, particularly in cases involving self-harm where Article 2 is engaged. Recent examples of use of the HRA 1998 by the claimant can be found in cases such as *R (on the application of Tracey) v Cambridge University Hospitals NHS Foundation Trust*[1] (Article 8) and *Coombs v Dorset NHS Primary Care Trust*[2] (Article 2).

1 [2014] EWCA Civ 822, [2014] 3 WLR 1054.
2 [2012] EWHC 521 (QB), [2012] Med LR 438.

CONCLUSION

1.131 This chapter has been concerned with an overview of the law: it is hoped that it has formed a sufficient basis for study of the more detailed and practical content of the book.

EDITORIAL NOTE ON THE GENERAL MEDICAL COUNCIL

The General Medical Council

1.132 The General Medical Council (GMC) is the professional regulatory body for medical practitioners. It was established under the Medical Act

1858. Its purpose was to protect the public and secure the exclusivity of the medical profession. All the GMC's functions derive from a statutory requirement for the establishment and maintenance of a register. The current statute that regulates the GMC is the Medical Act 1983 (the MA 1983), which has undergone consolidation with many amendments since.

1.133   The purpose of the GMC is set out in s 1A of the MA 1983:

'The main objective of the General Council in exercising their functions is to protect, promote and maintain the health and safety of the public'.

1.134   The past decades have seen a broadening of the GMC's function from one of preserving medical professional exclusivity and concomitant professional privileges, to one of promoting patient safety through regulation of doctors by registration and licensing, validation and revalidation. It was only as relatively recently as the Medical (Professional Performance) Act 1995 that the GMC became concerned with medical competence.

1.135   The MA 1983 contains detailed provisions and enabling provisions concerning professional regulation including: education and registration; fitness to practise and medical ethics; and privileges.

1.136   The GMC exercises a form of clinical governance by developing the concept of 'registers' to include: the register (provisional and full registration) for holders of primary qualifications; the general practitioner register; and, the specialist register. The register contains information as to whether a registered practitioner holds a licence to practise.

1.137   Through the device of registration the GMC thus can regulate the competence of the medical profession by undergraduate education and post-graduate training, licence to practise and revalidation.

1.138   Section 35 of the MA 1983 confers powers on the GMC to advise the medical profession on conduct, performance or ethics. The core professional advice is found in *Good Medical Practice*. It contains basic principles of medical professional practice which apply to all registered practitioners whether or not licensed to practise, in all professional situations whether or not clinical[1]. It provides as follows:

'Professionalism in action

1 Patients need good doctors. Good doctors make the care of their patients their first concern: they are competent, keep their knowledge and skills up to date, establish and maintain good relationships with patients and colleagues, are honest and trustworthy, and act with integrity and within the law.

2 Good doctors work in partnership with patients and respect their rights to privacy and dignity. They treat each patient as an individual. They do their best to make sure all patients receive good care and treatment that will support them to live as well as possible, whatever their illness or disability.

3 Good medical practice describes what is expected of all doctors registered with the General Medical Council (GMC). It is your responsibility to be familiar with Good medical practice and the explanatory guidance which supports it, and to follow the guidance they contain.

4 You must use your judgement in applying the principles to the various situations you will face as a doctor, whether or not you hold a licence to practise, whatever field of medicine you work in, and whether or not you routinely see patients. You must be prepared to explain and justify your decisions and actions'.

1 For an example of the conduct of an expert witness see *Pool v General Medical Council* [2014] EWHC 3791 (Admin) concerning a psychiatrist who accepted instructions to prepare a report concerning the fitness to practise of a paramedic. The court stated as follows:

'The Panel was entitled to find that the Appellant was not an expert in the field of general adult psychiatry and had failed to restrict his opinion to areas in which he had expert knowledge or direct experience and to matters that fell within the limits of his professional competence. The Panel was also entitled to find that he had failed to give adequate reasons for his professional opinions and failed to display an adequate understanding of the role and responsibilities of an expert witness. The Panel's findings of fact on these matters were not wrong. The Panel were entitled to find that that misconduct resulted, in the circumstances of this case, in an impairment of the Appellant's fitness to practise. The Panel was also entitled to regard the misconduct as serious when considering the appropriate sanction…' (Lewis J at paragraph 52).

1.139   There are other specific guidelines available; such guidelines are not a professional code of conduct nor are they exhaustive. However, serious or persistent failure to follow GMC guidance will put a doctor's registration at risk. Such guidelines can be used as a framework to inform appropriate standard in matters of professional conduct and professional performance arising in other forensic contexts.

1.140   It is the jurisdiction concerning fitness to practise and medical ethics that has most impact on patient care. The MA 1983 now sets out a unitary concept of fitness to practise and its impairment in relation to conduct, performance, and ethics. Section 35C(2) provides as follows:

'A person's fitness to practise shall be regarded as "impaired" for the purposes of this Act by reason only of:
  (a) misconduct;
  (b) deficient professional performance;
  (c) a conviction or caution in the British Islands for a criminal offence, or a conviction elsewhere for an offence which, if committed in England and Wales, would constitute a criminal offence;
  (d) adverse physical or mental health;
  (da) not having the necessary knowledge of English (but see section 2(4));
  (e) a determination by a body in the United Kingdom responsible under any enactment for the regulation of a health or social care profession to the effect that his fitness to practise as a member of that profession is impaired, or a determination by a regulatory body elsewhere to the same effect'.

1.141   The MA 1983 does not define fitness to practise or its impairment. 'Misconduct' is not confined to acts or omissions in the course of professional functions. Formerly there were three separate but overlapping jurisdictions concerning serious professional misconduct, fitness to practise (by reason of ill health), and professional performance. These were brought together in 2004.

The GMC can initiate an investigation in response to a complaint or on its own initiative.

1.142   The fitness to practise procedures of the GMC divide broadly into two stages: investigation and adjudication. They are complex and are set out in The General Medical Council (Fitness to Practise) Rules Order of Council 2004. The GMC has published helpful guidelines *Indicative Sanctions Guidance for the Fitness to Practise Panel.*

1.143 On receipt of information about a doctor an officer of the GMC will consider if it constitutes an impairment of fitness to practise. The information can be wide ranging. Events more than five years old will normally not be investigated unless considered to be in the public interest. The GMC may conclude the case, or refer it for further investigation or adjudication. The actions available are wide-ranging and flexible with some degree of informality so that the GMC can deal with the doctor appropriately and proportionately. Such actions include letters of advice, warnings, and undertakings.

1.144 Adjudication is by Fitness to Practise Panel on consideration of the evidence. The procedures are formal, adversarial and usually held in public. Findings on disputed fact are determined on the civil standard of proof, the balance of probability. This is controversial since disputed facts which in another forum would give rise to criminal liability are not determined by the criminal standard of 'beyond reasonable doubt'. The sanctions available are: erasure from the register; suspension from the register; conditions imposed on registration; and warnings.

1.145 The sanctions are directed at protection of the public, and are not punitive of the doctor though they may concern registration on which the practitioner depends for his livelihood. The GMC procedures do not provide remedies for the complainant or bestow private law rights. However, GMC procedures by findings of fact or adjudications can assist in relation to a claim for compensation arising out of the same events.

1.146 Doctors have a right of appeal to the High Court against any decision by a panel to restrict or remove their registration. The Professional Standards Authority for Health and Social Care may also appeal against certain decisions if they consider the decision was too lenient.

Decisions of the GMC are susceptible to judicial review.

1.147 Appeal is concerned with the merits of the decision whereas review is concerned with the decision making process. In the context of the decisions of the GMC the court has stated:

'The test on appeal is whether the decision of the Fitness to Practise Panel can be said to be wrong. That to my mind follows because this is an appeal by way of rehearing, not review. In any event grave issues are at stake and it is not sufficient for intervention to turn on the more confined grounds of public law review such as irrationality. However, in considering whether the decision of a Fitness to Practise Panel is wrong the focus must be calibrated to the matters under consideration. With professional disciplinary tribunals issues of professional judgment may be at the heart of the case... As to findings of fact, however, I cannot see any difference from the court's role in this as compared with other appellate contexts. As with any appellate body there will be reluctance to characterise findings of facts as wrong. That follows because findings of fact may turn on the credibility or reliability of a witness, an assessment of which may be derived from his or her demeanour and from the subtleties of expression which are only evident to someone at the hearing. Decisions on fitness to practise, such as assessing the seriousness of any misconduct, may turn on an exercise of professional judgment. In this regard respect must be accorded to a professional disciplinary tribunal like a Fitness to Practise Panel. However, the degree of deference will depend on the circumstances'[1].

1 Cranston J in *Cheatle v General Medical Council* [2009] EWHC 645 (Admin) at para 15.

1.148 The MA 1983 imposes a duty on the GMC to make regulations in respect of licence to practise and revalidation. Mere registration is insufficient to permit practitioners to practise medicine; practitioners must be licensed and undergo regular revalidation. All licensed doctors must demonstrate on an ongoing basis that they are up to date and fit to practise in their chosen field and able to provide a good level of care.

1.149 Section 44C(1) of the MA 1983 provides:

'A person who holds a licence to practise as a medical practitioner, and practises as such, must have in force in relation to him an indemnity arrangement which provides appropriate cover for practising as such'.

The GMC has in recent decades thus moved from serving and preserving professional interests to protecting and promoting public interest. It demonstrates the professional priorities fit for purpose for the modern era, the consumer age.

The GMC provides an excellent website from which further detailed information can be obtained.

CHAPTER 2

NHS complaints procedures

Sir Robert Francis QC

James Berry

INTRODUCTION

2.1   While this book is primarily concerned with clinical negligence (a breach of duty causing injury compensated by money) all clinical negligence lawyers should be familiar with patient complaints procedures. Patients may complain about a far wider range of issues than are likely to found a negligence claim, but used properly, they have the capacity to avoid claims altogether or help make them better informed and dealt with more efficiently and fairly.

2.2   Clinical negligence claims are, in essence, a legal expression of a patient's dissatisfaction with medical treatment he has received and a demand for a remedy for an injury suffered as a result. Many clinical negligence claimants will have initially raised that dissatisfaction by way of an informal complaint to the medical professional or institution concerned or by way of a formal complaint. By contrast, many patient concerns never give rise to a clinical negligence claim: for instance claims about discourtesy shown by staff, or hospital cleanliness, and waiting times, are areas that are the subject of complaints.

2.3   Vast numbers of complaints are made and processed in the NHS every year: in 2012/13 there were over 174,872 formal complaints about NHS provider organisations in England, of which 52,303 were about some aspect of clinical treatment[1]. Events which can give rise to a negligence claim are a small proportion of the events which can give rise to a complaint. In the same year 10,129 negligence claims were notified[2]. The number of complaints is not necessarily an adverse reflection on the overall quality of the service provided by the NHS. As stated by the Health and Social Care Information Centre in its annual statistical report:

'An organisation that has good publicity, that welcomes complaints as an opportunity to learn and to improve services, and that has a non-defensive approach in responding to complaints may be expected to receive a higher number of complaints than an organisation with poor publicity and a defensive approach in responding'[3].

1 Health and Social Care Information Centre *Data on Written Complaints in the NHS 2013–2014* http://www.hscic.gov.uk/catalogue/PUB14705/data-writ-comp-nhs-2013-2014-rep.pdf. See also Clywd, Hart *Review of the NHS Hospitals Complaints System – Putting Patients Back in the Picture* (October 2013) p 9.
2 http://www.nhsla.com/aboutus/Documents/NHS%20LA%20Annual%20Report%20 and%20Accounts%202013-14.pdf.
3 See above.

2.4   While lawyers often have little to do with NHS complaints, those who act for either side in clinical negligence litigation or professional disciplinary cases need to be familiar with the complaints procedures and what can be achieved through them.

2.5   Making a complaint can serve a number of purposes for a patient who has, or believes he has, been adversely affected by medical treatment. It will often be an end in itself. Someone affected by what they perceive to be a less than expected standard of care, or an adverse outcome may simply want to find out precisely what happened and the reasons for that. For the patient and his lawyer the response to the complaint may provide a factual narrative which may assist in the investigation of any potential negligence claim, but the purpose of the procedure is not to establish legal liability. The mere fact that a complaint is upheld does not establish legal liability or an entitlement to a legal remedy. In other cases complainants will want those responsible to recognise their perceived failings, offer redress in the form of an apology and, most importantly for many complainants, to demonstrate that lessons have been learned from what went wrong, and action taken to ensure as far as possible that the undesired events do not occur again. For some that will be sufficient to dissuade them from pursuing a legal claim.

2.6 In some cases complainants will want those they believe to be responsible to be held to account for what went wrong. A complaint under the NHS complaints procedure considered in this chapter will never in itself be assured of bringing about such a result. A complainant cannot require a healthcare provider to discipline its staff and in many cases it will be considered undesirable or inappropriate to do so, even where an avoidable incident has occurred. It is now recognised that the development and maintenance of a safety culture will be hindered by too ready a resort to disciplinary measures. Even where a complaint does result in a healthcare provider taking disciplinary measures, it may well consider itself under a duty of confidentiality owed to the employee. If a complainant is dissatisfied with an apparent absence of disciplinary action the only practical recourse is to make a further complaint to relevant practitioner's professional disciplinary regulator such as the General Medical Council or the Nursing and Midwifery Council.

2.7 The organisation to whom the complaint is addressed has much to gain from it. First and foremost a complaint offers an early opportunity to resolve a patient's concerns and put right anything that has gone wrong in their treatment or care. Making sure a complaint is dealt with promptly, thoroughly and fairly, involving the complainant fully in a transparent process, is the best way of resolving the patient's concerns. Equally, handling the complaint badly can allow additional harm or distress to be inflicted on the patient or those close to him, and increase the chances of litigation, reputational damage, and of allowing poor service delivery to continue. Complaints are an invaluable resource which a well run hospital Trust welcomes as a major tool in improving safety and quality of its service.

2.8 While there are legal requirements to be met in the processing of a complaint in the NHS, a lawyer asked to provide advice to a complainant, a service provider or an involved healthcare professional needs to have regard not only to the relevant law, but also policy guidance and accepted practice. A failure to take the whole context into account may lead to a complainant not understanding fully their entitlements, and to a service provider or its professional employees acting in a detrimental manner, which may attract regulatory action.

2.9 This chapter considers mainly the procedure for making formal complaints about a patient's experience or treatment in an NHS setting in England. It explores internal complaints procedures and the procedure for complaining to the Health Services Commissioner (or Ombudsman). It is not concerned with the complaints procedures that apply with respect to private healthcare providers, nor does it address the procedure for complaining about individual practitioners to the regulatory body. Finally, this chapter is not concerned with serious incident investigations, which must be commenced regardless of whether a complaint is made[1].

1 See the NHS National Patient Safety Agency's *National Framework for Reporting and Learning from Serious Incidents Requiring Investigation* (2010).

RECENT HISTORY AND PROPOSALS FOR REFORM

2.10 In March 2015 the Public Administration Select Committee said about complaints handling that:

'Complainants need to feel heard, whether they are patients, relatives or staff. They deserve the opportunity to contribute to learning in the system that will prevent a repeat of the same failure. Instead, they too often feel their issue is managed or avoided, to minimise reputational damage to individuals and organisations, or to avoid financial liability. The system is unacceptably complicated, with an unresolved tension between the desire for an open "no blame" culture and the demand for the clear accountability the public is entitled to expect from a public service. There is a clear requirement for a single body to provide a single focus for accountability for driving local improvement'[1].

1 Public Administration Select Committee *Investigating clinical incidents in the NHS* (27 March 2015) House of Commons HC 886 p 32 para 74, available at http://www.publications. parliament.uk/pa/cm201415/cmselect/cmpubadm/886/886.pdf.

2.11 This is but one of the more recent of a stream of official reports denouncing the NHS complaints handling system and recommending change. It was not until 1996 that a comprehensive NHS complaints system was put in place. That system provided for complaints to be investigated and resolved by the hospital complained about. It also provided for an independent review by an independent panel and an appeal to the Health Services Ombudsman[1]. Since then there has been a constant stream of reports identifying deficiencies in the complaints system and proposing reform.

1 For a historical overview of the system before 2005, see PHSO *Making things better* (9 March 2005), House of Commons HC 413) pp 1–4 and 23–32.

2.12 Following a protracted review between 1999 and 2003, the Department of Health proposed a new uniform national system which would transfer the appeal process to the Commission for Healthcare Audit and Inspection[1]. Regulations were promulgated in 2004 partially giving effect to this proposal.

1 Department of Health *NHS complaints reform, making things right* (April 2002).

2.13 In 2004 in the Fifth Report of the Shipman Inquiry, Dame Janet Smith criticised the lack of fair procedures and impartiality, and a failure to investigate complaints properly or give adequate explanations, among other failings[1]. In 2005 the Health Service Ombudsman published her own review of the complaints system which was scathing in its criticism of the way in which it operated. The Ombudsman considered the system was fragmented, did not centre on the needs of patients, lacked sufficient competent staff to run it, the right leaders, culture and governance, and just remedies[2]. She made recommendations designed to correct these deficiencies, including a set of national standards. Among these she recommended:

- 'fit for purpose, thorough, rigorous and evidence based investigations of complaints with clear and well explained decisions';
- 'a culture of openness and non-defensiveness which welcomes complaints as a way of remedying mistakes and improving service';
- 'leadership by senior managers who live out this commitment'[3].

She considered that the second stage should be delivered by the new healthcare regulator, the Healthcare Commission (HCC).

1 Shipman Inquiry *Safeguarding Patients: lessons from the past – Proposals for the Future* (9 December 2004, House of Commons, Cm 6394).
2 *Making things better* para 23.
3 *Making things better* para113.

2.14 The current system is largely based on the Ombudsman's 2005 recommendations, except that the HCC stage was abolished after its operation became the subject of sustained criticism.

2.15 In the aftermath of the Mid-Staffordshire scandal the consequent inquiries demonstrated that the system, which is still in place at the time of writing, was insufficient to prevent a badly-run hospital Trust failing to deal with complaints in a manner consistent with the purpose of the regulatory requirements. In particular there were frequent failures to address effectively the concerns raised by complainants or to act on the deficiencies that were brought to light. The requirements for reporting on complaints did not prevent the Board of the Trust remaining ignorant of the true scale of the problems being faced by patients. The independent inquiry commented that

'A poor complaints system has a negative impact on the patients and others who seek to use it. Inadequate responses cause distress and may exacerbate bereavement. Complainants are left desperate for answers to their questions ...'

2.16 It was recommended that

'The Board should review the Trust's arrangements for the management of complaints and incident reporting in the light of the findings of this report and ensure that it:

- provides responses and resolutions to complaints which satisfy complainants;
- ensures that staff are engaged in the process from the investigation of a complaint or an incident to the implementation of any lessons to be learned;
- minimises the risk of deficiencies exposed by the problems recurring; and
- makes available full information on the matters reported, and the action to resolve deficiencies, to the Board, the governors and the public'[1].

1 For an account of the management of complaints at Stafford see the report of the *Independent inquiry into care provided by Mid-Staffordshire NHS Foundation Trust January 2005–March 2009* vol 1 pp 19–20, 27, 258–274 (24 February 2010) HC375-1.

2.17 In 2011, following the first Mid-Staffordshire Inquiry's report, the House of Commons Health Select Committee published a report on the 2009 complaints system[1]. It recommended a review of the system to bring about an improvement of the patient experience. It pointed to unwarranted variations in the systems adopted by different organisations. It noted that the

'NHS complaints system sometimes compounds and exacerbates the negative experiences of patients. In such situations, patients have little choice but to give up or turn to the legal system'[2].

It also recommended that 'one organisation should be responsible for maintaining an overview of complaints handling in the NHS, setting and monitoring standards, supporting change, and analysis of complaints data'[3].

1 Health Select Committee *Complaints and Litigation* (28 June 2011) House of Commons, HC 786-1.
2 Health Select Committee *Complaints and Litigation* paras 1–3.
3 http://www.publications.parliament.uk/pa/cm201012/cmselect/cmhealth/786/78611. htm.

2.18 The report of the Mid-Staffordshire NHS Foundation Trust Public Inquiry identified the reluctance of people to complain, in part because of the fear of the consequences, and the need for better support for all complainants, higher priority for feedback, learning and the use of the warning signs offered by complaints, and a greater emphasis on independent investigation[1]. A number of recommendations were made including the provision of readily accessible and multiple methods of registering complaints, the removal of actual or potential litigation as a barrier to processing of a complaint, the equivalent treatment of concerns not formally expressed as complaints, arms length investigations for serious complaints, readily available advice and support, and the wider and more specific publication and sharing of information about complaints[2].

1 Report of the *Mid-Staffordshire NHS Foundation Trust Public Inquiry* vol 1 pp 245–265, 278–287.
2 Report of the *Mid-Staffordshire NHS Foundation Trust Public Inquiry* vol 1 pp 285–387.

2.19 In its response to this report the government commissioned a further review of NHS hospital complaints handling by the Rt Hon Ann Clywd MP and Professor Tricia Hart. In their report, they recommended measures for training complaints handlers, the improvement of basic information available to patients and in complaints handling[1]. More recently Healthwatch England has published a critical report on the complaints system and a proposed set of standards for advocacy services[2]. While the government has largely accepted the recommendations of all these reports in principle, the precise nature of any reforms they propose is awaited.

1 Clywd, Hart *A Review of the NHS Hospitals Complaints System – Putting Patients Back in the Picture* (October 2013).
2 Healthwatch England *Suffering in Silence* (October 2014) http://www.healthwatch.co.uk/ sites/healthwatch.co.uk/files/hwe-complaints-report.pdf; *Independent Complaints Advocacy Standards to support the commissioning, delivery and monitoring of the service* (February 2015) http://www.healthwatch.co.uk/sites/healthwatch.co.uk/files/healthwatch_advocacy_ standards_10022015.pdf.

2.20 In the meantime the House of Commons Public Administration Select Committee has added its contribution, suggesting among other things that there should be a Minister for government policy on complaints handling[1]. That Committee published a comprehensive report on 28 April 2014 calling for the Parliamentary and Health Services Ombudsman (PHSO) to be replaced with a more user friendly 'citizen's Ombudsman' with the power to start investigations, including into the NHS, on its own initiative rather than in response to a complaint[2]. The PHSO, the Local Government Ombudsman and Healthwatch England have published a vision of what a good complaints handling looks like and intend to work with the Department of Health Complaints Programme Board to develop tools to measure the impact of complaints processes for complainants[3].

1 Public Administration Select Committee *More Complaints Please!* (14 April 2014) House of Commons HC 229.
2 Public Administration Select Committee *Time for a People's Ombudsman* (28 April 2014) House of Commons HC 655.
3 PHSO *My expectations for raising concerns and complaints* (November 2014) http://www.ombudsman.org.uk/__data/assets/pdf_file/0010/28774/Vision_report.pdf.

2.21   In a yet further report, referred to above, the Public Administration Select Committee has recommended that there should be

'a new, permanent, simplified, functioning, trusted system for swift and effective local clinical incident investigation conducted by trained staff, so that facts and evidence are established early, without the need to find blame, and regardless of whether a complaint has been raised'.

2.22   In evidence to the Committee, the Secretary of State for Health expressed support for consideration of a body similar to the Air Accidents Investigation Branch[1] for cases where there is a dispute or where there is a lack of trust or where the relationship has broken down and where an expert view is rapidly needed.

1 Public Administration Select Committee *Investigating clinical incidents in the NHS* (27 March 2015) House of Commons HC 886, p 47, para 132. Dr Michael J Powers, QC proposed such a body to the Health Select Committee in December 2008 http://www.publications.parliament.uk/pa/cm200809/cmselect/cmhealth/151/151we30.htm.

LEGAL FRAMEWORK

2.23   The system for complaints about treatment in the NHS is underpinned by legislation. The Secretary of State for Health may by regulation make provision for the handling and consideration of complaints about: (a) the exercise of any of the functions of an English NHS body or a cross-border SHA; (b) the provision of health care by or for such a body; (c) the provision of services by such a body or by any other person in pursuance of arrangement made under NHS legislation; and (d) anything done by the NHS Commissioning Board or a clinical commissioning group in the exercise of their public health functions[1].

1 Health and Social Care (Community Health and Standards) Act 2003, s 113 as amended.

2.24   The current complaints regime is set out in the Local Authority Social Services and National Health Service Complaints (England) Regulations 2009[1] (the Complaints Regulations) which, for these purposes, came into force 1 April 2009, and Health Service Commissioners Act 1993 (the 1993 Act).

1 SI 2009/309. The National Health Service (Concerns, Complaints and Redress Arrangements) (Wales) Regulations 2011, SI 2011/704 apply to complaints with respect to NHS organisations in Wales. Complaints about the public health functions of local authorities are governed by comparable arrangements under the NHS Bodies and Local Authorities (Partnership Arrangements, Care Trusts, Public Health and Local Healthwatch Regulations 2012, SI 2012/3094, which came in to force on 1 April 2013.

LOCAL COMPLAINTS

Informal complaints

2.25 Many complaints are made informally, for example to ward staff, or orally to the Patient Support and Liaison Service (PALS) office at the hospital and are resolved without formality. The Complaints Regulations do not purport to prohibit this and indeed encourage the swift resolution of concerns where this is possible. Therefore generally hospital procedures and policies will, and should, provide for staff to be able to resolve concerns raised with them informally.

Who may be the subject of a complaint?

2.26 For the purposes of this chapter, complaints may be made about the following 'responsible bodies':

- an NHS body and about either the exercise of its functions; or the exercise of any health-related functions of a local authority that are discharged by an NHS body under an agreement pursuant to s 75 of the National Health Service Act 2006;
- a clinical commissioning group or the National Health Service Commissioning Board about the exercise by it of any functions in pursuance of arrangements made under s 7A of the National Health Service Act 2006;
- a primary care provider about the provision of services by it under arrangements with an NHS body; or
- an independent provider about the provision of services by it under arrangements with an NHS body.

Who may complain?

2.27 The Complaints Regulations only apply to certain complainants. That said, the range of complainants is broadly defined[1] and it includes:

- persons who receive or have received services from a responsible body; or
- a person who is affected, or likely to be affected, by the action, omission or decision of the responsible body;
- a person who is affected by an expert psychiatric report prepared for family court proceedings by a consultant employed by an NHS Trust is unlikely to be found to come within these provisions[2];
- a representative of one of the above classes of complainant.

1 SI 2009/309, reg 5(1).
2 *R (on the application of TA) v North East London NHS* [2011] EWCA Civ 1529, paras 22, 23, 28, 29.

2.28 A 'representative' is someone who makes a complaint on behalf of someone who[1]:

- has died;
- is a child;

- is unable to make the complaint themselves because of lack of capacity, whether physical or mental (within the meaning of the Mental Capacity Act 2005); or
- has requested the representative to act on their behalf.

1 See reg 5(2).

2.29   Where the complaint is made on behalf of a child, it must only be considered where the responsible body is satisfied that there are reasonable grounds for the complaint being made by the representative rather than the child himself. Where the responsible body is not so satisfied, it must provide written reasons to the representative[1]. This allows, but does not compel, a responsible body to decline to receive a complaint from a representative when the child is assessed as having the capacity to make his own complaint, presumably in accordance with the principles of *Gillick v West Norfolk & Wisbech Area Health Authority*[2] but this provision is not expressly limited to such a case. The responsible body is obliged to identify reasons for allowing the complaint to be made by a representative in preference to the child personally and therefore to start from an assumption that the child should be enabled to make his own complaint unless there are good reasons for it to be made on his behalf. For example a child, while being *Gillick* competent, might be unduly distressed by the process or might have to be made privy to information which it would not be in his best interests to receive. This rule should not be used to prevent a complaint being dealt with at all.

1 See reg 5(3).
2 [1986] AC 112.

2.30   Where the responsible body is satisfied that the representative of a child or complainant lacking capacity is not conducting the complaint in their best interests, the complaint must not be (further) considered under the Complaint Regulations. The responsible body must provide written reasons to the representative[1]. This appears to have the alarming consequence that where a legitimate complaint is being pursued in a manner which is contrary to the interests of the child or person lacking capacity, the processing of the complaint must be stopped. There is no provision allowing for the responsible body to ensure that a different representative is appointed to pursue the matter properly.

1 See reg 5(4).

What may they complain about?

2.31   What the complainant (or their representative) may complain about is not defined in the Complaint Regulations, and therefore a complaint can be made about any of the matters specified in the enabling legislation[1]. Regulation 8, however, sets out which complaints are not required to be dealt with in accordance with the Regulations. These include complaints:

- made by another responsible body;
- made by an employee of a NHS body about any matter relating to their employment or made about superannuation;
- that are made orally and resolved to the complainant's satisfaction by the next working day;

- that are repetitious, in the sense of being about a matter which has been resolved or investigated (under the Regulations or a variety of other specified statutory provisions);
- that arise out of an alleged failure to comply with a Freedom of Information Act 2000 request.

Otherwise complaints may be made about the exercise of any functions of an English NHS body, the provision of health care by or for such a body, and the provision of services by such a body or any other person in pursuance of arrangements made by the body under the National Health Service Act 2006, s 75[2].

1 Health and Social Care (Community Health and Standards) Act 2003, s 113 as amended.
2 Health and Social Care (Community Health and Standards) Act 2003, s 113.

2.32 Save for oral complaints that are resolved by the next working day, the responsible body must notify the complainant as soon as is reasonably practicable of a decision not to deal with his complaint and give reasons.

The mechanism

2.33 Responsible bodies must make their own arrangements for dealing with complaints, and those arrangements must be made in accordance with the Regulations. The arrangements for dealing with complaints must be such as to ensure that[1]:

- complaints are dealt with efficiently and properly investigated;
- complainants are treated with respect and courtesy;
- complainants receive, so far as is reasonably practical, assistance to enable them to understand the procedure in relation to complaints (or advice on where they may obtain such assistance), and timely and appropriate response.

Moreover, the arrangements must be such that complainants are told the outcome of the investigation and that action is taken in the light of the outcome if necessary.

1 Local Authority Social Services and National Health Service Complaints (England) Regulations 2009, reg 3(1), (2).

2.34 It follows that there is no one system throughout the NHS, and complainants have to inform themselves of the arrangements made by the responsible body to which they wish to complain. The advice on the NHS England website is to ask a member of staff, look on the hospital or trust's website or contact the complaints department[1]. The Department of Health is working with NHS England to include in the terms of the standard commissioning contract an obligation to display information about the complaints process. The Care Quality Commission (CQC) now examine complaints handling as part of their hospital inspection regime[2]. These developments are likely to lead in time to a more standardised approach to complaints handling.

1 www.nhs.uk/choiceintheNHS/Rightsandpledges/complaints/Pages/NHScomplaints.aspx.
2 http://www.engage.dh.gov.uk/francisresponse/recommendation/promoting-desire-to-receive-and-learn-from-complaints/.

2.35   Where one responsible body receives a complaint which, had it been sent to another responsible body, would be a complaint which would fall to be handled by that body, the two bodies must co-operate for the purposes of handling the complaint and ensuring that the complainant receives a co-ordinated response to the complaint. Each body is under a duty to seek to agree which should take the lead in the coordination and in communicating with the complainant. Further they must cooperate in providing relevant information to each other and in attending any meetings that may be required[1].

1 Local Authority Social Services and National Health Service Complaints (England) Regulations 2009, reg 9.

Time limits

2.36   Complaints under the Complaints Regulations must be made no later than 12 months after[1]:

- the date on which the matter which is the subject of the complaint occurred; or
- if later, the date on which the matter which is the subject of the complaint came to the notice of the complainant.

1 See reg 12(1).

2.37   There is a general discretion for the responsible body to disapply the time limit where that body is satisfied[1] that:

- the complainant had good reasons for not making the complaint within that time limit; **and**
- notwithstanding the delay, it is still possible to investigate the complaint effectively and fairly.

1 See reg 12(2).

HOW TO COMPLAIN

2.38   Responsible bodies are required to make information available to the public about their arrangement for dealing with complaints and how further information about those arrangements may be obtained[1].

1 See reg 16.

2.39   Some NHS bodies will have dedicated complaint forms available on their website or in hard copy, but they are not required to do so, nor are complainants required to use such forms that are available. Complaints may be made orally, in writing or electronically[1]. Where the complaint is made orally, the onus is upon the responsible body to make a written record of the complaint and to provide a copy of that record to the complainant[2].

1 See reg 13(1).
2 See reg 13(2).

First steps

2.40 Upon receiving a complaint, the responsible body must provide an acknowledgment within three working days. This can be done orally, or in writing[1]. At the time of acknowledgment, the responsible body must offer to discuss the following with the complainant at a time to be agreed with the complainant[2]:

(1)   the manner in which the complaint is to be handled; and
(2)   the period ('the response period') within which the investigation of the complaint is likely to be completed and the response is likely to be sent to the complainant.

Where the complainant does not take up the offer of such a discussion, the responsible body must still determine the response period and notify the complainant in writing[3].

1 See reg 13(6).
2 See reg 13(7).
3 See reg 13(8).

The investigation

2.41 The responsible body must investigate a complaint in a manner that is appropriate to resolve it speedily and efficiently and must keep the complainant informed as to the progress of the investigation, as far as reasonably practicable[1]. It should be noted that a complaint which amounts to or includes an allegation that a serious incident has occurred should be investigated as such in accordance with NHS England's Serious Incident Framework, which states[2]:

'Serious incidents identified (or alleged) through the complaints route, or any other mechanism, must be treated in line with the principles in this Framework to ensure that it is investigated and responded to appropriately'.

Communications with the complainant may be sent electronically where he has consented to being communicated with electronically and has not withdrawn that consent[3].

1 See reg 14(1).
2 NHS England, *The Serious Incident Framework* (2015) para 1.3
3 Local Authority Social Services and National Health Service Complaints (England) Regulations 2009, reg 15(1).

The response

2.42 After completing the investigation, the responsible body must send the complainant a written response as soon as practicable. That response must be signed by the responsible person and it must include three things[1]:

(1)   first, a report containing:
  •   an explanation of how the complaint has been considered; and
  •   the conclusions reached in relation to the complaint, including any matters for which the complaint specifies, or the responsible body considers, that remedial action is needed;

(2)   second, confirmation as to whether the responsible body is satisfied that any action needed in consequence of the complaint has been taken or is proposed to be taken;

(3)   third, details of the complainant's right to take their complaint to the Health Service Commissioner (ie the Health Service Ombudsman) under the 1993 Act.

1 See reg 14(2).

2.43   The response must be sent to the complainant within six months of the day on which the complaint was received. That period can be extended by agreement between the responsible body and the complainant before the expiry of the six-month period. If the responsible body does not provide a response within six months or an agreed longer period, the responsible body must[1]:

- notify the complainant in writing accordingly and explain the reason why; and
- send the complainant in a written response as soon as reasonably practicable.

1 See reg 14(4).

Monitoring and annual reports

2.44   The responsible body must record the following information[1]:

- each complaint received;
- the subject matter and outcome of each complaint; and
- where the responsible body gave a projected time for the completion of the complaint[2], whether the investigation report was sent to the complainant within that period (or any amended period).

1 See reg 17.
2 See reg 13(7)(b).

2.45   The responsible body must also prepare an annual report[1]. The annual report must be available to any person upon request. That report must specify:

- the number of complaints received;
- the number of complaints which the responsible body decided were well-founded;
- the number of complaints which the responsible body has been informed have been referred to the Health Service Commissioner to consider under the 1993 Act.

1 Reg 18.

2.46   The report must also specify:

- the subject matter of complaints received;
- any matters of general importance arising out of those complaints, or the way in which the complaints were handled;
- any matters where action has been or is to be taken to improve services as a consequence of those complaints.

2.47 Where the responsible body is an NHS body, primary care provider or independent provider providing services under arrangements with a clinical commissioning group or the National Health Service Commissioning Board, a copy of the annual report must be sent by the responsible body to the Clinical Commissioning Group or Commissioning Board in question.

SUPPORT AND ASSISTANCE FOR COMPLAINANTS

Patient Advice and Liaison Service (PALS)

2.48 The function of PALS has been described by the government in these terms:

'... staff will listen and provide relevant information and support to help resolve users' concerns quickly and efficiently, there and then, if at all possible. They will liaise with staff and managers, and, where appropriate, with other PALS services, health and related organisations, to help resolve complaints so avoiding the need for patients to make a formal complaint in most cases. They will also act as one of the gateways to independent advice and advocacy support for people wanting to pursue formal complaints and act as a force for change and improvement within the organisation as a whole'[1].

1 *Making things right* (2003) (see above) para 3.37.

2.49 Most hospitals provide a PALS service to help support and provide information to patients. This office will often be willing to intervene with ward staff to explore whether a concern can be addressed informally. Some hospitals combine their PALS service with the complaints handling service. It has been argued that this gives rise to a clear conflict of interest. It has been recommended that PALS should be 're-branded' to make it clear what services it provides, and that patients should not be made to feel they have to make a complaint through PALS[1]. On the other hand the Health Select Committee recommended that the role of PALS should be enhanced as the first line of contact for complainants[2].

1 Clywd, Hart, pp 12, 33, 37.
2 Health Select Committee 2011 report (see above).

Independent Advocacy Services (ICAS)

2.50 In spite of the intentions behind the complaints system, it can be a daunting and complex process for many, who are deterred from pursuing their concerns, leaving them without any resolution of their issues and the system deprived of information which could lead to improvement. In the opinion of Healthwatch England the system is 'utterly bewildering for people' and its failure is compounded by a 'lack of consistent and easy to access support and advocacy services'[1].

1 Healthwatch UK statement 20 March 2014 http://www.healthwatch.co.uk/news/health-and-care-complaints-system-utterly-bewildering-people.

2.51 The Secretary of State was placed under a duty in 2001 to make independent advocacy services, defined as services by way of 'representation or otherwise' available to complainants. This service was to be independent so far as was practicable from the organisation against which the complaint was raised[1]. The service under this provision was set up as from September 2003 by a series of contractual arrangements with providers for different parts of the country.

1 Health and Social Care Act 2001, s 12, inserting s 19A into the National Health Service Act 1977.

2.52 As part of the 2013 health service reforms, local authorities are required to make such arrangements as they think appropriate for the provision of independent advocacy services to provide assistance to any person intending to make a complaint under a procedure operated by a health service body or an independent provider[1]. In practice local authorities are making a wide variety of arrangements for this service of varying quality[2], and complainants have to rely on information offered by NHS providers and local authorities as to how to access such services as exist. Healthwatch England has proposed a set of standards for advocacy services and requested the government to consider changes to regulatory requirements to accommodate these, but they are proposed for implementation in any event[3].

1 Local Government and Public Involvement in Health Act 2007, s 222A, inserted by Health and Social Care Act 2012, s 185.
2 Healthwatch England has expressed concern at how little known are many advocacy services: Bradley, *Letter to the Secretary of State* (19 June 2013). http://www.healthwatch.co.uk/sites/default/files/healthwatch_england_letter_to_dh_20062013_v2.pdf. See also their critical report on complaints services *Suffering in Silence* (October 2014) http://www.healthwatch.co.uk/sites/healthwatch.co.uk/files/hwe-complaints-report.pdf.
3 Healthwatch England, *Independent Complaints Advocacy Standards* to support the commissioning, delivery and monitoring of the service (February 2015) http://www.healthwatch.co.uk/sites/healthwatch.co.uk/files/healthwatch_advocacy_standards_10022015.pdf.

COMPLAINTS TO THE HEALTH SERVICE COMMISSIONER

2.53 The Health Service Commissioner for England (who is in fact the Parliamentary and Health Service Ombudsman) has an important role in the NHS complaints structure and has broad powers which include a power to review and in some cases investigate matters about which a complaint has been made to a health service provider. The Commissioner is a creature of statute, namely the Health Service Commissioners Act 1993.

2.54 The Commissioner may investigate (ss 2, 2A and 2B):

- certain Special Health Authorities (defined in s 2(5));
- NHS trusts managing a hospital, or other establishment or facility in England;
- NHS foundation trusts;
- the NHS Commissioning Board;
- Clinical Commissioning Groups;
- persons (individuals or bodies) providing family health services under a contract with the NHS Commissioning Board (under ss 84, 100 or 117 of the National Health Service Act 2006);
- persons (individuals or bodies) undertaking to provide pharmaceutical services under the 2006 Act;

- individuals performing in England primary medical services (ie GPs) or primary dental services in accordance with arrangements made under ss 92 or 107 of the 2006 Act (except where those services are performed as employees of, or on behalf of, a health service body or an independent provider);
- individuals providing local pharmaceutical services in accordance with arrangements made under a pilot scheme established under s 134 of the 2006 Act except as employees of, or otherwise on behalf of, a health service body or an independent provider;
- persons (individuals or bodies) providing services under arrangements with health service bodies or family health service providers (ie independent providers);
- persons providing direct payment services.

Commissioner's remit

2.55 Generally, the Commissioner may investigate a complaint made to her by or on behalf of a person who has sustained injustice or hardship in consequence of[1]:

- a failure in a service provided by a health service body;
- a failure of such a body to provide a service which it was a function of the body to provide; or
- maladministration connected with any other action taken by or on behalf of such a body.

1 Health Service Commissioners Act 1993, s 3.

2.56 The definition of maladministration is a broad one that includes maladministration by the body in question, a person employed by that body, a person acting on behalf of that body, or a person to whom that body has delegated any functions[1]. Complaints concerning clinical judgment may be investigated, but the Commissioner is not obliged to apply the legal standards for clinical negligence such as the *Bolam/Bolitho* test to his consideration, although he should set out in his reports the basis on which he has found that any suggested failure or service has or has not been established[2].

1 Health Service Commissioners Act 1993, s 3(1ZA).
2 *Atwood v The Health Service Commissioner* [2008] EWHC 2315 (Admin), [2009] 1 All ER 415.

2.57 The Commissioner has a general discretion to determine whether to initiate, continue or discontinue an investigation and whether a complaint is duly made[1].

1 Health Service Commissioners Act 1993, s 3(2), (3).

2.58 The Commissioner is also entitled to apply any reasonable interpretation to the complaint received from a complainant, and is not bound in law to apply an objective view of the type a court would apply to a commercial document. While he may decide to investigate a systemic issue implied by the complaint he is not obliged to do so[1]. Indeed there is no power to investigate issues which are not raised by the complaint, but arise from evidence obtained in the course of an investigation, and a decision to do so may be open to judicial review[2]. It is therefore important that complainants set out explicitly the issues which it is desired that the Commissioner investigate.

1 *R (on the application of Morris) v Parliamentary and Health Service Ombudsman* [2014] EWHC 4364 (Admin).
2 *R (on the application of Cavanagh) v Health Service Commissioner for England* [2005] EWCA Civ 1578, [2006] 1 WLR 1229.

Where the Commissioner may not investigate

2.59   The Commissioner may conduct an investigation in respect of any action taken by a health service body in operating a procedure established to examine complaints (s 7(3B)). Subject to that general power, there are a number of matters that the Commissioner may not investigate.

2.60   The Commissioner may not conduct an investigation where the complainant already has access to an alternative remedy including[1]:

- an inquiry under s 84 of the National Health Service Act 1977 (presumably now an inquiry under the Inquiries Act 2005, as s 84 has been repealed);
- a right of appeal, reference or review to or before a tribunal constituted by or under any enactment or by virtue of Her Majesty's prerogative, unless the Commissioner is satisfied that in the particular circumstances it is not reasonable to expect that person to resort or have resorted to it;
- a remedy by way of proceedings in any court of law, unless the Commissioner is satisfied that in the particular circumstances it is not reasonable to expect that person to resort or have resorted to it. It is debateable whether this excludes a complaint to the Commissioner where there is a possibility of a clinical negligence claim. The remedy in such an action is compensation for the injury suffered as a result of negligence. What a complainant may seek in a complaint is an explanation and an apology, and an undertaking of remedial action for service deficiencies which may not amount to negligence in themselves. Therefore the approach of the Commissioner may be to consider whether it is reasonable to expect a person seeking a non-pecuniary remedy to bring a legal action.

1 Health Service Commissioners Act 1993, s 4.

2.61   The Commissioner may not conduct an investigation in respect of action taken by a Primary Care Trust in the exercise of its functions:

- under the National Health Service (Service Committees and Tribunal) Regulations 1992[1], or any instrument amending or replacing those regulations;
- under regulations made under s 126 or 129 of the National Health Service Act 2006 by virtue of s 17 of the Health and Medicines Act 1988 (investigations of matters relating to services)[2].

1 SI 1992/664.
2 Health Service Commissioners Act 1993, s 6.

2.62   Further the Commissioner may not conduct investigations in respect of:

- action taken in respect of appointments or removals, pay, discipline, superannuation or other personnel matters in relation to service under the National Health Service Act 2006;
- action taken in matters relating to contractual or other commercial transactions, except for matters relating to NHS contracts as defined by the National Health Service Act 2006, s 9;
- matters arising from arrangements for the provision of direct payment services;
- matters arising from arrangements between a health service body and an independent provider for the provision of services by the provider;
- matters arising from arrangements between a family health service provider and an independent provider for the provision of services by the independent provider;
- complaints in respect of action taken in any matter relating to arrangements made by a health service body and a family health service provider for the provision of family health services, the action is taken by or on behalf of the body or by the provider, and the complaint is made by the provider or the body[1].

1 Health Service Commissioners Act 1993, s 7.

Who may complain to the Commissioner

2.63   Complaints may be made to the Commissioner by an individual or by a body of persons (whether incorporated or not). A complaint may not, however, be made by a public authority[1].

1 Health Service Commissioners Act 1993, s 8.

Basic requirements of a complaint

2.64   There are three mandatory requirements for any complaint to the Commissioner to be entertained[1]:

- the complaint must be made in writing;
- the complaint must be made by the person aggrieved themselves, or by an appropriate individual or body where the person aggrieved has died or is for any reason unable to act for himself;
- the complaint must be made within a year after the day on which the person aggrieved first had notice of the matters alleged in the complaint. The Commissioner may extend time if she considers it reasonable to do so. An example would be where the complainant had complained to the responsible body timeously, that body took over one year to deal with the complaint and, dissatisfied with the outcome, the complainant lodged a complaint with the Commissioner promptly.

1 Health Service Commissioners Act 1993, s 9.

Self-referrals by health service bodies

2.65   A health service body may refer a qualifying complaint to the Commissioner itself. That referral must be made within one year of the date on which it received the complaint. Once the Commissioner has accepted the referral of the complaint, it is deemed to have been made to the Commissioner[1].

1 Health Service Commissioners Act 1993, s 10.

Investigations

2.66 Where the Commissioner proposes to conduct an investigation into a complaint she must give the opportunity to comment on the allegations to[1]:

- the health service body, family health service provider or independent provider concerned;
- any other person who is alleged in the complaint to have taken or authorised the action complained of.

1 Health Service Commissioners Act 1993, s 11(1), (1A).

2.67 Other than the requirement that the investigation is to be conducted in private[1], the procedure for conducting an investigation is a matter left to the Commissioner's discretion in each case[2]. The Commissioner therefore has a wide remit in which she may:

- determine whether any person may be represented (legally or otherwise) in the investigation;
- pay to the person by whom the complaint was made and to any other person who attends or supplies information for the purposes of an investigation expenses they have incurred and allowances by way of compensation for the loss of their time; and
- obtain information from such persons and in such manner, and make such inquiries, as he thinks fit.

1 Health Service Commissioners Act 1993, s 11(2).
2 Health Service Commissioners Act 1993, s 11(3)(b).

2.68 In gathering evidence for his investigation, the Commissioner may require[1]:

- any officer or member of the health service body concerned; or
- any other person who in his opinion is able to do so,

to supply information or produce documents relevant to the investigation.

1 Health Service Commissioners Act 1993, s 12.

2.69 This broad power has teeth, because the Commissioner has the same powers as the court in respect of the attendance and examination of witnesses and the production of documents. Where the Commissioner's requirement for information or documents is not satisfied, he may certify an offence to the court if he considers that[1]:

- a person has obstructed him or any of his officers in the performance of his functions without lawful excuse; or
- a person is guilty of any act or omission in relation to an investigation which, if that investigation were a proceeding in the court, would constitute contempt of court.

The matter is then dealt with by the court as if the person had committed the offence of obstruction or contempt of court in relation to the court itself.

1 Health Service Commissioners Act 1993, s 13.

2.70 Information obtained by, in the course of, or for the purposes of an investigation shall not be disclosed except for the purposes of the investigation and any report to be made in respect of it, save in other specified situations. Of most obvious importance is the situation where the information in question is to the effect that any person is likely to constitute a threat to the health or safety of patients as permitted by subsection (1B). If that be the case, the Commissioner may disclose the information to any persons to whom he thinks it should be disclosed in the interests of the health and safety of patients. The Commissioner must inform the person in question that he has disclosed the information and to whom[1]. The PHSO suggests that this provision restricts persons receiving drafts for comment of reports she intends to publish from disclosing information contained in it:

'You and the organisation may share the draft report with people who can help you comment on its accuracy and content (for example, a family member or professional adviser), but by law you and the organisation complained about must not make the contents public'[2].

1 Health Service Commissioners Act 1993, s 15.
2 http://www.ombudsman.org.uk/about-us/being-open-and-transparent/what-happens-to-the-information-you-giveus#b3.

2.71 A legal opinion submitted in evidence to and published by the Public Administration Select Committee as part of its clinical incidents investigation inquiry has suggested that the PHSO may be mis-interpreting the statute in extending it to apply to complainants, and alternatively that such an interpretation may constitute a breach of Article 10 of the European Convention on Human Rights[1]. While there has been no judicial decision on the meaning of this section, it is suggested that the Ombudsman's advice as set out above goes further than the statute can have intended. Inevitably her reports will contain information which has been provided by the complainant. It is difficult to see why this statutory provision should in itself inhibit a complainant from disclosing such information in any way the law does not otherwise prohibit. However, even without the provision a body such as an Ombudsman is likely to be entitled to share other information she has obtained and opinions she has formed for the legitimate purpose of obtaining comment on condition that it is kept confidential until such time as it is published. This is no more than the courts themselves require when offering the parties to litigation advance sight of a draft judgment before it is handed down.

1 http://data.parliament.uk/WrittenEvidence/CommitteeEvidence.svc/EvidenceDocument/Public%20Administration/NHS%20Complaints%20and%20Clinical%20Failure/written/18516.html.

Investigation Report[1]

2.72 The Commissioner must send a report of his investigation to:
- the person who made the complaint;

- any member of the House of Commons who assisted in the making of the complaint;
- to the health service body, family health services provider or independent provider in question;
- any person who is alleged in the complaint to have taken or authorised the action complained of.

Where the Commissioner decides not to conduct an investigation pursuant to a complaint he must send a statement of his reasons for not doing so to the same list of persons. Where an investigation is not completed within 12 months a statement explaining the reason for the delay must be sent to the complainant[2].

The Commissioner may also send the report or statement to such other persons as he thinks appropriate.

1 Heath Service Commissioners Act 1993, s 14.
2 Health Service Commissioners Act 1993, s 14(2HA), inserted by Health Service Commissioner for England (Complaint Handling) Act 2015, s 1 (coming into effect on 26 May 2015).

2.73 Where the Commissioner considers that the person aggrieved has sustained injustice or hardship that has not been and will not be remedied he may lay a special report on the case before each House of Parliament. These special reports are additional to the annual report on the performance of his functions that the Commissioner is required to lay before each House of Parliament.

DISSATISFACTION WITH THE INVESTIGATION PROCESS OR REPORT

2.74 Where the complainant is not satisfied with the investigative process or the investigation report he may be able to apply for judicial review of the investigating body. Where the complaint is being dealt with in the local procedure, the court might consider that the appropriate route is first to complain to the Health Service Commissioner. A complainant might not always be expected to complain to the Commissioner before applying for judicial review, but this is likely to be the advisable first step in almost all cases.

2.75 While the Health Service Commissioner is a public body whose decisions are susceptible to judicial review, it will be clear from the analysis above that the 1993 Act affords the Commissioner a broad discretion in how to conduct her investigations. The courts have consistently recognised that the Commissioner's investigatory powers are very widely drawn[1]. A dissatisfied complainant would therefore have to establish an error of law or clear irrationality on the Commissioner's part in order to succeed in a claim for judicial review. In *R (on the application of Jeremiah) v Parliamentary and Health Service Ombudsman* Collins J said:

'The law, as set out by both the Act and its interpretation in previous decisions, is that the hurdle which has to be surmounted by any claimant seeking to persuade a court that an exercise of discretion by the Ombudsman is unlawful is a very high one indeed. The relevant leading decision is *R v Parliamentary Commissioner for Administration, ex p Dyer* [1994] 1 WLR 621 where Simon Brown LJ, as he then was, giving the judgment of the Divisional Court made it clear that the width of the discretion was, as he put it, made 'strikingly clear' by the legislature. That is a reference to the provision which is now in section 3(5) that the Commissioner should act in accordance with his own discretion. He said that it would always be difficult to mount an effective challenge on what may be called the conventional ground of *Wednesbury* unreasonableness. While manifest absurdity perhaps did not have to be shown, it would be almost as difficult to demonstrate that the Commissioner had exercised one or other of his discretions unreasonably in the public law sense …'[2].

1 See eg *R (on the application of Mencap) v Parliamentary and Health Service Ombudsman* [2011] EWHC 3351 (Admin).
2 [2013] EWHC 1085 (Admin), at para [30]. Endorsed by Jay J in *R (on the application of Morris) v Parliamentary and Health Service Ombudsman* [2014] EWHC 4364 (Admin) at [35].

FURTHER USE OF REPORTS AND INFORMATION DISCLOSED TO THE COMPLAINANT BY THE INVESTIGATING BODY

2.76   Once the complainant has been provided with a report of his complaint[1], whether by the NHS body in question or by the Healthcare Commissioner, it is his to do with as he pleases. The complainant can release the report into the public domain if he wishes to. So too can the complainant use the report as part of his investigations for a potential claim in clinical negligence. There will be no obligation on the NHS body in question (or the Commissioner) to disclose to the complainant any documents underlying the report until proceedings have been issued and the obligation to give disclosure of relevant material arises under CPR Part 31.

1 For the position before the report is finalised see above.

2.77   Complaints can therefore be used as a means of gathering evidence and assessing the credibility of the NHS body's rebuttal of the complaint. Moreover, those who intend to apply for Legal Services Commission Funding must have made a complaint before applying for that funding, save in exceptional circumstances.

PRIVATE PATIENTS

2.78   Where a patient receives NHS-funded treatment in a private hospital or clinic, the complaints procedure set out in this chapter applies. Where the treatment is private, that procedure has no application and the patient will have to use the procedure operated by the clinician or hospital or clinic in question. Some private providers are signed up to the voluntary Independent Healthcare Advisory Service code.

POLICY REQUIREMENTS AND GUIDANCE ON COMPLAINTS IN THE NHS

2.79   In considering the merit of a complaint, and whether it is being or has been processed appropriately, the policy context and relevant guidance can – and arguably should – be brought to bear. Even documents which express aspirations rather than legal obligations arguably stand as representations to the public about how they can expect their health issues and their complaints to be treated.

The NHS Constitution

2.80   The NHS Constitution[1] contains a collection of rights to which patients, staff and the public are entitled. There is a statutory requirement on all NHS bodies and providers, including the CQC and Monitor, private sector organisations providing NHS services, and the Secretary of State to have regard to it. The NHS Commissioning Board, clinical commissioning groups and Health Education England are obliged to promote it[2]. Many of these are derived from other legal sources but some are free standing. A failure to comply with a patient's right recognised by the Constitution is capable of being the subject of a complaint. The Constitution also contains 'pledges' which are matters which the NHS is 'committed to achieve' and are therefore matters to which a provider Trust is obliged to aspire but which it is under no legal duty to achieve. A failure to honour a pledge in a manner adversely affecting a patient might form the basis of a complaint[3].

1 The NHS Constitution for England. The current edition at the time of writing is dated 26 March 2013, but remains under review following the Mid-Staffordshire Public Inquiry Report.
2 Health Act 2009, ss 1–7; National Health Service Act 2006, ss 1B, 13C, 14P inserted by Health and Social Care Act 2012, ss 2, 23, 26.
3 The rights and pledges for patients are listed at pages 6-10 of the Constitution. The handbook (see below, page 5) explains that pledges are not legally binding and cannot be guaranteed for everyone all of the time. It is suggested that while this may mean they cannot form the basis of legal proceedings, there is no reason why in appropriate circumstances a breach of a pledge cannot justify a complaint.

2.81   The Constitution also includes seven Principles which, it is suggested, should be had regard to in the evaluation of issues and concerns raised in a complaint. In summary the Principles are[1]:

1   'The NHS provides a comprehensive service available to all irrespective of gender, race, disability, age, sexual orientation, religion and various other matters';
2   'Access to NHS services is based in clinical need, not an individual's ability to pay';
3   'The NHS aspires to the highest standards of excellence and professionalism';
4   'The NHS aspires to put patients at the heart of everything it does'. Under the Principle it is stated that:

> 'The NHS will actively encourage feedback from the public, patients and staff, welcome it and use it to improve its services'.

This suggests that the NHS should behave in a way which welcomes complaints and uses them to improve its services. Indeed the Government has recognised that feedback from patients is essential as the service improvement is dependent on feedback'[2]. In its response to the Mid-Staffordshire Public Inquiry report it said[3]:

> 'An effective trust board will promote a culture of openness, recognise the value of patient comments and complaints, and make it easy for patients, their families and carers to give feedback. An effective trust board will also be open about and publish regular information about the complaints it receives and the action it is taking as a result'.

Therefore there is a clear public interest in an effective complaints system being made available to all users of the NHS;

5   'The NHS works across organisational boundaries and in partnership with other organisations, in the interests of patients, local communities and the wider population'.

In the context of complaints it could be argued this raises an expectation that a complaint about a course of treatment provided by a series of different NHS bodies should be dealt with as one, as, indeed is required by at least the spirit of the complaints regulations;

6   'The NHS is committed to providing best value for taxpayers' money and the most effective, fair and sustainable use of finite resources';

7   'The NHS is accountable to the public, communities and patients that it serves.' Under this heading it is stated that:

> 'The system of responsibility and accountability for taking decisions in the NHS should be transparent and clear to the public, patients and staff. The Government will ensure that there is always a clear and up to date statement of NHS accountability for this purpose'[4].

The Statement requires Provider to support accountability to patients by:

'... having clear procedures for dealing with patient feedback and complaints'[5].

1 Handbook to the NHS Constitution pp 3–4.
2 Handbook to the NHS Constitution [2013] p 16.
3 http://www.engage.dh.gov.uk/francisresponse/recommendation/promoting-desire-to-receive-and-learn-from-complaints.
4 The current Statement of Accountability is to be found in the *Guide to the Healthcare System in England including the Statement of Accountability for England*, Department of Health, May 2013).
5 *Guide to the Healthcare System in England including the Statement of Accountability for England*, p 18 where an overview is offered of the organisations to which a complaint may be made, p 28.

2.82   There is a list of 'Values' which 'should underpin' everything the NHS does[1]. These include the following which are relevant to the handling of complaints:

- 'we fully involve patients, staff, families, carers, communities and professionals inside and outside the NHS. We put the needs of patients and communities before organisational boundaries. We speak up when things go wrong';
- 'we earn the trust placed in us by insisting on quality and striving to get the basics of quality of care – safety, effectiveness and patients' experience – right every time. We encourage and welcome feedback from patients, families, carers, staff and the public. We use this to improve the care we provide and build on our successes';
- 'we ensure that compassion is central to the care we provide and respond with humanity and kindness to each person's pain, distress, anxiety or need. We search for the things we can do, however small, to give comfort and relieve suffering. We find time for patients, their families and carers, as well as those we work alongside. We do not wait to be asked, because we care';
- 'we strive to improve health and wellbeing and people's experiences of the NHS';
- 'we ... make sure nobody is excluded, discriminated against or left behind. We accept that some people need more help, that difficult decisions have to be taken – and that when we waste resources we waste opportunities for others'.

1 *Guide to the Healthcare System in England including the Statement of Accountability for England* p 5 from which the quotations in the list following are extracts.

2.83 In relation to complaints handling the Constitution contains a number of 'rights':

1 a right to have any complaint made about the NHS acknowledged within three days and 'properly investigated';
2 a right to discuss the manner in which the complaint is to be handled, and to know the period within which the investigation is likely to be completed and the response sent;
3 a right to be kept informed of progress and to know the outcome of any investigation into the complaint, including an explanation of the conclusions and confirmation of any action needed;
4 a right to take the complaint to the PHSO if not satisfied with the way the complaint has been dealt with by the NHS;
5 a right for a person to make a claim for judicial review it he believes that he has been directly affected by an unlawful act or decision of an NHS body;
6 a right to compensation when harmed by negligent treatment.

2.84 There are a number of 'pledges' made in relation to complaints:

● to ensure you are treated with courtesy and you receive appropriate support throughout the handling of a complaint; and the fact that you have complained will not adversely affect your future treatment (pledge);
● to ensure that when mistakes happen, to acknowledge them, apologise, explain what went wrong and put things right quickly and effectively (pledge); and
● to ensure that the organisation learns lessons from complaints and claims and uses these to improve NHS services (pledge)[1].

1 *The NHS Constitution*, p 10; *Handbook to the NHS Constitution* pp 80–88.

2.85 Staff are offered the 'pledge' that the NHS will encourage and support them in raising concerns at the earliest reasonable opportunity about safety, malpractice or wrong doing at work, and in responding to and where necessary investigating concerns raised and will act consistently with the Public Interest Disclosure Act 1998[1].

1 *The NHS Constitution*, p 13. The provisions of the 1998 Act are now to be found in the Employment Rights Act 1996, principally in Part IVA, ss 43A–43L, Part V s 47B, and s 103A. Note that employers are now vicariously liable for acts of victimisation by a fellow worker relating to protected disclosures: s 47B(1A)–(1E) as inserted by the Enterprise and Regulatory Reform Act 2013, s 19(1); *Handbook to the NHS Constitution* p 120.

2.86 This being the NHS a relatively short Constitution (16 pages) is accompanied by a Handbook of guidance running to 146 pages[1]. This provides further information about the contents of the Constitution, such as the legal authority of the rights referred to, and explanations of the principles, values, rights and pledges.

1 *The Handbook to the NHS Constitution for England* (Department of Health, 26 March 2013) published in accordance with the Health Act 2009, ss 1 and 5.

NHS Litigation Authority Guidance

2.87 In guidance published in 2007 the NHSLA exhorted trusts and doctors to offer expressions of sympathy and explanations to patients when treatment has produced an adverse result:

'… it is both natural and desirable for those involved in treatment which produces an adverse result, for whatever reason, to sympathise with the patient or the patient's relatives and to express sorrow or regret at the outcome. Such expressions of regret would not normally constitute an admission of liability, either in part or in full and it is not our policy to prohibit them, nor to dispute any payment, under any scheme, solely on the grounds of such an expression of regret

Explanations: … In this area, too, NHSLA is keen to encourage both clinicians and NHS bodies to supply appropriate information whether informally, formally or through mediation. Care needs to be taken in the dissemination of explanations so as to avoid future litigation risks, but, for the avoidance of any doubt, NHSLA will not take a point against any NHS body or any clinician taking NHS indemnity, on the basis of a factual explanation offered in good faith before litigation is in train. We consider the provision of such information to constitute good clinical practice, and provided that facts, as opposed to opinions, form the basis of the explanation, nothing is likely to be revealed which would not subsequently be discloseable in the event of litigation'[1].

1 Public Inquiry report vol 3, p 1482.

2.88 In 2009 the Guidance was changed to read as follows:

'It is both natural and desirable for clinicians who have provided treatment which produces an adverse result, for whatever reason, to sympathise with the patient or the patient's relatives; to express sorrow or regret at the outcome; and to apologise for shortcomings in treatment. It is most important to patients that they or their relatives receive a meaningful apology. We encourage this, and stress that apologies do not constitute an admission of liability. In addition, it is not our policy to dispute any payment, under any scheme, solely on the grounds of such an apology.

Explanations: Patients and their relatives increasingly ask for detailed explanations of what led to adverse outcomes. Moreover, they frequently say that they derive some consolation from knowing that lessons have been learned for the future …

… Explanations should not contain admissions of liability. For the avoidance of doubt, the NHSLA will not take a point against any NHS body or any clinician seeking NHS indemnity, on the basis of a factual explanation offered in good faith before litigation is in train. We consider that the provision of such information constitutes good clinical and managerial practice.

To assist in the provision of apologies and explanations, clinicians and NHS bodies should familiarise themselves with the guidance on being open, produced by the [NPSA] … this circular is intended to encourage scheme members and their employees to offer the earlier, more informal, apologies and explanations so desired by patients and their families'[1].

1 Public Inquiry report vol 3, p 1483.

2.89 The advice was endorsed by all the major medical defence organisations and regulators in a statement published with the NHSLA guidance:

'For many years we have advised our members that, if something goes wrong, patients should receive a prompt, open, sympathetic and above all truthful account of what has happened. Any patient who has had the misfortune to suffer through an error of whatever nature should receive a full explanation and a genuine apology. We encourage members to adopt this approach. There are no legal concerns about taking this course of action: it is quite different from admitting liability'[1].

1 Public Inquiry report vol 3, p 1484.

2.90   The advice was reiterated in a leaflet published in December 2013:

'Saying sorry is not an admission of legal liability; it is the right thing to do. The NHSLA is not an insurer and we will never withhold cover for a claim because an apology or explanation has been given'[1].

1 NHSLA *Saying Sorry* (December 2013) http://www.nhsla.com/Claims/Documents/ Saying%20Sorry%20-%20Leaflet.pdf.

2.91   In 2014 the NHSLA stated in its guidance on the statutory duty of candour:

'Clinical staff may worry that being open with patients may compromise the ability to deal with a claim if one is subsequently made by the patient. In reality candour is all about sharing accurate information with patients and should be encouraged. The facts are the facts and staff should be encouraged and supported to help patients understand what has happened to them.

Where staff should be more cautious is where the facts are not yet known or where they are being asked to speculate beyond what is known. It can be more damaging to a relationship with the patient to speculate inaccurately than to investigate and find the facts and then provide the extra information'[1].

1 NHSLA, *NHS Litigation Authority Guidance on Candour*, November 2014 http://www.nhsla. com/OtherServices/Documents/NHS%20LA%20-%20Duty%20of%20Candour.pdf.

2.92   Guidance issued by the National Patient Safety Agency encouraged candour in these terms:

'Being open involves:

- acknowledging, apologising and explaining when things go wrong;
- conducting a thorough investigation into the incident and reassuring patients, their families and carers that lessons learned will help prevent the incident recurring;
- providing support for those involved to cope with the physical and psychological consequences of what happened'[1].

1 Public Inquiry report vol 3, p 1484; *Being Open: communicating patient safety incidents with patients, carers and their families* (November 2009) National Patient Safety Agency, pp 2, 6.

Duty of candour[1]

2.93   The guidance quoted above suggests that whatever may have been the common law position, there was an expectation imposed on the NHS and its component parts that where something unexpected had gone wrong with a patient's treatment, a full and frank explanation of what had happened would be offered to the patient. However, it was clear from the evidence obtained by the Mid-Staffordshire inquiries that this was not the reality in at least some parts of the system. In response to recommendations made by the inquiries on this issue, the government introduced a statutory 'duty of candour'. The duty of candour is found in the Health and Social Care Act

2008 (Regulated Activities) Regulations 2014[2], reg 20, which came into force on 27 November 2014 for NHS bodies, and 1 April 2015 for all other persons and organisations registered with CQC[3].

1 Otherwise known as 'Robbie's Law' after a long campaign by Will Powell, the father of Robbie who died in 1990. In 1998, the Court of Appeal in *Powell v Boladz* [1998] Lloyd's Rep Med 116, held that there was no legal duty of candour on an NHS doctor to tell the truth to the father of a dead child patient about the circumstances of death. The campaign was supported by AvMA: see http://cri.sagepub.com/content/20/1-2/32.full.
2 SI 2014/2936.
3 Health and Social Care Act 2008 (Regulated Activities) (Amendment) Regulations 2015, SI 2015/64, reg 10(2).

2.94   Regulation 20(1) provides that 'registered persons', ie all persons and organisations registered by CQC[1], must act in an open and transparent way in dealings with relevant persons in relation to care and treatment provided to service users in carrying out a regulated activity.

1 SI 2014/2936, reg 2; Health and Social Care Act 2008, ss 8–15.

2.95   A 'relevant person' means a patient or a person lawfully acting on a patient's behalf where the patient: (i) has died; (ii) is a child under 16 who is not competent to make a decision; or (iii) is over 16 and lacks capacity[1].

1 SI 2014/2936, reg 20(7).

2.96   Only regulated activities engage the duty of candour. Regulated activities are defined in Sch 1 to the Regulations and include:

- provision of personal care, such as assistance with eating and washing, for the elderly, sick or disabled;
- provision of residential accommodation for people receiving personal care, or receiving treatment for substance misuse;
- treatment of disease, disorder or injury by a health care professional, which is defined in Sch 1, para 4(4);
- assessment or treatment of people detained under the Mental Health Act 1983;
- surgical procedures carried out by a health care professional, which includes all pre-operative and post-operative care associated with those procedures;
- diagnostic and screening procedures such as X-rays or ultrasound scans;
- blood and organ donation;
- transport in a vehicle designed to carry a person requiring treatment;
- medical advice given over the phone in emergency situations;
- maternity and midwifery services;
- terminations of pregnancy;
- services provided in a slimming clinic, under the supervision of a medical practitioner;
- nursing care, including care provided in a person's own home;
- insertion of intrauterine contraceptive devices, by or under supervision of a health care professional.

2.97   **What is 'acting in an open and transparent way'?** The Regulations provide no definition, but reg 21(a) states that for the purposes of compliance with the Regulations, persons providing regulated activities must have regard to guidance issued by the CQC. The CQC's, initial guidance[1] adopted the definitions of openness and transparency used in the Mid-Staffordshire NHS Foundation Trust Inquiry report inquiry, namely:

- 'openness' means enabling concerns and complaints to be raised freely without fear and questions asked to be answered;
- 'transparency' means allowing information about the truth about performance and outcomes to be shared with staff, patients, the public and regulators.

1 CQC, Guidance for NHS Bodies (November 2014) p 38. The statutory guidance issued more recently (CQC, Guidance for providers on meeting the regulations, March 2015) does not repeat these definitions, but does not contradict them: see p 79.

2.98   Regulation 20(2)–(6) sets out mandatory steps that must be followed by an NHS body as soon as reasonably practicable after it becomes aware that a notifiable safety incident has occurred, namely an incident that:

- is unintended or unexpected; and
- occurs in respect of a service user during the provision of a regulated activity; and that
- in the reasonable opinion of a health care professional could result in or appears to have resulted in: (a) the death of the service user; or (b) severe harm, moderate harm, or prolonged psychological harm[1].

It will be noted that there is no requirement for the harm to have materialised, only that it could result from the regulated activity or appears to have done so.

1 Regulation 20(7).

2.99   The different degrees of harm are also defined in reg 20(7) as follows:

(1)   'severe harm' is a permanent lessening of bodily, sensory, motor, physiologic or intellectual functions, including removal of the wrong limb or organ or brain damage, that is related directly to the incident and not related to the natural course of the service user's illness or underlying condition;

(2)   'moderate harm' is significant but not permanent harm that requires a moderate increase in treatment, meaning an unplanned return to surgery, an unplanned readmission, a prolonged episode of care, extra time in hospital or as an outpatient, cancelling of treatment, or transfer to another treatment area (such as intensive care);

(3)   'prolonged psychological harm' is psychological harm which a service user has experienced, or is likely to experience, for a continuous period of at least 28 days.

2.100   Where a patient's death relates directly to the regulated activity rather than to the natural course of the patient's illness or underlying condition, it must be treated in the same way as severe harm.

2.101   Where the degree of harm is not yet clear but may fall into the above categories, the CQC guidance states that the relevant person must be informed of the notifiable safety incident in line with the requirements of the regulation[1].

1 CQC *Guidance for providers on meeting the regulations* (March 2015) p 80.

2.102   The first mandatory step when an incident has occurred is to notify the relevant person about the incident as reasonably practicable[1]. The CQC guidance suggests that notifications must be given within 10 working days. Notification must be given in the following prescribed way under reg 20(2)(a) and 20(3):

- it must be given in person by a representative of the NHS body;
- it must give an account (which to the best of the NHS body's knowledge is true) of all the facts that body knows about the incident at the date of the notification;
- the NHS body must advise what further inquiries are believed to be appropriate;
- the NHS body must apologise[2];
- it must be recorded in a written record that is kept securely.

1 Regulation 20(2).
2 Defined as 'an expression of sorrow or regret in respect of a notifiable safety incident': CQC *Guidance for providers on meeting the regulations* (March 2015) Annex C.

2.103   The way in which an apology must be given is carefully prescribed in reg 20(7) as an expression of sorrow or regret in respect of the notifiable safety incident. This is presumably to prevent empty apologies that fail to acknowledge how the harm was caused. The apology need not go so far as to include an admission of liability to comply with the duty of candour. As the NHSLA guidance referred to above explains, apologies are to be encouraged and are not an admission of liability.

2.104   An oral notification must be followed by a written notification that includes the results of any further enquiries made, although it is clear from the CQC guidance the NHS body should not wait until enquiries are complete before providing a written notification[1].

There are various circumstances in which an NHS body is not required to send a written notification[2].

1 Regulation 20(4).
2 Regulation 20(5).

2.105   As well as complying with the notification requirements, the NHS body is also under a duty to provide 'reasonable support' to the relevant person in relation to the incidence pursuant to reg 20(2)(b). The CQC guidance expands on 'reasonable support', referring to the duty to treat people with respect and empathy and to provide information about support groups, counselling and complaints procedures.

2.106   It is a criminal offence under reg 22(1)(c) for a health service body not to comply with elements of the duty of candour, namely the notification requirement under reg 20(2)(a) and the requirement to give that notification in accordance with the prescribed criteria. It follows that it is not an offence to fail to comply with the other requirements of the duty of candour above (eg the general requirement to be open and transparent or to provide a written notification). Breach of the duty of candour is a summary offence, punishable by a fine not exceeding £2,500[1].

1 Level 4 on the standard scale, Criminal Justice Act 1982, s 47.

2.107   A health service body has a defence under reg 22(4) if it can prove that it took all reasonable steps and exercised all due diligence to prevent the breach of the regulations.

2.108   The duty of candour does not create any *individual* duties on healthcare staff. However, in October 2014, a joint statement headed 'Openness and honesty – the professional duty of candour' was issued by Chief Executives of the General Medical Council, General Dental Council, General Chiropractic Council, General Optical Council, General Osteopathic Council, General Pharmaceutical Council, Nursing and Midwifery Council and the Pharmaceutical Society of Northern Ireland. The Chief Executives reminded their registrants that:

'Health professionals must be open and honest with patients when things go wrong. This is also known as "the duty of candour". …this is an essential duty for all professionals working with patients. Although it may be expressed in different ways within our statutory guidance, this common professional duty clarifies what we require of all the professionals registered with us, wherever they work across the public, private and voluntary sectors.'

So while an individual cannot commit the offence of failing to comply with the statutory duty of candour, he may be answerable to his professional regulator for the same failing.

2.109   With respect to complaints, it is observed that the duty of candour applies regardless of whether or not a complaint about treatment or care is made by or on behalf of a patient. Compliance with the duty of candour will not prevent the affected patient making a complaint about the matter, indeed the information volunteered by the NHS body may be used as the basis of a complaint. In many cases, however, the offer of full information, an explanation and an apology may well be all the patient requires and may avoid the patient needing to make a complaint.

CONCLUSION

2.110   The history of complaints procedures in the NHS shows that the handling of them has been bedevilled over many years by defensive or incompetent handling, poor support for complainants, and a lack of learning from them. Nonetheless a complaint may be helpful to many who merely want their concerns resolved, and to those with more serious issues who want information before deciding what to do next. The system is complicated and is in the process of yet another period of change, so care is required in ensuring that any advice given is up to date and correct. The final report of the House of Commons Health Committee before the 2015 General Election made the following recommendation[1]:

'We recommend that the complaints system be simplified and streamlined by establishing a single "branded" complaints gateway across all NHS providers. This should be available online, but not exclusively so. There should be adequate resourcing to enable complaints to be examined, identified, and directed speedily to the appropriate channel'.

2.110 *Chapter 2*

As this chapter has shown, such a reform would undoubtedly remove a great deal of the potential for confusion that currently exists.

1 House of Commons Health Committee 'Complaints and Raising Concerns' HC350 (13 January 2015) para 31.

Sir Robert Francis QC chaired the Mid-Staffordshire Hospital Inquiries, is a board member of the CQC and President of the Patients Association.

CHAPTER 3

The UK medical defence organisations and the NHS Litigation Authority

Dr John S F Holden

John Mead

This chapter was written in two parts. The section on medical defence organisations was by John Holden, the section on the NHS Litigation Authority was by John Mead (para **3.96** onwards).

GENERAL INTRODUCTION

3.1   The first part of this chapter begins in 1858 and traces the establishment, evolution and modern function of the medical defence organisations in the UK. The second part of the chapter begins in 1990 with the introduction of NHS indemnity and describes the establishment and modern function of the NHS Litigation Authority in 1995.

THE UK MEDICAL DEFENCE ORGANISATIONS

Introduction

3.2   The first part of this chapter describes the generic nature and role of a medical defence organisation (MDO) within the UK, illustrated by reference to the three organisations: the Medical Defence Union (MDU), the Medical Protection Society (MPS) and the Medical and Dental Defence Union of Scotland (MDDUS) (nowadays an established UK-wide organisation). The three organisations are fundamentally similar, but the following sections include descriptions of key differences.

3.3   The following account has been aided by reference to the websites of the three MDOs[1] and in particular the respective annual reports for 2012. Otherwise, specific documents have been individually referenced.

1 www.mddus.com; www.themdu.com; www.medicalprotection.org/uk.

3.4   The MDOs find themselves at the hub of modern healthcare for the simple reason that they exist for the benefit of their members, who in turn owe their existence to the patients for whom they care. The sections that follow inevitably refer to a large number of bodies including the General Medical Council (GMC), General Dental Council (GDC) and National Clinical Assessment Service and processes (such as coronial inquests and the NHS complaints process) that are described in detail elsewhere in this book. These paragraphs, therefore, do not duplicate those fuller descriptions, but simply describe the relevant aspects as they impact upon the members of MDOs.

3.5   Dr Robert W Forrest, Convener of the MDDUS (1902–1910) stated:

'No member of the profession, however he may have enjoyed immunity from attack and however confident he may be of the care with which he discharges his duties, can claim to be free from charges and claims made against him. Such claims are made when they are least expected and deserved'[1].

Those sentiments remain true a century later. To facilitate understanding of the nature and purpose of the modern MDOs, the circumstances of their creation are reviewed.

1 See, for a full history, Muir and Bell *A Century of Care – A History of the Medical and Dental Defence Union of Scotland* (MDDUS, 2002).

Historical background

3.6   The Medical Act 1858 was enacted 'to regulate the qualifications of practitioners in medicine and surgery', introducing clarity to the concept of a legally qualified medical practitioner. The Act established 'The General Council of Medical Education and Registration of the United Kingdom', known then simply as 'The Council'. Registrars were appointed to maintain and publish a register of suitably qualified practitioners. The Council was also charged with publishing a British Pharmacopeia. The benefit to patients was that they could identify registered doctors, and to this day the modern GMC exists fundamentally to register doctors to practise medicine in the UK and to protect, promote and maintain the health and safety of the public by ensuring proper standards in the practice of medicine.

3.7   The Dentists Act 1878 introduced a dental register. Only dentists listed in the dentists' register could use the title 'surgeon dentist' or 'dental surgeon'.

3.8   In 1883 the British Medical Journal reported a charge of manslaughter against two Dulwich practitioners, following the death of a child. The magistrate dismissed the case as vexatious. Unsurprisingly, the case generated anxiety, causing the President of the Royal College of Physicians, Sir William Jenner, to establish a committee to collect subscriptions to assist with the legal expenses incurred by the two doctors. In a further case, Dr David Bradley of Chesterfield was wrongly convicted of assaulting a female patient in his surgery. He served 8 months in prison before receiving a pardon. The committee funds enabled all three doctors to return to practice, but the outrage generated in the medical community following Dr Bradley's wrongful conviction led directly to the establishment of the Medical Defence Union in 1885. Following the resignation of some MDU members, the London and Counties Medical Protection Society (now known simply as the Medical Protection Society) was established in 1892.

3.9   A clinical negligence claim against Dr Murray of Leith, in relation to his management of an infected finger, led to the establishment of the Medical and Dental Defence Union of Scotland in 1902. As the British Dental Journal noted in 1903, the fundamental differences between Scottish and English law and judicial procedures merited, at that time, a purely Scottish defence organisation. The modern MDDUS is, of course, well established as a UK-wide organisation.

3.10   The MDU first admitted dental practitioners in 1948. The MPS subsequently established its own wholly-owned subsidiary Dental Protection Limited, followed by the Dental Defence Union, a specialist division of the MDU, in 1994.

Mutual status

3.11   The Department for Business, Innovation and Skills recognises 'mutual' as an umbrella term for several different ownership models. The defining characteristic of a mutual organisation is that 'the organisation is owned by, and run for, the benefit of its members, who are actively and directly involved in the business – whether its employees, suppliers, or the community or consumers it serves, rather than being owned and controlled by outside investors'[1]. The MDO mutual model is generally as stated by the MPS:

'We are a mutual organisation, meaning that we are owned by our membership. All subscriptions paid by members are retained by the business; we have no shareholders to answer to, so members' money is invested solely for their benefit'[2].

1 Department for Business, Innovation and Skills *A Guide to Mutual Ownership Models* (November 2011) at p 2.
2 Medical Protection Society *The Right Choice* (2012) at p 4.

3.12 The benefits of membership of the three MDOs, as mutual not-for-profit organisations, are discretionary. Ultimately the extent of assistance is determined by the respective Boards of Management under the individual Memorandum and Articles of Association.

Medical defence organisations and insurance

3.13 The public, lay and health professionals often speak or write loosely, inter-changing the terms 'insurance' and 'indemnity'. The MDOs are not insurance companies and the following account is provided to facilitate a fuller understanding of the evolution and current functioning of the MDOs.

3.14 The Insurance Companies Act 1974 contains no definition of 'contract of insurance'. In *MDU v Department of Trade and Industry*[1], the court considered whether an MDU member against whom a claim was made could require the MDU to consider whether to conduct proceedings on his behalf and provide him with indemnity and whether membership constituted a contract of insurance. The court held that the member did not have a right to have proceedings conducted by the MDU on his behalf or to be given an indemnity and although the member acquired a benefit it did not satisfy the requirements for a contract of insurance[2].

1 [1979] 2 WLR 687.
2 Summary of the case by 3 Verulam Buildings; for further detail see http://www.3vb.com/userfiles/pdfs/Newsletter_Autumn_2008.pdf.

3.15 Although the MPS, as described above, is a mutual company, it established MPS Risk Solutions Limited (an insurance company authorised by the Prudential Regulation Authority and regulated by the Financial Conduct Authority and the Prudential Regulation Authority) as a wholly-owned subsidiary to address the corporate malpractice insurance needs of doctors and other health professionals[1]. In June 2012, MPS Risk Solutions Limited withdrew from the insurance market, to enable MPS to focus on its core business of providing discretionary indemnity. All policies have expired and the main purpose of MPS Risk Solutions Limited now is 'to focus on providing the highest standard of service for claims management, in respect of those incidents that have been notified and accepted under policies that were previously in force'[2].

1 Medical Protection Society *The Right Choice* (2012) at p 14.
2 www.mpsrs.co.uk (2015).

3.16 Soon after the millennium, the MDU introduced a professional insurance indemnity policy (although the MDU was not itself an insurance company). Although the non-claims assistance to MDU members continued solely under a discretionary model, claims assistance now had contractual and discretionary elements. The policy operated on a claims-made basis. Dr Christine Tomkins, the MDU's Chief Executive, described the inter-relation between the insurance policy and discretionary assistance to the House of Lords European Union Committee in 2008, and the minutes provide a helpful summary of the situation at that time[1]. Although Dr Tomkins was reported as stating 'we believe that doctors should have similar cover if they move provider or cease to practise for whatever reason', the MDU announced in 2013 that from 1 April 2013, as members renewed their membership, they would no longer be issued with an insurance policy, as going forward the full range of member services and benefits would be provided exclusively from MDU funds. The explanation given by Dr Tomkins was that in a 'prevailing economic and regulatory environment where low investment returns are the norm, we (the MDU) believe insurance no longer represents the best value for money for members'.

1 http://www.publications.parliament.uk/pa/ld200809/ldselect/ldeucom/30/08110604.htm.

3.17   Whilst the MDU remains a mutual company owned by its members, MDU Services Ltd (a wholly-owned subsidiary of the MDU) is an insurance intermediary, authorised and regulated by the Financial Conduct Authority (FCA) for insurance mediation and consumer credit activities only.

Discretionary indemnity versus insurance

3.18   The three MDOs are mutual organisations that provide assistance to their members on the basis of 'occurrence', meaning members may seek assistance of the respective MDO so long as they are, or were, a member at the time of the incident in question.

3.19   Occurrence-based indemnity is often cited by MDOs as a defining advantage over the insurance 'claims made' model (which requires an insurance policy to be in place at the time the claim is made) as practitioners leaving an insurance company will need to buy run-off cover, or negotiate purchase of a 'nose-payment' (whereby the new indemnifier may agree to provide retrospective indemnity).

3.20   It is generally postulated by MDOs that the very nature of discretion enables the organisation to extend assistance without being fettered by the inflexibility of an insurance product whose rigidity may not be able to accommodate the complex and rapid changes in clinical practice and society itself. The MDOs do not currently charge an excess or cap cover. Further, MDOs have knowledge and expertise built up over more than a century and provide to their members medico-legal advice and assistance over and beyond simple indemnity for claims in clinical negligence, as described below. Such extended benefits are generally considerably more limited, or non-existent, in the insurance market and if provided would normally attract additional payment.

Demographic aspects

3.21   The MPS describes itself as the world's leading mutual defence organisation, based upon an excess of 280,000 members in more than 40 countries. The main jurisdictions covered, outwith the UK, are Ireland, South Africa, New Zealand, Hong Kong, Singapore, Malaysia, the Caribbean and Bermuda, Kenya and others. The MPS does not permit permanent membership in all countries, most notably the USA and Canada (except to students on electives).

3.22   The MDU describes itself as the leading medical defence organisation in the UK, based on a membership which includes more than half the doctors in the UK. The MDU confines its membership to the UK and Ireland, although short-term indemnity is available for teaching or supervised training purposes except in the USA, Australia, Canada, Bermuda, Israel, Hong Kong, Nigeria or Zimbabwe.

3.23   The MDDUS concentrates on the separate legal jurisdictions that exist within Scotland, England, Wales and Northern Ireland and does not offer indemnity outside these countries. MDDUS, as its name suggests, has its historical roots in Scotland and continues to maintain its preeminent share among Scottish doctors and dentists. Prior to the early 1990s membership was confined to Scottish graduates or those working in Scotland, but in recent years growth is predominantly due to an increase in English members. The 2012 annual report states that over 17 per cent of English GPs are MDDUS members (compared to 9 per cent in 2006), with a total membership in excess of 35,000, more than 50 per cent of whom practise outside Scotland.

3.24   All three MDOs provide worldwide indemnity for Good Samaritan acts. A Good Samaritan act is generally understood as the provision of clinical services, without charge, at an incident arising as an emergency when the member is a bystander, rather than participating within their normal contracted duties or clinical practice. Common examples include attendance at a road traffic accident or a public event, where the practitioner is a spectator.

The requirement for indemnity or insurance

3.25   There are no current express statutory requirements or provisions dealing with professional indemnity arrangements for registered medical practitioners or those seeking registration with the GMC. Indeed, there is no compulsory statutory requirement for any doctor to be a member of an MDO or even to have professional indemnity or insurance arrangements[1]. However, since 1997, the GMC in its core guidance *Good Medical Practice* has placed a professional duty on doctors to have such arrangements in place. Paragraph 63 states that registered doctors must make sure that they have adequate insurance or indemnity cover so that their patients will not be disadvantaged if they make a claim about the clinical care a practitioner has provided in the UK[2]. Therefore, practitioners in the UK whose work is indemnified by their employer or covered by NHS need not belong to an MDO to satisfy this requirement. However, as MDOs regularly point out in their educational and marketing activities, the wise practitioner will seek the wider benefits of an MDO, which are described below.

1 http://www.gmc-uk.org/doctors/information_for_doctors/14195.asp.
2 General Medical Council *Good Medical Practice* (2013), para 63.

3.26   Standard 1.8 of the GDC's publication *Standards for the Dental Team* states that 'You must have appropriate arrangements in place for patients to seek compensation if they suffer harm'. The only types of cover that the GDC recognises are:

- dental defence organisation membership, either personally or via an employer's membership;
- professional indemnity insurance held by the practitioner or the employer;
- NHS/Crown indemnity.

3.27   The GDC does not require dentists to have their own policy and/ or defence organisation membership, but stresses the merits of defence organisation membership in terms of the additional support and advice, particularly during GDC fitness to practise investigations[1].

1 http://www.gdc-uk.org/Dentalprofessionals/Standards/Documents/Guidance%20on%20 indemnity%20(Sept%202013).pdf.

Membership

3.28   Registered practitioners (and in the case of medical practitioners, holders of a licence to practise) may apply for membership. The applicant will usually be asked to agree to disclosure of a letter of good standing from any previous MDO, which will be considered, in conjunction with the applicant's declaration of any previous claims, complaints, regulatory, disciplinary or relevant criminal matters, as part of an underwriting process.

Subscriptions

3.29   General practitioners contracted to provide NHS services are not generally covered by NHS indemnity. GP subscriptions are normally set according to the number of sessions the GP works. Junior hospital doctors will normally pay a subscription according to their stage of training. Compared to the GP rate, the subscription will normally be relatively modest, as the NHS normally indemnifies such doctors against claims, so the risks borne by the MDO are those that are unrelated to clinical negligence. The subscription normally allows junior doctors a modest private income, such as may be generated from signing certificates and incidental documents.

3.30   Consultants pay subscriptions that are actuarially determined according to their speciality and private non-indemnified earnings, taking into account the historical claims experience of the organisation for the speciality. Consultants whose work is exclusively NHS indemnified will usually pay a basic subscription that provides the non-claims related benefits of membership, (although in practice the basic subscription may permit and indemnify a modest private income).

3.31 Since 1 April 2013, Local Education and Training Boards (LETBs) have taken on the functions of Postgraduate Medical Deaneries in England. Some of the 13 LETBs now arrange block indemnity for GP speciality trainees (GPST) in England directly with an MDO, after considering tenders. The MDO indemnifies the individual GPST against claims arising from the GP placement. NHS indemnity is retained during hospital placements but the individual GPSTs usually continue to receive the additional benefits of membership of the relevant MDO.

Education and marketing

3.32 MDOs increasingly provide educational material to their members. The more traditional means of a journal (delivered by post), lectures, seminars and workshops persist and retain a useful function, but are increasingly supplemented by online resources in the form of advice sheets, articles, e-newsletters and journals, videos and podcasts.

3.33 Education is more than a simple marketing strategy. Practitioners who are aware of the potential jeopardies that they potentially face when working (be it a claim, complaint, coroner's inquest, criminal allegation, GMC investigation or disciplinary investigation) are wiser, especially if they are more mindful of simple methods to minimise the risk of criticism; whether by keeping better records, making appropriate use of a chaperone, or better communication. Consequently, the practitioner is not only more informed but also poses less risk to the patient, who in turn is safer, more reassured and content, and less likely to express dissatisfaction. As a result practitioners will need less formal assistance from their MDOs, whose financial reserves will have less demands put upon them, ultimately constraining the future subscription members will need to pay. Further, the public purse benefits whenever a formal investigation is prevented. Therefore, an MDO's education program is good for the patient and society as well as the member and the MDO.

3.34 Practitioners are more likely to change MDO than they were a generation ago, but brand loyalty is strong. The MDOs are commercial competitors and seek to recruit both neophyte and established practitioners. The medical and dental schools are key sources of recruits. Students may join one or all MDOs but at qualification will harden their choice to a single MDO. Increasingly, as described above, MDOs compete to recruit new members in bulk by tendering for GPST members via the LETBs. The challenge is then to retain the member when they enter general practice as a salaried practitioner or partner – a challenge hardened by the possibility that the partnership may have existing group membership of another MDO.

24-hour advisory helpline

3.35 A member's first contact with their MDO is usually via the telephone advice line. MDOs recognise the value their members attach to this resource. The vast majority of contacts occur during the working day but the availability of 24-hour medico-legal advice reassures members. The initial contact is normally with a medico-legal adviser (MLA), or dento-legal adviser (DLA), who may be supported by colleagues with a background in nursing or practice management. Whilst many calls are concluded with verbal advice, the advice line is the portal for most new written files. The range of advice and assistance is described below.

Medico-legal advisers and dento-legal advisers

3.36   MLAs are registered medical practitioners who are expected to participate in the GMC's re-validation process and to retain a licence to practise as MLAs. Most have previous clinical experience as a general practitioner or a hospital-based specialist, holding postgraduate qualifications such as Membership of the Royal College of General Practitioners or a specialist college such as the Royal College of Surgeons or Royal College of Physicians and increasingly, higher clinical doctorate degrees. Most MLAs already possess, or acquire early in their medico-legal career, an undergraduate or postgraduate legal degree. Increasingly, MLAs have also completed vocational legal training, and a few have also practised as a solicitor or barrister. Many MLAs have a higher degree in medical law. Increasingly, MLAs are Members (or Fellows) of the Faculty of Forensic and Legal Medicine of the Royal College of Physicians (FFLM), that was inaugurated in 2006.

3.37   DLAs have a similar background to MLAs, albeit with clinical experience in dentistry rather than medicine. DLAs often continue to undertake some clinical work. Currently, DLAs are not eligible to become Members of the FFLM, but may apply to be examined for the Faculty's newly introduced Diploma of Legal Medicine.

The role of the medico-legal adviser and dento-legal adviser

3.38   MLAs and DLAs participate in the telephone advice rota, as above, but the majority of an MLA's time is spent on a range of written files, as described below.

3.39   A small number of members become very distressed during GMC or disciplinary investigations in particular. The MLA is well placed to support the member and ensure that the member is consulting their GP and obtaining occupational health guidance and by flagging up specific agencies such as the BMA's 'Doctors for Doctors' service[1].

1 http://bma.org.uk/practical-support-at-work/doctors-well-being/about-doctors-for-doctors.

3.40   The role of the adviser in relation to claims files varies across the three MDOs. Some advisers work exclusively in non-claims related work, alongside medical or dental colleagues who are committed entirely to claims. Other advisers have a dual role, working in conjunction with claims handlers. All advisers work closely with solicitors (whose role is described below).

3.41   Advisers participate in educational activities across the full spectrum, from medical and dental students to general practitioners and specialists, which include workshops, seminars, formal lectures and specialist conventions, often with support from marketing colleagues. Advisers also contribute to the individual MDO's own publications, including journals, newsletters and press releases, and externally to the medical press. Occasionally advisers will be interviewed on radio or television in relation to topical medico-legal matters.

With experience and seniority advisers may also participate in additional roles such as underwriting, risk-management and liaison with external agencies.

Legal services

3.42   Legal services are a major expense but play a key role within the wider function of an MDO. In recent years MDOs have developed in-house legal divisions. The major saving for MDOs is VAT. However, the number, flow and complexity of cases cannot be absolutely predicted. Consequently, the MDOs require the assistance of external specialist legal firms, negotiating rates within a service level agreement. In-house and external solicitors will instruct barristers from specialist chambers, where appropriate.

Assistance to members

3.43   The need for medico-legal advice grows year on year. In 2012, the MDDUS advisory team handled 5 per cent more member contacts (telephone, email and letters) than the previous year, continuing a seven-year rise.

3.44   Members may seek assistance with a variety of matters. The fundamental requirements are that the practitioner is a member of the relevant MDO at the time of the incident in question and that the nature of the assistance falls within the remit of the MDO.

3.45   The MDOs publish indicative membership guides to inform members of what is normally included and not included in their membership. The key element is that the incident should arise from the *bona fide* practice of clinical medicine, although ultimately all assistance is at the discretion of the individual board of management.

3.46   Assistance to members is broadly 'non-claims' or 'claims' (although of course many non-claims matters have the potential to evolve into a claim). 'Non-claims' matters are sub-divided as follows. The distinctions are arbitrary as they may overlap, morph or evolve into more than one category.

Non-claims assistance

Advice

3.47   Many telephone requests for advice are straightforward and are closed at the end of the call. Such calls include advice on disclosure of records, consent and confidentiality. Some scenarios are complex and challenging and may generate a written file, allowing time for considered advice to be given and, where appropriate, a formal legal opinion to be sought. The advice line is the main initial portal for the following specific categories of assistance.

Crime

3.48   Crime is an uncommon reason for members to contact an MDO, but criminal allegations have considerable personal impact upon a medical or dental practitioner and the additional potential to generate disciplinary and regulatory processes.

3.49   The most common criminal scenarios that members face are unrelated to their clinical practice – drink-driving, altercations in night-clubs and domestic scuffles – and would not normally attract direct assistance from an MDO. However, the adviser has the opportunity to ensure members know when they are obliged to inform the GMC[1] (and other bodies such as the NHS England Local Area Team, in relation to the Performers List Regulations). This opportunity is significant in terms of damage limitation, as the police have historically informed the GMC when a practitioner is charged according to an agreement between the GMC and the Association of Chief Police Officers[2]. This meant that a failure to inform the GMC pro-actively risked an investigation and potential criticism by the GMC both for the incident itself and the failure to disclose. The Home Office is currently reviewing the circumstances in which the police share information with regulatory bodies at the early stages of a criminal investigation in England, Wales and Northern Ireland, as described in the GMC strategy and policy circular, April 2014[3].

1 http://www.gmc-uk.org/guidance/ethical_guidance/21184.asp.
2 http://www.cps.gov.uk/legal/assets/uploads/files/mou.pdf.
3 http://www.gmc-uk.org/16___The_Home_Office_review_of_police_disclosure_of_pre_conviction_information_about_doctors.pdf_56433195.pdf.

3.50   Individual MDOs exercise discretion as to whether a member is assisted with a GMC investigation subsequent to a non-clinically related criminal matter.

3.51   Criminal investigations may arise from allegations of inappropriate sexual contact with a patient in a clinical context; mainly involving a male doctor and a female patient, but not exclusively. Such allegations are serious matters for a medical or dental practitioner, who if found guilty are likely to receive a custodial sentence.

3.52   Some allegations are vexatious and many arise from simple misunderstandings, such as a failure to explain why a particular examination is required. Miscommunication is not confined to chest, breast and pelvic examination; even fundoscopy, in a darkened room, with close proximity between a doctor and patient can alarm a vulnerable patient. Clear explanations, obtaining consent, recording the history and need for the examination and the examination itself are not only good practice but also reduce the risk of unwarranted criticism. In particular the adoption of, and adherence to, a chaperone policy in line with the GMC's guidance on intimate examinations and chaperones is paramount[1].

1 http://www.gmc-uk.org/guidance/ethical_guidance/21168.asp.

3.53   The first a doctor may know of an allegation is a dawn visit to their home by the police. A GP is likely to be suspended under the Performers Lists Regulations[1], and a hospital doctor excluded under the Trust's Conduct, Capability and Health procedure. A short-notice GMC Interim Orders Panel is almost inevitable. Interim suspension would be expected. Conditions upon the doctor's practice would be an excellent outcome. Media attention is likely. These processes may generate further historic allegations from other patients who may identify their experience with the reported detail, especially in cases where a pattern to a doctor's behaviour emerges.

1 National Health Service (Performers Lists) (England) Regulations 2013, SI 2013/335.

3.54   Even if an allegation is vexatious or without foundation, it may take 18 months or more for a criminal process to be discontinued, by which time a doctor may be relatively de-skilled, or even expelled from a partnership under the terms of a partnership agreement. Consequently, doctors and dentists in this position should seek partnership, employment or contractual advice from the British Medical Association (BMA) or British Dental Association (BDA) at an early stage.

3.55   Even if a doctor or dentist is acquitted by the criminal court, a subsequent GMC or GDC investigation is almost inevitable. Whereas the jury at the criminal trial will have been asked to consider whether a doctor is guilty, beyond reasonable doubt, of a specific criminal charge(s), the regulatory bodies' remit is much wider, and at a standard of proof akin to a civil standard. Consequently, even an acquitted practitioner remains at serious risk of a determination of impairment and a sanction of suspension or erasure from the register if any of the significant facts are found proven by the regulator.

3.56   Following the death of a patient a practitioner may be approached by a police officer. Usually the officer is acting on behalf of the coroner, but the possibility of an investigation into gross negligence manslaughter should be considered. The wise practitioner will contact their MDO before making any statement. Duty solicitors rarely have the experience to understand the nature and implications of crime arising from clinical practice and its interface with the regulator. If the interview is to be under caution then it is of paramount importance that a suitably experienced solicitor is present. MDOs have access to expert solicitors 24 hours a day (although in practice most police interviews under caution take place by appointment during working hours).

3.57   Further to existing sanctions, the government announced in June 2014 the intention, subject to Parliamentary approval, to introduce new criminal offences of ill-treatment and wilful neglect, with effect anticipated in 2015. All three MDOs participated in the consultation in 2014. The MDU expressed the view that professional regulators provide sufficient safeguards, as the threshold for finding impaired fitness to practise is set at the civil standard, and that consequently 'there is no need of an additional criminal sanction, especially one with a higher threshold of proof'. The MPS expressed the view that the proposed sanctions will cause healthcare professionals to become more fearful of criticism such that they will be 'less open and willing to admit genuine errors to either patients or management' making 'healthcare less responsive and accountable to patients'. The Department of Health countered these arguments by pointing out that not all health and social care professionals are regulated and stressing the importance of holding organisations to account in addition to individuals. Penalties for individuals will reflect those attached to the offence of wilful neglect of persons without capacity as set out in the Mental Capacity Act 2005, s 44. Organisations will be subject to fines and/or the issuing of publicity orders and remedial orders, similar to those available in the Corporate Manslaughter and Corporate Homicide Act 2007 in relation to convictions of corporate manslaughter. The new offences will apply, in England and Wales, to the provision of adult health and social care in all formal health or adult social care settings[1].

1 https://www.gov.uk/government/uploads/system/uploads/attachment_data/file/319042/Ill-treament_or_wilful_neglect_consultation_response.pdf.

General Medical Council and General Dental Council

3.58   Doctors and dentists fear an investigation by their regulatory body, as an adverse outcome may blight or end a career. Indeed, the possibility of a regulatory complaint during a career is rising year on year. The MDDUS Annual Report 2012 describes a 41 per cent increase in the number of GMC cases handled on behalf of its members and a GDC increase of 67 per cent, but 96.5 per cent of GMC cases and 86.8 per cent GDC cases (in the year 2011) concluded with no sanctions imposed against MDDUS members. Overall, in 2012, 10 per cent of GMC cases reached a fitness to practise panel, of which the outcomes were[1]:

- suspension: 31 per cent;
- erasure: 26 per cent;
- no impairment: 23 per cent;
- conditions: 9.5 per cent;
- warning: 6 per cent;
- impairment; no further action: 3 per cent;
- voluntary erasure: 1 per cent;
- undertakings: 0.5 per cent.

Whilst these figures are reassuring, practitioners are nevertheless encouraged to contact their MDO at the earliest stage of a regulatory investigation, as the initial response may be critical to the outcome.

1 http://www.gmc-uk.org/2012_Annual_Statistics.pdf_53844772.pdf.

3.59   The Office of the Health Professions Adjudicator (OHPA) was established by the Health and Social Care Act 2008, with the intention that OHPA would take over fitness to practise hearings from the GMC from 1 April 2011. The coalition government decided in late 2010 not to go ahead with the OHPA programme. The Health and Social Care Act 2012 subsequently abolished OHPA. Instead, the Medical Practitioners Tribunal Service (MPTS) was launched in 2012, with the aim of strengthening professional and public confidence in the impartiality, fairness and transparency of hearings.

3.60   The MPTS provides a hearings service that is fully independent in its decision-making. Its adjudicatory role is separate from the investigatory role of the GMC. The MPTS is funded by the GMC, but accountable to Parliament and to the GMC Council for delivery of its objectives. The GMC retains its role as investigator and prosecutor in fitness to practise hearings. The MPTS has its own offices in Manchester, separate from both the GMC's London and Manchester offices. Hearings are now entirely held in Manchester.

3.61   Following changes to the GMC rules, a GMC case manager may in certain cases require details of the witnesses (including the practitioner) on whom they intend to rely and signed witness statements setting out the substance of their evidence. Furthermore a witness's written statement will normally stand as evidence in-chief, limiting the witness's oral evidence to cross-examination by the opposing party, re-examination by the party who called them to give evidence and questions from the panel. However, a practitioner currently has the residual opportunity to appear in front of a panel and give evidence.

3.62   His Honour David Pearl, Chair of the MPTS, said to the MDDUS in March 2013 that 'the changes will also allow for better case management – which is key to ensuring hearings are run more efficiently. Case managers will make binding decisions on what evidence can be presented, cutting out lengthy legal argument'. The Chair also stated:

'I think there is also an argument for allowing the MPTS to impose cost sanctions on both the GMC and defence if there are unnecessary delays. This is common in other tribunals and works effectively'.

Such developments await a fuller assessment with the passage of time, but reflect a greater embracement by the MPTS of a civil process.

Complaints: local resolution

3.63   The most common criticisms practitioners receive of their clinical practice are complaints, representing, in 2012, 21 per cent of calls to the MDDUS seeking advice. The NHS complaints process is addressed in a separate chapter, but a number of aspects are especially pertinent to MDOs.

3.64   The Local Authority Social Services and National Health Service Complaints (England) Regulations 2009[1] simplified the NHS complaints process in England, introducing a simpler two-tier (rather than three) system: local resolution (via the NHS provider directly, or the relevant Clinical Commissioning Group or NHS England) and the Parliamentary and Health Service Ombudsman. Whereas it was previously possible to close the NHS complaints process when an intention to litigate was intimated, the 2009 Regulations allow a claim to be pursued in parallel with an NHS complaint. This change provides a free facility to test a claim, creating an additional challenge for both practitioner and MDO when a solicitor acts as a patient's representative within the complaints process.

1 SI 2009/309.

3.65 Every complaint should be taken seriously and handled with sensitivity and respect. Indeed, the GMC requires registered doctors to respond promptly, fully and honestly to those who express dissatisfaction and where appropriate to apologise[1]. The challenge is how to provide a sincere and pertinent response without compromising the defence of a claim. The importance of practitioners seeking the early advice and assistance of their MDO cannot be over emphasised. Usually, where an apology is relevant, the key lies in making a genuine and heartfelt apology for any breach (such as a failure to seek a second opinion or to request an investigation) but without touching upon aspects of causation. Indeed, such considerations are often properly outwith the ability of an individual practitioner to comment upon and further, are the remit of experts and ultimately the court, in the event of a claim.

1 General Medical Council *Good Medical Practice*, 2013, para 61.

Complaints: the Ombudsman

3.66 The Ombudsman is now the second tier of the NHS complaints process across the UK, represented by the Parliamentary and Health Service Ombudsman (England), the Public Services Ombudsman for Wales, the Scottish Public Service Ombudsman and the Northern Ireland Ombudsman's Office. In England, The Health Service Commissioner (or Health Service Ombudsman) for England was first established under the National Health Service Reorganisation Act 1973 and the office opened for business on 1 October 1973. However, the Ombudsman now draws power almost wholly from the Health Service Commissioners Act 1993.

'When Things go Wrong': the duty of candour

3.67 'Virtually every clinician knows the sickening feeling of making a bad mistake ... You know you should confess, but dread the prospect of potential punishment and of the patient's anger'[1].

The *Compact Oxford English Dictionary* describes candour as 'the quality of being open and honest'. It refers to the Latin origin 'candor', meaning 'whiteness, purity'. The late JH (Cardinal) Newman remarked that 'openess and candour are rare qualities in a statesman'. It is outwith the remit of this chapter to comment on that observation, but clearly candour is a professional obligation upon doctors and dentists. The reactive component of candour is reflected in the duty of a practitioner to respond to a complaint (see above). The pro-active element – when something goes wrong – is that which has become more specifically associated with the term 'candour'. There is nothing new about the concept in UK healthcare, except perhaps the use of the word 'candour' itself. Indeed, Kate Allsopp stated in the MDU's 1986 annual report that 'For over 50 years the MDU has advised doctors and dentists, that if something goes wrong, patients are entitled to a prompt, sympathetic and above all truthful account of what has happened'. Yet, it was not until the 1998 edition of *Good Medical Practice* that the GMC indicated the steps a doctor should take 'If things go wrong'[2]. The current GMC guidance states:

'You must be open and honest with patients if things go wrong. If a patient under your care has suffered harm or distress, you should:

   a   put matters right (if that is possible)
   b   offer an apology
   c   explain fully and promptly what has happened and the likely short-term and long-term effects'[3].

1 Wu 'Medical Error: the Second Victim' (320) British Medical Journal 726–727.
2 General Medical Council *Good Medical Practice*, 1998, paras 16 and 17.
3 General Medical Council *Good Medical Practice*, 2013, para 55.

3.68   Since April 2013 NHS and non-NHS providers of services (other than those commissioned under primary care contracts) have had a contractual duty of candour, following an amendment to the NHS Standard Contract's Service Conditions, obliging doctors and dentists working in hospitals and other non-primary care contracted services to support their employing provider in the delivery of that duty by following local procedures. The contractual test of harm is an incident that results in moderate harm, severe harm, or death according to the National Patient Safety Agency definitions for grading patient safety incidents, within the NHS document *Seven Steps to Patient Safety*[1]. The contractual requirements relating to the duty of candour are set out in Service Condition 35. The NHS Commissioning Board document *2013/14 NHS Standard Contract – Technical Contract Guidance* contains an associated national quality requirement in Schedule 4 Part B. Annex 4 of the document provides guidance on how to implement and enforce the contractual requirements. In essence, this requires the contracted service provider to ensure that patients (or their family or carer) are told about patient safety incidents that affect them, receive appropriate apologies, are kept informed of investigations and are supported to deal with the consequences[2].

1 www.nrls.npsa.nhs.uk/resources/collections/seven-steps-to-patient-safety/?entryid45=59787.
2 www.england.nhs.uk/wp-content/uploads/2013/02/contract-tech-guide.pdf.

3.69   Whilst registered doctors have had a longstanding professional duty of candour, as described above, there has been increasing pressure for this duty to be extended since 1996, following the death of Robbie Powell from Addison's disease[1]. MDOs have long taken the view that the professional duty of candour (as stated by the GMC) was sufficient. However, the Mid Staffordshire NHS Foundation Trust Public Inquiry (the Francis Inquiry), February 2013[2], recommended that in relation to harm to patients a statutory duty of candour be imposed not only on healthcare providers, but also registered medical practitioners and other registered professionals 'who believe or suspect that treatment or care provided to a patient by or on behalf of any healthcare provider by which they are employed has caused death or serious injury to the patient'. The recommendation was that the professional would have a duty 'to report their belief or suspicion to their employer as soon as is reasonably practicable' (recommendation 181). Further, the Inquiry recommended that it:

'should be made a criminal offence for any registered medical practitioner, or nurse, or allied professional or director of an authorised or registered healthcare organisation:

- knowingly to obstruct another in the performance of these statutory duties;
- to provide information to a patient or nearest relative intending to mislead them about such an incident;
- dishonestly to make an untruthful statement to a commissioner or regulator knowing or believing that they are likely to rely on the statement in the performance of their duties (recommendation 183)'.

The Inquiry recommended that the Care Quality Commission (CQC) should police observance of the duty.

1 www.avma.org.uk/data/files/robbies_story__updated_july_2008.pdf.
2 www.midstaffspublicinquiry.com/report.

3.70   Following the Francis Inquiry and a series of reviews[1] the government proposed a much wider statutory duty of candour than the existing contractual duty of candour on organisations that provide services under the NHS Standard Contract. The Care Bill will place a specific duty on the Government to include a duty of candour on providers[2] registered with the CQC. The consequence, if the passage of the Bill is as planned, will be that a statutory duty of candour must always be one of the registration requirements placed on CQC registered providers (both healthcare and adult social care providers). The duty of candour itself is to be set out in secondary legislation in regulations. At the time of writing, following a recent consultation, the registration requirements will be part of a consolidated package of regulations to be introduced in October 2014.

1 Including the initial Government response (*Patients First and Foremost*, March 2013), a CQC consultation (June 2013), the Berwick Review (August 2013), a detailed Government review (*Hard Truths: the Journey to Putting Patients First'*, November 2013 and the Dalton Williams review.
2 The proposed statutory duty of candour would apply to England only. *Putting Things Right* (2011) already places a duty upon NHS organisations in Wales to be open that harm may have occurred.

3.71   What may these proposals mean for MDOs and their members? For the individual practitioner it was, at face value, reassuring that the government's review *Hard Truths: the Journey to Putting Patients First*, in November 2013 did not intend to introduce any candour related offences on individuals. However, the proposed regulations state that the statutory duty of candour falls to 'the registered person' – defined as a person who is the service provider or registered manager in respect of the registered activity. Therefore, in small organisations such as GP partnerships, the differentiation between a duty upon an organisation and an individual may be meaningless. We await the outcome and the implications for the individual practitioner.

3.72   The Department of Health consultation[1] states that the professional regulatory bodies are in the process of strengthening references to candour in their guidance and will review their guidance to the misconduct panels to ensure they consider whether practitioners have raised concerns promptly.

1 Department of Health, Introducing the Statutory Duty of Candour – a Consultation on Proposals to Introduce a New CQC Registration Regulation, March 2014.

3.73   What seems clear is that the distinction between organisations and individuals will be blurred. There may be more complaints to the GMC or GDC about individual members of MDOs, with a potential increase in clinical negligence claims. Certainly, practitioners must ensure that they adhere to their regulatory duties of candour and are encouraged to contact their MDO for advice when a patient safety incident occurs. The MDOs have a supportive and constructive role in advising their members, including advice on drafting a letter to a patient or conducting significant event analysis and other reflective activities, such as writing a contemporaneous account, which the MDO can keep on file pending a more formal process, once satisfied that nothing more active is necessary.

Coroner's inquests

3.74 Most doctors (and the rare dentist) will at some time in their career be required to provide a report for the coroner and perhaps attend an inquest to give evidence. MDOs have an important role in supporting members through the process.

3.75 Good advice on drafting a report may avoid the need for a coroner to call a practitioner to attend an inquest. If the practitioner is called to attend, the MLA can assist by ascertaining whether the practitioner is called as a witness to fact or as a properly interested person. In practice this is not always initially clear. The point is of particular relevance, as reg 9(2)(h) of the National Health Service (Performers Lists) (England) Regulations 2013 requires general practitioners called as a properly interested person to inform their NHS England Local Area Team.

3.76 If a practitioner is called as a properly interested person he is entitled to representation. The MLA has an important role in ascertaining whether the member is perceived to be vulnerable to criticism by the family or the coroner and whether the family, or any other party is legally represented. Where appropriate the MDO may arrange for legal representation of general practitioners and specialists who have attended the deceased patient in a non-NHS capacity. Trusts will normally arrange legal representation for hospital doctors and any community practitioner who is NHS indemnified. Where there is conflict between the interests of the Trust and an individual practitioner, the relevant MDO may agree separate representation.

3.77 The coroner may conclude that preventative action to avoid further deaths should be taken. If so, an individual member or their practice may be the recipient of a Regulation 28 (previously Rule 43) report of the Coroners (Investigations) Regulations 2013[1]. The MDO has a key role in assisting members formulate, under reg 29, a considered and reflective response clearly outlining remedial proposals within the requisite 56 days. Criticism by a coroner constitutes criticism within an official inquiry and requires a registered doctor to inform the GMC[2]. A well-constructed response may mitigate potential criticism by the GMC.

1 SI 2013/1629.
2 http://www.gmc-uk.org/guidance/ethical_guidance/21184.asp.

Disciplinary process

3.78 Disciplinary investigations are very distressing for practitioners. They tend to arise at short notice and are often poorly particularised. The concerns may relate to an individual's conduct, performance or health or, not uncommonly, a combination of these. The allegations or concerns may initially appear to arise from an isolated incident, but often a picture of complex dysfunction manifests itself, frequently extending back over a number of years. There may be a long history of difficult relations both between the subject of the investigation and colleagues and the subject and management. A parallel investigation by the GMC is not unusual. There may well be an overlapping background of clinical complaints or claims in clinical negligence. Sometimes an initial concern evaporates quickly but frequently investigations drag on, often over a number of years.

3.79 Disciplinary concerns frequently focus on a practitioner's conduct. An MDO's area of expertise is professional conduct, arising from the *bona fide* clinical care of patients. Allegations such as poor time keeping, bullying and theft are matters of personal conduct and as such an MDO will encourage a member to seek the advice (where the practitioner is a member) of the BMA, BDA or Hospital Consultants and Specialists Association (HCSA). In practice, personal and professional conduct aspects are less easily differentiated and often co-exist and overlap. Accordingly, the adviser may helpfully (with the member's permission) liaise with the BMA, BDA or HCSA.

3.80 The adviser uses skill and experience to establish clarity about the allegations, the key individuals (such as the case manager and case investigator), and may attend investigatory meetings, often at short notice, in support of a member. The early identification of the appropriate procedure is of fundamental importance.

3.81 NHS organisations in England have been required, since 2005, to have local procedures for handling concerns about the conduct, performance and health of medical and dental employees, (excluding those who perform PCT Medical Services for the exercise of those functions, as far as they are covered by the Primary Care List System), that are consistent with the national framework *Maintaining High Professional Standards in the Modern NHS*. The process was agreed with the BMA and BDA, and replaced circular HC(90)9, as well as the Special Professional Panels ('the three wise men') provided for in HC(82)13 and abolished the right of appeal to the Secretary of State held by certain practitioners under para 190 of the Terms and Conditions of Service. It was also agreed that the framework should be issued to NHS Foundation Trusts as advice, and in practice Foundation Trusts often elect to adopt MHPS[1].

1 In Wales WHC (90)22 is still active, although it is understood that protracted discussions regarding introducing MHPS are ongoing.

3.82 Frustrations surround the practical application of MHPS. MHPS gives a superficial impression of addressing misconduct, but on closer examination it: (1) makes no distinction between personal and professional misconduct; and (2) indicates that doctors and dentists employed in the NHS will be disciplined for misconduct under the same locally based procedures as other staff. There is a perception that Trusts seek to pursue matters as 'conduct', and the MLA has a role in resisting this approach where inappropriately applied.

3.83 Medical and dental general practitioners in England are subject to disciplinary procedures under the National Health Service (Performers Lists) (England) Regulations 2013[1]. The Regulations contain an element that complicates the interface between regulatory and performers lists investigations, which often run in parallel or series with each other. The 2013 Regulations (in contrast to the previous 2004 Regulations) state that where a regulator has suspended a practitioner (except in relation to health) they must be removed from the performers list. No distinction is made between an interim decision (where the facts have not ben considered, merely consideration given to whether interim sanctions are necessary to protect patients whilst the concerns are investigated) and a substantive suspension. It is understood that this departure from the 2004 Regulations is the result of poor drafting and NHS England is working with the Department of Health to reconsider the issue.

1 SI 2013/335.

Clinical negligence claims

3.84   Medical and dental practitioners tend to fear becoming the subject of a claim in clinical negligence, but in practice a claim is generally considerably less stressful for the individual clinician than a GMC investigation, or even many complaints.

3.85   There is a general perception that the number of claims involving members of MDOs is increasing in recent years, but matters must be closely considered within the context of legislative changes[1]. Lord Justice Jackson published the final report of his fundamental review of the rules and principles governing the costs of civil litigation in January 2010. Some of the recommendations were incorporated into the Legal Aid, Sentencing and Punishment of Offenders Act (LASPO) 2012, implemented from 1 April 2013, which reforms civil litigation funding and costs in England and Wales. The changes are set out in the primary legislation (LASPO) and secondary legislation, which includes the Civil Procedure Rules. The reforms apply across civil litigation, but have notable relevance in clinical negligence. Significant changes, well summarised by the Ministry of Justice[2], include the following:

- conditional fee agreements (CFAs) have been used extensively for many years. CFAs remain available in civil cases, but the additional costs involved (success fee and insurance premiums) are no longer payable by the losing side. If a 'success fee' is charged it will be payable by the winning party. Usually, for the claimant. This will be from the damages recovered;
- no win, no fee damages based agreements (DBAs), previously applicable in tribunals (such as employment tribunals) are available as a means of funding civil litigation cases for the first time. Under a DBA a successful claimant's lawyer may take a fee as a percentage of their client's recovered damages;
- claimants' damages are protected in that the fee that a successful claimant has to pay the lawyer – the lawyer's 'success fee' in CFAs, or 'payment' in DBAs – is capped at 25 per cent (for clinical negligence matters) of the damages recovered, excluding damages for future care and loss;
- general damages for non-pecuniary loss such as pain, suffering and loss of amenity are increased by 10 per cent;
- a new regime of 'qualified one way costs shifting' ('QOCS') is introduced in personal injury cases which caps the amount that claimants may have to pay to defendants. Claimants who lose, but whose claims are

conducted in accordance with the rules, are protected from having to pay the defendant's costs;

- a new sanction on defendants to encourage earlier settlement of claims.

1 'In the last five years, NHS spending has grown by 12 per cent. In the same period, liabilities for negligence have actually doubled. With the current rate of growth, they will take only six years to reach around £50 billion. The Medical Defence Union thinks that is unsustainable...' (Lord Sharkey 20 January 2015 HoL column 1202).
2 https://www.justice.gov.uk/civil-justice-reforms as updated at 7 November 2014.

What do these changes mean for claims frequencies?

3.86 In 2012 the MDDUS reported a 35 per cent rise in claims intiated over the year compared to 2011, including a 42 per cent rise in general practitioner claims. In the same period, claims intiated against general dental practitioners increased by 53 per cent. Whilst some of the growth was attributable to a rise in membership (8 per cent rise in total membership in 2012) there was also an increase in claims frequency.

3.87 In 2012, the MDU observed an increase of 20 per cent in the number of new claim notifications, compared with an average 8.6 per cent increase each year for each of the preceding four years, 2008–2011. The MDU considered that a key reason for the rise was the increase in CFAs, climbing from 5 per cent of cases funded in this way in 2004 to 48 per cent in 2012. The MDU indicated that it would monitor the impact of Lord Justice Jackson's recommendations to see if the aim of better proportionality between damages and costs would be achieved.

3.88 The MPS considered, in its 2012 Annual Report, the extent to which the acceleration of claims may be attributed to the legal reforms, noting the apparent signing up by claimant solicitors of as many clinical negligence claims as possible prior to 1 April 2013, as LASPO 2012 significantly restricts the level of costs recoverable from an unsuccessful defendant. The MPS observed an apparent 'pull forward' of claims and a possible increase in claims due to publicity drives of claimant solicitors as a final push before LASPO 2012 became effective in April 2013.

What has been the impact of the changes, so far as can be determined?

3.89 The MDDUS reported a further rise in claims in 2013 (against a background of a rise in membership numbers of 9.6 per cent), but observed a very sharp difference between Scotland and the rest of the United Kingdom. Scottish medical and dental members experienced far fewer claims, and medical members experienced far less expensive claims (the difference, it is believed, is deeply rooted in a number of societal and cultural factors). On a positive note, from the perspective of an MDO, just under 70 per cent of claims against MDDUS members that concluded in 2013 were closed with no payment being made.

3.90 The MDU reported, in 2013, a rise in demands upon its claims and legal services for the seventh year running, opening over 20 per cent more new medical claims than in 2012, with a rise of 10 per cent in dental claims. The MDU indicated its perception that the steep rise in claims was again attributable to the legal changes of April 2013, believing that claimant solicitors, in anticipation of the need to reduce fees in future, 'had rushed to take on claimants under the old CFA whereby clients had no interest in costs and solicitors could recover an uplift by way of a success fee from the defendant'. The MDU further observed that claimant solicitors 'continue to notify cases under the old arrangements, prolonging the disproportionately high costs the legal charges are intended to address'.

3.91 Similarly, the MPS 2013 annual report, states 'We are still tracking our experience of post-April (2013) cases to determine the impact it is having both in relation to claim frequency and also claimant lawyer behaviour, but in the meantime we expect to continue receiving notifications of pre-April 2013 cases for some time'.

3.92 The MDOs publish their annual reports in the summer following the relevant year, so at the time of writing the 2013 reports are the most up to date documents available for scrutiny. It is therefore rather early to make any profound comment on the effect of LASPO 2012 on claims frequency. However, in the 2013 annual report the MDU indicate:

'In the last quarter of 2013 claims against dentists slowed – a glimmer of hope, perhaps, that the effects of the Jackson reforms, and in particular the scrapping of the old conditional fee (or 'no win no fee') arrangements are starting to be felt'.

Time will tell.

Consultation and change

3.93 The MDOs regularly liaise with the GMC and GDC, and respond to consultation papers circulated by the regulators and government departments and agencies. Recent consultations have included 'wilful neglect' and 'duty of candour', which are described above.

The medico-legal framework within which modern healthcare operates is subject to constant change. A major development in recent years has been the establishment of the Care Quality Commission (CQC), already referred to in the context of the duty of candour, above.

Care Quality Commission

3.94 The CQC is the independent regulator of health and social care in England, with a remit to ensure that hospitals, care homes, dental and GP surgeries, and all other care services in England provide people with safe, effective, compassionate and high-quality care, and to encourage the service providers to make improvements. The CQC registers health and adult social care services, performing regular inspections, which may be unannounced. The CQC also protects the interests of vulnerable people, including those whose rights are restricted under the Mental Health Act 1983. The CQC works closely with local councils and other agencies, inspecting children's services jointly with Ofsted, youth offending services with HMI Probation, and prison healthcare with HMI Prisons.

3.95   Providers of health and adult social care must comply with the Health and Social Care Act 2008 (Regulated Activities) Regulations 2010[1], and the Care Quality Commission (Registration) Regulations 2009[2]. These two pieces of legislation set out the essential standards of quality and safety, consisting of 28 regulations and associated outcomes in relation to the experiences that the CQC expect people to have as a result of the care they receive. When checking compliance the CQC focuses on the 16 regulations within Part 4 of the Health and Social Care Act 2008 (Regulated Activities) Regulations 2010, as these most directly relate to the quality and safety of care.

Although both sets of regulations came into force on 1 April 2010 it remains early to determine the full impact of the CQC upon medical and dental members of MDOs.

1 SI 2010/781.
2 SI 2009/3112.

NHS INDEMNITY

3.96   MDOs have encountered many changes over the last century and more, but perhaps the greatest development was the introduction of NHS indemnity in 1990.

The role of the NHS Litigation Authority

Introduction

3.97   Established on 20 November 1995, the NHS Litigation Authority (NHS LA) owes its origin to the introduction of NHS Indemnity and to the subsequent establishment of NHS trusts in England in the early 1990s.

Clinical Negligence Scheme for Trusts (CNST)

3.98   This scheme became effective on 1 April 1995. All Trusts in England may join CNST and as at April 2013 membership stood at 100 per cent, at which level it has been for over ten years. The excesses initially applied were abolished with effect from 1 April 2002, which means that cover is ground-up in all cases. This is not an insurance scheme but rather a financial pooling arrangement. Contributions are based upon number and speciality of staff, compliance with risk management standards and increasingly, claims experience. The scheme covers incidents on or after 1 April 1995 (or whenever the relevant Trust joined). With effect from 1 April 1998 all claims have been handled direct by a dedicated team at NHS LA. CNST is a comprehensive scheme involving pooling of funds, patient safety and learning activities and claims handling. Uptake of 100 per cent is a testament to its popularity and success. From April 2013, independent providers of NHS healthcare have been entitled to join CNST, for their NHS activities.

Establishment of NHS LA

3.99   The NHS LA is part of the NHS, being a Special Health Authority established by statutory instrument with effect from 20 November 1995[1].

Initially, its sole function was to administer the Clinical Negligence Scheme for Trusts, which in practical terms entailed supervising the scheme managers. Almost immediately, however its tasks were increased significantly.

1 SI 1995/ 2800.

What is the NHS LA?

3.100 NHS LA is a Special Health Authority and an arms-length body of the Department of Health. It is a not-for-profit part of the NHS but not (as some may believe) an insurance company.

The NHS LA'S aims and objectives are listed in its Framework Document:

'The Secretary of State's overall aims for the Authority in administering the Schemes are to promote the highest possible standards of patient care and to minimise the suffering resulting from any adverse incidents which do nevertheless occur. In particular, the Authority will contribute to these aims by its efficient, effective and impartial administration of the Schemes, and by advising the Secretary of State on any changes that may be needed in the light of experience in running the Schemes and of changing circumstances'.

The above paragraph clearly demonstrates the breadth of the NHS LA's area of engagement, extending to clinical risk management and advice to the Secretary of State. It is very notable that the NHS LA owes a duty to NHS patients.

3.101 The Framework Document continues:

'Subject to this overriding aim, the specific objectives of the Schemes are:

Maximising resources available for patient care

    (i)   to minimise the overall costs of clinical negligence to the NHS and thus maximise the resources available for patient care, by defending unjustified actions robustly, settling justified actions efficiently, and creating incentives to reduce the number of negligent incidents'.

As an organisation, the NHS LA is ultimately accountable to Parliament. This is clearly appropriate for a body which is part of the NHS, administers substantial sums of public money and is involved in a great deal of high-profile litigation.

The conduct of litigation

3.102 The NHS LA commenced handling claims in 1996. Immediately it became apparent that 'the absolute need was for the litigation in respect of clinical negligence to be brought under effective control'[1]. External solicitors instructed by health authorities and Trusts ranged from the very good to the deplorable. Huge sums of money were being lost to the NHS as a consequence of the previous fragmented and largely uncontrolled system.

1 NHS LA Report and Accounts for 1999.

3.103 At the same time as the NHS LA was coming to grips with problems on the cases it had acquired, Lord Woolf published (in July 1996) the final version of his report *Access to Justice*. He devoted an entire chapter to medical negligence litigation, describing it as an area in which 'the civil justice system was failing most conspicuously to meet the needs of litigants'[1]. His conclusions were very much in line with the NHS LA's own findings: delay, disproportionate costs, the prolonged maintenance of untenable positions by both sides, and suspicion and lack of co-operation between the parties.

1 *Access to Justice*, chapter 15, 2.

3.104 Lord Woolf welcomed the establishment of the NHS LA as 'undoubtedly a positive move'[1] and noted that its chairman had already committed the NHS LA to 'support any steps taken to improve the legal process'[2]. Furthermore, Lord Woolf stated that he had 'no doubt that the more systematic and professional approach to claims management which the NHS LA is encouraging will help to achieve the necessary change of culture'[3], ie to bring about fundamental improvements in the conduct of clinical negligence litigation.

1 *Access to Justice*, chapter 15, 9.
2 *Access to Justice*, chapter 15, 11.
3 *Access to Justice*, chapter 15, 33.

3.105 How did the NHS LA bring about improvements in the conduct of claims? First, it played a major part in devising the Pre-action Protocol for the Resolution of Clinical Disputes, one of only two protocols ready for implementation on 26 April 1999, the date on which Lord Woolf's reforms came to fruition. This protocol aims, amongst other things, to minimise mistrust between the parties, encourage greater openness, reduce delay and costs and diminish the need for litigation by encouraging early disclosure of records and detailed letters of claim.

3.106 Second, the NHS LA took firm control of the litigation process by making it abundantly clear to defence solicitors that the old ways, which were rightly criticised by Lord Woolf and which were apparent on so many inherited files, were no longer acceptable. Delays by the defence are not tolerated, and numerous positive initiatives have been implemented:

1   where liability is indefensible, every effort is made to quantify the claim fairly, as quickly as possible, with a view to putting forward settlement terms;
2   unnecessary expert reports are avoided;
3   where evidence indicates that a claim is defensible, the matter is brought on for hearing promptly. The NHS LA is committed to supporting the NHS by defending resolutely unmeritorious claims;
4   periodical payments are encouraged. These benefit both claimants and defendants;
5   dialogue with those representing the claimant is actively sought;
6   a very firm line on excessive costs is taken;
7   health bodies are encouraged to offer apologies and explanations to patients and their relatives;
8   if more than one NHS body is involved in the same claim, and they are unable to resolve the dispute between themselves, the NHS LA will arbitrate.

Safety and Learning Service

3.107   A new Safety and Learning service is being developed. This has been influenced by key reports presented by Robert Francis QC (Mid Staffordshire), Sir Bruce Keogh, Professor Donald Bewick, Ann Clwyd MP and Professor Tricia Hart. Initial concentration has been upon learning from claims, and helping members to identify trends in their claims experience. An extranet has been developed, which gives members live access to their data via the NHS LA claims system and enables them to target specific areas to prevent harm to patients and staff. This facility also offers members access to a safety and learning library, good practice guidance on safety, case studies and links to external material. Over time, it will allow members to benchmark themselves against other trusts and to share information and learning through an online forum.

3.108   Specialist advisory groups on maternity and surgery issues have been established: these areas provide, respectively, the most expensive and largest number of claims in NHS LA's portfolio. An analysis of Ten Years of Maternity Claims was published in 2013[1].

1 www.nhsla.com.

National Clinical Assessment Service (NCAS)

3.109   This joined NHS LA on 1 April 2013, having previously been hosted by NPSA and NICE successively. Unlike its earlier status as a semi-independent organisation, NCAS is an integral part of NHS LA.

NCAS has a number of roles, all of which complement the existing functions of NHS LA:

- helping employers to resolve concerns about the professional practice of doctors, dentists and pharmacists working in the NHS and independent healthcare sector;
- providing expert support and advice, clinical assessment and training to the NHS and other healthcare organisations;
- supporting organisations by providing case investigations and case manager training.

Recent developments

3.110   From 1 April 2013 independent providers of NHS healthcare have been eligible to join CNST for their NHS work. Over fifty such organisations signed up in the first year, including most of the major companies.

3.111   On 1 April 2013 the Legal Aid, Sentencing and Punishment of Offenders Act 2012 took effect: the abolition of legal aid for most cases and a new fee regime were implemented. New costs rules under the CPR (qualified one way costs shifting and the regime on recoverability of success fee and insurance premium) were also introduced. There are conflicting considerations: the cost of litigation for the defendant is reduced but the risk of litigation for the claimant also reduced.

3.112   Numbers of new clinical negligence claims reported to NHS LA have risen very significantly:

- 2009/10: 6,652
- 2010/11: 8,655
- 2011/12: 9,143
- 2012/13: 10,129

This is an increase of 52.2 per cent in four years. By far the most important factor behind these figures is the system of costs recoverability in place prior to 1 April 2013 under which claimants' lawyers could seek an uplift of up to 100 per cent on their base fees from the defendant if operating under a Conditional Fee Agreement (CFA), also known as 'No Win, No Fee'. It remains to be seen what effect the more equitable recovery rules, introduced following recommendations from Sir Rupert Jackson, will have.

3.113   The scale of fees paid to claimants' solicitors on cases closed in one recent financial year (2012/2013) is illustrated by the following figures:

- fees paid to claimant firms: £205.3m;
- fees paid to defendant firms: £49.4m[1].

In other words, of the total of £254.7m paid on costs by NHS LA on this group of cases, some 80 per cent went to claimant firms. Admittedly, the claimant figure includes cases which were resolved without NHS LA having to instruct one of its own panel firms, but the broad picture is both alarming and disproportionate and clearly illustrates why the Jackson reforms were required.

1 Note: this comparison does not take into account any preparatory work by the NHS LA.

3.114   Total claims expenditure by NHS LA in recent years was as follows:

- 2011/12 Clinical: £1,095m; Non-clinical: £182m;
- 2012/13 Clinical: £1,117m; Non-clinical: £141m.

Even though total outlay in each of these financial years was in excess of £1 billion, this was less than 1 per cent of the overall NHS budget.

3.115   Despite rises in both claim numbers and expenditure, NHS LA's efficiency increased during this period. The average time taken to resolve clinical negligence claims fell from 1.45 years in 2009/10 to 1.25 years in 2012/13. These figures include all the complex brain-damage cases which necessarily take much longer to conclude, so the average time to resolve more straightforward cases is less than 1.25 years.

Total expenditure on administration, per claim, was just £546 in 2012/13. Defence legal costs, as a percentage of total damages paid, were only 10.8 per cent in the same financial year.

The future

3.116   There are many challenges ahead including expansion of the Safety and Learning service, updating and upgrading the NCAS portfolio, resisting ever larger and more imaginative schedules of loss and ensuring that valid claims continue to be paid promptly and fairly. With a track record of almost 20 years of achievement, NHS LA looks forward with confidence. And on 1 April 2013 the biggest changes ever affecting the economic drivers of clinical negligence litigation were implemented and the consequences of these changes are awaited.

EDITORIAL NOTE: COST OF LITIGATION

3.117 The cost of clinical negligence litigation is of public concern[1]. It has been raised in Parliament:

The following table shows the payments paid out by the NHS LA in settlement of clinical negligence claims both in absolute terms and as a percentage of the Department's total departmental expenditure limit (TDEL) in each of the last 10 years for which data are available.

Payments made by NHS LA in respect of clinical negligence claims against the NHS:

Year	Total Payments	(TDEL) Outturn	Percentage
	£'000	£'000	
2004–05	502,893	69,000,000	0.7%
2005–06	560,308	76,000,000	0.7%
2006–07	579,390	81,000,000	0.7%
2007–08	633,325	84,000,000	0.8%
2008–09	769,226	91,000,000	0.8%
2009–10	786,991	98,000,000	0.8%
2010–11	863,398	100,000,000	0.9%
2011–12	1,277,372	103,000,000	1.2%
2012–13	1,258,880	105,000,000	1.2%
2013–14	1,192,538	110,000,000	1.1%

(House of Lords, Written answer: 6 January 2015: Column WA182)

And:

NHS: Clinical Negligence

Asked by Lord Sharkey

To ask Her Majesty's Government what are the causes of the £3.1 billion increase in the National Health Service's potential liabilities for clinical negligence to £25.7 billion between 31 March 2013 and 31 March 2014.

The Parliamentary Under-Secretary of State, Department of Health (Earl Howe) (Con): My Lords, there are several factors behind this increase. These include the rise in numbers of patients cared for and the complexity of their care. In addition, there has been a general rise in litigation across a number of sectors, including the NHS, which is driven in part by no-win no-fee agreements. High costs incurred by claimants in bringing civil litigation have also played a role in the increasing clinical negligence cost and associated provisions.

Lord Sharkey (LD): In the last five years, NHS spending has grown by 12%. In the same period, liabilities for negligence have actually doubled. With the current rate of growth, they will take only six years to reach around £50 billion. The Medical Defence Union thinks that is unsustainable and has suggested reducing liabilities by changing the law. It suggests allowing courts to take account of the fact that the NHS and local authorities can provide some of the treatments required by successful claimants. Does the Minister agree that this is part of the way forward?

Earl Howe: My Lords, moneys paid in settlement of clinical negligence claims cannot be reclaimed or recycled in the way that my noble friend appears to suggest because, in the nature of NHS care, it is free from the patient's perspective...

(House of Lords, 20 January 2015: Column 1202)

1 See for example 'Medical negligence costs 'threat' to National Health Service' Financial Times, Sarah Neville and Alistair Gray (10 February 2015).

3.118   The Law Reform (Personal Injuries) Act 1948, s 2(4) provides as follows:

'In an action for damages for personal injuries (including any such action arising out of a contract), there shall be disregarded, in determining the reasonableness of any expenses, the possibility of avoiding those expenses or part of them by taking advantage of facilities available under the National Health Service Act 1977 or the National Health Service (Scotland) Act 1978, or of any corresponding facilities in Northern Ireland'.

3.119   The general principle is that a claimant is entitled to recover for his loss only; damages are intended to put the claimant in the position he would have been in had the tort not occurred. A defendant is only liable for the loss he has caused. There is a rule against double recovery and there is a duty to mitigate loss.

3.120   The 1948 Act thus is a statutory exception to the well-established common law principles for computing damages. Its effect *may be* to permit windfall damages in respect for the cost of future care and medical treatment, **where these are provided by the health service**. Sadly the NHS still falls short in the provision of services to those who suffer the most grievous injuries. The government has no plans to repeal this statutory provision.

CHAPTER 4

Clinical negligence and human rights

Philip Havers QC

Rachel Marcus

Kate Beattie

INTRODUCTION

4.1   The Human Rights Act 1998 (HRA 1998) seeks to give further effect to rights and freedoms guaranteed under the European Convention on Human Rights (the ECHR). This is achieved in four main ways.

4.2   First, so far as it is possible to do so, primary legislation and subordinate legislation must be read and given effect in a way which is compatible with the Convention rights[1]. If it is not possible to do so, a higher court may make a declaration of incompatibility[2]. The declaration does not affect the validity, continuing operation or enforcement of the provision in respect of which it is given, but it enables a Minister to take remedial action to make amendments to the legislation to remove the incompatibility.

1 HRA 1998, s 3.
2 HRA 1998, s 4.

4.3   Second, it is unlawful for a public authority (which includes a court or tribunal) to act in a way which is incompatible with a Convention right[1]. A person who claims that a public authority has acted (or proposes to act) in a way which is incompatible with a Convention right may bring proceedings against the authority or rely on the Convention right or rights concerned in any legal proceedings, if he is (or would be) a victim of the unlawful act[2].

1 HRA 1998, s 6.
2 HRA 1998, s 7.

4.4   Third, UK courts and tribunals determining a question which has arisen in connection with a Convention right must take account of judgments of the European Court of Human Rights[1].

1 HRA 1998, s 2.

4.5   Fourth, a minister in charge of a Bill before Parliament must make a statement to the effect that the provisions of the Bill are compatible with the Convention rights or must explain why, despite incompatibility, the government nevertheless wishes to proceed with the Bill[1].

1 HRA 1998, s 19.

4.6   For the purposes of the HRA 1998, the Convention rights mean the rights and fundamental freedoms set out in Sch 1 to the Act. These include Article 2 (the right to life), Article 3 (the prohibition of torture) and Article 8 (the right to respect for private and family life).

A claim under the HRA 1998 may be brought as part of a claim in negligence, and in the same claim form, or separately.

4.7   In the first part of this chapter the rights protected by the ECHR which are most likely to be engaged in a clinical context are examined, as is how they may relate to existing causes of action.

The second part of this chapter considers the areas of causation and quantification of damage.

The third and final part of this chapter addresses the impact of the HRA 1998 on the procedural aspects of bringing or defending a claim in negligence against a clinical practitioner or establishment.

THE ARTICLES OF THE CONVENTION

Article 2

4.8   Article 2(1) of the ECHR provides:

'1. Everyone's right to life shall be protected by law. No one shall be deprived of his life intentionally save in the execution of a sentence of a court following his conviction of a crime for which this penalty is provided by law'.

4.9 The state's responsibility to protect life encompasses not only the negative obligation not to take life but also positive obligations on the state to take appropriate steps to safeguard the lives of those within its jurisdiction (the 'substantive' obligation)[1].

1 *LCB v United Kingdom* (1999) 27 EHRR 212 at para 36; *Keenan v United Kingdom* (Application 27229/95) (2001) 33 EHRR 913 at para 88; *Edwards v United Kingdom* (Application 46477/99) (2002) 12 BHRC 190 at para 54.

4.10 The substantive obligation comprises: (i) a general duty on the state to put in place a legislative and administrative framework designed to provide effective deterrence against threats to the right to life; and (ii) an operational duty in certain circumstances to take appropriate steps to safeguard the lives of those within its jurisdiction, including a positive obligation to take preventative operational measures to protect an individual whose life is at risk.

4.11 Where agents of the state potentially bear responsibility for loss of life, the state has an obligation to ensure that the events in question are subject to an effective investigation (the 'procedural' obligation).

Beginning of life

4.12 For the purposes of Article 2, the courts have held that neither a fetus[1] nor an embryo[2] has a right to life protected by Article 2. A fetus prior to the moment of birth does not have independent legal rights[3]. This does not affect the legal protection afforded by domestic criminal law to the fetus in certain circumstances[4]. There is, however, no clear ruling from the European Court of Human Rights as to when the right to life begins, the court holding that this is an issue within the state's margin of appreciation[5].

1 *Vo v France* (Application 253924/00) (2004) 40 EHRR 259.
2 *Evans v Amicus Healthcare Ltd* [2004] EWCA Civ 727, [2005] Fam 1. At para 106, Arden LJ said that neither Convention jurisprudence nor English law provides a clear-cut answer to the question at what point human life attains the right to protection by law. In the Strasbourg proceedings, the Grand Chamber stated that embryos do not have a right to life within the meaning of the ECHR, Article 2: *Evans v United Kingdom* (2007) 46 EHRR 728, paras 55–56, although the applicant had not pursued her complaint under Article 2. In *Paton v United Kingdom* (1981) 3 EHRR 408 the European Commission of Human Rights held that on its true construction Article 2 was apt only to apply to persons already born and cannot apply to a fetus.
3 *In re F (in utero)* [1988] Fam 122; *Re MB (an adult: medical treatment)* [1997] 2 FLR 426; see also *Evans v Amicus Healthcare Ltd* [2004] EWCA Civ 727, [2005] Fam 1 at para 19 per Thorpe and Sedley LJJ. See also *Paton v British Pregnancy and Advisory Service* [1979] QB 276; *C v S* [1987] 1 QB 135; *Burton v Islington Health Authority* [1993] QB 204. For discussion of the status of the unborn child, see Grubb et al (eds) *Principles of Medical Law* (3rd edn, 2010) paras 10.29–10.41.
4 The unborn child is protected by the criminal law.
5 *Vo v France* (2004) 40 EHRR 259 at para 82; *A v Ireland* (Application 25579/05) (2010) 53 EHRR 429; *X v United Kingdom* (Application 8416/79) 13 May 1980, adm dec; *H v Norway* (Application 17004/90) 19 May 1992, 73 DR 155, adm dec; *Boso v Italy* (Application 50490/99) 5 September 2002, adm dec.

4.13 It is not permissible to bring a claim for 'wrongful life'. Such a claim by a child will be refused on the grounds that it is contrary to public policy, with the courts holding that this would violate the recognition of the sanctity of life, which underpins the common law[1].

1 *McKay v Essex Area Health Authority* [1982] QB 1166, CA. In *Reeve v United Kingdom* (Application 24844/94) 30 November 1994, adm dec, the European Commission of Human Rights held that the prohibition on claims for 'wrongful life' did not violate the ECHR, Article 6.

Right to die

4.14 The right to life under Article 2 does not impose a positive obligation to protect a right to die[1].

1 *R (on the application of Pretty) v DPP (Secretary of State for the Home Department intervening)* [2001] UKHL 61, [2002] 1 AC 800; *Pretty v United Kingdom* (2002) 35 EHRR 1, [2002] 2 FCR 97. Accordingly there was no violation of Article 2 where the DPP had refused to undertake not to prosecute in a case where a sufferer of motor neurone disease wished her husband to assist in her suicide.

Positive obligations

4.15 It is a general principle that positive obligations flowing from Article 2 should be interpreted in a way which does not impose an impossible or disproportionate burden on the authorities[1].

1 *Osman v United Kingdom* (2000) 29 EHRR 245 at para 116.

General duty to have legislative and administrative framework

4.16 The positive obligation to take all appropriate steps to safeguard life for the purposes of ECHR, Article 2 entails a primary duty on the state to put in place a legislative and administrative framework designed to provide effective deterrence against threats to the right to life[1]. This includes effective criminal law provisions to deter the commission of offences against the person, backed up by law-enforcement machinery for the prevention, suppression and sanctioning of breaches of such provisions[2].

1 In *R (on the application of Middleton) v West Somerset Coroner* [2004] 2 AC 182 at para 2, Lord Bingham of Cornhill described Article 2 as imposing a substantive obligation 'to establish a framework of laws, precautions, procedures and means of enforcement which will, to the greatest extent reasonably practicable, protect life'.
2 *Osman v United Kingdom* (2000) 29 EHRR 245 at para 115; *Keenan v United Kingdom* (Application 27229/95) (2001) 33 EHRR 913 at para 88; *Edwards v United Kingdom* (Application 46477/99) (2002) 12 BHRC 190 at para 54; *Van Colle v Chief Constable of Hertfordshire Police* [2008] UKHL 50, [2009] 1 AC 225 at para 28 per Lord Bingham of Cornhill.

4.17 Article 2 does not as such guarantee a right to have criminal proceedings instituted against third parties, but the effective judicial system required by Article 2 may, and under certain circumstances must, include recourse to the criminal law[1].

1 For example, where the infringement of the right to life or to personal integrity is caused intentionally. However, if death was not caused intentionally, a criminal law remedy may not be required and the obligation may be satisfied if civil, administrative or even disciplinary remedies are available. In the specific sphere of medical negligence, for example, the obligation may be satisfied if the legal system affords victims a remedy in the civil courts; disciplinary measures may also be envisaged: *Tarariyeva v Russia* (Application 4353/01) (2006) 48 EHRR 609 at para 75; *Calvelli v Italy* (Application 32967/96) 17 January 2002, Grand Chamber, at para 51. See further *Savage v South Essex Partnership NHS Foundation Trust* [2008] UKHL 74, [2009] AC 681 at paras 91–92 per Baroness Hale of Richmond.

4.18 In the clinical field, the positive obligation to protect life under Article 2 requires the state to make regulations compelling hospitals, whether private or public, to adopt appropriate measures for the protection of patients' lives[1]. This involves ensuring that competent staff are recruited, that high professional standards are maintained and that suitable systems of working are put in place[2]. The European Court of Human Rights has suggested that there is no reason why the requirement to regulate the activities of public health institutions and afford remedies in cases of negligence should not encompass medical orderlies and/or technical auxiliary staff, in so far as their acts may also put the life of patients at risk, the more so where patients' capacity to look after themselves is limited[3].

1 *Savage v South Essex Partnership NHS Foundation Trust* [2008] UKHL 74, [2009] AC 681 at para 44 per Lord Rodger of Earlsferry; *Erikson v Italy* (2000) 29 EHRR CD 152; *Calvelli v Italy* (Application 32967/96) 17 January 2002, Grand Chamber at para 49; *Tarariyeva v Russia* (Application 4353/01) (2006) 48 EHRR 609 at para 74; *Dodov v Bulgaria* (Application 59548/00) (2008) 47 EHRR 932 at para 80.
2 *Savage v South Essex Partnership NHS Foundation Trust* [2008] UKHL 74, [2009] AC 681 at para 44 per Lord Rodger of Earlsferry. In *Association X v United Kingdom* (Application 7154/75) 12 July 1978, adm dec, the European Commission of Human Rights was satisfied that system of control and supervision established by the state in relation to vaccination against infectious diseases was sufficient to comply with the obligation under Article 2.
3 *Dodov v Bulgaria* (Application 59548/00) (2008) 47 EHRR 932 at para 81.

4.19 Where such mechanisms have been put in place, the courts do not consider that 'casual' acts of negligence, errors of judgment on the part of a health professional or negligent coordination in the treatment of a patient are of themselves sufficient to constitute a breach of any positive obligations under Article 2[1]. However, the Strasbourg Court has determined that where a woman whom it found was 'victim of a flagrant malfunctioning of the hospital departments [and] was deprived of the possibility of access to appropriate emergency care', this was enough to conclude that the state failed in its substantive obligations under Article 2[2].

1 *Savage v South Essex Partnership NHS Foundation Trust* [2008] UKHL 74, [2009] AC 681 at para 45 per Lord Rodger of Earlsferry; *Powell v United Kingdom* (2000) 30 EHRR CD 362 at 364; *Dodov v Bulgaria* (Application 59548/00) (2008) 47 EHRR 932 at para 82; *R (on the application of Goodson) v Bedfordshire and Luton Coroner (Luton and Dunstable Hospital NHS Trust, interested party)* [2004] EWHC 2931 (Admin), [2006] 1 WLR 432 at para 59 per Richards J.
2 *Şentürk v Turkey* (Application 13423/09) (2013) 60 EHRR 92, reviewed in [2013] EHRLR 439. The Strasbourg Court also found a violation of the procedural obligation under Article 2.

Systems obligations

4.20 It has been suggested that English law and the English legal system are not defective in terms of meeting the 'systems' obligations under Article 2[1]. However, the precise nature and full extent of the obligation to ensure that 'suitable systems of work are put in place'[2] is yet to be tested.

1 *Rabone v Pennine Care NHS Foundation Trust* [2012] UKSC 2, [2012] 2 AC 72 at para 93 per Baroness Hale.
2 *Savage v South Essex Partnership NHS Foundation Trust* [2008] UKHL 74, [2009] AC 681 at para 45 per Lord Rodger of Earlsferry.

4.21 Thus, while human rights arguments relying on Article 2 are unlikely to add anything to an ordinary claim in negligence arising out of the death of a patient, they may do where 'systemic' failures are alleged[1], for example where it can be argued that a hospital has failed to put in place procedures to protect the lives of patients.

4.21 *Chapter 4*

1 For example, *R (on the application of Humberstone) v Legal Services Commission (The Lord Chancellor intervening)* [2010] EWCA Civ 1479, [2011] 1 WLR 1460 (the resources and operational systems of the ambulance service; *R (on the application of Takoushis) v Inner London North Coroner* [2005] EWCA Civ 1440, [2006] 1 WLR 461 (hospital triage system).

4.22 An issue may arise under Article 2 where it is shown that the state authorities put an individual's life at risk through denial of health care which they had undertaken to make available to the population generally[1]. In *Şentürk v Turkey*[2] the court also found that there was a violation of the substantive limb of Article 2 where domestic law did not provide for the provision of medical treatment in an emergency where the patient could not pay.

1 *Cyprus v Turkey* (Application 25781/94) (2001) 35 EHRR 731 at para 219; *Nitecki v Poland* (Application 65653/01) 21 March 2002, adm dec.
2 *Şentürk entürk v Turkey* (Application 13423/09) (2013) 60 EHRR 92, reviewed in [2013] EHRLR 439.

4.23 However, the European Court of Human Rights has rejected the proposition that it is a violation of Article 2 for the state authorities to refuse funding for a particular drug[1]. Nor can Article 2 be interpreted as requiring access to unauthorised medicinal products for the terminally ill to be regulated in a particular way[2].

1 *Nitecki v Poland* (Application 65653/01) 21 March 2002, adm dec; *Cyprus v Turkey* (Application 25781/94) (2001) 35 EHRR 731, para 219; *Pentiacova v Moldova* (2005) 40 EHRR SE23; *Gheorghe v Romania* (Application 19215/04) 22 September 2005, adm; and *Wiater v Poland* (Application 42290/08) 15 May 2012, adm dec; *Hristozov v Bulgaria* (Applications 47039/11 and 358/12) 13 November 2012. These arguments have also been considered under ECHR, Article 8; see further *Sentges v Netherlands* (Application 27677/02) 8 July 2003, adm dec; *Pentiacova v Moldova* (funding of haemodialysis).
2 In *Hristozov v Bulgaria* (Applications 47039/11 and 358/12) 13 November 2012, the Strasbourg Court held that there was no violation of Article 2 in respect of access to an unauthorised experimental anti-cancer drug which was not authorised in any country but was allowed in some other countries for 'compassionate use.

Duty to take preventative operational measures

4.24 The state is under a positive obligation to take preventive operational measures to protect persons at real and immediate risk to life[1].

This duty most clearly applies to prisoners and to others in state detention (for example police or immigration detention).

1 *Osman v United Kingdom* (1999) 29 EHRR 245.

4.25 In the clinical context, this operational obligation has been held to apply in the cases of psychiatric patients who are detained in a public hospital[1] and informal psychiatric patients at risk of suicide[2]. The positive obligation may also arise where the authorities are engaged in moving elderly residents out of a care home[3].

1 *Savage v South Essex Partnership NHS Foundation Trust* [2008] UKHL 74, [2009] AC 681.
2 *Rabone v Pennine Care NHS Foundation Trust* [2012] UKSC 2, [2012] 2 AC 72; *Reynolds v United Kingdom* (Application 2694/08) [2012] All ER (D) 176 (Mar). It is recognised that those detained in mental hospitals under the Mental Health Act 1983 pose a high suicide risk and in those circumstances the hospital authorities are bound by the substantive obligations under Article 2 to take reasonable care to ensure that such patients do not commit suicide, by putting

114

in place systemic precautions against it. If those precautions fail then the state's Article 2 procedural obligations will be triggered: *R (on the application of Antoniou) v Central and North West London NHS Foundation Trust* [2013] EWHC 3055 (Admin) at para 77.
3 *Watts v United Kingdom* (2010) 51 EHRR SE5 (adm dec), cited with approval in *Rabone* at para 96. In domestic cases the courts have been prepared to assume that Article 2 applies to such decisions; see *R (on the application of Thomas) v Havering London Borough Council* (2008) 152 Sol Jo (no 35) 28; *R (on the application of Haggerty) v St Helens Council* [2003] EWHC 803 (Admin); *R (on the application of Dudley) v East Sussex County Council* [2003] All ER (D) 296 (Apr). For recent consideration of similar issues under ECHR, Article 8, see *R (on the application of Chatting) v Viridian Housing* [2012] EWHC 3595 (Admin).

4.26 In the generality of cases involving medical negligence, however, the operational obligation is unlikely to arise[1]. But the jurisprudence of the operational obligation is 'young'[2], and as such the categories of individual to whom the obligation may be held to apply is yet to be fully tested. The obligation may be applied by the courts to additional situations where one or more of the relevant factors of assumption of responsibility, vulnerability and the level of risk are met[3].

1 In *Rabone v Pennine Care NHS Foundation Trust* [2012] UKSC 2, [2012] 2 AC 72, Lord Dyson referred to 'a general rule that no operational duty is owed by the state in the field of medical treatment in public hospitals' (at para 26) and noted that the European Court of Human Rights 'has stated that in the generality of cases involving medical negligence, there is no operational duty under Article 2' (at para 33).
2 *Rabone* at para 25 per Lord Dyson.
3 For an example in a different context, namely a vulnerable child known to social services, see *R (on the application of Kent County Council) v HM Coroner for Kent* [2012] EWHC 2768 (Admin). The Strasbourg Court has considered the positive operational obligation in the context of emergency services and emergency relief measures. See *Furdik v Slovakia* (Application 42994/05) 2 December 2008; *Budayeva v Russia* (Applications 15339/02, 21166/02, 20058/02 and 15343/02) (2008) 59 EHRR 59 at para 137.

4.27 The standard demanded for the performance of the operational duty is one of reasonableness[1]. Accordingly, a failure to take reasonable measures which could have had a real prospect of altering the outcome or mitigating the harm is sufficient to engage the responsibility of the state[2].

1 *Osman v United Kingdom* (2000) 29 EHRR 245 at para 116; *Rabone v Pennine Care NHS Foundation Trust* [2012] UKSC 2, [2012] 2 AC 72 at para 43 per Lord Dyson.
2 *Savage v South Essex Partnership NHS Foundation Trust* [2008] UKHL 74, [2009] AC 681; *Opuz v Turkey* (Application 33401/02) (2009) 50 EHRR 695 at para 136.

Investigative obligation

4.28 Article 2 also requires an effective independent judicial system to be set up so that the cause of death of patients in the care of the medical profession, whether in the public or the private sector, can be determined and those responsible made accountable, known as the procedural obligation under Article 2[1].

1 *Calvelli v Italy* (Application 32967/96) 17 January 2002, Grand Chamber at para 49; *Šilih v Slovenia* (2009) 49 EHRR 37 at para 194.

4.29 The UK's obligations in this latter regard are met by the existence of criminal, civil and coronial proceedings which should provide an effective means of investigation into a death which occurs in hospital or where medical professionals are implicated (*Goodson*[1], *Takoushis*[2] and, mutatis mutandis, *R (on the application of Middleton) v West Somerset Coroner*[3]).

1 *R (on the application of Goodson) v Bedfordshire and Luton Coroner (Luton and Dunstable Hospital NHS Trust, interested party)* [2004] EWHC 2931 (Admin), [2006] 1 WLR 432.
2 *R (on the application of Takoushis) v Inner London North Coroner* [2005] EWCA Civ 1440, [2006] 1 WLR 461.
3 [2004] UKHL 10, [2004] 2 AC 182.

4.30   There is no separate procedural obligation to investigate under the ECHR where a death in hospital raised no more than a potential liability in negligence[1]. But where issues of resources and operational systems arise, there may be an obligation under Article 2 proactively to undertake an enhanced investigation[2]. The Article 2 procedural obligations are also automatically triggered in the case of the death (including suicide) of a mental patient detained in hospital under the Mental Health Act 1983. But in such circumstances the procedural obligation under Article 2 did not require the state to perform an immediate and independent investigation into the circumstances of the death prior to an inquest[3].

1 *R (on the application of Goodson) v Bedfordshire and Luton Coroner (Luton and Dunstable Hospital NHS Trust, interested party)* [2004] EWHC 2931 (Admin), [2006] 1 WLR 432.
2 *R (on the application of Humberstone) v Legal Services Commission (The Lord Chancellor intervening)* [2010] EWCA Civ 1479, [2011] 1 WLR 1460.
3 *R (on the application of Antoniou) v Central and North West London NHS Foundation Trust* [2013] EWHC 3055 (Admin).

4.31   Where the Article 2 obligation applies, it requires that there be a prompt examination of the case without unnecessary delays[1]. Promptness is particularly necessary in cases concerning death in a hospital setting for the future safety of all users of health services[2].

1 In *McDonnell v United Kingdom* (Application 19563/11) (2015) Times, 9 January, the European Court of Human Rights found a violation of Article 2 by reason of excessive investigative delay in the case of a death in custody in a Belfast prison in March 1996. The inquest proper into the death did not begin until April 2013, more than 17 years later.
2 *Šilih v Slovenia* (2009) 49 EHRR 37 at paras 195–196. Rapid examination of such cases is important for the safety of users of all health services: see *Byrzykowski v Poland* (Application 11562/05) (2006) 46 EHRR 675 at para 117; *Şentürk v Turkey* (Application 13423/09) (2013) 60 EHRR 92 at para 82; *Oyal v Turkey* (Application 4864/05) (2010) 51 EHRR 713 at para 77.

Death of third parties

4.32   It should be noted that Article 2 may also be engaged where the death is not that of the patient: claims may be brought, for example, against a mental health provider who has, through allegedly negligent clinical judgment, failed to prevent the death of a third party at the hands of a patient. The case would be analogous to that of *Osman*[1], where the complaint was the failure of a state authority to detain the individual who carried out the killing.

1 *Osman v United Kingdom* (1999) 29 EHRR 245. For further consideration of the *Osman* test in respect of threats from third parties, see *Van Colle v Chief Constable of Hertfordshire Police* [2008] UKHL 50, [2009] 1 AC 225; *Van Colle v United Kingdom* (Application 7678/09) (2013) 56 EHRR 23; *R (on the application of Palmer) v Her Majesty's Coroner for the County of Worcestershire* [2011] EWHC 1453 (Admin), [2011] LGR 952.

Article 3

4.33   Article 3 provides:

'No one shall be subjected to torture or to inhuman or degrading treatment or punishment'.

The prohibition is absolute: there can be no justification for inflicting such treatment on an individual. However, the court has determined that ill-treatment must attain a certain level of severity before it qualifies as inhuman or degrading treatment under the ECHR. Whether it does so will depend on all the circumstances of the case, such as the duration of the treatment, its physical and/or mental effects, and the victim's own physical and mental characteristics[1].

1 *Keenan v United Kingdom* (Application 27229/95) (2001) 33 EHRR 913.

The threshold of inhuman or degrading treatment

4.34 The European Court of Human Rights has determined that, in an appropriate case, a lack of appropriate medical care may amount to inhuman or degrading treatment contrary to Article 3[1]. Moreover, suffering from physical illness may be covered by Article 3 where it is exacerbated by the treatment received from state authorities[2]:

'The suffering that naturally flows from naturally occurring illness, physical or mental, may be covered by Article 3, where it is, or risks being, exacerbated by treatment, whether flowing from conditions of detention, expulsion or other measures, for which the authorities can be held responsible'.

The caveat in the second part of this sentence is an important one, as may be seen below.

1 See *Keenan v United Kingdom* (Application 27229/95) (2001) 33 EHRR 913 at [111].
2 *Pretty v United Kingdom* (2002) 35 EHRR 1.

4.35 In considering whether a patient's Article 3 rights have been breached, the court will first determine whether the treatment received reaches the 'threshold' necessary to constitute inhuman or degrading treatment.

4.36 The assessment of this minimum level of severity is a relative one, depending on all the circumstances of the case, such as the duration of the treatment, its physical and mental effects and, in some cases, the sex, age and state of health of the victim[1].

1 *Price v United Kingdom* (Application 33394/96) (2002) 34 EHRR 1285.

4.37 As for the concept of degrading treatment, the European Court of Human Rights has in its case law described it as treatment such as to arouse feelings of fear, anguish and inferiority capable of humiliating or debasing the victim and possibly breaking their physical or moral resistance[1].

1 *Keenan v United Kingdom* (Application 27229/95) (2001) 33 EHRR 913 at [110].

4.38 In deciding whether treatment is degrading, the effect on the victim is not the only consideration: the court will also look at the purpose of such treatment. In other words, whether its object is to humiliate and debase the person concerned and whether, as far as the consequences are concerned, it adversely affected his personality in a manner incompatible with Article 3. However, the absence of any such purpose cannot conclusively rule out a finding of a violation of Article 3[1].

1 *Sanchez v France* (Application 59450/00) (2006) 45 EHRR 1099 at [118]; see also *Price v United Kingdom* (Application 33394/96) (2001) 34 EHRR 1285 at [30].

The responsibility of the state

4.39 In *Pretty*[1] the court itself drew a distinction between a case where the state itself removes access to care (as in *D v United Kingdom*[2], where an asylum seeker was to be removed to a country where no effective medical treatment was available), which could found a breach of Article 3, and where the state has not itself inflicted any ill-treatment on the applicant.

1 *Pretty v United Kingdom* (2002) 35 EHRR 1 at [53].
2 (1997) 24 EHRR 423.

4.40 It is important to note that even though there can be no justification for treatment reaching the threshold of Article 3, the courts have made it very clear that:

'Article 3 was not designed for circumstances ... where the challenge is as to a health authority's allocation of finite funds between competing demands'[1].

1 *R v North West Lancashire Health Authority, ex p A* [2001] 1 WLR 977.

Expanding the boundaries of clinical negligence?

4.41 Traditionally it was thought that clinical negligence could not found a claim under Article 3. In *R v North West Lancashire Health Authority, ex p A*[1] Buxton LJ insisted that Article 3 only addresses 'positive conduct' by public officials. In *R (on the application of Howard) v Secretary of State for Health*[2], Scott Baker J thought that clinical negligence, however gross, could not found a claim under Article 3.

1 [2000] 1 WLR 977.
2 [2002] EWHC 396 (Admin), [2002] 3 WLR 738 at 759.

4.42 However the court, it appears, has taken a more generous view of what amounts to a breach of Article 3 than domestic courts have done. In *MS v United Kingdom*[1] the UK judge had held that although the defendant had owed the applicant a duty of care, and that that duty had been breached, it had not caused the applicant any physical or psychological injury. The action in negligence therefore failed on causation and loss. In any event, any loss (a delay of 31 hours in hospitalising the applicant) had been absolutely minimal and could only lead to minimal damages. The judge also rejected the claim based on the HRA 1998 on the ground, inter alia, that the situation did not meet the minimum level of severity inherent in Article 3 of the Convention. On appeal, the court agreed that the situation had fallen far short of treatment in contravention of Article 3: the applicant had been lawfully detained and his basic needs had been met. The fact that he had spent an extra 12–24 hours at the police station did not make the situation so appalling as to breach Article 3. It was found to be unrealistic to suggest that a delay of a given number of hours (the applicant's counsel having conceded that the delay was considerably less than 31 hours) in some way caused that number of hours of psychosis.

1 (Application 24527/08) (2012) 126 BMLR 168.

4.43 However, the European Court held that prolonged detention without appropriate psychiatric treatment had diminished the applicant's human dignity. The court held that the conditions the applicant had to endure (shouting, taking off all of his clothes, banging his head on the wall, drinking from the toilet and smearing himself with food and faeces) met the threshold of degrading treatment for the purposes of Article 3[1].

1 It is important to note that the court did not find that there was a breach of the duty to provide an effective remedy under Article 3: the domestic courts had examined the matter under Article 3 and the UK courts' assessment was not invalidated by the fact that this court has reached the contrary conclusion on the applicant's Article 3 complaint. Nevertheless, the applicant was awarded €3,000 in respect of non-pecuniary damage.

4.44   This, at first blush, looks like it gives a cause of action under Article 3 where clinical negligence simply would not, and thereby gives scope for claims in similar cases where delay in treatment led to a loss of dignity amounting to degrading treatment for the patient. The decision caused some consternation amongst commentators in the UK for that reason: would it enlarge the scope of the type of treatment for which patients could complain? And was it in reality using Article 3 as an economic and social right to a certain type of treatment regardless of the resources available? Would simple delay in medical treatment also amount to a breach of Article 3 if the effect on the claimant were grave enough?[1]

1 Interestingly, the NHS-sponsored website 'Human Rights in Healthcare' (dormant since January 2013 due to withdrawal of funding) gives a considerable list of the types of treatment it considers could come under Article 3: neglect/carelessness, eg bed sores, not being fed properly; poor conditions in hospitals or care homes; washing or dressing without regard to dignity; excessive force used to restrain; authorities failing to protect individuals from abuse; malnutrition and dehydration. It will be noted that not all of these would be capable of founding a clinical negligence claim, in circumstances where there is no head of recoverable loss.

Article 3 and detention

4.45   However, in *MS v United Kingdom*[1] the court found it relevant to mention that:

'throughout the relevant time, the applicant was entirely under the authority and control of the State. The authorities were therefore under an obligation to safeguard his dignity, and are responsible under the Convention for the treatment he experienced'.

In other words, despite the controversy caused by the decision, *MS* could be interpreted as a case where a positive duty arose not just because of the simple fact of MS's medical condition but because he was detained.

1 (Application 24527/08) (2012) 126 BMLR 168.

4.46   This follows the by-now traditional approach whereby, where an individual is detained, different considerations apply because the state is under an obligation to protect the health of persons deprived of their liberty[1]. The state is not just under an operational duty to put in place adequate systems to protect a person's welfare and prevent a breach of Article 3, but also under a positive duty to prevent the detainee suffering inhuman or degrading treatment. This means that a detainee will be able to claim mental suffering and anguish occasioned by inadequate provision of healthcare in detention centres, even if the suffering falls short of the sort of physical or psychological injury which would ordinarily sound in negligence.

1 *Hurtado v Switzerland* Opinion of the Commission of 28 January 1994, Series A no 280-A,
pp 15–16 and 79; *Keenan v United Kingdom* (Application 27229/95) (2001) 33 EHRR 913 at [111].

4.47   In these detention cases, the court will consider whether the
applicant needed regular medical assistance, whether he was deprived of
the assistance and, if so, whether this amounted to treatment contrary to the
ECHR, Article 3[1].

1 *Farbtuhs v Latvia* (Application 4672/02) 6 June 2005; *McGlinchey v United Kingdom* (Application
50390/99) (2003) 37 EHRR 821.

4.48   In *Holomiov v Moldova*[1] the applicant did not receive the medical
treatment recommended for him whilst in detention for over four years,
although he did receive some medical care. The court found that his suffering
'serious kidney diseases entailing serious risks for his health' during a long
period of detention without appropriate medical care reached the threshold
of severity required by Article 3, and that the denial of appropriate medical
care was therefore a breach of the ECHR. This was despite the defendant
state's argument that the claimant had been offered medical treatment
'within the "modest possibilities" of the prison medical service'.

1 (Application 30649/05) (2007) 47 EHRR 327.

4.49   This echoes the development in English domestic law from *Knight v
Home Office*[1], where Pill J found that the care to be expected in a prison was
not the same as that in a psychiatric hospital, to *Brooks v Home Office*[2], which
established that the claimant prisoner was entitled to the same standard of
obstetric care as if she were at liberty. No prison or detention centre can now
realistically run a defence to a claim under Article 3 based on resources.

1 [1990] 3 All ER 237.
2 (1999) 48 BMLR 109.

Article 3 and mental health

4.50   Where a patient is detained under a mental health section rather than
in prison or police detention, the court has made it clear that 'the position
of inferiority and powerlessness which is typical of patients confined in
psychiatric hospitals calls for increased vigilance in reviewing whether the
ECHR has been complied with[1].

1 *Herczegfalvy v Austria* (Application 10533/83) (1992) 15 EHRR 437 at [82]; *Naumenko v Ukraine*
(Application 42023/98) (2004) ECHR 68.

4.51   A number of factors must be considered when determining whether
a treatment is of sufficient severity to engage Article 3. These include the
nature and context of the treatment, the manner in which it is administered,
its duration, its physical and mental effects, and whether it is intended to
humiliate or debase. Capacity is also a relevant factor but is not crucial[1].

1 *R (on the application of B) v S* [2006] EWCA Civ 28.

Compulsory treatment

4.52   In *Keenan*[1] the court said that:

'in respect of a person deprived of his liberty, recourse to physical force which has not been made strictly necessary by his own conduct (ie disproportionate) diminishes human dignity and is in principle an infringement of the right set forth in Article 3. Similarly treatment of mentally ill persons may be incompatible with the standards imposed by Article 3 in the protection of human dignity, even though that person may not be capable of pointing to any specific ill-effects'.

This means that, for example, poorly carried out control and restraint or confinement in the mental health context might found a breach of Article 3 even where there is no injury or loss that would sound in a claim for negligence.

1 *Keenan v United Kingdom* (Application 27229/95) (2001) 33 EHRR 913.

4.53   However, as a general rule any treatment which can be 'convincingly shown' to have been therapeutically necessary will not be a breach of Article 3.

In *R (on the application of B) v S*[1] it was found that compulsory treatment did not violate either Article 3 or Article 8 because the patient lacked capacity to consent to treatment and because his doctor had shown that treatment was a therapeutic necessity: it was quite proper for the court to place appropriate weight on the opinions of the treating clinicians. The standard of proof formulated in Article 3 as 'convincingly shown' is a high standard that lies between the two English standards of proof laid down in civil ('the balance of probabilities') and criminal law ('beyond reasonable doubt').

1 *R (on the application of B) v S* [2006] EWCA Civ 28.

4.54   It is interesting that, whilst the court accepts that in principle 'the established principles of medicine' are decisive in determining the therapeutic necessity for medical treatment, it reserves to itself the right to 'satisfy itself that that medical necessity has been convincingly shown to exist'. This sounds very like an echo of the *Bolitho* refinement to the *Bolam* test applied by the English courts[1].

1 *Bolitho v City and Hackney Health Authority* [1993] 4 Med LR 381; *Bolam v Friern Hospital Management Committee* [1957] 2 All ER 118, [1957] 1 WLR 582.

4.55   For example, in *Nevmerzhitsky v Ukraine*[1] the government had failed to provide a medical report or evidence to show that it had followed its own procedures on force-feeding detainees. Because the government had not demonstrated that force-feeding was medically necessary, it could only be assumed that it was arbitrary and not in the applicant's best interests. Force-feeding without medical justification and against the prisoner's will was therefore a violation of Article 3.

1 (Application 54825/00) (2005) 19 BHRC 177.

4.56   The domestic courts have already held that, when considering the appropriateness of treatment prospectively, although weight is to be placed on the opinions of the treating clinicians, the courts should undertake a 'full merits review' of the appropriateness of treatment, including cross-examination of the doctors involved[1]. The same will be true of a retrospective claim involving a breach of Article 3 which is combined with a clinical negligence claim.

1 *R (on the application of Wilkinson) v Responsible Medical Officer Broadmoor Hospital* [2001] EWCA Civ 1545, [2002] 1 WLR 419.

Article 8

4.57 Article 8 provides:

'1. Everyone has the right to respect for his private and family life, his home and his correspondence.

2. There shall be no interference by a public authority with the exercise of this right except such as is in accordance with the law and is necessary in a democratic society in the interests of national security, public safety or the economic well-being of the country, for the prevention of disorder or crime, for the protection of health or morals, or for the protection of the rights and freedoms of others.'

'Private life' covers the 'physical and psychological integrity of the person'[1] and it is in this regard that Article 8 may be invoked in relation to medical treatment.

1 *Pretty v United Kingdom* (2002) 35 EHRR 1; *X and Y v Netherlands* (Application 8978/80) (1985) 8 EHRR 235.

4.58 Article 8 may include positive obligations to ensure effective respect for private life, as well as the negative obligation on the state to refrain from interference[1].

1 See in the medical context *Passannante v Italy* (Application 32647/96) (1998) 1 July, ECHR (Admissibility Decision).

4.59 Any act or omission by healthcare professionals which affects that integrity may engage Article 8. In *GB and RB v Moldova*[1] the court found that although a domestic court had not expressly referred to Article 8 in making a finding of medical negligence, its findings were in essence of a violation of the article.

1 (Application 16761/09) [2012] ECHR 2079 (18 December 2012).

4.60 Further, delay in providing medical care can contravene Article 8 where the state has a duty to provide care and where excessive delay could have a serious impact on the patient's health[1].

1 See *Passannante v Italy*, where there was a five-month delay for a neurological appointment in the public health system (and a private appointment would be available in four days). However, on the facts of this case no damage to health was alleged so there was in fact no duty on the state.

4.61 However, although Article 8 has in theory the potential significantly to expand the kinds of claims that may be brought against healthcare professionals and institutions[1], the effect of Article 8 in a clinical negligence context has to a certain extent been limited. Part of this has to do with the justifications available under Article 8(2), in particular those to do with resources; these are dealt with below.

1 See, for example, *AB v Leeds Teaching Hospitals NHS Trust*, sub nom *Re Organ Retention Group Litigation* [2004] EWHC 644 (QB) at [298]: even though not all the claimants succeeded in their action for negligence, Gage J stated that they would be likely to succeed under Article 8.

4.62   However, the UK courts have also been reluctant to allow Article 8 to be used to extend the duty in negligence[1].

Likewise, the causing of psychiatric harm to an individual will not of itself found a claim under Article 8 in circumstances which could not found a claim in negligence.

1 For example, in *Lawrence v Pembrokeshire County Council* [2007] EWCA Civ 446 the Court of Appeal confirmed the conclusion of the House of Lords in *D v East Berkshire Community Health NHS Trust* [2005] UKHL 23, that the duty of care owed to children in child protection cases precluded the imposition on local authority and health professionals of a duty of care to the parents, and that Article 8 did not force an extension of that duty. See also the European Court's decision in *Clunis v United Kingdom* (Application 45049/98) (2001) 11 September (Admissibility Decision), where it was determined that there was no direct link between the measures which, in the applicant's view, should have been taken by Camden and Islington Health Authority and the prejudice caused to his psychiatric well-being attendant on the realisation of the gravity of his act, his conviction and subsequent placement in a mental hospital without limit of time. See also *AB v Leeds Teaching Hospitals NHS Trust* [2004] EWHC 644 (QB), where the court refused to allow a cause of action to be constructed where none existed in tort.

4.63   In *Anufrijeva v Southwark London Borough Council*[1] Lord Woolf CJ held that, whilst damages may be recoverable where the infringement of a right under the HRA 1998 'has the incidental effect of causing psychiatric harm', causing psychiatric harm to the claimant by maladministration on the part of a public authority was not itself an infringement of Article 8; this was because it was not known that the acts of maladministration complained of were likely to cause such harm to a 'particularly susceptible individual in circumstances where this was not reasonably to be anticipated'[2]. It was held that the 'egg-shell skull principle forms no part of the test of breach of duty under the HRA or the Convention'. However it is of course true that even in a claim for negligence some personal injury must be reasonably foreseeable if a claim for psychiatric harm is to succeed[3]; and that, absent any duty to prevent reasonably foreseeable personal injury, the 'eggshell skull' rule will not apply. The test for breach of duty which will be applied in an Article 8 claim appears, therefore, to be no broader or narrower than that used in negligence.

1 [2003] EWCA Civ 1406, [2004] QB 1124.
2 Upholding the defendant's appeal in the case of N in this conjoined appeal and giving the judgment of the court at [143]
3 *Page v Smith* [1996] AC 155.

4.64   However, it should be noted that the right to 'private life', and the 'physical and psychological integrity' it protects, contains within it the concept of the human dignity of the individual, which calls for an 'enhanced degree of protection'[1]. This means that actions by clinical practitioners which come nowhere near being negligent in clinical terms might in theory engage Article 8(1). It is conceivable, for example, that in certain circumstances placing a vulnerable patient on a mixed ward would be a violation of her dignity and therefore a breach of Article 8, even though she had undergone no negligent treatment. Similar considerations of enhanced protection would obtain in the treatment of disabled patients or any 'critically dependent on the help of others'[2].

1 See the judgment of Munby J in *A v East Sussex County Council* [2003] EWHC 167 (Admin) at [86] ff.
2 [2003] EWHC 167 (Admin) at [93].

4.65   Further, the responsibilities of the state towards detained persons will mean that is it easier to found a duty in Article 8 in respect of their medical care: the court couches this in terms of an 'assumption of responsibilities by the authorities' for the health of an individual[1].

1 See *Clunis* citing, for example, *D v United Kingdom* (Application 30240/96) (1997) 24 EHRR 423.

Consent

4.66   Any treatment contrary to the wishes of a patient will interfere with his rights under Article 8[1]. Further, the court has found that access to health information is vital for the exercise of personal autonomy protected by Article 8[2]: in effect finding that Article 8 protects the right to informed consent[3]. It is therefore possible to envisage an Article 8 claim on the basis of a lack of informed consent added to the claim form in a *Chester v Afshar* type claim[4]. Indeed, since the first drafting of this chapter the Supreme Court has in the case of *Montgomery* described the way in which:

'Under the stimulus of the Human Rights Act 1998, the courts have become increasingly conscious of the extent to which the common law reflects fundamental values. As Lord Scarman pointed out in *Sidaway's* case, these include the value of self-determination (see, for example, *S (An Infant) v S* [1972] AC 24, 43 per Lord Reid; *McColl v Strathclyde Regional Council* 1983 SC 225, 241; *Airedale NHS Trust v Bland* [1993] AC 789, 864 per Lord Goff of Chieveley). As well as underlying aspects of the common law, that value also underlies the right to respect for private life protected by article 8 of the European Convention on Human Rights. The resulting duty to involve the patient in decisions relating to her treatment has been recognised in judgments of the European Court of Human Rights, such as *Glass v United Kingdom* (2004) 39 EHRR 15 and *Tysiac v Poland* (2007) 45 EHRR 42'.

The court found that:

'The doctor is therefore under a duty to take reasonable care to ensure that the patient is aware of any material risks involved in any recommended treatment, and of any reasonable alternative or variant treatments. The test of materiality is whether, in the circumstances of the particular case, a reasonable person in the patient's position would be likely to attach significance to the risk, or the doctor is or should reasonably be aware that the particular patient would be likely to attach significance to it'.

1 *Glass v United Kingdom* (Application 61827/00) (2004) 39 EHRR 341.
2 *RR v Poland* (Application 27617/04) 26 May 2011: 'the effective exercise of this right (of access to information about her or his health) is often decisive for the possibility of exercising personal autonomy, also covered by Article 8 of the Convention, by deciding, on the basis of such information, on the future course of events relevant for the individual's quality of life (eg by refusing consent to medical treatment or by requesting a given form of treatment).'
3 See also *VC v Slovakia* (Application 18968/07) (2011) 59 EHRR 985.
4 Issues of consent – and particularly where capacity is disputed – will be most highly relevant in mental health or in best interest cases. Article 8 has had a significant impact in both these fields but the issues raised there are unlikely to arise in most clinical negligence contexts and are beyond the scope of this chapter.

4.67   Article 8 will be engaged by a decision as to how to pass the closing days and moments of one's life and how one managed one's death, as this touches in the most immediate and obvious way a patient's personal autonomy, integrity, dignity and quality of life[1]. The procedural obligations implicit in Article 8 require that there be a presumption in favour of involving a patient in a decision whether to place a DNACPR notice on her hospital notes.

1 *Tracey v Cambridge University Hospital NHS Foundation Trust* [2014] EWCA Civ 822, [2014] 3 WLR 1054; *Pretty v United Kingdom* (2002) 35 EHRR 1 and *Glass v United Kingdom* (Application 61827/00) (2004) 39 EHRR 341.

Justification: resources

4.68   However, the justifications that may be advanced under Article 8(2), and the wide margin of appreciation given to the state in matters involving Article 8, mean that it is only in very limited circumstances that the court will be willing to find that circumstances which would not give rise to a remedy in national law will give rise to one under the ECHR.

Article 8 cannot found a right, for example, to a specific treatment, or for funding for a specific treatment.

4.69   The court will have regard to the fair balance that has to be struck between the competing interests of the individual and of the community as a whole[1] and has held that 'while it is clearly desirable that everyone has access to a full range of medical treatment, including life-saving medical procedures and drugs, the lack of resources means that there are, unfortunately, in the contracting states many individuals who do not enjoy them, especially in cases of permanent and expensive treatment'[2].

This means that, in contrast to the position under Articles 2 and 3, a defendant may argue that it was constrained to act in a certain way by limited resources.

1 *Powell and Rayner v United Kingdom* (Application 9310/81) (1990) 12 EHRR 355; *Evans v United Kingdom* (Application 6339/05) (2007) 46 EHRR 728; and *Dickson v United Kingdom* (Application 44362) (2007) 46 EHRR 927.
2 *Pentiacova v Moldova* (2005) 40 EHRR SE23.

4.70   The state, of course, enjoys a margin of appreciation in establishing what is a fair balance. The court will start from the general principle that 'matters of healthcare policy are within the margin of appreciation of the domestic authorities, who are best placed to assess priorities, use of resources and social needs'[1]. Where there is no consensus among contracting states as to the relative importance of the interest, or the best means of securing it, particularly where there are sensitive moral or ethical issues, the margin will be wider; the same goes where the state has to strike a balance between competing private and public interests or ECHR rights[2].

1 *Shelley v United Kingdom* (Application 23800/06) 4 January 2008, adm dec; *Hristozov v Bulgaria* (Applications 47039/11 and 358/12) 13 November 2012.
2 *H v Austria* (Application 57813/00) [2012] 2 FCR 291.

4.71   However, where 'a particularly important facet of an individual's existence or identity is at stake', the court considers that that margin will be restricted[1]. In other words, it is likely to be a defence to a complaint that a certain treatment was not embarked upon when NHS or – for example – prison resources did not permit it[2]. This will be particularly so in applications for exceptional funding[3].

1 *Lopes-Ostra v Spain* (1995) 20 EHRR 277 at para 51.
2 See *Pentiacova v Moldova* (2005) 40 EHRR SE23.
3 As in, for example, *R (on the application of Condliff) v North Staffordshire Primary Care Trust* [2011] EWCA Civ 910, [2012] 1 All ER 689.

4.72 Further, the court has found that the state is entitled to regulate the access of patients to experimental treatment (and set out the various public interests in so doing)[1]. This means that most challenges to decisions which are made on the basis of cost will not succeed if those decisions adhere to the frameworks set out by regulations or guidance[2]; the same will apply if a claim in clinical negligence is in reality a complaint against funding priorities or decisions.

1 *Hristozov v Bulgaria* (Applications 47039/11 and 358/12) 13 November 2012.
2 Or unless they are irrational in the traditional *Wednesbury* sense, as was found in *R (on the application of Rogers) v Swindon NHS Primary Care Trust* [2006] EWHC 171 (Admin) and the decision on appeal [2006] EWCA Civ 392.

4.73 Lack of resources will not, however, be an excuse when it comes to a one-off payment of damages: the court has found that a state-owned hospital could not plead impecuniosity in failing to make an appropriate award, and could have made professional medical negligence insurance compulsory in order to be sufficiently covered to pay victims[1].

1 *GB and RB v Moldova* (Application 16761/09) [2012] ECHR 2079 (18 December 2012). See also below in relation to quantum.

THE CAUSATION AND QUANTIFICATION OF DAMAGE

4.74 The guiding English case on damages under the HRA 1998 remains *R (on the application of Greenfield) v Secretary of State for the Home Department*[1]. In that case the House of Lords made it clear, first, that a claim for damages under the Act is one entirely separate to a claim in negligence: the Act, said Lord Bingham (at para 19), 'is not a tort statute' and a claimant cannot recover a tortious measure of damages. The purpose of the Act was to give claimants the same remedies in English courts as those available in Strasbourg, and not better ones. Accordingly, in awarding damages in a human rights claim, the courts should have regard to Strasbourg precedents and not those of the English courts.

1 [2005] UKHL 14, [2005] 1 WLR 673.

4.75 A claimant does not, merely by virtue of settling a civil claim in negligence, lose the right to bring a claim for damages under the HRA 1998[1].

1 In the absence of express renunciation of the Article 2 claim: *Rabone v Pennine Care NHS Foundation Trust* [2012] UKSC 2, [2012] 2 AC 72.

4.76 Although, theoretically, the European Court of Human Rights insists that there be a 'clear causal link' between the violations of the ECHR as the basis of the complaint and the damage caused, the court's approach to causation has at times been rather looser than that of the English courts.

4.77 The test of causation for an Article 2 claim differs from that in negligence. In *Osman v United Kingdom*[1], the Strasbourg Court referred to whether, judged reasonably, the authorities failed to take measures within the scope of their powers which, judged reasonably, might have been expected to avoid that risk[2]. It has been suggested that the test is whether the protective measures 'could have had a real prospect of altering the outcome'[3]. As noted in the previous edition of this work, this is akin to the notion of the 'loss of a chance' which is familiar within the common law but not accepted as a basis for liability in clinical negligence[4].

1 (1998) 29 EHRR 235 at para 116.
2 See also *Rabone v Pennine Care NHS Foundation Trust* [2012] UKSC 2, [2012] 2 AC 72 at paras 42, 107; *Van Colle v Chief Constable of Hertfordshire Police* [2008] UKHL 50, [2009] 1 AC 225 at para 30 per Lord Bingham of Cornhill.
3 *Van Colle v Chief Constable of Hertfordshire Police* [2007] EWCA Civ 325 per Anthony Clarke MR at para 83. This point was not considered in the House of Lords.
4 See *Hotson v East Berkshire Area Health Authority* [1987] AC 750 at 783 per Lord Bridge: 'There is a superficially attractive analogy between the principle applied in such cases as *Chaplin v Hicks* [1911] 2 KB 786 (award of damages for breach of contract assessed by reference to the lost chance of securing valuable employment if the contract had been performed) and *Kitchen v Royal Air Force Association* [1958] 1 WLR 563 (damages for solicitors' negligence assessed by reference to the lost chance of prosecuting a successful civil action) and the principle of awarding damages for the lost chance of avoiding personal injury or, in medical negligence cases, for the lost chance of a better medical result which might have been achieved by prompt diagnosis and correct treatment. I think there are formidable difficulties in the way of accepting the analogy'.
   On loss of a chance in clinical negligence, see further *Gregg v Scott* [2005] UKHL 2, [2005] 2 AC 176.

4.78   Article 13 of the ECHR requires domestic legal systems to make available an effective remedy empowering the competent national authority to address the substance of an 'arguable' complaint under the ECHR[1].

1 *Z v United Kingdom* (2001) 34 EHRR 3.

4.79   However, what will constitute an effective remedy (or 'just satisfaction') will differ according to the article of the ECHR that is engaged and the facts of the case. In some cases, this will mean compensation; in others, the mere finding of a violation of the claimant's rights under the ECHR will be enough.

4.80   According to *Greenfield*[1], the court should consider whether an award of damages would be 'just and appropriate'. A claimant will not recover damages at all if a mere finding of a violation of his ECHR rights would be just satisfaction of her claim.

1 *R (on the application of Greenfield) v Secretary of State for the Home Department* [2005] UKHL 14, [2005] 1 WLR 673.

4.81   When the court does award compensation, it will do so under two heads: 'pecuniary damage', and 'non-pecuniary damage'.

'Pecuniary damage'

4.82   As long as a 'clear causal link' exists between the violation(s) and the pecuniary damage alleged, the court will award compensation even when the damage 'cannot be calculated precisely' or its assessment 'involve[s] a degree of speculation'[1]. In these cases, the court does not insist that each head of claim be 'duly documented' in detail, but will award compensation 'on an equitable basis'.

1 See *Öneryıldız v Turkey* (2005) 41 EHRR 20 at para 166.

'Non-pecuniary damage'

4.83   Again, the court will award damage according to its own 'equitable assessment'. In so doing, it will have regard to its own case law in similar cases.

4.84   The jurisprudence of the court indicates that different considerations will apply under each Article of the ECHR. These are canvassed below.

Article 2

4.85   It is clear that the European Court considers that where there has been an omission to act by a public authority leading to a victim's death, an enforceable right to compensation by the surviving relatives is an essential part of the remedy[1], both on behalf of the deceased and in compensation for their own 'anguish'[2]. The 'clear line of authority' to this effect was recognised by the Supreme Court in the case of *Rabone*[3].

1 See *Edwards v United Kingdom* (Application 46477/99) (2002) 12 BHRC 190 at para 101.
2 See *Öneryıldız v Turkey* (2005) 41 EHRR 20 at para 152.
3 *Rabone v Pennine Care NHS Foundation Trust* [2012] UKSC 2, [2012] 2 AC 72 per Dyson.

4.86   In *McGlinchey v United Kingdom*[1] the Strasbourg Court reiterated its position that, for breaches of Articles 2 and 3, compensation for the non-pecuniary damage flowing from the breach should in principle be part of the range of available remedies[2], and stated that 'the court itself will often award just satisfaction, recognising pain, stress, anxiety and frustration as rendering appropriate compensation for non-pecuniary damage'.

1 (Application 50390/99) (2003) 37 EHRR 821 at para 62ff.
2 See also *Z v United Kingdom* (2001) 34 EHRR 3 at [109].

4.87   Further, a surviving relative does not necessarily need to be the spouse or parent of a minor deceased in order to recover what are in effect 'bereavement' damages. For example, the parent of an adult son[1] and the brother of the deceased have recovered damages[2]. In *Önen v Turkey*[3] damages were awarded to the applicant (whose parents and brother had died) and ten surviving siblings for anguish and distress suffered as a result of failure to investigate.

1 *Ogur v Turkey* (Application 21594/93) (1999) 31 EHRR 912.
2 *Cakici v Turkey* (Application 23657/94) (1999) 31 EHRR 133.
3 (Application 22876/93) 14 May 2002.

4.88   Thus, the ECHR significantly extends the kind of damage and injury for which a claimant in a clinical negligence action may claim:

(1)   first, a claimant might be able to claim damages for a delay in treatment which did not have any effect on his condition or prognosis but which caused distress and suffering which, whilst crossing the Article 3 threshold, could not be diagnosed as a recognisable physical or psychological injury;

(2)   second, relatives can recover for their own 'anguish' without having to satisfy the criteria governing their status as secondary victims;

(3)   third, relatives of the deceased may recover 'bereavement' damages even where the deceased was not a spouse or child under 18, as is required by the Fatal Accidents Act 1976, s 1A;

(4)   fourth, sums awarded by the court for bereavement in some cases greatly exceed those available to claimants under the Fatal Accidents Act 1976.

This means that, where there has been a death or life-threatening injuries, in theory a wider category of claimants is entitled to recover damages for a wider category of damage than would otherwise be available under English law.

4.89   In the clinical context, awards of £5,000[1] and £10,000[2] have been made by the domestic courts to relatives of deceased patients where a breach of the operational obligation has been found.

1 Awards of £5,000 each to the parents in *Rabone*.
2 *Savage v South Essex Partnership NHS Foundation Trust* [2010] EWHC 865 (QB), [2010] HRLR 24. In *Reynolds v United Kingdom* (Application 2694/08) [2012] All ER (D) 176 (Mar), an award of €7,000 was made for a violation of Article 13 in conjunction with Article 2.

Article 3

4.90   Where the threshold of severity of suffering has been passed, the assessment by the court of a claimant's suffering for the purpose of awarding damages is carried out on what it calls 'an equitable basis', and does not involve any detailed consideration of causation: invariably it states that it considers that the applicant 'must have been caused a certain amount of anxiety and suffering' and awards damages accordingly. The considerations which will affect the amount of damages will be different in each case: see, for example, *Istratii v Moldova*[1], where one of the three prisoner applicants not only suffered pain and anxiety from the authorities' failure to offer him timely medical assistance (in failing to call an ambulance for three hours after emergency treatment became necessary), but was also humiliated by being handcuffed whilst in hospital and was exposed to a further danger to his health by being moved back into detention after surgery. He was accordingly awarded €6,000: €2,000 more than one applicant and €1,000 more than the other.

1 (Applications 8721/05, 8705/05 and 8742/05) 27 March 2007.

Article 8

4.91   Given that claims under this article are so disparate, it is difficult to give any guidance, even if a clinical situation were held to give rise to a claim under Article 8. It may be noted that in the case of *N* (under the conjoined appeals in *Anufrijeva v London Borough of Southwark*) the Court of Appeal stated that where a breach of Article 8 'has the incidental effect of causing psychiatric harm, that fact can properly be reflected in an award of damages'[1].

1 [2003] EWCA Civ 1406, [2004] QB 1124 at para 143.

4.92   However, the court will also award damages where a claimant has suffered such things as 'frustration and anxiety as a result of feelings of frustration and injustice', where this is not sufficiently compensated by a finding of a violation of the ECHR[1]. In other words, awards under Article 8 may go far beyond what would be recoverable in tort. Indeed, if the court finds that the domestic award for clinical negligence is insufficient it may find that an applicant has not lost their victim status and find a breach of Article 8[2].

1 See *Venema v Netherlands* (2004) 39 EHRR 5, where the claimants were jointly awarded €15,000 for the violation of their right to respect for family life.
2 *GB and RB v Moldova* (Application 16761/09) 18 December 2012.

PROCEDURE

4.93   It is clear that the provisions of Article 6, which secure the right to a fair trial, have potential impact in the field of clinical negligence as they do in all areas of litigation. A full examination of that impact is beyond the scope of this chapter; however, the following areas are particularly pertinent in clinical negligence matters.

Healthcare providers as public authorities

4.94   Under the HRA 1998, a claim may only be brought against a public authority. Section 6 of the HRA 1998 makes it unlawful for a public authority to act in a way which is incompatible with a Convention right. Section 6(3) of the HRA 1998 provides that a public authority includes:

(1)   a court or tribunal, and
(2)   any person certain of whose functions are functions of a public nature.

4.95   Human rights issues may therefore be engaged in a clinical negligence case in two ways: either as a substantive human rights claim, no doubt alongside a claim in negligence, or because the courts must take into account human rights principles when considering a case before them.

4.96   It is clear that NHS bodies are public authorities for the purposes of the HRA 1998 and that those providing private medical treatment are not and so do not have any duties to their patients under the HRA 1998.

4.97   There is as yet no authority on whether other providers of health services, such as GPs, are public authorities for the purposes of the HRA 1998, but the authors of this chapter consider it likely that they would be regarded as public authorities if providing treatment through the NHS.

4.98   It seems clear, following the decisions in *R (on the application of Johnson) v Havering London Borough Council*[1] and *YL v Birmingham City Council*[2] that private contractors providing services on behalf of the NHS will not be subject to the HRA 1998. However, if a claim against a private body appears to involve matters which would engage one of the articles of the ECHR, there may be a human rights claim available against the body contracting out those services for failing to secure or supervise the protection of ECHR rights by the private provider[3].

1 [2007] EWCA Civ 26.
2 [2007] UKHL 27. Section 145 of the Health and Social Care Act 2012 reverses the effect of the *YL* decision in respect of residential care provided under the National Assistance Act 1948.
3 See *Storck v Germany* (Application 61603/00) (2005) 43 EHRR 96 at paras 101–103.

4.99   The scope of the HRA 1998 is further extended by the approach that, where Article 2 is engaged, the positive obligation on the state to safeguard the lives of those within its jurisdiction applies 'in the context of any activity, whether public or not, in which the right to life may be at stake'[1].

1 *Öneryildiz v Turkey* (2005) 41 EHRR 20 at para 71.

4.100   This means that where a patient has suffered treatment which would amount to a breach of his rights under the ECHR had it been inflicted by an NHS body, the state's responsibility may still be engaged. For example, the death of a patient in the care of the medical profession, whether in the public or private sector, will engage the state's responsibility to investigate 'so that the cause of death of patients in the care of the medical profession, whether in the public or the private sector, can be determined and those responsible made accountable'. It may also disclose a failure by the state to 'make regulations compelling hospitals, whether private or public, to adopt appropriate measures for the protection of patients' lives'[1].

1 See *Tarariyeva v Russia* (Application 4353/01) (2006) 48 EHRR 609 at para 74, and the cases cited therein: *Vo v France* (2004) 40 EHRR 259 at para 89; *Calvelli v Italy* (Application 32967/96) 17 January 2002, Grand Chamber at para 49; and *Powell v United Kingdom* (45399/09) (2000) 30 EHRR CD 36.

Standing

4.101   Only the 'victim' of an act by the public authority may bring a claim under the HRA 1998[1]. The complainant must show that he was 'actually' and 'directly' affected[2].

1 HRA 1998, s 7(1). Section 7(7) provides that a person is a victim of an unlawful act only if he would be a victim for the purposes of Article 34 of the Convention if proceedings were brought in the European Court of Human Rights in respect of that act.
2 However, the 'directly affected' requirement is not to be applied in a rigid or inflexible way.

4.102   The definition of a victim is a wide one: anyone with a 'legitimate material interest' or 'moral interest' in the outcome of the claim, or even someone who is 'closely affected' enough by the matters giving rise to the alleged violation, may claim under the ECHR.

4.103   In some cases, the existence of laws or measures may be sufficient to entitle an individual to claim to be a victim of a violation, without having to allege that such measures were in fact applied to him[1].

In other words, a potential claimant in an action for clinical negligence will always have standing to bring a claim under the HRA 1998.

1 *Dudgeon v United Kingdom* (1982) 4 EHRR 19; *Klass v Germany* [1978] 2 EHRR 4; *Malone v United Kingdom* (1985) 7 EHRR 14; *Campbell v United Kingdom* (1993) 15 EHRR 137.

Victims under ECHR Article 2

4.104   In domestic case law, the question of victim status has been considered in a number of domestic Article 2 claims. In *Savage*, Lord Scott made *obiter* comments throwing some doubt on whether a close family member could claim to be a victim of the Article 2 positive obligation[1]. The point was subsequently considered in *Morgan v Ministry of Justice*[2], where Mr Justice Supperstone noted that the Strasbourg Court took a broad view for the purposes of determining whether a person is capable of claiming to be a 'victim' of a breach of Article 2 of the Convention but that each case was to be determined on its particular facts. In *Rabone*, the Supreme Court put to rest Lord Scott's doubt in *Savage* about victims of Article 2 breaches[3].

1 *Savage v South Essex Partnership NHS Foundation Trust* [2008] UKHL 74, [2009] AC 681 at para 5.
2 [2010] EWHC 2248 (QB)
3 *Rabone v Pennine Care NHS Foundation Trust* [2012] UKSC 2, [2012] 2 AC 72 at paras 46–48 per Lord Dyson, who noted that Lord Scott's comments seemed to have been made without the benefit of a consideration of the Strasbourg jurisprudence on the point.

4.105 It is convenient to note here that it has been determined that, as there is no general right in law for relatives of a deceased person to sue for their losses arising out the death, the rule within the Fatal Accidents Act 1976 which bars relatives of the deceased from making a claim for loss of dependency under the Act where the deceased's claim was determined or settled within his lifetime is not contrary to the Article 6 right to a fair trial[1]. In *Swift v Secretary of State for Justice*[2], the Court of Appeal held that the Fatal Accidents Act 1976, s 1(3)(b), which disentitles cohabitees who have been living with the deceased for less than two years from claiming damages for loss of dependency, was not incompatible with Article 14 (the prohibition on discrimination) in conjunction with Article 8.

1 *Thompson v Arnold* [2007] EWHC 1875 (QB).
2 [2013] EWCA Civ 193, [2013] 3 WLR 1151.

Limitation

4.106 The limitation period under the HRA 1998 is one year, but the court has a discretion to extend the time limit to such period as it considers equitable in all the circumstances[1]. However, this is subject to any stricter time limit imposed by another rule of law.

1 In *Bedford v Bedfordshire County Council* [2013] EWHC 1717 (QB), [2014] LGR 44, in a claim for breach of Article 8 brought by the claimant in relation to an assault and injuries he suffered while accommodated at a children's home, Jay J referred that 'the fact that the limitation period under the HRA is one year, not three years, and that it is clearly the policy of the legislature that HRA claims should be dealt with both swiftly and economically. All such claims are, by definition, brought against public authorities and there is no public interest in these being burdened by expensive, time-consuming and tardy claims brought years after the event' (at para 76).

IMPACT OF THE HRA 1998 IN OTHER AREAS OF MEDICAL LAW

4.107 The ECHR now plays a very significant role in many areas of health care law other than clinical negligence: for example, in mental health law, inquests, disciplinary proceedings, 'best interests' and 'access to treatment' cases consideration of the human rights implications of the case is now inescapable. Whilst such areas are beyond the scope of this chapter, it is not inconceivable that the principles developed in such cases may play a role in determining the scope and content of the duty owed by a clinical provider to a patient[1].

1 For example, the Supreme Court judgment in *P v Cheshire West and Chester Council* [2014] UKSC 19, [2014] AC 896, a case with significant ramifications for determining whether arrangements made for the care and/or treatment of a person lacking capacity to consent to those arrangements amounts to a deprivation of liberty. The Supreme Court held that the test for deprivation of liberty is whether a person is subject to continuous supervision and control, and is free to leave. It is expected that the case will result in an increase in requests for authorisation of deprivation of liberty for patients in hospitals. Deprivation of liberty and the ECHR, Article 5 are outside the scope of this chapter and readers are referred to texts on mental health law and mental capacity as appropriate.

CHAPTER 5

Compensation schemes

Dr Anthony Barton

INTRODUCTION

5.1   This chapter considers schemes for compensation for medical accidents:

(1)   the National Health Service Redress Act 2006; and
(2)   various proposals for no-fault compensation.

THE NHS REDRESS ACT 2006

Introduction

5.2   The NHS Redress Act 2006 (NHSRA 2006) is entirely concerned with clinical negligence. The statute represents an attempt to address the problems of clinical negligence litigation. According to the NHS Litigation Authority (NHSLA) in 2006, £560 million was paid out in connection with hospital-based clinical negligence, the contingent liability estimate is £8.22 billion. These figures do not even include general practice.

5.3   *Chapter 5*

Background

5.3   There has been widespread long-standing concern about clinical negligence litigation: delay; disproportionate cost; poor success rate; excessive legal fees; complexity; and limited access to justice. In May 2001 the National Audit Office published the report 'Handling Clinical Negligence Claims in England'[1]. The report acknowledged the 'enormous human and financial costs of clinical negligence'; the report recognised that there were four key bodies involved: the Department of Health, the NHSLA, the Lord Chancellor's Department (as it was then), and the Legal Services Commission. In particular, the report identified the problems concerned with the management of small- and medium-sized claims.

1 'Handling clinical negligence claims in England' a report by the Comptroller and Auditor General, National Audit Office, May 2001.

5.4   In August 2001 the Department of Health published 'Clinical negligence: what are the issues and options for reform?'[1]. It was a call for ideas. The Chief Medical Officer established an advisory committee representing broad interests. The paper was wide ranging and was concerned with such issues as: complaints and clinical negligence; the process and basis of compensation; the nature of any inquiry; responsiveness to patient concerns; the quality and cost of managing claims.

1 'Clinical negligence: what are the issues and options for reform?' Department of Health, August 2001.

5.5   In May 2002 the House of Commons Committee of Public Accounts published its report 'Handling Clinical Negligence Claims in England'[1]. The report identified some specific issues:

(1)   reducing the incidence of clinical negligence;
(2)   addressing patient needs;
(3)   speeding up the handling of claims;
(4)   reducing the cost of dealing with claims.

1 'Handling clinical negligence claims in England' House of Commons Committee of Public Accounts, Thirty-seventh Report of Session 2001-2002, HC 280 (May 2002).

5.6   The Committee heard oral evidence from witnesses who were senior officers of the Department of Health, the Legal Services Commission, the NHSLA, and the Lord Chancellor's Department. A written memorandum was admitted that included the assertion: 'The problems of clinical negligence litigation are inextricably linked to the flaws of the legal aid system'[1].

1 'Handling clinical negligence claims in England' House of Commons Committee of Public Accounts, Thirty-seventh Report of Session 2001–2002, HC 280 (May 2002), Memorandum submitted by Dr Anthony Barton.

5.7   In June 2003 the Department published the Chief Medical Officer's report 'Making Amends'. It was a consultation paper setting out proposals for reforming the approach to clinical negligence in the NHS. The report was generally critical of tort law and proposed to 'move the role of tort from its current central position to the outer perimeter of the NHS' (wherever that may be). The report appeared to confuse the procedural and substantive

134

aspects of civil litigation. The report contained 19 recommendations. Recommendation one was as follows:

'An NHS Redress Scheme should be introduced to provide investigations when things go wrong; remedial treatment, rehabilitation and care where needed; explanations and apologies; and financial compensation in certain circumstances'.

Eligibility criteria for compensation would be:

(1)   serious shortcomings in the standard of care;
(2)   harm that could have been avoided;
(3)   the adverse outcome was not the result of natural progression of an illness.

With respect, these criteria appear strikingly similar to the requirements of proof of fault and causation under any tort based system.

5.8   Recommendation two was as follows:

'The NHS Redress Scheme should encompass care and compensation for severely neurologically impaired babies, including those with severe cerebral palsy'.

The proposal was effectively for a no-fault system for 'severe neurological impairment related to or resulting from the birth'; however, moral arbitrariness was inevitable in that the proposed scheme excluded 'genetic or chromosomal abnormality'. Moreover the report did not address disability which was related to antenatal or post partum events, or non-neurological impairment.

5.9   The other 17 recommendations were wide ranging, consequential, commonsense, unexceptionable provisions. Recommendation 17 is worthy of mention; it was as follows:

'The costs of future care included in any award for clinical negligence made by the courts should no longer reflect the cost of private treatment'.

This recommendation would effectively repeal the Law Reform (Personal Injury) Act 1948, s 2(4); this statutory provision means that the availability of treatment under the NHS should not be taken into consideration when compensating the cost of future care. Compensation under common law tort principles is restorative; the effect of this outdated statutory provision is to inflate the cost of compensation.

The NHS Redress Act 2006

5.10   The preamble of the NHSRA 2006 establishes tort-based liability as the necessary condition for obtaining redress:

'An Act to make provision about arrangement for redress in relation to liability in tort in connection with services provided as part of the health service in England or Wales; and for connected purposes.'

The legislation is concerned exclusively with 'qualifying liability in tort' and affirms Parliament's view that fault-based liability should remain the basis of compensation for clinical mishaps; the early proposal for a limited no-fault scheme for brain-damaged babies was quietly dropped. The legislation addressed only recommendation one of 'Making Amends'; the rest were discarded.

5.11 The statute is important legislation, since it potentially affects NHS hospital patients; the intention is to extend its operation to primary care. The underlying policy of the NHSRA 2006 is to provide a genuine alternative to litigation. The Act does not affect any private law rights. It is wholly concerned with the process of compensation; it does not alter the basis of compensation. It is procedural, not substantive.

5.12 The NHSRA 2006 proposes a redress package where there has been clinical negligence in hospital. The redress package must include: an offer of compensation; explanation; apology; and report of action to prevent similar occurrences. The redress package may include care or treatment. The package can be accepted with waiver of the right to sue, or rejected. The redress scheme is to be run by the NHSLA.

5.13 The proposed redress scheme is a consensual process, not a judicial process; redress is offered, not awarded. Proceeding under the redress scheme is voluntary. Proceedings under the redress scheme and civil legal proceedings are mutually exclusive: they cannot be conducted at the same time. Legal rights are suspended but remain intact during the redress process when legal liability is assessed; legal liability is not adjudicated upon by the scheme's procedure since it is not a tribunal. Legal rights are only determined if any offer is made and accepted as part of a compromise agreement.

5.14 The NHSRA 2006 is enabling legislation and the detail of its operation will be set out in regulation. However, indications of its likely operation may be gleaned from Parliamentary debate and in supporting documentation[1]. For example, there are indications that:

(1) the scheme proposes that any offer made will be without prejudice, that if it is rejected it may not be taken as evidence of liability in any legal proceedings;

(2) the upper limit for monetary compensation will be £20,000;

(3) legal privilege will not be asserted in respect of the investigation report.

1 See for example the Explanatory Notes accompanying the Bill, the Explanatory Notes accompanying the NHSRA 2006, and the Full Regulatory Impact Assessment documents accompanying the Bill.

Commentary on the NHS Redress Act 2006

5.15 The NHSRA 2006 is fundamentally misconceived. Treatment is a matter of patient entitlement, not legal remedy. Out of court settlement should and does happen anyway. The Act's focus on blame and compensation does not reflect patient priorities.

5.16 The legislation envisages an integrated one stop shop run by the health service. The health service would investigate itself. The redress scheme is over-ambitious, combining incompatible and conflicting functions; it will produce a confusion of processes. It will mix inquisitorial and adversarial, fact finding with fault finding, open with privileged. The opposition proposal that there should be a two-stage process for the investigation in the NHSRA 2006 – the first stage an open independent fact finding inquiry; the second stage an in-house privileged fault finding assessment – was unsuccessful. This natural division of procedures would have bestowed functional coherence and efficacy on the investigation process.

5.17   Since the NHSRA 2006 is concerned with 'qualifying liability in tort', any investigation would ordinarily attract legal privilege. The proposed investigation combines fact finding with fault finding without formal separation. Assurances have been given that the investigations will be open and will not be privileged. There is thus a fundamental incoherence between the open investigation of liability and the making of any offer on a without prejudice basis. If a without prejudice offer is accepted then it may be that there are no difficulties in disclosing the investigation report since legal rights have been determined: it may not really matter whether any settlement is made with or without admission of liability. Where an investigation has taken place and an offer is not made or if a without prejudice offer is made and is not accepted, then the applicant's legal rights are intact. Where legal rights are intact, any investigation of liability would ordinarily remain legally privileged according to usual principles. The operation of legal privilege in relation to the investigation report under the scheme is not at all clear.

5.18   The idea of the NHSRA 2006 is to move away from adversarial attitudes in litigation, yet the Act proposes to provide free legal advice during the redress process. It is an attempt to bolster the credibility of the scheme which lacks independence. It threatens to replicate the problems of the litigation system without the closure and finality of a judicial process. Free legal advice is not to be confined to the end of the redress investigation, in connection with any offer or settlement when legal rights might be determined. Until that point legal rights are suspended: they are neither asserted nor defended.

5.19   The redress scheme affords a prospect of monetary compensation in an open-ended, demand-led, risk-free, cost-free system with free legal advice available. By contrast, any litigation process necessarily imposes some eligibility criteria through the commercial discipline of legal costs, whether by the availability of legal representation or the risk of exposure to liability for the defendant's legal costs. The redress scheme proposes a free ticket for speculative claims. The then Minister asserted that the 'vast majority of opportunistic claims [would] be easily rejected' because payment would only be made where there was negligence[1]. With respect, it is difficult to see that the requirement of proof of fault and causation can mean that claims under the scheme will be 'easily rejected'; these requirements present the very difficulties that are at the heart of clinical negligence litigation. In short, the cost of the scheme has not been properly assessed; the problem of assessing eligibility of claims for redress has not been recognised or considered.

1 Jane Kennedy, HC Official Report written answers col 963W (24 April 2006).

5.20   The conceptual basis of the redress scheme was described in Parliamentary debate thus:

'... we have a set of powers which will establish a heterogeneous scheme that amounts legally and practically to a dog's breakfast: one that involves investigation, fact finding, fault finding, arranging treatment and awarding compensation. I made the point earlier that this effectively amounts to a replication of the machinery of the courts, but without the independence or procedural safeguards that the courts afford to a litigant'[1].

1 Earl Howe, HL Official Report Grand Committee col GC359 (21 November 2005).

5.21 The legislation has been generally welcomed for its good intentions, even if its rationale is somewhat muddled, and for acknowledging the problems of clinical negligence litigation; however, it has been widely seen as a wasted opportunity. The scheme of the legislation has not been given effect in England.

NHS redress in Wales

5.22 The NHS redress scheme was given effect in Wales by the first piece of primary legislation to be passed by the Welsh Assembly: the NHS Redress (Wales) Measure 2008. The National Health Service (Concerns, Complaints and Redress Arrangements) (Wales) Regulations 2011[1] provide the detail of the implementation of the scheme.

1 SI 2011/704.

NO-FAULT COMPENSATION

Introduction

5.23 Clinical negligence is governed by the general law of negligence. The central concept underlying liability for negligence is that compensation requires proof of fault (breach of duty), causing injury. The liability to pay compensatory damages falls on the person whose negligent act or omission has caused the injury. There are thus two distinct elements to the tort of negligence:

(1) breach of duty; and
(2) causation.

It is fault-based liability and contrasts with strict liability and no-fault liability.

5.24 Any rational system of liability for clinical accidents imposes the requirement of medical investigation and clinical audit. A fault-based system imports additional concepts of professional accountability and deterrence. It may also serve our societal need to attribute blame and obtain an apology when things are perceived to have gone wrong. There is a widely held belief that the system of compensation for clinical negligence operates also to maintain standards of clinical practice.

5.25 Clinical negligence litigation has inherent difficulties for the claimant. Proof of breach of duty usually requires expert opinion. Proof of causation requires consideration of the effect of a negligent medical intervention (or non-intervention) on a disease process and the hypothetical question as to what would have happened in the absence of fault. These difficulties have been recognised by the court:

'But, whether we like it or not, the law which only Parliament can change, requires proof of fault causing damage as the basis of liability in tort. We should do society nothing but disservice if we made the forensic process more unpredictable and hazardous by distorting the law to accommodate the exigencies of what may seem hard cases'[1].

However, there are many examples to illustrate the saying 'hard cases make bad law'.

1 *Wilsher v Essex Area Health Authority* [1988] 1 All ER 871, per Lord Bridge at 883.

5.26 Despite ever-increasing cost to the health service, there is a widespread belief that litigation is failing as a system for obtaining compensation for victims of clinical negligence. Proof of negligence is inherently difficult. The legal process is lengthy, complex and expensive. There are concerns about access to justice. The relatively high cost of recovering compensation compared to the value of compensation recovered demonstrates the economic inefficiency of litigation. Too often the main beneficiaries of litigation appear to be lawyers. These concerns have been considered in reports by the National Audit Office and in Parliament[1].

1 'Handling clinical negligence claims in England' a report by the Comptroller and Auditor General, National Audit Office (May 2001); 'Handling clinical medical claims in England' House of Commons, Committee of Public Accounts, Thirty-seventh Report of Session 2001–2002, HC 280 (May 2002).

5.27 Numerous solutions have been proposed to address the unsatisfactory state of clinical negligence litigation. These can conveniently be classified as procedural or substantive. Procedural reforms entail changes to the process of compensation: these include replacing the litigation process by arbitration, mediation, or conciliation. The NHSRA 2006 is an example. Other proposals include investigative and disciplinary tribunals which have power to award compensation. Substantive reforms entail changes to the basis of compensation: these include operating a presumption of negligence in cases of medical accidents (effectively reversing the burden of proof) and removing the need to prove breach of duty (no-fault compensation).

5.28 This distinction between the basis of compensation and the process of compensation for the adverse consequences of medical treatment is fundamental. There is also the separate question of liability for compensation: who pays? These distinctions must be borne in mind when considering proposals for reform. Any system providing compensation for adverse consequences of medical treatment requires clear definition of what sorts of events and conditions are within its criteria for compensation.

Historical review

5.29 The unsatisfactory state of the litigation system for compensating medical accidents has long been recognised. It has led to repeated calls for the introduction of a no-fault compensation system by such diverse interests as politicians, patient groups and the British Medical Association (BMA).

Such proposals generally envisage not merely change in the substantive law enabling compensation to be awarded without proof of fault, but also procedural change in that it is awarded by a tribunal from a central fund; changes in the basis and process of compensation, and in the identity of the compensator. A valuable, though somewhat dated, discussion of the problems of compensation for medical injury can be found in the Pearson Report[1]. The terms of reference were as follows:

'To consider to what extent, in what circumstances and by what means compensation should be payable in respect of death or personal injury (including ante-natal injury) suffered by any person in the course of employment; through the use of a motor vehicle or other form of transport; through the manufacture, supply or use of goods or services; on premises belonging to or occupied by another or otherwise through the act or omission of another where compensation under the present law is recoverable only on proof of fault or under the rules of strict liability, having regard to the cost and other implications of the arrangements for the recovery of compensation, whether by way of compulsory insurance or otherwise'.

1 *Royal Commission on Civil Liability and Compensation for Personal Injury* (March 1978) CM 70f, Ch 24.

5.30 The report gave limited though specific consideration to medical accidents:

'The main difficulty in the way of a no-fault scheme is how to establish causation, since the cause of many injuries cannot be identified … Even with our definition of medical injury we were forced to conclude that in practice there would be difficulty in distinguishing medical accidents from the natural progression of a disease or injury, and from a foreseeable side effect of treatment … It is easy to distinguish the completely unexpected result from that which was expected. The grey areas in between pose serious difficulties in knowing where to draw the line'.

The Pearson Report was not able to recommend a no-fault scheme for medical accidents. It described this as a 'difficult' decision and said that the arguments were 'finely balanced'. It observed that it might have to review its conclusions in the future.

5.31 In 1974, New Zealand introduced a comprehensive compensation scheme for personal injury by accident, including medical accidents. It is a state scheme. Injury is defined to include physical and mental consequences of any accident.

5.32 Sweden has two voluntary insurance schemes: the patient insurance scheme concerned with accidents arising out of medical treatment; and the pharmaceutical insurance scheme concerned with the adverse effects of medicinal products. These are confined to physical injury; other exclusions also operate. The schemes are intended to supplement the tort system; however, there can be no double recovery. Finland also has introduced a limited no-fault scheme for medical accidents.

5.33 The BMA has advocated a system of no-fault compensation since 1983. It described the present litigation system based on tortious liability as 'harmful, unpredictable and unjust', mainly because it damages the therapeutic relationship but also because of the lack of availability of justice.

5.34   In late 1990 there were two Bills presented to Parliament – the Compensation for Medical Injury Bill (Ms Harriet Harman) and the NHS (Compensation) Bill (Mrs Rosie Barnes). Both envisaged state-funded compensation 'without having to prove negligence'. Neither received government support.

5.35   In December 1990, the Royal College of Physicians published its report 'Compensation for Adverse Consequences of Medical Intervention'. The report considered various options, including tortious liability, no-fault compensation and needs-based disability income and also acknowledged the difficulties of the requirement of proof of causation in a no-fault scheme. However, it considered that any such scheme introduced 'inequities', since the award of compensation to people with identical needs would depend on whether their condition arose from a medical intervention or was a natural process. It considered that the only permanent solution was a 'comprehensive disability income scheme for all illnesses and injury-related disability irrespective of causation'. However, in the context of political and economic reality it proposed a limited no-fault scheme.

5.36   The BMA continues to support a no-fault scheme. Individual Members of Parliament and judges from time to time call for such a scheme. Whatever the government, it has rejected such proposals as economically unrealistic, politically misconceived and legally flawed:

'Proponents of no-fault compensation have yet to show why compensation in healthcare should be regarded as essentially different from negligence and compensation in other walks of life, where claims are resolved through the usual legal process'[1].

And more recently:

'Some argue that, as it takes a long time for medical negligence cases to be heard, it is unfair on the litigant, and that a supposedly quicker no-fault scheme is the answer. The Government cannot agree with that. To pay compensation when no-fault has been established would, to some extent, belittle the harm caused to others through a negligent act. It would also treat medical accidents in a different way from other personal injuries, and it may often be just as difficult to establish that the medical treatment had caused the injury as to prove that someone had been negligent.

Even under a no-fault liability scheme, causation would still have to be established. That is not always easy, and can be as difficult as establishing negligence ... There is also a risk that a no-fault culture could, over time, diminish clinical accountability ...'[2].

1 Mr Tom Sackville MP, HC Official Report Vol 267, col 639 (22 November 1995).
2 Mr Paul Boateng MP, HC Official Report Vol 310, col 457 (8 April 1998).

5.37   In 2003 the Chief Medical Officer published a consultation paper 'Making Amends', which set out proposals for reforming the approach to clinical negligence in the NHS. The proposals included a limited no-fault scheme for brain damaged babies. It was intended to provide the basis for the NHSRA 2006. However, the proposal was quietly dropped from the face of the Bill. The NHSRA 2006 is confined to tort-based liability.

No-fault compensation in practice

5.38   There are a small number of discrete no-fault compensation schemes that operate in specific and limited circumstances. These include statutory and voluntary schemes, and settlements.

5.39   The Vaccine Damage Payments Act 1979 provides for payments to be made out of public funds in cases where severe disability occurs as a result of vaccination against certain diseases. Causation must be proven on the balance of probability. Initially many payments were made; however, more recently there has been increased medical understanding that injuries following vaccination were not necessarily caused by the vaccine. Barely a handful of payments are now made each year.

5.40   The Association of the British Pharmaceutical Industry has two schemes for compensation for injury as a result of participation in research: one applies to clinical trials, and the other to medical experiments in non-patient human volunteers. Neither compensation scheme requires proof of fault. The Association of British Healthcare Industries also operates such compensation schemes. An EC Directive provides that in relation to clinical trials any ethics committee shall consider the 'provision for indemnity or compensation in the event of injury or death attributable to a clinical trial' in preparing its opinion[1].

1 Directive 2001/20/EC, Article 6, para 3(h).

5.41   The government has on occasion made ex gratia payments to victims of mishap. These include haemophiliacs who contracted HIV from transfusion of blood products and victims of variant Creutzfeld-Jakob disease.

5.42   The operation of legal aid may have provided a de facto no-fault compensation scheme when claims are settled for commercial reasons regardless of merit in order to avoid irrevocable costs. In such situations compensation may occur regardless of cause as well as fault.

Conclusion

5.43   No-fault compensation schemes envisage the payment of compensation to the victim of a medical accident without proof of fault from a central fund. Such schemes enjoy some support based on an incomplete understanding of medical litigation: it is important to distinguish between the basis of compensation and the process of compensation. They are unlikely ever to be put into operation for economic, legal, and policy reasons. Payment according to need already exists in the form of the welfare state; the electorate has demonstrated its lack of support for such a scheme by voting for lower taxes. The system of fault-based compensation has much more to commend itself and seems likely to prevail. It has been endorsed in the NHSRA 2006.

CHAPTER 6

Funding clinical negligence claims

Dr Anthony Barton

INTRODUCTION

6.1   Access to justice and the rule of law are the hallmarks of a civilised
society. The exercise of private law rights provides, but does not ensure,
medical professional accountability. Clinical negligence cases are known for
their cost, technically complex subject matter and unpredictable outcome.
Litigation is expensive and attended by risk. Private funding is too expensive
and risky for most people; most cases have been funded other than by the
claimant. The majority of cases have been funded by legal conditional fee
agreements, and a minority funded by legal aid. Before the event insurance
has an increasing role.

6.2   On 1 April 2013 the Legal Aid, Sentencing and Punishment of
Offenders Act 2012 (LASPO 2012) was implemented. This legislation
represents the biggest change in clinical negligence, not in the substantive
law but in the economics of legal practice. It regulates the funding of clinical
negligence litigation. Most cases can now be funded by:

- conditional fee agreements (CFA);
- damages based agreements (DBA);

143

- before the event insurance (BTE);
- legal aid.

Conditional fee agreements, before the event insurance, and legal aid are well established; damages based agreements have been introduced by LASPO 2012. Cases are not likely to be privately funded.

BACKGROUND

6.3   In recent years there has been concern with regard to two aspects of the economics of access to justice: the expenditure of civil legal aid, and civil litigation costs. There has been increasing privatising of access to justice with the growth of the conditional fee system (with concomitant reduction of legal aid) under the Access to Justice Act 1999[1]. The conditional fee system overall has been successful in providing access to justice, but the balance of litigation risk between claimant and defendant had been distorted in favour of claimants so that defendant costs were excessive and disproportionate[2].

1 See *Privatizing Access to Justice* by Dr Anthony Barton, Adam Smith Institute (April 2000).
2 See *Access to Justice: Balancing the Risks* by Dr Anthony Barton, Adam Smith Institute (August 2010).

6.4   The excessive and disproportionate costs of civil litigation threatened to bring the law into disrepute. Two decades ago the Court of Appeal observed:

'It is no answer that there are public authorities or insurance associations that are footing the bill. The National Health Service has better things to spend its money on than lawyers' fees and the cost of medical insurance is a matter of public concern'[1].

1 *AB v John Wyeth and Brother Ltd* [1994] 5 Med LR 149, per Stuart-Smith LJ at 153.

6.5   On 3 November 2008 the then Master of the Rolls, with the support of the Ministry of Justice, appointed Lord Justice Jackson to lead and conduct a fundamental, independent and wide ranging review into the costs of civil litigation (the *Jackson* report)[1]. The terms of reference were:

'... to review the rules and principles governing the costs of civil litigation and to make recommendations in order to promote access to justice at proportionate cost ... to review case management procedures; to have regard to research into cost and funding; to consult widely; to compare our costs regime with those of other jurisdictions ...'

1 *Review of Civil Litigation Costs: Final Report*, The Stationery Office (December 2009).

6.6   The *Jackson* report made a number of major recommendations; the core proposals which affected clinical negligence litigation included:

- conditional fee agreements: these were recognised as the major contributor to disproportionate costs. The two key drivers of costs were: (i) the lawyer's success fee; and (ii) the after the event insurance. These were additional liabilities (in addition to base costs and damages) which were recoverable from an unsuccessful defendant. The success fee and the ATE insurance premium should cease to be recoverable from unsuccessful opponents.

- qualified one way costs shifting (QOCS): ATE insurance premiums add to the cost of litigation; this can be reduced by removing the need for ATE insurance by qualified one way costs shifting such that the claimant is not required to pay the defendant's costs if the claim is unsuccessful, but the defendant will be required to pay the claimant's costs if the claim is successful.

6.7 Some of the recommendations of the *Jackson* report required primary legislation. However, the recommendation and assertions in the report have been controversial and have not been universally welcomed[1].

1 See *Access to Justice: Balancing the Risks* by Dr Anthony Barton, Adam Smith Institute (2010).

6.8 The *Jackson* report made observations about legal aid which were outside its terms of reference:

'Legal aid is still available for some key areas of litigation, [including] in particular clinical negligence … It is vital that legal aid remains in these areas. However, the continued tightening of financial eligibility criteria, so as to exclude people who could not possibly afford to litigate, inhibits access to justice in those key areas. In my view any further tightening of the financial eligibility criteria would be unacceptable. It is not within my terms of reference to make recommendations about eligibility for legal aid and I do not do so. However, I would place on record my firm view that it would be quite wrong to tighten the eligibility criteria further, so that an even larger percentage of the population falls outside the legal aid net'[1].

The effect of legal aid on the economics of civil litigation has long been recognised by the courts:

'… legal aid helps those who lose cases, not those who win them. Legal aid makes out and out grants to those who lose cases. It only makes loans to those who win them'[2].

1 Part 2, chapter 7, para 3.2 at p 68.
2 *Davies v Eli Lilly & Co* [1987] 3 All ER 94 at 97, Sir John Donaldson MR.

6.9 The *Jackson* report made observations about the conditional fee system:

'Any person, whether rich or poor and whether human or corporate, is entitled to enter into a CFA and take out ATE insurance. All that such a person needs to do is to find willing solicitors and willing insurers …'[1].

Instead of celebrating the universality of access to justice according to the merits of the claim (instead of limited access according to financial eligibility for legal aid, with often perfunctory regard for the merits), the *Jackson* report considered it to be a 'flaw' that there was 'no eligibility test for entering into a CFA, provided that a willing solicitor can be found'[2]. There are eligibility criteria for CFAs, namely the merits as imposed by a system of payment by result: economic reality and commercial discipline.

1 Part 2, chapter 10, para 4.8 at p 109.
2 Part 2, chapter 10, para 4.12 at p 110.

6.10 Civil legal aid has been subject to scrutiny in Parliamentary debate:

'… Legal aid does not ensure access to justice for deserving cases, as most people are not eligible. Instead, it provides access to lawyers for an eligible minority. Legal aid lacks independence. Funding is granted on the advice of the applicant's lawyer, so there is a clear conflict of interest that may encourage over-optimistic advice, to put it kindly, or speculative litigation, putting it less kindly. Legal aid lacks fairness. Successful defendants cannot recover legal costs. Legal aid puts the claimant in a no-lose position and the health service defendant in a no-win position. It may be cheaper to settle a claim regardless of merit, to avoid irrecoverable legal costs – a practice known as legal aid blackmail...

Legal aid lacks accountability. Funding decisions involving public money are privileged and confidential, and are not subject to public scrutiny...

The record of legally aided claims involving health care is dismal, as I said. In some instances, that has promoted unsubstantiated health claims and scares based on junk science, threatening the health of the nation's children. Too often, lawyers are the only beneficiaries of publicly funded legal action. Scarce resources are diverted from patient care to lawyers' fees, all in the name of justice and all paid for by the taxpayer.

The solution to the problem of clinical negligence litigation lies in the realm of funding. Legal aid has brought relief to many people, but it is a popular misconception to equate legal aid with access to justice. Access to justice is not best delivered by the legal aid system'[1].

1 Andrew Lansley MP HC Official Report Vol 447, col 41 (5 June 2006).

6.11 The government published a consultation with a view to the further reform of legal aid[1]. The Judges' Council of England and Wales published a response[2] which contained the following statements:

'In practice, the majority of clinical negligence cases are legally aided' (para 40, p 9).

And:

'... it must be highly questionable whether there is any other 'viable' alternative to legal aid' (para 43, p 10).

And:

'Whilst there are no data for the breakdown of this figure between cases that were legally aided and those that were not ...' (para 44, p 10).

And:

'The absence of viable funding arrangements for clinical negligence claims might be mitigated were there any proposals for dealing with all such claims in other ways ...' (para 46, p 11).

These statements do not accord with answers to Parliamentary questions[3]:

Mr Slaughter: To ask the Secretary of State for Health how many cases brought against the National Health Service Litigation Authority were funded by (a) legal aid, (b) a conditional fee agreement and (c) by other forms of funding in each of the last three years; and how many in each category resulted in a compensation payment. [28807]

Mr Simon Burns: The NHS Litigation Authority (NHSLA) supplied the information in the following table:

Numbers of overall claims settled by the NHSLA by year and by funding arrangement, including the subset of those claims that were settled with damages						
Settlement year	Legal Aid funded	Legal Aid funded and settled with damages	Conditional fee arrangement funded	Conditional fee arrangement funded and settled with damages	Before the event insurance or self funded	Before the event insurance or self funded and settled with damages
2007–08	1,806	1,168	5,135	3,589	1,204	782
2008–09	1,690	1,091	5,065	3,611	1,183	673
2009–10	1,822	1,263	5,843	4,270	1,509	925

1 *Proposals for the Reform of Legal Aid in England and Wales,* Consultation Paper CP12/10 (November 2010).
2 Response of a Sub-Committee of the Judges' Council to the Government's Consultation Paper Cp12/10, *Proposals for the Reform of Legal Aid in England and Wales* (11 February 2011).
3 Commons Written Answer, 8 December 2010: volume 520, part 87 at column 341W.

6.12   The centuries old 'loser pays' costs rule or 'costs follow the event' rule has imposed commercial discipline on litigation (see below); it does not generally apply in legal aid claims which enjoy costs protection. The rule imposes some mutuality in the risks of litigation; it apportions the risks between the parties and affords some protection against costs blackmail – where cases are settled not according to merits, but to avoid unrecoverable costs. The effect of this rule is to deter claimants from bringing and defendants from defending actions they are likely to lose[1]. Hopeless claims and defences are discouraged and a willingness to compromise is induced[2]. This sensible rule promotes the settlement of cases according to their merits and discourages speculative litigation. The costs rule is derived from rules of court and case law: it does not have any specific basis in primary legislation.

1 *Roache v NewsGroup Newspapers Ltd* [1996] EMLR 161.
2 *Ridehalgh v Horsefield* [1994] Ch 205.

6.13   The *Jackson* report recommended that the usual 'loser pays' rule should be replaced by QOCS for certain types of claim including personal injury and clinical negligence. This proposal was the subject of comment in the course of the passage of the LASPO Bill in Parliament:

'… I am talking about perverse incentives under QOWCS to pursue weaker claims, and that is obviously particularly true in clinical negligence cases. ATE insurers act as an important brake on clinical negligence cases, screening out claims, as we have seen, that might otherwise be brought under the QOWCS scheme. QOWCS does not provide a deterrent to such cases. Indeed, if anything, it incentivises them as the impact assessment suggests. That is because QOWCS removes the check on claimants' enthusiasm, represented by the risk of meeting the defendant's costs, albeit covered by ATE. Even if they fail, such speculative cases will result in considerable extra costs to the NHSLA.

A calculation has shown that the actual additional cost to the NHS will be quite dramatic …

… the perverse incentive under QOWCS to pursue weaker claims in the general absence of the costs risk of losing …

… The impact assessment, however, makes it clear that the assumptions are based on the current level of cases, and that they do not take account of the incentivisation to pursue more cases under QOWCS …'[1].

The proposed QOCS was not part of the LASPO Bill, and so changing the operation of the centuries old costs follow the event rule did not have detailed Parliamentary scrutiny.

1 House of Commons. 13 September 2011 (afternoon), Column 530; Legal Aid, Sentencing and Punishment of Offenders Bill, Public Bill Committee, Andy Slaughter MP.

6.14   The passage of the LASPO Bill in the House of Lords was unfortunate. A leading clinical negligence author and publisher commented as follows:

'The striking feature about the Lords debates on clinical negligence was the poor quality of argument and the many errors of fact which betrayed a lack of understanding on basic issues. Peer after peer insisted that clinical negligence litigation would not be possible without legal aid even though 82 per cent of cases are funded by means other than legal aid. Well, with due respect, their Lordships were merely following the judiciary! The triumph of propaganda over evidence…'[1].

The Parliamentary debates contained a misconception: the commercial success of the privatisation of access to justice was scarcely recognised, and it was said that the removal of legal aid would deny access to justice.

1 Legal Aid, Sentencing and Punishment of Offenders Bill: clinical negligence – poor quality Lords debate – reform needed: democracy deserves better, justice deserves better! By Geoffrey Hall, barrister in *Medical Negligence*, 25 April 2012.

LEGAL AID, SENTENCING AND PUNISHMENT OF OFFENDERS ACT 2012

6.15   This statute is more wide ranging than suggested by its title; the preamble includes:

'An Act to make provision about legal aid; to make further provision about funding legal services; to make provision about costs and other amounts awarded in civil… proceedings; to make provision about referral fees in connection with the provision of legal services …'

The relevant parts of the Act concern legal aid (Part 1), and litigation funding and civil litigation costs (Part 2). The parts of the Act which deal with the reform of costs were modelled largely on the proposals of the *Jackson* report. However, with regard to legal aid, the scheme of the legislation disregarded the observations of the *Jackson* report and created the conditions for the privatisation of access to justice.

LEGAL AID

6.16   The availability of civil legal aid is defined generally under LASPO 2012; civil legal services are available to an individual if they are described in Part 1 of Sch 1 and the Director of Legal Aid Casework has determined that the individual qualifies. Legal aid is not generally available for clinical negligence cases. Paragraph 23 of Sch 1 provides an exception for clinical negligence cases only in respect of neurological injury where the victim is severely disabled and the negligence occurred before birth, during birth or in the first eight weeks after birth (or after 37 weeks if born before 37 weeks).

6.17 The Director's determination whether an individual qualifies for legal aid is in accordance with defined eligibility criteria based on the individual's financial resources, and the direction and guidance published by the Lord Chancellor ('Lord Chancellor's Guidance')[1]. The Lord Chancellor's Guidance sets out some of the factors that caseworkers should take into account in deciding applications for civil legal services.

1 Lord Chancellor's Guidance under section 4 of Legal Aid, Sentencing and Punishment of Offenders Act 2012.

6.18 The detail in relation to types of legal services, criteria and determinations in respect of qualification for legal aid is provided by regulation[1]. Clinical negligence is no longer treated as a special case category; funding clinical negligence cases is no longer ring fenced. Clinical negligence cases do not enjoy any priority or privilege in respect of public funding. The general merits criteria apply to clinical negligence cases. In particular, unsuitability of a clinical negligence case for funding by CFA is a standard criterion for determination by the Director[2]. There are criteria which must be satisfied for representation: the cost benefit criteria and the prospects of success criterion[3]. The cost benefit criteria set out ratios of likely damages to likely costs according to the prospects of the case[4]. The stronger the case, the less stringent the damages/costs ratio. The prospects of success criterion is only met if the prospects of success are at least 'moderate', or if borderline and the case is of 'significant wider public interest' or has 'overwhelming importance to the individual'[5].

1 See The Civil Legal Aid (Merits Criteria) Regulations 2013, and the Civil Legal Aid (Procedure) Regulations 2012.
2 The Civil Legal Aid (Merits Criteria) Regulations 2013, reg 39; note CFA has an extended meaning to include CFAs and DBAs.
3 The Civil Legal Aid (Merits Criteria) Regulations 2013, reg 41.
4 The Civil Legal Aid (Merits Criteria) Regulations 2013, reg 42.
5 The Civil Legal Aid (Merits Criteria) Regulations 2013, reg 43.

6.19 LASPO 2012 provides for exceptional funding including in relation to inquests in certain circumstances[1].

1 Legal Aid, Sentencing and Punishment of Offenders Act 2012, s 10(4).

CONDITIONAL FEE AGREEMENTS

6.20 CFAs have been permitted since July 1995 as an exception to the prohibition against maintenance and champerty, and as an exception to the indemnity principle. They are regulated by the Courts and Legal Services Act 1990 (as amended by LASPO 2012)[1] and subsidiary legislation[2]. Under a CFA a solicitor may charge his client an uplift of 100 per cent of his base fee in the event of a successful claim, and nothing should the claim fail. The success fee is recovered from the successful client and is capped at 25 per cent of damages for pain and suffering, and past loss (but not damages for future losses). Clinical negligence cases funded by CFAs are subject to QOCS (see below).

1 Legal Aid, Sentencing and Punishment of Offenders Act 2012, s 44.
2 The Conditional Fee Agreements Order 2013, SI 2013/689.

DAMAGES BASED AGREEMENTS

6.21   DBAs are now permissible for clinical negligence cases as an exception to the prohibition against maintenance and champerty under LASPO 2012[1]. Under a DBA, lawyers are not paid if they lose a case but may take a percentage of the damages recovered for their client as their fee if the case is successful. The maximum payment that the lawyer can recover from the claimant's damages is capped at 25 per cent of damages (excluding damages for future care and loss) in personal injury cases (other percentage caps apply to other types of claim).

1 Legal Aid, Sentencing and Punishment of Offenders Act 2012, s 45; the Damages-Based Agreements Regulations 2013, SI 2013/609.

6.22   Successful claimants using DBAs will recover their solicitors' base costs and disbursements from defendants in the usual way, but the claimant will be responsible for paying from their damages any shortfall between the solicitors' costs paid by the losing defendant and the agreed DBA fee and will also be required to pay any shortfall in respect of disbursements. Lawyers acting under a DBA will be required to comply with the indemnity principle[1], which means that their fee would be restricted to what is due under the DBA fee: if the DBA fee is less than the solicitors' costs would be in the absence of a DBA, a losing defendant would only be liable to pay the DBA fee.

1 According to the indemnity principle a client is not entitled to recover under an order for costs more than the amount payable by him to his solicitor. See also CPR 44.18 and, in particular, CPR 44.18(2)(b).

THE COSTS RULE AND QUALIFIED ONE WAY COSTS SHIFTING

6.23   The award of costs is within the discretion of the court; the court can award costs against the world at large[1]. The usual rule is that the costs follow the event, known familiarly as the 'loser pays' rule; this rule should apply unless there is good reason to disapply it[2]. The operation of this rule is that the loser pays the winner's costs in addition to the loser's own costs.

1 *Aiden Shipping Co Ltd v Interbulk Ltd* [1986] AC 965, and Senior Courts Act 1981, s 51.
2 CPR 44.2(2)(a).

6.24   Although not part of LASPO 2012 itself, QOCS is part of the operation of the scheme of the Act. The operation of the usual costs rule does not now apply in certain types of cases including personal injury, clinical negligence and fatal accident cases. Under QOCS[1]:

'… orders for costs made against a claimant may be enforced without the permission of the court but only to the extent that the aggregate amount in money terms of such orders does not exceed the aggregate amount in money terms of any orders for damages and interest made in favour of the claimant'.

There are exceptions to QOCS where the claim has been struck out[2]; or where the claim has been found to be fundamentally dishonest, and in other circumstances[3]. QOCS is said to be modelled on the costs protection of the legal aid scheme. However, there is an important difference: a successful defendant in a legally aided claim can in some circumstances recover costs from state funds. Under the QOCS regime a successful defendant has no remedy.

1 CPR 44.13; 44.14.
2 CPR 44.15.
3 CPR 44.16.

AFTER THE EVENT INSURANCE

6.25 ATE insurance is taken out after the actionable event has occurred. The insurance market has matured after nearly two decades; however, the introduction of QOCS has effectively removed the need to protect against the risk of adverse costs in the event of the claim failing after issue of proceedings. In clinical negligence litigation after LASPO 2012, the main exposure for costs is for disbursements and the risk of CPR Part 36 adverse costs (where, for example the defendant's offer is not beaten). With the exception of clinical negligence expert reports, ATE insurance premiums are not recoverable[1].

1 Legal Aid, Sentencing and Punishment of Offenders Act 2012, s 46.

6.26 In clinical negligence cases only, the risk of incurring the cost of expert reports, limited to liability and causation, may be underwritten by ATE insurance, the premiums for which are payable by the unsuccessful defendant. The premium will be recoverable in cases valued above £1,000[1].

1 The Recovery of Costs Insurance Premiums in Clinical Negligence Proceedings (No 2) Regulations 2013, SI 2013/739.

BEFORE THE EVENT INSURANCE

6.27 BTE insurance was not part of the scheme of LASPO 2012; it insures against the risk of potential future legal costs and liabilities; it is taken out before an actionable event has occurred. When taken out, BTE insurance is often purchased as an add-on to existing insurance policies (usually motor or home insurance) although it is available as a stand-alone product. Many consumers who purchase BTE insurance are often not aware of the coverage it provides and may not make use of it. It is increasingly used to fund clinical negligence cases (see above).

CONCLUSION

6.28 The central challenges in clinical negligence litigation concern not the substantive law but the rules and practice on funding access to justice. Recent years have seen a move away in funding clinical negligence cases from entitlement to state funded legal aid for a small sector of the population according to financial eligibility often with modest success, to a system of access to justice available for all according to the merits of their claim. The success of privatising access to justice can be judged by the increasing number of clinical negligence claims, and the increasing success rates of such claims. It remains to be seen if the success of the privatised system of access to justice can be sustained in the post-LASPO 2012 era.

POSTSCRIPT

6.29   Mr John Baron (MP for Basildon and Billericay) recently asked the following question in the House of Commons. A written answer has now been supplied (17 June 2015).

'Mr John Baron: [1567] To ask the Secretary of State for Health, how many cases brought against the NHS Litigation Authority were funded by (a) legal aid, (b) a conditional fee agreement and (c) other forms of funding in each of the last five years; and how many cases in each category resulted in compensation payments.

Ben Gummer: The information is shown in the tables attached.'

The table below shows the number of clinical negligence claims by type of funding and NHS Litigation Authority (NHS LA) notification year, as at 31 May 2015.

NHSLA notification year	Legal Aid	Unsettled as at 31/5/15	Number resulted in a compensation payment as at 31/5/15	Conditional fee agreement	Unsettled as at 31/5/15	Number resulted in a compensation payment as at 31/5/15	Other funding	Unsettled as at 31/5/15	Number resulted in a compensation payment as at 31/5/15
2014–15	448	361	30	7,647	5,339	1,089	2,964	2,005	397
2013–14	733	363	155	8,743	3,080	3,305	2,125	631	674
2012–13	885	306	292	7,384	1,195	4,133	1,673	173	763
2011–12	1,122	242	560	5,906	350	4,026	1,949	76	1,067
2010–11	1,379	154	816	4,846	101	3,523	2,304	53	1,350

Source: NHS LA. *Date:* June 2015

The author assesses cases, and advises on cases funded by conditional fee agreements.

CHAPTER 7

The coroner's inquest

Christopher P Dorries OBE

Dr Alan Fletcher

INTRODUCTION

7.1   There are few more emotive events than the death of a patient that is attributable to clinical negligence. They have a profound effect on the bereaved and also the healthcare staff involved in the patient's care. Many of

153

these cases lead to a coroner's investigation, of which the inquest is a crucial part.

7.2 The coroner's inquest has an ancient heritage, having been established in 1194, in the reign of King John to 'keep the pleas of the Crown'. The person who found a body from a death thought to be sudden or unnatural was required to raise the 'hue and cry' and to notify the coroner. Original roles of managing treasury have become less prominent over time.

7.3 The office of coroner has a unique position in the English legal system. Like many historically-based offices, it has matured and evolved but never lost its central purpose, which is to ascertain the facts surrounding death and reach a conclusion on the circumstances and cause. The law, practice and procedure of coronership are now provided by the Coroners and Justice Act 2009, the Coroners (Investigations) Regulations 2013[1] and the Coroners (Inquests) Rules 2013[2], supplemented where appropriate by decisions of the higher courts.

The legislation establishes a Chief Coroner, Senior Coroner, Area Coroner and Assistant Coroner. The appointment of a Chief Coroner together with his published guidance and law sheets should promote consistency across the different jurisdictions[3]. Previously coroners were acting largely in professional isolation; their decisions were subject only to judicial review and rarely to the fiat of the Attorney General. Coroners' decisions remain subject to judicial review.

1 SI 2013/1629.
2 SI 2013/1616.
3 *The Chief Coroner's Guide to the Coroners and Justice Act 2009* (Crown Copyright 2013); see also *Guide to Coroner Services* (Ministry of Justice, February 2014).

7.4 The inquest is an inquisitional process where the coroner conducts an investigation on behalf of the Crown. The coroner's purpose is to answer four questions: who the deceased was, how he came by his death and where and when he died. It is therefore clear that the inquest is a fact-finding exercise and not a fault-finding exercise, although the distinction can sometimes be difficult to see. The evidence established at inquest can provide important new information to inform future clinical negligence claims and test argument. That said, it should be noted that the coroner's inquest is an inquisitorial, not an adversarial, court as in criminal and civil cases and the arguments are under the close control of the coroner.

7.5 Interested parties have different perceptions of the inquest's formal proceedings. The bereaved have a unique opportunity to listen to evidence from those involved in the deceased's care and to ask pertinent questions directly (under the watchful eye of the coroner). Attending doctors' perceptions vary from dismissive regard, usually from a position of ignorance of the legal subtleties, to utter terror with a fear that professional registration will be jeopardised by a misplaced word. The press look to inquests as a rich source of emotive news, especially if medical treatment was less than ideal. Finally, solicitors have an opportunity to test and review the evidence for potential clinical negligence claims.

7.6   There were 499,331 deaths in England and Wales in 2012 with 221,721 (44.4 per cent) cases reported to coroners. Of these, post mortem examinations were made on 94,814 deceased and 32,542 inquests were opened[1]. The trends are interesting: the proportion of deaths reported remains constant but the number of post mortem examinations has steadily fallen, whereas the number of inquests has slowly increased (from 4.9 per cent of all deaths in 2002 to 6.5 per cent in 2012). The latter figures may not appear to be a significant rise but inquests involve a considerable amount of time and a considerable number of people.

1 Coroners Statistics 2012, Ministry of Justice Statistics Bulletin May 2013. Note that whilst 32,542 inquests were opened in 2012, only 30,123 were closed, which means that the system is failing to keep up with itself. See also para **7.72** as to the number of inquests held before a jury.

7.7   Referrals to a coroner are made according to elegantly worded criteria:

'where there is reason to suspect the death was violent, unnatural or of unknown cause, or where the death occurred in prison or otherwise in state detention'.

Most do not involve aspects where care or treatment was grossly substandard, but many do. The legal test of whether potentially clinically negligent issues are investigated by a coroner means knowledge on the part of those referring is essential *before* a case is referred. It is this key step that determines whether a case is investigated; put simply, the coroner can only investigate what he is told about. Many doctors who report deaths to the coroner lack knowledge of medico-legal matters; it is an area that is rarely covered in depth during their training.

7.8   In this chapter we consider in more detail the matters of jurisdiction, reportable deaths, the inquest, conclusions and prevention of future death reports, so that the reader is informed of the up-to-date legal position and how this relates to clinical negligence.

JURISDICTION

7.9   The coroner's jurisdiction to investigate a death arises under the Coroners and Justice Act 2009 (CJA 2009), s 1. This requires that the body is lying within the coroner's area *and* that the coroner has reason to suspect that:

- the deceased died a violent or unnatural death; or
- the cause of death is unknown; or
- the deceased died whilst in custody or otherwise in state detention.

By CJA 2009, ss 4 and 6, the investigation must include an inquest unless the pathologist conducting the post-mortem examination under s 14 concludes that the death is natural, and this is accepted by the coroner before an inquest is opened *and* the coroner thinks it unnecessary to continue: see para **7.12** below. A pathologist may consider a cause of death to be 'natural' in circumstances where the law considers the death 'unnatural'. This may occur, for example, where there has been a therapeutic omission (eg a diabetic patient is not given insulin at all, or an asthmatic patient is not treated in time):

'... cases may well arise in which human fault can and properly should be found to turn what would otherwise be a natural death into an unnatural one, and one into which, therefore, an inquest should be held'[1].

1 Simon Brown LJ in *R v Poplar Coroner, ex p Thomas* [1993] 2 All ER 381 at 389, CA.

Presence of a body

7.10   The body must lie physically within the coroner's geographical area, wherever the death occurred, unless:

- a transfer of jurisdiction is agreed between two coroners under the CJA 2009, s 2 (eg a vehicle collision in area A, patient taken to trauma unit in area B and dies there; it would be usual for coroner A to take the case back);
- the Chief Coroner has made an order transferring the case under the CJA 2009, s 3;
- the Chief Coroner has authorised an investigation under the CJA 2009, s 1(5), notwithstanding the absence of a body, because there is reason to believe that the death occurred in or near the coroner's area and the body is destroyed, lost or absent. This most commonly arises when a body has been cremated, but where later information suggests an investigation is necessary.

Note that a stillbirth does not fall within the coroner's jurisdiction although it may be necessary to investigate whether or not the child truly was stillborn.

Reason to suspect

7.11   The phrase 'reason to suspect' means that the coroner must have formed a genuine suspicion, based on an objective assessment, upon something of substance. Until that stage is reached, the duty to investigate is not engaged.

Violent/unnatural

7.12   In general, a violent or unnatural death will be self evident, but one point arises which will be of particular interest to the medical negligence practitioner. The 2001 case of *Touche*[1] made clear that a death which otherwise appears to be from a natural cause should be regarded as unnatural if the death was either:

- contributed to by neglect[2];
- a wholly unexpected death from natural causes resulting from a culpable human failure[3].

Where there is reason to suspect such an intervening event, or some other intervening factor, whilst a 'natural' cause of death may be given by a pathologist, the coroner will find it necessary to continue the investigation under the CJA 2009, s 4(1): see para **7.9** above.

1 *R v Inner North London Coroner, ex p Touche* [2001] QB 1206. See also *Canning v HM Coroner for the County of Northampton* [2006] EWCA Civ 1225.

2 See para **7.93** ff concerning the meaning of 'contributed to by neglect' in the coronial sense.
3 Described as a death that 'should plainly never have happened'.

Cause unknown

7.13   Where the cause of death remains unknown after post-mortem examination, necessary medical tests and reasonable investigation, the coroner must hold an inquest as part of the investigation.

Died in custody/state detention

7.14   Where a death occurs in custody or otherwise in state detention the coroner must hold an investigation, and an inquest as part of that investigation, even if the death arises from a purely natural cause. The criteria are widely defined:

- a prisoner serving a sentence who is removed to a hospital because of illness and dies there, even if not under guard, will still be regarded as 'in custody'[1];
- the phrase 'otherwise in state detention' has brought a considerable widening of the requirement to hold an inquest by encompassing (*inter alia*) those detained under the Mental Health Act 1983 and those subject to a deprivation of liberty safeguarding (DoLS) authority[2].

1 *R v HM Coroner for Inner North London, ex p Linnane* [1989] 1 WLR 395.
2 Introduced into the Mental Capacity Act 2005 through the Mental Health Act 2007 for those suffering from a mental disorder or disability of the mind (eg dementia) who lack capacity to give consent to the arrangements made for their care and for whom some deprivation of liberty is considered to be in their best interests to protect them from harm. Such a patient will normally be in a hospital or nursing home.

Investigations: the three-stage process

7.15   It is important to understand that the CJA 2009 has brought significant change to the way in which a coroner will assess whether a particular death requires an inquest, although the legal criteria for holding an inquest remain broadly the same as before, 'state detention' apart. There is now a 'three-stage process' available to the coroner, although not every case will need to involve all three stages.

Preliminary inquiries

7.16   The coroner may make preliminary inquiries to establish whether any formal investigation is necessary. This might commonly be because a death is reported where the cause is initially unknown but is likely to be ascertained by inquiries either of the deceased's attending doctor(s) or by way of post-mortem examination. If the death is not found to be unnatural by the coroner based on all the reported facts, the results of inquiries and the pathologist's findings (which may at the initial stage just be a short cause of death), the coroner will sign an appropriate form of notification to the Registrar declining further interest in the case and advise the family accordingly. Such preliminary inquiries are likely to last no more than three or four days.

Investigation without inquest

7.17 Sometimes referred to as a 'formal investigation', to distinguish it from preliminary inquiries, there is in fact little official distinction. There is no formal opening of such an investigation and a post-mortem examination may still be undertaken. This situation will most commonly arise where there has been a post-mortem examination but the results of further tests such as histology, bacteriology or toxicology are awaited.

7.18 Alternatively, the coroner may be making inquiries into (as yet unestablished) allegations of poor care. In an investigation the coroner is empowered to issue papers allowing the burial or cremation to proceed and 'certificates as to the fact of death' which may assist the family in proving death to financial institutions, so when these are needed the coroner will move from preliminary inquiry to investigation. Discontinuance of an investigation without inquest (s 4) requires a written explanation if requested by an interested person and (perhaps strangely) requires that a post-mortem examination has been held[1].

1 The statutory position is not clear. Coroners are taking the view that the wording of the CJA 2009, s 4(4) amounts to a requirement for a post mortem, otherwise where is the power to discontinue? Taking into account the Coroners (Investigations) Regulations 2013, reg 17 and Form 2, this is a reasonable interpretation. See also para 80 of the Chief Coroners Guide to the Coroners and Justice Act (www.judiciary.gov.uk/wp-content/uploads/JCO/Documents/coroners/guidance/chief-coroners-guide-to-act-sept2013.pdf).

7.19 Investigation with inquest: where the cause of death is plainly unnatural the coroner may well omit the earlier stages and move straight to the opening of an inquest as part of the investigation. Alternatively, once the results of a preliminary inquiry or (formal) investigation are known, it may be apparent that an inquest is required, and one will be opened.

REPORTABLE DEATHS

7.20 It is an obvious but important point that a coroner can only decide whether to investigate based on the quality and detail of the information given, and also whether a death is reported at all. The well-meaning observer may be puzzled as to why, in the face of published and easily accessible guidance, referrals are not accurate in every case. In fact, studies have shown accuracy is disappointingly low[1], for a variety of reasons.

1 Start et al 'Clinicians and the coronial system: ability of clinicians to recognise reportable deaths' (1993) 306 BMJ 1038–41 and also Start et al 'General practitioners' knowledge of when to refer deaths to a coroner' (1995) 45 British Journal of General Practice 191–93.

7.21 The large majority of deaths are reported by doctors; most of the remainder are reported by the police in cases of unexpected deaths outside healthcare, some by Registrars under reg 41[1], and a very few by funeral directors or informed relatives.

1 Registration of Births and Deaths Regulations 1987, reg 41.

7.22 Until the Coroners and Justice Act 2009, there was no statutory duty on a doctor to report a death. It remains to be seen whether the now statutory obligation to report will lead to more accurate referral, but it is doubtful that there will be an early visible change because the reasons for inaccuracy persist. These include: lack of knowledge of the law; failure to appreciate that an apparently natural death may arise in an unnatural way (see para **7.12**); and even efforts to cover up some error or act, as in the case of Dr Harold Shipman[1]. It is hoped that the recent report by Francis into the events at Mid Staffordshire NHS Foundation Trust[2] will lead to more instances of cases being brought to the attention of the coroner where death has occurred and concerns regarding care are raised.

1 The Third Report of The Shipman Inquiry, chaired by Dame Janet Smith DBE at https://www.gov.uk/government/uploads/system/uploads/attachment_data/file/273227/5854.pdf.
2 The Mid Staffordshire NHS Foundation Trust Public Inquiry, chaired by Robert Francis QC. http://www.midstaffspublicinquiry.com.

7.23 There is published guidance to remind doctors that they have a duty to be open and comprehensive in their dealings with the coroner. The General Medical Council requirements include[1]:

'You must comply with the legal requirements where you work for reporting deaths to a coroner (England, Wales and Northern Ireland) or procurator fiscal (Scotland)'.

1 Treatment and care towards the end of life: good practice in decision making (GMC, 2010) at para 86.

7.24 The importance of proper completion of the medical certificate as to cause of death (MCCD) was emphasised in *R v Sood*[1], where the Court of Appeal upheld the conviction of a doctor who had deliberately made a false entry on the certificate and had therefore made a false declaration.

1 *R v Sood* [1998] 2 Cr App Rep 355.

7.25 Section 1(2) of the CJA 2009 identifies the deaths that the coroner has a duty to investigate:

(1) where the deceased died a violent or unnatural death;
(2) where the cause of death is unknown, or
(3) where the deceased died while in custody or otherwise in state detention.

It follows that where there is cause to suspect that any of these criteria are fulfilled, a death should be reported to the coroner.

7.26 The particular criterion that is most challenging to doctors is what makes a death 'unnatural'. For clarification, in terms of potential negligence, the criterion may be expanded to include:

- an apparently 'natural' death which might have been contributed to by neglect[1];
- a death from natural causes resulting from a culpable human failure[2];
- a patient suffering from a life-threatening condition where, because of a failure in medical treatment, the death was not prevented;
- an apparently 'natural' death becoming unnatural by causative or intervening events[3];

- an otherwise natural disease brought about by the deceased's employment;
- a death where considerations of the European Convention on Human Rights, Article 2 arise, such as the failure of an organisation to put in place a necessary system[4].

It will be clear after reviewing this list that clinical negligence could be potentially involved in only some of the scenarios. Those that are relevant are considered in more detail, with examples, below.

1 See para **7.93** ff.
2 See para **7.12**.
3 See para **7.13**.
4 See para **7.62**.

7.27 The coronial concept of neglect is dealt with in detail at para **7.93** ff. The reporting doctor must recognise the potential for a causal link. This is challenging, especially if he was part of the team that oversaw care, and possibly contributed to the gross failure. It is more likely that relatives will raise concerns, sometimes to the point of refusing to accept the medical certificate or to register the death. Nevertheless, at such an emotive time, one can imagine the relatives' dilemma when wishing to proceed with funeral arrangements and/or if they have a strong wish to avoid post-mortem examination. It may be wise for an attending doctor to report a case where an allegation has been made, as the coroner's inquiry or investigation is likely to establish the correct facts, avoiding later dispute.

7.28 The culpable human failure is usually conspicuous, where it occurs. Examples include wrong site surgery or a fatal dosing error or a complete failure to monitor where this would be routine. In such cases, medical staff will usually recognise this, and report the death to the coroner without delay. Nevertheless, the need to preserve evidence (equipment or data) is often overlooked before referral, where in some circumstances a police investigation may follow.

7.29 A failure of medical (or surgical) treatment may occasionally overlap with culpable human failure but may also include so-called 'recognised complications'. Many attending doctors struggle to understand why such cases should be reported to a coroner, because to do so feels like an admission of error or a slight on clinical acumen. Examples include post-operative infection, rupture of a coronary artery during angioplasty or (commonly) anastomotic leak after bowel surgery. Coroners will weigh up the evidence and decide on an individual basis whether further investigation is needed. Whether a procedure was elective or emergency may well be relevant.

7.30 The intervening events that can lead to a natural death becoming unnatural are varied and limited only by the imagination. Consider a failure to monitor, as in *Touche*[1], a death during restraint or a mis-reporting of a laboratory or radiology result that leads to a failure to diagnose a cancer before it is too late to undergo curative treatment.

1 *R (on the application of Touche) v Inner London North Coroner* [2001] EWCA Civ 383.

7.31   In addition to the above, many doctors do not recognise the need to report a death due to a prior accident, whenever it occurred. Such cases include historic trauma from industrial accidents or traffic collisions but also 'accidents' due to medical negligence in the past. This is especially challenging if the events occurred in a different hospital and records are unavailable or scanty.

MEDICAL EXAMINERS

7.32   At the time of writing, the death certification reforms advocated by Dame Janet Smith in the Shipman Inquiry have not yet been implemented. A central component of the reforms will involve the establishment of a new workforce of independent, fully-trained medical examiners, whose job will be to ensure that deaths are correctly reported to the coroner in a timely manner, and also to ensure accuracy of MCCD completion. Raising clinical governance concerns will also be a core function, with the views of the bereaved considered in every case. Properly implemented, this system will have a unique opportunity to highlight cases of clinical negligence interest, especially through referral for coroner consideration, although the coroner's focus is inevitably subtly different. It is hoped these reforms will be implemented in the near future and their effect carefully scrutinised.

THE SCOPE OF THE INQUEST

7.33   Under the CJA 2009, s 5(1), the purpose of the coroner's investigation is to ascertain:

- who the deceased person was;
- how, when and where the deceased came by his/her death;
- particulars required by the Births and Deaths Registration Act 1953 (such as date and place of birth).

Section 5(2) adds (in summary) that where the European Convention on Human Rights, Article 2, is engaged (as to which see para **7.58** ff), then 'how' is to be read as including ascertaining in what circumstances the deceased came by his/her death.

7.34   In more practical terms, the inquest is simply an inquiry, held in public, with a remit that is limited to establishing the cause and circumstances (the 'how') of the death, as well as more basic details such as identity. The question is not one of attributing blame or guilt for the death, but of finding the truth in an event that can then speak for itself. This is a very important point when considering cases of clinical negligence: sometimes the non-attribution of blame can be frustrating to bereaved families and their representatives in the face of compelling evidence.

7.35   The fundamental legal premise of the inquest was described in the leading case of *R v HM Coroner for North Humberside and Scunthorpe, ex p Jamieson*[1]:

'An inquest is a fact-finding inquiry conducted by a coroner with or without a jury to establish reliable answers to four important but limited factual questions. The first of these relates to the identity of the deceased, the second to the place of his death, the third to the time of death. In most cases these questions are not hard to answer but in a minority of cases the answer may be problematical. The fourth question, and that to which evidence and inquiry are most closely directed, relates to how the deceased came by his death'.

1 *R v HM Coroner for North Humberside and Scunthorpe, ex p Jamieson* [1995] QB 1.

7.36   The question of 'how' the deceased came by his death, in its basic form, goes beyond the medical cause, and is generally understood as meaning 'by what means' did the death occur, a narrower question than either 'why' or 'in what circumstances'. An authoritative explanation was given in the 1994 case of *Homberg*[1]:

'Although the word "how" is to be widely interpreted, it means "by what means" rather than "in what broad circumstances"[2]. In short, the inquiry must focus on matters directly causative of death and must indeed be confined to these matters alone.

… the duty to inquire "how" does not to my mind properly encompass inquiry also into the underlying responsibility for every circumstance which may be said to have contributed to the death'.

Nonetheless, the court accepted that a coroner would often need to inquire into acts and omissions which were directly responsible for the death.

1 *R v HM Coroner for Western District of East Sussex, ex p Homberg, Roberts and Manners* (1994) 158 JP 357.
2 Contrast this with the language of 'in what circumstances' where the ECHR, Article 2 is engaged: see para **7.33**.

7.37   All this is not as restrictive as it may first sound. In the case of *Dallaglio*[1], heard only shortly after *Jamieson*, the court held:

'[164] The court [in the *Jamieson* judgment] did not however rule that the investigation into the means by which the deceased came by his death should be limited to the last link in the chain of causation. That would not be consistent with conclusion 14[2] … and it would defeat the purpose of holding an inquest at all if the inquiry were to be circumscribed in [this manner]. It is for the coroner conducting an inquest to decide on the facts of a given case at what point the chain of causation becomes too remote to form a proper part of his investigation'.

1 *R v Inner West London Coroner, ex p Dallaglio* [1994] 4 All ER 139 at 164.
2 Referring to General Conclusion no 14 in *R v HM Coroner for North Humberside and Scunthorpe, ex p Jamieson* [1995] QB 1.

7.38   The same judgment acknowledged that the actual inquiry made at an inquest would often stretch wider than might strictly be needed for the purposes of a conclusion[1], noting that how much wider was pre-eminently a matter for the coroner. In a notable example of the breadth of inquiry necessary, the Court of Appeal made clear in the 2005 case of *Takoushis*[2] that the remit of an inquest included making a thorough investigation of a hospital system which was potentially relevant to the death.

1 Note that what was previously called the 'verdict' is now referred to as the 'conclusion', thus removing an adversarial word from the inquest. See para **7.80** ff about conclusions.
2 *R (on the application of Takoushis) v Inner London North Coroner* [2005] EWCA Civ 1440.

7.39   Pavlos Takoushis jumped into the River Thames and drowned. He had been a long-term schizophrenic patient, periodically treated in psychiatric hospitals. On the day that he died, he obtained permission to leave his ward to visit a Day Unit in the grounds. He did not return. Later the same day he was seen preparing to jump off a bridge into the River Thames. He was taken to a nearby hospital where, on triage, he was assessed as at 'high risk of self harm'. He was categorised to be seen within ten minutes but was not. By the time an appropriate person attended he had left the hospital. He succeeded in killing himself a short time later.

7.40   The matter went before the High Court and then the Appeal Court on an application that the inquest remit had been too narrow and had not properly investigated whether a systemic failure had allowed the circumstances to occur. This case did not 'engage' the European Convention on Human Rights (ECHR), Article 2 in the sense of requiring a *Middleton*-type inquest[1], but the Court of Appeal held:

'[49] The question is whether those circumstances were fully investigated in the way contemplated in both *Jamieson* and *Dallaglio*[2]. Such an investigation surely involved investigating both what the system at the hospital was and how it operated on the day in question. The coroner recognised that, but in our view did not investigate the system in sufficient detail ... he did not investigate how the system was to work [after initial triage] and did not consider, for example, what was to be done and in particular what safeguards were in place if for some reason the patient could not be seen in the target time'.

1 See para **7.60**.
2 *R v HM Coroner for North Humberside and Scunthorpe, ex p Jamieson* [1995] QB 1 and *R v Inner West London Coroner, ex p Dallaglio* [1994] 4 All ER 139.

7.41   In summary, the remit of an inquest (even where ECHR, Article 2 is not engaged) is as wide as the coroner deems necessary in order to make a proper inquiry into the particular death. But this is not to say that the remit is limitless. In 2009 the Court of Appeal held:

'It was not incumbent on the coroner to investigate, still less state his conclusion in relation to, every issue raised ... however peripheral to the main questions to be determined ... The coroner was only required to investigate those issues which were, or at least appeared arguably to be, central to the cause of death[1]'.

1 *R (on the application of Allen) v HM Coroner for Inner North London* [2009] EWCA Civ 623 at paras 33 and 40. In fact this was a case where Article 2 was engaged.

7.42   Where the ECHR, Article 2[1] is engaged by the inquest, the word 'how' has the wider interpretation of ascertaining 'in what circumstances' the deceased came by his death (see CJA 2009, s 5(2)). This phraseology has its roots in the notable case of *Middleton*[2], which first held that such an expanded inquest would normally be the state's way of fulfilling its investigative obligation under Article 2.

1 See para **7.60** ff.
2 *R (on the application of Middleton) v West Somerset Coroner* [2004] UKHL 10.

7.43   The difference may be seen as simply a matter of words, but the intention in *Middleton* was clear, that the Article 2-compliant inquest (a '*Middleton* inquest') had a wider remit, going further back down the chain of causation than its simpler counterpart (the '*Jamieson* inquest'). But that has not proved to be the case. The remit of the *Jamieson* inquest has expanded to all but meet the *Middleton* inquest. Given the coroner's wide discretion as to scope, the distinction in remit is almost completely blurred. The Chief Coroner, sitting as a judge of the High Court, noted in the 2012 *Kent County Council* case that 'the extent to which the narrower form of inquest ... would differ materially from a *Middleton*-type inquest is, perhaps, debatable'[1].

1 HHJ Peter Thornton QC in *R (on the application of Kent County Council) v HM Coroner for Kent)* [2012] EWHC 2768 (Admin) at para 65.

7.44   Further, in the 2013 Court of Appeal case of *Sreedharan*[1] it was noted:

'[18vii] There is now in practice little difference between the *Jamieson* and *Middleton*-type inquest as far as inquisitorial scope is concerned. The difference is likely to come only in the verdict and findings'.

1 *R (on the application of Sreedharan) v County of Greater Manchester Coroner* [2013] EWCA Civ 181 at para 18(vii). See also *Chief Constable of Devon and Cornwall Police v Coroner for Plymouth, Torbay and South Devon* [2013] EWHC 3729 (Admin).

THE INQUEST PROCESS

7.45   The inquest is an inquisitorial process, with no parties, pleadings or allegations. The various 'interested persons' have no right to call a witness or make an address as to the facts. All witnesses are called by the coroner to help the court find the truth of how the deceased came by his death. It must be a forceful and independent inquiry, sometimes doggedly pursuing a kernel of truth that is elusive or even deliberately hidden:

'It is the duty of the coroner as the public official responsible for the conduct of inquests, whether he is sitting with a jury or without, to ensure that the relevant facts are fully, fairly and fearlessly investigated ... He must ensure that the relevant facts are exposed to public scrutiny ... He fails in his duty if his investigation is superficial, slipshod or perfunctory'[1].

1 *R v HM Coroner for North Humberside and Scunthorpe, ex p Jamieson* [1995] QB 1 at General Conclusion 14.

7.46   Not infrequently, the inquisitorial process can appear decidedly adversarial, with all the appearances of a trial and facts fiercely disputed, despite the fact that the inquest is not a testing ground for a future civil case. The inquest is an inquiry, not a trial; the coroner decides the evidence and the lines of inquiry subject to the law. There are no parties, only interested persons. The coroner's court can grant no remedies, and cannot award costs. Its determinations and conclusions on the evidence are not binding,:

'Their clients are not ... parties to adversarial litigation. Their only legitimate interest is one shared by the coroner – to investigate and discover the true circumstances of the death'[1].

1 *R v HM Coroner for West District of East Sussex, ex p Homberg* (1994) 158 JP 357.

7.47   Nonetheless, conclusions of unlawful killing or that the death has been 'contributed to by neglect'[1] may be sought in an almost open fashion. The coroner has to steer the proceedings through these perils, sometimes taking the evidence of a significant number of witnesses over days or even weeks, instructing expert witnesses to appear and help the court. In listening to the evidence, the coroner will not forget that a significant part of his task is to consider whether a 'report to prevent future deaths'[2] is necessary at the end of the inquest.

1 See para **7.80** ff on conclusions.
2 Report to prevent future deaths: CJA 2009, Sch 5, para 7 and the Coroners (Investigations) Regulations 2013, regs 28 and 29: see para **7.102** ff.

7.48   Transparency is an increasingly important part of the inquest process, and disclosure of documents obtained in the course of the investigation is now the norm[1]. Proceedings, including the opening of the inquest and any pre-inquest reviews, must now be recorded and available to those involved[2]. At the same time, the coroner's powers of investigation have increased substantially with the introduction of the 'Schedule 5 notice'[3] which can compel a potential witness to give a statement or report, enforce production of documents or items and then require the witness to attend at court and give evidence.

1 The Coroners (Investigations) Regulations 2013, reg 13 provides for disclosure. Regulation 15 provides exceptions: where there is a statutory or legal prohibition to disclosure; the consent of the owner or copyright author cannot reasonably be obtained; the request is unreasonable; the document relates to criminal proceedings whether contemplated or commenced; the coroner considers the document irrelevant to the investigation.
2 Coroners (Inquests) Rules 2013, r 26.
3 A notice served under the CJA 2009, Sch 5, para 1 or 2.

7.49   Whilst an inquest must be open to the public, the right to ask questions of witnesses is limited to those who are designated as 'interested persons'. The appropriate list is set out in the CJA 2009, s 47 and includes:

- a wide range of family members, any personal representative, insurer or beneficiary under a policy on the deceased's life;
- a spouse, civil partner or partner (defined as the two persons living together in an enduring relationship at the time of the death);
- a person who may by their act or omission have caused or contributed to the death -- or the employer of such a person.

7.50   The opening of an inquest may take place within a few days of the death where the cause is readily apparent as unnatural, for example a suicide or traffic collision, but may be delayed if the circumstances are less clear and the outcome of tests or inquiries is awaited (see para **7.17**). The opening is relatively brief, dealing primarily with identification of the deceased, but must still be held in public and recorded.

7.51   The coroner will most likely commence the proceedings with an explanation of the purpose of the inquest and will confirm to the family that they have a right to ask questions of the witnesses after the coroner has done so. After verifying the basics of full name and date of birth etc, the coroner will question the witnesses on oath, allowing other interested persons to do so in turn. No one may address the court as to the facts[1] although submissions as to law can be made. A submission on the conclusion is considered a submission on the law and some reference to the facts and evidence is permissible[2]. After the evidence is complete the coroner will summarise the facts, giving his conclusion with reasons as appropriate.

1 Coroners (Inquests) Rules 2013, r 27.

2 See *R v Southwark Coroner, ex p Hicks* [1987] 1 WLR 1624, and *R v HM Coroner for East Berkshire, ex p Buckley* (1993) 157 JP 425.

7.52 Only about 25 per cent of families attending more significant inquests have legal representation. This can result in the unfortunate sight of several state institutions appearing before the coroner (perhaps an ambulance service, NHS Trust and a local authority), each with representation effectively at the taxpayer's expense whilst the family sit alone, without the resources to obtain representation.

7.53 Witnesses can be compelled to give evidence[1]. However, whilst a witness must generally answer proper questions put to them, there is a protection available[2] because the witness is not obliged (at the coroner's direction) to answer a question that may tend to incriminate himself. Note that the word 'incriminate' refers to criminal matters, not civil or professional disciplinary matters. Further, there are limited exceptions to compellability, such as a journalist protecting his source and claims of public interest immunity. Many of the latter would now fail given the decision in the 2013 *Worcestershire Coroner* case[3].

1 See para **7.51**.
2 Coroners (Inquests) Rules 2013, r 22.
3 *Worcestershire County Council v HM Coroner for the County of Worcestershire* [2013] EWHC 1711 (QB).

7.54 In this case the coroner sought release of management reviews and information reports which the Local Safeguarding Children Board had obtained in the course of a Serious Case Review. The Board resisted and claimed public interest immunity on the basis that the various agencies giving information for the SCR would be inhibited by knowledge that the document might be released to others. The High Court held that disclosure should be given to the coroner as the need for a full and appropriately detailed inquest firmly outweighed the claim for immunity. However, disclosure was only to the coroner so that he might identify relevant witnesses or lines of inquiry; disclosure to others was a different matter.

7.55 The Chief Coroner issued his Law Sheet No 3[1] in connection with the case, indicating that the benefit of the decision for coroners was the extent to which they could justifiably ask for material which they reasonably believed might assist in their investigation.

1 The Chief Coroner has issued a number of law sheets and guidance notes for coroners which are publically available at http://www.judiciary.gov.uk/related-offices-and-bodies/office-chief-coroner/guidance-law-sheets.

7.56 Under the CJA 2009, s 5(3), neither the coroner nor any jury may express an opinion on any other matter than those set out in s 5(1) (who-how-when-where etc), although the subsection goes on to say that this is subject to the coroner's duty in Sch 5, para 7 to the Act to make a report to prevent future deaths where necessary. Whilst this is primarily a restriction for the conclusion of an inquest, the coroner must be mindful of the requirement during his inquest as well.

7.57   Finally, the advocate representing a family or other interested person at an inquest should be careful to give the client a thorough briefing before the inquest, and not just on the morning of the hearing when anxiety levels are likely to be such that little will be taken in. The client should understand the limitations of the inquest but appreciate the benefits that the hearing will bring. A thorough debriefing after the inquest is just as important, to make sure the client understands and has appreciated the additional information that the inquest will almost inevitably have uncovered.

THE IMPACT OF ECHR, ARTICLE 2

7.58   The Human Rights Act 1998 gave effect to the ECHR in domestic law. The Convention raises both explicit and implicit duties/obligations on the state, which have become an important issue for the inquest. It is almost inevitable that the interpretation of the ECHR and Article 2 in particular will continue to widen as time passes.

7.59   Article 2, which states, briefly, that everyone's right to life shall be protected by law, is the most fundamental provision of the Convention and is not confined to intentional killing[1]. The article also requires the state to take appropriate steps to safeguard life, which includes the proper planning and control of actions[2].

1 *McCann v United Kingdom* (1995) 21 EHRR 97 at paras 154–155.
2 *McCann v United Kingdom* (1995) 21 EHRR 97 at para 150.

7.60   Article 2 contains duties and an implied obligation:

- a **negative** duty that the state refrain from taking life[1];
- a **positive** duty that the state protect life by:

    — ensuring that there is 'a framework of laws, precautions, procedures and means of enforcement which will, to the greatest extent reasonably practicable, protect life'[2]; and
    — taking appropriate steps (the so called '**operational** duty') to safeguard those whose life is at risk, which will only arise where an individual life is specifically at risk in particular circumstances;

- an (implied) '**procedural obligation**' to initiate an effective public investigation by an independent official body'[3] into deaths where there is *prima facie* case that the state has breached one of the two duties.

1 Except as set out in the Article.
2 *R (on the application of Middleton) v West Somerset Coroner* [2004] UKHL 10 at para 2.
3 *R (on the application of Middleton) v West Somerset Coroner* [2004] UKHL 10 at para 3.

7.61   The investigation arising under the procedural obligation must meet certain criteria[1]: it must be independent, effective and reasonably prompt, have a sufficient element of public scrutiny, and involve the next of kin appropriately. The 2004 case of *Amin*[2] described further requirements of a compliant investigation:

- ensuring that the full facts are brought to light;
- exposing culpable and discreditable conduct and that those responsible are identified and brought to account;

- that any unjustified suspicion of wrongdoing is allayed;
- identifying and rectifying dangerous practices and procedures;
- ensuring that lessons are learnt that may save the lives of others;
- safeguarding the public and reducing the risk of further breaches of Article 2.

1 *Jordan v United Kingdom* (2001) 37 EHRR 2 at paras 102–109.
2 *R (on the application of Amin) v Secretary of State for the Home Department* [2004] 1 AC 653 at para18.

7.62 *Middleton*[1] held that in this country the 'effective public investigation' would generally be the inquest[2]. In order to comply with the requirements of the ECHR, the remit of an inquest would extend in cases where Article 2 was engaged from 'how' the deceased came by his death to 'how and in what circumstances'. Hence an extended remit inquest is known as a '*Middleton* inquest'. It was also held that such an inquest 'ought normally to culminate in an expression of the jury's conclusion on the disputed factual matters at the heart of the case'.

1 *R (on the application of Middleton) v West Somerset Coroner* [2004] UKHL 10.
2 See also *R (on the application of Antoniou) v Central and North West London NHS Foundation Trust* [2013] EWHC 3055 (Admin).

When Article 2 comes into effect at an inquest

7.63 Article 2 will be engaged where there is an arguable case that the state may have breached the duties set out at para **7.60** above. A breach of the negative duty (not to take life) will generally be clear, and a police shooting or restraint death will inevitably involve a *Middleton* inquest. It may be harder to identify a breach of one of the two parts of the positive duty, which might include taking reasonable steps to have a system in place that will protect life ('a framework of ... procedures' etc).

7.64 There is a duty on the state to protect the lives of those whom it chooses to detain because of their vulnerable position. This includes detained psychiatric patients as well as prisoners. This requires the employment of competent staff and systems of work which will meet the general risks to life[1].

1 *Savage v South Essex Partnership NHS Foundation Trust* [2008] UKHL 74.

7.65 There is also the 'operational duty' arising on knowledge of a particular risk to an individual, detained or not, where the state[1]:

- knew (or ought to have known) of a real and immediate[2] risk to the individual life; *and*
- failed to take steps within their power which might reasonably have been expected to negate the risk. This expectation cannot be one which imposes an impossible burden on the state[3] and must have regard to the resources available[4].

1 For example there may be a general duty upon a hospital to provide a safe environment with no obvious ligature points, and to train staff appropriately. The operational duty would be knowledge of a particular risk of death to a specific individual.
2 Meaning 'present and continuing' rather than 'imminent': *Re Officer L* [2007] UKHL 36. Also described as a stringent test: *R (on the application of Kent County Council) v HM Coroner for Kent)* [2012] EWHC 2768 (Admin) at para 43.

3 *Osman v United Kingdom* (1998) 29 EHRR 245.
4 *Re Officer L* [2007] UKHL 36.

7.66   Thus a death in prison engages Article 2, as does a police shooting or the suicide of a detained psychiatric patient. But what of the psychiatric patient not under detention? And perhaps of frequent interest to a medical negligence practitioner, what about the patient who dies in a medical hospital when they should not have done?

The psychiatric patient

7.67   In 2012 it was held that the operational duty to protect a psychiatric patient from suicide was not restricted to those detained under the Mental Health Act 1983. But there is no general duty to prevent everyone from committing suicide[1].

1 Lord Rodger in *Savage v South Essex Partnership NHS Foundation Trust* [2008] UKHL 74.

7.68   In the 2012 case of *Rabone*[1] an informal patient was at high risk of suicide. If she had tried to leave the ward she would have been held back and detained under the Mental Health Act 1983. In fact she was given leave from the hospital for the weekend against her parent's wishes when 'no reasonable doctor would have allowed her to go home in the circumstances'. The court held that the differences between the two categories of psychiatric patient should not be exaggerated and that in this case there were particular features that brought the non-detained patient within the operational duty:

- the patient's extreme vulnerability;
- that the hospital had assumed control over her, even though she was not detained;
- the exceptional nature of the risk.

1 *Rabone v Pennine Care NHS Foundation Trust* [2012] UKSC 2 at para 28.

7.69   The European Court of Human Rights made a similar finding very shortly after *Rabone* in *Reynolds v United Kingdom*[1]. The deceased was again a voluntary patient, but the court found that there had been a breach of Convention rights, citing the decision in *Rabone*.

1 *Reynolds v United Kingdom* 2694/08 [2012] ECHR 437. The judgment contains a brief but useful summary of the law.

The physically ill patient

7.70   It will generally be much harder to persuade the court that Article 2 will be engaged where the deceased was a physically ill patient in a general medical hospital. Of course, the state has an overall duty to put suitable systems of work in place, to ensure competent staff are recruited and that high professional standards are maintained[1]. But there cannot be an operational duty towards every patient whose life is known to be at risk

'[364] ... where a contracting state had made adequate provision for securing high professional standards among health professionals and the protection of the lives of patients, [the court] cannot accept that matters such as errors of judgment ... or negligent coordination among health professionals in the treatment of a particular patient are sufficient of themselves to call a contracting state to account from the standpoint of its positive obligations under Article 2 of the Convention to protect life[2]'.

1 *Savage v South Essex Partnership NHS Foundation Trust* [2008] UKHL 74.
2 *Powell v United Kingdom* (2000) 30 EHRR CD 362 at para 364.

7.71 In *Savage*[1] it was held that 'casual acts of negligence by hospital staff will not give rise to a breach of Article 2'. In *Humberstone*[2] the court accepted that faults of a systemic nature, such as a failure to provide suitable facilities or adequate staff or appropriate systems of operation, could raise a specific obligation to conduct an investigation but said that this would not include cases where the only allegations were of 'ordinary' medical negligence. It was also said that 'it will be necessary to ensure that allegations of individual negligence are not dressed up as systemic failures'.

This takes the position of earlier hospital cases, which found that only very serious negligence or concerns about a medically orchestrated cover up, could engage the operational duty for a death in medical care[3].

1 *Savage v South Essex Partnership NHS Foundation Trust* [2008] UKHL 74 at para 45.
2 *R (on the application of Humberstone) v Legal Services Commission (The Lord Chancellor intervening)* [2010] EWCA Civ 1479 at para 58.
3 See *R (on the application of Khan) v Secretary of State for Health* [2003] EWCA Civ 1129 and *R (on the application of Takoushis) v Inner London North Coroner* [2005] EWCA Civ 1440.

JURIES

7.72 In 2012 there were 30,123 inquests concluded by coroners, of which only 472 (or 1.6 per cent) were held before a jury[1]. Nonetheless, cases held before a jury are almost invariably longer and more complex, and not only because of the type of case requiring a jury.

1 Coroners Statistics 2012, Ministry of Justice Statistics Bulletin May 2013.

Reasons for a jury

7.73 Section 7(2) of the CJA 2009 sets out three situations where an inquest *must* be held before a jury:

- the deceased died in custody or otherwise in state detention and the death was violent/unnatural or the cause remains unknown[1]. Note that custody or state detention is quite widely interpreted (see para **7.14**), and now, given the cases of *Savage*, *Rabone* and *Reynolds* (see paras **7.67–7.71**), it will be interesting to see whether the deaths of some non-detained psychiatric patients are regarded as falling within the provision;
- the death resulted from the act or omission of a police officer[2] in the purported execution of his duty. This wording is slightly different from that in the Coroners Act 1988 which spoke of 'an injury caused by an officer' etc. In one sense the new wording is wider because it does not require the officer to directly cause the injury. But under the 1988 Act, if a person was killed by a police car on patrol then one would naturally assume that this was an injury caused by an officer. It remains to be seen whether the point will be taken that 'resulted from the act or omission'

implies a more qualitative test as to whether the death was the result of an officer being at fault. Experience suggests that most coroners will interpret the wording quite widely and cautiously, holding any such inquest with a jury;

- the death was caused by a notifiable accident, poisoning or disease[3]. This is further defined in the CJA 2009, s 7(4) and generally relates to deaths reportable to the Health and Safety Executive (HSE) by employers etc under the Reporting of Injuries, Diseases and Dangerous Occurrences Regulations 2013[4], more commonly known as 'RIDDOR'. Such a report must be made under reg 6(1) of RIDDOR if a person dies of a work-related accident, defined by reg 2(2) as an accident attributable to:

    — the manner of conducting an undertaking;
    — the plant or substances used for the purposes of an undertaking; or
    — the condition of the premises used for the purposes of an undertaking or any part of them.

Note that the deceased does not have to be at work; it is sufficient if a passer-by dies of a 'work related accident' such as falling scaffolding or faulty electrics. There are various exemptions (in reg 14) so, for example, where a surgeon at work during an operation accidentally cuts a major blood vessel, leading to the patient's death, that is not a reportable event. Nor would a patient committing suicide in a hospital be reportable to the HSE.

1 A death in custody or otherwise in state detention that is known to arise from a natural cause will still require an inquest, but not before a jury: CJA 2009, s 4(2)(b).
2 Or member of a service police force ie Army, Navy or RAF but not others such as the Civil Nuclear Constabulary who have officers (often armed) with the powers of a constable: CJA 2009, s 48.
3 This does not mean the list of diseases notifiable to Local Authority Proper Officers under the Health Protection (Notification) Regulations 2010, SI 2010/659, such as cholera.
4 SI 2013/1471.

7.74   Under the CJA 2009, s 7(3), the coroner also has a discretion to hold an inquest before a jury. Such a discretion must be exercised judicially and may take into account that a coroner sitting alone can give a reasoned decision whereas a jury could not[1]. Other matters that should be taken into account are said to be the views of the family and any resemblance to the mandatory provisions[2].

1 *R (on the application of Collins) v HM Coroner Inner South London* [2004] EWHC 2421.
2 *R (on the application of Paul) v Deputy Coroner of the Queen's Household and Assistant Deputy Coroner for Surrey; R (on the application of Al-Fayed) v same* [2007] EWHC 408 (Admin).

7.75   Juries are picked on exactly the same basis as at the Crown Court, ie a list of random names supplied by the Jury Central Summoning Bureau. However, a coroner's jury consists of between seven and eleven persons, rather than the more famous twelve.

7.76   The jury are responsible for making all the factual findings of the inquest conclusion whilst the coroner is responsible for directing the jury as to the law and summing up the evidence. The jury will be allowed to ask questions of the witnesses (albeit most likely in a strictly controlled manner). Whilst the coroner will initially require a unanimous conclusion, in time he may allow the jury to return[1] a majority conclusion with no more than two disagreeing, so with the smallest jury allowed of just seven this could be a 5:2 decision.

1 Traditionally a jury 'return' a conclusion (previously a verdict), whilst a coroner sitting alone 'records' a conclusion.

Summing up

7.77 In deciding which conclusions should be left open to the jury the coroner will hear any submissions as to *the law* that the advocates wish to make, in the absence of the jury. By rule 27[1] no person may address the coroner or any jury as to *the facts*. Perhaps the test of when an advocate is incorrectly addressing the coroner as to the facts is whether the advocate is seeking to persuade the coroner that a particular fact is true or false. However, unnecessary repetition of the facts to emphasise them or refresh them in the coroner's mind will also be unwelcome.

1 Coroners (Inquest) Rules 2013, r 27.

7.78 The decision on conclusions will be made first on the basis of the well-known *Galbraith*[1] principle: whether, taking the evidence at its highest, a reasonable jury properly directed, *could* reach that particular conclusion to the required standard of proof. However, following the 2012 *West Yorkshire Coroner* case[2], the Chief Coroner issued advice[3] that when coroners are deciding whether to leave a particular verdict to a jury, a dual test should be applied (the so called *Galbraith plus* test):

- the pure *Galbraith* question 'is there sufficient evidence upon which a jury properly directed could properly reach a particular conclusion?';
- plus a further question 'would it be safe on the evidence for the jury to reach this conclusion?'.

1 *R v Galbraith* [1981] 1 WLR 1039.
2 *Secretary of State for Justice v HM Deputy Coroner Eastern District of West Yorkshire* [2012] EWHC 1634 (Admin), following and developing previous cases such as *R v HM Coroner for Exeter and East Devon, ex p Palmer* [1997] EWCA Civ 978; *R v Inner London Coroner (South District), ex p Douglas-Williams* [1998] EWCA Civ 101 and more recently *R (on the application of Longfield Care Homes Ltd) v HM Coroner for Blackburn* [2004] EWHC 2467.
3 See http://www.judiciary.gov.uk/related-offices-and-bodies/office-chief-coroner/guidance-law-sheets/.

7.79 Rule 33 of the Coroners (Inquests) Rules 2013 stipulates that the coroner must direct the jury as to the law and provide the jury with a summary of the evidence, ie sum up the case. In brief, a summing up will consist of:

- reminding the jury of the purpose of an inquest;
- explaining the limitations placed by s 5(3) and s 10(2)[1];
- going through the questions to be answered in the record of inquest form;
- outlining the specific conclusions which the jury are to consider and any relevant law;
- explaining the necessary standard of proof;
- summarising the important points of evidence;
- advising the jury how they might go about assessing the evidence;

- a full and careful direction on any issues of causation;
- a direction that the conclusion must be unanimous (initially);
- brief advice as to how the jury's task might be approached.

Conclusions, whether left for a jury to consider or reached by a coroner sitting alone, are dealt with in the following paragraphs.

1 See para **7.85**.

CONCLUSIONS

7.80   In order to reduce the adversarial image of the inquest, the CJA 2009 and the associated secondary legislation no longer use the word 'verdict' and instead use other terminology:

- determination: the questions in the CJA 2009, s 5(1), setting out the who-how-when-where of the death[1];
- findings: formal particulars required by the Births and Deaths Registration Act 1953 such as date and place of birth;
- conclusion: either one of the traditional 'short-form' conclusions such as 'accidental death' or 'suicide', or a narrative conclusion setting out the court's decision as to important facts, or both.

These three phrases are together (and confusingly) known as the conclusion[2].

1 By s 5(2), where necessary to avoid a breach of ECHR rights, 'how' will be read as 'how and in what circumstances': see para **7.62**.
2 The three phrases being called 'the conclusion' is uniform practice although there is no statutory basis. The Chief Coroners Guide to the Act clearly uses the word 'conclusions' at paras 163–170 but avoids using it as a generic description other than in the heading to the section: http://www.judiciary.gov.uk/wp-content/uploads/JCO/Documents/coroners/guidance/chief-coroners-guide-to-act-sept2013.pdf

7.81   The use of the word 'findings' in relation to registration particulars is another potential area of confusion and should not be confused with the court's general 'findings of fact' which may be set out by the coroner in any summary/decision at the end of the case.

7.82   Advocates should remember, and should explain very clearly to their clients, that the conclusion of the coroner or jury is only one element of the proceedings. Rightly, the CJA 2009 tries to emphasise the importance of the investigation, of which the inquest is only a part and the conclusion an even smaller part, albeit an important and difficult part. Too often an inquest is judged wholly by its 'verdict', with little regard for the detailed investigative process that has led up to that point and the often immensely useful information that has been discovered en route.

7.83   Even in 1971, the Broderick Report[1] recognised this issue, commenting that there is a difference between a form of proceedings which affords others the opportunity to judge an issue, and one which appears to judge the issue itself. The inquest was not designed to judge the issues and make findings of blame or guilt but is frequently, quite wrongly, expected to fulfil this role.

1 Report of the Committee on Death Certification and Coroners, September 1971, Cmnd 4810.

7.84 The 'record of inquest' form, the court document recording the overall findings of the inquest, requires the following information to be found by the coroner or any jury:

- the name of the deceased;
- the medical cause of death;
- the determination (who-how-when-where);
- the conclusion (whether short-form or narrative);
- the findings (registration particulars).

7.85 There are two specific restrictions on the conclusion. Section 5(3) of CJA 2009 states that neither the coroner nor jury may express an opinion on any matter other than the questions set out in s 5(1) (the who-how-when-where etc[1]). Second, s 10 states that a determination as to the questions in s 5(1) may not be framed in such a way as to appear to determine any question of criminal liability on the part of a named person[2], or civil liability. However, note that these restrictions apply only to the conclusion of the inquest[3] and not to the conduct of the investigation, of which the inquest is part. Thus the coroner may explore issues which bear upon civil liability but may not reach a conclusion appearing to determine that liability.

1 But this is stated to be subject to the requirements of the CJA 2009, Sch 5, para 7, the prevention of future deaths, as to which see para **7.102** ff.
2 Thus the inquest can reach a conclusion of 'unlawful killing', however obvious the killer's identity may be, as long as his name is not stated in the conclusion. It may have been used quite openly in the actual proceedings.
3 Technically this is stated to relate only to the determination but is always taken to include any short-form or narrative conclusion as well.

7.86 The standard of proof applying to most inquest conclusions is 'on the balance of probabilities' otherwise known as 'more likely than not'. However, conclusions of suicide and unlawful killing require the higher standard of proof that the coroner or jury are 'sure' of the necessary criteria. This was previously known as 'beyond reasonable doubt'. Note that beyond a reasonable doubt does not mean beyond any doubt at all, a reasonable doubt has been defined as 'a doubt to which you can give a reason as opposed to a mere fanciful sort of speculation'[1].

1 *R v Yap Chuan Ching* (1976) 63 Cr App Rep 7.

Short form conclusions

7.87 The so-called 'short form conclusions' are listed in the notes to the record of inquest form shown on the reverse of that document. They include:

- accidental death/misadventure;
- alcohol related*;
- drug related*;
- industrial disease;
- lawful/unlawful killing;
- natural causes;
- road traffic collision*;
- stillbirth; and
- suicide.

The asterisked conclusions are new in the CJA 2009.

7.88 The remaining short form conclusion is the 'open conclusion' which is often the subject of misunderstanding. This is the conclusion that may be returned when a coroner or jury find that the evidence does not meet the criteria for another conclusion to the required standard of proof: it does not therefore have a standard of proof of its own. Note that the open conclusion is a conclusion in its own right; it does not mean that the inquest can be re-opened at some time in the future[1]. An open conclusion would require a unanimous decision of the jury (initially at least) just as any other conclusion.

1 To do so would require an order of the High Court upon judicial review, like any other conclusion of an inquest.

7.89 Whilst discouraged[1], it is possible for a coroner/jury to use a short form conclusion that is not on the notes to the record of inquest form. There may be some discussion as to what is an alternative short form conclusion and what is a narrative conclusion but phrases such as 'died from a complication of a necessary surgical procedure' might more adequately express the common mix of very significant natural disease and mishap from a known complication of a procedure.

1 The Chief Coroner has published guidance which, whilst accepting that the list is not exclusive, indicates that 'straying from the list will usually be unwise'. See http://www.judiciary.gov. uk/about-the-judiciary/office-chief-coroner/guidance-law-sheets/index.

Narrative conclusions

7.90 A more common, and acceptable, alternative to the short form conclusion is the narrative conclusion, a short factual account of how the death came about, more akin to 'findings' than a 'label'. Obviously the restrictions of the CJA 2009, ss 5(3) and 10(2) must still be observed[1]. Narrative conclusions were almost unknown 10–12 years ago but are now commonplace: there were more than 4,000 such conclusions in 2012 out of just over 30,000 inquests concluded.

1 See para **7.85**.

7.91 Although previously used by a number of coroners, legitimisation came with the 2004 case of *Middleton*[1], which first recognised the Article 2 inquest. The *Longfield Care Homes*[2] case of the same year recognised and described how the narrative could be used in non-Article 2 inquests:

'[29] … the comments made by the House [in *Middleton*] are not restricted to verdicts in cases of death where the State may have had a hand and are of general application.

[31] In cases where the death results from more than one cause of different types, a narrative verdict will often be required. It is here. The jury's findings can be encapsulated by a verdict such as the following …

"Mrs Hall died of bronchopneumonia resulting from dementia. Her death was probably accelerated by a short time by the effect on her pneumonia of injuries sustained when she fell through an unattended open window, which lacked an opening restrictor, in the lounge of Longfield Residential Home on 16 April 2003"'.

1 *R (on the application of Middleton) v West Somerset Coroner* [2004] UKHL 10 at paras 36 and 37.
2 *R (on the application of Longfield Care Homes Ltd) v HM Coroner for Blackburn* [2004] EWHC 2467 (Admin).

7.92 One advantage of the narrative conclusion is that it enables the coroner/jury to set out what could *not* be determined just as much as what *has* been found. For example, the court might find 'Mr Smith suspended himself by a rope from a beam within the garage of his home but the question of intent remains unclear'. The Chief Coroner's guidance makes it clear that narrative conclusions must not be lengthy.

Contributed to by neglect

7.93 Although more common with short form conclusions, the wording 'contributed to by neglect' may be added to or incorporated in any conclusion. The wording, sometimes incorrectly referred to as a rider[1], arises from the well-known case of *Jamieson*[2]. Neglect in this context is a narrowly defined legal concept, not to be confused with negligence. Originally described as 'lack of care', it was at first taken to mean that the death had occurred because of a failure to look after the deceased properly, causing starvation or exposure etc.

1 Riders were abolished by the Coroners Act 1980.
2 *R v HM Coroner for North Humberside and Scunthorpe, ex p Jamieson* [1995] QB 1.

7.94 The case of *Jamieson* involved a prisoner who had died by a self-inflicted hanging. The family were concerned that his care in prison was poor and that adequate measures had not been taken by the authorities to prevent the suicide, seeking a [then] verdict of 'lack of care'. The case progressed in due course to the Court of Appeal, where Sir Thomas Bingham MR gave a definitive judgment, effectively unchallenged to this day.

Asserting that a better term was 'neglect', the court held:

'Neglect in this context means a gross failure to provide adequate nourishment or liquid, or provide or procure basic medical attention or shelter or warmth for someone in a dependent position (because of youth, age, illness or incarceration) who cannot provide it for himself. Failure to provide medical attention for a dependent person whose physical condition is such as to show that he obviously needs it may amount to neglect. So it may be if it is the dependent person's mental condition which obviously called for medical attention'.

7.95 The court went on to emphasise that the proper test is what the person's condition appeared to be, not what it actually was:

'In both cases the crucial consideration will be what the dependent person's condition, whether physical or mental, appeared to be'.

7.96 Most recently examined in the *Commissioner of Police*[1] case in 2003, neglect as a conclusion remains clearly defined. Although the words in *Jamieson* are not to be read as if contained in an enactment, nor applied over-literally[2], the principles remain essentially intact, in that there must be a basis for finding that:

- the deceased's condition was known, or should have been known, to be such that action was necessary;
- the fact that action was not taken amounts to a gross failure;
- the failure to take action had a clear and direct causal connection with the death.

1 *R (Commissioner of Police for the Metropolis) v HM Coroner for Southern District of Greater London* [2003] EWHC 1829 Admin.
2 *R (on the application of Nicholls) v HM Coroner for City of Liverpool* [2001] EWHC (Admin) 922.

The impact of Article 2 on conclusions

7.97   In *Middleton*[1] the court held that:

'[20] To meet the procedural requirement of Article 2, an inquest ought ordinarily to culminate in an expression, however brief, of the jury's conclusion on the disputed factual issues at the heart of the case'.

Such a requirement will more often than not require a narrative conclusion, or perhaps a short form conclusion with a narrative in combination[2]. In *Middleton* the court suggested the following was the appropriate [then] verdict:

'The deceased took his own life, in part because the risk of his doing so was not recognised and appropriate precautions were not taken to prevent him doing so'

The court went on to describe this as:

'… a judgmental conclusion of a factual nature, directly relating to the circumstances of the death. It does not identify any individual nor does it address any issue of criminal or civil liability. It does not therefore infringe either rule 36(2) or rule 42[3]'.

1 *R (on the application of Middleton) v West Somerset Coroner* [2004] UKHL 10.
2 *R (on the application of P) v HM Coroner for Avon* [2009] EWCA Civ 1367 where the court had to ascertain both whether the death (in custody) was a suicide/accident and then the nature of the deceased lady's care in prison.
3 The old Coroners Rules 1984, rr 36 and 42 contained the same restrictions as the CJA 2009, s 5(3) and s 10(2).

7.98   At the time, the force of the wording in the court's suggested conclusion was met with some surprise. However, subsequently the wording of narratives for both Article 2 and non-Article 2 inquests has strengthened and it is not uncommon for narratives to identify factual issues that are described as 'a failure' or even 'a serious failure'.

7.99   In the 2009 Article 2 case of *Lewis*[1] the Court of Appeal considered whether there was a duty upon a coroner to identify causative factors that could only be described as 'possible' rather than (as would more normally be the case) 'probable'. The circumstances were that the deceased had been found hanging in his prison cell but the officer had neither a key nor a tool to cut down the prisoner, nor were the appropriately coded radio calls made to indicate the urgency of the situation to others. By the time entry was gained the prisoner was certainly dead but it could not be determined whether immediate action would have saved him, hence survival was said to be a *possibility* but could not be described a *probability*.

1 *R (on the application of Lewis) v HM Coroner for Mid and North Shropshire* [2009] EWCA Civ 1403.

7.100   The family's advocate had argued that there was a duty for the inquest to make findings on whether survival would have been a *possibility* in the circumstances. The Court of Appeal held that:

- a coroner has a *duty* to leave matters to the jury if there is evidence upon which they can conclude that the act/omission was at least *probably* causative (ie the normal situation);
- a coroner has *a power but not a duty* to leave matters to the jury if there is evidence upon which they can conclude that the act/omission was *possibly* but not probably causative.

This has relevance to the coroner's duty to make a Report to Prevent Future Deaths where appropriate, as to which see the following section.

7.101   Nonetheless, even the conclusion in an Article 2 compliant inquest is not limitless. In the case of *Smith*, the Supreme Court said[1]:

'[81] An inquest will not be the appropriate vehicle for all inquiries into state responsibility for loss of life … An inquest can properly conclude that a soldier died because a flak jacket was pierced by a sniper's bullet. It does not seem to me, however, that it would be a satisfactory tribunal for investigating whether more effective flak jackets could and should have been supplied by the Ministry of Defence'.

1 *R (on the application of Smith) v Secretary of State for Defence* [2010] UKSC 29, per Lord Phillips at para 81.

REPORTS TO PREVENT FUTURE DEATHS

7.102   The avoidance of future deaths is a major rationale of the inquest in avoiding the repetition of inappropriate conduct and in encouraging beneficial change[1].

1 *R v Inner South London Coroner, ex p Douglas Williams* [1999] 1 All ER 344.

7.103   The CJA 2009, Sch 5, para 7 and the Coroners (Investigations) Regulations 2013, regs 28 and 29 authorise the Report to Prevent Future Deaths (PFD) and state that:

- where a coroner finds that information arising from an investigation gives rise to a concern that circumstances creating a risk of other deaths will continue to exist, or will occur in the future;
- so that in his/her opinion action should be taken to prevent the recurrence/continuation of the circumstances or to eliminate/reduce the risk of death created by those circumstances;
- then he/she *must* make a report to a person who may have the power to take necessary action.

7.104   This is not restricted to matters raised in evidence. It may relate to an issue apparent from papers received at an early stage of the coroner's investigation. The report can be made before the inquest takes place if all the information is known[1]. Nor does the concern have to relate to deaths in similar circumstances.

1 Such a course would be rare but might happen where there was some urgency about the report and agreement between the interested persons.

7.105   The report (on a template created by the Chief Coroner's Office) will be sent to the appropriate person or authority who may have power to take the necessary action. It will be copied to the 'interested persons' and necessary agencies such as the Care Quality Commission.

7.106   The authority or person receiving the report must reply within 56 days, setting out their proposed action or explaining why they do not intend to take action. Such correspondence will again be shared with interested persons and is likely to become public[1]. Those who have not replied to reports will be named publicly in the Chief Coroner's regular report on PFDs[2].

1 The coroner may send a copy to 'any person who he believes may find it useful or of interest' but in any event the Chief Coroner's Office now publicise reports (which must be copied to the Chief Coroner).
2 But this is the only direct sanction for not replying, obviously Hospital Trusts or Government Departments etc may subsequently face challenging questions from others.

7.107   Often wrongly referred to as 'recommendations', the coroner's power is to make a report of what has happened to an appropriate person or authority, perhaps with a request that certain issues or practices be reviewed.

7.108   In the six months from 1 October 2012 to 31 March 2013 coroners issued 235 PFD reports, maintaining a slight upward trend. As with previous figures, just over a third related to hospital deaths (79).

CHAPTER 8

Preparation of medical evidence

David Black

SUMMARY
Introduction   **8.1**
Sources of factual evidence   **8.2**
   Witness statements of the claimant and/or those claiming on his
     behalf   **8.2**
   Witness statements of others who are able to give an account of the
     circumstances   **8.6**
   Witness statements of third parties   **8.8**
   Lay documentary evidence   **8.9**
   Transcripts of coroner's inquest   **8.10**
   Reports into untoward incidents and complaints   **8.12**
   Newspaper and television reports   **8.15**
   National bodies   **8.16**
   The medical records   **8.17**
   Going through the records with the claimant   **8.35**
   Expert opinion evidence   **8.36**
The purpose of expert evidence   **8.45**
The selection of the expert   **8.51**
The perfect expert?   **8.57**
Keeping the experts informed   **8.62**
Experts' fees   **8.63**
Instructing the expert   **8.73**
Interpreting the expert evidence   **8.78**
Expert assistance in drafting the Particulars of Claim   **8.87**
Expert assistance in evidence preparation from pleadings to trial   **8.92**
Pre-trial and trial preparation   **8.98**
Precedent 1: Application on behalf of a patient for hospital medical records
    for use when court proceedings are contemplated   **8.100**
Precedent 2: Specimen letter to doctor about cancellation fees   **8.101**

INTRODUCTION

8.1   It is axiomatic that the *medical* evidence on liability[1] in any clinical negligence action is of paramount importance. This chapter looks at the preparation of medical evidence from the claimant solicitor's viewpoint. In natural sequence, this falls into the following categories:

- factual evidence;
- expert opinion of likely factual circumstances;
- expert opinion on various factual bases regarding breach of duty;
- expert opinion on causation of injuries caused[2] or materially contributed to the alleged breach(es) of duty.

1 In this chapter 'liability' includes both breach of duty and causative loss.
2 See Chapter 15 on Causation.

SOURCES OF FACTUAL EVIDENCE

Witness statements of the claimant and/or those claiming on his behalf

8.2   Whether the claimant's witness statement is relevant to the *medical* evidence necessary to establish the claim depends upon the circumstances. The simple fact of an injury in relation to medical treatment may assist in proof of liability. Statements as to injuries and their history are more likely to be relevant to quantum. Their provenance must be recorded as accurately as possible from the claimant and any one else whose first-hand evidence may support the sequence of symptoms, signs, what they observed and what they were told at the time.

8.3   Where it is alleged there was a negligent failure of informed consent[1], it is necessary to set out carefully the words spoken, by whom and when. Any matters which caused the claimant concern or anxiety ahead of the consenting process need to be particularised, together with justification or reason for that anxiety. Did the person obtaining consent provide an opportunity for the patient/claimant to ask questions? Did the claimant ask any questions and, if so, what were they and what answers were received? Was a partner or friend present at the consultation and, if so, what evidence are they able to give? Literature may have been provided or a video shown. The instructed expert needs to consider all these materials. Moreover the claimant will also need to state what he would have done with the information it is alleged should have been given[2].

1 See Chapter 11 on Consent.
2 *Chester v Afshar* [2004] UKHL 41, [2005] 1 AC 134.

8.4   Lay witness statements may also be relevant to breach of duty. They are particularly important where there is a potential or actual conflict between what the care providers have said in the records and the claimant's account.

8.5   The claimant's witness statement[1] is likely to stand as evidence in chief and it should contain:

- a detailed chronology of the factual history as the claimant remembers it. It should include the claimant's account of his symptoms and signs. Where possible events should be fortified by recollection of incidental matters, meeting other people, and those present. Even the state of weather and the clothes worn may help to create a credible picture of the relevant occasion;

● a careful study with the solicitor of the medical records (see below) to ensure as far as possible consistency of dates and times with the contemporaneous medical notes. Where differences are irreconcilable it is wise to draw these out *in the witness statement* rather than have them emerge during evidence in court[2].

1 CPR 8A PD 7.
2 Some differences between the claimant's history and the defendant's on the basis of the contemporaneous records may have a critical effect on the merits of the case.

Witness statements of others who are able to give an account of the circumstances

8.6 Relatives, friends and others may be able to provide details which will help the experts and the court determine the facts. The same principles apply as to the claimant's witness statement. How did the claimant look? What did he say? Where and when did things happen? Who else was present?

8.7 The events after the point of injury or death may be as important as those before, as they may offer perspective, explanation, or correction besides being supportive of the necessary causal nexus to the injury or to the death.

Witness statements of third parties

8.8 There is no privity in a witness. All must be considered: ambulance personnel, police, recordings of emergency calls made to the out-of-hours service, the NHS 111 number, receptionists, patients in adjacent beds, even staff of the hospital/defendant – though this may present practical difficulties.

Lay documentary evidence

8.9 Occasionally a diary or contemporaneous notes are useful to corroborate dates and events. Call histories, text messages, and e-mails may be available: some may be important should there be a conflict of fact or timing. A trawl of social media sites to look for corroborating or damaging evidence may prove worthwhile.

Transcripts of coroner's inquest[1]

8.10 The public factual investigation into a death is a potentially fruitful source of evidence for a civil action. Evidence is taken on oath and at an early stage. Lawyers experienced in such cases can often extract evidence relevant to the coroner's investigation as well as material important for subsequent proceedings.

1 See Chapter 7 on the coroner's inquest.

8.11 Apart from the death certificate and post-mortem reports, a transcript of the evidence at the inquest should be obtained. Normally the coroner will provide a CD of the evidence given at the inquest. It should be listened to and/or a transcript of the evidence given should be made. There is a duty on coroners to record proceedings and interested persons may have copies. Whilst the status of such transcripts may be in issue at a civil trial, they will almost certainly assist witnesses' recollection for statements prepared at a much later time. Transcripts may be important for cross examination.

Reports into untoward incidents and complaints

8.12 Disclosure should be requested of any internal investigation or enquiry documents, such as a Serious Untoward Investigation Report (otherwise known as SUI report). Occasionally a court order will be necessary. These investigations will not be kept with the records but, if they exist, a claimant is generally entitled to them. Difficulties can arise in determining the status of documents coming into existence for more than one purpose. The test is what the dominant purpose of the document was at the time it was created. Where the dominant purpose of an accident report is the avoidance of future accidents, the report will not be privileged, even though a subsidiary purpose is for use in anticipated litigation[1]. In *Lask v Gloucester Health Authority*[2] a hospital accident report, prepared as required by NHS circular, was held not to be privileged, even though one of the purposes of such reports, mentioned in the circular, was for submission to lawyers in the event of a claim. It will generally be impossible for a hospital to argue that investigation or enquiry documents are privileged. As O'Connor J said in *Lask* (at p 383):

'the prevention of ... accidents must be, in a hospital of all places, at least of equal importance as the provision of material for the solicitor'.

1 *Waugh v British Railways Board* [1980] AC 521, [1979] 2 All ER 1169, HL.
2 [1991] 2 Med LR 379.

8.13 In *Hewlett Parker v St George's Health Care NHS Trust*[1] the court ordered disclosure of the NHS complaints file. The complainant can use the report and, once proceedings have been issued, obtain the documents underlying the report under CPR 31.

1 [1998] MLC 0072.

8.14 The argument frequently adumbrated that investigations of fact should not be hampered or prejudiced by concern about findings being used in civil proceedings has taken a further set back by the decision of the Court of Appeal in *Rogers v Hoyle*[1]. Reports are *prima facie* admissible in evidence and do not fall within CPR 35; the court will give such weight to them as is appropriate.

1 *Rogers v Hoyle* [2014] EWCA Civ 257, [2014] 3 All ER 550.

Newspaper and television reports

8.15 Whilst these may be less useful to the parties, it would be foolhardy to dismiss this source of evidentiary material. Sometimes statements are made to the press or to live media which may compromise the claimant or an opponent's position.

National bodies

8.16 National studies may provide useful information. All are anonymised, but the circumstances surrounding individual cases may enable the identification of similar cases, if not the one in question. The most important are:

(1) CEMD: Report on Confidential Enquiries into Maternal Deaths in the United Kingdom[1];
(2) CESDI: Confidential Enquiry into Stillbirths and Deaths in Infancy. Established in 1992. Reports annually[2];
(3) NCEPOD: Report of the National Confidential Enquiry into Patient Outcome and Death produces two or three reports a year, usually on specific topics.

1 December 2014.
2 5th Annual Report, 1 July 2014.

The medical records[1]

8.17 Of course, the medical records are a vital source of reference and information for the parties and the court. It is usually not too difficult to obtain these before the issue of proceedings using the Pre-Action Protocol for the Resolution of Clinical Disputes, but CPR 31 may be used if necessary.

1 This term includes all records: documents, letters, printouts (both hardcopy and computer records) relating to investigation, treatment and care by all care professionals and ancillary services such as haematology, clinical chemistry, radiology and other imaging and all the specialist therapies.

8.18 Medical records include GP records, and notes held by private hospitals, private health providers and other NHS hospitals. There may be issues of confidentiality and data protection, but copies of the claimant's medical records can be obtained whatever their provenance. The most obvious targets are the medical records of the caregivers and the hospital or practice identified as potentially at fault. An application for disclosure against a person who is not a party to proceedings is permitted under the Senior Courts Act 1981, s 34 or the County Courts Act 1984, s 53.

Hospital records

8.19 These are usually in A4 folders and divided into sections, although some of the documents are larger so there is some variation in the nature of these sections and their order. The following types of records, depending upon the treatment given, are to be expected:

- admission record sheet: personal details, date/time of admission, record number, name of consultant, ward: often in the form of computer print-out;
- notes made in A&E: first a 'clerking' note (usually made by junior doctor) with full history and examination;

- daily progress notes, with details of tests, conversations, changes in treatment plan etc;
- typed discharge summary (may be dated weeks or months after discharge);
- out-patient medical notes;
- Nursing Kardex (also known as Nursing Process) are nursing notes which are often as important as medical notes. Nurses tend to be more forthright and frequently name the medical staff whose identity may not be ascertainable from manuscript medical notes. Dates/times, usually down right-hand margin and signatures down left margin;
- nurses' charts: temperature, pulse, blood pressure, respiration, fluid balance etc;
- test and investigation results: sometimes on small sheets of computer print-out stuck sequentially on to an A4 'backing sheet' for each category, eg biochemistry, haematology, imagery request forms and reports. These investigations may be hardest to copy and hardest to understand. The instructed experts should explain the purpose of tests and significance of the results;
- prescription/treatment sheets: showing what drugs have been prescribed and administered. Usually in form of computer print-out;
- correspondence: such as GP referral letters, letters to GP after outpatient visit, letters to other hospitals/doctors. Correspondence may provide a quick insight to the case as summaries are common;
- clinical records from related professionals, eg physiotherapy, social work, psychological assessment: may not be kept with the main records. If these are relevant to the claim, they may need to be specifically requested;
- X-rays and other imagery needs to be obtained since independent opinion may differ from the reports in the records. CTs, MRIs and ultrasound investigations can be conveniently obtained on DVDs with the associated programmes for them to be viewed;
- anaesthetic record: on a separate sheet. The front looks rather like admission sheet. The first part is filled in by the anaesthetist when the patient is seen before operation. The bottom part records drugs given for pre-med and during operation. On the back may be a chart for blood pressure etc;
- consent forms for operations;
- ITU (intensive therapy unit) 'big' charts: with details of observations, measurements, tests. These will be A1 or even A0 in size and are best professionally copied;
- labour and delivery:
  (1) there are separate 'progress of labour' sheets on which entries are made by both midwives and doctors; sometimes hospitals have booklets with numbered pages on which antenatal and postnatal labour notes are made;
  (2) cardiotocograph (CTG) traces. These are continuous electronic double trace recordings of fetal heart (top line) and maternal contractions (bottom line). There may be several. Some can be very long (10–20 feet). They look like an old fashioned barometric trace. The more modern machines record 'real time' on the trace. The conventional paper speed is 1cm/minute. This is most important evidence and often gets 'lost'. Professional copies of

these traces must be made on continuous paper as detail and timings will have to be examined;

(3)   partogram: manual record in chart form of progress of labour (usually A3 size);

(4)   if the mother had a 'co-operation' card during pregnancy, that should be returned to her after birth. The card should be obtained from her. It has the usual identifying details of the patient plus details of (blood and other relevant) tests, brief entries for each antenatal visit and information about the birth;

(5)   neonatal unit charts: containing details of observations and tests (often A3 size).

8.20   Good medical records usually have structured format along the lines of:

* C/O – complains of;
* HPC – history of present complaint;
* Direct questions system by body system;
* PMH – past medical history;
* O/E – System examination;
* Summary – perhaps a differential diagnosis, suggested investigations, provisional lines of treatment.

General practitioners' records

8.21   The notes kept by GPs are very variable in quality. Since the 1990s records have been computerised, though earlier records (which may still be relevant) were contained in an envelope on which was recorded the patient's name, date of birth and successive addresses. Inside the envelope the records would include:

* FP7 records cards, doctor's notes;
* reports, eg from local hospitals of test/investigation results;
* letters, eg from hospital outpatient clinics or in-patient discharge summaries.

8.22   Solicitors should ensure that a full set of GP records are provided including:

* up-to-date computerised records;
* any 'Lloyd George' handwritten records of all consultations prior to the entries being electronically recorded;
* reports from local hospitals, eg A&E reports; and
* all correspondence including letters to and from the patient, referral letters to hospitals and letters from the patient's treating consultants and/or discharge summaries.

8.23   GPs are sometimes willing to lend original records to solicitors to inspect, copy and return (promptly and by secure means). Old FP7 records are sometimes difficult to copy because of contrast difficulties. It is essential, however, that great care is taken to ensure that records are copied fully and in order.

Organising medical records

8.24   Many firms employ nurses or doctors to sort records, identify missing/illegible/badly copied items and perhaps prepare a summary for the fee earner. A number of nurses and doctors offer this service on a freelance basis to firms who do not have in-house staff. The work is skilled (and chargeable, either as fee-earning work if done in-house or as a disbursement if sent out). A nurse or doctor is likely to do a quicker and better job than a lawyer on any large or complex set of records. The pressure for greater efficiency in billable hours is likely to lead to a more widespread practice in the use of a nurse or a doctor to review and sort the records, particularly in more complex cases.

8.25   Both solicitors (and subsequently counsel) must know and understand the key parts of the records. There are three separate problems:

(1)   having sufficient medical background knowledge to put the notes in context;
(2)   deciphering the notes; and
(3)   piecing together the key bits of information which tend to be scattered throughout the notes.

8.26   To help with the first problem any specialist solicitor (or barrister) must have a decent medical section in their library. Apart from basic medical texts, a dictionary or two and some anatomy 'picture books', there is a mass of information available on the internet and CD-ROM. 3D images or models are very useful to help understand 3D subjects such as obstetrics, orthopaedics and neurosurgery.

8.27   Doctors are reputed to have illegible handwriting. In reality the handwriting may not be particularly bad, but because many records are handwritten and contain a quantity of abbreviations and hieroglyphics, deciphering can be a struggle. It is best to avoid the temptation of relying solely upon the (typed) non-contemporaneous correspondence for an account of key events, just because it is readily legible. If something untoward did happen, the wish to rewrite the past may have taken hold by the time the letter is dictated.

8.28   Old editions of medical textbooks help in establishing evidence of contemporary standards, although the most up-to-date learning is essential on causation issues.

The Medical Directory is published annually and the *Medical Register* is available from the GMC online. They are useful to identify practitioners and their specialist standing and whether a current licence to practise is held.

The Medical Directory is published annually. It is the medical *Who's Who*. Entry is not compulsory but many practitioners, especially the more senior ones, are listed. The entries frequently include details of previous posts and publications. There are useful lists at the back of the *Directory* of health authorities, trusts and hospitals.

8.29   In organising and preparing the records, checks may need to be conducted against the originals and, in respect of the key records, they should be. Originals will often provide a much better insight into relevant events by revealing the colour and appearance of the entries. Sometimes the photocopying will not extend to the dates in the left margin of the nursing notes or will show only the last of the two digits for the day of the month which creates confusion. In one case the parties were misled when the hole puncher had obliterated the first digit[1]. In any event the records may be incomplete and an application for specific disclosure may have to be made[2].

1 *Johnson v John and Waltham Forest Health Authority* (1998) MLC 0244, CA.
2 CPR 31.12.

8.30   The organised bundle of records should be paginated, indexed and divided into sections:

- order of GP notes: computerised records of attendances, record cards in date order followed by correspondence, discharge summaries, test/investigation results, also in date order;
- order of hospital records. This varies from case to case: the aim is to approximate as closely as possible the way the originals would (or should) have been kept: admission sheet, medical notes, nursing Kardex, nurses' charts, test/investigation results (if numerous, they should be split into separate categories such as 'haematology', 'biochemistry'), correspondence, with each section in date order. If there have been several admissions, the process needs repeating for each;
- pagination is essential, but the method is a matter of choice. Some prefer to start each separate section from page 1 (rather than number the whole bundle from 1–420) to make addition of late arrivals less disruptive. A working pagination is required. Whilst it is desirable to avoid later repagination, that is a better option than leaving the disclosed records unpaginated once they have been organised;
- the indexed, paginated set of the original copies must be retained by the solicitor as the primary set of the records. Secondary copies will have to be made from these 'originals' for the client, experts, counsel and others.

8.31   Preparing a referenced chronology is the best way to understand the entire history and to assist the expert who will be instructed. It is suggested that this should be prepared using three columns:

- date/time;
- page reference;
- events: reference to the claimant's statement and other evidence (eg inquest transcript in a fatal case) can be included. Additionally, typed transcripts of key pages of the records (inserted as facing pages) will be useful to everyone, including the trial judge, if the matter goes to trial. Help may be necessary for an accurate transcript of manuscript notes. The expert may help and some experts put in their reports their own transcripts of the records. It may be necessary to ask the defendant to fill the gaps[1].

1 Normally defendants will oblige. In case of difficulty, CPR 35.9 gives the court power to direct a party who has access to information which is not reasonably available to the other party (here, access to the author of the illegible handwriting or incomprehensible abbreviations) to prepare, file and serve a document recording the information.

8.32   The Department of Health is committed to a 'duty of candour'[1] in complaints resolution. This has been implemented following the Francis report into Mid Staffordshire Hospitals[2]. This may ease the difficulties in eliciting responses to queries in negligence cases from patients/interested parties.

1 Sometimes known as 'Robbie's Law': *Powell v Boladz* [1998] Lloyd's Rep Med 116, CA (distinguished in *AB v Leeds Teaching Hospital NHS Trust* sub nom *Re Organ Retention Group Litigation* [2004] EWHC 644 (QB), [2005] QB 506 (Gage J)).
2 The report of the Mid Staffordshire NHS Foundation Trust Public Enquiry forwarded by Robert Francis QC reported at HC 947.

8.33   The medical history of many cases is told in several sets of records: GP records plus those from two or three hospitals. A referenced chronology will make sense of the likely sequence of events.

8.34   Not unusually, the disclosure can be voluminous. It is of enormous importance that it is all inspected carefully and the solicitor can be confident everything has been disclosed.

It is the duty of both solicitors and counsel to consider the medical records and not leave this important function to experts.

Going through the records with the claimant

8.35   It is necessary to go through the notes with the client (and/or any important witnesses). Understandably, some clients find this upsetting. The process can certainly jog memories and the client's statement may need revising. It is essential to identify any irreconcilable differences between the client's account of events and what the records say. The differences may remain irreconcilable. It is sensible to know as soon as possible where there is actual conflict. The conflict may not carry much importance beyond implicit criticism of the claimant for memory failure. Occasionally the difference is important. The records carry a great deal of weight: omissions in the records are less damaging to a claimant than outright conflict. Conflict on a major issue may destroy the merits of the case unless there is evidence in support of the client's version, or other evidence to show that the records are wrong.

Expert opinion evidence

8.36   The courts look to the medical experts to define proper standards of medical practice. It is a defence to an allegation of breach of duty for the doctor to show the treatment was in accordance with approved medical practice; even a practice approved and followed only by a minority of the profession[1].

1 *Bolam v Friern Hospital Management Committee* [1957] 2 All ER 118, [1957] 1 WLR 582.

8.37   Establishing such a practice existed (and that it was followed) is usually, but not invariably, a defence to a breach of duty allegation. It is the job of the judge additionally to satisfy himself that the practice is reasonable. A practice that exposes a patient to an unnecessary (and therefore unjustifiable) risk of harm is likely to be found unreasonable. Adherence to it will not provide a defence[1]. The judiciary remain remarkably reluctant in medical cases – compared to other professional negligence cases – to find an approved practice unreasonable. Nevertheless professionally approved practice is not sufficient to defend a claim of negligence if it cannot withstand logical analysis[2] and the court is the final arbiter.

1 *Hucks v Cole* [1993] 4 Med LR 393. Although it was reported in 1993, this Court of Appeal case was in 1968.
2 *Bolitho v City and Hackney Health Authority* [1998] AC 232, [1997] 4 All ER 771.

8.38   Usually expert opinion evidence is required *on the facts* as may be disclosed following investigation as above. An exception of importance is that expert evidence is occasionally helpful – if not necessary – *as to the facts*. For example, the records by the attendant doctor may set out an account of the history of a young child with an exanthematous rash, restless behaviour and/or altered conscious state, but make no note of temperature. A suitable expert using this account and the developing history thereafter may be able to help the court with *an opinion* as to what (as a matter of fact) the temperature is likely to have been.

8.39   In the final analysis it will be for the court to determine the facts (with or without the assistance of expert evidence) and the expert should be careful to shy away from any apparent acceptance of 'facts' as they may appear to him, let alone make any assumptions as to what they might be.

8.40   Opinion evidence pursuant to CPR 35 has to be in writing and the permission of the court is required for it to be given on a party's behalf. That is usually in the form of an expert report[1] but it may also include opinion evidence from standard textbooks. The latter is usually prayed in aid by the expert rather than adduced as standalone evidence.

1 See Chapter 14.

8.41   Expert evidence in clinical negligence cases falls into two distinct areas:

(1)   liability: the setting out of the range of acceptable standards of care at the time and in the relevant circumstances and the analysis of factual scenarios in relation to standards;
(2)   causation: the analysis of cause of the medical outcome about which complaint is made by looking at the relevance of any departure from acceptable standards of care. Strange though it may seem to the medical laity, the defence is often raised that although it is accepted there was a departure from acceptable standards of practice, it made no difference to the outcome of the case and the claimant bears the burden of showing that it did.

8.42   It is rarely wise for an expert to provide an opinion on both liability and causation, even if he is able to do so. Standards of care are not often in issue between the experts on a given sets of facts, although the facts themselves may be in issue. Standards of care depend upon time (date), place and circumstances. Textbooks and protocols play a major role, as standards vary only slowly over time. Although there will be a range of 'acceptable' standards, it is the lower end of the acceptable range in which the claimant's solicitor is interested, for to succeed it must be established that the care at the relevant time fell below that level.

8.43   Frequently causation requires a different speciality from breach of duty. An expert on issues of breach of duty in emergency medicine is unlikely to have the specialism necessary for dealing with issues of causation, such as whether an act or omission made any material contribution to the spread of a cancer. Even were that to be so, it would be better to call separate experts.

8.44   Causation evidence is much more complex both in medicine and in law. Textbooks are rarely helpful here. Above all, being based on scientific evidence, the determination of causation is dependent upon the latest learning on the subject and contemporary learned literature. This is the ground on which most contested cases are fought.

THE PURPOSE OF EXPERT EVIDENCE

8.45   The expert's purpose should be to *help the litigant, his lawyers and the court get it right*. Solicitors, unless also medically qualified, need expert help at an early stage on risk assessment. An expert can be asked to consider the records and then prepare and provide a brief overview on the potential merits of a case. If, on the preliminary assessment, the expert feels that there is likely to be a case to answer then the expert should be asked to prepare and provide a detailed and comprehensive report.

8.46   In the preparation of medical evidence on liability, the solicitor has a number of important tasks. These include obtaining and assembling the factual evidence, finding the right experts and giving them clear instructions. Clear guidance must be provided to the doctors as to their duties and what is expected of them. The right questions need to be asked and guidance on relevant areas of the law should be given[1]. It is essential that the expert has all relevant information and knows precisely what he is required to do.

1 See Chapter on the Medical Report.

8.47   Whilst the time frame of each case differs, below is an example as to the typical occasions on which an expert's help may be needed in a multi-track case:

Time since first	Action needed instructed
0–3 months	Risk assessment/preliminary report
6–9 months	Full report
9–12 months	Conference with claimant, counsel and other experts to focus issues for Particulars of Claim
	Check Particulars of Claim before service
12–15 months	Comment on defence
15–18 months	Provide 'dates to avoid' when trial date being fixed
18–21 months	Comment on factual witness statements
	Revise own report for exchange. Perhaps attend conference

Time since first	Action needed instructed
21–24 months	Comment on defence liability reports
	Advise on questions to defence experts to clarify their reports
	Answer questions (from defendant) on own report
24–27 months	Participate in discussions with defence experts. Report back
27–30 months	Pre-trial preparation and trial

8.48   Careful control needs to be kept over the appointment of experts in order to minimise costs, having regard to proportionality principles and to ensuring proper use is made court time. The practice of concurrent evidence or 'hot tubbing' is being actively promoted. This encourages a dialogue between the judge and two experts together, as well as encouraging experts to publish joint statements on agreed and non-agreed issues to narrow down the issues between them. A judge will frequently allow both experts to give evidence together, allowing them to assess, side by side, the merits of each position and reasons for their differences. This will also help to reduce court time.

8.49   The courts exercise their case management powers to control the number and use of experts. Generally, even in the most high-value cases, only one expert for each speciality will be allowed. In *Aleyan v Northwick Park NHS Trust*[1] Buckley J noted that the High Court Masters appeared to have agreed that wholly exceptional circumstances are needed in clinical negligence situations before more than one expert in the same discipline would be permitted. A useful case for solicitors to rely upon in support of a request for more than one expert on any given speciality is the reported case of *ES v Chesterfield and North Derbyshire Royal NHS Trust*[2]. This was a claim for cerebral palsy as a result of peri-natal asphyxia. In that case the claimant's solicitors were able to persuade the court that evidence should be allowed from two obstetric experts.

1 (1999) MLC 0150.
2 (2004) MLC 1051, (2004) Lloyds Rep Med 90, CA.

8.50   The court rules are clear that permission should only be granted for expert evidence from necessary experts from the relevant specialisms. Under the present rules[1] there is requirement to submit a budget for expert reports when directions questionnaires are submitted to the court. This then enables the district judge, when considering directions, to assess the potential cost of an expert's report and whether such a report is not only relevant but proportionate to the issues in question. The parties' solicitors do need to submit an accurate costs budget either at the same time as lodging a directions questionnaire or in any event no later than seven days prior to a Case Management Conference. Failure to do so may result in no costs being recoverable save for court fees[2]. It is important to ensure therefore that costs budgets are completed accurately. Costs budgets need to include anticipated cost of instructing experts.

1 CPR 35.4(2).
2 *Mitchell v News Group Newspapers Ltd* [2013] EWCA Civ 1537 and *Denton v TH White Ltd; Decadent Vapours Ltd v Bevan; Utilise TDS Ltd v Davies* [2014] EWCA Civ 906, [2014] 1 WLR 3926.

THE SELECTION OF THE EXPERT

8.51   Help may be required from an expert at a very early stage as to the appropriate speciality, though this is usually apparent on the disclosed facts. Whilst it would be unusual when selecting an expert to opine upon standards of another specialist's area of expertise there are occasions when this is desirable, if not necessary. In some areas of practice there is an overlap, for example between the spinal surgeon and the neurosurgeon. Investigation and treatment of the same condition may differ between specialisms. This may serve to assist a case of lack of informed consent or an argument that the operative procedure undertaken could no longer be justified.

8.52   Care has to be taken not to instruct a distinguished academic who may not be conversant with acceptable practice in a district hospital. Generally experts of consultant status should be instructed, as they are likely to have greater knowledge and gravitas than 'junior' doctors. They can also speak to the standards junior doctors in training are expected to meet.

8.53   Learner drivers, pilots in training, physicians and surgeons have to learn on the job. The *standard* to which they are to be judged, however, is that of the competent professional undertaking the procedure. There is no discount allowable in defence for the inexperienced.

8.54   Were a defence of lack of skill to be allowed it would permit health authorities to escape poor practice with impunity. Whilst there may be some judicial sympathy for the novice, none should undertake – or be permitted to undertake without close supervision – any procedure for which he is not competent.

8.55   Solicitors practising in clinical negligence will have a network of experts from which to make a selection. Exploration of medical case law, counsel practising in the field and some agencies may give guidance on where to seek help.

8.56   In a case of any complexity, more than one expert may be needed for both breach of duty and causation issues, for example:

- alleged mismanaged labour resulting in brain-damaged baby: obstetrician to report on question of breach of duty (was the labour mismanaged?), paediatrician to opine on causation (are the child's handicaps caused by the obstetric management, for example resulting in fetal hypoxia during labour?), neuroradiologist to advise what any USS, CT or NMRI imaging says about cause and timing of the injury;
- alleged injuries to babies and children: paediatrician. There are specialisms within specialisms: paediatric neurology, paediatric surgery, paediatric endocrinology, paediatric cardiology etc. If the case concerns the treatment of a neonate, an opinion will be required from a neonatologist. A report on quantum (long-term prognosis, recommendations for treatment, therapies, special education and so on) might be best from a developmental paediatrician. Overlap is inevitable;

- brain damage or paralysis: neurologist or neuropsychiatrist (if the brain damage has caused behavioural and personality changes). The cause of the brain damage may determine the choice of expert on liability, eg anaesthetist if the client collapsed under general anaesthetic;
- allergic reactions (which come in a wide variety of forms not restricted to skin rashes or vomiting, for example alleged anaphylactic reaction to anaesthetic drugs): immunologist may be able to advise (perhaps after further testing) on whether there was an allergic reaction to a particular substance or drug. Depending upon the cause of the allergic reaction other specialisms will be required to report on breach of duty.

THE PERFECT EXPERT?

8.57   The perfect expert will be experienced and knowledgeable. He will be an eminent doctor and a good communicator, both verbally and on paper. It is wise to check that the expert has a wealth of medico-legal experience. It is also sensible to ensure that the expert is still in current practice (or, at least, was in practice at the time of the alleged negligence) as opposed to an expert who is long since retired.

8.58   An eminent expert is more likely to prevail over other parties' experts at experts' meetings and to impress the judge at trial. He is also less likely to be afraid of 'ruining his career' by giving evidence for a claimant. But beware the 'ivory tower' problem: distinguished professor from nationally recognised centre applying that centre's high standards when judging the adequacy of treatment at a local general hospital.

8.59   The expert should be independent. The courts are very keen to ensure that justice must be objectively 'seen to be done' and although conflicts of interests are not black and white, the conflict may be too significant for permission to adduce the expert's evidence

8.60   An expert no longer has immunity from suit[1]. Whilst as a matter of practice successful actions in professional negligence against experts are likely to be few and far between, a civil action can now be taken against an expert in relation to comments and points made in expert reports. The experts will, of course, need to ensure that they are extremely thorough in the way they formulate their views and express their opinion.

1 *Jones v Kaney* [2011] UKSC 13, [2011] 2 AC 398.

8.61   The general rules are:

- not to instruct an expert too close to home: certainly not someone who works at the hospital or for the defendant against whom the allegations are made. Think twice about instructing the local surgeon who has given help over the years by providing reports in accident cases: clinical negligence work is very different;
- to keep a database of experts used in the past and note those who might be useful again. There are a number of sources of information including the Expert Witness Institute, the Academy of Experts and The Law Society. Of course, counsel may be able to advise on the names of

experts it would be appropriate to instruct. Law reports of similar cases may provide details of experts who did and who did not impress the trial judge. For arcane areas of medicine, an online search of medical literature will show who has published on the topic;

- to match the specialism of the breach of duty expert to the doctor being criticised. So, for example, instruct a GP, not a hospital specialist, to deal with breach of duty in a GP negligence case;
- to ensure the breach of duty expert was in practice in the field at the time of the events complained of and has experience of the treatment or procedure which the case is about;
- to ensure the causation expert, who does not need to have been in practice at the time, is currently practising in the field and is familiar with the up-to-date research;
- the expert must be able to write clearly and as succinctly as possible. The report must be consistent, logical and clear in the expression of opinion.

KEEPING THE EXPERTS INFORMED

8.62 It is a complaint of experts that some solicitors have scant regard to the pressures under which they work. Common sense and courtesy require that due consideration be given to minimising their burdens:

- do not send a bulky set of notes out to an expert without first asking if the expert is willing to accept instructions;
- be clear about what the expert is being asked to do, the timescale and what will be done with the report upon its receipt;
- if the case settles, let the experts know;
- consult the experts before fixing a trial date; some request a witness summons, others may need to be served them;
- acknowledge to the expert that medico-legal work is demanding and time-consuming: gratitude is as important as payment.

EXPERTS' FEES

8.63 Experts expect to be remunerated for their efforts and there should be no delay in the payment of their professional fees.

8.64 Apart from the general power to control the number of experts and the power to appoint a single joint expert, the court may, under the CPR, limit the amount of experts' fees and expenses which may be recovered from any other party: CPR 35.4. The court has no power to cap the fees payable to the expert by the instructing solicitor, but capping the amount recoverable from the other side has a moderating effect. There is a requirement by the courts to file a costs budget in all multi-track cases and to explain the reasoning for any increases.

This is particularly relevant in clinical negligence actions as it is often the case that addendum and supplementary expert reports are required to clarify issues and to answer opposing side's questions.

8.65   Experts can expect to be asked to extend time for payment of their fees. They may not like or want that, but doing so does not compromise an expert's independence and otherwise the instructions may go elsewhere.

8.66   For these reasons it is best to agree the basis of fee payment with the expert from the start. A solicitor is responsible for paying the proper fees of an expert instructed on behalf of the client, whether or not the solicitor is paid by the client. Unless they have agreed in advance to do so, experts are under no obligation to await the outcome of costs assessment.

8.67   Unless a reliable estimate of the expert's fees can be made, it is generally sensible to get an estimate and have this approved by the client before going ahead. The client should understand what money he is being asked to spend. In any event a solicitor must seek the client's authority for any unusual or expensive step[1].

1 CPR 48.8(2)(c) and CPR PD 48 para 2.9.

8.68   The solicitor's agreement to pay an expert a specified fee (for a report or court attendance) can be overturned on costs assessment; that is to say, the solicitor remains liable to pay the expert as agreed, but on costs assessment the court may decide the unsuccessful defendant, who has to pay the costs, is not liable for the full amount of the fee.

8.69   Some experts, when a case settles shortly before trial, seek 'cancellation fees'. This is a fee not favoured by costs judges, nor (unsurprisingly) by paying parties. Why, it is argued, should a medical expert, being a busy and distinguished person with more work available than he can fit in, a queue of private patients waiting for cancellations and a mound of medico-legal reports to prepare, be paid for a court attendance that in the end was unnecessary? Where is the financial loss? There is very little case law on this. The case frequently cited is the unreported 1986 case, *Reynolds v Meston*[1]. In that case a consultant neurologist, an ophthalmic surgeon and a clinical psychologist were allowed the cancellation fees they had claimed (£300, £300 and £250 respectively) when a case was cancelled 24 hours before the hearing.

1 (24 February 1986, unreported), Bingham J.

8.70   Details as to any cancellation fees should be set out in the original letter of instruction to ensure certainty on costs. Even if the expert provides details as to his cancellation fees there is no certainty that any cancellation fees will be recoverable from the opponent in the event of a successful claim. The significant issue will be that of any departure from costs that have been budgeted.

8.71   The BMA gives guidance on cancellation fees[1]. Bingham J stressed that each case for payment must be judged on its own merit but also said:

'The court is undoubtedly very much assisted by the expert evidence of medical and other witnesses at the peak of their professions. If such men are to respond to invitations to give expert evidence in court and to keep time free for that purpose, it is right that they should not run the risk of a last minute cancellation which would leave them substantially out of pocket. No doubt such witnesses are very conscious of a public duty to assist those finding themselves in the unfortunate position of this plaintiff. But there comes a point at which response to public duty cannot make demands beyond a certain limit on the personal goodwill of any expert, however eminent. It would, therefore, be very unfortunate if witnesses such as these were deterred from making their services available and if the court were dependent on the evidence of those who had no very pressing demands on their time'.

1 2014 Guidance on Fees: http://bma.org.uk/practical-support-at-work/pay-fees-allowances/fees/fee-finder/fee-finder-legal-aid-expert-witness.

8.72 In practice it is difficult for a solicitor to persuade a costs judge to order the defendant to pay an expert's cancellation fee save where the expert's booked trial attendances had to be cancelled very late *and* the expert provides the solicitor with a clear letter explaining why no other remunerative work could be slotted into the gap thus created (see the precedent at para **8.102** for a letter to an expert about cancellation fees). So if a solicitor agrees to pay an expert's cancellation fee on a more generous basis, the solicitor (or the client out of damages) may end up footing the bill. It is recommended the defendant's solicitors (on or after exchange of expert reports) are notified of any cancellation fee arrangements which have been made with the experts. Then, whatever other arguments they may raise, they cannot complain that they would have settled the case a couple of days earlier had they known what cancellation fees were at stake.

INSTRUCTING THE EXPERT

8.73 Before sending detailed instructions to an expert, check the following:

- Is the expert willing to accept instructions?
- When will the report be ready?
- What will it cost?
- Are there the funds to pay for it?
- Has the client agreed?
- In legal aid cases, does the certificate cover obtaining this report?
- In ATE cases, does the insurer agree to fund it?

8.74 It is a difficult line to tread between irritating the expert with tedious lengthy letters yet managing to provide the necessary factual and legal information. Experienced experts do not need any lectures on basic legal principles. The instruction letter should comply with the Guidance for the Instruction of Experts in Civil Claims 2014.

8.75 The expert must be sent a copy of the organised medical records (as above), a detailed statement from the proposed claimant and instructions as to what is required of him. That way the expert can pay attention to what is really needed. Experts who know instructions are well prepared will be more inclined to accept them and to do the instructing solicitor favours when they are desperately needed.

8.76 The expert needs to opine on the range of acceptable standards of care and whether or not they have been met in the factual circumstances alleged. If the defendant advances an alternative factual basis then the expert should

198

address that basis too. No opinion should be expressed upon which factual basis is correct, though if an expert takes the view on medical grounds that the defendant's fact basis is unlikely to be correct, then he should say so. It is for the lawyers to decide whether any shortcomings amount to negligence or breach of duty, not the expert. Inappropriate questions or poorly framed questions (particularly if the expert has little medico-legal experience) may lead to troublesome answers such as 'there but for the grace of God...' or 'this is the kind of mistake any doctor could make and cannot in my view be negligent...'.

8.77 Experienced medico-legal experts appreciate that the standard of proof in a civil case is the balance of probabilities; experts coming new to civil work may not. Their previous medico-legal experience may be restricted to criminal work.

INTERPRETING THE EXPERT EVIDENCE

8.78 Ensure that:

- the report is comprehensible by the intelligent lay person;
- the issues have been addressed;
- a contingent opinion is given on any conflicting factual scenarios; and
- the references relied upon are attached and relevant.

8.79 If the report is *positive*, analyse it carefully and critically. Does the report provide reasoned answers to points which might be made against the expert's conclusions, as well as those in favour? It is a reasonable indication the report is realistic, if it does so. Paragraph 1.2(5) of the Practice Direction which supplements CPR 35 requires an expert to summarise the range of opinion (where one exists on the matters dealt with in an expert report) and give reasons for his own opinions.

8.80 A *negative* report also merits careful analysis. Look out for points such as:

- 'Nowadays, this condition is relatively easy to treat using ... but in 2012 ...' Call for published references. Checks in standard texts to see if a pre-2012 reference to the then 'unavailable' treatment can be found;
- 'This condition cannot be diagnosed without special equipment.' What special equipment? Why was it not available? If the equipment is expensive, why was the patient not referred to a specialist centre where such equipment was available?
- 'In a proportion of cases the femoral shaft does split when it is being drilled for the prosthesis.' If this is a known risk, what are the known precautions? Were these taken? Was the patient warned of the risk? Is there a lack of informed consent case?
- 'Although the treatment given was far from satisfactory I do not think this affected the outcome as ... [the original condition] ... frequently results in severe limitation of movement'. In what proportion of cases does severe limitation of movement result? Call for published references. Was the client truly in a 'poor prognosis' category, judged,

for example, by age or progress/cause of the original condition? Did the far from satisfactory treatment contribute to the poor outcome?

8.81 When deciding whether to proceed with a case after having received an unfavourable report some questioning is necessary to be sure of both the adverse opinion and the reasoning for it. Even if, after probing, the expert reconsiders and provides a more favourable response one should be cautious. One must be wary as to the prospects of the expert simply reverting back to his original position following joint discussions with the other side's expert.

8.82 The change of opinion provided by an expert would not in itself be sufficient grounds for dismissing him and commissioning a new expert[1]. There must be 'reasonable grounds' to show that the expert's change of mind is not supported by the evidence or prevailing opinion. This case also ties in with the provisions of CPR 35.3 (the overriding duty to the court) and CPR 35.1 (the requirement to limit expert evidence to that reasonably required to resolve proceedings). In short if it cannot be shown that an expert has unreasonably departed from his view, flying clearly in the face of the evidence available and accepted opinion in the field, then that report will be sufficient to assist the court with the proceedings and the claimant will in all probability not be allowed permission to seek another report.

1 *Stallwood v David* [2006] EWHC 2600 (QB), [2007] 1 All ER 206.

8.83 When faced with an expert who has changed his opinion, the case of *Reid v Superior Seals Ltd*[1] may be helpful. In this case it was held that there is still some scope to change to another expert. It needs to be established through enquiries that the expert has no real basis to have changed his mind. In effect this would require enquiries of the expert to be made and for the expert to list his reasons for the change of mind. If the expert's views prove to be sustainable then that probably will be the end of the case. However if there is an argument that the expert has simply folded under pressure or wilfully turned his opinion against your client's case, then the court can accept that the evidence is flawed and unlikely to meet the test of CPR 35.3 to assist the court. At this point the expert report may be dispensed with and a new opinion sought.

1 [2008] CLY 267.

8.84 In *Edwards-Tubb v JD Weatherspoon plc*[1] and *Beck v Ministry of Defence*[2] litigation privilege attached to the first report was required to be waived under CPR 35.4 by order of the court as a condition of instructing a further opinion and report by the claimant's solicitor following an unfavourable report from their previously instructed expert. Under CPR 35.11 the defence were then entitled to rely upon the first unfavourable report as supporting evidence in their own case. There is also the question of a conduct costs penalty for so called 'expert shopping' in respect of any reports gained. It was suggested by the Court of Appeal in the *Edwards* case that it should be standard practice to require the waiver of privilege over an expert report if permission is to be granted to commission a new report.

1 [2011] EWCA Civ 136.
2 [2003] EWCA Civ 1043, [2005] 1 WLR 2206.

8.85   If a reliable expert provides a negative report which withstands probing, then the claim cannot proceed. This will be disappointing for the client, who may find negative advice upsetting and unpalatable. The client may find a meeting with the expert (with or without counsel) helpful. It is most unfair to the client to keep false hopes alive, as well as being unfair to the doctors whose treatment has been criticised to have the threat of litigation still hanging over them.

8.86   If further enquiries indicate the expert is not reliable, or what he says does not entirely hold water, or if the claim is of high value, a second opinion should be sought, though funding it may prove difficult.

EXPERT ASSISTANCE IN DRAFTING THE PARTICULARS OF CLAIM

8.87   When there is positive liability evidence, there is merit in arranging a 'pre-Particulars of Claim' conference with counsel, experts and client in all but the most straightforward cases. It is highly advisable in a case with multiple liability experts or when instructing an expert not familiar with medico-legal reporting to hold such a conference. There is more to being a good expert witness than writing a good report. The factual basis upon which the expert opinion evidence is founded must be clearly understood by all, as it has to be pleaded.

8.88   Central to the presentation of the medical evidence at trial is the understanding and awareness each expert must have of the written views of all the other experts in the case. Counsel should be instructed well in advance to provide time to read into the case properly and to prepare a draft Particulars of Claim as a discussion document. This should be circulated to all participants in advance of the conference, optimising the use of the time and providing focus.

8.89   *Keep notes* (and/or audio recording, with permission) and take the trouble to dictate a detailed note of the discussion. This note should be checked and approved by the experts and counsel. It can take a long time to prepare a note (it is not a simple matter of dictating a summary of what was said, in the order it was said), but it is essential for future reference and may save the additional expense of counsel preparing a written opinion. Costs judges can be reluctant on costs assessment to allow the time taken preparing a conference note, so it is worth dictating at the same time a file note explaining why this item of preparation is essential (and time-consuming).

8.90   *Invite the client (or the litigation friend)* to the conference, telling the experts and counsel the client will be there. Most clinical negligence claimants feel they have been short-changed on forthright medical explanations. Apart from the factual input which the client can often provide at conference, the opportunity to hear distinguished doctors discussing the case openly can go a long way towards restoring faith in the medical profession.

8.91   After the conference, counsel should prepare a final draft version of the Particulars of Claim to be checked by the experts before it is served. CPR

22.1 requires the facts in the Particulars of Claim to be verified by a statement of truth signed either by the claimant (or litigation friend) or the claimant's lawyer. So when asking the experts to check the final version of the Particulars of Claim, it is important to explain to them the importance of checking that the relevant factual history has been accurately pleaded, as well as asking them to confirm they support each of the allegations of negligence.

EXPERT ASSISTANCE IN EVIDENCE PREPARATION FROM PLEADINGS TO TRIAL

8.92   After the service of the defence and directions have been given, timetabling of further help from the experts should be undertaken.

8.93   Provision should be made for an expert conference prior to exchange of expert evidence once factual witness statements have been exchanged. The experts may need to revise their reports in the light of the witness statements. The experts should be persuaded to do any draft revision of their reports prior to the conference. Any further 'fine tuning' can be done at the conference. It is crucial to remember that experts are almost always giving evidence upon a factual basis (as opposed to an opinion *about* the facts). The exchange of witness statements will make clear (if the pleadings do not) if there are any significant factual issues. The experts must be prepared to give their opinions upon the alleged different factual bases advanced by the parties.

8.94   When expert evidence has been exchanged there are 28 days to put written questions to the defence experts in order to clarify their reports[1]. Ask your experts at once for their views on the defence reports and consider them with counsel. It is a tight timetable and it may be necessary to apply to the court for an extension of time if questions are to be asked of any of the defence experts. An expert's answers to CPR 35.6 questions are treated as part of the expert's report.

1 See CPR 35.6 and CPR 36 PD para 5.1.

8.95   Once expert reports have been exchanged then as a matter of course the court will almost always order that there should be discussion between the parties' medical experts. The parties' experts of like discipline should liaise with their 'opposite number' with a view to discussing their respective reports and then preparing and providing a joint report highlighting areas of agreement and disagreement.

8.96   The court has the power to specify the issues for discussion and it is important that this is done so that the expert's brief is clear. As a matter of course an agenda is prepared setting out the specific questions that the experts are to discuss. Having prepared the agenda, it should be forwarded to the defendant's solicitors for their consideration and approval before it is finalised and sent to the experts. A discussion between the experts will have to be scheduled. Such a discussion does not have to be at a face-to-face meeting. More often than not it will take place on the telephone. If discussions take place at a face-to-face meeting the issue of who (apart from the experts) attends that meeting seems surprisingly contentious. The judiciary seem to favour excluding everyone apart from experts. If a lawyer is present this should simply be to answer legal points. Following discussions between experts they will need to prepare and provide a joint report showing the issues upon which they agree and those on which they disagree, together with a summary of their reasons for disagreeing. Experts will then need to each sign the joint report.

8.97   Following the preparation of the joint reports a much clearer view as to the merits may be taken. This is the high point of the medical evidence before trial and it is the time to 'take stock' of the merits. In practice many cases will settle after receipt by the parties of the joint reports from their experts.

PRE-TRIAL AND TRIAL PREPARATION

8.98   Save for some cases of high value and those with causation difficulties, very few clinical negligence cases go to trial.

8.99   If the case is not settled, the really hard work of trial preparation must commence. Arrangements must be made to ensure all the expert and lay evidence which is not agreed will be available for trial. *Inter alia*, this means:

- checking and agreeing bundles of evidence for court;
- reminding witnesses of the trial dates and making sure they have copies of their witness statements and access to any other relevant documentation;
- booking the experts not only for the court days when they will be giving their own evidence, but to be in court when their defence 'opposition number' gives evidence, to help counsel with cross-examination;
- considering (again) the need to witness summons any experts. Some practitioners favour issuing and serving a witness summons on their experts to preserve priority over other commitments;
- organising the necessary pre-trial conferences;
- reminding the experts that they may be required to assist with points before/after each day the trial is running as the evidence unfolds;
- making sure every possible means of contacting the experts is known so as to be able to notify them of last-minute developments or settlement. Often in the run up to trial, important things happen in the evening so try to do better than the hospital departmental phone number;
- checking the defendant's solicitors have been notified of any 'cancellation fee' arrangements with the experts; and, finally
- checking there is money in account to pay for the experts.

PRECEDENT 1

Application on behalf of a patient for hospital medical records for use when court proceedings are contemplated

8.100   This should be completed as fully as possible

Insert:

Hospital

Name

and

Address

TO : Medical Records Officer

Hospital

1   Full name of patient (including previous surnames)
    (a)   Address now
    (b)   Address at start of treatment
    (c)   Date of birth (and death, if applicable)
    (d)   Hospital reference number (if available)
    (e)   NI number (if available)
2   This application is made because the patient is considering
    (a)   a claim against your hospital as detailed in para 7 overleaf
    YES/NO
    (b)   Pursuing an action against someone else
    YES/NO
3   Department(s) where treatment was received
4   Name(s) of consultant(s) at your hospital in charge of the treatment
5   Whether treatment at your hospital was private or NHS, wholly or in part
6   A description of the treatment received, with approximate dates
7   If the answer to Q2(A) is 'Yes' details of
    (a)   the likely nature of the claim
    (b)   grounds for the claim
    (c)   approximate dates of the events involved
8.   If the answer to Q2(B) is 'Yes' insert
    (i)   the names of the proposed defendants
    (ii)   whether legal proceedings yet begun YES/NO
    (iii) if appropriate, details of the claim and action number.
9   We confirm we will pay reasonable copying charges.
10   We request prior details of
    (i)   photocopying and administration charges for medical records
    YES/NO
    (ii)   number of and cost of copying X-ray and scan films
    YES/NO

11   Any other relevant information, particular requirements, or any particular documents not required (eg, copies of computerised records).

Signature of Solicitor

Name

Address

Ref

Telephone Number

Fax number

Please print name beneath each signature.

Signature by child over 12 but under 18 years also requires signature by parent

Signature of patient

Signature of parent or next friend if appropriate

Signature of personal representative where patient has died

PRECEDENT 2

Specimen letter to doctor about cancellation fees

8.101

Dear Doctor ....,

There are difficulties about cancellation fees, from the point of view of my firm and my client, which I need your help to resolve.

A successful claimant will get most (not all) of his costs paid by the defendant, on top of the damages award. If these costs cannot be agreed inter partes, they must be assessed by a court official ('Costs Judge'). A detailed bill is drawn and representatives of the claimant's and defendant's solicitors attend before the Costs Judge to argue what should reasonably and properly be paid.

On assessment, the Costs Judge may:

allow certain items of the successful claimant's bill in whole or in part against the paying party (defendant); or

allow certain items of the claimant's bill in whole or in part against the claimant (meaning they are paid out of the damages); or disallow certain items altogether.

If I agree to pay you cancellation fees, which are challenged by the defendant and the Costs Judge upholds the challenge, the fees must either be paid by my client or my firm.

Costs Judges (and paying party's solicitors) are extremely reluctant to agree cancellation fees of any kind. In practice it is difficult to persuade a Costs Judge that a cancellation fee should be paid for court appearance cancelled more than a week in advance.

So please can you set out in a letter (which may be shown to the Court and the defendant's solicitors):

(1) the level of your hourly/daily fee for Court attendance and the level of cancellation fee you seek, including details of the 'sliding scale' – increasing towards the full level of 'appearance' fee, the shorter the time before the trial that the cancellation occurs; and

(2) why your particular practice means that you do not in fact have other remunerative work such as seeing patients or drafting medico-legal reports, which could be 'slotted in', in the event of a late cancellation of the trial fixture.

Yours sincerely,

CHAPTER 9

The medical report and duties of the expert witness

Dr Evelyn M M Pollock

INTRODUCTION

Admissibility of opinion evidence

9.1   It is a substantive rule of evidence that witnesses may not give evidence of opinion but only of fact. (There are some obvious exceptions to this rule, such as where a witness describes a person's age, or the speed of a vehicle or the state of the weather.) A witness may only speak of facts which he personally perceives/has perceived not of inferences drawn from those facts. The evidence given by an expert witness is an exception to the substantive rule. Expert opinion is admitted because the drawing of certain inferences calls for an expertise which the tribunal of fact simply does not have. As long ago as 1553 it was said:

'If matters arise in our law which concern other sciences or faculties we commonly apply for the aid of that science or faculty which it concerns. This is a commendable thing in our law. For thereby it appears that we do not dismiss all other sciences, but our own, but we approve of them and encourage them as things worthy of commendation'[1].

1 Saunders J in *Buckley v Rice-Thomas* (1554) 1 Plowd 118 at 124

Civil Procedure Rules 1998, Practice Directions and Guidance for the Instruction of Experts to Give Evidence in Civil Claims 2014

9.2   In this chapter the Civil Procedure Rules 1998 in relation to experts and assessors (CPR 35) are set out in full in Appendix A; the Practice Directions (PDs) to CPR 35 (PD 35) are set out in full in Appendix B. Guidance for the Instruction of Experts to give Evidence in Civil Claims 2014, referred to in this chapter as 'the Guidance', is set out in Appendix C.

THE DUTIES OF EXPERTS

9.3   Prior to the introduction of the CPR, guidance about the duties and responsibilities of experts was to be found in case law[1]. Experts are now governed by CPR 35 if they give, or have been instructed to give or prepare expert evidence for the purpose of proceedings in a court in England and Wales (CPR 35.2). Where an expert has been instructed only to advise, and it is not intended that such advice be adduced in litigation, that expert is not bound by CPR 35. This will apply to an expert who has been instructed only to advise even after commencement of proceedings. However, CPR 35 will bind an expert formerly instructed only to advise who is then later instructed to give or prepare evidence for the purpose of civil proceedings.

1 See for a good example *National Justice Cia Naviera SA v Prudential Assurance Co Ltd, The Ikarian Reefer* [1993] 2 Lloyd's Rep 68.

9.4   The admissibility of expert evidence lying outside of CPR 35 was considered recently by the Court of Appeal in the case of *Rogers v Hoyle*[1]. The appellant argued that a report prepared by the Air Accident Investigation Branch (AAIB), into a fatal light aircraft accident in which a passenger in the aircraft died, and the pilot was seriously injured, was inadmissible as it did not comply with a number of the requirements of CPR 35. In particular, the author was not identified, no permission to adduce the AAIB report as expert evidence had been sought or given, the Part 35 requirements for the instruction of experts had not been observed and there was no expert's statement.

The Court of Appeal held that the procedural rules for expert evidence of CPR 35 did not preclude the admissibility of the AAIB report. CPR Part 35 did not purport to be a comprehensive and exclusive code regulating the admission of expert evidence in civil proceedings. Instead, it regulated the use of a particular category of expert evidence, namely the evidence of experts 'who had been instructed to give or prepare expert evidence for the purpose of proceedings'.

1 *Rogers v Hoyle* [2014] EWCA Civ 257.

9.5   Expert evidence which is prepared for another purpose is not regulated by CPR 35 and the common law continues to apply to this category of expert evidence. While at common law all expert evidence had to be given orally, documentary hearsay evidence is now admitted by statute and this includes documentary hearsay evidence of expert opinion.

It was observed in *Hoyle* that, in practice, to date, the courts have received expert evidence outside the confines of CPR 35: see *DN v Greenwich London Borough Council*[1] and *Multiplex Constructions (UK) Ltd v Cleveland Bridge UK Ltd (No 6)*[2].

1 [2004] EWCA Civ 1659.
2 [2008] EWHC 2220 (TCC).

9.6   In CPR 35 and in the Guidance a number of duties of experts are identified:

(1)   the expert has an overriding duty to help the court on matters which lie within his expertise (CPR 35.3; 35 PD para 2.2, Guidance 9). This duty overrides any obligation to the person instructing the expert or by whom he is paid;

(2)   experts should be aware of the overriding objective that courts deal with cases justly (CPR 1.1). This includes dealing with cases proportionately, expeditiously and fairly (Guidance 10);

(3)   experts should provide opinions which are independent regardless of the pressures of litigation. Experts should not take it upon themselves to promote the point of view of the party instructing them or engage in the role of advocates (Guidance 11);

(4) experts should confine their opinions to matters which are material to the disputes between the parties and provide opinions only in relation to matters which lie within their expertise. Experts should indicate without delay where particular questions or issues fall outside their expertise (Guidance 12);

(5) the expert's report must state the substance of all material instructions, whether written or oral, on the basis of which the report was written (CPR 35.10(3));

(6) experts should take into account all material facts before them at the time that they give their opinion. Their reports should set out those facts and any literature or any other material on which they have relied in forming their opinions. They should indicate if an opinion is provisional or qualified, or where they consider that further information is required or if, for any other reason, they are not satisfied that an opinion can be expressed finally and without qualification (Guidance 13).

9.7 The facts upon which an expert's opinion is based must be proved by admissible evidence. It is the expert's opinion on the facts as stated that is required, not his opinion of the facts. If the expert has been misinformed about the facts or has taken irrelevant facts into consideration or has omitted to consider relevant ones, the opinion is likely to be valueless[1].

1 *R v Turner* [1975] QB 834 at 840, CA; *Re J (Contact)* (17 August 2007, unreported), Family Division.

9.8 When addressing questions of fact and opinion experts should keep the two separate and discrete. They must state those facts (whether assumed or otherwise) upon which their opinions are based. They must distinguish clearly between those facts which they know to be true and those facts which they assume (Guidance 56). Not infrequently, in medical cases, the primary facts will be in dispute. In these circumstances the experts should express separate opinions on each factual hypothesis put forward. They should not express a view in favour of one or other disputed version of the facts unless, as a result of a particular expertise and experience, they consider one set of facts as being improbable or less probable, in which case they may express that view and should give reasons for holding it (Guidance 57). Where indicated (for example if at the time the expert writes the report it is clear that medical records or results of investigations or the like are missing), the expert should state that his opinion may need to be qualified should additional information come to hand. Experts should inform those instructing them without delay of any change in their opinions on any material matter and the reason for it (Guidance 14).

9.9 However, the expert can, to some extent, advise on the factual evidence needed to meet the opposing party's case. In *Stanley v Rawlinson*[1], which involved the collapse of a wall between two adjoining properties, Tomlinson LJ said this:

'Experts are often involved in the investigation and preparation of a case from an early stage. There is nothing inherently objectionable, improper or inappropriate about an expert advising his client on the evidence needed to meet the opposing case, indeed it is often likely to be the professional duty of an expert to proffer just such advice. The opinion of an expert is often if not usually dependent upon the precise nature of a factual situation which he must to some extent assume to have existed.

There is nothing improper in pointing out to a client that his case would be improved if certain assumed features of an incident can be shown not in fact to have occurred, or if conversely features assumed to have been absent can in fact be shown to have been present'.

1 [2011] EWCA Civ 405.

Experts' qualifications

9.10   A witness may not give his opinion on matters which the court considers call for the special skill or knowledge of an expert unless he is an expert in such matters. The details of experts' qualifications to be given in reports should be commensurate with the nature and complexity of the case (Guidance 53). It may be sufficient merely to state academic and professional qualifications. However, where highly specialised expertise is called for, experts should include accurate details with regard to particular training and/or experience that qualifies them to provide that highly specialised evidence. If the expert gives detail as to the split of his work between claimant and defendant that too must be stated correctly[1].

The expertise of an expert in the context of professional fitness to practise hearings was the subject of the court's scrutiny[2]:

'His principal criticism of the Appellant was that he purported to give an expert opinion in the case of an individual who was appropriate for treatment by a general adult psychiatrist when the Appellant was not on the Specialist Register in the category of general adult psychiatry, but was on the Register in the category of Psychiatry of Learning Disability. He was also critical of the fact that the Appellant did not have membership or Fellowship of the Royal College of Psychiatrists. The Appellant had not had any higher professional training in psychiatry and had not held a substantive post in the National Health Service. He had not published in any peer-reviewed journals …

One of the principal arguments being advanced on behalf of the Appellant was that a person could acquire expert knowledge either from formal training or from experience gained in the course of work.'

'The Panel was entitled to find that the Appellant was not an expert in the field of general adult psychiatry and had failed to restrict his opinion to areas in which he had expert knowledge or direct experience and to matters that fell within the limits of his professional competence. The Panel was also entitled to find that he had failed to give adequate reasons for his professional opinions and failed to display an adequate understanding of the role and responsibilities of an expert witness'.

1 See *Rhodes v West Surrey and NE Hampshire Health Authority* [1998] Lloyd's Rep Med 246.
2 *Pool v GMC* [2014] EWHC 3791 (Admin), Lewis J at paras 8, 9 and 52.

The independence of experts and conflicts of interest

9.11   Since under CPR 35.3 the expert has an overriding duty to the court rather than to the parties, the employee of a party involved in litigation *can* be an independent expert[1]. If a party is proposing to use the expert evidence of an employee it should be given an opportunity to demonstrate that the employee has the relevant experience and is aware of the primary duty to the court when giving expert evidence.

It should be noted that in *Liverpool Roman Catholic Archdiocesan Trustees Inc v Goldberg (No 3)*[2] it was said that a professional relationship between a litigant and an expert prevented the expert from having the necessary independence to be called an expert witness. This case was subsequently disapproved by Lord Phillips of Worth Matravers MR in *R (on the application of Factortame) v Secretary of State for Transport, Local Government and the Regions (No 8)*[3] (see below) and was probably wrongly decided.

1 See *Field v Leeds City Council* [2000] 17 EG 165, CA in which an employee of the council was allowed to give evidence on its behalf and *DN v Greenwich London Borough Council* [2004] EWCA Civ 1659, in which an educational psychologist was held to be entitled to give expert evidence on his own behalf as to why, in his opinion, his conduct did not fall below the relevant standard of care.
2 [2001] 1 WLR 2337.
3 [2002] EWCA Civ 932, [2003] QB 381.

9.12   The modern approach seems not to prohibit experts who have an interest but that there must be a declaration of such interest. Independence is a matter of degree and the rule against bias of natural justice ('nemo iudex in sua causa') is too stringent. This was the approach adopted by Lord Phillips MR in the *Factortame* case. He said, at para 70:

'It is always desirable that an expert should have no actual or apparent interest in the outcome of the proceedings in which he gives evidence, but such disinterest is not automatically a precondition to the admissibility of his evidence. Where an expert has an interest of one kind or another in the outcome of the case, this fact should be made known to the court as soon as possible. The question of whether the proposed expert should be permitted to give evidence should then be determined in the course of case management. In considering that question the Judge will have to weigh the alternative choices open if the expert's evidence is excluded, having regard to the overriding objective of the Civil Procedure Rules'.

9.13   In *Toth v Jarman*[1] the Court of Appeal gave guidance concerning the disclosure of potential conflicts of interest affecting expert witnesses. The claimant, whose son had died as a result of a defendant general practitioner's alleged negligent treatment, sought damages for psychiatric injury. The Medical Defence Union (MDU) who acted for the defendant instructed an expert to report. That expert's evidence was favourable to the defendant and, at trial, was preferred by the judge to the claimant's expert evidence. On appeal the claimant alleged there had been a material non-disclosure by the defendant's expert of a conflict of interest arising out of the fact that, at the time his report was written, he was a member of the Cases Committee of the MDU (the Cases Committee being the arm of the MDU that takes decisions on whether to defend any given action). Dismissing the appeal. the court held that the practice of the Cases Committee to exclude an expert involved in the litigation from discussions about the case meant that membership of the Committee would not automatically disqualify that expert from being an expert witness. It is evident from the judgment of the Court of Appeal that a party who intends to rely upon an expert must disclose both to the court and to the opposing party any conflict of interest on the part of the expert, unless it is 'obviously immaterial'. Unfortunately the Court of Appeal did not define what might constitute an 'immaterial' conflict of interest. It is submitted that a conflict of interest can only be immaterial if it cannot reasonably be said to have the potential to interfere with an expert's fundamental duty to give evidence independent of the party instructing him or the pressures of litigation (the overriding duty). Clearly, what a party wants to avoid is the potential for an argument being raised, either at trial or afterwards, that an expert instructed on its behalf has subconsciously displayed bias. (Such arguments can carry considerable weight[2].) It is submitted, therefore, that the prudent course of action is for the expert to declare, at as early a stage in the proceedings as possible, *any* conflict of interest he might have and let the court determine (either at the request of the opposing party or of its own initiative) whether the conflict of interest is so material that the party concerned should not be permitted to rely upon that expert's evidence.

1 [2006] EWCA Civ 1028, [2006] 4 All ER 1276.
2 See *Mellor v Sheffield Teaching Hospitals NHS Trust* [2004] EWHC 780 (QB), para 230 and *Hardman v Riddell* [2004] EWHC 1691 (QB).

9.14   In *Toth v Jarman*[1] the Court of Appeal suggested that consideration be given to requiring an expert to make a statement at the end of his report along the following lines:
(1)   that he has no conflict of interest of any kind other than any which he has disclosed in his report;
(2)   that he does not consider that any interest which he has disclosed affects his suitability as an expert witness on any issue on which he has given evidence;
(3)   that he will advise the party by whom he is instructed if, between the date of his report and the trial, there is any change in circumstances which affects his answers to (1) or (2) above.

1 [2006] EWCA Civ 1028, [2006] 4 All ER 1276.

9.15   In *Meat Corporation of Namibia Ltd v Dawn Meats (UK) Ltd*[1] each side had permission to rely on the evidence of one 'meat industry' expert. The claimant gave its (then) expert witness, Mrs B, privileged and confidential information based on her expressed interest in acting for them. Mrs B then changed her mind (citing a diary clash). Some time later, Mrs B was instructed by the defendant. The claimant applied to the court to have Mrs B's evidence excluded on the grounds that she had received confidential and privileged information from them and that she was now acting as a consultant for Dawn Meats. She therefore lacked independence. Mann J reviewed the relevant case law and held, on the facts, that the information received would not influence Mrs B's evidence and that her undertaking not to disclose the claimant's confidential and privileged information was a sufficient safeguard. The court was therefore satisfied that Mrs B could give evidence and refused the claimant's application.

The claimant cited the Court of Appeal's position in *Toth v Jarman*[2] to support its argument that 'where an expert has a material or significant conflict of interest, the court is likely to decline to act on his evidence, or indeed to give permission for his evidence to be adduced'.

The court in *Meat Corporation of Namibia Ltd* emphasised that the finding of a conflict of interest was not a black and white issue, the materiality of which could be decided between the parties; potential issues should be brought to the court's attention at the earliest possible opportunity[3].

1 [2011] EWHC 474 (Ch).

2 [2006] EWCA Civ 1028, [2006] 4 All ER 1276.
3 See *EXP v Barker* [2015] EWHC 1289 (QB) where an expert instructed by the defence had failed to disclose previous professional association with the defendant neuroradiologist, the court stated in assessing the evidence: 'Where the core issue in a case turns, as it does here, on the court's ability to evaluate the competing and finely balanced medical judgements of rival experts, the court's confidence in the independence and impartiality of the respective experts must play an important role' (para 73).

9.16   In the absence of a duty of confidence it is contrary to public policy for an expert to agree not to act for another party[1].

1 *Lilly Icos LLC v Pfizer Ltd* (17 August 2000, unreported), Ch D; LTL 26.1.2001.

THE MANAGEMENT OF EXPERT EVIDENCE BY THE COURT

9.17   Through the CPR the court has total control over the use of expert evidence. It may give directions about expert evidence under CPR 35 or under PD 28 (fast track cases) or PD 29 (multi track cases). The Court of Appeal is unlikely to interfere in case management decisions involving expert evidence unless it is satisfied that the decision of the judge in the lower court was 'clearly wrong'[1].

1 *Ahmed v Stanley A Coleman & Hill* [2002] EWCA Civ 935 '… it is essential for the satisfactory operation of the new CPR regime that the authority of the judges in the lower court case management issues should not be undermined by decisions of this court unless this court considers their decisions were clearly wrong or that they have gone wrong in law or there is some serious procedural mishap'.

9.18   Whether or not any expert evidence at all is required to resolve the issues in any particular case is a matter for the court. No party may call an expert or put in evidence an expert's report without the permission of the court (CPR 35.4(1)). A party applying for permission either to call an expert or put in evidence an expert's report must identify (CPR 35.4(2)):

(a)   the field in which expert evidence is required and the issues which the expert evidence will address; and
(b)   where practicable the name of the proposed expert.

If permission is granted it shall be in relation only to the expert named or the field identified under CPR 35.4(2). The order granting permission may specify the issue which the expert evidence should address (CPR 35.4(3)).

Numbers of experts

9.19   While the court does not have power to limit the number of experts a party may instruct, it does have power to limit the number of experts a party may call at trial. Expert evidence should be restricted to that which is reasonably required to resolve the proceedings (CPR 35.1).

9.20   In *S v Chesterfield and North Derbyshire Royal Hospital NHS Trust*[1] (a cerebral palsy case) the claimant appealed from a case management decision that each party be limited to one expert in the field of obstetrics. The claimant had sought permission to call two expert obstetricians to deal with breach of duty, on the grounds that since two of the doctors who had treated the claimant's mother were now practising as consultant obstetricians the defendant would be putting forward evidence from these two obstetricians as well as from the independent obstetric expert instructed on its behalf and would therefore have an unfair advantage. The Master took the view that there was no unfairness since the evidence of the treating obstetricians could be differentiated and isolated from that of the expert. Allowing the claimant's appeal, the Court of Appeal held that the Master had been wrong in his view. It considered that the three witnesses for the defence would cover a much wider spectrum of personal experience than the single expert permitted for the claimant. It was inevitable and indeed appropriate for a witness of fact who happened to be a professional to give evidence of his actions based on his professional experience and expertise. The additional cost and added length to the trial of allowing the claimant to call a second expert was proportionate and just. CPR 35 limited expert evidence as to what was reasonably required to resolve the proceedings in issue. What was reasonable in any particular context would inevitably be fact-sensitive and the overriding objective had to be considered. The present case was of high importance to the parties, of high monetary value and complexity. Therefore the most important of the considerations in CPR 1.1(2) was that the parties should be on an equal footing. The court stated that it '…was only in exceptional circumstances such as those pertaining in the instant case that two [experts] would be permitted'.

1 [2003] EWCA Civ 1284.

9.21   In *Kirkman v EuroExide Corpn (CMP Batteries Ltd)*[1] liability was admitted. In the determination of damages the question before the court was how the claimant's workplace accident had affected the date of the appointment for a pre-booked reconstruction operation on his knee. Each party relied on one expert to answer that question. In addition the claimant was permitted to rely on a statement from an orthopaedic surgeon (B), an expert in his own right since the relevant part of B's statement had been an expression of fact and not an expression of opinion. The Court of Appeal observed that the principle of 'equality of arms' had not been intended to amount to an absolute rule, but rather a general rule to ensure that the overriding objective that cases be dealt with justly would be obeyed.

1 [2007] EWCA Civ 66.

9.22   To date, claimants seeking to use the arguments in *S v Chesterfield and North Derbyshire Royal Hospital NHS Trust*[1] have largely been unsuccessful. In *Beaumont v Ministry of Defence*[2] (another cerebral palsy case) the claimant submitted that they should be permitted to rely on two obstetric experts since the defendant's factual obstetric witness was by now a consultant obstetrician who on occasion acted as an expert witness and who would inevitably base his opinion on his expertise. The Master refused the claimant's application. The claimant appealed. The appeal was dismissed on the ground that the circumstances of the case were not 'exceptional'. Further, the court stated that the 'weight of numbers' would not be the decisive factor when evaluating the expert evidence.

1 [2003] EWCA Civ 1284.
2 [2009] EWHC 1258 (QB).

Expert evidence must be in written form

9.23   There is a general requirement that expert evidence be given in the form of a written report (CPR 35.5). The content and form of the expert report is discussed at para **9.58** ff.

Exchange of published literature/scholarly information

9.24   In *Wardlaw v Farrar*[1] the Court of Appeal observed that the standard form of order made by the High Court Masters of the Queen's Bench Division in relation to disclosure of scholarly information by medical experts should be followed in all courts. In the current form of order used by QBD Masters Roberts and Cook[2], it is stated at para 12:

'Any unpublished literature upon which any expert witness proposes to rely shall be served at the same time as service of his report together with a list of published literature. Any supplementary literature upon which any expert witness proposes to rely shall be notified to all other parties at least one month before trial. No expert witness shall rely upon any publications that have not been disclosed in accordance with this direction without the permission of the trial judge on such terms as to costs as he deems fit'.

1   [2003] EWCA Civ 1719, [2003] 4 All ER 1358.
2   www.justice.gov.uk/downloads/courts/queens-bench/clinical-negligence-model.doc.

JOINT EXPERTS

9.25   Where two or more parties wish to submit expert evidence on a particular issue the court may direct that the evidence on that issue is to be given by a single joint expert (CPR 35.7(1)). Joint selection of an expert should be distinguished from joint instruction of an expert.

A jointly selected expert

9.26   A jointly selected expert is one who is chosen (usually by one side providing a list of proposed experts and the other side deciding whether to object to any of those named) by both sides but who is instructed by one side only. The instructing party is entirely responsible for the expert's fees and is entitled to assert legal professional privilege over the report[1].

1   *Carlson v Townsend* [2001] EWCA Civ 511.

A jointly instructed expert

9.27   A jointly instructed expert receives instructions from both sides. Both parties contribute to the expert's fees (unless the court directs otherwise) and are entitled to the expert's report.

The parties should try to agree joint instructions to single joint experts but in default of agreement, each party may give instructions. If separate instructions are given they should be copied to the other instructing parties (CPR 35.8, Guidance 37).

9.28 The use of a jointly instructed expert, in the setting of a contested clinical negligence action, may generate problems. This is particularly so if there is more than one school of thought on the central issues. In *Oxley v Penwarden*[1] the Court of Appeal overturned the decision of a circuit judge limiting evidence on causation to the instruction of a single joint expert. The court observed that: 'If there was more than one school of thought on the issues in dispute the court would effectively decide the issues without the opportunity for challenge'[2].

1 [2001] CPLR 1 (a vascular surgery case).
2 See also *Simms v Birmingham Health Authority* (2000) 58 BMLR 66 (a cerebral palsy case) in which an order for the joint instruction of a neonatologist was overturned.

9.29 In *Peet v Mid Kent Healthcare NHS Trust*[1] the Court of Appeal suggested that in clinical negligence disputes the balance between proportionality and expense could be achieved (even where the sums at stake were substantial) by allowing the parties to call their own experts on the medical issues but to direct the joint instruction of experts to deal with the non-medical issues. In reality in high-value clinical negligence cases it is still common for each party to call their own expert evidence in relation to major heads of damage such as nursing care/aids and equipment and to reserve the instruction of joint experts for less valuable heads.

1 [2001] EWCA Civ 1703, [2002] 1 WLR 210.

Communication by one party with a jointly instructed expert

9.30 Paragraph 43 of the Guidance states:

'Single joint experts should not attend any meeting or conference which is not a joint one, unless all the parties have agreed in writing or the court has directed that such a meeting may be held and who is to pay the experts' fees for the meeting'.

9.31 In *Peet v Mid Kent Healthcare NHS Trust*[1] the claimant sought permission to have a non-medical, single joint expert to attend a conference with counsel, in the absence of the other party. The Court of Appeal refused permission on the ground that all contact with a single joint expert should be transparent; the report of the joint expert would usually be the only evidence the expert would give and one party could not fairly be permitted to test it before trial without the involvement of the other party.

1 [2001] EWCA Civ 1703, [2002] 1 WLR 210.

9.32 In the recent case of *Edwards v Bruce & Hyslop*[1], the claimant's solicitors had been in contact with the single joint expert without the defendant's knowledge or consent. The defendant obtained an expert report from a different expert. The judge gave the defendant permission to rely on the new report because he concluded that there had been secret communications between the claimant's solicitors and the single joint expert which had created an unusual and unsatisfactory situation so that the single joint expert's position was no longer tenable. The claimant appealed the decision to a more senior judge. The appeal was refused.

1 [2009] EWHC 2970 (QB).

9.33   It should be noted that there is no restriction on communicating with a single joint expert, without the other party being present, for purely logistical reasons. In *Thorpe v Fellowes Solicitors LLP*[1] a jointly instructed expert, Dr C, had attempted to speak to the claimant's solicitors about the summons, and the timing of his appearance at court. The solicitors had refused to take his calls. At para 53 of the judgment Mrs Justice Sharpe said this:

'Though he [Dr C] had attempted to speak to the claimant's solicitors about the summons, and the timing of his appearance at court, they had refused to speak to him, presumably in the mistaken belief that it would not be proper for them to do so. The restrictions on one side seeing joint experts in conference to which the court referred in *Peet v Mid-Kent Healthcare Trust* [2001] EWCA Civ 1703, of course do not apply to speaking to them for what might broadly be described as logistical reasons'.

1 [2011] EWHC 61 (QB).

Challenging the report of a jointly instructed expert

9.34   In *Daniels v Walker*[1] (a case involving the joint instruction of quantum experts) the Court of Appeal gave guidance as to the approach to be adopted where one party was unhappy with the conclusions of the jointly instructed expert[2]:

(1)   where a single joint expert has been agreed by the parties and the court has directed that expert to report, a party who is unhappy with that expert's conclusions will not be permitted to call further expert evidence by way of their own expert unless it would be unjust pursuant to the overriding objective not to allow it so to do;

(2)   if, for reasons which were not 'fanciful', a party was dissatisfied it should put questions to the expert before challenging the joint report subject to the court's discretion;

(3)   in the majority of cases it would be wrong to seek permission to call new expert evidence where a modest sum was involved, since this might be disproportionate. Where substantial sums were involved it was perfectly reasonable for a party to seek its own evidence;

(4)   in the event that a party obtained its own expert report and the issue arose as to whether that evidence could be called at trial, no decision should be taken until after a meeting of the experts. Oral evidence should be given as a matter of last resort.

1 [2000] 1 WLR 1382.
2 See also *Cosgrove v Pattison* [2000] All ER (D) 2007 for factors to be taken into consideration by the court when exercising the discretion to allow additional expert evidence after a jointly instructed expert has reported.

WRITTEN QUESTIONS TO EXPERTS

9.35   CPR 35.6 makes specific provision for the further questioning, in writing, of experts whether it be an expert instructed by another party or a single joint expert appointed under CPR 35.7. Written questions may be put without the court's permission, once only, within 28 days of service of the expert's report, for the purpose only of clarification (unless the court gives permission or the other party agrees). The reply of the expert to the questions becomes part of that expert's report. In the light of the time limit for asking questions medical experts must review their counterpart's report immediately it is received. If the expert considers that any aspect of that report requires clarification in writing, it is imperative that he indicates that fact as soon as possible to the instructing solicitor and gives details of the questions to be asked.

9.36   Conversely, where a request for clarification of a medical report is properly made by one party it must be considered promptly by the other party. The CPR do not specify a time within which an answer to a request must be given, but the spirit of the rules would suggest that failure to provide an answer within a reasonable time will invoke some sanction.

9.37   If an expert fails to answer a question put to him properly the court has two sanctions: it may order that the party may not rely on the evidence of that expert or it may order that the party may not recover the fees and expenses of that expert from any other party (CPR 35.6(4)). No sanction is specifically provided in the rules to deal with failure by a jointly instructed expert to reply but such failure may reduce the evidential value of the expert's evidence.

Written questions to experts improper or excessive/onerous questioning

9.38   A failure to answer a question has to be distinguished from the situation where an expert declines to answer a question on the basis that the question does not seek to clarify his report, or is improper questioning (eg on an area of evidence which is not dealt with in his report and/or which is outside his area of expertise) or is excessive/onerous questioning. The CPR do not clarify what is meant by 'for clarification' nor on how the expert should deal with excessive or onerous questions which are tantamount to cross examination in writing. It is possible to ask about matters not in the expert's report (as long as they are within the expert's expertise) with the consent of the other side or the court's permission[1]. If in doubt, the expert should first discuss the questions with those instructing him and, if appropriate, those asking the questions. Attempts should be made to resolve the matter without recourse to the court (Guidance 67). However, if such attempt proves fruitless, then those instructing should ask the court for directions.

1 See the case of *Mutch v Allen* [2001] EWCA Civ 76.

9.39   Experts may themselves file a written request with the court for directions (Guidance 67).

Discussions between experts

9.40   Under CPR 35.12, the court may, at any stage, direct that there be discussion between the experts and the preparation of a subsequent statement for the court showing those issues which are agreed, those which are not agreed, and the reasons why. In multi track cases discussions may be face to face, but the practicalities or the proportionality principle may require discussions to be by telephone or video conference (Guidance 72).

9.41   The parties, their lawyers and experts should cooperate to produce the agenda for any discussion between experts, although primary responsibility for the preparation of the agenda should normally lie with the parties' solicitors (Guidance 73). The agenda should indicate what matters have been agreed and summarise concisely those which are in issue (Guidance 74).

9.42   Instructing solicitors must not instruct an expert to avoid reaching agreement (or to defer doing so) on any matter within the expert's competence. Experts are not permitted to accept such instructions (Guidance 75).

9.43   The parties' lawyers may only be present at discussions between experts if all the parties agree or the court so orders[1].

1 *Peet v Mid Kent Healthcare NHS Trust* [2001] EWCA Civ 1703, [2002] 1 WLR 210.

9.44   The content of the discussion between experts should not be referred to at trial unless the parties agree (CPR 35.12(4)).

9.45   At the conclusion of any discussion between experts a statement should be prepared (Guidance 77) in which the following should be set out:

(1)   a list of issues that have been agreed including, in each instance, the basis of the agreement;
(2)   a list of issues that have not been agreed including, in each instance, the basis of disagreement;
(3)   a list of any further issues that have arisen that were not included in the original agenda for discussion;
(4)   a record of further action, if any, to be taken or recommended including as appropriate the holding of further discussions between experts.

The joint statement should be agreed and signed by all the parties to the discussion as soon as practicable (Guidance 79). A statement made pursuant to CPR 35(12) is not privileged. This principle will apply to a joint statement provided for use in mediation[1].

1 *Aird v Prime Meridian Ltd* [2006] EWCA Civ 1866 '… The statement was a joint statement made pursuant to CPR r 35(12) and was not privileged. It did not acquire without prejudice status because it had been used in mediation …'.

9.46   Where experts reach agreement on an issue during discussions, the agreement shall not bind the parties unless the parties expressly agree to be bound by the agreement (CPR 35.12(5)). It is submitted that in reality there will be practical difficulties if the parties do not agree that they will be bound by any agreement. Certainly any party who is considering refusing to be bound by an agreement should give such refusal careful consideration and be able to explain their refusal should it become relevant to the issue of costs (Guidance 80).

9.47   Even if agreement is reached it is still open to the parties to challenge the factual basis upon which that agreement was reached, particularly if different facts emerge at trial. Where there is, on the face of it, a conflicting factual dispute, the better way would be to pose separate questions based on the different factual scenarios so that it is clear upon which factual basis the experts have agreed their opinion.

Attendance of experts at court

9.48   Experts instructed in cases have an obligation to attend court if called upon to do so, and accordingly should ensure that those instructing them are always aware of their dates to be avoided and take all reasonable steps to be available (Guidance 83). Experts should normally attend court without the need for the service of witness summonses, but on occasion they may be served to require attendance (CPR 34). The use of witness summonses does not affect the contractual or other obligations of the parties to pay experts' fees (Guidance 84).

Experts' fees

9.49   The primary liability to pay expert's fees is a matter of contract. While the contractual fee cannot be contingent on the outcome of the case, fees will be subject to assessment at the end of the case.

The court has the power to limit the amount of an expert's fees and expenses that the party who wishes to rely on the expert may recover from another party (CPR 35.4(4)). An expert who has caused significant expense to be incurred through flagrant disregard of his duties to the court may be ordered to pay those (recovered) fees[1].

1 *Phillips v Symes (No 2)* [2004] EWHC 2330 (Ch), [2005] 1 WLR 2043.

PRIVILEGE AND EXPERT REPORTS

9.50   Until an expert's report is disclosed to the other side, instructions to the expert as well as the report will be protected by legal professional privilege and the court will not make an order compelling disclosure[1]. By disclosing a report, whether voluntarily or pursuant to directions, a party waives privilege. Disclosing the final version of an expert's report does not waive privilege in earlier drafts of his report[2].

1 *Worrall v Reich* [1955] 1 QB 296. See the Court of Appeal judgment in *Watts v Oakley* [2006] EWCA Civ 1905.
2 *Jackson v Marley Davenport Ltd* [2004] EWCA Civ 1225, [2004] 1 WLR 2926.

9.51   As discussed at para **9.6**, an expert's report must contain a statement setting out the substance of all material instructions (whether written or oral) on the basis of which the report was written (CPR 35.10(3)). The purpose of this rule is to ensure that the factual basis upon which an expert has been instructed is transparent. What constitutes 'instructions' can have significant, practical importance. An expert's 'instructions' are not limited only to a letter of instruction but would include materials such as earlier reports and witness statements supplied to the expert as part of the instructions[1]. CPR 35.10(4) goes on to say that the court will not order disclosure of the expert's instructions or disclosure of any specific documents unless it is satisfied that there are reasonable grounds for believing the statement of instruction in the report is inaccurate or incomplete. It follows, therefore, that a party who is served with an expert's report is not allowed routinely to call for all the documents referred to in the report. Rather, that party will be entitled to do so only if there are reasonable grounds to consider that the expert's statement is inaccurate or incomplete.

1 *Lucas v Barking, Havering and Redbridge Hospitals NHS Trust* [2003] EWCA Civ 1102, [2004] 1 WLR 220.

THE CONSEQUENCES OF INSTRUCTING A SUBSTITUTE EXPERT

9.52 The consequences of instructing a substitute expert will depend on what procedural stage the litigation has reached.

In *Beck v MOD*[1] (a clinical negligence case) the claimant alleged he had received negligent treatment for a psychiatric illness. After issue of proceedings each party was given permission to rely on one psychiatrist. The direction did not name specific experts but specified only that each party could instruct one expert 'in that discipline'. The defendant instructed expert A. Subsequently the defendant lost confidence in expert A and instructed expert B. The defendant requested that the claimant be examined by B. The claimant refused to be examined unless the defendant disclosed expert A's report. The Court of Appeal held that a condition of the second examination was disclosure of expert A's report. The defendant did not need permission to rely on Dr B because of the wide wording of the order (the defendant already had an order allowing one psychiatrist and it was not limited to a named person).

At para 35 Lord Phillips said this:

'The answer in this case and in any case where a similar situation arises is … that the permission to instruct a new expert should be on terms that the report of the previous expert be disclosed. Such a course should both prevent the practice of expert shopping, and provide a claimant in the position of Mr Beck with the reassurance that the process of the court is not being abused. In this way justice will be seen to be done'.

1 [2003] EWCA Civ 1043.

9.53 *Hajigeorgiou v Vasilou*[1] was not a personal injury/clinical negligence case, but was concerned with expert evaluation of a restaurant business. The defendant relied on expert Mr A. Directions were given that each party rely on one valuation expert (unnamed).

The Court of Appeal held that, since the court order identified the experts only by their field of expertise (and not by name), the defendant required no permission from the court to change from Mr A to Mr B. For that reason the possibility of ordering disclosure of Mr A's report (as a condition of allowing the defendant to rely on Mr B) did not arise.

However, in *Hajigeorgiou* while the second part of the court's decision was obiter there was a clear decision that, where the court has a power to attach such a condition to an order, which is needed by the party changing expert, it should do so. At para 29 Dyson J said this:

'The principle established in *Beck* is important. It is an example of the way in which the court will control the conduct of litigation in general, and the giving of expert evidence in particular. Expert shopping is undesirable and, wherever possible, the court will use its powers to prevent it. It needs to be emphasised that, if a party needs the permission of the court to rely on expert witness A in place of expert witness B, the court has the power to give permission on condition that A's report is disclosed to the other party or parties, and that such condition will usually be imposed. In imposing such a condition, the court is not abrogating or emasculating legal professional privilege; it is merely saying that, if a party seeks the court's permission to rely on a substitute expert, it will be required to waive privilege in the first expert's report as a condition of being permitted to do so'.

1 [2005] EWCA Civ 236.

9.54 All of the cases considered so far concerned privileged post issue reports. In *Edwards-Tubb v JD Wetherspoon plc*[1] (a personal injury case) the claimant nominated three possible expert orthopaedic surgeons, none of which the defendant's insurers objected to, and chose one to give a report (Mr Jackson). The claimant went on to disclose a medical report from a different expert (Mr Khan) who had not been on the original list of nominees. The defendant asked the court to order the disclosure of the first report as a condition of allowing the claimant to rely on a report by someone not on the pre-action list.

The Court of Appeal held that the power to impose a condition of disclosure of an earlier report is available where the change of expert occurs pre-action as much as it is when it occurs in the course of proceedings. It is a matter of discretion, but it is a power which should ordinarily be exercised where a change occurs after the parties have embarked upon the pre action Protocol and thus engaged with each other in the process of the claim.

1 [2011] EWCA Civ 136.

9.55 The decision relied on the distinction between experts instructed to advise privately and experts instructed to give or prepare expert evidence for the purposes of proceedings. Where a party elects to take initial advice on the viability of his claim before embarking on the Protocol, the same justification does not exist for removing privilege. An expert consulted at that time, and not instructed to prepare a report for use in court, is in a different position and outside CPR 35.2.

At para 32, Hughes LJ considered the consequences of disclosure of an earlier report. He said this:

'I would draw attention to the consequences of disclosure on any earlier report. CPR 35.11 provides: "Where a party has disclosed an expert's report, any party may use that expert's report as evidence at the trial".

Without more, that means that the party to whom the earlier report is disclosed can simply put it in evidence and its author is not available to be tested. That will sometimes be perfectly appropriate. ... But there may be some cases in which it is a disproportionate consequence. The party who is abandoning reliance on the report may have good reason, especially in a serious case, for needing to test or explore the strength of its contents. Whilst it is important not unnecessarily to expand the scope of litigation or of satellite disputes, courts should, I believe, be ready in occasional cases where the circumstances genuinely require it to entertain argument that such testing will be necessary. Where, in such a case, it is necessary to do so to do justice, the court should be ready to consider requiring of the party to whom such a report is disclosed that he call the expert if he wishes to rely on it. I agree that this may occasionally generate a further need for case management, but it seems to me a necessary precaution in some cases if the party to whom the report is disclosed is not to be presented with a potentially unfair tactical advantage'.

IMMUNITY OF EXPERTS

Immunity from civil suit

9.56 Expert witnesses within the meaning of CPR 35 (those selected, instructed and paid for by a party) do not have immunity from suit for negligence or breach of contract[1]. Experts do, however, have immunity from suit in defamation.

1 *Jones v Kaney* [2011] UKSC 13.

Immunity from disciplinary proceedings

9.57 The case of *General Medical Council v Meadow*[1] concerned the immunity of an expert from disciplinary proceedings. The Court of Appeal held unanimously that a fitness to practise panel *did have* the appropriate jurisdiction and, as a result, Professor Meadow was not immune from disciplinary proceedings.

1 [2006] EWCA Civ 1390.

THE FORM AND CONTENT OF THE EXPERT'S REPORT

9.58 In clinical negligence disputes expert medical opinion may be needed:

(1) to address breach of duty of care and causation of damage;
(2) to determine the patient's condition and prognosis; and
(3) to assist in the evaluation of quantum.

9.59 There are two distinct forms of medical report:

(1) the report on liability and causation; and
(2) the report on condition and prognosis.

What follows is written from the point of view of the claimant, though the format of each type of report is appropriate for whichever side it is prepared.

Formalities

9.60 An expert's report should comply with CPR 35 PD 1 and with the Guidance for the Instruction of Experts to give Evidence in Civil Claims 2014, which are set out in full in Appendices B and C respectively of this chapter.

9.61 CPR 35 PD 3.1 requires that the expert's report should be addressed to the court and not to the party from whom the expert has received his instructions.

9.62   CPR 35 PD 3.2 states that an expert's report must:

(1)   give details of the expert's qualifications;
(2)   give details of literature or other material which the expert has relied on in making the report;
(3)   contain a statement setting out the substance of all facts and instructions given to the expert which are material to the opinions expressed in the report or upon which those opinions are based;
(4)   make clear which of the facts stated in the report are within the expert's own knowledge;
(5)   say who carried out any examination, measurement, test or experiment which the expert has used for the report, give the qualifications of that person, and say whether or not the test or experiment has been carried out under the expert's supervision;
(6)   where there is a range of opinion on the matters dealt with in the report:

  (a)   summarise the range of opinion, and
  (b)   give reasons for his own opinion;

(7)   contain a summary of the conclusions reached;
(8)   if the expert is not able to give his opinion without qualification, state the qualification; and
(9)   contain a statement that the expert:

  (a)   understands their duty to the court and has complied with that duty; and
  (b)   is aware of the requirements of Part 35, this practice direction and the Protocol for Instructions of Experts to give Evidence in Civil Claims.

9.63   An expert's report must be verified by a statement of truth. The form of the statement of truth should be as follows:

'I confirm that I have made clear which facts and matters referred to in this report are within my own knowledge and which are not. Those that are within my own knowledge I confirm to be true. The opinions I have expressed represent my true and complete professional opinions on the matters to which they refer'.

9.64   Proceedings for contempt of court may be brought against a person if he makes, or causes to be made, a false statement in a document, verified by a statement of truth, without an honest belief in its truth (CPR 32.14). Further information about statements of truth is contained in CPR 22 and the practice direction which supplements it.

9.65   As discussed in para **9.11**, it would seem prudent that the expert discloses at as early a stage as possible, any conflict of interest which he might have.

The medical report: condition and prognosis

9.66   A medical report as to condition and prognosis may be required by the claimant at the pre-issue stage if the claimant is going to make an offer to settle. Where the claimant is relying on the evidence of a medical practitioner the claimant must attach to or serve with his particulars of claim a report from a medical practitioner about the personal injuries which he alleges in his claim (CPR 35 PD 16.4(3)). Where the claimant's medical condition continues to change, an updated report may be required as litigation proceeds.

9.67 As a general principle it is sensible to avoid instructing as an expert any doctor who has treated the claimant. On occasion, by virtue of the particular injuries suffered, this may be difficult. There is, of course, no reason why one of the experts instructed on issues of liability and quantum should not also give an opinion of the present condition and prognosis of the claimant for the purpose of quantum.

9.68 No expert can properly give an opinion on the claimant's present condition and prognosis without the opportunity of an examination and, occasionally, some further investigation. Whilst the claimant usually does not object to an examination by the doctor instructed on his own behalf, it may be that an objection is taken to the medical expert nominated by the defendant to examine the claimant, or the further investigation he requires. The claimant is, however, under an obligation to afford the defendant reasonable opportunity for examination and should he decline to submit himself for examination the defendant may make an application to the court for an order staying the claimant's action until such time as he does submit to examination[1]. A claimant is not allowed to consent to an examination by anyone other than certain named experts[2].

1 *Edmeades v Thames Board Mills Ltd* [1969] 2 QB 67, [1969] 2 All ER 127, CA.
2 *Starr v National Coal Board* [1977] 1 All ER 243, CA.

9.69 As discussed at para **9.6**, an expert's report must contain a statement setting out the substance of all material instructions (whether written or oral) upon the basis of which the report was written (CPR 35.10(3)). It should summarise the facts and instructions given to the expert which are material to the opinions expressed in the expert's report or upon which those opinions are based. If the expert was instructed with the provision of draft witness statements those witness statements lose their privileged status because they form part of the expert's instructions (CPR 35.10(4)). This may cause particular problems in relation to the condition and prognosis report, since in most cases this report will be disclosed before the disclosure of factual witness statements. However, CPR 35.10(4) goes on to say that the court will not order disclosure of any specific documents unless it is satisfied that there are reasonable grounds for believing the statement of instruction in the report is inaccurate or incomplete. It is therefore important that the expert makes a full and accurate disclosure of his material instructions.

A suggested format for the condition and prognosis report

9.70 The following is suggested:

(1) typescript should be used, 1.5 or double spaced on A4 paper with 1-inch margins;
(2) the report should be addressed to the court;
(3) the title page should show:

(a)   the name of the claimant and his date of birth;

(b)   a short summary of the report;

(c)   the name, qualifications and appointment of the expert making the report;

(d)   the date and purpose of the report;

(e)   a statement of on whose behalf the report has been prepared;

(4)   a detailed list of literature or other material (eg medical records, reports, statements) upon which the opinion is based;

(5)   *the brief history*: it behoves the expert to listen to the claimant's story first. Sometimes this is clear and considerable detail is provided. In other cases the story is vague and numerous dates and events are forgotten. Any discrepancies in the history (which have not already been ironed out) should be noted separately and dealt with in conference with all the members of the team;

(6)   *the claimant's condition at the time of consultation*: the claimant's present symptoms and effect of any disability on daily living activities and work must be clearly established. It is not usual for the expert to lead the claimant when conducting the interview but it is sometimes necessary to ask specific questions because the claimant does not think to mention all relevant facts. Not infrequently, when eventually the claimant reads the report, it is returned because certain vital information has been omitted;

(7)   *the medical examination*: in addition to obtaining objective evidence of physical disability, the examination offers the expert an opportunity to assess the personality of the patient and form an opinion as to whether he is perhaps to some degree exaggerating symptoms and their effect. A qualitative assessment may be particularly important where date of knowledge and limitation issues arise;

(8)   *the investigations*: X-rays may be relevant and will always be so in orthopaedic cases. An up-to-date X-ray should be obtained if necessary. Consideration should be given to other sophisticated investigations such as CT scan and MRI. The expert should insist on seeing X-rays and must not rely on a radiologist's report. X-rays notoriously have a habit of going astray but it is usually worth persisting with requests for early films, and this is where good cooperation between expert and solicitor is often useful. The expert must say who carried out any examination test or experiment which the expert has used for the report, give the qualifications of that person and say whether or not the test or experiment has been carried out under the expert's supervision;

(9)   *the opinion*: first, it is important to establish the nature of the disability and correlate it with the claimant's symptoms. Factual statements should be made as to the likely cause of the disability without apportioning blame. An opinion has to be given on prognosis and it is likely that this will have to be stated in percentage terms. From a medical expert's point of view this is an inexact science and tends to amount to guesswork. Nevertheless, lawyers need this information when deliberating upon the quantum of damages (eg the increased risk of developing arthritis in a joint in future years) and some sort of estimate should be made, with qualifications where necessary. The accuracy of the prognosis should be stated and it should be mentioned if it is considered that a further review at some future date will be necessary;

(10) contain a statement setting out the substance of all facts and instructions given to the expert which are material to the opinions expressed in the report;

(11) contain a statement that the expert understands his duty to the court and has complied with, and will continue to comply with, that duty;

(12) contain a statement of truth.

The medical report: liability and causation

9.71 The expert instructed should have been provided with all the relevant primary material, including the witness statements of the claimant where indicated and those of other relevant witnesses. If the expert discovers that some vital document or X-ray or the like is missing, it is imperative that that fact is conveyed to the instructing solicitor as soon as possible so that steps can be taken to obtain the document and if necessary to apply to the court for an extension of time for service of the liability and causation report. Otherwise make it clear that review of opinion may be required should such information come to hand.

9.72 In some circumstances it will be advisable for the medical expert instructed to advise on liability and causation to see and examine the proposed claimant. Such examination may provide considerable assistance to the expert in assessing the demeanour and personality of the claimant, which may be important when addressing the issue of causation of damage.

9.73 The medical expert's opinion will necessarily be dependent upon the facts available to him. As the factual basis later changes or develops, so may his opinion. The expert should recognise this and qualify the opinion he expresses in his written report accordingly. This is particularly the case where he is requested to provide a written report before conference. Unless it is quite clear to the expert that there has been a breach of the duty of professional care, he is best advised to reserve his opinion until he has had the opportunity to consider more fully the matter in conference with the client and the other experts instructed at which time the facts upon which his opinion is to be based can be agreed or clearly identified.

The first-stage report

9.74 A written report is only necessary where it serves one or more of the following purposes:

(1) to apprise the lay client of the medical issues and the areas where, on the stated facts, and the accounts in the medical records, there appears to have been a departure from acceptable medical practice as it stood at the material time;

(2) to apprise, directly or indirectly, the public funding committee and/or the 'insurer';

(3) to apprise the solicitors and counsel of the essential medical issues as they appear to the expert and to give such guidance and instruction as may be thought necessary for those issues to be dealt with in an informed way in conference.

9.75   The first-stage report will not be disclosed to the other party. No particular format is essential. Adoption of the following guidance is advised:

(1)   typescript should be used, 1.5 or double spaced on A4 paper with 1-inch margins;

(2)   the report should be addressed to the court;

(3)   the title page should show:

    (a)   the name of the claimant and his date of birth;

    (b)   a short summary of the report;

    (c)   the name, qualifications and appointment of the expert making the report;

    (d)   the date and purpose of the report;

    (e)   a statement of on whose behalf the report has been prepared;

(4)   a detailed list of literature or other material (eg medical records, reports, statements) upon which the opinion is based. Do not make reference to counsel's written opinions or to conference notes;

(5)   a chronological account of the facts – as they appear from the source materials – set out such that random access may be made to any particular date or time. Frequently there will be discrepancies between the dates/times given by the lay client, his witnesses, and the various entries in the medical records. Most are likely to be of minor significance and ultimately these discrepancies should be reconciled to enable the pleadings to be consistent and to raise as few issues as possible. The lay client should not have his credibility reduced by irrational adherence to unsubstantiated dates and times, particularly where they have no or only minimal importance to the central issues in the case. The expert in this report may usefully draw attention to the chronological discrepancies and, if he so chooses, form and express a view as to the timing of the relevant events, whilst remembering that this part of the report should be reserved for the exposition of fact and not opinion;

(6)   the important events in the history should be identified and, where necessary, an account given of the relevant medical principles involved in the claimant's management. Where relevant an account of the natural history of the pathological process should be given for it often proves to be of critical importance. These are perhaps the most difficult tasks for the expert. He has to reduce his great learning and experience into simple quintessential propositions upon which his opinion will be founded. Relevant textbook authorities and learned articles should be cited and copies appended to the report for the pre-conference consideration of all those attending;

(7)   having set out the facts and the relevant fundamental medical principles, the final step is for the expert to express his opinion by formulating a conclusion on the standard and acceptability of all aspects of the care the claimant received. It is important for the expert to cover this ground widely. He should not confine his expression of opinion to those areas upon which the lay client has alighted as being the relevant areas of concern. If he has been provided with the reports from other experts it is useful for him to indicate any areas of disagreement such that these may later be explored in conference. Where there is a range of opinion on the matters dealt with by the report the expert must: (a) summarise the range of opinion; and (b) give reasons for his own opinion. Where

an opinion cannot be supported by literature, the expert should make it clear why he has reached a particular conclusion. If he has relied solely on his experience in coming to the conclusion this should be stated;

(8)   a brief curriculum vitae, including a list of publications should be included unless there are no publications relevant to the issues concerned which solicitors/counsel should have considered;

(9)   contain a statement setting out the substance of all facts and instructions given to the expert which are material to the opinions expressed in the report;

(10) contain a statement that the expert understands his duty to the court and has complied with, and will continue to comply with, that duty;

(11) contain a statement of truth.

The initial conference with counsel

9.76   The number of conferences and their timing will depend on the individual circumstances of the case. Most often an initial conference with counsel will be held at a fairly early stage to consider the merits of the case and to assist counsel with the drafting of the particulars of claim. A further conference may be needed prior to exchange of expert's reports and/or at an even later stage nearer to trial.

9.77   It may be appropriate that the experts dealing with present condition and prognosis also attend this conference. Although neither their reports nor their evidence will deal with the issues of liability and causation, those issues may well be within their area of expertise and it is absolutely essential to ensure that their views, if not expressed, accord with those of the experts primarily giving evidence on matters pertaining to liability.

9.78   Regardless of when any conference with counsel is held the expert should see the particulars of claim before that document is served in order to satisfy himself that the facts pleaded are accurate and that he can support the allegations made.

9.79   The initial conference with counsel has the following objectives:

(1)   collective analysis and interpretation of the medical records. It is frequently the case that it is only when the experts and lawyers are assembled together that the significance of entries in different parts of the notes is fully appreciated;

(2)   the identification of all the relevant medical records of which discovery is still to be given;

(3)   the resolution of (alternatively, the accounting for) discrepancies of date/time differences between the accounts of the lay client and witnesses and the dates and times recorded in the medical notes;

(4)   the clarification of other matters where lay and recorded medical accounts differ. The lay client may be convinced, for example, that he was not seen by a doctor. The notes may show he was apparently seen by a female doctor, whom in his distress he had mistaken for a nurse;

(5)   the determination of precisely what was done, assuming the medical records to be accurate;

(6)   the rationale for action/inaction at the various times in question. In the meritorious cases it is the investigation of the proposed defendant's rationale which throws into relief the negligence which hitherto would only have been suspected. The criteria for the action taken (based upon the pattern of symptoms and signs recorded in the notes and remembered by the claimant) may be such that it can be said that more timely intervention would probably have avoided the injury in respect of which complaint is made. An investigation requested may have been reported as abnormal but no notice taken of it, or, its import missed;

(7)   the identification/confirmation of the parties to the action;

(8)   the identification of the boundaries of contemporary standards of care. The conference provides the opportunity, often necessary, for the experts to be told or reminded of the relevant legal principles and the manner in which these are to be applied when looking at a particular specialist doctor's actions;

(9)   the identification of each and every negligent act and omission which the experts are prepared to support and which can be included in the particulars of claim;

(10) the limitation of the experts' expertise needs to be ascertained and other areas requiring specialist expertise identified. A decision has to be made upon whether the matter should proceed any further before this assistance is obtained;

(11) the consideration of the issues of causation. Clinical negligence cases, by their very nature, commonly give rise to issues of causation. The experts need to be reminded of the legal principles presently applicable and the extent to which they are willing and able to support the necessary causal nexus between the breach of duty alleged and the injury;

(12) the decision on the merits and the further steps to be taken;

(13) the identification of medical textbooks and learned articles upon which reliance may be placed.

9.80   It will be appreciated that by the conclusion of the initial conference with the experts the ground may have shifted appreciably from that set out in any first stage reports. An expert may be asked to amend any preliminary report in the light of the issues which it emerges are central to the case and to make other adjustments to his written opinion so as to reflect more closely the weight and tenor of the opinion he has given in conference. It is commonly the case that a view formed in the first stage (liability and causation) report requires extensive revision if not an about-turn on the opinion expressed once the expert has considered the matter more fully with the client, the other experts and the lawyers. There may also be a need for adjustment to the written report following exchange of the defence expert reports.

9.81   Where they are acquainted with the legal process, the experts will have no misgivings about making substantial changes to the report. The best time for these changes to be made is immediately after the conference when things are fresh in one's mind. It is better to persuade those experts who are unaccustomed to the legal process from committing themselves until they have had the benefit of discussing the whole matter in conference. An accurate note of the deliberations in conference may serve the dual purpose of both refreshing the experts (should there be any delay in the provision of their final reports) and counsel (should there be delay in the settling of the particulars of claim). A good attendance note may also serve as a sufficient advice (particularly if checked and endorsed by counsel) for the purpose of obtaining any requisite extension in the Public Funding Certificate. This saves counsel's time, delay and the incurrence of further and unnecessary costs in the provision of a written opinion simply reciting the advice already given in conference. Furthermore such unnecessary costs are not fairly recoverable between the parties.

The final report on liability and causation

9.82   This is the report which will be exchanged to the other side. It will be considered in great detail by the other side's expert, it will be considered in the agenda for the meeting of experts and it will be read by the judge before the trial begins. It should be written in a way which is factually accurate, logical and comprehensible.

9.83   In respect of this critical report the following corresponding guidelines are proposed:

(1)   as for the first-stage report (see para **9.74**);
(2)   as for the first-stage report;
(3)   as for the first-stage report save that it should not be apparent that the final report is one of a series. The relevant date on the final report is that upon which it was written;
(4)   a list of material relied upon as the basis for the opinion expressed should be included in the final report. As the parties should have had the benefit of exchanged witness statements before the final report is served, the list should include identification of the relevant statements;
(5)   there should be no or only small change to this section from the first stage report. However the detailed chronology should take account of:

    (a)   any revisions agreed as a consequence of the pleaded defence; the defence witness statements; the defendant's replies to requests for further information (previously further and better particulars and/or interrogatories);
    (b)   any further disclosure and inspection.

    Use page references where available. If the medical notes have not yet been paginated it is suggested that a pagination be agreed with the other side before the final report is written. Factual statements in the chronology which arise from the medical notes can be identified by reference to particular page numbers. If several experts are involved it is pointless to repeat the chronology in each report. Reference can simply be made to the report in which it has been decided the chronology should be contained. This places upon the expert assuming this responsibility the burden of ensuring that the chronology is accurate;

(6)   this should be unchanged from the first stage report. Every effort should be made to illustrate the relevant medical principles relied upon to assist in the education of the judge who may be coming to the technicalities of the case for the first time. The report is not written for the benefit of the other side's experts but for the court. It should not be assumed that medical principles and terminology will be understood

without explanation or definition. It may be necessary to append a glossary of medical terms;

(7) this remains as for the first-stage report;
(8) this remains as for the first-stage report;
(9) this remains as for the first-stage report;
(10) this remains as for the first-stage report;
(11) this remains as for the first-stage report.

Supplementary report

9.84 After mutual exchange of expert evidence the expert should be invited to consider the other side's expert evidence. A supplementary report for disclosure may be required. If any aspect of the expert's opinion has changed as a result of reading the other side's report(s) then the expert must state that that is the case in the supplementary report.

APPENDIX A

CPR Part 35 Experts and Assessors

[Reproduced with kind permission of Westlaw.]

9.85

Contents of this Part

Rule 35.1	Duty to restrict expert evidence
Rule 35.2	Interpretation and definitions
Rule 35.3	Experts – overriding duty to the court
Rule 35.4	Court's power to restrict expert evidence
Rule 35.5	General requirement for expert evidence to be given in a written report
Rule 35.6	Written questions to experts
Rule 35.7	Court's power to direct that evidence is to be given by a single joint expert
Rule 35.8	Instructions to a single joint expert
Rule 35.9	Power of court to direct a party to provide information
Rule 35.10	Contents of report
Rule 35.11	Use by one party of expert's report disclosed by another
Rule 35.12	Discussions between experts
Rule 35.13	Consequence of failure to disclose expert's report
Rule 35.14	Expert's right to ask court for directions
Rule 35.15	Assessors

35.1 Duty to restrict expert evidence

Expert evidence shall be restricted to that which is reasonably required to resolve the proceedings.

35.2 Interpretation and definitions

(1) A reference to an 'expert' in this Part is a reference to a person who has been instructed to give or prepare expert evidence for the purpose of proceedings.

(2) 'Single joint expert' means an expert instructed to prepare a report for the court on behalf of two or more of the parties (including the claimant) to the proceedings.

35.3 Experts – overriding duty to the court

(1) It is the duty of experts to help the court on the matters within their expertise.

(2) This duty overrides any obligation to the person from whom experts have received instructions or by whom they are paid.

35.4 Court's power to restrict expert evidence

(1) No party may call an expert or put in evidence an expert's report without the court's permission.

(2) When parties apply for permission they must provide an estimate of the costs of the proposed expert evidence and identify –

(a)   the field in which expert evidence is required and the issues which the expert evidence will address; and

(b)   where practicable the name of the proposed expert

(3) If permission is granted it shall be in relation only to the expert named or the field identified under paragraph (2). The order granting permission may specify the issue which the expert evidence should address.

(3A) Where a claim has been allocated to the small claims track or fast track, if permission is given for expert evidence, it will normally be given for evidence from only one expert on a particular issue.

(3B) In a soft tissue injury claim, permission –

(a)   may normally only be given for one expert medical report;

(b)   may not be given initially unless the medical report is a fixed cost medical report. Where the claimant seeks permission to obtain a further medical report, if the report is from a medical expert in any of the following disciplines –

  (i)   Consultant Orthopaedic Surgeon;

  (ii)   Consultant in Accident and Emergency Medicine;

  (iii) General Practitioner registered with the General Medical Council; or

  (iv)   Physiotherapist registered with the Health and Care Professions Council,

the report must be a fixed cost medical report.

(3C) In this rule, 'fixed cost medical report' and 'soft tissue injury claim' have the same meaning as in paragraph 1.1(10A) and (16A), respectively, of the RTA Protocol.

(Paragraph 7 of Practice Direction 35 sets out some of the circumstances the court will consider when deciding whether expert evidence should be given by a single joint expert.)

(4) The court may limit the amount of the expert's fees and expenses that the party who wishes to rely on the expert may recover from any other party.

35.5 General requirement for expert evidence to be given in a written report

(1) Expert evidence is to be given in a written report unless the court directs otherwise.

(2) If a claim is on the small claims track or the fast track, the court will not direct an expert to attend a hearing unless it is necessary to do so in the interests of justice.

35.6 Written questions to experts

(1) A party may put written questions about an expert's report (which must be proportionate) to –

(a)   an expert instructed by another party; or
(b)   a single joint expert appointed under rule 35.7.

(2) Written questions under paragraph (1) –

(a)   may be put once only;
(b)   must be put within 28 days of service of the expert's report; and
(c)   must be for the purpose only of clarification of the report,
unless in any case,

(i)   the court gives permission; or
(ii)   the other party agrees.

(3) An expert's answers to questions put in accordance with paragraph (1) shall be treated as part of the expert's report.

(4) Where –

(a)   a party has put a written question to an expert instructed by another party; and
(b)   the expert does not answer that question,

the court may make one or both of the following orders in relation to the party who instructed the expert –

(i)   that the party may not rely on the evidence of that expert; or
(ii)   that the party may not recover the fees and expenses of that expert from any other party.

35.7 Court's power to direct that evidence is to be given by a single joint expert

(1) Where two or more parties wish to submit expert evidence on a particular issue, the court may direct that the evidence on that issue is to be given by a single joint expert.

(2) Where the parties who wish to submit the evidence ('the relevant parties') cannot agree who should be the single expert, the court may –

(a)   select the expert from a list prepared or identified by the relevant parties; or

(b)   direct that the expert be selected in such other manner as the court may direct.

35.8 Instructions to a single joint expert

(1) Where the court gives a direction under rule 35.7 for a single joint expert to be used, any relevant party may give instructions to the expert.

(2) When a party gives instructions to the expert that party must, at the same time, send a copy to the other relevant parties.

(3) The court may give directions about –

(a)   the payment of the expert's fees and expenses; and

(b)   any inspection, examination or experiments which the expert wishes to carry out.

(4) The court may, before an expert is instructed –

(a)   limit the amount that can be paid by way of fees and expenses to the expert; and

(b)   direct that some or all of the relevant parties pay that amount into court.

(5) Unless the court otherwise directs, the instructing parties are jointly and severally liable for the payment of the expert's fees and expenses.

35.9 Power of court to direct a party to provide information

Where a party has access to information which is not reasonably available to another party, the court may direct the party who has access to the information to –

(a)   prepare and file a document recording the information; and

(b)   serve a copy of that document on the other party.

35.10 Contents of report

(1) An expert's report must comply with the requirements set out in Practice Direction 35.

(2) At the end of an expert's report there must be a statement that the expert understands and has complied with their duty to the court.

(3) The expert's report must state the substance of all material instructions, whether written or oral, on the basis of which the report was written.

(4) The instructions referred to in paragraph (3) shall not be privileged (GL) against disclosure but the court will not, in relation to those instructions –

(a) order disclosure of any specific document; or
(b) permit any questioning in court, other than by the party who instructed the expert,

unless it is satisfied that there are reasonable grounds to consider the statement of instructions given under paragraph (3) to be inaccurate or incomplete.

35.11 Use by one party of expert's report disclosed by another

Where a party has disclosed an expert's report, any party may use that expert's report as evidence at the trial.

35.12 Discussions between experts

(1) The court may, at any stage, direct a discussion between experts for the purpose of requiring the experts to –

(a) identify and discuss the expert issues in the proceedings; and
(b) where possible, reach an agreed opinion on those issues.

(2) The court may specify the issues which the experts must discuss.

(3) The court may direct that following a discussion between the experts they must prepare a statement for the court setting out those issues on which –

(a) they agree; and
(b) they disagree with a summary of their reasons for disagreeing.

(4) The content of the discussion between the experts shall not be referred to at the trial unless the parties agree.

(5) Where experts reach agreement on an issue during their discussions, the agreement shall not bind the parties unless the parties expressly agree to be bound by the agreement.

35.13 Consequence of failure to disclose expert's report

A party who fails to disclose an expert's report may not use the report at the trial or call the expert to give evidence orally unless the court gives permission.

35.14 Expert's right to ask court for directions

(1) Experts may file written requests for directions for the purpose of assisting them in carrying out their function.

(2) Experts must, unless the court orders otherwise, provide copies of the proposed request for directions under paragraph (1) –

(a)   to the party instructing him, at least 7 days before they file the requests; and

(b)   to all other parties, at least 4 days before they file them.

(3) The court, when it gives directions, may also direct that a party be served with a copy of the directions.

35.15 Assessors

(1) This rule applies where the court appoints one or more persons (an 'assessor') under section 70 of the Senior Courts Act 1981 or section 63 of the County Courts Act 1984.

(2) An assessor will assist the court in dealing with a matter in which the assessor has skill and experience.

(3) An assessor will take such part in the proceedings as the court may direct and in particular the court may direct an assessor to –

(a)   prepare a report for the court on any matter at issue in the proceedings; and

(b)   attend the whole or any part of the trial to advise the court on any such matter.

(4) If an assessor prepares a report for the court before the trial has begun –

(a)   the court will send a copy to each of the parties; and

(b)   the parties may use it at trial.

(5) The remuneration to be paid to the assessor for his services shall be determined by the court and will form part of the costs of the proceedings.

(6) The court may order any party to deposit in the court office a specified sum in respect of the assessor's fees and, where it does so, the assessor will not be asked to act until the sum has been deposited.

(7) Paragraphs (5) and (6) do not apply where the remuneration of the assessor is to be paid out of money provided by Parliament.

APPENDIX B CPR 35 PD: EXPERTS AND ASSESSORS

9.86   This Practice Direction supplements CPR Part 35

1. Part 35 is intended to limit the use of oral expert evidence to that which is reasonably required. In addition, where possible, matters requiring expert evidence should be dealt with by only one expert. Experts and those instructing them are expected to have regard to the guidance contained in the Guidance for the Instruction of Experts in Civil Claims 2014.

(Further guidance on experts is contained in Annex C to the Practice Direction (Pre-Action Conduct)).

35 PD.2 Expert Evidence – General Requirements

2.1 Expert evidence should be the independent product of the expert uninfluenced by the pressures of litigation.

2.2 Experts should assist the court by providing objective, unbiased opinions on matters within their expertise, and should not assume the role of an advocate.

2.3 Experts should consider all material facts, including those which might detract from their opinions.

2.4 Experts should make it clear –

(a) when a question or issue falls outside their expertise; and
(b) when they are not able to reach a definite opinion, for example because they have insufficient information.

2.5 If, after producing a report, an expert's view changes on any material matter, such change of view should be communicated to all the parties without delay, and when appropriate to the court.

2.6

(1) In a soft tissue injury claim, where permission is given for a fixed cost medical report, the first report must be obtained from an accredited medical expert selected via the MedCo Portal (website at: www.medco. org.uk).
(2) The cost of obtaining a further report from an expert not listed in rule 35.4(3C)(a) to (d) is not subject to rules 45.19(2A)(b) or 45.29I(2A)(b), but the use of that expert and the cost must be justified.
(3) 'Accredited medical expert', 'fixed cost medical report', 'MedCo', and 'soft tissue injury claim' have the same meaning as in paragraph 1.1(A1), (10A), (12A) and (16A), respectively, of the RTA Protocol.

35 PD.3 Form and Content of an Expert's Report

3.1 An expert's report should be addressed to the court and not to the party from whom the expert has received instructions.

3.2 An expert's report must:

(1) give details of the expert's qualifications;
(2) give details of any literature or other material which has been relied on in making the report;
(3) contain a statement setting out the substance of all facts and instructions which are material to the opinions expressed in the report or upon which those opinions are based;
(4) make clear which of the facts stated in the report are within the expert's own knowledge;

(5) say who carried out any examination, measurement, test or experiment which the expert has used for the report, give the qualifications of that person, and say whether or not the test or experiment has been carried out under the expert's supervision;

(6) where there is a range of opinion on the matters dealt with in the report –

   (a) summarise the range of opinions; and
   (b) give reasons for the expert's own opinion;

(7) contain a summary of the conclusions reached;

(8) if the expert is not able to give an opinion without qualification, state the qualification; and

(9) contain a statement that the expert –

   (a) understands their duty to the court, and has complied with that duty; and
   (b) is aware of the requirements of Part 35, this practice direction and the Guidance for the Instruction of Experts in Civil Claims 2014.

3.3 An expert's report must be verified by a statement of truth in the following form-

'I confirm that I have made clear which facts and matters referred to in this report are within my own knowledge and which are not. Those that are within my own knowledge I confirm to be true. The opinions I have expressed represent my true and complete professional opinions on the matters to which they refer'.

(Part 22 deals with statements of truth. Rule 32.14 sets out the consequences of verifying a document containing a false statement without an honest belief in its truth.)

35 PD.4 Information

4. Under rule 35.9 the court may direct a party with access to information, which is not reasonably available to another party to serve on that other party a document, which records the information. The document served must include sufficient details of all the facts, tests, experiments and assumptions which underlie any part of the information to enable the party on whom it is served to make, or to obtain, a proper interpretation of the information and an assessment of its significance.

35 PD.5 Instructions

5. Cross-examination of experts on the contents of their instructions will not be allowed unless the court permits it (or unless the party who gave the instructions consents). Before it gives permission the court must be satisfied that there are reasonable grounds to consider that the statement in the report of the substance of the instructions is inaccurate or incomplete. If the court is so satisfied, it will allow the cross-examination where it appears to be in the interests of justice.

35 PD 6 Questions to Experts

6.1 Where a party sends a written question or questions under rule 35.6 direct to an expert, a copy of the questions must, at the same time, be sent to the other party or parties.

6.2 The party or parties instructing the expert must pay any fees charged by that expert for answering questions put under rule 35.6. This does not affect any decision of the court as to the party who is ultimately to bear the expert's fees.

35 PD.7 Single joint expert

7. When considering whether to give permission for the parties to rely on expert evidence and whether that evidence should be from a single joint expert the court will take into account all the circumstances in particular, whether:

(a) it is proportionate to have separate experts for each party on a particular issue with reference to –

   (i)   the amount in dispute;
   (ii)   the importance to the parties; and
   (iii) the complexity of the issue;

(b) the instruction of a single joint expert is likely to assist the parties and the court to resolve the issue more speedily and in a more cost-effective way than separately instructed experts;

(c) expert evidence is to be given on the issue of liability, causation or quantum;

(d) the expert evidence falls within a substantially established area of knowledge which is unlikely to be in dispute or there is likely to be a range of expert opinion;

(e) a party has already instructed an expert on the issue in question and whether or not that was done in compliance with any practice direction or relevant pre-action protocol;

(f) questions put in accordance with rule 35.6 are likely to remove the need for the other party to instruct an expert if one party has already instructed an expert;

(g) questions put to a single joint expert may not conclusively deal with all issues that may require testing prior to trial;

(h) a conference may be required with the legal representatives, experts and other witnesses which may make instruction of a single joint expert impractical; and

(i) a claim to privilege makes the instruction of any expert as a single joint expert inappropriate.

35 PD.8 Orders

8. Where an order requires an act to be done by an expert, or otherwise affects an expert, the party instructing that expert must serve a copy of the order on the expert. The claimant must serve the order on a single joint expert.

35 PD.9 Discussions between experts

9.1 Unless directed by the court discussions between experts are not mandatory. Parties must consider, with their experts, at an early stage, whether there is likely to be any useful purpose in holding an expert's discussion and if so when.

9.2 The purpose of discussions between experts is not for experts to settle cases but to agree and narrow issues and in particular to identify:

(i)   the extent of the agreement between them;
(ii)   the points of and short reasons for any disagreement;
(iii)   action, if any, which may be taken to resolve any outstanding points of disagreement; and
(iv)   any further material issues not raised and the extent to which these issues are agreed.

9.3 Where the experts are to meet, the parties must discuss and if possible agree whether an agenda is necessary, and if so attempt to agree one that helps the experts to focus on the issues which need to be discussed. The agenda must not be in the form of leading questions or hostile in tone.

9.4 Unless ordered by the court, or agreed by all parties, and the experts, neither the parties nor their legal representatives may attend experts discussions.

9.5 If the legal representatives do attend –

(i)   they should not normally intervene in the discussion, except to answer questions put to them by the experts or to advise on the law; and
(ii)   the experts may if they so wish hold part of their discussions in the absence of the legal representatives.

9.6 A statement must be prepared by the experts dealing with paragraphs 9.2(i)–(iv) above. Individual copies of the statements must be signed by the experts at the conclusion of the discussion, or as soon thereafter as practicable, and in any event within 7 days. Copies of the statements must be provided to the parties no later than 14 days after signing.

9.7 Experts must give their own opinions to assist the court and do not require the authority of the parties to sign a joint statement.

9.8 If an expert significantly alters an opinion, the joint statement must include a note or addendum by that expert explaining the change of opinion.

35 PD.10 Assessors

10.1. An assessor may be appointed to assist the court under rule 35.15. Not less than 21 days before making any such appointment, the court will notify each party in writing of the name of the proposed assessor, of the matter in respect of which the assistance of the assessor will be sought and of the qualifications of the assessor to give that assistance.

10.2. Where any person has been proposed for appointment as an assessor, any party may object to that person either personally or in respect of that person's qualification.

10.3. Any such objection must be made in writing and filed with the court within 7 days of receipt of the notification referred to in paragraph 10.1 and will be taken into account by the court in deciding whether or not to make the appointment.

10.4. Copies of any report prepared by the assessor will be sent to each of the parties but the assessor will not give oral evidence or be open to cross-examination or questioning.

35 PD.11 Concurrent expert evidence

11.1 At any stage in the proceedings the court may direct that some or all of the experts from like disciplines shall give their evidence concurrently. The following procedure shall then apply.

11.2 The court may direct that the parties agree an agenda for the taking of concurrent evidence, based upon the areas of disagreement identified in the experts' joint statements made pursuant to rule 35.12 .

11.3 At the appropriate time the relevant experts will each take the oath or affirm. Unless the court orders otherwise, the experts will then address the items on the agenda in the manner set out in paragraph 11.4.

11.4 In relation to each issue on the agenda, and subject to the judge's discretion to modify the procedure –

(1)   the judge may initiate the discussion by asking the experts, in turn, for their views. Once an expert has expressed a view the judge may ask questions about it. At one or more appropriate stages when questioning a particular expert, the judge may invite the other expert to comment or to ask that expert's own questions of the first expert;
(2)   after the process set out in (1) has been completed for all the experts, the parties' representatives may ask questions of them. While such questioning may be designed to test the correctness of an expert's view, or seek clarification of it, it should not cover ground which has been fully explored already. In general a full cross-examination or re-examination is neither necessary nor appropriate; and
(3)   after the process set out in (2) has been completed, the judge may summarise the experts' different positions on the issue and ask them to confirm or correct that summary.

APPENDIX C GUIDANCE FOR THE INSTRUCTION OF EXPERTS TO GIVE EVIDENCE IN CIVIL CLAIMS 2014

Introduction

9.87   1. The purpose of this guidance is to assist litigants, those instructing experts and experts to understand best practice in complying with Part 35 of the Civil Procedure Rules (CPR) and court orders. Experts and those who instruct them should ensure they are familiar with CPR 35 and the Practice Direction (PD35). This guidance replaces the Protocol for the instruction of experts in civil claims (2005, amended 2009).

2. Those instructing experts, and the experts, must also have regard to the objectives underpinning the Pre-Action Protocols to:

a   encourage the exchange of early and full information about the expert issues involved in the prospective claim;

b   enable the parties to avoid or reduce the scope of the litigation by agreeing the whole or part of an expert issue before proceedings are started; and

c   support the efficient management of proceedings where litigation cannot be avoided.

3. Additionally, experts and those instructing them should be aware that some cases will be governed by the specific pre-action protocols and some may be 'specialist proceedings' (CPR 49) where specific rules may apply.

Selecting and instructing experts

The need for experts

4. Those intending to instruct experts to give or prepare evidence for the purpose of civil proceedings should consider whether expert evidence is necessary, taking account of the principles set out in CPR Parts 1 and 35, and in particular whether 'it is required to resolve the proceedings' (CPR 35.1).

5. Although the court's permission is not generally required to instruct an expert, the court's permission is required before an expert's report can be relied upon or an expert can be called to give oral evidence (CPR 35.4).

6. Advice from an expert before proceedings are started which the parties do not intend to rely upon in litigation is likely to be confidential; this guidance does not apply then. The same applies where, after the commencement of proceedings, experts are instructed only to advise (eg to comment upon a single joint expert's report) and not to prepare evidence for the proceedings. The expert's role then is that of an expert advisor.

7. However this guidance does apply if experts who were formerly instructed only to advise, are later instructed as an expert witness to prepare or give evidence in the proceedings.

8. In the remainder of this guidance, a reference to an expert means an expert witness to whom Part 35 applies.

Duties and obligations of experts

9. Experts always owe a duty to exercise reasonable skill and care to those instructing them, and to comply with any relevant professional code. However when they are instructed to give or prepare evidence for civil proceedings they have an overriding duty to help the court on matters within their expertise (CPR 35.3). This duty overrides any obligation to the person instructing or paying them. Experts must not serve the exclusive interest of those who retain them.

10. Experts should be aware of the overriding objective that courts deal with cases justly and that they are under an obligation to assist the court in this respect. This includes dealing with cases proportionately (keeping the work and costs in proportion to the value and importance of the case to the parties), expeditiously and fairly (CPR 1.1).

11. Experts must provide opinions that are independent, regardless of the pressures of litigation. A useful test of 'independence' is that the expert would express the same opinion if given the same instructions by another party. Experts should not take it upon themselves to promote the point of view of the party instructing them or engage in the role of advocates or mediators.

12. Experts should confine their opinions to matters which are material to the disputes and provide opinions only in relation to matters which lie within their expertise. Experts should indicate without delay where particular questions or issues fall outside their expertise.

13. Experts should take into account all material facts before them. Their reports should set out those facts and any literature or material on which they have relied in forming their opinions. They should indicate if an opinion is provisional, or qualified, or where they consider that further information is required or if, for any other reason, they are not satisfied that an opinion can be expressed finally and without qualification.

14. Experts should inform those instructing them without delay of any change in their opinions on any material matter and the reasons for this (see also paragraphs 64–66).

15. Experts should be aware that any failure to comply with the rules or court orders, or any excessive delay for which they are responsible, may result in the parties who instructed them being penalised in costs, or debarred from relying upon the expert evidence (see also paragraphs 89–92).

The appointment of experts

16. Before experts are instructed or the court's permission to appoint named experts is sought, it should be established whether the experts:

a   have the appropriate expertise and experience for the particular instruction;
b   are familiar with the general duties of an expert;
c   can produce a report, deal with questions and have discussions with other experts within a reasonable time, and at a cost proportionate to the matters in issue;
d   are available to attend the trial, if attendance is required; and
e   have no potential conflict of interest.

17. Terms of appointment should be agreed at the outset and should normally include:

a   the capacity in which the expert is to be appointed (eg party appointed expert or single joint expert);

b   the services required of the expert (eg provision of an expert's report, answering questions in writing, attendance at meetings and attendance at court);

c   time for delivery of the report;

d   the basis of the expert's charges (eg daily or hourly rates and an estimate of the time likely to be required, or a fixed fee for the services). Parties must provide an estimate to the court of the costs of the proposed expert evidence and for each stage of the proceedings (CPR 35.4(2));

e   travelling expenses and disbursements;

f   cancellation charges;

g   any fees for attending court;

h   time for making the payment;

i   whether fees are to be paid by a third party;

j   if a party is publicly funded, whether the expert's charges will be subject to assessment; and

k   guidance that the expert's fees and expenses may be limited by the court (note expert's recoverable fees in the small claims track cannot exceed £750: see PD 27 paragraph 7).

18. When necessary, arrangements should be made for dealing with questions to experts and discussions between experts, including any directions given by the court.

19. Experts should be kept informed about deadlines for all matters concerning them. Those instructing experts should send them promptly copies of all court orders and directions that may affect the preparation of their reports or any other matters concerning their obligations.

Instructions

20. Those instructing experts should ensure that they give clear instructions (and attach relevant documents), including the following:

a   basic information, such as names, addresses, telephone numbers, dates of incidents and any relevant claim reference numbers;

b   the nature of the expertise required;

c   the purpose of the advice or report, a description of the matter(s) to be investigated, the issues to be addressed and the identity of all parties;

d   the statement(s) of case (if any), those documents which form part of disclosure and witness statements and expert reports that are relevant to the advice or report, making clear which have been served and which are drafts and when the latter are likely to be served;

e   where proceedings have not been started, whether they are contemplated and, if so, whether the expert is being asked only for advice;

f   an outline programme, consistent with good case management and the expert's availability, for the completion and delivery of each stage of the expert's work; and

g   where proceedings have been started, the dates of any hearings (including any case/costs management conferences and/or pre-trial reviews), the dates fixed by the court or agreed between the parties for the exchange of experts' reports and any other relevant deadlines to be adhered to, the name of the court, the claim number, the track to which the claim has been allocated and whether there is a specific budget for the experts' fees.

21. Those instructing experts should seek to agree, where practicable, the instructions for the experts, and that they receive the same factual material.

Acceptance of instructions

22. Experts should confirm without delay whether they accept their instructions.

23. They should also inform those instructing them (whether on initial instruction or at any later stage) without delay if:

a   instructions are not acceptable because, for example, they require work that falls outside their expertise, impose unrealistic deadlines, or are insufficiently clear. Experts who do not receive clear instructions should request clarification and may indicate that they are not prepared to act unless and until such clear instructions are received;

b   they consider that instructions are insufficient to complete the work;

c   they become aware that they may not be able to fulfil any of the terms of appointment;

d   the instructions and/or work have, for any reason, placed them in conflict with their duties as an expert. Where an expert advisor is approached to act as an expert witness they will need to consider carefully whether they can accept a role as expert witness; or

e   they are not satisfied that they can comply with any orders that have been made.

24. Experts must neither express an opinion outside the scope of their field of expertise, nor accept any instructions to do so.

25. Where an expert identifies that the basis of his instruction differs from that of another expert, he should inform those instructing him.

26. Experts should agree the terms on which they are to be paid with those instructing them. Experts should be aware that they will be required to provide estimates for the court and that the court may limit the amount to be paid as part of any order for budgeted costs (CPR 35.4(2) and (4) and 3.15).

Experts' withdrawal

27. Where experts' instructions are incompatible with their duties, through incompleteness, a conflict between their duty to the court and their instructions, or for any other reason, the experts may consider withdrawing from the case. However, experts should not do so without first discussing the position with those who instruct them and considering whether it would be more appropriate to make a written request for directions from the court. If experts do withdraw, they must give formal written notice to those instructing them.

Experts' right to ask court for directions

28. Experts may request directions from the court to assist them in carrying out their functions (CPR 35.14), for example, if experts consider that they have not been provided with information they require. Experts should normally discuss this with those who instruct them before making a request. Unless the court otherwise orders, any proposed request for directions should be sent to the party instructing the expert at least seven days before filing any request with the court, and to all other parties at least four days before filing it.

29. Requests to the court for directions should be made by letter clearly marked 'expert's request for directions' containing:

a   the title of the claim;
b   the claim number;
c   the name of the expert;
d   why directions are sought; and
e   copies of any relevant documentation.

Experts' access to information held by the parties

30. Experts should try to ensure that they have access to all relevant information held by the parties, and that the same information has been disclosed to each expert in the same discipline. Experts should seek to confirm this soon after accepting instructions, notifying instructing solicitors of any omissions.

31. If a solicitor sends an expert additional documents before the report is finalised the solicitor must tell the expert whether any witness statements or expert reports are updated versions of those previously sent and whether they have been filed and served.

32. Experts should be specifically aware of CPR 35.9. This provides that, where one party has access to information that is not readily available to the other party, the court may direct the party who has access to the information to prepare, file and copy to the other party a document recording the information. If experts require such information which has not been disclosed, they should discuss the position with those instructing them without delay, so that a request for the information can be made, and, if not forthcoming, an application can be made to the court.

33. Any request for further information from the other party made by an expert should be in a letter to the expert's instructing party and should state why the information is necessary and the significance in relation to the expert issues in the case.

Single joint experts

34. CPR 35.7–8 and PD 35 paragraph 7 deal with the instruction and use of joint experts by the parties and the powers of the court to order their use. The CPR encourage the use of joint experts. Wherever possible a joint report

should be obtained. Single joint experts are the norm in cases allocated to the small claims track and the fast track.

35. In the early stages of a dispute, when investigations, tests, site inspections, photographs, plans or other similar preliminary expert tasks are necessary, consideration should be given to the instruction of a single joint expert, especially where such matters are not expected to be contentious. The objective should be to agree or to narrow issues.

36. Experts who have previously advised a party (whether in the same case or otherwise) should only be proposed as single joint experts if the other parties are given all relevant information about the previous involvement.

37. The appointment of a single joint expert does not prevent parties from instructing their own experts to advise (but the cost of such expert advisors will not be recoverable from another party).

Joint instructions

38. The parties should try to agree joint instructions to single joint experts, but in default of agreement, each party may give instructions. In particular, all parties should try to agree what documents should be included with instructions and what assumptions single joint experts should make.

39. Where the parties fail to agree joint instructions, they should try to agree where the areas of disagreement lie and their instructions should make this clear. If separate instructions are given, they should be copied to the other instructing parties.

40. Where experts are instructed by two or more parties, the terms of appointment should, unless the court has directed otherwise, or the parties have agreed otherwise, include:

a   a statement that all the instructing parties are jointly and severally liable to pay the experts' fees and, accordingly, that experts' invoices should be sent simultaneously to all instructing parties or their solicitors (as appropriate); and

b   a copy of any order limiting experts' fees and expenses (CPR 35.8(4)(a)).

41. Where instructions have not been received by the expert from one or more of the instructing parties, the expert should give notice (normally at least 7 days) of a deadline for their receipt. Unless the instructions are received within the deadline the expert may begin work. If instructions are received after the deadline but before the completion of the report the expert should consider whether it is practicable to comply without adversely affecting the timetable for delivery of the report and without greatly increasing the costs and exceeding any court approved budget. An expert who decides to issue a report without taking into account instructions received after the deadline must inform the parties, who may apply to the court for directions. In either event the report must show clearly that the expert did not receive instructions within the deadline, or, as the case may be, at all.

Conduct of the single joint expert

42. Single joint experts should keep all instructing parties informed of any material steps that they may be taking by, for example, copying all correspondence to those instructing them.

43. Single joint experts are Part 35 experts and so have an overriding duty to the court. They are the parties' appointed experts and therefore owe an equal duty to all parties. They should maintain independence, impartiality and transparency at all times.

44. Single joint experts should not attend a meeting or conference that is not a joint one, unless all the parties have agreed in writing or the court has directed that such a meeting may be held. There also needs to be agreement about who is to pay the experts' fees for the meeting.

45. Single joint experts may request directions from the court (see paragraphs 28–29).

46. Single joint experts should serve their reports simultaneously on all instructing parties. They should provide a single report even though they may have received instructions that contain conflicts. If conflicting instructions lead to different opinions (for example, because the instructions require the expert to make different assumptions of fact), reports may need to contain more than one set of opinions on any issue. It is for the court to determine the facts.

Cross-examination of the single joint expert

47. Single joint experts do not normally give oral evidence at trial but if they do, all parties may ask questions. In general, written questions (CPR 35.6) should be put to single joint experts before requests are made for them to attend court for the purpose of cross-examination.

Experts' reports

48. The content of experts' reports should be governed by their instructions and general obligations, any court directions, CPR 35 and PD35, and the experts' overriding duty to the court.

49. In preparing reports, experts should maintain professional objectivity and impartiality at all times.

50. PD 35, paragraph 3.1 provides that experts' reports should be addressed to the court and gives detailed directions about their form and content. All experts and those who instruct them should ensure that they are familiar with these requirements.

51. Model forms of experts' reports are available from bodies such as the Academy of Experts and the Expert Witness Institute and a template for medical reports has been created by the Ministry of Justice.

52. Experts' reports must contain statements that they:

a   understand their duty to the court and have complied and will continue to comply with it; and

b   are aware of and have complied with the requirements of CPR 35 and PD 35 and this guidance.

53. Experts' reports must also be verified by a statement of truth. The form of the statement of truth is:

'I confirm that I have made clear which facts and matters referred to in this report are within my own knowledge and which are not. Those that are within my own knowledge I confirm to be true. The opinions I have expressed represent my true and complete professional opinions on the matters to which they refer.'

54. The details of experts' qualifications in reports should be commensurate with the nature and complexity of the case. It may be sufficient to state any academic and professional qualifications. However, where highly specialised expertise is called for, experts should include the detail of particular training and/or experience that qualifies them to provide that specialised evidence.

55. The mandatory statement of the substance of all material instructions should not be incomplete or otherwise tend to mislead. The imperative is transparency. The term 'instructions' includes all material that solicitors send to experts. These should be listed, with dates, in the report or an appendix. The omission from the statement of 'off-the-record' oral instructions is not permitted. Courts may allow cross-examination about the instructions if there are reasonable grounds to consider that the statement may be inaccurate or incomplete.

56. Where tests of a scientific or technical nature have been carried out, experts should state:

a   the methodology used; and

b   by whom the tests were undertaken and under whose supervision, summarising their respective qualifications and experience.

57. When addressing questions of fact and opinion, experts should keep the two separate. Experts must state those facts (whether assumed or otherwise) upon which their opinions are based; experts should have primary regard to their instructions (paragraphs 20–25 above). Experts must distinguish clearly between those facts that they know to be true and those facts which they assume.

58. Where there are material facts in dispute experts should express separate opinions on each hypothesis put forward. They should not express a view in favour of one or other disputed version of the facts unless, as a result of particular expertise and experience, they consider one set of facts as being improbable or less probable, in which case they may express that view and should give reasons for holding it.

59. If the mandatory summary of the range of opinion is based on published sources, experts should explain those sources and, where appropriate, state the qualifications of the originator(s) of the opinions from which they differ, particularly if such opinions represent a well-established school of thought.

60. Where there is no available source for the range of opinion, experts may need to express opinions on what they believe to be the range that other experts would arrive at if asked. In those circumstances, experts should make it clear that the range that they summarise is based on their own judgement and explain the basis of that judgement.

Prior to service of reports

61. Before filing and serving an expert's report solicitors must check that any witness statements and other experts' reports relied upon by the expert are the final served versions.

Conclusions of reports

62. A summary of conclusions is mandatory. Generally the summary should be at the end of the report after the reasoning. There may be cases, however, where the court would find it helpful to have a short summary at the beginning, with the full conclusions at the end. For example, in cases involving highly complex matters which fall outside the general knowledge of the court the judge may be assisted in the comprehension of the facts and analysis if the report explains at the outset the basis of the reasoning.

Sequential exchange of experts' reports

63. Where there is to be sequential exchange of reports then the defendant's expert's report usually will be produced in response to the claimant's. The defendant's report should then:

a   confirm whether the background set out in the claimant's expert report is agreed, or identify those parts that in the defendant's expert's view require revision, setting out the necessary revisions. The defendant's expert need not repeat information that is adequately dealt with in the claimant's expert report;

b   focus only on those material areas of difference with the claimant's expert's opinion. The defendant's report should identify those assumptions of the claimant's expert that they consider reasonable (and agree with) and those that they do not; and

c   in particular where the experts are addressing the financial value of heads of claim (for example, the costs of a care regime or loss of profits), the defendant's report should contain a reconciliation between the claimant's expert's loss assessment and the defendant's, identifying for each assumption any different conclusion to the claimant's expert.

Amendment of reports

64. It may become necessary for experts to amend their reports:

a   as a result of an exchange of questions and answers;

b   following agreements reached at meetings between experts; or

c   where further evidence or documentation is disclosed.

65. Experts should not be asked to amend, expand or alter any parts of reports in a manner which distorts their true opinion, but may be invited to do so to ensure accuracy, clarity, internal consistency, completeness and relevance to the issues. Although experts should generally follow the recommendations of solicitors with regard to the form of reports, they should form their own independent views on the opinions and contents of their reports and not include any suggestions that do not accord with their views.

66. Where experts change their opinion following a meeting of experts, a signed and dated note to that effect is generally sufficient. Where experts significantly alter their opinion, as a result of new evidence or for any other reason, they must inform those who instruct them and amend their reports explaining the reasons. Those instructing experts should inform other parties as soon as possible of any change of opinion.

Written questions to experts

67. Experts have a duty to provide answers to questions properly put. Where they fail to do so, the court may impose sanctions against the party instructing the expert, and, if there is continued non-compliance, debar a party from relying on the report. Experts should copy their answers to those instructing them.

68. Experts' answers to questions become part of their reports. They are covered by the statement of truth, and form part of the expert evidence.

69. Where experts believe that questions put are not properly directed to the clarification of the report, or have been asked out of time, they should discuss the questions with those instructing them and, if appropriate, those asking the questions. Attempts should be made to resolve such problems without the need for an application to the court for directions, but in the absence of agreement or application for directions by the party or parties, experts may themselves file a written request to court for directions (see paragraphs 28–29).

Discussions between experts

70. The court has the power to direct discussions between experts for the purposes set out in the Rules (CPR 35.12). Parties may also agree that discussions take place between their experts at any stage. Discussions are not mandatory unless ordered by the court.

71. The purpose of discussions between experts should be, wherever possible, to:

a   identify and discuss the expert issues in the proceedings;
b   reach agreed opinions on those issues, and, if that is not possible, narrow the issues;
c   identify those issues on which they agree and disagree and summarise their reasons for disagreement on any issue; and

d   identify what action, if any, may be taken to resolve any of the outstanding issues between the parties.

They are not to seek to settle the proceedings.

72. Where single joint experts have been instructed but parties have, with the permission of the court, instructed their own additional Part 35 experts, there may, if the court so orders or the parties agree, be discussions between the single joint experts and the additional Part 35 experts. Such discussions should be confined to those matters within the remit of the additional Part 35 experts or as ordered by the court.

73. Where there is sequential exchange of expert reports, with the defendant's expert's report prepared in accordance with the guidance at paragraph 63 above, the joint statement should focus upon the areas of disagreement, save for the need for the claimant's expert to consider and respond to material, information and commentary included within the defendant's expert's report.

74. Arrangements for discussions between experts should be proportionate to the value of cases. In small claims and fast-tracks cases there should not normally be face to face meetings between experts: telephone discussion or an exchange of letters should usually suffice. In multi-track cases discussion may be face to face but the practicalities or the proportionality principle may require discussions to be by telephone or video-conference.

75. In multi-track cases the parties, their lawyers and experts should cooperate to produce an agenda for any discussion between experts, although primary responsibility for preparation of the agenda should normally lie with the parties' solicitors.

76. The agenda should indicate what has been agreed and summarise concisely matters that are in dispute. It is often helpful to include questions to be answered by the experts. If agreement cannot be reached promptly or a party is unrepresented, the court may give directions for the drawing up of the agenda. The agenda should be circulated to experts and those instructing them to allow sufficient time for the experts to prepare for the discussion.

77. Those instructing experts must not instruct experts to avoid reaching agreement (or to defer doing so) on any matter within the experts' competence. Experts are not permitted to accept such instructions.

78. The content of discussions between experts should not be referred to at trial unless the parties agree (CPR 35.12(4)). It is good practice for any such agreement to be in writing.

79. At the conclusion of any discussion between experts, a joint statement should be prepared setting out:

a   issues that have been agreed and the basis of that agreement;
b   issues that have not been agreed and the basis of the disagreement;
c   any further issues that have arisen that were not included in the original agenda for discussion; and

d   a record of further action, if any, to be taken or recommended, including if appropriate a further discussion between experts.

80. The joint statement should include a brief re-statement that the experts recognise their duties (or a cross-reference to the relevant statements in their respective reports). The joint statement should also include an express statement that the experts have not been instructed to avoid reaching agreement (or otherwise defer from doing so) on any matter within the experts' competence.

81. The joint statement should be agreed and signed by all the parties to the discussion as soon as practicable.

82. Agreements between experts during discussions do not bind the parties unless the parties expressly agree to be bound (CPR 35.12(5)). However, parties should give careful consideration before refusing to be bound by such an agreement and be able to explain their refusal should it become relevant to the issue of costs.

83. Since April 2013 the court has had the power to order at any stage that experts of like disciplines give their evidence at trial concurrently, not sequentially with their party's evidence as has been the norm hitherto: PD 35 paragraphs 11.1–11.4 (this is often known as 'hot-tubbing'). The experts will then be questioned together, firstly by the judge based upon disagreements in the joint statement, and then by the parties' advocates. Concurrent evidence can save time and costs, and assist the judge in assessing the difference of views between experts. Experts need to be told in advance of the trial if the court has made an order for concurrent evidence.

Attendance of experts at court

84. Those instructing experts should ascertain the availability of experts before trial dates are fixed; keep experts updated with timetables (including the dates and times experts are to attend), the location of the court and court orders; consider, where appropriate, whether experts might give evidence via video-link; and inform experts immediately if trial dates are vacated or adjourned.

85. Experts have an obligation to attend court and should ensure that those instructing them are aware of their dates to avoid and that they take all reasonable steps to be available.

86. Experts should normally attend court without the need for a witness summons, but on occasion they may be served to require their attendance (CPR 34). The use of witness summonses does not affect the contractual or other obligations of the parties to pay experts' fees.

87. When a case has been concluded either by a settlement or trial the solicitor should inform the experts they have instructed.

Experts and conditional and contingency fees

88. Payment of experts' fees contingent upon the nature of the expert evidence or upon the outcome of the case is strongly discouraged. In *ex parte Factortame (no 8)* [2008] QB 381 at [73], the court said 'we consider that it will be a rare case indeed that the court will be prepared to consent to an expert being instructed under a contingency fee agreement'.

Sanctions

89. Solicitors and experts should be aware that sanctions might apply because of a failure to comply with CPR 35, the PD or court orders.

90. Whether or not court proceedings have been commenced a professional instructing an expert, or an expert, may be subject to sanction for misconduct by their professional body/regulator.

91. If proceedings have been started the court has the power under CPR 44 to impose sanctions:

a   cost penalties against those instructing the expert (including a wasted costs order) or the expert (such as disallowance or reduction of the expert fee) (CPR 35.4(4) and CPR 44).

b   that an expert's report/evidence be inadmissible.

92. Experts should also be aware of other possible sanctions

a   In more extreme cases, if the court has been misled it may invoke general powers for contempt in the face of the court. The court would then have the power to fine or imprison the wrongdoer.

b   If an expert commits perjury, criminal sanctions may follow.

c   If an expert has been negligent there may be a claim on their professional indemnity insurance.

Civil Justice Council

August 2014

CHAPTER 10

The conduct of proceedings

Marek Bednarczyk

Master David Cook

INTRODUCTION

10.1   The Legal Aid, Sentencing and Punishment of Offenders Act 2012 (hereinafter described as LASPO 2012) and the amendments to the Civil Procedure Rules 1998 ('CPR'), both brought into effect from 1 April 2013, have the aim of achieving a major cultural change in how litigation is conducted. Some lawyers have commented that the new regime appears to be harsh. No breach of the CPR will now be tolerated, unless the breach is trivial, and punishments meted out to defaulting parties will be draconian. Supporters of the changes may argue, however, that the new regime is simply robust and it is no longer acceptable for parties – especially those with professional representation – to ignore the CPR and the directions of the court. Furthermore, it may be argued that the rising costs of litigation have to be curbed and litigants must have the principle of proportionality in the forefront of their thoughts when contemplating commencement of proceedings and thereafter the pursuit of such proceedings.

10.2   The overriding objective as set out at CPR 1.1 was revised as from 1 April 2013 so that it is not simply the case that the courts have to take into account the need to ensure that cases are dealt with justly; they also have to ensure that cases are pursued 'at proportionate cost' and with due regard to the need to enforce 'compliance with rules, practice directions and orders'.

1 CPR 1.1(2)(f).

10.3   As part of the process of curbing costs the new regime seeks to make ATE insurance redundant by 'qualified one way costs shifting'. An unsuccessful claimant in a personal injury or clinical negligence case (subject to certain qualifications) will effectively no longer be ordered to pay the successful defendant's costs. ATE premiums are no longer recoverable *inter partes* for cases pursued under the new regime, save in a clinical negligence case a proportion of the ATE premium (relating to liability and causation expert evidence) may be recoverable *inter partes*. Success fees in conditional fee agreement (CFA cases) will no longer be paid by the loser, but subject to certain restrictions the success fee will be funded via the claimant's damages (although a claimant's future losses are to be protected from any deduction with regard to the success fee).

Costs budgeting in multi-track cases (where reliance on Precedent H costs estimates will be mandatory) will be a formidable weapon in the judiciary's arsenal aimed at controlling costs and maintaining proportionality.

10.4   A number of judicial decisions following the implementation of the reforms on 1 April 2013 have highlighted how breaches of the CPR will no longer be tolerated and solicitors may ignore the CPR at their peril. The Court of Appeal's decision in *Mitchell v News Group Newspaper Ltd*[1] was an early and startling example of how far the courts are willing to go in enforcing the CPR and punishing lawyers for a breach which is deemed more than trivial. The facts of that case concern the failure by the claimant's solicitors to lodge in advance of the case management conference a Precedent H costs estimate. That failure resulted in the court deeming that the only expenses to be claimed by the defaulting party were in relation to court fees. Whilst that case involved a defamation action, the application of the principle of compliance with the CPR has universal application.

1 [2013] EWCA Civ 1537.

10.5   The case of *Mitchell* undoubtedly led to more applications for extensions of time and more attempts by parties to take advantage of their opponent's breach. In July 2014 the Court of Appeal in *Denton v TH White Ltd; Decadent Vapours Ltd v Bevan; Utilise TDS Ltd v Davies*[1] sought to clarify the approach to relief from sanction under CPR 3.9 and provided a three-stage test. This test emphasises the need for judges to consider whether the breach is serious or significant, why the breach occurred and all the circumstances of the case so as to deal justly with the application for relief. The Court of Appeal also warned parties not to pursue bad points and to seek instead to co-operate with each other.

1 [2014] EWCA Civ 906.

10.6   Avoidance of trials, and indeed the avoidance of litigation, appears to be another aim of the new regime. As mentioned in the previous version of this chapter, trials in clinical negligence cases have become increasingly rare events. Post 1 April 2013 parties are encouraged to consider ADR at every stage, and failing to respond to a party's request for mediation has been deemed to be unreasonable conduct sufficient to warrant a costs sanction (see *PGF II SA v OMFS Co 1 Ltd*[1]).

1 [2013] EWCA Civ 1288, [2014] 1 All ER 970.

10.7 Experts over the last six years have not escaped the impact of change. The Court of Appeal in *Jones v Kaney*[1] decided that the time had come to remove the long-standing principle that experts were immune from suit.

1 [2011] UKSC 13.

10.8 'Hot tubbing' of experts, that is the provision for concurrent expert evidence at trial, is now part of CPR 35. Experts involved in legal aid cases even prior to the major change in legal aid scope (also brought in on 1 April 2013) were affected by the Legal Services Commission (now the Legal Aid Agency or LAA) attempts to reduce experts' fees in legal aid matters. This has been a growing problem for legal aid practitioners who at times struggle to find a suitable expert willing to accept legal aid rates. It appears that similar restrictions on fees for defendant experts have not been imposed by the NHS Litigation Authority (NHSLA).

10.9 Lord Justice Jackson specifically called for the retention of legal aid for civil litigation[1], but government cutbacks have prevailed. As from 1 April 2013 very few cases involving allegations of clinical negligence will receive legal aid funding. Essentially, claims involving brain injury at birth causing serious disability may continue to receive funding from the LAA (other types of clinical negligence cases perhaps involving adults for example may receive legal aid funding but only if the cases are deemed 'exceptional').

1 *Review of Civil Litigation Costs: Final Report* (December 2009) at Part 2, Chapter 7, para 3.2, p 68.

10.10 In addition there are now damages-based agreements (DBAs), although it appears that the Damages-Based Agreements Regulations 2013[1] have not made such agreements particularly attractive to clinical negligence practitioners.

LASPO 2012, of course, also introduced a ban on referral fees in personal injury cases which obviously aims to remove the presence of case management companies (CMCs) which had proliferated prior to 1 April 2013.

1 SI 2013/609.

10.11 A welcome reform from the claimant's perspective was the increase in non-pecuniary general damages (for pain, suffering and loss of amenity). The increase of 10 per cent was meant to compensate claimants for losing the ability to claim success fees from an opponent in a case where the claimant was successful[1] and applies to cases which settle or where judgment is given after 1 April 2013, save that where there is a funding agreement which pre-dates 1 April 2013 the increase is to be ignored.

1 Considered in *Simmons v Castle* [2012] EWCA Civ 1288.

THE NEED FOR LITIGATION

10.12 Access to justice is a fundamental desire for all litigants not least for clinical negligence claimants. A clinical negligence case is of course a personal injury claim in a professional negligence context. Claimants may be deeply affected by the issue of professional negligence. Claimants expect professionals and hospitals to be accountable.

10.13   The desires of claimants may exceed the simple aim of monetary compensation and the litigator must explain the limits of the litigation system at the outset. Compensation is the primary aim of all clinical negligence cases and the pursuit of such compensation may be justified if the legal merits and the costs benefit analysis are supportive. Searches for truth and the provision of profound apologies from erring clinicians alone do not justify litigation albeit they may be a welcome by-product of the process. It should be added that the successful resolution of a dispute via ADR can also bring similar benefits.

10.14   Compensation is a worthy and much needed goal. Money may not restore health but it lessens the blow of injury and can win financial security. Other remedies may be pursued but monetary compensation remains the fundamental goal in clinical negligence cases.

MATTERS TO CONSIDER PRE-ISSUE

Funding

10.15   The rules in relation to CFAs are strictly enforced against solicitors in order to protect the client. Any solicitor who does not follow the guidance set down by the Court of Appeal in *Garrett/Myatt*[1] will run the risk of potentially winning his client's claim for damages and then losing all the profit costs. It is essential to undertake careful checks on BTE insurance prior to pursuing a CFA and obtaining ATE insurance.

1 *Garrett v Halton Borough Council; Myatt v National Coal Board* [2006] EWCA Civ 1017, [2007] 1 All ER 147.

10.16   If the client does have BTE insurance then that in itself creates a problem if the solicitor is not on the insurers' nominated panel. In clinical negligence cases it is not unknown for insurers to be more flexible about agreeing to appoint a specialist solicitor even if they are not on their existing panel. If the non-panel solicitor is appointed then careful consideration of the insurer's terms and conditions needs to be undertaken. A careful analysis of the policy terms and conditions is required. The courts have been critical of insurers who have attempted to restrict their insured's choice of solicitor.

10.17   The Court of Appeal in *Brown-Quinn v Equity Syndicate Management Ltd*[1] strongly criticised the BTE insurers for attempting to prevent their insured from instructing a solicitor of their own choice. Where BTE insurance contracts included restrictions on an insured's choice of legal representative, this was considered a breach of the Insurance Companies (Legal Expenses Insurance) Regulations 1990[2], reg 6.

1 [2012] EWCA Civ 1633.
2 SI 1990/1159.

10.18   The Court of Appeal took the view that, whilst insurers could seek to limit the hourly rate for a non-panel solicitor, that would be acceptable only if it did not curb the freedom of choice guaranteed by Directive 2009/138[1]. Practitioners facing a BTE insurer who refuses to countenance their insured choosing that non-panel solicitor should draw the insurer's attention to this Court of Appeal decision.

1 Directive 2009/138/EC of the European Parliament and of the Council of 25 November 2009
   on the taking-up and pursuit of the business of Insurance and Reinsurance (Solvency II).

10.19   The client will be directly liable for the costs of the action despite
their insurers' indemnity. Potential breaches of the indemnity principle in
BTE cases need to be considered and avoided.

10.20   In the event that all reasonable enquiries as to the existence of BTE
insurance have been undertaken and the outcome of the search confirms that
there is no such cover in place then alternative funding needs to be pursued.

10.21   The attack on claimant's solicitor's costs (the 'costs war') and in
particular the issue of the indemnity principle remains a cause for dispute.
Other types of defect could also be exploited by the paying party, for example,
where there was no valid retainer and therefore no entitlement to costs[1].

1 *Sharon Fox v Graham Birks* (unreported, 2010) (Lawtel), but cf *Kathleen Scott v Transport for
   London* (2009) (Lawtel).

10.22   The vexed question of solicitor and own-client costs (which are not
recoverable *inter partes*) was considered by the Court of Appeal in *Motto v
Trafigura Ltd*[1]. One of the issues related to the work undertaken by a solicitor
in connection with a CFA and ATE insurance. The Court of Appeal's decision
frankly caused dismay among practitioners who are well aware of the need
to assist clients with funding issues and ATE insurance. Many lawyers would
argue that to advise a client on these matters is just as important as advising
on the prospects of success in a case and other legal matters. The Court of
Appeal, however, considered this type of work to be an item of solicitor and
own-client costs and not recoverable *inter partes*.

Prior to this decision it appeared that the Senior Courts Costs Office was split
on the issue, as some Masters allowed such work to be recovered *inter partes*
and others did not.

1 [2011] EWCA Civ 1150, [2012] 2 All ER 181.

10.23   Under the new regime solicitors will be potentially claiming part
of a claimant's damages to cover their success fee and the unrecoverable
element of the ATE premium (which will not be recoverable *inter partes* even
in clinical negligence matters). The client remains liable to the solicitor for
unrecovered costs. Formerly these may have been waived, but solicitors may
choose to recover these from their clients.

10.24   Solicitors have to take into account the contents of the Solicitors
Regulation Authority (SRA) handbook. The SRA handbook sets out 10
mandatory principles which apply to all solicitors. This includes the
requirement to act in the best interests of each client and to provide a proper
standard of service to the client. Chapter 1 of the handbook deals with client
care and explains what outcomes must be achieved when acting for a client.
O(1.6) states:

'You only enter into fee agreements with your clients that are legal and which you
consider are suitable for the client's needs and take account of the client's best
interest'.

In addition O(1.13) states:

'Clients receive the best possible information, both at the time of engagement and when appropriate as their matter progresses, about the likely overall cost of their matter'.

10.25   When considering 'indicative behaviours' the SRA handbook states that if a solicitor acts in a certain way, that may show they have achieved the outcomes and have therefore complied with the principles. When dealing with a client's matter a solicitor therefore should show that they have explained any arrangements 'such as a fee sharing or referral arrangement, which are relevant to the client's instructions' (IB(1.4)). When dealing with fee arrangements with a client a solicitor will be complying with the principles and outcomes if they can show that where they are acting for a client under a fee arrangement governed by statute, such as a conditional fee agreement, they have given the client 'all relevant information relating to that arrangement' (IB(1.17)). A solicitor acting for a publicly funded client should show that they have explained how the client's publicly funded status affects the costs (IB(1.18)).

10.26   Chapter 6 of the SRA handbook deals with the issue of introductions to third parties. The section dealing with indicative behaviours stipulates that any referral to a third party that can only offer products from one source be made only after the client has been informed of this limitation (IB(6.2)).

10.27   As part of the CFA process appropriate consideration will also be required with regard to how disbursements are to be funded during the course of the action. Funding is available from a number of sources and appropriate advice on any disbursement funding agreement will need to be given to the client prior to the implementation of that agreement. Compliance with the SRA principles and outcomes and due regard to indicative behaviours will be required in such circumstances. Some practices may prefer to self fund, but the burden of disbursements, especially in clinical negligence claims, should not be underestimated.

10.28   A ban on referral fees in personal injury cases (including clinical negligence) was introduced by LASPO 2012 on 1 April 2013. The SRA issued a warning notice to the profession on 11 October 2013. The SRA stated in their notice:

'We know that the ban on referral fees has raised difficult issues in relation to its application and interpretation. We are also aware that, because of the wording of LASPO, it is possible for firms to have arrangements that involve the introduction of personal injury work without being in breach of LASPO'.

The SRA notice went on to highlight the fact that practitioners may be breaching principles or failing to achieve the SRA outcomes if they, for example, agreed with an introducer to deduct money from a client's damages, or failed to properly advise clients about the costs and how their claim should be funded. The notice refers to enforcement action and states:

'Whilst we are committed to working constructively with firms and practitioners, we will take enforcement action against those that fail to address the issues and risks associated with referral arrangements, particularly where those arrangements are detrimental to the interests of clients'.

10.29   In 2007 legal aid remained a crucial form of funding for clinical negligence matters. Many firms, however, even at that stage with a LSC franchise were finding that increasingly their legally aided clients tended to be children rather than adults. Many potential adult clients of course fell outside the rigid financial eligibility limits.

As from 1 April 2013 the scope of legal aid with regard to clinical negligence was narrowed dramatically.

10.30   Pursuant to LASPO 2012, Sch 1, Pt 1, para 23, legal aid may be provided in relation to a claim for damages in respect of clinical negligence which caused a neurological injury to an individual and as a result that individual is 'severely disabled', but only where two conditions may be met. The first condition is that the clinical negligence occurred while the individual was in his or her mother's womb or during or after the individual's birth, but before the end of the following period, namely, if the individual was born before the beginning of the 37th week of pregnancy the period of eight weeks beginning with the first day of what would have been that week and if the individual was born during or after the 37th week of pregnancy the period of eight weeks beginning with the day of the individual's birth. The second condition required under para 23 is that the services to be provided are to the individual or to that individual's personal representatives if the individual has died. In practice it is likely that only children cases involving serious brain injury at birth will be funded through legal aid. Few clinical negligence cases will obtain legal aid post-1 April 2013.

10.31   In legal aid cases applications for legal aid (especially in high-value claims) remain significantly more complex and comprehensive than in the past. In the event that the practice wishes to recover the costs of its work in a matter prior to the grant of legal aid it will be necessary to set up an appropriate funding agreement, which must be distinguished from a CFA in order to be valid.

10.32   However, in the light of the decision of the Court of Appeal in *Trafigura*, as mentioned above, work specifically relating to assisting a client with an application for legal aid would be challenged as solicitor and own-client costs, and therefore not recoverable *inter partes*.

10.33   Funding in high-value clinical negligence cases is now provided in tranches for each stage in the case. Practitioners still need to provide detailed applications in support of further funding to the LAA, but the system is less onerous than in the past. Proper information and advice on legal aid and its burdens as well as its benefits must be given to the client to assist them and to ensure compliance on audit taking into account the contents of the SRA Handbook.

10.34   Other sources of funding may be seen in clinical negligence cases albeit they are increasingly rare, namely trade union funding and private client funding.

10.35   All the different forms of funding indicated above will colour the approach of dealing with a case simply through the fact that particular terms and conditions on scope of action and on financial limitation will arise depending upon the source of funding. Case management techniques will need to be exploited to ensure appropriate compliance throughout the case. It is good practice to explain all limitations and conditions to clients so that they can appreciate how their form of funding will affect matters as the case progresses. This helps to manage the client's expectations and should ensure a more efficient pursuit of the case.

Which track?

10.36   There are three tracks: small claims track, fast track, and multi-track. The scope of each track within the CPR is set out in CPR 26.6.

10.37   The current limit means that any personal injury claim worth £1,000 or less in relation to general damages will fall into the small claims track. Claims above that limit, but where the overall financial value is not more than £25,000, will currently fall within the fast track.

10.38   Fast track clinical negligence cases will be pursued in the county court. Cases which are not far above the fast track limit of £25,000 may not be pursued in the High Court. However that may not be the case if the claim satisfies the requirements of CPR 7A PD 3(3.6):

'3.6 If a claim for damages or for an unspecified sum is started in the High Court, the claim form must:

(1)   state that the claimant expects to recover more than £100,000 (or £50,000 or more if the claim is for personal injuries); or

(2)   state that some enactment provides that the claim may only be commenced in the High Court and specify that enactment; or

(3)   state that the claim is to be in one of the specialist High Court lists (see CPR Parts 49 and 58–62) and specify that list'.

10.39   In addition, CPR 29 PD 2 specifically states that professional negligence cases and fatal accident cases are suitable for trial in the Royal Courts of Justice. Therefore a clinical negligence claim which is currently below £50,000 but above £25,000 may be commenced in the Royal Courts of Justice. Masters at the High Court will take into account the complexities of the issues involved even if the value of the claim may be below £50,000. It is understood though that this would only apply in exceptional circumstances (where the issues relating to breach and/or causation were very complex).

10.40   The High Court and County Court Jurisdiction (Amendment) Order 2014[1] came into force on 22 April 2014 to coincide with the introduction of the single county court. The sum below which money claims must be started in the county court increased from £25,000 to £100,000. Nonetheless personal injury claims of £50,000 or more may still be commenced in the High Court. In practice a straightforward clinical negligence claim of up to £350,000 commenced in the High Court in London would probably be transferred at an early stage to the county court.

1 SI 2014/821.

Who is the claimant?

10.41 As clinical negligence claims include a claim for personal injuries they fall into the definition as set out in CPR 2.3(1):

'… "claim for personal injuries" means proceedings in which there is a claim for damages in respect of personal injuries to the claimant or any other person or in respect of a person's death, and "personal injuries" includes any disease and any impairment of a person's physical or mental condition …'.

In many claims the nature of the claimant is normally a straightforward issue.

10.42 In a fatal accident case the claimant may be a dependant of the deceased, or simply the next of kin (who has no personal dependency). Consideration will have to be given at the outset to any formalities that will need to be pursued, such as the obtaining of a grant of probate or letters of administration (if there is no will).

10.43 Cases involving children who, owing to permanent brain damage, will always lack mental capacity need to be distinguished from those cases where the only cause for incapacity is that the claimant is under the age of majority. The Office of Public Guardian (OPG) will need to be involved in the former but not in the latter.

10.44 As from October 2007 the full provisions of the Mental Capacity Act 2005 (MCA 2005) became operational. The MCA 2005 sets out a single test for assessing whether a person lacks capacity to take a particular decision at a particular time. Pursuant to the MCA 2005, s 2:

'… a person lacks capacity in relation to a matter if at the material time he is unable to make a decision for himself in relation to the matter because of an impairment of, or a disturbance in the functioning of, the mind or brain'.

10.45 The MCA 2005, s 3(1) states that a person is unable to make a decision for himself if he is unable:

'(a) to understand the information relevant to the decision;
(b) to retain that information;
(c) to use or weigh that information as part of the process of making the decision, or
(d) to communicate his decision (whether by talking, using sign language or any other means)'.

Using simple language or visual aids to assist a person in making a decision is acceptable. Even if a person is able to retain information relevant to a decision for a short period only, it does not prevent a person from being regarded under the MCA 2005 as being able to make the decision.

10.46 It is good practice when dealing with a prospective litigation friend to give early advice on their potential personal liability. At the stage when proceedings will be commenced a certificate of suitability in form N235 will need to be completed by the litigation friend, and that requires the litigation friend to give an undertaking in relation to costs. That undertaking is currently in the following terms:

'I undertake to pay any costs which the above named claimant may be ordered to pay in these proceedings subject to any right I may have to be repaid from the assets of the claimant'.

10.47   It is appropriate to warn the litigation friend that they have a responsibility in pursuing an action in a reasonable manner, failing which they may face a personal liability to pay the opponent's costs if the court considers it just and appropriate to do so. Most litigation friends will have no problem in giving that undertaking provided they have been warned of the need to act reasonably.

10.48   A very helpful and brief guide to the OPG can be found in the Professional Negligence Bar Association *Facts and Figures* Book[1].

1 PNBA *Facts and Figures* (2014) pp 273–286.

10.49   If a solicitor has concerns at the outset that the patient will not have a competent litigation friend then an approach to the Official Solicitor will be required.

10.50   There may be occasions when a litigation friend needs to be replaced. The court's power to change a litigation friend and to prevent a person acting as a litigation friend is provided by CPR 21.7 and CPR 21 PD 4.

Who is the defendant?

10.51   Claims against general practitioners are usually pursued against the treating doctor in question, albeit the partnership may also be cited. The treating doctor may not be identified on face of record or the negligence may involve many doctors over many years or the doctors concerned may be assistants or associates. It may be more appropriate to sue the practice: see *Whetstone (t/a Whelby House Dental Practice) v Medical Protection Society Ltd (sued as Dental Protection Ltd)*[1]. In a claim against an NHS hospital, however, the treating doctor is not usually cited as an individual. The Trust or Health Authority will be the primary defendant.

1 [2014] EWHC 1024 (QB).

10.52   However, with NHS reorganisation, identifying the correct defendant can be problematic in some cases. A solicitor was once compelled to cite some 25 different potential defendants, notwithstanding considerable endeavours, in seeking confirmation from the NHSLA that they would unequivocally accept that one sole defendant was liable in the matter[1].

1 Personal communication.

10.53   In private treatment cases the responsible clinician must be identified. It may be necessary to pursue both the private hospital as well as the clinician involved.

10.54   In most NHS cases the identity of the opponent will be clear and the NHSLA will take over conduct of the case pursuant to the Clinical Negligence Scheme for Trusts (CNST).

However, the situation is different if the NHS is not involved. In *A v Ministry of Defence*[1] the Court of Appeal held that there were no grounds to justify the imposition of a non-delegable duty of care on the Ministry of Defence to ensure that appropriate skill and care would be exercised in a hospital to which it had sub-contracted the role of providing appropriate secondary health care treatment in Germany for service personnel and their families.

1 [2004] EWCA Civ 641.

10.55 It is worth considering in this context the Supreme Court decision in *Woodland v Essex County Council*[1]. This case involved a personal injury claim by a school pupil. The claimant was injured when she attended a swimming lesson in school hours. Sadly the claimant, a young girl then aged 10, got into difficulties in the swimming pool and was found 'hanging vertically in the water'. Although she was resuscitated she suffered serious hypoxic brain injury.

At first instance Langstaff J struck out the allegation against Essex County Council that they owed the claimant a 'non-delegable duty of care'. At the time the school group of which the claimant was a member had been taught by a swimming teacher and a lifeguard, neither of whom were employed by the education authority. Their services were provided by an independent contractor.

1 [2013] UKSC 66, [2014] AC 537.

10.56 The Court of Appeal affirmed Langstaff J's decision by a majority, but the matter then went on appeal to the Supreme Court which held contrary to the lower courts that in this particular case there was a non-delegable duty of care which was owed to the claimant by the education authority.

10.57 In the judgment of the Supreme Court Lord Sumption (with whom Lord Clarke, Lord Wilson and Lord Toulson agreed) reviewed the law on 'non-delegable duties of care'. Lord Sumption considered the decision of the Court of Appeal in *A v Ministry of Defence*. Lord Sumption considered that the decision in *A v Ministry of Defence* was correct, but that was because the essential element in his view was not (as suggested in the case of *A v Ministry of Defence*) whether the defendant had control of the environment in which the injury is caused, but rather whether the defendant had 'control over the claimant for the purpose of performing a function for which the defendant has assumed responsibility'. Therefore in the case of *A v Ministry of Defence* the MOD was not responsible for the negligence of a hospital with whom it contracted to treat soldiers and their families. There was no delegation of any function which the MOD had assumed personal responsibility to carry out and no delegation of any custody exercised by the MOD over the soldiers and their families.

10.58 Lord Sumption also commented that the Court of Appeal had also been right in its decision in *Farraj v King's Healthcare NHS Trust*[1] to dismiss a claim against a hospital which had employed an independent laboratory to analyse the tissue sample for a patient who was not being treated by the hospital and was therefore not in its custody or care. Lord Sumption, relying upon the comments of Dyson LJ in *Farraj*, stated that the rationale of any non-delegable duty owed by hospitals is that:

'The hospital undertakes the care, supervision and control of its patients who are in special need of care. Patients are a vulnerable class of persons who place themselves in the care and under the control of the hospital and, as a result, the hospital assumes a particular responsibility for their wellbeing and safety'.

Lord Sumption asserted that courts should be sensitive about imposing unreasonable financial burdens on those providing critical public services.

1 [2009] EWCA Civ 1203.

10.59 However, in the case of *Woodland* Lord Sumption stated that he thought it was appropriate to recognise the existence of a non-delegable duty in that case taking into account the long-standing policy of law aimed at protecting those who are both inherently vulnerable and highly dependent on the observance of proper standards of care (ie school pupils) and taking into account that parents are required by law to entrust their child to a school where they may have no knowledge of or influence over the arrangements that the school may make to delegate specialised functions and where their liability for the negligence of independent contractors arises where those contractors perform functions which the school has assumed for itself a duty to perform generally in school hours and on school premises. Lord Sumption also highlighted other limits on liability in his judgment.

10.60 Therefore, notwithstanding the decision of the Supreme Court in *Woodland*, the law for clinical negligence matters is as set out in *A v Ministry of Defence* and *Farraj*. The health service is concerned with the provision of medical care and assumes a personal duty of care whether it provides such care itself or by outsourcing or subcontracting.

Assessing the claimant's case

10.61 The requirement to assess and re-assess the merits of a claim focuses the attention of the practitioner throughout an action and should govern the advice given to the client at the different stages of an action.

10.62 Cases under LASPO 2012 will have to meet the standard criteria set out in the Civil Legal Aid (Merits Criteria) Regulations 2013[1], reg 39. This regulation provides that an individual may qualify for legal representation only if the LAA director is satisfied that:

(1)   the individual does not have access to other potential sources of funding (other than a conditional fee agreement) from which it would be reasonable to fund the case; and
(2)   the case is unsuitable for a conditional fee agreement; and
(3)   there is no person other than the applicant for legal aid, including a person who might benefit from the proceedings, who can reasonably be expected to bring the proceedings; and
(4)   the applicant for legal aid has exhausted all reasonable alternatives to bringing proceedings including any complaint system, ombudsman scheme or other form of alternative dispute resolution; and finally

(5)   there is a need for representation taking into account the nature and complexity of the issues, the existence of other proceedings and the interests of other parties to the proceedings and the proceedings are not likely to be allocated to the small claims track.

1 SI 2013/104.

10.63   Therefore the discretionary element in the funding code with regard to pursuit of a formal complaint via the NHS Complaints Procedure has now gone. It now appears mandatory that in a clinical negligence case that potentially will be in scope under LASPO 2012 the applicant will have to pursue a formal complaint.

Furthermore, a legally aided individual seeking full representation will only obtain that if reg 39 is met and the costs benefit criteria set down at reg 42 are also met.

10.64   Regulation 42 provides that where a case is primarily a claim for damages or other sum of money and is not of significant wider public interest then:

(a)   if the prospects of success in the case are very good, the director must be satisfied that the likely damages exceed likely costs;

(b)   if the prospects of success in the case are good, the director must be satisfied that the likely damages exceed likely costs by a ratio of 2:1; or

(c)   if the prospects of success in the case are moderate the director must be satisfied that likely damages exceed likely costs by a ratio of 4:1.

As under the Funding Code the definition of 'very good' prospects of success equates to a case which has an 80 per cent or more chance of obtaining a successful outcome. A case which has 'good' prospects of success means a case where there is a 60 per cent or more chance (but less than an 80 per cent chance) of obtaining a successful outcome. A case which can be categorised as 'moderate' is a case which has more than a 50 per cent chance of success (but less than a 60 per cent chance).

10.65   It appears, however, that applications for children with birth injuries may still be capable of being pursued subject to reg 39 being satisfied. Regulation 40 deals with the criteria for determinations for 'investigative representation'. Assuming reg 39 is satisfied, then the director will grant legal aid subject to the following criteria being met:

(a)   the prospects of success of the case are unclear and substantial investigative work is required before those prospects can be determined;

(b)   the director has reasonable grounds for believing that, once the investigative work to be carried out under investigative representation is completed, the case will satisfy the criteria for full representation and, in particular, will meet the costs benefit criteria in reg 42 and the prospects of success criterion in reg 43; and

(c)   subject to sub-para (2), if the individual's claim is primarily a claim for damages or other sum of money in which the likely damages do not exceed £5,000, the case must be of significant wider public interest.

Subparagraph 2 which is mentioned in reg 40 simply deals with multi-party actions. If the claim forms part of a multi-party action, only the lead claim within that action is capable of being a case of significant wider public interest.

10.66   It is also crucial that careful assessment of quantum is undertaken at the same time as an assessment of breach of duty and causation. Evidential gaps need to be highlighted and steps taken to eliminate such gaps. By the time that proceedings are about to be pursued, the well-prepared practitioner will have obtained most of the evidence in the case subject to funding issues and the need to pursue the matter by way of a split trial.

10.67   Split trials are well known to be favoured by the LAA. Defendants, however, may see advantages in trying to argue for a full trial on all issues and it is relatively commonplace now for the issue of a split trial to be argued vigorously at the first CMC. In accordance with CPR 29 PD 5.3(7) the court will have to consider:

'whether it will be just and will save costs to order a split trial or the trial of one or more preliminary issues.'

10.68   Certainly in the short term there will be very few cases where, from the claimant's perspective, CPR 29 PD 5.3(7) does not apply. The defendant may well, however, argue that there is a risk that costs will be duplicated and a claimant cannot at the outset rely on the court finding favour with the claimant's arguments on this issue. In addition to the issue of split trials, a practitioner will need to consider at the very start of a case whether it is likely to be one where periodical payments need to be seriously considered. CPR 29 PD 3A states:

'3A. Attention is drawn to Practice Direction 41B supplementing Part 41 and in particular to the direction that in a personal injury claim the court should consider and indicate to the parties as soon as practicable whether periodical payments or a lump sum is likely to be the more appropriate form for all or part of an award of damages for future pecuniary loss'.

10.69   CPR 41B PD 1 sets out the factors to be taken into account when considering periodical payments and confirms when an order may be made and the criteria that the court must take into account when concluding that a periodical payment order needs to be put in place. In addition, this practice direction also considers other issues concerning assignment or charge, variation and settlement including requirements where the settlement or compromise is on behalf of a child or a patient.

10.70   Although it is accepted that consideration of matters such as split trials and periodical payments do not necessitate a detailed analysis at this stage the issues should still be considered and clients advised in view of the potential implications for costs and the conduct of proceedings.

Limitation

10.71   This issue is dealt with more extensively in Chapter 12. The practitioner, however, will need to consider whether in the statement of case to be advanced details relevant to the issue of limitation should be pleaded. Although CPR 16.4 sets out requirements on what should be included in the particulars of claim (which is amplified in the practice direction to that rule) there is no mandatory requirement that the claimant should plead relevant facts on limitation. However, in practice it is likely that the issue will already have been addressed in correspondence, especially if the Pre-Action Protocol Procedure has been implemented. Of course in CPR 29 PD 5.3(7) the court at the first case management conference will have to consider whether it is appropriate to order a split trial of one or more preliminary issues, which can naturally include the issue of limitation. When assessing risk factors in any case for the purposes of considering a CFA the issue of limitation is bound to be of key importance. Indeed, if there is an arguable defence on limitation, the practitioner may not be willing to pursue the matter at all save in exceptional cases.

The clinical negligence protocol

10.72 The full text of the Pre-Action Protocol for the Resolution of Clinical Disputes can be seen in the *White Book*[1]. Compliance with the Pre-Action Protocol is a matter that the court will take into account on allocation. Non-compliance will have to be justified.

1 *Civil Procedure* (Sweet & Maxwell, 2014) Vol I, C3A-001–C3-030.

Settling claims pre-issue

10.73 Substantial multi-track cases are unlikely to be settled without the issue of proceedings. In cases involving children and/or protected parties proceedings will need to be pursued in order to obtain court approval for any settlement above a prescribed level and therefore the commencement of proceedings may be desirable in any event.

10.74 Obtaining formal interlocutory judgment on behalf of a claimant may be of benefit because it provides some certainty of outcome for the matter. A defendant may resile from any pre-action admissions made, and therefore formalising the position with regard to liability through the commencement of proceedings and the obtaining of interlocutory judgment is a benefit. Provisions in CPR 14.1A apply to admissions made before commencement of proceedings. Admissions made after a letter of claim is received are presumptively binding. A party seeking to resile from a pre-action admission will need either the consent of the other party or formal permission from the court to allow the withdrawal of the admission.

10.75 The Pre-Action Protocol for the Resolution of Clinical Disputes encourages parties to avoid litigation when settlement is still being actively explored and discourages a party from issuing a claim prematurely.

10.76 Limitation has often been an obstacle to settling cases without the need for court proceedings. The NHSLA and other defendant bodies will consider agreeing to extend by mutual agreement limitation in order to facilitate settlement without the expense of formal proceedings. It is, of course, essential that the terms of such an extension are set out in writing and are clear and unequivocal and binding on both sides. In view of the natural desire of litigators to avoid any dispute on limitation, there is an attraction to issuing proceedings in order to avoid such a dispute. In fast track matters where quantum is the only issue a sensible agreement on limitation may be pursued with a view to saving costs.

10.77 Part 36 offers should obviously be made prior to the issue of proceedings where practicable. The timing of such an offer is a matter of judgment. Defendants who wish to settle a claim will inevitably make early offers as a matter of routine. The claimant may wish to put forward a Pt 36 offer at the same time as serving the letter of claim if there are good arguments in favour of that step being taken in relation to tactics and practicalities.

Reasonable negotiations with an opponent ought to be considered and pursued where practicable.

10.78 The Recovery of Costs Insurance Premiums in Clinical Negligence Proceedings (No 2) Regulations 2013[1] relate only to clinical negligence cases where a costs insurance policy is taken out on or after 1 April 2013. Provisions in force in the CPR prior to that date relating to funding arrangements do not apply. Therefore it appears that a notice of funding (N251) post-1 April 2013 is no longer required.

1 SI 2013/739.

10.79 However, the new practice direction, CPR 48 PD 4.1, at section 4.1 deals with new provisions in relation to clinical negligence claims. It is incumbent upon a party seeking costs to request that the judge includes a provision requiring the payment of an amount in respect of all or part of the premium of the ATE policy to be recoverable. It appears that if no such provision is included in the final order, the cost of the premium will not be recoverable.

10.80 The NHS complaints procedure ought to be followed by a potential claimant in appropriate cases and this was a practice positively encouraged by the LSC. The complaints process may prove to be a useful fact finding exercise. Admissions of fact can be made by clinicians and trusts in the process of the investigation into a complaint. Information from the complaints process can be very useful when a litigator needs to provide a formal risk assessment on a matter.

10.81 The coronial process is also another means whereby a litigator can pursue a fact finding exercise. The outcome of the coroner's inquest can assist in direct negotiations with the defendant in order to obtain early admissions and a resolution to the claim without the need for commencement of proceedings.

STARTING PROCEEDINGS

10.82 This section deals with the pursuit of proceedings from issue of proceedings to allocation and the first CMC covering case management and the relevant procedures for fast track and multi-track cases.

Time

10.83 The calculation of the appropriate periods of time doing any act which is specified by the CPR and its Practice Directions and/or by any judgment or order of the court is set out in CPR 2.8.

10.84 It has been noted that within the rules there are inconsistencies in relation to the issue of time. Some rules state variously that a party must do so 'at least', 'no later than', 'not less than' or 'not more than' a certain number of days before that event. In this respect the draftsmen of the rules have been criticised for not achieving standardisation and simplification of the Rules of Court[1].

1 *White Book* (2014) Vol 1, p 41, Editorial.

Service

10.85 CPR 6.3 provides confirmation of the methods of service that can be utilised.

Practitioners should note that pursuant to CPR 6.23(5) and CPR 6A PD 4 service by fax may be permitted and it is sufficient written indication that a party will accept service by fax where a fax number is set out on the writing paper of the solicitor acting for a party to be served. However, service by electronic means other than by fax requires the parties seeking to serve a document to first ask the party to be served whether there are any limitations (eg formatting matters) to the recipient's agreement to accept service by such means.

10.86 Documents which are served in accordance with CPR 6 will be deemed to have been served on the day shown as provided at CPR 6.26.

10.87 Where the claim form is served by the claimant a certificate of service must be filed with the court within 21 days of service of the claim form and the claimant may not be able to obtain judgment in default under CPR 12 unless the certificate of service has been filed in accordance with CPR 6.17.

10.88 It should be further noted that the normal method of service is now service by the court (CPR 6.4) which has been a normal provision in the county court rather than the High Court. In practice it is likely that a defendant by the time that proceedings need to be served has already instructed solicitors to accept service on their behalf and practitioners will not rely upon the court to effect service in such circumstances. The form of the certificate of service required by the rules is as set out at CPR 6.29.

10.89 Where a claim form is served by the court, the court must also send pursuant to CPR 6.17 the notice which will include the date when the claim form is deemed to be served under CPR 6.14.

10.90 In the event that service is initially effected by fax or by e-mail it is still good practice to ensure that a hard copy of the document is served by DX or post.

10.91   Under the current CPR 6.16 the court may dispense with service of the claim form in exceptional circumstances.

The claim form (CPR 7 and CPR 16)

10.92   The same type of claim form (N1) is used whether proceedings are issued in the High Court or the county court. The claim form and the particulars of claim should be marked 'Clinical Negligence' (CPR 16 PD 9.3).

10.93   Pursuant to CPR 7.5 the general rule is that a claim form must be served within four months after the date of issue (if service is outside the jurisdiction the period of service is six months). If the defendant has nominated solicitors to accept service of proceedings then the claim form must be served on those nominated solicitors, together with – for pre-1 April 2013 cases – notice of funding in form N251 (CPR 44 PD 13, now supplemented but not replaced by the new practice direction 44 which deals with, among other things, qualified one way costs shifting). In a publicly funded (ie legal aid) case a notice of issue/amendment should also be served at the same time.

10.94   An application to extend the time for service of the claim form must be made within the relevant period (either four months or six months), but the court will only make an order extending the period if:

(a)   the court has been unable to serve the claim form; or
(b)   the claimant has taken all reasonable steps to serve but has been unable to do so; and
(c)   the claimant has acted promptly in making the application for an extension of time.

Such an application will need to be supported by evidence and may be made without notice (CPR 7.6). However it should be noted that it is permissible for the parties to agree an extension of time for service of the claim form outside the period specified in CPR 7.5. The parties may rely upon CPR 2.11 but that requires the extension to be in writing, albeit this could be by exchange of letters rather than an agreement set out in a single document.

10.95   Protective proceedings may be issued without the need for separate particulars of claim or a schedule of loss. Indeed, where a split trial is being pursued it may be impractical to do other than serve a general preliminary schedule of loss in any event.

10.96   Although the particulars of claim may be endorsed on the claim form it is invariably the case that separate particulars of claim are drafted and served in clinical negligence cases. If the claim form is served first without accompanying particulars of claim then the latter document may be served within 14 days after service of the claim form, provided it is not later than four months (or six months if serving outside the jurisdiction) from the date of issue (CPR 16 PD 3.2).

10.97   In normal cases the four month rule is a long stop and it would not therefore be appropriate to wait until the four-month period has almost elapsed to serve the claim form and then expect to have another 14 days to serve the particulars of claim. It has been observed that the rules sometimes create a trap for the unwary claimant[1].

1 See *Kesabo v African Barrick Gold plc* [2013] EWHC 3198 (QB).

10.98 It may be possible to serve the claim form and then, subject to agreement with the defendant, serve the particulars of claim at a later date outside the 14-day period mentioned above. The court has powers pursuant to CPR 3.1(2)(a) to extend time for service of the particulars of claim. The parties may also agree an extension even after the initial period of service has elapsed[1]. Of course, it is best to agree a consent order with the opponent in good time before the relevant period of four months or six months has elapsed. In accordance with CPR 2.11 the parties may agree to vary time limits provided it is by written agreement. However, obtaining a sealed order is undoubtedly the best option to avoid any scope for misinterpretation of the agreement reached (especially taking into account the matters set out at para **10.96** ff above).

1 *Totty v Snowden, Hewitt v Wirral and West Cheshire Community NHS Trust* [2001] EWCA Civ 1415, [2001] 4 All ER 577.

10.99 CPR 16.2 sets out the mandatory requirements for the contents of a valid claim form. This includes the requirement that there should be a concise statement of the nature of the claim, together with a specification of the remedy which the claimant seeks and, where the claimant is making a claim for money, a statement of value in accordance with CPR 16.3. The claim form also should comply with the requirements of CPR 16 PD 2. The latter sets out rules on, among other things, the details of the defendant's name and address to be included in the claim form.

10.100 The requirements of a statement of value to be included in a claim form are set out in full in CPR 16.3. In a claim for personal injuries, the claimant must state in the claim form whether the amount which he expects to recover as general damages for pain, suffering and loss of amenity is either not more than £1,000 or more than £1,000. In addition the claimant must indicate whether in overall terms he expects to receive not more than £10,000, or more than £10,000 but not more than £25,000, or more than £25,000 or that he cannot say how much he expects to recover. If the claim form is to be issued in the High Court then where the claim is for personal injuries the claimant must state that he expects to recover £50,000 or more (albeit as previously stated a clinical negligence case worth in excess of £25,000 may still be commenced in the High Court in London, provided that the issues are so complex that the case is exceptional).

10.101 The claim form, if served separately from the particulars of claim, should of course include a statement of truth that complies with CPR 22. If the particulars of claim are served later, then that document should also include a statement of truth.

10.102 When particulars of claim are served on a defendant, whether they are contained in the claim form served with it or served subsequently, they must be accompanied by a form for defending the claim together with a form for admitting the claim and a form for acknowledging service in accordance with CPR 7.8. If the claimant is using the procedure set out in CPR 8 (see below) then clearly there are no requirements to include the forms relating to defending or admitting a claim but the defendant should still receive a form for acknowledging service.

10.103 Proceedings are started when the court issues a claim form at the request of the claimant (see CPR 7.2) but where the claim form as issued was received in the court office on a date earlier than the date on which it was issued by the court the claim is effectively 'brought' for the purposes of the Limitation Act 1980 and any other relevant statute on that earlier date (CPR 7A PD 5). The date on which the claim form was received by the court will be recorded by a date stamp either on the claim form held on the court file or on the letter that accompanied the claim form when it was received by the court. Parties proposing to start a claim which is approaching the expiry of the limitation period should recognise the potential importance of establishing the date the claim form was received by the court and should themselves make arrangements to record the date. If possible the claimant's solicitor should arrange for proceedings to be issued on the day that they are lodged at the court in order to avoid any subsequent argument.

10.104 Where it is sought to start proceedings against the estate of a deceased defendant where probate or letters of administration have not been granted, the claimant should issue the claim against 'The Personal Representatives of AB deceased'. The claimant should then, prior to the expiry of the period for service of the claim form, apply to the court for an appointment of a person to represent the estate of the deceased (CPR 7A PD 5.5).

Alternative procedure for claims (CPR 8)

Child or protected party, or consent judgment for provisional damages

10.105 It may be necessary to obtain court approval of a settlement reached on behalf of a protected party or a minor before commencement of proceedings and in that situation CPR 8 needs to be followed. In addition, if a settlement reached prior to the commencement of proceedings includes a claim for provisional damages then it will be necessary to obtain judgment pursuant to CPR 8 and CPR 8A PD 3. The relevant claim form is N208 and the contents of the claim form are prescribed in CPR 8.2. In accordance with the rules the claim form will need to include confirmation of the question which the claimant wants the court to decide or the remedy which the claimant is seeking and the legal basis for that remedy. The claim form must obviously state that CPR 8 applies and that the claim is suitable for the Pt 8 procedure.

10.106 In accordance with CPR 8A PD 7 evidence will normally be in the form of a witness statement or an affidavit and the claimant may rely on the matters set out in his claim form provided it has been verified by a statement of truth. It may be more appropriate to provide the minimum information in form N208 and then prior to the Part 8 hearing serve a statement which takes into account CPR 21 especially CPR 21 PD 6. It should be noted that pursuant to CPR 21 PD.6.4 (1) an opinion on the merits of the settlement or compromise given by counsel or solicitor acting for the child or patient should, except in very clear cases, be obtained.

10.107   In addition a copy or record of any financial advice must also be supplied to the court. In view of the sensitivity of much of this information, a separate bundle for the court should be prepared and lodged which effectively will be for the court's eyes only. CPR 8.5, however, requires that the claimant files any written evidence on which he intends to rely when he files his claim form and further that the evidence must be served on the defendant with the claim form. However, in practice certain confidential documents which may be available for the court can be referred to in the claim form, but not served on the defendant. Indeed, if an approval application proceeds in the High Court then the clinical negligence Masters will expect to receive a bundle for the approval hearing reasonably in advance, but the Masters would not expect that all the evidence to be considered by the court would have been filed with the claim form at the outset (hence practice does not necessarily sit easily with CPR 8.5).

10.108   The defendant must file an acknowledgement of service in the relevant practice form not more than 14 days after service of the Part 8 claim form.

Responding to the particulars of claim

10.109   As provided by CPR 10.3, the general rule is that the period for filing an acknowledgement of service by a defendant where the defendant is served with a claim form which states the particulars of claim are to follow is that the acknowledgement should be filed 14 days after service of the particulars of claim and in any other case 14 days after service of the claim form. The defendant should use form N9 to acknowledge service.

10.110   As provided by CPR 15.4 the general rule is that the period for filing a defence is 14 days after service of the particulars of claim or, if the defendant files an acknowledgement of service under CPR 10, 28 days after service of the particulars of claim. The defendant and the claimant may agree that the period for filing a defence specified in CPR 15.4 shall be extended by a period of up to 28 days (CPR 15.5). In this situation, where the defendant and the claimant agree to extend the period for filing a defence, the defendant must notify the court in writing of that agreement. There is no express provision for parties to agree an extension beyond the said period of 28 days; should the defendant require more time, then an application to the court for an order extending time for filing a defence beyond 28 days will be required. If a defendant issues a reasonable application for an extension and the claimant unreasonably opposes it then the claimant may be open to an adverse costs order.

10.111   When the defendant files a defence a copy should be served on the claimant by the court. If a claimant wishes to file a reply to the defence then he must file his reply when he files his directions questionnaire and serve his reply on the other parties at the same time as he files it (CPR 15.8). The claim will be automatically stayed if it is not defended or admitted in a situation where at least six months have expired since the end of the period for filing a defence as specified in CPR 15.4 and where no defendant has served or filed an admission or filed a defence or counterclaim and the claimant has not entered or applied for judgment under CPR 12 (default judgment) or CPR 24 (summary judgment). However, where a claim is stayed under the relevant rule (CPR 15.11), any party may apply for the stay to be lifted.

10.112 A party may not file or serve any statement of case after a reply without the permission of the court (CPR 15.9).

Statements of case (CPR 16)

10.113 A 'statement of case':

(a) means a claim form, particulars of claim where these are not included in a claim form, defence, Part 20 claim, or reply to defence; and

(b) includes any further information given in relation to them voluntarily or by court order.

If a claimant pursues the Part 8 procedure then CPR 16 does not apply (CPR 16.1).

10.114 It is now more common for draft particulars of claim to have been annexed to a short letter of claim as part of the Pre-Action Protocol for the Resolution of Clinical Disputes. By the time formal proceedings have to be commenced, the draft particulars of claim may have undergone further revision following a review of the case with counsel in the light of the defendant's reasoned response. In appropriate cases a pre-issue conference may have been held and the revision to the particulars of claim agreed with the claimant's experts. This process may assist in reducing the need for post-service amendments to the particulars of claim.

10.115 The mandatory requirements of a particulars of claim are set out at CPR 16.4(1), which states that the particulars of claim must include:

'(a) a concise statement of the facts on which the claimant relies;

(b) if the claimant is seeking interest, a statement to that effect and the details set out in [CPR 16.4(2)];

(c) if the claimant is seeking aggravated damages or exemplary damages, a statement to that effect and his grounds for claiming them;

(d) if the claimant is seeking provisional damages, a statement to that effect and his grounds for claiming them; and

(e) such other matters as may be set out in a practice direction'.

Indeed CPR 16 PD 4.1 sets out additional requirements for personal injury claims. The claimant's date of birth and brief details of the claimant's personal injuries must be contained in the particulars of claim. Furthermore, the claimant must attach to his particulars of claim a schedule of details of any past and future expenses and losses which he claims. The claimant must also attach to the particulars of claim a report from a medical practitioner 'about' the claimant's personal injuries which he alleges in his claim. The rule does not specify whether the report should concern breach of duty, causation, or condition and prognosis. Fatal accident claims are considered at CPR 16 PD

5 and the direction requires that the claimant should state in his particulars of claim that it is a case brought under the Fatal Accidents Act 1976 and it should identify the dependants on whose behalf the claim is made and the date of birth of each dependant and details of the nature of the dependency claim. The direction also states that the fatal accident claim may include a claim for damages for bereavement and a claim brought pursuant to the Law Reform (Miscellaneous Provisions) Act 1934 on behalf of the estate of the deceased. Reference to the issue of periodical payments ought to be made taking into account the requirements of CPR 41. Of course, as from 1 April 2005 the courts were empowered to make an order in relation to periodical payments by virtue of the Courts Act 2003, s 100. CPR 41.5(1) states that in a claim for damages for personal injury each party in its statement of case may state whether it considers periodical payments or a lump sum a more appropriate form for all or part of an award of damages and in the event that such a statement is given the party must provide relevant particulars of the circumstances which are relied upon. The court also has the power to order a party to make such a statement (CPR 41.5(2)) and the court may also order a party to provide further particulars if the statement given appears to be insufficient (CPR 41.5(3)).

10.116   CPR 22 requires the particulars of claim to be verified by a statement of truth. This requirement also applies to the schedule of loss by virtue of CPR 22 PD 1.4(3). The words 'clinical negligence' should also be shown on top of every statement of case, as previously stated, in accordance with CPR 16 PD 9.3.

10.117   In most clinical negligence cases the particulars of claim will be set out separately and not endorsed on the claim form. Usually the particulars of claim will be served with the claim form or within 14 days of service (see paras **10.96–10.98** above).

10.118   In his defence a defendant must state, pursuant to CPR 16.5(1):

'(a) which of the allegations in the particulars of claim he denies;
(b) which allegations he is unable to admit or deny, but which he requires the claimant to prove; and
(c) which allegations he admits'.

Blanket denials are, of course, unacceptable and CPR 16.5(2) states that where the defendant denies an allegation he must state his reasons for doing so and if he intends to put forward a different version of events from that given by the claimant he must state his own version. A defendant who fails to deal with an allegation but has set out in his defence the nature of his case in relation to the issue to which that allegation is relevant shall be taken to require that allegation to be proved (CPR 16.5(3)). Otherwise a defendant who fails to deal with an allegation shall be taken to admit that allegation (CPR 16.5(5)).

10.119   The defendant also needs to comply with the general rules set out in the accompanying practice direction at CPR 16 PD 10 and in personal injury claims the defendant will also need to comply with CPR 16 PD 12. The defendant is therefore required to consider the medical report relied upon by the claimant as referred to or annexed to the particulars of claim.

In the defence the defendant must indicate whether he agrees or disputes the report or whether he neither agrees nor disputes but has no knowledge of the matters contained in the medical report. If the defendant disputes any part of the medical report then he must give his reasons for doing so in his defence. Where the defendant has obtained his own medical report on which he intends to rely, then a copy of that should be attached to the defence. The defendant will also have to provide a counter schedule where a claimant has provided a schedule of past and future expenses and losses. The defendant will need to state whether he agrees, disputes or neither agrees nor disputes the contents of the claimant's schedule (or indeed states that he has no knowledge of the contents) but where any items are disputed the defendant needs to supply alternative figures where appropriate (CPR 16 PD 12.2). The defence will need a statement of truth (CPR 16 PD 11) and the counter schedule, if served separately, should also have a statement of truth (CPR 22 PD 1.4(3)). A defendant must also provide details of the expiry of any relevant limitation period relied upon (CPR 16 PD 13). The purpose of the changes advanced by the CPR with regard to statements of case was to ensure that cases were put clearly and thoroughly allowing both sides to properly evaluate their positions. Unqualified denials from defendants therefore are not acceptable under the CPR.

10.120 A claimant who does not file a reply to the defence shall not be taken to admit the matters raised in the defence. The claimant who, however, files a reply to a defence but fails to deal with the matter raised in the defence shall be taken to require that matter to be proved. A reply of course is optional. It may become necessary, if the claimant considers it appropriate to allege facts in answer to the defence which had previously not been set out in the particulars of claim.

Case management – preliminary stage (allocation)

10.121 In the county court the parties who are legally represented will receive a notice giving details of the court's requirements for filing the directions questionnaire (in the fast track and multi-track form N181 is to be used). CPR 26.3 was amended so that with effect from 1 April 2013 changes were put into place which would impact upon the responsibilities imposed on parties and on the court with regard to case management. The revised rule allows the court to make a provisional decision as to the allocation of the case to an appropriate track confirmed in a notice of proposed allocation (form N149C for the multi-track and form N149B for the fast track). Following service on the parties of the said notice the parties are required to file the documents required by the notice, in particular completing a 'directions questionnaires' (no longer obviously an allocation questionnaire, as provisional allocation will already have been undertaken). A notice of provisional allocation to the multi-track is now issued in all cases in the Royal Courts of Justice.

10.122 Each party will have to file the completed directions questionnaire with the court by the due date. This date cannot be varied by agreement between the parties. Failure to file the questionnaire will result in the court issuing an order for strike out if the questionnaire is not filed within seven days of the date of the order (CPR 26.3(7A)).

10.123   After 1 April 2013 mistakes will be punished severely. There is now greater emphasis on co-operation between the parties and CPR 26 PD 2.3(1) requires the parties to complete the directions questionnaire and consult one another and co-operate on the exercise. Form N181 states that all proposed directions for fast track cases must be based on CPR 28, and for multi-track cases directions are to be found on a website[1]. In clinical negligence cases this will require in a multitrack case the use of the 2012 model directions revised by Master Roberts and Master Cook. It will be necessary to consider a one month stay in order to attempt to settle the claim either by way of formal discussion or by alternative dispute resolution (CPR 26.4(1)). If the parties subsequently require additional time the court may grant a further four week stay upon receipt of a letter from the parties requesting extra time. More than one extension may then be granted (CPR 26.4(3); CPR 26 PD 3). Should the case be settled during the stay, then a consent order from the parties will be sufficient to lift the stay (CPR 26 PD 3.4), as would an application for approval or a notice of acceptance.

1 http://www.justice.gov.uk/courts/procedure-rules/civil/standard-directions/list-of-cases-of-common-occurrence.

10.124   The questionnaire also requires information to be provided in relation to location of trial and compliance with Pre-Action Protocols. In the section dealing with case management information the party must indicate whether they intend to apply for any particular orders such as summary judgment. Fortunately the requirement to file and serve a disclosure report in form N263 is not required in personal injury cases. Details of factual witnesses need to be provided and information given in relation to the experts that the party wished to use at the trial or final hearing. The party will need to indicate whether copies of the experts' reports have been served on the opponent and whether the party considers the case is suitable for a single joint expert in any particular field. The party will also need to indicate the appropriate form of track for the matter and provide brief reasons for their choice in the event that the track chosen would not be the normal track for that type of claim. The party will also need to provide information to assist in the fixing of the trial including an estimate for the final hearing in days or hours. The form confirms that the party should seek to agree directions wherever possible and the form should be accompanied by a draft list of directions.

Costs budgeting

10.125   The questionnaire confirms with regard to costs that if the claim is likely to be allocated to the multi-track, form Precedent H must be filed in accordance with CPR 3.13. The rule provides that, unless the court otherwise, orders all parties (except litigants in person) must file and exchange budgets as required by the rules or as the court otherwise directs. Each party must file and exchange budgets by the date specified in the notice served under CPR 26.3(1) or, if no such date is specified, then seven days before the first case management conference.

10.126   In the light of the fact that CPR 3.14 imposes a draconian order for failure to file a budget, it would be best for practitioners to file their Precedent H costs estimates with the directions questionnaire in all cases. Practitioners need to be reminded that CPR 3.14 states that, unless the court otherwise orders, any party which fails to file a budget despite being required to do so will be treated as having filed a budget comprising only the applicable court fees.

10.127 The Court of Appeal, as stated above, supported this sanction in the case of *Mitchell v News Group Newspapers Ltd*[1] although that decision now needs to be considered in the light of *Denton v TH White Ltd; Decadent Vapours Ltd v Bevan; Utilise TDS Ltd v Davies*[2], where the Court of Appeal advanced a three-stage test for consideration when judges are asked to deal with applications for relief from sanctions.

1 [2013] EWCA Civ 1537.
2 [2014] EWCA Civ 906.

10.128 The strict requirements of a Precedent H budget or costs estimate is considered in detail in the revised rules and the new practice direction CPR 3E PD. It should be noted that recoverable costs of initially completing Precedent H shall not exceed the higher of £1,000 or 1 per cent of the approved budget (CPR 3E PD 3).

10.129 Furthermore, all other recoverable costs of the budgeting and costs management process shall not exceed 2 per cent of the approved budget (CPR 3E PD 3). The parties will need to seek to try and agree their budgets which will be divided into phases. It has to be said that the phases in Precedent H do not accord with the normal manner of working of practitioners, who will clearly have to adapt to cope with the new requirements.

10.130 As stated at CPR 3E PD 3 (section 7.4) the court will not undertake a detailed assessment in advance, but rather will consider whether the budgeted costs fall within the range of reasonable and proportionate costs. With regard to costs incurred before the date of any budget (ie effectively past costs) the court may not approve such costs, but may record its comments on those costs and should take those costs into account when considering the reasonableness and proportionality of all subsequent costs (CPR 3E PD 3, section 7.4).

10.131 The practice direction emphasises that if significant developments in the litigation warrant a revision of the costs budget (either upwards or downwards), then each party shall revise its budget accordingly. Amended budgets will be submitted to the other parties for agreement and in default of agreement those amended budgets will be submitted to the court together with a note explaining the changes made and the reasons for those changes and detailing the objections of any other party. The court then will approve, vary or disapprove the revisions and thereafter each party will re-file and re-serve the budget in the form approved with re-cast figures annexed to the order approving it.

10.132 There is no doubt that the issue of costs budgeting will represent a major challenge to practitioners dealing with cases that have been issued after 1 April 2013. It should be noted, however, that the court has power to order costs budgets to be filed and served in all cases even those where proceedings were issued prior to 1 April 2013.

10.133   The Masters at the High Court in a case where the court has yet to order a split trial will expect the parties to provide a costs budget based on a split trial and a second budget based on a trial on all issues.

The previous exemption with regard to costs budgeting has gone and the revised practice direction CPR 3E PD 1 now requires costs budgeting in all cases of less than £10 million in value (the previous threshold of £2 million has gone).

10.134   The questionnaire also allows a party to provide additional or extra information which may well be appropriate in clinical negligence cases. CPR 26 PD 2.2 states that the court will not take such information into account unless the document containing it either confirms that all parties have agreed that the information is correct and that it should be put before the court or confirms that the party who has sent the document to the court has delivered a copy to all the other parties, hence the need to serve a copy of the allocation questionnaire on the opponent. CPR 26 PD 2.3 sets out the requirements in relation to the need for the parties to consult one another and cooperate in the completion of the allocation questionnaires in giving other information to the court. The directions form states that the party should try to agree the case management directions (further details appear in the practice directions which supplement CPR 28 dealing with the fast track and CPR 29 dealing with the multi-track). However, the process of consultation must not delay the filing of the directions questionnaires.

Allocation to track

10.135   In most cases the court will expect to have enough information from the statements of case and the directions questionnaires provided by the parties to be able to allocate the claim to a track and to give appropriate case management directions (CPR 26 PD 4.2(1)). The court may decide to issue an order requiring one or more parties to provide further information within 14 days if the court takes the view that inadequate information has been provided in the questionnaire. The court has a duty to pursue active case management and therefore part of that duty will include the summary disposal of issues which do not need full investigation and trial (CPR 1.4(2)(c)). The court's powers include the provision to allow for striking out a statement of case or part of a statement of case and under CPR 24 giving summary judgment where a claimant or a defendant has no reasonable prospect of success. However, if the claimant indicated in the directions questionnaire that they intended to seek summary judgment then in that circumstance the claimant ought to have issued an application either before or when filing the directions questionnaire. If no such application is made even though the claimant indicated that they would be making such an application then the court will fix a directions hearing (CPR 26 PD 5.3(3)).

10.136   A directions hearing should be held in accordance with CPR 26 PD 6. The court will give the parties at least seven days' notice of the hearing in form N153. A legal representative who attends a directions hearing should, if possible, be the person responsible for the case and must in any event be familiar with the case in order to allow them to be able to provide the court with the necessary information to make appropriate decisions about directions and case management and have sufficient authority to deal with any issues that are likely to arise (CPR 26 PD 6.5).

10.137 If a party is guilty of some default in connection with the directions procedure then the court may order that party to pay on the indemnity basis the costs of any other party who has attended the hearing, and to assess summarily the amount of those costs and order them to be paid forthwith or within a stated period. The court may order that if the party does not pay those costs within the time stated then his statement of case will be struck out. Non-attendance at the directions hearing may also lead to an order being made striking out the defaulting party's statement of case (CPR 26 PD 6.6).

10.138 The principles behind allocation are set out at CPR 26 PD 7. The scope of each track is set out in CPR 26.6. The general rules relating to allocation are set out at CPR 26.7 and further matters relevant to allocation are set out in CPR 26.8. It is for the court to assess the financial value of a claim (CPR 26 PD 7.3) and where the court believes that the amount the claimant is seeking exceeds what he may reasonably be expected to recover, the court may make an order under CPR 26.5(3) directing the claimant to justify the amount claimed by him (see also CPR 26 PD 7.3(2)).

10.139 CPR 26 PD 9 sets out the relevant rules relating to allocation in a fast track matter. The court will allocate a claim to the fast track unless it believes that it cannot be dealt with justly on that track. The court should have regard in particular to the extent to which expert evidence may be necessary and whether the trial is likely to last more than a day. The court also needs to take into account the limits likely to be placed on disclosure. The court will regard a day as being a period of five hours for the purposes of the likely length of trial. However the possibility that a trial might last longer than one day is not necessarily a conclusive reason for the court to allocate or to re-allocate a claim to the multi-track. The claim may be allocated to the fast track or ordered to remain on that track although there is to be a split trial.

10.140 The relevant rules in relation to a multi-track case are set out at CPR 26 PD 10, albeit the direction does not apply to any claim which is being dealt with at the Royal Courts of Justice. Rules on the venue for allocation and case management in multi-track matters are set out at CPR 26 PD 10.2. Case management of a claim which is allocated to the multi-track will normally be dealt with at a civil trial centre. The practice direction, however, states that case management will be subject to CPR 29 and in the practice direction supplementing that Part and that will be considered in detail below.

The fast track

10.141 Part 28 sets out the requirements for conducting a fast track case (as from 1 April 2013 these cases would include claims of a value of £10,000 or more up to and including £25,000). The procedure was designed to take straightforward cases to trial within a short and reasonable time scale of not more than 30 weeks from the giving of directions (CPR 28.2).

10.142   The court will set directions for the conduct of the fast track and fix a trial date or trial period (the latter not to exceed three weeks) (CPR 28.2). The matters to be dealt with by the directions will include disclosure of documents, service of witness statements and service of expert evidence (CPR 28.3). Standard fast track directions can be seen set out at CPR 28 PD 9 and particular care will need to be taken in dealing with the standard direction for expert evidence. As confirmed at CPR 28 PD 3.2, the court will seek to tailor its directions to the needs of the case and the steps of which it is aware that the parties have already taken to prepare the case. In particular the court will have regard to the extent to which any Pre-Action Protocol has or (as the case may be) has not been complied with. The court's primary concern in giving directions at allocation will be to ensure that the issues between the parties have been identified and that the necessary evidence is available and disclosed. The typical timetable the court may give for the preparation of a case can be seen at CPR 28 PD 3.12, but this too will need to be considered carefully and adapted to suit a clinical negligence case.

10.143   The parties in a fast track case will have to contend with the court's general approach, which is to limit expert evidence to that which is essential (CPR 35.4) and to limit oral expert evidence and exclude it all together whenever possible by relying on a written report complying with CPR 35 (CPR 35.5). The potential problems this may cause in a clinical negligence case are obvious and appropriate representations will need to be made to the court to allow the effective use of expert evidence.

10.144   Variation of fast track directions is covered at CPR 28.4 and CPR 28 PD 4. Of course, the new provision at CPR 3.8(4) allowing parties to agree in writing to an extension of time up to 28 days (provided the hearing date is not put at risk) is relevant here too. Where a party is dissatisfied with a direction given or other order made by the court, he may appeal or apply to the court for it to reconsider its decision. The correct approach is to appeal the decision if it was given at a hearing; if the direction was given on paper, the party dissatisfied with that direction should apply to the court to reconsider its decision. This will usually be dealt with by way of a hearing by the judge who gave the direction or another judge of the same level. The court will give all parties at least three days' notice of the hearing (CPR 28 PD 4.3).

10.145   Should there be a failure to comply with case management directions then the party entitled to apply for an order against the party in default must apply without delay but should warn the other party first of his intention to make such an application (CPR 28 PD 5.2). However, parties need to co-operate, and variation pursuant to CPR 3.8(4) will be acceptable. The parties were encouraged by the Court of Appeal in *Denton* not to take bad points against each other. The court will seek to ensure that the trial will not be postponed and will only allow a failure of compliance with the directions to lead to postponement if the circumstances of the case are 'exceptional' (CPR 28 PD 5.4).

10.146   Unless the court has decided to dispense with pre-trial check lists, they will be sent to the parties in form N170 together with a notice of the date for the return of the pre-trial check list (form N171). Although the CPR do not require that the parties exchange their completed pre-trial check lists, the parties are nonetheless encouraged to do so (CPR 28 PD 6.1(4)). The court will give directions on listing and may decide to hold a hearing under CPR 28.5(4). The court must give directions in relation to confirmation of the trial date specifying the place of trial and providing a time estimate. The trial date must be fixed with the assumption that it will start and conclude on the same day (CPR 28 PD 7.1(1)). The parties should receive at least three weeks' notice before the hearing (unless the court directs that shorter notice should be given (CPR 28.6(2)). Additional directions may also be given, including the preparation of a trial bundle and any other matter required to prepare the case appropriately for trial. A direction giving permission to use expert evidence will stipulate that permission has been granted for oral evidence or permission is given to rely upon reports or both and the order will name the experts concerned. The court will not make a direction giving permission for an expert to give oral evidence unless it believes it is necessary in the interests of justice to do so (CPR 28 PD 7.2(4)(b)). In the event that there has been no 'without prejudice' meeting or other discussions between the experts in the action, the court may grant permission conditionally on such a discussion taking place, and a report being filed before trial. If a party fails to file a pre-trial check list then the court will issue an order against that party in default stating that unless they serve the pre-trial checklist within a specified period of time their statement of case will be struck out (CPR 28 PD 6.5(1)).

10.147 Unless the trial judge otherwise directs, the trial will be conducted in accordance with any previous order made in the action (CPR 28.7). It is assumed that the judge will have read the papers in the trial bundle and may dispense with an opening address (CPR 28 PD 8). The court has power to confirm or vary any timetable previously given in the action and to restrict evidence and cross examination. Witness statements may stand as evidence in chief (CPR 28 PD 8.4). At the conclusion of the trial the judge will normally summarily assess the costs of the claim in accordance with CPR 44.6 and CPR 45, section vi, which deals with fast track file costs. In the event that the trial is not finished on the day for which it is listed, the judge will normally sit on the next court day to complete the case.

The multi-track

10.148 As from 1 April 2013 a new rule has been added at CPR 29.1(2). This new rule states that when drafting case management directions both the parties and the court should take as their starting point any relevant model directions and standard directions which can be found on line (see para **10.123** above) and these directions should be adapted as appropriate to the circumstances of the particular case. In accordance with CPR 29.2, when the court allocates the case to the multi-track, it will give directions for the management of the case and set out a timetable for steps to be taken between the giving of the directions and the trial and may fix a case management conference or a pre-trial review or both and give such other directions relating to the management of the case as it sees fit. The court will also fix the trial date or the period in which the trial is to take place as soon as practicable and notice will be provided to the parties for the date or period and the parties will be told the date by which they are to file a pre-trial checklist.

10.149 If the court fixes a case management conference (or a pre-trial review) then the parties' legal representatives (assuming there are any) who have familiarity with the case and sufficient authority to deal with any issues that are likely to arise, must attend the case management conference (or pre-trial review). It should be noted that at some county courts it is expected that all the parties will attend with their representatives. Therefore the claimant's solicitor and counsel, as appropriate, and the claimant himself will need to be in attendance. Similarly the defendant's solicitor and counsel will need to attend, together with a representative of the NHSLA where appropriate, or the defendant in person with their defence union representative. To assist the court, the parties and their legal advisers should ensure that all documents (including witness statements and experts' reports) that the court is likely to ask to see are brought to the hearing. Consideration should also be given as to whether the parties should attend (as previously indicated certain courts require a full attendance and if there is any doubt on this it is best to check with the court direct). The parties should also consider preparing a case summary, not normally exceeding 500 words in length, to be prepared by the claimant and agreed with the other parties if possible. The case summary should set out a brief chronology of the claim, the issues of fact which are agreed or in dispute, and the evidence needed to decide them (CPR 29 PD 5.7(1)). The parties and their advisers are encouraged to try to agree directions prior to the case management conference; this may obviate the need to have a hearing in appropriate cases. In appropriate cases the case management conference may be conducted by way of a telephone conference or indeed a video conference. Telephone hearings are dealt with at CPR 23A PD 6. Video conferencing is considered at CPR 23A PD 7.

10.150 Practice Form 52 covers all types of High Court action and is therefore rather cumbersome. As already stated there is a new rule as from 1 April 2013 (CPR 29.1(2)), which states that when drafting case management directions both the parties and the court should take as their starting point any relevant model directions and standard directions which can be found online (see para **10.141** ff above). The court will also consider the issue of periodical payments at the outset when undertaking case management (CPR 29 PD 3A). The court may also consider whether the case ought to be tried by a High Court judge. The directions set at the case management conference may be varied in accordance with CPR 29 PD 6. If the directions were given at a hearing, then the parties seeking to amend the direction may have to pursue an appeal. In the event that the directions were given on paper then, as with the fast track procedure, the party should apply to the court to reconsider its decision and a hearing will then be fixed. The parties are of course empowered to vary the timetable by written agreement pursuant to CPR 2.11 and CPR 3.8(4). However, the parties must apply to the court if they wish to vary the date which the court has fixed for the case management conference, a pre-trial review, the date for the return of a pre-trial check list, the trial date or the trial period (CPR 29.5). If the changes sought by the parties do not fall within CPR 2.11 (taking into account CPR 29.5 or CPR 3.8(4)) the parties must apply to the court for a variation if the changes are agreed by consent. The court may make an order in the agreed terms or in other terms without a hearing, albeit it may direct that a hearing is to be listed to deal with the variation. Compliance with the court's order for directions in relation to service of witness statements and experts' reports should be followed in all cases. A failure to comply with the directions will have serious consequences.

10.151 CPR 32.10 provides that a witness statement or witness summary which is not served within the time specified by the court would not allow the party in breach to call their witness to give oral evidence unless the court gives permission. CPR 35.13 stipulates that a party who fails to disclose an expert's report may not use the report at the trial or call the expert to give evidence orally unless the court gives permission. These provisions need to be seen in the light of *Mitchell v News Group Newspapers Ltd*[1] and two cases that followed *Mitchell*.

1 [2013] EWCA Civ 1537.

10.152 In *Durrant v Chief Constable of Avon and Somerset Constabulary*[1] the Court of Appeal overturned a decision of Birtles HHJ which had granted relief to the defendant from sanction for non-compliance with a court order in relation to service of witness statements. The judge, however, did not have the benefit of the Court of Appeal's judgment in the case of *Mitchell*. In the leading judgment of Richards LJ it was emphasised that, whilst the Court of Appeal would not lightly interfere with case management decisions, it was vital that decisions under CPR 3.9 which failed to follow the robust approach laid down in the *Mitchell* case should not be allowed to stand, since if they were allowed to stand they would undermine the message sent out in *Mitchell*.

1 [2013] EWCA Civ 1624.

10.153 In a more recent case Mr Justice Turner considered a claimant's failure in complying with an order for sequential exchange of witness statements[1]. Mr Justice Turner commented in his judgment that this case 'provides yet another example of a litigant treating an order of the court as if compliance were an optional indulgence'. The claimant had failed to file or serve any witness statements or skeleton arguments, despite earlier orders made by the court. The judge took the view that the claimant was in error in failing to inform the court of the difficulty the claimant would face in complying with the order to serve and file witness evidence. Second, the claimant should have made an application to extend the time for compliance as soon as practicable and in any event before the deadline for compliance had passed. The judge relied upon the decision in *Mitchell* and indeed in the case of *Durrant v Chief Constable of Avon and Somerset Constabulary*. The court concluded there was no evidence of any good reason for the delay. The judge also took the view that the defendant was 'unduly timid' in not making an application to the court specifically in respect of the claimant's default. In any event the claimant was to be debarred from adducing the factual evidence it wished to use to support its arguments at trial as a consequence of its failure to comply with the court's earlier order for directions.

1 *MA Lloyd & Sons Ltd v PPC International Ltd* [2014] EWHC 41 (QB).

10.154 Applications for extension of time must be made in good time before the deadline has passed. Prompt applications will be considered appropriately by the court, but a significant delay in applying to vary an order will not be regarded favourably. Of course, thanks to CPR 3.8(4) 28-day extensions in writing can now be agreed by the parties, provided the hearing date is not put at risk.

10.155 Much has been written about *Mitchell* and *Denton* and the issues relating to applications for relief. A very helpful review of case law focusing on applications for relief from sanctions can be seen in *Civil Procedure*[1].

1 2014 Autumn Supplement at pp 26–45.

10.156 Any failure to comply with case management directions will allow a party to make an application for an order against the defaulting party, subject to the warning issued by the Court of Appeal in *Denton* requiring co-operation between the parties and the avoidance of parties taking bad points against each other. The party seeking to apply for an order against the party in default should do so without delay, though a warning to the other party of their intention to do so should be given first. The court will be concerned not to allow any postponement of the trial unless the circumstances are exceptional. Any postponement will have to be for the shortest possible time. The court will be determined to ensure rapid progress in the action even in the event of a postponement. The Masters at the High Court will expect parties to use common sense and act in accordance with their duty under CPR 1.3 to co-operate with each other and to assist the court with the overriding objective. The Masters will strongly discourage opportunistic applications. If a sanction is already provided by the rules no further application to impose sanctions will be required. The onus will be upon the defaulting party to apply for relief from sanction or an extension of time.

Costs estimates and costs capping

10.157 The Court of Appeal held that cost capping orders are essentially case management decisions depending heavily on the judge's perception of the needs of his case and it was only possible therefore to provide general statements about when, and in what circumstances, a costs capping order should be made[1]. With regard to costs estimates the Court of Appeal confirmed that these were crucial and a capping exercise cannot proceed unless the court has estimates on which to work. The Court of Appeal stated that where an estimate has been ordered and the costs sought on assessment differed by more than 20 per cent from that estimate, paras 6.5a and 6.6 of the 'Costs Practice Direction' (CPR 43 PD) provide that the discrepancy must be explained and may be taken into account in deciding whether the costs claimed are disproportionate or unreasonable. However, the party cannot be punished on assessment just because his costs differ from the estimate if there are good reasons for that difference. The Court of Appeal accepted that, although costs capping orders were attractive in theory, in practice they present formidable problems for the judiciary. The court also stated that the very high costs of civil litigation in England and Wales are of concern not merely to the parties in the *Willis* case, but also as far as the whole litigation system is concerned.

1 *Willis v Nicolson* [2007] EWCA Civ 199.

10.158 The court recommended that if a party wished to make an application for a capping order then it should do so at the earliest point possible. In the *Willis* case the appellant had issued his application relatively close to the date of trial. The Court of Appeal referred to the judgment of Gray J[1], where the learned judge stated: 'the purpose of a capping order is to enable the capped party to plan ahead the appropriate level of expenditure to bring the case to a trial at a cost which is in line with the amount of the cap'. The Court of Appeal also noted that, apart from timing, another practical issue that would have to be considered would be the time spent by a costs judge in analysing a case and providing a judgment on the appropriate cap to be ordered. That process could be 'as expensive and time consuming as a final assessment itself'. The Court of Appeal took the view, however, that the most obvious candidates for cost capping would be personal injury cases and that further guidance on costs capping should be provided but probably from the Civil Procedure Rules Committee rather than from the Court of Appeal. Cost capping applications in the Royal Courts of Justice in relation to clinical negligence cases have been considered by the Masters on a number of occasions. Usually the Masters would initially, where appropriate, order an estimate to be prepared and once that is served and lodged the matter would normally be referred to a costs Master at the SCCO. It is understood that in practice few, if any, clinical negligence claims have been subject to costs capping orders.

1 *Henry v BBC* [2005] EWHC 2503 (QB), [2006] 1 All ER 154 at [39].

Case management of multi-track matters in the Royal Courts of Justice

10.159 As previously stated, following receipt of the defence or following the transfer of a case to the Royal Courts of Justice (after a defence has been received) the case will normally be allocated to the multi-track on paper. The specialist clinical negligence Masters at the court will then fix a date for a case management conference. Unless there is a substantial degree of agreement it is unlikely that the Masters will hold a telephone case management conference, but if all the directions are agreed and a suitable consent order is drawn then the matter may be dealt with by post or e-mail, although a telephone conference may be held if there are issues to be discussed but that will not result in a hearing of more than 30 minutes.

10.160 The parties need to ensure that all the necessary papers are sent to the Master in good time to assist the Master in being able to determine any issues that arise between the parties. A draft of the proposed directions should be sent to the Master by e-mail and the party which seeks the telephone hearing should then make appropriate arrangements with the telephone conference provider. The Masters at the High Court will expect parties to use the 2015 directions[1].

1 See para **10.123** fn 1.

10.161 The draft order should be sent to all parties in the action in sufficient time for them to consider it before the case management conference. It helps the court if the draft order is double spaced with wide margins, to allow for corrections at the time that the order is made.

10.162 Certain elements of the suggested model directions include some passages in italics or in bold or normal text which set out matters which are there to assist the parties. In both the 2014 and 2015 annotated model directions is a warning which states:

'You must comply with the terms imposed upon you by this order otherwise your case is liable to be struck out or some other sanction imposed. If you cannot comply you are expected to make formal application to the court before any deadline imposed upon you expires'.

It will also be noted that, for example, periodical payments are referred to and the parties are advised that at the first CMC they should be prepared to give their provisional view as to whether the case is one in which a periodical payments order might be appropriate.

10.163 Although in due course the claimant may need to obtain a report from a financial adviser in relation to the issue of periodical payments, it is unlikely that a specific order in that regard will be made at the CMC.

10.164 As can be seen from the model directions a court will favour sequential exchange with regard to expert evidence on quantum, condition and prognosis. Many claimants' solicitors perhaps would still prefer simultaneous exchange of such reports but the presumption is certainly that sequential exchange will be ordered. The solicitor who is the co-author of this chapter is of the view that defendants in substantial cases will tend to obtain their own reports in any event, and it is not clear whether in overall terms this provision provides equal benefits to both sides.

10.165 The effect of the standard direction and the usual practice with regard to experts' discussions are that solicitors do not attend experts' discussions. Notwithstanding the observations of Tuckey LJ in the *Hubbard* case[1] and the potential issue over ECHR Article 6 compliance (the right to a fair trial), there has been no practice direction.

1 See *Hubbard v Lambeth Southwark and Lewisham Health Authority* [2001] EWCA Civ 1455.

10.166 Both the 2014 and 2015 versions of the model directions emphasise, like the earlier versions, that discussions between experts are not mandatory. The parties are to consider whether there is likely to be any useful purpose served in holding a discussion and should be prepared to agree that no discussion is in fact needed. The model directions also require that a draft agenda be prepared – assuming that a discussion between the experts is merited – which directs the experts to the remaining issues relevant to the experts' discipline as identified in the statements of case. However the use of an agenda is not mandatory. It is also suggested that there should be a preamble to the agenda, reminding the experts of the standard of proof and the *Bolam* test. The experts should also be reminded in the preamble that they should not seek to determine factual issues nor should the experts stray outside their field of expertise. It is suggested that the preamble also include a comprehensive list of supplementary materials which each expert has seen, although it would be assumed that the experts would have been provided with all the relevant notes at the outset. Providing one's experts with a bundle of relevant materials for the purpose of experts' discussions may well assist so that the experts can have ready access in a convenient format to the relevant materials.

10.167 The 2014/2015 directions also request that, with regard to service of the updated schedule of loss and the counter schedule, the parties should exchange schedules in a form which enables the counter schedule to be based on the claimant's schedule, ie by delivering a disc with the hard copy or by sending it as an e-mail attachment.

10.168 The 2014/2015 directions also include provision for alternative dispute resolution (ADR). They require the parties to consider ADR at all stages. Previously the model directions merely required the parties to consider whether the case was capable of resolution by ADR and provided a date when that consideration should take place. The 2014/2015 model directions helpfully confirm that ADR includes round table conferences at which the parties attempt to define and narrow the issues in the case, including those to which expert evidence is directed and in addition it covers early neutral evaluation, mediation and arbitration. The Masters at the High Court have noted that the parties have on occasion found the change to the model order unsettling having previously worked to a fixed date for ADR. The Masters at the High Court consider that there is no reason why the parties should not continue to do so. The new wording in the model order is designed to emphasise the need to keep ADR at the forefront of a party's mind throughout the litigation process. It is certainly the impression of the Masters at the High Court that ADR is now being used in a greater proportion of cases than ever before.

10.169 The 2014/2015 directions also provide for an application to be made, usually no later than six weeks after the CMC, to Queen's Bench Judges Listing in London for a listing appointment for a trial period for the hearing. The procedure for fixing a trial in the Royal Courts of Justice differs from practice elsewhere.

10.170 The 2014/2015 directions allow for the restoration of the case management conference prior to trial, although if all directions have been complied with and there are no further directions to be made the further CMC can be vacated by consent preferably by providing the Master with as much notice as possible. (Only some 50 per cent of cases proceed to the restored CMC.) Master Cook's current view is that the reference to pre-trial directions or a final CMC should be removed from the model order. On too many occasions practitioners do not inform the Master that they do not need directions or that the claim has settled wasting court time. Sending a consent order to the Masters Support Unit (MSU) will not result in the further CMC being vacated unless a specific request is made (the consent order should include an express provision vacating the further CMC). Master Cook is also of the view that it should be sufficient for the model order to provide for permission to restore, especially taking into account the increased emphasis on parties complying with rules, practice directions and orders. Practitioners should note the additional comments in italics relating to pre-trial directions which can be seen in the 2014 model directions (very slight changes have been made to the 2015 version in that regard).

10.171   Practitioners should also note that as the 2014/2015 model directions will provide permission to restore the application for further directions, the parties will be able to make an expedited application to the Masters provided that the time estimate for their application is 30 minutes or less. A joint letter from the parties stating that the application will take no longer than 30 minutes, and giving three dates on which both parties are available, should be provided to the court. The application will then be listed by the Master at 10.00 am on the first available of those dates, otherwise matters which will require more than 30 minutes should be applied for as a private room appointment in the usual way.

10.172   Following the implementation of the more robust approach by the court with regard to compliance for exchange of witness statements and the like court time was increasingly taken up with numerous applications for extensions of time. As a result in the 2014 model directions there was a new provision to allow the parties, by prior agreement in writing, to extend time for a direction in the order by up to 28 days and without the need to apply to the court; this is now enshrined in CPR 3.8(4). Both the 2014 and 2015 model directions require that if the parties need more than 28 days, then any agreed extension of time must be submitted to the court by e-mail including a brief explanation of the reasons, confirmation that it will not prejudice any hearing date and with a draft consent order provided in Word format. The court will then consider whether a formal application and hearing is necessary.

10.173   Telephone hearings in appropriate circumstances will be acceptable to the court. It should be noted that the extension of telephone hearings brought about by the revised version of CPR 23A PD 6 (effective from 6 April 2007) applies to all 'telephone conference enabled' courts. The Royal Court of Justice (RCJ) in fact is not a telephone conference enabled court. There is no doubt that the directions provide a framework for the case management of an action which contrasts significantly to the procedures which had been in place prior to the introduction of the CPR. There is no doubt that the use of the suggested model directions and the practice developed by the specialist Masters at the RCJ assists all parties in the efficient pursuit of their cases.

10.174   The Masters at the RCJ will expect counsel and/or the conducting solicitor to be in attendance at the first CMC (but not usually the parties themselves), although agents need to be appropriately considered as alternatives provided that they are well briefed. As already stated, the Masters will expect the parties to have provided well in advance a draft consent order, preferably agreed and in a suitable format as described above. The case summary should be as short as possible, covering the age of the claimant, what went wrong and with what result and where the parties are in relation to experts and the timetable for the case. Separate chronologies are useful especially if there is an application to be made in relation to extension of time or strike out. In more substantial matters a skeleton argument may be lodged in advance of the CMC but the Masters again request that these skeletons are as brief as possible. It should be added that the requirements which the parties should meet will usually be set out in the order for a CMC or a costs management hearing. In costs management hearings the Master will expect to be provided with a composite summary of the total costs for each stage of the proceedings and a list of cost issues.

10.175 It is rarely the case that spending time on preparing an appropriate consent order for a timetable is unproductive. It is important to know the availability of one's experts before committing them to a timetable which is frankly impractical. Real life tends to intrude on the best laid plans, and discussing the proposed timetable with one's experts and counsel may well be helpful and prevent a situation where at some point in the future an application for an extension of time will need to be made. At the first CMC the claimant should always seek an order for interim judgment if it is appropriate to do so, although this may prove problematic and practitioners should consider making separate applications especially if the matter will be strongly contested. An application for a substantial payment for alternative accommodation may cause difficulties as a result of the impact of periodical payments.

10.176 Following the CMC the claimant's solicitor will need to draw and file the order made by the time specified in the draft order initialled by the Master. Obviously once a trial window, or more rarely a fixed date, is obtained then witness summonses should be served on the experts (and as appropriate lay witnesses) at the earliest opportunity. Needless to state, the key dates set out in the directions should be diarised and an application made to Queen's Bench Judges Listing on or before the date given in the directions for an appointment to fix. Practitioners should also note the matters set out in the model directions (under trial directions) relating to the procedure in obtaining a 'trial period' rather than a fixed date. The comments in italics in the model directions state that in order to accommodate the parties' need for certainty as to dates for experts to attend, Queen's Bench Judges Listing will, if an approach is made close to the beginning of the trial period, confirm the date for the trial to begin as the first date of the trial period. Indeed, Listing will also consider, for example, a second-day start in the trial window.

Preliminary issue of limitation

10.177 This matter is dealt with elsewhere at length. It has already been seen that the court will need to consider at the first CMC whether a preliminary issue needs to be tried, which would clearly include an issue such as limitation. Specific directions can then be given for the determination of that issue (CPR 29 PD 5.3(7)).

PURSUIT OF PROCEEDINGS POST FIRST CMC TO PRE-TRIAL REVIEW

Disclosure (CPR 31)

10.178 The model directions mentioned above provide for standard disclosure by list/category to be effected by the set date and any initial request for inspection or copy documentation is to be made within seven days of service of the list. Practice form N265 should be used. It should be noted that CPR 31.6 requires a party to disclose only the documents on which he relies and the documents which adversely affect his own case, adversely affects another party's case or supports another party's case (together with any documents which may be required to be disclosed by a relevant practice direction). The procedure for standard disclosure is set out at CPR 31.10. This confirms what the list should indicate and stipulates that the list must include a disclosure statement. As from 1 April 2013 CPR 31.5 was amended. It includes additional requirements in relation to disclosure of electronic documents, albeit at CPR 31.5(2) it states: 'unless the court otherwise orders, paragraphs (3) to (8) apply to all multi-track claims, other than those which include a claim for personal injuries'. The reference to paras (3) to (8) relate to the requirements for reporting in relation to electronic documents, which do not apply to personal injury (including therefore clinical negligence) cases.

10.179   The parties must undertake a reasonable search for documents (CPR 31.7). In the light of the practice of obtaining disclosure from a defendant in relation to the relevant medical records prior to issue it may be the case that there will be few issues relating to disclosure at this stage of the proceedings. However, all practitioners will have had experience with defendants where key documentation has apparently gone missing or has been destroyed. Cases where records have been deliberately altered do occur and appropriate application of the CPR to deal with these problems needs to be pursued robustly. Evidence that goes missing inevitably prejudices the claimant to a greater extent than it prejudices the defendant. In certain cases, however, the defendant may have concerns in relation to the adequacy of the claimant's disclosure, especially with regard to documents relevant to special damages. An application for specific disclosure may be made pursuant to CPR 31.12. The court will have to balance one party's right to a fair hearing with another party's right to privacy.

10.180   The parties' duty of disclosure continues during the course of the proceedings (CPR 31.11). This means that in a clinical negligence case where the claimant's medical records are clearly relevant to the issues in the action, then those records will need to be regularly updated and disclosed to the opponent during the course of the proceedings. Indeed if relevant documents come to a party's notice at any time during the proceedings they must immediately notify every other party (CPR 31.11(2)). If the party wishes to inspect documents referred to in the expert's report of another party then, prior to issuing an application, a request should be made for inspection of the documents and inspection should be provided by agreement unless the request is unreasonable (CPR 31A PD 7 and CPR 31.14(2)).

Witness statements and depositions (CPR 22 and 32)

10.181   The court has wide powers to control evidence by giving directions which may exclude evidence and limit cross examination (CPR 32.1). The general rule is that any fact which needs to be proved by the evidence of a witness is to be proved at trial by oral evidence (CPR 32.2). As from 1 April 2013 a new rule has been added, namely CPR 32.2(3) which deals with evidence of witnesses and states that the court may give directions identifying or limiting the issues to which factual evidence may be directed and also may give directions identifying the witnesses who may be called or whose evidence may be read, or limiting the length or format of witness statements. In Jackson LJ's final report dealing with civil litigation costs he was critical of the wastage of costs incurred as a result of lengthy and irrelevant witness statements, hence the revised rule provides additional powers to the court to give directions in relation to witness evidence. However, evidence may be allowed by video link or other means (CPR 32.3). A witness statement containing the evidence which the witness would be allowed to give orally will be served as the court directs (CPR 32.4).

10.182   A witness statement must comply with the requirements set out in CPR 32 PD 17 and must be verified by a statement of truth in accordance with CPR 22 and CPR 32 PD 20. In the event that the witness makes a false statement without an honest belief in its truth then contempt proceedings may be brought against that witness (CPR 32.14).

10.183   A party who is required to serve a witness statement but is unable to obtain one may apply without notice for permission to serve a witness summary instead (CPR 32.9).

10.184   'Hearsay' is defined in CPR 33.1 as a statement made otherwise than by a person while giving oral evidence in proceedings which is tendered as evidence of the matters stated and references to hearsay include hearsay of whatever degree. If a party intends to rely on hearsay evidence at trial then the party needs to comply with the Civil Evidence Act 1995, s 2(1)(a) (CPR 33.2).

10.185   The party who has served a witness statement which he wishes to rely upon at trial must call the witness to give oral evidence at trial unless the court orders otherwise or he puts in the statement as hearsay evidence (CPR 32.5). Where a witness is called to give oral evidence his statement will stand as evidence in chief unless the court orders otherwise. Provided the court gives permission the witness may amplify his statement and give evidence in relation to new matters which have arisen since his statement was served. It should be noted that if a party who has served a witness statement has not called that witness to give evidence at trial or put the witness statement in as hearsay evidence, then any other party may put that witness statement in as hearsay evidence (CPR 32.5(5)).

10.186   The preparation of witness statements can be difficult for both sides in a clinical negligence case. The aim to have the statement in the own words of the witness is laudable but often impractical. Traps can lurk in a statement which may afford fertile grounds for cross examination at trial. Although defendants' statements prepared for witnesses who are clinicians are meant to deal with matters of fact, the temptation for defendants must be to include opinion evidence which will support the overall defence to a claim. On the other hand a claimant may wish to call a treating doctor to provide oral factual evidence in his case and this should be permitted provided that the clinician's evidence was clearly evidence of fact as confirmed by the Court of Appeal in *Kirkman v EuroExide Corpn (CMP Batteries Ltd)*[1]. In that case the district judge at first instance had allowed the claimant to rely on his clinician's witness evidence as factual evidence rather than opinion evidence. The defendant appealed the district judge's decision and the circuit judge upheld that appeal. The circuit judge was concerned that if the claimant was allowed to call factual evidence from a clinician, then essentially the claimant's expert witnesses would outnumber the defendants. The Court of Appeal subsequently reviewed the case and concluded that the opinion of the district judge had been correct. The clinician's evidence was clearly evidence of fact. The Court of Appeal recognised that at trial under cross examination the clinician might be drawn into expressing an expert opinion but 'it must be a matter for the trial judge's discretion ... to permit such a development'[2].

1 [2007] EWCA Civ 66.
2 [2007] EWCA Civ 66 per Smith LJ at [21].

10.187 CPR 32 also deals with notices to admit facts and notices to admit or produce documents. A party may serve a notice on another party requiring him to admit the facts, or the part of the case that the serving party specified in the notice served. Such a notice must be served no later than 21 days before trial. Where the other party makes any admission in response to the notice the admission may be used against him only in the proceedings in which the notice to admit is served and by the party who served the notice. The court may allow a party to amend or withdraw any admission made by him on such terms as it thinks just (CPR 32.18). There may be costs implications for a party who failed to admit facts that he ought to have admitted. In such a case the court will have to consider all the circumstances which are to be taken into account when exercising its discretion as to costs (CPR 44.3) and to consider the relevant factors which need to be taken into account in deciding the amount of costs to be ordered (CPR 44.3(4)).

10.188 Each party shall be deemed to admit the authenticity of a document disclosed to him under Part 31 unless he serves notice that he wishes the document to be proved at trial. The notice must be served by the latest date for serving witness statements or within seven days of disclosure of the document, whichever is later (CPR 32.19). This emphasises the importance of scrutinising carefully the list of documents served by a party in an action in order to establish whether a notice to admit or produce documents should be issued forthwith following disclosure and inspection. It should be noted that the practice direction that accompanies CPR 32 provides little in amplification to either CPR 32.18 or CPR 32.19.

Witnesses and depositions (CPR 34)

10.189 CPR 34 deals with the use of witness summonses to secure the attendance of the witness at the trial or prior hearing. It also sets out the rules on the use of depositions which may be required if the witness will not be able to give oral evidence at trial. It is understood that the rules on the taking of depositions come into play only rarely and their use will not be considered in detail below.

10.190 A witness summons is a document issued by the court requiring a witness to attend court to give evidence or produce documents to the court (CPR 34.2). The witness summons must be in the relevant practice form which is currently form N20. It is necessary to serve a separate witness summons for each witness. The summons may require a witness to produce documents to the court either on a date fixed for a hearing or such date as the court may direct.

10.191 A witness summons is issued on the date entered on the summons by the court. A party does not need permission to issue a witness summons normally but will need permission if the summons is to be issued less than seven days before the date of trial. If a party wishes to issue a summons for a witness to attend court to give evidence or to produce documents on any date except the date fixed for trial or to give evidence or to produce documents at any hearing except the trial then permission from the court will also be required. The summons has to be issued at the court where the case is proceeding or where the hearing in question will be held (CPR 34.3).

10.192 As already indicated, the general rule is that a witness summons is binding if it is served at least seven days before the date on which the witness is required to attend before the court or tribunal, unless the court orders otherwise (CPR 34.5). The court will serve the witness summons unless the party issuing the summons specifically requests in writing that service should be effected by the party himself. If the court is to serve the witness summons then the party on whose behalf it is issued must deposit in the court office the money to be paid or offered to the witness pursuant to CPR 34.7 (previously known as 'conduct money'). Personal service is not mandatory but there may be circumstances when it would be preferable for personal service to be effected (for example in a situation where the witness may be reluctant to attend or has failed to confirm that they will attend).

10.193 CPR 34.7 stipulates that at the time of service of a witness summons the witness *must* be offered or paid a sum reasonably sufficient to cover his expenses in travelling to and from court and an appropriate sum by way of compensation for 'loss of time'. It is always prudent to serve witness summonses on an expert witness (indeed on any key witness) at the earliest opportunity to ensure their attendance at trial[1].

1 Further details can be seen in the useful editorial note in the *White Book* (2014) Vol 1, para 34.7.1.

Depositions

10.194 There may be rare occasions when it will be necessary and appropriate to obtain a deposition from a witness who will be unable to attend the trial and where other means of introducing that evidence would prove prohibitively expensive. CPR 34.8 provides that a party may apply for an order for a person to be examined before the hearing takes place. An order under this rule would be for the witness (that is the 'deponent') to be examined on oath before a judge or an examiner of the court or a person appointed by the court. At the time of service of the order the defendant must be offered or paid a sum reasonably sufficient to cover his expenses in travelling to and from the place of examination and an appropriate sum by way of compensation for loss of time (which will be on the same basis as the allowances provided for normal witnesses when a witness summons is served). The conduct of the examination of the deponent is set out at CPR 34.9 and essentially requires that the examination must be conducted in the same way as if the witness were giving evidence at a trial. Naturally the evidence given by the deponent should be recorded in full and a copy of the deposition should be sent to the party who had obtained the order for the examination of the witness and to the court. The party who obtained the order must also arrange to have a copy of the deposition served on all the other parties to the action. The party seeking to use the deposition at a hearing must follow the provisions of CPR 34.11, which stipulates that the party intending to put in evidence a deposition at a hearing must serve notice of his intention to do so on every other party to the action and the notice must be served at least 21 days before the date fixed for the hearing. The procedure to follow where a person is examined outside the jurisdiction is set out at CPR 34.13. Consideration must be given to the practice direction that accompanies CPR 34 which provides for more detailed rules and guidance on the use of depositions (CPR 34A PD 4).

Expert evidence

10.195 The Civil Justice Council Guidance for the Instruction of Experts to Give Evidence in Civil Claims (which replaced the previous Code of Guidance) is set out in full at the end of CPR 35 PD[1]. The guidance aims to provide a steer on good practice and to set appropriate standards for experts. The guidance supplements CPR 35 and CPR 35 PD but does not replace them. The guidance emphasises that experts must not serve the exclusive interests of those who retain them but rather the expert must comply with their overriding duty to the court as required by CPR 35.3.

1 The guidance was updated in August 2014 and the new guidance can be seen in the Autumn 2014 Supplement of Civil Procedure at pp 85–97.

10.196 Expert evidence will only be allowed if it is reasonably required to resolve the proceedings (CPR 35.1). Indeed a party may not put in expert evidence or call an expert to give oral evidence without permission from the court (CPR 35.4). The court has the power to limit or cap experts' fees as appropriate. The court is also under a duty to restrict expert evidence (CPR 35.1). In clinical negligence cases this duty should not be slavishly followed. In *S v Chesterfield and North Derbyshire Royal Hospital NHS Trust*[1] the claimant was allowed two opinion experts where the defendant had two from the same discipline as witnesses of facts. The Court of Appeal took into account the fact that the claim was worth approximately £1.5 million and the issues were complex. The overriding objective – to deal with cases justly (as per the old version of CPR 1.1) – supported the decision to allow the claimant to rely on two experts in the circumstances.

1 [2003] EWCA Civ 1284.

10.197 Of course, the overriding objective has been changed as from 1 April 2013 and the court will have to consider that when cases are to be treated justly it must be at 'proportionate cost'.

The court now has the power to direct that experts of like discipline shall give their evidence concurrently. This power emanates from CPR 35 PD.11 which also explains the procedure that should apply. In Australia where the procedure has been followed, it was described as 'hot tubbing'. Practitioners should be alert to the possibility of hot tubbing, although some practitioners may take the view that that process may generate more unpredictable outcomes than the old regime.

10.198   The form and content of an expert's report are set out in CPR 35 PD 3.2. See Chapter 9.

Discussions between experts

10.199   The court has the power of course to direct that a discussion takes place between experts (at any stage in the proceedings) for the purpose of identifying and discussing the expert issues in the proceedings and where possible to reach an agreed opinion on those issues. The court may specify the issues which the experts need to discuss and direct that following a discussion between the experts they prepare a statement for the court showing those issues on which they agree and those issues on which they disagree, providing a summary of their reasons for disagreeing. However, the content of the discussion between the experts shall not be referred to at trial unless the parties agree. If the experts reach an agreement on an issue during their discussions that agreement shall not bind the parties unless the parties expressly agree to be bound by that agreement (CPR 35.12).

10.200   The suggested model directions relating to experts' discussions is considered above at para **10.165**. There is no doubt that concerns with experts' discussions remain widespread. The parties' legal representatives will be concerned at the prospect of the experts' discussions because the outcome of that event can make or break their case. The court may be concerned in the light of the costs arising from such discussions, especially where there is vigorous debate on the content of the agenda for that discussion. Experts appear to be divided on the issue of the attendance of lawyers at the discussion. Some experts would be hostile to any lawyer being present, whereas other experts will welcome their presence. Experts' discussions should not be an opportunity for one expert to 'bully' the other into submission. This is not a fanciful concern, as practitioners know from their own experience that force of personality is a significant factor and that some experts are more robust in those terms than others. The introduction of the use of a moderator between the parties' experts at discussions may assist in providing an additional means of control to ensure that a fair discussion takes place. Recording discussions (whether lawyers are present or not) may also assist. The presence of lawyers at such discussions – provided that they behave in accordance with the old model direction – would be another mechanism to ensure fairness.

10.201   The Guidance for the Instruction of Experts also covers the issue of discussions between experts. At para 73 it recommends that in multi-track cases the parties, their lawyers and experts should cooperate to produce the agenda for any discussion between experts, although primary responsibility for the preparation of the agenda should normally lie with the parties' solicitors. The agenda should indicate what matters have been agreed and summarise concisely those which are in dispute. The protocol suggests that it is often helpful for it to include questions to be answered by the experts and goes on to state that if the parties cannot reach agreement on the agenda then the court may give directions for the drawing up of the agenda. The model direction also provides for the preparation of an agenda for the experts' discussions as discussed at para **10.166**. The current model directions require provision of a preamble to the experts' agenda which sets out the relevant legal tests for the experts to consider and confirms that it would be helpful for the agenda to include a comprehensive list of the materials which each expert has seen, perhaps in the form of an agreed supplementary bundle (and it is assumed that the experts will also have been provided with a bundle of medical notes). Notwithstanding the model direction covering the provision of unpublished literature and the provision of a list of published literature, experts may have left preparation for the discussion late in the day and so they may bring with them to the discussion literature which has not been previously disclosed. That represents a clear breach of the model direction and could justify an adjournment of the discussion or at the very least the setting up of a further discussion to explore properly the issues raised by that literature if the issues raised by the new documentation are sufficiently significant to justify that step being taken. The whole thrust of the CPR is to avoid parties ambushing each other but regrettably such ambushes still occur.

10.202   If a party fails to disclose an expert's report then they will not be able to use the report at the trial or call the expert to give evidence orally unless the court gives permission (CPR 35.13).

10.203   An expert may wish to write to the court to ask for directions in appropriate cases to assist him in carrying out his function as an expert. Such a written request to the court, however, should be copied to the party instructing the expert at least seven days before he files the request and to all other parties at least four days before he files the request with the court (CPR 35.14). Such applications appear to be very rare in practice.

10.204   Neither CPR 35 nor the practice direction accompanying it deal with the issue of amendment of experts' reports but that is considered at length in the Guidance for the Instruction of Experts. At para 62 the guidance states that an expert should not amend his report in a manner which distorts his true opinion. Amended reports should include reasons for amendments (para 64 of the protocol) where the amendment effectively amounts to a significant alteration of the expert's original opinion. Furthermore, should an expert change his opinion following an experts' discussion, a simple signed and dated note to that effect is (so the protocol states) generally sufficient. This is incorporated into the model direction which includes the provision that 'if an expert radically alters his or her opinion, the joint statement should include a note or addendum by that expert explaining the change of opinion'. Interestingly the Guidance also states that experts should normally attend court without the need for the service of witness summonses but on occasion they may be served to require attendance (para 84)[1].

1 The solicitor co-author favours experts being issued with witness summonses and being able to evidence service.

10.205   Although it may rarely be required, practitioners should also consider whether, following receipt of the joint statement following the experts' discussion, formal questions are to be put for clarification purposes. An application to the court for a direction in that regard will be required although it should be explored whether the matter can be dealt with by way of a consent order.

Schedule of loss

10.206   The suggested model directions include provision for the claimant to serve by a given date their final schedule of loss and damage costed to the date of trial. In the event that the experts' discussion impacts upon quantum (as it is bound to do where experts' discussions include quantum experts) then the updating of the schedule of loss may need to be postponed pending the outcome of the experts' discussions. Alternatively it may be necessary to revise the schedule prior to trial. Although this may have been considered at the CMC, in practice the fixing of a date for the experts' discussions can prove problematic and the outcome of discussions may well not become available until sometime after the date which has been fixed for service of the final schedule. If it is not possible to agree a variation of the timetable with regard to service of the schedule of loss, then an application for further directions will be needed. As stated elsewhere the Masters at the High Court prefer a fully costed schedule served at an earlier date. Post 1 April 2013 there will be less indulgence for parties failing to comply with the directions.

Alternative dispute resolution

10.207   As stated above at para **10.168** there is a standard direction in the model directions for the parties to consider alternative dispute resolution (ADR). It would be most unusual if a claimant took the view that ADR should not be put forward as a proposal to the opponent. In practice it is probably the case that the only issues concerning ADR involve the question as to at what stage in the proceedings ADR should be pursued, and second in what form it should be pursued.

Pre-trial review

10.208   In multi-track cases CPR 29.7 provides that if, on receipt of the parties' pre-trial checklists, the court decides to hold a PTR, or to cancel a PTR which has already been fixed, then it will serve a notice of its decision at least seven days before the date fixed for the hearing or as the case may be the cancelled hearing. The direction in the suggested model directions dealing with the PTR issue in multi-track cases is discussed at para **10.170** above. Where the parties have fully complied with the directions and there are no further directions to be made the CMC/PTR can be vacated by consent. In other cases the PTR or adjourned CMC will be an opportunity to review what directions have yet to be undertaken and what new directions, if any, will be required in order to prepare the action for trial. The PTR may also afford a further opportunity for settlement before the full trial costs are incurred. If the action is proceeding outside the Royal Courts of Justice then practitioners will need to know what specific requirements their own court may have in relation to attendance at the PTR, as this could again include a requirement that all parties are to be in attendance (especially important if it is reasonable to take the opportunity of a PTR to consider settlement).

PRE-TRIAL MATTERS

10.209 In this section consideration will be given to such matters as interlocutory hearings, funding issues, pre-trial conferences with counsel, dealing with the updating of the claimant's schedule of loss, offers to settle and settlement.

Interlocutory hearings

Fast track

10.210 Interlocutory hearings in the fast track are likely to be rare. At or before allocation the parties should apply for summary judgment and/or for alternative directions to those that have been set by the court. If a party needs to apply for permission to amend its case, that should be done as soon as possible so as to minimise the need to change the timetable (CPR 28 PD 2.8). At listing any directions needed should be limited to fine tuning the timetable and the necessary preparation for trial (for example covering the agreed trial timetable). If one party is in default in relation to following the set timetable, the other party who is entitled to apply for an order must do so without delay (CPR 28 PD 5.2), but should first warn his opponent of his intention to do so. Applications which are often seen in multi-track cases such as applications for interim payments will probably be rare, if not non-existent, in fast track cases.

Multi-track

10.211 This section will look at the most common applications in clinical negligence cases which may require consideration at an interlocutory hearing but will not look at all possible applications. It is unlikely in a clinical negligence case that a practitioner will be facing an application disputing the court's jurisdiction (covered by CPR 11). Practitioners may, on occasion, wish to enter default judgment, but if the defendant is dealing with the matter appropriately that should be a rare occurrence although it is covered by CPR 12 and the corresponding practice direction. Similarly the issue of setting aside/varying a default judgment is unlikely to come up regularly in practice. This is, however, covered by CPR 13. Adding or subtracting parties to litigation and dealing with issues relevant to group litigation is covered by CPR 19. Discontinuance is dealt with by CPR 38. On rare occasions a practitioner may have to apply to change the party's solicitor pursuant to CPR 42 or to deal with issues concerning disclosure in CPR 31. None of these applications will be considered in detail in this section. However, the applications which will be considered in some detail below include applications relating to: adjournment; amendments of case; further information; summary judgment and applications for interim payments and variation of the court's timetable; and finally applications relating to experts' meetings.

10.212   The general rules relating to interlocutory applications can be seen in CPR 23. The general rule is that an applicant must file an application notice unless that is not required by the appropriate rule or practice direction. The court may also dispense with that requirement in appropriate cases (CPR 23.3). The application must be served on each respondent unless that is not required by the rules or the relevant practice direction (CPR 23.4). The practice direction accompanying the rule provides further guidance on applications including the procedures to follow with regard to telephone hearings (CPR 23.6) and the requirements for the provision of evidence and certain types of application (CPR 23.9) and finally in relation to consent orders (CPR 23.10). In practice the clinical negligence Masters at the Royal Courts of Justice are increasingly making orders during telephone hearings, but will only do so if a draft of the proposed order is supplied as an e-mail attachment and in Word format, in which case the final order can be sealed and sent out by the court, usually to the claimant's solicitor for service on the defendant. In all other cases sufficient copies should be provided to the MSU (Masters Support Unit) for sealing with the original draft signed by the Master.

Adjournment

10.213   Pursuant to CPR 3.1(2) the court has power to adjourn or bring forward a hearing. The court will have regard to the overriding objective in order to deal with the case justly and at proportionate cost (CPR 1.1). As previously stated CPR 29 PD 7(5) stipulates that in cases where the court has no option but to postpone the trial, it will do so for the shortest possible time and will give directions for the taking of the necessary steps in the meantime as rapidly as possible. Where the action is proceeding in the Royal Courts of Justice and the case has been listed for trial, an application for adjournment must be made to the judge in charge of the non-jury lists. Applications for adjournment have to be regarded as an application of the last resort and such applications may well fail if the court takes the view that there are no compelling reasons for adjournment. Of course such an application for an adjournment should be on notice and supported by evidence.

10.214   It is, of course, a well-established principle that the court should aim to see an early resolution to all the issues in an action. The principle of finality remains crucial, though there may be cases where the uncertainty of outcome is such that postponement of final resolution of an issue may be in the interest of justice[1].

1 *Cook v Cook* [2011] EWHC 1638 (QB).

Amendments

10.215   CPR 17.1 provides that a party may amend his statement of case at any time before it has been served. After service a party may amend only with the consent of the parties or with permission of the court (CPR 17.1(2)). If an application is required to remove, add or substitute a party then the procedure set out in CPR 19.4 must be followed. Rules relating to endorsing amending statements of case and using appropriate colours to show the different amendments are covered in CPR 17 PD 2. However, it may be appropriate not to show the original amendments unless the court orders otherwise. In rare cases where a party has amended the statement of case without needing permission and serves the amended copy on an opponent the latter may issue an application to disallow the amendment if the application is issued within 14 days of service of the amended statement of case (CPR 17.2).

10.216 If permission to amend is needed from the court then CPR 17.3 provides that the court may give directions as to service of the amended case and give directions as to what amendments, if any, are required to any other statement of case in the action. If a claimant therefore amends the particulars of claim the court is likely to permit the defendant to amend their defence as appropriate.

10.217 The applicant seeking an amendment will normally have to file the amended statement of case within 14 days of the order and if the amendment is substantial the statement of case should be re-verified by a further statement of truth (CPR 17 PD 1.4).

10.218 The party who amends will almost invariably be ordered to bear the costs of the amendment and pay any consequential costs arising from it. Depending on the nature and timing of the amendment those costs may be very significant indeed. An amendment at trial where, but for the amendment, the trial would have been lost should enable a defendant to claim their costs of the action down to the date of the amendment[1]. In certain cases, however, the court may award costs in favour of the party seeking the amendment. This is possible in a case where a party unreasonably refuses to consent to an amendment, thereby provoking an application[2].

1 *Beoco Ltd v Alfa Laval Co Ltd* [1995] QB 137.
2 *La Chemise Lacoste SA v Sketchers USA Ltd* [2006] EWHC 3642 (Ch).

10.219 Amendments where the relevant limitation period has ended may be allowed, but only if the new claim arises out of the same facts or substantially the same facts as can be seen in the claim which is already being pursued (CPR 17.4). The court may also allow an amendment to correct a genuine mistake concerning the capacity of a party where the mistake was not only genuine but also where that mistake would not have caused any reasonable doubt as to the correct capacity of the party (CPR 17.4(3)).

Further information (CPR 18)

10.220 Pursuant to CPR 18.1 the court may make an order, at any time, that a party should clarify any matter which is in dispute in the proceedings or give additional information in relation to any such matters whether or not the matter is contained or referred to in a statement of case. However, before an application is made to the court a party should seek clarification or information by way of a written request to their opponent providing the opponent with a reasonable time period for their response (CPR 18 PD 1). Detailed guidance on the contents of such a request and the making of an application relating to the request can be seen in CPR 18 PD 1 and CPR 18 PD 5. A response should be verified by a statement of truth (CPR 18 PD 3). The relevance of the provisions in CPR 18 is obvious and consideration should be given following receipt of the statement of case as to whether a request pursuant to CPR 18 should be made. In other instances, for example, a defendant may wish to use the provisions of CPR 18 to raise questions relating to quantum. However, fishing expeditions will not be allowed by the court, nor will the court entertain requests which essentially go solely to cross examination as to credit[1]. An order made pursuant to CPR 18 needs to follow the precedent order set out at Practice Form 58.

1 *Thorpe v Chief Constable of Greater Manchester Police* [1989] 1 WLR 665.

Summary judgment (CPR 24)

10.221 If the claimant has no real prospect of succeeding on the claim or on any particular issues in the claim or where a defendant has no real prospect of successfully defending the claim or an issue in the claim and there is no other compelling reason why the case or issue should be disposed of at trial, then the court may grant summary judgment (CPR 24.2). A party needs to show some chance of success on an issue (albeit a 'real' rather than a fanciful chance) in order to defeat such an application. The procedure to follow in making such an application is set out in CPR 24 PD 2. Normally the claimant will apply for summary judgment once the acknowledgement of service or defence has been filed (CPR 24.4). This should also be, as previously stated, before or when the directions questionnaire is filed. Written evidence may be relied upon in support of the application in accordance with CPR 24.5 and CPR 24 PD 2. The latter provisions also cover the issue of service of evidence in reply. The general rule is that written (not oral) evidence will be permitted at the hearing (CPR 32.6). The court may give directions on the management of a case following a determination of the application for summary judgment and those directions may include a direction on filing and service of a defence (CPR 24.6). The court may also attach conditions when making an order, although the application of such a conditional order in a clinical negligence case appears of little relevance. In practice applications for summary judgment will be rarely made and only perhaps in the most obvious cases, bearing in mind that the court may be reluctant to take the view that a party has no chance of success on an issue.

Interim payments (CPR 25)

10.222 Applications for interim payments in multi-track cases will be seen regularly. However, the claimant's receipt of legal aid or welfare benefits could be jeopardised unless steps are taken to avoid any prejudicial effects from obtaining a sizeable interim payment. Interim payments for specific equipment for a disabled claimant or to pay for care should not jeopardise the claimant's receipt of legal aid or means-tested benefits. However, a substantial interim payment which is unspecific and general may have an adverse effect upon a client's position with regard to receipt of benefits or legal aid. Care needs to be taken to avoid such an unfortunate occurrence. Setting up a special needs trust (ie a personal injury trust) may protect the claimant's means-tested benefits and such a trust may need to be set up during the case not just at the end of the action.

10.223 Alternatively, keeping the monies in court for future use with permission of the court and the Public Guardianship Office (PGO) may be an appropriate way of dealing with funds in a case where the claimant is legally aided and/or in receipt of means-tested benefits. Assuming that any potential practical problems can be remedied any practitioner should be seeking early interim payments to assist their client especially in substantial matters. The general procedure for making an interim payment application is covered by CPR 25.6. Applications should be issued after the acknowledgement of service has been filed. Such applications need to be served at least 14 days before the application is to be heard and must be supported by evidence. If the respondent to the application seeks to rely upon written evidence in reply then that also needs to be served on the parties at least seven days before the hearing. If an applicant wishes to then file/serve further evidence in response to the other party's evidence then that should be filed/served at least three days before the hearing.

10.224   It should also be noted that pursuant to CPR 25 PD 1.2 the permission of the court must be obtained before making a voluntary interim payment in respect of a claim by a child or protected party.

10.225   When making an application for an interim payment for damages the evidence adduced in support of the application should cover:

- the sum of money sought by way of interim payment;
- the items or matter in respect of which the interim payment is sought;
- the sum of money for which the final judgment is likely to be given;
- the reasons for believing that the conditions set out in CPR 25.7 are satisfied; and
- in claims for personal injuries, details of special damages and past and future loss; and
- where the claim is under the Fatal Accidents Act 1976, details of the persons on whose behalf the claim was made, together with details on the nature of their claim (CPR 25B PD 2).

10.226   As indicated above, the court will only make an order for an interim payment if certain conditions set out in CPR 25.7 are satisfied, namely that the defendant has admitted liability or that judgment for damages to be assessed has been granted or if the matter went to trial substantial damages would be obtained by the claimant. However the court should not make an order of more than a reasonable proportion of the likely amount of the final judgment (CPR 25.7(4)).

10.227   Practitioners need to be aware of the potential problems in obtaining a substantial interim payment for an alternative property[1]. A judge would usually make a conservative preliminary estimate of the likely final award and, whilst erring on the side of caution, the judge would then order an interim payment which allowed a comfortable margin in case the judge's preliminary estimate turned out to be too generous.

1 *Eeles v Cobham Hire Services Ltd* [2009] EWCA Civ 204. See also *Spillman v Bradfield Riding Centre* [2007] EWHC 89 (QB).

10.228   The court would also be cognisant of the fact that an interim payment order should not effectively shackle the trial judge, whose discretion in making a final damages award should not be fettered. The option of awarding a periodical payments order (PPO) meant that any court would have to take into account how an interim order might affect a PPO. Lady Justice Smith held that whilst the court has power to order an interim payment, that discretionary power is however not unfettered. It is restricted by virtue of CPR 25.7(4). In other words, the court has no power to make an order for more than 'a reasonable proportion' of the likely amount of the final judgment. In a case in which a PPO is likely to be made, the amount of the final judgment is the actual capital sum awarded (ignoring the PPO itself). It was noted that if a judge makes too large an interim payment then that sum is lost for all time for the purposes of founding a PPO.

10.229   The first step was for the court to consider the likely awards for the heads of damage which are bound to be ordered as lump sums. The court considered that other heads of damage such as future loss of earnings, costs of care, case management, therapies, equipment, increased holiday costs and the Court of Protection costs were potentially the subject of PPOs. A judge should stop at a figure which he is satisfied is likely to be awarded as a capital sum. He may award a reasonable proportion of that figure. It may be reasonable to award a high proportion of that figure provided that the estimate has been a conservative one.

10.230   In some cases, however, the judge may be confident that the trial judge will capitalise additional elements of the future losses so as to produce a greater lump sum award. In such a case a larger interim payment can be justified. This will be achieved in cases where the claimant can clearly demonstrate a need for an immediate capital sum probably to fund the purchase of accommodation.

10.231   A judge nonetheless should have a 'high degree of confidence' that such a course is appropriate and that a trial judge would endorse the capitalisation undertaken. The Court of Appeal's decision in *Eeles*[1] has been followed in a number of cases since 2009[2].

1 *Eeles v Cobham Hire Services Ltd* [2009] EWCA Civ 204. See also *Spillman v Bradfield Riding Centre* [2007] EWHC 89 (QB).
2 *Mabiriizi v HSBC Insurance (UK) Ltd* [2011] EWHC 1280 (QB); *FP v Taunton & Somerset NHS Trust* [2011] EWHC 3380 (QB).

10.232   In the case of a child or patient the monies may be left in court so that the litigation friend may use the fund as and when appropriate, subject to approval from the district judge/Master and where relevant the PGO.

10.233   The relevance of the recoupment regulations need to be appreciated, however, in the context of an interim payment application. CPR 25B PD 4 states that in a claim for personal injuries where an application for an interim payment is being pursued and where the issue of relevant welfare benefits received is relevant to the case, then the defendant should obtain from the Secretary of State a certificate of recoverable benefits. A copy of the certificate should be filed at the hearing of the application for an interim payment and the order made should set out the amount by which the payment made to the claimant has been reduced in accordance with the provisions of the Social Security (Recovery of Benefits) Act 1997, Sch 2, as amended. The payment made to the claimant will be the net amount, but the interim payment for the purposes of the final judgment figure in the interim payment application will be the gross amount.

Variation of timetable (CPR 3 and CPR 29)

10.234   This is discussed at some length at para **10.144** (fast track) and paras **10.150** ff and **10.170** (multi-track). It is perhaps worth emphasising that CPR 3.8(3) states where a rule, practice direction or court order: (a) requires a party to do something within a specified time; and (b) specifies the consequence of failure to comply, the time for doing the act in question may not be extended by agreement between the parties.

10.235   If additional time is needed to allow for service of witness statements and experts' reports then this is likely to require court approval (unless CPR 3.8(4) can be used to obtain a 28-day extension which is to be evidenced by an agreement in writing). CPR 32.10 states that if a witness statement or a witness summary for use at trial is not served in respect of an intended witness within the time specified by the court then the witness may not be called to give oral evidence unless the court gives permission[1].

1 *MA Lloyd & Sons Ltd v PPC International Ltd* [2014] EWHC 41 (QB).

Summary assessment of costs following an interlocutory hearing

10.236   Where the court orders a party to pay costs to another party (other than fixed costs) it may either make a summary assessment of the costs or order detailed assessment of the costs by a costs officer, unless any rule, practice direction or other enactment provides otherwise (CPR PD 8). It should be noted that in the 2014 edition of the *White Book* the old rules (ie pre-dating 1 April 2013) can be seen following CPR 48 and CPR PD 28A).

10.237   CPR 44 PD 9.8 provides, however, that the court will not make a summary assessment of the costs of a receiving party who is an assisted person.

10.238   The court will not make a summary assessment of the costs of the receiving party who is a child or patient within the meaning of CPR 21 unless the solicitor acting for the child or patient has waived the right to further costs, although the court may make a summary assessment of costs payable by a child or patient (CPR 44 PD 9.9).

10.239   Clearly in the event of an application being pursued where legal aid is not involved, then the court may well make a summary assessment of costs and the parties are under a duty to assist the judge in making that summary assessment. Each party who intends to claim costs must prepare a written statement of the costs he intends to claim giving the necessary information detailing the costs incurred on the lines set out in form N260.

10.240   The statement of costs must be signed by the party or his legal representative (CPR 44 PD 9.5). Where a litigant is an assisted person or is represented by a solicitor in the litigant's employment, the statement of costs need not include the certificate appended at the end of form N260 (which confirms the costs being claimed are not greater than those costs which the solicitor's client is liable to pay).

10.241   It should be noted that if a party fails, without reasonable excuse, to comply with the requirement to serve an appropriate statement of costs (which should be served no less than 24 hours before the date fixed for the hearing) then the court will take such matters into account in deciding what order to make about the costs of the claim, hearing or application and about the costs of any further hearing or detailed assessment hearing that may be necessary as a result of that failure (CPR 44 PD 9.6).

10.242   Where there is a case involving additional liabilities (as in a conditional fee agreement case) then the summary assessment of the costs will deal solely with the base costs and not the additional liabilities, unless the summary assessment is at the conclusion of the proceedings (ie following a fast track trial). As far as interlocutory matters are concerned, where the litigant is or may be entitled to claim an additional liability then the statement filed and served need not therefore reveal the amount of that liability (CPR 44X PD 3).

Cases after 1 April 2013 which, of course, do not have old style ATE policies will not be subject to these old rules.

FUNDING ISSUES

Legal aid

10.243   Prior to the major reforms of legal aid in April 2013 it was already the case that the LSC would rarely, if ever, fund fast track cases to trial. The pressure on the LSC by successive governments inevitably meant that fewer caseworkers were able to deal with cases in depth. This led to the streamlining of the funding system for legal aid cases and special case plans became broader and more generalised. Funding was provided in tranches, which meant that fewer applications were needed for amendment of a legal aid certificate.

10.244   Whether the case relates to a pre- or post-1 April 2013 matter, the practitioner needs to ensure that the client's certificate is appropriately amended to provide the necessary scope and funding to allow the action to proceed to trial. This will need to include the necessary authorities for the use of leading counsel and junior counsel as appropriate. Practitioners do need to review regularly the costs position in an action and make appropriate and timely applications to the LSC/LAA for increased funding, usually by way of revised special case plans or if the revision is relatively limited, by a reasonably detailed letter.

10.245   The Civil Legal Aid (Remuneration) Regulations 2013[1] includes provision that the Lord Chancellor pay for expert service at the rates set out in the table in reg 10.

Practitioners have faced considerable difficulty in obtaining services from an appropriate expert in a clinical negligence case, in view of the LSC/LAA's funding restrictions and that situation will continue.

1 SI 2013/422.

10.246 It is the case that higher rates may be permitted in 'exceptional circumstances' as explained in Sch 5 to the 2013 Regulations. This permits the LAA to allow higher rates, for example, in the field of paediatric neurology, albeit the rates are still appreciably lower than the rates often requested by experts in this field.

The concept of achieving a level playing field between the parties is sadly ignored in legal aid cases.

10.247 With the use of 'risk rates' for LSC/LAA contracts, the practitioner will need to review carefully prospects of success since failure in the case will make a significant financial impact on the practitioner (although of course not as great as that of a failed CFA case). However, a solicitor's duty to his client must take precedence and the solicitor will therefore have to pursue a case even where there is a relatively modest chance of success (albeit better than 50/50), subject to the matter complying with the LSC funding code and, for matters arising after 1 April 2013, the contents of 2013 Regulations.

Conditional fee agreements

10.248 For cases pre-dating 1 April 2013 different but equally important requirements will be seen in a CFA case where ATE insurance is in place. The necessary authorities will need to be obtained and reports on merits given. Where staged premiums apply then appropriate early notice will need to have been provided to the opponent confirming that staged premiums apply in the action. It is also sensible to repeat the warnings to the opponent prior to the relevant stages arising, in order to encourage the opponent to consider the cost advantages of early settlement. The overall cover afforded by the ATE provider needs to be reviewed at different stages, especially at the crucial stage prior to trial. It is necessary to consider the estimates given by the opponent in order to assist in the assessment of how much cover is required. Timely applications for increased cover must be made. For cases which are pursued after 1 April 2013 the practitioner will need to follow the requirements of their ATE provider and the new demands of costs budgeting (perhaps cost capping) will need to be borne in mind.

10.249 It is not clear whether the new emphasis on proportionality will produce a situation where further action in the case cannot be justified on a costs/benefit analysis basis. If the case becomes uneconomic to run thanks to say an imposed budget will it be possible for a practitioner to withdraw from the case? These potential problems will need to be drawn to the client's attention before a new-style CFA is put in place, so that the client is put on notice of such problems and appreciates their potential consequences. There is little doubt that the impact of costs budgeting represents a new risk factor for practitioners.

Before the event insurance

10.250   In BTE insurance cases similar considerations will also apply and the insurer may have extensive and rigid requirements which, if ignored, will place the claimant and his solicitor in peril. In cases where BTE is available it was in the past rarely the case that funding would be adequate enough to take the matter to trial because the indemnity limits were usually relatively small and therefore top-up cover was needed. At times obtaining top-up cover could prove problematic to say the least. A CFA usually needed to be put in place for the next stage of the case to work in conjunction with the ATE top-up cover provided.

10.251   It appears that the new regime in place since 1 April 2013 will provide a benefit in relation to qualified one way costs shifting that will affect BTE cases initially pursued under the old rules. This may mean that indemnity limits (which previously might not have been sufficient to take the case all the way through to trial) may now be viewed as sufficient, taking into account the effect of qualified one way costs shifting. Prior to 1 April 2013 it was not unusual for a case which benefited from BTE insurance effectively running out of funding which then required, as indicated above, a practitioner to pursue the matter via a CFA with ATE top-up cover. For cases affected by the reforms put into effect on 1 April 2013 the situation does indeed appear quite different and it remains to be seen what problems, if any, emerge as a consequence.

Private client

10.252   Prior to 1 April 2013 it was very rare for a case to be pursued to trial on a private client basis. If such a rare event occurred, however, it was essential that insurance to protect the client from a loss was obtained, if possible. Advising a client of modest means to proceed to trial would seldom be appropriate especially if no insurance was available to cover the client for a loss at trial.

10.253   It is likely that with the reforms introduced on 1 April 2013 there will continue to be very few private client clinical negligence cases being pursued. It is theoretically possible for a client to decide to pay for a solicitor privately after 1 April 2013 in order to avoid any deduction from their damages, but it is anticipated that this scenario will seldom be seen in the future as the advantages of a post-1 April 2013 CFA probably still outweigh its disadvantages.

Updating the schedule of loss

10.254   Save in very complex cases, the task of the claimant's lawyer at this stage is simply to update the schedule and re-calculate the figures, including interest, taking into account the trial date and any further expenses incurred by the claimant from the date when the previous schedule had ended to the current date.

10.255   The model directions (see para **10.167** above) request that the schedule of loss is in the form whereby the counter schedule can be based on it (the opponent should be given an electronic version of the schedule, or it should be sent to the opponent by e-mail).

10.256   If the action is being pursued to a split trial then the schedule attached to the particulars of claim will be irrelevant at this stage in the proceedings. If the claimant has from the outset sought a split trial then it is likely that the schedule attached to the particulars of claim at the outset would have been limited to past losses, which could be easily quantified without quantum expert input, and only the heads of future losses would have been set out in summary. The court may, on occasion, order service of a fuller provisional schedule at the first CMC even where a split trial has been ordered. Clearly such a provisional schedule will need to be based on a number of qualified assumptions. If a split trial is pursued the court will not seek to obtain an updated schedule from the claimant in the circumstances. It should be noted that the Masters at the Royal Courts of Justice are likely to take the view that an accurate valuation of the claim should be obtained at the earliest opportunity. Schedules citing 'to be assessed' (TBA) are to be discouraged. Masters will take the view that the defendant is entitled to know the approximate value of the claim it faces regardless of there being a split trial.

10.257   In substantial cases, even where quantum has been investigated prior to service of proceedings there may be a need to re-draft substantially the initial schedule in the light of developments, especially with regard to exchange of lay and expert witness evidence which may be very relevant to quantum. The outcome of experts' discussions usually impacts not insignificantly on the issue of quantum. The directions for updating the schedule should therefore be based on the assumption that the service of the updated schedule should take place after joint statements have been procured. In practice delays with experts can affect service of the updated schedule. Post 1 April 2013 any changes to the directions regarding the schedule will require a further application to the court for new directions.

10.258   As yet there is no specific direction on the form of the schedule and counter schedule (subject to the points raised above). In substantial cases the preparation of the schedule is indeed a team effort. Forensic accountants may be used to prepare whole schedules, which should then be refined by counsel and/or the solicitor. It is increasingly common that solicitors and/or counsel draft their own schedules. Clearly there may be complex issues relating to quantum, for example in difficult pension cases when forensic accountancy input will be required. For the purposes of financial advice, input from a forensic accountant will also be needed on investment and periodical payments.

10.259   In *R v Secretary of State for Transport*[1] the Court of Appeal considered whether the action by accountants in providing forensic accountancy services to litigants on a contingency fee basis amounted to an infringement of the Courts and Legal Services Act 1990, s 58. In earlier proceedings the claimants had successfully challenged their exclusion from fishing in British waters and had been awarded damages. The matter then went to Master Wright at the Supreme Court Costs Office who considered that there was no breach of s 58 and therefore the arrangement was not champertous. The court was quite satisfied that the CLSA 1990, s 58 applied only to conditional fee agreements between clients and 'litigators', ie in relation to the provision of advocacy in litigation services. Although the court would not be prepared to consent to an expert being instructed on a contingency fee basis in normal circumstances (as such an arrangement was likely to undermine their objectivity), in the present case the court could not see any difficulty in the accountants providing accountancy support services rather than providing expert witness evidence. The court therefore was satisfied that the accountants' conduct in the proceedings did not offend public policy.

1 *R (on the application of Factortame) v Secretary of State for Transport, Environment and the Regions* [2002] EWCA Civ 932.

Offers to settle (CPR 36)

10.260 New rules on Pt 36 offers came into force on 6 April 2007. CPR 36.14 underwent yet a further change as from 1 April 2013[1], and the latest changes date from 6 April 2015.

1 They are not covered in this Chapter.

SETTLEMENT OF CLAIMS

Non-OPG cases

10.261 Cases involving a competent adult claimant may be concluded by an appropriately worded consent order signed by the parties' representatives. The contents of such an order need to comply with the requirements of CPR 40.2 and CPR 40.6. An appropriate order needs to be drawn up in the terms agreed between the parties and should be expressed as being 'by consent' and it must be signed by the legal representatives acting for each of the parties to whom the order relates (CPR 40.6(7)). Parties may wish to follow the Tomlin form of order, but such an order is not necessary where all that is required is an order that one party shall pay money to the other. A hybrid Tomlin order may be ineffective and it is not unknown for courts to reject consent orders if they are inappropriately drafted. Prior to settlement, and before an order is prepared, consideration should be given to the history of the action and the existence of any earlier costs orders. For example the claimant seeking a settlement where a past order for costs was made against the claimant should attempt to agree with the defendant that the order be reversed if at all possible. If an order for costs has been reserved then the consent order should state clearly on its face that the defendant is to pay the claimant the costs of that order previously reserved as part of the costs of the whole action. Provision should also be included for a payment on account of costs. In a case where periodical payments are not appropriate the consent order is likely to be in very straightforward terms.

10.262 Cases involving children who are not protected parties, and where there is therefore no role for the Court of Protection and the OPG, cannot be settled without court approval pursuant to the requirements of CPR 21 and its accompanying practice direction. Of course settlement of claims where proceedings have not been issued, but where the claimant is a child, has to follow the procedure set out at CPR 8.

10.263   Where settlement or compromise arises after proceedings have been commenced then CPR 21 PD 6 applies, requiring an application to be made for the court's approval of the agreement reached. The court must be satisfied that the parties have considered whether the damages should wholly or partly take the form of periodical payments. If the settlement includes provision for periodical payments then the application for approval must set out the terms of the settlement or compromise and have attached to it a draft consent order which fulfils the requirements of CPR 41.8 and CPR 41.9 (CPR 21 PD 6.3(2)).

10.264   The court must be supplied with an opinion on the merits of settlement or compromise given by counsel or the solicitor acting for the child and a copy or record of any financial advice.

10.265   The judgment on settlement in respect of a claim under the Fatal Accidents Act 1976 must be apportioned between the persons by or on whose behalf the claim has been brought (CPR 21 PD 7). A claim on behalf of a dependent child sees the monies apportioned to that child invested on his behalf in accordance with CPR 21.10 and CPR 21.11 and in addition CPR 21 PD 8 and CPR 21 PD 9. In order to approve an apportionment of money to a dependent child the court will have to take into account the matters set out at CPR 21 PD 7.4, which include consideration of any future loss of earnings and the extent and nature of the dependency involved.

10.266   With regard to investment on behalf of the child, CPR 21 PD.9 sets out the procedure that needs to be followed. In many cases involving relatively modest damages the appropriate order would be for the placement of the child's monies in the special investment account. The litigation friend may make an application to a Master or district judge for further investment directions and indeed for a request for use of monies for the benefit of the child prior to the child reaching the age of majority. Subject to advice from the claimant's legal team and financial adviser, the court may approve the terms of a trust and any appropriate investment regime to be set up in conjunction with that trust. Practitioners should also note the option of investing part of the protected parties fund in an Equity Index Tracker Fund (EITF). This is a form of unit trust managed by Legal & General on behalf of the Ministry of Justice. The Chief Financial Officer will make this option available to claimants including children who have been awarded £10,000 or more and are under 13 years of age at the time of the investment hearing. In general terms the investment in EITF would be up to a maximum of 70 per cent of the claimant's award and a minimum of 30 per cent. The claimant will be entitled to sell all of the units once they have reached their 18th birthday following transfer of ownership of the fund into the child's name.

Court of Protection/OPG cases

10.267   If the claimant (whether adult or child) is a protected party, then the Court of Protection/OPG will need to be involved at the earliest opportunity once it becomes clear that any funds are going to be received on behalf of the patient (subject to the different approach in cases involving damages of less than £50,000). As previously stated, the obligation to notify the Court of Protection arises before the appointment of a deputy.

10.268 Previously (ie before October 2007) it was necessary to obtain approval from a Master of the Court of Protection where a protected party's claim for damages was to be settled. This is no longer necessary, as discussed above.

10.269 After proceedings have been commenced and where settlement approval is required because the claimant is a protected party, then the provisions of CPR 21 PD 6 apply and must be followed. The steps described above with regard to obtaining PGO approval of a settlement (prior to the commencement of court proceedings) also apply where proceedings have been started. It may assist if, prior to the court approval hearing, a deputyship order has been made but it is not mandatory and the consent order can be worded to indicate that such an application is to be made within a reasonable time.

10.270 The control of money recovered by or on behalf of a protected party is considered at CPR 21 PD 8 and CPR 21.11. CPR 21 PD 8.1 provides that:

'The court:

(a) may direct the money to be paid into the High Court for investment,
(b) may also direct that certain sums be paid direct to the child or protected beneficiary, his litigation friend or his legal representative for the immediate benefit of the child or protected beneficiary or for expenses incurred on his behalf, and
(c) may direct the applications in respect of the investment of the money be transferred to a local district registry'.

In the event that a claim for past care and expenses has been included in the claim on behalf of the parents of the protected party, then consideration will need to have been given for the appropriate sum that should be advanced to the parents. The court will therefore have to consider what would be a just and reasonable sum to deduct from the protected party's damages in order to meet the parents' claim. This matter does need careful discussion with the parents, especially in cases where some discount on the damages has been negotiated.

THE TRIAL

10.271 The following represents some points from the solicitor's perspective.

Trial bundle

10.272 This is also discussed in detail elsewhere but it cannot be over emphasised that it is essential to take great care in the preparation of the trial bundle.

Attendance at court by solicitor

10.273 Costs restrictions may be an obstacle to the conducting solicitor attending the trial with counsel, especially if the client is already represented by leading and junior counsel. It is not uncommon for the conducting solicitor to attend only part of the trial, perhaps the first day and the last, with a junior member of the firm attending to 'sit behind counsel'. Ideally in a major claim the conducting solicitor should be in attendance throughout the trial and should be prepared to take an active part in the case. Provided that a solicitor during the course of the trial brings points to counsel's attention in a discreet and constructive and positive manner, this input will no doubt be gratefully received. Dealing with witnesses both lay and expert and ensuring the correct running order of witnesses is part of the solicitor's duty. Diligent solicitors will ensure their attendance at pre- and post-trial conferences regardless of funding issues.

Negotiations and final orders

10.274 Negotiations during trial may occur and the solicitor must involve himself directly in that process. In addition the drafting of any final order needs careful consideration by the solicitor together with counsel. Costs issues may be difficult at the end of a trial. In children or protected party cases care should be shown when considering the provision in an order confirming that the solicitor and counsel for the claimant waive their right to claim costs over and above those that they recover from the losing opponent. Unwary solicitors and counsel have found to their cost that 'no good deed goes unpunished' and effectively such an order can mean that substantial solicitor and own client costs cannot be recovered.

10.275 Furthermore where earlier adverse costs orders have been made then negotiation may produce an agreement between the parties that such orders are reversed, waived or at least modified to the client's advantage. Costs orders which have been reserved will need naturally to be finalised. In legal aid cases the wording in the final order should reflect whether the Legal Aid Act 1988 applies (but this would be in very old cases) or whether the certificate was issued pursuant to the Access to Justice Act 1999. Cases involving certificates issued after 1 April 2013 will obviously be under LASPO 2012.

10.276 If a party receives a judgment which brings into play the costs provisions of Part 36 then an application should be made to the trial judge for the appropriate order.

Appeals

10.277 In multi-track cases judgment is usually reserved. If the judgment, when handed down, proves adverse careful discussion with counsel on the merits of an appeal needs to be undertaken. Unless the prospects of a successful appeal are poor, permission to appeal should always be sought in accordance with CPR 52 and its accompanying practice direction.

AFTER TRIAL

Detailed assessment

10.278   The issue of costs and detailed assessment is dealt with in more detail elsewhere. In a fast track trial detailed assessment will be irrelevant as the costs will be summarily assessed following trial in accordance with CPR 46. In a multi-track action the usual order will be for detailed assessment of the winner's costs on the standard basis in default of agreement, if the winner is the claimant. If qualified one way costs shifting applies in a post-1 April 2013 case, then a winning defendant will not normally benefit from a costs order. The procedure for detailed assessment is set out in CPR 47 and its practice direction, which introduced a number of significant changes. For example, where the winner's costs do not exceed £75,000 (see CPR 47 PD 14) the case will be subject to the procedure for provisional assessment as detailed at CPR 47 PD 14.

Of course, the emphasis on costs budgeting may also change the way in which costs are dealt with at the conclusion of the case. Will there be a need for detailed assessment if, for example, the successful party has concluded the action and their costs fall within the approved budget?

10.279   It is submitted that all practitioners should gain some experience at least in attending detailed assessment hearings and indeed in acting as the primary advocate at such hearings as well as dealing with the process of objections and replies and negotiations. The solicitor who has been successful in winning damages for their clients and obtaining a favourable costs order will undoubtedly have worked hard to achieve these results and they should continue to argue their case within the costs process as well. Substantial costs relating to the costs of detailed assessment may also be recovered by the solicitor, which would justify their continued involvement in that process.

10.280   The requirement that the paying party pays interest on costs following judgment should not be overlooked. If the paying party fails to make an early and substantial payment on account (for whatever reason) the amount of recoverable interest may be substantial.

10.281   Interest under the Judgments Act 1838, s 17 or the County Courts Act 1984, s 74 runs from the date on which the event giving rise to the entitlement to costs occurred or from such date as the court may order. In cases which have gone to trial that will clearly be the date of judgment. In cases requiring court approval, interest will run from the date approval is granted. It should be noted that CPR 44.2, which deals with the court's discretion as to costs, also provides for the court having a discretion with regard to awarding interest on costs from or until a certain date, including a date before judgment (CPR 44.2(6)). If a Pt 36 offer is accepted by a claimant then a deemed 'standard basis' costs order arises (CPR 44.9). Interest therefore runs from the date of acceptance in such a situation. Oddly CPR 44.9 is silent where a defendant accepts an offer, but CPR 36.10 does state:

'where a Part 36 offer is accepted within the relevant period the claimant will be entitled to his costs of the proceedings up to the date on which the notice of acceptance was served on the offeror'.

Interest should therefore run on costs as from the date that the defendant accepts the claimant's offer.

10.282 In legal aid cases care should be taken as there are significant differences between the assessment of costs where the matter is governed by the Legal Aid Act 1988 and the Access to Justice Act 1999. There may still be some very old cases which fall under the Legal Aid Act 1988 and where the certificate was issued prior to February 1994. In old Legal Aid Act 1988 cases parties were not allowed to avoid detailed assessment unless the receiving party accepted any offer in relation to costs in full and did not seek to pursue a separate assessment of the legal aid only costs (although the SCCO occasionally adopted a different approach in practice). After February 1994 it has been possible to agree the *inter partes* costs and obtain a legal aid only assessment. The introduction of the Access to Justice Act 1999, however, complicated matters further in legal aid cases and in a successful case only inter partes costs may be recovered and no separate legal aid only costs can be claimed in normal circumstances. A solicitor may elect to be paid by the legal aid authority in place of seeking *inter partes* costs but this is unlikely to be attractive in a clinical negligence case. In certain limited circumstances the legal aid authority may agree to assess and pay costs incurred which have not been recoverable *inter partes*. In December 2014 a new tender process was opened by the LAA for clinical negligence (as well as some other areas of legal aid work) which may lead to further firms deciding to give up clinical negligence legal aid work.

10.283 Once the costs process has been concluded and monies have been accounted for as necessary and all formalities followed, the case can then be closed. In cases involving competent adults the papers must be retained for at least six years. If the case involves a child (who is not a protected party) then the papers may be destroyed once the child reaches the age of 24 years. In patient cases, however, a date for destruction cannot effectively be set thus requiring the solicitor to retain his client's papers indefinitely.

CONCLUSION

10.284 In the previous edition of this publication it was noted in the concluding paragraphs to this chapter that between April 1999 and April 2007 CPR had undergone 44 revisions. By May 2015 the CPR had been amended 80 times. Any litigator with some 20 years post-qualification experience will have experienced momentous changes in litigation practice and procedure over that period. The pace of change has been relentless. Practitioners have continued to experience a degree of anxiety arising from the uncertainty created by that relentless change. In the light of the matters dealt with in this revised chapter it is unlikely to be the case that anxiety levels will fall over the next few years.

10.285 Although the tide has apparently turned against claimants, in the light of changes to the CFA regime, other changes, including the more robust approach to case management and costs budgeting, may well affect defendants in equal measure. Whilst the increased powers of the court may be perceived positively by the judiciary, the added heavy burden of active case management on individual judges will perhaps be another less than attractive consequence of the recent far-reaching reforms. In the light of the above, few would be bold enough at present to attempt to predict what litigation will look like in ten years' time or, for that matter, even five years from now.

CHAPTER 11

Consent

Andrew Hockton

AUTONOMY/SELF-DETERMINATION

11.1   The principle of autonomy or self-determination is fundamental to medical law. There are many formulations. The locus classicus remains the judgment of Cardozo J in *Schloendorff v Society of New York Hospital*[1].

323

'Every person being of adult years and sound mind has a right to determine what shall be done with his own body.'

Further examples are as follows:

'Any treatment given by a doctor to a competent patient which is invasive (ie which involves any interference with the physical integrity of the patient) is unlawful unless done with the consent of the patient: it constitutes the crime of battery and the tort of trespass to the person'[2].

'An adult who ... suffers from no mental incapacity has an absolute right to choose whether to consent to treatment, to refuse it or to choose one rather than another of the treatments being offered ... this right of choice is not limited to decisions which others might regard as sensible. It exists notwithstanding that the reasons for making the choice are rational, irrational, unknown or even non-existent ... The fact that "emergency cases" apart, no medical treatment of an adult patient of full capacity can be undertaken without his consent, creates a situation in which the absence of consent has much the same effect as refusal'[3].

'An adult patient has an absolute right to refuse to consent to medical treatment for any reason, rational or irrational, or for no reason at all, even where that decision may lead to his death'[4].

The principle of autonomy underpins the Mental Capacity Act 2005, whereby a person must be assumed to have capacity unless it is established that he lacks capacity (s 1(2)).

1 (1914) 105 NE 92.
2 *Airedale NHS Trust v Bland* [1993] AC 789 at 882.
3 *Re T* [1992] 3 WLR 782, at 786G–H, per Lord Donaldson.
4 *Re MB* [1997] 2 FLR 426 at 432.

RIGHT TO BODILY INTEGRITY

11.2   The principle of self-determination is underpinned by the European Convention on Human Rights. Physical integrity is an aspect of the right to respect for private life which is protected under Article 8 of the Convention. In *Pretty v UK*[1], it was stated that:

'In the sphere of medical treatment, the refusal to accept a particular medical treatment might, inevitably lead to a fatal outcome, yet the imposition of medical treatment, without the consent of a mentally competent adult, would interfere with a person's physical integrity in a manner capable of engaging the rights protected under Article 8.1 of the Convention'.

The decision of the Strasbourg Court in *Pretty v UK* on the engagement of Article 8 was adopted by the House of Lords in *R (on the application of Purdy) v Director of Public Prosecutions (Society for the Protection of Unborn Children Intervening)*[2] (departing from the decision of the House of Lords in *R (on the application of Pretty) v Director of Public Prosecutions (Secretary of State for the Home Department Intervening)*[3]).

1 Application 2346/02 [2001] UKHL 61, (2002) 66 BMLR 147.
2 [2009] UKHL 45, [2010] 1 AC 345.
3 [2002] 1 AC 800, HL.

11.3   Articles 2 and 3 of the Convention have also been invoked in cases involving medical treatment. With reference to the right to life under Article 2, Robert Walker LJ stated that[1]:

'every human being's right to life carries with it, as an intrinsic part of it, rights of bodily integrity and autonomy – the right to have one's own body whole and intact and (on reaching an age of understanding) to take decisions about one's body'.

1 In *Re A (minors) (conjoined twins: separation)* [2000] Lloyd's Rep Med 425 at 494.

THE RIGHT OF THE PATIENT TO DEMAND TREATMENT

11.4 The right to refuse treatment does not necessarily connote a right to demand it. As was stated in *R (on the application of Burke) v General Medical Council*[1]:

'The proposition that the patient has a right to refuse treatment is amply demonstrated by the authorities cited by Munby J [2005] QB 424, paras 54–56, under the heading "Autonomy and self-determination". The corollary does not, however, follow, at least as a general proposition. Autonomy and the right of self-determination do not entitle the patient to insist on receiving a particular medical treatment regardless of the nature of the treatment. In so far as a doctor has a legal obligation to provide treatment this cannot be founded simply upon the fact that the patient demands it. The source of the duty lies elsewhere'.

1 [2005] 3 WLR 1132, CA at 1148.

11.5 The nature of the doctor's duty was clarified in *Burke*[1]. In particular, at para 50, Lord Phillips MR stated:

'So far as the general position is concerned, we would endorse the following simple propositions advanced by the GMC. (i) The doctor, exercising his professional clinical judgment, decides what treatment options are clinically indicated (ie will provide overall clinical benefit) for his patient. (ii) He then offers those treatment options to the patient in the course of which he explains to him/her the risks, benefits, side effects, etc involved in each of the treatment options. (iii) The patient then decides whether he wishes to accept any of those treatment options and, if so, which one. In the vast majority of cases he will, of course, decide which treatment options he considers to be in his best interests and, in doing so, he will or may take into account other, non-clinical factors. However, he can, if he wishes, decide to accept (or refuse) the treatment option on the basis of reasons which are irrational or for no reasons at all. (iv) If he chooses one of the treatment options offered to him, the doctor will then proceed to provide it. (v) If, however, he refuses all of the treatment options offered to him and instead informs the doctor that he wants a form of treatment which the doctor has not offered him, the doctor will, no doubt, discuss that form of treatment with him (assuming that it is a form of treatment known to him) but if the doctor concludes that this treatment is not clinically indicated he is not required (ie he is under no legal obligation) to provide it to the patient although he should offer a second opinion.

51. The relationship between doctor and patient usually begins with diagnosis and advice. The doctor will describe the treatment that he recommends or, if there are a number of alternative treatments that he would be prepared to administer in the interests of the patient, the choices available, their implications and his recommended option. In such circumstances the right to refuse a proposed treatment gives the patient what appears to be a positive option to choose an alternative. In truth the right to choose is no more than a reflection of the fact that it is the doctor's duty to provide a treatment that he considers to be in the interests of the patient and that the patient is prepared to accept'.

The principle that neither the court or patient can order a doctor to provide a particular form of treatment was reviewed and confirmed (at para 18) by Lady Hale in *Aintree University Hospitals NHS Foundation Trust v James*[2].

1 [2005] 3 WLR 1132, CA at paras 49–55.
2 [2013] UKSC 67, [2014] AC 591.

VALID CONSENT

11.6 In order to be valid, consent must be voluntarily given by a person who is appropriately informed (either the patient or a person with parental responsibility where the patient is under 18) and who has the requisite capacity either to consent to or refuse treatment. Consent may be expressed or implied. There is no requirement that it be in writing, although model consent forms have now been in use for a number of years. The use of the forms is good practice where intervention such as surgery is planned. The significance of the consent form is evidential. As Popplewell J stated in *Taylor v Shropshire Health Authority*[1]:

'For my part I regard the consent form immediately before operation as pure window dressing in this case and designed simply to avoid the suggestion that a patient has not been told. I do not regard the failure to have a specialised consent form at the time to be any indication of negligence'.

1 [1998] Lloyd's Rep Med 395.

11.7 It is not enough to get a patient to sign a pro forma expressing consent to a procedure with no explanation. The doctor must explain the implications of the procedure[1]. The explanation should be in terms which the patient can understand[2].

1 *Chatterton v Gerson* [1981] 1 All ER 257 at 265J.
2 *Abbas v Kenney* [1996] 7 Med LR 47.

IMPLIED CONSENT

11.8 Consent may be implied or inferred from a patient's conduct. In *O'Brien v Cunard SS Co*[1], a passenger on a boat who had stood in a line of passengers waiting to see a surgeon and who held her arm out for a smallpox inoculation, was held to have consented. In dismissing her action, Knowlton J stated:

'If the claimant's behaviour was such as to indicate consent on her part, [the surgeon] was justified in his act, whatever her unexpressed feelings may have been'.

1 [1891] 28 NE 266 (Supreme Judicial Court of Massachusetts).

11.9 Silence on the part of the patient will not necessarily constitute consent. In *Schweizer v Central Hospital*, Thompson J stated that[1]:

'consent may be implied where circumstances dictate that it is clearly indicated and it is manifest that the will of the patient accompanies such consent'.

1 (1974) 53 DLR (3d) 494.

11.10 Where the patient is incompetent consent cannot be inferred. Prior to the Mental Capacity Act 2005, the doctrine of necessity was invoked to treat incompetent patients in their best interests (as explained by Lord Goff in *Re F (mental patient: sterilisation)*[1]). Section 5 of the Act now provides a statutory power to treat patients who lack capacity in their best interests.

1 [1989] 2 All ER 545.

SUFFICIENT INFORMATION

Negligence/battery

11.11   Valid or real consent requires a broad understanding on the part of the patient of the nature and purpose of the procedure[1]. Failure to provide sufficient information may give rise to an action in battery which is actionable per se: without proof of damage.

1 *Chatterton v Gerson* [1981] QB 432 at 443.

11.12   Alternatively, and more commonly, where insufficient information is provided to a patient by a doctor an action may lie in negligence for breach of duty. The leading case on the nature and extent of the duty on doctors to provide information to their patients is now *Montgomery v Lanarkshire Health Board*[1]. Previous case law may be regarded as being of largely historical interest although, no doubt, issues will arise for some time as to the extent to which pre-*Montgomery* cases fall to be assessed by reference to a different test. For the reasons set out below, *Montgomery* is best regarded as reflecting well-established principles rather than signalling a new departure. In the case of *Sidaway v Board of Governors of the Bethlem Royal Hospital*[2], (until *Montgomery*, regarded as the leading case in this area), the House of Lords (or, at least, Lord Diplock) the House of Lords decided that the legal standard to be applied in assessing whether a doctor was negligent in relation to the provision of advice about treatment was that contained in the *Bolam* test[3]: a doctor would not be held to have acted negligently if he acted in accordance with a reasonable body of medical opinion. Much has been made of the fact that in *Sidaway* the majority (although on careful reading the different speeches are somewhat more nuanced) rejected the approach of Lord Scarman, who, having considered the doctrine of informed consent as applied in the American case of *Canterbury v Spence*[4], and the Canadian case of *Reibl v Hughes*[5], concluded that the law:

'must recognise a duty of the doctor to warn his patient of risk inherent in the treatment which is proposed; and especially so, if the treatment be surgery. The critical limitation is that the duty is confined to material risks. The test of materiality is whether in the circumstances of the particular case the court is satisfied that a reasonable person in the patient's position would be likely to attach significance to the risk. Even if the risk be material, the doctor will not be liable if upon a reasonable assessment of the patient's condition he takes the view that a warning would be detrimental to the patient's health'.

1 [2015] UKSC 11.
2 [1985] AC 871.
3 *Bolam v Friern Hospital Management Committee* [1957] 2 All ER 118.
4 464 F 2d 227.
5 (1980) 114 DLR (3d)

11.13   Lord Diplock stated that[1]:

'The merit of the *Bolam* test is that the criterion of the duty of care owed by a doctor to his patient is whether he acted in accordance with a practice accepted as proper by a body of responsible and skilled medical opinion ... in English jurisprudence the doctor's relationship with his patient which gives rise to the normal duty of care to exercise his skill and judgment to improve the patient's health in any particular respect in which the patient has sought his aid, has hitherto been treated as a single comprehensive duty covering all the ways in which a doctor is called upon to exercise his skill and judgment in the improvement of the physical or mental condition of the patient for which his services either as a general practitioner or specialist have been engaged. This general duty is not subject to dissection into a number of component parts to which different criteria of what satisfied the duty of care apply, such as diagnosis, treatment, advice (including warning of any risks of something going wrong, however skillfully the treatment is carried out). The *Bolam* case itself embraced failure to advise the patient of the risk involved in electric shock treatment as one of the allegations of negligence against the surgeon as well as negligence in the actual carrying out of treatment in which that risk did result in injury to the patient. The same criteria were applied to both those aspects of the surgeon's duty of care...

My lords, no convincing reason has in my view been advanced before Your Lordships that would justify treating the *Bolam* test as doing anything less than laying down a principle of English law that is comprehensive and applicable to every aspect of the duty of care owed by a doctor to his patient in the exercise of his healing functions as respects that patient'.

1 [1985] AC 871.

11.14 Detailed analysis of the different emphases in the speeches given by their Lordships in *Sidaway* is now somewhat redundant. In *Montgomery v Lanarkshire Health Board*[1], the Supreme Court decisively endorsed the principle of 'informed consent' (the Scarman approach, as modified in *Rogers v Whittaker*). There was, in any event, reason to think that there was little difference in substance between the *Bolam* test and the 'prudent patient' test adopted by Lord Scarman in *Sidaway* by reason of the content of contemporary guidelines from bodies such as the General Medical Council (GMC) that emphasised the duty to obtain 'informed consent': only the sort of inquiry envisaged by the prudent patient test would arguably, in any event, satisfy the *Bolam* test. The doctor must disclose all material risks. A risk is material when a reasonable person, in what the physician knows or should know to be the patient's position, would be likely to attach significance to the risk or cluster of risks in deciding whether or not to forgo the proposed therapy.

1 [2015] UKSC 11, [2015] All ER (D) 113.

11.15 Prior to *Montgomery*, in England and Wales, at least, the *Bolam* test had largely ceased to be regarded as providing the appropriate yardstick for measuring the sufficiency of information for the purposes of consent (although it was applied in cases such as *Gold v Haringey Health Authority*[1], *Blyth v Bloomsbury Health Authority*[2] and the Scottish case of *Moyes v Lothian Health Board*[3]). In *Pearce v United Bristol Healthcare NHS Trust*[4], Lord Woolf stated that the doctor should normally inform a patient of 'a significant risk which would affect the judgment of a reasonable patient.' This appears to be indistinguishable from the 'prudent patient' test (and closer to the leading Australian case of *Rogers v Whittaker*[5] where the *Bolam* test was rejected). In *Wyatt v Curtis*[6], the Court of Appeal applied the law as stated in *Pearce*. In *Creutzfeldt-Jacob Disease Litigation (No 1)*[7] the court held that 'informed consent' was not a concept recognised in English law. In the light of *Montgomery*, this is no longer a correct statement of the law.

1 [1988] QB 481.
2 [1993] 4 Med LR 151.
3 [1991] 1 Med LR 463.
4 (1999) 48 BMLR 118.
5 [1992] 3 Med LR 331.
6 [2003] EWCA Civ 1779.
7 (2000) 54 BMLR 174.

11.16 Failure to warn of a particular risk has long been considered to be potentially negligent even where a body of doctors would not warn: the practice had to be reasonable and/or responsible[1]. The *Bolitho* decision was anticipated in *Sidaway*. In commenting on a passage from the Canadian case of *Reibl v Hughes*[2], Lord Bridge stated:

'But I do not see that this approach involves the necessity "to hand over to the medical profession the entire question of the scope of the duty of disclosure, including the question whether there has been a breach of that duty". Of course if there is a conflict of evidence as to whether a responsible body of medical opinion approves of non-disclosure in a particular case, the judge will have to resolve that conflict. But even in a case where, as here, no expert witness in the relevant field condemns the non-disclosure as being in conflict with accepted and responsible medical practice, I am of the opinion that the judge might in certain circumstances come to the conclusion that disclosure of a particular risk was so obviously necessary to an informed choice on the part of the patient that no reasonably prudent medical man would fail to make it'[3].

1 *Bolitho v City and Hackney Health Authority* [1998] AC 232.
2 (1978) 89 DLR (3d) 112.
3 [1985] AC 871 at 900D.

11.17 It has been stated that a clinician must take reasonable care to give a warning which is adequate in scope, content and presentation, and take steps to see that the warning is understood[1]. In *Al Hamwi v Johnston and North West London Hospitals NHS Trust*[2], a case about obstetric advice, Simon J stated (at paras 44 and 45) that the advice should be balanced and tailored to the individual patient. In this context, reference was made to the 'useful guidance' on this subject contained in the paper published by the GMC currently, *Consent: patients and doctors making decisions together*:

'30. In assessing the risk to an individual patient, you must consider the nature of the patient's condition, their general health and other circumstances. These are variable factors that may affect the likelihood of adverse outcomes occurring.

31. You should do your best to understand the patient's views and preferences about any proposed investigation or treatment, and the adverse outcomes they are most concerned about. You must not make assumptions about a patient's understanding of risk or the importance they attach to different outcomes. You should discuss these issues with your patient.

32. You must tell patients if an investigation or treatment might result in a serious adverse outcome, even if the likelihood is very small. You should also tell patients about less serious side effects or complications if they occur frequently, and explain what the patient should do if they experience any of them.'

In *Birch v University College Hospitals NHS Trust*[3], the court held that the duty to inform a patient of significant risks would not be discharged unless and until a patient was made aware that fewer or no risks were associated with another alternative and available treatment. The principle of patient autonomy was affirmed in *Chester v Afshar*[4].

In *Meiklejohn v St George's Healthcare NHS Trust, Homerton University Hospitals NHS Foundation Trust*[5] the court affirmed that the duty to advise and warn about diagnosis, treatment, and possible side-effects is to be assessed in accordance with the practice of a responsible body of doctors. There was, however, no duty to warn of a possible alternative diagnosis that was not reasonably suspected (para 62). In the light of *Montgomery* this decision should now be treated with caution.

Montgomery v Lanarkshire Health Board[6]: Mrs Montgomery, who was diabetic, gave birth to a baby with severe disabilities caused by complications due to a difficult vaginal delivery. The main argument in Mrs Montgomery's case was that, had she been given appropriate advice about the risk of shoulder dystocia, which was increased as a result of her diabetes, she would have elected to have a caesarean section and avoided damage. The Supreme Court summarised (at para 87) the legal position on consent, as follows:

'The correct position, in relation to the risks of injury involved in treatment, can now be seen to be substantially that adopted in *Sidaway* by Lord Scarman, and by Lord Woolf MR in *Pearce*, subject to the refinement made by the High Court of Australia in *Rogers v Whitaker*, which we have discussed at paras 70–73. An adult person of sound mind is entitled to decide which, if any, of the available forms of treatment to undergo, and her consent must be obtained before treatment interfering with her bodily integrity is undertaken. The doctor is therefore under a duty to take reasonable care to ensure that the patient is aware of any material risks involved in any recommended treatment, and of any reasonable alternative or variant treatments. The test of materiality is whether, in the circumstances of the particular case, a reasonable person in the patient's position would be likely to attach significance to it.'

The 'therapeutic exception' is maintained. The doctor is entitled to withhold from the patient information as to a risk if he reasonably considers that its disclosure would be seriously detrimental to the patient's health (para 88).

The significance of a risk is likely to reflect a variety of factors besides its magnitude: for example, the nature of the risk, the effect which its occurrence would have upon the life of the patient, the importance to the patient of the benefits sought to be achieved by the treatment, the alternatives available, and the risks involved in those alternatives. The assessment is therefore fact-sensitive, and sensitive also to the characteristics of the patient (para 89).

The decision in *Montgomery* confirms that 'informed consent' is now a part of the law in England, Wales and Scotland (per Baroness Hale at para 107). It restates the basic principle that autonomy is based on the patient's right to make decisions about his or her body.

1 *Lybert v Warrington Health Authority* [1996] 7 Med LR 71.
2 [2005] EWHC 206 (QB), [2005] Lloyd's Rep Med 309.
3 [2008] EWHC 2237 (QB), (2008) 104 BMLR 168.
4 [2004] UKHL 41.
5 [2014] EWCA Civ 120.
6 [2015] UKSC 11, [2015] All ER (D) 113.

PROFESSIONAL GUIDELINES

11.18   The GMC sets out in *Good Medical Practice* core guidance of standards expected of every doctor. This is expanded in detailed guidance from the GMC on consent contained in *Consent: patients and doctors making decisions together*. Various principles are set out in details, including:

1. All healthcare involves decisions made by patients and those providing their care. This guidance sets out principles for good practice in making decisions. The principles apply to all decisions about care: from the treatment of minor and self-limiting conditions, to major interventions with significant risks or side effects. The principles also apply to decisions about screening.

2. Whatever the context in which medical decisions are made, you must work in partnership with your patients to ensure good care. In doing so, you must:

   (a) listen to patients and respect their views about their health
   (b) discuss with patients what their diagnosis, prognosis and treatment involve
   (c) share with patients the information they want or need in order to make decisions
   (d) maximise patients' opportunities, and their ability, to make decisions for themselves
   (e) respect patients' decisions

Consent guidance: Partnership

3. For a relationship between doctor and patient to be effective, it should be a partnership based on openness, trust and good communication. Each person has a role to play in making decisions about treatment or care.

4. No single approach to discussions about treatment or care will suit every patient, or apply in all circumstances. Individual patients may want more or less information or involvement in making decisions depending on their circumstances or wishes. And some patients may need additional support to understand information and express their views and preferences.

5. If patients have capacity to make decisions for themselves, a basic model applies:

   (a) The doctor and patient make an assessment of the patient's condition, taking into account the patient's medical history, views, experience and knowledge.
   (b) The doctor uses specialist knowledge and experience and clinical judgement, and the patient's views and understanding of their condition, to identify which investigations or treatment are likely to result in overall benefit for the patient. The doctor explains the options to the patient, setting out the potential benefits, risks, burdens and side effects of each option, including the option to have no treatment. The doctor may recommend a particular option which they believe to be best for the patient, but they must not put pressure on the patient to accept their advice.
   (c) The patient weighs up the potential benefits, risks and burdens of the various options as well as any non-clinical issues that are relevant to them. The patient decides whether to accept any of the options and, if so, which one. They also have the right to accept or refuse an option for a reason that may seem irrational to the doctor, or for no reason at all,
   (d) If the patient asks for a treatment that the doctor considers would not be of overall benefit to the patient, they do not have to provide the treatment. But they should explain their reasons to the patient, and explain any other options that are available, including the option to seek a second opinion.

6. If patients are not able to make decisions for themselves, the doctor must work with those close to the patient and with other members of the healthcare team. The doctor must take into account any views or preferences expressed by the patient and must follow the law on decision-making when a patient lacks capacity.

The Consent guidance gives detailed guidance on information and capacity issues.

11.19 Non-compliance with professional guidance is not necessarily negligent but may provide persuasive evidence as to what constitutes a reasonable standard of care. Similarly, where there is evidence that a defendant accepts that at the material time he personally felt that he owed a duty to warn of a particular risk, although theoretically not dispositive of the question as to whether such a duty exists, such evidence, in practice, will be[1].

1 See *Smith v Tunbridge Wells Health Authority* [1994] 5 Med LR 334.

WITHDRAWAL OF CONSENT

11.20   A withdrawal of consent will invalidate the lawfulness of any treatment. In *Ciarlariello v Schacter*[1], the claimant who suffered an adverse reaction following a diagnostic cerebral angiogram, sued the doctor for battery, having during the procedure asked him to stop and then told him to continue. Cory J stated:

'An individual's right to determine what medical procedures will be accepted must include the right to stop a procedure. It is not beyond the realm of possibility that the patient is better able to gauge the level of pain or discomfort that can be accepted or that the patient's premonitions of tragedy or morality may have a basis in reality. In any event, the patient's right to bodily integrity provides the basis for the withdrawal of a consent to a medical procedure even while it is underway. Thus, if it is found that the consent is effectively withdrawn during the course of the procedure then it must be terminated'.

It was further stated that the withdrawal of consent will depend up the patient's capacity, which may be affected by sedation or other medication. Accordingly, an assessment of capacity will be required and, it is suggested, that the right to withdraw consent is not absolute but may be overruled where its effect is life-threatening or poses serious problems to the patient's health.

1 (1983) 100 DLR (94th) 609 (SCC).

CAPACITY

Mental Capacity Act 2005

11.21   Valid consent presupposes capacity to consent. In the case of adults there is both at common law and pursuant to statute a presumption as to capacity.

The issue of capacity now falls to be determined by reference to the principles set out in the Mental Capacity Act 2005 (MCA 2005) (the bulk of which came into effect on 1 October 2007).

11.22   Broadly-speaking the MCA 2005 reiterates and expands upon well-established principles of common law in relation to the assessment of capacity, but also introduces important measures relating to the appointment of lasting powers of attorney[1], the appointment of deputies to make decisions on behalf of incompetent patients[2], specific provisions relating to advance decisions to refuse treatment[3], the appointment of independent mental capacity advocates[4] and the establishment of the Court of Protection and the Public Guardian (which will take over the jurisdiction of the Family Division in relation to the treatment of incompetent patients).

1 MCA 2005, ss 9–14.
2 MCA 2005, ss 15–21.
3 MCA 2005, ss 24–26.
4 MCA 2005, ss 35–41.

11.23   The MCA 2005 places a renewed emphasis (further underlined in a Code of Practice, intended as guidance to those assessing capacity[1]) upon the requirement to involve patients and those close to them in the decision-making process with regard to medical treatment. This broadly reflects the best practice already prescribed by professional bodies such as the General Medical Council and the BMA.

1 Issued by the Lord Chancellor on 23 April 2007 in accordance with ss 42 and 43 of the Act.

11.24 A number of guiding principles are set out in the MCA 2005, s 1, which provides that:

'(2) A person must be assumed to have capacity unless it is established that he lacks capacity.

(3) A person is not to be treated as unable to make a decision unless all practicable steps to help him to do so have been taken without success.

(4) A person is not to be treated as unable to make a decision merely because he makes an unwise decision.

(5) An act done, or decision made under this Act for or on behalf of a person who lacks capacity must be done, or made, in his best interests.

(6) Before the act is done, or the decision is made, regard must be had to whether the purpose for which it is needed can be as effectively achieved in a way that is less restrictive of the person's rights and freedom of action'.

11.25 Under the MCA 2005, s 2(1) a person lacks capacity in relation to a matter if at the material time he is unable to make a decision for himself in relation to the matter because of an impairment of, or a disturbance in the functioning of, the mind or brain.

The MCA 2005, s 2(2) provides that it does not matter if the impairment or disturbance is permanent or temporary.

11.26 Under the MCA 2005, s 2(3) a lack of capacity cannot be established merely by reference to:

'(a) a person's age or appearance, or
(b) a condition of his, or an aspect of his behaviour, which might lead others to make unjustified assumptions about his capacity'.

11.27 The provisions of the Act broadly restate and expand upon the position at common law but with renewed emphasis upon the flexible nature of the test and upon the safeguards necessary to ensure that decisions are not based upon pre-conceptions about capacity based upon appearance. The two-stage test of capacity under the MCA 2005, s 2(1) requires, first, proof that the person has an impairment of, or a disturbance in the functioning of his mind or brain. The second stage involves an assessment as to whether the impairment or disturbance means that the person is unable to make a specific decision when it needs to be made.

11.28 Paragraph 4.12 of the Code of Practice states that examples of an impairment or disturbance in the functioning of the mind or brain may include the following:

(1) conditions associated with some forms of mental illness;
(2) dementia;
(3) significant learning disabilities;
(4) the long-term effects of brain damage;

(5) physical or medical conditions that cause confusion, drowsiness or loss of consciousness;
(6) delirium;
(7) concussion following a head injury; and
(8) the symptoms of alcohol or drug use.

The references to *appearance* and *condition* under the MCA 2005, s 2(3) are intended to be broad (see para 4.8 of the Code of Practice, discussed below).

11.29 The MCA 2005 restates the position at common law that capacity is not a question of the degree of intelligence or education of the person concerned. Some may permanently lack capacity due to mental illness or retarded development. Others who would normally have capacity may be deprived of it by temporary factors such as unconsciousness, confusion, pain or drugs used in treatment[1] or by some phobia[2].

1 *Re T (adult: refusal of treatment)* [1992] 3 WLR 782 at 796F.
2 *Re MB (medical treatment)* [1997] 2 FLR 426.

11.30 The MCA 2005, s 2(4) provides that any question of capacity falls to be decided on the balance of probabilities.

11.31 The MCA 2005, s 2(5) provides that no power which a person (D) may exercise under the Act is exercisable in relation to a person who lacks capacity or where D reasonably thinks that a person lacks capacity, is exercisable in relation to a person under 16. However, by virtue of s 18(3) the powers may be exercised in relation to a person (P) even though P has not reached 16, if the court considers it likely that P will still lack capacity to make decisions in respect of that matter when he reaches 18.

Assessment of capacity

11.32 At common law, in determining a patient's capacity, the court applied the three-stage test adopted by Thorpe J in *Re C*[1]. The patient must be able to:

(1) comprehend and retain the relevant information;
(2) believe it;
(3) weigh it in the balance so as to arrive at a choice.

1 [1994] 1 All ER 891.

11.33 The test has now been codified. The Mental Capacity Act 2005, s 3 (in effect from 1 October 2007) provides that:

'(1) For the purposes of section 2 a person is unable to make a decision for himself if he is unable:

    (a) to understand the information relevant to the decision,
    (b) to retain that information,
    (c) to use or weigh that information as part of the process of making the decision, or
    (d) to communicate his decision (whether by talking, using sign language or any other means).

(2) A person is not to be regarded as unable to understand the information relevant to a decision if he is able to understand an explanation of it given to him in a way that

is appropriate to his circumstances (using simple language, visual aids or any other means).

(3) The fact that a person is able to retain the information relevant to a decision for a short period only does not prevent him from being regarded as able to make the decision.

(4) The information relevant to a decision includes information about the reasonably foreseeable consequences of:

(a) deciding one way or another, or
(b) failing to make the decision'.

11.34   The new definition of capacity is intended to expand on, rather than abolish, the existing tests at common law[1]. Whilst all practical steps should be taken to assist a patient in making a decision, the risk of undue influence must be avoided. Persuasion must not overbear the independence of the patient's decision (*Re T (adult: refusal of treatment)*[2]).

In *Re L (vulnerable adults with capacity: court's jurisdiction)*[3] the Court of Appeal affirmed earlier cases in which it was established that the Mental Capacity Act 2005 had not ousted the inherent jurisdiction of the court to deal with cases which fell outside the Act in order to protect vulnerable adults who were subject to constraint or undue influence.

1 Law Com no 231, para 3.23.
2 [1992] 4 All ER 649 at 662.
3 [2012] EWCA Civ 253, [2013] Fam 1, [2012] 3 WLR 1439.

11.35   The MCA 2005 is accompanied by a comprehensive Code of Practice. Those specified under the MCA 2005, s 42(4) (including treating doctors and those assessing capacity) are under a duty to have regard to the Code. Under s 42(5) courts or tribunals conducting criminal or civil proceedings must take into account the provisions of the Code, where relevant.

11.36   The Code emphasises the fact that an assessment of capacity must be based on a person's ability to make a specific decision at the time it needs to be made, and not his ability to make decisions in general. There may be a temporary loss of capacity. A person may lack capacity to make one decision but not another (paras 4.4–5).

11.37   Given the broad correspondence between the new test and the formulation in *Re C*, there continues to be reference to pre-statute case law. A helpful summary of the relevant provisions at common law was provided by Butler-Sloss LJ in *Re MB (an adult, medical treatment)*[1] (in a case involving a Caesarian section, and with the proviso that in any given case the court's decision will depend upon the facts):

(1)   every person is presumed to have capacity to consent to or to refuse medical treatment unless and until that presumption is rebutted;
(2)   a competent woman who has the capacity to decide may, for religious reasons, other reasons, for rational or irrational reasons or for no reason at all, choose not to have medical intervention, even though the consequence may be the death or serious handicap of the child she bears or her own death. In that event the courts do not have the jurisdiction to declare medical intervention lawful and the question of best interests objectively considered does not arise;

(3)   irrationality is here used to connote a decision which is so outrageous in its defiance of logic or of accepted moral standards that no sensible person who has applied his mind to the question to be decided could have arrived at it. As Kennedy and Grubb point out[2], it might be otherwise if a decision is based on a misperception of reality (eg the blood is poisoned because it is red). Such a misperception will be more readily accepted to be a disorder of the mind. Although it might be thought that irrationality sits uneasily with competence to decide, panic, indecisiveness and irrationality in themselves do not as such amount to incompetence, but they may be symptoms or evidence of incompetence. The graver the consequences of the decision, the commensurately greater the level of competence is required to take the decision[3];

(4)   a person lacks capacity if some impairment or disturbance of mental functioning renders the person unable to make a decision whether to consent to or refuse treatment. That inability to make a decision will occur when:

(a)   the patient is unable to comprehend and retain the information which is material to the decision, especially as to the likely consequences of having or not having the treatment in question;

(b)   the patient is unable to use the information and weigh it in the balance as part of the process of arriving at a decision. If as Thorpe J observed in *Re C* (above), a compulsive disorder or phobia from which the patient suffers stifles belief in the information presented to her, then the decision may not be a true one. As Lord Cockburn CJ put it in *Banks v Goodfellow*[4]:

'... one object may be so forced upon the attention of the invalid as to shut out all others that might require consideration.';

(5)   the 'temporary factors' mentioned by Lord Donaldson MR in *Re T* (above) (confusion, shock, fatigue, pain or drugs) may completely erode capacity but those concerned must be satisfied that such factors are operating to such a degree that the ability to decide is absent;

(6)   another such influence may be panic induced by fear. Again, careful scrutiny of the evidence is necessary because fear of an operation may be a rational reason for refusing to undergo it. Fear may also, however, paralyse the will and thus destroy the capacity to make a decision.

1   [1997] 2 FLR 426 at 436–7.
2   Kennedy and Grubb *Medical Law* (3rd edn, 2000).
3   *Re T (Adult Refusal of Treatment)* [1992] 3 WLR 782; *Sidaway* [1985] AC at 904 and *Gillick v West Norfolk and Wisbech Area Health Authority* [1986] AC 112 at 169 and 186, [1986] 1 FLR 224 at 234 and 251.
4   (1870) LR 5 QB 549 at 569.

BEST INTERESTS

Incompetent adults

11.38   The position at common law is that no one is able to give consent on behalf of an incompetent adult. Doctors are under a legal duty to treat incompetent patients in accordance with the best interests principle[1]. The best interests test is now enshrined in the MCA 2005, s 1(5). The MCA 2005, s 4 sets out in detail the basis upon which the test should be applied:

'(1) In determining for the purposes of this Act what is in a person's best interests, the person making the determination must not make it merely on the basis of:

   (a) the person's age or appearance, or

   (b) a condition of his, or an aspect of his behaviour, which might lead others to make unjustified assumptions about what might be in his best interests.

(2) The person making the determination must consider all the relevant circumstances and, in particular, take the following steps.

(3) He must consider:

   (a) whether it is likely that the person will at some time have capacity in relation to the matter in question, and

   (b) if it appears likely that he will, when that is likely to be.

(4) He must, so far as is reasonably practicable, permit and encourage the person to participate, or to improve his ability to participate, as fully as possible in any act done for him and any decision affecting him.

(5) Where the determination relates to life-sustaining treatment he must not, in considering whether the treatment is in the best interests of the person concerned, be motivated by a desire to bring about his death.

(6) He must consider, so far as is reasonably ascertainable:

   (a) the person's past and present wishes and feelings (and, in particular, any relevant written statement made by him when he had capacity),

   (b) the beliefs and values that would be likely to influence his decision if he had capacity, and

   (c) the other factors that he would be likely to consider if he were able to do so'.

1 *Re F* [1990] 2 AC 1.

11.39   The best interests checklist is intended to be both broad and flexible. The Joint Committee of both Houses, in its response to the Mental Capacity Bill, stated that:

'We acknowledge that consideration of best interests requires flexibility, by allowing and encouraging the person [lacking capacity] to be involved to the fullest possible extent but also enabling the decision-maker to take account of a variety of circumstances, views and attitudes which may have a bearing on the decision in question. This flexibility is particularly important in cases of partial or fluctuating capacity. Determining best interests is a judgment, requiring consideration of what will often be conflicting or competing concerns, while seeking to achieve a consensus to decision-making'.

11.40   A key feature of the legislation is the requirement under the MCA 2005, s 1(3) that all practicable steps be taken to help a person to make a decision before he is found to be incapable of doing so.

11.41   Chapter 5 of the Code of Practice contains a summary of steps to be taken in assessing best interests. These include establishing the views of the person who lacks capacity and avoiding discrimination. An interesting question arises as to whether the MCA 2005 introduces a 'substituted judgment' test adopted in most American courts or merely requires the views of the incompetent patient to be taken into account as one of the factors in determining best interests. Domestic case law on this issue has been somewhat inconsistent. The subjective approach to establishing best interests based upon the presumed wishes of the patient has been used in cases involving property and the affairs of incompetent patients[1]. However, an important passage in the *Bland* case stated[2]:

'I wish however to refer at this stage to the approach adopted in most American courts, under which the court seeks, in a case in which the patient is incapacitated from expressing any view on the question whether life-prolonging treatment should be withheld in the relevant circumstances, to determine what decision the patient himself would have made had he been able to do so. This is called the substituted judgment test, and it generally involves a detailed inquiry into the patient's views and preferences: see eg *Re Quinlan* (1976) 355 A 2d 647, and *Superintendent of Betchertown State School v Saikewicz*, 370 NE 2d 417. In later cases concerned with PVS patients it has been held that, in the absence of clear and convincing evidence of the patient's wishes, the surrogate decision-maker has to implement as far as possible the decision which the incompetent patient would make if he was competent. However, accepting on this point the submission of Mr Lester, I do not consider that any such test forms a part of English law in relation to incompetent adults, on whose behalf nobody has the power to give consent to medical treatment. Certainly in *Re F* [1990] 2 AC 1 your Lordships' House adopted a straightforward test based on best interests of the patient; and I myself do not see why the same test should not be applied in the case of PVS patients, where the question is whether life-prolonging treatment should be withheld. This was also the opinion of Thomas J in *Auckland Area Health Board v Attorney General* [1993] 1 NZLR 235, a case concerned with the discontinuance of life support provided by ventilator to a patient suffering from the last stages of incurable Guillain-Barre syndrome. Of course, consistent with the best interests test, anything relevant to the application of the test may be taken into account; and if the personality of the patient is relevant to the application of the test (as it may be in cases where the various relevant factors have to be weighed), it may be taken into account as was done in *Re J (a minor) (wardship: medical treatment)* 1991 Fam 33. But where the question is whether life support should be withheld from a PVS patient, it is difficult to see how the personality of the patient can be relevant, though it may be of comfort to his relatives if they believe, as in the present case, and indeed may well be so in many other cases, that the patient would not have wished his life to be artificially prolonged if he was totally unconscious and there was no hope of improvement in his condition'.

1 *Re D (J)* [1982] Ch 237 at 244 per Megarry V-C.
2 *Airedale NHS Trust v Bland* [1993] AC 789 at 871H–872E per Lord Goff.

11.42 In *Aintree University Hospitals NHS Foundation Trust v James*[1], Lady Hale drew the distinction between the best interests test and the *Bolam* test, and approved the observation made by the Court of Appeal in *Re SL (adult patient) (medical treatment)*[2] that logically there can only be one best option.

'The advantage of a best interests test is that it focused upon the patient as an individual, rather than the conduct of the doctor, and took all the circumstances, both medical and non-medical, into account (paras 3.26, 3.27). But the best interests test should also contain 'a strong element of "substituted judgment", taking into account both the past and present wishes and feelings of patient as an individual and, and, also the factors which he would consider if able to do so (para 3.28)'.

Lady Hale concludes that this is still a best interests rather than a substituted judgment test, but one which accepts that the preferences of the person concerned are an important component in deciding where his best interests lie (para 24 of *James*).

1 [2013] UKSC 67.
2 [2001] Fam 15, [2000] 2 FCR 452.

Best interests and withdrawal of treatment

11.43 In *Re J*[1] Lord Donaldson stated (at 46B following) that the question of withdrawal of treatment should be looked at from the assumed point of view of the patient rather than from the point of view of the decider. Taylor LJ stated, at 55F:

'I consider the correct approach is for the court to judge the quality of life the child would have to endure if given the treatment and decide whether in all the circumstances such a life would be so afflicted as to be intolerable to that child. I say "to that child" because the test should not be whether the life would be intolerable to the decider. The test must be whether the child in question, if capable of exercising sound judgment, would consider the life tolerable'.

1 *Re J* [1991] Fam 33.

11.44   Lord Phillips MR in *R (on the application of Burke) v GMC*[1] drew a distinction between cases such as *Re J*, where treatment can prolong life for an indeterminate period but only at a cost of great suffering, and other cases 'where a patient has lost competence in the final stages of life and where ANH may prolong these final stages, but at an adverse cost so far as comfort and dignity are concerned, sometimes resulting in the patient's last days being spent in a hospital ward rather than at home, with family around' (para 58). Lord Phillips (at para 62) took issue with the suggestion that the 'touchstone' of best interests should be intolerability and stated that:

'The test of whether it is the best interests of the patient to provide or continue ANH must depend on the particular circumstances. The two situations that we have considered above are very different. As to the approach to be adopted in the former, this court dealt with that in *Re J* and we do not think it is appropriate to review what the court there said in a context that is purely hypothetical.

63. As to the approach to best interests where a patient is close to death, it seems to us that the judge himself recognised that "intolerability" was not the test of best interests. At paragraph 104 he said where the patient is dying, the goal may properly be to ease suffering and, where appropriate, to "ease the passing" rather than to achieve a short prolongation of life.

We agree. We do not think it possible to attempt to define what is in the best interests of a patient by a single test, applicable in all circumstances'.

1 [2005] Lloyd's Rep Med 403.

11.45   In *Wyatt v Portsmouth Hospital NHS Trust*[1] the Court of Appeal carried out an extensive review of the case law on best interests (in particular *Re B (a minor) (wardship: medical treatment)*[2] and *Re J* above) and agreed with Hedley J at first instance that the concept of 'intolerable to that child' from *Re J* should not be seen as a gloss on, much less a complementary test to, best interests. It is a valuable guide in the search for best interests in this kind of case'. The Court of Appeal summarised the position thus:

'87. In our judgment, the intellectual milestones for the judge in a case such as the present are, therefore, simple, although the ultimate decision will frequently be extremely difficult. The judge must decide what is in the child's best interests. In making that decision, the welfare of the child is paramount, and the judge must look at the question from the assumed point of view of the patient (*Re J*). There is a strong presumption in favour of a course of action which will prolong life, but that presumption is not irrebuttable (*Re J*). The term "best interests" encompasses medical, emotional, and all other welfare issues (*Re A (male sterilisation)* [2000] 1 FLR 549). The court must conduct a balancing exercise in which all the relevant factors are weighed (*Re J*) and a helpful way of undertaking this exercise is to draw up a balance sheet (*Re A*).

88. Inevitably, whilst cases involving the treatment of children will fall into recognised categories, no two cases are the same, and the individual cases will, inevitably, be

highly fact specific. In this context, any criteria which seek to circumscribe the best interests tests are, we think, to be avoided. As Thorpe LJ said in *Re S* "it would be undesirable and probably impossible to set bounds to what is relevant to a welfare determination"'.

In *Aintree University Hospitals NHS Trust v James* Lady Hale reviewed the above authorities and referred also to para 5.31 of the MCA Code of Practice, which states

'All reasonable steps which are in the person's best interests should be taken to prolong their life. There will be a limited number of cases where treatment is futile, overly burdensome to the patient or where there is no prospect of recovery'.

On the facts in *James*, Lady Hale concluded:

'39 The most that can be said, therefore is that in considering the best interests of this particular patient, at this particular time, decision-makers must look at his welfare in the widest sense, not just medical but social and psychological; they must consider the nature of the medical treatment in question, what it involves and its prospects of success; they must consider what the outcome of that treatment is likely to be; they must try to put themselves in the position of the individual patient and ask what his attitude to the treatment is or would be likely to be; and they must consult others who are looking after him or interested in his welfare, in particular for their view of what his attitude would be'.

In particular, Lady Hale said that it is setting the goal too high to say (as the Court of Appeal had) that treatment is futile unless it has 'a real prospect of curing or at least palliating the life-threatening disease or illness from which the patient is suffering'. A treatment may bring some benefit to the patient even though it has no effect on the underlying disease or disability (para 43).

1 [2005] EWCA Civ 1181, [2005] Lloyd's Rep Med 474.
2 [1981] 1 WLR 1421.

11.46   In *An NHS Trust v (1) A (2) SA*[1], a dispute arose between members of a patient's (A's) family and doctors as to whether to withdraw treatment. In opposing the withdrawal of treatment the family relied in part upon the presumed wishes of the patient who was held to lack capacity. The Court of Appeal held that the views of the family and presumed views of the patient were 'highly material factors' but not determinative of best interests (para 59). The court reiterated the fact that the best interests test is not the same as the *Bolam* test. It encompasses a broad assessment of the patient's welfare and is not confined to medical issues[2].

1 [2005] EWCA Civ 1145, [2006] Lloyd's Rep Med 29.
2 *Re A (male sterilisation)* [2000] 1 FLR 549.

11.47   The decision of the Supreme Court in *James* has now affirmed that, whilst the patient's views are important, they are not determinative of the issue of best interests.

ADVANCE DECISIONS/DIRECTIVES

11.48   The MCA 2005 contains important provisions relating to advance decisions about future treatment made by adults (s 24).

11.49   An advance decision is not valid if withdrawn while the patient has capacity, or where the patient has conferred decision-making powers in relation to the treatment on a donee under a lasting power of attorney or done anything clearly inconsistent with the advance decision (MCA 2005, s 25(2)).

11.50   A number of further safeguards are provided under the MCA 2005, s 25:

'(4) An advance decision is not applicable to the treatment in question if:

    (a)   that treatment is not the treatment specified in the advance decision,

    (b)   any circumstances specified in the advance decision are absent, or

    (c)   there are reasonable grounds for believing that circumstances exist which P did not anticipate at the time of the advance decision and which would have affected his decision had he anticipated them.

(5) An advance decision is not applicable to life-sustaining treatment unless:

    (a)   the decision is verified by a statement by P to the effect that it is to apply to that treatment even if life is at risk, and

    (b)   the decision and statement comply with subsection (6).

(6) A decision or statement complies with this subsection only if:

    (a)   it is in writing,

    (b)   it is signed by P or another person in P's presence and by P's direction,

    (c)   the signature is made or acknowledged by P in the presence of a witness, and

    (d)   the witness signs it, or acknowledges his signature, in P's presence'.

11.51   An advance decision which is valid and applicable to the treatment in question is treated as the decision of a patient who has capacity at the time it is made. A person who reasonably believes that an advance directive is valid and applicable to treatment, does not incur liability for the consequences of withdrawing or withholding treatment (MCA 2005, s 26(3)). The court may make a declaration as to the validity and applicability of an advance decision. Importantly, nothing in an advance directive stops a person from providing life-sustaining treatment while a decision as respects 'any relevant issue' is sought from the court (MCA 2005, s 26(5)). Clarity is needed as to the nature of any treatment that is refused (*W Healthcare NHS Trust v H*[1]). In *Re M (adult patient) (minimally conscious state: withdrawal of treatment)*[2], Baker J, sitting in the Court of Protection, emphasised that an advance decision must address specifically the circumstances in which it will be binding.

1 [2004] EWCA Civ 1324, [2005] 1 WLR 834.
2 [2011] EWHC 2443 (Fam), [2012] 1 WLR 1653.

11.52   The scope of the MCA 2005, s 26(5) is unclear. It appears to be unqualified. If so, this might mean that in emergency cases treatment apparently inconsistent with the terms of an advance decision (in, for example, cases involving Jehovah's Witnesses) might be given pending determination by the court as to the effect of the directive. This provision may, somewhat surprisingly, in certain circumstances qualify the effect of cases such as *Malette v Shulman Hotel*[1] where a doctor was held liable in battery where he administered an emergency blood transfusion to an unconscious adult patient in the knowledge that the patient carried a Jehovah's Witness card requesting no blood transfusions under any circumstances. Can the mere issue of proceedings in these circumstances change the status of the act, rendering lawful what would otherwise be unlawful? This seems an improbable proposition but the MCA 2005, s 26(5) clearly suggests that this may be the case. It is difficult, however, to reconcile this position with basic common law principles. Two passages in *Airedale NHS Trust v Bland*[2] are pertinent. First, Lord Mustill (at 890C) on the nature of declaratory relief:

'The declarations will simply apply the law as it now stands to the undisputed facts of the present case. By upholding them the House will bind all courts charged in the future with a similar task to approach it in the same way. The declarations will not however alter the legal status of the proposed conduct from what it would have been even if no declarations had been sought, nor will it make any change in the existing law'.

Second, Lord Goff, in a passage in which he explains that an advance directive or prior refusal of consent to treatment by an unconscious patient should be given effect so long as especial care is made to ensure that the prior refusal is properly to be regarded as being applicable, applying the basic principle of patient autonomy (see 893H following):

'To presume that the incompetent person must always be subjected to what many rational and intelligent persons may decline is to downgrade the status of the incompetent person by placing a lesser value on his intrinsic human worth and vitality'.

Arguably, s 26(5) has no application where the terms of an advance decision are clear and valid (in other words where there is clearly an actual advance directive as opposed to one that is merely 'apparent').

1 [1991] 2 Med LR (Ont CA).
2 [1993] AC 789.

LASTING POWERS OF ATTORNEY/DEPUTIES

11.53 In certain circumstances, a donee of a lasting power of attorney can make decisions about treatment on behalf of patients who lack capacity (MCA 2005, s 11(7)). But this power does not authorise the giving or refusing of consent to the carrying out or continuation of life-sustaining treatment, unless the instrument used to create the power contains an express provision to that effect (MCA 2005, s 11(8)). Furthermore the court may revoke the power where the donee behaves or proposes to behave in a way which is not in the patient's best interests (MCA 2005, s 22(4)).

11.54 The court may also under the MCA 2005, s 16 appoint a deputy to make decisions on behalf of an incompetent patient, including decisions about giving or refusing consent to the carrying out or continuation of treatment: s 17(1)(d). A deputy may not be given power to make a decision on behalf of a patient which is inconsistent with a decision made, within the scope of his authority and in accordance with the Act, by the donee of a lasting power of attorney (MCA 2005, s 20(4)).

A deputy may not refuse consent to the carrying out or continuation of life-sustaining treatment (MCA 2005, s 20(5)).

CHILDREN

11.55   It is trite law that a doctor is not entitled to treat a patient without the consent of someone who is authorised to give that consent. If he does so, he will be liable in damages for trespass to the person and may be guilty of a criminal assault (*Re R (a minor) (wardship: medical treatment)*[1]).

1 [1992] 1 FLR 190 at 196.

11.56   As a general rule anyone with parental responsibility for a child can give valid consent for treatment. A child means anyone under the age of 18 (Children Act 1989 (ChA 1989), s 105). Under the ChA 1989, s 3(1), parental responsibility is defined as meaning:

'All the rights, duties, powers, responsibility and authority which by law a parent of a child has in relation to the child and his property'.

11.57   The ChA 1989, s 2(5) states that more than one person may have parental responsibility for the same child at the same time.

11.58   The right of parents to make decisions about treatment on behalf of their children is a dwindling right that must be exercised in the child's best interests. In the leading case of *Gillick v West Norfolk Area Health Authority*[1] Lord Fraser adopted the words of Lord Denning MR in *Hewer v Bryant*[2]:

'... The legal right of a parent to the custody of a child ends at the 18th birthday: and even up till then, it is a dwindling right which the courts will hesitate to enforce against the wishes of the child, and the more so the older he is. It starts with a right of control and ends with little more than advice'.

1 [1986] 1 AC 112.
2 [1970] 1 QB 357 at 369.

11.59   Parental rights are derived from parental duty and exist only so long as they are needed for the protection of the person and property of the child[1]. Parental rights do not exist for the benefit of the parent. They exist for the benefit of the child and are justified only in so far as they enable the parent to perform his duty towards the child[2]. For this reason it is, at least, possible that treatment which is not, in fact, in a child's best interests might constitute an assault, notwithstanding the fact that parental consent to it has been obtained. In the Court of Appeal in *Re F*[3], Lord Donaldson assumed that a doctor would commit assault where he performed a sterilisation operation on a minor, which was not in the minor's best interests, notwithstanding the presence of parental consent[4].

1 *Gillick v West Norfolk Area Health Authority* [1986] 1 AC 112 at 184B per Lord Scarman.
2 *Gillick v West Norfolk Area Health Authority* [1986] 1 AC 112 at 170D per Lord Fraser.
3 [1990] 2 AC 1 at 20A–C.
4 See also discussion on this issue in the Australian case of *Secretary Department of Health and Community Services v JWB & SMB* (1992) 175 CLR 218 per McHugh J at 316.

11.60   Parents also have rights under Article 8 of the European Convention on Human Rights. The right to agree to treatment is an aspect of family life[1]. Any parental right in this context is subject to the best interests principle. The court may overrule parental rights where it is in a child's best interests to do so[2].

1 *Nielson v Denmark* (1989) 11 EHRR 175 at para 61.
2 *Johansen v Norway* (1997) 23 EHRR 33.

11.61 In *NHS Trust A v Mrs M*[1], the President expressed doubt, in a case involving an adult in a persistent vegetative state, that a family had separate rights from the rights of the patient and that, if relevant, they cannot outweigh the positive obligation of the state to maintain the patient's life.

1 [2001] Lloyd's Rep Med 28.

11.62 The best interests principle is enshrined in Article 3(1) of the UN Convention on the Rights of the Child 1989, which states that:

'In all actions concerning children, whether undertaken by public or private social welfare institutions, courts of law, administrative authorities or legislative bodies, the best interests of the child shall be a primary consideration'.

Gillick competence/children under 16

11.63 A *Gillick* competent child under the age of 16 may give valid consent on his or her own behalf. The question as to whether or not a child is *Gillick* competent is a question of fact. *Gillick* competence is a developmental concept. It is likely to be viewed now with specific regard to the principles contained in the MCA 2005 although, save in regard to the situation set out in para 18(3), this does not apply to a person under 16. As a general rule, *Gillick* competence requires sufficient maturity and understanding to understand the nature and implications of proposed treatment. The more serious the treatment, the greater the degree of understanding that will be required in order to prove consent:

'It seems to me verging on the absurd to suggest that a girl or boy aged 15 could not effectively consent, for example, to have a medical examination of some trivial injury to his body or even to have a broken arm set. Of course the consent of the parents should normally be asked but they may not be immediately available. Provided the patient, whether a boy or girl, is capable of understanding what is proposed, and of expressing his or her own wishes, I see no good reason for holding that he or she lacks capacity to express them validly and effectively and to authorise the medical man to make the examination or give the treatment which he advises'[1].

1 *Gillick v West Norfolk Area Health Authority* [1986] 1 AC 112 at 169B per Lord Fraser.

11.64 However, Lord Fraser further qualified the circumstances in which a doctor would be justified in giving advice about contraception to a child under 16 by reference to the child's best interests. On this analysis, the scope of consent of a *Gillick* competent child is circumscribed by reference to the best interests principle. Lord Scarman further stated that the patient should have sufficient maturity to understand the moral, social and emotional impact of any decision. Additionally, the doctor must be satisfied that the circumstances are such that 'he ought to proceed without parental knowledge and consent'.

In *R (on the application of Axon) v Secretary of State for Health (Family Planning Association intervening)*[1] the court applied *Gillick* and held that there was no infringement of the Article 8(1) rights of a young patient's parents where confidential information about advice or treatment of the young person on sexual matters was withheld from them.

1 [2006] EWHC 37 (Admin), [2006] 2 WLR 1130.

Children of 16 and over

11.65   In relation to children aged 16 and over, there is by law a presumption of capacity to consent to treatment of most sorts (excluding donation of organs or blood or other procedures which do not constitute treatment or diagnosis)[1]. The Family Law Reform Act 1969, s 8 provides:

'(1) The consent of a minor who has attained the age of sixteen years to any surgical, medical or dental treatment which, in the absence of consent, would constitute a trespass to his person shall, be as effective as it would be if he were of full age; and where a minor has by virtue of this section given an effective consent to any treatment it shall not be necessary to obtain any consent for it from his parent or guardian.

(2) In this section "surgical, medical or dental treatment" includes any procedure undertaken for the purposes of diagnosis, and this section applies to any procedure (including, in particular, the administration of an anaesthetic) which is ancillary to any treatment as it applies to that treatment.

(3) Nothing in this section should be construed as making ineffective any consent which would have been effective if this section had not been inactive.'

1 *Re W (a minor) (medical treatment: court's jurisdiction)* [1993] Fam 64; also reported as *Re J* [1992] 3 Med LR 317.

Refusal of consent

11.66   Current case law draws a distinction between the minor's capacity to consent to treatment and the capacity to refuse treatment (which can be overruled by parents or the court upon an application of the best interests principle). This case law may now need to be treated with caution by reason of the MCA 2005, at least in relation to children aged between 16 and 18. In *Re R (a minor) (wardship: consent to treatment)*[1], the court held that the refusal of consent of a *Gillick* competent 15-year-old child could be overruled. Lord Donaldson MR stated that:[2]

'(1) No doctor can be required to treat a child, whether by the court in the exercise of its wardship jurisdiction, by the parents, by the child or anyone else. The decision whether to treat is dependent upon an exercise of his own professional judgment, subject only to the threshold requirement that, save in exceptional cases usually of emergency, he has the consent of someone who has authority to give that consent. Informing that judgment the views and wishes of the child are a factor whose importance increases with the increase in the child's intelligence and understanding.

(2) There can be concurrent powers to consent. If more than one body or person has a power to consent, only a failure to, or refusal of, consent by all having that power will create a veto.

(3) A "*Gillick* competent" child or one over the age of 16 will have a power to consent, but this will be concurrent with that of a parent or guardian.

(4) "*Gillick* competence" is a developmental concept and will not be lost or acquired on a day to day or week to week basis. In the case of mental disability, that disability must also be taken into account, particularly where it is fluctuating in its effect.

(5) The court in the exercise of its wardship or statutory jurisdiction has power to override the decisions of a "*Gillick* competent" child as much as those of parents or guardians.

(6) Waite J was right to hold that R was not "*Gillick* competent" and even if R had been, was right to consent to her undergoing treatment which might involve compulsory medication'.

1 [1992] Fam 11, [1992] 3 Med LR 342.
2 [1992] Fam 11, [1992] 3 Med LR 342 at 26E.

11.67   In *Re W*[1] Lord Donaldson MR further reviewed the effect of consent in a case involving a 16-year-old minor:

'There seems to be some confusion in the minds of some as to the purpose of seeking consent from a patient (whether adult or child) or from someone with authority to give that consent on behalf of the patient. It has two purposes, the one clinical and the other legal. The clinical purpose stems from the fact that in many instances the co-operation of the patient and the patient's faith or at least confidence in the efficiency of the treatment is a major factor contributing to the treatment's success. Failure to obtain such consent will not only deprive the patient and the medical staff of this advantage, but will usually make it more difficult to administer the treatment. I appreciate that this purpose may not be served if consent is given on behalf of, rather than by, the patient. However, in the case of young children knowledge of the fact that the parent has consented may help. The legal purpose is quite different. It is to provide those concerned in the treatment with a defence to a criminal charge of assault or battery or a civil claim for damages for trespass to the person. It does not, however, provide them with any defence to a claim that they negligently advised a particular treatment or negligently carried it out'.

1 [1993] Fam 64, also known as *Re J (a minor)* [1992] 3 Med LR 317.

11.68   Lord Donaldson went on to describe the consent of the minor over 16 as a 'flak jacket' which protects doctors from claims by the litigious (in place of the 'key-holder' analogy in *Re R* 'because keys can lock as well as unlock'). He affirmed that the refusal of consent of a minor over 16 could be overridden by parents or the court.

11.69   These authorities have attracted much criticism but have invariably been applied in subsequent cases, particularly, in circumstances where the competent minor's refusal of consent has placed his or her life at risk. The reluctance of society 'to allow an infant to martyr himself'[1] has been the guiding principle for intervention where the life of the child is at stake.

1 *Re E* [1993] 9 BMLR 1 at 9 per Ward J.

11.70   The provisions of the MCA 2005 relating to advance directives and lasting powers of attorney do not relate to minors (those under 18). The MCA 2005, s 2(5) specifies (subject to s 18(3)) that no power under the Act may be exercised in relation to a person under 16. The Act and the Code are unclear as to whether or not the court can continue to overrule the views of a competent minor aged between 16 and 18. The Code (at para 12.14) indicates that the Court of Protection would have no jurisdiction to review the decision of a competent minor aged between 16 and 18 but that the Family Division will still have jurisdiction. Assuming that the Family Division has jurisdiction, it is unclear how it could override the provisions of the Act which specify that:

(1)   a person is not to be treated as unable to make a decision merely because he makes an unwise decision (s 1(4)); and that

(2)   a lack of capacity cannot be established merely by reference to a person's age (s 1(3)(a)).

MENTAL HEALTH ACT 1983

11.71   The MCA 2005, s 28 provides that nothing in the Act authorises anyone to give a patient treatment for a mental disorder or to consent to a patient's being given treatment for mental disorder if his treatment is regulated by the Mental Health Act 1983 (MHA 1983), Pt 4. A number of amendments to the MHA 1983 have been made by the Mental Health Act 2007 (MHA 2007).

11.72   An extensive review of the MHA 1983 is beyond the scope of this chapter. Section 57 as amended by the MHA 2007, s 12, contains provisions relating to the most serious form of treatment which can only be given if the patient consents and three independent people (one of whom must be a registered medical practitioner, not the 'responsible clinician' or person in charge of the treatment in question) have certified in writing that the patient is capable of understanding the nature, purpose and likely effects of the treatment in question and has consented to it. Section 58 provides that certain forms of treatment require the patient's consent or written certification from an independent medical practitioner that, having regard to the likelihood of its alleviating or preventing a deterioration in the patient's condition, the treatment should be given (see MHA 2007, s 12(3) for amendments to the certification requirements).

11.73   In *R (on the application of N) v Dr M*[1], it was held that any alleged breach of a patient's rights under the ECHR, Article 6, based on the manner in which the certification process was conducted would fall away on the judge deciding the disputed facts for himself on an application for judicial review. There was no requirement under Article 6 for the judge to hear oral evidence[2].

1 [2002] EWCA Civ 1789, [2003] MHLR 157.
2 See also *R (on the application of B) v Dr SS (Responsible Medical Officer), Second Opinion Appointed Doctor and the Secretary of State for Health* [2006] EWCA Civ 28.

11.74   Specific provisions are contained in the MHA 1983, ss 62 and 63, as amended by the MHA 2007, s 12(5) and (6), in relation to urgent treatment. Section 62A contains detailed provisions for treatment on recall of community patients or revocation of orders. Under s 62, ss 57 and 58 shall not apply to any treatment which is immediately necessary to save the patient's life or inter alia (not being irreversible) is immediately necessary to prevent a serious deterioration in his condition (see paras 16.40 and 16.41 of the Code of Practice). Under s 63 the consent of a patient shall not be required for any medical treatment given to him for the mental disorder from which he is suffering, not being treatment falling within s 57 or 58, if the treatment is given by or under the direction of the approved clinician in charge of the treatment (MHA 2007, s 12(5)). The definition of 'medical treatment' under the MHA 1983, s 145 was further broadened by the MHA 2007, s 7 to include nursing, psychological intervention and specialist mental health habilitation, rehabilitation and care. Under s 145(4) as amended, any reference to medical treatment, in relation to mental disorder, shall be construed as a reference to medical treatment the purpose of which is to alleviate, or prevent a worsening of, the disorder or one or more of its symptoms or manifestations. This further definition gives statutory support to the approach in the leading case of *B v Croydon Health Authority*[1], where the Court of Appeal held that medical treatment, as defined by the MHA 1983, s 145(1) (prior to the amendment), included a range of acts ancillary to the core treatment not all of which had to be, in themselves, likely to alleviate or prevent a deterioration of the disorder. In *Nottinghamshire Healthcare NHS Trust v RC*[2], it was held that the administration of a blood transfusion to a Jehovah's Witness who suffered from personality disorders which caused him to self-harm amounted to treatment to 'prevent the worsening of the disorder or one or more of its symptoms or manifestations' within the meaning of s 63. Treatment in the form of tube feeding to alleviate the symptoms of mental disorder, in the form of a refusal to eat in order to inflict self-harm, was held to be just as much a part of treatment for the disorder as that directed to remedying its underlying cause[3].

1 [1995] 1 All ER 683.
2 [2014] EWCOP 1317, [2014] Med LR 260.
3 See *R v Collins and Ashworth Hospital Authority, ex p Brady* [2000] MHLR 17; *R v Ashworth Hospital Authority, ex p B* [2005] UKHL 20, [2005] 2 All ER 289.

BATTERY

11.75   Treatment without consent may amount to the tort of battery. Battery is a form of trespass to the person and is actionable per se. Unless damage or loss is proved any damages are likely to be notional.

11.76   In *Chatterton v Gerson*[1] the tort of battery was deemed an inappropriate vehicle for claims for clinical non-disclosure (which are usually brought in negligence; for an example of a successful action in trespass see *Appleton v Garrett*[2] where the claimants recovered aggravated damages in trespass for unnecessary treatment). The confusion as to whether or not a 'hostile intent' was required in cases of battery appears to have been decided by the speech of Lord Goff in *Re F*[3] where he states that:

'In the old days it used to be said that, for a touching of another person to amount to a battery, it had to be a touching "in anger" (see *Cole v Turner* (1704) 6 Mod 149, *per* Holt CJ); and it has recently been said that the touching must be "hostile" to have that effect (see *Wilson v Pringle* [1987] QB 237, 253). I respectfully doubt whether that is correct. A prank that gets out of hand: an over-friendly slap on the back; surgical treatment by a surgeon who mistakenly thinks that the patient has consented to it – all these things may transcend the bounds of lawfulness, without being characterised as hostile. Indeed the suggested qualification is difficult to reconcile with the principle that any touching of another's body is, in the absence of lawful exercise, capable of amounting to a battery and a trespass. Furthermore in the case of medical treatment, we have to bear well in mind the libertarian principle of self-determination which, to adopt the words of Cardozo J (in *Schloendorff v Society of New York Hospital* (1914) 105 NE 92, 93) recognises that:

"Every human being of adult years and sound mind has a right to determine what shall be done with his own body; and a surgeon who performs an operation without his patient's consent commits an assault ..."'.

1 [1981] QB 432.
2 [1997] 8 Med LR 75.
3 [1992] 2 AC 1 at 73B.

11.77   Although often used in reference to both assault and battery, 'assault' denotes an act by which a person intentionally or recklessly causes another to apprehend immediate unlawful violence[1].

1 *Fagan v Metropolitan Police Commissioner* [1969] 1 QB 439; *R v Venna* [1976] QB 421 at 429; *Smith v Chief Superintendent Woking Police Station* (1983) 76 Cr App R 234; *R v Ireland; R v Burstow* [1998] AC 147.

11.78   Any touching of another person, however slight, might amount to a battery[1]. In *Wilson v Pringle*[2], Croom-Johnson LJ stated that where emergency treatment is provided to an unconscious patient, rather than invoke a doctrine of implied consent, 'It is better simply to say that the surgeon's action is acceptable in the ordinary conduct of everyday life, and not a battery'. In other words, the treatment constitutes one of the exceptions (such as lawful sporting activity) to conduct which would otherwise be tortious. This approach was not followed by Lord Goff in *Re F*[3] who invoked the doctrine of necessity and stated (in common with Lord Donaldson MR in the Court of Appeal in *Re F* at 12D) that surgical treatment carried out in a mistaken belief as to a patient's consent might be unlawful.

1 *Collins v Wilcox* [1984] 1 WLR 1172–1178.
2 [1987] 1 QB 237.
3 [1992] 2 AC 1 at 74B.

11.79   This issue is now governed by the MCA 2005, s 5 which provides that:

'(1) If a person ('D') does an act in connection with the care or treatment of another person ('P'), the act is one to which this section applies if:

(a) before doing the act, D takes reasonable steps to establish whether P lacks capacity in relation to the matter in question, and

(b) when doing the act, D reasonably believes:

    (i)   that P lacks capacity in relation to the matter, and

    (ii) that it will be in P's best interests for the act to be done.

(2) D does not incur any liability in relation to the act that he would not have incurred if P:

(a) had had capacity to consent in relation to the matter, and

(b) had consented to D's doing the act.

(3) Nothing in this section excludes a person's civil liability for loss or damage, or his criminal liability, resulting from his negligence in doing the act.

(4) Nothing in this section affects the operation of sections 24 to 26 (advance decisions to refuse treatment).'

Defence to battery

11.80   Consent in broad terms to the procedure involved constitutes a defence to battery. In *Chatterton v Gerson*[1], Bristow J defined the concept, described as 'real' consent in these terms;

'in my judgment what the court has to do in each case is to look at all the circumstances and say, "Was there a real consent?" I think justice requires that in order to vitiate the reality of consent there must be a greater failure of communication between doctor and patient than that involved in a breach of duty if the claim is based on negligence. When the claim is based on negligence the plaintiff must prove not only the breach of duty to inform but that had the duty not been broken she would not have chosen the operation. Where the claim is based on trespass to the person, once it is shown that the consent is unreal, then what the patient would have decided if she had been given the information which would have prevented vitiation of the reality of her consent is irrelevant.

In my judgment once the patient is informed in broad terms of the nature of the procedure which is intended, and gives her consent, that consent is real, and the cause of the action on which to base a claim for failure to go into risks and implications is negligence, not trespass. Of course, if information is withheld in bad faith, the consent will be vitiated by fraud'.

1 [1981] 1 All ER 257.

11.81 The above passage must now, of course, be read in the light of the decision of the House of Lords in *Chester v Afshar*[1] (which might somewhat qualify the causative distinction between the two actions). However, the distinction between the two actions remains. Battery is an intentional tort. Most claims for injuries arising from medical treatment involve negligence or carelessness. The courts have discouraged actions framed in battery. The stigma attached to a finding of criminal assault is felt to be inappropriate where doctors, albeit negligent, act in good faith[2]. In *Border v Lewisham and Greenwich NHS Trust (formerly South London Healthcare NHS Trust)*[3] the Court of Appeal rejected an amendment on appeal to plead assault. The case, however, illustrates the importance of obtaining express or implied consent for the insertion of an IV cannula, notwithstanding that neither in the choice of site (potentially lymphoedematous arm) nor in the conduct of the procedure was the doctor negligent. Acting in the best interests of a patient is no defence, even in an emergency procedure if the patient is competent and able to give consent.

1 [2004] UKHL 41, [2005] 1 AC 134.
2 *Chatterton v Gerson* [1981] 1 All ER 257, where Bristow J followed comments made in the Ontario Court of Appeal in *Reibl v Hughes* (1978) 21 OR (2d) 40.
3 [2015] EWCA Civ 8.

11.82 In *Hills v Potter*[1], where the action included a claim in battery for injuries sustained following an operation for neck deformity on the basis that the claimant had been inadequately advised about the risks of surgery, Hirst J found:

'As to the claim for assault and battery, the plaintiff's undoubted consent to the operation which was in fact performed negatives any possibility of liability under this head, *see Chatterton v Gerson*. I should add that I respectfully agree with Bristow J in deploring reliance on these torts in medical cases of this kind, the proper cause of action, if any, is negligence'[2].

1 [1983] 3 All ER 716.
2 At 653D/E. Note: this approach was approved by Lord Scarman in *Sidaway v Board of Governors of Bethlem Royal Hospital and the Maudsley Hospital* [1985] 1 AC 871 at 883E.

FRAUD

11.83 Fraud will vitiate consent where it leads to a misunderstanding as to the nature and quality of the procedure. In *R v Tabassum*[1] it was held that the apparent consent of women to a breast examination by the defendant who falsely led them to believe that he was medically qualified was vitiated by fraud as to the nature and quality of the conduct. In *R v Richardson*[2] it was held that a patient's ignorance of the fact that the doctor who treated him was suspended from practice did not vitiate his consent. However, there does not appear to have been any argument in *Richardson* as to whether there was fraud in relation to the nature and quality of the conduct in question.

1 [2000] Lloyd's Rep Med 404.
2 [1998] 2 Cr App Rep 200.

CHAPTER 12

Limitation of actions

Caroline Harrison QC

OVERVIEW

12.1 At common law claims are actionable indefinitely. Limitation of actions is, in English law, the product of statute. Since the time of King Henry VIII, if not before, Parliament has enacted a variety of statutes setting limits to the period within which a claimant is entitled to commence a legal action[1]. Different periods have been set for different kinds of claim. In 1623, a six-year limit was introduced for claims founded on what would now be termed tort or contract[2].

The present legislation seeks to strike a balance between competing interests: to promote certainty and avoid the litigation of stale claims, whilst allowing certain actions to proceed where the strict application of time limits would result in unfairness to a claimant.

1 1540, 32 Hen VIII c 2, which concerned actions for the recovery of property. Roman law, in general, did not recognise lapse of time as affecting a right of action, once vested. In AD 424, Theodosius II enacted that a limitation period of 30 years should apply to actions which had hitherto been perpetual.
2 By the Statute of Limitations 1623, s 2, 21 Jac 1, c 16. Time did not run against a person under disability.

12.2   Thus, it has been said that the purpose of statutes of limitation is threefold:

(1)   to protect defendants from being vexed by stale claims relating to long past incidents about which their records may no longer be in existence and as to which their witnesses, even if they are still available, may well have no accurate recollection;
(2)   to encourage claimants to institute proceedings as soon as it is reasonably possible for them to do so (but without encouraging precipitate litigation); and
(3)   to ensure that a person may with confidence feel that after a given time he may regard as finally closed an incident which might have led to a claim against him[1].

1 See the Report of the Edmund Davies Committee, *Limitation of Actions in Cases of Personal Injury* (Cmnd 1829, 1962); and *Birkett v James* [1978] AC 297, HL at 331, per Lord Edmund Davies.

12.3   A defendant is entitled to the protection of the statutes of limitation where the claim against him is commenced after the expiry of the limitation period. In the general run of clinical negligence cases, the claimant must begin his claim within a period of three years from the date of the mishap[1], but there are numerous exceptions to this, which are considered in detail below. Whilst the commencement of a claim means in practice the issue of a claim form[2], an action is 'brought' within the meaning of the Limitation Act 1980 (LA 1980), s 11(3) when the claimant's request for the issue of a claim form, together with the court fee, is delivered to the court office, and not when the claim form is subsequently issued by the court[3]. When, on the last day of the period, the court office is closed, the time is extended to the first day on which the office reopens[4]. In computing time, the day during which the cause of action arose is excluded, and the day on which the proceedings are brought is included[5].

1 LA 1980, s 11(4)(a).
2 CPR 7.2.
3 See *Barnes v St Helen's Metropolitan Borough Council* [2006] EWCA Civ 1372, [2007] 1 WLR 879. The request was received by the court within office hours, within the limitation period; however, owing to industrial action the claim form was not issued until after expiry. The action was brought within the limitation period. The rationale of this is that a claimant's risk should cease once he has taken the steps required by the Act, and he should not be vulnerable to failures within the court's own administration, see *Page v Hewetts Solicitors* [2012] EWCA Civ 805. This may be an increasingly important provision, because court administrative failures seem to be on the increase, with two examples from the Salford Business Centre reaching the Court of Appeal between May and July of 2014 alone (*Stoute v LTA Operations* [2014] EWCA Civ 657 and *Edward Power v Meloy Whittle Robinson Solicitors* [2014] EWCA Civ 898). See also para 5.1 of the Practice Direction to CPR Pt 7: where the claim form as issued is

received in the court office on a date earlier than the date on which it is issued by the court, the claim is brought for the purposes of the Limitation Act 1980 and any other relevant statute on that earlier date. This means that if issuing anywhere near the expiry of primary limitation, claimants' solicitors should be alert to the potential need for evidence to prove exactly *when* and how a request was lodged at court.

4 *Pritam Kaur v S Russell & Sons Ltd* [1973] QB 336, CA.
5 See *Marren v Dawson Bentley & Co Ltd* [1961] 2QB 135, where the plaintiff was injured in an accident on 8 November 1954. Havers J held that a writ issued on 8 November 1957 was not barred by the Limitation Act 1939, s 2(1).

12.4   The current principal statute of limitations is the LA 1980. This contains no provisions specific to actions for clinical negligence. The relevant provisions are those governing actions founded on tort or contract, together with special rules applicable in cases of personal injuries or death, and rules which postpone the running of the period in cases of legal disability (ie where the claimant is under 18 years old or lacks the necessary mental capacity[1]) and cases of concealment. A simplified overview of the relevant provisions is given in Table **12.1**.

TABLE 12.1

Personal injury claims arising out of negligence, nuisance or breach of duty:	
Primary period	
Three years from accrual of cause of action, or, if later, from 'date of knowledge'.	
Extensions	
1	Legal disability: three years from end of disability.
2	Concealment: three years from discovery of concealment, or from when claimant could with reasonable diligence have discovered it.
3	Discretion: court has power to override time limit where equitable to do so.
Other claims:	
Primary period	
Six years from accrual of cause of action: or, in negligence claims only, three years from 'starting date'* if that period expires later than the six years, but subject to overall limit of 15 years from last act of negligence.	
Extensions	
1	Legal disability: six years from end of disability.
2	Concealment: six years from discovery of concealment, or from when claimant could with reasonable diligence have discovered it.

1 Within the meaning of the Mental Capacity Act 2005, see CPR 21.1(2)(c).

12.5   In general, the law on limitation is procedural rather than substantive. The expiry of a limitation period does not extinguish the cause of action, but operates to bar the remedy. However there are exceptions to this. For example with regard to defective products (such as medical devices or pharmaceutical products[1]) and where the cause of action arises at sea[2]. In large group actions the imposition of a cut-off date is essential for efficiency and the proper conduct of such substantial litigation. A cut-off date does not, however, operate as a limitation period for those who fail to meet the deadline, but rather is a procedural requirement[3].

1 The LA 1980, s 11A(3) provides a ten year long-stop for actions in respect of defective products, thus extinguishing the right of action.
2 See the Athens Convention Relating to the Carriage of Passengers and their Luggage by Sea 1974, especially article 16; and also *Feest v South West Strategic Health Authority* [2014] EWHC 177 (QB) (Mercantile, Bristol). The Athens Convention provides for a limitation period of two years from the date of disembarkation, and the right of action is extinguished if the claim is not brought within that time. Thus if passengers on a cruise ship, for example, were injured by the inept medical management of a serious outbreak of food poisoning, then the Athens Convention would apply.
3 *AB v John Wyeth & Brother Ltd* [1993] 4 Med LR 1, CA. The rules governing group litigation are to be found in CPR 19.10–19.15. CPR 19.13 gives the management court power to specify cut-off dates, but permission for late joinder may be given.

WHEN A CAUSE OF ACTION ACCRUES

12.6 The general rule is that time begins to run against a claimant from the date when his cause of action accrues to him. A 'cause of action' is simply a factual situation the existence of which entitles one person to obtain from the court a remedy against another person[1]. The first date on which that factual situation comes into existence is the date of accrual of the cause of action.

1 *Letang v Cooper* [1965] 1 QB 232, CA, per Diplock LJ.

12.7 A cause of action founded on tort is not complete until the claimant suffers damage[1]. Thus, in a case of clinical negligence, the date of accrual of the cause of action is normally the date when the claimant suffers injury. Difficult factual questions can arise where the injury is at first imperceptible so that the date of the injury cannot readily be ascertained. In such cases, it is a question of fact and degree at what point the claimant has suffered material damage by reason of physical changes in his body. Changes within the principle *de minimis non curat lex* ('the law is not concerned with trifles') are ignored, but anything greater than this is regarded as substantial damage[2].

1 Except in the case of torts actionable per se, ie without proof of damage, such as trespass to the person.
2 *Cartledge v E Jopling & Sons Ltd* [1963] AC 758 at 779, per Lord Pearce; see also at 772, damage 'beyond what can be regarded as negligible', per Lord Reid; and at 774, 'real damage as distinct from purely minimal damage', per Lord Evershed.

12.8 In practice, the bulk of clinical negligence cases are claims for damages for personal injuries. However, such cases are not the only possible instances of negligence liability in the medical profession. Damages may be sought for loss of a solely financial nature (usually termed 'economic loss') where the negligent report or statement complained of and relied upon was given to a known recipient for a specific purpose of which the maker was aware[1]. Where a doctor makes a report on a patient to a prospective employer, a negligent misstatement may cause such loss. If the misstatement is unduly optimistic as to the patient's state of health, loss may be suffered by the employer. If it is too negative, the patient may be the loser[2]. An insurance company may suffer loss by relying on a negligent report by a doctor who examines a person proposing for life assurance. However, in practice, such cases are extremely difficult to bring successfully, and require either a 'special relationship' or an assumption of responsibility (for causing economic loss)[3]. Where the damage is in the nature of economic loss, difficulties of a conceptual nature can arise in ascertaining the date of occurrence of the damage[4].

1 *Caparo Industries plc v Dickman* [1990] 2 AC 605, HL.
2 The 'patient' in *Kapfunde v Abbey National plc* [1999] IRLR 583, CA failed to get the job because Dr Daniel incorrectly said that her history of sickle cell anaemia would be likely to result in a higher than average level of absences from work because of illness. The Court of Appeal held that Dr Daniels did not owe the plaintiff a duty of care.
3 See generally *Jackson and Powell on Professional Liability* (7th edn, Sweet & Maxwell), paras 2-041 to 2-048 and 13-011. Although the writer of a reference or medical report is obliged to exercise reasonable care (see *Spring v Guardian Assurance plc* [1993] 2 All ER 273), liability of a medical practitioner for economic loss to third parties is exceptionally hard to establish, see eg *London Borough of Islington v University College London Hospital NHS Trust* [2005] EWCA Civ 596 and *West Bromwich Albion Football Club v El-Safty* [2006] EWCA Civ 1299.
4 If, for example, an insurer issues a policy on the life of a person who is in poorer health than was reported, it might be thought that the economic loss occurs only when the patient dies, so giving rise to a claim under the policy (indeed, in the case of a term assurance there may be no loss at all if the patient, though ailing, outlives the term). But it may be a more accurate analysis to state that the economic loss occurs when the policy is issued, since at that time the insurers have taken on an obligation more onerous than expected. It is impossible to give straightforward guidance on this complex area of law, and each case will turn on its own particular facts, but it is clear from the leading case of *Nykredit Mortgage Bank plc v Edward Erdman Group Ltd (No 2)* [1997] 1 WLR 1627, HL that a cause of action can accrue before actual financial losses have crystalised (see further para **12.9** and fn 1 to that para).

12.9 Clinical negligence claims may be mishandled by lawyers so that the claim is lost because of some procedural default. The question that arises then, is when does the cause of action accrue? In a case where the claim had been struck out for want of prosecution, and the negligent solicitor was then sued, the court held that the loss was not sustained until the clinical negligence action was struck out[1]. It is now clear that question of when damage is first sustained is essentially a factual question[2]. There are two principles which are relevant to determining the answer to the question: (a) actual damage is any detriment, liability or loss capable of assessment in money terms, and included liabilities which might arise on a contingency; (b) a useful formulation was to consider 'when was the claimant worse off financially by reason of a breach of the duty of care than he otherwise would have been?'. The claim in the original action is a chose in action; the claim against the solicitor is for the diminution in the value of the chose (which may be worthless before the original action is struck out).

1 *Hopkins v MacKenzie* [1995] PIQR P43, CA. That decision was subsequently considered to be inconsistent with the decision of the House of Lords in *Nykredit Mortgage Bank plc v Edward Erdman Group Ltd (No 2)* [1997] 1 WLR 1627, in which Lord Nicholls had approved the proposition that 'damage' in economic loss claims meant any detriment, liability or loss capable of assessment in money terms and included liabilities which may arise on a contingency (though note the judgment of the House of Lords in *Law Society v Sephton & Co* [2006] UKHL 22, [2006] 2 AC 543, at paras 18–20 and 30, on the question of contingent liabilities). For the power to strike out a statement of case, see CPR 3.4.
2 *Susan Berney v Thomas Saul (t/a Thomas Saul & Co)* [2013] EWCA Civ 640, where the Court of Appeal held it was not necessary to try and reconcile the arguably inconsistent approaches of *Hopkins*, *Khan v Falvey* [2002] PNLR 28, CA and *Hatton v Chafes (a firm)* [2003] EWCA Civ 341, [2003] PNLR 24. The court applied *Forster v Outred & Co* [1982] 1 WLR 86 and *Nykredit*.

12.10 Where a claim is based on breach of contract, the cause of action is complete when the contract is broken, irrespective of the date when damage results to the claimant[1]. Where, therefore, a doctor acts in contravention of his contractual duty to his patient, time runs from the date of the breach.

Most such duties relate to the mode of performance of a particular act at a particular time. However, where the contractual duty in question is of a continuing nature, the claimant can rely on the breach latest in time. This is most likely to arise in the context of an omission to act, when the duty to rectify the omission may continue until the act becomes impossible to carry out or until the contractual relationship is terminated[2]. For example, if a GP fails to advise a private patient, whom he puts on a course of drugs, of the risks of drinking alcohol while taking the drugs, he would be under a continuing duty to rectify his failure by giving the correct advice. This duty would continue until fulfilled or until the course of treatment ends.

1 *Howell v Young* (1826) 5 B & C 259. For a case considering the contractual and tortious position where medical services were provided by a consultant orthopaedic surgeon to a footballer by arrangement with the football club under a BUPA policy, see *West Bromwich Albion Football Club Ltd v El Safty* [2007] PIQR P7, CA. This may also be relevant to claims for cosmetic procedures, and claimants may also need to consider the potentially different remedies available in contract and tort.
2 The relevant legal reasoning was considered at some length in a solicitors' negligence case, *Midland Bank Trust Co Ltd v Hett, Stubbs & Kemp* [1979] Ch 384. Further discussion of this kind of issue is to be found in the cases on the duty of architects to keep their design of a building under review: *Brickfield Properties Ltd v Newton* [1971] 1 WLR 862, CA, and more recently *New Islington Health Authority v Pollard Thomas & Edwards* [2001] PNLR 515 (Dyson J). See also the cautionary remarks of Bingham LJ in *Eckersley v Binnie* (1988) 18 Con LR 1 at 146–147.

12.11   Interesting questions previously arose as to a doctor's duty to inform his patient that he has broken his contract. There is authority that a contracting party who knows he has made an error which may have dangerous consequences is under an implied duty to inform the other party, irrespective of whether the contract continues or not[1]. However, this has all now been overtaken by the statutory duty of candour which has come into force[2], which will require a doctor to inform a patient of any 'notifiable safety incident' as soon as practicable after becoming aware of it (by reg 20).

1 *Stag Line Ltd v Tyne Shiprepair Group Ltd, The Zinnia* [1984] 2 Lloyd's Rep 211. Staughton J held that there was such a duty, but nevertheless described it as 'a novel concept'. Contrast *Wood v Jones* (1889) 61 LT 551. See also the vigorous obiter dicta of Sir John Donaldson MR in *Naylor v Preston Area Health Authority* [1987] 2 All ER 353, CA at 360, cf *Lee v South West Thames Regional Health Authority* [1985] 2 All ER 385, CA at 389–390. The notion of a free-standing duty of candour, irrespective of the doctor-patient relationship, was rejected in *Powell v Boladz* [1998] Lloyd's Rep Med 116, CA (distinguished in *Re Organ Retention Group Litigation* [2005] 1 QB 506 (Gage J)).
2 The Health and Social Care Act 2008 (Regulated Activities) Regulations 2014, SI 2014/2936. These Regulations are the culmination of the consultation process which followed the Report of the Mid-Staffordshire NHS Foundation Trust Public Inquiry, February 2013 (The Francis Report).

12.12   Injuries caused to a child by acts done before his birth (and even before his conception) are the subject of special provisions in the Congenital Disabilities (Civil Liability) Act 1976. Liability under the Act is regarded as liability for personal injuries sustained by the child immediately after his birth[1]. This means that the ordinary limitation provisions apply as from the date of birth. The practical effect is that the period of limitation runs during the child's minority and then for three years, ie until the child's 21st birthday[2].

1 Congenital Disabilities (Civil Liability) Act 1976, s 4(3).
2 See para **12.39** as to the extension of the limitation period whilst a minor.

PERSONAL INJURY CASES[1]

12.13   The LA 1980, s 2 imposes a limitation period for an action founded on tort of six years from the date on which the cause of action accrued. However, by the LA 1980, s 11 a three-year period applies to actions for damages for negligence or other breach of duty[2] where the damages claimed consist of or include damages in respect of personal injuries[3]. 'Personal injuries' is defined as including any disease and any impairment of a person's physical or mental condition[4].

1 LA 1980, ss 11–14.
2 Whether the duty exists by virtue of a contract or of provisions made by or under a statute or independently of any contract or any such provision, and including a duty in the law of nuisance: LA 1980, s 11(1).
3 The time limits when the injuries are fatal are dealt with in para **12.38**.
4 LA 1980, s 38(1).

12.14   The six-year period provided by the LA 1980, s 2 applies to tort generally. Section 11 applies to actions for personal injury arising from accidents caused by negligence, nuisance or breach of duty. The House of Lords has held that it also applies to intentional torts such as trespass, including sexual assaults[1]. Some injury claims may be made under the Human Rights Act 1988, but by s 7(5)(a) of that Act the limitation period for such claims is one year from the act complained of. However, the court has an unfettered discretion to extend time[2].

1 *A v Hoare* [2008] UKHL 6, where the House departed from its previous decision in *Stubbings v Webb* [1993] AC 498, which had held the converse.
2 Unfettered in the sense that s 33 of the LA 1980 does not apply, but obviously the court must exercise its discretion judicially. See *Rabone v Pennine Care NHS Foundation Trust* [2012] UKSC 2; *D v Commissioner of Police for the Metropolis* [2012] EWHC 309 and *XYZ v Chief Constable of Gwent Constabulary* (unreported) QBD 2 April 2014.

12.15   The LA 1980, s 11 is so worded that if only part of a claim is for personal injuries, the three-year period will apply to the whole action. When deciding whether a claim consists of or includes damages in respect of personal injuries it is necessary to analyse the substance of the allegation being made. In *Ackbar v CF Green & Co Ltd*[1] the claimant was injured when travelling in his own lorry as a passenger. He was unable to recover compensation from the driver because the insurance did not extend to passenger liability. Although the claimant suffered loss by reason of his injuries, his claim against his insurance brokers for failing to obtain proper insurance was held not to be a claim where the damages consisted of or included 'damages in respect of personal injuries'. It was, therefore, not subject to the three-year limit. Thus if, for example[2], a doctor omits relevant material from a report made for the purposes of litigation, and the injured claimant recovers reduced damage as a result, the claimant's subsequent claim against the doctor to recover the shortfall would not be an action 'in respect of' personal injuries. In *Ackbar* it was observed that an action against former solicitors for the mishandling of a personal injury claim is a claim for economic loss, so that s 11 would not apply. That is consistent with the analysis in *Hatton v Chafes (a firm)*[3] as to the true nature of the cause of action. By contrast, in *Bennett v Greenland Houchen and Co*[4], a claim against former solicitors who negligently conducted the defence of proceedings to enforce a restrictive covenant in a contract of employment, as a result of which the claimant contended that he had become clinically depressed and suffered consequential financial loss, was held to be a claim in respect of personal injuries[5]. The appropriate test has been put succinctly, 'what is the action all about?'[6]

1 [1975] QB 582. But see *Howe v David Brown Tractors (Retail) Ltd* [1991] 4 All ER 30, CA, where the three-year limit was held to apply to a claim for loss of profits by a firm owned by the injured claimant. *Ackbar* was distinguished in *Norman v Aziz* [2000] PIQR P72, CA, where s 11 applied to a *Monk v Warbey* type action against the owner of a motor vehicle. *Ackbar*, in contrast, was a 'derivative' claim concerned with a breach of duty independent of the accident.
2 As illustrated by *McGrath v Kiely and Powell* [1965] IR 497; and *Oakes v Hopcroft* [2000] Lloyds Rep Med 394, where the initial claim was compromised.
3 [2003] EWCA Civ 341, [2003] PNLR 24, but see also para **12.9**.
4 [1998] PNLR 458, CA.
5 See also *Gaud v Leeds Health Authority* (1999) Times, 14 May, CA: a claim by an employee against his former employer for failing to advise him as to the benefits he was entitled to on suffering personal injury in the course of his employment was a claim for negligent advice rather than a personal injury claim.
6 *KR v Bryn Alyn Community (Holdings) Ltd* [2003] EWCA Civ 783, [2003] QB 1441 at 1454, per Auld LJ citing *Ackbar*, *Howe* and *Walkin*. See also the discussion in *Jackson and Powell on Professional Liability* (7th edn, Sweet & Maxwell), paras 5-089 to 5-096.

12.16 Claims for wrongful conception may be brought by a female claimant for damages in respect of her husband's failed vasectomy or her own failed sterilisation, or by a male claimant in respect of a failed vasectomy. In *Walkin v South Manchester Health Authority*[1], the female claimant claimed damages for the financial consequences of a failed sterilisation (with no claim for damages for personal injury). It was held by the Court of Appeal that this was a claim for 'damages in respect of personal injuries'. There was 'impairment' within the meaning of the LA 1980, s 38(1), which arose at the moment of conception. The claim for the economic costs arose from that impairment. This is so whether the claim is brought in respect of negligent advice or negligent surgery. The issue is one of substance rather than pleading[2].

1 [1995] 1 WLR 1543. In *Pattison v Hobbs* (1985) Times, 11 November, a two-judge Court of Appeal suggested that a claimant could limit the claim for damages to financial loss to come within the six-year limitation period under the LA 1980, s 2. In *Allen v Bloomsbury Health Authority* [1993] 1 All ER 651, Brooke J stated that claims limited to the financial cost of bringing up the child would be a claim for foreseeable economic loss caused by negligent advice or misstatement, to which it was hard to see the LA 1980, s 11 applying. These observations are unlikely to be correct, certainly in the context of wrongful conception claims, following the decision in *Walkin*. In the cases of *Pounds v Eckford Rands (a firm)* [2003] Lloyd's Rep PN 195, QB, and *Shade v Compton Partnership* [2000] PNLR 218, QB, the personal injury elements were removed by amendment, so as to overcome the limitation defence (doubting *Oates v Hart-Reade & Co* [1999] PIQR P120 on the point). Those were cases in which the personal injury element was a modest part of the overall claim. See, however, *Hatton v Chafes (a firm)* [2003] EWCA Civ 341, [2003] PNLR 24, and *Polley v Warner Goodman & Street* [2003] EWCA Crim 1013, [2003] PNLR 40, in which it was held that a claimant cannot defeat the statute of limitations by claiming only in respect of damage which occurs within the limitation period if he has suffered damage from the same wrongful act outside that period.
2 See *Walkin* [1995] 1 WLR 1543 at 1551H, per Auld LJ. There might be limited claims by male claimants arising out of failed vasectomies in which it could be argued that the only loss claimed is purely financial: see *Pattison v Hobbs* (1985) Times, 11 November, CA. Since *Walkin* the House of Lords has given judgment in *McFarlane v Tayside Health Board* [2000] 2 AC 59: in the case of a failed vasectomy, damages for the cost of maintaining a healthy child are irrecoverable, being pure economic loss. In *Godfrey v Gloucestershire Infirmary NHS Trust* [2003] Lloyd's Rep Med 398, an unwanted birth claim based on alleged inadequate information to make an informed decision about termination of pregnancy, Leveson J held that the claim for the cost of supporting the severely injured child was for damages consisting of or including damages in respect of personal injuries. That was a separate issue from whether it was a claim for damages for pure economic loss.

12.17 The House of Lords affirmed that claims for damages for failure to address dyslexia and thereby ameliorate the effects of the condition are claims for personal injuries[1].

1 *Adams v Bracknell Forest Borough Council* [2005] 1 AC 76, approving *Robinson v St Helens Metropolitan Borough Council* [2003] PIQR P128, CA. In *Younger v Dorset and Somerset Strategic Health Authority* [2007] LS Law Med 489 (Southampton County Court) psychological harm falling short of a psychiatric illness, consequent on negligent misdiagnosis of coeliac disease which resulted in the claimant remaining on a gluten-free diet which was completely safe, did not amount to a personal injury. *Robinson* was distinguished, drawing a distinction between loss of enjoyment of life or amenity that arises from one's physical make up or a failure to ameliorate one's physical condition, and a loss of amenity which arises simply from external circumstances.

12.18 The three-year period runs from the date on which the cause of action accrued[1], or the 'date of knowledge' (if later) of the person injured[2]. The 'knowledge' referred to is, broadly, knowledge of facts sufficient to bring an action against the wrongdoer. The policy of this provision is to alleviate the hardship that would be suffered by a claimant who failed to start his action in time because he was unaware that he had been injured by someone's negligence.

1 As to accrual of a cause of action see paras **12.6–12.7** and **12.10**, above.
2 LA 1980, s 11(4).

12.19 The extent of the knowledge necessary to start time running against the claimant is closely defined in the LA 1980, s 14(1). The 'date of knowledge' is defined as the date on which a person first has knowledge of the following facts:

(a) that the injury in question was significant; and
(b) that the injury was attributable in whole or in part to the act or omission which is alleged to constitute negligence, nuisance or breach of duty; and
(c) the identity of the defendant; and
(d) if it is alleged that the act or omission was that of a person other than the defendant, the identity of that person and the additional facts supporting the bringing of an action against the defendant.

Knowledge that any acts or omissions did or did not, as a matter of law, involve negligence, nuisance or breach of duty is irrelevant.

12.20 The appellate courts have reached a strict construction of the actual and constructive knowledge provisions set out in LA 1980, s 14(2) and (3). These are now construed wholly objectively so that, for example, idiosyncratic characteristics of a claimant which might previously have been taken into account under s 14(3) are now disregarded under that section, but are instead considered under s 33. This accords with the statutory language and creates a greater degree of certainty as to when a claimant will be fixed with knowledge. It has been judicially observed that this approach offers greater protection to the legitimate interests of defendants, with s 33 remaining available as a flexible mechanism whereby justice can be done in the circumstances of the individual case.

Knowledge

12.21 The relevant test may now be stated with greater confidence than for many years, following the Supreme Court's decision in the '*Atomic Vets*' case[1]. Although the judges divided four to three, the majority (Lords Wilson, Walker, Brown and Mance) explicitly endorsed the analysis of Lord Wilson. Lord Wilson himself approved the approach of Lord Donaldson MR in *Halford v Brookes*[2], where it was held that a claimant is likely to have acquired knowledge of the facts specified in s 14 when he first comes 'reasonably to believe' them. Lord Wilson would have preferred the phrase 'reasoned belief' rather than 'reasonable belief', but did not want semantics to cloud jurisprudence based on *Halford*. This position emphasises that the belief does not have to be 'correct' in the sense of being based upon accurate facts which are potentially capable of proof, but rather that it is a reasoned (albeit possibly wrong) position, derived from the claimant's experiences (ie what he saw, heard, read and as a result what he considered to be the position). This is emphatically not the same as having the evidence with which to substantiate that belief in court, and Lord Wilson said that it was 'heretical' to argue that a claimant who has issued proceedings for damages for personal injury could yet still lack the relevant knowledge for the purpose of s 14[3].

1 *Ministry of Defence v AB* [2012] UKSC 9.
2 *Halford v Brookes* [1991] 1 WLR 428 at 443, CA.
3 This was the view of the minority, who said that until the claimants had received the Rowlands report in late 2007, some two years after proceedings were issued, time had not started to run, per Lord Phillips.

12.22 As to the degree of confidence with which a belief must be held in order to satisfy s 14, Lord Wilson approved the approach of Lord Nichols in *Haward v Fawcetts*[1] which is that the belief must be held 'with sufficient confidence to justify embarking on the preliminaries to the issue of a claim form, such as submitting a claim to the proposed defendant, taking legal or other advice and collecting evidence'[2].

1 [2006] UKHL 9.
2 The investigation upon which the claimant should reasonably embark is into whether in law he has a valid claim and if so how that claim can be established in court. The focus is on the moment when it is reasonable for the claimant to *embark* on such an investigation. The claimant may well take legal advice before his belief is held with the requisite degree of confidence, and therefore it does not necessarily follow that the claimant had the requisite knowledge by the date on which he first took legal advice, but such an inference may well be justified (Lord Wilson in '*Atomic Vets*' [2012] UKSC 9 at para 12, where he approved *Sniezek v Bundy (Letchworth) Ltd* [2000] PIQR P213, CA).

12.23 In *Nash v Eli Lilly & Co*, the Court of Appeal accepted that once a claimant has the requisite knowledge the limitation period starts to run and nothing which occurs thereafter (such as an expert opinion which casts doubt on the claimant's understanding) will suspend or stop time continuing to run[1].

1 [1993] 4 All ER 383 at 393. And see also Lord Wilson in *Atomic Vets* at para 25, where he said that the veterans had s 14 knowledge long before proceedings were issued, notwithstanding that even in 2012 they still did not have expert evidence which could credibly prove causation.

Significant injury

12.24   Knowledge that an injury is significant is qualified by the LA 1980, s 14(2), which provides that an injury is significant if the person whose date of knowledge is in question would reasonably have considered it sufficiently serious to justify his instituting proceedings for damages against a defendant who did not dispute liability and was able to satisfy a judgment. The law on what 'significant' means is now clear following the House of Lords decision in *A v Hoare*[1]. The test is wholly objective. Lord Hoffmann said (para 39) 'the test is external to the claimant and involves no inquiry into what he ought reasonably to have done. It is applied to what the claimant knew or was deemed to have known but the standard itself is impersonal'[2]. This was noted and approved by Lord Wilson in *Atomic Vets*[3]. The possible effect of a claimant's injuries, for example the inhibitory effect of the abuse in historic sexual abuse claims, is taken into account under s 33, but not, now, under s 14[4].

1 [2008] UKHL 6.
2 However, note also that there is a difference between claimants who were injured at birth, and so have never known a different condition, and people who are injured in adulthood. Claimants injured at birth are given much greater latitude as to what constitutes 'significant injury'. See *Whiston v London SHA* [2010] EWCA Civ 195 and *Khairule v North West SHA* [2008] EWHC 1537 (QB).
3 *Ministry of Defence v AB* [2012] UKSC 9, paras 46–47.
4 See also para **12.35**.

Attributability

12.25   While the claimant must have knowledge of the essence of the act or omission to which the injury is attributable, it is not necessary for him to know the precise terms in which negligence or breach of duty would be alleged. By the LA 1980, s 14(1), it is expressly provided that knowledge that any acts or omissions did or did not, as a matter of law, involve negligence, nuisance or breach of duty is irrelevant. It has been held that it is sufficient for the claimant to have a broad knowledge that his injuries are attributable to the defendant's acts or omissions, without being aware of the specific acts or omissions[1].

1 *Wilkinson v Ancliff (BLT) Ltd* [1986] 1 WLR 1352, CA. *Nash v Eli Lilly & Co* [1993] 4 All ER 383, per Purchas LJ at 398: 'knowledge of the essence of the act or omission to which the injury is attributable'. In *Haward v Fawcetts (a firm)* [2006] UKHL 9, Lord Nicholls stated that 'knowledge' for the purposes of s 14A (latent damage) meant 'knowledge of the facts constituting the essence of the complaint of negligence'.

12.26   The claimant must also have knowledge that the injury was caused by that act or omission: it must be causally relevant knowledge[1]. But the test is one of factual rather than legal causation.

1 See *Hallam-Eames v Merrett Syndicates Ltd* [1996] 7 Med LR 122, per Hoffmann LJ: 'the act or omission of which the plaintiff must have knowledge must be that which is causally relevant for the purposes of an allegation of negligence ...'.

12.27   In many clinical negligence claims, the causal relationship between injury and act or omission may be far from clear and is often difficult to prove. Despite this the law is tolerably clear that the threshold is relatively low. In *Atomic Vets* Lord Wilson endorsed the Court of Appeal's approach in

Spargo v North Essex District Health Authority[1] and said that attributable for the purposes of s 14 means merely that there is a real possibility that the act or omission caused the injury. In *Spargo* Brooke LJ summarised the principles as follows:

'(1) The knowledge required to satisfy section 14(1)(b) is a broad knowledge of the essence of the causally relevant act or omission to which the injury is attributable;

(2) "Attributable" in this context means "capable of being attributed to", in the sense of being a real possibility;

(3) A plaintiff has the requisite knowledge when she knows enough to make it reasonable for her to begin to investigate whether or not she has a case against the defendant. Another way of putting this is to say that she will have such knowledge if she so firmly believes that her condition is capable of being attributed to an act or omission which she can identify (in broad terms) that she goes to a solicitor to seek advice about making a claim for compensation;

(4) On the other hand, she will not have the requisite knowledge if she thinks she knows the acts or omissions she should investigate but in fact is barking up the wrong tree[2]; or if her knowledge of what the defendant did or did not do is so vague or general that she cannot fairly be expected to know what she should investigate; or if her state of mind is such that she thinks her condition is capable of being attributed to the act or omission alleged to constitute negligence, but she is not sure about this, and would need to check with an expert before she could be properly said to know that it was'[3].

1 [1997] 8 Med LR 125. See also Lord Wilson in *Atomic Vets* [2012] UKSC 9 (para 2).
2 See, for example *Rowbottom v Royal Masonic Hospital* [2002] EWCA Civ 87, [1994] 4 All ER 439 at 448.
3 [1997] 8 Med LR 125 at 130. See *O'Driscoll v Dudley Health Authority* [1998] Lloyd's Rep Med 210, CA, for a claim involving cerebral palsy at birth in which the plaintiff when aged 18 had the requisite knowledge, at a time before reading her medical expert's report. Simon Brown LJ observed that principles (3) and (4) were antithetical situations. (4) Represents a state of mind short of a firm belief which takes a potential claimant to a solicitor. He added that the reference in (4) to the 'need to check with an expert' is a reference to the need for an expert's opinion before even the claimant can be said to know that the attributability of her condition to a particular act or omission is a real possibility. In *Roberts v Winbow* [1999] Lloyd's Rep Med 31, CA, it was decided that time started to run from the date when the claimant knew that a lesser part of her injuries was attributable to the defendant, and not when she later discovered that the greater part was also so attributable.

12.28 In *Atomic Vets* the majority of the Supreme Court held that the claimants had knowledge of attributability notwithstanding that the state of scientific knowledge was limited and they still had no credible evidence to prove causation around 60 years after the explosions. The court held that although the understanding of the veterans about the precise type of radiation to which they had been exposed may have been wrong (some types not being capable of causing the chromosomal damage of which the claimants complained), that did not amount to 'barking up the wrong tree' in the *Spargo* sense. All that was required was a 'real possibility' of attributability.

Identity of defendant

12.29 Where a claimant is misinformed as to the identity of the defendant, that may result in the claimant lacking the necessary knowledge for the purposes of the LA 1980, s 14[1]. The misinformation does not have to be deliberate or amount to a breach of duty. How long it then takes to complete the appropriate enquiries, so that actual or constructive knowledge is acquired, is a question of fact in each case[2]. However, a claimant will be fixed with knowledge of the identity of the correct defendant if he should reasonably have ascertained it without the need for external (eg legal) help[3].

1 *Cressey v E Timm and Son Ltd* [2005] EWCA Civ 763, [2005] 1 WLR 3926, an employers' liability claim, applying *Simpson v Norwest Holst Southern Ltd* [1980] 1 WLR 968. The judgment of Rix LJ discusses further issues arising out of the word 'identity'.
2 See *Cressey* [2005] 1 WLR 3926, CA, para 28. Rix LJ felt that knowledge was unlikely to be postponed for long.
3 *Henderson v Temple Pier Ltd* [1998] 1 WLR 1540.

12.30   In a case where it is alleged that the act or omission was that of a person other than the defendant, the necessary knowledge includes the identity of that other person and the additional facts supporting the bringing of an action against the defendant[1]. This provision may be of assistance to a claimant wishing to sue a private hospital but unaware of the identity of the treating doctor and his relationship with the hospital[2]. On the other hand, time will run when the relevant NHS Trust has been identified, irrespective of knowledge of the identities of individual clinicians.

1 LA 1980, s 14(1)(d). See *Nash v Eli Lilly & Co* [1993] 4 All ER 383 at 400–401, for discussion of the position in product liability actions where difficulties might be experienced in identifying corporate defendants, and the application of constructive knowledge.
2 In *Halford v Brookes* [1991] 3 All ER 559, Lord Donaldson MR stated that s 14(3) does not assist the claimant who knows that his injuries are caused by one or other of two known defendants, but could not have been caused by both: the claimant should then sue both in the alternative.

12.31   As knowledge that any acts or omissions did or did not as a matter of law involve negligence, nuisance or breach of duty is irrelevant, it follows that the provision of incorrect legal advice will not postpone the claimant's date of knowledge[1]. Similarly irrelevant for these purposes will be a claimant's belief about the state of the law, resulting in an impression that he does not have a claim[2].

1 *Farmer v NCB* (1985) Times, 27 April 1985, CA.
2 *Rowe v Kingston-Upon-Hull City Council* [2003] EWCA Civ 1281, [2004] PIQR P16, para 20, a claim based on alleged failure to diagnose dyslexia.

Constructive knowledge

12.32   If the criteria defining the date of knowledge were applied by reference only to the actual knowledge of the particular claimant under consideration, the time limit would operate in favour of claimants with a high degree of ignorance and against those of a more inquiring disposition. The LA 1980 therefore attributes to the claimant such knowledge as he might reasonably have been expected to acquire from facts ascertainable by him, whether on his own or with such medical or other expert advice as it is reasonable for him to seek. However, a person is not fixed with knowledge of a fact ascertainable only with the help of expert advice so long as he has taken all reasonable steps to obtain (and, where appropriate, to act on) that advice[1].

1 LA 1980, s 14(3).

12.33 There has over the years been a degree of confusion as a result of seemingly conflicting decisions of the Court of Appeal as to the correct construction of the LA 1980, s 14(3) and the extent to which the individual characteristics of the claimant should be taken into account when deciding what observations and enquiries it was reasonable for him to have made. At one extreme was the decision in *Nash v Eli Lilly & Co*, which incorporated a partly subjective element into the exercise[1]. At the other, was *Forbes v Wandsworth Health Authority*[2] where the majority expressed the view that the s 14(3) test was purely objective, and that the prevention of stale claims overrode other policy considerations.

1 [1993] 4 All ER 383.
2 [1997] QB 402.

12.34 In *Adams v Bracknell Forest Borough Council*[1] the House of Lords had to consider a claim brought 14 years after the conclusion of his school education, by a 30-year-old man who alleged that he had suffered injury through the defendant's failure throughout his school education, to recognise and take steps to ameliorate the effects of his dyslexia. The House approved *Forbes* and ruled that the test of constructive knowledge was objective. The criterion to apply was the standard of reasonable behaviour of a person suffering from untreated dyslexia. The House held that the claimant should have taken steps to investigate his claim much earlier than he did, and that his claim was time barred. Lord Hoffmann observed:

'It is true that the plaintiff must be assumed to be a person who has suffered the injury in question and not some other person. But, like Roch LJ in *Forbes* [1997] QB 402, 425 I do not see how his particular character or intelligence can be relevant. In my opinion, section 14(3) requires one to assume that a person who is aware that he has suffered a personal injury, serious enough to be something about which he would go and see a solicitor if he knew he had a claim, will be sufficiently curious about the causes of the injury to seek whatever expert advice is appropriate[2].

In principle, I think that the judge was right in applying the standard of reasonable behaviour to a person assumed to be suffering from untreated dyslexia. If the injury itself would reasonably inhibit him from seeking advice, then that is a factor which must be taken into account'[3].

Lord Phillips agreed with Lord Hoffmann's opinion as to the correct test. Lord Scott stated:

'The reference in section 14(3) to "knowledge which he might reasonably have been expected to acquire" should, in my opinion, be taken to be a reference to knowledge which a person in the situation of the claimant, ie an adult who knows he is illiterate, could reasonably be expected to acquire. Personal characteristics such as shyness and embarrassment, which may have inhibited the claimant from seeking advice about his illiteracy problems but which would not be expected to have inhibited others with a like disability, should be left out of the equation. It is the norms of behaviour of persons in the situation of the claimant that should be the test'[4].

1 [2005] 1 AC 76.
2 At para 47.
3 At para 49.
4 At para 71.

12.35 *Adams* and s 14(3) have been clarified by the House of Lords in *A v Hoare*[1] where Lord Hoffmann explained that the key points were that s 14(2) defines the knowledge which a person is to be regarded as having by reference to factors entirely 'external' to the claimant; whereas s 14(3) requires the court to consider what it was reasonable for a person in the claimant's position to have *done*. Under s 14(3) the court should consider the injuries sustained by the claimant. The example he gave was to say that it would not be reasonable to expect a blind person to have acquired knowledge by reading. However it was clear that individual characteristics which may have inhibited a particular claimant from bringing his claim earlier, would be disregarded if they would not have affected a 'reasonable person' with the claimant's injury. At para 35 Lord Hoffmann said:

'...I cannot accept that one must consider whether someone "with [the] plaintiff's intelligence" would have been reasonable if he did not regard the injury as sufficiently serious. That seems to me to destroy the effect of the word "reasonably". Judges should not have to grapple with the notion of the reasonable unintelligent person. Once you have ascertained what the claimant knew and what he should be treated as having known, the actual claimant drops out of the picture'.

This test has been applied in two subsequent Court of Appeal cases in the context of industrial disease claims[2].

1 [2008] UKHL 6, at paras 38–44.
2 *Johnson v Ministry of Defence* [2012] EWCA Civ 1505 and *Collins v Secretary of State for Business Innovation and Skills* [2014] EWCA Civ 717. In *Johnson* the Court of Appeal held that a reasonable person in the claimant's position would have realised that the hearing problems he first began to notice in 2001, when he was 61 years old, might have been caused by the very loud noises to which he was exposed at work between 1965 and 1979 (when he was aged 25–39 years). A reasonable person with the claimant's hearing loss should have consulted his GP in 2001. The claimant was fixed with constructive knowledge by the end of 2002. He started his claim in 2010. In *Collins* the claimant was exposed to asbestos as a dock worker between 1947 and 1967 (when he was aged 23–43 years). In 2002 he was diagnosed with lung cancer. He made no enquiries about the possible cause of this. He was discharged in remission in 2008. In 2009 he saw an advert from a firm of solicitors about possible compensation for asbestos exposure at his docks between 1940 and 1980. In 2012 he launched a claim for compensation for his lung cancer. The Court of Appeal held that a reasonable person in the claimant's position would have made enquiries by mid-2003 as to possible causes of his lung cancer and whether there was any link to his former occupation. He was thus fixed with constructive knowledge by that time.

Section 14(3) proviso

12.36　A claimant will not be fixed with knowledge of a fact ascertainable only with the help of expert advice so long as he has taken all reasonable steps to obtain (and, where appropriate, to act on) that advice.

12.37　A lawyer is not an expert for this purpose[1]. In *Henderson v Temple Pier Co Ltd*[2], the Court of Appeal held that advice given by a solicitor could come within the proviso only if it related to matters of fact on which expert advice was required. Having identified the person answerable in law for injuries, naming that party would not, save in the most exceptional circumstances, be a fact ascertainable only with the help of expert advice. The proviso did not give an extended period of limitation to a person whose solicitor acted dilatorily in acquiring facts ascertainable without particular expertise. How to identify the difference between knowledge of facts sufficient to start the limitation clock ticking (ie the 'essence' of a claim, and a 'real possibility' of attributability) and the collection of sufficient evidence necessary to be able to plead and prove the case to the required legal standard, is a 'moot point'. This area of tension was discussed by Lord Walker in *Atomic Vets* (at paras 51–58), and it is likely that this issue will require some further exploration and clarification by the courts in due course.

1 *Fowell v National Coal Board* [1986] CILL 294, (1986) Times, 28 May, CA.
2 [1998] 1 WLR 1540.

DEATH OF CLAIMANT/FATAL ACCIDENTS

12.38 If the injured person dies before the expiry of the three-year period applicable to an action by him, the limitation period applicable to an action on behalf of his estate[1] is three years from the date of death or from the date of the personal representative's knowledge, whichever is later[2]. The time limit for bringing an action on behalf of dependants under the Fatal Accidents Act 1976 is three years from the date of death or from the date of knowledge of the person for whose benefit the action is brought, whichever is later[3]. Dependants who acquired the necessary knowledge on different dates are therefore subject to different time limits[4].

1 By virtue of the Law Reform (Miscellaneous Provisions) Act 1934.
2 See LA 1980, s 11(5)–(7). Where the deceased was statute-barred at death under s 11(4), or the personal representative becomes statute-barred after the death under s 11(5), application to disapply under s 33 may be made (with appropriate modifications under s 33(4) and (5)).
3 LA 1980, s 12(2). But no action under the Fatal Accidents Act 1976 may be brought if the death occurred at a time when the person injured had already lost his right of action: LA 1980, s 12(1). In deciding whether the deceased's action was statute-barred no account shall be taken of the possibility of that time limit being overridden under s 33. The dependants themselves may seek discretion to disapply under s 33, but only in personal injury claims: s 33(2). See also s 33(5), whereby regard is had to the reasons for the dependants', and not the deceased's, delay.
4 LA 1980, s 13.

CLAIMANT UNDER A LEGAL DISABILITY

12.39 A person is under a disability if he is an infant, ie under the age of 18 years[1], or of unsound mind[2], ie lacks capacity (within the meaning of the Mental Capacity Act 2005) to conduct legal proceedings[3]. This restrictive definition has the consequence that a person is not under a disability for these purposes if he is incapable of managing his property and affairs solely by reason of a physical disability. If, on the date when a right of action accrued, the person to whom it accrued was under a disability, the action may be brought at any time before the expiry of six years or, for personal injury cases, three years from the date when he ceased to be under a disability or died (whichever first occurred)[4]. This extension for disability takes effect notwithstanding the expiry of the 15-year long stop period.

1 Family Law Reform Act 1969, s 1.
2 LA 1980, s 38(2). This provides an exhaustive definition: see *Chagos Islanders v AG* [2003] EWHC 222 at paras 612–613, Ouseley J (leave to appeal was refused [2004] EWCA Civ 997). The *Chagos Islanders* case concerned the previous definition of incapacity under the Mental Health Act 1983, but the case decided that the statutory definition is determinative, and this will survive later amendments to the LA 1980.
3 Mental Capacity Act 2005, s 1 confirms the presumption of capacity; and s 2 provides that a person lacks capacity in relation to a matter if at the material time he is unable to make a

decision for himself in relation to the matter because of an impairment of, or a disturbance in the functioning of, the mind or brain. For detailed consideration of the Mental Capacity Act 2005 and capacity generally see Chapter 11 on Consent. For detailed consideration of the issue of capacity see *Masterman-Lister v Brutton & Co* [2003] 1 WLR 1511, CA. The test is 'issue-specific'. Per Chadwick LJ: 'For the purposes of Order 80 – and now CPR Pt 21 – the test to be applied, as it seems to me, is whether the party to legal proceedings is capable of understanding, with the assistance of such proper explanation from legal advisers and experts in other disciplines as the case may require, the issues on which his consent or decision is likely to be necessary in the course of those proceedings' (para 75). Note also the judgment of Kennedy LJ that, 'It is common ground that all adults must be presumed to be competent to manage their property and affairs until the contrary is proved, and that the burden of proof rests on those asserting incapacity'. The issue-specific test for capacity in *Masterman-Lister* was endorsed in *Dunhill v Burgin* [2014] UKSC 18. In *Dunhill* the claimant sustained severe head injuries in a road traffic accident. The injuries robbed her of capacity. This was not appreciated by her solicitors, who failed to arrange for a litigation friend and also allowed the claim to be settled (without any approval process) for only £12,500, which was a gross undervalue. The Supreme Court held that the proper test for capacity was by reference to the true case that the claimant actually had, rather than the case which her negligent lawyers *thought* that she had. Thus because the claimant had not in fact had capacity to conduct the claim, and should have had a litigation friend from the outset, the settlement was invalid under CPR Pt 21.10, and should be set aside.

4 LA 1980, s 28(1), (6). However, when a right of action which has accrued to a person under a disability accrues, on the death of that person while still under a disability, to another person under a disability, no further extension of time is allowed by reason of the disability of the second person: s 28(3). In *Headford v Bristol and District Health Authority* [1995] 6 Med LR 1, [1995] PIQR P180 (writ issued 28 years after material event), the Court of Appeal considered that there could be exceptional cases where a writ issued within the limitation period on behalf of a person under a disability might be struck out as an abuse of process (this was not such a case). It was noted that s 28(1) contained no provision comparable to s 33.

12.40   In personal injury cases, the extension on the ground of disability only applies when the disability exists at the date when the right of action accrues. If a person is of sound mind at the time when the right of action accrues, but subsequently becomes of unsound mind, the supervening incapacity does not prevent the ordinary limitation period running against him[1]. Hence there is no extension for an injured claimant who is under a disability only at his date of knowledge[2]. However, where a claim is for damages for tortious negligence, not including damages for personal injuries, there is an extension for disability if all the following conditions are fulfilled[3]:

(1)   the action is commenced before the expiry of 15 years from the last act of negligence[4];
(2)   the period of three years from the 'starting date'[5] expires later than the period of six years from the accrual of the cause of action;
(3)   on the starting date, the claimant[6] was under a disability;
(4)   on the date when the cause of action accrued, the claimant[7] was not under a disability.

In this event the extension is for three years from the date when the claimant[8] ceased to be under a disability or died, whichever first occurred.

1 See *Purnell v Roche* [1927] 2 Ch 142, an action for foreclosure on a mortgage.
2 But see para **12.42** ff for the court's discretionary power to extend the limitation period.
3 See the LA 1980, s 28A.
4 Note that, in contrast with the position under the LA 1980, s 28, the 15-year long stop limits this disability extension.
5 As defined in the LA 1980.
6 Or any person in whom the cause of action was vested before him: LA 1980, ss 14A(5) and 28A(1)(b).

7 Or other person to whom it accrued: LA 1980, ss 28(1) and 28A(1)(c).
8 Or any person in whom the cause of action was vested before him: see n 6, above.

CONCEALMENT

12.41   Where any fact relevant to the claimant's right of action has been deliberately concealed from him by the defendant[1], the period of limitation does not begin to run until the claimant has discovered the concealment or could with reasonable diligence have discovered it[2]. For this purpose, deliberate commission of a breach of duty in circumstances in which it is unlikely to be discovered for some time amounts to deliberate concealment of the facts involved in that breach of duty[3]. It does not, however, include failure to disclose a negligent breach of duty that the defendant was not aware of committing[4]. It should be noted that concealment does not postpone the running of the limitation period for claims under the Fatal Accidents Act 1976[5].

1 Or the defendant's agent, or any person through whom the defendant claims or such a person's agent: LA 1980, s 32(1).
2 LA 1980, s 32(1). These provisions were intended to give effect, subject to some modifications, to a recommendation of the Law Reform Committee that the relevant provision of the Limitation Act 1939 should be reformulated so as to express its true legal purport as decided by the courts. The main cases were *Kitchen v Royal Air Force Association* [1958] 1 WLR 563, CA; *Clark v Woor* [1965] 1 WLR 650; *Applegate v Moss* [1971] 1 QB 406, CA; *King v Victor Parsons & Co (a firm)* [1973] 1 WLR 29, CA. Whether they do so is open to question. A similar extension applies (inter alia) where the action is based on the fraud of the defendant. In *Sheldon v RHM Outhwaite (Underwriting Agencies) Ltd* [1996] AC 102, the House of Lords decided that s 32(1)(b) applied both where concealment occurred at the time of the accrual of the cause of action, and where the concealment took place only at a later time.
3 LA 1980, s 32(2).
4 *Cave v Robinson Jarvis & Rolf* [2002] UKHL 18, [2003] 1 AC 384, overruling *Brocklesby v Armitage and Guest* [2002] 1 WLR 598, CA. See *Williams v Fanshawe Porter & Hazelhurst* [2004] 1 WLR 3185, CA, a claim alleging solicitors' negligence arising out of a clinical negligence claim. Failure to inform the client about a consent order releasing a party and subsequent dismissal of application to rejoin, amounted to deliberate concealment within s 32(1)(b). Motive was irrelevant. Consideration was given to the nature of the solicitor-client relationship, and the professional duty to disclose facts (para 14). By contrast, in *Skerratt v Linfax Ltd* [2003] EWCA Civ 695, [2004] PIQR P10, the claimant had signed a form of disclaimer before using a go-kart track, by which he believed he was riding at his own risk. The claimant could not rely on s 32 to allege deliberate concealment by the defendant of a cause of action.
5 This is the effect of the LA 1980, s 12(3).

DISCRETION TO OVERRIDE TIME LIMITS

12.42   The court has a discretionary power to disapply the time limits set by ss 11 and 12 of the LA 1980, which apply in cases of personal injury or death[1]. The power is exercisable where it appears to the court that it would be equitable to allow a claim to proceed having regard to the degree to which:

(1)   the provisions of ss 11[2] or 12 prejudice the claimant[3]; and
(2)   any decision of the court on the application to disapply would prejudice the defendant[4].

1 LA 1980, s 33(1).
2 Ie the three-year period from the date of accrual of the cause of action or from the date of knowledge if later, as extended where appropriate in cases of disability or concealment: see LA 1980, s 33(8).

3 Or any person whom he represents: LA 1980, s 33(1)(a).
4 Or any person whom he represents: LA 1980, s 33(1)(b).

12.43 Following *Walkley v Precision Forgings Ltd*[1] it had long been understood that if a claimant started an action in time but failed for some reason to proceed with it, he would not be allowed after the expiry of the three years to pursue a second action by virtue of the court's power to disapply the limit. In such circumstances he had been prejudiced not by the provisions of the LA 1980, s 11, but by his failure to proceed with the first action. Subsequent decisions attempted to limit *Walkley* to its particular facts[2]. More recently, in *Horton v Sadler*[3] the House of Lords departed from its decision in *Walkley*, holding that it was based on unsound reasoning and had resulted in fine distinctions and unsatisfactory jurisprudence. Lord Bingham stated:

'Counsel for the appellant submitted that the effect of section 11 is to provide the defendant with a time limit defence in any proceedings brought after the expiry of the three-year period. When section 33(1) refers to consideration whether it would be equitable to allow "an action" to proceed it is referring to such an action. It is prejudice to the plaintiff by application of section 11 to that action to which section 33(1)(a) refers, and that action to which the court may direct that the provisions of section 11 shall not apply. Thus the question for the court under section 33 is always whether it is equitable or inequitable as between the parties to override the time bar which, if relied on by the defendant, will, unless disapplied by order of the court, defeat the action which the plaintiff has ex hypothesi brought out of time. This analysis is, as I think, plainly correct'[4].

1 [1979] 1 WLR 606, HL.
2 See *Shapland v Palmer* [1999] 3 All ER 50, CA, where a claimant had issued proceedings in a personal injury action against a different defendant after the expiry of the primary limitation period, the court had power to disapply s 11 under s 33, even though the claimant had already issued similar proceedings against another defendant within the primary limitation period but had failed to serve those earlier proceedings; *Piggott v Aulton* [2003] EWCA Civ 24, [2003] PIQR P22, an action against an estate where no representative had been appointed was discontinued, and the second action against the representative was not against the same defendant; *Adam v Ali* [2006] EWCA Civ 91, [2006] 1 WLR 1330, an action begun out of time (where the limitation point was not taken) was subsequently struck out, but a new claim issued was allowed to proceed under s 33.
3 [2006] UKHL 27, [2006] 2 WLR 1346.
4 [2006] UKHL 27, [2006] 2 WLR 1346 at [21]–[22].

12.44 In *Davidson v Aegis Defence*[1] a claim was started within time but not pursued, and a second claim form was issued out of time. The Court of Appeal upheld a judge's finding that there had been prejudice to the defendants after the expiry of the limitation period and s 11 was not disapplied. The Court of Appeal reviewed several appellate decisions which the claimant had argued were in conflict, and said that the applicable guidance was set out by Smith LJ in *Cain v Francis*[2]:

'It seems to me that, in the exercise of the discretion, the basic question to be asked is whether it is fair and just in all the circumstances to expect the defendant to meet this claim on the merits, notwithstanding the delay in commencement. The length of the delay will be important, not so much for itself as to the effect it has had. To what extent has the defendant been disadvantaged in his investigation of the claim and/or the assembly of evidence, in respect of the issues of both liability and quantum? But it will also be important to consider the reasons for the delay. Thus, there may be some unfairness to the defendant due to the delay in issue but the delay may have arisen for so excusable a reason, that, looking at the matter in the round, on balance, it is fair and just that the action should proceed. On the other hand, the balance may go in the opposite direction, partly because the delay has caused procedural disadvantage and unfairness to the defendant and partly because the reasons for the delay (or its length) are not good ones'.

1 [2013] EWCA Civ 1586, see especially at para 10.
2 [2008] EWCA Civ 1451, see especially at para 73.

12.45   The discretion under the LA 1980, s 33 is wide and unfettered[1]. A number of decisions consider whether the burden on a claimant seeking to rely on s 33 is a 'heavy' or onerous one. However, the Court of Appeal has now said this is inappropriate and unhelpful, and all that could be said is that the burden of making out the s 33 criteria in his favour, falls on a claimant because it was he who was seeking to be exempted from the normal consequences of failing to issue proceedings in time[2]. The Court of Appeal will not interfere with a decision at first instance, unless the judge has failed to follow the directions of the section or has reached what was plainly and obviously the wrong conclusion[3].

1 *Horton v Sadler* [2006] UKHL 27, [2007] 1 AC 307; *A v Hoare* [2008] UKHL 6.
2 *Clifford Sayers v Lord & Lady Chelwood* [2012] EWCA Civ 1715.
3 *Conry v Simpson* [1983] 3 All ER 369, CA; *Gregory v Ferro (Great Britain) Ltd* [1995] 6 Med LR 321, CA; *KR v Bryn Alyn Community (Holdings) Ltd* [2003] EWCA Civ 783, [2003] QB 1441, per Auld LJ at para 69. See *Ashe Construction Ltd v Burke* [2003] EWCA Civ 717, [2004] PIQR P11, where 'the exercise of discretion went to the extremity of its margins' (per Potter LJ). In *McGhie v BT plc* [2005] EWCA Civ 48 the judge erred in the exercise of his discretion under s 33 where his decision was based on the fact that the claimant had been devoted to his job and had acted reasonably, which was not the statutory test that had to be applied under s 33. The issue of proportionality had been referred to but not evaluated and no reference was made to the balance of prejudice. See also *McHugh v Gray* [2006] EWHC 1968 (QB), [2006] LS Law Medical 519, where there were no grounds to interfere with the exercise of the discretion by the judge. The comparative weight to be applied to the factors in s 33 was a matter for the trial judge. Statute provided no indication as to the relative importance of those factors.

12.46   The LA 1980 directs the court to have regard to all the circumstances of the case and in particular to:

(a)   the length of, and the reasons for, the delay on the part of the claimant;
(b)   the extent to which, having regard to the delay, the evidence adduced or likely to be adduced by the claimant or the defendant is or is likely to be less cogent than if the action had been brought within the time allowed by ss 11 or 12;
(c)   the conduct of the defendant after the cause of action arose, including the extent (if any) to which he responded to requests reasonably made by the claimant for information or inspection for the purpose of ascertaining facts which were or might be relevant to the claimant's cause of action against the defendant;
(d)   the duration of any disability of the claimant arising after the date of the accrual of the cause of action;
(e)   the extent to which the claimant acted promptly and reasonably once he knew whether or not the act or omission of the defendant, to which the injury was attributable, might be capable at that time of giving rise to an action for damages;
(f)   the steps, if any, taken by the claimant to obtain medical, legal or other expert advice and the nature of any such advice he may have received.

12.47 There is extensive, and recent, appellate authority concerning the nature of the s 33 exercise, and its inter-relationship with s 14. The guidance given by the Court of Appeal in *KR v Bryn Alyn Community (Holdings) Ltd*[1] has now been overturned by the House of Lords' decision in *A v Hoare*[2]. Now the courts are required to construe the s 14 criteria strictly and objectively, and should consider any particular features of the individual claimant which might go to explain the delay, under s 33. The essence of the exercise is whether a fair trial is still possible[3]. The bare fact of prejudice to a defendant from lifting the time bar is not a relevant factor, because this is always balanced by the equal and opposite prejudice that a claimant will lose the ability to achieve full compensation[4]. A claim against a solicitor for the negligent management of litigation is always a claim for the loss of a chance, and is inevitably worth less than 'primary litigation' against the original tortfeasor for full compensation. Thus whilst the existence of a potential claim against a negligent solicitor is a relevant factor, it will rarely be determinative. However, it is a relevant factor to consider the relative strengths and weaknesses of the claim, as well as value and proportionality[5].

1 [2003] EWCA Civ 783, [2003] QB 1441.
2 [2008] UKHL 6, see in particular Lord Carswell at para 70.
3 See *Cain v Francis* [2008] EWCA Civ 1451. This may still be the case even where the events complained of (in this case, allegedly state-sponsored torture) occurred approximately 60 years before the issue of the claim form, see *Mutua v Foreign & Commonwealth Office* [2012] EWHC 2178 (QB).
4 *Roberts v Commissioner of Police of the Metropolis* [2012] EWCA Civ 799
5 *Collins v Secretary of State for Business Innovation and Skills* [2014] EWCA Civ 717.

Section 33(3)(a)

12.48 The Court of Appeal has now made it clear that because the court is required to consider 'all the circumstances of the case' it is obliged to take into account the effect of the *entire* period of delay between the breach of duty and the issuing of the claim form[1]. This includes any time which has elapsed before a claimant could even have known he had a claim[2]. In *Collins* Jackson LJ noted that a claimant and defendant may want to rely on pre-limitation delay for different purposes. The claimant may say that post-limitation delay has had no effect on the cogency of evidence, because it was already weak and incomplete before time expired. Whereas the defendant may argue that pre-limitation delay gave rise to serious difficulties in defending the claim, and thus *any* additional delay severely exacerbates these difficulties. Prompt notification of a claim to the defendant may assist a claimant, even in cases of significant delay[3]. The words 'on the part of the plaintiff' in the LA 1980, s 33(3)(a) indicate that the court is engaged in a subjective enquiry[4]. A number of factors which would be inappropriate under s 14 can be considered by the court when exercising its discretion under s 33: for example, a claimant's lack of understanding of his legal rights (which, as has been seen, is expressly excluded when considering date of knowledge by the terms of s 14(1))[5]. The longer the delay the less likely the court will be inclined to disapply because, other things being equal, the greater will be the difficulties in achieving a fair trial[6]. Each case, however, will turn on its own facts.

1 *Donovan v Gwentoys Ltd* [1990] 1 WLR 472, HL; *Atomic Vets* in the Court of Appeal [2010] EWCA Civ 1317.
2 *Price v United Engineering Steels Ltd* [1998] PIQR P407, CA; *Collins v Secretary of State for Business Innovation and Skills* [2014] EWCA Civ 717.

3 For example, *Ward v Foss* (1993) Times, 29 November, CA; *Hind v York Health Service NHS Trust* [1998] PIQR P235, a case where a doctor was untraceable, and the defendant's inadequate procedure for keeping track of junior doctors who moved on to new appointments was commented upon. Contrast *Donovan v Gwentoys Ltd* [1990] 1 WLR 472, HL; *Dale v British Coal Corpn* [1992] PIQR P373, CA.
4 *Coad v Cornwall and Isles of Scilly Health Authority* [1997] 1 WLR 189, CA. The fact of continuing medical treatment may be relevant: see *Driscoll-Varley v Parkside Health Authority* [1991] 2 Med LR 346, a s 14 case, which must now be regarded as wrongly decided under that section.
5 *Mutua v Foreign & Commonwealth Office* [2012] EWHC 2178 (QB).
6 *KR v Bryn Alyn Community (Holdings) Ltd* [2003] QB 1441, CA; *Cain v Francis* [2008] EWCA Civ 1451.

Section 33(3)(b)

12.49 This may be the most significant factor in the exercise of the discretion under the LA 1980, s 33[1]. The approach in *Hartley* (that if delay did not seriously affect the evidence, the claim should be allowed to proceed) was endorsed by Lord Carswell in *Horton v Sadler*[2]. This is consistent with the Court of Appeal's judgments in *Cain v Francis*[3] and *Davidson v Aegis*[4]. It is not essential that a defendant should call evidence of the particular respects in which witnesses' recollections are impaired[5]. The existence of clinical records, and the importance of expert opinion on the outcome of the case, will often be relevant[6].

1 *Hartley v Birmingham CDC* [1992] 2 All ER 213, CA. If records are missing as a result of the defendant's own fault, this is a relevant factor, see *S v Camden LBC* [2009] EWHC 1786 (QB) and *Mutua v Foreign & Commonwealth Office* [2012] EWHC 2178 (QB). For an analysis of how the lack of cogency argument may affect claimants and defendants differently, see *Thompson v Brown Construction (Ebbw Vale) Ltd* [1981] 1 WLR 744, HL per Lord Diplock at 751.
2 [2006] UKHL 27.
3 [2008] EWCA Civ 1451.
4 [2013] EWCA Civ 1586.
5 *Stanley Price v United Engineering Steels Ltd* [1998] PIQR P407, CA. But see also *Farthing v North East Essex Health Authority* [1998] Lloyd's Rep Med 37, CA. In *Griffin, Lawson and Williams v Clwyd Health Authority* [2001] EWCA Civ 818, [2001] PIQR P31, where there had been three years' delay between the date of knowledge and issue of the writ, there was no adequate explanation for the delay, and the judge was upheld in finding that the cogency of the evidence had been seriously and adversely affected by the delay: 'there was evidence which the judge was entitled to accept – no-one suggested it was untrue – that the hospital had been closed in 1994; therefore understandably workers had dispersed; there had been a whole series of structural changes in the management of the hospital … In such a case it is very easy for a judge to find prejudice simply on the face of the evidence' (per Buxton LJ, para 45). Contrast *Farraj v Kings Healthcare NHS Trust* [2006] PIQR P29, where the cogency of the evidence had not been severely affected where detailed witness statements had been served by the Part 20 defendant. In *Ashe Construction Ltd v Burke* [2004] PIQR P11 there was a seven-year delay, in a case involving safe system of work, where it was possible to have a 'respectably fair trial'.
6 Eg *Bentley v Bristol and Weston Health Authority* [1991] 2 Med LR 359; *Hind v York Health Service NHS Trust* [1998] PIQR P235; *Pearse v Barnet Health Authority* [1998] PIQR P39. But see *Hammond v West Lancashire Health Authority* [1998] Lloyd's Rep Med 146, CA, destruction of X-rays after claim notified, so that prejudice to the defendant was significantly discounted.

Section 33(3)(c)

12.50 This covers procedural conduct, after the cause of action arose. However, failure to keep a claimant informed as to treatment and reasons for outcomes may be relevant here[1]. The continuance of negotiations has been held to be potentially relevant, as have offers of interim payments[2] and a defendant's failure to take adequate steps to investigate or make enquiries regarding the alleged abuse[3]. However the threshold for a defendant's 'conduct' being considered relevant appears to be relatively high[4].

1 As in *Atkinson v Oxfordshire Health Authority* [1993] 4 Med LR 18.
2 *Marshall v Martin* (10 June 1987, unreported), CA. An admission of liability may be a relevant consideration, though apparently not without more, so as to amount to a waiver: *Kathryn Cotterrell v Leeds Day (a firm)* (21 December 1999, unreported), Buckley J.
3 *Maga v Trustees of Birmingham Archdiocese of the Roman Catholic Church* [2009] EWHC 780 (QB).
4 In *Mutua v Foreign & Commonwealth Office* [2012] EWHC 2178 (QB) McCombe J acknowledged that some documents had been destroyed and that there was evidence that both the UK and Kenyan governments had attempted to limit investigations into the alleged abuses, and whilst these were relevant to s 33 generally, they fell far short of being relevant 'conduct' within s 33(3)(c).

Section 33(3)(d)

12.51 'Disability' refers to a person under disability by reason of being an infant or patient within the meaning of the Mental Health Act 1983 as amended[1]. It does not refer to physical disability (which may, however, be taken into account when considering all the circumstances of the case)[2]. The subsection is concerned with supervening disability[3].

1 *Yates v Thakeham Tiles Ltd* [1995] PIQR P135, CA; *Pearse v Barnet Health Authority* [1998] PIQR P39. See further para **12.39** above.
2 Whilst the Limitation Act 1980, s 38(2) provides an exhaustive definition of 'disability' (see *Chagos Islanders v AG* [2003] EWHC 222, Ouseley J) so that poverty and illiteracy could not amount to a disability, those are matters which the court could take into account having regard to all the circumstances of the case. See also *Yates* [1995] PIQR P135, CA, above.
3 *Thomas v Plaistow* [1997] PIQR P540, CA. Infancy cannot supervene.

Section 33(3)(e)

12.52 This subsection is concerned with the claimant's conduct once he actually knew that his injury was attributable to the act or omission of the defendant, but judged against objective standards of promptitude[1].

1 See *Dale v British Coal Corporation* [1992] PIQR P373. The conduct of the claimant and his advisers will be relevant: *Thompson v Brown Construction (Ebbw Vale) Ltd* [1981] 1 WLR 744, HL. See *Das v Ganju* [1999] Lloyd's Rep Med 198, (1999) 48 BMLR 83; *Corbin v Penfold Ltd* [2000] Lloyd's Rep Med 247; *Steeds v Peverel Management Services Ltd* [2001] EWCA Civ 419; and *Horton v Sadler* [2006] UKHL 27, [2006] 2 WLR 1346.

Section 33(3)(f)

12.53 This requires consideration of the steps taken by the claimant, and the nature of the advice given[1] but does not have the effect of overriding legal professional privilege[2]. Although some cases say that the claimant will not be fixed with delay on the part of his lawyers, in *Horton v Sadler*[3] the House of Lords said that a claimant *does* bear some responsibility for his solicitor's delays. Fear of victimisation in whistleblowing claims is also unlikely to amount to a good reason for delay[4].

1 The various factors are discussed in the speech of Lord Diplock in *Thompson v Brown Construction (Ebbw Vale) Ltd* [1981] 1 WLR 744 at 751–752, HL. The court will need to know whether legal advice received was favourable to the claimant's alleged cause of action: *Jones v G D Searle & Co Ltd* [1979] 1 WLR 101, CA. See *Bentley v Bristol and Weston Health Authority* [1991] 2 Med LR 359, for a case involving changed medical and legal advice.

2 *Tatlock v GP Worsley & Co. Ltd* (22 June 1989, unreported), CA.
3 [2006] UKHL 27.
4 *Rihani v J Wareing & Son* (10 February 2000, unreported), CA.

12.54 In *Adams v Bracknell Forest Borough Council* Lord Hoffmann approved the observations of Sir Murray Stuart-Smith in *Robinson v St Helens Metropolitan Borough Council* as carrying great weight:

'The question of proportionality is now important in the exercise of any discretion, none more so than under section 33. Courts should be slow to exercise their discretion in favour of a claimant in the absence of cogent medical evidence showing a serious effect on the claimant's health or enjoyment of life and employability. The likely amount of an award is an important factor to consider, especially if, as is usual in these cases, they are likely to take a considerable time to try'[1].

Although referring directly to failure to diagnose dyslexia claims, those comments have general application to claims of substance and complexity.

1 [2005] 1 AC 76, para 54.

12.55 In addressing the respective degrees of prejudice the effect on the claimant of the operation of the limitation period, and on the defendant of losing an accrued limitation defence, will often be counter-balancing. The true issue for a defendant has therefore been identified as the prejudice arising from having to defend a stale claim. So, in addition to quantum of damages and costs, the court will have regard to the strength of the claimant's substantive case in the action[1]. If the claim is a poor case lacking in merit there may be significant and relevant prejudice to the defendant if the limitation period is disapplied[2]. The court will also pay regard to any potential claim which the claimant may have against his solicitors. Even if the claimant has an unanswerable claim against his own solicitors, he may nevertheless be regarded as prejudiced, since (inter alia) if the action is not allowed to proceed he may be personally liable for the costs and may suffer further delay in finding new solicitors and suing those at fault[3]. But if that prejudice is slight compared with the prejudice the defendants would suffer in having to meet a stale claim, then the existence of such a claim against the claimant's solicitors may be decisive in causing the court to refuse to disapply the time limit[4]. Since it is legitimate to take into account that the claimant may have a claim against his own solicitor, it follows that it is legitimate to take into account that the defendant is insured, for, if the defendant is deprived of his limitation defence, he will have a claim upon his insurers[5]. It has also been stated that the court may have regard to the insurance position of other defendants who have been sued in time[6]. It may also be relevant to take into account any public funding position[7].

1 *Dale v British Coal Corpn* [1992] PIQR P373, CA.
2 *Nash v Eli Lilly & Co* [1993] 4 All ER 383 at 404, though their Lordships did not share the view of the Court of Appeal in *Hartley v Birmingham City District Council* [1992] 1 WLR 968, that the benefit of the LA 1980 defence should necessarily be described as a windfall where a defendant's ability to defend was unaffected by the delay.
3 *Thompson v Brown Construction (Ebbw Vale) Ltd* [1981] 1 WLR 744, HL. See also *Ramsden v Lee* [1992] 2 All ER 204, CA. There may be further prejudice in that the claimant's solicitors will know the weaknesses in his case against the original tortfeasor whereas that tortfeasor may not know of them: *Hartley v Birmingham City District Council* [1992] 1 WLR 968, CA.
4 *Donovan v Gwentoys Ltd* [1990] 1 WLR 472, HL.
5 *Hartley v Birmingham City District Council* [1992] 1 WLR 968, CA. In *Kelly v Bastible* [1997] 8 Med LR 15, the Court of Appeal considered the fact that the defendant was insured with the

MDU was relevant under s 33; the insurer and defendant should be treated as a composite unit, even in cases where the claimant would have no claim against his legal adviser. In line with the old cases on striking out for want of prosecution, the courts have been prepared to consider changes in insurance arrangements as a relevant factor: *Baig v City and Hackney Health Authority* [1994] 5 Med LR 221; but see also *Smith v Leicestershire Health Authority* [1998] Lloyd's Rep Med 77, CA at 91.

6 *Liff v Peasley* [1980] 1 WLR 781 at 789.
7 *Halford v Brooks* [1991] 3 All ER 559, CA at 577. This works both ways, because a change in the funding arrangements which may prejudice a defendant (eg the availability of CFA funding instead of legal aid, as a result of which the defendant would face an additional cost if the claimant succeeded) are also potentially relevant, see *Smith v Ministry of Defence* [2005] EWHC 682 (QB).

12.56 The court, in exercising its discretion, will give some weight to the consideration that a professional negligence action is a serious matter for a medical practitioner and that such actions ought to be dealt with expeditiously[1].

1 See *Johnson v North Staffordshire Health Authority* (5 February 1995, unreported). But see the observations of Beldam LJ in *Dobbie v Medway Health Authority* [1994] 1 WLR 1234 at 1246.

CONTRIBUTION

12.57 Where contribution is claimed under the Civil Liability (Contribution) Act 1978, s 1 the time limit is two years from the date on which the right to recover contribution accrued[1]. The right accrues in the case of a judgment given in any civil proceedings on the date judgment is given, and in the case of an award made in any arbitration on the date of the award[2]. Where a person makes or agrees to make payment by way of settlement, the right accrues on the earliest date on which the amount to be paid is agreed[3].

1 LA 1980, s 10(1).
2 LA 1980, s 10(3). No account is taken of any judgment or award given or made on appeal in so far as it varies the amount of damages awarded against the person claiming.
3 LA 1980, s 10(4).

12.58 In *Knight v Rochdale Healthcare NHS Trust*[1] a surgeon agreed to settle a claim for damages brought by a former patient, which was later embodied in a consent order. He then sought indemnity from other parties. It was held that where there had been a firm agreement which did not require the making of a consent order, time ran from the moment the agreement was entered into. It was observed that the position would have been different where the agreement required the making of a consent order before it took effect. This must also be true of cases which require court approval under CPR 21.10.

1 [2003] EWHC 1831 (QB), [2004] 1 WLR 371 (Crane J).

12.59 A consent judgment for damages to be assessed, followed by a judgment for payment of an agreed sum was considered in *Aer Lingus plc v Gildacroft Ltd*[1]. The Court of Appeal held that time ran from the date of the judgment on quantum. Although the LA 1980, s 10(3) makes no express reference to the ascertainment of quantum, it was to be implied that time ran from the date of the judgment or award ascertaining damages rather than the date liability was established or admitted (thereby creating parity with s 10(4)).

1 [2006] EWCA Civ 4, [2006] 1 WLR 1173.

12.60   In the case of a person under a disability, the two-year period is subject to the provisions of the LA 1980, s 28[1]. The time limit then expires two years from the date when the claimant ceased to be under a disability or died (whichever first occurred)[2]. Similarly, where there has been concealment, the two year period only starts to run when the claimant has discovered the fact relevant to the right of action or could with reasonable diligence have discovered it[3]. There is no discretionary power to extend the period under the LA 1980, s 33[4].

1 LA 1980, s 10(5). For the operation of s 28 and disability more generally, see para **12.39** ff.
2 LA 1980, s 10(5) and s 28(5).
3 LA 1980, s 10(5) and s 32(1). For concealment and s 32, see para **12.41**.
4 LA 1980, s 10(5).

NEW CLAIMS IN PENDING ACTIONS

12.61   A new claim made in the course of an action is deemed to be a separate action and to have been commenced in the case of a new claim made in or by way of Part 20 proceedings on the date on which that claim was commenced; and in the case of any other new claim on the same date as the original action[1]. A new claim means any claim by way of set-off or counterclaim, any claim involving either the addition or substitution of a new cause of action or the addition or substitution of a new party, as well as claims made in or by way of Part 20 proceedings.

1 LA 1980, s 35(1).

12.62   The court may not, generally, allow a new claim to add or substitute a new cause of action or a new party (other than an original set-off or counterclaim) in the course of any action after the expiry of any time limit under the LA 1980[1]. That general rule is subject to the following limited exceptions.

1 LA 1980, s 35(3). An original set-off or counterclaim is one made by a party who has not previously made any claim in the action.

12.63   The LA 1980, s 33 discretion to disapply is expressly preserved in actions for personal injuries or death[1].

1 LA 1980, s 35(3).

12.64   The addition or substitution of a new cause of action will be allowed where the new cause of action arises out of the same or substantially the same facts as the claim in respect of which the party applying for permission has already claimed a remedy in the proceedings[1]. Whether a new claim arises out of substantially the same facts as the prior claim is a matter of impression, derived from a reasoned assessment of the essential facts[2].

1 LA 1980, s 35(5)(a) and CPR 17.4(2). See *Goode v Martin* [2001] EWCA Civ 1899, [2002] 1 WLR 1828. In *Charles Church Developments Ltd v Stent Foundations Ltd* [2006] EWHC 3158 (TCC), [2007] 1 WLR 1203, the rationale for CPR 17.4 was said to justify an expanded interpretation of the rule, whereby a claimant would be allowed to amend to plead a new cause of action against the first defendant based on facts pleaded by the second defendant. Whether the court would allow that course depended on all the circumstances, including what was fair to the defendant.
2 See *Chantrey Velacott v Convergence Group plc* [2005] EWCA Civ 290.

12.65   The addition or substitution of a new party will be allowed if the relevant limitation period was current when the proceedings were started and the addition or substitution is necessary for the determination of the original action[1]. However the court will not allow the substitution of the new party where that will have the effect of launching a new claim against a new party, even if it arises out of the same facts[2]. The addition or substitution shall not be regarded as necessary for the determination of the original action unless the new party is substituted for a party whose name was given in any claim made in the original action in mistake for the new party's name[3]; the claim cannot properly be carried on by or against the original party unless the new party is added or substituted as claimant or defendant[4]; or the original party has died or had a bankruptcy order made against him and his interest or liability has passed to the new party[5].

1 LA 1980, s 35(5)(b) and CPR 19.5(2).
2 In *Nemeti v Sabre Insurance Co Ltd* [2013] EWCA Civ 1555, injured passengers sought to substitute the estate of the driver in negligence, in a claim where they had already sued the deceased driver's insurers directly under the European Communities (Rights against Insurers) Regulations 2002. The attempt failed.
3 LA 1980, s 35(6)(a) and CPR 19.5(3)(a).
4 LA 1980, s 35(6)(b) and CPR 19.5(3)(b).
5 CPR 19.5(3)(c).

PROCEDURE/BURDEN OF PROOF

12.66   In order to take advantage of the protection afforded by the expiry of the limitation period, the defendant must expressly plead the statute in his defence[1]. The defence should be pleaded expeditiously. Whether a late application to raise limitation will be granted lies in the discretion of the court[2]. In a very clear case the defendant can apply to strike out the statement of case as disclosing no reasonable grounds for bringing the claim, or perhaps as an abuse of process[3]. Such an application should be made as soon as possible and, where possible, before allocation[4].

1 By para 13.1 of the Practice Direction to CPR 16, the defendant must in his defence give details of the expiry of any relevant limitation period relied on.
2 See *Ketteman v Hansel Properties* [1987] AC 189, HL, and *Lewis v Hackney London Borough Council* [1990] 2 EGLR 15, CA.
3 See CPR 3.4(2)(a) and (b) and the Practice Direction to CPR 3. See *Ronex Properties Ltd v John Laing Construction Ltd* [1983] QB 398, CA (under the RSC).
4 See para 2 of the Practice Direction to CPR 23.

12.67   Having been raised in the statements of case, either party can apply for the defence of limitation to be tried as a preliminary issue[1]. This is often the preferable course as it may have the effect of saving costs, and is consistent with the overriding objective of the CPR. There is ample opportunity for the court itself to give directions for the hearing of the issue of limitation under its powers of case management[2]. Occasionally, the issue may be left to the trial of the action[3].

1 See CPR 23 governing applications.
2 CPR 1.4 requires the court to further the overriding objective by actively managing cases. Active case management includes identifying issues at an early stage; deciding promptly which issues need full investigation and trial; and deciding the order in which issues are to be resolved. For the specific provisions relating to case management of cases allocated to the multi-track see CPR 29 and its Practice Direction.

3 In *Fletcher v Sheffield Health Authority* [1994] 5 Med LR 156, CA, the issues of limitation could not readily be separated from the issues of causation and negligence, so that the limitation point was ordered to be decided at trial.

12.68 A defendant is under no obligation to raise a limitation defence. The parties are free to agree that a limitation point will not be relied upon, and in certain circumstances a defendant might be held to be estopped by his conduct from relying upon a limitation defence, as where, for example, he misled the claimant into not starting his action in time[1].

1 See, generally, *Kaliszewska v John Clague & Partners* (1984) 5 Con LR 62; *Westlake v Bracknell District Council* [1987] 1 EGLR 161; but see also *Sheldon v RHM Outhwaite (Underwriting Agencies) Ltd* [1994] 4 All ER 481, CA; revsd [1996] AC 102, HL. To the contrary effect, it may also be argued that to allow estoppel to defeat a limitation defence could in certain circumstances run contrary to the reasoning of *Cartledge v E Jopling & Sons Ltd* [1963] AC 758, HL, as cited again by the House of Lords in *Pirelli General Cable Works Ltd v Oscar Faber & Partners* [1983] 2 AC 1 at 13, that Parliament expressly provided for fraud and mistake in the Limitation Act 1939 (now 1980), so must have intended that there should be no other exceptions based on any difficulty of discovering the facts giving rise to the cause of action. It is well established that where estoppel is relied upon, the acts said to support the estoppel must be clear and unequivocal: see, for example *Seechurn v ACE Insurance* [2002] EWCA Civ 67, [2002] 2 Lloyd's Rep 390, a claim on a disability policy, where the defendant was not estopped from raising limitation in its defence. The mere continuation of negotiations will rarely be sufficient for these purposes.

12.69 Where limitation is to be tried as a preliminary issue, care must be taken in drafting the terms of the order, to ensure that the preliminary issue is identified with adequate precision[1]. Where the parties intend that the only finding which will be *res judicata* is the date of knowledge, and that incidental findings of fact are to be open for reconsideration on further evidence at the trial of the main action, that should be made clear[2].

1 See *Robinson v St Helens MBC* [2003] PIQR P9, CA, at [44].
2 *Adams v Bracknell Forest Borough Council* [2005] 1 AC 72, at [24].

12.70 The burden of proof in relation to the LA 1980, s 14(1) (actual knowledge) rests upon the claimant once the defence of limitation has been raised. Likewise, in relation to s 14(3) (constructive knowledge)[1]. In cases where a claimant seeks to have the limitation period disapplied under s 33 the onus lies upon him to show that in the particular circumstances of the case it would be equitable to make an exception[2].

1 It was held by Colman J in *Parry v Clwyd Health Authority* [1997] PIQR P1 that the burden of proving constructive knowledge is on the defendant. However, in *Crocker v British Coal Corpn* (1995) 29 BMLR 159 Mance J considered that whilst there may be an evidential burden on the defendant, the legal burden remains on the claimant (which it is submitted accords with the usual rules of evidence): 'There cannot be opposing legal onuses on opposite parties on the single issue whether there was or was not knowledge within the three-year period'. See also *Cartledge v E Jopling & Sons Ltd* [1962] 1 QB 189, CA; *London Congregational Union Inc v Harriss & Harriss (a firm)* [1988] 1 All ER 15, CA; and *Darley Main Colliery Co v Mitchell* (1886) 11 App Cas 127.
2 *Thompson v Brown Construction (Ebbw Vale) Ltd* [1981] 1 WLR 744 at 752, HL; *Long v Tolchard & Sons Ltd* [2001] PIQR P18; *KR v Bryn Alyn Community (Holdings) Ltd* [2003] EWCA Civ 783, [2003] QB 1441, per Auld LJ at [74].

CHAPTER 13

Product liability for medicinal products

Charles Gibson QC

Geraint Webb QC

James Purnell

379

INTRODUCTION

13.1   This chapter focuses on the issue of civil liability for injuries caused, or allegedly caused, by medicinal products[1]. Liability for injuries associated with the use of medicinal products is complex and frequently emotive. No prescription medicine is free from the risk of serious adverse effects for certain patients; science can strive to minimise the risks of a medicine, but it will rarely be possible scientifically to separate the beneficial therapeutic effects of an active ingredient from the risks posed by that active ingredient. Moreover, knowledge as to both the benefits and risks of a medicinal product, or class of such products, will evolve and change over time; the risk/benefit profile of a medicine may be reassessed, positively or negatively, over time. The concept of safety is a relative one[2] and the risk/benefit profile of a medicine may itself be influenced by the availability or otherwise of alternative treatments or, indeed, by changing perceptions as to the risks inherent in the condition for which the medicine is indicated.

1 The current contributors are indebted to the authors of this Chapter in the previous edition: Ian Dodds-Smith, Michael Spencer QC and Dr Jacqueline Bore; and to Lucy McCormick for her valuable assistance in the research and preparation for this edition.
2 Cf Lord Mance, in a different context concerning liability under the Factories Act 1961, s 29, in *Baker v Quantum Clothing Group Ltd* [2011] UKSC 17 at para 64 'Whether a place is safe involves a judgment, one which is objectively assessed of course, but by reference to the knowledge and standards of the time. There is no such thing as an unchanging concept of safety'.

13.2   The experience of thalidomide in the early 1960s gave rise to demands, particularly within Europe, for greater regulatory control of medicines and sparked off the contentious debate about the basis upon which companies that research and market medicinal products should be liable for any injury caused, or allegedly caused, by those products. Increased regulatory control was introduced in the UK in the form of the Medicines Act 1968. Regulatory control has been extended to every aspect of the marketing of medicinal products and now also to investigational products supplied for clinical research. European initiatives to harmonise the standards against which assessments take place have now been supplemented by entirely new mechanisms for the grant of authorisations to market human medicines. Medicines are now among the most highly regulated of all products, the applicable regulatory regime being aimed at safeguarding public health and achieving an appropriate balance between the benefits and risks of medicinal products. In terms of civil liability, the thalidomide experience directly informed the debate which resulted, eventually, in the adoption of the Product Liability Directive[1].

1 Council Directive 85/374/EEC.

13.3   The field of product liability is primarily concerned with the liability of the producer and accordingly that is the focus of this chapter. Nonetheless, the issue of product liability for medicinal products is so closely intertwined with both the regulatory regime and with the role of the professional intermediary that a discussion of product liability for medicinal products cannot properly ignore either issues; accordingly, the regulatory context and the role of other professional intermediaries is considered, briefly, below. Medical devices are governed by their own regulatory regime, which we do not seek to deal with in this chapter; nevertheless, the framework relating to civil liability discussed below applies both to medicinal products and medical devices.

13.4   The principal causes of action for imposing civil liability for defective products in England and Wales are founded upon: (i) the Consumer Protection Act 1987 (the CPA 1987), implementing Council Directive 85/374/EEC of 25 July 1985 (the Product Liability Directive)[1]; (ii) negligence; and (iii) breach of contract, each of which is considered further below. The result is that product liability for medicinal products concerns a mélange of contractual and tortious principles. There is a relative absence of judicial decisions on the impact of these principles upon the activities of the industry.

1 [1985] OJ L210/29.

13.5   Over the past 50 years, England and Wales has seen a number of cases, or threatened cases, involving medicinal products and medical devices said to have caused injury. The 1960s saw claims in relation to thalidomide; the late 1970s and 1980s brought claims involving hormone pregnancy tests, oral contraceptives, Debendox, Opren, pertussis vaccine, prednisolone, intra-uterine devices, benzodiazepines, and blood products; the 1990s saw cases concerning contrast media (Myodil), human insulin, human growth hormone, steroids, contraceptive implants (Norplant), minocyclines, third generation oral contraceptives, Lariam malaria tablets and Measles, Mumps and Rubella vaccines (MMR); the 2000s brought claims in respect of SSRIs

(Seroxat), and anti-convulsants (alleged visual field defects in relation to Sabril and alleged birth defects and developmental delay in relation to Epilim), whilst claims are currently on foot in relation to PIP breast implants and metal-on-metal hip implants.

13.6 It remains the case, however, that whilst a few of these claims have resulted in settlement[1], no case against a commercial manufacturer has yet been taken to judgment on all aspects of liability in England and Wales[2] and the claimants' claims have been unsuccessful in many of the major claims[3]. Similarly, it is notable that although the CPA 1987 came into force in 1988, there have been few reported decisions regarding Part 1 of the CPA 1987 at all and the courts of England and Wales have yet to grapple with the proper interpretation of the Directive's key concepts of 'defect' and the 'development risk defence' in the context of a prescription medicine.

1 See, for example, the settlement of the Opren litigation (NLJ 18 December 1987 at 1183). Cases concerning alleged side effects of long-term use of prednisolone in the 1960s and 1970s for juvenile rheumatoid arthritis (see Scrip no 1212, 10 June 1987, p 2) were also settled immediately prior to trial. Cases involving the contrast medium Myodil, were settled by Glaxo-Wellcome a few months before trial, with just over 400 patients from an original cohort of over 3,500 sharing £7m and recovering their reasonable costs (see Daily Telegraph, 1 August 1995).
2 In 2002, claims concerning third generation oral contraceptives collapsed following a judgment of the court on the first issue to be considered which found that, on the balance of probabilities, such contraceptives did not increase the risk of thrombo-embolic disorders beyond the risk associated with second generation products (*XYZ v Schering Healthcare Ltd* [2002] EWHC 1420 (QB)).
3 See, for example, the MMR Litigation, the second generation oral contraceptives litigation (which collapsed after the trial of a preliminary issue) and the Fetal Anti-Convulsant (FAC) Litigation (which collapsed prior to trial).

13.7 As at the time of writing, the one exception (albeit not in a case involving a prescription medicine), and something of a lone voice in this field, is the judgment of Burton J in *A v National Blood Authority*[1], the group litigation brought on behalf of 112 claimants who had received blood transfusions or blood products which had been infected with hepatitis C virus from the blood of donors. The decision of Burton J provided the first and, to date, the most detailed consideration of the statutory product liability regime in England and Wales, and in particular the concepts of defect and development risk. The decision has been the subject of considerable academic criticism, but has yet to receive any detailed consideration by the higher courts[2]. Whatever the merits of the decision, it is important to note that the case did not concern a medicinal product subject to statutory regulation and available only on prescription.

1 [2001] Lloyd's Rep Med 187.
2 Although cases brought under Part 1 of the CPA 1987 have been considered in the Supreme Court, House of Lords and Court of Appeal, they did not make any reference to *A v National Blood Authority* [2001] Lloyd's Rep Med 187 (see the House of Lords and Supreme Court decisions in *O'Byrne v Aventis Pasteur MSD Ltd* [2008] UKHL 34, [2010] UKSC 23 (limitation period); and the Court of Appeal in *Tesco v Pollard* [2006] EWCA Civ 393, *Piper v JRI (Manufacturing) Ltd* [2006] EWCA Civ 1344 and *Ide v ATB Sales Ltd* [2008] EWCA Civ 424). In the other lengthy group litigation brought under Part 1 of the CPA 1987 which has proceeded to trial, there was no consideration of the decision in *A v National Blood Authority* because the case was decided on a preliminary issue of causation: see the oral contraceptive group litigation *XYZ v Schering Health Care Ltd* [2002] EWHC 1420 (QB).

13.8   The absence of reported decisions in relation to product liability for medicinal products reflects, at least in part, the complexity of this area of litigation. Invariably, medicinal product litigation is conducted on a group basis or, at least, in litigation with multiple parties. Such litigation has the tendency to be protracted, expensive and raises complex questions. On any view, the nature of these products and the conditions they are used to treat would make the simplest of systems, where compensation depended only upon showing causation, difficult enough, for their adverse effects are frequently difficult to distinguish from the adverse progression or the recrudescence of the underlying condition for which the product was given. Their adverse effects are sometimes said to appear many years after use and not in the patient but in her offspring. Moreover, the difficulties are accentuated where, as is common, a person has taken many different products for separate conditions or a series of similar products from different manufacturers for one condition. Merely identifying the product used years after the event has proved impossible for some claimants[1].

1 In *Mann and Close v Wellcome Foundation Ltd* (20 January 1989, unreported) QBD, the claimants ultimately conceded that there was insufficient evidence to establish that the defendant's subsidiary (Calmic Ltd) had supplied the relevant neomycin spray alleged to have caused deafness and the case against the manufacturer defendants failed.

13.9   Scientists seek to perfect the architecture and performance of statistical studies for the purpose of seeking reliably to identify the adverse effects of medicinal products. However, the enormous potential for bias entering into the collection of epidemiological data, and the existence of confounding factors correlating positively both with an increased likelihood of the product being prescribed and an increased incidence of the condition under consideration, make interpretation of such data very difficult. This is particularly so where low levels of risk are under consideration[1]. The courts have made it clear that reports of epidemiological studies are not of themselves admissible evidence of the facts of the risks reported in them (see *H v Schering Chemicals Ltd*)[2], although they can be introduced into evidence through expert testimony. Where they are introduced in this way, however, there may often remain an issue, particularly where a relative risk or odds ratio derived from epidemiological studies is two or less, as to whether it is possible to conclude that the association is more than a relationship of chance[3]. The courts have supported the application of the Bradford Hill criteria, which set out various criteria relating to epidemiological evidence against which to test the hypothesis that a causal relationship exists between the use of a product and injury[4]. In the US the difficulties of untested causal theory being presented to juries as scientific fact led the Supreme Court to develop the *Daubert* doctrine[5], under which expert scientific testimony is only admissible if it rests on a reliable foundation in terms of the underlying methodology and is relevant to the issues in question. Reliability was to be judged in part by considering matters such as peer review and acceptance in the specialist scientific community concerned. In England the issues of fact are decided by a judge who is presumed to be alert to reliability and relevance and, although similar factors may influence the court in deciding what weight to attach to the testimony of an expert witness, admissibility is not usually an issue. A fuller analysis is set out in the Causation section below, under the heading 'The role of epidemiology and statistics'.

1 At a conference organised by the Royal Society of Medicine on 17–19 July 1989 concerning oral contraceptives and breast cancer, Professor S Shapiro commented that a relative risk of 1–2 is 'beyond the resolving power of the epidemiologic microscope'.
2 *H v Schering Chemicals Ltd* [1983] 1 All ER 849, [1983] 1 WLR 143.
3 *Vadera v Shaw* (1999) 45 BMLR 162 at 173–174, CA and *XY v Schering Healthcare Ltd* [2002] EWHC 1420 (QB); *Novartis Grimsby Ltd v Cookson* [2007] EWCA Civ 1261; see also the obiter discussion on the value of epidemiological evidence in *Sienkiewicz v Greif (UK) Ltd* [2011] UKSC 10, [2011] 2 AC 229.
4 See Hill 'The environment and disease: association of causation?' (1965) 58 Proc Roy Soc Med 295–300, utilised by French J in *Reay and Hope v British Nuclear Fuels plc* [1994] 5 Med LR 1 at 13.
5 *Daubert v Merrell Dow Pharmaceuticals Inc* 509 US 579 (1993). The Supreme Court has now applied the rule to non-scientific but technical expert testimony in the landmark case *Kumho Tire Co v Carmichael* 526 US 137 (1999).

13.10 Proving causation – both general causation (that the medicine is capable of causing the alleged injury in principle) and causation in the individual case (that the claimant's own alleged injury was in fact caused by the medicine) – is therefore a major problem for claimants, whether their claim is based on negligence or founded on the CPA 1987. It often dwarfs all other problems[1].

1 In *Loveday v Renton and Wellcome Foundation Ltd* [1990] 1 Med LR 117, the court found that the plaintiffs had failed to establish a causal relationship between the use of pertussis vaccine and brain damage in young children. In *D and R v Schering Chemicals Ltd* (2 July 1982, unreported) QBD, the claimants sought leave to discontinue cases alleging malformations had been caused by exposure to the hormone pregnancy test Primodos in utero after exchange of extensive expert evidence, on the basis that – as their leading counsel put it – there was no real possibility of establishing that the products were teratogenic as alleged.

13.11 The difficulties faced by claimants in these cases have led to calls for product liability for medicinal products to be taken completely outside the existing contractual and tortious law system so that compensation is based upon an insurance-based 'no fault compensation scheme'[1]. However, given the supremacy of EU law in this area, as illustrated in *Skov v Bilka*[2], it is probable that such a scheme would require wholesale amendment, if not dismantling, of the present scheme of liability for defective products contained in the Product Liability Directive. Article 13 of the Directive only preserves special liability systems in force when the Directive was adopted[3].

1 Diamond and Laurence 'Product Liability in Respect of Drugs' in D'Arcy and Griffin (eds) *Iatrogenic Diseases* (3rd edn, 1986) pp 117–123.
2 Case C-402/03.
3 This does not preclude Member States introducing special liability systems regarding matters which are not governed by the Directive: see the ECJ decision in *Novo Nordisk Pharma GmbH v S* (Case C-310/13, 20 November 2014). The claimant sought disclosure from a pharmaceutical company on the adverse effects of a medicinal product containing insulin for the treatment of diabetes. Applying a provision of the German drug liability regime only introduced in 2002 (the Directive was notified in 1985), the claim for information succeeded. The ECJ concluded that the German liability system for pharmaceutical products was a 'special liability system' within the meaning of Article 13, which the national legislator was permitted to develop beyond the date of the notification of the Directive. The consumer's right to require the manufacturer of a product to provide him with information on the adverse effects of that product is not among the matters governed by the Directive and thus falls outside the scope of the Directive and did not compromise the effectiveness of the system provided for under the Directive or the objectives pursued by the Directive.

13.12 In addition to such scientific and legal difficulties, claimants have historically faced funding difficulties in attempting to bring medicinal product liability claims. The days of medicinal product group litigation funded by the Legal Aid Board and, latterly, the Legal Services Commission appear to be at an end. The cost and complexity of this type of litigation rendered it largely unattractive for funding on a conditional fee agreement basis, not least because of the potential liability for adverse costs. It remains to be seen whether claimant firms will be able to utilise the 'Jackson reforms' and, in particular, the introduction of qualified one-way costs shifting[1] to their clients' advantage.

1 CPR 44.13–44.17.

13.13   The last medicinal product liability group action to be brought with the benefit of public funding in England and Wales, the Fetal Anti-Convulsant Group Litigation (the FAC Litigation), provides an illustrative (and by no means isolated[1]) example of the complexity and scale of this type of litigation. The litigation was commenced in 2003 by litigation friends on behalf of children born to mothers suffering from epilepsy, who were prescribed anti-epileptic drugs whilst pregnant. In each case, the claimants alleged that they were born with disabilities as a consequence of fetal exposure to sodium valproate. After numerous interlocutory and satellite hearings (including the successful judicial review of a withdrawal of public funding, a refusal of an application for a trial of preliminary issues[2] and the denial of certain expert evidence in relation to the 'fair apportionment of risk'[3]) and after service of over 100 expert reports in 12 disciplines, public funding was finally withdrawn in 2010, three weeks before the commencement of an 18-week trial. The claims were finally discontinued in May 2011, eight years after the commencement of the litigation.

1 For a history of the demise of and the problems that beset the MMR Group Litigation, see: 'The Rise and Fall of the MMR Litigation: A Comparative Perspective', Chapter 6 in Goldberg *Medicinal Product Liability and Regulation* (2013). For a summary of the history and collapse of the Benzodiazepine Litigation, see the Court of Appeal decision in *AB v John Wyeth* [1997] PIQR P385, upholding the decision of Ian Kennedy J striking out the claims for abuse of process in the light of withdrawal of funding by the Legal Aid Board.
2 [2007] EWHC 1860 (QB), per Andrew Smith J.
3 *Multiple Claimants v Sanofi Sythelabo Ltd (Fetal Anti-Convulsant Litigation)* [2007] EWHC 1860 (QB), (2007) 98 BMLR 192.

THE REGULATORY CONTEXT

Overview

13.14   The pharmaceutical industry is one of the most highly regulated industries in the world. Strict regulatory controls, structures and procedures exist worldwide and govern all aspects of the lifecycle of a medicinal product from its initial development and assessment in pre-clinical and clinical trials, to its licensing and approval for human use, through to measures governing its manufacture, sale and marketing and regulating its post-marketing safety and risk/benefit.

13.15   In the UK, a system of regulatory controls was first put in place following the thalidomide experience in the early 1960s. Over the period, regulatory requirements and controls have been transformed beyond recognition and the system that has operated since 1995 (when European legislation establishing new procedures for the grant of marketing authorisations was implemented in the UK) bears hardly any resemblance to the one that came into effect in the early 1970s in the aftermath of the thalidomide tragedy.

13.16   Save for limited circumstances when a medicinal product is exempted[1], a medicinal product may be supplied only if it has been granted a marketing authorisation. A marketing authorisation will only be granted if the product is found to have met appropriate standards of quality, safety and efficacy in its approved uses following detailed consideration of the available data by those with appropriate medical and scientific expertise within the relevant regulatory authority. A marketing authorisation will only be granted or continued where a medicine is assessed as having a positive risk/benefit profile ie the benefits associated with use of the product outweigh the potential risks.

1 For example: Member States may make a medicinal product for human use available for compassionate use to a group of patients with a chronically or seriously debilitating disease or whose disease is considered to be life-threatening, and who cannot be treated satisfactorily by an authorised medicinal product (EC Regulation 726/2004 (OJ L136, 30.4.2004 p 1) Articles 83(1) and (2)); Member States may temporarily authorise the distribution of an unauthorised medicinal product for human use in response to the suspected or confirmed spread of pathogenic agents, toxins, chemical agents or nuclear radiation any of which could cause harm (EC Directive 2001/83 (OJ L311, 28.11.2001, p 67) Article 5(2)); a Member State may authorise a medicinal product to be placed on the market for justified public health reasons which is authorised in another Member State (EC Directive 2001/83, Article 126a(1)).

13.17   The types of information to be supplied with and about the product by means of patient information leaflets (PILs) and summaries of product characteristics (SPCs)[1] are prescribed by legislation and the content of SPCs and PILs in relation to any particular medicine is determined by the regulatory authority, which must approve such documents before the product is marketed. The marketing authorisation holder for a medicinal product is required to comply with various regulatory obligations, including pharmacovigilance requirements and obligations as to the reporting of adverse drug reactions.

1 In other texts these may be referred to as SmPCs.

13.18   Pharmacovigilance within the EU is a tri-partite operation:

(1)   At the highest level, the European Medicines Agency (EMA), a decentralised agency of the European Union located in London, is responsible for the protection and promotion of public and animal health, through the evaluation and monitoring of medicines for human and veterinary use. The European Medicines Agency was set up in 1995[1] and until 2004 was known as the European Agency for the Evaluation of Medicinal Products. It was renamed by EC Regulation No 726/2004 as the European Medicines Agency and had the acronym EMEA until December 2009. In particular, the EMA is responsible for the scientific evaluation of medicines that fall within the scope of the centralised authorisation procedure. This procedure results in a single marketing authorisation that is valid in all EU countries, Iceland, Liechtenstein and Norway. The centralised procedures are compulsory in those

countries in relation to certain categories of human medicines such as those for treatment of cancer, diabetes, neurodegenerative diseases and auto-immune diseases. For medicines falling outside these categories producers have the option of submitting an application for a centralised marketing authorisation to the EMA as long as the medicine concerned is a significant therapeutic, scientific or technical innovation, or if its authorisation would be in the interest of public or animal health. The EMA carries out a number of tasks including pharmacovigilance, scientific advice and the maintenance of pan-European databases such as EudraVigilance (a database for the reporting and evaluation of suspected adverse reactions), EudraCT (database of all clinical trials of investigational medicinal products) and EudraPharm (database of medicinal products authorised, including information contained in SPCs, PILs and labelling).

(2)   Each EU Member State has its own procedures for the authorisation, within its own territory, of medicines that fall outside the scope of the centralised authorisation procedure. A company can apply for authorisation of such medicines in more than one EU country at a time under a decentralised procedure or, alternatively, under a mutual-recognition procedure. National medicine regulatory bodies operate pharmacovigilance at Member State level. Member States must operate a pharmacovigilance system to collate information on the risks of medicinal products including evaluating adverse reactions, considering risk minimisation and taking regulatory action[2]. In the UK, that function is performed by the Medicines and Healthcare Products Regulatory Agency (MHRA), an executive agency of the Department of Health.

(3)   The marketing authorisation holder must operate its own pharmacovigilance system, evaluate all information scientifically, consider options for risk minimisation and prevention and take appropriate measures as necessary[3]: including, inter alia, an appropriately qualified person responsible for pharmacovigilance; a pharmacovigilance system master file; and a risk management system for each medicinal product, monitoring and updating the risks.

1   Pursuant to EC Regulation No 2309/93.
2   EC Directive 2001/83 (OJ L311, 28.11.2001, p 67) on the Community code relating to medicinal products for human use, Article 101(1) and (2).
3   EC Directive 2001/83, Article 104(1) and (2).

The licensing authority

13.19   With regard to human medicines, the licensing authority carries out its executive functions through a regulatory authority which was created for the purpose of regulating all the activities related to human medicinal products in the UK including the grant, renewal, variation, suspension and revocation of licences and certificates. The regulatory authority was initially a branch of the Department of Health and Social Security (DHSS), known as the Medicines Division (MD). The DHSS was later split into DH and DSS in 1988, and the executive arm of the licensing authority (MD) became a branch of the DH. This executive branch (MD) was authorised to discharge all the functions of the licensing authority. The Medicines Division was later re-organised in April 1989 into an agency, known as the Medicines Control Agency (MCA)[1]. In April 2003, the MCA was further re-organised following its merger with the Medical Devices Agency and the body is known today as the Medicines and Healthcare Products Regulatory Agency (MHRA)[2].

1 Created in April 1989, established in July 1991 and achieved trading fund status on 1 April 1993 (the Medicines Control Agency Trading Fund Order 1993, SI 1993/751). The Trading Fund Order set out details of the functions of the MCA.
2 The Medicines and Healthcare Products Regulatory Agency Trading Fund Order 2003, SI 2003/1076.

13.20 Previously, the licensing authority was advised by a series of committees. The Medicines Commission (MC) was established in December 1969[1] and was responsible for advising on all matters relating to the implementation of the Act. The licensing authority was also advised by the Committee on Safety of Medicines (CSM), an independent committee that provided advice on the quality, efficacy and safety of medicines. The CSM itself had a range of subcommittees[2] providing more detailed advice on matters such as adverse drug reactions and clinical trials. Following a re-organisation of the advisory structure in October 2005, the functions of the CSM and the Medicines Commission with regard to human medicines were merged and transferred to the newly established Commission on Human Medicines (CHM).

1 Medicines Act 1968, s 2.
2 These committees included the Subcommittee on Toxicity, Clinical Trials and Therapeutic Efficacy, the Subcommittee on Chemistry, Pharmacy and Standards (CPS), the Subcommittee on Adverse Reactions and the Subcommittee on Biologicals.

Monitoring the safety of marketed products

13.21 Data relating to the safety of marketed medicines are available to the regulatory authority from multiple sources including spontaneous reports from healthcare professionals (and now members of the public), the marketing authorisation holder, other regulatory authorities, worldwide published literature, coroners and academic researchers and institutes.

13.22 In carrying out its assessment of the evidence, the regulatory authority and the committees are not reliant solely on information provided by the marketing authorisation holder in assessing a product's safety profile/warnings. More often than not, it is the case that because healthcare professionals report adverse drug reactions (ADRs) relating to a medicine only to the regulatory authority, it is the regulatory authority that provides the marketing authorisation holder with anonymised spontaneous reports of ADRs and it is the regulatory authority that draws the attention of the marketing authorisation holder to a specific publication (often sent by the investigators to the regulatory authority in advance of its submission or publication) concerning drug safety. Furthermore, for cases that require follow up, healthcare professionals are often more inclined to provide further information to the regulatory authority than to the marketing authorisation holder.

When appropriate, the manufacturer may be asked to provide a report either evaluating all the data available to it on the risks and benefits of the product or focussing on a particular safety issue.

13.23 The World Health Organisation (WHO) and many regulatory authorities produce medicine safety bulletins and these are routinely screened by the regulatory authority to ensure that alerts which have not already been identified are reviewed in the context of use of the relevant medicine(s) in the UK. The medical and scientific literature also contains much information which is relevant to medicine safety. It is therefore systematically screened by the regulatory authority to ensure that published case reports and medicine safety studies are identified and included in the signal generation procedures and assessments made.

13.24 In addition, data may sometimes be available from other sources which could be used in the assessment of medicine safety or as a basis for specific studies. Examples include routinely collected data on mortality or disease incidence eg from the Office of National Statistics or from disease registries.

13.25 As laid down in pharmacovigilance guidelines for EU Member States, there is also close interaction on medicine safety issues between the regulatory authorities of EU Member States. In particular, such interaction occurs through meetings of the Pharmacovigilance Working Party of the Committee for Medicinal Products for Human Use (CHMP) and via a Rapid Alert System[1] for the exchange of important or urgent information.

1 The Rapid Alert System (RAS) alerts Member States and the Commission to pharmacovigilance data for medicinal products which indicate that action could be needed urgently to protect public health. It was set up so that information concerning safety hazards which may result in major changes to the marketing authorisation status or withdrawal of a product could be exchanged between the Member States and the Commission with the appropriate degree of urgency.

The precautionary approach

13.26 In determining what, if any, action is appropriate in the light of new safety data, the regulatory authority adopts a 'precautionary approach'. This is a key regulatory principle by which action (such as the provision of warnings) is taken to address the risk of potential adverse effects, where there is a reasonable suspicion that the effect may be associated with use of the medicinal product, even if the evidence does not establish a causal relationship. In 2000, the European Commission defined the 'precautionary approach' as having application in: 'those circumstances where scientific evidence is insufficient, inconclusive or uncertain and there are indications through preliminary objective scientific evaluation that there are reasonable grounds for concern that the potentially dangerous effects on the environment, human, animal or plant health may be inconsistent with the chosen level of protection'[1].

1 EU Commission, Communication from the Commission on the Precautionary Principle, COM (2000) 1, 2 February 2000.

13.27 In the context of the assessment of the risks from a medicine, a precautionary approach does not mean a priori that warnings should be provided or other action taken in response to each and every report of an adverse effect allegedly associated with a medicinal product, irrespective of the quality of the data. In deciding whether regulatory action is appropriate in the light of new data, the regulatory authority will take account of all the available information regarding the medicinal product (including preclinical data, possible mechanisms of action, class-related effects, epidemiological data and data from clinical trials) and the information regarding the adverse effect (including the medical history of the patient, temporal relationship to drug administration, the quality of data and assessment, alternative causes and the effect of re-challenge if there was one) to assess whether the new evidence amounts to a qualitative and/or quantitative change in risk. That assessment is a matter of judgment. The decision-maker must judge what level of risk is an acceptable risk, taking all factors into consideration and implementing suitable measures to try to manage that risk.

13.28 The type and quality of evidence supporting a change in warnings may vary depending on the overall circumstances. Usually the regulatory authority will not require a change in warnings unless: (a) there is reasonable evidence of an association; and (b) the risk is not covered by existing warnings. However, in assessing what action may be appropriate, the regulatory authority will adopt a precautionary approach and consider whether any delay in taking action may have a serious impact on public health. If, for example, a very rare but extremely serious side effect is identified based on a few case reports then that may be sufficient to require a warning or other regulatory action (such as withdrawal of the product from the market) to be taken on a precautionary basis because of the risk to public health. The precautionary approach therefore provides the regulatory authority with flexibility to take action if necessary in the interests of public health, even if the evidence supporting such action is limited. In relation to a class of products with active ingredients in the same pharmacological or chemical class, the precautionary approach may dictate the inclusion of class warnings in the prescribing information of all products in the class where a potential risk has been identified in one medicine[1].

1 For example, the inclusion of class warnings of the possible risk of suicidality in all SSRIs following the identification of a risk with one product, paroxetine.

Assessment of risks and benefits

13.29 Underpinning the continuous process of review of medicinal products throughout their lifecycle, is the recognition that all medicines carry risks as well as provide benefits to the patients. No medicine is 100 per cent safe, and all medicines have side effects. A licence will only be granted or renewed if there is deemed to be a positive balance of risks and benefits[1] (in other words, the benefits of the product outweigh the risks) or the product is, in the MHRA's own words, 'acceptably safe'[2]. Determining the safety of a product is a holistic approach that calls for an integrated assessment of the clinical and laboratory adverse effects associated with the product in terms of their frequency, seriousness, severity, reversibility and outcome, and determining whether the risk can be mitigated by warnings on any risk factors. That assessment is complex and takes into account a range of factors including the nature of the disease or condition to be treated, the type of patient and the duration of treatment. It is important to appreciate that regulators approve or disapprove a drug on the basis of risk/benefit at a population level and not at an individual patient level. Consequently, risk/benefit will be favourable for a certain class of patients, but not necessarily for all, of the patients or all the subgroups of patients (eg males versus females or children versus the elderly) with the relevant illness or disease. Where risk/benefit for a particular subgroup is unfavourable, the licensing authority may restrict or contraindicate the use of the medicine in that group of patients.

1 This principle was implicit in the need to assess safety, quality and efficacy in accordance with Directive 65/65/EEC, but was made explicit in Directive 75/318/EEC which required, in the context of the evaluation of an application for a marketing authorisation, that 'Therapeutic advantages must outweigh potential risks'.
2 MHRA guidance 'Medicines & Medical Devices Regulation: What you need to know', April 2008: http://www.mhra.gov.uk/home/groups/comms-ic/documents/websiteresources/con2031677.pdf.

Data sheets or summary of product characteristics (SPCs)

13.30   The data sheet or summary of product characteristics (SPC) is designed and intended to provide the physician with the key information necessary for the safe and effective use of a medicine. Critically, it is a dynamic document that evolves with time as experience with the wider use of the medicine concerned increases and better defines its efficacy and safety and any populations at risk. For all practical purposes, it is the most important regulatory document relating to a medicinal product.

13.31   The content of the SPC is strictly regulated: it must contain certain prescribed information set out in the manner required in the legislation. A draft SPC was at all material times required to be submitted to the regulatory authorities as part of the application for a product licence/marketing authorisation. Once the application is determined to be approvable, the next task is to approve the prescribing information for physicians. The regulatory authority, in light of the dossier accompanying the application, would carefully scrutinise the terms of the SPC.

13.32   The SPC forms part of the product licence/marketing authorisation issued by the licensing authority. Its contents cannot, therefore, be amended without a variation application that requires approval of the regulatory authority. Any promotion of the medicine must be consistent with the information contained in the SPC. The product licence/marketing authorisation defines the basis upon which companies may market the relevant product and includes all information which should be made available to health professionals; this is a legally binding document and pharmaceutical companies breach its terms, stray outside it or amend it without regulatory approval at their peril. Depending on its significance, breaching the terms could attract financial or custodial penalties and/or revocation of the product licence/marketing authorisation.

In September 2009, the European Commission issued its latest revision to the guideline on SPC[1].

1 Notice to Applicants, Volume 2C, A Guideline on Summary of Product Characteristics, September 2009, Revision 2.

13.33   Copies of SPCs are made available to healthcare professionals from reference sources such as the Association of the British Pharmaceutical Industry (ABPI) Data Sheet Compendium[1] or monographs which are usually updated annually. In addition, since 1999, SPCs and PILs (see below) have been available to healthcare professionals online at a dedicated website updated daily known as the electronic Medicines Compendium[2]. All information on the website is provided by pharmaceutical companies and is approved by the regulatory authorities.

1   Published by Datapharm Communications Ltd.
2   www.medicines.org.uk/emc/, the medicines information website provided by Datapharm Communications Ltd.

Patient information leaflets

13.34   A patient information leaflet (PIL) is 'a leaflet containing information for the user which accompanies a medicinal product'[1] which provides the patient with key information necessary for the safe and effective use of a medicine. It is not promotional. The language must be simple and non-technical, easily readable and readily understood by lay people. The amount of information that is included calls for a delicate balance between the provision of adequate information to support patients using the medicine appropriately and excessive information that may dilute other important messages in the text. Furthermore, the wording of the PIL should encourage appropriate use and adherence to treatment without giving rise to anxiety or unnecessarily frightening the patient.

1   Directive 92/27/EEC, Article 1.

13.35   With changing attitudes to the provision of information directly to patients, PILs have, over the years, become progressively more detailed. Early guidance issued by the ABPI in 1987/1988 described the role of the PIL as 'to reinforce and amplify the information already given by the doctor and the pharmacist'[1] and to 'improve patient understanding of the use of their medicines'[2]. The focus of early PILs was therefore to remind patients on appropriate usage of the medicine (such as how to take, store and use it). Over time, as increased weight has been placed on the active involvement of patients in decisions regarding their own health, there has been a trend towards the provision of more detailed safety information in PILs. The current requirements are set out in the Human Medicines Regulations 2012[3], Part 13, together with Schs 24 and 27 thereto.

1   ABPI Working Party report dated October 1987.
2   ABPI guidance 'Patient Information: Advice on the drafting of leaflets', March 1998. Revised guidance issued in 1992 described the PIL as an aid to the patient in the correct use of the product.
3   SI 2012/1916.

Pharmacovigilance

13.36   Pharmacovigilance is the term usually applied to post-marketing surveillance of the safety of medicines on the market. There is no universally accepted definition of pharmacovigilance, but the most widely quoted description is the WHO definition of 'the science and activities relating to the detection, assessment, understanding and prevention of adverse effects or any other drug related problems'[1], which encompasses the use of pharmaco-epidemiological studies. The European Medicines Agency (EMA) defines pharmacovigilance as the process of monitoring, evaluating and improving the safety of medicines in use.

1 This term is used in Volume 9A of the Rules Governing Medicinal Products in the European Union: Pharmacovigilance for medicinal products for human use, and the ICH E2E guideline.

13.37   Gradually, pharmacovigilance has begun to involve the assessment of the wider safety of medicines. Pharmacovigilance now also concerns the identification of substandard medicines, medication errors, lack of efficacy, use of medicines for indications that are not approved (off-label use) and for which there is an inadequate scientific basis, case reports of acute and chronic poisoning, assessment of medicine-related mortality, abuse and misuse of medicines and adverse interactions of medicines with chemicals, other medicines and food.

13.38   The medicine development process has its limitations in fully characterising the safety of a new medicine. No new medicine, however rigorously tested, can be guaranteed to be 'safe' and universally effective at the time of its approval. This is the reason for the emphasis on surveillance of the safety of the product during its clinical use after it has been approved for marketing. New and unexpected safety concerns are routinely expected to emerge, and frequently do, after the approval. The safety of an approved medicine may be different when used for a new indication or in different dose forms (because frequently, the safety profile of a medicine may differ following its administration by a different route). Even the most rigorously tested medicines are never without risk.

The regulatory requirements for pharmacovigiliance

13.39   The domestic requirements are contained in the Human Medicines Regulations 2012, Part 11, entitled 'Pharmacovigilance'. These impose dual obligations on both the licensing authority and the UK marketing authorisation holder. The obligations are necessarily broadly stated. The focus is on the maintenance and regular audit of a pharmacovigilance system[1], the reporting and assessment of pharmacovigilance data[2], monitoring data to detect any relevant changes in relation to the product[3], and the submission and assessment of periodic safety update reports (PSURs)[4].

1 See the Human Medicines Regulations 2012, regs 178 and 182.
2 Regulations 185 and 187.
3 Regulations 189 and 190.
4 Regulations 191 and 195.

13.40   The regulatory requirements have developed rapidly since the mid-1990s and today most pharmaceutical manufacturers have large departments devoted to monitoring the safety of the medicines they produce on a worldwide basis. The pharmacovigilance system is overseen by a 'qualified person' who is responsible for ensuring that appropriate procedures and systems are in place. Separate regulatory obligations govern the submission to the authorities of reports of serious ADRs and the preparation and submission of Periodic Safety Update Reports (PSURs) which review the safety experience with marketed products. Information about medicine safety is derived from a number of sources including ADRs and reviews of the published scientific literature. The effect of these systems is that the safety of medicines is kept constantly under review.

Evaluating and communicating risk

13.41 Where, as a result of the surveillance systems outlined above, a signal[1] of a potential hazard emerges, the safety of the medicine should be kept under constant surveillance and its risk/benefit profile regularly re-evaluated, both by the marketing authorisation holder as well as by the regulatory authority. The potential hazard must be identified, confirmed and quantified using all available sources of information. Steps should be taken to investigate potential safety hazards. What action may be appropriate will depend on the particular circumstances and the nature of the hazard, but may range from continuing to monitor adverse event reports to sponsoring studies to investigate the possible hazard (if practicable). The clinical risks are placed in perspective against the benefits of the medicine during an active re-evaluation of the medicine and appropriate action(s) taken.

1 A safety signal is an alert of a potential safety issue based on all available sources, or as in the following WHO definition, based on reporting of individual cases: 'Reported information on a possible causal relationship between an adverse event and a drug, the relationship being unknown or incompletely documented previously. Usually more than a single report is required to generate a signal, depending on the seriousness of the event and the quality of the information' (Safety of Medicines: A guide to detecting and reporting adverse drug reactions, WHO, Geneva 2002).

13.42 There are very few medicines that have been approved and which have not had their prescribing information amended by the regulatory authority and/or voluntarily by the marketing authorisation holder following their routine clinical use. Amendments are frequently necessary because of novel safety issues that have emerged, both qualitative (new safety issue) and/or quantitative (greater than expected prevalence or severity) in nature. Such amendments may take the form of restricting the use, altering (usually downwards) the dose schedule, describing risk factors, recommending specific measures to monitor the patients or elaborating on undesirable effects.

13.43 Depending on the complexity of the issue, the data and the concerns surrounding the issue, it may be necessary for the regulatory authority to set up special ad hoc expert groups to evaluate the data[1]. It is thus possible that, although the risk may have changed only little, or not at all, over a period of time, labelling changes become progressively more detailed and complex as the evidence to support the relevant assessment becomes more reliable.

1 For example, the groups set up to review the safety of hormone replacement therapy, third generation contraceptive pills and drug-induced prolongation of the QT interval of electrocardiogram.

13.44 Where there is a need to communicate safety related information to physicians quickly, the licensing authority may do this in several ways. One is to publish an item in the safety bulletin of the regulatory authority. This was previously known as 'Current Problems in Pharmacovigilance', but was replaced in 2007 by a publication called 'Drug Safety Update'. The other, reserved for more urgent communications, is to send out a 'Dear Doctor' letter. In order to co-ordinate and harmonise their responses to any consequences and queries from stakeholders, this letter can be sent by the regulatory authority (usually the CSM/CHM in the UK) or by the company, but always in collaboration and consultation between the two. However, marketing authorisation holders need the approval of the regulatory authority before they can send out these letters, the text of which also requires regulatory approval.

Reporting of adverse drug reactions by healthcare professionals

13.45 The UK was one of the first two countries in the world to introduce a spontaneous reporting system for gathering data on the safety of medicines in clinical use, the so-called 'Yellow Card Scheme', introduced in 1964. This scheme was originally restricted to receiving reports only from doctors, coroners and dentists, but was extended in April 1997 to include hospital pharmacists. The scheme has now been extended to allow reporting by other healthcare professionals (November 1999 and October 2002) and patients and their carers (January 2005).

13.46 In the UK, healthcare providers have a professional duty to report adverse events by voluntarily submitting these spontaneous reports (on a yellow reporting form[1]), to the regulatory authority and/or to the marketing authorisation holder (but have no legal obligation to do so). In contrast, marketing authorisation holders have a legal obligation (a condition of the granting of a marketing authorisation) to report specific types of adverse reactions that they become aware of to the MHRA via a company 'Yellow Card'.

1 The General Medical Council guidance on Good Medical Practice, para 14(h), states that doctors must report suspected adverse medicine reactions in accordance with the relevant reporting scheme. Similarly, the BMA has issued a guide on adverse event reporting, which states, under Recommendations, that 'It is the professional duty of all healthcare professionals to report all suspected ADRs associated with black triangle products and all serious ADRs associated with established products using the Yellow Card Scheme' (Reporting Adverse Medicine Reactions: A Guide for Healthcare Professionals' (May 2006)).

Reporting of adverse drug reactions by marketing authorisation holders

13.47 Regulations require the marketing authorisation holder to keep the regulatory authority informed of the safety of their products, with criminal and/or regulatory penalties for non-compliance. In the UK, one of the most important provisions in all licences (for the conduct of pre-approval clinical trials as well as for post-approval marketing of medicines) is the requirement that the holder of the licence must inform the licensing authority of any data or information that cast doubt on the safety of the medicinal product[1].

1 See the Human Medicines Regulations 2012, reg 75.

13.48 The reporting obligations have changed over time, but in general marketing authorisation holders have an obligation to report serious[1] unpredictable (later referred to as unexpected) adverse drug reactions on an expedited basis. When reports of adverse drug reactions are received, these are followed up to establish causality, severity, seriousness, outcome and risk factors so as to determine if the ADR is reportable. There are no set procedures for follow up of an adverse event report but it is usually done by whoever (the marketing authorisation holder or the regulatory authority) receives the report first, keeping the other one informed.

1 MAIL 41 defined 'serious' as those reactions which are fatal, life-threatening disabling or incapacitating. MAIL 49 extended the definition to include those that result in hospitalisation or prolong hospitalisation.

Intensive monitoring of medicines

13.49   Since November 1975 (MAIL 10), all new medicines[1] in the UK have been subject to intensive monitoring under the so called 'Black Triangle' scheme, pursuant to which all such new medicines are marked with an inverted black triangle (▼) next to the name of the product in all prescribing and/or promotional material. When the regulatory authority is content with the safety profile gathered during the first 2–4 years, a recommendation is made for the medicine to be removed from intensive monitoring; in essence removing the inverted black triangle (▼). When necessary, because concerns remain after 2–4 years, the duration of the period for requiring the inverted black triangle (▼) may be extended for the product concerned for as long as necessary. Although the black triangle has been in place in the UK for many years, for the first time in other EU countries, the black triangle started appearing in the package leaflets of the medicines concerned from the autumn of 2013. It will not appear on the outer packaging or labelling of medicines[2].

1 The black triangle (▼) may be re-instated in the case of established products having significant new indications or routes of administration and entirely novel combinations of potent medicinal substances. These products are denoted by an asterisk next to the Black Triangle (▼*). Formulations which are novel in terms of release characteristics, salt or chirality may also attract an inverted black triangle (▼).
2 http://www.mhra.gov.uk/Safetyinformation/Howwemonitorthesafetyofproducts/Medicines/BlackTriangleproducts/index.htm.

European requirements

13.50   Similar schemes for the reporting of suspected adverse drug reactions existed in other European countries. However, before 1990 there were significant variations between Member States (and also from other major regulatory regions such as the United States and Japan) in terms of reporting requirements generally. Neither were there any consistent requirements for periodic reporting of adverse events from clinical trials or post-authorisation safety studies. In recognition of the need for a harmonised approach, Directive 93/39/EC[1] introduced a new pharmacovigilance regime. European legislation and guidance issued by the Council for International Organizations of Medical Sciences[2] (CIOMS) has done much to harmonise these national differences in pharmacovigilance.

1 Directive 93/39/EC amended Directive 75/319/EC which had not, until then, included any specific provisions in relation to the reporting of adverse events.
2 CIOMS was set up by WHO and UNESCO in 1949 to provide a forum (known as Working Groups) for academics, regulators and the industry to come together to discuss high

profile scientific, ethical, legal or social issues of mutual interest. Although CIOMS is non-governmental and the final Reports produced by its various Working Groups have no legal or regulatory force, these Reports have ultimately influenced medicine regulation and guidelines promulgated by regulatory authorities.

13.51   In addition to harmonising the rules relating to the reporting of adverse events, Directive 93/39/EC and the UK implementing regulations required the marketing authorisation holder to establish a centralised pharmacovigilance system and to appoint a 'Qualified Person' (QP) with personal responsibility for the establishment and maintenance of that system.

13.52   Directive 93/39/EC also introduced the PSUR[1] which required the marketing authorisation holder to provide to the licensing authority at prescribed intervals, a report on the licensing status of the product in the global market, including detailed information on medicine safety, with a systematic analysis and evaluation of the risk/benefit profile of the product based on cumulative data from all sources, including national and international publications, as well as a report on any consequences in terms of the approved licence particulars. The PSUR included detailed records of all suspected adverse reactions (and not just those that were classified as serious).

The requirements of Directive 93/39/EC were incorporated into UK law by the Medicines for Human Use (Marketing Authorisation etc) Regulations 1994[2].

1 Prior to this date CIOMS guidelines had recommended the preparation of summary safety reports ('International reporting of periodic drug-safety update summaries' (1992)) which foreshadowed PSURs.
2 SI 1994/3144.

13.53   In October 2005, new rules[1] were introduced requiring marketing authorisation holders to prepare a risk management plan prior to the marketing of newly authorised products. Such plans aim to anticipate, and contain measures to manage, any likely risks.

1 Article 8(3)(ia) of Directive 2001/83/EC, as amended by Directive 2004/27/EC, which was required to be implemented into national legislation by 30 October 2005. Implementing requirements set out in Guideline On Risk Management Systems For Medicinal Products For Human Use, November 2005.

13.54   Member States are responsible for enforcing these obligations and monitoring compliance through inspections of marketing authorisation holders. The licensing authority is able to take urgent action, where appropriate, if safety concerns are raised. For example, it can suspend the marketing authorisation for a product or it can issue an 'urgent safety restriction' (USR)[1] to inform healthcare professionals about changes as to how or in what circumstances the medicine may be used. This USR can be formalised by a variation to the authorisation or it can be lifted later if the review of the data so warrants. The licensing authority can take action on a national basis or it can refer the matter to the CHMP for consideration on a Europe wide basis.

1 USRs were initially introduced in relation to marketing authorisation holders by Commission Regulation (EC) No 541/95 of 10 March 1995 concerning the examination of variations to the terms of a marketing authorisation. Commission Regulation (EC) No 1084/2003 of 3 June 2003

gave competent authorities the right to take urgent safety restrictions. This was implemented into the UK by the Medicines for Human Use (Fees and Miscellaneous Amendments) Regulations 2003, SI 2003/2321. Under the Human Medicines Regulations 2012, reg 80, it is an offence if the market authorisation holder fails to implement an urgent safety restriction imposed by the licensing authority. Further, regulation 196 is headed 'Urgent action' and sets out a number of ways in which the licensing authority may take urgent action as a result of the evaluation of data resulting from pharmacovigilance activities.

CLAIMS UNDER THE CONSUMER PROTECTION ACT 1987

The Product Liability Directive

13.55   The Council of Europe began work on a draft Convention on Liability for Defective Products in 1970 but by the time the so-called 'Strasbourg Convention' was open for signature the European Commission had produced its own preliminary draft Directive on the same subject, with the result that many states, including the UK, decided to seek agreement over the Directive before taking any final steps to change their own law. It took a further ten years to finalise the Directive.

13.56   The Directive[1] was adopted under former Article 100 (EEC)[2] on the basis that the differences in the laws of liability on producers in respect of their products had a distorting effect on competition. This legal basis meant that the Directive required unanimous agreement, which requirement necessitated compromises to be reached between the Member States. It also means that the Directive is not solely concerned with the protection of the consumer; it is also fundamentally concerned with competition between producers and the functioning of the common market. Thus, the Directive's first recital asserts that the 'approximation of laws of the Member States concerning the liability of the producer for damage caused by the defectiveness of his products is necessary because the existing divergences may distort competition and affect the movement of goods within the common market'.

1 The full title of which is 'Council Directive of 25th July 1985 on the approximation of the laws, regulations and administrative provisions of the Member States concerning liability for defective products'.
2 Now Article 115 of TFEU, by which directives are issued 'for the approximation of such legal provisions as directly affect the establishment or functioning of the Common Market'. In *Allen v Depuy International Ltd* [2014] EWHC 753 (QB), Stewart J relied upon this basis of the Directive in part of his reasoning for rejecting the extra-territorial scope of the CPA 1987 to consumers who had suffered harm in New Zealand and South Africa. He concluded (para 32(i)): 'I find it difficult to see how Article 115 TFEU could provide a basis for legislating to make EU producers liable to consumers outside the EU. As [the Defendant] submitted, there is no prospect of harmonising the rules in relation to consumers worldwide or to the protection to which those consumers are entitled'.

13.57   The Directive therefore represents a compromise between the interests of the consumer and those of the producer. That compromise was not reached quickly[1]. Much of the history of the debate can be traced through the travaux préparatoires. The initial calls for reform were undoubtedly influenced by the thalidomide experience in the early 1960s and the early proposals leaned towards a policy of absolute liability heavily biased in favour of the consumer[2]. Over time, however, the move against absolute liability gathered momentum, leading to proposals for defences for producers to be introduced into the mix, including what later became the 'development risk defence' (now Article 7(e)). Arguments in favour of the introduction of this defence focused on both equity (how is it possible to justify the manufacturer's liability for a product which at the time it was manufactured was considered not defective in the light of the state of science and technology?[3]) and economic considerations (to extend producer product liability to development risks constitutes a barrier to innovation – particularly in those branches of industry where research and development play an important part). It was argued that absolute liability would impose a very heavy liability on producers, would put a brake on innovation and would push up costs for consumers; equally, it was recognised that innovation was of vital importance for the European economy and that, in the light of the international distribution of labour, Europe must concentrate on technologically advanced products[4]. Ultimately, disagreement on the balance to be struck between the rights of the injured person to receive compensation and the need not to stifle innovation by producers led to a compromise that allows Member States to deviate from the basic provisions of the Directive in certain limited, but important, respects.

1 For further detail on the gestation of the Directive see Stapleton *Product Liability* (1994) pp 45–65; Miller and Goldberg *Product Liability* (2nd edn, 2004), p 211 ff; Whittaker *Liability for Products* (2005) pp 431–440.
2 The Commission's first Proposal for a Council Directive concerning liability for defective products on 9 September 1976, Official Journal C 241/9 of 14.10.76.
3 Report of the Legal Affairs Committee, 17 April 1979, at p 16 para 19 (PE 57.516/fin).
4 Opinion of the Committee on Economic Affairs, 4 November 1977, at pp 26–27.

13.58   The following précis of the evolution of the Directive was provided by Advocate General Tesauro in his Opinion of 23 January 1997 in *Commission v UK*[1], a case brought by the Commission alleging that the UK Government had failed properly to implement the Directive:

'In contrast [to the original Commission Proposal] the Directive as it was adopted by the Council opted for a system of strict liability which was no longer absolute, but limited, in deference to a principle of the fair apportionment of risk between the injured person and the producer, the latter having to bear only quantifiable risks, but not development risks which are, by their nature, unquantifiable. Under the Directive, therefore, in order for the producer to be held liable for defects in the product, the injured party is required to prove the damage, the defect in the product and the causal relationship between defect and damage, but not negligence on the part of the producer… The producer, however, may exonerate himself from liability by proving that the 'state of the art' at the time when he put the product into circulation was not such as to cause the product to be regarded as defective…'.

1 Case C-300/95 at para 19.

13.59   It is the Directive itself which sets the appropriate balance between the competing interests of producers and consumers of defective products. This precludes departures from that balance by a Member State giving greater protection to one such interest. The Directive fixes the position of consumers and suppliers to ensure a level playing-field for business. It therefore precludes any reinterpretation which affects the balance imposed by the Directive.

13.60   In three cases to date the ECJ has ruled unequivocally that Member States are not to be permitted to 'gold plate' or 'over-implement' the Directive so as to impose a greater degree of consumer protection than that provided for by the Directive itself[1]. Two of the cases were brought by the Commission against Member States (France and Greece) alleging failure to implement the Directive properly on the ground that their implementing legislation went further in protecting persons injured by defective products than was permitted by the Directive. The third case involved a preliminary question raised by a Spanish court, in litigation brought by a person who had contracted HIV from blood supplied by the defendant hospital, regarding whether the Directive precluded Member States from restricting rights granted to consumers by legislation which pre-dated the enactment of the Directive.

1 Cf *Commission v France* (C-52/00); *Commission v Greece* (C-154/00); and *Gonzàlez Sanchez v Medicine Asturiana SA* (C-183/00).

13.61   The ECJ ruled in each decision that the Directive not only permitted the restriction of rights for consumers, but in fact required such restriction as a result of the purpose for which the Directive was enacted: '[T]he Directive seeks to achieve, in the matters regulated by it, complete harmonisation of the laws, regulations and administrative provisions of the Member States'[1].

1 *Commission v France* (para 24); *Commission v Greece* (para 20); *Sanchez* (para 23-32). However, as can be seen from the Directive's 18th recital, Directive 85/374 does not seek exhaustively to harmonise the sphere of liability for defective products beyond the matters regulated by it (see ECJ decisions in *Dutrueux and caisse primaire d'assurance maladie du Jura* (Case C-495/10, 21 December 2011) para 21; and *Novo Nordisk Pharma GmbH v S* (Case C-310/13, 20 November 2014), para 24).

13.62   The Directive, in its eventual form, therefore is to be understood to represent a careful balance between the competing interests of consumers, manufacturers and their insurers. This has been repeatedly emphasised by the ECJ in seven decisions concerning the Directive: *Commission v UK*[1], *Commission v France*[2], *Commission v Greece*[3], *Skov AEg v Bilka Lavprisvarehus A/S*[4], *Sanchez v Medicina Asturiana SA*[5], *Commission v France*[6] and *Boston Scientific Medizintechnik GmbH v AOK Sachsen-Anhalt*[7].

1 Case C-300/95 [1995] ECR I-2663.
2 Case C-52/00 [2002] ECR I-3827.
3 Case C-154/00 [2002] ECR I-3879.
4 Case C-402/03 [2006] ECR I-199.
5 Case C-183/00 [2002] ECR I-3901.
6 C-177/04 [2006] ECR I-2461.
7 Case C-503/13 *Boston Scientific Medizintechnik GmbH v AOK Sachsen-Anhalt – Die Gesundheitskasse* [2015] All ER (D) 88 (Mar), ECJ.

13.63   But as Advocate General Tesauro noted in his Opinion in *Commission v UK*[1], the hard-fought battle over the wording of the Directive does not provide all the answers as to the nature and scope of product liability law within the EU; the scope for interpretation as to the proper meaning and effect of the Directive by the courts in giving 'practical implementation' to the Directive remains a key factor:

'In this connection, it is worth pointing out that in the United States the case-law showed a propensity for absolute liability on the part of the producer, especially in the pharmaceuticals sector. However, the "indiscriminate expansion of substantive tort liability" resulting from this case-law, as a result of which there was held to be liability in every case whatever the cost and the state of the art defence was rejected, brought about a crisis on the insurance market which was so serious that some economic activities could no longer obtain insurance cover. Owing to this, there have recently been signs of a reversal of this trend both in the case-law and in legislation and a return to the rules of strict, rather than absolute, liability: see Priest's observations, The current insurance crisis and modern tort law, in 96 Yale Law Journal 1589 (1987); ibid., La controrivoluzione nel diritto di reponsabilità da prodotti negli Stati Uniti di America, in Foro italiano 1989, IV, p. 119 et seq. In the latter article, the author gives a warning to legal circles in Europe which it is well to bear in mind: "The California Supreme Court in Brown and the new legislation of New Jersey have begun to reappraise the premises of the rule of strict liability in the products liability sector. It will be important to see whether, in giving practical implementation to the Community Directive of 25 July 1985, adopting the standard of strict liability twenty-five years after it was introduced in the United States, the European States will accept the original theoretical premises of that system which subsequently caused a crisis in the USA or whether, on the other hand, they will accept the counter-revolution which has just begun"'.

1 At footnote 9 to the 18th paragraph.

13.64   As the Advocate General noted, an appreciation of the genesis of the Directive reveals that much of the political wrangling over the decade leading up to the adoption of the Directive was concerned with this very question, namely whether the Directive should provide for a quasi-absolute liability model, such as that originally adopted by the US, and that, ultimately, such a model was rejected by the European legislature. Given the compromise position which the Directive reflects, it is the role of the courts of Member States to construe the wording of the Directive itself when applying national legislation which implements the Directive, remembering that it is the Directive itself which was intended to strike a balance between the competing policy arguments.

13.65   Accordingly, the recitals to the Directive emphasise that the Directive strikes what is termed 'a fair apportionment of risk'. The broad-textured wording of the Directive, as adopted, requires the national courts of Member States, applying national implementing legislation, to approach product liability claims on a case-by-case basis having regard to all of the circumstances relevant to each case. The result is that national courts are left with very considerable discretion when it comes to assessing the requisite standard of safety – that which a person is entitled to expect the product to provide – on the facts of each case.

13.66   Finally, it is worth noting that although the Directive is frequently referred to, by both commentators and courts, as imposing 'strict liability' on producers, the final balance achieved is perhaps better characterised as a system of 'no fault liability'[1].

1 'Most worrying in the context of a search for rationales to support the alleged shift to stricter liability for products is the ambiguity with which the term 'strict liability' is often used', see generally Jane Stapleton *Product Liability* (1994) pp 6 and 219–230.

13.67   Whilst the Directive brings the legal position of the producer closer to the position of the person who sells a product direct to the consumer, the post-Directive position of a manufacturer of medicinal products in the UK remains more favourable than that of the pharmacist selling a product to the patient, who will be liable in contract, and this remains the subject of considerable comment. While the thalidomide tragedy was the catalyst for proposed changes in the law, it is by no means clear that claimants would have been markedly better off had no fault liability, as now implemented, applied to their claims.

13.68   The Directive envisaged that it could not at that time achieve total harmonisation, so recital 18 recorded that it is 'therefore necessary that the Council receive at regular intervals, reports from the Commission on the application of this Directive, accompanied, as the case may be, by appropriate proposals'. Article 21 therefore requires the Commission to present a report to the Council on the application of the Directive every five years (the last report was in 2011). Nevertheless, the various reviews of the Directive, its provisions and national rights of derogation by the European Commission, have not led to a proposal from the Commission to change any aspect of the law, other than to reverse the exclusion of primary agricultural products from its scope[1]. This is despite intensive lobbying by consumer groups to make it more 'claimant friendly'[2]. In its report of January 2001[3], the Commission observed that, more than a decade after the coming into force of the Directive, it had given rise to few decided cases, either in national courts or the ECJ. It concluded that, since any modifications to the Directive should be grounded on objective factual bases, '… it would be premature to envisage any changes to the current liability system under Directive 85/374'. The most recent Commission reports (of 2006 and 2011) both concluded that the Directive appeared to maintain 'the balance between the producers' interests and consumer interests as regards liability for defective products. The Commission takes the view that the differences that may arise do not create significant trade barriers or distort competition in the European Union' and made no proposals for change[4].

1 The reviews and reports are: (i) EC Commission First Report (1995): 'First Report on the Application of the Council Directive on the Approximation of Laws, Regulations and Administrative Provisions of the Member States concerning Liability for Defective Products (85/374/EEC)' Com(95)617 final (13 Dec 1995); (ii) EC Commission Green Paper (1999) 'Liability for Defective Products' Com(1999)396 final (28 Jul 1999); (iii) EC Commission Second Report (2001) 'Report from the Commission on the Application of Directive 85/374 on Liability for Defective Products' Com/2000/0893 final (2001); (iv) Lovells Report (2003) 'Product Liability in the European Union: a Report for the European Commission' (Feb 2003); (v) Fondazione Roselli Report (2004) 'Analysis of the Economic Impact of the Development Risk Clause as provided by Directive 85/374/EEC on Liability for Defective Products' (April 2004); (vi) EC Commission Third Report (2006) 'Third report on the application of Council Directive on the approximation of laws [etc]' COM(2006) 496 final (14 Sept 2006); (vi) EC Commission Fourth Report (2011) 'Fourth report on the application of Council Directive on the approximation of laws [etc]' COM(2011) 547 final (8 Sept 2011).
2 EC Commission First Report (1995).
3 EC Commission Second Report (2001).
4 See EC Commission Fourth Report (2011) at p 11.

Consumer Protection Act 1987

Construing the CPA 1987

13.69   The Directive (Council Directive 85/374/EEC) is an instrument of EU law. The provisions of a directive may not be invoked in litigation between private parties as the direct source of an obligation imposed on one party and a correlative right conferred upon the other (sometimes called the rule of 'no horizontal direct effect'). As between private parties, the provisions of the Directive provide no cause of action enforceable at the suit of the claimant. It is the national implementing legislation which, in each Member State, provides the individual claimant with his cause of action against a producer.

13.70 The CPA 1987 was enacted on 15 May 1987, and Part 1 came into force on 1 March 1988. The Act follows the text of the Directive closely in most respects:

'... where any damage is caused wholly or partly by a defect in a product, every person to whom subsection (2) below applies shall be liable for the damage (section 2(1))

...there is a defect in a product for the purposes of this Part if the safety of the product is not such as persons generally are entitled to expect; and for those purposes '*safety*', in relation to a product, shall include safety with respect to products comprised in that product and safety in the context of risks of damage to property, as well as in the context of risks of death or personal injury (section 3)

13.71 Section 1(1) of the Act provides that the CPA 1987 'shall have the effect for the purpose of making such provision as is necessary in order to comply with the Product Liability Directive and shall be construed accordingly.' Section 1(1) of the CPA 1987 therefore reinforces the assumption, which would follow from the duty of sincere cooperation, that Parliament intended to implement the Directive fully and correctly.

13.72 In *A v National Blood Authority*[1], the parties concentrated on the terms of the Directive, on the basis that insofar as the wording of the CPA 1987 differs from the equivalent Articles in the Directive, it should not be construed differently from the Directive. Consequently, the court agreed that 'the practical course was to go straight to the fount, the Directive itself'[2]. Whilst the pragmatism of this approach is undoubtedly attractive, as a matter of law, the English court must seek to construe the CPA 1987 in light of the wording and the purpose of the Directive, but, ultimately, it is the law as set out in the CPA 1987 which must be applied[3]. If the court, applying the proper principles of statutory interpretation under English law, were to find that any provision of the CPA 1987 was in conflict with or deviated from the intention of the Directive such that the two were irreconcilable, then the court would have to give effect to the wording of the CPA; it would not be open to the court to ignore the statutory provision, *contra legem*, and apply the wording of the Directive[4].

1 [2001] Lloyd's Rep Med 187.
2 [2001] Lloyd's Rep Med 187, at para 2.
3 See further 'Product liability and the effect of directive' (2001) 26 EL Rev (June) 213, where Professor Anthony Arnull, Barber Professor of Jurisprudence at Birmingham University and consultant editor of the *European Law Review*, described Burton J's approach as putting the position 'too strongly': 'The interpretation of provisions of national law is a matter for the competent national courts, subject to compliance with their duty to perform that task, as far as possible, in the light of the wording and the purpose of relevant provisions of Community law.'
4 This factor may be of particular importance where a court is concerned with construing those provisions of the CPA 1987 which seek to deal with the interface between the application of the CPA 1987 and other statutes; see, for example, CPA 1987, s 6(3) concerning the application of the Congenital Disabilities (Civil Liability) Act 1976, s 1.

Products affected

13.73   Pursuant to s 50(7), the CPA 1987 does not apply to a product supplied to another in the course of the producer's business before the Act came into force on 1 March 1988; this provision refers to the actual product that caused the injury and not to the date the first product of that description was put into circulation by the producer.

13.74   The title 'Consumer Protection Act' is something of a misnomer. A claimant does not have to be a consumer to claim under the Act and the product does not have to be a consumer product. In a personal injury claim there is no 'consumer' requirement of any type[1].

1 The sole 'consumer' restriction applies in cases of property damage; CPA 1987, s 5(3) (and see Article 9 of the Directive) provides that a person will not be liable for loss of or damage to any property which, at the time it was lost or damaged was not '(a) of a description of property ordinarily intended for private use, occupation or consumption and (b) intended by the person suffering the loss or damage mainly for his own private use, occupation or consumption'.

13.75   Not only all finished medicinal products, but also any component part or raw material, fall within the definition of 'a product' under the CPA 1987. Moreover, the Act will impact upon any natural product (eg herbal or blood product) which, while not strictly 'manufactured' still has 'essential characteristics' attributable to an industrial or other process[1]. It does not affect the manufacturer's liability just because the product is given away as a sample or is a research product, even if supplied free of charge, provided the product was supplied to another in the course of business (see CPA 1987, s 4(1)(c)). Nor would it be a good reason to conclude that a product was not supplied in the course of business just because it was supplied to a medical research charity or body such as the Medical Research Council. In contrast, where a product is stolen, the producer has a defence because he did not 'supply' the product. Equally, injury due to exposure to products or raw materials in the workplace prior to the putting of the product into circulation will continue to be governed by existing laws.

1 *A v National Blood Authority* [2001] Lloyd's Rep Med 187.

13.76   The CPA 1987 does not apply in respect of consumers who suffer damage outside the EEA and who have no connection with the EEA and where marketing and supply of the defective product was outside the EEA. Thus, in *Allen v Depuy*[1], Stewart J rejected the argument that the CPA 1987 could apply to patients who had suffered adverse reactions to hip implants which had been designed and manufactured in England. None of the patients had any connection with England: the hip implant operations were all undertaken in South Africa or New Zealand and all symptoms, revisions and treatment sustained by the claimants were outside England. This part of the judgment was *obiter*, because Stewart J concluded that English law did not apply to that case as a matter of private international law. However, had English law been applicable, he held that the CPA 1987 would not have applied. His reasons in summary were: (i) that it was difficult to see how Art 115 TFEU could provide a basis for legislating to make EU producers liable to consumers outside the EU; (ii) that there was nothing in the language of the CPA 1987 or the Directive to suggest territorial effect beyond the UK/

EU/EEA; and (iii) the facts of the present cases were simply insufficiently connected to the EEA to bring the claims within the scope of the CPA 1987[2].

1 [2014] EWHC 753 (QB).
2 For the subsequent decision regarding whether claims for compensatory damages were recoverable under New Zealand law, see [2015] EWHC 926 (QB), per Simler J.

Persons liable

13.77 Liability under the CPA 1987 is imposed on 'producers'. Whereas fault liability focuses upon the conduct of the manufacturer and asks whether it was reasonable, the CPA 1987 focuses upon the product, and imposes liability on the manufacturer if the product was defective and if none of the statutory defences are applicable. The producer may be anyone from a major pharmaceutical company to a hospital pharmacist making up a limited amount of product from bought-in materials[1]. It also follows that a company manufacturing under contract for the product licence holder may be subject to liability, regardless of its lack of involvement in research and development of the product. It may therefore be more exposed than when its liability was governed only by negligence principles and it must carefully consider the terms of its supply contracts. Similar considerations apply to persons manufacturing and supplying under licence, but essentially relying upon the licensor's know-how.

1 C-203/99 *Veedfald v Amstkommune* [2001] ECR I-3569.

13.78 The manufacture of medicinal products frequently involves several different stages from preparation of the basic product to final assembly and packaging of the finished dosage form. Neither the Directive nor the CPA 1987 defines precisely what constitutes an act of manufacture but there is obviously a risk that anyone involved in preparing the finished dosage form could be joined in proceedings as a 'manufacturer'. This could include a person putting a product manufactured by another into a 'blinded' dosage form for use in a clinical trial sponsored by such person. It is less clear that a person merely packaging the product would be treated as a manufacturer as his 'product' is not comprised in another (see CPA 1987, s 1(2)), although he might be liable in negligence for defects in the packaging he supplied that rendered the final product defective[1]. The ECJ in *O'Byrne v Sanofi Pasteur MSD Ltd*[2] considered that a product left the 'manufacturing' process operated by the producer when it entered 'a marketing process in the form in which it is offered to the public in order to be used or consumed.' This suggests that packaging, including inserting appropriate product information, might be regarded as part of the process of manufacture.

1 For the purposes of labelling with the manufacturer's name, Directive 92/27/EEC defines manufacturer in a way that encompasses both total and partial manufacture and various processes of packaging.
2 Case C-127/04 *Declan O'Byrne v Sanofi Pasteur MSD Ltd and Sanofi Pasteur SA* [2006] ECR I-1313.

13.79 Primary liability is extended beyond the manufacturer himself and embraces any person who by putting his name, trademark, or other distinguishing feature on the product (eg 'brand-naming') represents himself to be the producer. Any person who imports a product into the EU for supply in the course of a business is also deemed to be a producer so that the injured person does not have to commence litigation outside the EU in order to seek compensation. Finally, where the injured person cannot identify the producer of the product, the person who supplied the product to the injured person is treated as the producer unless he is able within a reasonable time to answer the request of the injured person to identify one or more of the persons who fall within the definition of 'producer' of the product or at least the person who supplied him with the product (see CPA 1987, s 2(2) and s 46 for the definition of a supplier). The Advocate-General in *O'Byrne* thought that what was required by the Directive was merely that the supplier should identify his supplier or the ultimate producer 'immediately he is sued'. His opinion left open the question of whether the CPA 1987 is consistent with the Directive in inserting the requirement that a request first be made for the supplier to identify the producer or his supplier.

13.80   Once in receipt of the identity of the immediate supplier, the claimant may repeat his request until he either establishes the identity of the producer or importer or finds a supplier unable to identify his immediate supplier, who may then be treated as though he were the producer. The implication is that retailers and wholesalers supplying generic products sourced from a variety of companies could be exposed to liability if they do not keep adequate records. Such records may have to be kept for much longer than ten years, after which a consumer's rights under the CPA 1987 are extinguished (see Article 11 of the Directive and the CPA 1987, Sch 1, para 1), since the national systems of procedural law of Member States may allow potential defendants to remain ignorant of the fact of a claim for some years after it is made[1].

1 For example in the Republic of Ireland where claims may be issued but not served for several years on the basis of successive applications made ex parte.

13.81   It follows that more than one person in the chain of supply of medicinal products may be liable under the CPA 1987 for the same injury. The manufacturer of the finished product, the manufacturer of any defective raw material and the product licence holder importing the product from outside the EU may all be exposed and will be liable on a joint and several basis (ie the injured person can sue any of them and recover full compensation) but that liability is without prejudice to national rights of contribution or indemnity between each person liable (see CPA 1987, s 2(5) and Article 5 of the Directive).

13.82   Many medicinal products are imported from outside the EU and arguably under fault liability the importer would only be exposed in very limited circumstances (for example, in respect of patent defects in the product), but not those where special research or testing to confirm safety would be necessary. In contrast, under the CPA 1987 the importer may be liable to pay compensation to the injured person and rely upon a right to recover indemnity from his foreign supplier through specific contractual provision or by operation of law. Such indemnities may be of equal importance to 'own-branders'. However, it is not clear whether a company procuring the manufacture of medicinal products to his own specification and applying his own brand name can avoid the implicit representation that he is the manufacturer by stating elsewhere in the labelling that the product was manufactured by another or merely 'manufactured specially for him'. Suffice it to say, this provision worried pharmacists sufficiently for the Pharmaceutical Society to seek an assurance from the Department of Health that dispensing from bulk (which under the Medicines Act labelling legislation requires the pharmacist to label the container with his name and address) would not expose the pharmacist to liability as if he were a producer. The Department did not believe that the Society had cause for concern, but it is notable that the manufacturing/marketing interface was placed by the ECJ in *O'Byrne*[1] at the point at which the product is in its final form, as offered to the public. Certainly this provision is very likely to be of importance to the major supermarkets and retail chemist chains whose product 'get-up' is designed to foster brand identity and where statements qualifying the inference that the product is their own are not prominent. In fact, requirements relating to labelling of all medicinal products (including dispensed products) and package leaflets require all products to have leaflets noting the name and address of the manufacturer (as well as the product licence-holder) unless this information appears on the outer packaging or on the immediate packaging[2].

1 Case C-127/04 *Declan O'Byrne v Sanofi Pasteur MSD Ltd and Sanofi Pasteur SA* [2006] ECR I-1313.
2 Directive 2001/83/EC, OJ L 311 28/11/2001, see Article 58.

The concept of 'defect'

13.83 The cornerstone of the Directive is the definition of a defective product (see Article 6(1)), which reads:

'A product is defective when it does not provide the safety which a person is entitled to expect taking all circumstances into account including:

    (a) the presentation of the product
    (b) the use to which it could reasonably be expected that the product would be put
    (c) the time when the product was put into circulation.'

13.84 Thus the Directive provides for a single catholic definition of a defect, having regard to its lack of safety and not to its fitness for purpose[1], which is intended to be applicable to any and every 'movable' product which is commercially supplied[2]. As the scope of the Directive is not limited to 'consumer products'[3], the product safety standard provided by Article 6 of the Directive must be capable of being applied to all moveable products from common or garden products to the most highly specialised, complex and unusual of products.

1 As emphasised by the 6th recital to the Directive: 'to protect the physical well-being and property of the consumer, the defectiveness of the product should be determined by reference not to its fitness for use but to the lack of the safety which the public at large is entitled to expect'.
2 The original 1985 Directive's definition of 'product' in Article 2 excluded primary agricultural products and game, although individual Member States were permitted to derogate from Article 2 by including those matters within the definition of 'product' (pursuant to former Article 15(1)(a)). This was amended in 1999 by Directive 1999/34, as a result of the BSE crisis in the mid-1990s, so that the current definition of 'product' no longer excludes primary agricultural products and game.
3 The only 'consumer' restriction is in relation not to the type of product, but in a case of property damage, to the type of property which is damaged (see Article 9). In the case of a claim for personal injury, therefore, there is no 'consumer' element requirement at all.

13.85 The definition of the safety standard provided by the Article 6 test of 'defect' is therefore framed in broad terms. As part of the reviews of the Directive undertaken on behalf of the Commission in accordance with Article 21 of the Directive, consideration has been given as to whether the concept of defect might be defined with greater precision, but it has been recognised that any such greater precision might restrict the ability of national courts to deal with claims under the Directive on a case-by-case basis[1].

1 See Lovells Report (2003) (pp 48–49).

13.86 The standard of safety which a person is 'entitled to expect' is a principle which is incapable of precise definition, just as concepts of 'negligence' and 'fault' have always escaped precise definition. The court is bound to take account of *all* the circumstances. This presumably means all *relevant* circumstances and requires the court to determine what is and what is not relevant. Article 6 also provides for certain mandatory circumstances to be taken into account which it comes to the exercise of the court's objective judgment in setting the appropriate safety standard; among those circumstances, it is bound to have regard to the matters listed under points (a) to (c) of Article 6(1); and, pursuant to Article 6(2), the court must not find a given product to be defective for the sole reason that a better product has subsequently been put into circulation.

13.87 Within these broad horizons, however, the open-textured character of the prescribed safety standard provides the court with a very considerable degree of flexibility in relation to the matters to which it can properly have regard so as to enable it to perform its duty, on a case-by-case basis, of ensuring that the appropriate safety standard is set on as fully an informed basis as possibly having regard to the facts pertaining to the specific product in question.

13.88 One reading of Article 6(1) is that the court steps into the shoes of the notional 'person' and that, through the eyes of that notional person, takes all circumstances into account when assessing the safety which he, that notional person, is entitled to expect of the product in question. An alternative reading is that it is the court which must take all circumstances into account in determining the level of safety which the notional person is entitled to expect the product to provide and that no issue of imputing any particular knowledge to that notional person arises. It is submitted that the latter reading is to be preferred as a matter of construction.

13.89 Section 3(1) of the CPA 1987 is cast in different terms to Article 6 of the Directive. Section 3(1) provides that 'there is a defect in a product for the purposes of this Part if the safety of the product is not such as persons generally are entitled to expect' and then CPA 1987, s 3(2) provides that 'in determining for the purpose of subsection (1) above what persons generally are entitled to expect in relation to a product all the circumstances shall be taken into account…'.

13.90 There are clear differences between the English language version of the Directive and the manner in which it has been transposed into English law by the CPA 1987. The first obvious difference is the Directive's use, in Article 6, of 'a person' as against the CPA's use of 'persons generally'.

13.91 Second, whilst the wording of the Directive uses a single fluid definition of 'defect', namely that the product must provide 'the safety which a person is entitled to expect, taking all circumstances into account,…', the CPA 1987 deals with defect in two stages: (i) a product is defective if it does not have the safety which persons generally are entitled to expect and (ii) all circumstances shall be taken into account (by the court) when determining the safety that persons generally are entitled to expect.

13.92 The difference in the wording and structure of the test between the Directive and the CPA 1987 poses the question as to whether the test provided by the Directive has been accurately transposed into domestic law by the CPA 1987 or whether there are any material differences.

It is suggested that the CPA's rendering of 'persons generally' is consistent with the meaning of the Directive as long as that term is understood consistently with the sense carried by an indefinite pronoun; in other words, it is a reference to a non-existent notional person – 'one' and not a reference to the actual general public[1].

1 It is also to be noted that the 7th recital to the Directive refers to the safety standard which the 'public at large' is entitled to expect (close to the CPA 1987 wording of 'persons generally'), rather than 'a person'.

13.93 The court must set the safety standard on a fully informed basis having regard to all the circumstances and no circumstances should be left out of the equation on the basis that the notional person might not possess knowledge of relevant circumstances. In the context of prescription medicines, it is suggested that regard must necessarily be had to the circumstances pertaining to the class of patients prescribed with the medicine.

13.94 The emphasis of the test should be firmly placed on the question as to the standard of safety which persons generally are *entitled* to expect the product in question to provide[1]. Thus, this moves the test away from the court attempting to make any assumptions or findings about the information or knowledge which persons generally (in the sense of the actual general public) may or may not have about the product in question.

1 It is suggested that the correct approach to the test of defect is to focus on what the consumer is *entitled* to expect: see further Stapleton 'Restatement (Third) of Torts: Product Liability, an Anglo-American Perspective' (2000) 39 Washburn LJ 363, 377; Miller and Goldberg *Product Liability* (2nd edn) para 10.22; and Stapleton, 'Liability for Drugs in the US and EU: Rhetoric and Reality' (2007) 26 Rev Litig 991–1033 in which she refers throughout to the issue as one of '*legal entitlement*' (see eg 1008).

13.95 The test is not a jury question to be determined by reference to the views of the man on the Clapham omnibus. Rather, the phrases 'a person' and 'persons generally' are all short-hand terms intended to convey the requirement for the court to determine the objective standard of safety which 'one', in the sense of the notional person, is entitled, as a matter of law, to expect the product in question to provide[1]. Unlike the man on the Clapham omnibus, in determining the safety to which persons generally are entitled to expect, the court has the benefit of the totality of the evidence relating to '*all circumstances*' which the parties are able to put before it. This is a privileged position which enables the court to take into account information which extends well beyond the knowledge of any actual, or notionally reasonable, individual.

1 But see also the ECJ's reference to 'the reasonable expectations of the public at large' in its ruling in Case C-503/13 *Boston Scientific Medizintechnik GmbH v AOK Sachsen-Anhalt – Die Gesundheitskasse* [2015] All ER (D) 88 (Mar), ECJ.

13.96   It is submitted therefore that it is wrong to characterise the task of the court as the expectation of an 'informed bystander' or by describing the judge as 'an informed representative of the public at large'. The latter suggestion by the German academic, Dr Harald Bartl, was referred to with approval by Burton J in *A v National Blood Authority*[1], but it is a formulation which, it is submitted, is apt to lead a court into error: the court should not assume the position of the public at large and should not concern itself with what knowledge should be imputed to the public at large or what knowledge should be deemed to be possessed by the public at large.

1 At para 31 (see also para 56).

13.97   Thus, it is submitted that a degree of caution should be applied to the decision of Burton J in *A v National Blood Authority* wherein, when expressing his conclusion as to the 'legitimate expectation' of the public, he placed considerable weight on what in his belief consumers actually would or would not expect in relation to the purity of blood products[1]. Having quoted Dr Bartl, Burton J went on to state that:

'... in my judgement it is impossible to inject into the consumer's legitimate expectation matters which would not by any stretch of the imagination be in his actual expectation. He will assume perhaps that there are tests, but his expectations will be as to the safeness of the blood. In my judgment it is inappropriate to propose that the public should not "expect the unattainable" in the sense of tests or precautions which are impossible – at least unless it is informed as to what is unattainable or impossible, as it is to reformulate the expectation as one that the producer will not have been negligent or will have taken all reasonable steps...'

1 At paras 55 and 56. It is, however, to be noted that elsewhere Burton J did expressly recognise that the level of safety below which a product must fall to qualify as defective is 'not what is actually expected by the public at large, but what they are entitled to expect' (para 26). Burton J also went on to suggest obiter that 'drugs with advertised side effects' may fall into a category of products which have harmful characteristics such that 'no complaint may be made' because no-one can legitimately expect from them a degree of safety that they do not and cannot possess (para 28).

13.98   As set out above, it is submitted that the standard of safety is not to be set by reference to the *actual* expectations of the notional consumer. The court should not seek to assume the role of an informed user of the product. It is not through the eyes of the user that one determines the objective standard of safety, albeit that the objective standard necessarily has regard to the circumstances pertaining to the user. The safety standard is to be set according to the safety which persons generally are *entitled* to expect the product to provide. It may well be correct, depending on the circumstances, to conclude that persons are not entitled to expect a product to provide a level of safety which that type of product simply cannot provide. It is the role of the judge to have regard to factors which might not be within the actual contemplation of the consumer. It is in this regard that the reference to the phrase 'legitimate expectation' is inapposite and potentially misleading.

'Legitimate expectation' in the context of administrative law may indeed be concerned with 'actual' expectations, but that is not the test provided for by the scheme of the Directive and the CPA 1987[1].

1 However, it is to be noted that in the recent ECJ ruling in Case C-503/13 *Boston Scientific Medizintechnik GmbH v AOK Sachsen-Anhalt – Die Gesundheitskasse* [2015] All ER (D) 88 (Mar), ECJ, at para 37, the court referred to recital 6 of the Directive as requiring the assessment of defect to be carried out having regard to the 'reasonable expectations of the public at large', albeit that at para 38 it is clear that the test is one of the safety which 'the public at large is entitled to expect'; see also the Opinion of the Advocate General in that case, particularly paras 28–30.

13.99   In summary, it is submitted that the following points as to the test of 'defect' can be drawn from the English text of the Directive and are reflected in the CPA 1987:

- the test sets an objective standard: the issue of defect is not to be determined by reference to the level of safety which a particular claimant considers that the product should provide;
- the language emphasises the depersonalised and objective nature of the judgment that has to be made as to the appropriate safety standard;
- the language emphasises the concept of legal *entitlement*. The test is not concerned with the level of safety which a person, or persons generally, or the public at large, *actually expect* or anticipate that the product provides or *ought* to provide. In other words, the test is not concerned with discerning the views in fact held (legitimately or otherwise) by a person, a consumer, the general public, or any sub-set of the general public, but rather is concerned with the safety which a notional person – 'one' – is legally *entitled* to expect the product to provide;
- the Directive does not use the term 'legitimate expectation'[1]. Rather, the emphasis is on the safety standard to which a person, or the public at large, is 'entitled'[2]; the concept of 'legitimate expectation' may, potentially, be misleading;
- there is no textual basis for any suggestion that any relevant circumstances should be left out of account, whether by reason of the fact that those circumstances might not be known to 'persons generally' or should not be imputed to 'a person' or for any other reason.

1 This was the phrase adopted by Burton J in the hepatitis C litigation: '... 'Legitimate expectation', rather than 'entitled expectation' appeared to all of us to be a more happy formulation (and is analogous to the formulation in other languages in which the directive is published)' (at para 31). But there is no further explanation in the judgment to support the assertion that 'legitimate expectation' is analogous to the formulation in other languages. The wording of the Directive requires the court to determine the standard of safety to which a person is entitled and it is submitted that the question of legal entitlement is the critical test. Substituting that test with one of 'legitimate expectation', which places the emphasis on expectation rather than entitlement is potentially unhelpful and misleading; cf the ECJ's ruling in Case C-503/13 *Boston Scientific Medizintechnik GmbH v AOK Sachsen-Anhalt – Die Gesundheitskasse* [2015] All ER (D) 88 (Mar), ECJ and the footnote to para **13.98**.
2 Article 6(1).

The formulation of the alleged defect

13.100   The burden is on the claimant to prove that a product is defective. To do so, the claimant must demonstrate that the product did not provide the safety which persons generally are entitled to expect taking all circumstances into account. The test is to be determined at the material time, which will almost invariably be at the time that the producer put the product into circulation[1].

1 Article 6(1)(c); CPA 1987, s 3(2)(c).

13.101   The way in which the allegation of defect is formulated has to be very carefully considered by claimants and defendants and the court. It is essential that the same definition of the defect is maintained consistently for the purpose of analysing each of the following issues of law and fact that fall for determination in any particular case[1]:

- in relation to defect – whether there is a defect in the product pursuant to Article 6/s 3;
- in relation to causation – whether the same alleged defect caused the damage alleged;
- in relation to any defence – for example, whether the same defect was not capable of being discovered at the material time for the state of the art defence provided by Article 7(e)/s 4(1)(c)[2].

1 It is to be noted that the judgment of Burton J in *A v National Blood Authority* [2001] Lloyd's Rep Med 187 has been the subject of academic criticism for failing to maintain a consistent definition of the defect alleged in that case. Professor Stapleton has commented 'For the purposes of Article 6, the judge allowed each claimant to define the 'defect' in the stand-alone sense of the simple physical state of the individual product, namely the virus in the blood in the individual bag that the claimant received, and not the risk in all bags... Yet for the purpose of Article 7(e) Justice Burton used a different formulation of 'defect', namely the generic risk in all bags. He asserts 'if there is known risk, ie the existence of the defect is known'... This approach not only offends basic rules of consistency in statutory interpretation, but if the 'defect' is formulated as the mere generic risk of infection the claimants cannot establish the causal relationship between defect and damage as required by Article 4 of the Directive: the risk of infection does not cause infection...' in Stapleton 'Liability for Drugs in the US and EU: Rhetoric and Reality' (2007) 24 Rev Litig 991.
2 In *Hufford v Samsung Electronics (UK) Ltd* [2014] EWHC 2956 (TCC), HHJ David Grant rejected, in respect of a fire claim, the proposition that the claimant had to specify with accuracy or precision the defect in the product that he seeks to establish. It was enough that he proved the existence of a defect in broad or general terms such as 'a defect in the electrics of the motor car'. It is submitted that whilst this may be a permissible approach to adopt in relation to cases such as fire claims arising out of electrical goods which have been destroyed, in cases involving medicinal products as a matter of practice claimants will be required to particularise the defect in the product with greater specificity, not least because the claimant always bears the burden of proof in relation to the existence of a defect and causation.

The circumstances to be taken into account

13.102   The test of defect is not a test of absolute safety. Safety is a relative concept and this is recognised by the provision of a suitably flexible test. Both Article 6 of the Directive and the CPA 1987, s 3 *require* the court to take 'all circumstances' into account; the CPA 1987 uses the mandatory 'shall'. Among those circumstances, the court is bound to include, and perhaps have particular regard to, the matters listed under Article 6(1)(a)–(c). However, the list is non-exhaustive, as clearly indicated by the word 'including'[1]. The illustrative list provided by s 3(2)(a)–(c) is more expansive than that provided by the Directive, but it is submitted that the two provisions are compatible in all material respects.

1 As Burton J observes, para 34 of his judgment in *A v National Blood Authority* [2001] Lloyd's Rep Med 187, the French text uses the word 'notamment' and the German text uses the word 'inbesondere' both of which can be translated at 'in particular' or 'especially'. Both terms, like

'including', connote a non-exhaustive list. We are aware of no support for the assertion that the examples should be construed *ejusdem generis*.

13.103 Despite the mandatory requirement of the Directive and the CPA 1987 to take into account 'all circumstances', it is apparent that there may still be debate as to whether it is nevertheless impermissible to take certain circumstances into account. In *A v National Blood Authority*, Burton J determined that the words 'all the circumstances', whilst not exclusive, were not unlimited: they were to be considered as all *relevant* circumstances. He concluded that the first stage in assessing defectiveness was to identify the harmful characteristic which caused the injury. The next step was to decide whether the product was 'standard' (performing as intended by the producer) or 'non-standard' (differing from the standard product because of the inclusion of a harmful characteristic by reason, for example, of a manufacturing or process design defect)[1] – a categorisation which he preferred to the traditional tripartite categorisation of 'design defect' 'manufacturing defect' 'warnings defect'. In the case of non-standard products, Burton J stated:

'…I conclude that the following are not relevant [circumstances]: (i) avoidability of the harmful characteristic – ie impossibility or unavoidability in relation to precautionary measures; (ii) the impracticability, cost or difficulty of taking such measures; and (iii) the benefit to society or utility of a product (except in the context of whether – with *full information* and *proper knowledge* – the public does and ought to accept the risk)'[2].

Burton J concluded that blood infected with hepatitis C was non-standard; that the public had not taken it to be socially acceptable for non-standard units of blood to infect patients with hepatitis C (the knowledge of the medical profession being irrelevant to that consideration); that the public at large were entitled to expect that the blood transfused to them would be free from infection; and that the blood which infected each of the claimants was therefore defective for the purpose of Article 6.

1 Paragraph 36.
2 Paragraph 68.

13.104 It is important to recognise that the court in *A v National Blood Authority* was dealing with a process design issue – a 'non-standard product'[1] – but even so, Burton J's exclusion of circumstances which he deemed impermissible to take into account has, without doubt, proved highly controversial[2]. When it comes to 'standard' products, it is exceedingly difficult to see how risk/utility (risk/benefit) or the 'unavoidability' of a risk of harm could properly be considered to be irrelevant circumstances[3]. Nowhere is this clearer than in relation to medicinal products which may, at the same time, be life-saving as well as posing serious, unavoidable, risks to certain patients[4]. Indeed, in the case of a regulated product such as a medicinal product, the risk/benefit assessment is, *de facto*, a requirement imposed by the legislature (initially by Parliament and now at an EU level) as a pre-condition of obtaining the necessary marketing authorisation.

1 Burton J noted the potentially different issues arising in relation to 'standard' products: 'I can accept that resolution of the problem of the defective standard product will be more complex than in the case of a non-standard product…' at para 73.
2 See, for example, Miller and Goldberg *Product Liability* (2nd edn) para 10.86, p 385; Fairgrieve and Howells 'Rethinking Product Liability: A Missing Element in the European Commission's

Third Review of the European Product Liability Directive' (2007) 70(6) MLR 962 at 968; Stapleton 'Bugs in Anglo-American Products Liability' 53 South Carolina LR 1225 at 1251.
3 In relation to a 'standard product' Burton J suggested, obiter, that it was 'obviously relevant' to compare any other comparative products, but that 'there is no room in the basket for (i) what the producer should have done differently; and (ii) whether the producer could or could not have done the same as the others did' (para 71). It is not clear what a comparison of alternative products achieves other than to provide a surrogate marker for what a producer should or could have done differently in designing his product and/or a surrogate marker for a 'risk/utility' analysis.
4 Professor Stapleton makes the point by reference to aspirin: '… But if we ignore the overall social utility of the standard product, which in the case of aspirin is universally acknowledged to be massive, how can aspirin's nondefectiveness be established given that, from the perspective of the victim, its cost outweighed its benefit? The court's attempt to bridge this gap in its approach is the mere assertion that "standard products, if compared at all, will be compared with other products on the market". But this is, of course, a utility measure: a product's defectiveness being measured by any availability substitutes on the market that have more successfully avoided the risk!' 'Bugs in Anglo-American Products Liability' 53 South Carolina LR 1225 at 1251.

13.105 It is also difficult to see how a prohibition on the consideration of the risk/benefit profile of a medicinal product in the assessment of the safety which people are entitled to expect fits with the words of CPA 1987, s 3(2)(a) namely 'the purposes for which the product has been marketed'. These words must, on any proper construction, include the primary purpose for which a medicinal product is marketed: for the potential benefits that they provide for healthcare. It is the role of the regulatory authority to manage the inherent and unavoidable risks posed by medicines and to ensure that such products provide a level of safety which is acceptable to society. It is submitted that such factors must fall squarely within the circumstances which the court is expressly obliged to take into account.

13.106 It is also to be noted that Burton J accepted that regard should be had to the issue of the social acceptability of risks posed by certain products[1]. He found that the risk of blood being infected with hepatitis C was not known by the consumer, that there was no 'public understanding or acceptance of the infection of transfused blood by hepatitis C' and that 'it was certainly, in my judgment, not known and accepted by society that there was such a risk which was thus not 'sozialadäquat' (socially acceptable).' Thus, he concluded blood was not the kind of product which by its very nature carried a risk, inherent and generally known, which 'consumers can be taken to have chosen to expose themselves to in order to benefit from the product'[2]. But he expressly recognised that 'drugs with advertised side-effects may fall into this category'[3].

1 Ian Kennedy J seems to have adopted this approach in *Richardson v LRC Products Ltd* [2000] Lloyd's Rep Med 280, in which he concluded that a split condom was not defective, finding that 'Naturally enough the user's expectation is that a condom will not fail. There are no claims made by the defendants that one will never fail and no-one has ever supposed that any method of contraception intended to defeat nature will be 100 per cent effective.'
2 Paragraph 55, citing Professor Howells.
3 Paragraph 31.

13.107 Whilst questions of 'social acceptability' may well have a part to play in relation to a consideration of 'all the circumstances', the concept may perhaps be of only limited assistance in many cases. In particular, social acceptability depends upon the level of knowledge that the public might have in relation to a particular product. The general public come into regular contact with products such as knives, or matches, or gas and may be taken to accept the risks posed by such products, but they do not come into regular contact with many other products, such as blood products, which also carry risks. The test prescribed by the Directive and the CPA 1987 does not require the court to speculate as to whether the risks of such products would or would not be socially acceptable if known about, but rather, what standard of safety the public is *entitled* to expect such products to provide, having regard to all the circumstances. It is very difficult to see why those relevant circumstances would not include the risk/benefit profile of the product and the avoidability of the risk; indeed, the 'social acceptability' of the risks of everyday products will itself be a product of the public having regard to precisely these types of consideration.

13.108   Similarly, when it comes to medicines, the test of 'social acceptability' can provide only limited assistance. Certain medicines, such as paracetamol, will be commonly known to the public, along with certain of its associated risks, but the general public will not know of the existence of, let alone be alive to the specific risks of, the vast majority of prescription-only medicines. Moreover, producers cannot protect themselves by 'advertising' the risks of prescription-only medicines, given the tight regulatory restrictions imposed in relation to the advertising of prescription medicines in any event. Indeed, the public's assumed knowledge of the risks of a medicine may well be based upon whether the risks of that medicine have hit the headlines; but the media reports of such risks may not accurately reflect the underlying science[1] and may even give rise to an unjustified (from a scientific perspective) public response – the drop in the uptake of MMR in the 1990s being a case in point. Such factors cannot properly be relied upon to determine the safety standard which, as a matter of law, persons generally are *entitled* to expect a product to provide.

1 As noted by Sedley LJ in *B (Child)* [2003] EWCA Civ 1148, para 36.

13.109   What is, perhaps, of relevance in relation to 'social acceptability' in the context of medicines is that it is well known that, as a class of products, medicines carry the risk of adverse effects and society has elected to accept the risks of medicines and to control such risks through a regulatory regime. There can be no further requirement to prove that each and every side effect of each and every medicinal product has been 'made known to the public at large with full information', nor 'was a matter of public knowledge', nor 'socially accepted'. Such requirements could never be satisfied.

13.110   In the context of medicinal products, it is submitted that the circumstances to be taken into account when determining the safety that persons generally are entitled to expect will typically include, subject to the precise characterisation of the alleged defect in the individual case, some or all of the following:

- the context of the regulatory regime governing all aspects of medicines, including prescription medicines;
- the risk/benefit profile of the medicine and whether the medicine was, at the material time, clinically indicated for a class of patients;
- the fact that the medicine may only be available to a patient on prescription from an authorised healthcare professional who is

under a professional duty, and who owes a legal duty to the patient, to ensure that the patient is prescribed with the medicine only if it is clinically indicated for the treatment of that patient having regard to the individual factors pertaining to that patient, as well as to ensure that the patient is appropriately advised as to the benefits and risks of the medicine;

- the information supplied by the producer via SPCs to prescribers as well as the information which might reasonably be expected to be available to prescribers from other sources about the product;
- the information which it is reasonable to expect will be supplied with and/or about the product to patients by prescribers or other healthcare professionals;
- the information which is supplied to patients directly via the PIL.

The regulatory regime

13.111 No prescription medicine is free from the risk of serious adverse effects for certain patients. This fact is well recognised by society and, via the legislature, society has chosen to respond to those risks by the adoption of a system of regulation by an independent regulatory authority. Medicines are amongst the most highly regulated of all products both in terms of regulatory scrutiny of the product itself and in terms of the control of supply, particularly those available on prescription only. Accordingly, save for the limited circumstances when a medicinal product is exempt from these requirements, a prescription-only medicinal product may be supplied only if it has been granted a marketing authorisation, which authorisation will only be granted if the product is found to have met appropriate standards of quality, safety and efficacy in its approved uses (indications) following detailed consideration of the available data by those with appropriate medical and scientific expertise within the regulatory authority.

13.112 As explained above, a marketing authorisation will only be granted or continued where a medicinal product has a positive risk/benefit profile ie the benefits associated with the use of the product outweigh the potential risks. The types of information to be supplied with and about the product by means of PILs and SPCs are prescribed by legislation and the content of SPCs and PILs in relation to any particular medicine is determined by the regulatory authority, which must approve such documents before they are put into circulation. The marketing authorisation holder for a medicinal product is required to comply with various regulatory obligations, including in relation to the reporting of adverse drug reactions, which are considered by the regulatory authority as part of its continuing review of the product, the information supplied with and about the product and its risk/benefit profile.

13.113 As academic commentators have noted, whilst a failure to comply with regulatory standards will frequently constitute a criminal offence, conversely compliance with statutory and regulatory requirements such as those set out in the Medicines Act 1968 and the Human Medicines Regulations 2012 ought, it is submitted, to be a significant, but not determinative factor, in relation to the assessment of defect[1]. The fact that the risk/benefit profile of a prescription medicine has been independently assessed and evaluated by the regulatory authority, with access to teams of independent experts, ought, it is submitted, to carry considerable weight in the context of any assessment of the safety which persons generally are entitled to expect of that medicine[2].

1 See, for instance, Miller *Product Liability and Safety Encyclopaedia* para **III** **[255]**; Freeman 'Assessing Manufacturers' Liability in Highly Regulated Industries' (2001) 5 Lovells' European Product Liability Review 25; Miller and Goldberg *Product Liability* (2nd edn) paras 10.76 and 10.77; Goldberg *Medicinal Product Liability and Regulation* (2013) pp 138–139. See also *Lambson Aviation v Embraer Empressa Brasiliera de Aeronautica SA* [2001] All ER (D) 152 (Oct), per Tomlinson J at para 17 *'in heavily regulated industries such compliance carries 'considerable but not decisive weight''*; see also *Albery-Speyer & Budden v BP Oil Ltd and Shell Oil Ltd* (1980) 124 Sol Jo 376, CA in which, in a different context, the Court of Appeal expressed its reluctance to lay down standards higher than those prescribed by Parliament.
2 See also Dr Richard Goldberg 'Paying for Bad Blood' 10 Med Law Rev 165 in his criticism of Burton J's decision in *A v National Blood Authority* (at 183): 'Although Burton J has rejected the risk-utility test for hepatitis C, the irony in respect of such community-used natural resources would seem to be that the circumstances in which the expectation is not one hundred per cent are going to be situations where the public are aware that a risk-benefit assessment has been made to put the product on the market... It is thus submitted that the public expectation in these circumstances is shaped by risk-benefit assessment'.

13.114 Equally, the fact that the regulatory authority will have determined: (i) what restrictions should be imposed as a condition of the grant of marketing authorisation; (ii) what contra-indications or 'Uses' limitations should be provided; and (iii) each and every word of the information and warnings which should be provided with and about the product via SPCs and PILs, will also be factors which ought, it is submitted, to carry considerable weight in relation to the court's assessment of the safety persons generally are entitled to expect under the CPA 1987. Indeed, the role of the regulatory authority itself encompasses the need to ensure that a medicinal product provides the safety which the legislature requires a medicine to meet – which may be considered to be relevant to the safety which a person generally is entitled to expect.

13.115 There may be circumstances in which the regulatory authority makes an error, and it subsequently transpires that a product should not have been granted a marketing authorisation by reason of its negative risk/benefit profile or, alternatively, that the warning about a particular side effect was inadequate at a particular point in time. Similarly, circumstances change; it may be that the authorisation and warnings were appropriate on the basis of the available data at the material point in time, but that further data have subsequently become available which result, or ought to result, in a changed approach to the marketing authorisation and/or warnings.

13.116 Thus, whilst the existence of regulatory authorisation and approval of warnings will not be determinative as to the issue of defect under the CPA 1987, where a product remains on the market with a positive risk/benefit assessment and particularly where warnings have not been materially amended by the regulatory authority, a court may well have regard, it is submitted, to the fact and significance of that assessment in relation to the issue of defect under the CPA. In such cases, it may be anticipated that the claimant may face some difficulty in demonstrating why, notwithstanding the regulatory authority's assessment of the positive risk/benefit profile and approved warnings, the product should not be deemed to be as safe as persons generally are entitled to expect.

The risk/benefit profile

13.117 Leaving aside the case of a production error resulting in a defective batch of product, a claim that a prescription medicine is defective by reason of the adverse effect(s) *per se* (as opposed to by reason of the warnings and indications provided with and about the medicine) is likely to amount to a claim that the medicine is defective by reason of its chemical formula. The benefits and risks of the medicine are inherent in its chemical formula. It is very difficult to see the basis upon which such a claim could ever properly be made out in circumstances in which the medicine possesses a positive risk/benefit profile and so remains clinically indicated for the treatment of certain patients. To put it another way, a medicinal product may give rise to a severe risk of injury and yet not be 'defective' merely because of that risk having regard, as part of the circumstances, to its potential benefits and the clinical needs which it meets. Thus, a form of chemotherapy treatment, for example, may pose very serious risks of adverse effects, but yet meet the risk/benefit profile from a regulatory perspective and, it is submitted, meet the threshold of safety set by the CPA 1987, s 3(1). It is submitted that, save, perhaps, in exceptional circumstances, persons generally would not properly be entitled to expect a medicinal product with a positive risk/benefit profile and which is clinically indicated for the treatment of certain patients to provide a level of safety which is unattainable in practice, namely one which divorces the therapeutic benefits provided by the chemical formulation from the risks of adverse effects which are equally inherent in that formulation. In the words of one leading academic: 'Unlike durable goods, drugs cannot be designed in an alternative fashion, at least not in the light of current technological capabilities'[1].

1 Green 'Statutory Compliance and Tort Liability: Examining the Strongest Case' (1997) 30 U Mich JL Reform 461, 471, quoted by Miller and Goldberg *Product Liability* (2nd edn) at para 10.99, p 392. There may be some exceptions, for example, where a 'combination medicine' containing more than one active ingredient could have the component elements changed or where a medicine is supplied at a concentration which is higher than is required to provide a therapeutic dose.

13.118 Conversely, where a medicine has a negative risk/benefit profile such that it is not clinically indicated for the treatment of any class of patients, then, in such circumstances, it is suggested that the medicine may potentially be deemed to be inherently defective, rather than defective by reason of its warnings.

13.119 The above analysis is consistent with the position reached in the US Restatement, Third, Torts: Product Liability, section 6(c) which defines the limited circumstances in which a prescription medicine can be held to be defective by reason of the adverse effects inherent in its design:

'A prescription drug or medical device is not reasonably safe due to defective design if the foreseeable risks of harm posed by the drug or medical device are sufficiently great in relation to its foreseeable therapeutic benefits that reasonable healthcare providers, knowing of such foreseeable risks and therapeutic benefits, would not prescribe the drug or medical device for any class of patients'.

Warnings

13.120 Article 6 requires the court to have regard to all the circumstances, including '(a) the presentation of the product' and '(b) the use to which it could reasonably be expected that the product would be put'. These requirements are articulated more fully in the CPA 1987, s 3(2): '(a) the manner in which, and the purposes for which, the product has been marketed, its get-up, the use of any mark in relation to the product and any instructions for, or warnings with respect, doing or refraining from doing anything with or in relation to the product' and '(b) what might reasonably be expected to be done with or in relation to the product'.

13.121 In the case of a medicinal product licensed by a regulatory authority, the 'manner in which' the product is marketed within the meaning of s 3(2)(a) encompasses the fact that the product is marketed pursuant to the grant of marketing authorisation by the licensing authority charged with the authorisation of medicines. It is also the regulatory authority which controls and defines the 'purposes for which' a medicinal product is marketed within the meaning of s 3(2)(a) by virtue of the marketing authorisation granted. Similarly, the SPC and PIL, which provided the 'instructions for, or warnings with respect to, doing or refraining from doing anything with or in relation to the product' (s 3(2)(a)), are both subject to detailed control by the regulatory authority.

Information supplied to prescribers

13.122 Prescription medicines are licensed to be only available to individuals for whom the benefit and risk of the use of the product has been individually assessed by appropriately qualified and approved medical practitioners. The SPC provides a primary means by which those prescribers are informed as to the appropriate use of a prescription medicine. The SPC contains 'instructions' and 'warnings' with respect to the product within the meaning of CPA 1987, s 3(2)(a) and is aimed directly at those who, by reason of the regulatory regime, are the only people who can authorise the product to be supplied to a patient.

13.123 The fact that a medicinal product might only be supplied on prescription by an authorised prescriber forms part of the circumstances which must be taken into account in relation to 'what might reasonably be expected to be done with or in relation to the product' as required by CPA 1987, s 3(2)(b) whilst the instructions and warnings contained in the SPC must be taken into account under s 3(2)(a). Moreover, the SPC will not be the only source of information available to the prescriber. Independent guidelines concerning medicines are often available to prescribers, as well as various independent reference materials published for the benefit of prescribers. The information and warnings contained in the SPC will, or should, have assisted the prescriber to have reached a decision as to whether a particular patient should be commenced upon, or maintained upon, a particular medicine regime, or whether a different regime is more appropriate.

13.124 The role played by prescribers in relation to prescription medicines is central to the regulatory regime which governs the supply of prescription medicines. This principle pre-dates the Directive and its existence has not been affected by the Directive[1].

1 See further Miller and Goldberg *Product Liability* (2nd edn) paras 12.45–12.50, pp 452–454. See also Hodges *Product Liability: European Law and Practice* para 3-048.

13.125 The 'learned intermediary principle' forms part of the circumstances which the court must take into account as part of the assessment of defect, falling squarely within the requirement to have regard to 'what might reasonably be expected to be done with or in relation to the product' as set out in CPA 1987, s 3(2)(b) and which is derived from and consistent with Article 6(1)(b), namely the requirement to have regard to the use to which it could reasonably be expected that the product would be put. Both the Directive and the CPA 1987 expressly require the court to make an assessment based on what might 'reasonably' be expected in this regard.

13.126 In *A v National Blood Authority*, it was held that the consumer did not know that blood being supplied to him was not 100 per cent clean and that there was not any public understanding or acceptance of the infection of transfused blood by hepatitis C. There were no warnings and no material publicity. Doctors and surgeons knew, but did not tell their patients unless asked and were very rarely asked[1]. In those circumstances, Burton J held that 'the knowledge of the medical profession, not materially or at all shared with the consumer, is of no relevance'[2]. The position would be different, it is submitted, in the case of a medicinal product which is only available on prescription by learned intermediaries and is accompanied by product information, approved by the regulatory authority, informing prescribers of any restricted use of the product and PILs providing warnings to patients to consult their doctors. This was not an issue which was addressed by Burton J in *A v National Blood Authority*[3].

1 Paragraph 55.
2 Paragraph 80.
3 See Miller and Goldberg *Product Liability* (2nd edn) paras 12.48–12.49, pp 453–454, quoting with approval the concerns of Dr Hodges in 'Compensating Patients' (2001) 117 LQR 528, 532. As Dr Hodges put it 'it could be a relevant Article 6 circumstance that the product was used and was intended to be used, only where learned intermediaries would interpose between the producer and consumer, and that it was generally recognised to be the function of such intermediaries to warn consumers as fully as should be necessary of the risks involved in the selection for use of a particular product, often from a number of other products'.

Better products subsequently put into circulation

13.127 The Directive provides that a product shall not be considered defective for the sole reason that a better product was subsequently put into circulation (Art 6(2)). A similar provision is found in the CPA 1987, s 3(2). The issue of whether a particular medicinal product is defective depends upon whether it could properly be termed defective at the time when the actual product was put into circulation. The product must be judged by reference to circumstances prevailing at the date of its putting into circulation by the producer regardless of whether subsequent scientific advances have enabled others to license and supply a product with an improved safety profile for the same indication. However, once an improved product is available, the continued supply of those older generation products might in theory present problems for their manufacturers. In practice, of course, it may still be possible to claim advantages for the older products, either for specific groups of patients, or more generally, on the basis of the greater clinical experience that will have been acquired in relation to such older products. A further point is worth noting in relation to prescription medicines: where the risk/

benefit profile of medicinal product A (perhaps a first generation medicine) falls to be reassessed following the introduction of medicine B (perhaps a second generation variant), the existence of the alternative B, offering an improved risk/benefit profile, may itself have an impact upon the regulatory authority's assessment of the risk/benefit profile of medicine A and could, in principle, result in medicine A being assessed as having a negative risk/benefit profile; in such circumstances Article 6(2)/s 3(2) may well be of particular importance.

Development risks defence

13.128 The initial draft version of the product liability directive included liability for so-called 'development risks'. However, several Member States, including the UK, raised concerns as to the effect this would have on innovation and technology and pressed for the inclusion of a specific 'development risks defence'; this proved to be a particularly contentious issue during the negotiations surrounding the drafting of the Directive. Ultimately, however, a development risks defence was included, at Article 7(e), but Member States were provided with an option to omit this defence when drafting national implementing legislation. Article 7(e) provides that:

'The producer shall not be liable as a result of this Directive if he proves… that the state of scientific and technical knowledge at the time when he put the product into circulation was not such as to enable the existence of the defect to be discovered'.

13.129 Section 4(1)(e) of the CPA 1987 provides a defence where the defendant can prove:

'that the state of scientific and technical knowledge at the relevant time was not such that a producer of products of the same description as the product in question might be expected to have discovered the defect if it had existed in his products while they were under his control'.

The wording of s 4(1)(e) differs from that of Article 7(e) in potentially significant ways, prompting a challenge by the Commission as to the UK's implementation of the Directive. The ECJ dismissed the Commission's challenge in *Commission v United Kingdom*[1] and, in doing so, provided guidance in relation to Article 7(e), discussed further below.

1 Case C-300/95 [1997] ECR I-2649.

13.130 The implications of this defence have been criticised as reintroducing concepts of negligence into a no fault liability regime. However, the Directive represents a compromise between the conflicting interests of consumer and producer. There are also differences between a claim in negligence, which focuses on the alleged acts and/or omissions of the particular producer and the development risks defence under the Directive/CPA 1987 which provides for an objective test, disconnected from the actual acts or omissions of the particular defendant. Further, whereas in negligence the burden is upon the injured person to prove that the manufacturer should have been aware of the defect given the state of the art at the time he supplied the product, under the Directive/CPA 1987 the burden of proof is reversed and it is the producer who must make out the defence.

13.131 The USA has similarly grappled with the competing policy considerations in relation to some form of development risks defence. One argument frequently made in favour of such a defence is that if a producer is strictly liable for injury caused by defects in its products, regardless of the care which it takes, or which its sector takes, to avoid such defects, then the unintended consequence may be to reduce, rather than promote, consumer protection. The inhibitory effects on research of product liability litigation in certain therapeutic areas, notably vaccines and contraception, has also been well documented in the past in the USA[1]. The majority of jurisdictions in the US do now allow for some equivalent to a development risk defence, incorporating a concept of reasonableness or 'practical technological feasibility'. In California, the Court of Appeals has declared that under strict liability principles as applied to design defects in products such as pharmaceuticals, there is in practice no real difference between the negligence standard and the strict liability standard, with open recognition of the policy considerations underpinning this position:

'Perhaps a drug might be made safer if it was withheld from the market until scientific skill and knowledge advanced to the point at which additional dangerous side effects would be revealed. But in most cases such a delay in marketing new drugs – added to the delay required to obtain approval for release of the product from the Food and Drug Administration – would not serve the public welfare. Public policy favours the development and marketing of beneficial new drugs, even though some risks, perhaps serious ones, might accompany their introduction, because drugs can save lives and reduce pain and suffering'[2].

1 See eg *Brown v Superior Court* 751 P2d 479, 479-480 (Cal Sc, 1988); Charlotte Smith Siggins 'Strict Liability for Prescription Drugs: Which Shall Govern – Comment K or Strict Liability Applicable to Ordinary Products?' (1986) 16 Golden Gate ULR 309, 325–327. See The Economist, 8 October 1988, p 59 and Scrip no 1367, 7 December 1988, p 16. Note too that the perceived exposure for doctors prescribing Norplant in the UK led them largely to cease prescribing, which in turn led to the discontinuation of the product in the UK (see The Times, 30 April 1999). This was despite the collapse of the product liability litigation a few weeks before trial.

2 *Brown v Superior Court* (Supreme Court of California) 1988, 44 Cal (3d) 1049. Compare rejection of the defence in an asbestos case – *Beshada v Johns-Manville Products Corpn* (1982) CCH Prod Liab Rep P9344, 90 NJ 191, 447 A 2d 539.

13.132 It is estimated that the larger pharmaceutical companies already spend 16 per cent of their annual turnover on research and development[1]. Research and development is ultimately a compromise that takes account of what is scientifically and commercially practical and nowhere is the position more acute than in the research of new medicinal products.

1 See Office of Fair Trading *Market Study on The Pharmaceutical Price Regulation Scheme* (2007), para 3.14.

13.133 In relation to a medicinal product the alleged 'defect' is frequently identified by reference to a causal association, whether the capacity of the medicine to cause an adverse event *per se* (a design defect) or the failure to provide an adequate warning of such a capacity (a warnings defect). The issue of pre-marketing clinical trials and post-marketing pharmacovigilance is there at the heart of many medicinal product liability actions.

13.134 Although drugs are tested on laboratory animals before being administered to humans, the extrapolation of such results to man is a difficult task, even if one is satisfied that the most suitable animal models have been found. Frequently, as the laboratory work must be in a limited number of animals, it will identify a problem only where the numerical chance of an adverse reaction occurring is high and only then where the particular species used for testing mimics the response of man to the drug. The question quickly becomes 'What incidence of adverse effect is it reasonable to try to detect?' The same issue arises at the clinical research stage. As Professor William Asscher has remarked:

'Even with the drugs used for the treatment of common disorders, clinical experience may be limited to use in 2–3,000 patients by the time a new drug receives its licence. The rationale for this policy is that the hazards of a new drug are more likely to be discovered when it is used extensively in clinical practice, rather than under the artificial circumstances of a clinical trial'[1].

1 A W Asscher, Paper entitled '*Developments in Risk Assessment and Management*' presented at a conference on Risk in Medicine, 28–29 April 1988, London.

13.135 Where a risk may be small numerically but severe in impact, it remains impracticable to detect it by clinical research: it is simply not possible to recruit to studies sufficient volunteers to give studies the statistical power to produce reliable results. Information about a product is gained from healthy volunteer studies and clinical trials but in practice no programme of testing that is feasible, commercially or practically, will enable a manufacturer to say that he has isolated all possible risks. The real test is widespread marketing and pharmacovigilance.

13.136 However, after a rare adverse effect becomes manifest from such marketing, a claimant might argue that, even if clinical research to identify that effect was impracticable, the defect would have been observed if the drug in question had been tested in very large numbers of primates rather than the limited numbers of rodents and other smaller laboratory animals that it is normal to test drugs upon. It is suggested that a court is not likely to be concerned with what might be hypothetically possible, as opposed to what is possible in practice and s 4(1)(e) encapsulates the need for an approach based upon reasonable practicability by reference to what a notional producer 'might be expected to have discovered'.

13.137 Even after marketing, however, it may be impossible in practice to 'discover' a causal association for many years. The detection of rare adverse events may require very large numbers. The nature of scientific endeavour is that a single study is rarely, if ever, likely to be able to lead to the discovery of a causal association between a medicine and a particular outcome. Multiple studies will be required to identify associations, test hypotheses as to causal associations, enable relative risks to be calculated, consider issues of confounding, dose effects etc. The development of scientific knowledge tends to be an incremental and iterative process[1]. Indeed, 'repeatability' is an essential requirement of epidemiology: a single study, however well conducted, will rarely, if ever, be capable of enabling a causal association to be 'discovered'. Rather, such causal associations and risks are 'discovered' as a result of the weight of scientific evidence which develops over a period of time; multiple studies of different designs and in different study populations will typically be necessary to demonstrate the requisite 'repeatability' to permit a causal association to be established.

1 '[A] new theory, however special its range of application, is seldom or never just an increment to what is already known. Its assimilation requires the reconstruction of prior theory and the re-evaluation of prior fact, an intrinsically revolutionary process that is seldom completed by a single man and never overnight' Thomas Kuhn *The Structure of Scientific Revolutions* (1962) p 7.

13.138 Important questions therefore arise as to the nature of the 'discovery' with which the development risk defence is concerned: is the 'discovery' that of a causal association, or some lesser 'discovery', such as the 'discovery' of an association (which may or may not be causal), or even with the 'discovery' of a hypothesis of a causal association? Furthermore, are Article 7(e)/s 4(1) (e) concerned with what 'the state of scientific knowledge' in the sense of the existence of the relevant *know-how* to enable a notional producer to generate the data which would be required to enable a causal association to be discovered, such as by conducting appropriate trials and studies (as is typically argued by claimants)? Or is the test concerned with whether 'the state of scientific knowledge' is such as to enable the existence of a causal association to be discovered having regard to the *data* which are in fact available at the relevant time? These and other questions remain, as yet, unanswered by the courts.

13.139 The only substantive consideration of Article 7(e) by the ECJ has been in *Commission v United Kingdom*[1] in the context of the Commission's application for a declaration that the UK government had failed to implement the Directive. The Commission failed in its challenge.

1 Case C-300/95 [1997] ECR I-2649.

13.140 Analysis of the reasoning of the ECJ is assisted by the detailed consideration given by Advocate General Tesauro to the background and purpose of the Directive as a whole and Article 7(e) in particular. The ECJ and the Advocate General reached the same conclusions on certain central issues. Nevertheless, the judgment of the ECJ is silent on certain matters on which the Advocate General expressed an opinion and therefore a degree of caution needs to be exercised in this regard.

13.141 The focus of the Commission's complaint was that whilst Article 7(e) of the Directive did not frame the 'state of the art defence' by reference to the perspective of producers, CPA 1987, s 4(1)(e) required an English court to consider whether the state of scientific and technical knowledge at the relevant time was not such that a 'producer of products of the same description as the product in question might be expected to have discovered the defect…'. The Commission's position was, in essence, that the CPA 1987 provided a lower threshold than the Directive and that the burden under s 4(1)(e) could be discharged by proving an absence of negligence on the part of the defendant producer – a producer would merely have to show that it could not have discovered the defect had it complied with industry norms and standards[1]. Conversely, the Commission's interpretation of the Directive was, in effect, that if a single person anywhere in the world was capable of discovering the defect then that would defeat the development risk defence.

1 See paras 17 and 36 of ECJ judgment.

13.142 The UK government contended that s 4(1)(e) captured the proper meaning of Article 7(e), namely, that it lays down an 'objective' test in the sense that the 'state of scientific and technical knowledge' does not refer to what the producer in question actually knows or does not know, but to the state of knowledge which a producer of the class of the product in question, understood in a generic sense, may objectively be expected to have. The UK relied upon the 7th recital's reference to a 'fair apportionment of risk', permitting the producer to exonerate himself from liability if he discharged the evidential burden to prove exonerating circumstances, as showing 'an intention on the part of the Community legislator to afford the producer real, effective defences, the effectiveness of which would be destroyed if the Commission's interpretation were to be accepted'[1]. The force of this submission appears to have been accepted by both the Advocate General and the ECJ[2].

1 Advocate General's Opinion, para 10.
2 See, for example, para 24 of the ECJ judgment.

13.143 Having reviewed the evolution of the Directive and the move from the original 'absolute' liability policy underpinning the original Commission Proposal to the more balanced provisions of the final Directive, the Advocate General concluded that the effect of Article 7(e) was that 'the producer… may exonerate himself from liability by proving that the 'state of the art' at the time when he put the product into circulation was not such as to cause the product to be regarded as defective. This is what Article 7(e) of the Directive provides'[1].

1 Advocate General's Opinion, para 19.

13.144 The ECJ endorsed this construction of the Directive, at paras 26–30 of its judgment holding that:

'First, as the Advocate General rightly observes … since that provision refers to "scientific and technical knowledge at the time when [the producer] put the product into circulation", Article 7(e) is not specifically directed at the practices and safety standards in use in the industrial sector in which the producer is operating, but, unreservedly at the state of scientific and technical knowledge, including the most advanced level of such knowledge, at the time when the product in question was put into circulation.

Second, the clause providing for the defence in question does not contemplate the state of knowledge of which the producer in question actually or subjectively was or could have been appraised, but the objective state of scientific and technical knowledge of which the producer is presumed to have been informed'[1].

As the ECJ makes clear, Article 7(e) is concerned 'unreservedly' with the actual state of knowledge pertaining at the relevant time. It does not avail the producer to show that he complied with relevant industry standards or practices, if, in fact, the material knowledge was available at the relevant time; but the logical corollary, presumably, is that it cannot avail the claimant to show that the necessary knowledge was not available at the relevant time by reason of any failure on the part of the defendant producer to act in accordance with relevant practices or procedures. Such matters are the preserve of negligence. Article 7(e) is not concerned with negligence, but is an objective test based upon the actual state of knowledge of which the producer is presumed to have been informed at the relevant time; it is not concerned with the subjective issues pertaining to what the defendant producer did or did not do, nor what the defendant producer did or did not know; still less what the defendant producer should have done or should not have done. Equally, it does not avail a claimant to say that the defendant producer could have done more to bring into existence data or knowledge which were not in fact in existence at the relevant time[2].

1 ECJ judgment, paras 26 and 27
2 In *A v National Blood Authority* Burton J considered the ECJ's decision in *Commission v UK* (Case C-300/95) and concluded that 'The article [Article 7(e)] is not concerned with the conduct or knowledge of individual producers…' (at paragraph 49(i)). Later in the judgment when considering, *obiter*, the application of Article 7(e) to 'standard products' the learned judge commented, however, that 'Negligence, fault and the conduct of the producer or designer can be left to the (limited) ambit of Article 7(e)…' (para 73). Insofar as the latter statement was intended to suggest that Article 7(e) is concerned with the conduct of the individual defendant producer, it is respectfully submitted that this is not correct and that the earlier analysis is to be preferred as a correct statement of the law.

13.145 A Member State is not permitted to impose any requirement on a producer to demonstrate subjective factors such as the taking of reasonable research and development steps as a precondition to establishing a defence under Article 7(e). In *Commission v France* [1] the ECJ upheld the Commission's complaint that France had incorrectly transposed Article 7(e) by inserting a requirement that a producer could only rely on the Article 7(e) defence if he can prove that 'he has taken appropriate steps to avert the consequences of a defective product' (para 49). The reasoning of the ECJ was that the Directive seeks to achieve 'complete harmonisation of the laws, regulations and administrative provisions of the Member States' in relation to matters regulated by the Directive and that whilst Article 15 of the Directive permitted a Member State to derogate from the development risks defence, 'it does not authorise them to alter the conditions under which the exemption is applied'. Thus it was impermissible for a Member State to adopt the Article 7(e) defence in an amended form as France had attempted to do: see paras 42–49 of the ECJ's judgment. It is submitted that just as it is impermissible for the legislature of a Member State to insert a condition into Article 7(e) referable to the subjective steps taken by a producer, so too would it be impermissible for a national court of a Member State to attempt to insert any such condition.

1 Case-52/00 I-3827.

13.146 The ECJ's reference (para 27) to 'the objective state of scientific and technical knowledge of which the producer is presumed to have been informed' and its conclusion that 'it is implicit in the wording of Article 7(e) that the relevant scientific and technical knowledge must have been accessible at the time when the product in question was put into circulation'[1] echo closely the Advocate General's opinion that 'the state of knowledge must be construed so as to include all data in the information circuit of the scientific community as a whole, bearing in mind, however, on the basis of a reasonableness test the actual opportunities for the information to circulate'[2]. Both the Advocate General and the ECJ therefore rejected the Commission's contention that the defence provided by Article 7(e) will necessarily be defeated if it can be shown that there was 'one person, irrespective of his country and language, who was capable of discovering the defect in the product'[3]. The ECJ did, however, recognise that the issues concerning when the requisite knowledge might be said to be accessible were not straightforward, contrary to the Commission's position, and would have to be determined by national courts, if necessary with references to the ECJ. When examining the criterion of discoverability provided for by CPA 1987, s 4(1)(e), the Advocate General accepted that this test could be regarded as 'an objectively verifiable and assessable parameter'.

1 ECJ judgment, para 28. See also footnote 12 to para 20 of the Advocate General's Opinion (at I-2659) where he makes clear that the test is not what the producer did know, but what he ought to be deemed to have known 'if a chemist or pharmacologist has to keep up to date with the characteristics of a given substance, similar knowledge will be required for present purposes of an industrialist producing pharmaceuticals containing the same substances'.
2 Advocate General's Opinion, para 24.
3 See footnote 13 of the Advocate General's Opinion (page I-2660) and paras 28–33 of the ECJ judgment.

13.147 It is interesting to note that the Advocate General's opinion suggests that the producer's defence will not necessarily be defeated even in circumstances in which the defect has *in fact* been discovered by a third party[1] if the relevant data are not reasonably accessible. Far less, it might be submitted, can the defence be defeated in circumstances in which the relevant data were not only inaccessible at the relevant time, but did not in fact exist at the relevant time. Thus, in the context of the epidemiological enquiry, it is presumably arguable that the test laid down by Article 7(e) is not concerned with whether the state of scientific and technical knowledge at the relevant time was such as to enable the trials or studies to be conducted which could have generated the necessary data from which a causal association might have been demonstrated, but rather with whether the state of scientific and technical knowledge at the relevant time was such as to enable a causal association to be demonstrated having regard to the data which were in fact in existence and reasonably accessible to the notional producer at that time.

1 As was the case in the Advocate General's example of the Manchurian scientist (para 23 of his Opinion).

13.148 In his Opinion the Advocate General also envisaged a position in which 'new studies and new discoveries may initially be criticised and regarded as unreliable by most of the scientific community, yet subsequently after the passage of time undergo an opposite process of 'beatification', whereby they are virtually unanimously endorsed'. In the Advocate General's opinion the producer could not rely upon the defence in a situation in which 'there is a risk that is not certain and will be agreed to exist by all only ex post'[1]. However, the ECJ did not comment upon such a situation nor endorse the comments of the Advocate General on this point and it is arguable that the Advocate General's comment is open to misinterpretation. Article 7(e) is not concerned with *the risk* that a product is defective; it is concerned with whether the state of scientific and technical knowledge at the relevant time was not such as to enable '*the existence of the defect*' to be discovered; it is not the knowledge which would enable the existence of a *risk* of a defect to be discovered which is in issue.

1 Advocate General's Opinion, para 21.

13.149   It must also be borne in mind that the Advocate General was not addressing the specific context of medicinal products; the Directive deals with all moveable products. In the context of medicinal products, epidemiology almost invariably requires 'the passage of time' to elapse to enable reliable conclusions to be reached as to whether an association amounts to a causal association; it is generally only with the passage of time that studies of the requisite power can be undertaken and the necessary data be generated. If the requisite data to demonstrate a causal association are not extant at the relevant time then the existence of data amounting to a 'risk' of a causal association ought not, it is submitted, to be equated with the discovery of a causal association. Taking short cuts in epidemiology can have serious consequences and courts are likely to be astute to self-serving claims by the 'leading researchers' to have demonstrated a causal association at face value. The dangers of such an approach are self-evident but can be well illustrated by the claims of the now discredited research at the heart of the MMR/MR product liability litigation; 'new discoveries may initially be criticised and regarded as unreliable by most of the scientific community' for good reason[1].

1 Conversely, there may, of course, be cases in which the necessary data or knowledge is available, but the appropriate inference has not been drawn. A classic illustration of the latter situation is *Abouzaid v Mothercare (UK) Ltd* [2000] All ER (D) 2436, in which the tendency of the elastic straps to snap back and of the capacity of a metal buckle to cause injury were known facts, but the producer had simply failed to appreciate the existence of the risk.

13.150   It is also to be borne in mind that, in the case of a medicinal product, the regulatory authority has been empowered, at an EU level, to authorise the warnings provided with and about the medicine for the purposes of securing the protection of public health. Thus, the standard of proof that would be required by the regulatory authority, properly directing itself, in order to be persuaded as to the risk/benefit profile of a medicine or as to whether a particular warning should be included may provide a useful benchmark for the court. It is submitted that the state of scientific and technical knowledge must mean, at the very least, the existence of data of sufficient quality to have permitted the regulatory authority, properly directing itself, to have concluded that the medicine possessed a negative risk/benefit profile, or to have concluded that a particular warning was appropriate, as the case may be. Data falling short of the evidential quality required by the regulatory authority for the relevant purpose are unlikely to be capable of satisfying the test that the state of scientific and technical knowledge was such as to enable the medicine to be inherently defective by reason of its design or such as to identify the inadequacy of a warning within the meaning of s 4(1)(e)/Article 7(e). This does not, of course, amount to a 'pre-emption defence'[1], for regulatory authorities may not have been in possession of all material extant data at the relevant time and, in any event, are capable of making errors.

1 Support for a regulatory compliance defence has been raised by representatives of the pharmaceutical industry in Europe, and noted in the 2003 Lovells study on product liability in the EU, and in the Third Commission Report (2006) and the Fourth Commission Report (2011). The view expressed (although without any opinion or recommendation by the Commission) is that the liability regime of the Directive does not sufficiently take into account the strict regulation of medicinal products, resulting in an overlap of regulation and tort law, with the risks of excessive liability and deterrence from research and development. However, this putative defence divides opinion, with the counterview being that exposure to tortious liability incentivises producers in their pharmacovigilance effort, to provide prompt reporting of adverse reactions. It is notable that in the US the concept of an FDA Pre-emption Policy was rejected by the US Supreme Court in *Wyeth v Levine* 129 S Ct 1187 (2009); although, conversely,

in relation to generic medicines the pre-emption defence was permitted in later cases of *PLIVA Inc v Mensing* 131 S Ct 2567 (2011) and *Mutual Pharmaceutical Co Inc v Bartlett* 133 S Ct 2466 (2013): see the discussion of federal pre-emption and prescription drugs in Goldberg *Medicinal Product Liability and Regulation* (2013).

13.151 Similarly, the ECJ passed no comment on, and did not endorse, the opinion of the Advocate General that 'the producer has to bear the foreseeable risks, against which he can protect himself by taking either preventive measures by stepping up experimentation and research investment or measures to cover himself by taking out civil liability insurance against any damage caused by defects in the product'. It may well be the case, as Burton J appears to have assumed[1], that the Advocate General was intending to refer to a situation in which the state of knowledge does not permit the producer to discover the existence of a defect in an individual product (eg that the particular bag of blood was contaminated with hepatitis C), albeit that it is possible to discover that the product line carries a generic risk (of contamination with hepatitis C). In certain such circumstances then, as the Advocate General states, the foreseeable risk of a finding of defect has to be borne by the producer and it is up to him as to whether he increases research in an attempt to design out that defect, or whether he insures against the risk or whether he provides a warning as to the existence of the risk (if permitted to do so) or whether he takes the product off the market.

1 See *A v National Blood Authority*, paras 74 and 77. It should be noted, however, that Burton J may have elided the opinion expressed by the Advocate General as to 'known risks' with the actual judgment of the ECJ. The latter does not follow the former in considering the situation of 'risks' as opposed to 'defects': as to the elision, see paras 74–78.

13.152 Article 7(e) is not, however, concerned with whether a risk of a defect is foreseeable or not. Rather, as stated above, it is concerned with whether the state of the scientific and technical knowledge at the relevant time is such, or is not such, as to enable the *existence* of the defect itself to be discovered. If, at the relevant time, the most advanced level of scientific and technical knowledge does not permit it to be concluded that the medicine is capable of causing that adverse effect, then, it is submitted, the producer ought to succeed on his defence under Article 7(e) as the state of knowledge does not permit the *existence* of the defect to be discovered.

13.153 If it were the case that the mere discovery of a *risk* that a product might be defective was sufficient to deny a producer the defence, then the implications would be significant. In respect of unregulated products the consequence would be that producers could only seek to protect themselves by expanding the warnings provided with the product to include warnings as to all such possible risks, however apparently unlikely, for fear that one or more such risk might subsequently prove to be correct, with the danger that the utility of the warnings to the consumer would be undermined. In respect of a highly regulated product such as a medicinal product, the producer is not free to introduce warnings unilaterally; any warnings must be approved by the regulatory authority, which must be satisfied that the evidence is sufficient to justify such a warning.

13.154 The ECJ's omission to comment, in a factual vacuum, upon the types of issues raised by the Advocate General as to how Article 7(e) might operate in practice is significant. In contrast, the ECJ did endorse the conclusion of the Advocate General as to the issue of the 'accessibility' of the material data: 'the 'state of knowledge' must be construed so as to include all data in the information circuit of the scientific community as a whole, bearing in mind, however, on the basis of a reasonableness test the actual opportunities for the information to circulate'[1]. Even where the existence of a defect has in fact been discovered, a test of reasonableness is applied in relation to whether such information of the discovery should itself be deemed to be discoverable.

1 ECJ judgment, para 24.

13.155 Ultimately, the Commission failed in its claim that the result intended by Article 7(e) would not be achieved by the application of the CPA 1987, s 4(1)(e). Whilst the Advocate General considered that the wording of s 4(1)(e) contains a potential ambiguity 'in so far as it refers to what might be expected of the producer, it could be interpreted more broadly that it should', he concluded that there was no irredeemable conflict between that provision and Article 7(e)[1]: '... I do not consider that the reference to the 'ability of the producer' despite its general nature, may or even must (necessarily) authorise interpretations contrary to the rationale and the aims of the Directive'. Further, he noted that 'consideration of the producer is central not only to the rules of the Directive taken as a whole, but also to Article 7(e), which, although it does not mention him, is aimed at the producer himself, as the person having to discharge the burden of proof... From this angle, the provision of the Act merely expresses in a clear way a concept which is implicit in the Community provision'.

1 And the ECJ found there to be no irredeemable conflict.

13.156 In summary, therefore, in requiring the court to have regard to whether the state of scientific and technical knowledge at the relevant time was not such that a producer of products of the same description as the product in question might be expected to have discovered the defect, CPA 1987, s 4(1)(e) should be construed as requiring the court: (i) to make a finding of fact as to what, in fact, the state of scientific and technical knowledge was at the relevant time in relation to material issues, divorced from any subjective considerations as to the actual acts or omissions of the defendant producer; and (ii) to make a finding of fact on the basis of an objective test, again divorced from any subjective considerations as to the actual acts or omissions or knowledge of the defendant producer, as to whether the state of scientific and technical knowledge at the relevant time was 'accessible' in the sense that an objective producer operating in the same field as the defendant might have been expected to have discovered the defect.

13.157 It is to be noted that Burton J considered that 'the CPA 1987 inappropriately sought to enact in s 4(1)(e) "a producer of products of the same description as the product in question" ...'[1]. However, it is respectfully submitted that that is the test that has been laid down by Parliament and it is that test which the court is bound to apply (in accordance with the duty of consistent interpretation and CPA 1987, s 1(1)). Furthermore, as *Commission v UK* demonstrates, s 4(1)(e) is capable of providing an 'objectively verifiable and assessable parameter, which is in no way influenced by considerations of the subjective knowledge of the producer or by his organisational and economic requirements'[2]; s 4(1)(e) is capable of being construed as to be compatible with Article 7(e)[3]. It is suggested, therefore, that s 4(1)(e) can be read consistently with Article 7(e) and incorporates an implicit and necessary requirement as to the perspective from which the test of discoverability of the defect, including the accessibility of the state of knowledge, should be determined.

1 *A v National Blood Authority*, para 76.
2 Paragraph 28 of the Advocate General's Opinion.
3 ECJ judgment paras 33–38.

13.158 The application of the test will not be straightforward in the case of a medicinal product. Difficult considerations arise as to the criteria which the court should apply when determining whether the data which exist at the relevant time are or are not such as to enable the existence of the defect to be discovered at that point in time. *Commission v UK* provides no assistance on this point. It is suggested that there are two primary issues: the first is to determine the elements of the defect which must be capable of being 'discovered' in the medicinal context, in order to permit a finding to be made that the 'defect' was capable of being discovered at the relevant time; the second issue is one of verification, namely how the court is to verify whether the data in existence at the relevant time would have permitted the existence of the defect to be discovered.

13.159 In a 'defective design' case in which a medicinal product has been provisionally[1] found to be defective by reason of its capacity to cause a particular adverse effect such that the medicine is not clinically indicated for the treatment of any class of patients by reason of its negative risk/benefit profile, then the test is likely to turn on whether the state of scientific and technical knowledge at the relevant time was or was not such as to enable the capacity of the medicine to cause the particular outcome to be discovered. Depending on the precise facts, such a case is likely to require the producer to demonstrate that the state of scientific and technical knowledge at the relevant time was not such as to enable the existence of the relevant causal association(s) to be discovered, and in most cases this is likely to turn on an epidemiological analysis of the data which were extant and accessible at the relevant time.

1 If the producer discharges the burden placed upon him by s 4(1)(e)/Article 7(e) it will have the effect of rendering the product not 'defective'. See the Opinion of Advocate General Tesauro in *Commission v UK* at para 19: 'The producer, however, may exonerate himself from liability by proving that the 'state of the art' at the time when he put the product into circulation was not such as to cause the product to be regarded as defective. That is what Article 7(e) of the Directive provides'.

13.160 In the case of a defect by reason of inadequate warnings, it is likely to be the case that the producer must establish that the data which were extant and accessible at the relevant time did not permit the fact of the inadequacy of the warning to be discovered. If the medicine is defective because the SPC failed to warn that the medicine was capable or might be capable of causing a particular adverse effect, then the question will be whether the data at the material time enabled that causative factor to be discovered.

13.161 The standard of proof may vary depending on the nature of the precise defect found. It may be inappropriate to wait until all epidemiologists (or perhaps even the majority of epidemiologists) have agreed on the existence of a causal association, but, on the other hand, the court is unlikely to accept potentially self-serving claims by the 'leading researchers' to have demonstrated a causal association at face value. Equally, a court is unlikely to conclude that the state of scientific knowledge was such as to enable the existence of the defect to be discovered at the relevant time if, at that time, the researchers who have undertaken the 'most advanced level of research which has been carried out at the time' are themselves not claiming that their data establish the existence of the causal association which founds the defect.

13.162 In the case of a medicinal product which is found to be defective by reason of inadequacy of warnings, the state of scientific and technical knowledge must mean, at the very least, the existence of data of sufficient quality to have permitted the regulatory authority, properly directing itself, to have agreed to the inclusion of the 'adequate' warning such that the product would not have been defective by reason of the inadequate warning which founds the defect. Data falling short of the evidential quality required by the regulatory authority for the purpose of approving a warning on a precautionary basis are unlikely, it is submitted, to be capable of satisfying the test that the state of scientific and technical knowledge was such as to enable the inadequate warning defect to be discovered within the meaning of CPA 1987, s 4(1)(e)/Article 7(e).

CLAIMS IN NEGLIGENCE

Introduction

13.163 If a claimant has a claim under the CPA 1987 and in negligence then, if the claimant cannot succeed under the CPA, a claim in negligence is unlikely to add anything[1]. Thus claims in negligence are typically only brought in medical product liability cases where the cause of action under the CPA 1987 is not available (for example, because of the long stop). The most difficult hurdle for claimants in proving their case is usually causation and this will be proved in the same way and to the same standard in both fault and no fault liability. If a CPA 1987 claim fails on causation then it will follow inevitably that a negligence claim would also have failed.

1 Claims have frequently been brought solely under the CPA 1987; see for example: *Richardson v LRC Products Ltd* [2000] Lloyd's Rep Med 280, the oral contraceptive group litigation *XYZ v Schering Health Care Ltd* [2002] EWHC 1420 (QB), *Piper v JRI (Manufacturing) Ltd* [2006] EWCA Civ 1344, *Ide v ATB Sales Ltd* [2008] EWCA Civ 424, and the Fetal Anti-Convulsant Litigation (*Multiple Claimants v Sanofi Sythelabo Ltd* [2007] EWHC 1860 (QB)). In *Worsley v Tambrands Ltd* [2000] PIQR P95, the claim was brought under the CPA 1987 and negligence, but the fact that the box and leaflet were not 'defective' was determinative. In *Pollard v Tesco Stores* [2006] EWCA Civ 393, the claim was brought under the CPA 1987 and negligence, but as Laws LJ stated (at para 13) 'this case is one of breach of statutory duty or nothing'.

Duty of care

13.164 It is the duty of every person in the chain of supply of a product to take reasonable care to avoid causing injury to the consumer by their careless act or failure to act, ie by their negligence[1]. The degree of care involved must have regard to the seriousness of the consequences of failure[2]. On this basis all those dealing in medicinal products are vulnerable to claims. To succeed under fault liability the injured person must prove not only that they have been injured by the product and that the relevant person has been negligent but also that, but for the negligent act or omission, the claimant would not have suffered the injury or it would have been reduced. The burden of proving each of these ingredients of liability lies with the claimant and the standard of proof required is the 'balance of probabilities'. Medical monitoring claims of the type frequently pursued in the US courts where patients have not yet suffered overt injury from a product associated with a harmful propensity, but allege anxiety and mental anguish at the thought they might later suffer injury, have not, as yet, been litigated to judgment in the UK (albeit that so-called 'worried-well' claims are, at the time of writing, being advanced within the PIP breast-implant group litigation). However, the courts in related fields have made it clear that physical changes alone that fall short of impairment of health and are asymptomatic cannot found a claim requiring proof of damage[3]. Moreover, anxiety through awareness of being at risk of injury must amount to a recognised psychiatric injury and be a foreseeable consequence of the defendant's fault before a claim in tort can succeed. Some claimants did succeed in proving this in the Creutzfeld-Jakob disease litigation where there was a fear of contracting CJD from use of human growth hormone processed from material found to be carrying the prion[4]. In *Boston Scientific Medizintechnik v AOC Sachsen-Anhalt*[5] the ECJ held that, in respect of persons fitted with a pacemaker which was part of a group containing a 'potential defect', all products forming part of that group may be classified as defective within the meaning of the Product Liability Directive, without the need to establish that the individual product has the relevant defect and, further, that damage caused by surgical removal of such a product constitutes damage or personal injury.

1 *Donoghue v Stevenson* [1932] AC 562, HL.
2 *Paris v Stepney Borough Council* [1951] AC 367, [1951] 1 All ER 42, HL.
3 *Rothwell v Chemical & Insulating Co Ltd* [2008] 1 AC 281 (usually cited as *Johnston v NEI International Combustion Ltd* [2007] UKHL 39) and *AB v Tameside & Glossop Health Authority* [1997] 8 Med LR 91. See also *Greenway v Johnson Matthey plc* [2014] EWHC 753 (QB) in which claims involving sensitisation to platinum salts failed on the basis that the claimants did not suffer actionable injury. The presence of the antibodies were not in themselves harmful. As such, the restrictions placed on the claimants' employment by reason of the presence of the antibodies was pure economic loss and not recoverable.
4 *CJD Litigation (Group B Plaintiffs v MRC)* 41 BMLR 157.
5 Case C-503/13 *Boston Scientific Medizintechnik GmbH v AOK Sachsen-Anhalt – Die Gesundheitskasse* [2015] All ER (D) 88 (Mar), ECJ.

13.165 In the absence of decided cases in England and Wales, the application of negligence principles to the producer of medicinal products depends on extrapolation from cases arising in other industries. It is clear, however, that at every step in research and marketing he must take such care as the reasonably skilful manufacturer would take and his conduct will at all times be measured against the prevailing state of scientific and technical knowledge ('the state of the art')[1]. Where an enterprise is inherently dangerous, liability can arise even where it may be said that it involved 'work which was both at and beyond the frontier of professional knowledge'[2]. In the context of prescription medicines, the Ontario Court of Appeal, holding the manufacturer of oral contraceptives liable for failing adequately to warn of the risk of a stroke, stated as follows[3]:

'A manufacturer of prescription drugs occupies the position of an expert in the field; this requires that it be under a continuing duty to keep abreast of scientific developments pertaining to its product through research, adverse reaction reports, scientific literature and other available methods. When additional dangerous or potentially dangerous side-effects from the drug's use are discovered, the manufacturer must make all reasonable efforts to communicate the information to prescribing physicians'.

1 *Vacwell Engineering Co Ltd v BDH Chemicals Ltd* [1971] 1 QB 88, [1969] 3 All ER 1681; and *Stokes v Guest Keen & Nettlefold (Bolts and Nuts) Ltd* [1968] 1 WLR 1776 at 1783, applied in *White v Holbrook Precision Castings* [1985] IRLR 215, CA, and *Smith v P&O Bulk Shipping* [1998] 2 Lloyds Rep 81. In the context of prescription medicines in the US, see *Dorsett v Sandoz, Inc* 699 F Supp 2d 1142 at 1163 (CD Cal 2010) and *Motus v Pfizer, Inc* 196 F Supp 2d 984 at 990 which held that a manufacturer of drugs has a duty to warn physicians 'about any known or reasonably knowable dangerous side effects'; upholding *Carlin v Superior Court* 920 P 2d 1347 at 1354 (Cal 1996) which held that 'drug manufacturers need only warn of risks that are actually known or scientifically knowable'.
2 *Independent Broadcasting Authority v EMI Electronics Ltd and BICC Construction Ltd* (1980) 14 BLR 1 at 27, HL.
3 *Buchan v Ortho Pharmaceuticals (Canada) Ltd* (1986) 25 DLR (4th) 658.

13.166 Failure to exercise care in research and design of the product or in manufacture of it or in labelling and warning through product information of possible risks associated with normal use – and conceivably foreseeable misuse – may lead to liability in negligence[1]. A manufacturer's duty is not limited to assessing for safety those parts of the product that he has researched and developed himself. It may extend to raw materials supplied by others[2].

1 *Cartwright v GKN Sankey Ltd* [1972] 2 Lloyd's Rep 242 at 259; *Wallhead v Ruston Ltd & Hornsby Ltd* (1973) 14 KIR 285; *Fuller v Baxenden Chemical Co Ltd* (1 February 1985, unreported), QBD; *E Hobbs (Farms) Ltd v Baxenden Chemical Co* [1992] 1 Lloyd's Rep 54 and *Devilez v Boots Pure Drug Co Ltd* (1962) 106 Sol Jo 552. See also *McMullin v ICI Australian Operations Pty Ltd* (1997) 72 FCR 1 and *ACC v Glendale Chemical Products Pty Ltd* [1999] ATPR 41-672. See also *Wright v Dunlop Rubber Co Ltd* (1972) 13 KIR 255. See also *Buchan v Ortho Pharmaceutical (Canada) Ltd* (1986) 25 DLR (4th) 658.
2 *Taylor v Rover Co Ltd* [1966] 2 All ER 181 at 186 and *Winward v TVR Engineering Ltd* (4 March 1986, unreported), QBD.

The role of the intermediary

13.167 It was thought at one time that the duty of care to the ultimate consumer only applies where there is 'no reasonable possibility of intermediate examination'[1]. However, the meaning of 'intermediate examination' has been severely qualified in decisions of the courts and, as a result, it is probably correct to say that, if a product is defective, the possibility of intermediate examination will only assist the manufacturer if he could reasonably have anticipated that the examination conducted by the intermediary would be of such a type as to reveal the defect[2]. Where such an examination is anticipated a duty of care may not arise at all. The intervention of a regulatory authority, prescriber or a pharmacist in the supply of a medicinal product, therefore, raises the question of whether that intervention could reasonably be expected to have isolated the defect. Clearly, a latent defect such as a design defect would often not be apparent and the intervention of such third parties will not automatically insulate the manufacturer from liability. In contrast, failure by an intermediary to isolate an obvious defect such as a packaging failure which has led to deterioration in the product or its sterility, could, on particular facts, give rise to a defence that a duty of care on the part of the manufacturer did not arise or will be sufficient to sever the causal link between the creation of the risk by the manufacturer and the injury it causes. Difficult questions of law may arise in the case of an allegation of 'failure to warn' (see para **12.206**) concerning a prescription-only product. The reasonable expectation that the prescribing physician (or specialist to whom the patient may be referred) will exercise his knowledge and skill in deciding whether and how to prescribe a product, may affect the determination of whether a duty of care is owed at all to a particular patient.

1 *Donoghue v Stevenson* [1932] AC 562 at 599.
2 *Griffiths v Arch Engineering Co (Newport) Ltd* [1968] 3 All ER 217 and *Hurley v Dyke* [1979] RTR 265, HL.

The standard of care

13.168 Absence of reasonable care is an essential ingredient in the tort of negligence and adherence to the common practice of the industry is accordingly a useful starting point in defending an action in negligence because it is admissible evidence of what a reasonably prudent manufacturer would do under the same circumstances[1]. However, it is certainly open to the court to hold that common practice does not amount to a proper precaution to avoid foreseeable risk[2]. The type of information that must accompany an application for a marketing authorisation is now harmonised within the European Union, but the requirements refer to types of research. They still leave room for some discretion, both on the part of the regulatory authorities and the manufacturer, as to what is appropriate for a particular type of product. Guidelines from time to time issued by regulatory authorities and the industry itself reflect and explain standard practice[3]. The fact that a manufacturer has complied with such requirements is not, therefore, to be treated as an automatic defence to a claim in negligence. The court may find that the manufacturer knew that the general requirements were not directly applicable to the research into the product in question and additional research should have been done. This may be particularly pertinent to the application of preclinical animal testing guidelines, given the known physiological differences between humans and laboratory animals that make the use of particular animal species unsuitable for certain drug testing. Equally, it is safe to assume that, in the absence of a considered basis for divergence, non-compliance with common practice and guidelines aimed at promoting safety is unlikely to be held consistent with the exercise of proper care.

1 *Marshall v Lindsey County Council* [1935] 1 KB 516, CA and *Whiteford v Hunter* [1950] WN 553 HL.
2 *Morris v West Hartlepool Steam Navigation Co Ltd* [1956] AC 552, [1956] 1 All ER 385, HL; *Cavanagh v Ulster Weaving Co Ltd* [1960] AC 145, [1959] 2 All ER 745, HL; *Brown v Rolls Royce Ltd* [1960] 1 All ER 577, [1960] 1 WLR 210, HL; *Thompson v Smiths Shiprepairers (North Shields) Ltd* [1984] QB 405, [1984] 1 All ER 881; and see Miller and Goldberg *Product Liability* (2nd edn, 2004) para 14.146.
3 See for instance the Code of Practice for the Pharmaceutical Industry (2nd edn, 2012).

Compliance with regulatory standards

13.169 Compliance with statutory requirements is better evidence that the duty to take proper care has been discharged[1]. The rationale of any regulation is that it enshrines the legal standard of care at the time when the regulation is promulgated. On the other hand, compliance cannot be regarded as conclusive, for the courts have consistently held that statutory regulations do not supersede the general duty to take whatever care is appropriate in the particular circumstances[2]. Accordingly, the licensing of the product is not of itself a defence to any claim. Indeed Article 25 of Directive 2001/83/EC notes that a marketing authorisation under European law 'shall not affect the civil and criminal liability of the manufacturer and where applicable, of the marketing authorisation holder'[3]. Even where the Directives or Regulations do prescribe a detailed standard, eg in relation to certain aspects of labelling, compliance cannot be treated as decisive. A manufacturer's obligation under the common law duty of care is not exhausted upon compliance with the statute[4].

1 Medicinal products must comply with the requirements currently provided for by the Human Medicines Regulations 2012.
2 *Bux v Slough Metals Ltd* [1974] 1 All ER 262, [1973] 1 WLR 1358, CA, regarding the safe system of working with non-ferrous metals.
3 Directive 65/65/EEC [1965] OJ 22/369 (as amended). Directive 2001/83/EC [2001] OJ L311/67.
4 See the Australian Vioxx litigation *Merck Sharp & Dohme (Australia) Pty Limited v Peterson* [2011] FCAFC 128 in which the court held that compliance with the regulatory regime did not discharge the medicine manufacturer's duty of care in negligence.

13.170 In practice, however, the licensing of a product and a manufacturer's compliance with all applicable regulations will often be a difficult hurdle for a claimant to overcome. Where regulations in question cover precisely the circumstances which give rise to the complaint, the courts have shown themselves slow to substitute their own version of reasonableness in relation to activities which are closely regulated by Parliament[1]. Moreover, the control exercised by the competent regulatory authority may, indirectly, be evidence that the manufacturer's research or prescribing information was acceptable on the grounds that an independent body, such as the CSM or more recently the CHM, had reviewed the same data and information and reached the same conclusion as the manufacturer on the probable safety of the product or, as the case may be, the adequacy of the prescribing information put in the SPC[2].

1 *Albery-Speyer & Budden v BP Oil Ltd and Shell Oil Ltd* [1980] JPL 586, CA; (1980) 124 Sol Jol 376, CA in the context of injury as a result of exposure to lead in petrol, the claims were dismissed on the grounds that the defendant had complied with regulations prescribed by Parliament.
2 Cf *Thompson v Johnson and Johnson Pty Ltd* [1992] 3 Med LR 148, [1991] 2 VR 449, SC of Victoria, App Div. in a case concerning the warnings of the risk of toxic shock syndrome caused by tampons, the Court held that the response of the regulator, although not determinative, was a 'significant factor to have regard to'. See also *R v Licensing Authority Established Under Medicines Act 1968, ex p Smith, Kline & French Laboratories Ltd* [1990] 1 AC 64, at 108 per Lord Templeman; and *R v Code of Practice Committee of the Association of the British Pharmaceutical Industry, ex p Professional Counselling Aids Ltd* (1990) 10 BMLR 21 per Popplewell J at para 32.

13.171 Failure to meet regulatory requirements will place the manufacturer in a very vulnerable position because the injured person will argue that, independent of any criminal sanctions imposed because of the breach, the breach is also admissible evidence in a civil case based on negligence.

Liability for independent contractors

13.172 If a pharmaceutical company chooses to instruct another to carry out preclinical or clinical research work or to manufacture or package a product, rather than use its own resources, the question arises whether the company is liable in tort for any injury or damage caused by the negligence of the other. The general rule is that an employer is not responsible for the negligence of his independent contractor, provided reasonable care was exercised in appointing that contractor by establishing the adequacy of the facilities and reputation of the contractor for careful performance of work. There are, however, ill-defined exceptions to this rule that seek to categorise certain duties as 'non-delegable' where they involve 'extra-hazardous' acts[1].

1 *Alcock v Wraith* (1991) 59 BLR 20, CA, and *Periquito Hotels v Allied Services Construction Ltd* (25 March 1996, unreported). See also *Woodland v Essex County Council* [2013] UKSC 66.

CLAIMS IN CONTRACT

Introduction to contractual remedies

13.173 Contractual remedies against producers are generally of limited relevance to individuals who suffer drug-related injuries. There is normally no contract between the pharmaceutical manufacturer and the ultimate recipient of their product. When a drug is prescribed under an NHS prescription, there will be no contract with either the pharmacist or the doctor who wrote the prescription[1]. As the medicinal products most likely to be associated with injury are those available only through the intervention of a prescriber, and the majority of prescriptions are dispensed under the NHS, a contractual claim for injury caused by a medicinal product is likely to be comparatively rare. In the circumstances, where a patient believes that he has been injured by a medicinal product, his cause of action against persons involved in its supply – the manufacturer/marketing authorisation holder, wholesaler, pharmacist, or prescriber – is likely to be in negligence or under the CPA 1987 (as regards the manufacturer or any supplier who cannot identify his supplier or the manufacturer).

1 Because the pharmacist has a statutory duty to give the drug to the patient on presentation of a prescription and the appropriate prescription charge: *Pfizer Corporation v Minister of Health* [1965] 2 WLR 387 and *Appleby v Sleep* [1968] 2 All ER 265, [1968] 1 WLR 948, DC.

13.174 However, when medicines are sold by a retailer to a consumer over-the-counter, a contractual claim can arise; such a claim can move back up the chain of supply to the wholesaler, and ultimately give rise to a claim for an indemnity from the manufacturer[1]. The same is true for private prescriptions, although those represent a very small proportion of all prescriptions made. A further potential exception is in the context of research, where the manufacturer may contract with volunteers[2]. In relation to medical devices, some private hospitals and/or surgeons undertaking private work do contract to supply the medical devices directly to the patient and so, in such cases, the surgeon may face a claim in contract as the supplier of an allegedly defective device.

1 Such claims for indemnity may, however, be limited by exclusion clauses in the contract governing the supply.

2 This area became the focus of particular attention following the serious adverse reactions of a group of healthy volunteers to an experimental product 'TGN1412' at the Northwick Park Hospital in March 2006 (research called 'First in Humans'). The drug, which was manufactured by German pharmaceutical company TeGenero, was being tested as a potential treatment for certain autoimmune diseases and leukaemia. The direct responsibility for the administration of the research product lay with the contract research organisation Parexel. Parexel became the target of legal proceedings after TeGenero declared bankruptcy. It is thought that Parexel negotiated a settlement with the volunteers out of court.

13.175 Unlike in some US jurisdictions, statements made in promotional material issued by the manufacturer do not, of themselves, provide the user with a quasi-contractual remedy based on an implied warranty that the statements were true[1].

1 *Lambert v Lewis* [1978] 1 Lloyd's Rep 610 at 628.

13.176 If the consumer does have a contract, then the ordinary rules of contract will apply. Moreover, if the product does not correspond with its description, or is not of satisfactory quality, there might be a breach of the Sale of Goods Act 1979[1].

1 Section 14(2) and s 14(3), as amended.

Sale of Goods Act 1979

13.177 The Sale of Goods Act 1979 (as amended) implies certain conditions into contracts of sale which cannot be excluded in the case of consumer sales and can only be excluded in commercial sales if the exclusion is 'reasonable'. The effect of these conditions is, first, that the seller will be liable independent of fault on his part for injury suffered by the buyer if the product is not of satisfactory quality and, secondly, that the seller will be liable if the product was of satisfactory quality for some purposes, but not for the particular purpose that the buyer made known to the seller in circumstances where the buyer was relying on the skill and judgment of the seller. Similar terms are implied by the Supply of Goods and Services Act 1982 into a contract for the performance of a service in the course of which a product is administered.

13.178 Where goods supplied under contract are 'defective' in either sense, it is no defence for the seller to argue that he has exercised all reasonable care in the supply of such goods[1]. Such liability has always been 'strict'. It is the existence of, and not the discoverability of, or reason for, the defect in the product which renders the seller liable for the resulting damage caused. It is relatively straightforward to establish liability in the event of actual 'manufacturing defects', such as the contamination of a particular batch of medicines. Moreover, there is no doubt that liability may arise out of the inadequate nature of the labelling or instructions for use rather than the inherent design of the product itself[2]. This issue has been clarified by the introduction of the Sale of Goods Act 1979, s 14(2D) which provides that in contracts for the sale or supply of goods, the relevant circumstances to be taken into account by the court in deciding whether the goods are of adequate quality or fitness for purpose should include any public statements on the specific characteristics of the goods made about them by the seller, the producer or his representative, particularly in advertising or labelling[3].

1 *Frost v Aylesbury Dairy Co Ltd* [1905] 1 KB 608, CA.

2 *Wormell v RHM Agriculture (East) Ltd* [1986] 1 All ER 769, [1986] 1 WLR 336; applied in *Amstrad plc v Seagate Technology Inc* (1997) 86 BLR 34.
3 As introduced by the Sale and Supply of Goods to Consumers Regulations 2002, reg 3. Further changes introduced by those Regulations provide for public statements not to be relevant circumstances where for example they are shown by the seller to have been withdrawn or not relied upon (s 14(2E)).

13.179 Accordingly, the buyer of a defective medicinal product available over-the-counter or sold pursuant to a private prescription could sue the pharmacist who sold it, provided it was the buyer who was injured. However, in the case of a sale on prescription, the pharmacist may be able to show that the injured person relied upon the prescriber rather than the pharmacist for the choice of product, making any claim based upon breach of the implied condition of fitness for purpose unrealistic. A further issue is how much information a pharmacist must obtain in order to assess whether the medicine is fit for the purpose for which it is being bought within the meaning of SGA 1979, s 14(3). If a pharmacist fails to elicit sufficient information from a particular consumer about potential contraindications – high blood pressure, diabetes and so on – then if it emerges the medicine is not fit for purpose he may in certain circumstances find himself strictly liable for any consequent injuries.

13.180 Moreover, since most drugs have some side-effects, it can be difficult to establish that a medicine that has caused an adverse reaction has breached the implied condition of satisfactory quality. The Sale of Goods Act 1979, s 14(2A) provides the following definition:

'… goods are of satisfactory quality if they meet the standard that a reasonable person would regard as satisfactory, taking account of any description of the goods, the price (if relevant) and all the other relevant circumstances'.

13.181 Section 14(2B) provides examples of the criteria against which the satisfactory quality of goods may be assessed. These include 'fitness for all the purposes for which goods of the kind in question are commonly supplied' (s 14(2B)(a)) and 'safety' (s 14(2B)(d)). The nature of medicinal products (where safety is a relative concept) arguably makes it unreasonable for a consumer, having knowledge that drugs carry unavoidable risks which may be entirely due to the genetic makeup of the individual consumer, to expect them to be free of all side-effects. The extensive system of licensing such products will also be relevant to any determination as to whether the product meets the relevant statutory standards (satisfactory quality etc).

Use other than by the contracting party

13.182 It should be noted that defective products under the Sale of Goods legislation only arises between persons in a contractual relationship and ignores any of the persons involved with the use of the product who are not purchasers, such as a purchaser's friends or family who may use a product and be injured while doing so. However, there may be scope to argue in appropriate circumstances that the purchaser was acting as agent for the consumer.

Contributory negligence?

13.183 In principle, contributory negligence by the buyer is not a defence to an action based in contract[1]. The law proceeds on the basis that the seller promised that he would provide a product which was of satisfactory quality and fit for purpose and if he did not provide such a product he should be liable to compensate the buyer. However, where concurrent tortious and contractual duties to take care exist, a line of cases suggest that contributory negligence by the consumer may be relied upon by the defendant in certain circumstances, at least for the purpose of reducing the level of compensation recoverable[2].

1 *Basildon District Council v J E Lesser (Properties) Ltd* [1985] QB 839, [1985] 1 All ER 20.
2 *Forsikringsaktieselskapet Vesta v Butcher* [1989] AC 852, [1989] 1 All ER 402, HL. But see also the Australian case *Astley v Austrust Ltd* (1999) 73 ALJR 403. *Barclays Bank plc v Fairclough Buildings Ltd (No 2)* [1995] IRLR 605, CA. See also Law Commission Report 219 of 1993.

LIABILITY OF THE PRODUCER IN PRACTICE

Common types of alleged defect

13.184 There are various ways of categorising types of defects. As noted above, Burton J in *A v National Blood Authority*[1] adopted a 'standard product' and 'non-standard product' categorisation, but it is more common to refer to a three-fold categorisation[2] of 'design defects', 'manufacturing defects' and 'marketing/warnings defects' or a four-fold categorisation which adds a separate category of 'process design defects'. We consider these different forms of defect claims below, both in relation to fault liability and no-fault liability allegations, adopting the three-fold categorisation below and including 'process design defects' within manufacturing defects.

1 [2001] Lloyd's Rep Med 187.
2 The categorisation of defect play a more crucial role in US tort law, which has developed a difference between manufacturing defects, design defects and instruction defects. This distinction found its genesis in case law, but was expressly incorporated into the Third Restatement, published in 1998 (s 2(a)(b)(c): Categorisation of Product Defects).

Manufacturing defects

13.185 Where a product is defective because there has been some irregularity in the process of manufacture, with the result that it fails to meet the manufacturer's own specification for the product (rendering it a 'non-standard' product in Burton J's taxonomy), it may be said to have a process design, processing or manufacturing defect. Process design failures can occur at any stage of the manufacturing process, from the production or acceptance of defective or contaminated raw materials, through to contamination caused by packaging materials or procedures (such as the migration of chemicals from plastics or inks[1]) or even to the insertion of incorrect patient information. Cases of contamination, mistakes of formulation and filling and incorrect patient information (particularly earlier versions of amended PILs) do occur[2]. *A v National Blood Authority*[3] provides an example of a process design defect case insofar as it amounted to the failure of the system to detect and quarantine contaminated blood products.

1 Packing contamination having been a particular problem in the food and drinks industry, such as the ITX contamination of Nestlé baby milk: as reported in The Guardian, 23 November 2005.
2 See '*Patients get rogue drug after mix-up*' in The Guardian, 29 June 1985 – involved accidental filling by Organon of ampoules of hydrocortisone sodium succinate (used in shock treatment) with vecuronium bromide (used in anaesthesia). The recall of all batches of Viracept (an anti-HIV treatment) across Europe because of contamination with a genotoxic substance was reported by the MHRA in June 2007 and led to the suspension of the product's centralised marketing authorisation.
3 [2001] Lloyd's Rep Med 187.

13.186   If injury does result from such a defect, the manufacturer's position may well prove to be difficult. Even in relation to negligence claims, the courts have tended to recognise that the injured person may face great difficulty in showing by reference to a complex production and delivery process, precisely where the manufacturer failed to take reasonable care, with the result that negligence has, in effect, been inferred and the burden placed on the manufacturer to rebut the inference[1]. A manufacturer may be hard pressed to rebut such an inference, even by proof that he took reasonable care in operating a comprehensive and generally safe system of manufacture which complied with GMP Guidelines[2].

1 *Hill v James Crowe (Cases) Ltd* [1978] 1 All ER 812 and *Carroll v Fearon* (1998) Times, 26 January, CA.
2 Directive 2003/94/EC and MHRA Rules and Guidance for Pharmaceutical Manufacturers and Distributors (2014).

13.187   Further, it is to be noted that a manufacturing issue may not affect every product of the relevant type and, further, it may be impossible to identify whether the individual product does or does not suffer from the relevant defect. The difficulty may be particularly pronounced in cases of implanted medical devices where explantation by surgery may be required in order to determine whether the implanted product does or does not contain the defect. In *Boston Scientific Medizintechnik v AOC Sachsen-Anhalt*[1] the ECJ recently determined, in respect of persons fitted with a pacemaker which was part of a group containing a 'potential defect', that all products forming part of that group may be classified as defective within the meaning of the Product Liability Directive, without the need to establish that the individual product has the relevant defect and, further, that damage caused by surgical removal of such a product constitutes damage or personal injury. So called 'worried-well' claims have also been advanced in relation to potentially defective breast implants in the PIP breast implant group litigation.

1 Case C-503/13 *Boston Scientific Medizintechnik GmbH v AOK Sachsen-Anhalt – Die Gesundheitskasse* [2015] All ER (D) 88 (Mar), ECJ.

13.188   The position may be different if the defect was one which ought to have been identified by intermediate examination by, for example, the pharmacist. In such a case the manufacturer may properly argue that the causal link has been severed. It will also be different if the 'contamination' can be said to be outside the manufacturer's ability to avoid given the prevailing state of scientific knowledge. An example might be the existence of HIV in blood products prior to the recognition of the virus or the means to screen blood or heat treat products.

13.189 Under the CPA 1987 the user will be entitled to expect products to meet the standard of safety which would be achieved had the product been made according to specification and, if a product is not properly made and causes injury, liability is likely to follow. In its evidence of 1974 to the Royal Commission on Civil Liability and Compensation for Personal Injury the ABPI accepted that responsibility for such injuries should fall 'unequivocally on the shoulders of the manufacturer'. In practice the record of the industry on quality control is an excellent one[1]. In *A v National Blood Authority*[2], the fact that no system of quality control capable of identifying the contamination existed at the time the defect was introduced into the product was held not to be a relevant factor in assessing the level of safety which persons generally were entitled to expect[3].

1 See '*Memorandum of Evidence of the Association of the British Pharmaceutical Industry to Pearson Commission and to Law Commission*' Working Paper No 64.
2 *A v National Blood Authority* [2001] Lloyd's Rep Med 187.
3 Burton J relied upon the '*German Bottle Case*', BGHZ 129 9 May 1995 in which the German Federal Supreme Court said 'The fact that it is not possible to detect and repair such defects in the bottle does not alter the consumer's expectation.'

13.190 To reduce their exposure to such claims, it is crucial for manufacturers to maintain and implement an appropriate procedure for recall. While it is a condition of the grant of a marketing authorisation that such procedures exist[1], a claim in negligence could arise because a company did not follow it properly, even if – as might be the case with a recall based on realisation of a design defect – the initial supply of the product would not have attracted liability[2]. In principle, the failure of a third party to act upon a properly advertised and organised recall might allow the manufacturer to argue that the injury in any particular case was caused not by the defect in the product but by the intervening negligence of the third party, but it is worth noting that, as far as claims under the CPA 1987 are concerned, Article 8(1) of the Directive provides that, without prejudice to national laws governing contribution and indemnity, the liability of the producer 'shall not be reduced when the damage is caused both by a defect in the product and by the act or omission of a third party'.

1 See reg 59 and reg 77 of the Human Medicines Regulations 2012/1916.
2 *Walton v British Leyland (UK) Ltd* (1978) Times, 13 July. Referenced in *Products Liability Casebook* (1984, Lloyds of London Press Ltd).

13.191 It should be noted, however, that the producer has a defence under the CPA 1987 if the defect which caused the damage did not exist at the time when the product was supplied (see Article 7(b) and CPA, s 4(1)(d)). Therefore, if on the evidence it is probable that the defect arose after supply[1] by reason of the actions of a third party, perhaps through poor storage, the application of inappropriate labelling, or the removal of product information from the package subsequent to supply, then the defence may be applicable. Inadequate labelling for specific markets and deterioration through improper storage have been a concern in relation to parallel importing and the defence could be relevant here. Equally, some doctors may continue practices of directing pharmacists to remove patient leaflets from original packs and, indeed, some family planning clinics substitute their own leaflets for those of manufacturers when prescribing contraceptive preparations and products.

This could be of significance as manufacturers' leaflets tend to contain increasingly comprehensive information and warnings.

1 For a successful application of the defence under the CPA 1987, s 4(1)(d), see *Piper v JRI (Manufacturing) Ltd* [2006] EWCA Civ 1344.

13.192 In terms of fault liability, manufacturers of raw materials or component parts must take care to see that their products do not suffer from any manufacturing defects, but difficulties can arise because often such products can be used for a variety of purposes and in many different situations. The manufacturer supplying them does not always know the use to which his product will be put. His basic obligation is, therefore, to deliver a product manufactured to the correct specification[1] and to take appropriate steps to guard against the risk of his product causing personal injury or damage to other property when used in reasonably foreseeable ways. If an inappropriate use was clearly foreseeable he might be obliged under fault liability principles to issue a warning as to the limits of his product's suitability.

1 Mere supply in accordance with specification may not be sufficient as specifications are rarely comprehensive; in particular specifications rarely include parameters in relation to contaminants which are not expected or anticipated. See for example, the Benzene Litigation *Britvic Soft Drinks v Messer UK Ltd* [2002] EWCA Civ 548 where a detailed specification for a raw material, carbon dioxide, include parameters in relation to a variety of contaminants which the producer had envisaged might be present in the end product at trace levels, but did not include a specific limit on benzene, which the producer did not anticipate might be present and was, in fact, present only because of a defect in the production process; 'compliance' with a specification in such circumstances will not necessarily absolve the producer from liability.

13.193 Under the CPA 1987, if the defective nature of the finished product arises from a deficiency in a raw material or component part, the producer of the relevant material or part component will be liable jointly with the producer of the finished product. In such circumstances there would exist no liability on the part of producers of other component parts that were not defective. However, the peculiar difficulties for manufacturers of raw materials and components are recognised by the Directive in that such producers have a specific defence if they can show that the defect in their product was wholly attributable to the design of the finished product or to compliance, by the producer of the raw material or component part, with instructions given by the producer of the finished product (see Article 7(f) and the CPA 1987, s 4(1)(f)). The position of such manufacturers is therefore largely protected unless they fail to meet the specification.

13.194 The final stages of the manufacturing process also give rise to risks of liability, particularly in relation to defects arising from packaging and labelling. Under fault liability principles the manufacturer must take reasonable care in developing his packaging and may be exposed to liability in respect of defects which, for instance, render the product subject to deterioration or contamination, whether from packaging itself of external sources. Under no fault liability, the definition of a defective product requires consideration of 'get-up' (see s 3(2)(a)) which would appear wide enough to encompass the quality of and design of packaging, for example whether it is child-proof.

13.195 In *Pollard v Tesco Stores*[1], a packaging design claim was brought on behalf of an infant who ingested dishwasher powder from a Tesco own brand dishwasher powder bottle. The bottle cap was a child-resistant closure. However, it did not comply with the British Standard in that it failed to provide the proper minimum torque required to unscrew the cap without squeezing. The Court of Appeal held that there was no defect under the CPA 1987 or breach of duty in negligence by Tesco or the bottle manufacturer. The chemical constitution of the dishwasher powder fell short of the mandatory requirement for a child-resistant closure cap to be fitted. The claimant contended that since the defendants had fitted that type of cap anyway, they should be held liable in circumstances where it did not comply with the relevant standard. Laws LJ, giving the only judgment of the Court of Appeal, disagreed 'since there is no trace of any reference to the British Standard on the bottle, packaging or get up of this product, and no reason to suppose that members of the public such as Mrs Pollard would have appreciated that any public authority had pronounced upon the matter'. This was a case concerning voluntary national standards. A medicinal product, by contrast, is far more likely to be governed by mandatory regulatory requirements. However, it serves as an illustration that the concept of defect under the CPA 1987 may not necessarily correlate precisely with the concept of a safe product under the General Product Safety Directive[2].

1 [2006] EWCA Civ 1393.
2 Directive 2001/95/EC, which provides that a product shall be presumed safe when it conforms to voluntary national standards which transpose European standards (Article 3(2)).

13.196 Interesting questions have also arisen in relation to the design of tamper free – or more properly tamper evident – containers, given the increased incidence of intentional tampering and blackmail of health care companies so graphically illustrated by the Tylenol incident in the USA[1]. The manufacturer may argue that he took reasonable care to see that the integrity of the product was not compromised prior to the time it left his control and that he has a statutory defence under the CPA 1987 because it was not defective when he supplied it. However, if such seals are technically and economically practicable to incorporate, it might be argued that the product has a design defect and does not offer the safety people are generally entitled to expect.

1 In 1982, seven people were reported dead after taking Tylenol capsules. An unknown suspect put lethal amounts of cyanide into Tylenol capsules. It is thought that the tampering occurred once the product had reached the shelves.

Design defects

13.197 Clearly any product may suffer from a design defect which makes it intrinsically unsafe for the majority of foreseeable users, regardless of whether it has been manufactured correctly according to the manufacturer's specification. The concept of safety has always been difficult to apply to medicinal products where safety is, more than ever, relative. However, in principle, under fault liability the manufacturer has to decide whether the level of risk associated with a product is acceptable, bearing in mind the benefits. The task of the manufacturer is to take all reasonable steps to exclude the risks that are avoidable and by appropriate user/prescribing information minimise the risks that remain.

13.198 In this regard, it may be relevant to distinguish between allergic/ idiosyncratic reactions and liability for extreme reactions to a medicinal product that is known to cause injury of the type suffered by the patient in question. If the adverse reaction itself was due to idiosyncrasy, which by definition is an abnormal and sporadic response and of an unpredictable nature, then the manufacturer may be better able to demonstrate that he exercised reasonable care and/or that the product should not be deemed to be defective by reason of such a response. On the other hand if the injury sustained is not due to idiosyncrasy and is of a type, given the design of the product, which the manufacturer ought reasonably to have foreseen as a real risk and therefore should have made the subject of a warning, the fact that the patient possibly suffered an extreme reaction peculiar to him may not assist the manufacturer. He may be liable for all the consequences of pain and suffering that flow from the initial injury even if such injury was exacerbated by an abnormal physical susceptibility on the patient's part[1].

1 *Smith v Leech Brain & Co Ltd* [1962] 2 QB 405, [1961] 3 All ER 1159 and see also *Robinson v Post Office* [1974] 1 WLR 1176 and *Page v Smith* [1994] 4 All ER 522, CA; rvsd *Page v Smith* [1995] 2 All ER 736, HL.

13.199 If it turns out that a medicinal product does suffer from a design defect, the outcome of an action in negligence (whether in relation to an idiosyncratic or an extreme reaction) will depend upon whether the court finds that the manufacturer ought to have foreseen that the dangerous nature of the product was a probable outcome of its design. Under English law, the conduct of the manufacturer is to be judged by reference to his actual scientific knowledge or his constructive knowledge, ie the means of knowledge reasonably available to him when the product was under development – the so-called 'state of the art'. This actual knowledge may derive from his pre-clinical work and clinical trials (and, possibly, research conducted by associated companies) but he will also be treated as having constructive knowledge of the international literature relating to the compound in question or the class of compounds.

13.200 Many of the significant claims in the UK and elsewhere in the last 40 years have concerned products with design defects or alleged design defects:

- the incidence of phocomelia following exposure in utero to thalidomide (Distaval) led to claims of design defect is the classic example, yet thalidomide continues to be used successfully in treating certain conditions such as leprosy and a form of the compound was approved centrally on 14 June 2007 for the treatment of certain patients suffering from multiple myeloma[1]. As the amount of unlicensed use of thalidomide grew, the MCA issued guidelines for use which remained 'exceptional'[2];
- oculomucocutaneous syndrome and other problems were experienced by patients prescribed practolol (Eraldin) and ICI set up a voluntary scheme of compensation in 1975 as a result;
- litigation arose in the late 1970s in the UK based on an alleged link between the use of hormone pregnancy tests and teratogenic effects manifest in the newborn[3];
- litigation in the 1980s concerned the alleged association between use of pertussis vaccine and brain damage, between benoxaprofen (Opren)

and liver damage[4] and between neomycin spray and hearing defects when the product was administered to burns[5];

- in the 1990s, allegations of design defect were central to litigation concerning both third generation oral contraceptives and MMR vaccine.

1 See CHMP release of 29 March 2007 concerning Revlimid (lenalidomide). On 23 April 2009, The National Institute for Health and Clinical Excellence issued a Final Appraisal Determination (FAD) approving lenalidomide, in combination with dexamethasone, as an option to treat patients who suffer from multiple myeloma who have received two or more prior therapies in England and Wales.
2 CSM/MCA, Current problems in Pharmacovigilance Vol 20, May 1994, p 8.
3 *D and R v Schering Chemicals Ltd* (2 July 1982, unreported) QBD.
4 See NLJ 18 December 1987 at 1183 and the personal review of the issues by Dr Ian Shedden, previously vice-president of Lilly Research Laboratories, published in Scrip no 1284, 19 February 1988, p 30.
5 See *Mann and Close v Wellcome Foundation Ltd* (20 January 1989, unreported) QBD.

13.201   Almost all significant product liability litigation involving medicinal products has, to date, related essentially to design defects or warnings rather than processing defects[1], although those advising claimants are always on the lookout for 'hot lots' where it appears that the adverse effects complained of follow the administration of certain lots of the product more frequently than would be expected by chance. Although not involving a commercial manufacturer, there has been significant litigation surrounding the administration to about 2,000 children of human growth hormone extracted from the pituitary glands of cadavers between 1959 and 1985. The treatment took place under the supervision of the Medical Research Council (MRC) and a number of patients contracted Creutzfeldt-Jakob disease. In 1996 Morland J issued his judgment on a preliminary issue of whether it was negligent to proceed with the treatment programme during the whole period. He found that from the spring of 1977 the MRC had been negligent in providing human growth hormone derived from human cadavers to any new 'non-hypoglycaemic' patients[2]. Accordingly, he found that patients treated after that date became entitled to compensation. Significantly, the judge went on to hold[3] that the MRC should also have foreseen a risk of psychiatric damage arising from fear that patients might be diagnosed with this disease and that, therefore, independent of proof of current bodily injury, recovery of damages should be allowed:

'It was reasonably foreseeable that if the worst fears were realised and death from CJD occurred, Hartree HGH recipients both those of normal fortitude and those more vulnerable might suffer psychiatric injury. I cannot see in the facts and circumstances of this litigation why public policy including social and economic policy considerations should exclude them from compensation.'

1 See, for example, the MMR/MR vaccine litigation, the oral contraceptive litigation, and the Fetal Anti-Convulsant litigation.
2 *N v Medical Research Council and Secretary of State for Health* [1996] 7 Med LR 309.
3 *Group B Plaintiffs v Medical Research Council* (1997) 41 BMLR 157.

13.202   The acceptance of anxiety claims of this type is a significant development. In other cases in the USA, this in turn has led in some States to legally controversial claims for medical monitoring, whereby compensation is recovered for periodic testing to detect early onset of latent disease, or at least for monitoring from when the claimant first develops symptoms[1]. In *Boston Scientific Medizintechnik v AOC Sachsen-*

Anhalt[2] the ECJ recently held, in respect of persons fitted with a pacemaker which was part of a group containing a 'potential defect', that all products forming part of that group may be classified as defective within the meaning of the Product Liability Directive, without the need to establish that the individual product has the relevant defect and, further, that damage caused by surgical removal of such a product constitutes damage or personal injury. In England and Wales, the courts in related fields have made it clear that physical changes alone that fall short of impairment of health and are asymptomatic cannot found a claim requiring proof of damage[3]. So called 'worried-well' claims are currently being advanced in the PIP breast implant group litigation.

1 See *Bourgeois v A P Green Industries, Inc* 716 So 2d 355 (La 1998) and *Metro-North Commuter R R Co v Buckley* 521 US 424, 117 S Ct 2113 (1997). In the Shiley heart valve class action settlement (which encompassed foreign claimants) payments were also made despite the absence of injury (see the Guardian, 24 March 1992).
2 Case C-503/13 *Boston Scientific Medizintechnik GmbH v AOK Sachsen-Anhalt – Die Gesundheitskasse* [2015] All ER (D) 88 (Mar), ECJ.
3 *Rothwell v Chemical & Insulating Co Ltd* [2008] 1 AC 281 (usually cited as *Johnston v NEI International Combustion Ltd* [2007] UKHL 39) and *AB v Tameside & Glossop Health Authority* [1997] 8 Med LR 91. See also *Greenway v Johnson Matthey plc* [2014] EWHC 753 (QB), para **13.164**, fn 3 above.

13.203   Invariably in such litigation allegations about inadequate research on the part of the manufacturer are made. There is, however, a limit in English law to liability for design defects. If a manufacturer does everything that can reasonably be expected of him, but still does not discover the existence of a defect, then under negligence principles this 'development risk' falls upon the consumer rather than the manufacturer. As a general principle, it must be emphasised that a defect of design can arise quite independent of negligence. The courts made it clear long ago that if strict liability was to be imposed upon manufacturers in these circumstances, it was for Parliament so to enact[1]. In cases concerning deafness said to have resulted from the use of neomycin spray Waterhouse J (obiter) rejected the suggestion that pharmaceuticals belong to the category of things dangerous per se[2]. In any event, it now appears likely that, even if such an extension of the law were enacted by Parliament, this would be incompatible with the Product Liability Directive and liable to be struck down on the principles of *Commission v UK, Commission v France*[3], *Commission v Greece*[4] and *Skov v Bilka*[5].

1 *Read v J Lyons & Co Ltd* [1947] AC 156, [1946] 2 All ER 471, HL.
2 See *Mann and Close v Wellcome Foundation Ltd* (20 January 1989, unreported) QBD.
3 Case C-52/00 *Commission v France* [2002] ECR I-3827.
4 Case C-154/00 *Commission v Greece* [2002] ECR I-3879.
5 Case C-402/03 *Skov v Bilka*.

13.204   No fault liability under the CPA 1987 is likely to be the favoured approach by claimants to design defects. If a product does prove to be unsafe when used in the way apparently intended or according to its normal instructions for use, it is likely to be found defective[1]. However, liability will not automatically arise because the Directive (see Article 7(e)) allows a defence for the producer where 'the state of scientific and technical knowledge at the time when [the producer] put the product into circulation was not such as to enable the existence of the defect to be discovered'. Most Member States have retained this 'development risks defence'.

1 See *Abouzaid v Mothercare (UK) Ltd* (2001) Times, 20 February, CA, where the Court of Appeal found that the design of a product whose harmful characteristics could readily be remedied was defective under the CPA 1987.

13.205 It should be noted that the CPA 1987 implicitly contemplates a situation where a producer has a defence to liability in circumstances where he acquired knowledge of a harmful characteristic of his product before its administration but after its date of supply by him. A claim in negligence may, however, arise for failure to use that after-acquired knowledge reasonably by issuing warnings or (depending upon the hazard in question) organising a recall. Such issues were relevant to the carefully organised initiative of the Aspirin Foundation in notifying the trade, doctors and patients of the suspicion that the use of aspirin in young children had been associated with an increased risk of developing Reye's syndrome, at the time they discontinued 'junior' formulations of that popular analgesic[1].

1 See HC Official Report vol 102 cc 815–823 (24 July 1986).

Marketing defects and warnings

13.206 The absence of satisfactory product information can turn an intrinsically safe product into an unsafe product and, given the nature of its products, the 'failure to warn' claim is very familiar to the pharmaceutical industry. The interest in consent issues and disclosure of risks by doctors to patients can only increase this type of litigation[1].

1 See, for instance, *Sidaway v Board of Governors of the Bethlem Royal Hospital and the Maudsley Hospital* [1985] AC 871, [1985] 1 All ER 643, HL; see also *Chester v Afshar* [2004] UKHL 41.

13.207 As regards fault liability, part of any duty of care found to be owed by a manufacturer to a consumer is undoubtedly to formulate and supply adequate information about the product, so that it can be used safely. The essence of a warning is that it allows the user to confront and avoid the hazard which it describes. The location and prominence of warnings, as well as their existence, may be important particularly with products promoted direct to the public. If the manufacturer supplies a proper warning in his technical information about the product and the user or intermediary ignores that warning, then the causal link between the manufacturer's action in putting the product on the market and the injury to the user is broken and no liability will result[1].

1 See, for instance, *Worsley v Tambrands Ltd* [2000] PIQR 95 and *Foster v Biosil* (2000) 59 BMLR 178.

13.208 It is settled English law, however, that the duty of care relating to the supply of information may, in certain circumstances, be discharged by supplying the relevant information to a responsible intermediary[1]. In the field of medicinal products available on prescription, the doctor is such an intermediary, although the concept has been challenged in Canada in a case where the issue of a warning direct to patients using oral contraceptives was found to be practicable and necessary[2]. In *Reyes v Wyeth Laboratories*[3], a Texas case concerning the contraction of paralytic polio following vaccination with live attenuated polio vaccine, the learned intermediary principle was held not to apply to large scale public health campaigns such as mass vaccination, where it was said that nurses administered the vaccine without making the usual personalised assessment of risks and benefits typical of a decision to administer a prescription only medicine. However, the doctrine was recently applied by the Texas Supreme Court in *Centocar, Inc v Hamilton*[4], which ruled that a manufacturer of a medicinal product fulfils its duty to warn patients of a product's risks by providing adequate warnings to the prescribing physician. The prescribing physician is best suited to weigh the risks and benefits of the prescription medicine.

1 *Holmes v Ashford* [1950] 2 All ER 76, CA and *Kubach v Hollands* [1937] 3 All ER 907.
2 *Buchan v Ortho Pharmaceutical (Canada) Ltd* (1984) 46 OR (2d) 113. See also *Dow Corning Corporation v Hollis* (1995) 129 DLLR (4th) 609.
3 498 F 2d 1264 (5th Circuit, 31 July 1974).
4 *Centocar, Inc v Hamilton* 372 SW 3d 140 (Tex 2012).

13.209 In the UK, the basic rule is reflected in the Human Medicines Regulations 2012, reg 294, which provides that a person may not advertise a product to practitioners qualified to prescribe unless those practitioners have been supplied with a succinct statement of the entries in the summary of product characteristics about prescribed matters[1]. Information to prescribers is traditionally supplied by inclusion of product information in the compendium of products prepared by the Association of the British Pharmaceutical Industry and supplied free to all registered medical practitioners. If a manufacturer wishes to rely upon the right to supply information only to prescribers, it is important to ensure that such information is adequate. The Human Medicines Regulations 2012, reg 260 and Sch 27 set out the contents that must appear on package leaflets.

1 See the Human Medicines Regulations 2012, Sch 30, para 9.

13.210 The need for, and adequacy of, warnings in relation to medicinal products will depend upon a number of factors but primarily upon the magnitude of the risk both in terms of the numerical chance of it occurring and the seriousness of the injury that might result. The manufacturer may justifiably take into account the knowledge he knows the reasonable prescriber will have from other sources, but that does not mean the manufacturer can justify a general failure to warn on the grounds that the industrious prescriber could have obtained the information from elsewhere, if only he had searched properly. In practice, for many years[1] doctors in the UK obtain information from a variety of sources, including established reference sources such as The *British National Formulary*[2] and MIMS – the Monthly Index of Medical Specialities[3]. It would appear that these sources may be more influential than the manufacturer's Summary of Product Characteristics but the latter's status under European law means that its contents are frequently the focus of litigation.

1 See for instance Eaton G and Parish P (1976) Journal of the Royal College of General Practitioners (Suppl no 1) 22, 64-68 and Miller R R (1974) 8 Drug Intelligence and Clinical Pharmacology 81–91.
2 Published by the British Medical Association and The Pharmaceutical Society of Great Britain and supplied to all NHS doctors.
3 An independent monthly publication of the Haymarket Press sent free to full-time GPs and heads of hospital pharmacy departments.

13.211 In principle, however, to show a causal link between any alleged 'failure to warn' by the manufacturer and the injury sustained by the claimant, it would be necessary to show that the prescriber relied upon the manufacturer's prescribing information and his actions would have been different were it not for the postulated breach of duty in relation to the supply of adequate product information. The Benzodiazepine Litigation collapsed in the light of the difficulties the claimants faced proving not only that the warnings about the alleged dependence potential of the benzodiazepines in question were negligent but also that alleged injuries were withdrawal symptoms as opposed to the recrudescence of the underlying disorder. The litigation was struck out as an abuse of process following the withdrawal of funding by the Legal Aid Board. One of the issues considered relevant to the decision was the formidable problems the claimants faced with regard to causation: few if any of the claimants had evidence from the general practitioners that they would have taken a different course if the defendant had given more adequate advice and warnings[1].

1 This issue was also raised in the oral contraceptives litigation *XYZ v Schering Health Care Ltd* [2002] EWHC 1420 (QB). Had generic causation been established, one of the issues which the court would have determined was whether the claimants would have been prescribed third generation combined oral contraceptive pills but for the defect (including inadequate warnings), which would have included consideration of the potential benefits in respect of matters other than venous thrombo-embolism which the product was perceived to bring. However, this issue did not fall to be determined as the product was held to be not defective on a trial of the prior issue of generic causation.

13.212 Possibly the most difficult problem in developing prescribing information is, however, deciding the cogency of the evidence that is required to justify a contra-indication or warning of possible adverse effects. In this regard, it may not always be appropriate for a manufacturer to wait for a risk to be proven before inserting a warning. In determining the level of suspicion that should trigger a warning the manufacturer must take into account a variety of factors including the benefit to be derived from the drug and the alternative treatment possibilities. The less serious the illness to be treated, the greater the onus, it is argued, upon the manufacturer to advise the doctor, and through him the patient, of the possibility of a serious adverse reaction even if the evidence of hazard in man is only flimsy or is based on animal evidence of questionable extrapolability. On this principle, a high standard will be expected in relation to the duty to warn about potential adverse events where the product in question is used to prevent disease in healthy people or a physiological state such as pregnancy. A Canadian Court applying English law principles has emphasised that where medical evidence exists which indicates the possibility of a serious adverse effect, it is not reasonable for the manufacturer to ignore that information because he finds it unconvincing[1]. Equally, this does not mean that the manufacturer cannot exercise some judgment about the validity of data adverse to his product and, indeed, as prescribing information is developed by industry scientists for prescribers, it might be argued that provided, when developing that information, the manufacturer's medical and scientific staff adopt an approach that would be supported by a respectable body of scientific opinion, neither they personally, nor the manufacturer, will have been negligent. In practice, many manufacturers seek to record 'associations' or 'reports' without conceding any causal connection between the use of the product and the reported event. Ultimately, however, in prescription only medicines, it is the regulator who must be persuaded as to the appropriateness of any warning.

1 See *Buchan v Ortho Pharmaceutical (Canada) Ltd* (1984) 46 OR (2d) 113. An immediate obligation to disclose, suspicion of hazard was found in *Wells v Ortho Pharmaceutical Corpn* 615 F Supp 262 at 294 (ND Ga 1985). See also *McColl v Strathclyde Regional Council* 1983 SLT 616 in relation to possible carcinogenic risks of fluoridation of water supply.

13.213 Even if the defect was 'unknowable' when a product was first designed and marketed, an injured person may still be able to show that at some later date the manufacturer was in a position to establish the existence of the defect, as a result perhaps of new information available in the technical literature or reports of adverse events involving that type of product. This situation was the basis of ICI's liability in *Wright v Dunlop Rubber Co*[1] where the court found that although ICI did not initially realise that a chemical they were supplying to Dunlop was a carcinogen, they later should have taken note of increasing evidence that it had this property. There is increasing importance attached by manufacturers and the regulatory authorities to systematic post-marketing surveillance, especially in the case of the products of biotechnology where traditional 'screening' methods at the research stage are inapplicable. Withdrawal from the market in the face of the results of such surveillance is now quite frequent and often controversial[2].

1 *Wright v Dunlop Rubber Co Ltd* (1972) 13 KIR 255, CA. See also *Ralph v Yamaha Motor Co Ltd* (5 July 1996, unreported).
2 For example, Les Laboratoires Servier discontinued its fenfluramine products for use in obesity in September 1997 after data available in the USA suggesting a possible link with heart valve lesion (see Scrip no 2288, 19 September 1997 at p 17). Merck's withdrawal of its anti-arthritis product, Vioxx, following an analysis of research on a different indication which revealed a higher incidence of coronary events than had previously been recorded was accompanied by reports that it had set aside US$1 billion as a provision for the legal costs of defending consequent product liability claims.

13.214 Positive statements about safety made through promotional material and statements by company representatives when promoting products may affect the status of product information. An otherwise adequate warning may be judged ineffective if issued against the background of promotional statements which seek to deny the existence of any danger that is the subject matter of the warning[1]. The 'dilution of warnings' in this way may lead to liability on the part, not only of the manufacturer, but also possibly advertising agencies and others who have developed or approved the promotion in question.

1 See, for instance, *Love v Wolf, Parke Davies & Co* 38 Cal Rptr 183 (1964).

13.215 In relation to no fault liability, the Directive makes it clear that instructions for use and warnings will have a major bearing upon whether the product is deemed to offer the safety that the public are entitled to expect. In describing the considerations relevant to the existence of a defect, the CPA 1987, s 3(2) raises, along with 'all the circumstances', the purposes for which the product is marketed and the manner of its marketing. Equally, it is considered that the courts will look closely not only at instructions and warnings supplied with the product but also the wider activities of the producer in promoting his product which would appear to be covered by the expression 'manner of marketing'. Expectations of safety may inadvertently be created by advertising that information provided with, or in connection with, the product may not satisfactorily qualify. Title VIII of Directive 2001/83/EC now contains the EU code on the advertising of medicinal products for human use[1] and both the MHRA and the ABPI, through the Prescription Medicines Code of Practice Authority, are increasingly vigilant in monitoring the accuracy of advertising with a view to ensuring that the safety and efficacy of products are not 'over-sold'; exceptionally, there may be criminal prosecution[2]. Advertising for products available over-the-counter requires prior approval under the Codes of Practice of the Proprietary Association of Great Britain[3].

1 Directive 2001/83/EC, [2001] OJ L311/67 implemented in the UK now by the Human Medicines Regulations 2012
2 *R v Roussel Laboratories and Good* (1988) 153 JP 298, CA, and the Association of the British Pharmaceutical Industry Code of Practice for the Pharmaceutical Industry 2012.
3 The Proprietary Association of Great Britain (PAGB) Medicines Advertising Codes 2009.

13.216 In relation to all these matters the CPA 1987 would not appear directly to undermine the principle that the informational activities of the manufacturer of medicinal products can properly be concentrated upon an intermediary – the prescriber. More generally, it is suggested that although a high standard of product information will be required there can be no absolute standard for such information and it is difficult to see how its adequacy can be judged by anything other than the same concept of the safety that persons generally, or a person, is entitled to expect, given the state of scientific knowledge. A decision to add a warning after reassessment of the literature will not be taken automatically as an admission of prior defect or negligence[1].

1 See *Hart v Lancashire and Yorkshire Rly Co* (1869) 21 LT 261 at 263.

13.217 Patient information is a continuing issue in Europe. Articles 58–69 of Directive 2001/83/EC, as amended, require manufacturers to include a package leaflet with all medicinal products unless certain obligatory information can be contained on the packaging. The obligatory information includes at Article 59.1:

> '(c) a list of information which is necessary before the medicinal product is taken…
> (d) the necessary and usual instructions for proper use…
> (e) a description of the adverse reactions which may occur under normal use of the medicinal product…'

13.218 A leaflet was required for all products first licensed after 1 January 1994 and for existing products when the product licence was first renewed after that date. The marketing authorisation holder must obtain an approval for its text from the Competent Authority before supplying it with a product. Although the entries are required to be compatible with the SPC, there remains a lack of consensus as to how detailed such entries should be for some matters such as contra-indications and side-effects. In the UK, prior to the adoption of Directive 92/27/EEC, the ABPI[1] and the Department of Health[2] have argued that some selectivity is necessary in order to meet the principal aim of providing understandable information of practical benefit to the patient. Some commentators too have noted that life would be impossible if every practitioner, let alone every patient, were to be exposed to all available data and were expected to take all postulated risks into account before prescribing or using a drug[3].

1 Association of the British Pharmaceutical Industry 'Information to Patients on Medicines' (1987).
2 Evidence to the Select Committee of the House of Lords (HL Paper 77, 1990 HMSO).
3 Dukes & Swartz *Responsibility for Drug Induced Injury* (1988, Elsevier).

13.219 European legislation[1] now requires consultation with relevant consumer groups on the content of patient information leaflets and the MHRA requires that all new patient information leaflets are user tested. Where a patient information leaflet has been user tested, this factor may itself be relevant to the issue of the safety that persons generally are entitled to expect, at least in relation to the decision as to the form of a particular warning.

1 Council Directive 2001/83, Article 59.2 and the Human Medicines Regulations 2012. The European Commission has also published Guidance concerning consultations with target patient groups for the package leaflet (May 2006). See also the European Commission Guideline on the readability of the labelling and package leaflet of medicinal products for human use (12 January 2009).

13.220 For the moment, patient information leaflets in the EU have not sought to emulate the US-style documents listing every reported association, whether thought causative or not. It remains to be seen, however, whether in future product liability litigation patients will rely on the absence of warnings and information from the patient information leaflet, as compared to the SPC, to make out their case on defect, or whether the SPC supplied to prescribers will retain its primacy in this regard and what approach the court will take to any such claims.

13.221 The manufacturer's legal position will seldom be better than when he can show that the patient's safety expectations were directly qualified by supply of a patient-orientated package leaflet. On the other hand, the difficulties of making inherently technical information understandable cannot be underestimated and detailed information may serve only to confuse the patient.

13.222 *Worsley v Tambrands Ltd*[1] provides an interesting insight into the competing considerations inherent in the design of product information. In that case the claimant alleged (under the CPA 1987 and in negligence) that the tampon product was defective by virtue of inadequate warnings of the potential risk associated with tampon use in particular with regard to the risk and potentially life-threatening consequences of toxic shock syndrome (TSS). The factual circumstances of the case included the fact that the claimant had lost the information leaflet which came inside the box. The claimant had two main contentions:

(1) First, she contended that the defendant ought to have foreseen that the leaflet might not be kept and/or read and that as a consequence the health warning, including the list of likely symptoms and advice on how to react to them, ought to have been printed in full on the outside of the package. Ebsworth J disagreed:

'As a matter of common sense, I conclude that the duty of the manufacturer, and that which persons generally are entitled to expect in relation to the product, is that the box contains an unambiguous and clear warning that there is an association between TSS and tampon use and directs the menstruating woman to the internal leaflet for full details. TSS is a rare but potentially very serious condition which may be life threatening, but it is necessary to balance the rarity and the gravity. That balance is reasonably, properly and safely struck by the dual system of a risk warning on the box and a full explanation in the leaflet if the former is clearly visible and the latter is both legible and full.'

(2)   Second, the claimant contended that the leaflet was designed in such a way that it did not have a sufficient impact upon her, whereas the US warnings current in 1994 were more prominent, fuller and would have had an impact. Ebsworth J concluded:

'As a design, I accept that the United States model is better than the United Kingdom one. But that is not the point. The issue is not whether the U.K. pattern could have replicated the United States one (I am prepared to accept that it could, in the absence of evidence to the contrary), but whether the United Kingdom one falls below the statutory or common law standard by reason of its design and/or contents, and, if it did, whether a different design would have caused the claimant to have acted differently. The United Kingdom leaflet is, because it is multilingual, set out in the columns of relatively small print in blue type on white. There are four columns on the page which contains the English language warning. The symptoms of TSS are in bold type. I consider the original to be legible without undue effort. There is no evidence before me to suggest that multilingual documents are less likely to be read than single language ones. I would have thought that we are all used to them by now. I reject the argument that they fall below the standard which persons might generally be entitled to expect.'

1 [2000] PIQR P95.

13.223 Misuse is another important issue. In determining whether a product is defective, the CPA 1987 states that one consideration is what might reasonably be expected to be done with or in relation to the product (see s 3(2)(b)). Even under no fault liability there is no duty to warn of dangers that are obvious or a matter of common knowledge[1]. Although the position is somewhat unclear, it is thought that the law relating to liability for gross misuse by a patient will not change radically as a result of no fault liability, and indeed contributory negligence is retained (see Article 8(2) of the Directive and CPA 1987, s 6(4)), but the manufacturer will be well advised to consider issues of possible misuse, particularly in relation to products available over-the-counter[2].

1 *Bogle v McDonald's Restaurants Ltd* [2002] All ER (D) 436.
2 Even with products available only on prescription, the decision of the Frankfurt Appellate Court requiring more detailed warnings with an Orciprenalin aerosol for asthma illustrates the trend (see BGH, NJW 1989, 1542 FF).

13.224 However, if a manufacturer has encouraged, either directly or indirectly, uses other than those in the product information ('off-label' use), claimants will have an argument that such encouragement amounts to one of the circumstances which must be taken into account in determining what persons generally are entitled to expect. Even mere knowledge of off-label use by a manufacturer and inaction on his part prior to the product in question being put into circulation (such as failing to write an appropriate 'Dear Doctor' letter distancing himself from unsafe use) could potentially amount to a relevant consideration, as the circumstances set out in s 3(2)(a) include '…refraining from doing anything with or in relation to the product'.

CAUSATION

13.225 As stated above, in claims for injuries arising from allegedly defective medicinal products, causation usually provides a significant hurdle for claimants in proving their case. There is no distinction in the way in which causation is to be proved in fault and no fault liability regimes. The standard of proof is the same in both.

13.226 Article 4 of the Directive and CPA 1987, s 2(1) require a claimant to prove the damage, the defect and the causal relationship between the defect and the damage. Beyond this, however, the Directive prescribes no specific requirements as to how causation is to be established and thus a Member State is free to implement the Directive so as to leave issues of causation to be determined in accordance with the rules and norms applicable to the determination of civil liability matters within that jurisdiction.

13.227 Consideration has been given by the Commission to the question as to whether the Directive should be amended so as to provide a lower threshold for a claimant in relation to the burden of proof in establishing that the defect caused the damage. Several options were discussed in the Commission's Green Paper of 1999[1], including the possibility of inferring a causal relationship between defect and damage, or even inferring the existence of the defect where a claimant proves damage caused by a product. The Commission also looked at the possibility of stipulating the standard of proof required to establish the causal relationship between defect and damage, and proposed a probability of greater than 60 per cent[2]. Similarly, the 2003 Report for the Commission noted that the issue of the burden of proof *'continues to be controversial'*, with certain consumer representatives seeking a lessening of the burden on claimants. The Report noted the concerns expressed that to alter the burden of proof would upset the existing balance of the Directive and might encourage spurious claims[3]. In short, despite calls, there has been no amendment to the Directive in relation to the requirement that the claimant prove defect, damage and the causal connection between the two, whether in relation to the burden of proof, uniformity as to the causational requirements applied by Member States, or otherwise.

1 Commission Green Paper: Liability for Defective Products, Brussels, COM(1999) 396, para 3.2, pp 20–22.
2 Commission Green Paper: Liability for Defective Products, Brussels, COM(1999) 396, para 3.2, p 21.
3 'Product Liability in the European Union: A Report for the European Commission' (Lovells) Part 3 para 2.2(a), p 47.

13.228 The CPA 1987 itself provides no special rules on causation. It merely stipulates by s 2(1), that where any damage is caused 'wholly or partly' by a defect in a product, then the producer shall be liable for the damage. Common law principles will therefore apply. In this jurisdiction, causation in tort has commonly been accepted to constitute a two-fold inquiry as to whether: (i) the defendant's tortious conduct caused the damage as a matter of fact; and (ii) if so, whether the defendant is to be held liable for such damage as a matter of law. The first-stage factual enquiry may, in some cases, be capable of being satisfied by the application of the 'but for' test. The 'but for' test, however, has long been recognised as providing only a potentially exclusionary starting point to the causal inquiry; it may not provide a complete answer as to factual causation.

13.229 Where it is alleged that an exposure to a particular agent has caused a particular alleged condition, the factual enquiry is likely to be complex and the court is likely to require the assistance of expert evidence on a variety of scientific issues. The enquiry is likely to be of particular complexity when 'generic causation' is properly in issue, that is, in circumstances in which there is disagreement amongst the scientific community as to whether the agent in question is *capable* of causing the condition alleged as a matter of medical science. Such scientific inquiries in 'medical causation' can therefore assume a major significance in medicinal product liability claims. In certain cases there may be public health implications arising from any finding by the court on generic causation which may go well beyond the confines of the litigation itself, placing a particular burden on the parties to ensure that the court is presented with the best scientific evidence reasonably obtainable. The MMR litigation provides a notable example. The contentions advanced by Dr Wakefield in relation to the alleged causal link between MMR and autism (and other adverse effects) had a profound impact on the uptake of the MMR vaccine between 1998–2003[1], with consequential public health implications; the litigation collapsed before the court had to determine the claims, but any determination would have been likely to have affected the uptake (whether positively or negatively) of the vaccine.

1 Daily Telegraph, 27 November 2012 'MMR uptake rates finally recovered from Wakefield scandal figures show'.

13.230 Even if the claimant is able to discharge the burden of proof in relation to generic causation, he must still prove, on the balance of probabilities, that the product in question caused his condition in his individual case. In circumstances in which a condition occurs in the general population even in the absence of exposure to the agent in question, the authorities demonstrate the considerable difficulties which a claimant is likely to face in proving 'individual causation'[1].

1 See, for example, the failure of the claimant in the tobacco litigation *McTear v Imperial Tobacco Ltd* 2005 2 SC 1.

13.231 If the claimant is able to establish both elements of 'medical' causation, that is, that the agent is in fact capable of causing the condition alleged and, further, that the agent did in fact cause the condition in the individual claimant's case, then the relevant 'factual' causal steps still remain to be established. Thus, the claimant will need to establish the 'factual causation' requirement as to whether the breach of duty in question (as opposed to merely the chemical agent in question) caused the claimant's condition. This stage of factual causation may overlap with 'individual' medical causation, but will not necessarily be co-extensive with that enquiry as the defendant's tort will not necessarily equate exactly with the exposure to the agent in question. The tort must still be shown to have caused the injury alleged. For example, a tortious failure to provide protective equipment will not cause the damage if, as a matter of fact, the worker would not have worn the equipment in any event[1]; similarly, in a product liability pharmaceutical case, a prescription medicine may be 'defective' under CPA 1987, s 3 by reason of an alleged defect relating to the inadequacy of the information or warnings in an SPC or PIL, but it is submitted that the claim will fail as a matter of causation unless the claimant is able to demonstrate that he or she would not have been prescribed the medicine and/or would not have taken the medicine if the appropriate warning had been provided[2].

1 See *McWilliams v Sir William Arrol & Co* [1962] SC (HL) 70.
2 See *Worsley v Tambrands Ltd* [2000] PIQR P95; but cf the House of Lords' decision in *Chester v Afshar* [2005] 1 AC 134.

13.232 Even in a 'defective design' case, in which it is alleged that a medicinal product was 'inherently' defective by reason of its negative risk/ benefit profile, then the claim might still fail on causation if, on the facts, the prescribing doctor had warned the patient of the relevant risks but the patient had nevertheless elected to take the medicine.

13.233 Finally, in the event that factual causation is established, the court must have regard to whether the defendant is to be held responsible, in law, for causing or contributing to the claimant's condition. Various labels have been applied in this context for the purpose of limiting the scope of the defendant's liability to the claimant, but typically the inquiry may include considerations of whether the tort was the 'effective' or 'proximate'[1] cause of the injury, or whether there were 'intervening causes' amounting to a break in the chain of causation'. In addition, in negligence claims, it has been typical for the court to have regard to whether the injury was too 'remote' or not 'foreseeable'.

1 The label 'proximate causation', although commonly used, has been the subject of extensive criticism particularly in the US: see Stapleton 'Unpacking 'Causation' in Cane and Gardner (eds) *Relating to Responsibility* (2001) p 168; and in 'Legal Cause: Cause-in-Fact and the Scope of Liability for Consequences' (2002) 54 Vand L Rev 941; and in 'Choosing what we mean by 'Causation' in the Law' (2008) 73 Missouri LR 433. See also Professor Joseph Page in the introduction to *Torts: Proximate cause* (New York, 2003). The criticism prompted the framers of the new 2009 Third Restatement of Torts to advise US courts to abandon the term 'proximate causation' in favour of a categorisation of 'factual' causation and 'scope of liability for consequences of breach' (or 'scope causation').

13.234 The ECJ's ruling in *Boston Scientific Medizintechnik v AOC Sachsen-Anhalt*[1] is of interest both in terms of the requirements to prove the existence of a 'defect' and also in terms of causation: it would appear that a person implanted with a medical device which belongs to a series of products, some of which are defective, may succeed in establishing both that the product with which he was implanted was defective and that such defect caused personal injury or damage by reason of surgical explantation even where it transpires that the explanted product did not, in fact, possess the relevant defect.

1 Case C-503/13 *Boston Scientific Medizintechnik GmbH v AOK Sachsen-Anhalt – Die Gesundheitskasse* [2015] All ER (D) 88 (Mar), ECJ.

13.235 The House of Lords has described causation in law as informed by a 'value judgment' as to whether the defendant ought reasonably or fairly or justly be held liable for the damage in question. In *Kuwait Airways Corpn v Iraqi Airways Co (Nos 4 and 5)*, Lord Nicholls stated:

'... the inquiry is whether the plaintiff's harm or loss should be within the scope of the defendant's liability, given the reasons why the law has recognised the cause of action in question. The law has to set a limit to the causally connected losses for which a defendant is to be held responsible. In the ordinary language of lawyers, losses outside the limit may bear one of several labels. They may be described as too remote because the wrongful conduct was not the substantial or proximate cause, or because the loss was the product of an intervening cause… Familiar principles, such as foreseeability, assist in promoting some consistency of general approach. These are guidelines, some more helpful than others, but they are never more than this'[1].

1 [2002] UKHL 19, [2002] 2 AC 883 at 1091, para 70, per Lord Nicholls, adapting the language of Professor Stapleton in 'Unpacking 'Causation' in *Relating to Responsibility* p 168.

13.236 In the product liability context practitioners and academics frequently refer to a tri-partite division of causation, namely: (i) generic medical causation; (ii) individual medical causation; and (iii) a category of causation variously labelled 'effective causation'/'proximate causation' or 'fault causation' (in negligence).

13.237 A clear example of this tri-partite classification is demonstrated by the case of *McTear v Imperial Tobacco Ltd*[1]. In that case a claim in negligence was brought by a widow of a smoker who had died of lung cancer, against the tobacco company which manufactured the brand of cigarettes smoked by the deceased. It was alleged that the tobacco company was negligent on two bases, first in failing to provide adequate warnings, and secondly for continuing to manufacture and supply cigarettes despite awareness of their capacity to cause cancer. The claim was dismissed on the basis that the pursuer had failed to establish any of the three causal steps:

- in relation to generic causation, the Lord Ordinary held that it was not within judicial knowledge that cigarette smoking can cause lung cancer and this had to be proved. The scientific evidence adduced by the pursuer failed to discharge the burden of proof required to establish that cigarette smoking can cause lung cancer[2];
- in relation to individual causation, the epidemiological evidence adduced could not be used to establish causation in any individual case and the use of statistics applicable to the general population to determine the likelihood of causation in an individual case was wrong. Even if it was accepted that 90 per cent of lung cancers were caused by smoking, that evidence would not demonstrate that the deceased did not belong to one of the 10 per cent who contracted lung cancer by reason of factors other than smoking[3];
- finally, it was held that the pursuer had failed to establish 'fault causation'[4]. The pursuer failed to demonstrate that any negligence on the part of the defendants had caused or materially contributed to the deceased's lung cancer. The judge found that had the defendants not manufactured cigarettes, the deceased would still have started smoking when he did and would have continued to smoke for the same length of time and in the same quantities as he did in any event; he would simply have smoked an alternative brand of cigarette. Within this category, the judge also considered the issue of whether the deceased was *volens*.

1 [2005] CSOH 69, [2005] 2 SC 1; see in particular para 6.1, p 425 and, on 'fault' causation (or 'proximate' causation) paras 7.182, 7.183, 9.12 at pp 551, 552, 569.
2 See, in particular, paras 1.11, 6.149–7.171, 9.7, 9.9.
3 See, in particular, paras 6.25, 6.172–6.185 and 9.10.
4 Paragraphs 7.182, 7.183 and 9.12.

Generic causation

13.238   As set out above, a claimant must demonstrate that exposure to the medicinal product is capable of causing the particular injuries which the claimant alleges. If the product cannot be shown to be capable of causing the injuries alleged, the action will fail at the first stage of the analysis of causation. It is only if it is capable of causing the injuries alleged (generic causation), and did in fact cause the injuries alleged (individual causation), that the court need proceed to 'proximate' causation. Indeed, if as a matter of fact the product is adjudged not capable of causing the alleged effects, then the court need not even consider whether the product is defective for the purpose of determining the outcome of the litigation. The approach taken in *XYZ v Schering Health Care Ltd (Combined Oral Contraceptive Litigation)*[1] provides an example of this point in operation. The case was a trial of seven lead cases in group litigation against pharmaceutical companies in respect of venous thromboembolism, which the claimants alleged were caused by taking the defendants' third generation combined oral contraceptives. The case was decided on one issue: whether the claimants could prove that third generation combined oral contraceptives carried an excess risk of venous thromboembolism which was twice that carried by second generation combined oral contraceptives[2]. The court held the claimants failed on this first issue. As a result, the court was not required to consider whether the product was defective or not.

1 [2002] EWHC 1420 (QB).
2 As to the reasons for the need, in that case, to establish a doubling of the risk see further para **13.250** below.

13.239   There is a clear distinction between causation in most individual cases of personal injury and generic issues in a medicinal product liability claim. There is a very different type of judicial and inferential reasoning process involved in the latter. This is because the latter will frequently be concerned with the generic causation issue: is the product *capable* of causing the injury? This is a question that is the province of scientific enquiry and rooted in epidemiology.

The role of epidemiology and statistics

13.240   In the absence of there being an established biological pathway, the issue of generic causation will inevitably turn on a scientific enquiry as to the capability of the agent to cause the outcome, because the only known way of determining whether the agent has the capacity to cause the outcome is by reference to statistical and epidemiological evidence. Statistics and epidemiology are thus central to the determination of this question. Statistical methods in particular involve the formal mathematical calculation, analysis and interpretation of large amounts of numerical data. Epidemiological methods involve the same approach, ie analysis and interpretation, but of clinical and other data, rather than numerical data alone. The court is here concerned with specialist inferences, rather than the type of ordinary inferential reasoning which informs the assessment of individual causation issues where findings of fact can be made and can be relied upon to support a conclusion on causation. Generic causation is not concerned with individual findings of fact derived from a factual matrix, but with what answers science can provide to issues which are only capable of being assessed by means of the specialist analysis of large quantities of data.

13.241   Thus, by way of example, the drinking of coffee might be (and has been) observed to be associated with cardiac disease. But it is uniquely by way of epidemiological research and statistical analysis that it could eventually be demonstrated that this association could not be demonstrated to be causal and was more likely to be the product of confounding by indication: cigarette smokers drink more coffee. A court which has the benefit of epidemiological and statistical evidence as to the extant data will be in a far stronger position to conclude whether, on the balance of probabilities, the association is causal.

13.242   Epidemiology is the study of disease and disease attributes in defined populations. It is concerned with aetiology and distribution of disease. The purpose of epidemiological studies is to make an assessment: (a) whether there is any association between an agent (such as is contained in a medicinal product) and the injuries alleged; and (b) whether any such association is causal. Epidemiological reasoning is primarily concerned with refuting a hypothesis rather than proving a theory. However, by virtue of the former, the latter may come to be established. The safety of a medicinal product can never be 'proven', instead, the hypothesis of 'no harm' ('the null hypothesis') is either refuted or not having regard to the data available. In other words, the assessment of the probability of association is undertaken by examining the improbability of there being no association.

13.243   Epidemiological studies include studies designed to test the probability of outcomes between two groups being ascribed to chance. These studies produce probability values (P-value). A P-value of 5 per cent or less (0.05) is considered, by convention, to be 'statistically significant'. Thus, if the assessment of a study observation or result (called 'a point estimate') produces a probability value (a P-value) above 5 per cent (P>0.05), that observation or result is interpreted as having arisen by chance. If a study produces a probability value of 5 per cent or less (P<0.05) this is indicative of a real difference between the two groups and the null hypothesis is rejected, for that study, accordingly.

13.244   An essential part of the process of assessing the statistical significance of the results (point estimates) from research studies is the calculation of confidence intervals around the point estimate, which have the effect of indicating its precision. Epidemiologists seek to indicate the precision of the observed point estimate by reference to confidence intervals. Confidence intervals provide a range of values about the observed effect size. It is conventional to create confidence intervals at 95 per cent, meaning effectively that 95 per cent of the time the confidence intervals will contain the true value of the variable of interest (ie the tested outcome). For most purposes, if the lower confidence interval is unity (1), or less than unity, then the result (point estimate) is not statistically significant and chance as an explanation for the result has not been rejected. This corresponds to hypothesis testing with P-values.

13.245 Epidemiology is not solely concerned with statistical significance. Having found in their study that the result (or a result) is statistically significant and unlikely to be due to chance or to methodological problems such as bias or confounding (the cancer and coffee-drinking example above), epidemiologists then assess whether that association has a causal basis by applying criteria designed to assist the epidemiologist to reach a robust and accurate conclusion. Typically, the criteria employed are the Bradford Hill criteria, which include the following:

- Strength of association: the stronger the association, the less likely it is due to chance;
- Consistency: the data are comparable to the results of other studies;
- Specificity: the effect denotes a discrete entity;
- Temporal relationship: cause and effect must be related in time – cause must precede effect;
- Biological gradient: the greater the exposure the greater the effect;
- Biological plausibility: is there a plausible mechanism?
- Coherence: is a causal relationship in keeping with what is known about the postulated cause and effect?
- Experimental evidence: can the observations be reproduced?
- Analogy: do similar causes produce similar effects?

Thus, for example, one study which had very small numbers and was methodologically weak and poorly-conducted could nevertheless produce a point estimate. Of course, with small numbers, such a point estimate would be bound to be surrounded by extremely wide confidence intervals. But provided the result of interest was statistically significant, applying the above criteria to it the epidemiologist would be able to analyse and explain the reliability of the result. Even in the absence of methodological weaknesses, wide confidence intervals and the absence of other properly conducted and analysed studies replicating the same finding would suggest to an epidemiologist/biostatistician that one could not put any real reliance or confidence in the result, ie of the point estimate representing a true causal value (eg that factor x doubles the incidence of disease y in that study population). In such circumstances, a court would be unlikely to conclude, on the basis of that study, that factor x is more likely than not to be capable of causing disease y.

13.246 It is for the court to determine, having heard the totality of the evidence, whether causation is established on a balance of probabilities. This point was addressed by Stuart-Smith LJ in *Loveday v Renton*[1] (the Pertussis vaccine case):

'Mr Brodie has submitted that a distinction is to be drawn between scientific proof and clinical proof, which he equates to proof on balance of probability. He contends that the effect of the evidence is that while the proposition for which he contends is not scientifically proved it is clinically proved. It is true that some of the plaintiff's witnesses… use these expressions sometimes coupling the former with 95 per cent confidence. Lawyers are familiar with different standards of proof as, for example, that required in criminal as opposed to civil cases. But I have not found Mr Brodie's submission of great assistance for a number of reasons. First, I do not think there is any generally accepted standard of scientific proof, nor is it clear who has to be satisfied to such a standard. The addition of the words '95 per cent confidence' is a confusion of thought derived from the statistical concepts of 95 per cent confidence intervals and probability values... they are not concerned with standards of proof, but the probability of chance. Secondly, the expression 'clinical proof' appears to be used to mean two different things. First, it is used in the sense of making a diagnosis in a particular case. Quite clearly if a clinician is to make a diagnosis in a given case that a child is suffering from permanent brain damage caused by pertussis vaccine, he can only do so on the basis that he has already reached the conclusion that pertussis vaccine can cause brain damage... The decision then depends upon the clinician's judgment as to whether or not the clinical signs and symptoms and the history relating to the patient meet certain criteria determined by the clinician in question. It also appears to be used as the standard of proof in determining to the clinicians' satisfaction whether the vaccine can cause brain damage. Ultimately this is the question for the court and in my mind the only significance of this topic is that when considering a witness's assertion that he is or is not satisfied of a certain fact, the court must bear in mind that he may be applying too low or too high a standard of proof.'

1 [1990] 1 MLR 117 at 124–125.

13.247   A similar approach was taken by French J in *Reay v British Nuclear Fuels plc*:

'The fact that an epidemiologist or another scientist would or would not find an association and/or a cause to be established to his satisfaction is, of course, most helpful to a judge but only within the limits imposed by their respective disciplines ...[1]'.

1 [1994] 5 Med LR 1 at 10.

13.248   In *XYZ v Schering Health Care Ltd*[1], Mackay J summarised the court's approach on generic causation as follows:

'But there must come a time in this case when, having received all the assistance that epidemiology has to offer me, I part company with it and embark on the final judicial journey of assessing, as best I can, on all the evidence...

In this second stage of my journey I will be armed with all the assistance that I can acquire from epidemiology but I will no longer be bound as it seems to me, by its rules and conventions...I will have emerged from that forest into broader more open country where the simpler concept of the balance of probabilities rules....

The Claimants say that I should look at all the evidence in the case both that which is and that which is not statistically significant taken on its own and form my judgement from it. I believe that submission is right.

I have, of course, to decide each of these cases on the balance of probabilities.'

1 [2002] All ER 437.

13.249   The case of *XYZ v Schering Health Care Ltd* provides a pertinent example of trying to reconcile the common law standard of proof with the standards used in epidemiology in medicinal product litigation, by the use of the concept of doubling the relative risk. Relative risk is the ratio of the incidence of a disease in a population exposed to the agent as against the incidence of disease in a population that has not been exposed.

13.250   In *XYZ v Schering Health Care Ltd*, the court took generic causation as a preliminary issue (albeit one that required a trial over 42 days). The issue in that case was whether third generation combined oral contraceptives (COC3) caused the claimants to suffer venous thromboembolism (VTE). The parties and the court took the first issue as being whether the claimants could prove that COC3 carried a true excess risk of VTE which was more than twice that carried by the second generation. The reason for the formulation of that issue was set out by the judge at para 21:

'The reason why the claimants accept through Lord Brennan QC that this first issue is capable of disposing of the claims should be set out. It is not because an increase of less than 2 would fail to render the product defective within the meaning of the Act, though the Defendants would so argue if they had to. It is for reasons of causation that he accepts this burden, correctly in my view. If factor X increases the risk of condition Y by more than 2 when compared with factor Z it can then be said, of a group of say 100 with both exposure to factor X and the condition, that as a matter of probability more than 50 would not have suffered Y without being exposed to X. If medical science cannot identify the members of the group who would and who would not have suffered Y, it can nevertheless be said of each member that she was more likely than not to have avoided Y had she not been exposed to X. There is a statistical formula which expresses this concept, but in this case I intend to resort to words where I can, both from a preference for language over symbols and because I am conscious that this judgment should be accessible, above all to the women who bring these claims.'

13.251 After hearing the evidence, the judge assessed the relative risk at about 1.7. Accordingly, on the basis of the issue as framed, the claim failed. The judge therefore concluded that it was 'not strictly necessary for me to make a finding as to whether the RR of 1.7 itself translates into a relationship of true cause and effect or is a merely statistical appearance.'

13.252 The use of doubling the risk has been argued and applied in subsequent cases[1]. For example, in *Novartis Grimsby Ltd v Cookson*[2], a case concerning occupational exposure to carcinogens causing carcinoma of the bladder, the dispute was whether the cancer was caused by the tortious occupational exposure, or by the claimant's cigarette smoking. Smith LJ stated at para 74:

'The evidence of Mr Barnard which the Recorder accepted was that occupational exposure accounted for 70 per cent to 75 per cent of the total. Put in terms of risk, the occupational exposure had more than doubled the risk due to smoking. In my view, if Mr Feeny is right and the correct test for causation in a case such as this is the 'but for' test and nothing less will do, that test is plainly satisfied on the facts as found. The natural inference to draw from the finding of fact that the occupational exposure was 70 per cent of the total is that, if it had not been for the occupational exposure, the respondent would not have developed bladder cancer. In terms of risk, if occupational exposure more than doubles the risk due to smoking, it must, as a matter of logic, be probable that the disease was caused by the former.'

1 See also the claimants' argument in *Ministry of Defence v AB* [2010] EWCA Civ 1317, the nuclear test veterans' claim which was determined on the basis of the limitation defence. Part of the assessment in refusing to exercise the discretion to extend the limitation period under the Limitation Act 1980, s 33 was the fundamental difficulties that lay in the claimants' way in respect of causation. The claimants accepted that they could not show that tortious exposure to radiation had increased the risk of injury by anything approaching two fold. But they hoped to be able show at least a doubling of the risk by demonstrating that the risk arising from radiation will interact synergistically with that arising from any other potential cause which may be present in the individual case. The Court of Appeal determined that there was no realistic prospect of the claimants establishing this (decision ultimately upheld in the Supreme Court [2012] UKSC 9, [2013] 1 AC 78).
2 [2007] EWCA Civ 1261.

13.253 In *Sienkiewicz v Greif (UK) Ltd*[1], the Supreme Court conducted what was in the event an *obiter* debate about the use of epidemiological evidence and the theory of doubling the risk in the context of a mesothelioma claim which was subject to the *Fairchild* exception. The Supreme Court was unanimous that in cases where the *Fairchild* exception applies there was no room for the 'more than doubles the risk' approach to causation. However, the Supreme Court considered the use of epidemiological evidence more widely, including its use in the US in *Merrell Dow Pharmaceuticals Inc v Havner*[2], a decision of the Supreme Court of Texas involving a claim brought against the manufacturer of the prescription medicine Bendectin, alleging birth defect caused by the mother's ingestion of the medicine during pregnancy. The claimants sought to establish causation by epidemiological evidence which they contended demonstrated that taking the medicine more than doubled the risk of such birth defects. In that case, the Texas Supreme Court held that:

'The use of scientifically reliable epidemiological studies and the requirement of more than a doubling of the risk strikes a balance between the needs of our legal system and the limits of science'[3].

1 [2011] UKSC 10, [2011] 2 AC 229 (SC).
2 953 SW 2d 706.
3 At 718 per Phillips CJ.

13.254 In discussing the use of epidemiological evidence more widely, the Supreme Court disclosed differences of opinions:

- Lord Phillips considered that there was no scope for the application of the doubling the risk test in cases where two agents have operated cumulatively and simultaneously in causing the onset of a disease[1]. In such a case the rule in *Bonnington Castings v Wardlaw*[2] applies[3]. However, he saw no reason in principle why the doubling the risk test should not be applied in the case of a dose related disease, where an innocent exposure came first and there may be an issue as to whether this was sufficient to trigger the disease or whether the subsequent tortious exposure contributed to the cause[4]. In addition, he saw no reason in principle why the test should not be used in a case where there are competing alternative, rather than cumulative, potential causes of an injury[5];
- Lord Rodger indicated that statistical evidence demonstrated the chances of contracting the disease, but did not prove on a balance of probabilities what was the actual cause as a matter of fact[6];
- Lady Hale agreed that the doubling the risk approach had no place in *Fairchild* exception cases. She doubted whether it was an appropriate approach to causation in other cases, but accepted that statistical associations were, if well-researched, a valuable source of evidence[7];
- Lord Brown made no comment on the test;
- Lord Mance considered that whether epidemiological evidence could by itself prove a case was a question best considered not in the abstract but in a particular case[8];
- Lord Kerr emphasised that the use of epidemiological data for the purpose of establishing a specific proposition in an individual case should be treated with great caution. He referred to '*a real danger that so-called 'epidemiological evidence' will carry a false air of authority*'[9];
- Lord Dyson agreed that it was not necessary to decide whether there are any circumstances in which, as a matter of English law, causation could be proved on the basis of epidemiological evidence alone. However, he

ventured that there was no *a priori* reason why, if the epidemiological evidence was cogent enough, it should not be sufficient to prove the case without more[10].

1 Paragraph 90.
2 [1956] AC 613.
3 Namely, the claimant bears the burden of proving, on the balance of probabilities, that the breach caused or materially contributed to the injury. Where there are separate causes, it is enough if one of those causes arose from the breach of the defendant. The claimant does not have to prove that this cause would of itself have been enough to cause him injury. What is a material contribution is a question of degree.
4 Paragraph 91.
5 Paragraph 93. It should be noted that Lord Phillips' analysis (at para 74) of the use of epidemiological evidence *in XYZ v Schering Health Care Ltd* [2002] EWHC 1420 appears to proceed from a misstatement of the facts of that case and, possibly, a misunderstanding of the reasons behind the application of the doubling of risk test in that case; see further Professor Goldberg's criticism of Lord Phillips' reasoning in *Medicinal Product Liability and Regulation* (2013) pp 92–93.
6 Paragraph 156.
7 Paragraphs 172 and 173.
8 Paragraph 192.
9 Paragraphs 205–206.
10 Paragraphs 221 and 222.

13.255 It is questionable how much of this is relevant to the issue of proving generic causation in a case involving a medicinal product, particularly in cases of prescription medicines, where effectively the only evidence that the claimant can produce is epidemiological. In any event, the mere existence of a statistically significant association does not prove causation, which is precisely why epidemiologists apply the Bradford Hill criteria. Lord Rodger's speech provides the most useful summary for present purposes[1]:

'Finally, nothing which I have said is intended to discourage the use of epidemiological evidence or to depreciate its value in cases where a claimant has to prove his case on the balance of probabilities. Far from it. Obviously, for example, epidemiology is likely to lie behind much of the evidence on which a court determines whether an exposure has materially increased the risk of the claimant developing a disease. Epidemiological evidence may also be relevant when deciding whether it would have been reasonable for a defendant to take precautions to avoid the risk of the claimant suffering a particular injury – say, the side-effect of a drug. And, of course – it must be emphasised once more – epidemiological and statistical evidence may form an important element in proof of causation. I have simply emphasised the point made by *Phipson on Evidence*, 17th ed (2010), para 34-27, that, unless a special rule applies, "Where there is epidemiological evidence of association, the court should not proceed to find a causal relationship without further, non-statistical evidence". In other words, since, by its very nature, the statistical evidence does not deal with the individual case, something more will be required before the court will be able to reach a conclusion, on the balance of probability, as to what happened in that case. For example, where there is a strong epidemiological association between a drug and some condition which could have been caused in some other way, that evidence along with evidence that the claimant developed the condition immediately after taking the drug may well be enough to allow the judge to conclude, on the balance of probability, that it was the drug that caused the claimant's condition. Of course, in any actual dispute, the epidemiological evidence may be contested. The judge will then have to decide which expert view he accepts and how reliable the evidence is – whether, for example, the study has been properly constructed and, in particular, what the confidence intervals are. In that respect epidemiological evidence is no different from other evidence.'

1 Paragraph 163.

13.256   A recent example of a court rejecting causation notwithstanding a relative risk of 'about two' in the context of medicinal products is the Australian federal appeal decision in *Merck Sharp & Dohme (Australia) Pty Ltd v Peterson*[1]. The claimant alleged that Vioxx caused the claimant to suffer a myocardial infarction. The claimant succeeded at first instance on the basis that the epidemiological evidence demonstrated that Vioxx doubled the risk of myocardial infarction across the population as a whole and had materially contributed to the claimant's heart attack. The decision was overturned on appeal. The epidemiological evidence did not distinguish between individuals with no history of heart disease and those with such a history. In the claimant's case there were other competing potential causes (age, gender, hypertension, hyperlipidaemia, obesity, left ventricular hypertrophy and a history of smoking). These circumstances diminished the strength of the epidemiological evidence, which simply served to demonstrate that Vioxx was one of many factors that may have caused the claimant's heart attack.

1 [2011] FCAFC 128.

13.257   In *AB v Ministry of Defence*[1] (the *Atomic Veterans* group litigation), the claimants claimed damages for tortious exposure to radiation resulting in an increased risk of injury. The case was disposed of at a preliminary hearing (on appeal to the Supreme Court) on the issue of limitation. However, a considerable amount of argument in the case concerned the claimants' prospects of establishing causation. As a result of the epidemiological evidence, by the time of the hearings the claimants accepted that they could not show that tortious exposure to radiation had increased the risk of injury by two fold, but they alleged that they would be able to show at least a doubling of the risk by demonstrating that the risk arising from radiation had interacted synergistically with other factors. Both the Court of Appeal and the Supreme Court considered that this fell well short of establishing causation according to established principles of English law.

1 [2012] UKSC 9.

Individual causation

13.258   If the court concludes that the medicinal product is capable of causing a particular alleged injury then the court will need to proceed to determine whether that alleged injury was in fact caused, or materially contributed to, by exposure to the product in the case of the individual claimant who alleges such injury. In the first instance, it will be necessary in each case for the claimant to establish that he or she suffers from the particular injury alleged. As to this issue, the court should have the benefit of clinical expert evidence. In making a diagnosis the clinician should consider the clinical history and presentation of the claimant and then, exercising his or her judgment based on clinical experience and diagnostic criteria, whether the claimant should be diagnosed as suffering from the condition/injury in question.

13.259   If the court concludes that a claimant is properly to be diagnosed with a particular condition then the court must proceed to determine the issue of attribution: whether the condition was caused or materially contributed to in this individual case by exposure to the medicinal product as alleged. This may require the court to return to a consideration of issues of generic causation. Even if the court is satisfied that exposure to the medicinal product is capable of causing a particular condition, the court may nevertheless have to consider whether the exposure in the individual case (for instance, by reference to the dose taken and/or the temporal connection between exposure and onset of the relevant condition) is capable of causing the alleged condition. Additionally, the court will have to consider the expert evidence which addresses other possible causes of the condition in the individual case as well as, returning to epidemiology, the background incidence of the particular condition.

13.260 Irrespective of whether the epidemiological evidence permits the court to make a finding that the agent in question is capable of causing a particular outcome as a matter of generic causation, it is not possible to extrapolate from such population studies to an individual case so as to prove, on the basis of such evidence, that the agent did in fact cause the outcome in the particular claimant's case. A clear illustration of this is provided by *McTear v Imperial Tobacco Ltd*[1]. The court noted that the evidence was that only a relatively small minority of smokers contract lung cancer, but that smoking could be an important cause. The court accepted that:

'epidemiology cannot provide information on the likelihood that an exposure produced an individual's condition… The fact that cases and non-cases can emerge both from the unexposed and the exposed groups show that the likelihood of the individual occurrence cannot be reliably predicted from his or her exposure group membership alone'.

The judge noted that in the state of modern science there was no way of telling whether in an individual case a lung cancer was caused by cigarette smoking[2].

1 [2005] 2 SC 1 at paras 6.172–6.208.
2 At para 6.184.

'Proximate' causation – non-medical individual causation

13.261 In *McGhee* it had been suggested that where a substance is known to cause the injury complained of, and the defendant negligently exposed the claimant to that substance there may be causation. Whilst the burden of proof was not reversed the majority decision was based on an increase in risk being treated in the same way as material contribution and the defendant must show that another factor was as likely or more likely to have caused the injury in the case in question[1]. The decision in *McGhee* has been the subject of detailed judicial consideration in a number of recent cases in the House of Lords, resulting in a relaxation of the strict requirements for proof of causation in certain closely defined circumstances, in the cases of *Fairchild v Glenhaven Funeral Services Ltd*[2] and *Barker v Corus*[3].

1 This was a view expressed by a minority in the House of Lords in *McGhee v National Coal Board* [1972] 3 All ER 1008, [1973] 1 WLR 1, HL.
2 [2003] 1 AC 32.
3 [2006] UKHL 20.

13.262 In the case of *Fairchild*, the House of Lords decided that a person who had contracted mesothelioma after wrongful exposure to asbestos at different times by more than one negligent employer could sue any of them, notwithstanding that he could not prove which exposure had actually caused the disease – because all had materially contributed to his disease by increasing the risk of him contracting the disease. Their Lordships looked again at the case of *McGhee* and the concept of increasing the risk of a disease and rejected the dictum of Lord Bridge in the case of *Wilsher*[1], namely that:

'The conclusion I draw from these passages is that *McGhee v National Coal Board* [1973] 1 WLR 1 laid down no new principle of law whatever. On the contrary, it affirmed the principle that the onus of proving causation lies on the pursuer or plaintiff. Adopting a robust and pragmatic approach to the undisputed primary facts of the case, the majority concluded that it was a legitimate inference of fact that the defenders' negligence had materially contributed to the pursuer's injury. The decision, in my opinion, is of no greater significance than that and to attempt to extract from it some esoteric principle which in some way modifies, as a matter of law, the nature of the burden of proof of causation which a plaintiff or pursuer must discharge once he has established a relevant breach of duty is a fruitless one.'

1 *Wilsher v Essex Area Health Authority* [1988] 1 All ER 871 at 881j.

13.263 In *Fairchild* the House of Lords expressly decided, contrary to Lord Bridge's analysis quote above, that *McGhee* had modified the nature of the burden of proof of causation, but only in the sort of circumstances pertaining in those cases where the damage could only have been caused by one agent (unlike the facts in *Wilsher* itself) to which the claimant had been exposed and he had been exposed to that agent by a number of different tortfeasors and he could not show which exposure was responsible. Lord Bingham summarised his view of the effect of the *McGhee* decision:

'... it was expressly held by three members of the House (Lord Reid at page 5, Lord Simon at page 8 and Lord Salmon at pages 12–13) that in the circumstances no distinction was to be drawn between making a material contribution to causing the disease and materially increasing the risk of the pursuer contracting it. Thus the proposition expressly rejected by the Lord Ordinary, the Lord President and Lord Migdale was expressly accepted by a majority of the House and must be taken to represent the ratio of the decision, closely tied though it was to the special facts on which it was based.'

He concluded this part of his speech by saying:

'As is apparent from the conclusions expressed in paragraph 21 above, I cannot for my part accept this passage in Lord Bridge's opinion as accurately reflecting the effect of what the House, or a majority of the House, decided in *McGhee*, which remains sound authority. I am bound to conclude that this passage should no longer be treated as authoritative.'

This view of the effect of the decision in *McGhee* was shared by all other members of the court save for Lord Hutton.

13.264 In all their speeches the Court emphasised that the relaxation of the strict requirements of the 'but for' test had to be confined to the sort of special facts found in that case and in *Fairchild* itself. However, they left open the possibility of development of the principle in other circumstances, albeit that considerable caution would be required. Thus, Lord Hoffmann in his speech observed:

'That does not mean that the principle is not capable of development and application in new situations. As my noble and learned friend Lord Rodger of Earlsferry has demonstrated, problems of uncertainty as to which of a number of possible agents caused an injury have required special treatment of one kind or another since the time of the Romans. But the problems differ quite widely and the fair and just answer will not always be the same. For example, in the famous case of *Sindell v Abbott Laboratories* (1980) 607 P 2d 924 the plaintiff had suffered pre-natal injuries from exposure to a drug which had been manufactured by any one of a potentially large number of defendants. The case bears some resemblance to the present but the problem is not the same. For one thing, the existence of the additional manufacturers did not materially increase the risk of injury. The risk from consuming a drug bought in one shop is not increased by the fact that it can also be bought in another shop. So the case would not fall within the *McGhee* principle. But the Supreme Court of California laid down the imaginative rule that each manufacturer should be liable in proportion to his market share. Cases like this are not before the House and should in my view be left for consideration when they arise. For present purposes, the *McGhee* principle is sufficient. I would therefore allow the appeals.'

13.265 *Fairchild* did not resolve whether liability should be joint and several, although it was presumed that this would be the rule and this was the approach taken in practice. Nor did it deal with competing causes which were non-negligent or were the consequence of the claimant's own negligence. Furthermore, Lord Rodger in his speech allowed the possibility of application of the relaxed approach where the agents to which the claimant had been exposed were not the same but at least operated in a similar fashion. In *Barker v Corus UK Ltd* (and conjoined cases)[1], another mesothelioma case with similar facts to *Fairchild*, the House of Lords considered a number of these issues. It decided that the damages were to be apportioned among those responsible for the wrongful exposure according to their relative degree of contribution to the chance of the person contracting mesothelioma. On the issue of competing agents which were different Lord Hoffmann said:

'In my opinion it is an essential condition for the operation of the exception that the impossibility of proving that the defendant caused the damage arises out of the existence of another potential causative agent which operated in the same way. It may have been different in some causally irrelevant respect, as in Lord Rodger's example of the different kinds of dust, but the mechanism by which it caused the damage, whatever it was, must have been the same. So, for example, I do not think that the exception applies when the claimant suffers lung cancer which may have been caused by exposure to asbestos or some other carcinogenic matter but may also have been caused by smoking and it cannot be proved which is more likely to have been the causative agent.'

1 [2006] UKHL 201. Section 3 of the Compensation Act 2006 has reversed the decision of the House of Lords in *Barker*, at least for mesothelioma cases, by establishing joint and several liability in such cases, thereby enabling claimants, or their estate or dependants, to recover full compensation from any liable person, leaving that person to seek contribution from other negligent persons.

13.266 The question arises as to the significance, if any, these decisions may have for cases involving medicinal products. Often in such cases, a primary issue is the general causation question of whether the product was capable of causing the damage alleged. In *Fairchild* one of the reasons for relaxing the strict requirement for causation was the fact that the agent in question, asbestos, was an established carcinogen. Indeed, it was the known cause of the claimants' mesothelioma. Neither of those conditions applies in a typical pharmaceutical liability case. It was the undisputed capacity of asbestos to cause mesothelioma which constituted the raised risk to which the claimants in *Fairchild* were exposed. In a pharmaceutical case, generic medical causation is almost always one of the very issues which has to be established. If, however, the propensity for the product to cause the injury is not in issue, and the issue is which of a number of manufacturers it was that caused the damage, again it is doubtful that *Fairchild* will assist for the reasons given in the quotation from Lord Hoffmann's speech in the case set out above. It is also notable that the House clearly identified the dangers involved in judicial development of the common law in this area. All of the speeches in *Fairchild* were liberally scattered with warnings, typical of which is that of Lord Nicholls who said:

'I need hardly add that considerable restraint is called for in any relaxation of the threshold 'but for' test of causal connection. The principle applied on these appeals is emphatically not intended to lead to such a relaxation whenever a plaintiff has difficulty, perhaps understandable difficulty, in discharging the burden of proof resting on him. Unless closely confined in its application this principle could become a source of injustice to defendants. There must be good reason for departing from the normal threshold 'but for' test. The reason must be sufficiently weighty to justify depriving the defendant of the protection this test normally and rightly affords him, and it must be plain and obvious that this is so. Policy questions will loom large when a court has to decide whether the difficulties of proof confronting the plaintiff justify taking this exceptional course. It is impossible to be more specific'.

13.267 The House of Lords subsequently declined to apply the *Fairchild* principle to clinical negligence cases[1]. It was also rejected by the Court of Appeal and Supreme Court in the Atomic Veterans group litigation. At first instance, Foskett J was prepared to contemplate the possibility that the Supreme Court would extend the *Fairchild* principle so as to equate causing an increase of risk with causing injury. However, this argument was dismissed on appeal, where it was held that there was no foreseeable possibility that the Supreme Court would be willing to extend the *Fairchild* exception to cover conditions which have multiple potential causes some of which have not been identified. The *Fairchild* principle only applies to cases where the cause of the condition is known. It does not apply where all that can be said is that exposure to the tortious substance is one of several possible causes[2]. In the Supreme Court, it was stated that in the light of *Sienkiewicz v Greif (UK) Ltd*[3], the Court of Appeal was plainly correct[4].

1 *Gregg v Scott* [2005] 1 AC 176.
2 See the Court of Appeal [2010] EWCA Civ 1317 at para 154.
3 [2011] UKSC 10.
4 See Lord Phillips at para 157.

13.268 The question arises as to whether it would be legitimate for the court to adopt a similar, more relaxed approach to proof of causation in a claim brought under the CPA 1987. It may be questioned whether the approach to causation adopted in *Fairchild* could be said to result in the demonstration of a causal relationship at least in a traditional sense. Indeed, a number of their Lordships said expressly that it did not. Thus, Lord Nicholls observed:

'In an area of the law already afflicted with linguistic ambiguity I myself would not describe this process of legal reasoning as a 'legal inference' or an 'inference of causation'. This phraseology tends to obscure the fact that when applying the principle described above the court is not, by a process of inference, concluding that the ordinary 'but for' standard of causation is satisfied. Instead, the court is applying a different and less stringent test. It were best if this were recognised openly.'

13.269 Additionally, it might be argued that relaxation of the legal requirement to prove causation would be inappropriate in the context of the CPA 1987. The Directive is the result of an extensive consultation exercise among interested parties across the whole of the EU and represents a careful balance between the interests of the consumer and the interests of manufacturers of goods. Relaxation of the need for the consumer to prove breach of duty is counterbalanced by a clearly stated requirement for the consumer to prove causation. That is part of the balanced protection for the manufacturer which the EU has seen fit to make a requirement for all Member States to include in their national laws, and arguably it would be wrong for the national courts of a Member State to relax the usual requirements for CPA 1987 claims[1]. Arguably, too, it could be unfair, and in this developing area of the law the House of Lords has repeatedly stated the need for fairness. Lord Hoffmann in *Fairchild* stated:

'The concepts of fairness, justice and reason underlie the rules which state the causal requirements of liability for a particular form of conduct (or non-causal limits on that liability) just as much as they underlie the rules which determine that conduct to be tortious. And the two are inextricably linked together: the purpose of the causal requirement rules is to produce a just result by delimiting the scope of liability in a way which relates to the reasons why liability for the conduct in question exists in the first place.'

1 However, the recent ruling of the ECJ in *Boston Scientific Medizintechnik GmbH v AOK Sachsen-Anhalt*, ECJ, 5 March 2015, Case C-503/13 (particularly paras 41 and 42) might be seen as pressing the concept of 'a fair apportionment of risks' towards what might be seen from an English perspective as a relaxation of traditional principles of proof of defect and causation.

LIMITATION

Introduction

13.270 English law provides that a person must bring his claim within reasonable time ('the limitation period'). The law arises from the Limitation Acts 1939–1980. A claim in contract to recover loss cannot in general be pursued after six years from the date of the breach of contract. The breach normally takes place, at the latest, when the product is delivered under a contract of sale to the buyer. In cases founded on the law of tort (such as negligence) the limitation period is generally six years from the date of damage (see generally **Chapter 12**.)

13.271 However, in the case of personal injuries allegedly caused by a product, where the claim is based either on a breach of duty arising by virtue of a contract or on a breach of duty to take care, the claim will be time-barred three years after the date the claimant knew or should have known of the damage, that it was significant, that the injury was attributable to the defect in the product, and the identity of the person responsible for the defect in the product[1]. Knowledge of attribution may be established where a claimant's subjective belief that his injury is capable of being attributed to the breach

of duty/defective product is held with sufficient confidence to make it
reasonable for him to begin to investigate whether he has a valid claim[2]. In a
case arising out of the *Opren* litigation, it was stated that under the Limitation
Act 1980, s 14(1)(b) the act or omission of which the claimant must have
knowledge is the provision of an unsafe drug capable of causing the damage
complained of/or in failing to discover its defective nature so as to protect
such patient[3]. For the avoidance of doubt, it is not possible to achieve a six-
year limitation period in a claim for injuries by framing the claim in contract[4].

1 Limitation Act 1980, s 11 and s 14(1).
2 *Ministry of Defence v AB* [2012] UKSC 9.
3 *Nash v Eli Lilly & Co* [1992] 3 Med LR 353, CA.
4 See the wording of s 11(1), also *David Bond v Livingstone & Co* [2001] PNLR 30.

13.272 The Limitation Act 1980[1] makes specific provision at s 11A for claims
in respect of defective products under the CPA 1987. It retains the basic three
year limitation period as in other cases of personal injury but, unusually,
also provides for a ten-year 'longstop'. As to the 'longstop', this provides
that an action under the CPA 1987 shall not be brought after the expiration
of the period of ten years from the date on which the producer put the actual
product[2] which caused the damage into circulation, unless the injured person
has begun legal proceedings against the producer in the meantime. This
operates as a substantive extinction of the legal right of action rather than a
procedural time bar. For this purpose the ECJ has held that a product is 'put
into circulation' when it is taken out of the manufacturing process operated
by the producer and enters a marketing process in the form of which it is
offered to the public in order to be used or consumed[3].

1 As amended by the CPA 1987.
2 Not the date upon which the class of product was first marketed.
3 Case C-127/04 *O'Byrne v Sanofi Pasteur MSD Ltd* [2006] All ER (EC) 674, [2006] 1 WLR 1606,
   ECJ; see also C-358/08 *Aventis Pasteur SA v OB* [2010] All ER (EC) 522, [2010] 2 CMLR 415, ECJ.

The longstop and the wrong defendant

13.273 In *Horne-Roberts v SmithKline Beecham plc*[1] 'proceedings against the
producer' was interpreted by the Court of Appeal to include proceedings
against a person mistakenly identified as the producer, so that substitution
of the actual producer was permitted more than ten years after he put the
product into circulation. The claimant incorrectly sued Merck thinking that
they had manufactured the batch of MMR vaccine with which he had been
administered. In fact, it had been manufactured by SmithKline Beecham. By
the time that the claimant sought to substitute SmithKline Beecham as the
defendant, the ten-year longstop had expired. The Court of Appeal held that
the original defendant had been wrongly identified, but it had always been
intended for the claimant to sue the manufacturer of the identified vaccine.
This was a mistake which was covered by the Limitation Act 1980, s 35(6)
and CPR 19.5 and accordingly there was power to substitute the defendant
even after the expiry of the ten-year period.

1 [2001] EWCA Civ 2006, [2002] 1 WLR 1662.

13.274 However, in *Aventis Pasteur SA v OB*[1], the ECJ held that a 'producer'
could not be substituted as the defendant after the expiry of the ten-year

period if proceedings were not instigated within that period against a person who is a producer within the meaning of Article 3. It matters not if an injured person wrongfully attributes the status of producer to a person or genuinely intended to sue the producer but in fact sued the wrong person. In these circumstances, it would seem that it is not now possible to use the Limitation Act 1980, s 35 as a basis for substituting defendants in product liability claims on the grounds of mistake after the expiry of the ten-year long stop. However, the ECJ said that if proceedings were instigated within the relevant period against a wholly owned subsidiary of the 'producer', the 'producer' may be able to be substituted after the expiry of the ten-year period. Further, a supplier would be treated as a 'producer' unless it informs the injured person of the identity of the supplier promptly and of its own initiative. Therefore, if proceedings were instituted against a supplier within the ten-year period who failed to inform the injured person of the manufacturer's identity, this could be treated as if proceedings had been instituted 'against a producer'.

1 Case C- 358/08 [2010] 1 WLR 1375, ECJ.

13.275 The Supreme Court came to consider this guidance in *OB v Aventis Pasteur SA*[1]. Its approach was to construe ECJ's allusion to whether the supplier was a subsidiary of the 'producer' as directing attention to factors which may point to a close connection between the two companies. The Supreme Court therefore had to consider whether the manufacturer was in fact controlling its subsidiary and determining when it put its product into circulation. The fact that one was a wholly owned subsidiary was not sufficient on its own to justify substitution after the expiry of the ten-year period. It was only one, by no means decisive, factor to be taken into account by the domestic court when assessing how closely the subsidiary was involved with its parent's business as a producer. In all the circumstances of the *Aventis* case, it was found not to be appropriate for the High Court to order substitution.

1 [2010] UKSC 23.

13.276 The 10-year longstop is intended at least in part to make it easier for manufacturers to insure against liability. It is key for manufacturers to maintain proper records so that the position of their insurer is not prejudiced through inability to show that the product at the centre of a claim was supplied more than ten years ago. The longstop can have harsh consequences for those consumers whose conditions take several years to manifest themselves. Moreover, for claimants there may be no immediate way of knowing whether the time limit is about to expire. However, even if the longstop has passed, some claimants may still be able to make a claim in negligence. The concept of a product having a 'liability life' is quite novel to English law, but is common in the USA.

Children and parties lacking capacity: persons under a disability

13.277 Special rules apply for children and for individuals who lack capacity (within the meaning of the Mental Capacity Act 2005) to conduct legal proceedings; these are persons under a disability[1]. In the case of a child, the three-year time limit would begin from the date of their 18th birthday. In the case of a protected party, the three-year time limit would not begin to run until he gained capacity[2]. However, children and protected parties are not exempt from the ten-year 'longstop' in respect of CPA 1987 claims[3].

1 Limitation Act 1980, ss 28(7), 38(2).
2 Although note that if the claimant acquires lucidity for even a brief period, time will begin to run. Once time begins to run, it cannot stop: *Prideaux v Webber* (1661) 1 Lev 31 263. This is counterbalanced to some degree by the provision in the Limitation Act 1980, s 33(3)(d) expressly exhorting the court to take into account any period of disability in deciding whether or not to dis-apply time limits.
3 It was initially pleaded in the fetal anti-convulsant litigation that the ten-year longstop could not apply to persons under a disability because of the provisions of the European Convention on Human Rights, incorporated into English law by the Human Rights Act 1998, but this was not pursued.

Death of the claimant

13.278 In a case where the damages claimed by the claimant consist of or include damages in respect of personal injuries to the claimant or any other person, the injured person died before the expiration of the three-year period, and a claim surviving for the benefit of the deceased's estate is brought under the Law Reform (Miscellaneous Provisions) Act 1934, then for that period there is substituted a limitation period of three years from whichever is the later of: (a) the date of death; and (b) the date of the personal representative's knowledge.

Repeated exposure

13.279 Interesting questions may arise where repeated exposures to a product have occurred. Very often treatment is over a long period and the claimant will be unable to identify which administration(s) actually caused the injury. Given the approach of the House of Lords in *Fairchild v Glenhaven Funeral Services*[1] and in *Barker v Corus*[2] it may be that the courts will treat any use of the product within the ten-year period as making a material contribution to the cause of the injury, provided that repeated exposure is capable of contributing to the injury, ie that (unlike in *Fairchild*) the science does not show that the injury is caused only by a single exposure. The application of the *Fairchild* principle to product liability proceedings generally will require its express extension.

1 *Fairchild v Glenhaven Funeral Services Ltd* [2003] 1 AC 32.
2 *Barker v Corus* [2006] UKHL 201.

Discretion to disapply time limits

13.280 The court has a discretionary power to disapply the three-year time limit in actions in respect of personal injuries or death. The court may permit the claim to proceed if it would be equitable to do so, balancing the prejudice caused to the claimant against the prejudice which the defendant will suffer if it is deprived of the limitation defence. The discretion is unfettered, and the court is entitled to take into account all the circumstances of the case, together with six specific features set out at s 33(3). In particular, it is now established that it may take into account the merits of the case and whether the claim has a reasonable prospect of success[1]. It has been said that there is no public policy presently requiring a different approach to the exercise of discretion in group actions[2], although this may be a matter that ought to be considered by legislation[3]. There is no discretion to disapply the 'longstop'[4].

1 *Ministry of Defence v AB* [2012] UKSC 9; see also *Horton v Sadler* [2006] UKHL 27.
2 In *Ministry of Defence v AB* [2012] UKSC 9, Lord Wilson (with whom Lords Walker, Brown and Mance agreed on this point), rejected the minority view that the existence of other claims in the group that were not time-barred should affect the determination of the preliminary issue of limitation in respect of those claims that were (see paras 15 and 27).
3 *Nash v Eli Lilly & Co* [1992] 3 Med LR 353, CA.
4 Limitation Act 1980, s 33(1A).

PROCEDURE

Pre-action

13.281 In principle, claims for disease and illness arising out of medicinal products are subject to the Pre-Action Protocol for Disease and Illness Claims[1]. This Protocol is similar to the Pre-Action Protocol for Personal Injury Claims, and provides for early notification of claims, a detailed letter of claim and a recommended three-month response period. However, the Protocol is not intended to cover those cases which are dealt with as a 'group' or 'class' action and as a result many medicinal product liability claims will not be formally subject to the Protocol. In any event, as a matter of good practice, litigants should endeavour to comply with the spirit of the Protocol. In the case of multi-claimant litigation, it is often the case that the court is asked to exercise its case management powers at an early stage, perhaps when only a few of the claims in prospect have been issued. The court may then dictate how, when and in what court the remaining claims should be issued, whether letters of claim should be sent and responses provided and what supporting documents should accompany the claims.

1 See para 2.4 of the Protocol.

Multi-party claims

13.282 Litigation arising out of adverse drug reactions very often involves a large number of claimants, and this poses particular problems relating to the handling of the claims for all parties. The CPR 1998 contain specific provisions relating to group actions, to be found in Part 19, Section III, headed 'Group Litigation'. In particular, the court has discretion to make a Group Litigation Order (GLO) to provide for case management of claims which give rise to common or related issues of fact and law[1]. GLOs were introduced in May 2000, and at time of writing some 85 GLOs have been made[2]. There is no minimum number of claims before a GLO can be made, but if the court is not satisfied that there is likely to be a significant number of claims then the application for a GLO may fail[3]. It is important to note that the purpose of a GLO is for the determination of an issue or issues which is or are common across all claims or at least groups of claims within the overall group. In a scenario where there are many similar claims but no common issue as such, it may be more appropriate to make a consolidation order, or simply a direction that all related claims be heard by the same judge[4]. A further potential option for avoiding a multiplicity of proceedings is the use of the rules in Section II of Part 19 concerning 'representative parties'. However, this is rarely used as it is only available where the class of litigants have the same interest in a cause of action[5].

1 CPR Pt.19, as amplified by PD 19B.
2 See the Ministry of Justice website for up-to-date list: http://www.justice.gov.uk/courts/rcj-rolls-building/queens-bench/group-litigation-orders.
3 See *Austin v Miller Argent (South Wales) Ltd* [2011] EWCA Civ 928 per Jackson LJ at para 35: 'The court will not make a GLO before it is clear that there is a sufficient number of claimants, who seriously intend to proceed and whose claims raise common or related issues of fact and law'.
4 See for example *Hobson v Ashton Morton Slack Solicitors* [2006] EWHC 1134 (QB), in which the court refused to grant a GLO because no group litigation issue had been sufficiently identified.
5 *Emerald Supplies Ltd v British Airways plc* [2010] EWCA Civ 1284.

Applying for a Group Litigation Order

13.283   A GLO can be made of the court's own motion[1], but is more usually the result of an application by the claimants or defendants to a potential group action. Before applying for a Group Litigation Order (GLO) the solicitor acting for the proposed applicant should consult the Law Society's Multi Party Action Information Service in order to obtain information about other cases giving rise to the proposed GLO issues. An application for a GLO may be made at any time before or after any relevant claims have been issued – the required contents of the application form are found at CPR PD 19B. Unusually, before an order can be made, the approval is necessary of the President (in the Queen's Bench Division and on circuit), the Chancellor (in the Chancery Division), or the Head of Civil Justice (in the county court). This may be sought before or after the hearing of the application for the Group Litigation Order.

1 CPR 19B PD 11.

Content of the GLO

13.284   A GLO must contain directions about the establishment of a register (the 'group register') on which the claims managed under the GLO will be entered, as well as specifying the GLO issues which will identify the claims to be managed as a group, and specifying the court (the 'management court') which will manage the claims on the group register. It may also, in relation to claims which raise one or more of the GLO issues: direct their transfer to the management court; order their stay until further order; and direct their entry on the group register. It may also direct that from a specified date claims which raise one or more of the GLO issues should be started in the management court and entered on the group register; and give directions for publicising the GLO. Such provisions are designed to corral all such claims into one court and before one managing judge. The judge may (and usually does) specify cut-off dates after which no claims may be added to the court without permission of the court.

Effect of the GLO

13.285 The effect of a GLO is that, where a judgment or order is made in a claim on the group register in relation to one or more of the GLO issues, that judgment is binding on the parties to all other claims that are on the group register at the time of the judgment or order and the judge may give directions on the extent to which it shall also be binding on claims which subsequently join the group register[1].

1 CPR 19.12.

Publicising the GLO

13.286 A copy of the GLO must be provided to the Law Society and to the Senior Master of the Queen's Bench Division[1]. This will publicise the news to the legal profession via the Law Society's Multi Party Action Information Service and the court service website. As to raising awareness of the litigation and acquiring further claimants from the general public, there is no specific guidance available. However, this will usually take the form of newspaper advertisements. There is no requirement to have an advertisement approved by the court, but it is good practice for any advertising to be so approved[2]. Any publicity must comply with the Solicitors Code of Conduct and in particular must 'be accurate and not misleading'[3]. Care is likely to be required in respect of a medicinal product which is still on the market and available for use, for example, with regard to the risks to patients in coming off the medicine. It is also possible (with the defendant's co-operation) to integrate the defendant's customer helpline or customer complaints department into the process for identifying potential claimants.

1 CPR 19B PD.19.
2 See for example the form of order approved in the CF Arch cru financial mis-selling litigation, which provided the lead solicitors with 'permission to place a notice in the form at Schedule 2 to this order on its website, on the website www.archcruclaims.org, in the Law Society Gazette, on social media sites to include Facebook, in the financial press and in at least one newspaper of national circulation in the UK, the costs of which shall be dealt with at the conclusion of the CF Arch cru Group Litigation'.
3 Chapter 8 of the Code of Conduct (Version 9, published 1 April 2014).

Group litigation in practice

13.287 There is great flexibility in how group litigation may be managed and directions should be tailored to the specific needs of a particular set of claims. Almost invariably, it is necessary for the Claimants' solicitors to form a group and choose one of their number to take the lead in applying for a GLO, and later in litigating the GLO issues. The GLO Register is usually maintained by the lead solicitors acting for the claimants, but may also be maintained by the defendants or by the court.

13.288 The court will frequently impose a 'cut-off date' by which claims must join the GLO. This can raise questions about the extent to which a claimant may join at a later date. One approach is to manage a group of 'latecomers' as a separate 'Group B' within the GLO, staying them until the outcome of 'Group A's' claims. Strictly speaking, the cut-off date is a case management measure and does not directly affect the law on limitation. However, seeking to join the GLO at a later date, or pursuing separate proceedings, may in certain circumstances raise issues of abuse of process. The Court of Appeal in *Taylor v Nugent Care Society*[1] held that it was not an abuse of process of the court for a claimant to proceed with his claim notwithstanding that he had commenced proceedings that raised issues covered by a group litigation order and was refused permission to join the group action out of time. If the claimant brought proceedings that ran parallel to the group action, the court was entitled to manage the proceedings in a way that took account of directions enforced upon the parties to the group action. This may well involve staying such a claim (even though they do not form part of the group action) until completion of the group action.

1 [2004] 1 WLR 1129.

13.289 In *Candice Holloway v Transform Medical Group (CS) Ltd*[1] the High Court refused an application by 17 women to join the register of claims in the PIP Group Litigation concerning allegedly defective implants used in breast augmentation surgery after the cut-off date imposed by the court for any new claims to be added. The solicitors had failed to have the claims joined to the register before the cut-off date; failed to make an application for an extension before the cut-off date; and having taken the decision to make the application, failed to do so until 10 months had elapsed. The court held that the cut-off date was a sanction, CPR 3.9 applied, and the applicants were required to obtain relief from sanction. Relief from sanction was refused. The failures were deemed serious and sustained. There was no good reason for the failures and nothing was done to meet the deadline. To grant relief from sanction would be to undermine the discipline of the litigation.

1 [2014] EWHC 1641 (QB).

13.290 The court has a discretion as to how to handle statements of case. By CPR PD19.14.1, the court is specifically empowered to direct that the GLO claimants set out 'Group Particulars of Claim'. To a degree formal pleadings may be replaced by Schedules of Information or questionnaires. A common compromise is for the courts to order that test cases or lead cases should be pleaded in full, but that only limited information need be provided for the remaining claims, by means of a Schedule.

13.291 The courts have given directions to ensure that the defendants to the litigation are put into the position where they can properly investigate individual cases expeditiously. It is now common for the court to direct (usually by agreement) that a claimant serves a consent to inspect medical records and copies of any medical records in their possession, with the claim form or the individual particulars of claim. Further, the courts have ordered claimants to waive their right of confidentiality in respect of their treating doctors, to enable the defendants to approach those treating doctors to ask questions concerning the complainant's medical history: indeed, the courts have gone further on the particular facts of a case and required the claimant not only to give such consent, but also to waive any rights they may have in pursuing a treating doctor, to avoid the possibility of a treating doctor refusing to speak to a defendant on the grounds that he or she may be joined into the action by the claimant as a result of what might have been said[1].

1 *AB v John Wyeth & Brother Ltd* [1993] 4 Med LR 1, CA and *Shaw v Skeet Aung Sooriakumaran* [1996] 7 Med LR 371.

Preliminary issues

13.292 The attraction of a trial of preliminary issues to all the claims in a multi-claimant case is that it appears to offer a way out from the possibility of having endless trials based on individual facts. However, preliminary issues need to be approached with particular caution in the context of group litigation. The trial of a preliminary issue of general causation was proposed in the hormone pregnancy test cases, but this approach was rejected by the Court of Appeal[1]. Moreover, preliminary issues on matters of breach of duty were not seen by Ognall J as practical in the blood product litigation, nor by Ian Kennedy J in the benzodiazepine litigation, nor by Andrew Smith J in the FAC litigation. In practice the courts have tended to progress group actions through the medium of lead cases but it will always be relevant to consider whether the litigation can be most efficiently and justly disposed of by the trial of one or more preliminary issues.

1 *Hyman and Williams v Schering Chemicals Ltd* (1980) Times, 9 June, CA.

Lead claims and test cases

13.293 The lead or test case approach is often the best medium through which to examine the issues common to the group. Lead cases were tried, for example, in *A v National Blood Authority*[1] and *XY v Schering Healthcare Ltd*[2]. The lead case approach means that real claims which illustrate the legal and factual issues which the members of the group must prove to succeed in their claims will be tried; the other claims in the group being stayed at an early stage, usually after exchange of pleadings but sometimes even earlier. However, issues can arise in relation to the extent to which the lead cases are truly representative of the issues arising in the group of claims. In the MMR/MR litigation, a sizable minority of former claimants later complained that their cases were so different from the lead cases that were chosen to represent the group that they should not have been bound by the court's determinations, nor the LSC's decisions on funding.

1 [2001] Lloyds Rep Med 187.
2 [2002] EWHC 1420 (QB).

Costs generally

13.294 It is trite to say that the costs of multi-claimant litigation are likely to be very significant, both in respect of the investigation of the general scientific and state of the art issues and the issues raised in individual cases such as causation[1]. In the *Opren* cases Hirst J provided for this by ordering that where particular claimants incurred costs either personally or through the legal aid fund in pursuing lead actions, or thereby become liable to pay costs to the defendants, every other claimant should contribute rateably on a per capita basis. This novel solution to a problem never before considered by the courts was upheld by the Court of Appeal (see *Davies v Eli Lilly*[2]). The *Opren* form of costs sharing order has been adopted in many subsequent cases, with later adaptations approved by the Court of Appeal in *Sayers v SmithKline Beecham plc*[3], the MMR/MR group litigation, to take account of the position of claimants who discontinue their claim before any trial of common issues has taken place. The general rule is now reflected in CPR 46.6. The presumption is a relatively strong one: in *BCCI SA v Ali*[4], all five test claims (representing over 300 claims) failed. Despite findings of dishonesty by some of the test claimants, the court ordered that the claimants' costs should be shared equally by all 300+ claimants, as there had been an understanding to that effect.

1 The MMR/MR litigation was reported by the Legal Services Commission to have cost over £15 million in claimants' costs alone up to the point at which funding was withdrawn after exchange of expert reports.
2 *Davies v Eli Lilly & Co* [1978] 3 All ER 94, [1987] 1 WLR 1136, CA.
3 *Sayers v Smithkline Beecham plc; XYZ v Schering Healthcare Ltd; Afrika v Cape plc* [2001] EWCA Civ 2017, [2002] 1 WLR 2274s.
4 [2000] 2 Costs LR 243.

Costs budgeting

13.295 It should be noted that as GLOs are automatically allocated to the multi-track, they are *prima facie* subject to the costs budgeting provisions. There is presently an exception for claims worth over £10 million, which may apply to many product liability actions. In any event, there is a discretion to disapply costs budgeting, and the court might be persuaded to do so. Where costs budgeting does apply, the authors suggest that the court is unlikely to require individual costs budgets for every individual case that is part of a GLO[1]. For example, the court may be willing to accept one Precedent H dealing with the common costs to be incurred by the solicitors, and a further Precedent H setting out typical costs for a typical individual case. However, it would be wise to seek the court's approval of this course before the deadline for filing costs budgets.

1 See *Lotus Cars Ltd v Mecanica Solutions Inc* [2014] EWHC 76 (QB), where the court found that it was acceptable to provide a combined costs budget for three cases. Although this case concerned joined cases, not a GLO, Master Kay Q.C commented that 'Of course each case must be treated on its own merits but in the case of large group actions where the management of the various cases is to be treated as common and is dealt with accordingly there is no sensible reason why the costs budgeting should always be considered separately and some good reasons why it should not'.

Funding

13.296 CPR 3.19(2)(m) gives the court the power to order a defendant to provide a witness statement setting out their insurance position, allowing the court to assess whether they have adequate insurance to fund its participation in the litigation to the completion of trial[1]. Claimants' solicitors are entitled to a reasonable cash flow from the defendants once the general issue of liability has been admitted or determined in the claimants' favour.

1 *PIP Breast Implant Litigation* [2013] EWHC 2643 (QB).

The future for group actions

13.297 On 11 June 2013, the European Commission published a non-binding recommendation urging Member States to enable groups of victims to bring court actions more efficiently ('collective redress') when seeking injunctions or compensation for violations of EU competition and any other substantive EU laws. The proposals include a suggestion that governments should create non-profit-making representative entities to bring collective actions on behalf of groups, and that the claimant's funding arrangements must be declared at the outset. Most significantly, the Recommendation suggests that collective claims should be based on the 'opt-in' principle requiring the express consent of the individuals or companies claiming to have been harmed; this represents the current UK practice in product liability claims for medicinal products. The Recommendation asks Member States to put in place appropriate measures within two years at the latest.

CHAPTER 14

Damages awards: lump sums and periodical payments

Jennifer Stone

INTRODUCTION

14.1   This chapter in the last edition of this book commenced by introducing
what was at the time, the *totally new legislative framework*, in relation to future
losses created by the statutory periodical payments regime. That regime

was underpinned by the Courts Act 2003 and has had a significant impact upon the format of damages awards, most particularly in respect of claims involving high value future losses. Structured settlements, a consensual arrangement, were replaced by periodical payments when the above Act came into force on 1 April 2005.

The law now requires that in cases with future pecuniary loss, the courts should consider whether to award periodical payments in respect of those losses. Further, the courts have the power to impose periodical payments on the parties at trial. However, the lump sum, despite all its imperfections, is still appropriate in many cases.

14.2   This chapter, notwithstanding its detail, can offer only a superficial view of financial planning for clinical negligence cases. Every case is different and the potential financial solutions manifold. For many clients there is no such thing as a right answer, merely a range of acceptable solutions. The theory of damages does not always reflect the financial planning realities faced by either claimants or defendants in negotiation or post-settlement.

14.3   This chapter aims to provide a practical perspective on the use of periodical payments, investment of lump sums and the rules regarding state benefits and assistance. All financial planning options possess advantages and disadvantages, and it is hoped that the chapter provides a broad understanding of the issues involved.

DEVELOPMENT OF THE LEGISLATION

14.4   Lump sum damages have long been perceived as an imperfect system of compensating personal injury claimants. At the risk of stating the obvious, lump sum damages for future loss are calculated using a multiplicand, and a multiplier, which incorporates a discount rate.

14.5   The multiplicand is an estimate, resulting from expert evidence, of the future annual losses or costs which claimants are likely to incur as a result of their injuries.

It is necessary to estimate the number of years for which the losses are likely to continue. Where an individual has suffered catastrophic injuries, this will involve medical experts providing a prognosis on life expectancy. Medical experts will often differ as to their estimates.

14.6   If the multiplicand is multiplied, without any discount, by the number of years of life expectancy, the resulting lump sum would over-compensate the claimant (in general, although negative discount rates are not unknown). The theory of lump sum damages is that once invested, it will provide exactly the right amount every year by drawing on both income and capital, and will be exhausted by the end of the period of loss. In other words, from the date of the award, a battle commences between the capital and investment returns (assumed presently to be 2.5 per cent above inflation), and annual expenditure, with the award becoming exhausted at the time of the claimant's death.

14.7   In *Wells v Wells*[1] the House of Lords held that a court, when awarding a lump sum for personal injuries, must assume that the claimant would invest the lump sum in Index-Linked Government Securities (ILGS). ILGS is considered to be a low-risk investment vehicle in comparison to equities. Therefore it produces, on average, a net discount rate less than that of equities. In theory, therefore, a personal injury investor is not expected to take a high level of risk with investment. Of course, life is not so simple, and rare is the case where the claimant has the luxury of relying on index-linked gilts for investment returns. Whether claimants are always apprised of the risks involved in alternative forms of investment prior to settlement is questionable.

1 [1999] 1 AC 345.

14.8   The current assumption is that the lump sum, when invested in ILGS, will produce a return equivalent to 2.5 per cent per annum in excess of the Retail Prices Index (RPI). However, the present discount rate of 2.5 per cent does not reflect (and never has since it was set by the Lord Chancellor in 2001) the real return available from ILGS. The catalyst for the setting of that rate came from the House of Lords decision in *Wells v Wells*, which recognised that recipients of personal injury awards are not ordinary investors, and should not therefore, be exposed to investment risk in order to obtain a real return on their awards. The required returns on closer analysis means in present, broad terms, a return net of tax (say 1 per cent), inflation (3 per cent), and the costs of investment management (about 1.5–2.00 per cent per annum). In total, a gross return of over 8 per cent is required, which is not at all easy to achieve, and is certainly not consistent with *Wells*, nor with an assumed cautious approach to investment risk. To complicate matters further, this nominal required rate of return of 8 per cent does not allow for earnings-based future costs increasing in excess of RPI over the longer term.

14.9   The Lord Chancellor reviewed the discount rate post-*Wells*, in June 2001, and set the still current rate of 2.5 per cent. It is clear that there has long been a significant mismatch between the theory, as opposed to the reality, of investing lump sum awards. The system of lump sum compensation has attracted much criticism and unsurprisingly the discount rate has been under attack for many years as being unrealistically high. The current and ongoing consultation process in relation to the discount rate, commenced in 2012 by the Ministry of Justice, is arguably long overdue. The consultation followed significant pressure, principally from the Association of Personal Injury Lawyers.

Are periodical payments a better alternative? Put simply, periodical payments provide for a guaranteed future income stream based on the losses sustained by the claimant, without risk as to mortality or investment. Those risks, when taken together, are very substantial. As will be seen below, periodical payments, following judicial scrutiny, are linked to earnings-related inflation, which over many years has been greater than price inflation, as measured by the RPI.

Bearing in mind that the discount rate is based on price inflation as opposed to earnings inflation, the periodical payments regime serves to highlight the inadequacies and risks of the once and for all lump sum.

14.10   The lump sum and its associated problems were outlined by Lord Scarman over 30 years ago in the case of *Lim Poh Choo v Camden and Islington Area Health Authority*[1], when he stated:

'The course of litigation illustrates, with devastating clarity, the insuperable problems implicit in a system of compensation for personal injuries which (unless the parties agree otherwise) can yield only a lump sum assessed by the court at the time of Judgment. Sooner or later, and too often later rather than sooner, if the parties do not settle, a court (once liability is admitted or proved) has to make an award of damages. The award, which covers past, present and future injury and loss, must, under our law, be a lump sum assessed at the conclusion of the legal process. The award is final: it is not susceptible to review as the future unfolds, substituting fact for estimate. Knowledge of the future being denied to mankind, so much of the award as is to be attributed to future loss and suffering (in many cases the major part of the award) will almost surely be wrong. There is only one certainty: the future will prove the award to be either too high or too low'.

1 [1980] AC 174.

14.11   Structured settlements, the predecessor to periodical payments, arose in the UK in the late-1980s. The early structured settlements were Byzantine in their bureaucracy, and were seen to restrict the wider use of such settlements. Compensation for personal injury has come a long way since then.

14.12   The first structured settlement in the UK was implemented in 1989 in the case of *Kelly v Dawes*[1]. Since then, a number of initiatives and legislative changes have occurred, leading us to the current system whereby periodical payments can be imposed by the court. It is perhaps worth outlining a brief history of the legislative attempts to move away from the lump sum.

1 (1990) Times, 27 September, [1990] CLY 1724.

14.13   The Law Commission published Consultation Paper 125 in October 1992 and, having received wide-ranging responses, recommended many changes to the structured settlement system in Paper No 224 published in September 1994. Having considered the responses to the consultation paper, the Law Commission stopped short of giving the court the power to impose structured settlements on one or other of the involved parties.

14.14   A number of legislative changes followed. First came the introduction of the Finance Act 1995, which gave provision in the Income and Corporation Taxes Act 1988 to secure the tax-free nature of structured settlements. It enabled defendant insurers to purchase structured settlement annuities on behalf of claimants. An annuity is an income stream purchased in exchange for a capital sum. The annuity providers made tax-free payments direct to the claimant. However, the Finance Act 1995 did not cover all possible circumstances in which structured settlements might arise, hence further provision was made in the Finance Act 1996.

14.15   Next came the Damages Act (DA) 1996, which was intended to establish structured settlements firmly in the legislation as the safest form of 'investment' in the UK. It led to the provision of 100 per cent protection of structured settlement payments under what was then the Policyholders Protection Act.

As a result of the Finance Acts 1995 and 1996, and the DA 1996, the process for establishing structured settlements in suitable cases was greatly simplified, and the security of payment was guaranteed in the event that the annuity provider (usually an insurance company) ceased to exist.

14.16 Following this push to establish support for structured settlements in the legislation, take-up remained surprisingly low. The perceived major flaw in the system was that structured settlements could only be implemented by consent between the parties. Despite the ground-swell of support in many quarters, both claimant and defendant practitioners often viewed structured settlements with suspicion.

Arguably, without suitable advice on the benefits of structured settlements, the natural preference of claimants was in favour of a lump sum award. Time and again structured settlements were not considered in cases that were eminently suitable for their inclusion within damages awards.

14.17 *Wells v Wells*[1] was a landmark case in the history of personal injury. Lord Steyn outlined in his judgment a potential resolution to the problems:

'The solution is relatively straightforward. The court ought to be given the power of its own motion to make an award for periodical payments rather than a lump sum in appropriate cases. Such a power is perfectly consistent with the principle of full compensation for pecuniary loss. Except perhaps for the distaste of personal injury lawyers for a change to a familiar system, I can think of no substantial argument to the contrary, but the judges cannot make the change. Only Parliament can solve the problem'.

1 [1999] AC 345.

14.18 In March 2000, the Lord Chancellor published the consultation paper 'Damages: The Discount Rate and Alternatives to Lump Sum Payments'. Other initiatives followed, including Structured Settlements: Report of the Master of the Rolls' Working Party.

14.19 The Master of the Rolls' Working Party's report on structured settlements was published in August 2002. The purpose of the Working Party was to provide comprehensive, balanced and informed views. It was chaired by Brian Langstaff QC (as he then was), and comprised representatives from the relevant sectors. The Working Party's view on lump sums was as follows:

'The one thing that is certain about a once and for all lump sum award in respect of future loss is that it will inevitably either over-compensate or under-compensate. This will happen particularly where the claimant survives beyond the life expectancy estimated at the date of trial, or alternatively dies earlier. It will frequently be the case in practice that there is over-compensation in six figure sums, or, correspondingly, that a combination of increased life expectancy, the cost of care, and (it may be) the cost of new but necessary medical treatments is such that the sum needed exceeds anything that might have been awarded at the date of trial'.

They went on to state:

'Further, the method of compensation on a "once and for all" basis is most frequently made by the multiplication of the annual loss, assessed at the time of the award, by a multiplier which is derived from assumptions as to investment performance (as we have pointed out above), which may be vulnerable to future movements in interest rates and which assumes that the cost of provision of services and the specialised needs that the seriously injured may require will rise in accordance with the RPI rather than the National Average Earnings Index, or at some other rate'.

They concluded:

'Accordingly, we prefer a system that is better able to meet future needs as and when they arise. Such a system may also have its defects – as we shall go on to point out – but we believe the advantages outweigh them'.

14.20   The outcome from the Working Party was the implementation of CPR Practice Direction 40(c) relating to structured settlements, whereby cases with future losses in excess of £500,000 required consideration as to whether a lump sum or structured settlement was a more appropriate form of award. The Practice Direction related only to minors or patients (now protected parties/beneficiaries), and was subject to the DA 1996, hence the consensual basis remained. That said, it represented a sensible step in the right direction, and required the parties in prescribed cases to obtain proper advice.

14.21   This was quickly overtaken by the result of the Lord Chancellor's further Consultation Paper *Damages for Future Loss: Giving the Courts the Power to Order Periodical Payments for Future Loss and Care Costs in Personal Injury Cases*. This Consultation Paper concluded as follows:

'That in most circumstances periodical payments are, in principle, the more appropriate means for paying compensation for significant future financial loss. Periodical Payments better reflect the purpose of compensation, which is to restore the claimant's prior position. They also place the risks associated with life expectancy and investment on defendants rather than claimants'.

14.22   The outcome of this consultation was the Courts Act 2003, ss 100–101 which provides the courts with the power to impose periodical payments on the parties.

The tax-free nature of periodical payments, whether provided by a self-funding body or by the purchase of an annuity, is enshrined in the Income Tax (Trading and Other Income) Act 2005, ss 731–733.

Courts Act 2003

14.23   Consensual structured settlements were replaced on 1 April 2005 by periodical payments.

On that date the provisions of the Courts Act 2003 relating to payment of damages for future pecuniary loss came into force. The courts now have the power to order those losses to be paid periodically, whether wholly or in part, if that approach is found to be in the best interests of the claimant.

14.24   The new legislation amended the DA 1996 and significant amendments have been made to the Civil Procedure Rules 1998, in particular to Parts 36 and 41. The rule changes are supplemented by new provisions in their respective practice directions.

14.25 Practice Direction 40(c) relating to structured settlements was swept away. There is now no lower limit to the value of a claim where periodical payments may be appropriate. That limit used to be set at £500,000 in terms of future loss under the structured settlements practice direction. Cases of maximum severity will always fall to be considered, but claims of much lesser value now come within scope. What, for example, of the unsophisticated claimant with modest earnings loss? That type of individual may be best compensated by regular income, thus avoiding worries over management or, worse still, early dissipation of a lump sum.

14.26 The DCA's paper 'Guidance on Periodical Payments', issued shortly after the new regime came into effect, was indicative of a *fundamentalist* approach, based on a *bottom up* assessment of the claimant's needs. In theory this means that the order for periodical payments provides for the claimant to be paid the appropriate amounts for his need (usually life), escalating in line with RPI unless the court orders otherwise. It follows that there is no need for speculative estimates or extended disputes about life expectancy, as payments will be based on the claimant's annual needs and will be payable as long as necessary.

14.27 An example of this would be a child with cerebral palsy aged seven with a life expectancy to age 45 according to the defendant's expert, and 55 according to the claimant's. The care and case management costs are agreed to increase in cost at the age of 19 from £35,000 per annum to £95,000 per annum. Under the lump sum route, life expectancy would need to be agreed or adjudicated, in order that an appropriate lump sum is paid. With periodical payments, once the multiplicands are agreed or the subject of judicial finding, the idea would simply be to pay those annual amounts for the lifetime of the individual.

14.28 Many years into the regime, it is widely accepted amongst experienced practitioners that it is necessary still to calculate the lump sum in each case. That way, it is possible to evaluate offers inclusive of periodical payments made during negotiation with reasonable accuracy. The multiplier/multiplicand route still holds great weight, and can be used as a yardstick in settlement negotiations.

14.29 On reflection, following decided cases and also a lack of development of an annuity market, some of the DCA guidance has been shown to be misguided. For example, the implementation of the periodical payments regime coincided with the withdrawal from market of the two insurance companies providing appropriate annuities.

Although a new annuity provider entered the market, the cost of its RPI-linked annuities was usually far in excess of the lump sum equivalent award, hence that approach was most unattractive to defendants. Further, the indexation litigation (of which much more below) rendered RPI-linked annuities effectively redundant. The annuity market in relation to periodical payments has not recovered, save for some preliminary interest by a conglomerate of interested insurers.

There are other issues with periodical payments that neither the pre-legislative consultations nor the DCA guidance identified, which have implications for clinical negligence practitioners, and which are explored later in this chapter.

PERIODICAL PAYMENTS – THE LEGISLATION

CPR Part 41 and CPR PD 41B

14.30   CPR Part 41 relates to the court's powers under the DA 1996, s 2(1) to order that *all or part* of a personal injury damages award is to take the form of periodical payments. Early consideration of periodical payments by the parties and the court is prescribed by the broadly drafted CPR 41.5–41.7:

41.5 Statement of Case

(1) In a claim for damages for personal injury, each party in its statement of case may state whether it considers periodical payments or a lump sum is the more appropriate form for all or part of an award of damages and where such statement is given must provide relevant particulars of the circumstances which are relied on.

(2) Where a statement under paragraph (1) is not given, the court may order a party to make such a statement.

(3) Where the court considers that a statement of case contains insufficient particulars under paragraph (1), the court may order a party to provide such further particulars as it considers appropriate.

Court's Indication to the Parties

41.6 The court shall consider and indicate to the parties as soon as practicable whether periodical payments or a lump sum is likely to be the more appropriate form for all or part of an award of damages.

Factors to be taken into account

41.7 When considering:

    (a)   its indication as to whether periodical payments or a lump sum is likely to be the more appropriate form for all or part of an award of damages under rule 41.6; or
    (b)   whether to make an order under section 2(1)(a) of the 1996 Act

The court shall have regard to all the circumstances of the case and in particular the form of award which best meets the claimant's needs, having regard to the factors set out in Practice Direction 41B'.

Practice Direction 41B states as follows:

'Factors to be taken into Account (Rule 41.7)

1. The factors which the court shall have regard to under rule 41.7 include:

(1) the scale of the annual payments taking into account any deduction for contributory negligence;

(2) the form of award preferred by the claimant including:

    (a)   the reasons for the claimant's preference; and
    (b)   the nature of any financial advice received by the claimant when considering the form of award; and

(3) the form of award preferred by the defendant including the reasons for the defendant's preference'.

14.31   For the parties and the court, such early consideration is not an unsophisticated exercise. Statements of case should be drafted on the basis of the parties' reasoned preferences being to hand. From the claimant's perspective, Practice Direction 41B anticipates the availability of expert financial advice. It may be difficult for the legal team to advise the claimant without such input. Overall, there must be sufficient information to allow the court to indicate the most appropriate form of damages, whether that is a lump sum, periodical payments, or a mixture of both. If the required information is unavailable at that early stage, it would be wise to delay taking expert advice.

In spite of the above, in practice, periodical payments have been firmly in the territory of the cases of highest value. How periodical payments fit within an award of damages can usually only properly be considered once quantum investigations are complete and a schedule of loss is to hand.

14.32   Contributory negligence and its effect on the form of award is specifically dealt with by Practice Direction 41B. Presumably, the similar effect of litigation risk discount falls to be considered accordingly. Some practitioners still take the view that a discounted award is best paid by way of lump sum, so as to be as flexible as possible in meeting the claimant's needs.

This is not always the case, however, as year-on-year tax-free payments can be of great benefit, particularly where the effects of the compromise may be compounded by uncertain life expectancy and an inappropriate discount rate.

14.33   The regime also applies to circumstances where the court considers that part of the award should continue after the claimant's death. CPR 41.8(2) states:

'Where the court orders that any part of the award shall continue after the claimant's death, for the benefit of the claimant's dependants, the order must also specify the relevant amount and duration of the payments and how each payment is to be made during the year and at what intervals'.

14.34   Practice Direction 41B explains that this applies in situations where a dependant would have had a claim under the Fatal Accidents Act 1976 if the claimant had died at the time of the accident. The DCA guidance notes provide the example of a court ordering damages for care costs that last for the claimant's lifetime *and* part of the damages for future loss of earnings that should be paid after the claimant's death, until his child has reached the age of 18. An important factor that the court will have to take into account is that awards pursuant to CPR 41.8(2), and paid periodically after the claimant's death, will not be tax free, as the tax exemption applies only to payments in the hands of the claimant or someone receiving payments on behalf of the claimant. It is likely that very few awards have been made on this basis.

14.35   Overall, however, expert financial advice can help clarify the merits of the options available. The claimant will have had the benefit of being advised on a risk-free alternative to the lump sum settlement. So often in the recent past, consideration of a structured settlement or periodical payments very late in the claim (and to the surprise of the claimant) led to rejection of what might have been a more appropriate settlement.

CPR Part 36 and CPR PD 36A

14.36 Whether claimant or defendant, formulating, evaluating or clarifying an offer under CPR 36.5, it is likely that some expert financial input will be necessary.

Although the pure lump sum payment is preserved, Part 36 offers can be very sophisticated. It is provided for in the rule that offers may be made on the basis of a smaller lump sum in conjunction with periodical payments. That accompanying lump sum would usually comprise general damages and past losses, but may be supplemented by capitalised heads of future loss.

14.37 The provisions relating to lump sums accompanying an offer of periodical payments are straightforward and provide for flexibility, whether the defendant's offer to pay or the claimant's to accept. The claimant or defendant *may* state how the lump sum is constructed. There may be capitalised heads of future loss in addition to general damages and past losses.

14.38 As regards the periodical payments element of an offer from either side, CPR 36.5(4) requires considerable detail. Duration and amount of payments must be specified. Payments relating to care and other annual lifelong needs must be shown separately to loss of income. Payments for renewable capital items such as vehicles or equipment must also be distinguished from other types of periodical payments. Claimants may only accept the whole of the defendant's offer and cannot accept the lump sum leaving the periodical payments to be decided at a later stage.

14.39 The possible permutations under CPR Part 36 are manifold. Costs therefore will inevitably be more complex. With such a mix and match of periodical payments and lump sums, the parties may call on the help of a financial expert, but what of the judge at trial? The Rules Committee takes the simple view that the trial judge would have the benefit of knowledge of the substantive proceedings so would be best placed to deal with costs issues.

14.40 After almost a decade of the statutory periodical payments regime, practical experience has shown that Part 36 offers have not caused too much by way of difficulty. It is uncommon to find offers made on a lump sum basis, particularly where periodical payments would be the normal approach to settlement. For example, a claim based on full liability, in relation to a claimant with lifelong needs on account of birth injury – in those circumstances, the court would be unlikely to approve a lump sum award. Generally speaking, following the indexation cases, the court would normally expect settlements to be inclusive of periodical payments, where the claimant is a minor or a protected party.

14.41   Lump sum awards can be appropriate in certain cases, for example, where there is a very significant reduction on account of liability, but expert financial advice would usually form an important part of the Approval bundle.

Variation of periodical payments

14.42   The Damages (Variation of Periodical Payments) Order 2005[1], sets out how the periodical payment regime fits with provisional damages. *Variation* applies only to claims issued post-1 April 2005. As with provisional damages, variation is restricted in its use. A low take-up rate was identified in Parliamentary debate during the genesis of the legislation. Nevertheless, the court has the power pursuant to article 2 of the Order to make variable orders:

'If there is proved or admitted to be a chance that at some definite or indefinite time in the future the claimant will:

    (a)   as a result of the act or omission which gave rise to the cause of action, develop some serious disease or suffer some serious deterioration, or

    (b)   enjoy some significant improvement, in his physical or mental condition, where that condition had been adversely affected as a result of that act or omission.

The court may, on the application of a party, with the agreement of all the parties, or of its own initiative, provide in an order for periodical payments that it may be varied'.

1 SI 2005/841.

14.43   Variation differs from provisional damages in that the potentially improving claimant comes within scope. Although improvers will be few and far between, some may in fact end up with increased periodical payments: what of the bedridden claimant whose improvement brings some mobility? There may well be increased care and equipment costs to maximise that mobility.

Experience of the periodical payments regime has illustrated that the ongoing costs of a deputy have come under scrutiny in this regard. The overall approach to this head of loss has become more sophisticated over recent years, resulting in much increased claims. Defendants have sought, in cases where there is a chance that the claimant's capacity might return, to cater for that eventuality, by way of medical reviews from time to time. In such cases, there is the possibility that periodical payments might vary by ceasing altogether.

14.44   It is important to distinguish variation from increases or decreases in periodical payments as provided for in CPR 41.8(3). Variation relates to a *chance* of change in *medical condition*, as opposed to changes in condition or circumstances that are agreed between the parties or the subject of a judicial finding.

Reasonable security

14.45   Under the DA 1996, s 2(3) the court will order or approve a periodical payments order only if it is satisfied that continuity of payment under the order is *reasonably secure*.

14.46   The definition of *reasonably secure* is found at the DA 1996, s 2(4)[1].

'2(4) For the purpose of subsection (3) the continuity of payment under an order is reasonably secure if:

   (a)   it is protected by a guarantee given under section 6 of the Schedule to this Act;
   (b)   it is protected by a scheme under section 213 of the Financial Services and Markets Act 2000 (compensation) (whether or not as modified by section 4 of this Act); or
   (c)   the source of payment is a government or health service body'.

1   As substituted by the Courts Act 2003, s 100(1).

14.47   The DA 1996, s 2(4)(c) is clarified in the Damages (Government and Health Service Bodies) Order 2005[1]. Designation under the Order removes the need for a ministerial guarantee to be given under the DA 1996, s 2(4)(a).

1   SI 2005/474.

14.48   The DA 1996, s 2(4)(c) should have been simple to apply, but there were difficulties, which have since been resolved. During late 2005, the two cases of *YM* and *Kanu*[1] ran into troubled waters. The defendant NHS Trust, which had converted to Foundation status, was not covered by the NHS Residual Liabilities Act 1996. Such a trust can become insolvent and, as the provider of periodical payments, the case could not proceed to approval until the security issue had been resolved.

1   [2006] EWHC 820 (QB).

14.49   The position of Foundation Trusts in relation to periodical payments alerted legal teams to wider issues. What would result if an NHS Trust already funding periodical payments, converted to Foundation status? Most trusts were expected to follow that route, and since then, the Health and Social Care Act 2011 stated an intention for all hospitals to be part of a Foundation Trust, or a Foundation Trust in its own right by April 2014. As at May 2014, 147 Foundation Trusts were in existence.

14.50   In *YM* and *Kanu*, the Secretary of State for Health was made a party to the action by the judge. In addition to the ministerial guarantee that can underpin periodical payments, the application of the NHS (Residual Liabilities Act) 1996, in relation to Foundation Trusts required clarification. Section 1 of that Act states:

'1. (1) If a National Health Service trust, a Health Authority or a Special Health Authority ceases to exist, the Secretary of State must exercise his statutory powers to transfer property, rights and liabilities of the body so as to secure that all of its liabilities are dealt with'.

14.51 *YM* was approved by Mr Justice Forbes on 30 January 2006. A model order was produced to deal with the resulting terms of settlement. Various scenarios were considered by the court. First, should a foundation trust become insolvent, it was suggested in argument that the Department of Health would be unlikely to turn its back on a failing Trust and should, therefore, put the National Health Service Litigation Authority (NHSLA) in funds. That authority should consequently meet any remaining liability under a periodical payments order. The NHSLA would be named in the order as source of payment, for the purposes of security, but would not be a party to the action. This is not to be confused with a DA 1996, s 2(4)(a) *ministerial guarantee*. Such a guarantee has not as yet been given, apparently because no guidelines exist as to how one should be made.

14.52 Second, the NHS (Residual Liabilities) Act 1996 covers present NHS Trusts. On conversion to Foundation status, the Trust would enter into an agreement with the NHSLA as regards cover in the event of insolvency. A lump sum would be payable to the NHSLA should the Foundation Trust leave the Clinical Negligence Scheme for Trusts (CNST[1]). The NHSLA would then administer and pay outstanding periodical payment order liabilities. Existing periodical payment or structured settlement liabilities are also covered by one or other of the above procedures.

1 The Clinical Negligence Scheme for Trusts handles all clinical negligence claims against member NHS bodies where the incident in question took place on or after 1 April 1995 (or when the body joined the scheme, if that is later). Although membership of the scheme is voluntary, all NHS Trusts, (including Foundation Trusts) and Primary Care Trusts (PCTs) in England currently belong to the scheme (www.nhsla.co.uk).

14.53 Aside from NHSLA cases, where the security issue has been resolved, problems remain as regards indemnifying bodies such as the Medical Defence Union and the Medical Protection Society. Therefore the areas of general practitioner negligence and that relating to the growth area of private medicine, cannot presently be considered automatically secure for the purposes of s 2(3).

14.54 The Medical Defence Union, although an indemnifying body, operated an insurance-based scheme until 1 April 2013. Claims reported before that date would be dealt with under the terms of the agency agreement made with the insurers involved (SCOR UK Company Ltd and International Insurance Company of Hannover). Both insurers are regulated by the Financial Conduct Authority, hence are secure in terms of the DA 1996, s 2(4) (b).

In other words, should the relevant insurer become insolvent and default on its liability under a periodical payments order, the Financial Services Compensation Scheme would meet that ongoing liability in full in its stead.

The insurance-based scheme will no doubt continue to feature over the next few years in relation to cases initiated before April 2013. After that date claims will be dealt with on the basis of discretionary indemnity from the Medical Defence Union's own resources.

14.55   The insurance scheme requires further scrutiny, due to the applicable level of indemnity, set at £10 million. At first glance that appears more than sufficient to meet most high-value claims in this field. However, periodical payments paid over a long period and proofed against inflation by an earnings-related measure, might reach an accumulative total greater than the indemnity. If that were the case, payments would cease once the indemnity was exhausted. It would be difficult for the court to be satisfied of the continuity of payments being reasonably secure in such circumstances. The test, however, is one of reasonableness, and using reasonable assumptions as to likely earnings inflation and life expectancy, it is possible to provide forecasts to assist the court. If sufficient headroom between the possible accumulative total and the indemnity is the result, the court may be able to approve the periodical payments order. A further point to bear in mind is that the lump sum that would accompany periodical payments and, in addition, both sides' legal costs would need to be deducted from the indemnity as a starting point. The net indemnity for the purposes of periodical payments would therefore be substantially less than £10 million.

14.56   Now that the insurance scheme is no more, the position as regards security in the sense of the DA 1996, s 2(3) is far from clear, as the Medical Defence Union will be meeting all claims notified post-1 April 2013 from its own resources on the basis of discretionary indemnity. In the guidance issued by the Department for Constitutional Affairs (DCA) at the outset of the periodical payments regime, para 36 states as follows:

'Section 2(4) does not cover periodical payments self-funded by the Motor Insurer's Bureau, medical defence organisations, offshore insurers or private defendants, as none of these payments attract statutory protection under the FSCS'.

14.57   However, para 39 of the DCA Guidance goes on to state the following:

'This does *not* mean that the courts cannot order periodical payments against these defendants and insurance bodies. They may be able to provide statutorily secure periodical payments by purchasing an appropriate annuity from a life office for the benefit of the claimant, thus attracting the full protection of the FSCS under Section 4 (1) and (2) of the 1996 Act … Alternatively, it is open to these bodies to satisfy the Court that they can offer a method of funding other than one of those deemed secure under section 2(4) that is reasonably secure'.

14.58   Developments since the Guidance was published include the court holding that the Motor Insurers Bureau is secure in the sense that it can self-fund periodical payments from its own resources. The case of *Thacker v Steeples and MIB*[1] considered the issue and the Bureau was held by the court to be reasonably secure because:

— it has longevity and significant resources;
— it is a collective of 80 motor insurers. If one fails, MIB would simply increase the levy on remaining 79;
— the MIB is the body through which the government satisfies its obligation to ensure compensation for victims of uninsured and untraced drivers under Article 4 of European Directive on Motor Insurance. Therefore, morally and politically it is unlikely that the government would allow the MIB to dissolve, without its continuing liabilities being provided for.

1 (16 May 2005, unreported), see Lawtel Quantum AM 0900821 and [2005] 3 Kemp News 5.

14.59 Whether or not the Medical Defence Union, the Medical Protection Society or the other, smaller, indemnifying bodies can satisfy the court in the sense of the required reasonable security, is unclear. By analogy with the *Thacker* decision, and without going in to a detailed history of those bodies and forensically examining their respective assets and funding arrangements, it might be argued that the longevity and resource points might be met.

14.60 Beyond that, a direct comparison between the MIB and the above indemnifying bodies is not possible, due to the differing nature of the respective organisations. However, as the Medical Defence Union and the Medical Protection Society appear to be robust, the court may take the view that self-funded periodical payments are secure. As regards reasonable security, a note of caution was sounded, however, by Mackay J in the case of *Bennett v Stephens*[1]. The case was in the context of a road traffic accident, but the judge's analysis of the resources backing the insurer, which was not automatically reasonably secure, sets a high bar, and gives an indication of the level of judicial scrutiny that will be applied in similar cases:

'However, if I make a periodical payment order and continuity of payment is broken and those payments cease, the claimant's position here would be a disastrous one. He would have no further recourse to the defendants, to whom he will have given a legal discharge as a consequence of making of the order, he will have no recourse to any compensation scheme or guarantee. He will be left with desperate measures seeking to set this Order aside many years hence, or making a claim against his solicitors.

While therefore, I am only required by the statute to consider whether the proposed order is reasonably secure, I am not required to find that it is entirely secure or free of all risk, it seems to me that my satisfaction has to reach a high level, given what is involved and I must finish up satisfied on something higher than a mere balance of probabilities…

So, the primary obligation to fund a periodical payments order lies with Farraday. It is as I said, a major reinsurer in its own right, doing very substantial business in the Lloyds market, regulated by Lloyds and the FSA … it is a wholly owned subsidiary of Berkshire Hathaway Inc, a substantial and well known United States corporation. It is itself fully reinsured in respect of the risks of which now effectively the insurer, the lead reinsurer being Munich Re, itself one of the world's largest reinsurers with a market capitalisation in excess of £21 billion and a 2009 operating profit of more than €2.5 billion. The following reinsurance market behind it is composed of reinsurers of repute.

If matters rested there, however, I would be reluctant to pronounce myself satisfied under Section 2(3). Without in any way denigrating the current status or stability of Farraday as a going concern, taller trees than it have fallen in the financial forest before now and, unless it could claim the backing of Section 2(4) which it cannot as I am presently invited to assume, I would hesitate to say that I could sufficiently discount the risk that it might fail sometime in the next 50 years or so, which is the period I have to consider covered by the proposed order in this case'.

1 [2010] EWHC 2194 (QB).

14.61 The required standard of security is reasonableness, not perfection. If a funding mechanism could be constructed either by trust or similar vehicle providing certain safeguards, then it may well be that the reasonable security test as set by Mackay J is passed. The safeguards in relation to such a scheme might be:

—   the scheme's sole purpose is to fund the periodical payments liability;
—   the nature of the vehicle is that it is irrevocable and the indemnifying body cannot call upon any of the assets to be repaid unless and until the scheme's liabilities have been met;
—   the appointment of an independent trustee/member of the scheme, preferably with expertise in representing claimants' interests;
—   prudent and conservative actuarial assumptions used in calculating the sum to be paid into the scheme by the indemnifying body when considering new periodical payment liabilities. For example, the discount rate calculated net of tax (as opposed to the normal gross approach); the assumption of normal life expectancy in circumstances of impairment; and the assumption that liability under a periodical payment order increases in relation to earnings related inflation;
—   the requirement of an annual actuarial valuation of the entire scheme to prevent deficits arising;
—   amendment of the scheme can only be made in circumstances which will not (in the view of the actuary), adversely affect the ability to meet its obligations;
—   any funds invested, should be managed on a cautious basis in terms of investment risk.

As things stand presently, it is worth emphasising that periodical payments and their numerous and very significant advantages may be denied to claimants, where medical practitioners are indemnified as above.

Assignment or charge of right

14.62   The DA 1996, s 2(6) prevents the assignment or charge of the right to receive periodical payments unless the court that made the original order is satisfied that there are special circumstances that make it necessary. This is intended to avoid the possibility of claimants receiving less than the true value of the award as a result of their assigning their right to receive the payments in return for a lump sum. The US experience has been that a large secondary industry has arisen in the market, known as 'factoring'.

14.63   The restrictions on claimants' ability to assign periodical payments do not affect their ability to borrow future income. Unsecured loans are permissible, but not secured loans that put the claimant's right to receive payments at risk.

Fatal accidents

14.64   Fatal accident claims are included within the periodical payments regime, ensuring that, where appropriate, dependants receive tax-free periodic income. The DA 1996, s 7 incorporates fatal accidents within its definition of *personal injury* and in addition, refers to quantification of those claims, pursuant to the Fatal Accidents Act 1976 and the Law Reform (Miscellaneous Provisions) Act 1934.

Judicial Studies Board

14.65   The Judicial Studies Board training paper, *Periodical Payments under the Damages Act 1996*, was authored by His Honour Judge Oliver-Jones QC and Master Ungley and was circulated to the judiciary in July 2005. The following excerpt from the Lord Chancellor's Department Consultation Paper 2002 concluded the JSB training paper:

'So it will be for the courts to develop the principles and guidelines for deciding which form of damages for future loss (and care costs) should take … we hope that the courts will normally order periodical payments in cases of significant future loss. If they do, the majority of cases will do so against that background. Although the parties will be free to agree a lump sum, and no doubt many will, it will be harder for a party to insist on a lump sum where the other party wishes to settle for reasonable periodical payments; so we hope that periodical payments will become the norm for settlements too'.

14.66   Procedural judges have been aware since publication of the JSB paper of the court's duty pursuant to CPR 41.6, to:

'Consider and indicate to the parties as soon as practicable whether periodical payments or a lump sum is likely to be the more appropriate form for all or part of an award of damages'.

14.67   The JSB paper confirms that the court's indication is simply that – an indication. It is not binding on the parties, or the trial judge. It is no more than a case management tool. Its purpose is not to force the parties into concessions that may change as cases progress. The training document offers no practical guidance as to what form the court's indication might take. It does, however, guide judges through the factors set out in CPR PD 41, but without instruction as to how much weight to attach to each of those factors.

It would probably be fair to say that despite the new procedural powers, judges when case managing were reluctant to apply the new rules. However, as hoped, the courts have developed the principles and guidelines which have shaped the periodical payment regime. A review of the key cases follows.

Case law

14.68   Decided cases have shaped the periodical payments regime to a very significant extent. Initial low take-up of settlements inclusive of periodical payments can perhaps be attributable in part to the slow pace at which the procedural judiciary warmed to its new powers. However, the principal cause was the indexation issue. This is illustrated by the cases, but in outline, periodical payments from the outset were seen as being targeted at care costs. Therefore, annual payments would be used to pay carers' earnings. Earnings-related inflation had historically outstripped prices inflation for many years. As periodical payments were linked to the RPI, there was grave concern that periodical payments would lag behind the increasing costs of care, year on year, resulting in a growing shortfall and substantial under compensation.

Godbold v Mahmood

14.69   Between 1 April 2005 and the distribution of the judicial training, two cases of significance were decided. The first, *Godbold v Mahmood*,[1] was heard by Mr Justice Mitting. Judgment was handed down on 20 April 2005. At that time the claimant, Mr Godbold, was 58 years old. He had suffered a significant head injury along with orthopaedic injuries. The judge ordered periodical payments in respect of recurring care and related costs:

'I am satisfied that a periodical payments order for recurring costs best meets the claimant's needs, having regard to the factors set out in the Practice Direction PD 41B.

The factors that have influenced me in favour of making a periodical payments order are: first, uncertainty as to the claimant's life expectancy … a periodical payments order eliminates uncertainty and so the risk of unfairness to the claimant or to the defendant.

Secondly, Mr Sturton's (the professional Receiver in the case) preference for a periodical payments order because it is easier to match expense to income and because the income stream is secure and not dependent on investment returns … the periodical payments order will be indexed … by reference to the increase in the retail prices index …'

The judge awarded loss of earnings as a lump sum as it would provide 'a substantial cushion against unexpected future events and expenditure'.

1 [2005] EWHC 1002 (QB).

14.70   In other words, the lump sum would be sufficient for flexibility and contingency. Mr Godbold was getting on in years, so the problems associated with RPI linkage might not bite to any significant degree, unless of course, he lives much longer than expected.

Walton v Calderdale

14.71   One month or so after *Godbold* came Mr Justice Silber's judgment in *Walton v Calderdale Healthcare NHS Trust*[1]. He ordered RPI-linked periodical payments for the claimant's care after he reached the age of 19. A lump sum valuation of £2.65 million had been agreed between the parties. Also agreed, but subject to approval, was an alternative settlement package inclusive of RPI-linked periodical payments. The accompanying lump sum was agreed, as was the annual periodical payment at £20,000 to age 19. Although care experts for both sides agreed that periodical payments from age 19 should be £50,548, the defendant trust thought otherwise.

1 [2005] EWHC 1053 (QB).

14.72   The defendant's position was that the correct annual sum should be £44,000. The argument was that the local authority would, to some extent, contribute to the claimant's care. Further support for the defendant's lesser figure was, apparently, to be found within the HM Treasury document entitled *Value for Money*.

14.73   The defendant produced no evidence in support of its contentions. The judge, predictably, awarded an annual payment, RPI linked in the sum as agreed between the care experts. The judgment sets out the five factors in Practice Direction 41B and expanded somewhat:

'Applying those principles to the facts of this case, each of those factors supports the claimant's contention that there should be periodical payments for future care for the claimant after he has reached the age of 19 as the litigation friend and mother of the claimant strongly supports periodical payments on the basis of advice she has received from an Independent Financial Advisor. She explains in her second witness statement that she is concerned that the claimant will live for another 70 or so years, if he was not to receive periodical payments, he might otherwise run out of capital and income which could pay for his care costs. I regard this as a sensible and cogent point as is the fact that a lump sum payment might not be large enough to compensate the claimant if there was to be a high rate of inflation in the future'.

Flora v Wakom

14.74   It was not until December 2005 that *Flora (Tarlochan Singh) v Wakom (Heathrow) Ltd*[1] provided some further judicial scrutiny of the periodical payments regime. The judgment relates to an interim application made by the defendant. The defendant issued an application to strike out those parts of the claimant's statement of case that sought to pursue a claim for periodical payments linked to Average Earnings Index (AEI), therefore disapplying RPI linkage. The application also sought to exclude the claimant's expert evidence supporting that aspect of his claim. The basis for striking out the application was that the claimant had no reasonable prospects of success.

1 [2006] EWCA Civ 1103.

14.75   Sir Michael Turner, the judge at first instance, dismissed the application as being procedurally misconceived. Although ultimately for the trial judge to decide, Sir Michael indicated that, in his view, if the courts allowed only RPI linkage, the result might be that periodical payments would never achieve widespread acceptance:

'It is my respectful opinion that the legislative attempt to meet the long felt need for a system of compensation for future losses and expenses may prove to be as dead in the water as the earlier attempt to do so consensually. It is hard to envisage circumstances in which the court would in effect, intentionally, deprive the current legislative attempt of practical effect'.

14.76   The defendant appealed. The Court of Appeal upheld the first instance decision. The court acknowledged that clear guidance could only be given once it was seised of real cases, in which the evidence had been admitted and the case argued.

14.77   The appellant's argument was that the court should only depart from RPI linkage in *exceptional* circumstances. The respondent argued for departure *whenever it appears just to do so*.

The court was referred to Hansard and other material relevant to the formulation of the Courts Bill, as aids to interpretation of the provisions of the Courts Act 2003 under consideration. The court found reliance on such material illegitimate or unhelpful in relation to the defendant's argument.

14.78 The court restated Lord Steyn's 100 per cent principle from *Wells v Wells*[1]: a victim of a tort was entitled to be compensated as nearly as possible in full for all pecuniary losses. Periodical payments linked to RPI might, therefore, breach that principle, in that full compensation would not be provided.

1 [1999] 1 AC 345.

14.79 At first instance, the judge separated the issue of inflation-proofing of lump sum awards through the discount rate, from that relating to periodical payments. Lord Justice Brooke underscored that separation:

'It is unnecessary in the context of this statutory scheme to make the kind of guesses that were needed in setting a discount rate. The fact that these two quite different mechanisms sit side by side in the same Act of Parliament does not in my judgment mean that the problems that infected the operation of the one should be allowed to infect the operation of the other'.

Arguments over affordability were, suggested the court, irrelevant. There is no doubt that the cost of settlements where periodical payments linked to an earnings related index will, over time, cost defendants more than RPI. The courts were not concerned with *affordability*.

A v B

14.80 The issue of a lump sum versus RPI-linked periodical payments in respect of future care came before Mr Justice Lloyd Jones in *A v B Hospitals NHS Trust* in October 2006[1]. The claimant was a child aged six with a life expectancy to his early 40's. The requirement was for a comprehensive care regime. The claimant's preference was for a lump sum award because of concerns as to the long-term effect of periodical payments linked to RPI. After considering the claimant's evidence in support of that preference, the judge summarised the issue with great clarity:

'... I consider that it is most unlikely that periodical payments linked to RPI will meet the future care costs in this case. On the contrary, I consider that there is a very strong probability that divergence between RPI and the actual cost of the provision of care will result in a massive shortfall of provision'.

The resultant award was a lump sum in respect of future care of £3,995,818.

1 [2006] EWHC 2833 (Admin).

Thompstone v Glossop Acute Services NHS Trust

14.81 The substantive arguments relating to indexation of periodical payments were heard in at first instance, in the case of *Thompstone v Glossop Acute Services NHS Trust*[1]. The claimant sought an order whereby RPI was substituted by a more appropriate index or measure, because RPI would not adequately protect the increasing cost of his care needs against inflation. In other words, the annual increase in the cost of paying wages would not be met by linkage to RPI, an index borne of consideration of the *notional basket of goods*, as consumed by the average family.

1 [2006] EWHC 2904 (QB).

14.82   In *Thompstone*, the claimant's experts' evidence provided the court with a reasoned and detailed consideration of three indices or measures and invited the court to substitute RPI with the most appropriate. Each is an official measure of earnings published by the Office for National Statistics (ONS):

(1)   the *Average Earnings Index* (AEI) is a long-established indicator of earnings growth based upon data from a survey of 8,400 employers covering 9 million employees. The AEI is based on information obtained from ONS' Monthly Wages and Salary Survey. Because it is based on aggregate data, it does not accurately reflect increases in pay for those, such as carers, who are at the lower end of the pay spectrum. Note however, that AEI has since been replaced by Average Weekly Earnings (AWE);

(2)   *Annual Survey of Hours and Earnings (ASHE) Median* is a measure of changes in the levels of average earnings, based on an annual 1 per cent survey of all PAYE employees (1 per cent = approx 240,000). It is a broad measure encompassing the make-up of earnings and hours worked for employees in all industries and occupations. As such, it is based on *aggregate* data which does not reflect increases in pay for carers;

(3)   *ASHE 6115* is a *disaggregated* measure, specifically recording changes in actual earnings of care assistants and home carers. Nine centile estimates across the earnings distribution are published at the occupational levels, providing hourly rates for different care packages.

14.83   The judge, pursuant to the DA 1996, s 2(9), substituted RPI with ASHE 6115, on the basis that it was fair and reasonable to do so. More particularly, the judge found that the 75th percentile of ASHE 6115 was closest to matching likely increases in the cost of the claimant's care.

The relevant hourly rate for Lee Thompstone's care regime, based in the north west of England, was closest to the rate fixed at that percentile. A higher percentile would likely be relevant for a claimant living in London or the Home Counties, or generally where greater hourly rates would apply. In the case of a very disabled claimant, requiring more specialist (and expensive) nursing care, a different measure of ASHE might be relevant, for example, a severely brain damaged child, requiring specialist paediatric nursing care.

Mrs Justice Swift made it clear that her decision applied to the facts of that case and was not to be taken as wider authority.

14.84   The defendants' arguments both in *Flora* and *Thompstone* certainly carry some weight. However, the Court of Appeal held that *affordability* is not something that courts can consider in the context of whether or not a periodical payments order should be made. Under a concept termed *distributive justice*, the defendant sought to persuade the court that the increase in cost that would result from earnings related periodical payments, would unfairly impact upon NHS patients generally. Mrs Justice Swift in *Thompstone* took the view that distributive justice was *affordability*, just by another name.

14.85 Similar decisions as to appropriate indexation of periodical payments were reached at first instance in the cases of *Corbett v South Yorkshire Strategic Health Authority*[1], *Sarwar v Ali and MIB*[2] and *RH v United Bristol Healthcare NHS Trust*[3]. *Corbett* and *RH* were conjoined with *Thompstone* at the Court of Appeal in November 2007.

1 [2006] EWCA Civ 1797.
2 [2007] EWHC 1255 (QB).
3 [2007] EWHC 1441 (QB).

Court of Appeal decision in Thompstone

14.86 The Court of Appeal handed down its judgment on 17 January 2008 in the four appeals of *Thompstone, De Haas, Corbett* and *RH*[1]. The appeals related to the index or measure that should be applied to calculate the annual increase in the respondent claimants' periodical payments. The court rejected the appellants' arguments and gave a resounding and unanimous affirmation of the respondent claimants' previous triumphs.

1 [2008] EWCA Civ 5.

14.87 The respondent claimants in the four appeals suffer from severe cerebral palsy as a result of negligence at or around the time of their birth. All four claimants have very high lifelong care requirements. The issue in question was whether periodical payments should be varied by reference to the RPI in accordance with the DA 1996, s 2(8) (as amended), or whether that sub-section should be modified, pursuant to s 2(9) of the Act, which allows the court to *disapply* or *modify* the effect of s 2(8).

14.88 On appeal, the appellants argued the following:

(a) using an earnings related measure would lead to differences in compensation between the lump sum system and periodical payments;

(b) ASHE 6115 was not an appropriate measure and lacked proximity to the claimant's carers' earnings;

(c) that the only form of modification permitted by the DA 1996, s 2(9) is modification of the RPI itself; and

(d) the principle of 'distributive justice' should be applied, as account should be taken of the significant costs of an earnings related measure to the NHS.

14.89 The Court of Appeal dismissed all four appeals on all issues and upheld the trial judges' decisions. The Court of Appeal made it clear that ASHE 6115 is an appropriate measure:

'We hope that as a result of these proceedings the National Health Service, and other defendants in proceedings that involve catastrophic injury, will now accept that the appropriateness of indexation on the basis of ASHE 6115 has been established after an exhaustive review of all the possible objections to its use, both in itself and as applied to the recovery of costs of care and case management. It will not be appropriate to reopen that issue in any further proceedings unless the defendant can produce evidence and arguments significantly different from, and more persuasive than, that which has been deployed in the present cases. Judges should not hesitate to strike out any defences that do not meet that requirement'.

14.90   The Court of Appeal grasped the opportunity to consider the correct approach to the exercise of this power to impose periodical payments against the wishes of the parties. The two facets of s 2(1), namely allocation of future losses between lump sum and periodical payments and how to index any periodical payment, are inextricably linked and should be considered together. The Court of Appeal provided guidance on how CPR 41.7 should be complied with, confirming a wide interpretation of a claimant's needs, not restricted to those claimed. Claimants' needs do not have to be 'foreseeable necessities'.

14.91   The court recognised that in a substantial case the claimant is likely to instruct and call an Independent Financial Adviser (IFA). If the claimant is advised by an 'experienced and responsible expert it is likely that great weight will be given to what that expert advises'.

It will also be a rare case where the defendant would need to call an expert to demonstrate that the form of order preferred by the claimant will not best meet their needs.

14.92   Both parties' preferences should be given equal weight by a judge but any decision should be based upon an objective assessment of what the claimant needs and not what they or the defendant wants.

14.93   Following this ruling it is clear that a well thought out financial package provided by a suitably qualified expert is likely to be approved. The amount of future losses to be allocated to lump sum or periodical payments (allocation) and which index or measure is appropriate for calculation of the uplift in the periodical payments (indexation) need to be considered in unison.

Other cases

14.94   There is no doubt that the *Thompstone* decision is by far the most important in relation to periodical payments, and has resulted in settlements inclusive of periodical payments becoming the norm in catastrophic cases. The *Thompstone* litigation in fact consisted of several cases. The terms of the respective complex Final Orders in those cases varied, and it was not until the *Thompstone* cohort was back before the court[1], that Sir Christopher Holland approved a standard form of periodical payment order.

1 [2008] EWHC 2948 (QB).

14.95   The model order has not been universally followed. Although clinical negligence cases against NHS Trusts utilise the standard, some insurers have developed slightly different models to accommodate their needs. For example, some insurers prefer the inclusion of a clause which enables reasonable access to the claimant so that medical evidence can be updated to assist with the reserving process.

14.96   Such an approach is covered here as it may apply in cases involving the Medical Defence Union, where the insurance scheme applies. In *Wallace v Follett*[1], the following clause was approved:

'The defence insurer shall be entitled to require the claimant to undergo medical examination at its request upon reasonable notice being given to the claimant at any time during the claimant's life time, such medical examinations to be limited to obtaining a medical opinion as to the claimant's general health in order to obtain a quotation for the purchase cost of an annuity to fund the periodical payments and/ or (not more frequently than once every seven years) for the express purposes of reviewing its reserve'.

1 [2013] EWCA Civ 146.

14.97   The cost of any such examination, to include any reasonable costs and any loss of earnings incurred by the claimant in attending the examination, shall be paid by the defence insurer. The claimant shall have permission to apply to the court in the event of reasonable concern as to the nature or extent of any such examination.

14.98   The Holland standard order provides for re-classification of the ASHE data. In 2010, the ONS split ASHE 6115 into ASHE 6145 and ASHE 6146, to distinguish care workers and home carers from senior care workers. ASHE 6115, the amalgam of the two, continues to be published in a separate table. The new classification from SOC 2000 to SOC 2010 caused difficulty in terms of its statistical reliability. In November 2012, the ONS published the ASHE data with a change in methodology, and in doing so did not publish a key piece of data, hence a solution was required. Mrs Justice Swift approved the required changes in one of the original cases in the *Thompstone* litigation, *RH v United Hospitals Bristol NHS Foundation Trust*[1]. The resulting standard form of periodical payment order is found at Appendix 1, along with an example calculation for annual indexation.

1 [2013] QB 229.

14.99   However, despite the towering importance of *Thompstone*, decided cases, some outside the clinical negligence sphere, have clarified separate discrete issues in relation to the development of the periodical payments regime. *Sarwar v Ali*[1] was important on several counts. First, Mr Justice Lloyd Jones showed that the court was willing to use its power to impose periodical payments against the wishes of a claimant with capacity. The case is also illustrative of how periodical payments can be used for heads of loss other than care and case management. Mr Ali's claim was compromised at 75 per cent liability. His retirement date, but for his injury, was broadly aligned with his post-accident life expectancy. Two periodical payments were ordered, one for care and case management costs, and the second for loss of earnings, the expert evidence being that by taking that approach, Mr Ali's very expensive care regime (due to his tetraplegia), would be met in full by earnings-related periodical payments, thus eliminating the 25 per cent liability shortfall. Further, the case shows that periodical payments are not the preserve of 100 per cent liability settlements. The interesting approach of combining two periodical payments to meet care needs, should not detract from proper consideration of periodical payments in a general sense, simply because of the removal of investment and mortality risks. The received wisdom of taking a traditional lump sum in circumstances of a liability reduction on the basis that an invested lump sum *might* make up the shortfall, is at best flawed. Personal injury awards are likely to be invested following a cautious approach to investment risk. Such an approach will limit returns, thus making little meaningful headway into any deficit.

1 [2007] EWHC 1255 (Admin).

14.100 In *Morton v Portal*[1], decided by Walker J, the effect of the DA 1996, s 2 was considered together with CPR 41.7 and Practice Direction 41B, in the context of a claimant of full age and capacity. The relevant legislative history and the comments of Lord Steyn in *Wells v Wells* were also taken into account. According to *Morton*, the claimant's preference as regards the format of the award is merely one of the factors in the Practice Direction, and does not give the claimant a trump card. Walker J said:

'… it seems to me that s 2(1) of the 1996 Act makes it perfectly clear that before making an order which awards damages for future pecuniary loss in respect of personal injury, the court is under an obligation to consider whether to make an order the damages are wholly or partly to take the form of periodical payments.

There is nothing to suggest that the agreement of the parties – either that the damages should be lump sum only, or that they should wholly or partly take the form of periodical payments – would remove that obligation. It follows that if the parties were to reach a contractual agreement in this regard the court would not be required to give effect to that contract'.

Walker J made clear that his views were provisional, and because of the circumstances of the case, he did not need to make any findings on the particular points that arose. That is perhaps unfortunate, as it would be very interesting to see how far he would intend the court's power to apply.

1 [2010] EWHC 1804 (QB).

14.101 *Farrugia v Burtenshaw*[1] is an interesting case in many respects, not least for consideration of variable periodical payments (to reflect provisional damages award), and whether in the circumstances, periodical payments could be considered to be secure. In addition, Mr Justice Jay ordered that it was entirely appropriate to award periodical payments for the costs of deputyship. He approved the annual uprating of such costs to be calculated and assessed by reference to the guideline hourly rates for solicitors.

1 [2014] EWHC 1036 (QB).

14.102 In summary, periodical payments have found judicial support for heads of future loss, other than care, but cases are not often reported. Since the *Thompstone* litigation, loss of earnings, rent payments (so as to avoid the problems resulting from the *Roberts v Johnstone* calculation), and the cost of deputyship, have been met by way of a periodical payments order. Also case law illustrates that foreign claimants, injured in this jurisdiction have had the benefit of periodical payments when living abroad, paid in the appropriate foreign currency, and uprated in line with earnings inflation in their own country. Wider usage is evident and entirely possible when the parties are willing to co-operate.

The Discount Rate Review

14.103 Lord Justice Brooke, when giving the lead judgment in the Court of Appeal in *Flora v Wakom*[1], and considering the traditional lump sum and periodical payments in the context of the DA, said:

'The fact that these two quite different mechanisms sit side by side in the same Act of Parliament does not in my judgment mean that the problems that infected the operation of the one should be allowed to infect the operation of the other'.

1 [2006] EWCA Civ 1103.

14.104   That was in 2006, very much at the beginning of the periodical payment regime and pre *Thompstone*. It is clear that he meant that the new regime should not be held back by being tied to RPI, as was (and is) the lump sum calculation. Since then, pressure has grown on the Lord Chancellor to review the discount rate under his powers pursuant to the DA 1996. Part of that pressure has been arguably because of the periodical payment regime highlighting the problems with the lump sum settlement. In other words, the reverse of the infection meant by Brooke LJ.

In October 2012, a consultation process was initiated by Kenneth Clarke, the Lord Chancellor. A further consultation process followed in early 2013.

14.105   At this stage, a reminder of the present position might be of use by way of reference. Personal injury case law underpins the use of low-risk investments when calculating the level of personal injury lump sum damages. The multiplier used in the calculation of personal injury damages is based upon the concept that a personal injury investor is not an ordinary investor and therefore should not be required to invest in assets which can demonstrate higher levels of investment risk.

14.106   As such, the initial calculation of the damages is based upon a discount rate which is currently set at 2.5 per cent per annum. In simple terms, the discount rate is based upon the claimant investing their lump sum damages into Index Linked Government Stock (ILGS) and achieving a 2.5 per cent real return (which is 2.5 per cent per annum above the RPI). Index Linked Government Stocks are considered to be one of the safest forms of investment. If, for example, inflation is, say, 2.5 per cent per annum, a nominal return of about 8 per cent per annum would be needed, to account for price inflation, tax and investment costs. Earnings related inflation would simply add to the gross return required, and such high annual returns would be extremely difficult to achieve on a smooth year-on-year basis, and in any event, significant investment risk would be unavoidable to target such returns.

14.107   The 2.5 per cent discount rate was set by the Lord Chancellor in 2001. This followed the House of Lords' judgment in *Wells v Wells*[1], as summarised by Lord Berwick:

'The plaintiffs are not in the same happy position. They are not "ordinary investors" in the sense that they can wait for long-term recovery, remembering that it was not until 1989 that equity prices regained their old pre-1972 level in real terms. For they need an income and a portion of their capital every year to meet their current cost of care. A plaintiff who invested the whole of his award in equities in 1972 would have found that their real value had fallen by 41 per cent in 1973 and a further 62 per cent in 1974. The real value of income on his equities had also fallen'.

1 [1999] 1 AC 345.

14.108   Clearly, given current interest rate conditions and the returns achievable on ILGS, this level of investment return is impossible to achieve in risk-free assets such as cash deposits and ILGS. This has more or less been the case since the discount rate was set, resulting in mounting pressure for the present review process.

As outlined above, there is a significant difference between price inflation and that relating to earnings.

14.109   Historical data supports the assumption that wages (whether for carers or other associated professionals) rise over the longer term by an amount in excess of inflation as measured by RPI.

The calculation of the lump sum, assuming a 2.5 per cent discount rate, does not take into account the fact that some future income requirements are likely to be subjected to a high degree of wage-related inflationary pressure rather than general prices pressure as measured by RPI.

14.110   Claimants with the benefit of periodical payments for such future wage-related losses are catered for in that they are able to have future loss periodical payments linked in payment to earnings-related measures such as ASHE 6115 (care assistants and home carers) and in some cases, periodical payments for other heads of future loss, such as earnings. This ensures that future income streams rise in line with the inflationary measure which is most appropriate. Not only does this alleviate the major risks associated with the conventional lump sum approach (investment and mortality), but it also deals with the issue of wage inflation for future recurring losses such as care, case management and loss of earnings.

14.111   Earnings, as measured in the UK, have, on average, risen by about 1.50 per cent faster than prices since the Average Earnings Index was introduced. However, it is accepted that the average difference between these two rates does conceal wide variations in individual years.

14.112   As stated above, periodical payments linked to an appropriate inflation-proofing measure have been helpful in redressing the imbalance caused by an RPI-linked discount rate being utilised to calculate earnings-related losses. That approach can only serve to increase the risks of investment to meet lifelong needs. In effect, a two-tier regime has emerged: those with periodical payments; and those compensated by the traditional lump sum approach, with all of the risks that the latter method involves. Comparison with the periodical payment regime illustrates how lump sum awards now fail to meet the principle of full compensation, sometimes known as the 100 per cent principle as described in *Wells v Wells*.

14.113   A helpful analysis was undertaken as recently as March 2012 by the Privy Council in the case of *Helmot v Simon*[1]. The case was based in Guernsey, where the DA 1996 and hence the periodical payment regime is inapplicable, as is the Lord Chancellor's decision on the discount rate. The Privy Council was invited to decide an appropriate discount rate to apply to a lump sum settlement, taking into account ILGS yields and the differential between normal price inflation and that related to earnings. Expert evidence in the case came from three witnesses, including a specialist forensic accountant, an economist and an actuary, formerly the Government Actuary, who had advised the Lord Chancellor in 2001 when the discount rate was fixed. At Court of Appeal level, the array of witnesses had been described as impressive as they could have been.

1 [2012] UKPC 5.

14.114 At para 52, Lord Hope in addressing the issue of whether different discount rates should apply to different heads of loss (which in effect answers the question, should any allowance be made for potential differences between RPI inflation and health care costs), referred to the 100 per cent principle (which underpins his judgment):

'... the victim of a tort is entitled to be fully compensated. If the evidence shows that inflation will affect different heads of loss in different ways and that the differential is capable of being evaluated, the court should not close its mind to different rates'.

To do that would risk giving the victim less than he is entitled to. The possibility of modifying the effect of tying future payments to the retail prices index was recognised by the DA 1996, s 2(9), as amended by the Courts Act 2003. It was endorsed by the Court of Appeal in *Flora v Wakom (Heathrow) Ltd*[1], on the ground that there was no indication in that section that Parliament had intended to depart from the principle that a victim of a tort was entitled to be compensated as nearly as possible for all pecuniary losses.

1 [2006] EWCA Civ 1103.

14.115 At para 53, his Lordship states that *over-elaboration in the carrying out of this exercise is to be avoided*, however:

'The decision of the House of Lords in *Wells v Wells* should not be seen as an indication that a single discount rate must always be adopted. It would be wrong to do that if the evidence shows that, if that were to be done, a given head of loss would not be fully compensated.

The evidence in the *Helmot* case, bearing in mind the credentials of the experts, was regarded by the Court as robust and went largely unchallenged. A summary of the evidence of Messrs Hogg (forensic accountant), Bootle (economist) and Daykin (actuary) is at paragraph 32 of Lord Hope's judgment, and is worth replicating in full:

"Mr Daykin referred in section 2 of his report of 6th May 2009 to the actuarial approach to the evaluation of loss of income and future costs, to which additional rigour had been introduced by the Ogden Tables. In para 2.3 he said that an actuary would approach the decision as to the appropriate discount rate by determining a risk-free rate of return, having regard to the yields available in the market on suitable very low-risk financial instruments which could produce cash flows similar to those which have to be valued and that the most appropriate securities would be UK ILGS. In para 2.8, he said that, taking the one-year average of ILGS with more than 15 years to maturity and allowing for an 11.4 per cent deduction for tax as proposed by Mr Hogg, the resulting discount rate was 0.86 per cent and that, before adjustment for the differential between Guernsey inflation and UK inflation, it should certainly not be more than 1 per cent per annum.

In para 2.9 he said that he agreed with Mr Hogg and Mr Bootle that a reasonable allowance to make for the future differential between Guernsey inflation and UK inflation was 0.5 per cent, so the adjusted discount rate for determining the multipliers in Guernsey should be no more than 0.5 per cent (ie 1.0 per cent less

0.5 per cent). In para 2.11 he said that in his reports to the Guernsey Social Security Department over a number of years he considered that an appropriate assumption for real earnings growth in Guernsey was 2 per cent per annum and that he still believed this to be an appropriate assumption. In para 2.12 he said that heads of damages which were considered to be likely to go up in line with Guernsey price inflation should be valued using a multiplier based on a discount rate of no more than 0.5 per cent per annum. Heads of damages relating to cash flows likely to go up in line with earnings in Guernsey, such as loss of earnings or costs of care, should be valued using a multiplier based on a discount rate of no more than -1.5 per cent"'.

14.116 The expert evidence as above led the Court of Appeal to order a discount rate of -1.5 per cent for earnings related losses, avoiding over-elaboration and inclusive of health care costs inflation. That approach was approved by the Privy Council. Although some of the figures vary between Guernsey and the UK generally, the differentials are small and the underlying methodology in the approach would be identical, should the courts in the UK ever consider the issue.

14.117 As stated above, periodical payments alleviate the problem in many cases. However, in those cases where periodical payments are not available, or where substantial financial flexibility is needed, resulting in a lump sum award alongside periodical payments, future losses related to earnings but compensated by reference to an unadjusted RPI-linked discount rate, will result in under-compensation.

14.118 *Helmot* aside, the most recent round of the consultation process included questions that implied consideration of an approach that is outwith the *Wells* principle. Two questions taken from the consultation as below exemplify this:

— whether the present parameters of the Lord Chancellor's power to set the discount rate should be changed and if so, how? Such change may reflect investment in a mixed portfolio of assets rather than ILGS. This may lead to a greater rate than 2.5 per cent, or a lower rate, depending on how the portfolio is defined;

— whether the use of periodical payments instead of lump sum awards should be encouraged and if so, how?

14.119 Taken together, those questions may amount to the discount rate either remaining unchanged, or revised downwards, but not to the extent that might be otherwise expected, following the *Helmot* analysis. The mixed portfolio of assets is clearly an entirely different assumption to the whole award invested in ILGS. Once the views of the powerful defendant lobby are taken into account, against the backdrop of austerity, any significant reduction in the discount rate may be unlikely.

14.120 Two issues arise from the consultation process. Should the discount rate remain the same or similar, based on a new assumption that claimants invest in mixed portfolios, investment risk must feature as part of that assumption. Personal injury claimants then fall into the category of ordinary investors. It follows that investment costs should become recoverable as a head of future loss.

14.121 Second, it may be argued that greater use of periodical payments should dilute the risk of the accompanying lump sums. But not all cases can be settled in that way. Also, how can greater use of periodical payments be encouraged? One method might be to consider periodical payments in lower value cases, and/or to use them to compensate heads of loss other than the traditional approach of care and case management. The ASHE dataset as compiled by the Office for National Statistics contains a wealth of information regarding earnings-related inflation. The above review of case law outlines how heads of future loss such as lost earnings, therapies and deputy costs might be met by periodical payments, properly proofed against inflation.

INDEPENDENT FINANCIAL ADVICE

14.122 Practitioners need to understand the potential role of an Independent Financial Adviser (IFA) in a clinical negligence claim. IFAs are authorised and regulated by the Financial Conduct Authority (FCA). Each IFA, as well as the firm they work for, is registered with the FCA, and their status can be checked on the FCA register at www.fca.gov.uk. Details of supervisory, disciplinary, and civil regulatory action taken by the FCA against individual IFAs can also be found on this website. Unfortunately there is no function to allow a search for a particular specialisation of the firm or the IFA.

14.123 Very few law firms are authorised to provide independent financial advice; the regulations are onerous and the costs of running such an in-house operation can be burdensome. All IFAs must carry the requisite professional indemnity cover as stipulated by the regulators.

14.124 Too many claimants in the UK receive an award of damages and, knowing no better, go to a financial practitioner who is not independent. This results in the claimant being offered a restricted range of products or advice, as opposed to the provision of proper and expert financial planning. It is incumbent upon the legal profession to guide clients towards Independent Financial Advisers; the hard work of the litigation can easily be undone by inappropriate or misguided financial advice.

14.125 It should be appropriate to instruct a specialist IFA to provide advice in any of the following circumstances:

Claimants:
(1)   the case requires assessment of the viability of periodical payments or a lump sum;
(2)   the deputy acting on behalf of a protected beneficiary requires expert investment advice for funds held at court;
(3)   the claimant is mentally capable and requires expert investment advice;
(4)   the claimant is mentally capable and their state benefits may be affected by receipt of the award;
(5)   a minor trust needs to be considered, which could result in the need for a financial report.

Defendants:

(1)   the case requires assessment of the viability of periodical payments or a lump sum;
(2)   the defendant may require tactical advice on the merits of an offer to settle.

14.126   In a case that requires an assessment of the viability of periodical payments and/or a lump sum, the IFA may be required to do a number of things:

(1)   detailed consideration of the relevant medical information, schedules and quantum reports;
(2)   meeting(s) with the claimant/defendant and/or their representatives;
(3)   a detailed appraisal of the claimant's current and future financial needs;
(4)   formulating a financial package which is best suited to meet those needs;
(5)   preparation of report(s) for the court in accordance with the relevant Practice Directions;
(6)   assistance with drafting the periodical payment order and agreement for consideration by the court;
(7)   attendance at conference(s);
(8)   appearance at court to give evidence.

14.127   When required to provide investment advice, the IFA should do the following:

(1)   explain to the claimant the terms under which advice may be provided;
(2)   discuss with the claimant their aims and objectives;
(3)   ensure the claimant is taken through a risk profiling exercise;
(4)   discuss with the claimant the financial planning service and relevant fees;
(5)   provide a written report with supporting documents outlining the IFA's advice;
(6)   ensure that this advice reflects the claimant's needs and preferences;
(7)   implement the plans once given the instruction to proceed from the claimant;
(8)   monitor and review the arrangements as necessary.

Practicalities: when and how to instruct an IFA

14.128   There can be no hard and fast rule as to when to instruct an IFA in a clinical negligence claim. In a case likely to involve an assessment of the viability of periodical payments, it would be wise to have around three to six months in hand, to ensure there is adequate time available for the IFA to report. In any event, quantum evidence should be largely complete at the time of instructing the IFA.

14.129   At the very minimum, the IFA will need to know the basic details as follows:

(1)   liability;
(2)   the client's living arrangements;

(3)   the client's current care arrangements;
(4)   whether the Court of Protection is involved (if so, whether a deputy has been appointed);
(5)   confirm the client's state benefit position, including care provision by local authority, Clinical Commissioning Groups, or Independent Living Fund, etc;
(6)   give details of interim payments and how they have been utilised, how much remaining;
(7)   state details of any offers to settle.

14.130   The IFA will need to see the following documents:

(1)   medical reports (both sides);
(2)   claimant's schedule of loss and defendant's counter schedule;
(3)   care reports (both sides);
(4)   advices from counsel;
(5)   witness statements relating to quantum;
(6)   CRU certificate.

14.131
As part of the letter of instruction, it is advisable to state timescales and bear in mind it may be necessary for the financial adviser to meet with the client and/or their representatives before providing a report. If dates are available for trial, conference/consultation or round-table meeting, provide these dates to the financial adviser, asking for the report to be available in advance. Also check the financial adviser's availability to attend conference/meeting/trial if required.

14.132
Last but not least, make enquiries as to how the IFA intends to charge for their work, and ask for a breakdown on the estimate of cost, based on the work expected of them.

PERIODICAL PAYMENTS: SUMMARY

14.133
In summary, the advantages and disadvantages of lump sums and periodical payments for claimants and defendants are as follows.

Lump sums

14.134   Claimant advantages:
(1)   the capital is accessible to the claimant; flexible investments may be established, which may accommodate unforeseen future financial requirements;
(2)   the capital may increase in value ahead of expectations;
(3)   tax efficient portfolios can be established through the provision of good quality advice;
(4)   the claimant has no ongoing link with the defendant;
(5)   on death, any remaining funds (subject to inheritance tax) are transferred to the claimant's estate; the lump sum is available for beneficiaries;

(6)   protection of investments is offered through the FSCS; the first £2,000 is paid, with 90 per cent of the rest to a maximum compensation of £48,000.

Claimant disadvantages:

(1)   there is no guarantee of positive returns within the investment fund (investment risk);

(2)   there is a risk of dissipation of the damages: unwise expenditure often occurs with unsophisticated claimants;

(3)   there is a risk of frugality with the damages as claimants may be anxious to save for their later years;

(4)   the claimant may live longer than expected, resulting in little or no money to cope with their needs beyond their predicted life expectancy;

(5)   investments can fluctuate in value, causing anxiety with vulnerable investors, particularly those with high income needs;

(6)   the investor will be vulnerable to future changes in taxation of investments;

(7)   the investment fund requires ongoing management, therefore charges are levied by advisers to cover this cost (which is not recoverable as part of the claim).

Defendant advantages:

(1)   a lump sum is a known cost and it is straightforward for reserving purposes;

(2)   the defendant is in a position to 'close the book' and move on without the necessity for carrying long-term liabilities.

Defendant disadvantages:

(1)   if the claimant dies early, the defendant has paid the claimant for losses which are not in fact incurred;

(2)   lump sum payments impact negatively on defendants' short-term cashflow.

Periodical payments

14.135   Claimant advantages:

(1)   income guaranteed by statute to be tax-free (Income Tax (Trading and Other Income) Act 2005, ss 731 and 733). The value of this freedom from tax depends on what the claimant's tax position would be with a lump sum, some of which is necessarily speculative as tax regimes can change;

(2)   linkage to ASHE 6115 to proof payments against earnings-related inflation, building in 100 per cent compensation;

(3)   guaranteed payments for agreed period (may be payable for life or fixed term, eg until retirement), providing peace of mind to claimant;

(4)   damages will never run out during period of future loss: removes anxiety over investment returns for claimant;

(5)   no investment management charges once periodical payments are implemented;

(6) 100 per cent protection of income for claimant: court will sanction use of periodical payments only in cases where satisfied as to security of payment and continuity of income (DA 1996, s 2(4) as amended).

Claimant disadvantages:

(1) once set up periodical payments are irrevocable; there is a distinct lack of flexibility for the claimant (although see assignment or charge of right earlier in the chapter);
(2) periodical payment income, if linked to anything other than ASHE 6115, is unlikely to keep pace with care costs (*A v B, Thompstone*, etc);
(3) claimant loses opportunity to take advantage of investment returns (opportunity cost);
(4) limited returns (if any) available on death of claimant;
(5) claimant retains an ongoing relationship with tortfeasor[1].

Defendant advantages:

(1) the defendant does not pay out the full damages at outset, thereby easing short-term cash-flow;
(2) if a claimant dies early, the defendant does not need to pay out future periodical payments.

Defendant disadvantages:

(1) the defendant cannot 'close the book', and must maintain an ongoing relationship with the claimant;
(2) if the claimant lives longer than expected, it is costly for the defendant;
(3) periodical payments can be difficult to reserve;
(4) the defendant may be required to link periodical payments to an index other than RPI, which may prove to be costly in the long term.

1 Cf Denzil Lush 'Damages for Personal Injury: Why some claimants prefer a conventional lump sum to periodical payments' (2005) London Law Review, December.

14.136 The role of the specialist IFA has always been in part to advise on the format of the award. In other words, what is the appropriate balance between capital in the form of the lump sum award, and income from periodical payments. The usual model of periodical payments for care and case management can be departed from (and bettered) in appropriate cases. If, for example, other heads of loss should be paid periodically, the IFA can then advise on the most suitable index or measure available.

14.137 Further, it is wise to bear in mind that in cases of significant value, general damages plus past losses will usually be insufficient to counter the problems inherent in *Roberts v Johnstone*[1], which allows only for interest on the additional capital tied-up in accommodation as a result of the claim. Real-life accommodation requirements, especially for claimants living in expensive areas, usually results in depleting other losses in order to make up the full costs of accommodation from capital.

1 [1989] QB 878.

14.138 So, is there a secret to mixing and matching lump sums with periodical payments in negotiation? Legal practitioners will be aware of the litigation risks in proceeding to trial. This will undoubtedly result in concessions being made in certain areas. In cases where life expectancy is agreed or virtually agreed, it is relatively simple to convert a lump sum accompanied by periodical payments into an equivalent lump sum value: simply multiply the periodical payments by the relevant multipliers, add to the accompanying lump sum and the equivalent lump sum value is produced.

14.139 The most suitable outcome is very much dependent on the circumstances of the case. For instance, a disabled lady in late middle age with full mental capacity and a risk averse nature to investment might be well suited to having the majority of her future losses paid by way of periodical payments. On the other hand, a claimant with a more robust attitude to risk and relatively little requirement for care might be better suited to the lump sum approach. Every claimant and their respective family is different. Two seemingly identical cases on paper could have entirely different 'best case scenario' financial solutions.

14.140 The judiciary has commented on the *allocation* issue, per Mackay J in the *RH* case (part of the *Thompstone* cohort):

'In my judgment, though this is not strictly speaking an approval exercise, in that the allocation will be the result of the order of the court, I see the court's role as ensuring that the allocation has proceeded on the basis of suitably qualified advice, which appears to have taken all relevant matters into account, from a source which has had the advantage of a free discussion with the family as to their hopes and fears for the future. That is what has happened here, in my judgment. Nor is there any suggestion to the contrary'.

14.141 Finally, the Court of Appeal concluded the following in *Thompstone*;

'There is now no dispute that, in deciding whether to make an order under section 2(1) the judge's overall aim must be to make whatever order best meets the claimant's needs. Part 41.7 might have been more clearly expressed but that is what it amounts to.

The parties also agree that the claimant's "needs" in Part 41.7 are not limited to the needs that he demonstrated for the purpose of proving the various heads of damage; they include those things that he needs in order to enable him (or those looking after him) to organise his life in a practical way'.

For example, if the claimant is not yet living in suitable accommodation, one of his immediate needs will be to buy somewhere to live. The damages assessed under the head of accommodation will not cover the whole of the costs of purchase and adaptation. So he will need enough capital to enable him to buy, adapt and equip a home. He may have other immediate needs, such as the purchase of a vehicle, for which damages have been agreed or awarded. He will certainly need a regular income stream from which to pay his continuing expenses, particularly for care. It may well be in his best interest that, rather than relying on the income from the investment of a lump sum, that income stream should be provided by a PPO, so that, when appropriately indexed, it will keep pace with the rise in the cost of provision. Many claimants are advised that, due to the uncertainties inherent in a long life in a disabled condition, they should seek a substantial capital sum for contingencies in addition to that required for their immediate and foreseeable needs; this will provide a degree of flexibility in the future. The claimant may also wish to purchase some facility for which damages have not been awarded at all or for which partial damages have been agreed on a compromise basis. Such a facility may not be a 'need' in the sense of being an absolute necessity (if it were, it would have been covered by the damages) but it may nonetheless be taken into account by the judge when assessing what order best meets the claimant's needs. In short, the claimant's needs are not limited to the provision of those things which are foreseeable necessities but must be considered in a wider and more general sense. The decision as to what form the order should take will be a balancing exercise of the various factors likely to affect the claimant's future life.

SUMMARY

14.142 Financial planning is a complex subject in clinical negligence cases, made even more difficult by the fact that practitioners are on constantly shifting sands. The development of the periodical payments legislation has ensured, more than ever, that financial advisers and lawyers need to understand a great deal about the cross-over of expertise required in their respective fields.

14.143 The experts can never be certain as to the correct financial solution at the time of settlement. This poses numerous difficulties for the advisers, legal and financial. A pragmatic approach is usually required as to the appropriate split between capital and periodical payments.

14.144 Sound financial planning requires a good understanding of a claimant's overall position. State benefits can be vital to boost income. If benefits are means-tested, a personal injury trust is essential if the claimant is not a protected beneficiary. Complex financial arrangements may occur in the event of direct payments from the local authority. A comprehensive overview will result in the best financial advice.

14.145 A well-balanced investment portfolio should always have a weighting of secure investments, whether cash, gilts or corporate bonds. Periodical payments linked to an earnings-related measure, such as ASHE 6115 can provide a much greater level of security with the added attraction of tax-free status. The trade-off is lost flexibility, as the periodical payments element of the award is irreversible. However, if the remainder of the award is in the form of capital, and the split between capital and income correct, flexibility should be more than sufficient.

14.146 Despite the *Thompstone* judgment in the Court of Appeal, many cases will still settle on a lump sum basis during negotiations. Awkward choices will need to be made by some claimants, particularly in cases where the litigation risk of going to trial is too high, and the defendant is recalcitrant over periodical payments. The need for expert financial advice has never been greater.

CASE STUDIES

Claimant periodical payment case study

14.147   Mrs P sustained profound neurological damage four years ago during an operation, due to the defendant NHS Trust's admitted negligence. She is now 45 years of age and has permanent paralysis affecting her left side, and she suffers a cognitive deficit such that she is unable to manage her own financial affairs. She will rely on care provided by others for the rest of her life. Mrs P's life expectancy is estimated by Dr R to age 75. Dr T, a specialist in the same field of medicine, takes a more pessimistic view, assessing life expectancy to age 70.

14.148   The parties considered the matter at a round-table settlement meeting, liability having already been resolved at 100 per cent. The largest element of Mrs P's award related to care and case management, the annual costs of which were agreed at £135,000 per annum. The remainder of Mrs P's annual losses were around £25,000 per annum for life. This excluded her loss of earnings and the losses related to *Roberts v Johnstone*[1] which it was agreed should be capitalised. The lump sum equivalent of the future annual losses (totalling £160,000 per annum) was £2,984,000 to age 70 and £3,390,400 to age 75.

1 [1989] QB 878.

14.149   The claimant's legal team secured an agreement such that care and case management was to be paid periodically, with the remainder of the future losses paid as a lump sum.

As life expectancy was uncertain, it made sense to have those future losses paid periodically. The reason for capitalising the remainder of the future losses was twofold; first, there was a risk of deterioration of her condition, and the claimant's adviser was of the opinion that it would be sensible to leave some flexibility in the finances to accommodate such changing circumstances; second, it was felt that the claimant should be given the opportunity potentially to benefit from the returns that could be available from the investment markets.

14.150   Periodical payments for the future costs of the deputy were also considered and put to the defendant as part of the negotiation process. The defendant was unwilling to agree to such a periodical payments order. It was considered that with the backing of appropriate expert evidence, the court would make an order on that basis, irrespective of the defendant's objection. However, given the favourable nature of the proposed settlement when viewed globally, weighed against the possible benefits of further periodical payments, and the risks of exposing the claim to judicial scrutiny, the claim was compromised as above.

Personal injury trust case study

14.151   The claimant, Mr C, aged 45, was injured in a road traffic accident five years ago. Although his right leg was saved from amputation, it was very badly damaged, and he is unable to return to his former job as a labourer in a house building firm. He also suffered psychologically as a result of the accident and it is unlikely he will return to any form of paid employment. His modest savings have been depleted and he is receiving state benefits. His legal team have secured a settlement from the defendant's insurer of £321,454 net of payment to the Compensation Recovery Unit.

14.152 Mr C is concerned about such a large sum of money and although he is a man used to living in a modest way, he informs his solicitor that he intends to spend all of the damages on buying a house. That way, he believes he will secure his future and not have to worry about the money. His solicitor is concerned for a number of reasons:

(1) her client will need to move to a different area away from his family and friends;
(2) he will tie up his award of damages in one asset, which provides no future financial flexibility;
(3) his income is unlikely to meet the running costs of such a property.

14.153 His solicitor refers the claimant to an independent financial adviser with experience of these cases. On discussing the situation with Mr C, the IFA identifies the following:

(1) Mr C is in receipt of means-tested state benefits;
(2) he would like to have additional income to boost his standard of living;
(3) he does not want to take large amounts of risk with his money;
(4) the claimant has the 'right to buy' his local authority property at a discount to its market value.

14.154 On receiving appropriate advice, the claimant proceeds as follows:

(1) a personal injury trust is established with the claimant's brother and sister-in-law as his trustees. Mr C will continue to receive means-tested state benefits, and he feels confident that with guidance from an IFA and his family members as trustees he will not be so concerned about managing a large sum of money;
(2) he uses £80,000 of the settlement to purchase his local authority property; a further £10,000 is used to improve the kitchen and bathroom;
(3) he gives £3,000 to his ex-wife and £1,000 to each of his son and daughter in respect of the past care they provided to him;
(4) £200,000 of the settlement is invested in a low-medium risk investment portfolio, spread between a variety of assets to reduce risk. It is designed to produce a steady income of £500 per month, plus provide the opportunity for long-term capital growth. The monthly income will top-up Mr C's state benefit income;
(5) the remainder of the settlement is held by the trustees in cash, as an emergency fund, should Mr C need to access it.

CHECKLIST

14.155

– Periodical payments – the legislation.

- Advantages/disadvantages of lump sums and periodical payments.
- What is an Independent Financial Adviser and what is their role.
- Periodical payments – the practicalities.
- Investment options for lump sums.
- State provision of benefits, care and accommodation.
- Protecting state benefits through personal injury trusts.
- How and why trusts may be used for minors and mentally incapable individuals
- Case studies including complex interaction of state benefits with damages awards.

APPENDIX

Summary of judgment in RH: Honourable Mrs Justice Swift

14.156 1 The case of *RH* was one of the original 'test' cases on the issue of the indexation of periodical payments. The periodical payments order in *RH* was made by Mackay J in July 2007 and was subsequently modified slightly at a hearing before Sir Christopher Holland in December 2008. Since then, the 'model order' based on Sir Christopher's modified order in *RH* has been used in every case involving the National Health Service Litigation Authority (NHS LA) in which a periodical payments order for care and case management has been made. To date 643 such orders have been made.

2 Periodical payments for care and case management in cases involving the NHS LA are index-linked by reference to the Annual Survey of Hours and Earnings (ASHE) 6115 published by the Office for National Statistics (ONS). The model order contains formulae based on the ASHE 6115 data to be used when calculating the annual increase in the periodical payments to be made to a claimant.

3 In 2010, the ONS changed its methodology, as a result of which certain data which were required to calculate the increases in the periodical payments payable to claimants in December 2012 were not available to the NHS LA. Periodical payments were made on the basis of the data that were available and claimants/Deputies were informed that balancing payments would be made, if appropriate, once the problem caused by the missing data had been solved.

4 With the assistance of the three experts who had been instructed for the claimant and the defendant in *RH* and other 'test' cases and who had both been involved in the development of the model order, the defendant/NHS LA succeeded in identifying a solution to the problem of the missing data. That solution and the proposed amendments to the order in *RH* (which amendments are to be replicated in the model order) have been carefully considered by the experts, together with solicitors and leading counsel, and are agreed by the parties in *RH*.

5 I am entirely satisfied that the proposed solution is fair and reasonable and will achieve justice as between the parties. I am satisfied also that the

proposed amendments are both necessary and appropriate to meet the problem which has arisen in giving effect to the existing order.

6 It is the NHS LA's intention to use the amended model order in all future cases where periodical payments orders for care and case management are made. It is also necessary that the amended provisions should be applied to all cases involving the NHS LA in which there are existing periodical payments orders for care and case management so as to enable the periodical payments made in December 2012 to be recalculated and any balance owing to claimants to be paid, and also so as to ensure that there is a process in place to deal with any similar problems that might arise in the future.

7 I would strongly encourage all claimants and Deputies in cases with existing periodical payments for care and case management to accept the NHS LA's proposal that the amended provisions of the model order should be applied to their case. Whilst it is open to an individual claimant or Deputy to object to that course and to contend that the problem that has arisen should be solved in some other way, he/she should be aware of the implications of doing so. If an objection is raised, the claimant or Deputy will have to be prepared to demonstrate, to the satisfaction of a Court and on the basis of sound expert evidence, circumstances such as:

(a)   the existence of some technical or other flaw in the solution that has been adopted in the case of *RH* which has gone undetected and will affect the future operation of the model order; and/or

(b)   an alternative proposed solution to the problem of the missing data which has very significant advantages over the solution adopted in *RH* such that a further amendment to the model order would be just and proportionate; and/or

(c)   some specific feature of the claimant's case that makes the solution adopted in *RH* unworkable.

In the event that the objection is dismissed, the claimant will be at risk of paying the costs of what may have been a very expensive exercise.

8 The NHS LA proposes to write to the claimant or Deputy in every case in which the NHS LA is involved and where there is an existing periodical payments order for care and case management:

(a)   identifying the problem that has arisen and explaining the way in which it intends to solve it;

(b)   enclosing and explaining the revised calculation and the financial consequences for the claimant;

(c)   enclosing a copy of the amended model order, with track changes so that the amendments can be clearly seen; and

(d)   informing him/her that the NHS LA intends to apply the provisions of the amended model order to the claimant's case in the future unless, within 28 days of receipt of the letter, the claimant or Deputy gives notice in writing to the NHS LA's solicitors that he/she disagrees with the proposed solution and/or the amendments to the order, setting out his/her proposed alternative solution, together with any relevant calculation(s) and/or proposed technical adjustments.

9 The proposals set out above do not of course apply to cases in which periodical payments orders for care and case management have been made and the NHS LA is not involved. I am told that there are many such cases currently in existence. The compensators in those cases include government and public bodies, insurers, the Motor Insurers' Bureau and Lloyd's syndicates. I am told that the form of periodical payments orders used in non-NHS LA claims varies, some being based on the NHS LA's model order and others not.

10 I would urge compensators in all cases where a periodical payments order for care and case management has been made and the NHS LA is not involved to review the terms of their existing order(s) and, in the event that the terms of the orders require it and the same problem of calculation arises, to seek acceptance by claimants and Deputies to amendments similar to those which have been made to the NHS LA model order.

Model form of order

Part 1 of the Schedule to the Order

14.157 Each sum payable under Part(s) 2 and 3 of this schedule is a 'periodical payment' subject to the conditions set out in paragraphs 1–8 of this part

1 Unless specifically stated, all the periodical payments under Part(s) 2 and 3 of this schedule will continue during the lifetime of the Claimant

2 No minimum number of periodical payments under Part(s) 2 and 3 of this schedule shall be made

3 Payment of the periodical payments under Part(s) 2 and 3 of this schedule will cease on the death of the Claimant

4 The final periodical payment under Part(s) 2 and 3 of this schedule will be pro-rated for so much of the final year that the Claimant had survived and any balance owing to the NHS LA or its successor will be repayable to it out of the Claimant's estate, subject only to deduction by the Claimant's estate of such sums as the Claimant's estate may be liable for in respect of the termination of the employment of any persons employed to care for the Claimant

5 The NHS LA shall be entitled to require the Claimant to produce evidence in a form reasonably satisfactory to the NHS LA that the Claimant remains alive before making any periodical payment

6 The periodical payments under Part(s) 2 and 3 of this schedule are to be made by BACS to the Court of Protection (or its successor) for the benefit of the Claimant under reference [   ] (where applicable)

7 Under Part(s) 2 and 3 of this schedule the NHS LA shall provide to the Claimant and/or the Deputy in writing:

7.1 At the time of each periodical payment an explanation of how it has been calculated;

7.2 If reclassification or a change of methodology occurs within the meaning of Part 3 of this Schedule then when a periodical payment is made or in the event of a deferred periodical payment as soon as practicable following such a reclassification or a change of methodology, the relevant calculation(s) under paragraph 6 and the numerical value of 'AR' as defined in paragraph 7.1.4 of that part applicable to any current and/or future periodical payment to be made under that part.

8 The NHS LA shall pay the relevant annual sums set out in Part(s) 2 and 3 of this schedule on 15 December of each year, save that:

8.1 If the Office for National Statistics ['ONS'] does not publish by 17th November in the relevant year all the relevant data and as a result the NHS LA is unable to perform the relevant calculations under Part(s) 2 and 3 to recalculate the periodical payment(s) due to the Claimant before 15 December of the relevant year, the NHS LA shall on 15 December of the relevant year make the periodical payment(s): (a) in the same sum as that paid in the previous year; or (b) in the increased/decreased sum recalculated in accordance with the relevant data for the previous year where in the relevant year the annual sum was due to be increased or decreased or commenced under the relevant sub-paragraph of paragraph 1 of Part(s) 2 or 3.

8.2 Any balancing payment due to the claimant or the NHS LA shall be made within 28 days after the publication of all the relevant data by the ONS.

8.3 The NHS LA shall pay interest at the then applicable Judgment Act rate on any outstanding periodical payment or part of a periodical payment not paid on 15 December in any year from 16 December in that year until full payment is made, except that in the circumstances contemplated in paragraphs 8.1–2 interest due on any balancing payment shall only be payable by the NHS LA from 28 days after publication of all the relevant data until full payment is made.

9 For the period from [the date when the future loss period accrues assuming periodical payments relate only to future loss] to [14 December of the relevant year when the periodical payments will commence] to represent the periodical payment under Part(s) 2 and 3 of this schedule for that period the Defendant do pay the sum of [£] ( ) due as the balance of the periodical payment for the above period and that sum shall be paid 4.00 pm on the [ ].

Part 2: The RPI-Linked Periodical Payments

1 The following present value annual sums as recalculated in accordance with paragraph 3 shall be paid in advance:

1.1 The annual sum of [£] ( ) payable on the 15th of December in each year from 15th December [ ] until 15th December [ ] inclusive, with the first such payment to be made on 15th December [ ].

1.2 The annual sum of [£   ] (   ) payable on the 15th of December in each year from 15th December [   ] until 15th December [   ] inclusive.

1.3 The annual sum of [£   ] (   ) payable on 15th of December in each year from 15th December [   ]

The expiry of one period and the commencement of another period under the above sub-paragraphs constitutes a 'step change' under this Schedule

2 The index to be applied is the United Kingdom General Index of Retail Prices for all items ['RPI'] published by the ONS (January 1987 = 100) or any equivalent or comparable measure which in the parties' reasonable opinion replaces such index from time to time. In the event of a dispute between the parties as to the appropriate alternative measure and/or the formulae to be applied in the event of a rebasing of RPI the same shall be determined by the court

3 Each periodical payment referred to in paragraph 1 *[1.1 to 1.3]* above shall be recalculated annually in November in each year prior to payment on 15th December of the same year from November [   ] in accordance with the following formula:

$$PP = C \times (NF/A)$$

3.1 Where

3.1.1 '*PP*' = the amount payable by way of periodical payment in each year, the first *PP* being the payment made on 15th December [   ]

3.1.2 '*C*' = the relevant annual sum set out in paragraph 1 *[1.1 to 1.3]* above respectively

3.1.3 '*NF*' = the index applicable to September in the year in which the calculation is being carried out, the first NF being in respect of September [   ]

3.1.4 '*A*' = the index applicable to [the index applicable to three months prior to the date of settlement or judgment]

Part 3: The ASHE 6115-Linked Periodical Payments

1 The following present value annual sums as recalculated in accordance with paragraphs 3–10 shall be paid in advance

1.1 The annual sum of [£   ] (   ) payable on 15th December in each year from [   ] until 15th December [   ] inclusive, with the first such payment to be made on 15th December [   ].

1.2 The annual sum of [£   ] (   ) payable on 15th December in each year from [   ] until 15th December [   ] inclusive.

1.3 The annual sum of [£   ] (   ) payable on 15th December in each year from [   ].

The expiry of one period and the commencement of another period under the above sub-paragraphs constitutes a 'step change' under this Schedule.

2 The relevant earnings data are the gross hourly pay for '*all*' employees given by the present Standard Occupational Category ['*SOC*'] for (Care assistants and home carers) ['*6115*'] at the relevant percentile shown below (currently in table 26.5a at the tab for '*all*' employees) of the Annual Survey of Hours and Earnings in the United Kingdom ['*ASHE*'] published by the ONS. The original relevant percentiles are:

2.1 [   ] percentile shall be applied to paragraphs [   ] above

2.2 [   ] percentile shall be applied to paragraphs [   ] above

First payment of periodical payments under each step

3 Unless paragraphs 5–10 below apply, the annual periodical payments referred to in paragraph 1 *[1.1 to 1.3]* above shall be recalculated in November prior to payment on the 15th December of the same year from November [   ] in accordance with the following formula

$$PP = C \times (NF/A)$$

3.1 Where

3.1.1 '*PP*' = the amount payable by way of periodical payment in each year being calculated in November and paid on the 15th of December the first '*PP*' being the payment on the 15th of December [   ].

3.1.2 '*C*' = the relevant annual sum set out in paragraph 1 *[1.1 to 1.3]* above respectively.

3.1.3 '*NP*' = the '*first release*' hourly gross wage rate published by the ONS for the relevant percentile of ASHE SOC 6115 for '*all*' employees for the year in which the calculation is being carried out, the first *NP* being the figure applicable to the year [   ] published in or around October [   ].

3.1.4 '*A*' = the '*revised*' hourly gross wage rate for the relevant percentile of ASHE SOC 6115 for all employees applicable to [   ] and published by the ONS in or around October [   ]. In the event of a correction by the ONS it will be the replacement '*revised*' figure issued by the ONS.

Subsequent payment of periodical payments under each step

4 Unless paragraphs 5–10 below apply, the annual periodical payments referred to in paragraph 1 *[1.1 to 1.3]* above shall be recalculated annually in subsequent years in November in each year prior to payment on the 15th December of the same year from November [   ] in accordance with the following formula

$$PP = C \times (NP + (NF - OP))/A$$

4.1 Where in addition to the definitions previously set out:

4.1.1 *'NF'* = the *'revised'* hourly gross wage rate published by the ONS for the relevant percentile of ASHE SOC 6115 for *'all'* employees for the year prior to the year in which the calculation is being carried out, the first *NF* being that applicable to the year [   ] and published in or around October [   ]

4.1.2 *'OP'* = the *'first release'* hourly gross wage rate published by the ONS for the relevant percentile of ASHE SOC 6115 for *'all'* employees for the year prior to the year in which the calculation is being carried out, the first *OP* being the figure applicable to the year [   ] published in or around October [   ].

Payments upon reclassification of the SOC or a change of methodology by the ONS

5 Reclassification for the purposes of paragraphs 6-9 below, and subject to paragraph 6.1.2, occurs when the ONS publishes for the same year *'revised'* hourly gross wage rates for both:

5.1 the previously applied SOC (for which the *'revised'* wage rate is defined as *'AF'* in paragraph 6.1.1 below) and

5.2 for a new SOC (for which the *'revised'* wage rate is defined as *'AR'* in paragraph 7.1.4 below) that includes those currently defined as *'home carers'* in ASHE SOC 6115

Or alternatively, where the ONS publishes *AR* for a new SOC that includes those currently defined as 'home carers' in the previously applied SOC but does not publish *AF* for the same year, then reclassification is nonetheless deemed to have occurred.

Unless the Court otherwise orders pursuant to paragraph 11 below, in either event the new SOC shall be applied.

6 The relevant annual sum referable to the sums at paragraph 1 *[1.1 to 1.3]* above following reclassification shall be known as *'CR'* and shall be calculated only in each year of reclassification, in accordance with the following formula

$$CR = C \times (AF/A)$$

6.1 Where in addition to the definitions previously set out

6.1.1 *'AF'* = the final published *'revised'* hourly gross wage rate for the relevant percentile of the previously applied SOC for *'all'* employees

6.1.2 If, for the year of reclassification, the ONS does not publish AF, then the 'first release' hourly gross wage rate published for the relevant percentile of the previously applied SOC for 'all' employees (which is defined as *'OPF'* in paragraph 7.1.3 below) shall be applied in its place

6.1.3 If reclassification has previously occurred then C will be the numerical value of CR calculated when reclassification last occurred

7 When reclassification occurs the first payment only shall be

$$PPR = (CR \times (NPR/AR)) + (C \times ((AF - OPF)/A))$$

The second bracket of the above formula shall not apply where at the time of reclassification, either (a) there has been no periodical payment made in the previous year or (b) where at that time a step change in the annual sum is due under paragraph 1 above and in those circumstances the first payment shall be calculated in accordance with the following formula

$$PPR = CR \times (NPR/AR)$$

Where reclassification has occurred on more than one occasion prior to the first payment then successive applications of paragraph 6 above must be carried out first to arrive at the present numerical value of CR and C shall represent the numerical value of CR previously calculated

7.1 Where in addition to the definitions previously set out

7.1.1 'PPR' = the amount payable by way of periodical payment in each year following reclassification

7.1.2 'NPR' = the 'first release' hourly gross wage rate published for the relevant percentile of the new SOC following reclassification for the year in which the calculation is being carried out

7.1.3 'OPF' = the final 'first release' hourly gross wage rate published for the relevant percentile of the previously applied SOC for 'all' employees

7.1.4 'AR' = the 'revised' hourly gross wage rate for the published percentile of the new SOC, which, when first published, is closest to AF, and the relevant percentile of the new SOC shall be the percentile to which AR corresponds

8 Until further reclassification the formula for calculating subsequent values of PPR shall be

$$PPR = CR \times (NPR + (NFP - OPR)/AR)$$

8.1 Where in addition to the definitions previously set out

8.1.1 'NFR' = the 'revised' hourly gross wage rate published for the relevant percentile of the new SOC following reclassification for the year prior to the year in which the calculation is being carried out

8.1.2 'OPR' = the 'first release' hourly gross wage rate published for the relevant percentile in the new SOC following reclassification for the year prior to the year in which the calculation is being carried out

9 Further reclassifications shall be dealt with in the same way by the application of paragraphs 5–8 above

10 For the purposes of this part a change of methodology occurs when the ONS publishes two sets of data for the applied SOC. In that event, the same process as set out in paragraphs 6–9 above shall be undertaken. However, in these circumstances references to

10.1 *'reclassification'* shall be treated as being a reference to *'a change of methodology'*,

10.2 *'the new SOC'* shall be treated as being a reference to *'the existing SOC using the new methodology'*, and

10.3 'the previously applied SOC' shall be treated as being a reference to 'the existing SOC using the old methodology'.

Miscellaneous

11 In the event of a dispute between the parties arising out of the application of this part, there be liberty to apply.

CHAPTER 15

Causation

Dr Anthony Barton

INTRODUCTION

15.1   The consideration of scientific material in the civil courts has been
the subject of comment.

'In some cases, perhaps particularly medical negligence cases, causation may be so shrouded in mystery that the court can only measure statistical chances'[1].

And:

'Such claims are increasing, and are likely to increase further: this case gives an alarming foretaste of the complexities which arise when a legal system based on the compensation for the injuries men suffer from their neighbors' wrongdoings is faced with the allegations of harm arising from distortions of the natural world which were unknown and unsuspected by the common lawyers who developed the law of tort. Such cases inevitably depend on the evidence of scientists, who have a totally different approach from the lawyers to such philosophical concepts as "causation" and "proof". Yet, however scientific the subject matter of the claim, and however recondite the evidence and the argument, the legal definitions must apply in a court of law; the problem for the lawyer is in making the scientist understand a totally different concept of proof required by the Court'[2].

And:

'Both scientists and attorneys begin with hypotheses. But interaction between the worlds of law and science in the courtrooms makes clear that they represent two very different traditions. Clashes are already common between the truth-seeking world of science and the justice-serving institutions of the law; they are likely to intensify in the future'[3].

1 *Hotson v East Berkshire Area Health Authority* [1988] UKHL 1, per Lord Bridge at 5.
2 Margaret Puxon QC FRCOG, commentary on *Reay v British Nuclear Fuels* [1994] 5 Med LR 1 at 54.
3 Richard C Leone, foreword to *Science at the Bar* by Sheila Jasanoff (1997) Harvard University Press.

15.2   The civil courts have to apply legal principles to scientific evidence in respect of claims concerning medicinal products, environmental toxins and medical liability. These claims can be complex. Some of the difficulty arises from the very different traditions of reasoning in science and the law. Scientific data are collected and analysed by scientists in order that they can make assertions which are meaningful to scientists. The conflict arises when these data, analyses and assertions are considered as evidence by the court in order to make a legal determination. Further complexity arises when the scientific evidence and understanding are incomplete. Moreover, the courts may depart from established legal principles in such cases to decide cases on policy considerations, where the balance of justice requires it.

THE LAW: THE RULES FOR DETERMINING CAUSALITY

15.3   In order to succeed in a civil action (whether under strict liability or negligence) a claimant has to demonstrate that the matter complained of caused or materially contributed to the injury suffered: this is the causal link. Causation is a question of fact. The rules for its determination are matters of law[1]. Causation is determined conventionally and traditionally according to: (1) the 'but for' test; or (2) the doctrine of material contribution. However, the court may depart from the generally accepted rules:

'The causal requirements for liability often vary, sometimes quite subtly, from case to case. And since the causal requirements for liability are always a matter of law, these variations represent legal differences, driven by the recognition that the just solution to different kinds of case may require different causal requirement rules…

… the essential point is that the causal requirements are just as much part of the legal conditions for liability as the rules which prescribe the kind of conduct which attracts liability or the rules which limit the scope of that liability'[2].

And:

'…Judge Posner put it pithily in *United States v Oberhellmann* 946 F 2d 50, 53 (7th Cir. 1991):

"Causation is a complex, contextually variable concept, in law as in life."

Lord Bingham made the same point in *R v Kennedy* [2007] UKHL 38 at [15]:

"Questions of causation frequently arise in many areas of the law, but causation is not a single, unvarying concept to be mechanically applied without regard to the context in which the question arises."

Lord Hoffmann in his chapter on causation in *Perspectives on Causation* (edited by Richard Goldberg, 2011), page 9, wrote:

"It might be easier if, instead of speaking of proof of 'causation', which makes it look as if we are dealing with one monolithic concept which can be defined as 'part of the history' or by NESS ['necessary element of a sufficient set'], we spoke of the 'causal requirements' of a legal rule. That would make it clear that causal requirements are creatures of the law and nothing more. The causal requirements of one rule may be different from those of another … To say, as in *Fairchild*, that the exposure to asbestos by the defendant must have increased the risk of mesothelioma is to state a causal requirement"'[3].

1 *Fairchild v Glenhaven Funeral Services Ltd* [2002] UKHL 22.
2 *Fairchild v Glenhaven Funeral Services Ltd* [2002] UKHL 22, per Lord Hoffmann at paras 52 and 54.
3 *IEG Ltd v Zurich Insurance plc UK Branch* [2013] EWCA Civ 39, per Toulson LJ at paras 25–27.

15.4 Causation is conventionally to be established independently of conduct at fault or defect in a product. However, the causal requirements to establish liability are conditioned by the facts of the whole case, including the conduct or product in question, and the nature of the injury. The burden of proof is on the plaintiff and the standard of proof is the civil standard of the balance of probabilities. The tort of negligence requires proof of damage to found an action (unlike contract, where a breach of duty can be actionable per se). It is trite law that damage is the gist of negligence.

The 'but for' test

15.5 According to the 'but for' test, but for the matter complained of, the injury would not have occurred. This test is also known as the 'what if' test and the 'counterfactual conditional'. This test of causation entails two inquiries: (1) a question of historical fact (what actually happened); and (2) a question of hypothetical fact (what would have happened but for the matter complained of). For example, where a casualty officer negligently refused to see a patient who died shortly afterwards of arsenic poisoning, there was no suitable antidote and so the negligence had not caused the death[1]. For example, where a doctor negligently failed to administer a test dose of anti-tetanus serum and the patient suffered an adverse reaction as a result of such injection, the adverse reaction would not have been manifest as a result of the test dose and so the negligence did not cause the injury[2].

1 *Barnett v Chelsea and Kensington Hospital Management Committee* [1969] QB 428.
2 *Robinson v Post Office* [1974] 2 All ER 737, CA.

15.6   The 'but for' test is robust and logical; it provides clear decisions, especially where the medical evidence is near complete. The discharge of the 'but for' test can have inherent difficulties for claimants in clinical negligence and pharmaceutical product liability because of factual complexity, for example: there is often an underlying condition or disease process which is itself changing; there may be several aetiological factors operating, of which the matter complained of is one; the alleged injury may be non-specific; the medical evidence may be incomplete. The difficulty is to identify the extent, if any, of the alleged compensatable injury and to distinguish it from any underlying pathological condition which is part of the natural history.

15.7   The court's application of the 'but for' test is strictly deterministic and is all or nothing in effect:

'In determining what did happen in the past a court decides on the balance of probabilities. Anything that is more probable than not it treats as certain'[1].

And:

'When the question is whether a certain thing is or is not true – whether a certain event did or did not happen – then the court must decide one way or the other. There is no question of chance or probability. Either it did or it did not happen. But the standard of civil proof is a balance of probabilities. If the evidence shows a balance in favour of it having happened then it is proof that it did in fact happen'[2].

And:

'While medical science may seldom permit a precise evaluation of risk in percentage terms, courts are often faced with the requirement to make findings as to risk notwithstanding and do so, often on the basis of little more than informed guesswork'[3].

And:

'... where on disputed evidence a judge reaches a conclusion on the balance of probabilities it will not usually be easy to assess a specific measure of probability for the conclusion at which he has arrived ... A judge deciding disputed questions of fact will not ordinarily do it by use of a calculator'[4].

1 *Mallett v McMonagle* [1970] AC 166, per Lord Diplock at 176.
2 *Davies v Taylor* [1974] AC 207, per Lord Reid at 212.
3 *Bryce v Swan Hunter Group* [1988] 1 All ER 659, per Phillips J at 671.
4 *Hotson v East Berkshire Area Health Authority* [1988] UKHL 1, per Lord Mackay at 8.

15.8   Future loss in negligence can be recovered as consequential damage only when the anterior liability of actual damage has been established. However, future loss or risk of injury cannot generally of themselves provide a cause of action. The law has different approaches to past events and future events. Past events, whether historical or hypothetical, are treated deterministically[1]. Future events are treated probabilistically. The probability of the occurrence of an event may have application in terms of the probability of cause if it has occurred in the past or quantification of damage if it is in the future. These distinctions between past events and future events, causation and damage are thus crucial in negligence. A claim for injury is actionable; a claim for threat of injury is not:

'Proof of damage is an essential element in a claim in negligence … Neither [does] the risk of future illness … amount to damage for the purpose of creating a cause of action, although the law allows [it] to be taken into account in computing the loss suffered by someone who has actually suffered some compensatable physical injury and therefore has a cause of action. In the absence of such compensatable injury, however, there is no cause of action under which damages may be claimed and therefore no computation of loss in which the risk … may be taken into account … The risk of future disease is not actionable …'[2].

For example, the presence of symptomless pleural plaques may signal the risk of asbestos-related disease such as asbestosis and mesothelioma. The court held that the pleural plaques were not compensatable damage and could not found a cause of action; accordingly the threat of future disease was not actionable[3].

1 *Hotson v East Berkshire Area Health Authority* [1988] UKHL 1.
2 *Johnston v NEI International Combustion Limited* [2007] UKHL 39, per Lord Hoffmann at [2].
3 *Johnston v NEI International Combustion Limited* [2007] UKHL 39.

15.9   Where the 'but for' test cannot be satisfied, claimants have sought to formulate their claim in terms of loss of chance (such claims are established in contract law). For example, the negligent failure to consider the possibility of avascular necrosis following a hip injury did not give rise to a loss of chance claim. The prospect of recovery if there had been no negligence at the material time was less than probable: the injury was considered inevitable so the claim had to fail[1]. The House of Lords considered recovery of damages for loss of chance in personal injury and medical negligence cases as follows:

'There is a superficially attractive analogy between the principle applied in such cases as *Chaplin v Hicks* [1911] 2 KB 786 (award of damages for breach of contract assessed by reference to the lost chance of securing valuable employment if the contract had been performed) and *Kitchen v Royal Air Force Association* [1958] 1 WLR 563 (damages for solicitors' negligence assessed by reference to the lost chance of prosecuting a successful civil action) and the principle of awarding damages for the lost chance of avoiding personal injury or, in medical negligence cases, for the lost chance of a better medical result which might have been achieved by prompt diagnosis and correct treatment. I think there are formidable difficulties in the way of accepting the analogy'[2].

There are fundamental differences between contract and tort in respect of damages.

1 *Hotson v East Berkshire Area Health Authority* [1988] UKHL 1.
2 *Hotson v East Berkshire Area Health Authority* [1988] UKHL 1, per Lord Bridge at 5.

15.10   Where the negligent delay in diagnosis of a malignancy resulted in the diminution of prospect of a favourable outcome such loss could not be compensated[1]. On the particular facts of that case it was a risk which had not materialised. It was proposed that a proportionate recovery approach should be adopted so that the reduction in the prospect of a favourable outcome should be reflected in the extent of liability and the measure of damages. This approach would mean that almost any breach of duty could be actionable:

'Almost any claim for loss of an outcome could be reformulated as a claim for loss of a chance of that outcome. The implications of retaining them both as alternatives would be substantial. That is, the claimant still has the prospect of 100% recovery if he can show that it is more likely than not that the doctor's negligence caused the adverse outcome. But if he cannot show that, he also has the prospect of lesser recovery for loss of a chance. If (for the reasons given earlier) it would in practice always be tempting to conclude that the doctor's negligence had affected his chances to some extent, the claimant would almost always get something. It would be a "heads you lose everything, tails I win something" situation…'[2].

This approach would have meant that total liability for probability of cause was replaced by partial liability for possibility of cause. A related formulation of loss was 'diminution of prospects' of cure or survival. The majority of the House of Lords rejected this approach:

'A robust test which produces rough justice may be preferable to a test that on occasion will be difficult, if not impossible to apply with confidence in practice …

… there is a danger, if special tests of causation are developed piecemeal to deal with perceived injustices in particular factual situations, that the coherence of our common law will be destroyed'[3].

There is liability for an adverse outcome caused by negligence, not for the loss of chance of a more favourable outcome.

1 *Gregg v Scott* [2005] UKHL 2.
2 *Gregg v Scott* [2005] UKHL 2, per Baroness Hale at para 224.
3 *Gregg v Scott* [2005] UKHL 2, per Lord Phillips of Worth Matravers at paras 170 and 172.

15.11　The law in cases of negligent omissions raises the issue of hypothetical fact as to how would the doctor have acted; this matter has come before the House of Lords[1]. If the hypothetical fact concerned a second omission, the court determines: (1) whether the relevant person would have taken the requisite action; and, if not, (2) whether the second hypothetical omission amounted to a breach of duty in determining liability[2]. There is thus a sequence of two questions: a simple question of hypothetical fact ('what would have happened?'); if the answer is negative then a more sophisticated question of whether the omission was negligent ('what should have happened?'). The two questions must not be conflated[3].

1 *Bolitho v City and Hackney Health Authority* [1998] AC 232.
2 *Joyce v Wandsworth Health Authority* [1995] 6 Med LR 60; and *Joyce v Wandsworth Health Authority* [1996] 7 Med LR 1.
3 *Gouldsmith v Mid Staffordshire General Hospital Trust* [2007] EWCA Civ 39.

15.12　The 'but for' test provides forensic certainty; however, it has also been perceived as producing a harsh outcome for claimants. The courts temper the rigour of this test by adopting a robust common sense approach. This is particularly so where the medical evidence cannot resolve completely the factual uncertainties:

'… when a man who has not previously suffered from a disease contracts that disease after being subjected to conditions likely to cause it, and when he shows that it starts in a way typical of disease caused by such conditions, he establishes a prima facie presumption that his disease was caused by those conditions … That presumption could be displaced in many ways. The respondents sought to show, first, that it is negatived by the subsequent course of the disease and, secondly, by suggesting [another condition] as an equally probable cause of its origins'[1].

The application of the causal test in the context of the factual complexities and conflicting considerations of a claim requires a robust, common sense approach:

'The extent to which "positive or scientific proof of causation" is required must be a matter of judgment in each case and depends on the evidence as a whole. There is also a significant difference between, on the one hand, relying on inference to establish both breach of duty and causation of loss and, on the other hand, relying on inference to find a causal connection between proven breach of duty and ensuing loss.

In the absence of any positive evidence of breach of duty, merely to show that a claimant's loss was consistent with breach of duty by the defendant would not prove breach of duty if it would also be consistent with a credible non-negligent explanation. But where a claimant proves both that a defendant was negligent and that loss ensued which was of a kind likely to have resulted from such negligence, this will ordinarily be enough to enable a court to infer that it was probably so caused, even if the claimant is unable to prove positively the precise mechanism. That is not a principle of law nor does it involve an alteration in the burden of proof; rather, it is a matter of applying common sense. The court must consider any alternative theories of causation advanced by the defendant before reaching its conclusion about where the probability lies. If it concludes that the only alternative suggestions put forward by the defendant are on balance improbable, that is likely to fortify the court's conclusion that it is legitimate to infer that the loss was caused by the proven negligence'[2].

1 *Gardiner v Motherwell Machinery and Scrap Co Ltd* [1961] 1 WLR 1424, per Lord Reid at 1429.
2 *Drake v Harbour* [2008] EWCA Civ 25, per Toulson LJ at [27] and [28].

The doctrine of material contribution

15.13   The doctrine of material contribution evolved in the 1950s and was further developed in the 1970s. The doctrine has been recently examined in detail (see below) and has been extended. The doctrine evolved around two House of Lords[1] cases concerning occupational diseases due to industrial dusts; the earlier case concerned pneumoconiosis due to silica dust and the latter one concerned dermatitis due to brick dust. In each case there was a single aetiological factor, either silica dust or brick dust.

1 *Bonnington Castings v Wardlaw* [1956] UKHL 1, [1956] AC 613 (and see also *Nicholson v Atlas Steel Foundry and Engineering Co* [1957] 1 All ER 776); *McGhee v National Coal Board* [1972] UKHL 11, [1972] 3 All ER 1008.

15.14   In both cases, as a matter of law, the dust came from two sources, one 'innocent' (not in breach of regulation or negligence) and one 'guilty' (in breach of regulation or negligence). In the pneumoconiosis case the exposure to dust sources was concurrent; in the dermatitis case the exposure to the dust sources consisted of consecutive episodes. In both cases the claimant was unable to establish that had there been no breach of duty he would not have sustained any injury. In short, he was unable to satisfy the 'but for' test. However, the court stated the law in simple terms:

'It would seem obvious in principle that a pursuer or plaintiff must prove not only negligence or breach of duty but also that such fault caused or materially contributed to his injury …'[1].

1 *Bonnington Castings v Wardlaw* [1956] UKHL 1 at 3, [1956] AC 613 at 620, per Lord Reid.

15.15   The court considered the difficulties facing a claimant in proving causation under the 'but for' test; these are set out here in detail for medical interest and to illustrate the principle:

'The medical evidence was that pneumoconiosis is caused by a gradual accumulation in the lungs of minute particles of silica inhaled over a period of years. That means, I think, that the disease is caused by the whole of the noxious material inhaled and, if that material comes from two sources, it cannot be wholly attributed to material from one source or the other … I cannot agree that the question is, which was the most probable source of the respondent's disease, the [innocent] dust from the pneumatic hammers or the [guilty] dust from the swing grinders? It appears to me that the source of his disease was the dust from both sources, and the real question is whether the dust from the swing grinders materially contributed to the disease. What is a material contribution must be question of degree. A contribution which comes within the exception *de minimis non curat lex* is not material, but I think that any contribution which does not fall within that exception must be material. I do not see how there can be something too large to come within the *de minimis* principle but yet too small to be material'[1].

It was possible to say that the inhalation of the silica attributable to breach of duty had contributed to causing the plaintiff's pneumoconiosis.

1 *Bonnington Castings v Wardlaw* [1956] UKHL 1 at 4, [1956] AC 613 at 621, per Lord Reid.

15.16   In *McGhee v National Coal Board*, the claimant faced similar difficulties; again these are set out for medical interest and to illustrate the principle:

'Dermatitis can be caused, and this dermatitis was caused, by repeated minute abrasions of the outer horny layer of the skin followed by some injury to or change in the underlying cells, the precise nature of which has not yet been discovered by medical science. If a man sweats profusely for a considerable time the outer layer of the skin is softened and easily injured. If he is then working in a cloud of abrasive brick dust [innocent exposure], as this man was, the particles of dust will adhere to his skin in considerable quantity and exertion will cause them to injure the horny layer and expose to injury or infection of the tender cells below. Then in some way not yet understood dermatitis may result. If the skin is not thoroughly washed as soon as the man ceases work that process can continue at least for some considerable time. This man had to continue exerting himself after work by bicycling home whilst still caked with sweat and grime [guilty exposure], so he would be liable to further injury until he could wash himself thoroughly. Washing is the only practicable method of removing the danger of further injury. The effect of such abrasion of the skin is cumulative in the sense that the longer a subject is exposed to injury the greater the chance of his developing dermatitis: it is for that reason that immediate washing is well recognised as a proper precaution'[1].

It was not possible to say whether or not the lack of a shower had in fact contributed to the contraction of the dermatitis.

1 *McGhee v National Coal Board* [1972] UKHL 11, [1972] 3 All ER 1008 at 1010, per Lord Reid.

15.17   In *McGhee* the House of Lords stated the law:

'It has always been the law that a pursuer succeeds if he can show that fault of the defender caused or materially contributed to his injury. There may have been two separate causes but it is enough if one of the causes arose from fault of the defendant. The pursuer does not have to prove that this cause would of itself have been enough to cause him injury'[1].

And:

'... the burden rests on the appellant to prove, on a balance of probabilities, a causal connection between his injury and the respondents' negligence. It is not necessary, however, to prove, that the respondent's negligence was the only cause of injury. A factor, by itself, may not be sufficient to cause injury but if, with other factors, it materially contributes to causing injury, it is clearly a cause of injury'[2].

1 *McGhee v National Coal Board* [1972] UKHL 11, [1972] 3 All ER 1008 at 1010, per Lord Reid.
2 *McGhee v National Coal Board* [1972] UKHL 11, [1972] 3 All ER 1008 at 1017, per Lord Salmon.

15.18   *Wilsher v Essex Area Health Authority*[1] was a clinical negligence case where the causal test was whether the negligent act 'caused or materially contributed' to the injury. The infant plaintiff was born nearly 12 weeks prematurely. A catheter was negligently located in a vein rather than an artery; this resulted in a false reading of the oxygen level resulting in excess oxygen being administered. Subsequently the infant was administered excess oxygen non-negligently. The main allegation was that the negligent administration of excess oxygen caused or materially contributed to the plaintiff's retinopathy of prematurity (then known as 'rentrolental fibroplasia). The evidence was that prematurity itself and a number of other conditions from which premature babies commonly suffer (eg apnoeia, hypercarbia, intraventricular haemorrhage, patent ductus arteriosus, all conditions which afflicted the plaintiff) were associated with retinopathy of prematurity.

1 *Wilsher v Essex Area Health Authority* [1987] UKHL 11, [1988] AC 1074.

15.19   The main importance of *Wilsher*[1] was the consideration of the doctrine of material contribution in a clinical negligence case, specifically in a case involving tortious exposure to a toxic agent, excess oxygen, involving a divisible injury in the context of multiple risk factors. The case is unfortunate; the state of the evidence was unsatisfactory so that a retrial was ordered. The reasoning of the court was unclear, and some of its analysis of earlier authorities is difficult to follow. The detailed critical review of the case is not rewarding.

1 *Wilsher v Essex Area Health Authority* [1987] UKHL 11, [1988] AC 1074.

15.20   The courts have applied the doctrine of material contribution more generally in clinical negligence cases:

'In my view one cannot draw a distinction between medical negligence cases and others. I would summarise the position in relation to cumulative cause cases as follows. If the evidence demonstrates on a balance of probabilities that the injury would have occurred as a result of the non-tortious cause or causes in any event, the claimant will have failed to establish that the tortious cause contributed. *Hotson* exemplifies such a situation. If the evidence demonstrates that "but for" the contribution of the tortious cause the injury would probably not have occurred, the claimant will (obviously) have discharged the burden. In a case where medical science cannot establish the probability that "but for" an act of negligence the injury would not have happened but can establish that the contribution of the negligent cause was more than negligible, the "but for" test is modified, and the claimant will succeed'[1].

1 *Bailey v Ministry of Defence* [2008] EWCA Civ 883, Waller LJ at para 46.

15.21   The older authorities allowed the claimant full compensation for the whole injury where the court made a finding of material contribution; there was little consideration of partial recovery for incremental injury where there was a material contribution in space[1] or in time[2]. There is a paradox: allowing full compensation where a claimant cannot satisfy both limbs of the 'but for' test; whereas a claimant who can discharge the 'but for' test only recovers for the incremental, attributable injury. Defendants as well as claimants are entitled to a just result[3].

1 *Cartledge v E Jopling & Sons* [1961] 2 Lloyd's Rep 61.
2 *Clarkson v Modern Foundries Ltd* [1958] 1 All ER 33.
3 *Thompson v Smith's Shiprepairers Ltd* [1984] 1 All ER 881; see also *Crookall v Vickers-Armstrong Ltd* [1955] 2 All ER 12.

15.22 It is a fundamental principle that a defendant should only be responsible for the damage he has caused. The extent of compensation in a case where causation has been determined according to the doctrine of material contribution has only recently been specifically considered:

'[The claimant] will be entitled to succeed if he can prove that the defendant's tortious conduct made a material contribution to his disability. But strictly speaking the defendant is liable only to the extent of that contribution ... The question should be whether at the end of the day and on consideration of all the evidence, the claimant has proved that the defendant is responsible for the whole or a quantifiable part of his disability. The question of quantification may be difficult and the court only has to do the best it can using its common sense ...'[1].

However, where the injury was not divisible and was caused by tortious and non-tortious factors the court did not consider apportionment appropriate:

'... in a case which has had to be decided on the basis that the tort has made a material contribution but it is not scientifically possible to say how much that contribution is (apart from the assessment that it was more than *de minimis*) and where the injury to which that has lead is indivisible, it will be inappropriate simply to apportion the damages across the board ... But my provisional view is that there should not be any rule that the judge should apportion the damages across the board merely because one non-tortious cause has been in play'[2].

And:

'While the law does not expect tortfeasors to pay for damage that they have not caused, it regards them as having caused damage to which they have materially contributed. Such damage may be limited in its arithmetical purchase where one can quantify the possibility that it would have occurred sooner or later in any event; but that is quite different from apportioning the damage itself between tortious and non-tortious causes. The latter may become admissible where the aetiology of the injury makes it truly divisible, but that is not this case'[3].

1 *Holtby v Brigham & Cowan* (2000) MLC 0531, per Stuart-Smith LJ at para 20.
2 *Dickens v O2* [2008] EWCA 1144, per Smith LJ at para 46.
3 *Dickens v O2* per Sedley LJ at para 53.

Increased risk of injury as material contribution to injury, and as the injury itself

15.23 The courts have in very limited circumstances allowed the claimant to succeed when he was unable satisfy the 'but for' test, to demonstrate that the injury was avoidable. Such cases involve situations where there was a clear breach of duty, and where the scientific evidence was incomplete. As a matter of policy the courts have considered the balance of justice favoured the injured claimant over the defendant who had breached his duty. However, the courts appeared to have gone further and have on occasion equated an increased risk of injury with material contribution to injury. In *McGhee* the court stated:

'Nor can I accept the distinction drawn ... between materially increasing the risk that the disease will occur and making a material contribution to its occurrence ... From a broad and practical viewpoint I can see no substantial difference between saying that what the respondents did materially increased the risk of injury to the appellant and saying that what the respondents did made the material contribution to his injury'[1].

And:

'In the circumstances of the present case, the possibility of a distinction existing between (a) having materially increased the risk of contracting the disease, and (b) having materially contributed to causing the disease may no doubt be a fruitful source of interesting academic discussion between students of philosophy. Such a distinction is, however, far too unreal to be recognised by the common law'[2].

This sort of reasoning has been described as the 'triumph of policy over logic'[3]. The position has been summarised by the Court of Appeal:

'In the context of insidious occupational diseases, because of the protective approach which the courts have taken towards the health of employees and the difficulty of knowing the particular moment of exposure which has caused the onset of the disease, the courts have in the past sometimes adopted a broader test of causation which is satisfied by establishing that the employer's misconduct materially increased the risk of the employee suffering the illness which he sustained: *Bonnington Castings Limited v Wardlaw* and *McGhee*'[4].

There are fine distinctions between *Bonnington* and *McGhee* (every 'guilty' particle was shown to be pathogenic in the former but not the latter) but the similarities are more striking than the differences. Over-analysis is not necessarily rewarding.

1 *McGhee v National Coal Board* [1972] 3 All ER 1008, per Lord Reid at 1011.
2 *McGhee v National Coal Board* [1972] 3 All ER 1008, per Lord Salmon at 1018.
3 Machin QC in *Medical Negligence* by Powers and Harris (eds) (2nd edn, 1994) at p 407.
4 *IEG Ltd v Zurich Insurance plc UK Branch* [2013] EWCA Civ 39, per Toulson LJ at para 24.

15.24   The developments in the doctrine of material contribution thus evade the logical rigour imposed by the 'but for' test:

'A benevolent principle smiles on these factual uncertainties and melts them all away'[1].

The departure from the 'but for' test in the form of the doctrine of material contribution is based on a fiction which enables claimants to succeed for policy considerations.

1 *Fitzgerald v Lane* [1987] All ER 455, per Nourse LJ at 464.

15.25   The Court of Appeal in *Wilsher* reviewed the speeches in *McGhee* and summarised the approach of the court in broad and general terms:

'If it is an established fact that conduct of a particular kind creates a risk that injury will be caused to another or increases an existing risk that injury will ensue; and if the two parties stand in such a relationship that the one party owes a duty not to conduct himself in that way; and if the first party does conduct himself in that way; and if the other party does suffer injury of the kind to which the risk related; then the first party is taken to have caused the injury by his breach of duty, even though the existence and extent of the contribution made by the breach cannot be ascertained'[1].

This provides a clear and simple statement of how the rule of causation departs from the 'but for' test. It does not provide assistance as to whether and when the court should depart from the 'but for' test.

1   *Wilsher v Essex Area HA* [1987] 1 QB 730, per Mustill LJ at 771 and 772.

15.26   For example, in a case involving mesothelioma from wrongful exposure to asbestos the claimant sued three former employers. The claimant was unable to satisfy the 'but for' test and to demonstrate material contribution to the condition. However, the claim was successful on the basis that the defendants 'increased the risk' of the deceased developing mesothelioma.[1]

1   *Bryce v Swan Hunter Group plc* [1988] 1 All ER 659.

15.27   The proper application of traditional rules for determining causation, namely the 'but for' test and the doctrine of material contribution, does not entitle the claimant to compensation where the claimant has contracted mesothelioma as a result of wrongful exposure to asbestos from several previous employments. Medical science does not generally enable the occurrence of the condition to be attributed to any identifiable exposure to asbestos. The matter has been recently before the House of Lords[1]; after detailed review of the authorities the court drew heavily on its reasoning in *McGhee*[2]. It decided the case on a number of bases: that the creation of a material risk satisfied the causal requirements for liability, or that exposure to a risk was equivalent to the making of a material contribution. On either view causation was taken to be proven.

1   *Fairchild v Glenhaven Funeral Services Ltd* [2002] UKHL 22.
2   *McGhee v National Coal Board* [1972] 3 All ER 1008.

15.28   The *Fairchild*[1] decision is not logically sustainable; the existence of a risk and its realisation are separate things, even if damage has occurred. Yet the reasoning (and that in *McGhee*) has been variously characterised as 'a fiction', 'a legal inference', 'a factual inference', 'common sense', 'not a new legal principle', 'a new legal principle' and 'robust and pragmatic'. The decision was based on policy of the balance of justice, rather than strict determination according to evidence.

1   *Fairchild v Glenhaven Funeral Services Ltd* [2002] UKHL 22.

15.29   The court was concerned that the relaxation in *Fairchild* of the usual test of causation should only be used in limited conditions and was not of general application:

'The principle applied on these appeals is emphatically not intended to lead to such a relaxation whenever a plaintiff has difficulty, perhaps understandable difficulty, in discharging the burden of proof resting on him. Unless closely confined in its application this principle could become a source of injustice to defendants. There must be good reason for departing from the normal threshold "but for" test[1].'

It is difficult to see the *Fairchild* extension applying in clinical negligence cases.

1 *Fairchild v Glenhaven Funeral Services Ltd* [2002] UKHL 22, per Lord Nicholls at para 43.

15.30 The extent of the application of the *Fairchild*[1] exception was recently considered. Where there were several exposures to noxious agents, some tortious and some non-tortious, resulting in a single injury the House of Lords held that it did not matter whether other exposures were non-tortious for there to be a finding of liability in respect of the tortious exposure[2]. The creation of the risk itself was treated as the damage caused[3]. However, there was some limitation on this extension of the exception in that the mechanism of injury caused by the noxious exposures should be similar for tortious and non-tortious exposures.

1 *Fairchild v Glenhaven Funeral Services Ltd* [2002] UKHL 22.
2 *Barker v Corus (UK) plc* [2006] UKHL 20.
3 *Barker v Corus (UK) plc* [2006] UKHL 20, per Lord Hoffmann at para 36.

Liability for damage: joint and several

15.31 The basic principle of compensation for tort is that the court should so far as is possible endeavour to restore the claimant to the position in which he would have been in but for the defendant's wrongful act. A defendant is only responsible for the damage he has caused.

15.32 There may be difficulties in determining liability and apportionment where there are several tortfeasors. The common law has devised rules on joint and several liability:

'... a fundamental principle in the law of damage. Where injury has been done to the plaintiff and the injury is indivisible, any tortfeasor whose act has been a proximate cause of the injury must compensate for the whole of it. As between the plaintiff and the defendant it is immaterial that there are others whose acts also have been a cause of the injury and it does not matter whether those others have or have not a good defence. These factors would be relevant in a claim between tortfeasors for contribution but the plaintiff is not concerned with that; he can obtain judgment for total compensation from anyone whose act has been a cause of his injury. If there are more than one of such persons, it is immaterial to the plaintiff whether they are joint tortfeasors or not. If four men, acting severally and not in concert, strike the plaintiff one after another and as a result of his injuries he suffers shock and is detained in hospital and loses a month's wages, each wrongdoer is liable to compensate for the whole loss of earnings. If there were four distinct physical injuries, each man would be liable only for the consequences peculiar to the injury he inflicted, but in the example I have given the loss of earnings is one injury caused in part by all four defendants. It is essential for this purpose that the loss should be one and indivisible; whether it is so or not is a matter of fact and not a matter of law'[1].

Where several persons are responsible for the same damage statutory rules for the apportionment of damage may apply[2].

1 *Dingle v Associated Newspapers Ltd* [1961] 1 All ER 897, per Devlin LJ at 916.
2 See the Law Reform (Contributory Negligence) Act 1945 and the Civil Liability (Contribution) Act 1978.

Divisible and indivisible injury: divisible and indivisible cause

15.33   The rules of joint and several liability can merge with questions of causality. This arises in relation to the concepts of divisibility and indivisibility of injury in respect of the damage and its cause. The court will depend on expert evidence. As a matter of medical science some conditions appear to be discrete (for example, death, pregnancy and birth, miscarriage, the existence of malignancy); these would correlate with 'indivisible' injuries. Other conditions appear to be cumulative (for example, dermatitis, pneumoconiosis, industrial deafness); these would correlate with 'divisible' injuries and their severity would tend to be related to the degree of exposure. Some conditions are caused by a single event even against a background of multiple exposures (for example, pregnancy and sexual intercourse, mesothelioma and asbestos). Some conditions appear to depend on a threshold of cumulative exposure before a material risk is attained (for example, malignancy and exposure to carcinogens).

15.34   Thus, even where a relationship of cause and effect is established, the nature of the relationship can give rise to difficulty in determining liability and apportionment. This applies especially where different causal factors, in both fact and law, are operating. Complex factual scenarios can arise involving several aetiological agents and several tortfeasors, acting sequentially, concurrently or synergistically. These raise matters of scientific evidence, usually based on incomplete information and understanding, to which the court must apply legal principles in order to determine liability.

15.35   The House of Lords has considered issues of apportionment where mesothelioma arose from a number of exposures to asbestos involving different employers. The court held that the attribution of liability should be limited to the relative degree of contribution to the chance of the disease being contracted, or in proportion to the fraction of the total exposure[1]. This reasoning resembles the American doctrine of apportioning liability according to the market share of a product. The decision conflicts with the common law principles of liability where several tortfeasors are responsible for a single injury. The reasoning of the court was that the potential injustice of fixing liability where causation could not be established according to traditional rules should be tempered by not applying the usual rules of joint and several liability.

1 *Barker v Corus (UK) plc* [2006] UKHL 20.

15.36   The Compensation Act 2006, s 3 was passed to reverse the decision in *Barker*[1] in respect of apportionment. This section is specifically and exclusively concerned with damages where mesothelioma has been caused by asbestos and there has been a tortious exposure by a responsible person against a background of other exposure, whether or not tortious. The responsible person is wholly liable for the damage, and jointly and severally liable with any other responsible person. This can have a draconian effect on an employer who was responsible only for a small proportion of the overall exposure of a claimant to asbestos. The rules on contribution and contributory negligence also apply.

1 *Barker v Corus (UK) plc* [2006] UKHL 20.

15.37 Where there was only a single tortious occupational exposure to asbestos against a background of environmental exposure the court held that the *Fairchild* exception applied rather than the 'doubles the risk' test; the claimant succeeded where, on the balance of probability, the defendant's breach of duty materially increased the risk that she developed mesothelioma[1]. Where there were several defendants responsible for tortious exposures following other exposure to asbestos resulting in lung cancer the court applied the reasoning of *Fairchild*[2].

1 *Sienkiewicz v Greif* [2011] UKSC 10.
2 *Heneghan v Manchester Dry Dock Ltd* [2014] EWHC 4190 (QB); mesothelioma and lung cancer in this case were considered 'legally indistinguishable' (at para 81).

Overview: causation in the law

15.38 The courts have traditionally rejected an over-analytical approach:

'The object of the civil enquiry into cause and consequence is to fix liability on some responsible person and to give reparation for damage done ... The trial of an action for damage is not a scientific inquest into a mixed sequence of phenomena ... It is a practical inquiry'[1].

And:

'Causation is to be understood as the man in the street, and not as either the scientist or metaphysician would understand it'[2].

And:

'Courts of law must accept the fact that the philosophic doctrine of causation and the juridical doctrine of responsibility for the consequences of a negligent act diverge. To a philosopher – a term which I use in no disparaging sense, for what is a philosopher but one who, inter alia, reasons severely and with precision? – to a philosopher, the whole legal doctrine of responsibility must seem anomalous'[3].

And:

'The impression that may well be left on the reader of the scores of cases in which liability for negligence has been discussed is that the courts were feeling their way to a coherent body of doctrine and were at times in grave danger of being led astray by scholastic theories of causation and their ugly and barely intelligible jargon'[4].

And:

'The nature of causation has been discussed by many eminent philosophers and also by a number of learned judges in the past. I consider, however, that what or who has caused a certain event to occur is essentially a practical question of fact which can best be answered by ordinary common sense rather than by abstract metaphysical theory'[5].

And:

'... the legal concept of causation is not based on logic or philosophy. It is based on the practical way in which the ordinary man's mind works in the everyday affairs of life. From a broad and practical viewpoint ...'[6].

The law thus traditionally adopts an approach to causation which is not based on philosophy or logic but instead embraces common sense and human intuition. This approach inevitably gives rise to difficulties when assessing data of a biostatistical or scientific technical nature in order to determine causation.

1 *Weld-Blundell v Stephens* [1920] AC 956, per Lord Sumner at 986.
2 *Yorkshire Dale Steamship Co v Minister of War Transport* [1942] AC 691, per Lord Wright at 706.
3 *Stapley v Gypsum Mines Ltd* [1953] AC 663, per Lord Asquith at 687.
4 *Overseas Tankship (UK) Ltd v Morts Dock & Engineering Co Ltd, The Wagon Mound* [1961] AC 388, per Viscount Simonds at 419.
5 *Alphacell Ltd v Woodward* [1972] AC 824, per Lord Salmon at 847.
6 *McGhee v National Coal Board* [1972] 3 All ER 1008, per Lord Reid at 1011.

15.39   In general the 'but for' test is applied where the conduct complained of consists of a discrete, identifiable act or omission and the medical evidence is complete; whereas the doctrine of material contribution may be applied where there are repeated tortious acts or exposures against a background of non-tortious acts or exposures where the injury is cumulative, and where the medical evidence is incomplete. However, the courts can vary the causal requirements for liability according to the facts of the case. Where the medical evidence is incomplete the issues before the court may involve dispute as to which of the various rules for determining causation is to be applied.

15.40   The more recent decisions of the courts have been helpful; they set out their reasoning and have been explicit where they have departed from established principle in preference for policy reasons; they have shown a readiness to identify unclear reasoning in earlier cases. They have been more deferential to scientific method. The courts have demonstrated how they depart from established principle. What is not predictable is whether, when, and why they depart from such principle. The court has conveniently summarised the position:

'Had the common law adhered to strict logic and principle, all the difficulties which bedevil cases such as these would not have arisen, and would not continue to arise. The disadvantage of strict adherence to logic and principle is that frank injustice may arise in certain types of case, and therefore the common law constantly strains at the leash of the intellectually pure approach. Policy considerations often serve to buttress the logic and principle of the reasoned outcome in any individual case, but there are circumstances where the application of such considerations cuts across the very principles in play.

In a case where medical causation is in issue, strict adherence to logic and principle would demand proof on the balance of probabilities either of the whole of the damage suffered or of a material part of it. For these purposes, there is no distinction between the whole and the part, provided that the part is significant. The clearest exposition of this principled approach is to be found in the opinion of Lord Reid in *Bonnington Castings* .... I will call this the conventional common law approach'[1].

And:

'The conventional common law approach began to be whittled away, and policy considerations perhaps inadvertently to intrude, as early as 1957. The precise, windy path the common law took need not be examined in detail. At this stage, I need only identify the end-point, by which I mean the point which the common law has reached which is furthest away from the conventional approach. That end-point has been described in these proceedings, and elsewhere, as the "*Fairchild*-extension". This extended principle undoubtedly arises in mesothelioma cases...'[2].

1 *Heneghan v Manchester Dry Dock Ltd* [2014] EWHC 4190 (QB), Jay J at paras 50 and 51.
2 *Heneghan v Manchester Dry Dock Ltd* at para 53.

INVESTIGATING CAUSE AND EFFECT

15.41   Even the simplest organism demonstrates individual variation: living things are unique, diverse, complex and unpredictable. There are inter-individual and intra-individual variations. Accordingly, it is not generally possible to define the general properties in any individual, let alone study a general relationship of cause and effect: the effect due to an extrinsic agent may be smaller than the intrinsic variation of the individual. This is the fundamental problem of the study of cause and effect in living things:

'Certain events tend to follow others in time. Some of these temporal associations have qualities that lead the observer to think of them as cause and effect – the earlier event being denoted the cause of the later. The repeated observation of sequences of similar events gives confidence that a particular effect is likely to succeed a particular cause. However, as Hume noted: "We are never able, in a single instance, to discover any power or necessary connection, any quality which binds the effect to the cause, and renders the one an infallible consequence of the other. We only find that one does actually, in fact, follow the other." What, then, leads us to think of certain relationships as causal and others as non-causal?'[1].

1 MacMahon and Trichopoulos *Epidemiology – Principles and Methods* (2nd edn, 1996) at p 19.

15.42   Philosophical treatises on the nature of causation have generally failed to provide a useful touchstone to help recognise causality in biological systems, whether for the scientist or the lawyer. However, John Stuart Mill described five basic principles of induction, Mill's Methods[1]: the method of agreement, the method of difference, the joint method of agreement and difference, the method of residues, and the method of concomitant variations. The method of difference is as follows:

'If an instance in which the phenomenon under investigation occurs, and an instance in which it does not occur, have every circumstance in common save one, that one occurring only in the former; the circumstance in which alone the two instances differ, is the effect, or the cause, or an indispensable part of the cause, of the phenomenon'.

This approach applied repeatedly and quantitatively appears to be the conceptual basis of analytical epidemiology (see below).

1 John Stuart Mill *A System of Logic* (1843).

Epidemiology: descriptive and analytical

15.43   One can attempt to investigate biological characteristics and effects by population study; the underlying reasoning is that individual variation is averaged out in a population. There is a hierarchy of types of population evidence: the anecdotal case report; the case series; ecological population studies; case control studies; cohort studies; self-controlled risk-interval relative incidence models. The first three are classified as descriptive epidemiology, whereas the latter three are classified as analytical epidemiology.

15.44 With respect to investigating causality, there are essentially two sorts of epidemiological evidence: descriptive studies and analytical studies. Descriptive studies describe phenomena; they raise questions of causation rather than answer them; they are hypothesis generating. They cannot provide probative evidence of causality. Analytical studies examine outcomes in an exposed population compared with a control population. The control population enables the occurrence of naturally occurring, spontaneous events to be investigated. Analytical studies enable cause and effect to be investigated; they are hypothesis testing. They can provide probative evidence of causality.

The null hypothesis

15.45 The empirical approach is to construct a hypothesis which is tested. The hypothesis is that there is no association between exposure and outcome, the 'null' hypothesis. The concept of proof is asymmetrical; verification of a theory by observation is not logically possible. Falsification avoids induction. For example, the assertion that all swans are white can be logically refuted by a single black swan but not logically proven by any number of white swans; an inductive proof would entail counting white swans provided that there were no black ones. The failure to refute the null hypothesis represents evidence of absence of an association rather than absence of evidence of an association. Absence of evidence is not evidence of absence.

15.46 The scientific approach has two stages which are sequential. The first stage is to demonstrate a statistical association by refuting the null hypothesis relying on deductive logic. The second stage is to infer that such an association is causal, relying on interpretation and inductive reasoning. The first stage is generally a condition precedent to the second stage.

Statistical association

15.47 The two-by-two table derived from analytical, comparator studies can be analysed numerically. The relative risk or odds ration can be calculated. The relative risk is derived from the cohort study and is the ratio of the risk of the disease in the exposed population to the risk of the disease in the unexposed population. The odds ratio derived from the case control study can be considered an approximation of the relative risk. A relative risk greater than unity denotes an association; a relative risk of unity denotes no association; a relative risk less than unity denotes a negative association.

If the probability of any association occurring by chance is less than 1 in 20 then the result is said to be 'significant' ($P<0.05$). This probability figure refers merely to the probability of the data. This 1 in 20 figure is an arbitrary but agreed value.

15.48 The aetiological fraction refers to the proportion of cases of disease in an exposed population which are associated with exposure to the agent under study. The aetiological fraction is calculated by the following formula:

Aetiological fraction = (relative risk – 1)/relative risk

A statistical association is purely a numerical value. It may arise from the following factors:

(1) chance;
(2) experimental method: bias;
(3) confounding factors;
(4) reverse cause, ie effect;
(5) a true causal relationship;
(6) combinations of the above.

Having measured an association the second stage is to interpret it, to consider if the association is causal.

Association or causation

15.49 In order to infer that a statistical association has a causal basis certain criteria are applied[1]. These are known as the Bradford Hill criteria. They include the following:

(1) strength of association: the stronger the association, the less likely it is due to chance;
(2) consistency: the data are comparable to the results of other studies; do experiment and observation produce similar results?
(3) specificity: the effect denotes a discrete entity, a 'fingerprint';
(4) temporal relationship: cause and effect must be related in time; the effect cannot precede a cause;
(5) biological gradient: the greater the exposure the greater the effect, a dose-response curve;
(6) biological plausibility: a value judgment, does it offend common sense? Is there a mechanism?
(7) coherence: is a causal relationship in keeping with what is known about the postulated cause and postulated effect?
(8) experimental evidence: can the observations be reproduced by experiment?
(9) analogy: do similar causes produce similar effects?

These criteria are essentially the application of common sense value judgments which convert a probabilistic assertion (ie a numerical association) into a deterministic one (ie a causal relationship). Cause must precede effect: *a temporal relationship is a necessary but not sufficient condition for causality.* The other criteria are neither necessary nor sufficient conditions for causality. The criteria enable an association to be interpreted. It is applying concepts of specificity, exclusivity and reproducibility to a relationship which has been numerically defined. The inference of causation thus depends on both statistical and biological evidence. This two-stage approach has received judicial approval which recognised that the Bradford Hill criteria were 'a useful means of evaluating epidemiological evidence'[2].

1 Hill *Environment and Disease: Association or Causation?* (1965) 58 Proc Roy Sac Med 295–300.
2 *Huxley v Elvicta Wood Engineering Ltd* [2001] Medical Litigation cases 0201, CA.

15.50 The distinction between association and causation can be problematical:

'It is a tenet of epidemiology that association is not synonymous with causation ... Unfortunately, the distinction between association and causation is frequently overlooked, and novel epidemiological findings are often referred to, particularly in the non-scientific press, as demonstrating a "link" between an exposure and some adverse health outcome, inviting the erroneous conclusion that a cause-and-effect relationship has been established. This confusion of association with causation can have important ramifications for policy decisions, compensation claims and the attitude of the general public towards epidemiology and other statistical sciences ... the difficulty that non-scientists have in distinguishing association from causation'[1].

And:

'... the tendency on the part of the public, encouraged by the media, to assume that association implies causation'[2].

1 Wakeford 'Association and Causation' RSS News, December 1994.
2 Doll 'Risk of Misleading' RSS News, February 1995.

Subsequence or consequence

15.51   The existence of a temporal relationship is a condition precedent to establishing a causal relationship. However, human intuition and mere common sense may tend to impart causality to a temporal relationship (the fallacy: post hoc ergo propter hoc):

'It is incident to physicians ... to mistake subsequence for consequence'[1].

Lawyers and journalists too must beware of confusing a causal relationship with a temporal relationship.

1 Dr Johnson 'Review of Dr Lucas's Essays on Waters' (1734).

Biological proof

15.52   Not all causal relations depend on statistical evidence for their demonstration. Biological evidence of specificity, exclusivity and reproducibility, without evidence of association, can denote a causal relationship, for example, as in Koch's postulates; however, such specificity, exclusivity and reproducibility must be of a very high order. Evidence of re-challenge is especially compelling. A wonderful, modern example is the exposition of the relationship between Helicobacter pylori and peptic ulcer[1]. It is a medical triumph. It shows that even in the latter half of the last century individual endeavour, if scientifically rigorous, could succeed against a contrary overwhelming orthodox medical view. It is to be contrasted with sorry tale of failure and opportunism associated with the supposed link between MMR vaccine and autism.

1 Allen 'What's the story H pylori?' (2001) 357 Lancet 694.

15.53   The existence of a mechanism of itself merely demonstrates biological plausibility rather than causality. It is a theoretical construct. It means that something could cause rather than does cause. The operation of the mechanism needs to be demonstrated by the existence of an association or other evidence in order for causality to be inferred:

'In the absence of convincing case reports or epidemiological studies, however, the mere demonstration of biological plausibility was felt to constitute insufficient evidence to accept or reject a causal relation'[1].

1 Stratton and others *Adverse Events Associated with Childhood Vaccines: Evidence bearing on Causality*. Vaccine Safety Committee, Division of Health Promotion and Disease Prevention, Institute of Medicine; National Academy Press, Washington DC (1994).

Overview: investigating causality

15.54 Inferring causality generally requires both quantitative and qualitative consideration of the relationship between exposure and outcome. Biological evidence assists in the interpretation of an association. Statistical evidence may demonstrate that biological mechanism operates causally rather than merely suggesting a theoretical possibility.

SCIENCE AND LAW COMPARED

15.55 Science and law may have different functions but share striking similarities. Both purport to provide rational, reasoned, independent, unbiased processes concerned with the objective assessment of evidence. The approach of the law to the issue of causation has traditionally been pragmatic and robust.

'... the lawyer's causal problems are not scientific inquests but are to be determined on common sense principles ... the lawyer ... [is] primarily concerned to make causal statements about particulars, to establish that on some particular occasion some particular occurrence was the effect or consequence of some other particular occurrence. Their characteristic concern with causation is not to discover connections between types of events, and so not to formulate laws or generalisations, but is often to apply generalisations, which are already known or accepted as true and even platitudinous, to particular concrete cases. In this and other respects the causal statements of the lawyer ... are like the causal statements most frequent in ordinary life: they are singular statements identifying in complex situations certain particular events as causes, effects, or consequences of other particular events. Such singular causal statements have their own special problems and it is these that most trouble the lawyer ... By contrast, in the experimental sciences by which so much of the philosophical discussion of causation has been influenced, the focus of attention is the discovery of generalisations and the construction of theories. What is typically asserted here is a connection between kinds of events, and particular causal statements have only the derivative interest of instances ...'[1].

1 Hart and Honore *Causation in the Law* (2nd edn, 1990) pp 9–10.

15.56 There are also striking differences. Scientific assertions when compared with determinations of legal causation have the following characteristics:

(1) they are population-based, not individual; general not particular;
(2) they are probabilistic, not deterministic;
(3) they are generally expressed as the refutation of the hypothesis and not a finding of fact or proof of an allegation;
(4) the evidence is not exhaustive, whereas an adjudication is determined according to the evidence available.

The courts, however, increasingly have to make causal determination of a general nature which are outside the known science. The legal process has to engage in hypothesis testing rather than merely applying established and accepted general causal relationships to any particular case.

15.57 The major distinction between legal determinations and scientific assertions lies in the concept of certainty. The legal concept of causation is deterministic: it is an expression of fiction of certainty, an absolute concept. The scientific concept of causation is probabilistic: it is an expression of the uncertainty of truth, an asymptotic concept.

The fundamental conceptual distinction has been recognised by epidemiologists, if not by some lawyers and journalists:

'Epidemiologists live with the uncertainty of statistical inference founded upon observational data. They should not forget that others may not share this appreciation'[1].

1 Wakeford 'Association and Causation' RSS News, December 1994.

15.58 Scientific and legal reasoning differ in their approach to evidence and proof of causation. The two are not directly comparable. For example, there has been concern expressed about the differing standards of proof of the civil courts and science. It is a recurring theme of the 'fallacy of the transposed conditional' (see **Chapter 16**), a tendency to confuse the probability of experimental data testing a hypothesis with the probability of the truth of the hypothesis tested by the experimental data.

15.59 For example, the requirement for the probability of data expressed as confidence interval of 95 per cent has been confused with a standard of proof. This is an arbitrary level of significance to denote reliability of the data. The 95 per cent figure does not refer to the probability of the truth of the assertion. It is not a standard of proof. This has been recognised by the courts:

'... I do not think there is any generally accepted standard of scientific proof, nor is it clear who has to be satisfied to such a standard. The addition of the words "95% confidence" is a confusion of thought derived from the statistical concept of 95% confidence intervals and probability values. They are not concerned with the standards of proof, but the probability of chance'[1].

And:

'The fact that epidemiologists or another scientist would or would not find an association and/or a cause to be established to his satisfaction is most helpful to a judge but only within the limits imposed by their respective disciplines ... I have to decide ... on the balance of probabilities'[2].

1 *Loveday v Renton* [1990] 1 Med LR 117, per Stuart-Smith LJ at 124.
2 *Reay v British Nuclear Fuels* [1994] 5 Med LR 1, per French J at 10.

15.60 In *Reay*, Professor MacMahon described the role of the epidemiologist:

'In the end, it must be recognised that the idea of cause is a probabilistic one. Rarely can we be certain that a causal relationship exists, but by assembling evidence from many different angles we may build a body of support sufficient to convince most reasonable people that it is more prudent to act as though the association were causal than to assume that it is not. The point in the accumulation of evidence at which this decision is reached depends in considerable part on the consequences of the alternative actions to be taken as a result of the judgment'[1].

A major difference in law and science lies in their application and finality:

'Scientific conclusions are subject to perpetual revision. Law, on the other hand, must resolve disputes finally and quickly ... rules of evidence [were] designed not for the exhaustive search for cosmic understanding but for the particularised resolution of legal disputes'[2].

And:

'The contrasts between law and science are often described in binary terms: science seeks truth, while the law does justice; science is descriptive, but law is prescriptive; science emphasises progress, whereas the law emphasises process. These simplified characterisations restate in varying ways the insight that fact-finding in the law is always contingent on a particular vision of (and mechanism for) delivering social justice. Scientific claims, by contrast, are thought to lack such contingency. Although its conclusions may be speculative, provisional, and subject to modification, science is ordinarily seen as set apart from all other social activities by virtue of its institutionalised procedures for overcoming particularity and context dependence and its capacity for generating claims of universal validity. Not surprisingly, then, comparisons between science and the law often celebrate science's unique commitment to systematic testing of observations and its willingness to submit its conclusions to critical probing and falsification'[3].

1 *Reay v British Nuclear Fuels* [1994] 5 Med LR 1 at 10.
2 *Daubert v Merrell Dow Pharmaceuticals Inc* 113 S Ct 2786 (1993), Justice Blackman.
3 *Science at the Bar* by Sheila Jasanoff (1997) Harvard University Press, p 7.

Causation: generic and individual

15.61   The application of data derived from population studies to the individual has inherent difficulties for both the lawyer and the clinician who are both primarily concerned with the individual:

'The causation issues dealt with in civil actions and by medical scientists are not the same. In a civil action the causation issue is typically whether the plaintiff's injuries were caused by agent X. Population-based studies by medical experts cannot answer the question of individual causation; they merely show whether an individual is at an increased risk if he or she is a member of a certain group, the broader question of whether a substance causes a statistically significant increased risk of disease is usually not in issue'[1].

1 Kapshandy T 'Proof of causation' (letter) (1992) 339 Lancet 876.

15.62   In determining the issue of causation due to a drug or a toxic agent, the court is faced with the sequential questions 'can X cause?' (generic causation) and 'did X cause?' (individual causation). If generic causation is determined in the negative, it is dispositive of the whole litigation.

15.63   In much of the product liability and toxic tort litigation, the causal issues are not established science: generic causation 'can it cause?' is in issue. The legal process must engage in hypothesis testing according to legal rules and reasoning. This was the situation in the pertussis vaccination case[1] where the parties agreed the determination of a preliminary issue as follows:

'Can or could pertussis vaccine used in the United Kingdom and administered intramuscularly in normal dosage cause permanent brain damage or death in young children?'

It was recognised by the court that the determination of causation was essentially a two-stage process:

'Quite clearly if a clinician is to make a diagnosis in a given case that a child is suffering from permanent brain damage caused by pertussis vaccine, he can only do so on the basis that he has reached the conclusion that pertussis vaccine can cause brain damage … [the] decisions in individual cases were made on this assumption. The decision then depends on the clinician's judgment as to whether or not the clinical signs and symptoms and the history relating to the patient meet certain criteria determined by the clinician in question'[2].

And:

'Assessment of causation in any individual case involved a two-stage exercise. One had first to consider whether or not a causal association had been established in relation to the study population as a whole. Only if one considered that a causal association was established would one then go on to consider whether it was more likely than not that the cause had played a role in the development of the disease … of the individuals. Any uncertainty which existed in relation to the general question of causation must be taken into account in assessing the "probability of causation" or "attributable risk" in respect of the individual'[3].

1 *Loveday v Renton* [1990] 1 Med LR 117 at 125.
2 *Loveday v Renton* [1990] 1 Med LR 117, per Stuart-Smith LJ at 125.
3 *Reay v British Nuclear Fuels* [1994] 5 Med LR 1, per French J at 23.

15.64   A finding of generic causation is merely a condition precedent for finding individual causation. It does not necessarily advance the individual claim. This is particularly so where the injuries alleged are not specific. How can it be said that an alleged injury is due to an agent rather than representing the background rate? The claimant's task is much easier where there is a specific 'fingerprint' injury such as a characteristic phenotype (for example, phocomelia and thalidomide) or, for example, a unique chromosomal, anatomical, cytological, biochemical or serological marker.

15.65   Where the court has made a finding of generic causation, it has employed such biological criteria as history of exposure, temporal relation, specificity of injury, plausible mechanism, analogy, and exclusion of alternative aetiology, to enable an inference of individual causation to be made[1].

1 See for example *Hill v Tomkins* (17 October 1997, unreported), QBD.

Science in court

15.66   The English courts are generally willing to embark on a detailed examination of evidence including epidemiology to determine causality:

'What he has to do is to prove that … his loss was caused by the defendant's negligence. To be a figure in a statistic does not by itself give him a cause of action'[1].

And:

'... the danger of using statistics as a basis on which to prove proximate cause and indicated that it was necessary as a minimum to produce evidence connecting the statistics the facts of the case ... To hold a defendant liable without proof that his action caused the plaintiff harm would open up untold abuses of the litigation system'[2].

1 *Hotson v East Berkshire Area Health Authority* [1987] 1 All ER 210, per Croom-Johnson LJ at 223.
2 Lord McKay citing a US case in *Hotson v East Berkshire Area Health Authority* [1987] 2 All ER 909 at 918.

15.67 The approach of the English court may be compared with the Irish court:

'... it is not possible ... for a ... court to take upon itself the role of a determining, scientific authority resolving disputes between distinguished scientists in any particular line of technical expertise. The function which a court can and must perform in the trial of a case in order to acquire a just result, is to apply common sense and a careful understanding of the logic and likelihood of events to conflicting theories concerning a matter of this kind'[1].

1 *Best v Wellcome Foundation* [1994] 5 Med LR 81 (Irish Supreme Court), per Finlay CJ at 98.

The balance of probability: the relative risk: the aetiological fraction

15.68 There is a tendency to correlate with respect to generic causation statistical concepts with the legal standard of the balance of probabilities:

'51% proof ... equates neatly with a relative risk of 2 – ie the plaintiff must show that exposure to, say, a mutagen more than doubled his risk of contracting the disease in question'[1].

And:

'... the burden of proof in civil action is more comparable with the relative risk (RR) or the aetiological fraction (EF), and several US courts have recognised this ...

It has been suggested that the >50% burden of proof in civil cases is met when the EF exceeds 0.5 (RR >2.0) because more than half the cases of the disease of interest in an exposed group were caused by exposure to agent X. While this is a more accurate analogy than the comparison to CI [confidence intervals], this comparison is also vulnerable. The late Sir Austin Bradford Hill pointed out many years ago that a statistically significant association is not equivalent to causation. Nor does the RR answer the issue of individual causation at issue in a tort action. If half the cases of the disease of interest in the exposed group may have been caused by agent X, half were not; and the study gives the jury and the judge no clue about which group the plaintiff falls into ...

Traditional notions of causation in epidemiology (ie RR >2.0 at 95% CI) are not at all incompatible with the burden of proof in civil tort actions ...'[2].

1 Meeran 'Scientific and legal standards of proof in environmental and personal injury cases' (letter) (1992) 339 Lancet 671.
2 Kapshandy 'Proof of causation' (letter) (1992) 339 Lancet 876.

15.69 Although the concept of balance of probability and aetiological fraction of half correlate numerically, they are conceptually different. The High Court considered this correlation:

'... the odds ratio or relative risk ... does not in any event exceed the figure 2, the figure beyond which it would have to go before it could be said that there is more chance than not that an individual picked from the sample had suffered a stroke by reason of the oral contraceptive taken.

Having considered the evidence reviewed above on a balance of probabilities I am not able to find that the plaintiff sustained her stroke by reason of the oral contraceptive prescribed for her!'[1]

1 *Vadera v Shaw* (22 November 1996, unreported), per Alliot J (emphasis added).

15.70   The court treated the relative risk as evidence of causation to be evaluated on the balance of probabilities, and not as substituting the legal test itself. This issue came before the Court of Appeal. The court stated as follows:

'... the judge concluded that it could not be established, applying the discipline of statistics to the available figures, that the association between a person taking Logynon and that person suffering a stroke was more than a relationship of chance. It followed (bearing in mind that the burden of proof on this issue rested with the plaintiff) that it could not be established on a balance of probabilities that this plaintiff suffered her stroke by reason of taking the Logynon.

It is as commonsense a conclusion as one could wish to say that if the connection between A and B cannot be shown with confidence to be other than a coincidence, then it cannot be held on a balance of probabilities that A caused B. This is not to allow scientists or statisticians to usurp the judge's function, but rather to permit him to use their skills to discern a connection, or lack of connection, between two phenomena'[1].

However, a 'connection between A and B' is demonstrated by a relative risk greater than unity, not 2. As for 'confidence', this is demonstrated by a confidence interval not including unity.

1 *Vadera v Shaw* (1998) 45 BMLR 162, Henry LJ.

15.71   In the combined oral contraceptive product liability litigation[1] there was an agreement between the parties, which was accepted by the court as 'correct', that the issue was whether the relative risk for venous thromboembolism of third generation pills compared with second generation pills was greater than 2. This was the basis on which causation was determined, relying on the concept of aetiological fraction:

'If factor X increases the risk of condition Y by more than 2 when compared with fn.- for Z it can be said, of a group of say 100 with both exposure to factor X and the condition, that as a matter of probability more than 50 would not have suffered Y without being exposed to X [but exposed to Z instead]. If medical science cannot identify the members of the group who would and who would not have suffered Y, it can nevertheless be said of each member that she was more likely than not to have avoided Y had she not been exposed to X [but to Z instead]'[2].

The relative frequency of occurrence of events in population study is converted to the probability of that event in an individual, so that where the probability is more than evens the balance of probability is considered to be discharged. The probability of the data is treated as if it is the probability of the truth of the allegation. Ironically, this sort of reasoning is a variety of what was described by Professor MacRae in the court itself as the 'fallacy of the transposed conditional'[3]. According to this sort of reasoning a relative risk of 2 or less would mean an aetiological fraction of less than half and so not discharge the balance of probability. However, an association denoted by a relative risk of greater than unity and less than two can be causal in nature. Indeed the court stated:

'... the above finding [relative risk of 1.7] both disposes of the first issue in a way which means that the claim must fail ... I would incline to a finding that there is an underlying causal connection at about that level of increased risk'[4].

The court having disposed of the issue of causation because the relative risk was less than 2 then found (obiter) that a relative risk of less than 2 denoted a causal relationship. A relative risk of 1.7 provides an aetiological fraction of 41 per cent, such that 41 of 100 women with the condition and exposed to the matter complained of would be able to attribute their condition to the matter complained of. These 41 women would not be compensated, whereas if the relative risk was just over 2 then 51 of 100 such women could be compensated. This does indeed appear to be compensation by the calculator.

1 *X, Y, Z v Schering Health Care Ltd* [2002] EWHC 1420 (QB).
2 *X, Y, Z v Schering Health Care Ltd* [2002] EWHC 1420 (QB) per Mackay J at [21].
3 *X, Y, Z v Schering Health Care Ltd* [2002] EWHC 1420 (QB) per Mackey J at [37].
4 *X, Y, Z v Schering Health Care Ltd* [2002] EWHC 1420 (QB) per Mackey J at [344].

15.72   The Supreme Court has explicitly approved the doubling of risk as satisfying the balance of probability:

'The "doubles the risk" test is one that applies epidemiological data to determining causation on balance of probabilities in circumstances where medical science does not permit determination with certainty of how and when an injury was caused. The reasoning goes as follows. If statistical evidence indicates that the intervention of a wrongdoer more than doubled the risk that the victim would suffer the injury, then it follows that it is more likely than not that the wrongdoer caused the injury...

Where there are competing alternative, rather than cumulative, potential causes of a disease or injury, such as in *Hotson*, I can see no reason in principle why epidemiological evidence should not be used to show that one of the causes was more than twice as likely as all the others put together to have caused the disease or injury'[1].

This approach achieves a pragmatic application of scientific probabilism with legal determinism. It provides an indication of where it is appropriate to apply the 'doubles the risk' test.

1 *Sienkiewicz v Greif* [2011] UKSC 10, per Lord Phillips at [72] and [93].

15.73   The Supreme Court provided some further guidance:

'... I see no scope for the application of the "doubles the risk" test in cases where two agents have operated cumulatively and simultaneously in causing the onset of a disease. In such a case the rule in *Bonnington* applies. Where the disease is indivisible, such as lung cancer, a defendant who has tortiously contributed to the cause of the disease will be liable in full. Where the disease is divisible, such as asbestosis, the tortfeasor will be liable in respect of the share of the disease for which he is responsible.

Where the initiation of the disease is dose related, and there have been consecutive exposures to an agent or agents that cause the disease, one innocent and one tortious, the position will depend upon which exposure came first in time. Where it was the tortious exposure, it is axiomatic that this will have contributed to causing the disease, even if it is not the sole cause. Where the innocent exposure came first, there may be an issue as to whether this was sufficient to trigger the disease or whether the subsequent, tortious, exposure contributed to the cause. I can see no reason in principle why the "doubles the risk" test should not be applied in such circumstances, but the court must be astute to see that the epidemiological evidence provides a really sound basis for determining the statistical probability of the cause or causes of the disease'[1].

Sienkiewicz demonstrates that there are several rules of law to determine causation; it is unclear as to why any one test applies to any set of facts.

1 *Sienkiewicz v Greif* [2011] UKSC 10, per Lord Phillips at [90] and [91].

Overview: science and law

15.74 The position has been explicitly recognised: the court has stated:

'... this approach, whereby the layman applying broad common sense draws an inference which the doctors as scientific witnesses are not prepared to draw, is one which is permissible'[1].

Causation is determined according to law, and law is manmade, whereas science is not. Given such judicial encouragement it is not surprising that medical and pharmaceutical claims are sometimes advanced on the basis of belief or hope, rather than evidence.

1 *Fairchild v Glenhaven Funeral Services Ltd* [2002] UKHL 22, per Lord Hutton at [100].

15.75 In recent years the courts have been used in attempts to find causal relationships new to established science. Despite huge expenditure, many actions, numerous claimants and much data, the legal process has not arrived at a single novel generic causal determination. Claims are advanced without any supportive peer reviewed probative published evidence, and in the face of unsupportive peer reviewed published probative evidence. There is absence of evidence, there is evidence of absence. The reasoning appears to be that because the absence of a causal relationship cannot be demonstrated by deductive logic, and absolute safety is unattainable, then related phenomena are taken to represent evidence of causality. Epiphenomena are over-interpreted. The distinction between descriptive and analytical epidemiology is disregarded. Possibility and probability become the same. After spending tens of millions of pounds of public money on this sort of litigation the Legal Services Commission concluded: 'The courts are not the place to prove new medical truths'[1].

1 Legal Services Commission 'Decision to remove funding for MMR litigation upheld on appeal' Press Statement, 1 October 2003

15.76 The judicial process has analysed and assessed scientific data according to principle where such evidence has been available to determine liability. The recent decisions of the House of Lords and the Supreme Court which involved deviations from principle in the interests of justice have involved cases where the underlying causal relationship between exposure and outcome was established, and the legal issue was finding primary liability where the evidence was incomplete.

PROXIMATE CAUSATION: FAILURE TO WARN

15.77 The relationship between a doctor and a patient is factually complex; the doctor's interaction with a patient can involve counselling, diagnosis and treatment. Likewise, a drug manufacturer's relationship with a patient is complex. There is a learned intermediary interposed between the manufacturer and the patient; however, this relationship can be qualified by patient information leaflets. Issues of proximate causation raise difficult issues of the hypothetical advice of the doctor and the hypothetical choice of the patient.

Hypothetical action of doctor to be proven on available evidence

15.78 Increasingly, medical negligence and product liability claims are framed in terms of defective or negligent warnings, whether in addition to or instead of allegation of negligent procedures or defective products[1]. Indeed, the eponymous *Bolam*[2] case included an allegation of negligent failure to warn. In such actions issues of proximate causation are raised. It raises difficult issues of historical fact: what the doctor actually advised. However, it is the issues of hypothetical fact which create the greatest difficulties. This involves such issues as how the doctor would have acted if he had been properly informed by an adequately worded datasheet; how the patient would have elected if he had been properly counselled by an adequately warned doctor.

1 See *Sidaway v Board of Governors of Bethlem Royal Hospital* [1985] AC 871; and *Benzodiazepine Litigation* [1996] 7 Med LR 267.
2 *Bolam v Friern Hospital Management Committee* [1957] 2 All ER 118.

15.79 At English law such questions of hypothetical fact are treated as facts to be proved according to the evidence applying the 'but for' test; since they are hypothetical they will usually have to be proven by inference rather than by direct evidence. However, such facts nonetheless must be proven on a case-by-case basis[1]. English law does not operate by evidential presumptions (albeit rebuttable presumptions) in determining hypothetical facts which enable an inference to be drawn such that what ought to be done would have been done (*omnia praesumunter rite et solemniter esse acta*). This is a presumption which operates in some US states.

1 See *McWilliams v Sir William Arrol & Co Ltd* [1962] 1 WLR 295; *Wigley v British Vinegars Ltd* [1964] AC 307.

The subjective patient test

15.80 The hypothetical election (ie if properly warned) of a patient inadequately warned is treated as a fact to be determined on a case-by-case basis. This is sometimes referred to as the 'subjective basis'[1]. This is contrasted with the 'objective basis' where the issue of hypothetical fact is determined according to the election of a hypothetical reasonable patient. This is the approach favoured in Canada.[2]

1 See *Smith v Barking Health Authority* [1994] 5 Med LR 285.
2 See *Buchan v Ortho Pharmaceuticals (Canada) Ltd* (1986) 25 DLR (4th) 658; *Reibl v Hughes* (1980) 114 DLR 3d 1; *Arndt v Smith* (1997) 35 CCLT (2d) 233.

15.81 The difficulty faced by the courts is because this retrospective evidence is likely to be self-serving:

'... in the end the matter must be one for decision on a subjective basis. This must plainly as a matter of principle be right, because the question must be: If this plaintiff had been given the advice that she should have been given, would she have decided to undergo the operation or not? However, there is a peculiar difficulty involved in this sort of case – not least for the plaintiff herself – in giving, after the adverse outcome of the operation is known, reliable answers as to what she would have decided before the operation had she been given proper advice as to the risks inherent in it. Accordingly, it would, in my judgment be right in the ordinary case to give particular weight to the objective assessment. If everything points to the fact that a reasonable plaintiff, properly informed, would have assented to the operation, the assertion from the witness box, made after the adverse outcome is known, in a wholly artificial situation and in the knowledge that the outcome of the case depends on that assertion being maintained, does not carry great weight unless there are extraneous or additional factors substantiated'[1].

1 *Smith v Barking Health Authority* [1994] 5 Med LR 285, per Hutchison J at 288 and 289.

15.82 The English courts have not shied away from the difficulty of evaluating evidence according to the 'subjective test' but taking into consideration the 'objective basis'[1].

1 See *Smith v Salford Health Authority* [1994] 5 Med LR 321; *Smith v Tunbridge Wells Health Authority* [1994] 5 Med ER 334; *McAllister v Lewisham and North Southwark Health Authority* [1994] 5 Med LR 343; *Newell v Goldenberg* [1995] 6 Med LR 371; *Coker v Richmond Twickenham and Roehampton Area Health Authority* [1996] 7 Med LR 58; *Lybert v Warrington Health Authority* [1996] 7 Med LR 71, CA.

15.83 A House of Lords decision evaded the 'but for' test in a failure to warn case[1]. The court disregarded the weight of English authorities, preferring a single majority decision of a foreign court[2]. Where there had been a negligent failure to warn and the patient was unable to state that she would have declined the operation at all the court held that the claim should succeed:

'To leave the patient ... without a remedy, as the normal approach to causation would indicate, would render the duty useless in the cases where it is needed most. This would discriminate against those who cannot honestly say that they would have declined the operation once and for all if they had been warned. I would find that result unacceptable. The function of the law is to enable rights to be vindicated and to provide remedies where duties have been breached. Unless this is done the duty is a hollow one, stripped of all practical force and devoid of all content, it will have lost its ability to protect the patient and thus to fulfill the only purpose which brought it into existence. On policy grounds therefore I would hold that the test of causation is fulfilled in this case'[3].

1 *Chester v Afshar* [2004] UKHL 41.
2 *Chappel v Hart* (1998) MLC 0067.
3 *Chester v Afshar* [2004] UKHL 41, per Lord Hope of Craighead, at para 87.

COMMENT AND CONCLUSION

15.84 Causation is an issue of fact to be determined according to evidence but the criteria for its determination raise issues of law. The burden of proof is on the claimant and the standard of proof is the balance of probabilities. The determination of the issue of causation is independent of the determination of negligent conduct or defective product. However, there is no universal test for causation in the law. The modern position has been conveniently summarised by the House of Lords:

'It is now, I think, generally accepted that the "but for" test does not provide a comprehensive or exclusive test of causation in the law of tort. Sometimes, if rarely, it yields too restrictive an answer ... More often, applied simply and mechanically, it gives too expansive an answer ... But in the ordinary run of cases, satisfying the but for test is a necessary but not sufficient condition of establishing causation ...'[1].

And:

'... there is a danger, if special tests of causation are developed piecemeal to deal with perceived injustices in particular factual situations, that the coherence of our common law will be destroyed'[2].

1 *Chester v Afshar* [2004] UKHL 41, per Lord Bingham of Cornhill at para 8.
2 *Gregg v Scott* [2005] UKHL 2, per Lord Phillips of Worth Matravers at para 172.

15.85 Certain cases have been decided on the basis of policy rather than principle because the justice of the case appeared to require it. The result, however, has been uncertainty and, with respect, judicial indiscipline. The case law provides ample illustrations of the maxim 'hard cases make bad law'. The House of Lords has stated:

'But, whether we like it or not, the law, which only Parliament can change, requires proof of fault causing damage as the basis of liability in tort. We should do society nothing but disservice if we made the forensic process still more unpredictable and hazardous by distorting the law to accommodate the exigencies of what may seem hard cases'[1].

It is for the courts to devise the rules that determine causation; the result is that development and distortion of the common law appear indistinguishable; flexibility and uncertainty become conflated; policy replaces principle. The determination of legal liability is a judicial function based on evidence.

1 *Wilsher v Essex Area Health Authority* [1988] 1 All ER 871, per Lord Bridge at 883.

CHAPTER 16

Epidemiology and statistics in litigation

Professor John N Newton

SUMMARY

INTRODUCTION

16.1   Epidemiology is the study of the distribution and determinants of health and illness in specified populations[1]. Since its earliest origin epidemiology has been, and remains, the scientific basis of public health practice. Statistics is the science and art of collecting, summarising and analysing data[1]. While nearly all epidemiology involves some statistics, they remain very different disciplines. This chapter will focus on epidemiology but with reference to relevant statistical concepts as necessary.

1 Last *A Dictionary of Epidemiology* (3rd edn, 1995).

16.2   Epidemiology emerged as a recognisable discipline with the London Epidemiological Society of the 1850s and John Snow's classic work on cholera. However, the foundations for this work had clearly been laid earlier by Graunt and then Farr who set up progressively more effective systems for the routine recording and compilation of numbers and causes of death[1]. Epidemiologists were predominantly concerned with infectious diseases until sometime after the Second World War, when attention turned from infections to the major chronic diseases, such as cancer and heart disease. The term 'modern epidemiology' was coined to refer to a set of methods developed by these post-war pioneer epidemiologists such as Sir Richard Doll[2], and which still make up the core of the discipline today[3].

1 Hennekens and Buring (eds) *Epidemiology in Medicine* (1987).
2 Peto and Beral 'Doll, Sir (William) Richard Shaboe (1912–2005)' *Oxford Dictionary of National Biography* (2009) (www.oxforddnb.com/view/article/95920).
3 Rothman and Greenland *Modern Epidemiology* (1998).

16.3   These methods were developed to provide a reliable framework for assessing the effect on the health of groups of people due to various potential hazards to health such as tobacco, radiation, diet or inherited predisposition. Sometimes the aim is simply to provide explanations for observed patterns of ill health but more often it is with a view to identifying those factors amenable to intervention. An early application of the new methods was to provide the evidence that cigarette smoking caused lung cancer long before the mechanism was understood, let alone demonstrated[1]. An epidemic of lung cancer was becoming apparent after the Second World War. A number of causes were suggested including occupation, and the effect of systematically surfacing roads with compounds derived from tar (a known carcinogen). The early studies showed that patients with lung cancer were much more likely to be smokers than those who did not smoke[1]. However, these case-control studies (as they are now known) from England, Germany and the USA were generally not believed because the methods were unfamiliar and relatively opaque. As a result Doll and colleagues set out to design a definitive follow-up or cohort study to provide more easily understood epidemiological evidence. It is worth noting that although more persuasive, the results of the cohort study of British Doctors[2] were quantitatively exactly the same as the studies available more than ten years earlier, confirming the validity of the case-control approach.

1 Doll and Hill 'A study of the aetiology of carcinoma of the lung' (1952) 2(4797) BMJ 1271–1286.
2 Doll and Hill 'Mortality in Relation to Smoking: Ten Years' Observations of British Doctors' (1964) 1(5396) BMJ 1460–1467 Conclusion.

16.4   Since then there have been numerous examples of epidemiological evidence providing the basis for action to safeguard health, through direct observation of what actually happens in human populations rather than by extrapolating from theories and experiments conducted in laboratories, or on small groups of experimental subjects in the field. The potential benefits of epidemiology are therefore considerable in understanding the risks associated with everyday life, environmental exposures and aspects of health care such as the safety of medicines or clinical devices. However, pitfalls abound in this field and epidemiological practice requires strict attention to underlying principles of good practice to produce valid results. For those using the results of these studies, including in relation to litigation, some understanding of these epidemiological concepts is essential to the correct interpretation and application of those results. Provision of that understanding is the aim of this chapter.

16.5 The problems associated with interpretation of epidemiology as evidence are mostly intrinsic to its nature. The approach relies on careful observation of patterns of occurrence of ill health and its causes in populations and exploits the natural variation that almost always exists within those populations. As Doll once said, if we all smoked it would have been very difficult to show that smoking caused lung cancer. Fortunately actual examples of near universal exposures are rare but are problematic for epidemiologists when they occur (for example after successful vaccination programmes almost all children will be exposed to the vaccine). The problems of interpretation in epidemiology have been well described[1] and will be covered in more detail later in the chapter. For example, it may be difficult to collect all the information required accurately and completely, and in a representative manner. Also, reliance on natural variation can make it very difficult to distinguish which of a number of factors that vary together is the true cause of the observed effect and which is the 'fellow traveller'. Finally, it has been pointed out that many important effects are quantitatively quite small and these can be very difficult to detect reliably[2]. However, most, if not all, of these problems can be overcome with good design and sound interpretation of the results. Epidemiology continues to provide important evidence in litigation and in public health practice.

1 Grimes and Schulz 'Bias and causal associations in observational research' (2002) 359(9302) Lancet 248–252.
2 Taubes 'Epidemiology faces its limits' (1995) 269(5221) Science 164–169.

16.6 A particular problem in establishing causal relationships from epidemiological studies is the fact that relevant studies are based on systematic interpretation of observations of events in the real world without any manipulation of those events by the investigator. This may be because the interventions are too complex (such as the effect of certain occupations) to be manipulated in a trial or the outcomes too long term (the effect of smoking on lung cancer takes 20 years to be apparent) or most commonly because it would be obviously ethically unacceptable to randomly allocate a group of people to, for example, drink above recommended limits or engage in unsafe sexual practices. However, this is not so much a criticism of epidemiology but recognition of the fact that many important questions (that might be relevant to litigation) are simply not amenable to experimental study. We cannot recreate the Big Bang to study the origins of the universe and we cannot randomly allocate families to live in areas of high radon or close to nuclear power stations to find out if it is dangerous to do so.

16.7 It is an interesting observation that in both litigation and public health practice, there is no ability to select the question at issue – it is a given – whereas in the world of funded academic science there is a bias towards selecting questions for study which are amenable to methods with high validity (especially randomised controlled trials) and therefore likely to meet the requirements of peer review. Thus, it is this author's view that there is often a poor match between the body of funded and published research and the requirement for evidence in litigation and in public health practice.

16.8   The limitations of randomised controlled trials are most obvious in the area of drug safety. Clinical trials undertaken before a drug is marketed demonstrate effectiveness and detect common side effects but cannot confirm safety. It is relatively common for more unusual or unsuspected side effects to only become apparent after the drug is marketed[1].

1 Rawlins 'Spontaneous reporting of adverse drug reactions' (1986) 59 (230) QJ Med 531–534.

16.9   Epidemiology has featured from time to time in litigation, perhaps most commonly in relation to establishing the effects of certain drugs, vaccines, medical devices or environmental exposures including occupational exposures. Some very significant cases involving drugs such as thalidomide, Debendox and third-generation contraceptives relied heavily on epidemiological evidence. But such evidence is not just relevant to drug safety issues: the effect of the MMR vaccine, silicone breast implants, and exposure to environmental tobacco smoke in the workplace have all been subject to litigation contested on the basis of epidemiological data. The application of statistics can crop up in almost any case of clinical negligence where quantitative data are at issue or the play of chance and probability are being considered.

16.10   Unfortunately, useful epidemiological evidence may only become available some years after a putative causal relationship has become the subject of litigation. In the case of silicone breast implants, by 1992 there were numerous reports of groups of women with silicone implants who had developed auto-immune disease of various kinds but there were no studies comparing the frequency of such disease in women with or without implants[1]. As a result the manufacturers found it very difficult to defend claims for compensation. However, many good quality epidemiological studies were initiated as a result of the concerns and have consistently failed to demonstrate an association between such implants and auto-immune disease[1]. When the outcome of these studies became apparent, one industry commentator responded:

'It would have been nice to have had this [evidence] $7 billion ago'.

1 Brown 'Epidemiology of silicone-gel breast implants' (2002) 13(3) Epidemiology S34–39.

DEFINITIONS, TERMINOLOGY AND APPROACH

Frequency

16.11   A basic element of epidemiology is some measure of how common the condition is in the population. It requires a careful count of disease occurrences in relation to the people and time spans in which they occur. This is not easy to achieve. Studies that count cases of disease without paying adequate attention to quantifying the population from which those cases are drawn can be very misleading.

Distribution

16.12 The next consideration will generally be to determine who within the population studied is getting the disease, where and when. This can be done by comparing rates in different populations, in the same population at different times or between subgroups of the same population at the same time. Consistent patterns of disease occurrence may then emerge.

Determinants

16.13 Studies of the distribution of disease tend to suggest a number of possible causal hypotheses. These can then be further investigated in studies designed to test those hypotheses. Conclusions can then be drawn about the underlying determinants of observed patterns of disease occurrence.

Exposures and diseases

16.14 Epidemiologists use a common terminology to describe the two elements of their hypotheses. Thus, all factors that might be altering the risk of a disease occurring are referred to as 'exposures'. These 'exposures' might include such diverse influences on health as radiation, smoking, using a particular drug, low income, being a vegetarian or reading the The Times newspaper. Exposure levels can also be quantified to generate a notional 'dose', for example in terms of the length of time a drug was taken or the number of cigarettes smoked per day or the extent of adherence to a particular diet etc. In the same way all constructs affected by exposures tend to be termed 'diseases' even though some of them may be more correctly described in other ways, for example as health outcomes, syndromes, or as variants of normal health.

Measures of risk

16.15 Measures of disease frequency are either incidence or prevalence rates. Both take into account the numbers of affected individuals and the size of the population from which they are derived:

- when counting cases of a disease with a relatively short time course (say an infectious disease or a malignant cancer) it is usually most helpful to know how many new cases occurred over a period of time. This is the **incidence rate**. Both the number of people observed and the length of time over which they were observed are important when calculating incidence rates. Incidence rates are most commonly used when trying to understand the causes of a disease;
- for long-lasting conditions (for example diabetes or arthritis) it may be more useful to know what proportion of the population are affected at any particular time. This is known as the **prevalence**. Prevalence is especially important in understanding the burden of illness in the population.

16.16   To allow comparison between populations, both incidence and prevalence are expressed using round numbers for the population size. Thus, whatever the number of people actually observed the incidence rate will be expressed as numbers of cases per 1,000, 10,000 or million per year, depending on the rarity of the condition. In turn, prevalence may be expressed as a percentage, as in '2 per cent of the population have diabetes', or, for less common conditions, per 1,000, per 10,000 etc. It is important to remember that prevalence is always a proportion not a rate.

16.17   Both incidence and prevalence can be thought of as measures of 'risk'. The first is a probabilistic assessment of the risk of a person developing the disease in a given time; the second is the risk that they will have the disease at any particular time.

16.18   In order to extrapolate from a published incidence rate or prevalence to an individual, it must be assumed that the person in question is similar to those in the observed population in all material ways. In practice, individual risk will vary a lot from person to person, perhaps due to inherited factors[1]. The population estimate of risk (obtained from a research study or survey) will at best be a measure of the average risk of people similar to the group as a whole in the measured characteristics (for example by age, sex and smoking status). It will only provide an approximate guide to an individual's risk and therefore the probability of causation in that individual. However, when applied appropriately to a group of people the incidence rate will accurately predict how many cases will occur over a period in the group as a whole. Thus, there will always be individuals within the group whose experience differs from the average. This phenomenon explains the anecdotal grandfather who smoked and drank his way to his 90th birthday without a day's illness.

1 Robins and Greenland 'The probability of causation under a stochastic model for individual risk' (1989) 45(4) Biometrics 1125–1138.

Measures of association

16.19   In order to investigate the determinants of ill health, epidemiologists first look for statistical associations between exposures and diseases. By definition, when an association exists the probability of the disease is different in the presence of the exposure from the corresponding probability in its absence[1]. An association in this sense implies some relationship between the exposure and the disease but not necessarily a causal one. However, it is logically impossible for an exposure to be a cause unless an association exists. If the occurrence rate of a disease is the same in an exposed group as it is in an otherwise similar group that is not exposed, then there is no association and that exposure cannot be a cause of the disease. In some situations the relevant causal association may be numerically very small and therefore difficult to measure (for example the increased risk of cancer due to exposure to environmental tobacco smoke) but if there is a causal relationship the association will still be there to be measured by a large enough study.

1 Hennekens, Buring *Epidemiology in Medicine* (1987) p 30.

16.20   Comparing the risk of disease in two groups usually requires measurement of the risk in each separately. For convenience of expression, the two results are combined in a summary measure that becomes a measure of the strength or importance of the association. The *ratio* of the two risks describes how much more likely one group is to develop the disease than the other. A high ratio implies a strong association. The *difference* between the risks shows how much greater the risk is in one group than the other.

16.21 The ratio measure is known as the '**relative risk**' and the difference measure is the '**attributable risk**'. The relative risk is the best measure of how closely the exposure is associated with the disease. The attributable risk gives an idea of how many cases of the disease are caused by the exposure in affected groups, and therefore what benefits might result from an effective intervention. The public health importance of an increase in the rate of a disease depends on how common it is in the population as well as the size of the increase.

EPIDEMIOLOGICAL METHODS

Descriptive studies

16.22 Epidemiological studies are either descriptive or analytical. **Descriptive studies** report the distribution of disease states without regard to cause[1]. Interpretation of observed patterns may give useful clues as to the underlying causes of the disease in question. However, before any conclusions are drawn these speculative ideas must be crystallised into formal hypotheses that can be tested **in analytical studies** (see below). Descriptive studies are therefore useful for hypothesis generation but not for testing hypotheses and are therefore rarely convincing as evidence in litigation. They do, however, provide important additional information in epidemiology when estimating the population burden of a risk (as in what proportion of lung cancers are due to smoking versus those due to radon exposure). Also, with certain rare exposures and diseases descriptive studies may be convincing in their own right and may be the only evidence available (perhaps because the putative cause was a drug that has been withdrawn from use).

1 Grimes and Schulz 'Descriptive studies: what they can and cannot do' (2002) 359(9301) Lancet 145–149.

16.23 There are a number of types of descriptive study. The simplest form is the **case report**. A number of cases reported together become a **case series**. These rarely rise above the level of anecdote but can occasionally trigger a line of investigation that bears fruit[1].

1 Sesoko and Kaneko 'Cough associated with the use of captopril' (1985) 145(8) Archives of Internal Medicine. 1524.

16.24 In the published literature case reports and case series are used:

- to document the limits of the natural history of unusual diseases, such as in the case of the so-called 'Elephant Man';
- to remind the reader of some already-known fact in a form that is easy to remember;
- to invite readers to report similar patients;
- to report a possible association that may warrant further investigation.

16.25 The problem here for epidemiologists is that the reported cases may not be representative of all cases of the disease in the population. What is true for them may or may not be true for other less 'interesting' cases. Thus, the fact that all the reported cases share an exposure does not guarantee that all cases occurring in the population from which they are drawn will have been so exposed. It may be that only the exposed cases came to the notice of the author or that only the exposed cases were reported. The cases may be **selected** in some way that is related to their exposure. The exposure then seems to be associated with the disease.

For example, a substantial proportion of cases of headache referred to a neurologist will be shown to have a brain tumour. This does not mean that all people with headache need to be scanned. The patients seen by neurologists are selected by GPs for referral because their clinical history suggests a possible tumour.

16.26 Case series can in certain circumstances be considered de facto epidemiological studies. This is only true if they are identified from defined populations in such a way that any case occurring in that population would have an equal chance of being included in the reported series (usually from an existing disease register). Examples include the author's own studies of the epidemiology of carcinoid tumours and myocardial infarction[1]. In particular the chance of inclusion in the study as a case must not be affected in any way by any of the exposures of interest. If it is, then the exposure in question will appear to be associated with the disease. This independence can be accomplished either by including *all* cases that fit a stated definition or by including a *random sample* of such cases.

1 Newton, Swerdlow, dos Santos Silva, Vessey, Grahame-Smith, Primatesta (et al) 'The epidemiology of carcinoid tumours in England and Scotland' (1994) 70(5) British Journal of Cancer 939–42; Volmink, Newton, Hicks, Sleight, Fowler, Neil 'Coronary event and case fatality rates in an English population: results of the Oxford myocardial infarction incidence study' The Oxford Myocardial Infarction Incidence Study Group (1998) 80(1) Heart 40–44.

16.27 It is important to stress that the conditions mentioned above are rarely met in practice so it is still important to treat case series with considerable scepticism. The well-known MMR study[1] published in the Lancet in 1998 and later withdrawn is a classic case in point. The cases were said to be consecutive referrals (which in itself is not an unbiased method of ascertainment) but in fact it was later shown that they were not even consecutive referrals, they were selected to fit the pre-existing hypothesis.

1 Wakefield, Murch, Anthony, Linnell, Casson, Malik (et al) 'Ileal-lymphoid-nodular hyperplasia, non-specific colitis, and pervasive developmental disorder in children' (1998) 351(9103) Lancet 637–641.

16.28 For case series and case reports, information on levels of exposure is lacking from a comparison group that does not have the disease. This limits the extent to which one can draw inferences about any association although unfortunately authors are often still tempted to do so. For example:

- an analysis of 75 hang-gliding accidents in the Austrian Tyrol showed that most accidents occurred between 11am and 3pm. The authors suggested that unfavourable thermic conditions were responsible for the timing of the accidents. They recommended that flying should be encouraged at other times of day. However, there is no comparison group. It would seem feasible, even likely, that uneventful flights would also mostly have occurred between 11am and 3pm;

- the Elephant Man may have smoked, played cards and read romantic novels but that is not why he had neuro-fibromatosis.

16.29 Most drugs that are withdrawn from the market on safety grounds are done so based on the results of case reports[1], although the role of more reliable study designs seems to be increasing. Case reports can therefore provide compelling evidence in certain situations. To a large extent the value of a case series (which is by its nature uncontrolled) depends on how common the exposure and the disease in question are in the general population. If both are known to be rare then reporting a small number of cases all of which share the exposure strongly suggests an association even without access to a control group. If either the exposure or the disease are common then the co-existence of the two is inevitable in a number of cases and reporting this is not informative. The following are examples of unusual exposures and unusual diseases occurring together:

- in 1981, in three Los Angeles hospitals, five young previously healthy homosexual men were found to have developed pneumocystis carinii pneumonia. This unusual coincidence led to the identification of the AIDS syndrome;
- initial observations in the USA showed that almost all cases of a newly-described condition eosinophilia myalgia syndrome had been taking a dietary supplement called L-tryptophan. Up to 2% of the population may have been taking L-tryptophan, but the fact that all the cases had been exposed to it was an important observation. It was later established that the form of drug consumed by the cases contained an unusual contaminant introduced during its manufacture. Withdrawal of L-tryptophan from the market halted the epidemic;
- randomised trials show little or no increase in reported side effects in patients taking statins compared with placebo, however a number of case reports have described the very rare condition acute rhabdomyolysis in patients taking statins and it is generally accepted that this is a causal relationship[2].

1 McNaughton, Huet and Shakir 'An investigation into drug products withdrawn from the EU market between 2002 and 2011 for safety reasons and the evidence used to support the decision-making' (2014) 4(1) BMJ Open; Clarke, Deeks and Shakir 'An assessment of the publicly disseminated evidence of safety used in decisions to withdraw medicinal products from the UK and US markets (2006) 29(2) Drug Safety: an international journal of medical toxicology and drug experience 175–181.
2 Mendes, Robles and Mathur 'Statin-induced rhabdomyolysis: a comprehensive review of case reports' (2014) 66(2) Physiotherapy Canada 124–132.

Cross-sectional studies

16.30 Cross-sectional studies collect information on exposure status and disease status simultaneously from a population of individuals. These can be helpful because the cases are more representative than those in case series. Also, good information is available on exposure levels in the population. The major problem with this design is that it is impossible to know whether exposure preceded the disease state or was a result of it, as in the example below. Cross-sectional studies are therefore most useful to study exposures that do not change over time, such as sex, race or specific genetic factors:

- teenagers with acne show high levels of anxiety and other mood disorders. For many years it was thought that acne was partly caused by 'stress', whereas it now seems more likely that the acne causes the patients' mood disorders.

16.31 Cross-sectional studies can be contrasted with longitudinal studies where observations on levels of exposure and diseases are made at different points in time, either in the same individuals or in groups with similar characteristics. The former (observations on the same individuals) are cohort studies and indeed the term longitudinal study is often used as a synonym for cohort study (see below).

Ecological studies

16.32 In ecological studies rates of diseases are examined in relation to the characteristics of the whole population. Exposure data on individuals within the population may not be available. This works particularly well when the exposure in question is an 'ecological' exposure or in some way affects the whole population more or less equally (for example temperature or hours of sunlight). Epidemiologists look for correlation between rates of disease and rates of exposure among the populations studied. Ecological studies have been important in nutrition studies, showing for example that countries with high saturated fat consumption tend to have high rates of cardiovascular disease and that high salt intake correlates with levels of hypertension. These studies do not prove that the individuals with these diseases have the high intake and indeed they may not. Although important, these studies frequently lead to lengthy debate about the interpretation of the results.

16.33 Ecological studies are difficult to interpret and subject to a number of potential problems, including the so-called ecological fallacy[1]. Unfortunately, relationships seen at the group level (northern areas have high mortality) may not be true relationships in individuals (if a person moves north it does not increase their mortality). There are a number of technical explanations for this[2] but they all lead to erroneous conclusions being drawn of the 'television aerials cause cancer' type (wealthy areas tend to have more TVs and more cancers). Also, by contrast, effects seen at the individual level may be masked or absent at the level of whole populations.

1 Greenland and Robins 'Invited commentary: ecologic studies – biases, misconceptions, and counterexamples' (1994) 139(8) American Journal of Epidemiology 747–760.
2 Greenland and Morgenstern 'Ecological bias, confounding, and effect modification' (1989) 18(1) International Journal of Epidemiology 269–274.

16.34 Examples of ecological studies:

- studies of rates of dental disease in counties of England showed that rates were lower in counties with high levels of naturally occurring fluoride in the water. Similar observations around the world led to the widespread use of fluoride to prevent tooth decay;
- for populations that are mostly white-skinned, rates of skin cancer can be shown to be greater in countries such as Australia and New Zealand,

than in countries that are further from the equator. This suggests that sun exposure on a white skin is a cause of skin cancer.

Secular trend analysis

16.35   Secular trend analysis is a type of ecological study in which changes in rates of disease over time are compared with changes in average exposure rates in that population. (Not to be confused with a longitudinal study which is another name for a cohort study, see below). For example:

- there was a steep decline in the rate of infant deaths in England and Wales after the introduction of the Midwives Act in 1902. This is thought to be due to improved supervision of births by qualified midwives and the subsequent avoidance of postnatal sepsis;
- death rates in Britain from tuberculosis substantially declined in the period from 1855 to 1950, ie before the introduction of specific therapy. This is thought to be due to improvements in general living conditions and sanitary reforms;
- the introduction of seat belt legislation in the UK was followed by a decline in deaths from head injuries.

16.36   Secular trend analysis faces a number of problems. One difficulty may be distortion in trends over time due to changes in the classification or rate of diagnosis of the disease in question. Also, it is often not known what lag time to expect between exposure and disease. Empirical methods that solve this problem by choosing a lag time in order to maximise the apparent association can be very misleading.

16.37   Perhaps the biggest problem facing any ecological or time trend design is the lack of specificity involved in making comparisons (sometimes called multiple collinearity). There will be many differences between groups defined geographically or over time. It may be impossible to know which of those differences may account for the observed differences in disease rates. For example, is the increase in gun crime in the UK in recent years due to increases in illicit drug use, a change of government, greater use of mobile phones, or none of these? There are more cases of allergy in children now than there were 30 years ago: is that caused by increasing levels of chemicals in our water supply, antibiotics changing our gut flora or trends in bedroom flooring materials?

16.38   Ecological studies can be reassuring where distinct changes in patterns of exposure are known and yet no matching change can be seen in the disease in question, as in the example below:

- Darby and Doll showed that there was no temporal association between measured levels of radiation fallout from weapons testing and rates of childhood leukaemia in three European countries between 1945 and 1985.

Surveillance systems

16.39   Surveillance systems are sometimes considered to be a particular kind of descriptive study[1]. Surveillance is defined as the ongoing, systematic collection of information and its dissemination to those who can take action as a result. Surveillance is an important form of protection for the population and is typically used to identify outbreaks of infectious diseases or unexpected side effects of drugs.

1 Grimes, Schulz 'Descriptive studies: what they can and cannot do' (2002) 359(9301) Lancet 145–149.

16.40 A strong surveillance system uses a variety of sources of data, such as routine death records or hospital records as well as specific notifications, to ensure that important patterns of events are not missed. Surveillance is said to be 'active' if information is explicitly sought by the group undertaking surveillance, for example by conducting surveys or periodically examining databases. Passive surveillance relies on notifications of events by others, for example the 'yellow card' system for reporting suspected adverse events in the UK[1].

1 Rawlins MD. Spontaneous reporting of adverse drug reactions. Q J Med. 1986;59(230):531-4.

16.41 Post marketing surveillance of drugs is an important exercise undertaken after drugs are licensed for use. Information is routinely analysed to identify rare side effects that were not identified during clinical trials. Established approaches include monitoring of GP databases such as the General Practice Research Database.

16.42 Passive surveillance may be incomplete (cases are missed). However, provided a constant proportion of cases is notified, trends may still be apparent. In practice, active surveillance is rarely possible at the level of whole populations.

Analytical studies

16.43 Descriptive studies usually suggest a range of interesting causal hypotheses for any given disease. It is then necessary to find out which, if any, of those hypotheses represent valid models of disease causation that should guide public health policy. Undertaking appropriately designed analytical studies is the only way to do that.

16.44 Ideally an experiment would be performed in which all factors that might affect the outcome of interest are controlled except for the exposure, which can then be varied under the control of the investigator. This ideal is rarely achievable in biological models because of the extent of variation between individual subjects. In relation to most important factors, there tends to be unpredictable variation in risk between subjects. In clinical trials the random allocation of subjects to receive an intervention is a good compromise. There will be variation in risk of disease within each group but on average the groups will be comparable except that one received the intervention and the other did not. The effect of exposure on outcome is then apparent provided the groups can be followed up reliably and for long enough:

- in a randomised controlled trial patients with a defined condition are randomly assigned to receive the treatment being investigated or a suitable comparator treatment. The results are then assessed in all patients without knowledge of which treatment each received. Any consistent differences in outcome between the groups should be due to differences in the two treatments. In every other way each group should be representative of the whole study population because they were randomly chosen.

16.45 Random allocation is a powerful technique but is not universally applicable. This is because there are many situations where it is not possible to control exposure for the purpose of a study (ie to assign factors randomly). This may be for ethical or practical reasons. It is unreasonable to randomly allocate subjects to receive 'lifestyle' exposures such as smoking, alcohol or sexual orientation. It would be impractical to attempt the random allocation of an exposure such as income, area of residence or occupation. Furthermore once an intervention has been shown to be effective it may be unethical to perform further randomised clinical trials to assess possible adverse events. Also, effects that occur a long time after exposure are very difficult to study in experiments because of the requirement for prior allocation.

Cohort studies

16.46 In situations where experiment is not possible, the next best thing is the cohort study, sometimes referred to as a 'natural experiment'. As for a clinical trial, the outcome in different exposure groups is compared except that in a cohort study the investigator does not control exposure. Subjects are recruited disease free on the basis of their exposure status. Subsequent disease status is then studied over a period. Because most diseases are rare very large numbers of subjects are often required and follow up may need to go on for years or even decades before possible associations are confirmed or excluded. One of the largest cohort studies in the world is the UK Biobank[1] which has successfully recruited 500,000 participants, examined them and stored samples of their blood and urine for subsequent analysis. It may take 30 years for the full value of this study to be realised and it was controversial from the outset for this reason[2].

1 www.ukbiobank.ac.uk.
2 'Barbour v UK Biobank: a project in search of a protocol?' (2003) 361(9370) Lancet 1734–1738.

16.47 Prospective cohort studies are most reliable because data on exposure is actively sought before disease status is known. The alternative is a retrospective cohort study, in which exposure data is collected from historical records and the subjects then 'followed up' to the present day. Retrospective studies are less reliable but produce results more quickly.

16.48 Cohort studies are particularly good for investigating associations between multiple diseases and a single exposure, for example in an occupational group. They are also necessary to determine the incidence rate of a disease in an exposed group, hence their alternative name 'incidence studies':

• in the long-running British Doctors Study, Richard Doll followed a large number of doctors prospectively for 40 years. Information on smoking and drinking habits was collected at the outset and at intervals during follow up. The effect of these exposures on cancer and heart disease was reported at different times.

Case-control studies

16.49   In a cohort study large groups of exposed and unexposed subjects are followed up in order to count and compare numbers of cases occurring in each group. In a case-control study the time-consuming and expensive follow-up process is dispensed with and to begin with only the cases of disease are identified. Some of these will be exposed and others will not. If the exposure is a cause of the disease the proportion of cases of disease that are exposed will be greater than the level of exposure in the general population. In order to determine the latter a sample of individuals are drawn from the unaffected population so that their exposure can be assessed. These controls should be similar, in respect of age, sex and other factors, to the cases but should be without the disease. Exposure levels in the cases can then be compared with those in the controls.

16.50   Case control studies are observational but also retrospective in that exposure status is determined after disease has developed. This makes them especially susceptible to errors of recall and other so-called information biases (see below). Also, the selection of appropriate cases and controls can be problematic. Any process of selection that favours particular groups may produce misleading estimates of exposure levels in the cases or in the population. Nevertheless case-control studies can be very helpful, for example:

- case-control studies showed that cases of the rare childhood condition Reye's syndrome were more likely to have been given aspirin shortly before the onset of their illness than children admitted to hospital with other febrile illnesses. For this reason, aspirin is no longer given to children.

Other study designs

16.51   Although case-control and cohort designs are the two fundamental approaches to analytical epidemiology there are many variations on these core designs developed to suit different settings. For example, in the case of assessing vaccine safety four different methods have been compared using a simulation[1]. These included a standard cohort approach and a 'nested' case-control within a cohort study. Basing or 'nesting' a case-control study in a cohort design improves validity because cases and controls are more representative and is more suitable for assessing the risk of rare events than a cohort design. Another approach compared was the self-controlled risk interval case series design[2]. This is a particular approach that can be used to assess the temporal link between an exposure such as vaccination and a suggested outcome such as onset of encephalitis. The method uses sets of time periods and compares the risk of the event occurring in the period soon after the event compared to at any other time including before the event. Only cases are required and so it is very efficient.

1 Glanz, McClure, Xu, Hambidge, Lee, Kolczak (et al) 'Four different study designs to evaluate vaccine safety were equally validated with contrasting limitations' (2006) 59(8) Journal of Clinical Epidemiology 808–818.
2 Whitaker, Hocine and Farrington 'The methodology of self-controlled case series studies' (2009) 18(1) Statistical Methods in Medical Research 7–26.

ISSUES OF VALIDITY

16.52   Powerful techniques though they are, epidemiological studies are subject to important constraints. Data collection, study design and data analysis all require careful attention if valid results are to be obtained. The rigour applied to the interpretation of those results is also very important to the validity of the conclusions. It is a sad fact that many published papers fail to meet adequate standards in some way even in high profile journals such as the Lancet. The editors of the Lancet said:

'Following the judgment of the UK General Medical Council's Fitness to Practise Panel on Jan 28, 2010, it has become clear that several elements of the 1998 paper by Wakefield et al are incorrect, contrary to the findings of an earlier investigation. In particular, the claims in the original paper that children were "consecutively referred" and that investigations were "approved" by the local ethics committee have been proven to be false'.

16.53   Published epidemiological studies must therefore be read with a critical eye, and carefully considered in the context of other work before the conclusions are accepted. The most precise instrument can be a 'blunt tool' in the wrong hands.

16.54   Validity can be compromised by problems of two general kinds. The first are due to the play of chance or other causes of natural variability between subjects. The second are due to factors in the design of the study. In both cases alternative explanations may account for the observed findings. The authors must have considered and convincingly discounted these alternatives if their conclusions are to be relied on.

Statistical significance, confidence intervals and power

16.55   The interpretation of observed differences between groups of subjects is the basis of epidemiology. In a cohort study a difference in disease rates between the exposed and non-exposed subjects may suggest an association. In a case-control study a difference in exposure rates in cases compared with controls may do the same.

16.56   It is stated above that the occurrence of disease in particular individuals is essentially unpredictable. However, as the number of individuals observed increases it becomes possible to predict the number of cases occurring in the group with increasing precision. By analogy, the result of a single toss of a coin is unpredictable. If a coin is tossed fairly 100 times it is a good bet that close to 50 per cent of results will be heads. If tossed a thousand times it is almost a certainty.

16.57   If a study does not include very many subjects then the proportion that become cases of disease may be very unpredictable. The results will suffer from a lot of 'noise' that will swamp any 'signal'. Statistical methods can predict the extent to which chance might be an explanation of the observed results, taking account of the numbers of cases and other information about the study. Thus, when a result is presented it should carry a statistical 'health warning'. This may be in the form of a *P*-value, the result of a significance test or a confidence interval. These are all measures of **precision** or **statistical significance**.

16.58   There are many pitfalls in the interpretation of these statistical health warnings. For example, a statistically significant result is commonly taken to be a result that has only a 1 in 20 chance of occurring in a study of this size if no association existed. If a number of studies are performed, or if a single study generates many results, it is easy to see that 'significant' results will occur not infrequently even if no association exists. Every time a 'significant' result is acted on one is effectively playing 'Russian roulette' with a revolver that has 20 spaces in the magazine and one bullet.

16.59   A confidence interval is nearly always preferable to a simple test of significance. It provides a range of values that would, if the study were repeated many times and similar methods used to calculate confidence intervals, be expected to contain the true result with a given probability. The lower limit of a confidence interval is equivalent to a test of significance. If it includes the null value the result is not significant. The null value is the value that represents no association between exposure and disease. It will be zero for a difference measure (ie the attributable risk) but will be 1.0 for a ratio measure (ie the relative risk).

16.60   The upper limit represents the level of association that can safely be rejected by the study. For example, a study may show that most likely there is no risk associated with a particular exposure but that if there is any risk it is fairly certain (95 per cent) that it is no greater than the value of the upper confidence limit. This is very important when trying to establish that an exposure is 'safe' (for example in the case of silicone breast implants). Because all studies will have some imprecision, confidence intervals will always demonstrate some 'spread'. It is therefore almost impossible to exclude a small increase in risk on statistical grounds. However, it is relatively easy to exclude large relative risks.

16.61   Errors due to lack of precision are of two main types. If a result due to chance variation is interpreted as showing an association where none actually exists that is said to be a 'Type I error'. Conversely, if a study fails to produce a result that achieves statistical significance it may be concluded that no association exists when in fact there is one. That is a 'Type II error'. Of course the 'true' situation is normally unknown but the probability of these errors can nevertheless be calculated.

16.62   The history of medical research suggests that both types of error are common. The current trend is for fewer but larger studies to be performed. These can produce definitive results with adequate precision and, therefore, acceptably low chances of Type I or Type II errors. The probability of these errors occurring can generally be predicted from the outset and studies designed accordingly, although this is not always done. The extent to which a study can be expected to produce results that are free from Type I or Type II errors is known as the **power** of the study. A powerful study will produce statistically precise results.

16.63 An important further consideration is that all the above statements about significance and power assume that the underlying data conform to the assumed statistical model. These models are generally derived from non-biological systems or purely theoretical mathematical constructs. For example, rare diseases are assumed to occur with a perfectly random distribution similar to the pattern of emissions from a radio-isotope over time (consider the chaotic rhythm of the clicks made by a Geiger counter). Actual data derived from human subjects are very likely to show greater unpredictable variation than the theoretical models would suggest (although they cannot show less). Thus, an estimate of precision such as a conventional confidence interval should be considered to be a *minimum* estimate of the potential for error. Robins and Greenland have pointed out in relation to litigation and compensation that because of the inevitable non-random (or stochastic) variation that exists between individuals the level of risk in any individual claimant is very difficult to estimate and is almost never going to be the same as the average[1].

1 Robins and Greenland 'The probability of causation under a stochastic model for individual risk' (1989) 45(4) Biometrics 1125–1138.

16.64 Finally, tests of significance assume that the study design is completely free from bias and confounding (see below). This is rarely the case.

Bias and confounding

16.65 Bias in epidemiology denotes deviation from the truth, but not necessarily prejudice[1]. There are many specific types of bias[2]. However, all these can usefully be thought of as either **selection biases** or **information biases**. Some authors include confounding as a form of bias although this author believes it should be considered separately.

1 Grimes and Schulz 'Bias and causal associations in observational research' (2002) 359(9302) Lancet 248–252.
2 Sackett 'Bias in analytic research' (1979) 32(1–2) Journal of Chronic Diseases 51–63.

16.66 **Selection bias** arises when the groups compared differ in some important respect for reasons related to the way they have been selected. Selection bias occurs when the inclusion or not of cases (or controls) in a study is in some way determined by their exposure status or a factor related to it[1]. Thus in a cohort study the groups may differ according to the exposure in question but also some other factor that alters their chance of developing the disease. For example, if the non-exposed subjects are volunteers recruited from newspaper advertisements they will tend to be healthier than the general population and therefore healthier than the exposed individuals, regardless of any effect of the exposure.

1 Last *A Dictionary of Epidemiology* (3rd edn, 1995).

16.67 **Information bias** arises when the complex processes of collecting data about cases or controls operate in subtly different ways for different groups. This can easily happen unless strict comparability of methods is enforced: for example, if a more assiduous search is made for cases among one group than another. The result is that either cases are wrongly classified as controls or vice versa, or perhaps more commonly the exposure status of either cases or controls is misclassified in some systematic way. For example, one form of information bias is recall bias in which cases of a disease are more likely to recall taking an implicated drug than controls who have no interest in or knowledge of the hypothesis.

16.68 To avoid selection bias in a cohort study, groups of subjects must on average be similar except for the exposure, and in a case-control study similar except for being a case or not. For example, in the Wakefield study of autism and measles the cases were not consecutive as stated in the paper; they were selected to be included because of their measles or status or vaccine history. To avoid information bias in a cohort study, information about disease must be obtained in a similar way for exposed and non-exposed groups, and in a case-control study information about exposure must be obtained in a similar way for cases and controls.

16.69 **Confounding** arises when some third factor is consistently associated with the exposure in question and is a cause of the disease[1]. Common confounding factors include age, sex, economic deprivation, smoking and diet. Any exposure that becomes more common as people age (for example playing bowls) will appear to be associated with most diseases. A study comparing a group of bowls players with a random sample of the population might easily conclude that the game was unhealthy unless differences in age between the two groups were taken into account.

1 Breslow and Day (eds) *Statistical methods in cancer research: Volume 1 - The analysis of case-control studies* (1980).

16.70 The difference between confounding and bias is that confounding is not a distortion of the truth. It represents a true result but not for the reason presumed by the investigator. Bowls players are more likely to be ill than the average person, but because they are older not because they play bowls. Confounding can be dealt with to an extent in various ways, either in the design or the analysis of a study. Bias is a more difficult problem to address. The results of a study afflicted by bias do not relate to any real association in the population. They are merely an artefact of that study.

16.71 All known causes of a disease have to be considered potential confounding factors and dealt with in the study design. Difficulties arise when there are unknown factors, which could be confounders (so called residual confounding). This phenomenon can only be dealt with convincingly by conducting a randomised trial. For example:

- a number of large cohort studies suggested that post-menopausal women who took hormone replacement therapy were protected from heart disease, even after taking account of all known potential confounding variables. However, there was still a strong suspicion that the women who took HRT differed in some way from those that did not take it, and that those differences were the true cause of differences in rates of heart disease. Subsequent randomised trials have indeed shown no benefit for HRT and heart disease.

INFERRING CAUSATION FROM ASSOCIATION

16.72   The final and often most challenging step in the epidemiological approach is a judgment as to whether an observed association represents a cause and effect relationship or not. A number of fundamental issues should be mentioned before specific approaches to making such judgments can be considered.

16.73   Causal relationships in biological systems are seldom straightforward. Galileo Galilei's concept of necessary and/or sufficient causes is not much used in epidemiology. Most exposures that can be shown to be associated with disease outcomes are neither necessary nor sufficient causes on their own. Epidemiologists tend to use terms such as 'predisposing', 'enabling', 'precipitating' or 'reinforcing' to explain the relationships that they uncover in their studies. The essential finding is that the presence of the 'cause' reliably increases or decreases the probability of the effect.

16.74   In many cases, robust data may show an important association between a cause and an effect when nothing may be known of the explanation for the association. For example:

- Lind had no idea why citrus fruits cured scurvy but from a simple set of experimental observations on the HMS Salisbury in 1753 he could show that they did;
- it was shown beyond doubt that thalidomide was teratogenic in the 1960s by direct observation of an association, since when more than 30 hypotheses have been advanced as a biological explanation but none has yet been proven[1].

1 Ito and Handa 'Deciphering the mystery of thalidomide teratogenicity' (2012) 52(1) Congenital Anomalies 1–7.

16.75   An approach that emphasises inputs and outputs rather than intermediate pathways has been called 'black-box epidemiology'[1]. Despite this somewhat disparaging epithet, such evidence can be intrinsically more reliable than evidence from artificial laboratory models or from animal studies[2]. Unlike epidemiological evidence the latter are not based on what is actually occurring in the population. Putative causal pathways derived from them are often merely informed guesswork.

1 Skrabanek 'The emptiness of the black box' (1994) 5(5) Epidemiology 553–555.
2 Lilienfeld and Stolley (eds) *Foundations of Epidemiology* (1994).

16.76   Weight of evidence from epidemiology alone can and should be decisive in certain circumstances[1], because epidemiology can provide information for action long before the mechanisms are understood. For example:

- studies in the 1950s showed that people with lung cancer were much more likely to be smokers than would be expected by chance. Only years later were the active components of tobacco smoke identified;
- the condition 'Toxic Shock Syndrome' a systemic life-threatening illness, was occurring much more commonly in women using newly-introduced 'super absorbent' tampons. The mechanism was unknown

but withdrawal of the tampons was effective in preventing further cases;

- case-control studies in the USA showed that children with viral infections who were given aspirin were more likely to develop a rare but serious illness known as Reye's syndrome. Since parents have been advised to use paracetamol instead of aspirin, numbers of cases of Reye's syndrome have fallen dramatically around the world. Years later the mechanism remains unknown.

1 Charlton 'Attribution of causation in epidemiology: chain or mosaic?' (1996) 49(1) Journal of Clinical Epidemiology 105–107.

16.77 All inference from epidemiology is based on inductive reasoning (as opposed to deductive logic) and therefore suffers from the problems exposed by empiricist philosophers such as Hume. The examples below illustrate the danger of extrapolating beyond observed data:

- a chicken found that every morning of its life the sun rose and the farmer's wife gave him some corn. One morning the sun rose and the farmer's wife wrung its neck. So much for inductive reasoning;
- a man jumped from the top of a very tall building. As he passed the 20th floor he was heard to call out 'so far so good'.

16.78 How can we be certain that relationships identified in study populations can safely be applied to other groups or in any sense considered to be universally true? Epidemiologists (and others) rely on arguments such as those put forward by Bertrand Russell, that there are certain natural laws that can be discovered and these allow extrapolation beyond what can be directly observed. If not, we would all be paralysed by uncertainty in everyday life let alone in science. However, mistakes can easily be made when extrapolating beyond observed data without supporting evidence. For example, when first imported into Europe, botanists advised that the tomato was almost certainly poisonous because the plant is closely related to the deadly nightshade[1] and indeed the berries of the related potato plant are toxic.

1 Goodwin and Goodwin 'The tomato effect. Rejection of highly efficacious therapies' (1984) 251(18) Journal of the American Medical Association 2387–2390.

16.79 If we must always extrapolate from a set of observed data to determine the general rule, it is vital that those data come from a sample constructed in such a way that relationships existing in the universal situation are likely to be accurately reproduced within the sample. For example, if there are equal numbers of men and women in most populations then study samples should also contain equal numbers of each. This quite simple concept underlies much epidemiological thinking and explains why so much emphasis is placed on constructing representative samples of cases and controls. If this simple rule is ignored the sample may be biased, in which case any amount of careful examination will not lead to reliable results.

16.80 In general, epidemiologists are very cautious in interpreting results. Time and again this humility has been shown to be appropriate. Bias, confounding and other errors seem to be almost universal phenomena. If a valid relationship exists then in time a body of evidence will emerge that is consistent with it. Single studies or reports from a single group of scientists are rarely accepted as proof of a hypothesis.

16.81 Support for a cautious, step-by-step, approach to epidemiology comes from other areas of science where fundamental uncertainties are being increasingly recognised. For example, chaos theory suggests that even very simple non-linear systems are intrinsically unpredictable. Most of the models involved in epidemiology are highly complex non-linear models. Any scientist who claims to be able to predict the outcome in such a situation because they fully understand all the material relationships is almost certain to be wrong.

'For every human problem, there is a neat, simple solution; and it is always wrong'[1].

1 H L Mencken.

16.82 In relation to litigation it is important to understand the difference between lay concepts of cause which tend to be tied up with the notion of volition[1]. In other words causes are generally thought of as active processes that result in some effect or other: 'someone must have done something to cause my problem'. However, epidemiologists and philosophers recognise that causes are just as likely to be static conditions as they are to be active processes. Examples of static conditions include sex, inherited factors, geography or social class. Individuals affected by a disease will tend to look first for an active cause as an explanation of their disease[2] and find it hard to accept that static conditions can also be important determinants. For example studies of men with brain tumours showed that their wives very often dated the onset of their husbands' condition to a head injury, although it is most unlikely that the injury was a true cause.

1 Susser 'What is a cause and how do we know one? A grammar for pragmatic epidemiology' (1991) 133(7) American Journal of Epidemiology 635–648.
2 Goldberg 'MMR, autism, and Adam' (2000) 320(7231) BMJ 389.

Formal approaches to assessing causation

16.83 Observed associations can be spurious, indirect or causal. Spurious associations are due to bias and indirect associations are due to confounding. It can be very difficult to be sure that an association is causal because the possibility of confounding due to unknown factors is hard to exclude other than in a randomised trial. However, as an aid to this judgment various criteria have been proposed. These can only be a guide to what remains a subjective process. The available evidence must always be considered as a whole and in context in order to arrive at a reasonable conclusion.

Koch's postulates

16.84 The most famous criteria for establishing a necessary cause may be Koch's postulates[1], first published in 1882 and intended to establish whether the tubercle bacillus was the true cause of the clinical condition we now call TB (then known as phthisis). The postulates are satisfied when:

- the agent is found in all cases of the disease;
- the agent is absent from all non-diseased individuals;

- the disease is reproducible in an animal model using a pure preparation of the agent.

1 Charlton 'Attribution of causation in epidemiology: chain or mosaic?' (1996) 49(1) Journal of Clinical Epidemiology 105–107.

16.85 Koch's postulates operate at the level of observed individuals not populations and can only be used when a pathognomonic lesion identifies the disease[1].

'One swallow does not make a summer, but one tophus makes gout and one crescent malaria'[2].

1 A pathognomonic lesion is a characteristic pathological entity that only occurs in cases of the disease.
2 William Osler, circa 1903.

16.86 Diseases identified by the presence of a cluster of characteristics and not by a pathognomonic lesion are called syndromes (autism or dementia being good examples). Koch's postulates cannot be applied to syndromes. This is because case definitions for syndromes can never be as reliable as a pathognomonic lesion (some observed 'cases' will not be true cases and some true cases will not be included as such). Koch's postulates will never be satisfied in these circumstances. For syndromes, causal relationships can only be explored at the level of populations using epidemiological methods. For example, Wakefield attempted to demonstrate that all children with autism had measles antigen in their gut but this was the wrong approach to assess such a relationship.

Bradford Hill's guidelines

16.87 Austin Bradford Hill was the eminent statistician who worked with Richard Doll to develop the methodology to show that smoking caused lung cancer. His eponymous 'criteria' were developed as a helpful standard for the interpretation of epidemiological studies of causation (see below). He himself always referred to them as guidelines or features, not criteria, emphasising the fact that they were intended to assist the exercise of judgment not substitute for it. Bradford Hill's landmark paper of 1965 was not completely original but incorporated ideas from earlier work including the US Surgeon General's report on smoking and health.

16.88 The nine guidelines proposed by Bradford Hill are somewhat similar in structure to Koch's postulates in that both require evidence of a strong association followed by subsidiary evidence of the importance of the putative cause as an explanation of that association. Bradford Hill's guidelines rely on a statistical association, whereas Koch demands a one to one association. Koch relies on experimental induction of disease by the agent for corroboration whereas Bradford-Hill looks for other evidence recognising that direct experimental evidence is unlikely to be available.

'Bradford Hill's guidelines for judgement of a causal association

- Temporal sequence: did exposure precede the outcome?
- Strength of association: how strong is the effect, measured as relative risk?
- Consistency of association: has the effect been noted by others?

- Biological gradient (dose-response): does more of the exposure result in more of the outcome?
- Specificity of association: does exposure lead to a distinct disease?
- Biological plausibility: does the association make sense in terms of known biological mechanisms of disease causation?
- Coherence with existing knowledge: is the association consistent with other available evidence?
- Experimental evidence: has a randomised-controlled trial been done?
- Analogy: is the association similar to others?

16.89 Of these criteria some are considered to be more important than others[1]. All authorities agree that there are two criteria which must be satisfied if a cause is to be accepted; these are therefore necessary conditions or conditions precedent. These are **association** with the effect and an appropriate **time order**. Thus, the criteria should only be applied once a statistical association has been established and it is meaningless to attempt to use them in the absence of such an association. Nevertheless, the need for evidence of association is sometimes ignored as a criterion because it was assumed in the Surgeon General's report, and the Bradford Hill paper, that an association had already been described. The importance of first identifying an association before applying Bradford Hill's or any other criteria cannot be overstated:.

'A causal factor must occur together with a putative effect. If no grounds for an association can be shown to exist, causality has been rejected and we proceed no further.' (Susser)

1 Grimes and Schulz 'Bias and causal associations in observational research' (2002) 359(9302) Lancet 248–252; Susser 'What is a cause and how do we know one? A grammar for pragmatic epidemiology' (1991) 133(7) American Journal of Epidemiology 635–648.

16.90 It is also logically impossible for a cause to occur after the effect, hence the need to establish an appropriate time order. If these two major criteria are satisfied, the question then becomes whether the effect occurs not only in conjunction with and following the cause, but also as a consequence of it. This last point is the most difficult to establish.

16.91 Susser proposes the following criteria, in addition to association and time order, as a development from the Bradford Hill list:

- **strength of association**: defined by the size of the relative risk demonstrated;
- **specificity of association**: defined as the association of a particular and well-defined cause with a particular and well-defined effect;
- **consistency**: defined by the presence of the association in a variety of studies, which are scientifically rigorous, performed in a variety of settings;
- **predictive performance**: defined as the ability of a causal hypothesis to correctly predict future events;
- **coherence**: defined as compatibility with pre-existing theory and knowledge.

16.92 Grimes and Schulz also choose strength of association and consistency as among the most important of Bradford Hill's 'criteria'. They suggest that specificity, biological plausibility, coherence and analogy are weak criteria.

16.93   It is unfortunate that in litigation it is very common for experts to refer only to Bradford Hill in assessing causation and rarely to more modern considerations of epidemiological evidence of causation[1].

1 Susser 'What is a cause and how do we know one? A grammar for pragmatic epidemiology' (1991) 133(7) Am J Epidemiol 635–648.

Epidemiological evidence and theoretical analysis compared

16.94   Arguments for and against possible causal relationships can be divided broadly into those based on theory (often derived from axiomatic arguments or inference from the results of laboratory studies of various kinds) and those based on direct observation of phenomena in human populations. As the fundamental sciences advance it might be expected that better theories would lead to greater reliance on coherence with basic scientific knowledge as a causal criterion[1]. In fact, it is not always obvious which type of evidence will be more persuasive in any given situation[2].

1 Weed and Hursting 'Biologic plausibility in causal inference: current method and practice' (1998) 147(5) American Journal of Epidemiology 415–425.
2 Vandenbroucke and de Craen 'Alternative medicine: a 'mirror image' for scientific reasoning in conventional medicine' (2001) 135(7) Annals of Internal Medicine 507–513.

16.95   For example, a group of clinical trials appeared to show that homeopathic remedies were effective[1]. However, it is known that these remedies are diluted to such an extent that none of the original compound can be present in most tablets. Most doctors would say that it is therefore theoretically impossible for such preparations to have an effect on a disease process. The trials were rejected as likely to be flawed. In this case theory was preferred over observed evidence.

1 Vandenbroucke and de Craen 'Alternative medicine: a 'mirror image' for scientific reasoning in conventional medicine' (2001) 135(7) Annals of Internal Medicine 507–513.

16.96   By contrast, physiological studies in volunteers have been used to develop a causal theory for the common condition of vasovagal syncope (fainting attacks)[1]. The theory predicted with some certainty that pacemakers would not help these patients. However, a clinical trial of pacemakers has shown an overwhelming benefit. In this case there are two opinions: the physiologists claim the trial is flawed and the clinical cardiologists claim the theory is wrong.

1 Vandenbroucke and de Craen 'Alternative medicine: a 'mirror image' for scientific reasoning in conventional medicine' (2001) 135(7) Annals of Internal Medicine 507–513.

16.97   Thus, apparently similar scientific evidence of various kinds is sometimes accepted and sometimes rejected. However, this is not mere caprice on the part of academic authorities. In the best analyses there is a structure to the approach, intended to maximise the likelihood of a correct interpretation in situations where the evidence is incomplete.

16.98   One useful analogy is that of the crossword[1]. The observed facts represent the clues. Existing theories derived from earlier observations represent the already completed entries. Any proposed new word must be a reasonable solution to the relevant clue. If it also fits neatly with earlier entries then it is more likely to be correct than other possible answers. If the new answer seems to solve the relevant clue very well but is inconsistent with an earlier answer we may go back and reconsider whether our earlier answer really was the right one.

1 Vandenbroucke and de Craen 'Alternative medicine: a 'mirror image' for scientific reasoning in conventional medicine' (2001) 135(7) Annals of Internal Medicine 507–513.

16.99 In relation to scientific studies, valid conclusions must be consistent with and supported by the observed facts. If they appear inconsistent with earlier conclusions or with hypothesised explanations then we may want to revise these. However, if as in the case of homeopathy we are certain that our pre-existing ideas are correct, we tend to look harder for alternative explanations for the new evidence instead.

Thus, the importance of new evidence is interpreted on its merits but also according to our prior beliefs about the question. If our prior beliefs are based on reliable evidence we do not reject them easily.

16.100 It remains true, however, that observed fact if reliably interpreted should always be more persuasive than hypothetical argument. Dr Spock's advice to lay babies on their front to sleep was based on an assumption that they might inhale their vomit if left on their backs. Evidence from clinical trials showed that this advice actually increased the risk of cot death. Subsequently, a public health campaign asking parents to lay children on their back and not their front at bedtime has reduced the rate of cot death considerably. If a prior belief is not based on reliable evidence it should be quickly rejected when reliable evidence to the contrary becomes available.

16.101 In conclusion, it is important to note that despite the need for subjective judgments in the interpretation of evidence, 'science is not just another belief system that can be replaced by any other belief at will'[1]. What Vandebroucke describes as 'unproven flights of imagination' are of little value if they do not bear any relation to what exists in reality. As evidence emerges in areas of incomplete knowledge different scientists may legitimately hold different opinions. However, all should be working to the same goal of uncovering some sort of meaningful truth supported by empirical evidence. Science is a pragmatic exercise. If the rules of evidence are not followed correctly predictions made will be wrong, and the scientific process will not 'work' for society.

1 Vandenbroucke and de Craen 'Alternative medicine: a 'mirror image' for scientific reasoning in conventional medicine' (2001) 135(7) Annals of Internal Medicine 507–513.

Biological plausibility and 'coherence' as causal criteria

16.102 Bradford Hill distinguished between biological plausibility and coherence whereas Susser treats them together. The principle behind both criteria is really the same. Epidemiological evidence is more persuasive when it is supported by evidence from non-epidemiological studies. However, there is some confusion about what is meant by a biologically plausible causal hypothesis.

16.103 Weed and Hursting suggest that there are three levels of biologically plausible mechanisms to support the causal nature of observed associations[1]. In ascending order of importance, they are 'hypothesised' or 'evidence-free' proposed mechanisms, 'evidence-supported' and finally 'coherent'.

1 Weed and Hursting 'Biologic plausibility in causal inference: current method and practice' (1998) 147(5) American Journal of Epidemiology 415–425.

16.104 According to Bradford Hill a biologically plausible causal association was merely one for which a reasonable mechanism could be hypothesised, but for which no biological evidence may exist (ie the lowest level). However in this form, the criterion of biological plausibility is considered very weak[1]. The absence of a plausible mechanism may simply reflect the limits of current knowledge.

1 Grimes and Schulz 'Bias and causal associations in observational research' (2002) 359(9302) Lancet 248–252.

16.105 Nor does the criterion work very well in the opposite direction. At least one plausible mechanism can be hypothesised for almost any association given the wealth of material to draw on in the literature, provided of course that no supporting evidence is required. The following quotes show that this is a widely held view:

'Incidentally, one of the authors' arguments in favour of this being a genuine association was plausibility. This is an almost worthless argument – doctors can find a plausible explanation for any finding'[1].

'The ability of imaginative investigators to reconcile any data with preconceived concepts is, in our experience, both amazing and unlimited'.

'The human mind is sufficiently fertile that there is no shortage of biologically plausible explanations or indirect evidence to support almost any observation'.

'Although virtually any set of observations can be made biologically plausible (given the ingenuity of the human mind and the vastness of the supply of contradictory biologic facts), some biologic observations can be highly persuasive, such as finding an enteric-coated potassium chloride tablet at the site of a perforated small bowel. Nonetheless, overinterpretation is a powerful temptation'.

1 Altman 'Statistical reviewing for medical journals' (1998) 17 Statist Med 2661–2674.

16.106 Therefore, if biological plausibility is to be used to argue that an observed association is a causal one, evidence to support the proposed mechanism is required. The stronger the evidence for the mechanism the greater the support. The most stringent interpretation is that an association should only be said to be biologically plausible if there is sufficient evidence to confirm every step of the pathway showing precisely how the factor influences the disease process in question. This is what Weed and Hursting refer to as 'coherence'[1].

1 Weed and Hursting 'Biologic plausibility in causal inference: current method and practice' (1998) 147(5) American Journal of Epidemiology 415–425.

NOTES ON THE USE OF EPIDEMIOLOGY AND STATISTICS IN LITIGATION

16.107 In November 1997 the Supreme Court of Texas published its findings in the case of *Merrell Dow v Havner and Havner*[1]. The court had considered whether there was any evidence that the drug Bendectin caused Kelly Havner to be born with a birth defect. They concluded that the evidence offered was legally insufficient to establish causation. This was the conclusion of a long series of hearings and appeals and a great deal of expert evidence on both sides. The reason for quoting this judgment in a book primarily aimed at UK lawyers is the particularly thoughtful and extensive discussion of many of the most important issues that arise in the use of epidemiology as evidence of causation.

1 (1997) 953 S.W.2d 706.

16.108   The Texas Supreme Court started by making the point at some length that experts must not only be experts in the relevant field, but must quote reliable studies and must quote them correctly with adequate critical appraisal of the underlying data:

'If the foundational data underlying opinion testimony are unreliable, an expert will not be permitted to base an opinion on that data because any opinion drawn from that data is likewise unreliable. Further, an expert's testimony is unreliable even when the underlying data are sound if the expert draws conclusions from that data based on flawed methodology. A flaw in the expert's reasoning from the data may render reliance on a study unreasonable and render the inferences drawn therefrom dubious. Under that circumstance, the expert's scientific testimony is unreliable and, legally, no evidence'.

There is then extensive discussion of the issue that a doubling of relative risk has been said by some to be equivalent to the 'balance of probabilities' test of causation. As the Texas Court put it:

'The "doubling of the risk" issue in toxic tort cases has provided fertile ground for the scholarly plow'.

16.109   The doubling of risk argument was also used in the UK in relation to the litigation on third generation contraceptives[1]. That case is interesting for a number of reasons not least because the epidemiological expert for the defendant was challenged on their understanding on basic concepts such as confounding. The author firmly believes that the size of the relative risk, the likelihood that the association is in general causal, and the issue of specific causation in the individual case are all independent matters to be assessed on their merits. The current trend to conduct large studies (such as the million women study) means that small excess risks of less than 2.0 are being accurately and reliably identified and that these risks will relate to genuine causal relationships. The establishment of specific causation in individual cases is a matter for the court, not for expert epidemiological opinion. There is thus a difference between the approach of the epidemiologist and of the lawyer; a relative risk of greater than unity can denote causality in epidemiology, whereas on occasion the court requires a doubling of risk – a conflation of the probability of the data required to denote causality with the probability required to prove the truth of the causal allegation.

1 Dyer 'Pill claimants accuse defendants' witness of 'cavalier' attitude' (2002) 2002-05-11 07:00:00. 1115 p.

16.110   Having dealt with the doubling of risk issue the Texas court went on to provide an extremely good summary of epidemiological methods and then to evaluate the epidemiological evidence in this case. The striking conclusion was that the court much preferred to rely on the body of published good-quality epidemiological studies (which showed no association) compared with clinical evidence or ad hoc analysis by the claimants' experts. Indeed the clinical evidence was pretty much dismissed as follows:

'A physician, even a treating physician, or other expert who has seen a skewed data sample, such as one of a few infants who has a birth defect, is not in a position to infer causation'.

16.111 Another case, this time from the UK, which raised a number of relevant issues was the very unfortunate case of Sally Clark[1]. The case will be well known to readers of this book. The statistical mistake made by the prosecution expert was to assume that the probability of two consecutive deaths was independent when he should have been aware that they were not. This is known as conditional probability: ie what is the probability of X conditional on the fact that Y has already occurred?

1 *R v Clark* [2003] EWCA Crim 1020, [2003] 2 FCR 447.

16.112 The second issue raised by the case was that of the prosecutor's fallacy. The fact that sudden infant death syndrome was rare should not have been given much weight in the judgment as all possible explanations of the facts were rare. The judgment should not have been made on the relative probability of double child murder (very rare) versus double cot death (very, very rare), but on the existence or not of tangible evidence to support each theory.

16.113 Finally, and perhaps most significant is the issue of 'the wrong expert'. It is not uncommon for clinical experts to be asked to give opinions on matters which are properly statistical or epidemiological. Because most clinicians use statistics in their practice, especially if they conduct research, there is a temptation to stray beyond their expertise. Even in the area of epidemiology there are many expert clinical epidemiologists who may not be familiar with the application of epidemiology to other areas such as large-scale population studies or to pharmacoviglance. Whatever the background of the expert it is crucially important now to support any opinion with cogent argument and relevant high-quality references to the literature.

16.114 The English courts have considered the basis of expert evidence and this has led to the following comments:

'In reaching my decision a number of processes have to be undertaken. The mere expression of opinion or belief by a witness, however eminent, that the vaccine can or cannot cause brain damage, does not suffice. The court has to evaluate the witness and the soundness of his opinion. Most importantly this involves an examination of the reasons given for his opinions and the extent to which they are supported by the evidence. The judge also has to decide what weight to attach to a witness's opinion by examining the internal consistency and logic of his evidence; the care with which he has considered the subject and presented his evidence; his precision and accuracy of thought as demonstrated by his answers; how he responds to searching and informed cross-examination and in particular the extent to which a witness faces up to and accepts the logic of a proposition put in cross-examination or is prepared to concede points that are seen to be correct; the extent to which a witness has conceived an opinion and is reluctant to re-examine it in the light of later evidence, or demonstrates a flexibility of mind which may involve changing or modifying opinions previously held; whether or not a witness is biased or lacks independence. Criticisms have been made by counsel of some of the witnesses called on either side and I shall have to consider these in due course'[1].

1 *Loveday v Renton* [1989] 1 Med LR 117 at 125, Stuart-Smith LJ.

16.115 The approach of the English courts is to consider carefully the evidential basis of an expert opinion:

'As to the analytical studies, the approach of the defendants' experts has been to discard the studies that did not pass tests of statistical significance and methodological purity and only to pay real heed to the studies remaining. This was despite Professor Doll's statement that he was not inclined to place too much weight on the issue of statistical significance. The plaintiffs' experts, on the other hand, had taken a rather less absolutist approach, attempting to put all the studies into the melting pot and giving studies more or less weight depending upon the issues of size of study, relative risk, *p*-value, possible bias, reputation of authors etc. The plaintiffs would adopt the suggestion of Professor Doll that epidemiology was a lot about "informed common sense" while Professor Howe had accepted that the overall views of the experts on both sides were reasonable and that it was a question of overall assessment and judgment upon which views might properly differ. Professor Thomas was inclined to think that a number of studies, each perhaps not in itself reliable, but tending in the same direction, could collectively provide a "prior". The plaintiffs submitted that this was a sound way of considering the other analytical studies and determining the consistency of the evidence with the Gardner study'[1].

1 *Reay v British Nuclear Fuels plc* [1994] 5 Med LR 1 at 17, per French J.

16.116 Evidence of absence and absence of evidence are distinct concepts. A claim can be defeated by showing that the evidence is insufficient to sustain an allegation of causation (absence of evidence). Additionally, and more convincingly, a claim can be defeated by showing evidence of lack of association, contradicting an allegation of causation (evidence of absence). Thus in the MMR vaccine controversy studies showing a relative risk of unity between the risk of autism and exposure to MMR vaccine, demonstrated the failure to refute the null hypothesis and provided powerful evidence that there was not a causal relationship[1].

1 Madsen, Hviid, Vestergaard, Schendel, Wohlfahrt, Thorsen (et al) 'A population-based study of measles, mumps, and rubella vaccination and autism' (2002) 347(19) New England Journal of Medicine 1477–1482.

CONCLUSION

16.117 Evidence that relies on epidemiology and statistics has been crucially important to the outcome of litigation in a number of cases in the UK and abroad. Most of these have been to do with product liability involving pharmaceutical manufacturers as defendants rather than individual claims of clinical negligence against doctors but there is scope for epidemiology and statistics to inform a much wider range of other cases, for example on exposure to certain risks in the workplace.

It is important that any use of such evidence takes account of the generic strengths and weaknesses of the class of study used as well as critical appraisal of the quality of the specific study or studies relied upon. Since the use of epidemiology as evidence is not commonplace in litigation, and may not be familiar to the court, it is important that experts have regard to their duty to assist the court in the interpretation as well as the presentation of that evidence. This means that they should almost always provide some general advice on the nature, use and interpretation of epidemiology (for example in establishing causation) as well as presenting their views on the epidemiological studies themselves. It is hoped that this chapter provides some additional help in that regard.

CHAPTER 17

Negligence in general practice

Dr Howard Thompson

17.1   Out of all the medical disciplines, general practitioners have a particularly trusted and, often over the long term, close relationship with their patients. Because of their expertise in dealing with a wide spectrum of medical problems, they are able to use their knowledge and experience to decide whether, among other things, onward referral to specialist care

593

is appropriate and advisable or not. An incorrect decision and consequent failure in this responsibility can have a devastating outcome for the patient.

INTRODUCTION

17.2   One hundred years ago an experienced Scottish judge, while hearing a case against an Edinburgh GP[1], commented on its rarity:

'This action is certainly one of a particularly unusual character. It is an action of damages against a medical man. In my somewhat long experience I cannot remember having seen a similar case before'.

1 *Farquhar v Murray* 1901 38 SLR 642, 3F 859–64.

17.3   Today, the medico-legal landscape could not offer a stronger contrast. In 2012–13, 10,129 claims of clinical negligence against National Health Service (NHS) bodies were received by the NHS Litigation Authority (compared with 9,143 claims in 2011–12), and £1.1177 billion was paid in connection with claims settled in 2012–13, an increase of 2 per cent over the previous 12 months[1]. Directly attributable costs of litigation are probably only a fraction of the total cost borne by the NHS as a result of positive and negative defensive practices in response to real or perceived risks of litigation[2].

1 *The National Health Service Litigation Authority: report and accounts 2012/13.*
2 Kessler, Summerton, Graham 'Effects of the medical liability system in Australia, the UK, and the USA' (2006) 368 Lancet 240–246.

17.4   Over 99 per cent of successful negligence claims are settled out of court through early negotiation and a variety of methods of alternative dispute resolution; approximately 40 per cent of all claims received are resolved without a damages payment[1]. In the decade between 1989 and 1998, a tenfold increase in the number of claims dealt with on behalf of GPs was observed by the Medical Protection Society, which estimated that 3.6 per cent of its GP membership worldwide was likely to face claims as a result of work undertaken in the previous 12 months[2].

1 *The National Health Service Litigation Authority: report and accounts 2012/13* (London, The Stationery Office, 2013) available at http://www.nhsla.com/aboutus/Documents/NHS%20 LA%20Annual%20Report%20and%20Accounts%202012-13.pdf..
2 Dyer 'GPs face escalating litigation' (1999) 318 BMJ 830.

17.5   This chapter discusses the nature of general practitioners' work, the contractual terms of their relationship with the NHS, standards of care and areas of practice prone to claims in negligence. Because trials against GPs in the UK are still relatively rare, given the high proportion which settle before reaching court, sources of information other than reported legal cases concerning substandard practice are also considered, including:

(1)   data on claims from UK defence societies and US insurers of primary care physicians; (paras **17.22–17.28**);
(2)   complaints about general practice (paras **17.29–17.31**);
(3)   official statements setting out unacceptable general practice (paras **17.32–17.34**).

THE NATURE OF GENERAL PRACTICE

17.6   Although general practice has been a growing and important part of UK health provision since the early nineteenth century, in 1948 the primary component of health care was thrust into a pivotal position with the inception of the NHS. This created a right for every citizen (and almost every resident) to be registered with a NHS general practitioner, who could be consulted free of charge. The NHS cemented an aspect of inter-professional etiquette that had arisen informally between doctors, which ensured that other than in emergencies (by attendance at hospital casualties), patients could consult hospital-based specialists only if they were referred by their GP[1]. In the context of almost complete GP registration of the resident UK population and significant differences in skills and costs associated with GP and hospital-based specialist care, the 'gate-keeper' and 'gate opener' functions conferred on GPs by exclusive referral rights have become critical components of the GP role within the NHS.

1 Loudon 'The principle of referral: the gatekeeping role of the GP' (2008) 58 British Journal of General Practice 128–130.

17.7   General practice medicine is characterised by high volumes of clinical activity. Some 90 per cent of all consultations that take place in the NHS occur in the general practice setting: approximately 8,000 patient encounters per GP per year, which in 2001 amounted to 261 million consultations. On average, patients remain registered with the same general practice for about 10 years, and they consult a GP on average five times a year, with many groups – especially children, women, the elderly and those who suffer from psychological and chronic medical conditions – having higher GP consultation rates[1]. The consultation rate increased from 3.9 consultations per patient per year in 1995 to 5.5 consultations per patient per year in 2008, by which time the total number of consultations in general practice in England had risen to over 300 million[2].

1 Jones, Britten, Culpepper, Gass, Grol, Mant, Silagy (eds) *Oxford Textbook of Primary Medical Care* (OUP, 2003) Vols 1 and 2.
2 http://www.rcgp.org.uk/policy/rcgp-policy-areas/~/media/Files/Policy/A-Z-policy/ Evidence_for_enhancing_leadership_skills.ashx.

17.8   In the Royal College of General Practitioner's response to the March 2014 budget, Dr Maureen Baker, Chair of the College said:

'There are over 340 million consultations in general practice per year – around 90 per cent of all patient contacts in the NHS'.

She went on to say that the share of government funding that general practice receives is at an all-time low of 8.39 per cent of the total NHS budget.

1 http://www.rcgp.org.uk/news/2014/march/budget-response.aspx.

17.9   The Royal College of General Practitioners characterises general practice as:

'... primarily focused on populations with a low prevalence of serious disease, so it is crucial that the physician develops concepts of health, function and quality of life as well as models of disease. This finds expression, first, in the preventative and health promotion activities of physicians and in risk management. It is also expressed in decisions made in palliative and terminal care. Family doctors are also increasingly challenged by the need to be conscious of healthcare costs. In caring for patients, general practitioners work with an extended team of other professionals in primary care, both within their own practice and in the local community, and also with specialists in secondary care, using the diagnostic and treatment resources available in hospitals. Thus primary care education must promote learning that integrates different disciplines within the complex team of the NHS'[1].

1 RCGP Curriculum 2010 – 1 The Core Curriculum Statement – Being a General Practitioner (Revised 14 August 2013) available at http://www.rcgp.org.uk/gp-training-and-exams/~/media/Files/GP-training-and-exams/Curriculum-2012/RCGP-Curriculum-1-Being-a-GP.ashx.

17.10 First point of contact, unsorted, personal, continuing medical care are the defining characteristics of general practice. The European arm of the World Organization of Family Doctors Association (WONCA) refers to a broad amalgam of aims and values that make up the work of GPs. Today, there is less continuity of patient contact than hitherto, as a result of development of new NHS primary care services outside the main GP contracts; these include out-of-hours services, walk-in and the NHS '111' telephone advice service. Secular trends, such as greater population mobility and the increasingly part-time commitment which NHS GPs make to their practice, contribute to curtailed continuity of GP-patient contact. Such developments also diminish the GP gatekeeper/opener function, although other changes, including shift in the locus of health care from expensive hospital to cheaper community settings, tend to reinforce the gatekeeper role[1]. Failure to refer patients in a timely and appropriate way is an important source of liability in actions sounding in negligence against GPs.

1 Cox 'GPs can no longer claim to be the "gatekeepers" of the NHS' (2006) 56 British Journal of General Practice 83–84.

17.11 *WONCA Consensus Definition of General Practice*[1]: General practitioners are specialist physicians trained in the principles of the discipline. They are personal doctors, primarily responsible for the provision of comprehensive and continuing care to every individual seeking medical care irrespective of age, sex and illness. They care for individuals in the context of their family, their community, and their culture, always respecting the autonomy of their patients. They recognise they will also have a professional responsibility to their community. In negotiating management plans with their patients they integrate physical, psychological, social, cultural and existential factors, utilising the knowledge and trust engendered by repeated contacts. General practitioners exercise their professional role by promoting health, preventing disease and providing cure, care, or palliation. This is done either directly or through the services of others according to health needs and the resources available within the community they serve, assisting patients where necessary in accessing these services. They must take responsibility for developing and maintaining their skills, personal balance and values as a basis for effective and safe patient care.

1 The European Definition of General Practice/Family Medicine – WONCA Europe 2005 edition available at http://www.woncaeurope.org/sites/default/files/documents/Definition per cent202nd per cent20ed per cent202005.pdf.

GENERAL PRACTICE IN THE NHS

17.12   In contrast to a doctor in private practice, who may be considered to have a contract of sorts with a patient each time he consults[1], the nature of the GP-patient relationship in the NHS is not one of contract: first, because registered patients are *owed* general medical services under the National Health Service Act 1977; and second, because GPs are obliged to provide their services pursuant to various Acts. There is no contractual relationship between GPs and NHS patients; the operative contracts are between the primary care provider and the commissioner, NHS England, Scotland, Wales or Northern Ireland, which by virtue of the terms of service involve the provider undertaking to ensure that a primary care performer (GP) is available at specified hours on weekdays for patients to consult (or to be visited by, if necessary). The legally enforceable *duty* between a GP performer and patient only materialises when the GP is requested to provide, or becomes aware of the need for, medical services of the sort provided by general practitioners. This duty covers permanent or temporary registrations and any NHS patient within the practice area whom the GP sees in an emergency who is unable to obtain treatment from his own doctor. The terms of service inaugurated by the 2004 Regulations continue to specify that patients who have been *refused* entry onto a GP list who live in the practice area, are entitled, within 14 days of that refusal, to be seen by a GP for immediately necessary treatment[2]. Clauses such as these highlight just how *different* work as an NHS GP is from work undertaken privately or in hospital practice.

1 Although the private doctor-patient relationship involves many of the elements of a contract, namely, an offer of services, acceptance of the services by a patient (for consideration), the courts have generally held that the relationship between doctor in private practice and patient, is best described as 'contractual in origin' rather than contractual in law. The reason for this is that doctors, like lawyers, generally cannot warrant a particular result, viz that a client will win a case or that a patient will be cured. All they can warrant is to provide treatment with reasonable skill and care, and this is usually the implied term of contracts between patients and doctors in the private sector. The result of treatment generally depends upon the problem which the patient is bringing to the doctor, the state of knowledge about this, and the treatments available. See Kennedy and Grubb *Medical Law: Text with Materials* (1994) pp 69–73.
2 The National Health Service (General Medical Services Contracts) Regulations 2004, SI 2004/291.

NEGLIGENCE IN GENERAL PRACTICE

17.13   Negligence in general practice involves failure to provide a reasonable standard of care in any aspect of the highly diverse terrain of clinical activity undertaken by GPs. The broad and multidisciplinary nature of GP care creates a myriad of potential pitfalls, amplified to some extent by the increased clinical and organisational complexity of modern practice.

17.14   The remuneration arrangements of GPs are complicated and derive from a number of sources, including allowances, incentives, capitation, and item of service payments. A framework of practice which remunerates visible and measurable activities of primary health care introduces certain biases into practice provision and opens it up to synergy with political and economic drives that aim to shift care away from expensive hospital provision to cheaper primary care settings (irrespective of patient preference or robust evidence of equivalent efficacy). Some of these arrangements are operated by agencies outside of the GP-consultant relationship, triaging patients between primary and secondary care services, in order to manage the flow of patients across the primary-secondary care interface. Triaging services are subject to error, and claims alleging mis-assessment of urgency or refusal to direct patients to more expensive secondary care treatments from which they would benefit would seem a possibility in future. Pronounced 'incentivisations' place strains on traditional approaches to clinical work and threaten the ability of GPs to make overall assessments of patients' predicaments based on close working contact with, and knowledge of, patients' overall situations. Incentivisations in the NHS are moving the focus of care away from the patients' agenda for consulting and the unravelling of their concerns, towards collection of clinical information – frequently unrelated to the patient's main complaint – required to meet pre-set (remunerated) targets.

17.15   Although claims of negligence against GPs are less likely to be pursued than similar actions against hospital doctors, Brazier finds that legal actions against GPs are becoming more common. The factor that worked to protect GPs in the past – the high esteem in which the public held them – was based to a significant extent on the long-standing and personal nature of the patient-GP relationship: 'a mistake is more likely to be forgiven and forgotten in context of a GP's continuing care than in an impersonal hospital atmosphere', and this meant patients were less likely to want to put a familiar doctor 'into the dock' when things went wrong[1].

1 Brazier M *Medicine, Patients and the Law* (2003) p 158.

17.16   At all times GPs should use considered judgment in the organisation and delivery of care, ensuring patients can be seen in the surgery or at home in a timely and appropriate manner during working hours. They are required to maintain their core clinical skills of listening, examining, diagnosing, prescribing and referring patients to hospital (and other community-based specialists). It is no defence against a charge of negligence that a receptionist or other member of staff failed to convey materially relevant information about a visit request, or that a deputy or locum failed to undertake a home visit[1]. This does not mean, of course, that every patient needs to be offered a home visit when requested but they should be visited if, with the information available to the GP, it is judged that the patient cannot come to the surgery and their health would significantly deteriorate without a home assessment by a GP; once it has been decided that a home visit is required it should be undertaken within a reasonable time interval. The principle demonstrated in *Davy-Chiesman v Davy-Chiesman*[2], relating to the fact that solicitors cannot avoid their responsibilities to the parties and the court, applies just as much to doctors in their relationship with their patients, staff, and any agency to which the patient might be referred. It is incumbent upon the doctor to bring his own experience to bear on matters and retain and exercise an independent judgment.

1 *Lobley v Going* (9 December 1985, unreported), CA, cited in Nelson-Jones R and Burton F *Medical Negligence Case Law* (Butterworths, 1995) pp 431–432.
2 [1984] Fam 48.

Professional indemnity

17.17   GPs are not covered by the NHS indemnity scheme that operates for hospital trust employees. However, the contracts that GPs have with the NHS require them to have adequate insurance cover. Failure to do so would be a breach of those contracts. The General Medical Council's booklet *Good Medical Practice* states, at para 63:

'You must make sure you have adequate insurance or indemnity cover so that your patients will not be disadvantaged if they make a claim about the clinical care you have provided in the UK'.

Partnership agreements often specify if costs of insurance are to fall on individual primary care performers or on the partnership.

17.18   At present, there are no express statutory requirements or provisions dealing with professional indemnity arrangements for registered medical practitioners or those seeking registration with the GMC. There is no compulsory statutory requirement for any doctor to be a member of a medical defence organisation or to have professional indemnity or insurance arrangements[1].

1 General Medical Council: 8 November 2011: http://www.gmc-uk.org/5___Insurance_and_ Indemnity.pdf_45922951.pdf ; Page 2, Para 4.

Vicarious liability/non-delegable duty

17.19   A primary care provider is vicariously responsible for the actions of a GP whom he employs; an employed GP may be sued as may employed practice nurses (and health care assistants (HCAs)). Primary care providers should be careful to delegate to practice nurses (and HCAs) only the tasks for which a nurse (or HCA) has been trained (and would normally be expected) to undertake. Some nurse practitioners have undergone additional training in diagnosis and prescribing, in which case they can be asked to undertake work of this sort, but only in the areas covered by their training. The primary care provider is responsible to the patient for ensuring that nurse practitioners, practice nurses and HCAs have been adequately trained for procedures that are delegated to them. Nurses, like GPs, are not compelled to be insured against liability. Liability insurance should be specified as a requirement in the terms and conditions of nurse employment contracts with practices. Many practices now cover all GPs and nurses working within the practice with a single indemnity policy.

17.20   Negligence claims against general medical and dental practitioners can raise problems. The health care professional may not be readily identified and the employment relationship with the practice may be unclear. Medical and dental practices have often obscured matters by saying they are not responsible for the conduct of the health professional concerned, who may have left the practice. Attempts to sue the practice are often met with unhelpful, delaying and deflecting tactics. A standard response from practices is to deny any responsibility for the provision of healthcare, saying that it is a matter for the individual healthcare professional concerned.

Patients are patients of the practice, and are not generally concerned by the remuneration and indemnity arrangements of the health carer, which are largely irrelevant to the patient.

17.21 Two recent cases have clarified the law and make it easier for injured patients to claim when injured by general medical practitioners and general dental practitioners. These cases establish a non-delegable duty in certain situations owed by the practice as the proposed defendant. A third, older case demonstrates the same principle in a non-medical context. These cases are:

- *Whetstone v Medical Protection Society*[1];
- *Woodland v Essex County Council*[2], and
- *Rogers v Night Riders (a firm)*[3].

It is difficult to see the relevance of the status of the health carer and his insurance arrangements when considering the liability of the practice; this appears to be the approach of the court.

1 *Whetstone (t/a Whelby House Dental Practice) v Medical Protection Society (Sued As Dental Protection Ltd)* [2014] EWHC 1024 (QB), especially paras 123–126.
2 [2013] UKSC 66.
3 [1983] RTR 324.

RISK FACTORS FOR NEGLIGENCE IN GENERAL PRACTICE

17.22 The legal principles that hold sway over provision of health care have arisen from the very small proportion of claims that reach the courts. The vast majority of claims against GPs are abandoned early or settled, prior to issue of formal proceedings, or after a writ has been served before (sometimes immediately before) the court stage; only 1–3 per cent reach a court hearing[1]. This percentage had reduced to less than 1 per cent, as reported in the NHSLA Report and Accounts of 2012–13. Complete sets of data are generally not available from UK defence societies on which well-powered studies of the factors associated with negligent general practice can be ascertained, but several studies have analysed US primary care malpractice data[2].

1 Mulcahy 'Threatening behaviour: the challenge of medical negligence claims' in Freeman and Lewis (eds) *Law and Medicine* (OUP, 2000) pp 81–105.
2 See Phillips, Bartholomew, Dovey (et al) 'Learning from malpractice claims about negligent, adverse events in primary care in the United States' (2004) 13 Qual Saf Health Care 121–126; Levinson, Roter, Malloly (et al) 'Physician-patient communication. The relationship with malpractice claims among primary care physicians and patients' (1997) 277 JAMA 553–559.

17.23 Several North American studies have considered the effect that the communicative style, such as the warmth, hostility, dominance and anxiety, as well as the age, of a doctor might have on their favourable or unfavourable claims profile. While the findings are not surprising, the references are set out below[1].

1 Ambady, Laplante, Nguyen (et al) 'Surgeons' tone of voice: a clue to malpractice history' (2002) 132 Surgery 5–9. Sloan, Mergenhagen, Burfield (et al) 'Medical malpractice experience of physicians' (1989) 262 JAMA 1 3291–3307; Ly, Dawson, Young (et al) 'Malpractice claims against family physicians. Are the best doctors sued more?' (1999) 48 J Fam Pract 23–29.

17.24   Analysis of UK defence societies' reports reveals that the following grounds are commonly at the root of legal claims in general practice:

(1)   failure to visit a patient at home when requested (eg for fever and/ or non-specific illness where the history suggests a possibly serious cause);

(2)   failures of communication, for instance between hospital and GP, in GPs not acting on the results of discharge summaries or test results such as an abnormal cervical smear result or infected wounds requiring not only antibacterial treatment but review and monitoring, or not carrying out treatments suggested by specialists. It is not adequate to rely on a patient as an intermediary between doctors[1]: the communication should be directly from one doctor to another[2];

(3)   failure to examine[3], or investigate[4], to refer to a specialist[5], or keep adequate contemporaneous medical records (see para **17.26** for official guidance on maintenance of adequate medical records);

(4)   errors in drug treatment, for instance known (though inadequately documented) drug allergies, where responsibilities for prescribing and monitoring medication, such as warfarin or methotrexate, are split, with GPs prescribing drugs on a regular basis but where the dose is titrated against the results of blood monitoring tests organised by hospital clinics which may not feed back the results: in this situation, poor co-ordination can lead to serious mistakes. In the case of patients referred to hospitals, GPs cannot claim that care that routinely comes under the purview of general practice has been delegated to a specialist; and

(5)   failures of practice management, such as poorly-trained reception staff offering advice to patients, whose questions or concerns should be dealt with by a nurse or GP.

1 *Chapman v Rix* (1960) Times, 22 December, HL; *Cole v Reading and District Hospital Management Committee* (1963) 107 Sol Jo 115.
2 *Dwyer v Rodrick* (1983) 127 Sol Jo 806; *Farquhar v Murray* (1901) 38 SLR 642.
3 *Patel v Adyha* (2 April 1985, unreported), CA; *Riddett v D'A'Arcy* (1960) 2 BMJ 1607.
4 *Connolly v Rubra* (1937) 1 Lancet 1005, CA.
5 *Connolly v Rubra* (1937) 1 Lancet 1005, CA.

17.25   The GMC gives the following advice regarding the recording of work clearly, accurately and legibly[1]:

- documents you make (including clinical records) to formally record your work must be clear, accurate and legible. You should make records at the same time as the events you are recording or as soon as possible afterwards;

- you must keep records that contain personal information about patients, colleagues or others securely, and in line with any data protection requirements;

- clinical records should include:
  (a)   relevant clinical findings;
  (b)   the decisions made and actions agreed, and who is making the decisions and agreeing the actions;
  (c)   the information given to patients;
  (d)   any drugs prescribed or other investigation or treatment;
  (e)   who is making the record and when.

1 GMC *Good Medical Practice* (London 2013).

17.26 Electronic patient records place important demands on GPs, virtually all of whom now record data from consultations directly into e-records. This requires good keyboard skills and familiarity and fluency with the software and operation of the e-record system, and correct coding of important clinical information to ensure relevant clinical information is visible and easily retrievable from within the record. Failure to update records with laboratory, imaging or screening test results, and omitting to act on important findings contained in hospital letters and discharge sheets, have always been potential sources of negligent harm to patients. But the arrival of e-records and electronic data transmission means that practices must now operate robust procedures to capture, review and interpret large amounts of electronic information. Electronic records offer many health care advantages in the way of information gain on the health profile of a registered population, and on the health care activities of GPs, but (as currently designed) they curtail what is easily presentable on an electronic screen to the consulting doctor. GPs therefore need to keep e-records up to date and methodically review the record when patients consult, to apprise themselves properly of the relevant past medical histories of their patients. Defence societies publish cautionary case histories arising from the legal claims they advise on, which focus on areas of practice they have found require special vigilance and attention and featuring claims arising from e-information processing.

17.27 Analysis of a thousand consecutive claims lodged against GP members of the Medical Protection Society after July 1996 showed that the most frequently-perceived cause (in 63.1 per cent of the cases) involved failure/delay in diagnosis, a quarter of which concerned malignant disease and 12 per cent circulatory conditions[1]. Of the 1,000 claims, 19.3 per cent related to alleged prescribing mistakes, the commonest of which – across all drug categories – involved failure to recognise or monitor adverse medication effects. Eighteen per cent of these involved prescription of incorrect or inappropriate medication, 12.5 per cent contraindicated drugs, and 12 per cent wrong dose of medication. In terms of drug groupings, steroids accounted for a fifth, other named groups (antibiotics, phenothiazines, hormone replacement, oral contraception, anti-epilepsy, opiates and lithium, non-steroidal anti-inflammatories and warfarin) each amounting to a few per cent of the total of prescribing-related claims. Forty-five per cent of the 1,000 claims related to failure to:

- refer for hospital admission: 11.8 per cent;
- refer to another speciality: 11.6 per cent;
- examine adequately: 6.9 per cent;
- maintain adequate medical records: 6.6 per cent;
- investigate adequately: 5.2 per cent;
- monitor adequately: 4.5 per cent;
- arrange an X-ray/scan: 3.7 per cent;
- act on an abnormal finding: 21 per cent;
- visit a patient at home: 1.7 per cent.

1 Silk 'What went wrong in 1000 negligence claims' Health Care Risk Report (London, Medical Protection Society, 2000) pp 14–16; Silk 'Findings from 1000 negligence claims – part two' Health Care Risk Report (London, Medical Protection Society, 2001) pp 13–15.

17.28 The importance of prescribing safely cannot be over-emphasised, as medication-related adverse events represent important and common causes of morbidity in primary care[1]. A prospective cohort study has shown that within four weeks of receiving a primary care prescription some 25 per cent of patients experience an adverse drug event of sorts, of which 11 per cent are judged preventable[2]. A systematic review and meta-analysis of 15 studies reported that a median 7.1 per cent of hospital admissions result from drug-related problems, of which 59 per cent are attributable to error[3], many of which are judged preventable by greater GP care and dispensing pharmacist vigilance[4].

1 Avery, Sheikh, Hurwitz (et al) 'Safer medicines management in primary care' (2002) 52 (Suppl) Br J Gen Pract S17–22.
2 Gandhi, Weingart, Borus (et al) 'Adverse drug events in ambulatory care' (2003) 348 N Engl J Med 1556–1564.
3 Winterstein, Sauer, Hepler (et al) 'Preventable drug-related hospital admissions' (2002) 36 Ann Pharmacother 1238–1248.
4 Royal, Smeaton, Avery, Hurwitz, Sheikh 'Interventions in primary care to reduce medication related adverse events and hospital admissions: systematic review and meta-analysis' (2006) 15 Qual Saf Health Care 23–31; Inc Joint Commission Resources *Think twice, save a life: the pharmacist's role in medication safety* (2004).

COMPLAINTS ABOUT GPS

17.29 From July 2004 until March 2009, the Health Care Commission was responsible for reviewing complaints about NHS services that had failed to be resolved by the GP practice complaints procedure, and by local investigation and discussion. Since March 2009 this has been the responsibility of the Parliamentary and Health Service Ombudsman (PHSO).

The PHSO reports that during the year 2011–12, of the 16,333 complaints received relating to the NHS, 4,399 were examined in closer detail. Of those, in 2,400 complaints no case for the NHS to answer was found.

In 950 complaints, although it was established that things had gone wrong, the NHS had already corrected these.

649 complaints were resolved without the need for formal investigation and 400 complaints were investigated. This compares to 351 complaints for the previous year.

Of the 400 investigated, 375 were fully resolved during the year, of which 60 per cent were fully upheld, 19 per cent were partly upheld and 21 per cent were not upheld.

Of the total number of complaints received by the ombudsman, 2,951 (ie 18 per cent) related to GPs. Of those complaints accepted for formal investigation, 82 (ie 21 per cent) related to GPs. Of those complaints against GPs that were investigated, 65 (ie 80 per cent) were upheld[1].

1 Parliamentary and Health Service Ombudsman: Listening and Learning 2011-2012 http://www.ombudsman.org.uk/__data/assets/pdf_file/0018/18126/FINAL_Listening_and_Learning_NHS_report_2011-12optimised.pdf.

17.30   The Medical Defence Union, in its paper 'Rising claims against GPs' (January 2010)[1], states that the most common allegation made against GPs was a failure to diagnose, which arose in 60 per cent of notified claims, followed by failure to refer (15 per cent) and medication errors (10 per cent). Claims were also becoming more expensive. In 1995 the MDU only paid compensation exceeding £1m to one patient following a GP claim. By contrast, in 2010, the MDU was notified of 13 claims against GP members valued at over £1m.

1 http://www.themdu.com/guidance-and-advice/guides/statutory-duty-of-candour/ statutory-duty-of-candour.

17.31   Two thirds of complaints about GPs reviewed by the Healthcare Commission, prior to the inception of the PHSO, concerned alleged GP failures in making timely and accurate diagnoses, but most of these were not upheld[1]. Where referral shortcomings were identified, the Commission referred the GPs involved to the National Patient Safety Agency[2] for re-training and 13 per cent of these GPs to the GMC for follow up under professional misconduct procedures. The Commission made the following five recommendations based on its independent review of unresolved complaints about GPs:

(1)   ensure local policies for removing patients from GP lists comply with legislation and relevant professional guidance;
(2)   ensure that records are kept in accordance with guidance by the GMC[3];
(3)   provide training to improve the communication skills of GPs and other staff working in general practices;
(4)   maintain a log of when patient records are sent to the Clinical Commissioning Group (CCG), another practice or the Family Health Services Appeals Authority; and
(5)   apologise to the complainant.

1 Commission for Healthcare Audit and Inspection Spotlights on complaints (2007).
2 In June 2012 the key functions and expertise for patient safety developed by the National Patient Safety Agency transferred to the NHS Commissioning Board Special Health Authority.
3 GMC *Good Medical Practice* (2013) p 9.

17.32   *Good Medical Practice for General Practitioners* was drawn up by the Royal College of General Practitioners and the General Practitioners Committee of the BMA in 2002 and revised in July 2008, to put into operation the GMC's 2001 ethical code of practice in the context of general practice. This document not only defines an excellent GP but also stipulates unacceptable general practice. Whilst a guide, 'unacceptable general practice' is not necessarily to be equated with negligence.

17.33   In terms of clinical skills, *Good Medical Practice for GPs* states that the unacceptable GP:

- has limited competence, and is unaware of where his or her limits of competence lie
- consistently ignores, interrupts or contradicts his or her patients
- fails to elicit important parts of the history
- is unable to discuss sensitive and personal matters with patients
- fails to use the medical records as a source of information about past events
- fails to examine patients when needed
- undertakes inappropriate, cursory, or inadequate examinations
- does not explain clearly what he or she is going to do or why

- does not possess or fails to use appropriate diagnostic and treatment equipment
- consistently undertakes inappropriate investigations
- shows little evidence of a coherent or rational approach to diagnosis
- draws illogical conclusions from the information available
- gives treatments that are inconsistent with best practice or evidence
- has no way of organising care for long-term problems or for prevention
- is dismissive, patronising or unsupportive towards patients who wish to take a responsible role in caring for their own condition
- has unsafe premises, eg hazardous chemicals or sharp instruments are inadequately protected'.

17.34   Regarding records, the writing of reports and ensuring colleagues are informed, the unacceptable GP:

- keeps records which are incomplete or illegible, and contain inaccurate details or gratuitously derogatory remarks
- does not keep records confidential
- does not take account of colleagues' legitimate need for information
- keeps records that cannot readily be followed by another doctor
- consistently consults without records
- omits important information from a report which he or she has agreed to provide, or includes untruthful information in such a report'.

Good Medical Practice for GPs also guides on matters such as access, availability and providing out-of-hours care to patients, making effective use of resources and keeping up-to-date[1].

1 Royal College of General Practitioners *Good Medical Practice for General Practitioners*, (2008).

Duty of candour

17.35   The Francis Report[1], published in February 2014, called for, among other things, the establishment of a statutory duty of candour on both providers of healthcare and individuals working within healthcare, requiring staff to disclose information to their employer where they believe poor care has resulted in death or serious injury to a patient, and making it a criminal offence for staff to try to prevent someone exercising this duty.

1 http://www.midstaffspublicinquiry.com/report.

17.36   The British Medical Association supports the principle underlying the idea of a duty of candour and believes that all NHS staff must be honest and transparent in everything that they do in order to best serve and protect their patients[1].

The General Medical Council (with the Nursing and Midwifery Council) has launched a consultation on new joint guidance regarding duty of candour, which it is hoped will be published in March 2015.

1 http:/bma.org.uk/working-for-change/the-changing-nhs/nhs-culture/duty-of-candour.

17.37   NHS organisations whose services are commissioned under a post-April 2013 standard NHS contract, with the exception of primary care services, already have a *contractual* duty of candour.

The new *statutory* duty of candour was introduced for NHS bodies, registered with CQC in England, from 27 November 2014 and will be extended to primary care in April 2015[1].

1 See the Health and Social Care Act 2008 (Regulated Activities) Regulations 2014, SI 2014/2936. Details may be found at: http://www.themdu.com/guidance-and-advice/guides/statutory-duty-of-candour/statutory-duty-of-candour.

INFORMED CONSENT IN GENERAL PRACTICE

17.38   From a practical point of view, consent may best be viewed as *a process of agreement* that takes place between patients and doctors, which helps to ensure patients can freely choose whether or not to undergo what is being proposed. Valid consent should be relevantly informed, not coerced, and given by a competent person after consideration of the associated risks and benefits, and after discussion of alternative possible interventions.

17.39   Consent is a pre-requisite for almost all clinical services, including:

(1)   touching a patient;
(2)   medical and surgical treatment;
(3)   patients taking part in research studies;
(4)   provision of innovative treatments;
(5)   the presence of friends, family or a chaperone in the consulting room;
(6)   providing immunisations, screening, minor surgery procedures;
(7)   disclosing medical information (including confidences) not routinely required for the medical care of patients, eg in the information transfer for purposes of insurance, reports or discussion with family or other agencies;
(8)   helping in the education of medical students or nurses (or others);
(9)   to authorise withdrawal of blood for laboratory tests or for donation;
(10) for tissue biopsy, typing or donation[1].

1 Department of Health Reference Guide to Consent for Examination or Treatment (Second Edition) (London, 2009) available at https://www.gov.uk/government/uploads/system/uploads/attachment_data/file/138296/dh_103653__1_.pdf.

17.40   Arguably, consent is also required to authorise publication of a patient's personal health care story, photograph or physiological tracing, whether anonymous or not. Consent may also be required for access to, and use of, personal patient information for the purposes of non-intrusive research[1]. CCG or NHS England audits of new General Medical Services (nGMS) and Personal Medical Services (PMS) activity – required for non clinical care reasons (eg verifying payments to GPs) – are generally not based on specific patient consent, but patients should be informed and given a chance to dissent from their records being accessed by third parties for such purposes:

'The BMA does not accept that it is routinely necessary for financial auditors to have access to identifiable patient information in order to verify the appropriate use of NHS resources. Similarly, the Association prefers that any person having access to identifiable health information should be bound by the rules of a statutory regulatory body, in order that appropriate means of redress are available should confidentiality be breached. However, not all health authority staff who currently undertake inspections to verify claims for payment have professional registration and this should be clear to patients.

The Association therefore supports the GMC's published view that patients must be informed prior to their records being used for financial audit:

1 About the purpose of such disclosures
2 That the auditor may or may not be medically qualified
3 That they have a right to object, and that such objections will be respected'. (*Access to General Practitioners' Records for Financial Audit* (GMC, November 1997))[2].

1 Iversen, Liddell, Fear, Hotopf, Wessely 'Consent, confidentiality, and the Data Protection Act' (2006) 332 BMJ 165–169; doi:10.1136/bmj.332.7534.165.
2 BMA *Confidentiality and Disclosure of Health Information* available at http://bma.org.uk. Enter 'Confidentiality and Disclosure of Health Information' in the search box.

17.41 In general practice settings, most consent is implied, ie agreement can reasonably be inferred from patient behaviour and conduct. Here, agreement is signified by actions, eg by a patient lying down on a couch and removing relevant garments to facilitate clinical examination. Someone who deliberately rolls up his sleeve in response to a GP who mentions the need for a procedure whilst picking up a syringe may be giving implied consent to venesection or to being immunised[1]. Implied consent depends upon patients appreciating the medical context of what is proposed. However, contextual understanding cannot always be assumed to be adequate: a woman who agrees to have her eyes examined ophthalmoscopically may not also realise that this could involve a male doctor approaching her face very closely in a darkened room, so the process should be clearly explained. Similarly, although a refugee mother may open her baby's mouth to receive oral polio drops in the belief it can only be protective, if she herself has previously not been immunised she cannot be assumed to be consenting to her own exposure to the live polio virus that will subsequently be excreted in her baby's faeces, possibly infecting her with a variant polio virus; such a possible consequence must be explained explicitly so that simultaneous, protective polio immunisation can be offered to the mother at the time that her baby is immunised. Implied consent does not obviate the need for relevant up-to-date information to be given to patients in the course of offering medical treatment.

1 See *Border v Lewisham and Greenwich NHS Trust (formerly South London Healthcare NHS Trust)* [2015] EWCA Civ 8.

17.42 Consent given after explicit discussion of attendant risks and benefits of treatment is known as express consent, as when a patient agrees verbally, or in writing, or by a clear and unambiguous gesture (such as by nodding or by giving a thumbs up sign), that he agrees to a course of action. The most commonly used form of express consent in general practice is verbal assent to an option verbally set out. Express consent in written form, signed and dated, is unusual in general practice, though many GPs and practice nurses may seek it prior to procedures such as immunisation, the fitting or removal of an intra-uterine device and before minor surgery in primary care.

17.43 In law, implied and express consent are equally valid. Legally, the major difference between the two is that express consent when recorded on a signed document provides durable, independent evidence that consent has been obtained. For procedures such as minor surgery, removal of IUCD or immunisation, express consent is preferred by some practices; it is considered required for release of medical information to a third party (eg solicitor, the police, or a medical insurance company). It may also be sensible to gain express consent prior to a procedure about which the patient has been wavering or feeling unsure, but only in order to record and signify that a decision has been made (not to pressurise or foreclose on such a decision).

17.44 The BMA lists the following elements as important to consider when assessing best interests:[1]

- the patient's own ascertainable wishes, feelings and values
- the patient's ability to understand what is proposed and weigh up the alternatives
- the patient's potential to participate more in the decision, if provided with additional support or explanations
- the patient's physical and emotional needs
- the risk of harm or suffering for the patient
- the views of the patient and family
- the implications for the family of treatment or non treatment
- relevant information about the patient's religious or cultural background
- evidence of the effectiveness of the proposed treatment, particularly in relation to other options
- the prioritising of options that maximise the patient's future opportunities and choices
- evidence concerning the likelihood of improvement with treatment
- evidence about the anticipated extent of improvement
- risks arising from delayed treatment or non-treatment'.

1 BMA Consent, Rights and Choices in Health Care for Children and Young People (2001) pp 4 and 35.

CHAPERONES

17.45 Allegations of indecent assault in clinical examinations almost invariably involve female patients and male doctors, but occasionally they may be levelled by a male patient against a male doctor. Permission should always be requested explicitly for intimate examinations (especially examinations of breasts and/or chest in women, pelvis, anus and rectum). There are two quite distinct rationales for the presence of a chaperone during an intimate examination. These are:

(a) to provide a sense of comfort and security to the patient, who may be undergoing an unpleasant and/or embarrassing examination; and

(b) to allow a third party to act as an observer of what takes place, in order to ensure that someone (other than the patient and doctor) may testify in the event of a patient feeling that there has been some impropriety in the conduct of the consultation or medical examination.

'A relative or friend of the patient is not an impartial observer and so would not usually be a suitable chaperone, but you should comply with a reasonable request to have such a person present as well as a chaperone'[1].

Female patients consulting a male GP should be offered an opportunity for a chaperone to be present during an intimate examination or the option of returning to see a lady doctor if possible. Whatever the mix of patient-doctor genders, the opportunity of a chaperone being present during an intimate examination is increasingly advocated[2].

1 GMC *Intimate Examinations and Chaperones* (March 2013) available at http://www.gmc-uk. org/Intimate_examinations_and_chaperones.pdf_51449880.pdf.
2 See Jones 'The need for chaperones' (1993) 307 BMJ 951–952; Speelman, Savage, Verburgh 'Use of chaperones by general practitioners' (1993) 307 BMJ 986–987; Jones 'Patients' attitudes to chaperones' (1985) 35 J R Coll Gen Pract 192–193; Royal College of Obstetricians and Gynaecologists. *Guidelines on Intimate Examinations* (London, RCOG, 1998); Anonymous 'Chaperones in the general practice surgery' MPS Casebook 1997; 8; Rosenthal, Rymer, Jones, Haldane, Cohen, Bartholomew 'Chaperones for intimate examinations: cross sectional survey of attitudes and practices of general practitioners' (2005) 330 BMJ 234–235 doi:10.1136/_ bmj.38315.646053.F7.

17.46   In the case of the first rationale, it is obvious that chaperones can only be admitted to the consulting room with the permission of the patient[1]. If the chaperone is a nurse, then the nurse can offer emotional comfort to a patient by discussing the procedure and allowing the patient to anticipate what will take place, what is likely to happen next and, where appropriate, by modification of clinical contact, eg by holding hands with the patient. Where the chaperone is not a nurse their role is less clear. Without clinical training and with no other special relationship with the patient, it is generally not appropriate for a non-nurse chaperone to make physical contact with the patient, and not appropriate for the chaperone to have direct vision of an intimate examination. It is therefore good policy for GP receptionists to act as chaperones only if they have received training for this role. A non-clinically qualified chaperone will not be able to provide an eyewitness report of a clinical examination, though they may be able to offer a general indication of the atmosphere of a consultation, its ethos and smooth running (or otherwise). On the other hand, a nurse who acts as a chaperone is more likely to be able to act as an eyewitness to the events that unfold.

1 Stern 'Gynaecological examination post-*Ledward*: a private matter' (2001) 358 Lancet 1896– 1898.

17.47   When an intimate examination is required, the GMC recommends that doctors should:

(1)   explain to the patient why an examination is necessary and give the patient an opportunity to ask questions;
(2)   explain what the examination will involve, in a way the patient can understand, so that the patient has a clear idea of what to expect, including any pain or discomfort;
(3)   get the patient's permission before the examination and record that the patient has given it;
(4)   offer the patient a chaperone;
(5)   if dealing with a child or young person, their capacity to consent to the examination must be assessed. If they lack the capacity to consent, parental consent must be sought;
(6)   give the patient privacy to undress and dress, and keep them covered as much as possible to maintain their dignity: do not help the patient to remove clothing unless they have asked you to, or you have checked with them that they want you to help[1].

1 GMC *Intimate Examinations and Chaperones* (March 2013) available at http://www.gmc-uk. org/Intimate_examinations_and_chaperones.pdf_51449880.pdf.

17.48 However, a survey of 260 GPs in one health authority area in 1993 found that only 35 per cent of male and 5 per cent of female GPs ever offered patients a chaperone. The Medical Defence Union, in its document 'Guide to Chaperones (2013)', states:

'Patients have a right to refuse a chaperone. If you are unwilling to conduct an intimate examination without a chaperone, you should explain to the patient why you would prefer to have one present. You may need to offer an alternative appointment, or an alternative doctor, but only if the patient's clinical needs allow this'[1].

1 http://www.themdu.com/guidance-and-advice/guides/chaperones.

17.49 The key points in the Medical Defence Union's advice to doctors regarding chaperones are:

(1)   chaperones are there to support the patient;
(2)   chaperones should routinely be offered before intimate examinations;
(3)   patients can refuse a chaperone;
(4)   note the patient's acceptance or refusal in the records[1].

1 Stern 'Gynaecological examination post-*Ledward*: a private matter' (2001) 358 Lancet 1896–1898.

17.50 Patients need good doctors. Good doctors make the care of their patients their first concern: they are competent, keep their knowledge and skills up to date, establish and maintain good relationships with patients and colleagues, are honest and trustworthy, and act with integrity and within the law[1].

1 GMC *Good Medical Practice* (2013).

APPENDIX: CASE REPORTS

Gow v Harker [2003] EWCA Civ 1160

17.51 This was an appeal by the defendant, Dr Harker, former general practitioner, in a clinical negligence action.

The trial judge had found in favour of Miss Gow, in that Dr Harker had adopted an unacceptable technique when she extracted blood from Miss Gow in the course of a routine blood test in June 1995 and that, because she inserted a needle into her patient's wrist at too steep an angle, she thereby pierced the claimant's wrist and its underlying structures, damaging the radial nerve. It came to light during the appeal that, on the evidence, there were so many improbabilities and at least one apparent impossibility that the judge had not addressed in his judgment adequately or at all, his judgment could not be upheld and justice required a retrial by a different judge. The appeal judges said there should be a stay on the action of two months in order to give the parties the chance to consider mediation. The trial had been limited to issues of liability. Issues of causation were deliberately not included in the directions for trial.

At the age of 11 years Miss Gow had been diagnosed as having a thyroid condition which necessitated her having regular blood tests. Miss Gow attended Dr Harker's surgery in June 1995 to have this test done. Miss Gow was able to give the judge a graphic account of what happened on this occasion. Dr Harker had virtually no memory of the attendance and had only made a brief note in her GP records, as one would expect for the taking of a routine blood sample, so she was largely dependent on telling the judge about her regular practice when taking blood tests.

Having failed to extract blood from either of her preferred sites on the inside of each of Miss Gow's elbows, she took blood from a vein on the back of Miss Gow's right wrist. This is common practice in taking routine blood samples in a GP surgery. Miss Gow said that the doctor had inserted the needle at an angle of 90° to the skin and with some force. She said that she had immediately felt severe pain in her fingers and hand. She cried out with pain, slumped forward in a cold sweat from her sitting position and almost blacked out while Dr Harker jumped back and let go of the syringe she had been using. Miss Gow said she saw the needle and syringe sticking out from her wrist 'like a dart stuck in a dartboard'. Dr Harker then pulled the needle out. Miss Gow said she then suffered intense pain over the weekend. She complained of numbness in the first and second fingers of her right hand and could not move her right arm.

She returned to the surgery after the weekend and saw another doctor. She said that all her fingers had swollen up, the back of her hand between the first and second fingers was also physically swollen and she could not turn or bend her wrist. In the doctor's contemporaneous note in the medical records for that appointment, he describes pain in the wrist and fingers but states 'no swelling or inflammation'.

Dr Harker, in her evidence, described her normal technique of taking blood from a vein on the back of the wrist. This is described in detail in the court report. Dr Harker had also worked as an anaesthetist for 15 months when she was probably performing up to ten venipunctures a day so she had plenty of experience of this type of technique. She had no recollection of Miss Gow crying out or expressing any pain or disquiet when the needle was inserted, nor did she recollect jumping back and leaving the needle in place. It was not true that only a small amount of blood flowed into the syringe as had been stated by Miss Gow. There was ample blood for the thyroid tests, which were successfully performed. One of the expert witnesses confirmed that for this test the amount of blood required would normally be between 3ml and 5ml and not the 1ml, which Miss Gow had said, had been drawn. Dr Harker confirmed that if the needle had gone into a nerve rather than the vein she would not have been able to extract any blood at all.

The expert evidence confirmed that the shallower the angle of approach of the needle, the less likely it was that the needle would go through the back of the vein. A normal approach would be 10–15° and anything over 25° would be unacceptable and certainly not as much as 90°.

There was a dispute between claimant and defendant with regard to the point of entry of the needle into the wrist. The experts agreed that on Miss Gow's account of the matter, no blood could have entered the syringe and all agreed that Dr Harker would have had to pull back on the plunger for blood to enter the syringe and on Miss Gow's account Dr Harker jumped back and let go as soon as she shrieked with pain, immediately upon entry of the needle into her wrist.

Apparently the trial judge did not address any of the issues relating to the site of the needle entry in the two accounts and nor was the fact addressed that 3–5ml of blood were required for a successful test, which did in fact take place. The appeal judges considered that if the trial judge had considered these points, he would have concluded that Miss Gow must have been mistaken in her evidence and when he turned to Dr Harker's evidence, any judge weighing the evidence thoroughly would have been bound to consider the inherent improbability of a doctor with as much experience of performing venipuncture, both as a GP and as an anaesthetist, attempting to take blood in the extraordinary way described by Miss Gow.

The appeal judges therefore concluded that they could not uphold the trial judge's judgment when on the evidence there were so many improbabilities and at least one apparent impossibility (the presence of a millilitre of blood in the syringe), elements of evidence that the judge simply did not address in his judgment adequately or at all.

The appeal judges therefore allowed the appeal and directed that there should be a stay on the action of a retrial for two months in order to give the parties a chance to consider the enlistment of a skilled mediator before any further costs were expended on the litigation. If the case did progress to a retrial, this should be by a different judge and should try both liability and causation on the same occasion.

Wardlaw v Farrar [2003] EWCA (Civ) 1719

17.52 This was an appeal by the claimant, Mr Wardlaw, in a clinical negligent action from a decision by the judge in the original trial, awarding Mr Wardlaw £1,000 damages against the defendant general practitioner, Dr Farrar, in respect of the death of his wife in September 1997.

On 14 September 1997 Mrs Wardlaw had consulted Dr Farrar but the trial judge found that the doctor had been negligent in his examination of Mrs Wardlaw. The doctor did not consider a diagnosis of pulmonary embolism (PE), which eventually resulted in Mrs Wardlaw's death, and he did not arrange her admission to hospital for further investigation.

She was seen by a locum doctor one week later when her admission to hospital was arranged. In the intervening period she remained in pain and suffered from breathlessness.

On admission to hospital, Mrs Wardlaw was treated with anticoagulation therapy for a suspected diagnosis of pulmonary embolism. Heparin was started. Five hours later, she sustained a sudden collapse, which was associated with increased pain and increased shortness of breath. The following day, a lung ventilation and perfusion scan was performed. That confirmed the presence of numerous small pulmonary emboli but no large emboli were evident. Heparin and warfarin stabilised Mrs Wardlaw's condition, so that by three days later it was considered that she might be released to go home during the following week. However her condition worsened and she died the following day in hospital, the cause of death being pulmonary embolism and deep vein thrombosis.

The medical expert for the defence stated that a delay between the two GP consultations of one week would have made no difference to the outcome of the case. The expert noted that the deceased had progressive pulmonary embolism despite adequate anticoagulation and considered that the lady's condition was therefore unresponsive to treatment.

The claimant's expert relied on an article published in the Lancet, which itself raised certain questions that had not been clarified by guidelines published by the British Thoracic Society.

The trial judge found that Dr Farrar's negligence was responsible for a week's pain and suffering during the delay in the admission to hospital but that that delay did not increase the risk of her death. The delay did not therefore materially contribute to her death. The judge had therefore awarded the claimant £1,000 damages in respect of his claim.

At the appeal, the appeal judges made observations relating to the use of learned articles or textbook passages during trials. The appeal judges listened to much evidence reiterated by counsel from the original trial and counsel for the appellant endeavoured to extract from the transcripts an entirely new argument, which had not been put to the medical experts at the trial, nor advanced by her predecessor to the trial judge. This was not entertained by the appeal judges.

The appeal judges were in agreement in dismissing the appeal.

Harding v Scott-Moncrieff [2004] EWHC 1733 (QB)

17.53   This was a claim by the claimant, Lady Harding, widow of the deceased Sir Christopher Harding, against Dr Scott-Moncrieff, a general practitioner.

Sir Christopher Harding died suddenly at his home at about 3.30pm on the afternoon of 13 December 1999. It was alleged that the defendant, Dr Scott-Moncrieff, who attended the deceased, was negligent in that prompt action by him would have saved Sir Christopher's life. He was 60 years old when he died and it was claimed that he would have continued to work until the age of 70 years.

There was acute disagreement between two eminent expert cardiologists as to the underlying cause of death and the prognosis.

Sir Christopher had felt unwell since about 3am on that date and the general practitioner, after being called, had attended at about 2.05pm. After examination he attempted to make arrangements for the patient to be admitted to a private hospital and for a private ambulance to collect him. The defendant's differential diagnosis included pulmonary embolus, myocardial infarction and infection. The defendant did not stay with his patient while the private ambulance was being awaited.

The defendant enquired at 3.20pm, by telephone, whether the ambulance was on its way but he was told that it might be another hour. Ten minutes later at 3.30pm, the defendant telephoned the au pair at Sir Christopher's home because he thought his patient might be deteriorating. As a result he rang for an NHS blue light ambulance to take the patient to St Mary's Hospital instead of King Edward VII Hospital.

The general practitioner experts, at their meeting, agreed that the above stated differential diagnoses, which they agreed were life threatening, required the doctor to remain with the patient as standard practice until the ambulance arrived. It was thus accepted that the defendant's failure to do this was a breach of duty. He was also found in breach of duty in failing to call a blue light ambulance in the first instance and also for acceding to the patient's wishes to go to a private hospital and not explaining the risks of doing so. He was also said to be in breach of duty for failing to administer either a diuretic or 300mg of aspirin at the patient's home before the ambulance arrived.

With regard to breach of duty, myocardial infarction carries a high risk of death for about 24 hours, although the risk diminishes during this time. Since the defendant's differential diagnosis included myocardial infarction and since the 24 hours starts from the onset of symptoms, that being 3.00am, all experts agreed that Sir Christopher should have been taken to hospital urgently.

The defendant stated that he did not regard Sir Christopher's condition as a medical emergency and he did not consider that there was any real risk of deterioration or sudden death in the next couple of hours. His concern was simply to get Sir Christopher into hospital that afternoon and it was presumably this belief that led him to accede to Sir Christopher's wish to go to private hospital without explaining the risks involved or the medical need for urgent transfer. All experts agreed that for a patient to make an informed choice of that sort he must be given the relevant information. All experts also agreed that the administration of a diuretic or aspirin was standard practice and should have been given unless aspirin had been contraindicated, which it was not in this instance.

The acute disagreement between the two eminent expert cardiologists not only related to the underlying cause of death but there was dramatic disagreement on prognosis. The claimant's expert was clear that Sir Christopher should have survived and been able to return to work after a period of convalescence until the age of 70 years if he wished. The defendant's expert cardiologist was adamant that he would have died roughly when he did whatever had happened.

On the evidence presented to him, the judge found a breach of duty in each of the failings above by the general practitioner. With regard to causation the judge had to differentiate between the opinions of the expert cardiologists, which as described above varied considerably. The judge gave full reasoning to support his decision to accept the evidence of the claimant's expert in that, had Sir Christopher been referred by blue light ambulance to NHS hospital in the first instance, he would have survived and been able to return to work.

Where the differential diagnosis of a patient's condition includes even only one serious and potentially life threatening diagnosis, it is essential that the attending GP takes immediate and appropriate action. While the patient might prefer private treatment and transport, acute medical conditions are virtually always best dealt with by using NHS facilities and transport. Transfer to a private hospital, if that is the preference, can take place at a later stage once the acute situation has been stabilised. In addition, in an acute medical situation, the GP should stay with the patient until handover takes place to the ambulance crew. If there is life-saving treatment which can be given to the patient while waiting for transport, such as in this case, this should always be available in the doctor's bag and given to the patient. It is also essential that where the patient's uninformed preferences with regard to transport and hospital admission vary from the recommendations of the attending doctor the doctor's view of the situation should be explained in detail so that the patient can make an informed choice.

Bowe v Townend [2005] EWHC 198 (QB)

17.54   In April 2000, the claimant, Mr Adrian Bowe, collapsed with a right-sided headache, left-sided weakness and speech defects. On admission to hospital a CT scan revealed acute changes of major right middle cerebral artery infarction but unfortunately his condition deteriorated. While in hospital, in May 2000, he had a transoesophageal echocardiogram that revealed that he had a large patent foramen ovale and atrial septal aneurysm. He was severely disabled because of his catastrophic stroke.

The claimant was claiming damages against his general practitioner, Dr Townend, alleging that the doctor had made a negligent misdiagnosis in January 1999, at which time the claimant had presented to Dr Townend with sudden loss of vision in the right eye followed by left-sided headache; there was also some blurring of vision in the temporal half of the right field. Dr Townend had diagnosed migraine. The claimant claimed that at this consultation, had a differential diagnosis been made, he would ultimately have been referred to a cardiologist who would have required a transoesophageal echocardiogram, which would have revealed Mr Bowe's condition and appropriate treatment would have avoided the catastrophic stroke that he had suffered.

In the claimant's history, he had been born in 1974, at which time he was diagnosed as having a congenital hole in the heart that had apparently healed spontaneously.

In 1997, another GP had referred Mr Bowe to a neurologist at the local hospital because of an episode of facial palsy and dysarthria. The neurologist diagnosed a transient ischaemic attack (TIA), which would have been very unusual in a man of 23 years. On further investigation all tests conducted were negative.

Mr Bowe alleged that at the consultation with Dr Townend in January 1999, had Dr Townend considered Mr Bowe's past medical history, the misdiagnosis would not have occurred. It was also observed that at this consultation Dr Townend, in the medical record, did not record the neurological examination that he conducted. The benefits of a full description of the examination include the benefit to those doctors who have occasion to treat the patient subsequently and also in the event of litigation a full note provides the best aide-memoir.

In the judge's consideration of causation, he stated that Dr Townend's failure was one of omission. Had Dr Townend made a differential diagnosis and consequently referred Mr Bowe to a specialist, whether a neurologist or an ophthalmologist, it is more likely than not that he would have been referred on to a cardiologist, who would have diagnosed on the balance of probabilities, after a transoesophageal echocardiogram, a patent foramen ovale and atrial septal aneurysm. Following these diagnoses, treatment with warfarin would have avoided the stroke and aspirin would have reduced the possibility of a stroke. The judge's final conclusion was that he found for the claimant on both negligence and causation.

An incorrect diagnosis made without consideration of other possible differential diagnoses, and particularly without apparent consideration of the past medical history, in this instance the cardiac defects that the patient was born with, can lead the doctor into having a false sense of security in making his diagnosis, and in so doing, potentially seriously compromise the patient's future health and well-being. In addition, there should always be full documentation in the GP record of a clinical examination.

McDonnell v Holwerda [2005] EWHC 1081 (QB)

17.55 The claimant, Sebastian McDonnell, suing by his mother and litigation friend Christina McDonnell, brought a claim against the defendant doctor, Dr Holwerda, his former GP, regarding events on Christmas Day 1997, when the claimant was four years old. As a result of the meningococcal septicaemia that he developed that day, he suffered a number of severe disabilities, including the loss of his right leg through amputation and the loss of a number of digits on both hands. The claimant's left leg was also badly affected.

The claimant's case was that the defendant, despite having seen the claimant twice on that day, failed to detect the extent to which a risk existed that he was suffering from a meningococcal septicaemia and/or meningitis, which risk required immediate referral to hospital. It was contended for the claimant that had she referred him he would have received earlier treatment and his disabilities would have been avoided.

During the course of the afternoon on the day in question, Sebastian became sufficiently unwell that his parents called the general practitioner, the defendant, who arrived reasonably promptly at about 5pm. The defendant examined the claimant, checked his temperature which was 40°C and concluded he might have gastroenteritis. She advised Calpol and a cool bath.

She stated that she did not think it was meningitis and told the family to call her again if necessary and in particular to look out for sensitivity to light and the presence of a rash.

Shortly before 9pm that evening the mother again telephoned the defendant, who arrived promptly. She was informed that the claimant had expressed sensitivity to light and as a result the main lights in the room were not on. She was informed that the claimant had a rash. The defendant concluded that there were no signs of meningitis, that he had a heat rash and the treatment should continue by way of fluids, paracetamol and keeping the child cool.

Later that night, because of the claimant's deteriorating condition, the family telephoned the hospital and were told to bring him in. Shortly after that call he started to fit and an ambulance was called. He arrived at the hospital at about 1.30am and was admitted as an emergency. A diagnosis of meningococcal septicaemia was rapidly made and he was treated with intravenous antibiotics, the first doses probably being given within ½–1 hour of his arrival in hospital.

In his judgment the judge considered that the mother was mistaken in her recollection, reflected by her answers in cross-examination, that she mentioned every symptom of the condition that she could then recall Sebastian had developed, on the telephone when asking the defendant to make a home visit on the first occasion. There is no doubt that she must have mentioned some of the symptoms in order for the visit to take place but that some of the symptoms, including probably the sensitivity to light, had developed at a later stage. There is no dispute that when the defendant left after the first occasion she advised the family to be alert for sensitivity to lights and if he had already developed this by that time she would not have given this advice. There was also a question with regard to Sebastian's temperature in relation to the fact that he was wearing a lot of clothing and was in close proximity to a hot air vent. At the time of the first visit the defendant advised against both of these in order to help to reduce his temperature. It is apparent that she took both a stethoscope and otoscope into the house but inexplicably not her bag. She apparently did not have her thermometer with her and used a strip thermometer offered by the mother. The defendant stated in her witness statement that on her first visit, 'he was not confused, he was not concerned by the lights on in the room, he had no neck stiffness nor a suspicious rash'. In her statement she observed, 'I only raised the issue of meningitis as this is a condition parents are often worried about'.

The judge stated that he accepted the evidence supported by the experts that the examination which the defendant carried out on the first visit was not below the standard expected of a reasonably competent GP, that her suggested diagnosis of gastroenteritis was reasonable and that her advice to the parent to monitor the situation and particularly to watch for specific symptoms was acceptable. At the time of the second visit, when the claimant considered that Sebastian had deteriorated, had developed a rash and did not like the light on in the room, the defendant considered, after examining him, that there had been some improvement, his temperature was now 38°C and as a result she advised the continuation of fluids and keeping him cool as well as more paracetamol. Although the doctor's attendance following the second call was prompt, she arrived without a thermometer, stethoscope or otoscope on this occasion. There was a dispute as to what clothing Sebastian was wearing at this time. The family maintaining that he was wearing only underpants and the defendant that he was wearing a T-shirt, which she had to lift to look at the rash. In order to see the rash clearly the doctor asked that the lights be put on in the living room and she stated in her evidence that he did not seem to mind this being done. She also said that the rash, when she saw it, was restricted to his right shoulder and that it disappeared completely on exerting pressure on the skin. Classically, the purpuric rash of meningitis does not fade when a glass is pressed against it. The doctor describes him as 'fully conscious' but in his judgment the judge stated that that did not shed any light on his overall alertness. In the absence of any signs of meningitis, including the fact that his neck was not stiff, the doctor concluded that the diagnosis was gastroenteritis.

Having heard the evidence of the GP expert witnesses, the judge was of the opinion that the defendant's examination of the patient on the second visit was inadequate and that she had adopted a brusque approach in her assessment of both his sensitivity to light and the existence of the rash. The judge accepted the claimant's expert witness's evidence that there were important deficiencies in the history that the defendant took from the family and that the defendant's examination was inadequate. Also a proper examination of a child's rash requires full undressing. The defendant should have looked 'everywhere'. Different parts of the rash may have different characteristics. The expert witness stated that he would expect a GP to know that some parts could blanch and others not. Further evidence that the defendant missed, related to excessive sensitivity to being touched as a sign of irritability as a significant factor in an assessment of risk for meningitis and meningococcal septicaemia. Further, the expert witness was of the opinion that the defendant should have examined the abdomen because 'when called back to a child with a high temperature you must examine the abdomen'. The experts agreed that if 'the family's account' was correct, treatment would have been given after arrival at hospital and would have commenced between 10.30–11pm. The judge concluded that this was correct. The judge's final paragraph in the court report is as follows: 'In the light of the above conclusions, I shall hear counsel on the necessary consequential orders and directions for the future conduct of the case'.

When called to see a sick child, even on a second visit, a GP must always be mindful of the potentially serious nature of a child with a high temperature and the rapidity with which a child's condition can deteriorate. The rash in a meningococcal infection may be variable on different parts of the child and so all areas should be examined. 'Brusqueness' is never acceptable in a doctor and a GP on a home visit should carry all necessary diagnostic equipment.

Burne v A [2006] EWCA Civ 24

17.56   This was an appeal by the defendant in a clinical negligence action, Dr Burne, a general practitioner, from a decision by the judge in favour of the claimant A at a trial limited to the issue of liability. A was born prematurely in

1991 with a hydrocephalic condition requiring a ventriculo-peritoneal shunt which was fitted at the age of 9 weeks.

In January 1998, when A was 6½ years old, he began vomiting or, as the mother described it, throwing up a lot of phlegm, and complaining of a headache. His mother telephoned Dr Burne. Over the telephone Dr Burne diagnosed an upper respiratory infection. The judge found that the mother had not mentioned the child's irritability, drowsiness and restlessness as well as vomiting, although she would have mentioned these had she been specifically asked about them. The following day when A was worse and continuing to deteriorate, an ambulance was called and in hospital it was found that the shunt had become blocked causing a heart attack and brain damage.

The judge had found for the claimant on the grounds that, had the general practitioner exercised a proper standard of skill and care when he first spoke to the mother on the telephone, A's symptoms would have been recognised as possibly indicative of a blockage in his shunt. Had this been realised, prompt specialist attention would have prevented the occurrence of damage.

The written and oral evidence of two expert witnesses on professional standards in general practice showed that they were both prepared to accept that the use of 'open' questions was a proper method of diagnosis and that if this were the case, Dr Burne's failure to obtain from the mother specific answers which would have alerted him to the possibility of a blocked shunt, was not professionally negligent. The judge did not accept that this was reasonable in the case of a sick child with A's known condition and history.

In view of the fact that Dr Burne had been supported in not asking closed questions of the claimant's mother by the expert witnesses, the appeal judges considered that the original trial judge had not applied the *Bolam* rule and quoted Lord Scarman as saying that this test does not permit the judge to make his or her own choice between two or more respectable schools of professional practice. The view of the appeal judges was that this was a case that must be referred to alternative dispute resolution before it was restored for re-trial and it was to be hoped that mediation would bring a swift conclusion to a tragic event.

This case demonstrates the difficulties surrounding a telephone conversation with a relative of the patient when the doctor cannot see the true clinical state of the patient. If the GP does not have access to the clinical record, he may be unaware of a past medical history which could give rise to an alternative diagnosis with potentially more serious consequences. Although the expert witnesses supported the general practitioner in not asking closed questions, it would certainly have made the clinical picture clearer for him to have done so.

Zarb v Odetoyinbo [2006] EWHC 2880 (QB)

17.57 The claimant, Mrs Zarb, claimed damages for alleged clinical negligence against her general practitioner, Dr Odetoyinbo. Her case was that in September 2001, at the age of 33 years, when she presented with bilateral sciatica and a history of back pain, he failed to make an immediate call to an orthopaedic surgeon or a same day referral in respect of the symptoms. The claimant later developed cauda equina syndrome (CES), resulting in permanent nerve damage and a resultant loss of normal function of the bowels and the bladder. She alleged that, because of the defendant's negligence, she developed CES as a result.

Following the consultation, the defendant wrote a referral letter to a consultant orthopaedic surgeon, the letter being dated two days after the consultation. Three days after the consultation, the claimant was admitted to the neurosurgical unit of the Royal London Hospital as an emergency via A&E at about 6am. The casualty officer noted that there was a long history of back pain for eight years and that the current pain had been getting worse over six days. She was unable to open her bowels or pass urine and she felt numb around the anus.

She was referred for a neurosurgical opinion and was seen by the specialist registrar something over four hours later. An MRI scan was requested, which revealed central disc prolapse. Later that night, a neurosurgeon performed a small L4 laminectomy and lateral flavectomy. The outcome of the operation was poor. The claimant was discharged about two weeks later, following which she had suffered total permanent loss of normal bladder function and sexual sensation as well as permanent loss of bowel function and severe back pain.

The expert neurosurgeons agreed that if the defendant had made a same day referral and that she had had immediate surgery, the back pain would, in all probability be similar to the back pain she in fact suffered following the operation three days later. They also agreed that if early surgery had taken place, the incontinence suffered by the claimant would in all probability not have occurred.

It was the claimant's case that the only reasonable and proper course for the defendant was immediate or same day referral. The bilateral sciatica that she was suffering was a sufficiently strong indicator of a risk of CES and that no other course was open to the defendant. The defendant's case was that immediate referral was not the only or even the proper course and that the referral he did make was a proper course, as the claimant did not say that she suffered loss of sensation in the perineum or any bladder or bowel dysfunction until the day of her admission to hospital.

Regarding causation, the claimant's neurology expert, in his evidence, made the point that had she been operated upon at any time before the time when the operation did take place, she would have had to consent to the operation, having had explained to her the risks of poor outcome in 10–15 per cent of such cases; and without knowing whether she was going to be one of the 6 per cent of bilateral sciatica sufferers who were going to go on to contract CES, it would have been a very difficult assessment of risk for her to undertake.

With regard to breach of duty, if the defendant had referred the claimant immediately and the neurosurgeon, to whom the claimant was referred, did not admit her but, provided that he advised her to return to hospital if and when she felt saddle anaesthesia or urinary or bowel dysfunction, it would not have been considered negligent. On that basis, if a GP effectively followed the same course in not making a same day referral but advising the patient to return to him or to hospital under the same conditions, this could not be considered to be negligent either.

Complications also occurred for two reasons. The first related to the fact that the judge held that guidelines, that were made available by the Royal College of General Practitioners in February 2001, would be a major obstacle to a finding that there had been a breach of duty in this case. In principle, it was possible that these guidelines might fail the *Bolam* test but it would be difficult to envisage the circumstances in which a judge would be bound to reach that conclusion. Second, the fact that the defendant's GP expert witness, in addition to having 27 years' experience, was a member of the management board of the Medical Defence Union (MDU) and that his instruction came from the MDU, who were acting for the defendant. It was suggested that he lacked or appeared to lack the independence necessary for the fulfilment of the duties of an expert witness giving evidence in court. The judge considered this but made no finding on this point.

There were some inconsistencies between the oral evidence of the claimant and the evidence of her husband, Mr Zarb. There were also inconsistencies between the evidence given by the claimant and that of the different doctors who attended her. The judge stated that, in his judgment, it was very improbable that all the contemporaneous notes taken by the different doctors, who saw the claimant around the time of the operation, should be mistaken and consistently mistaken as the claimant alleged. He followed this by stating that he had no hesitation in preferring the evidence of the defendant to that of the claimant and of her husband.

A point that the judge made was that a GP making a same day referral is unlikely to be in breach of his duty to his patient whatever effect such a practice might have upon his relationship with the surgeons and hospital to whom the referrals may be made, but it does not follow that a GP who trusts his own judgment and acts as the defendant did, would be in breach of his duty.

In summary, the judge stated, 'In my judgment the defendant was not in breach of his duty of care in his management of the claimant's illness in September 2001, and so the claim must fail'.

Holt v Edge [2007] EWCA Civ 602

17.58   This was an appeal by the claimant, Mrs Holt, against a decision by the trial judge, dismissing a preliminary issue as to liability and causation in her clinical negligence claim against the respondent defendant, Dr Edge, a general practitioner.

On a day in May 2001, the appellant had slipped in the shower at her home. She had suffered a spontaneous subarachnoid haemorrhage. Her husband telephoned the respondent's practice at a little before 4.00pm and spoke to the receptionist who noted that Mrs Holt had cramp in her neck, difficulty breathing and pins and needles in her arm. The receptionist spoke to Dr Stagg, the duty doctor, who said the appellant should be referred to the out-of-hours doctors service and the message was passed at 6.15pm. It was common ground that Dr Stagg should have conducted a telephone triage and that he was in breach of duty in not doing so.

The appellant was visited at her home at about 9.00pm that evening by the out-of-hours duty doctor who examined her and conducted a full neurological examination. He did not suspect any intracranial pathology but noted that the appellant's blood pressure was high and advised her to see her GP the following day. The following morning the appellant's husband telephoned the practice and the message that was taken was, '?whiplash yesterday, headache, vomiting, pain neck and back'. Dr Edge saw this and visited the appellant at home after 11am. He agreed with the out-of-hours doctor from the previous evening that she had suffered a musculoskeletal neck injury.

At the trial it was stated that Dr Edge should have asked Mrs Holt directly about the history of vomiting which was in the receptionist's note. The experts' joint statement recorded that if Dr Edge had been told about repeated vomiting, the appellant should have been referred to hospital.

Two days later the appellant attended the local A&E department. A CT scan done later that day revealed a subarachnoid haemorrhage. Three days later she was operated on, suffering a stroke in the course of the operation because the aneurysm in her brain ruptured.

The trial judge found that the admitted breach of duty by the respondent's practice of failing to ensure that the appellant was spoken to by a doctor in order to carry out telephone triage on the original day of injury, made no difference to the course of events. The judge found there was no breach of duty by Dr Edge when he attended Mrs Holt by failing to ask her about her history of vomiting of which he was aware. The judge reiterated the appellant's primary case that Mr Holt had furnished critical information about his wife's condition to Dr Edge, namely, pounding headaches and persisting vomiting which were the classic symptoms that would have required immediate referral to hospital.

The stroke that Mrs Holt suffered in the course of the operation was because the aneurysm in her brain ruptured in the course of being dissected by the surgeon, this being due to temporary clipping of the aneurysm. There is no criticism of the manner in which the operation was conducted.

The grounds for appeal in the first instance relate to the fact that Mr Holt did not speak to a doctor when he first telephoned the practice following Mrs Holt's injury and also that, had a competently administered telephone triage been carried out at that time, Mrs Holt would have been referred to the A&E department that afternoon for a prompt neurological assessment which would have led to diagnosis of her subarachnoid haemorrhage and earlier surgical intervention. Had Dr Stagg taken the call himself, his questions might very well have elicited more information than those of his receptionists but as the out-of-hours doctor some hours later did not make the diagnosis of subarachnoid haemorrhage the question arises, why should Dr Stagg have elicited any different information from that obtained by the out-of-hours doctor? The appeal judges agreed with the trial judge's finding that a telephone triage at about 4.00pm would not have elicited any reference to headaches and therefore there was no evidence that any reasonably competent general medical practitioner would have considered a neurological assessment to be necessary. There was none of the history of the classic presentation of a pounding headache shortly after subarachnoid haemorrhage and therefore no case for referring Mrs Holt immediately to hospital.

The appeal judges therefore determined that had Dr Stagg conducted a telephone triage himself, it would have made no difference. The out-of-hours doctor would still have attended during the evening and the subsequent outcome would have been no different. Accordingly, these grounds failed in the judgment of the appeal judges.

Other grounds of appeal relate to finding no breach of duty by Dr Edge when he failed to ask about a history of vomiting of which he was aware and also that he was in breach of duty by not referring Mrs Holt to the A&E department that day, which it was agreed would have led to the diagnosis of her subarachnoid haemorrhage and earlier surgical intervention. There was discussion by the appeal judges as to whether, and if so to what extent, questioning took place with regard to Mrs Holts' vomiting by either Dr Edge or the out-of-hours doctor but at the end of it the appeal judges decided that it was impossible to conclude that there was information in the hands of, or that was available to, Dr Edge that dictated immediate referral to hospital when he visited Mrs Holt and therefore these further grounds of appeal were judged to fail. The judges therefore dismissed the appeal.

It is always appropriate for telephone triaging to be conducted by a doctor or practice nurse and not a receptionist, who is unlikely to have had any formal training in medical history taking. It would be appropriate for the receptionist to take a message from the patient and for the doctor to call back, as often happens in GP out-of-hours services. It is not apparent why there was such a considerable delay between the initial taking of the message by the receptionist at about 4pm and it being passed to the out-of-hours service at 6.15pm. Rather than waiting until the out-of-hours service opened, as a general principle, a doctor at the practice, during core working hours, should be expected to deal with the patient's problem, or at the very least refer the patient to A&E.

Vance v Taylor [2007] EWHC 1602 (QB)

17.59   On Friday 17 August 2001, the claimant, Mr Gareth Vance, then aged 28 years, started to experience aching in his lumbar region. Two days later he was in so much pain, aggravated by any movement, that he was bedbound. He was taken to the A&E Department of the Middlesex Hospital; nothing abnormal was found. Two hours after he arrived, a doctor diagnosed 'acute back sprain' and prescribed analgesics, anti-inflammatories and a relaxant. The following day his condition had not improved and he began vomiting. On Tuesday 21 August, he started to sweat profusely.

The claimant's general practitioner, the defendant Dr Taylor, made a home visit later that day. He was told that Mr Vance had been vomiting but not that he had been sweating. There was no physical examination because of the pain that this would have caused but Dr Taylor did touch Mr Vance's feet as part of his concern to exclude paraplegia. He changed the medication and gave advice as to future conduct and management.

The vomiting ceased but, for a period of weeks, the history was one of continuous pain, often excruciating. There was apparently a discussion between Dr Taylor and Mr and Mrs Vance with regard to the availability of a domiciliary visit by an NHS physiotherapist. Dr Taylor explained that this was not possible under the NHS climate at that time and so, on 24 August, a private physiotherapist made a home visit and she then did daily visits throughout each week until the end of September and kept excellent contemporaneous records of findings, complaints and progress.

Progress was slow but towards the end of September he was able to walk 50 yards down the road and walk back again. During the time that Mr Vance was receiving treatment from the physiotherapist, at no time was his condition referred back to the defendant. He seemed to be content to leave his treatment wholly in the care of the physiotherapist. During the last week of September there was an increase in the pain that Mr Vance was experiencing. The physiotherapist was concerned about this and made direct contact with a consultant neurosurgeon in order to arrange admission to a private hospital for an MRI scan.

While awaiting the scan, Mr Vance arranged for a home visit by the defendant and, at that visit, the defendant's advice was for immediate admission to the West Middlesex Hospital. Mr Vance preferred to follow the route arranged by the physiotherapist.

The judge inferred from the experts, who gave evidence before him, that it was apparent with hindsight that it was a pity that Mr Vance did not take Dr Taylor's advice and had declined admission to NHS hospital, where he would have been fully investigated. Unfortunately, the private hospital assumed that Mr Vance's condition amounted to a disc problem and the MRI scan during the first week of October was directed at the lumbar spine. Although this revealed degenerative changes in some lumbar disc spaces, at the lower margin of the scan there was, what the consultant neuroradiologist described as 'a large cystic or necrotic mass in the right psoas extending to the right erector spinae. I think this is most likely to be a psoas abscess although malignancy is not ruled out'. Mr Vance was admitted to the private hospital.

About two weeks later, he had a consultation with a consultant in infectious diseases. Subsequently, malignancy was ruled out and a Staphylococcus aureus infection confirmed involving soft tissues and bone as well as a psoas abscess. Unfortunately, despite intensive administration of antibiotics, the infection inflicted damage such that Mr Vance required a left hip resurfacing operation in May 2002, a prolonged period off work and to be reconciled to the prospect of hip replacements in the future.

In the judge's consideration of the evidence of the expert witnesses, he considered that the defendant exercised entirely appropriate care and skill in his care of the patient at the stages at which the patient was seen by the defendant. In his comments and conclusion, the judge makes reference to the fact that Mr Vance had some chiropody on 11 August and that the chiropodist, having been using a scalpel, may have inadvertently caused the introduction of some infection into Mr Vance's foot which had led to the psoas abscess, but an infection had not been diagnosed until Mr Vance was under the care of the infectious diseases consultant towards the end of October. Mr Vance had fallen victim to a virulent infection with features in terms of history, presentation and extent that were unusual almost to the point of being unique. The judge stated that to make a claim of negligence out of these circumstances is in itself bold and even surprising, then to advance it against just one individual doctor, who was arguably only a minor contributor to the history, out of several doctors, is even more surprising, not least when it is acknowledged that to a significant degree that doctor's advice was good. The judge therefore found that the claimant had failed to prove his case.

Baxter v McCann [2010] EWHC 1330 (QB)

17.60   In this case, the claimants, the family members of the patient, Mrs Catherine Moores, were suing Mrs Moores' GP, Dr Kirsty McCann for clinical negligence. Mrs Moores had died in March 2003 because of an ovarian clear cell adenocarcinoma. The claimants alleged that her death was caused by the defendant, in failing to carry out a proper physical examination at an appointment in March 2001, which would, it was alleged, have demonstrated the tumour when it was at a stage at which it could and probably would have been successfully treated.

It was agreed that Dr McCann should have conducted a full pelvic examination, including a bimanual vaginal examination. It was also agreed between the parties that at the time of that examination Mrs Moores had a tumour, irregular in shape, of approximately 5–10 cms in diameter in the pelvis, probably behind the uterus. In para 39 the defendant says that she had conducted the three elements of: abdominal examination, vaginal speculum examination and bimanual examination but her clinical records for that consultation (para 35) only suggests by inference that these were all done, in that the stated information could only have been obtained by at the very least, a vaginal examination.

The tumour was not detected until October 2001 and it was removed in December 2001 when it was over 11cms in diameter and had infiltrated the bowel, liver and abdomen and the nodes in the lymphatic system.

The issues that arose related to both breach of duty and causation. With regard to breach of duty, did Dr McCann perform an appropriate and competent examination of Mrs Moores in March 2001 and, with regard to causation, if Dr McCann had performed a reasonably competent examination and if, as a result, diagnosis of the carcinoma was delayed, did that delay make any difference to Mrs Moores' outcome?

The claimants contended that, had the tumour been diagnosed at first presentation, Mrs Moores could have survived for at least five years. It was submitted on Dr McCann's behalf that the tumour at the time of initial presentation was already in such an advanced state that any failure to diagnose it then did not have any material effect on her outcome.

The judge heard evidence from expert witnesses on both sides and also referred to various papers relating to the diagnosis of pelvic tumours on bimanual examination and the fact that some pelvic masses, even of 5–10 cms in diameter, are frequently missed by gynaecologists. With regard to this point, the junior doctor in gynaecology who examined Mrs Moores in the clinic in September 2001 also failed to palpate the tumour.

The judge held, on the basis of the evidence that was presented to him, that Dr McCann did not act incompetently or negligently in not palpating the tumour and accordingly the claimants had failed to establish that Dr McCann was in any way negligent in her examination of Mrs Moores in March 2001, as a result of which it was unnecessary for the court to make any finding on causation and the judge declined to do so. For these reasons the judge dismissed the claim.

General practitioners are able to diagnose most conditions but they have to be aware that where they cannot make a diagnosis, if appropriate, they must still give the patient the benefit of onward referral for specialist consideration. Also, in examining the patient, the written account in the patient's records should describe clearly all aspects of that examination.

Marcus v Medway Primary Care Trust [2010] EWHC 1888 (QB)

17.61   This was a medical negligence claim by the claimant Sebastian Marcus who, in 2005, at the age of 31 years, suffered occlusion of the arteries of his left lower leg caused by embolisation from a lesion in the abdominal aorta. As a result of the occlusions he suffered ischaemia in the foot which caused very severe pain and resulted in a below knee amputation of the left lower limb in June 2005. The first defendant was the Medway Primary Care Trust and the second defendant was Dr Hussain.

The first defendant's employee, Dr Thom, a general practitioner, diagnosed ischaemia but failed to take the appropriate steps thereafter. The second defendant, Dr Hussain, a locum with the claimant's own general practitioner, failed to diagnose ischaemia at any time on the three occasions when he saw the defendant. Negligence was admitted by both defendants.

The issues on causation related to whether there would have been complete recovery or, amputation avoided, the leg remained permanently symptomatic. The issues related in the first instance to what was the latest date when intervention by a vascular surgeon would have saved the claimant's leg and what was the latest date at which anticoagulant medication would have preserved a compromised supply to the left lower limb and prevented further embolisation? In each case, if the date was before 14 April 2005, the claim on each basis failed. If the date was after 14 April but before 20 April the claim succeeded against only the second defendant. If the date was after 20 April then the claim succeeded against both defendants.

On 24 March the claimant saw a locum GP who noted a painful left foot and prescribed some analgesic medication. Because the claimant's foot pain continued to worsen, at 2.00am on 6 April, he attended the A&E Centre at Medway Maritime Hospital. It was noted in the records on this occasion that he had suffered pain and coldness of the left foot for seven months since a motorbike accident. He was referred to the Same Day Treatment Centre (SDTC) later that morning where he arrived soon after 10.00am and was triaged by a nurse. The nurse referred him to the duty doctor, Dr Thom, who in the records described tenderness in the foot but no critical ischaemia. He was referred for an X-ray of his left foot to exclude fractures and from there, referred on to his own GP for follow-up. Dr Thom's clinical records in the SDTC were poor as she had recorded the history on the X-ray request form and therefore the referral letter to the GP said simply, 'diagnosis: disorder of foot (left)'.

The claimant first saw the second defendant on 14 April, who in the record describes an ingrowing toenail and an infected blister. He prescribed an antibiotic and a painkiller. The claimant returned to the same doctor on 21 April and was given a sick note for one week to stay off work. He was also given a tube of antifungal cream for athlete's foot. The next consultation with the second defendant was on 28 April, when the doctor again documented ingrowing toenail, prescribed a different antibiotic and painkiller and referred the claimant to podiatry and to an orthopaedic surgeon. This letter was not dated until 5 May, a week later.

On this day, 5 May, the claimant consulted another doctor at the practice, who referred the claimant to a podiatrist. This referral was also dated 5 May.

The claimant was seen by the podiatrist on 12 May, who recorded the claimant's foot was ischaemic and immediately referred the claimant to the A&E department with a letter suggesting absent pulses in the leg and foot and the possibility of a deep vein thrombosis.

Later that day in the A&E department, although the notes say that he was referred to the surgical department, he in fact went back to the SDTC where, having seen another doctor, he was referred to the surgeons. He saw a junior surgical doctor early that evening and was later that evening seen by the surgical registrar who noted a gangrenous left big toe and 'acute on chronic ischaemia'. He was given heparin, an angiogram was arranged and he was admitted. Later that day the patient had transfemoral angiography and treatment for blocked arteries in the leg (thrombolysis). Attempts to clear the clot were unsuccessful and despite further attempts to clear the blockage a follow-up angiogram recorded 'no circulation recorded in the foot'. The left foot remained ischaemic and nonviable so a left below-knee amputation was carried out and he was subsequently provided with a prosthetic limb.

There was much discussion and disagreement among the medical experts with regard to the mechanism of the arterial blockages and the sequence in which they took place. Despite the varying evidence from the various experts, the judge finally accepted that anticoagulants could not have saved the leg unless given before 6 April 2005 and that thrombolysis and embolectomy would probably have failed if tried at any time on or after 14 April. Because of the nature and severity of the condition it is highly unlikely that the analgesia prescribed by the second defendant would have had any beneficial effect. The judge assessed that the only awards that he could give were general damages for pain and suffering for 28 days against the second defendant and 22 days against the first defendant. The judge concluded that this was a clear case where, on the balance of probabilities, the defendants could not have achieved the saving of his leg even if they had been as careful as they should have been.

Despite the fact that early referral by either of the defendants would probably not have saved the claimant's leg, nevertheless it is necessary to point out the error caused by relying too heavily on an irrelevant past medical history, in this case a motorbike accident, and the fact that neither defendant recognised the clinical signs presented to them by not appreciating or recognising correctly the absence of peripheral pulses in the leg and foot and by treating the beginnings of a gangrenous toe as an ingrowing toenail and athlete's foot. A week was even lost in the referral process because the second defendant did not write his referral letter until a week after the consultation that it related to. There was also considerable criticism of the standard of note taking by the first and second doctors that the claimant consulted, the first defendant's referral letter to the second defendant was also totally inadequate and there was unnecessary delay in sending hospital referral letters.

Ganz v Childs [2011] EWHC 13 (QB)

17.62   This was a medical negligence claim by the claimant, Morwenna Ganz, against the first defendant, Dr Giles, a general practitioner, the second defendant Dr Lloyd, an out-of-hours general practitioner and the third defendant, Kingston Hospital NHS Trust.

The events occurred in December 1999 when the claimant was then aged 14 years. She developed mycoplasma pneumonia and sustained irreversible brain damage. Her claim against the two general practitioners succeeded because, had she been sent to hospital earlier and had she received competent care, the circumstances that led to her irreversible brain damage would have been avoided or at least reduced such that the damage would not have occurred.

Her claim against the hospital failed because, while breach of duty had been established, it was impossible to prove when irreversible brain damage occurred during the material period.

In mid-December 1999, Morwenna was seen by several doctors at the surgery over a period of days with a cold and cough. She had a past history of asthma and was given appropriate treatment. Because Morwenna was becoming worse she was taken on the Friday evening to see a doctor working for the out-of-hours service because of fever and vomiting. Because of her parents' concern for her overnight, she was taken the following morning, Saturday, to the surgery where she saw Dr Childs. It seems Dr Childs was unaware and was not informed that Morwenna had been seen the previous evening by the doctors of the out-of-hours service.

Dr Childs' note in the medical records for that consultation appears to be quite extensive. Dr Childs felt she needed to exclude pneumonia and so arranged a blood count and a chest X-ray. These tests were to take place the following Monday. Dr Childs said later in her witness statement that, had she considered pneumonia a probability, she would have referred Morwenna to hospital the same day. She also said that the only way to get an urgent X-ray done was by 'sending her in'. It seemed she considered pneumonia to be so unlikely that admission that day was not justified. Her view was that the most likely diagnosis was a viral illness with gastritis and/or a dyspeptic reaction to oral steroids that had been taken for the asthma.

During the afternoon of that Saturday, according to Mr and Mrs Ganz, Morwenna became worse. She became more lethargic, more thirsty, tired and weak. Mrs Ganz apparently called the out-of-hours service at about 10.30–11.00pm on the Saturday and apparently the nurse talked her through the symptoms and said it was 'flu. She called again at about 1.00am. As a result of this, there was a telephone conversation between Dr Lloyd and Mrs Ganz at about 3.00am on the Sunday morning. Mrs Ganz explained the situation and how things had developed and, in answer to questions from Dr Lloyd, confirmed that there was no neck stiffness, headache, rash or photophobia. Dr Lloyd said that he thought they should wait to see how Morwenna was in the morning and that if she was 'on the mend', then the tests suggested by Dr Childs could take place the following day, Monday. If there was still no improvement then she should be taken to hospital in the morning. If she became worse overnight Dr Lloyd said he was available to visit during the night. It is accepted on Dr Lloyd's behalf that he should have attended following this telephone conversation. If he had done so it is accepted that Morwenna would have been admitted to hospital by about 5am or 6am that morning.

Morwenna's parents became increasingly concerned about her condition and so they made contact again with the out-of-hours service between 5am and 6am, although the records at the out-of-hours service show that this call was made at 07.49. Following this call another out-of-hours doctor arrived at the house at 08.35hrs. Following this visit Morwenna was promptly taken by ambulance to hospital.

The case against Dr Childs was that she ought to have arranged for Morwenna's admission to hospital following the consultation on the Saturday morning. Dr Childs said that had she known about the out-of-hours consultation the previous night and also had she been aware that Morwenna had suffered from double vision on the previous day, she would have performed a neurological examination and 'almost certainly' admitted Morwenna to hospital. The GP experts agreed Morwenna should have been referred to hospital that day and Dr Childs would seem to accept that had she been aware of the above information she should have arranged for Morwenna's hospital admission at that time.

In Morwenna's past history she had an episode of encephalitis while living in Brazil at aged 15 months and a possible further episode while living in Texas at the age of 5½ years. There was no mention of or reference to these items of past medical history in the records made about her by the practice with which she was currently registered. The only evidence was on the summary of treatment card from the previous practice, which would have been placed at the back of the sequence of Lloyd George cards in her record and would not therefore have been the first document seen by a doctor when Morwenna attended the surgery. Dr Childs stated that had she known of this past history she would have asked questions that might have revealed neurological matters, including the double vision, which would have led to hospital admission.

After much consideration of the evidence given by the GP expert witnesses in addition to all the other evidence, the judge was of the view that Dr Childs was in breach of duty to Morwenna in not making arrangements for her admission to hospital during the Saturday morning. Breach of duty was also established with regard to the second defendant Dr Lloyd, in that, in not seeing her at the time of his telephone conversation with her mother he missed the opportunity to clinically assess her which, had he done so, would have led him to admit her to hospital at that time. The claim against the third defendant failed because, whilst breach of duty was established, in that Morwenna did not receive the timely treatment that she ought to have done upon her arrival at hospital, it was impossible to prove when the irreversible brain damage occurred during the material period, although from the evidence of medical experts in paediatrics, paediatric neurology, anaesthetics and respiratory medicine it was very likely that irreversible brain damage started before admission to hospital.

This case demonstrates the need to consider information that may not be immediately apparent to the examining doctor, but hidden away in the medical record. Knowledge of the past medical history, particularly that which occurred when under the care of a previous practice, should be readily available and not be tucked in at the back of the envelope of notes. This system has now been substantially superseded with the advent of electronic records, in which the current system usually presents the doctor with on-screen warnings of significant current and past medical conditions when accessing the patient record.

As stated above, Dr Childs was of the view that, on the Saturday morning, had she been aware of the past medical history, more detail relating to symptoms such as, in this case, double vision, or the consultation with the on-call doctor during the previous evening, any of these would have prompted her to refer the patient to hospital and the devastating brain damage would most probably have been avoided.

With regard to Dr Lloyd's involvement, general practitioners need to be particularly wary with regard to giving advice to patients without seeing and examining them, particularly when the patient has been unwell for some days and, although several doctors have already been consulted, the patient's condition is worsening or at least not improving.

JD v Mather [2012] EWHC 3063 (QB)

17.63   This case was the trial of the issue of causation in a medical negligence claim by the claimant JD against the defendant, Dr Mather, his general practitioner. It relates to the claimant's nodular malignant melanoma.

The claimant first noticed the presence of a growth in his right groin in mid-2005 and presented to Dr Mather in March 2006. He had been worried about the growth and consulted the doctor because the lesion 'appeared to him to be growing, it was itching, and it had bled when he had scratched it'. He had mentioned all three features to the defendant. The defendant examined the area of the lesion closely but briefly and formed the opinion that it was a seborrhoeic wart. She reassured the claimant he had nothing to worry about.

Seven months later, in October 2006, the claimant visited the surgery again because of the lesion. He was seen by the defendant's father, also Dr Mather, who realised it was possibly a malignant melanoma. He removed it by curettage and sent it to hospital for histological examination. The report said that this was a nodular malignant melanoma in the vertical growth phase with a Breslow thickness of 5mm.

Breslow's depth was used as a prognostic factor in melanoma of the skin. It is a description of how deeply tumour cells have invaded. Currently, the standard Breslow's depth has been replaced by the AJCC (American Joint Committee on Cancer) depth. Originally Breslow's depth was divided into five stages according to thickness. These were as follows: Stage I > or = .75mm; II .75–1.5mm; III 1.51–2.25mm; IV 2.25–3mm; V > 3mm. AJCC staging introduces, in addition to Breslow's depth, superficial ulceration of the skin, whether the cancer has reached lymph nodes, and whether there has been any metastatic spread.

Because of the urgent referral by Dr Mather (Snr), JD was seen by a dermatologist at hospital eleven days later in October 2006. The dermatologist referred him to the Christie Hospital, a major cancer hospital in Manchester and he was seen there three days later. It was found that the curettage had left a remnant of the melanoma in the claimant's abdomen. Two weeks later this was excised. It was recorded that attached to the skin specimen was a specimen of groin dissection containing eight lymph nodes in the fat. Two out of the eight lymph nodes identified contained metastatic melanoma.

In November 2011, after the claim had been made, the defendant's solicitors admitted that she had been in breach of her duty of care in March 2006 but made no admission as to the nature or extent of any causative damage flowing from that negligence. There was no case against Dr Mather, her father, who had arranged the urgent referral to the hospital. Had the claimant been referred by the defendant to a specialist with a suspected malignant melanoma in March 2006 as she should have done, he would have been seen within two weeks and the tumour would have been excised.

The claimant's case originally, as put in the particulars of claim, was that 'excision and treatment at this time would have carried a likelihood of cure and survival'. There was a fall-back case that excision and treatment in March 2006 would at least have given the claimant a longer period of disease-free survival. The judge heard evidence from a histopathologist, a dermatologist and a clinical oncologist for each of both the claimant and the defendant and there was much consideration of all this evidence. A particular medical point that was made was that the full thickness of the lesion was not simply what was curetted in the first instance, because the full depth had not been removed until the remnant had been excised at hospital. The original lesion therefore was deeper than first indicated. With regard to the claimant's original case, the Breslow thickness in March 2006 was on the evidence of the experts likely to have been in the bracket 3–4mm and on the balance of probabilities there was also some malignant ulceration at that time. It was accepted that at initial presentation in March 2006, the tumour could well have spread, at least microscopically, to regional lymph nodes but it was not established that there would have been palpable regional lymph node involvement.

It was likely that in March 2006 the melanoma was at stage IIIb of the AJCC staging, namely, an ulcerated primary tumour with at least one regional nodal micrometastasis. By October 2006 it would have reached stage IIIc, an ulcerated tumour with two macroscopic regional nodes. Counsel were agreed that if that was the position in March 2006, the claimant's chances of surviving a further ten years were already less than 50 per cent, even if the tumour had been detected and excised then as it should have been. On this basis the principal claim must therefore be dismissed in accordance with the majority decision in *Gregg v Scott* [2005] UKHL 2 at [153].

As to the alternative claim, the judge found that, on the balance of probabilities, the failure to diagnose the tumour in March 2006 had caused the claimant's life expectancy to be reduced by three years. In his conclusion, the judge said that the claimant was therefore entitled to judgment for damages to be assessed but in respect of his alternative claim only and he invited submissions from counsel as to what would be appropriate.

At the claimant's original presentation to Dr Mather in March 2006, he complained that the lesion was itching, appeared to be growing and it had bled when he scratched it. Although not mentioned in the court report, it is highly likely that the lesion was also pigmented with a brown or black discoloration. The only other two observations that would make the lesion pathognomonic of melanoma would be a variation in the colour across its surface and an irregular edge to the lesion. As the melanoma at this time was probably at AJCC staging of IIIb, it is very likely that all these were present but were not recognised. Nevertheless, even given the stated presenting symptoms, Dr Mather should have considered malignant melanoma and referred him. It is surprising that Dr Mather (Snr) curetted it. Having realised that the lesion was possibly a malignant melanoma, it would have been more appropriate to refer directly to the dermatology clinic, as disruption of the lesion by curettage can potentially create difficulties in determining if any of the lesion has not been removed and possibly of causing cells to break away from the growth and be transported elsewhere in the body by the blood stream, thus causing metastatic spread.

Doy v Gunn [2013] EWCA Civ 547

17.64 This case was an appeal by the claimant Kieran Doy, a child whose mother was his litigation friend. The judgment of the original trial judge had been to dismiss the medical negligence claim against the defendant, Dr Gunn, a general practitioner. The claim alleged that if Kieran had been referred to hospital by the defendant on a date in March 2002, he would have been prescribed antibiotics and that would have prevented the development of bacterial meningitis, which had led to moderate mental handicap, global developmental difficulties, the absence of speech, double incontinence and a right hemiplegic cerebral palsy. The judge had made his judgment in December 2011.

Kieran had been born prematurely in January 2002 and had remained in hospital for over three weeks. In mid-March 2002, when less than two months old, Kieran was seen by a GP, a partner at the practice at which he was registered, after being unwell for two days and was diagnosed as suffering from colic and given an appropriate prescription. Three days later Kieran was seen by both the health visitor and another partner of the practice for his standard six-week check at the baby clinic. Later that day his mother says that she took him to the evening clinic at the practice, where he was seen again by the partner who had seen him three days previously.

During that evening Kieran's mother telephoned the local out-of-hours service about Kieran because of 'persistent constant crying for three hours'. The call was referred to Dr Gunn who was on duty that evening. Dr Gunn spoke to Kieran's mother on the telephone, following which Kieran was seen by Dr Gunn at the out-of-hours service base at Lowestoft Hospital. Dr Gunn diagnosed colic; her recorded clinical note is somewhat brief, as observed by the judge at the trial.

At the trial, the GP experts agreed that if the claimant's condition when seen by Dr Gunn was as described by the mother, then Dr Gunn ought to have referred Kieran to hospital that evening. Conversely, if the defendant's evidence with regard to Kieran's condition was accepted, then it was not mandatory for Kieran to have been referred to hospital and accordingly the issue of breach of duty resolved to the question of whether, on the balance of probabilities, the account given by the mother was to be relied upon.

The judge at the trial found that in many respects he could not accept the mother's account. She stated that Kieran's condition had deteriorated between the first consultation with the GP and three days later when he attended the six-week check-up. Over these three days she said that he had become more drowsy, crying or screaming a lot, drawing up his legs and refusing to feed or be comforted, but when he was seen by both the doctor and the health visitor for his six-week check-up, there is no evidence of any of these. The doctor's clinical record of the six-week check-up was very full and extensive and gave no hint of any ongoing problem. The mother also claimed that Kieran was seen that evening at the surgery by Dr Lloyd. Dr Lloyd denied this on the grounds that there was no entry in the child's GP clinical record relating to that (and she said that she would always have made an entry) and also there was no record of an appointment in the practice records. A chronology of the evening surgery, which was reconstructed from the records, left no gap within which Dr Lloyd could have seen Kieran.

Overall the judge accepted Dr Gunn's account in spite of his criticism of her inadequate note of the consultation and in this was supported by the evidence of bacteriological experts, which was that whilst Kieran was probably bacteraemic at the time of the consultation they could not say that it would have resulted in signs or symptoms indicative of established infection by then. The judge agreed with the experts on general practice that if Dr Gunn's account was accurate and Kieran's mother's was not, breach of duty was thereby ruled out.

The judge who gave the conclusion at the appeal stated that the judge at the trial had come to a clear conclusion about the consultation with Dr Gunn and the appeal judge did not find any material error in the trial judge's approach or findings. The appeal judge was satisfied that the trial judge was right to acquit Dr Gunn of negligence and he therefore dismissed the appeal. The other two appeal judges agreed.

The defendant in this instance, for her own part, only had what the trial judge described as an inadequate record to support her case, but her case was effectively supported by the records made by the other doctors and the health visitor who had all seen the child in the few days prior to hospital admission. The inconsistencies in the evidence of the mother also led the trial judge to prefer the evidence of the defendant.

CHAPTER 18

Emergency medicine

Dr Michael J Clancy

INTRODUCTION

18.1   The aim of this chapter is to describe the speciality and practice of emergency medicine in order to provide an understanding of the context

of that practice (and why some errors occur) and to describe some of the
common clinical areas of concern.

DESCRIPTION OF EMERGENCY MEDICINE

18.2   Emergency medicine is an established medical speciality with its own
defined training programmes, examinations and knowledge maintenance
programmes. The Royal College of Emergency Medicine was established to
advance education and research and the setting and monitoring of standards
in emergency medicine[1]. Previously known as casualty, then accident and
emergency medicine, it is now called emergency medicine (EM) in line with
international practice.

1 www.collemergencymed.ac.uk/training.

18.3   EM was defined by the International Federation for Emergency
Medicine in 1991 as:

'the field of practice based on the knowledge and skills required for the prevention,
diagnosis and management of acute and urgent aspects of illness and injury affecting
patients of all age groups with a full spectrum of undifferentiated physical and
behavioural disorders. It further encompasses an understanding of the development
of pre-hospital and in-hospital emergency medical systems and the skills necessary
for this development'.

18.4   Emergency medicine is the practice of care for patients experiencing
an acute deterioration in health that requires the expertise and resources of
a typical emergency department (ED). This means that the whole spectrum
of medicine is seen, from the newborn to the elderly, those with physical
and mental problems, and ranges in severity from the immediately life
threatening to those conditions that require reassurance and no follow up.

18.5   The purpose of the ED is to receive the undifferentiated patient (ie
the diagnosis has yet to be established), to resuscitate as needed, to diagnose,
treat and decide whether:

(1)   the patient needs to be admitted to an in-patient bed;
(2)   the patient needs a period of further observation in order to determine
       whether admission is needed or not (in a clinical decision unit/
       observation ward); or
(3)   the patient can be discharged with follow up (by primary care physicians
       or hospital outpatient departments) or without follow up.

Where EM is practised: the emergency department

Triage

18.6   This is where the initial assessment of the patient (who may have
arrived by ambulance or their own transport) is undertaken, in order to
judge the urgency of the case and where the patient is best cared for within
the department. The assessment includes a brief history, limited examination
and typically, for those brought by ambulance, measurement of heart rate,
blood pressure, level of consciousness, ECG as needed and relief of pain.

Patients may be assessed for their risk for falls (based for example on a history of confusion, poor balance, previous falls and poor mobility) and if assessed as high risk they are identified by a coloured wrist band and placed in a well-observed area with (ideally) higher numbers of nurses.

18.7 Patients who are critically ill or who have the potential to deteriorate will be transferred to the resuscitation room. Those who require to be cared for on a trolley will be transferred to the 'major' side of the ED; ambulatory patients will typically wait in the waiting area prior to transfer to the 'Minors' side. Children have their own dedicated triage, waiting and clinical area.

18.8 Increasingly, senior medical staff are participating in triage, supporting the correct distribution of patients by the recognition of potentially life-threatening conditions, the early interpretation of ECGs and the early ordering of tests. Triage capacity may be exceeded at times of high numbers of new arrivals, and patients may have to wait beyond the typical time of 15 minutes from their arrival by ambulance before they are assessed.

Resuscitation room

18.9 This is where assessment, investigation and treatment of the critically ill and those who could have life-threatening conditions occurs. Patients are cared for, ideally on a one-to-one nursing ratio, are continuously monitored and looked after by a team of doctors that typically includes a trained emergency physician and may involve specialists from the in-patient teams of the hospital. The resuscitation room is often busy with multiple cases, rapidly changing, and requires intense decision making.

Major

18.10 The 'major' side patients are usually cared for on a trolley, will have further observations made by the nursing team and will usually be seen first by doctors in training, with their care overseen by a trained emergency physician. Typical cases include patients with chest pain, abdominal pain, breathlessness, and the elderly patient with falls and confusion. This side of the department is often congested, with patients waiting to be seen and having been seen, waiting to be admitted.

Minors

18.11 The 'minors' side of the department is where patients who are ambulant and not thought to have life-threatening problems are seen (eg ankle sprains, wrist fractures and wounds). In many departments these patients will be seen by advanced nurse practitioners, who have undergone additional training and will look after these patients autonomously but with ready access to doctors if needed. Within the 'minors side' group there may be patients with serious conditions that were not initially apparent, and clinical staff need to be especially vigilant.

Paediatrics

18.12   Children (ie those 18 years old or younger) typically constitute 25 per cent of the ED workload. They are triaged separately and have their own dedicated waiting and clinical areas, with audio-spatial separation from adults. Standards are set out for their treatment[1]. Nursing care is supervised by registered paediatric nurses.

1 Standards for Children and Young People in Emergency Care Settings (3rd edn, 2012) RCPCH.

Clinical decisions unit/observation ward

18.13   This is a ward area where patients are admitted for a limited period:

(1)   in order to complete their care: this may include a period of observation (eg minor head injury), or treatment (eg mild asthma) and it is expected that these patients would be discharged within 24 hours, most sooner than this;

(2)   for further testing in order to establish the diagnosis and to determine the need for further care with either referral to the in-patient teams or to be discharged. Increasingly there are care pathways for common presentations that describe which investigations, treatments and observations are needed (eg low-risk chest pain, those suspected to have renal colic, asthma, headache, overdose)[1].

1 For examples see www.collemergencymed.ac.uk/Shop-Floor.

18.14   There is variation in how these units work but typically the three largest patient groups are:

(1)   elderly patients who present after falls and collapses, who after medical assessment typically need a period of observation and review by specialist nurses to assess their mobility and social care needs;

(2)   patients who have deliberately harmed themselves by taking overdoses, who do not require in-patient treatment but will require assessment of their mental health;

(3)   those who are acutely intoxicated, who may or may not be alcohol dependent, and those who suffer the complications of intoxication, eg assault and head injury.

This area is demanding of staff time, with typically 7–8 per cent of all patients attending the ED being cared for here with high patient turnover, typically 2–3 patients occupying each bed over a 24-hour period. This is based upon unpublished audit data at Southampton University Hospital.

Overcrowding

18.15   The ED becomes 'overcrowded' when the capacity of the department is exceeded. This can occur when there is large influx of patients, insufficient staff to see the patients in a timely manner, or delays in transferring patients out of the ED to an in-patient bed. Patients will then queue, with potential delays in diagnosis and treatment. There is clear evidence that the mortality for patients within the ED increases with overcrowding and that care is impaired (eg delays in the administration of antibiotics and analgesia and being transferred to intensive care units)[1].

1 Higginson 'Emergency department crowding' (2012) 29(6) Emerg Med Jnl 437–443.

How patients access EDs and where they fit within the NHS

18.16   Patients who experience an abrupt change in their health may:

(1)   attend a range of services (general practice, walk-in centres (WIC), minor injuries units (MIU), acute care centres) all of which can refer the patient to the ED;

(2)   seek telephone advice (they called 999, telephone advice lines or their primary care doctor) and may be advised to attend the ED; or

(3)   independently make the decision to attend the ED.

18.17   Most patients will not have seen a doctor before their attendance at the ED. Many arrive by their own means, but those attended by ambulance staff will have had an assessment (including a brief history, examination and recording of vital signs: heart rate, blood pressure, conscious level, oxygen saturation and respiration rate, blood sugar levels), and may have been administered drugs, intravenous fluids or oxygen. This assessment is recorded and shared at the time of the triage assessment, becomes part of the ED notes and is available to the receiving doctor. For those patients who are judged by the ambulance service to be critically ill or have the potential to become critically ill, there will be forewarning and these cases go directly to the resuscitation area.

18.18   Emergency departments sit between those services that care for patients outside of hospital (primary care, out-of-hours services, ambulance services, MIUs, WICs) and the hospital with its resources of specialist care: critical care/anaesthesia, acute medicine, paediatrics, orthopaedics and general surgery, together with the provision of diagnostic services and blood transfusion. EDs are thus part of a continuum of care and provide open access to healthcare at all times. When there are service provision difficulties in different parts of the health service, the consequences may be played out in the ED and impact on the care delivered. For example, overcrowding may be due to a lack of available in-patient and community beds, and increased attendances may be due to perceived or real out-of-hours service deficiencies.

18.19   The health service undergoes continuous revision of services, which will mean that not all supporting in-patient services are available on each site and that some patients will need to be transferred to other centres. The increasing centralisation of services for stroke, acute coronary syndromes, and major trauma means that the patient needs to be correctly identified and transferred to these centres.

The ED workforce

The medical workforce

18.20   Junior doctors will either be foundation year two doctors or those with more experience and in training programmes (usually the Acute Care

Common Stem programme (training years 1, 2 and 3) or general practice), and make up approximately 50 per cent of the ED medical workforce[1]. The patients they care for can have any medical problem, of any severity, and consequently they are often working at the limits of their knowledge and competence. These patients have typically not been seen by another doctor prior to attending the ED (ie a diagnosis has not been established) and the ED doctor will have the responsibility of working out what is wrong with the patient. There are large numbers of patients attending EDs, and the current performance targets[2] mean these doctors can feel under a considerable time pressure. They also have responsibility for determining whether the patient is to be discharged or admitted. This requires skills in referring patients clearly and precisely, negotiating authority gradients and often being responsible for ordering, coordinating and checking large numbers of tests. The ED is a challenging environment for juniors who work with large numbers of staff – nurses, radiographers, and in-patient teams – all of which are continually changing. In order to prepare these doctors for such work all departments should have a comprehensive induction programme and ready access to both senior support and written guidance.

1 The drive for quality – How to achieve safe, sustainable care in our Emergency Departments (May 2013) www.collemergencymed.ac.uk.
2 A&E clinical quality indicators: Implementation guidance and data definitions (December 2010), Department of Health.

18.21   Senior doctors include those trainees who are in the second part of their specialist training programme (ie training years 4, 5 and 6), staff grade and associate specialists, and consultants. These doctors both supervise juniors and see new patients. They typically supervise more than one area of the department, and focus on those areas that have patients with a high probability of serious disease: the resuscitation room, major side of the department, and those patients with recognised high-risk presentations (such as those with an unplanned return to the ED in 72 hours, those about to be discharged with chest and abdominal pain, headache, and children aged under three with a fever). These doctors are the key decision-makers in the department, and ideally each case seen by the junior is discussed with such a doctor. It is recognised by the NHS that there is a significant shortfall of these senior doctors[1] especially out of hours and this may impact on the quality of decision making. This major workforce challenge means that locum doctors are frequently used to support the service; they may not have worked in the department previously and may be unfamiliar with the staff, local systems and practice.

1 House of Commons Committee of Public Accounts: Emergency admissions to hospital (Forty-sixth Report of Session 2013–14).

Nurses and advanced nurse practitioners

18.22   Nurses form the largest part of the ED workforce, ensuring that patients are triaged (prioritised) and that patients of concern are identified early and discussed with the medical team. They ensure patients have had a set of observations made and that pain relief is provided. Increasingly nurses gain intravenous access, and order blood tests prior to clinical assessment. Advanced nurse practitioners (ANPs) have undergone additional training in order to see patients autonomously, ordering X-rays and tests as necessary and with access to medical advice if they need it. Typically the patients cared for in this way are those with minor illness and injury and in many departments the majority of such patients are seen by ANPs. Although ANPs work autonomously, they are accountable to the medical consultants who carry the professional responsibility for the care of these patients.

18.23 For some conditions needing a time-critical intervention by in-patient teams, specialist nurses from these teams are increasingly involved in the reception of these patients in the ED (eg those with chest pain who would potentially benefit from an angioplasty, those with symptoms and signs suggestive of a stroke who would benefit from thrombolysis and being cared for on a stroke unit).

The context of clinical practice

18.24 The large numbers of patients, the mindset changes needed by doctors to swap from one case to another (to go from a resuscitation case to the next minor injury case), the ability to hold on to several cases synchronously and be able to prioritise the minor from the serious make EM practice challenging[1]. Whilst junior doctors are working at the limits of their competence because of the range and urgency of cases, their seniors are facing a high density of decision making (the frequency with which questions have to be answered is amongst the highest in medicine[2]), supervising many cases, and ensuring that the whole department is working efficiently, and patients are flowing through it. All of this occurs in a noisy environment with multiple distractions (answering phones, nursing enquiries, patient enquiries) in departments that are increasingly overcrowded. Trusts are currently expected to achieve the target of 95 per cent of cases either admitted or discharged within four hours[3]. For these reasons clinical decision making in ED can be difficult.

1 Croskerry 'ED cognition: any decision by anyone at anytime' (2013) CEJM.
2 See Croskerry 'Achieving quality in decision making cognitive strategies and detection of bias' (2002) 9 Acad Emerg Med 1184–1204.
3 A&E clinical quality indicators: Implementation guidance and data definition (December 2010) Department of Health.

The referral process to other teams

18.25 The ED doctor, having decided that the patient will need (or is highly likely to need) admission, will then need to make the referral to the in-patient team. There is an opportunity for ambiguity as to exactly what is being requested: the ED doctor needs to be clear in what he is asking for. Is he asking for an opinion and advice? For the in-patient team to come and see the patient? Or to accept the patient for admission? The SBAR system[1] is designed to help remove this ambiguity by standardising the referral process. It specifies:

- Situation (who am I; who is the patient; what is wrong);
- Background (admission diagnosis; summary of treatment to date);
- Assessment (vital signs; I think the problem is…; I have done…); and
- Recommendation (What I would like you to do).

1 www.saferhealthcare.com/sbar/what-is-sbar.

Specific issues relating to EM practice

Record keeping

18.26 The notes must be legible, timed, signed and follow the traditional medical model with relevant positive and negative features of the presentation recorded. There should be a clear diagnosis or differential diagnosis, record of tests requested (and any results and their interpretation) and a management plan including a record of the referral process and any advice given. The responsibility to review the results of tests should lay with the test requester. However, in the ED setting, tests are requested the results of which may not be available at the time of referral and acceptance of the patient by the in-patient teams. The responsibility for the review of these results needs to be clearly defined and handed over to the in-patient team. For those patients who are discharged from the ED, the responsibility for the results of tests ordered lays with the ED staff. The large volume of patients[1], of which up to 50 per cent will have X-rays, and blood tests, means that robust reporting systems, audit and means of identification of abnormal results need to be in place.

1 There were 14 million visits to EDs in England 2014 (Accident and Emergency Performance England 2013–14, national and regional data. Research paper 14/22, April 2014) House of Commons library.

The risks of the handover

18.27 The changing of ED staff throughout every 24-hour period inevitably means that patients who are part way through their journey will need to be handed over to the incoming team. This handover needs to be detailed, with the doctor handing over being clear as to what has been done, the provisional diagnosis, the outstanding tasks remaining and what is to be done for that patient. To ask the incoming doctors to start at the beginning with these patients is unrealistic in the setting of a busy service. However, if the assessment by the handing over doctor is incorrect or incomplete, error is possible. This risk can be reduced by the handover being in front of the patient to the receiving doctor, who should start from the beginning if the patient does not follow the expected course or deteriorates.

18.28 The handover of a whole department to the incoming senior doctor needs to be structured to ensure that not only individual patients are handed over successfully but that any outstanding issues that may impact on the performance of the department are addressed. The Imperial College handover tool was specifically designed for this purpose[1].

1 The ABC of Handover (www1.imperial.ac.uk/cpssq/cpssq_publications/resources_tools/handover/).

Guidelines in the ED

18.29 Each department will have its own collection of guidelines that are trust based or from national organisations that set a standard or make recommendations for care of patients. Examples of the latter relevant to EM include NICE (eg head injury and cervical spine imaging guidelines), British Thoracic Society (the care of asthma and pneumothoraces), British Diabetic

Society (the care of diabetic ketoacidosis), Resuscitation Council (for cardiac arrest). The College of Emergency Medicine website[1] has an up-to-date collection of guidelines relevant to EM, including those generated by the College, individual departments as well as external sources. Such guidelines are updated regularly and EDs must ensure that their staff are educated about these guidelines and that they are easily accessible at all times.

1 www.collemergencymed.ac.uk/Shop-Floor/Clinical%20Guidelines/External%20Guidelines.

Communication with the patient and GP

18.30   It is essential that patients are involved in the decisions about their care. Staff need to explain the diagnosis, the risks and benefits of any tests and the treatment options. Patients should have a clear understanding of the anticipated clinical course and what to do if that is not the case. This should be recorded in the patient notes and supported by written advice sheets (which should cover the common presentations). Follow up arrangements (with primary care, hospital outpatients) should be made clear and written down. Each attendance at the ED requires a written communication with the patient's GP to inform them of the diagnosis, tests and results, treatment and follow up plans and any outstanding tasks. It is useful to supplement this communication with a fuller letter for those conditions which are serious (eg the diagnosis of cancer) and require clarity as to future clinical responsibility.

Types of error that happen in EDs

18.31   It is useful to consider three types of error:

- clinical error which would not have occurred if clinical standards had been adhered to;
- systems error which would not have occurred if there had been an effective and competent organisation of the ED; and
- error of judgment, ie when the wrong choice was made but this can only be seen retrospectively.

18.32   There are inherent features of EM practice that make error more likely: the high number of decisions that need to be made; diagnostic uncertainty; cognitive load; narrow time windows for assessment; multiple transitions of care; multitasking; interruptions; surge phenomena; fatigue; circadian dysynchronicity; sleep deprivation; novel and infrequently occurring conditions; and staffing shortages. These all impact on the way clinicians make decisions and can lead to failure to adhere to clinical standards and errors of judgment[1].

1 Croskerry (et al) *Patient Safety in Emergency Medicine* (2009).

18.33   Clinical errors may be subclassified[1] into:

(1)   diagnostic error, where there is failure in the process to take an appropriate history and examination, to consider the differential diagnosis and to systematically explore these possibilities or to order the appropriate tests and correctly interpret them;

(2)   treatment error, when the correct diagnosis is made but the treatment is incorrect, incomplete or delayed;

(3) judgment error, which is more likely to occur when the potential underlying causes of the presentation are numerous and include both benign and serious conditions, the frequency of the underlying condition is rare and where the common and readily available tests (in the ED) may not be diagnostic (and if negative become falsely reassuring). For this reason it is recommended that high risk groups (non-traumatic chest pain in adults (ie over the age of 17), febrile illness in children under a year old, unscheduled returns (with the same complaint) within 72 hours) should be reviewed by a senior prior to discharge (Indicator 8 of Quality Indicators for Emergency Care). The textbook presentations of specific conditions may be modified by drugs, age and other co morbidities, making achieving the correct diagnosis harder.

In order to limit this error a high level of clinical suspicion and an awareness of possible diagnoses are required.

1 Siff 'Legal issues in Emergency Medicine' in Tintinalli's *Practice of Emergency Medicine* at p 296.

18.34 There are specific groups of patients that are especially challenging:

- the elderly, who may have multiple other conditions and medications that affect their presentation, and who may not manifest the typical signs of the disease;
- the very young, who cannot vocalise, whose condition can change quickly, and for whom a benign diagnosis is more likely (compared to that of an adult);
- those affected by alcohol, who are not only difficult to assess, but more likely to suffer serious illness affecting a number of body systems;
- those who have the potential for more than one concurrent problem, eg the multiply-injured patient with several body systems concurrently affected, the cancer patient undergoing chemotherapy.

SPECIFIC AREAS OF CLINICAL PRACTICE

18.35 The very breadth of this speciality means that it is not possible to cover all areas. The following paragraphs focus on those symptoms and conditions recognised to be a frequent source of medico-legal concern. Texts that provide quick and accessible information on the practice of EM in the UK[1] and more detailed authoritative texts[2] can usefully be consulted to supplement the information provided here.

1 Wyatt (et al) *The Oxford Handbook of Emergency Medicine* (4th edn).
2 Rosens *Emergency Medicine. Concepts and clinical practice* (8th edn); Marx et al *Tintinalli's Emergency Medicine: A Comprehensive Study Guide* (7th edn).

18.36 Paragraphs **18.37–18.64** deal with a number of presenting symptoms that can be problematic for the clinician, using specific conditions to illustrate the issues. Paragraphs **18.65–18.104** cover topics/conditions that occur frequently in EM medico-legal practice.

Symptom: chest pain; specific conditions: acute coronary syndrome, pulmonary embolism

Chest pain

18.37 An increasing number of patients attend EDs with chest pain, such that it now constitutes 8 per cent of all attendances. The number of causes of chest pain is large, ranging from the life threatening to the self limiting and the frequency of the life-threatening conditions is low, eg myocardial infarction. The ED doctor has the tools of a focused and thoughtful history and examination together with ECGs, chest X-ray and blood tests to work out the diagnosis. Yet these tests can be normal at presentation in the patient with significant disease[1].

1 See NICE CG95 2010: Chest pain of recent onset: assessment and diagnosis of recent onset chest pain or discomfort of suspected cardiac origin.

Acute coronary syndrome

18.38 Cardiac chest pain is typically described as 'tight, heavy, crushing or pressure like', located over the centre of the anterior chest and may spread to the arms, jaw and upper abdomen and be associated with sweating, nausea and anxiety. This pain is typical of a spectrum of cardiac disease that ranges from angina (the patient's usual chest pain typically triggered by a certain level of exertion) through to unstable angina (pain coming on more easily or at rest) and myocardial infarction. Usually the examination of these patients is normal, which emphasises the importance of the patient's history.

18.39 Those patients presenting with cardiac sounding chest pain, lasting more than 20–30 minutes or with angina coming on more frequently or at rest will need detailed evaluation and a period of hospital observation. They should be in a monitored area, have intravenous access, their pain relieved, be given aspirin and with a defibrillator readily accessible. For patients with angina the ECG will not show the signs of cardiac muscle injury and if a previous ECG is available it will be unchanged. For those with unstable angina, the ECG may show some changes in T waves but is likely to be normal or unchanged from previous ECGs. Those suffering from a myocardial infarction may have either ST segment elevation or depression which will be new and different from previous ECGs. Changes in the ECG can be subtle, change over time and can be difficult to detect in the presence of pre-existing changes. Repeated ECGs are essential to detect changes over time. A normal ECG does not exclude significant recent pathology, whereas acute changes on the ECG are confirmatory: it is a confirmatory test, not an exclusionary test.

18.40 The troponin blood test is a measure of cardiac muscle injury and is raised when the patient has suffered a myocardial infarction. This rise is reliably detected 10 hours after the onset of pain or from when the pain was at its greatest.

18.41 Those patients with evidence of myocardial infarction associated with ST elevation will need to have prompt specialist consultation re thrombolysis/percutaneous coronary intervention which is recommended to be delivered within 90 minutes of arrival, and will subsequently be cared for on a coronary care unit ('CCU'). Those patients with ST depression type myocardial infarction will be cared for on CCU (and will not benefit from emergent PCI). Those patients with unstable angina are problematic, as their ECG may be normal/unchanged and the troponin test negative, yet they are at risk of myocardial infarction and need specialist care, with admission to CCU. This diagnosis hinges on the patient's history and an appreciation of the misleading nature of negative tests.

18.42   Those patients with cardiac-sounding chest pain but with a normal or unchanged ECG and no troponin rise when first seen form a growing group of patients who are admitted for serial ECGs and serial troponin testing to rule out myocardial infarction. These patients should be risk stratified (eg using the TIMI score) and low risk patients (defined as TIMI score 0–1) can be safely cared for in an ED observation ward/chest pain unit where further troponin testing will be undertaken (increasingly over periods shorter than 10 hours). Higher risk patients should be admitted to a monitored in-patient medical bed for further testing.

18.43   Patients suffering a myocardial infarction can be problematic because the diagnosis may not initially be obvious (they may present with upper abdominal pain or no pain at all), and the tests may initially be normal (50–60 per cent of patients will not have a diagnostic ECG on arrival and 17 per cent of those with eventual diagnosis of myocardial infarction have a normal initial ECG[1]).

1 Wyatt *The Oxford Handbook of Emergency Medicine* (4th edn).

Pulmonary embolism

18.44   This can be a difficult diagnosis to make because the symptoms may be diverse: weakness, breathlessness, syncope, dizziness, malaise as well as chest pain, and overlap with those of numerous other diseases. Physical examination may be normal, specifically the heart rate, blood pressure and oxygen saturation readings.

18.45   This helps explain why this diagnosis was missed 55 per cent of the time in a recent series of fatal cases[1]. Those patients who present critically ill (hypotensive and hypoxic) or with classical pleuritic chest pain are more likely to have the diagnosis made than those who are not physiologically deranged and have non-specific symptoms. For these patients to be detected requires a high level of clinical suspicion. Initial tests in the ED (eg ECG, chest X-ray and blood gases) may all be normal. The d dimer test, which is a measure of the breakdown products of blood clots, is sufficiently sensitive in low-risk patients (as determined risk stratification using the Wells score) that if it is negative, less than 1 per cent would have a pulmonary embolism, and this is considered an acceptable risk, such that further testing is not required. However, for those who are not low risk (Wells score >1), the d dimer test will miss a number of patients with a pulmonary embolus. Thus a negative test in moderate to high-risk patients may be falsely negative and falsely reassuring. These patients and those who are low-risk with a raised d dimer will need further investigation (typically with a CT pulmonary angiogram) and admission. Empiric heparinsation (blood thinning) is required for patients who may have a pulmonary embolus who are awaiting CTPA[2].

1 Pidenda (et al) 'Clinical suspicion of fatal pulmonary embolism' (2001) 120 Chest 791–795.
2 For a detailed discussion see ACEP Clinical Policy document: Critical Issues in the Evaluation and Management of Adult Patients Presenting to the Emergency Department with Suspected Pulmonary Embolism at www.acep.org/content.aspx?id=30060.

Symptom: headache; specific conditions: four types of headache

18.46   Many patients attend the ED with headaches but less than 1 per cent will have life-threatening organic disease[1]. Trying to establish which patient has serious disease is a major challenge given that there are many conditions that cause headache, that for each pathology the patient presentation may be highly variable and that the symptoms may have resolved by the time of presentation.

1 Barton 'Evaluation and treatment of headache patients in the emergency department: a survey' (1994) 34 Headache 91.

18.47   There are a number of conditions that must be actively considered by the doctor because of their seriousness and potential reversibility.

Subarachnoid haemorrhage (SAH)

18.48   SAH occurs when a weakened blood vessel bursts, causing a sudden severe headache (typically the worst the patient has experienced), usually at the back of the head. It may be associated with a transient loss of consciousness, with the patient making a full recovery and with resolution of their symptoms and they may exhibit signs of meningeal irritation. Alternatively they may have a persistent altered level of consciousness (SAH should always be in the differential diagnosis for comatose patients). For the diagnosis to be made the clinician needs to have considered the possibility, be aware that the headache may occur in areas other than at the back of the head, and may have resolved by the time they are seen. The difficulty in recognising this condition is reflected by the evidence that an estimated 20–50 per cent of these are missed on first presentation to a physician[1]. For this diagnosis to be made requires it to be first considered and further investigated by CT (which may show subarachnoid blood but which may be normal and especially if done more than 12 hours after onset). If the CT is normal a lumbar puncture looking for evidence of blood break down products in the CSF is needed (this is usually undertaken by the in-patient teams). A negative CT and lumbar puncture effectively rule out the possibility of SAH[2].

1 Mayer (et al) 'Misdiagnosis of symptomatic cerebral aneurysm: prevalence and correlation with outcome at four institutions' (1996) 27 Stroke 1558.
2 For further detailed discussion see Edlow (et al) 'Clinical policy: critical issues in the evaluation and management of adult patients presenting to the Emergency Department with acute headache' (2008) 52 Ann Emerg Med 407–436.

Meningitis

18.49   Meningitis usually presents with concurrent fever, photophobia and neck stiffness, but all these features may not be present and vary in intensity. This condition needs to be considered, especially in those who are immunocompromised and requires immediate administration of antibiotics and consideration of undertaking a lumbar puncture.

Carbon monoxide poisoning

18.50   Carbon monoxide (CO) poisoning may be accompanied by headache, nausea and vomiting. Typically a number of patients are affected from the same location and improve once removed from that location. The diagnosis is made by CO measurement, which is routinely available from blood gas analysis of venous blood.

Temporal arteritis

18.51   Temporal arteritis typically occurs in those over 50, who may have a unilateral headache, associated with pain in the jaw on eating, low grade fever and visual disturbances. The diagnosis is made by an elevated ESR, and treated by immediate commencement of steroids (to avoid sight loss) and urgent referral to an ophthalmologist.

Shunt malfunction

18.52   Those patients with a history of ventriculoperitoneal shunts who present with headache should be assumed to have a shunt malfunction or infection and should always be discussed with a neurosurgical specialist.

18.53   Generally those patients with headaches and any of the following high-risk features will need further investigation and typically admission[1]:

- sudden onset of headache;
- patient description of the headache as 'the worst ever';
- altered mental status;
- meningismus;
- unexplained fever;
- focal neurologic deficit on examination;
- symptoms refractory to appropriate treatment or worsening despite treatment;
- onset of headache during exertion;
- history of human immunodeficiency virus (HIV) infection or immunosuppression;
- ventriculoperitoneal shunt.

1 *Rosen's Emergency Medicine: Concepts and Clinical Practice* (8th edn, 2012) Chapter 20, Headache.

18.54   Patients with a headache that has *all* the following characteristics do not need further testing or imaging and may be candidates for discharge:

- that is similar in location and intensity to an established history of recurrent headache (eg migraine) or of minor severity and gradual onset (eg typical tension headache);
- with normal neurologic examination findings including mental status;
- with absence of fever or meningismus; and
- showing improvement with appropriate treatment.

Symptom: acute abdominal pain; specific condition: ectopic pregnancy

18.55   Acute abdominal pain is a common presentation, but the diagnosis of its cause can be difficult because:

(1)   there is a lack of reliable physical signs, especially in the elderly (who have a higher probability of serious disease) and the immunocompromised. Patients with serious abdominal disease may be apyrexial, with a relatively benign abdominal examination which misleads the doctor. Peritonitis is suggested by involuntary guarding. Pain caused by sudden release of pressure over the abdomen by withdrawal of the examiner's hand (rebound tenderness) is often regarded as a reliable sign of peritonitis yet more than one third of patients with surgically proven appendicitis do not have rebound tenderness;

(2)   failure to completely expose and examine the patient: this may lead to failure to examine the genitalia (torsion of the testes may cause predominantly abdominal rather than testicular pain), inguinal regions (site of obstructed herniae) and rectal examination, all of which can provide diagnostic information. The doctor should ensure that dignity and privacy of the patient is respected and that a chaperone is present;

(3)   the differential diagnoses range from life threatening (ruptured abdominal aorta, perforation, obstruction and bowel ischaemia) to benign (urinary tract infection, irritable bowel syndrome);

(4)   the abdominal pain may be a manifestation of a disease process outside the abdomen, eg myocardial infarction, basal pneumonia, diabetic keotacidosis;

(5)   there is a lack of any reliable individual tests for abdominal pathology, eg the white blood cell count is neither sensitive nor specific to be usefully discriminatory and abdominal X-rays are not sensitive for perforation.

Women of child bearing age presenting with abdominal pain should always have ectopic pregnancy considered. Children can be difficult to diagnose especially when non verbal, when appendicitis may be misdiagnosed as gastroenteritis, or a lower respiratory tract infection.

18.56   Pain relief should be provided to all patients as this enables the patient to give an undistracted history and to cooperate with the physical examination. The evidence is clear that it does not obscure the diagnosis[1].

1 Thomas SH et al 'Effects of morphine analgesia on diagnostic accuracy in emergency department patients with abdominal pain: a prospective randomized trial' (2003) 196 J AM Coll Surg 18.

18.57   The following conditions should be met before considering discharge of patients presenting to the ED with abdominal pain: normal vital signs, no concerning abdominal examination features, relief of nausea and pain, able to drink, clear discharge instructions relating to predicted clinical course and what to do if that course is not followed[1].

1 *Rosen's Emergency Medicine: Concepts and Clinical Practice* (8th edn, 2012) Chapter 27, Abdominal Pain.

Ectopic pregnancy

18.58   In the general population, ectopic pregnancy accounts for 2 per cent of first-trimester pregnancies; however, among women visiting the ED with vaginal bleeding or abdominal pain in the first trimester of pregnancy, the incidence of ectopic pregnancy is typically 10 per cent[1]. The history may be misleading with periods misinterpreted, the patient taking contraceptive precautions or denial of intercourse.

1 *Rosen's Emergency Medicine: Concepts and Clinical Practice* (8th edn, 2012) Chapter 178, Acute complications of pregnancy.

18.59   For these reasons a pregnancy test is required in all patients of childbearing age with a complaint of abdominal pain, irrespective of sexual history or reported contraception use. Women who present with syncope or hypotension (regardless of whether they have abdominal pain) should also be presumed to have a bleeding ectopic pregnancy. A positive test result may indicate intrauterine or extrauterine pregnancy or, rarely, molar pregnancy or cancer. Those with a positive test will need demonstration of an intrauterine pregnancy in order for the ectopic diagnosis to be excluded. Those in whom the diagnosis cannot be excluded and those who are hypotensive and pregnant will need an urgent gynaecology consultation[1].

1 See Ectopic pregnancy and miscarriage (NICE CG154, December 2012).

Symptom: low back pain; specific condition: cauda equina syndrome

18.60   Low back pain is a frequent symptom amongst the population but with a wide differential diagnosis, including serious pathology that does not involve the spine and the cord. Ninety-seven per cent of patients visiting a physician for evaluation of acute low back pain, defined as lasting less than six weeks, are ultimately diagnosed with mechanical or non-specific low back pain[1]. The vast majority of these are strain and degenerative in origin, but a few per cent have herniated disk, spinal stenosis, fracture, and congenital disorders.

1 *Rosen's Emergency Medicine: Concepts and Clinical Practice* (8th edn, 2012) Chapter 35, Back Pain.

18.61   However the serious emergency presentations of back pain include aortic dissection, cauda equina syndrome, epidural abscess or hematoma, ruptured or expanding aortic aneurysm, spinal fracture or subluxation with cord or root impingement. Urgent diagnoses include back pain with neurologic deficits, disk herniation causing neurologic compromise, malignancy, sciatica with motor nerve root compression, spinal fractures without cord impingement and vertebral osteomyelitis. For these diagnoses to be made in the small minority requires a systematic and comprehensive history together with a detailed examination, including rectal examination and gait. Specifically those patients with low blood pressure or fever may have life-threatening causes. The clinician needs to be sensitive to red flags (see below) and ensure the appropriate tests (including FBC, CRP/ESR and plain radiology) are undertaken.

18.62   Red flags include:

- recent significant trauma;
- recent mild trauma in patients older than 50 years;
- history of prolonged steroid use;
- history of osteoporosis;
- patients older than 70 years;
- children without clear mechanism: young children with no clear explanation for their back pain should have early and more extensive evaluation for infection and tumour;
- syncope, history of cancer in cancer patients; 80 per cent who report back pain have spinal metastases;
- low back pain worse at rest or night pain;
- unexplained weight loss;
- recent bacterial infection;
- unexplained fever (ie higher than 38°C);
- immunocompromised status;
- failure to improve after six weeks of conservative therapy;
- features of aortic dissection, ruptured aortic aneurysm;
- urinary retention, saddle anaesthesia, reduction/loss of rectal sphincter tone, bilateral leg neurological signs;
- focal back pain with fever.

18.63   Often there is a chronic history and the patient may have been seen by primary care previously and have reached the end of their capacity to cope, and may be awaiting outpatient investigation. These patients should not be assumed to have a benign cause and require the same approach if significant pathology is not to be missed. For those patients who are discharged, there will need to be clear instructions as to when to seek medical help, eg any sphincter disturbance, progression of paraesthesia or weakness and all should be followed up by their GP[1].

1 See: Low Back Pain: Early management of persistent non-specific low back pain (NICE CG88) May 2009.

18.64   Cauda equina syndrome consists of bilateral leg pain and weakness, urinary retention with overflow incontinence, faecal incontinence or decreased rectal tone, and 'saddle anesthesia'. It is a rare but rapidly progressive disabling complication usually caused by a large central herniated disk and less often by tumour or infection, and rarely by vascular pathology such as aorto-caval fistula. It requires early recognition (when the symptoms may be less obvious, with only elements of the syndrome) prompt investigation (an urgent MRI scan) and emergent surgery if long-term disability is to be avoided.

Head injuries

18.65   Patients with head injuries are potentially problematic because

- the patient's history may be limited or unavailable, due to the patient's reduced level of consciousness, and consequently key information (eg the patient's past history and medication) may be missing. Information from witnesses and paramedics can be key to the care of these patients;

- the reduced level of consciousness may be attributed to causes other than the head injury (eg alcohol) or other important medical causes not identified (eg hypoglycaemia);
- the detection of other injuries in the unconscious patient is harder because the patient may not be able to localise their symptoms or cooperate with the examiner. Spinal injuries, abdominal injuries and non limb-threatening orthopaedic injuries (eg finger dislocation, wrist fracture) may thus be missed;
- these patients are often immobilised to protect their spine and consequently if the clinician does not undertake a log roll to examine the patient's back, important injuries may be missed (injuries to the back of the head, spine and back of the torso);
- patients taking anticoagulants who sustain a head injury may have life-threatening intracranial haemorrhage that requires immediate reversal and neurosurgical intervention. The clinician needs to actively determine if head injured patients are taking such drugs (eg by contacting relatives, checking in patient notes);
- patients with severe head injuries (assessed using the Glasgow Coma Score ('GCS'), a measure of cerebral function) with a GCS lower than 8, and those with a falling GCS, may have threats to their life from airway, breathing and circulatory problems, as well as their head injury. This requires a prioritised team approach and meticulous care if all injuries are to be detected. These patients are at risk of hypoxia, hypercarbia, hypotension, and intracranial bleeding and will need to have their airway secured, and undergo repeated observation to detect any deterioration;
- the clinician should be aware that head injury may be a presentation of non-accidental injury in children;
- the elderly may present with a fluctuating level of consciousness due to a chronic subdural haematoma with a remote or no history of head injury.

18.66   The indications for CT scanning are:

- in adults with a GCS lower than 13/15 on initial assessment in the ED; with a GCS 13–14/15 at 2 hours post injury; suspected open or depressed skull fracture; any sign of a basal skull fracture; focal neurological deficit; post traumatic seizure; more than one episode of vomiting; patients who have sustained a head injury with no other indications for a CT and who are having warfarin treatment should have a CT within 8 hours of injury;
- children should have a CT if there is: suspicion of non-accidental injury; post traumatic seizure but no history of epilepsy; if on initial assessment a GCS lower than 14 or (for children under one year old) a GCS lower than 15; at two hours after the injury a GCS lower than 15; suspected open or depressed skull fracture; any sign of basal skull fracture; focal neurological deficit; for children under one year old the presence of bruise, swelling or laceration greater than 5cm on the head.

18.67   Children with a head injury and more than one of the following risk factors should undergo CT examination: loss of consciousness for longer than 5 minutes; abnormal drowsiness; three or more episodes of vomiting; dangerous mechanism; amnesia for longer than 5 minutes.

There is no role for skull X-rays.

18.68 It should be noted that head injured patients are liable to deterioration (seizures, vomiting, fall in GCS), and thus this should be anticipated at all times, including when they go to the CT scanner.

18.69 Neurosurgical consultations will be required for patients with the following: CT showing recent intracranial lesion; CT cannot be done locally; persistent coma with GCS of 9/15 after initial resuscitation; confusion for longer than 4 hours; deterioration in level of consciousness after admission; progressive focal neurological signs; seizure without full recovery; depressed skull fracture; definite or suspected penetrating injury; CSF leak or other sign of basal skull fracture.

18.70 The indications for admission are: a GCS of lower than 15; neurological deficit or post traumatic seizure; significant symptoms (severe headache, vomiting, irritability or abnormal behaviour); continuing amnesia more than 5 minutes after the injury; significant other medical problems; difficulty in assessment due to alcohol, drugs, or epilepsy; no one at home or safe home to go to.

18.71 Those who are alert and orientated are candidates for discharge, provided that they have a responsible adult who will observe them for any signs of deterioration, and have been provided with written advice[1].

1 See Head injury – Triage, assessment, investigation and early management of head injury in children, young people and adults (January 2014), NICE guidance 176.

The patient with multiple injuries

18.72 These patients present with injuries ranging from the life threatening to the self limiting, involving more than one body system, that are unlikely to have all been identified prior to arrival in the ED. To manage such patients requires a systematised prioritised approach[1] which guides the minimum standard of care, with the primary survey designed to identify life threatening airway, breathing, circulation and neurologic problems and a detailed secondary survey to detect all other injuries. This care is delivered by a team whose members have clear areas of responsibility. Such teams may be working together for the first time.

1 As advocated by ATLS (https://www.rcseng.ac.uk/courses/course-search/atls.html).

18.73 Problems that can arise include:

- lack of information about the patient (because they are unconscious, there are no relatives available), eg drugs, allergies and medical conditions that may have led to the injury: seizures, pacemaker etc;
- obvious and spectacular injuries that may distract from other more important injuries leading to their delayed detection;
- failure to ensure that all tests (blood tests, transfusion, CT scans, plain radiology, ultrasound) are requested, completed and that the results are obtained and correctly interpreted;

- failure to correctly prioritise the care of the patient, eg need to go directly to theatre for life-saving surgery rather than the CT scanner for imaging;
- failure to repeatedly reassess the patient in order to detect deterioration, as this is often a dynamic situation that may change rapidly;
- when multiple casualties are being cared for synchronously this may stretch the capacity of staff.

To successfully manage such patients and avoid these difficulties needs a consistent approach, prior training, good leadership, good communication and clear documentation.

Alcohol

18.74 Alcohol-related problems account for 15 per cent of the ED workload. These patients may be simply intoxicated, or more problematically alcohol may contribute to other presentations, eg head injury, deliberate self harm. Alcoholics are more prone to injury, haemorrhage, withdrawal seizures, hypoglycaemia and severe infections as well as having concurrent social and mental health problems. For these reasons these patients require meticulous attention if the doctor is not to be misled by the labelling of these patients by others ('he is simply drunk'), to identify all the body systems that can potentially be affected by alcohol and to recognise that alcohol is often only part of the presentation (eg the drunk with a reduced level of consciousness and a significant head injury). Alcoholics may present with the direct brain effects of alcohol (Wernicke's encephalopathy: ataxia, ophthalmoplegia, nystagmus, confusion) which are treatable with Vitamin B complexes and therefore important to recognise and treat[1].

1 See Alcohol-use disorders: physical complications (NICE CG100, June 2010).

Fractures and dislocations

18.75 In order for clinicians to manage these patients successfully they must have knowledge of the common fractures and dislocations and their associated problems, and these should be taught on department induction programmes. Identification is dependent on the patient's history, examination and imaging.

18.76 At each of these stages there may be failings:

- the history may be limited or unavailable due to a reduced level of consciousness, eg due to head injury or intoxication, making it harder to identify injuries. This requires the clinician to anticipate potential injuries based on limited information and to be diligent in searching for them;
- the examination may be too limited (eg examination of the wrist only rather than the whole limb in the patient who has fallen on an outstretched hand) and not in sufficient detail (eg not recording the neurovascular and tendon function). The clinician may be distracted by other more obvious but less important injuries, or fail to consider important potential complications (eg compartment syndrome);

- imaging may not be requested, wrongly requested (eg wrist views instead of scaphoid views for a scaphoid injury, failure to X-ray the joint above and below the injured area), requested correctly and misread (as normal or failure to detect all the abnormalities). Knowledge of the common fractures and dislocations should avoid these problems.

18.77 Treatment of fractures and dislocations requires pain relief using local or regional anaesthesia techniques or sedation (in an appropriate environment) prior to reduction. When a fracture or dislocation is reduced, X-rays must be taken to confirm this is the case and immobilisation provided by the use of plaster of Paris, slings and splints. The neurovascular status of the limb must also be recorded after the procedure. Patients require clear guidance as to the expected typical course for their injury and when to seek help, be comfortable and provided with analgesia and a follow up appointment.

18.78 The following are examples that demonstrate some common difficulties in diagnosis and treatment.

Cervical spine

18.79 For injury to the cervical spine and spinal cord to be detected requires the clinician to have both a high index of suspicion and to initially provide spinal immobilisation for the following patient groups[1]:

- those suspected of sustaining major trauma;
- minor trauma with spinal pain and or neurological symptoms/signs;
- altered consciousness after injury;
- a mechanism of injury with possible spinal injury (eg road traffic accident, high fall, diving);
- pre-existing spinal disease (eg rheumatoid arthritis, ankylosing spondylitis), as serious fractures or dislocations may follow apparently minor trauma.

1 Wyatt (et al) *The Oxford Handbook of Emergency Medicine* (4th edn).

18.80 Assessment of these patients may be problematic because

- the patient may be unable to give a history or cooperate with the examination (after head injury, intoxication, major distracting injuries elsewhere, effects of opiate analgesia);
- the clinician may be preoccupied by more pressing concerns with regard to the patient's airway, breathing and circulation; a spinal injury may fail to be considered;
- failure to complete a full physical examination (to log roll the patient and examine the whole of the spine and undertake rectal examination and full neurological examination) in order to detect a spinal injury.

18.81 The patient will typically have been transported on a spinal board and the patient should be moved off this at the earliest stage to avoid skin break down and pressure sores, unless CT scanning is planned within half an hour of arrival, when it is best to remain on the board and avoid the risks of repeated log rolling.

18.82   For patients who are fully alert, the Canadian C spine rule[1] provides a standard of care and indicates which patients require X-rays of the cervical spine (and those which do not, where immobilisation can be discontinued). Plain radiology of the cervical spine requires three views (AP, lateral and open mouth) with the cervicothoracic junction fully visualised on the lateral view. Any deviation from normality of these X-rays requires a senior review and likely further imaging. Those patients with normal X-rays, no neurology, and no disproportionate pain can be discharged, provided with analgesia and written guidance as to how to look after their neck over the coming weeks.

1 Stiell 'The Canadian c-spine rule for radiography in alert and stable trauma patients' (2001) 286(15) JAMA 1841–1848.

18.83   Those patients who have sustained multiple injuries, or have an altered level of consciousness, will have CT scans which provide comprehensive information and are less likely to be misinterpreted as they are reported emergently by radiologists. The presence of a spinal injury forewarns of other potential injuries both within the spine (10 per cent of cervical injuries are associated with spinal injury elsewhere) and outside (eg thoracic spinal injuries are associated with mediastinal injury). It is not possible to be confident that there is no cervical injury in those patients with altered levels of consciousness, major distracting injuries, or who have been given opiate analgesia who will require their spine to continue to be immobilised and handed over to the in-patient teams[1].

1 See Head injury – Triage, assessment, investigation and early management of head injury in children, young people and adults (January 2014) NICE guidance 176.

Shoulder dislocation

18.84   An anterior dislocation is usually obvious (by the deformity, pain and the radiology is easy to interpret). Neurovascular complications are more common with anterior dislocation than with posterior, with risk to the axillary artery and nerve and both must be examined for, and documented. Reduction may be achieved by use of Entonox, but more usually requires sedation. Post reduction films and documentation of neurovascular status are essential. With posterior dislocation (2–5 per cent of cases) the deformity is less obvious (50 per cent may be missed on initial presentation). X-ray interpretation is problematic as the dislocation does not lie in an obviously dislocated position but appears along the side of the glenoid (but in reality is located behind it), and there may be some internal rotation which makes the head of the humerus more rounded. These subtle signs that may not be appreciated. The axial view or lateral view will more obviously detect this dislocation.

18.85   Elbow dislocations are usually obvious, posteriorly located and injury to median, ulnar and radial nerve and brachial artery are possible, and there may be associated fractures of adjacent structures. Neurovascular status must be recorded prior to reduction as well as after, and post reduction films will be required.

18.86   Displaced surpacondylar fractures are more common in children with the risk of neurovascular injury, and compartment syndrome. These cases need prompt recognition and reduction if ischaemic contracture and neurological injury is to be avoided.

18.87 Forearm fractures may be associated with dislocations of the radial head and distal ulnar and require the clinician to be aware and ensure that the elbow and wrist joints are also imaged.

18.88 Falls on the outstretched hand may be associated with Colles and scaphoid fractures which are usually obvious. However with the same mechanism, the carpal bones of the wrist may be injured leading to dislocation of the lunate (part of the proximal row of carpal bones) and potential injury to the median nerve. This diagnosis may be delayed or missed because this dislocation is rare, the lunate bone is not fractured, and it is hard to see on the AP X-ray (easier on the lateral, where the relationship with the surrounding bones is abnormal). If there is a delay in diagnosis, reduction may be harder and may require an open procedure.

Scaphoid injury

18.89 Patients with traumatic wrist pain may have a scaphoid fracture. Examination of scaphoid should include detection of snuff box tenderness, axial compression pain, tubercle tenderness and reduced range of movement. Initial X-rays of the scaphoid bone may be normal (15 per cent). For those that are displaced, or associated with other injuries, they should be discussed emergently with an orthopaedic specialist. Undisplaced fractures should be immobilised in plaster and followed up by a specialist making the patient aware of the risks of non union and avascular necrosis. Those with apparently normal X-rays, but clinical features suggestive of scaphoid fracture, should be treated presumptively as cases of fracture, they require immobilisation either by plaster (traditionally this had been a scaphoid plaster but a recent evidence review suggests no benefit over a Colles type plaster) or splint (but there are no studies comparing splints to plaster) and further imaging (MRI) if symptoms persist when reviewed, typically after two weeks[1].

1 See Suspected Scaphoid Fractures (Flowchart) (September 2013) at www.collemergencymed. ac.uk/Shop-Floor/Clinical%20Guidelines/College%20Guidelines/.

Lower limb sprains and dislocations

18.90 Ankle dislocations are usually unstable and may be associated with skin ischemia and loss of foot pulses when they will need prompt reduction under sedation. Recording of the neurovascular status is therefore important.

18.91 Children rarely suffer ankle sprains; they are more likely to suffer an epiphyseal injury (and the X-ray appear normal) which may be unrecognised and untreated.

18.92 Dislocation of the knee is rare and requires major ligamentous disruption. Importantly it is associated with damage to the popliteal artery whose presentation may be delayed, ie there may be progressive reduction in blood flow that is only detectable by repeated examination.

Dislocation of the hip requires major force and is usually obvious. Importantly it is associated with damage to sciatic nerve, femoral nerve and artery and there is a risk of femoral head necrosis the longer it remains unreduced. These patients require accurate recording of neurovascular status and timely general anaesthesia to reduce the hip.

18.93   Patients with hip pain and a prosthesis require imaging of both the hip joint and full length of the prosthesis to detect dislocation or periprosthetic fractures.

18.94   Hip pain in the elderly after a fall is most likely due to fractures to the neck of femur or pubic ramus and these are seen on plain radiology. For those with disproportionate pain and an apparently normal hip X-ray further imaging should be considered (CT/MRI) for the detection of undisplaced sub-capital fractures.

18.95   Compartment syndrome is caused by a rise in tissue pressure within a fascial compartment secondary to injury with consequent impaired tissue perfusion. The early clinical signs are of disproportionate pain that is difficult to control with opiates, that is made worse by passive extension of the muscles that traverse the compartment which become swollen and firm. However the pain may not be evident because of reduced level of consciousness. Burning pain and parathesia precede diminished sensation; pallor and pulselessness are late signs. The presence of pulses and sensation should not be relied upon to exclude the diagnosis which needs always to be considered and can only be diagnosed by direct pressure readings of the compartment. Doctors are familiar with the compartments of the forearm and leg, but compartments exist in the thigh, buttock, hand and foot and are all sites at risk of compartment syndrome.

Wounds[1]

18.96   The injury is usually obvious but the doctor needs a structured approach for successful management:

- history: it is important to establish if the mechanism was blunt trauma (when it should be anticipated that the injury will be over a wider area than that of the wound with delayed onset of swelling) or due to cutting, where the injury will be more localised. The potential for wound contamination by foreign bodies (glass, soil, grit) and bacteria (eg from bites) will need to be considered. Those patients who are immunocompromised (eg diabetics, those taking steroids) will be at increased risk of infection. All patients should be asked about their tetanus status;
- examination of the wound requires adequate lighting and ideally a bloodless field. The wound should be described in terms of shape, size, depth, and body position. The doctor needs to consider the underlying structures that could be damaged and assess their function. For limb wounds joint movement, neurological function, vascular supply and tendon function will all need to be recorded;
- if a glass or metallic foreign body is a possibility, X-ray requests describing the location, and that a foreign body is being looked for (as

this requires a different radiographic technique) should be specified. For non radio-opaque foreign bodies (eg wood) ultrasound imaging should be requested;

- treatment of the wound requires anaesthesia, proper lighting, cleaning of the wound (by irrigation, physical removal of debris, or scrubbing) and inspection of the underlying structures. Tendon injuries may be partial with normal function and so the tendon should be assessed by direct inspection through its full range of movement in order to detect partial division. Finding foreign bodies can be difficult, as they may be embedded in tissue and blood covered, and may require senior help. Clinicians asking for a wound to be closed by another member of staff should be aware that this may not typically include an evaluation of the underlying structures, which is the responsibility of that clinician;
- wound closure is typically undertaken with repeated single sutures, or skin adhesives/ glue if wounds are non gaping and superficial. Those wounds that are heavily contaminated or with delayed presentation (ie more than 12 hours after the event) should not be closed (with the exception of the face) but have a planned review at 48 hours for consideration of delayed primary closure;
- antibiotics should be prescribed for bites, puncture wounds and those wounds with exposed tendons and joints. Tetanus immunisation and or provision of tetanus antibodies needs to be considered for each case;
- the patient will need elevation of the injured area, provision of analgesia and clear instructions as to when any sutures should be removed, what complications to look for (eg infection) and where to seek help.

1 *Tintinalli's Emergency Medicine* (7th edn) Emergency Wound Management Section 6.

Sepsis

18.97   Severe sepsis, which has a high mortality, is defined by the presence of two of the following: a temperature between 36 and 38°C; heart rate faster than 90/min; respiratory rate greater than 20/min; or a white cell count between 4 and 12 (to the power of 9/L) and signs of poor tissue perfusion in patients with presumed infection.

18.98   The diagnosis may be problematic because:

- the focus of infection may not be obvious;
- the onset may be insidious, and the presenting symptoms non specific: eg confusion and lethargy, syncope, breathlessness;
- the physical signs may be multiple and difficult to unite in a single diagnosis because sepsis affects many systems.

These patients require early recognition, prompt treatment with fluids and antibiotics and repeated close monitoring in order to detect deterioration. Those who do not respond (or transiently respond) will need urgent critical care support. The standard of care for these patients is provided by the Surviving Sepsis Campaign[1].

1 www.survivingsepsis.org/Guidelines.

Mental health

18.99 Psychiatric presentations comprise 1–2 per cent of all new ED attendances and may be seen by staff sometimes as unwelcome, being often complex, heavy consumers of staff time and energy and not infrequently exhibiting aggressive or disturbed behaviour.

18.100 In a busy ED it can be difficult to spend large amounts of time with a single patient, and despite recommendations regarding interview rooms these may not always be available.

18.101 The mental health clerking detail is commonly poor in ED notes, and without a prompt it is unlikely that doctors will record the key findings that inform risk. A structured proforma is essential, to ensure that a psychiatric history and mental state examination is recorded and a risk assessment of the patient is undertaken. This is especially true for those patients who have self harmed and may be at risk of suicide.

18.102 This enables a clear management pathway to be defined. Close liaison with psychiatry services is essential and a multidisciplinary team concerned with social, alcohol and drug problems is ideal.

18.103 The College of Emergency Medicine recommends[1] that:

- patients who have self-harmed should have a risk assessment in the ED;
- previous mental health issues should be documented in the patient's clinical record;
- a mental state examination (MSE) should be recorded in the patient's clinical record;
- the provisional diagnosis should be documented in the patient's clinical record;
- details of any referral or follow-up arrangements should be documented in the patient's clinical record;
- from the time of referral, a member of the mental health team should see the patient within an hour.

1 Mental Health in Emergency Departments – A toolkit for improving care, at www. collemergencymed.ac.uk/.

Paediatrics

18.104 Children (ie those under the age of 18) typically constitute 25 per cent of an ED workload. Care is overseen by consultant emergency physicians who have undergone training in the emergency aspects of paediatrics. However an increasing number of consultants are choosing to specialise in paediatric EM, having undergone additional training and having come from either a paediatric or EM background. Nursing care is typically delivered and supervised by registered paediatric nurses.

18.105 Junior doctors will see a substantial proportion of these patients, who can be particularly challenging because:

- the doctors may not have cared for children previously and had the chance to develop communication skills with children who are at different developmental stages;
- the presentations of serious disease can be subtle, and non specific. The overlap of presentation of benign conditions with the early presentations of serious disease is substantial;
- a child may not be capable of vocalising their symptoms;
- the rapidity with which symptoms and signs can change;
- the breadth and complexity of presentations including their often complex social components.

These factors make this a stressful group to look after, in an environment that is usually busy and noisy, and in which practical procedures such as cannulation can be difficult.

18.106   Therefore these doctors must:

- have dedicated focused teaching to cover the key presentations;
- undertake meticulous history and examination and documentation;
- recognise which patients will need to be discussed with a senior (middle grade and consultant staff) and have ready access to such a person. The CEM recommend that all children under the age of three with fever who are to be discharged are discussed with a senior;
- understand and have access to the guidelines that exist for the care of these patients[1].

1 See Paediatric EM guidance (NHS Institute for Innovation and Improvement) http://webarchive.nationalarchives.gov.uk/*/http://institute.nhs.uk for a comprehensive list of guidelines.

18.107   EDs will have good working relationships with the in-patient teams (which should be on the same site), community paediatricians and nurses. Excellent communication with primary care and health visitors is essential and all patients will have a GP letter for each attendance which will also be copied to the health visitor/school nurse/social worker as appropriate.

Paediatric resuscitation

18.108   Typically resuscitation in children is of a lower frequency compared to adults. Teams need to be activated quickly with a consistent response. The training and standard of care needed for these patients is specified by the APLS[1] and EPLS[2] courses. There are clear protocols for the common presentations (asthma, seizures, cardiac arrest, arrhythmias). Care needs to be taken with equipment and drugs that are weight specific.

1 www.alsg.org/uk/APLS.
2 www.resus.org.uk/pages/eplsinfo.htm

Child abuse

18.109   The recognition that the presentation could be one of child abuse or neglect requires a high level of awareness and sensitivity and must always be considered a possible diagnosis for any presentation. The role of the ED staff is to detect possible cases of abuse by a thorough history and complete physical examination, looking for other signs of injury, undertaken sensitively. Concerns can be raised by the pattern of injury, inconsistency in the history and delay in presentation. Collateral information will need to be gained from primary care/health visitor/social worker as well as checking the register of children that are of concern. Concerns of possible child abuse must be shared with a senior in the ED or directly with the paediatric team[1].

1 See Safeguarding Children and Young People (RCPCH, March 2014).

Parental concern

18.110   The doctor should be aware that the early signs of serious illness are often extremely subtle and that the parents know their own child better than any doctor can. The doctor should always defer to a more senior clinician when he is unable to convince both himself and the parents that the child is not seriously ill.

Feverish infant

18.111   This group may have a benign cause for their fever but there may also be a serious cause. Guidance provided by NICE states the conditions that need to be met for the safe discharge of such children, and who needs in-patient referral[1].

1 Feverish Illness in Children (NICE, CG160) May 2013.

CHAPTER 19

Endocrinology

Dr Mark Vanderpump

INTRODUCTION

19.1   Endocrinology is the medical speciality which includes the study of hormones and hormone producing glands. Hormones are chemical messengers which are released from endocrine glands and may have actions restricted to a specific target organ or widespread effects throughout the body. The word hormone was first used in 1905 by Irwin Starling (1866–1927)[1]. Until the nineteenth century treatment was often worthless as there was absolutely no knowledge of the nature of the disease. At that time it became understood that the central nervous system no longer controlled most bodily functions and Sharpey-Schäfer in 1895 had successfully described almost the complete endocrine system[2]. Sir William Bayliss in 1915 referred to cell processes which were a reflection of the understanding up to that time of body metabolism and the role of enzymes. Subsequent research aimed to identify new hormones and how they worked[3]. In 1921 insulin was extracted from the cells of the islets of Langerhans within the pancreas by a team from the University of Toronto comprising Banting, Best, McLeod and Collip, who proved that insulin and peptide hormone played a decisive role in regulating carbohydrate metabolism, and changed the treatment of diabetes. Insulin soon came to be produced commercially in large quantities[4].

1 Welbourne 'Endocrine diseases', in Bynum, Porter (eds) *Companion of Encyclopaedia of the History of Medicine* (1994) pp 484–511.
2 Schäfer 'Internal secretions' (1895) ii Lancet 321–324.
3 Bayliss *Principles of General Physiology* (1915).
4 Bliss *The Discovery of Insulin* (1987).

19.2   Hypofunction, hyperfunction and dysfunction are the three disturbances of the endocrine system. All the glands of the body can be affected by at least one of these disturbances and sometimes by all three, and those glands that secrete a variety of hormones may well exhibit quite complex combinations of all three. In the twenty-first century a hormone is a molecule secreted in a regulated fashion from one organ and acting on another. The definition is firmly based on the anatomy of the seventeenth century, the histology of the nineteenth and the physiology of the twentieth. Endocrinology thus includes the care of patients with diabetes mellitus, the thyroid gland, the parathyroid glands, the adrenal gland, the pituitary gland, the gonads including both ovaries and testes and disorders of bone metabolism. Diabetes is by far the most common of all endocrine diseases. Other common endocrine disorders are those of the thyroid gland (thyroid failure (hypothyroidism), overactivity (hyperthyroidism) and nodules). Pituitary disease, including Cushing's disease and acromegaly, is relatively rare.

DIABETES MELLITUS

19.3   Diabetes mellitus is the most common endocrine disorder and its prevalence is approximately 5 per cent of the UK population[1]. It is estimated that at least 10 per cent of the NHS budget is spent on diabetes. People with diabetes are more likely to be admitted to hospital and experience prolonged stays in hospital. Medical negligence claims involve misdiagnosis and poor diabetes care, where earlier intervention and treatment would have avoided or curtailed the complications of diabetes.

1 Diabetes in the UK 2010 Key statistics on Diabetes. Diabetes UK, 2010. http://www.diabetes. org.uk/Documents/Reports/Diabetes_in_the_UK_2010.pdf.

19.4   The diagnosis of diabetes is made on biochemical criteria by finding a raised fasting or random blood glucose or using a measure of longer term blood sugar levels called glycosylated haemoglobin (HbA1c). The two principal types of diabetes that are recognised are:

- type 1, which is an autoimmune disease where there is destruction of the insulin producing beta-cells in the islets of Langerhans by the immune system;
- type 2 diabetes is of a much longer duration prior to the diagnosis and is initially due to increasing insulin resistance and subsequently a loss of insulin production by the beta-cells, resulting in hyperglycaemia.

Type 2 diabetes is often associated with other features of the so-called metabolic syndrome which include hypertension, hyperlipidaemia and obesity often characterised as central obesity with a raised waist circumference. Diabetes is a risk factor for higher mortality, particularly cardiovascular mortality and also specific complications of diabetes known as microvascular complications involving the eyes (retinopathy), the nerves (neuropathy) and the kidneys (nephropathy).

19.5   Diabetes ketoacidosis (DKA) represents the metabolic consequences of insulin deficiency, glucagon excess, and counter-regulatory hormonal responses to stressful triggers in people with diabetes. DKA may be the initial presentation in approximately 25 per cent of adults with newly-diagnosed type 1 diabetes. Compared with children, the loss of insulin secretory capacity usually is less rapid in adults with type 1 diabetes. Thus, adults with type 1 diabetes typically have a longer estimated period prior to diagnosis and are likely to have a longer period with symptoms of hyperglycaemia (polyuria, polydipsia and fatigue) than children. In 2–12 per cent of adults, the clinical presentation is similar to that of type 2 diabetes (not initially insulin dependent), with autoimmune mediated insulin deficiency developing later in the course of disease. This is sometimes called latent autoimmune diabetes of adults (LADA). Type 1 diabetes requires lifelong insulin therapy.

19.6   The pathogenesis of diabetes distinguishes type 2 diabetes resulting from interaction between insulin resistance and beta-cell dysfunction from type 1 diabetes, in which the autoimmune destruction of pancreatic beta-cell leads to absolute insulin deficiency. The diagnosis of type 1 diabetes should be considered if ketonuria is detected, weight loss is marked or the patient does not have features of a metabolic syndrome or contributing illness. When diabetes is diagnosed in a younger person, the possibility that the diabetes is not type 1 diabetes should be considered if they are obese or have a family history of diabetes, particularly if they are of non-white ethnicity. Tests to detect specific autoantibodies or to measure C-peptide deficiency can be used to confirm the diagnosis of type 1 diabetes to discriminate type 1 from type 2 diabetes.

19.7   The clinical course of type 1 diabetes, including its treatment, metabolic outcomes and long-term clinical complications, has changed dramatically over the past 20 years. Treatment innovations including multiple daily treatment regimes, external subcutaneous insulin infusion with external pumps, new insulin analogues with more physiological pharmacokinetic characteristics and widespread self-monitoring, improved treatment of co-morbidities such as hypertension and dyslipidaemia have all contributed to dramatic improvements in the management of type 1 diabetes.

19.8   Type 2 diabetes usually manifests in later adult life and accounts for over 90 per cent of all cases. This type of diabetes develops mostly through a combination of resistance to the action of the pancreatic hormone insulin in the liver, muscle and fat and defective production of insulin from the beta cells within the pancreas. Most patients with type 2 diabetes are diagnosed in the relatively late stages of a long and complex pathological process. Disease onset is usually insidious and diagnosis is often delayed. Epidemiological studies have calculated that type 2 diabetes to have been present for at least four to seven years prior to its presentation[1]. As a result, diabetic microvascular complications may be present at the time of diagnosis of diabetes, and their frequency increases over time. Commonly, patients with type 2 diabetes report a family history of the condition. The lifetime risk associated with having a single parent with diabetes is approximately 15 per cent; it is 75 per cent or more if both parents are affected[2]. The genetics of most cases of type 2 diabetes involve a polygenic (multigene) inheritance. The prevalence of diabetes increases with age and in certain ethnic groups such as black Africans and south Asians. The weight gain that commonly occurs between the fourth and seventh decades of life increases insulin resistance, particularly if this adiposity is of central (abdominal) distribution. Low levels of physical exercise also predict the development of type 2 diabetes as exercise increases insulin sensitivity and can prevent obesity.

1 Balasubramanyam, Nalini, Hampe (et al) 'Syndromes of ketosis-prone diabetes mellitus' (2008) 29 Endocrine Reviews 292–302.
2 Turner, Cull, Frighi, Holman for the UK Prospective Diabetes Study (UKPDS) Group (1999) 'Glycemic control with diet, sulfonylurea, metformin, or insulin in patients with type 2 diabetes. Progressive requirement for multiple therapies' (UKPDS 49) JAMA 281: 2005–2012.

19.9   There are three major components to non-pharmacological therapy of blood glucose in type 2 diabetes, namely dietary modification, exercise and weight reduction. Regular physical activity is recommended for patients with type 2 diabetes since it may have beneficial effects on metabolic risk factors for the development of diabetic complications. Two of the major goals of diabetes therapy are to reduce hyperglycaemia and body fat. Obesity, especially abdominal obesity, is associated with insulin resistance, hyperinsulinaemia, hyperglycaemia, dyslipidaemia, and hypertension; these abnormalities tend to cluster and are often referred to as the 'metabolic syndrome'. Elements of the metabolic syndrome are strong risk factors for cardiovascular disease, and regular exercise in non-diabetic subjects has beneficial effects on virtually all aspects of the syndrome.

19.10   If target glycaemic control is not achieved, combined therapy with other oral hypoglycaemic agents or the early addition of insulin is considered. Regardless of the initial response to therapy, the natural history of most patients with type 2 diabetes established by the UK Prospective Diabetes Study (UKPDS) Group is for blood glucose concentrations and

HbA1c to rise over time[1]. The UKPDS suggested that worsening beta-cell dysfunction with decreased insulin release was primarily responsible for disease progression. Oral agents become less effective as beta cell function declines. More severe insulin resistance or decreased compliance with the dietary regimen also may contribute to progression. After a successful initial response to oral therapy, patients fail to maintain target HbA1c levels (less than 7 per cent) at a rate of 5–10 per cent per year. In the UKPDS, 50 per cent of patients originally controlled with a single drug required the addition of a second drug after three years and, by nine years, 75 per cent needed multiple therapies to achieve the target HbA1c value. It has been estimated that 50 per cent of patients with type 2 diabetes will ultimately require treatment with insulin within 15 years, particularly in those diagnosed at a younger age. Alternative therapies to insulin which are gut hormones that enhance insulin action (the incretins) have recently become available.

1 Turner, Cull, Frighi, Holman for the UK Prospective Diabetes Study (UKPDS) Group (1999) 'Glycemic control with diet, sulfonylurea, metformin, or insulin in patients with type 2 diabetes. Progressive requirement for multiple therapies' (UKPDS 49) JAMA 281: 2005–2012.

19.11   A ketosis prone form of diabetes, which was initially observed in young African Americans has emerged as a new clinical entity[1]. This syndrome of episodic diabetic ketoacidosis without the immunological markers of type 1 diabetes characterised by insulin dependence at the time of presentation as in the case of type 1 diabetes, but followed by absence of insulin requirements for years as observed in type 2 diabetes. This third type of diabetes is mostly observed in obese, adult Afro Caribbean and sub-Saharan African patients and other adult non-white diabetic populations. The absence of any defined pathophysiological mechanism has led the American Diabetes Association and World Health Organisation (WHO), to classify this entity as idiopathic type 1 or type 1B diabetes. Ketosis prone diabetes shows a strong male predominance, stronger family history, higher age and body mass index, and more severe metabolic decompensation than type 1 diabetes. In ketosis prone diabetes, discontinuation of insulin therapy with development of remission of insulin dependence, is achieved in 76 per cent of patients (non-insulin dependent), whereas only 24 per cent of patients remain insulin dependent. This form of diabetes is important to recognise as it can have significant implications for treatment of the condition[2].

1 Balasubramanyam, Nalini, Hampe (et al) 'Syndromes of ketosis-prone diabetes mellitus' (2008) 29 Endocrine Reviews 292–302.
2 Frank 'Diabetic retinopathy' (2004) 350 N Engl J Med 48–58.

Complications of diabetes

19.12   Morbidity from diabetes involves both macrovascular (atherosclerosis) and microvascular disease (retinopathy, nephropathy, and neuropathy). Interventions can limit end organ damage and are the focus of care for the patient with diabetes. Prevention of cardiovascular morbidity is the major priority for patients with diabetes, especially type 2; diabetes is considered equivalent to known coronary disease in predicting the risk of future cardiac events. Cardiovascular morbidity can be significantly reduced with management of hypertension and cholesterol and appropriate use of aspirin. Good glycaemic control can minimise risks for retinopathy, nephropathy and neuropathy in type 1 and type 2 diabetes.

19.13   The principal method of monitoring of diabetes is with the HbA1c. Glucose reacts with various proteins of the blood including haemoglobin and the glycated products can be measured to provide an index of the overall blood sugars during the life of the red blood cell, ie 90 days. Therefore the HbA1c level will give a guide to the overall blood sugar, although in the previous six to twelve weeks. The WHO has now recommended the use of HbA1c to diagnose diabetes. There is good evidence in both type 1 and type 2 diabetes that the level of HbA1c predicts both microvascular and macrovascular complications and that intensive treatment of diabetes to lower the HbA1c to target 48–53mmol/mol (6.5–7.0 per cent) can significantly reduce the onset of retinopathy, microalbuminuria and neuropathy. The interpretation of HbA1c needs to be taken with caution in some situations including those with haemoglobulinopathies such as thalassaemia or sickle cell anaemia or those with renal failure.

19.14   Chronic hyperglycaemia is thought to be the primary cause of diabetic microvascular complications[1] and the Diabetes Control and Complications Trial (DCCT) in patients with type 1 diabetes demonstrated the effects of better blood sugar control on the incidence of microvascular complications[2]. The DCCT assigned patients to conventional or intensive treatments and the results led to the recommendations that intensive therapy be recommended for all patients. Recent data suggest that after 30 years of type 1 diabetes the incidences of proliferative retinopathy, nephropathy and cardiovascular disease were 50 per cent, 25 per cent and 14 per cent respectively in the conventionally treated group. In the DCCT intensive treated group there were substantially lower incidences at 21 per cent, 9 per cent and 9 per cent respectively and fewer than 1 per cent had become blind, required kidney replacement or had an amputation because of diabetes during the 30 years from the onset of the study[3].

1 Frank 'Diabetic retinopathy' (2004) 350 N Engl J Med 48–58.
2 Diabetes Control and Complications Trial (DCCT) Research Group 'Effect of intensive diabetes management on macrovascular events and risk factors in the Diabetes Control and Complications Trial' (1995) 75 Am J Cardiol 894–903.
3 Diabetes Control and Complications Trial/Epidemiology of Diabetes interventions and complications research group 'Modern day clinical course of type 1 diabetes mellitus after 30 years duration' (2009) 169 Arch Intern Med 1307–1316.

19.15   Patients with diabetes are at increased risk for visual loss, related both to refractive errors (correctable visual impairment) and to the increased incidence of retinopathy over time. Approximately 50–75 per cent of patients with type 2 diabetes will be affected by mild retinopathy during their lifetime. Legal or total blindness is experienced by 20 per cent. The efficacy of laser photocoagulation surgery in preventing loss of vision is the major reason to screen regularly for diabetic retinopathy. The incidence of blindness is 25 times higher in patients with diabetes than in the general population. The prevalence of retinopathy increases progressively in patients with type 1 diabetes with increasing duration of disease and retinopathy occurs within three to five years after diagnosis and almost all patients are affected at 15–20 years[1]. Strict glycaemic control early in the course of the diabetes and photocoagulation for established disease are of primary importance in slowing the rate of progression of retinopathy in patients with very mild to moderate non-proliferative retinopathy. The incidence of severe visual loss is influenced by other forms of therapy including control of hypertension which also slows the rate of progression of diabetic retinopathy and reduces the risk of vitreous haemorrhage. Photocoagulation is the primary treatment for advanced retinopathy. Regression of proliferative retinopathy following pan-retinal photocoagulation is in part related to glycaemic control during the pre-treatment, treatment, and post-treatment periods. Early photocoagulation is not usually recommended except in the use of focal laser therapy for macular oedema as this therapy increases the frequency of visual improvement and diminishes the risk of visual loss[2]. Good visual acuity can be maintained with aggressive monitoring, and treatment when indicated.

1 Frank 'Diabetic retinopathy' (2004) 350 N Engl J Med 48–58.
2 Turner, Cull, Frighi, Holman for the UK Prospective Diabetes Study (UKPDS) Group (1999) 'Glycemic control with diet, sulfonylurea, metformin, or insulin in patients with type 2 diabetes. Progressive requirement for multiple therapies' (UKPDS 49) (1999) 281 JAMA 2005–2012.

19.16   Increased urinary protein excretion (microalbuminuria) is the earliest clinical finding of diabetic nephropathy. Diabetes is the most common cause of new patients requiring renal replacement therapy. Approximately 20–30 per cent of patients with type 1 diabetes will have microalbuminuria after a mean duration of diabetes of 15 years. Less than half of these patients will progress to overt nephropathy; microalbuminuria may regress or remain stable in a substantial proportion, probably related to glycaemic and blood pressure control. Recent studies have found that the renal prognosis of type 1 diabetes, including the rate of progression to end-stage renal disease, has dramatically improved over the last several decades[1]. In addition to the importance of glycaemic control, more aggressive blood pressure reduction, the use of angiotensin converting enzyme inhibitors and lipid lowering have been shown to reduce the rate of progression of diabetic nephropathy. The onset of overt nephropathy in type 1 diabetes is typically between 10 and 15 years after the onset of the disease. Those patients who have no proteinuria after 20–25 years have a risk of developing overt renal disease of only about 1 per cent per year. Over a median of 15 years from diagnosis of type 2 diabetes, nearly 40 per cent of patients develop albuminuria and nearly 30 per cent develop renal impairment[2]. The risk of development of nephropathy and the requirement for dialysis or renal transplant is significantly increased if there is associated hypertension and with duration of diabetes.

1 Diabetes Control and Complications Trial/Epidemiology of Diabetes interventions and complications research group 'Modern day clinical course of type 1 diabetes mellitus after 30 years duration' (2009) 169 Arch Intern Med 1307–1316.
2 Retnakaran, Cull, Thorne (et al) for the UKPDS Study Group 'Risk Factors for Renal Dysfunction in Type 2 Diabetes. UK Prospective Diabetes Study 74 (2006) 55 Diabetes 1832–1839.

Life expectancy in diabetes

19.17   People with diabetes have a lifespan around ten years shorter than those without diabetes, and the major cause of this increased mortality is macrovascular disease[1]. Until recently relatively few data existed on life expectancy or mortality in type 1 diabetes and most large cohort mortality studies include patients with both type 1 and type 2 diabetes.

1 Robb, Lawrenson 'Diabetes mellitus', in Brackenridge, Croxson, Mackenzie (eds) *Brackenridge's Medical Selection of Life Risks* (5th edn, 2006) pp 289–315.

19.18   Despite advances in care, UK mortality rates in the past decade continue to be much greater in patients with type 1 diabetes than in those without diabetes[1]. In a UK cohort from north east England an excess mortality was associated with diabetes, even in an area with high background death rates from cardiovascular disease. This excess mortality was evident in all age groups, was most pronounced in young people with type 1 diabetes, and was exacerbated by material deprivation[2]. In a Swedish cohort study of mortality in the 15–34-year-old age group there was a two-fold excess mortality in patients with type 1 diabetes[3].

1 Soedamah-Muthu, Fuller, Mulnier (et al) 'All-cause mortality rates in patients with type 1 diabetes mellitus compared with a non-diabetic population from the UK general practice research database 1992–1999' (2006) 49 Diabetologia 660–666.
2 Roper, Bilous, Kelly (et al) 'Excess mortality in a population with diabetes and the impact of material deprivation: longitudinal, population based study' (2001) 322 BMJ 1389–1393.
3 Waernbaum, Blohmé, Ostman (et al) 'Excess mortality in incident cases of diabetes mellitus aged 15 to 34 years at diagnosis: a population-based study (DISS) in Sweden' (2006) 49 Diabetologia 653–659.

19.19   Thus, despite advances in treatment, diabetes still carries an increased mortality in young adults, even in a country with a good economic and educational patient status and easy access to health care. Increasing hyperglycaemia increases the risk of cardiovascular mortality and is more profound in people with type 1 diabetes than in subjects with type 2 diabetes[1]. A recent follow-up study to the DCCT has produced evidence to support the view that intensive insulin therapy in patients with type 1 diabetes decreases the incidence of fatal and nonfatal cardiovascular events[2]. There is clearly marked variability and life expectancy is dependent on complications which develop with duration of diabetes which are clearly linked by glycaemic control as measured by the HbA1c. Tight blood sugar control without disabling rates of hypoglycaemia, if achieved before irreversible end-organ damage has occurred, reduces the incidence of microvascular disease and cardiovascular disease in patients with type 1 diabetes. Thus, intensive insulin therapy should be attempted in all appropriate patients with type 1 diabetes as early in the course of disease as is safely feasible. Both patient and physician education and support are required to perform this task safely. The optimal level of glycaemic control is uncertain. In general, the aim is for HbA1c value of 53mmol/mol (7 per cent) or lower in compliant patients in whom the benefits outweigh the risks. Specific blood sugar targets should be set for individual patients, weighing benefits related to life-expectancy and existing complications against the risk of hypoglycaemia.

1 Juutilainen, Lehto, Rönnemaa (et al) 'Similarity of the Impact of Type 1 and Type 2 Diabetes on Cardiovascular Mortality in Middle-aged Subjects' (2008) 31 Diabetes Care 714–719.
2 Cefalu 'Glycemic control and cardiovascular disease--should we reassess clinical goals?' (2005) 353 N Engl J Med 2707–2708.

19.20   Around 25 per cent of the adult type 1 diabetes population has persistent poor blood sugar control and thus are at increased risk of developing microvascular complications and increased mortality. Only a few studies have identified determinants and correlates of long-standing poor blood sugar control in type 1 diabetes[1]. There is evidence implicating genetic factors, as well as lower economic status, and psychological factors, including lack of motivation, emotional distress, depression and eating disorders. Ways of improving glycaemic control include strategies to enable self-management, for example motivational strategies, coping-orientated education, psychosocial therapies, and/or intensifying insulin injection therapy plus continuous subcutaneous insulin infusion. Long-standing poor blood sugar control therefore appears to be a heterogeneous and complex phenomenon, for which there is no simple, single solution. Comprehensive psycho-medical assessment in diabetes care may prove useful in tailoring interventions.

1 Devries, Snoek, Heine 'Persistent poor glycaemic control in adult type 1 diabetes. A closer look at the problem' (2004) 21 Diabet Med 1263–1268.

19.21 In people with type 2 diabetes, there is an increased risk for atherosclerosis due both to diabetes and to the frequent presence of other risk factors. Men and women with diabetes are at increased risk for developing cardiovascular disease (CVD) and of dying when CVD is present[1]. Men and women with diabetes have decreased life expectancy (seven to eight years less) compared to those without diabetes. At the time of diagnosis of type 2 diabetes, many people already have one or more risk factors for macrovascular disease (obesity, hypertension, dyslipidaemia, smoking) and many have evidence of overt atherosclerosis. A substantial reduction in cardiovascular mortality could be achieved by smoking cessation, daily low-dose aspirin for most patients, and aggressive treatment of hypertension and dyslipidaemia[2]. Although the benefit of tight blood pressure control has been confirmed in the UKPDS data[3], benefit from strict glycaemic control has not been conclusively demonstrated. The life expectancy of people with diabetes decreases with increasing duration of disease, poor glycaemic control, hypertension and proteinuria.

1 Franco, Steyerberg, Hu (et al) 'Associations of diabetes mellitus with total life expectancy and life expectancy with and without cardiovascular disease' (2007) 167 Arch Intern Med 1145–1151.
2 Turner, Millns, Neil (et al) 'Risk factors for coronary artery disease in non-insulin dependent diabetes mellitus: United Kingdom prospective diabetes study (UKPDS 23)' (1998) 316 BMJ 823–828.
3 UK Prospective Diabetes Study Group 'Tight blood pressure control and risk of macrovascular and microvascular complications in type 2 diabetes: UKPDS 38' (1998) 317 BMJ 703–713.

19.22 The UKPDS Risk Engine is a type 2 diabetes specific risk calculator based on 53,000 patient-years of data from the UKPDS, which also provides an approximate 'margin of error' for each estimate[1]. The UKPDS Risk Engine estimates the likelihood that a person with recently diagnosed type 2 diabetes, who has not had a cardiovascular disease event, will have one in the next defined period (usually five to ten years). This calculator has been designed predominately for clinical use to help patients and health care providers decide on the most appropriate management for individuals who develop type 2 diabetes. UKPDS Risk Engine outputs are the estimated risks and 95 per cent confidence intervals for a first coronary heart disease or stroke event within a given period.

1 Clarke, Gray, Briggs (et al) 'A model to estimate the lifetime health outcomes of patients with type 2 diabetes: the United Kingdom Prospective Diabetes Study (UKPDS) Outcomes Model (UKPDS 68)' (2004) 47 Diabetologia 1747–1759 (UKPDS Risk Engine version 2.0. http://www.dtu.ox.ac.uk/riskengine/).

Diabetes and pregnancy

19.23 Women with diabetes diagnosed for the first time during pregnancy are usually diagnosed during screening or by diagnostic oral glucose tolerance test around the middle of the pregnancy, as they have been labelled at high risk of having gestational diabetes due to risk factors identified at booking including older age, obesity, ethnicity and a family history[1]. Hyperglycaemia first recognised in early pregnancy is more often previously undiagnosed type 1 or type 2 diabetes and HbA1c is frequently elevated, which may not be the case in gestational diabetes mellitus. If type 1 diabetes is considered most likely insulin should be started immediately to prevent the unexpected development of ketoacidosis. Medical nutritional therapy with regular review of blood glucose monitoring results and fetal growth is successful in controlling hyperglycaemia in 80–90 per cent of patients with gestational diabetes. Insulin therapy is indicated for persistent maternal hyperglycaemia in order to prevent the complications, especially those related to compensatory hyperinsulinaemia and insulin macrosomia.

1 The Confidential Enquiry into Maternal and Child Health (CEMACH), Pregnancy in women with type 1 and type 2 diabetes 2002 and 2003, England, Wales and Northern Ireland. London: CEMACH, 2005: 1-98 (www.CEMACH.org.uk); National Institute for Health and Clinical Excellence 'Diabetes in Pregnancy: Management of diabetes and its complications from pre-conception to postnatal period' (2008) (www.NICE.org.uk/CG063).

19.24 Women presenting with type 1 diabetes in pregnancy are thought to be in the early phase of the diagnosis and lack the necessary beta-cell reserve, which leads to abnormal adaptation of carbohydrate, protein and metabolism. A pregnant woman with latent or undiagnosed type 1 diabetes requires sufficient insulin to compensate for increasing calorie needs, increasing adiposity, decreasing exercise and increasing anti-insulin hormones. The insulin dose required to remain normoglycaemia and prevent maternal ketosis may increase up to threefold in the course of pregnancy in type 1 diabetes.

19.25 Type 1 diabetes in pregnancy is associated with increased risks of maternal and fetal complications. In a Swedish study from 1982 to 1985, the perinatal mortality (3.1 per cent) and stillbirth rates (2.1 per cent) were up to five times those of the general population[1]. Since then and after the introduction of tight glycaemic control, outcomes of type 1 diabetic pregnancies are considered to have improved significantly. More recent studies on type 1 diabetic pregnancies have reported that stillbirth and perinatal mortality rates were still significantly increased, the risk for major malformations varied from 2 to 10 times normal, and the incidence of fetal macrosomia remained markedly increased, despite apparently good metabolic control with HbA1c levels close to the normal range. There is no clear explanation for the wide variation in perinatal outcomes for diabetic pregnancies. Differences in organisation of health care, socioeconomic factors, maternal characteristics, and patient compliance could account for some of the observed differences.

1 Persson, Norman, Hanson (2009) 'Obstetric and perinatal outcomes in type 1 diabetic pregnancies: A large, population-based study' (2009) 32 Diabetes Care 2005–2009.

19.26 Diabetic ketoacidosis is a serious metabolic complication in pregnant women with diabetes with a high mortality if undetected. Its occurrence in pregnancy compromises both the fetus and the mother profoundly. It usually occurs in the second and third trimesters because of increased insulin resistance. The incident rate of DKA in pregnancy and the corresponding fetal mortality rates have dropped significantly and according to recent reports the incidence is now between 1 to 3 per cent with fetal loss of 9 per cent. The mechanism by which maternal DKA affects the fetus is unknown. Ketoacids as well as glucose readily cross the placenta. Whether it is the maternal acidosis, hyperglycaemia, severe body fluid depletion or electrolyte imbalance that has the most detrimental effect on the fetus is unclear. The high mortality rate associated with DKA suggests a hostile intrauterine environment. Possible mechanisms include decrease in uteroplacental blood flow resulting in fetal hypoxia, maternal acidosis leading to fetal acidosis and electrolyte imbalance, maternal hypokalaemia and fetal hyperinsulinaemia which if severe could cause fetal hypokalaemia leading to fetal myocardial suppression and fatal arrhythmia. Maternal hypophosphatemia associated with DKA can also lead to impaired delivery of oxygen to the fetus.

19.27 The clinical presentation of DKA in pregnancy is similar to that in non-pregnant diabetics. Infection may or may not be apparent. However a significant minority may have glucose levels less than 12mmol/l. Factors contributing to increased risk of DKA in pregnancy include the fact that pregnancy is a state of insulin resistance and that insulin sensitivity has been demonstrated to be reduced for by as much as over 50 per cent through 36 weeks of gestation through an increase in insulin antagonistic hormones. For this reason the insulin requirement progressively rises during pregnancy, explaining the higher incidence of DKA in the second and third trimesters. Treatment includes aggressive volume of replacement, insulin infusion, careful attention to electrolytes and a search for and correction of precipitating factors. Once hyperglycaemia and acidosis is reversed and maternal stabilisation achieved, fetal compromise may no longer be evident. In essence an approach that incorporates uterorescusitation with internal stabilisation, hydration and reversal of hyperglycaemia and metabolic acidosis under combined medical and obstetric supervision, is the cornerstone of management of this condition.

19.28 Where a fetal death occurs, it is usually in the final weeks of pregnancy and in the context of poor glycaemic control, polyhydramnios and/or accelerated fetal growth[1]. The occurrence of fetal compromise of still birth when the fetus is normally grown or macrosomia, is most likely to result from chronic fetal hypoxia and/or fetal acidaemia secondary to maternal/fetal hyperglycaemia and fetal hyperinsulinaemia. The goal of obstetric surveillance is to identify those at risk in order to intervene in a timely and appropriate fashion to reduce perinatal morbidity and mortality. Babies of women with type 1 or type 2 diabetes are five times more likely to be stillborn and three times more likely to die in the first month of life compared to mothers without diabetes. Approximately 80 per cent of these losses are stillbirths, 80 per cent of these babies being structurally normal.

1 The Confidential Enquiry into Maternal and Child Health (CEMACH), Pregnancy in women with type 1 and type 2 diabetes 2002 and 2003, England, Wales and Northern Ireland. London: CEMACH, 2005: 1-98 (www.CEMACH.org.uk).

19.29 It is recommended that all women with gestational diabetes should be reviewed at six weeks after delivery when they should be counselled regarding contraception and future pregnancy planning[1]. Women with pre-existing diabetes (type 1 or type 2) are referred back to their pre-pregnancy care provider. Women with gestational diabetes are offered 75g oral glucose tolerance test between six and twelve weeks and non-attenders are followed up. The lifetime risk of developing type 2 diabetes after gestational diabetes is 30 per cent[2].

1 National Institute for Health and Clinical Excellence 'Diabetes in Pregnancy: Management of diabetes and its complications from pre-conception to postnatal period' (2008) (www.NICE. org.uk/CG063).
2 Diabetes in the UK 2010 Key statistics on Diabetes. Diabetes UK, 2010. http://www.diabetes. org.uk/Documents/Reports/Diabetes_in_the_UK_2010.pdf.

The management of the diabetic foot

19.30 Foot problems due to vasculopathy and neuropathy are a common and important source of morbidity in diabetic patients. Systematic screening examinations for neuropathy and vascular involvement of the lower extremities and careful inspection of feet may substantially reduce morbidity from foot problems. Clinical and subclinical neuropathy has been estimated to occur in 10–100 per cent of diabetic patients, depending upon the diagnostic criteria and patient population examined[1]. Diabetic neuropathy is classified into distinct clinical syndromes and there are a characteristic set of symptoms and signs which exist for each syndrome, depending on the component of the peripheral nervous system that is affected. The most frequently encountered neuropathies include:

- distal symmetric polyneuropathy is the most common type of diabetic neuropathy and is often considered synonymous with the term diabetic neuropathy. It is characterised by a progressive loss of distal sensation correlating with loss of sensory axons, followed, in severe cases, by motor weakness and motor axonal loss. Classic 'stocking-glove' sensory loss is typical in this disorder;
- individual cranial and peripheral nerve involvement causing focal mononeuropathies, especially affecting the oculomotor nerve (cranial nerve III) presenting with double vision and the median nerve presenting with carpal tunnel syndrome;
- asymmetric involvement of multiple peripheral nerves, resulting in a mononeuropathy multiplex;
- autonomic neuropathy which can result in erectile dysfunction, postural hypotension, nausea and vomiting due to gastroparesis, constipation or diarrhoea; carpal tunnel syndrome;
- thoracic and lumbar nerve root disease, causing polyradiculopathies.

1 Jeffcoate and Harding 'Diabetic foot ulcers' (2003) 361 Lancet 1545–1551.

19.31 Diabetic foot ulcers are a leading cause of non-traumatic amputation worldwide. Although accurate figures are difficult to obtain for the prevalence or incidence of foot ulcers the results of cross sectional community surveys in the UK show that 7 per cent (type 1 and type 2 combined) of people with diabetes had a history of active or previous foot ulcer. The lifetime risk for any diabetic patient is up to 15 per cent[1]. Of those with diabetic foot ulcers up to 20 per cent will require an amputation and most begin with a potentially preventable initial event. Neuropathy resulting in insensitivity, abnormal foot biomechanics and peripheral vascular disease (especially medium- and small-sized vessels) along with poor wound healing are the major contributors to the development of a foot ulcer in a diabetic patient.

1 Jeffcoate and Harding 'Diabetic foot ulcers' (2003) 361 Lancet 1545–1551.

19.32 Lower extremity disease, including peripheral arterial disease, peripheral neuropathy, foot ulceration, or lower extremity amputation, is twice as common in diabetic persons compared with non-diabetic persons and it affects 30 per cent of diabetic persons who are older than 40 years. Foot ulcers cause substantial emotional, physical, productivity, and financial losses. The most costly and feared consequence of a foot ulcer is limb amputation, which occurs ten to 30 times more often in diabetic persons than in the general population. Diabetes underlies up to eight out of ten non-traumatic amputations, of which 85 per cent follow a foot ulcer. It has been estimated that approximately 85 per cent of these amputations could be avoided by early detection of foot complications, timely intervention, involvement of the diabetic foot care team, good diabetes control, and patient education[1].

1 Cheer, Shearman and Jude (2009) 'Managing complications of the diabetic foot' (2009) 339 BMJ 1304–1307.

19.33 Many overlapping factors lead to foot ulceration. They put the foot at risk, precipitate a break in the skin or impair healing. The peripheral neuropathy of diabetes results in abnormal forces being applied to the foot, which diabetic ischaemia renders the skin less able to withstand. Other complications contributing to the onset of ulceration include poor vision, limited joint mobility and the consequences of cardiovascular and cerebrovascular disease. However the most common precipitant is accidental trauma especially from ill-fitting footwear. Once the skin is broken many processes contribute to defective healing. Infection is usually the consequence rather than the cause of foot ulceration but can cause substantial deterioration and delay in healing and clinicians should consider early use of antibiotics. Deterioration in a wound is more likely if assessment is delayed. The first principle is to treat any infection, the second is to establish whether any associated ischaemia is amenable to re-vascularisation, the third is to keep forces applied to the ulcerated part to a minimum and the fourth is to improve the condition of the wound or ulcer by wound bed preparation, topical applications and removal of callus. Once the wound has healed attention can be turned to the prevention of ulcer recurrence.

19.34 Primary prevention is the aim of diabetes management but secondary prevention is the goal of good foot ulcer care. Improved blood glucose control will reduce microvascular complications and reduction in cardiovascular risk factors will render the foot less susceptible to ischaemia from macrovascular disease. Routine surveillance will detect patients whose feet are at risk and they should receive targeted care. A previous lesion is strongly predictive of further ulceration. Efforts should be made to reduce abnormal pressure loading with focus on foot care, regular podiatry, self-examination and provision of emergency contacts. Rates and speed of healing are best in ulcers that are mainly a result of neuropathy. Despite good management healing rates in large multi-centre trials were 24 per cent at 12 weeks and 31 per cent at 20 weeks[1].

1 Margolis, Kantor, Berlin 'Healing of diabetic neuropathic foot ulcers receiving standard treatment: a meta-analysis' (1999) 22 Diabetes Care 6292–6295.

19.35   The longer term healing rate for diabetic foot ulcers varies widely but typically 80 per cent of ulcers are healed in six months and the average time to heal is eight weeks with optimal therapy. Patients with diabetes who develop one ulcer are more likely to get recurrent ulcers (40 per cent in three years) even with optimal management. For patients having a trans-metatarsal amputation there is a 68–93 per cent success of healing the wound, 14 per cent develop a new ulcer on the same foot in one year and 28 per cent eventually need a revision approximately to a higher level of amputations[1]. Approximately one-third will need an amputation on the contralateral leg at three years. Only 50 per cent of patients with diabetes are able to rehabilitate to a prosthesis and this failure rate is associated with age. Two thirds of patients having amputation die within five years and this correlates to other health scores and is related to cardiac, vascular, endocrine, renal function and correlates with age.

1 Pittet, Wyssa, Herter-Clavel (et al) 'Outcome of diabetic foot infections treated conservatively: a retrospective cohort study with long-term follow-up' (1999) 26 Arch Intern Med 851–856; Senneville, Lombart, Beltrand (et al) 'Outcome of diabetic foot osteomyelitis treated nonsurgically: a retrospective cohort study' (2008) 31 Diabetes Care 637–642.

19.36   Due to a multi-factorial aetiology the treatment of diabetic foot ulcers requires various treatment modalities and warrants a multi-disciplinary team approach including diabetologists, orthopaedic and vascular surgeons and podiatrists. Current therapeutic modalities are determined also by the underlying medical conditions that may complicate healing. The standard treatment modalities for low-grade ulcers are local wound care with dressing, vigorous and repeated debridement of callus and necrotic material and offloading (ie relieving pressure from the wound area). Broad spectrum antibiotics are given if ulcers appear to be clinically infected. Higher grade ulcers requiring evaluation and treatment of bone involvement (osteomyelitis) and improving circulation (by angioplasty or bypass surgery) if peripheral, large vessel disease exists. In cases that still progress and that develop gangrene, limited or major amputation is inevitable[1].

1 Jeffcoate and Harding 'Diabetic foot ulcers' (2003) 361 Lancet 1545–1551.

Charcot arthropathy

19.37   Charcot arthropathy is the name given to the diabetic form of neuropathic joint disease which most frequently involves joints in the foot such as the tarsus and tarsometatarsal joints followed by the metatarsophalangeal joints and the ankle. It is thought to occur due to a combination of mechanical and vascular factors resulting from diabetic peripheral neuropathy[1]. The effects of Charcot arthropathy are almost exclusively seen in the foot and ankle, and the diagnosis is commonly missed upon initial presentation. It has been well established that this complication of diabetes mellitus severely reduces the overall quality of life and dramatically increases the morbidity and mortality of patients. However, there are few high-level evidence studies to support management and treatment options. It is uncommon, affecting approximately one in 700 diabetic patients, with either type 1 or type 2 diabetes. These patients typically have longstanding diabetes (average duration 15 years) and peripheral neuropathy, and are in their sixth or seventh decade but rarely can occur in patients in their 20s. The clinical manifestations of Charcot's neuropathy can be variable. The patient may present with sudden onset of unilateral warmth, redness and oedema over foot or ankle, often with a history of minor trauma. Recurrent acute attacks may occur, or there can be a slowly progressing arthropathy with insidious swelling over months or years. Involvement of the foot is characterised by collapse of the arch of the mid foot and bony prominences in peculiar places.

1 Petrova, Edmonds (2013) 'Medical management of Charcot arthropathy' (2013) 15 Diabetes Obes Metab 193–197.

19.38   If the diagnosis is made before significant radiological damage has occurred, then successful treatment is much more likely. In the earlier stages of neuropathic arthropathy, in which oedema, redness and warmth are present, avoidance of weight-bearing on the affected joint should be recommended until resolution of the oedema and erythema occurs, with improvement of radiologic signs if present. A minimum of eight weeks without weight-bearing has been recommended for disease of the mid foot, progressing through partial weight-bearing in a cast brace to full weight-bearing in about four to five months. Good chiropody and well-fitting shoes are essential at this stage. The total contact cast for offloading and immobilisation is increasingly becoming the treatment of choice with or without an initial period of non-weight-bearing immobilisation. Late presentation may mean that joint disorganisation is severe and irreversible. Disease of the hindfoot and ankle appears to have a worse prognosis than disease of the midfoot. Common deformities seen are the 'rocker bottom foot' caused by collapse of the medial arch, medial convexity deformity caused by medial displacement of the talonavicular joint, and tarsometatarsal dislocation. Such deformities transfer weight-bearing to areas which tolerate it poorly and which may lack sensation thus ulceration and infection commonly ensue[1].

1 Petrova, Edmonds (2013) 'Medical management of Charcot arthropathy' (2013) 15 Diabetes Obes Metab 193–197.

Association of stress with type 2 diabetes

19.39   It has long been suggested that emotional stress plays a role in the aetiology of type 2 diabetes. Most studies have mainly focused on depression as a risk factor of the development of type 2 diabetes[1]. Depression is associated with poor health, behaviours such as smoking, reduced physical activity and increased calorie intake, but the risk of type 2 diabetes is also increased. Depression is also related to central obesity and potentially to impaired glucose tolerance. Depression is also associated with physiological abnormalities including activation of the hypothalamic-pituitary-adrenal axis, sympathoadrenal system and pro-inflammatory cytokines which can all induce insulin resistance and contribute to diabetes risk.

1 Mezuk, Eaton, Albrecht S (et al) (2008) 'Depression and type 2 diabetes over the lifespan' (2008) 31 Diabetes Care 2383–2390.

19.40 Diabetes may increase the risk of depression because of the sense of threat and loss associated with receiving this diagnosis and the substantial lifestyle changes necessary to avoid developing debilitating complications. In a meta-analysis of 42 publications[1], 13 met eligibility for depression predicting onset of diabetes and seven met criteria for diabetes predicting onset of depression. The conclusion was that depression was associated with a 6 per cent increased risk of type 2 diabetes but that type 2 diabetes was only associated with a modest increased risk of depression.

1 Mezuk, Eaton, Albrecht S (et al) (2008) 'Depression and type 2 diabetes over the lifespan' (2008) 31 Diabetes Care 2383–2390.

19.41 Stress usually refers to the consequence of the failure of an organism to respond appropriately to emotional or physical threats whether actual or imagined. Stress symptoms commonly include a state of alarm. Signs of stress can be defined at a cognitive, emotional, physical or behavioural level. Cognitive signs include poor judgement, low self-esteem, poor concentration and negative cognitions. Emotional signs include moodiness or even depression, feeling of anxiety, excessive worrying, irritability, agitation and feeling lonely or isolated. Behavioural symptoms can include eating disorders, sleep disorders, social withdrawal, procrastination or neglect to responsibilities, increased alcohol, smoking or drug consumption and nervous habits. The exhaustion phase during which bodily symptoms start to dysfunction or shut down may also include depression, as depression is commonly regarded as a form of exhaustion resulting from chronic emotional stress[1].

1 Bao, Meynen, Swaab 'The stress system and depression and neurodegeneration: Focus on the human hypothalamus' (2008) 57 Brain Res Rev 531–553.

19.42 Chronic emotional stress is an established risk factor for the development of depression. Longitudinal studies suggest that not only depression, but also general emotional stress and anxiety, sleeping problems, anger, and hostility are associated with an increased risk for the development of type 2 diabetes[1]. Emotional stress can increase the risk for development of type 2 diabetes through different pathways. Behavioural mechanisms as emotional stress were found to be associated with unhealthy lifestyle behaviours such as eating disorders, low exercise levels, smoking and alcohol abuse, which are all well-established factors of development of type 2 diabetes.

1 Pouwer, Kupper, Adriaanse 'Does emotional stress cause type 2 diabetes mellitus? A review from the European Depression in Diabetes (EDID) Research Consortium' (2010) 9 Discovery Medicine 112–118.

19.43 Chronic stress reactions and depression are often characterised by long term activation of the hypothalamic-pituitary-adrenal axis and a sympathetic nervous system which were found to be associated with the development of abdominal obesity and may explain why depression or chronic stress increases the risk of diabetes. Chronic stress can also initiate changes in immune system activity with clinical evidence that a rise in a concentration of pro-inflammatory cytokines and glucocorticoids, particularly cortisol, in response to chronic stress, and often in depression both contribute to behavioural changes associated with depression. In general, the research findings available support the notion that different forms of emotional stress are associated with an increased risk of development of type 2 diabetes.

19.44 Evidence from prospective and cross-sectional studies demonstrate that the presence of diabetes doubles the risk of co-morbid depression and this may affect up to one-quarter of the population of patients with diabetes. Concurrent depression is associated with a reduction in metabolic control, poor adherence to medication and diet regimens, a reduction in quality of life and increase in healthcare expenditure. In turn poor metabolic control may exacerbate depression and diminish response to antidepressant regimens. Conventional anti-depressant management strategies are effective and regimes tailored to the individual patient can enhance better glycaemic control which may also contribute to improvement in mood and perceptions of well-being[1].

1 Lustman, Clouse (2005) 'Depression in diabetic patients: the relationship between mood and glycemic control' (2005) 19 J Diabetes Complications 113–122.

In-patient diabetes care

19.45 One in ten people admitted to hospital has diabetes. A UK study reported high levels of clinical risk associated with in-patient diabetes care. One-third of hospitals surveyed did not have diabetes management guidelines for day surgery, endoscopy, barium studies or immediate management of the diabetic foot. Patients admitted with DKA were not immediately referred to the specialist team in one-third of hospitals. About half had no routine access to podiatry or dietetic care for in-patients with diabetes. The majority of UK hospitals either never adopted diabetes or insulin infusion protocols or had recently changed practice, and half do not endorse the use of in-patient subcutaneous insulin 'sliding-scales'[1].

1 Sampson, Brennan, Dhatariya, Jones, Walden 'A national survey of in-patient diabetes services in the United Kingdom' (2007) 24 Diabetic Medicine 643–649.

19.46 Hypoglycaemia is the most common adverse effect of intensive insulin therapy in both the out-patient and in-patient setting. Hypoglycaemia has a substantial clinical impact in terms of mortality, morbidity and quality of life. The biochemical definition of hypoglycaemia has used blood glucose concentrations less than 2.2mmol/l but avoidance of exposure to less than 3.0mmol/l is clinically desirable whereas exposure to glucose concentrations of 3.5–4.0mmol/l provided the glucose fall is then arrested is of little clinical significance. Because of the activation of counter regulatory responses plasma glucose concentrations less than 3.5mmol/l this intermediate number is a reasonable definition of hypoglycaemia for use in clinical practice.

19.47 Hypoglycaemia occurs frequently in patients with type 1 diabetes. The average patient suffers countless numbers of episodes of asymptomatic hypoglycaemia (which are not benign because they impair defences against subsequent falling plasma glucose concentrations), two episodes of symptomatic hypoglycaemia per week, and one episode of temporarily disabling hypoglycaemia per year[1]. The primary cause of hypoglycaemia in type 2 diabetes is injected insulin or diabetes medication such as those that raise insulin levels regardless of blood sugar including sulphonylureas.

The risk of hypoglycaemia is increased in older patients, those with longer diabetes duration and in those attempting strict glycaemic control. Patients taking insulin having the highest rates of self-reported severe hypoglycaemia with approximately levels of 25 per cent quoted in patients who have been taking insulin for more than five years[2].

1 Seaquist, Anderson, Childs, Cryer, Dagogo-Jack, Fish, Heller, Rodriguez, Rosenzweig, Vigersky, American Diabetes Association; Endocrine Society. (2013) 'Hypoglycemia and diabetes: a report of a workgroup of the American Diabetes Association and the Endocrine Society' (2013) 98 J Clin Endocrinol Metab 1845–1859.
2 Amiel, Dixon, Mann (et al) 'Hypoglycaemia in type 2 diabetes' (2008) 25 Diabetic Medicine 247–254.

19.48   The most common cause of hypoglycaemia in diabetes resulting in significant physical and psychological morbidity is iatrogenic, occurring with the use of insulin secretagogues or insulin therapy. The most common behavioural factor which precipitates individual episodes of severe hypoglycaemia that has been identified is missed or irregular meals. Time of day is also important in that even in the absence of pharmacological therapy the lowest plasma glucose of the day is just before the evening meal and unsuspected hypoglycaemia can occur at this time once drug therapy has started. Rates of hypoglycaemia with insulin vary according to the regimen and the stage of evolution of the person's diabetes. Rates of hypoglycaemia are higher in those on at least twice daily insulin regimes. A particular problem is nocturnal hypoglycaemia which can lead to disruption of sleep and delays in the correction of hypoglycaemia. Night-time is typically the longest period between self-monitoring of plasma glucose, between food ingestion, and the time of maximum sensitivity to insulin.

19.49   Severe hypoglycaemia has serious consequences particularly in the elderly. In a retrospective study of elderly patients (mean age 78 years) presenting to accident and emergency departments in the US, almost all patients presented with neuroglycopaenic symptoms and 49 per cent present with loss of consciousness[1]. Approximately 5 per cent were associated with stroke, myocardial infarction, transient ischaemic attack, injury or death, although the cause and effect relationship is not clear. Severe hypoglycaemia is associated with increased mortality with a retrospective review of 102 patients admitted to hospital with drug induced hypoglycaemic coma revealing a mortality rate of approximately 5 per cent. However it was not possible to confirm whether the deaths were due to hypoglycaemia in view of serious co-morbidities in all those cases.

1 Turchin, Matheny, Shubina (et al) 'Hypoglycemia and Clinical Outcomes in Patients With Diabetes Hospitalized in the General Ward' (2009) 32 Diabetes Care 1153–1157.

19.50   The relationship between the number and severity of hypoglycaemic episodes within hospital mortality was evaluated in a retrospective cohort study which analysed 4,368 admissions and 2,582 patients with diabetes hospitalised in the general ward of a teaching hospital[1]. Mortality among hypoglycaemic patients in this population was 3 per cent and there was a strong relationship between hypoglycaemia and in-hospital mortality. In-patient mortality increased as the number of hypoglycaemic episodes rose and a greater degree of hypoglycaemia was also associated with an increase in in-patient mortality. In view of this study and other previous studies recommendations are often made to nurse diabetic patients in the general wards more closely for the occurrence of hypoglycaemia and extra care should be taken to prevent hypoglycaemic events in this population already at high risk for adverse events, with particular attention being paid to matching the anti-hypoglycaemic regime to the nutritional intake.

1 Turchin, Scanlon, Matheny (et al) 'Hypoglycaemia and clinical outcomes on patients with diabetes hospitalised in the general ward' (2009) 32 Diabetes Care 1153–1157.

19.51 A study from Hull Royal Infirmary has demonstrated that patients with diabetes are monitored similarly whether nursing levels are high or low, but when hypoglycaemia was identified during periods of low nursing levels it took more than 30 minutes longer to confirm the recorded biochemical resolution of a hypoglycaemic event. It is therefore clear that ongoing education of nursing staff is paramount to ensure that there is an understanding of the importance of managing hypoglycaemia[1].

1 Turchin, Matheny, Shubina (et al) 'Hypoglycemia and clinical outcomes in patients with diabetes hospitalised in the general ward' (2009) 32 Diabetes Care 1153–1157; Dhatariya, Levy, Kilvert (et al) for the Joint British Diabetes Societies 'NHS Diabetes guideline for the perioperative management of the adult patient with diabetes' (2012) 29 Diabetic Medicine 420–433.

19.52 Metformin belongs to a class of drugs called biguanides and is an oral hypoglycaemic drug that directly improves insulin action. In the absence of contraindications, metformin is considered the first choice for oral treatment of type 2 diabetes and is initiated in the absence of contraindications, concurrent with lifestyle intervention, at the time of diabetes diagnosis. It is effective only in the presence of insulin, and its major effect is to decrease hepatic glucose output. In addition, metformin increases insulin-mediated glucose utilisation in peripheral tissues (such as muscle and liver), particularly after meals. Metformin also increases intestinal glucose utilisation and this effect could protect against hypoglycaemia. Metformin can lead to lactic acidosis. Lactic acidosis is the most common cause of metabolic acidosis in hospitalised patients and is associated with an elevated plasma lactate concentration. Impaired tissue oxygenation, leading to increased anaerobic metabolism, is usually responsible for the rise in lactate production. Symptoms of lactic acidosis are non-specific and may include anorexia, nausea, vomiting, abdominal pain, lethargy, hyperventilation and hypotension. Serious lactic acid accumulation occurs with superimposed shock or in the presence of predisposing conditions to metformin toxicity. Metformin-induced lactic acidosis can occur in patients with normal renal and hepatic function. The incidence of lactic acidosis in metformin users appears to be very low. In a review of 11,800 patients treated with metformin for a mean of about two years, only two patients developed lactic acidosis (incidence nine cases per 100,000 person-years of exposure)[1]. This finding is consistent with a systematic review of 347 randomised trials and prospective cohort studies representing 70,490 patient-years of metformin use and 55,451 patient-years in the comparator group in which there were no cases of lactic acidosis[2].

1 Calabrese, Coley, DaPos (et al) 'Evaluation of prescribing practices: risk of lactic acidosis with metformin therapy' (2002) 162 Arch Intern Med 434–437.
2 Salpeter, Greyber, Pasternak, Salpeter 'Risk of fatal and nonfatal lactic acidosis with metformin use in type 2 diabetes mellitus' (2010) 2010 Cochrane Database Syst Rev CD002967.

19.53   Despite its rarity, lactic acidosis related to metformin remains a concern because of the high case fatality rate. Most cases have occurred in patients with shock or tissue hypoxia or in the presence of several other predisposing conditions; all are relative or absolute contraindications to the institution of metformin therapy. These predisposing factors/contraindications include previous lactic acidosis, impaired renal function, which has been variably defined, liver disease or alcohol abuse, heart failure and circumstances of decreased tissue perfusion or haemodynamic instability due to infection or other causes.

19.54   The precise serum creatinine limits and estimated glomerular filtration rates (eGFR) thresholds for the safe use of metformin remain uncertain. In clinical practice, some experts use an eGFR of >30 mL/min as a threshold for the safe use of metformin. For a patient with an eGFR between 30 and 50 mL/min, typically the dose may be reduced by half. In addition, patients are advised to stop taking metformin if they have any illness, such as influenza, upper respiratory infection, or urinary tract infection. Metformin should be discontinued in patients who develop one of the predisposing factors listed above. When used according to current prescribing recommendations, the risk of metformin-induced lactic acidosis is close to zero. However, inappropriate prescription of metformin remains a common problem. A number of patients treated with metformin have one or more of the above contraindications (most often renal insufficiency or heart failure). The frequency with which this occurs has varied in different series, with a range of 14–27 per cent in most reports[1].

1 Horlen, Malone, Bryant (et al) 'Frequency of inappropriate metformin prescriptions' (2002) 287 JAMA 2504–2505.

19.55   The risk of lactic acidosis in the overall population of patients with type 2 diabetes treated with metformin is therefore low. Although patients with one or more of the predisposing factors cited above are most at risk, the incidence of lactic acidosis in these patients is not known and may be low in patients with borderline risk factors, such as well-compensated heart failure. This is an important issue because the benefits of metformin in the treatment of type 2 diabetes mellitus may outweigh the risk in such patients.

Pancreatic trauma

19.56   The pancreas is a compound exocrine and endocrine gland located in the retroperitoneum at the level of the 2nd lumbar vertebra. The pancreas is divided into five parts including the head, uncinate process, neck, body and tail. The head of the pancreas lies to the right of the superior mesenteric artery. The uncinate process is a variable postural lateral extension of the head that passes behind the retro pancreatic vessels and lies anteriorly to the inferior vena cava and the aorta. The neck is defined as the portion of the gland overlying the superior mesenteric vessels. The body and tail lie to the left of the mesenteric vessels. There is no meaningful anatomic division between the body and the tail.

19.57   Pancreatic function is divided into exocrine (production of gut enzymes which digest food in the intestine) and endocrine (production of circulating hormones such as insulin and glucagon). Due to the close anatomical and functional links between the exocrine and endocrine pancreas, any disease affecting one of these parts will inevitably affect the other. Any disease that damages the pancreas, or removal of pancreatic tissue including acute and chronic pancreatitis, pancreatic surgery, cystic fibrosis and pancreatic cancer, can result in diabetes. There is wide variability in the frequency with which this occurs, primarily determined by the degree of pancreatic insufficiency[1].

1 Jalleh, Williamson 'Pancreatic exocrine and endocrine function after operations for chronic pancreatitis' (1992) 216 Ann Surg 656–662.

19.58   Exocrine pancreatic secretion is composed of enzymes, water, electrolytes and bicarbonate which are delivered to the duodenum via the pancreatic duct of Wirsung and aid digestion. Endocrine pancreatic function includes the production of the hormones insulin, glucagon and somatostatin which are secreted by the islets of Langerhans, A cells and D cells respectively. Removal of 90 per cent of the mass of the pancreas can be performed without resulting in diabetes.

19.59   Injuries of the pancreas occur in about 3–5 per cent of all traumatic abdominal injuries. The diagnosis can be challenging, particularly in the setting of blunt trauma because symptoms and signs resulting from these injuries may not be obvious due to the retroperitoneal location of the pancreas. Initial evaluation of patients at risk is focused on the earliest possible identification of high grade injuries which often occur in the setting of other severe injuries and are associated with high mortality rates. The majority of injuries to the pancreas are of low grade and can be managed non-operatively[1].

1 Akhrass, Yass, Yaffe, Brandt (et al) 'Pancreatic trauma: a ten year multi-institutional experience' (1997) 63 American Surgeon 598–604.

19.60   About 75–85 per cent of blunt injuries to the pancreas are caused by motor vehicle collisions. The mechanism is typically due to the crushing of the fixed retroperitoneal organs between the vertebral column and steering wheel and seatbelt. Associated injuries include damage to the liver along with the duodenum, small bowel, colon and stomach. Because of the proximity of the major vascular structures including the aorta, vena cava and portal vein, injury to the pancreas can be associated with significant haemorrhage.

19.61   History and physical examination in pancreatic injuries are non-specific. A diagnosis is made by imaging studies typically CT scan of the abdomen or possibly exploratory laparotomy. Laboratory studies such as serum amylase and lipase are typically performed as part of routine trauma assessment. Serum amylase or lipase cannot be used to rule out or establish a diagnosis of pancreatic injury. An elevated amylase or lipase can be present in patients with blunt abdominal trauma who do not have pancreatic injury. There is a classification system to grade injury and although injury management does not correlate exactly with grade, injury scales provide a practical means by which to communicate the severity of injury. A grade 1 injury would be minor with contusion without duct injury or superficial laceration without duct injury.

19.62 Non-operative management of the pancreas or pancreatic injury is safe for patients with blunt grade 1 or grade 2 injuries of the pancreas (contusion, superficial laceration). Non-operative management consists of nutritional support and early enteral nutrition is preferred over intravenous nutrition for most injured patients. Most pancreatic injuries are low grade (grade 1 or grade 2) and most can be managed non-operatively[1]. After pancreatic trauma 50 per cent of deaths are early caused by bleeding and haemorrhagic shock and the remainder are due to late complications including sepsis, fistula formation and multi-organ failure. Morbidity and mortality increases with increasing grade for pancreatic injuries. Complications rates for pancreatic injuries range from 24–50 per cent. Complications include pancreatic fistula, pancreatic pseudocyst and intra-abdominal abscess.

1 Lin, Chen, Fang (et al) 'Management of blunt major pancreatic injury' (2004) 56 Journal of Trauma 774–778.

19.63 Little is known or described in terms of the long term implications following pancreatic injury. Pancreatic insufficiency can present with either endocrine loss such as diabetes or exocrine loss due to pancreatic enzyme insufficiency. Patients with pancreatic exocrine dysfunction cannot properly digest complex foods or absorb partially digested break-down products. Clinically significant protein and fat deficiencies do not occur until over 90 per cent of pancreatic function is lost. Fatty stores secondary to fat malabsorption are loose, greasy and foul smelling and are difficult to flush. Malabsorption of fat soluble vitamins (A, D, E, K) and vitamin B12 may also occur, although clinically symptomatic of vitamin deficiency is rare.

19.64 Glucose intolerance occurs with some frequency in chronic pancreatitis but overt diabetes usually occurs later in the course of the disease. Diabetes is also more likely to occur in patients with a family history of diabetes, suggesting an underlying decrease in pancreatic reserve or in insulin responsiveness. Diabetes that occurs in patients with pancreatic disease is usually insulin requiring. However, it is different from typical type 1 diabetes in that the pancreatic alpha cells, which produce glucagon, are also affected. As a result, there is an increased risk of hypoglycaemia, both treatment-related and spontaneous[1].

1 Czakó, Hegyi, Rakonczay(et al) 'Interactions between the endocrine and exocrine pancreas and their clinical relevance' (2009) 9 Pancreatology 351–359.

Risk of diabetes post pancreatic surgery

19.65 Recent studies using pancreas samples from human autopsies have provided evidence that glucose levels begin to rise when the extent of beta-cells has been reduced by approximately 50 per cent; the extent of beta-cell loss in patients with overt diabetes is reported to be approximately 65 per cent[1]. Pancreatic surgery (including pancreaticoduodenectomy) does not always appear to increase the risk of diabetes[2]. All patients with normal glucose tolerance before surgery are unchanged postoperatively. Insulin secretion is reduced by approximately 50 per cent after partial (either proximal or distal) pancreatectomy in patients with chronic pancreatitis, patients with pancreatic cancer and controls. High pre-operative body weight and elevated fasting glucose levels are associated with poor glycaemic control after partial pancreatectomy[1]. In a retrospective review over a six year period of 27 normoglycaemic patients who had no prior history of diabetes undergoing a pancreaticoduodenectomy (Whipple procedure), post-operative diabetes (defined as the need for oral hypoglycaemic agents or insulin) was recorded in ten. This study confirmed that progression to diabetes is very unlikely after a Whipple operation if the preoperative HbA1c value is in the normal range[3].

1 Menge, Schrader, Breuer (et al) 'Metabolic consequences of a 50 per cent partial pancreatectomy in humans' (2009) 52 Diabetologia 306–317.
2 Marczell and Stierer 'Partial pancreaticoduodenectomy (Whipple procedure) for pancreatic malignancy: occlusion of a non-anastomosed pancreatic stump with fibrin sealant' (1992) 5 HPB Surgery 251–260.
3 Hamilton and Jeyarajah 'Hemoglobin A1c can be helpful in predicting progression to diabetes after Whipple procedure' (2007) 9 HPB (Oxford) 26–28.

19.66   The development of diabetes greatly influences the prognosis and quality of life of patients with exocrine pancreatic diseases. It may cause life-threatening complications, such as hypoglycaemia, due to the lack of glucagon and the impaired absorption of nutrients, or the micro- and macrovascular complications may impair the organ functions. Diabetes mellitus is an independent risk factor of mortality in those with exocrine pancreatic diseases. The treatment of pancreatic diabetes, a distinct metabolic and clinical form of diabetes, requires special knowledge. Diet and pancreatic enzyme replacement therapy may be sufficient in the early stages. Oral hypoglycaemic agents are not usually recommended so if the diet proves inadequate to reach the glycaemic targets, insulin treatment with multiple injections is required. In the event of a proven impairment of the pancreatic exocrine function in diabetes mellitus, pancreatic enzyme replacement therapy is indicated. This may improve the nutritional condition of the patient and decrease the metabolic instability[1].

1 Czakó, Hegyi, Rakonczay(et al) 'Interactions between the endocrine and exocrine pancreas and their clinical relevance' (2009) 9 Pancreatology 351–359.

THYROID DISEASE

19.67   Thyroid hormones control the metabolism of cells, which is their speed of activity. If there is too little hormone, the body cells work too slowly; too much results in them working too fast. Fundamentally, the thyroid hormones regulate the rate of oxygen consumption. This metabolic action influences the utilisation of the main components of food (carbohydrate, protein and fat). Although thyroid hormones have a similar effect and influence the proper working of all body cells, their action is particularly evident in certain tissues and for certain functions. For example, the physical and brain development of a baby growing in the womb depend on the correct amount of thyroid hormones being present in the mother until the 12th week of the pregnancy when the baby's own thyroid gland begins to function. In a child too little hormone will slow up growth, whereas too much my make the child grow faster than normal. Thyroid hormones also have very noticeable effects on bone, fat, the heart and muscle amongst other organs.

Hypothyroidism

19.68   Hypothyroidism is the name given to the clinical condition that develops when there is inadequate secretion of thyroxine (T4) and to a lesser extent triiodothyronine (T3). Irrespective of the cause for the thyroid under activity the symptoms are in general the same, and their severity depends upon the degree of thyroid failure and upon its duration. Myxoedema is the word used to describe untreated hypothyroidism of advanced degree and of long standing, and was originally used to describe the thickened, cold skin often found in this state.

19.69   Hypothyroidism should be looked upon as a graded condition ranging from a slight impairment of thyroid function as shown by a rise in the serum thyrotrophin (TSH) level and few if any symptoms (mild thyroid failure or subclinical hypothyroidism) progressing through a greater reduction of thyroid hormones with more likelihood of symptoms, to complete thyroid failure that is symptomatic, clinically obvious and associated with very abnormal laboratory tests[1].

1 Clinical Knowledge Summaries. Hypothyroidism. National Institute for Health and Clinical Excellence 2011. http://cks.nhs.uk/hypothyroidism/management; Association of Clinical Biochemistry, British Thyroid Association and British Thyroid Foundation 'UK guidelines for the use of thyroid function tests' (2006): http://www.british-thyroid-association.org/info-for-patients/Docs/TFT_guideline_final_version_July_2006.pdf.

19.70   Symptoms of thyroid under activity include tiredness, feeling rundown, constipation and cold intolerance. People may gain some weight but seldom more than a few kilograms. Skin becomes drier and thicker; scalp hair may come out more than it used to. The voice becomes deeper in pitch. Daytime somnolence may occur if the person begins snoring due to obstructive sleep apnoea. Hearing can become dulled unbeknown to the affected person. Aches and cramps in the muscles are also common and in the night or on waking in the morning, people may experience pins and needles in their fingers and hands due to a nerve at the wrist becoming trapped (carpal tunnel syndrome). People with mild hypothyroidism, and even more so those with severe hypothyroidism, may become mentally disturbed, being depressed or anxious. These problems will improve gradually as the thyroid deficiency is corrected.

19.71   The symptoms of abnormal thyroid function in cases of mild thyroid failure are not clearly defined. Most evidence using studies of large numbers of healthy people in the community use symptom scores and the results are inconsistent. Certain symptoms such as dry skin, cold intolerance and tiredness appear more often in people with subclinical hypothyroid than in those with normal thyroid function. However, these findings are not useful in separating individual subjects and a quarter of the healthy population complain of symptoms that could be attributed to hypothyroidism.

19.72   Hashimoto's thyroiditis is an autoimmune disorder and is caused by the presence of certain antibodies that react with the cells of the thyroid gland. The diagnosis of Hashimoto's thyroiditis is based on finding thyroid peroxidase (TPO) antibodies in the blood. The level of these often increases as the disease progresses. In the later stages if the thyroid gland is destroyed and becomes atrophic, no thyroid tissue will be left and the level of these autoantibodies may fall to low or undetectable levels. Levothyroxine therapy to correct thyroid hormone deficiency may also reduce the level of autoantibodies with time. They develop more commonly in people with a particular genetic make-up and there is often a history of thyroid disease or other autoimmune disease in the person's immediate family or distant relatives. There is currently no evidence linking emotional or psychological stress to Hashimoto's thyroiditis most probably because of the long natural history of the disease requiring a large part of the gland to be damaged before thyroid function is compromised. Any major stress will have occurred many years before.

19.73   The association between hypothyroidism and clinical depression has been recognised for many years. This clinical depression often remits when the hypothyroidism is corrected, but in some patients, despite the correct replacement dosage of levothyroxine for several months, it persists. Persistent depression-like symptoms after correction of thyroid deficiency is a cause for people being dissatisfied with their response to levothyroxine treatment. It is of course essential that the correct replacement is being given and that the serum TSH is within the reference range. If people continue to feel generally unwell despite having received the correct amount of levothyroxine, it is possible that the ill health is due to a persistent degree of clinical depression, which merits treatment in its own right.

19.74   The best treatment for thyroid deficiency is replacement therapy with levothyroxine. Although man-made, medicinal levothyroxine is chemically identical to the natural hormone secreted by the thyroid gland. The dose of levothyroxine is adjusted according to how the person feels and the results of the laboratory tests. The recommended approach is a target of a serum TSH within the reference range. This strategy will prevent over-replacement and decrease possible harmful effects. The total daily dose in an adult with no functioning thyroid tissue is usually 100–150 micrograms. People treated for thyroid deficiency do not feel miraculously better overnight. The longer someone has had thyroid deficiency, the longer it will take to feel well again, and sometimes as long as six to nine months. It takes this length of time for the changes in the tissues to be reversed[1].

1 Royal College of Physicians 'The diagnosis and management of primary hypothyroidism' (June 2011): http://www.rcplondon.ac.uk/resources/clinical-resources/diagnosis-and-management-primary-hypothyroidism.

Hyperthyroidism

19.75   Overactivity of the thyroid gland, also known as hyperthyroidism or thyrotoxicosis, is a disease in which increased amounts of thyroid hormones (T4 and T3) are present in the bloodstream. The most common aetiologies of hyperthyroidism are Graves' disease (between 70–80 per cent), followed by toxic multinodular goitre (10–20 per cent). In Graves' disease the thyroid gland is subjected to excess stimulation by thyroid-stimulating antibodies[1]. Factors involved in the causation of Graves' disease include:

- often there is a familial or hereditary factor because autoimmune diseases of the thyroid gland and other organs or tissues tend to run in families;

- women at all ages are some ten times more likely than men to develop the condition. It has been suggested that the presence of female sex hormones may make the antibody attack more likely to occur, however it can rarely occur in children of any age;
- the fundamental cause of Graves' disease is the formation of antibodies that stimulate the thyroid cells to excess activity;
- an environmental factor, such as a viral infection or a stressful life event, is thought to trigger the immune system in those who are genetically susceptible, to produce the stimulating antibodies in Graves' disease.

1 Bahn, Burch, Cooper (et al) 'Hyperthyroidism and other causes of thyrotoxicosis: management guidelines of the American Thyroid Association and American Association of Clinical Endocrinologists' (2011) 21 Thyroid 593–646.

19.76   Graves' disease usually comes on slowly, and it may be several months before the person is ill, although rarely the onset is rapid over a few days or weeks. Tiredness is often an early symptom, to be followed by weight loss, palpitations or increased awareness of the heartbeat, nervousness and particularly irritability, tremor, sweating and heat intolerance. Physical weakness is common and often not realised with the upper muscles of the arms and legs most likely to be affected. Appetite may be better than usual and some people feel hungry all the time. Even with this voracious appetite there may be a considerable weight loss but this is very variable. Women may notice that their periods become less heavy, less frequent or stop completely as failure to ovulate is common. Laboratory tests usually give clear-cut confirmation of the diagnosis. The free T4 and the free T3 levels are raised above normal and the serum TSH level is undetectable. The majority of people with Graves' disease will have TSH receptor stimulating antibodies in their blood[1].

1 Association of Clinical Biochemistry, British Thyroid Association and British Thyroid Foundation 'UK guidelines for the use of thyroid function tests' (2006): http://www.british-thyroid-association.org/info-for-patients/Docs/TFT_guideline_final_version_July_2006.pdf.

19.77   The following treatment methods achieve satisfactory outcomes in over 90 per cent of patients with Graves' hyperthyroidism[1]:

- anti-thyroid drugs (thionamides) for 12–18 months which suppress the ability of the thyroid gland to make thyroid hormones;
- radioiodine which is concentrated in the thyroid cells and, by irradiation, destroys them;
- surgical removal of most of the thyroid gland (subtotal or near-total thyroidectomy).

1 Bahn, Burch, Cooper (et al) 'Hyperthyroidism and other causes of thyrotoxicosis: management guidelines of the American Thyroid Association and American Association of Clinical Endocrinologists' (2011) 21 Thyroid 593–646.

19.78   There are disparate but established practices in the management of Graves' disease in the UK[1]. There is also an increasing participation by patients in choice of therapy. The optimal outcome is for the patient to be off treatment and euthyroid. However, the available treatment modalities are associated with varying risks of either developing hypothyroidism or a relapse of thyrotoxicosis. The desire for euthyroidism is complicated by the fact that lower treatment failure rates are associated with higher rates of hypothyroidism.

1 Vanderpump (et al) on behalf of a Working Group of the Research Unit of the Royal College of Physicians and the Endocrinology and Diabetes Committee of the College and Society for Endocrinology 'Development of consensus for good practice and audit measures in the management of hypothyroidism and hyperthyroidism' (1996) 313 BMJ 539–544.

19.79 Although anti-thyroid drugs will usually render the person euthyroid, they may not provide a permanent cure. When the drug is stopped, the thyroid overactivity may gradually return over the next 3–24 months. In Graves' disease treatment for 12–18 months is associated with remission of 40–50 per cent in the 12–24 months after the end of a course of treatment. Most relapses occur within the first year and most of the remaining recurrences happen within five years but may continue to relapse many years after the episode of Graves' disease. In general, the standard policy in the UK is to offer an initial 18 month course of thionamide. If the patient relapses then definitive treatment such as radioiodine or surgery is considered. A second course of thionamide almost never results in remission. Up to 30–40 per cent of patients treated with a thionamide remain euthyroid ten years after discontinuation of therapy. If hyperthyroidism recurs after treatment with a thionamide, there is little chance that a second course of treatment will result in permanent remission. Young patients, smokers, those with large goitres, ophthalmopathy, or high serum concentrations of free T4 at diagnosis or TSH receptor antibody at the time of diagnosis or at the end of treatment are unlikely to have a permanent remission. Relapses are most likely to occur within the first year. Patients with multinodular goitres and thyrotoxicosis always relapse on cessation of anti-thyroid medication, and definitive treatment with radioiodine or surgery is usually advised. Long-term thionamide therapy at low dose is occasionally used as an option[1].

1 Abraham, Avenell, Watson (et al) 'A systematic review of drug therapy for Graves' hyperthyroidism' (2005) 153 Eur J Endocrinol 489–498.

19.80 In practice which treatment option used depends on several factors and circumstances, which must be discussed between the patient and their specialist. These include the aetiology of hyperthyroidism, age, gender, goitre size and whether it is causing compression or displacement of the trachea, choice and convenience to remain for 18 months under medical supervision for treatment with anti-thyroid drugs or whether a rapid, once-and-for-all cure is preferable. Other practical factors include social considerations such as if the person is pregnant or living with young children, the availability of an experienced specialist thyroid surgeon, the presence and severity of any eye complications and the experience of previous treatments that have been given for the condition. Potential complications of thyroidectomy include transient or permanent hypoparathyroidism and vocal cord palsy.

Stress in the aetiology of Graves' hyperthyroidism

19.81 The fundamental cause of Graves' disease is the formation of antibodies that stimulate the thyroid cells to excess activity. An environmental factor is thought to trigger the immune system in those who are genetically susceptible, to produce the stimulating antibodies in Graves' disease. There is abundant evidence for a familial or hereditary factor because autoimmune diseases of the thyroid gland and other organs or tissues tend to run in families. Genetic inheritance has been estimated to account for at least 50 per cent of the aetiology of organ specific autoimmune diseases such as Graves' disease. A recent careful analysis of concordance in Danish twins with Graves' disease estimated that 79 per cent of the liability for this disorder was attributable to genetic factors[1].

1 Brix, Kyvik, Christensen, Hegedus 'Evidence for a major role of heredity in Graves' disease; A population-based study of two Danish Twin cohorts' (2001) 86 J Clin Endocrinol Metab 930–934.

19.82 It is often asked by patients whether stress is the cause of autoimmune thyroid disorders because they note that the onset of Graves' disease, in particular, seems to occur following some major stress, such as bereavement, loss of a job, an accident, or some other major psychological upset. Indeed the second case of hyperthyroidism ever described by Parry in 1825 was a 21-year-old woman whose symptoms began four months after she had been thrown accidentally down the stairs in a wheelchair. This report has been followed by many more studies, some of which support the idea. The incidence of Graves' disease increased in Denmark during World War II, but did not in Ireland during the sustained civil war in that country during the period of 1980 through 1990. A study in Yugoslavia indicated that patients with Graves' disease had suffered on average more stressful episodes than control subjects, but previous similar studies have failed to show this relationship. Increased numbers of stressful life events were found in patients with Graves' disease prior to onset of the disease, compared to patients with toxic nodular goitre (a non-autoimmune aetiology) who had a similar number as control patients[1].

1 Falgarone, Heshmat, Cohen, Reach 'Role of emotional stress in the pathophysiology of Graves' disease' (2013) 168 Eur J Endocrinol R13–R18.

19.83 Such studies however are not without methodological complexities as all are performed retrospectively. Patients are interviewcd once euthyroid about events occurring twelve or more months previously. Since the onset of disease cannot be known with certainty subjects are asked to recall events either prior to the onset of symptoms (a rather vague time point) or to give the date of events relative to the date their thyrotoxicosis was diagnosed. Since hyperthyroidism itself might precipitate negative life events, for example marital breakdown, this temporal relationship is a key element of separating cause and effect. Clearly coping strategies and social support networks can be factors that modify the impact of life events.

19.84 Numerous human and animal studies have demonstrated that psychological and physiological stresses induce various immunological changes. These immune modulations may contribute to the development of autoimmunity as well as the susceptibility to autoimmune disease in genetically pre-disposed individuals. There is a complex interaction between the nervous, endocrine and immune systems and unravelling the pathways whereby stress may alter the course of autoimmunity is extremely difficult. Although indirect experimental support exists for such a mechanism, mediated through the stress hormones, given the diversity of the various environmental factors, presumably operating on different genetic backgrounds, it is difficult to establish the relative importance of each in the development of Graves' disease. It is clearly difficult from the available literature to put a precise value on the contribution of the various factors that result in an autoimmune condition such as Graves' disease declaring itself at a particular time. It is also unknown how long this condition had been present but it may have been present for at least six months prior to the diagnosis contributing to symptoms of stress and depression. People experience many acute and chronic stressful life events so it is not clear what would be unique about a particular event to have contributed to the development of an autoimmune disease at a specific time[1].

1 Tomer, Huber 'The etiology of autoimmune thyroid disease: A story of genes and environment' (2009) 32 J Autoimmun 231–239.

Thyroid cancer

19.85 The clinical presentation of thyroid cancer is usually as a solitary thyroid nodule or increasing goitre size. Although thyroid nodules are common, thyroid cancers are rare although there is epidemiological evidence that they are increasingly being detected through increasing use of neck ultrasound scans[1]. The four major histological types are papillary, follicular (both designated as well differentiated thyroid cancers), medullary and anaplastic. Papillary and follicular tumours which comprise of up to 90 per cent of the total thyroid cancers are amongst the most curable of cancers. They are rare in children and adolescents and their incidence increases with age in adults[2].

1 Davies, Welch 'Increasing incidence of thyroid cancer in the United States, 1973-2002' (2006) 295 JAMA 2164–2167.
2 Perros, Boelaert, Colley (et al) for British Thyroid Association 'Guidelines for the management of thyroid cancer' (2014) 81 Suppl 1 Clin Endocrinol (Oxf) 1:1–122.

19.86 Papillary thyroid cancer is the most common thyroid malignancy and worldwide constitutes 50–90 per cent of differentiated follicular cell-derived thyroid cancers. Most diagnoses of papillary thyroid cancer occur in patients aged between 13 and 50 years and the majority 60–80 per cent (occur in women). The long-term outcome of patients treated effectively for differentiated thyroid cancer is usually favourable. The overall ten year survival rate for middle age adults with differentiated thyroid carcinoma is 80–90 per cent. However, 5–20 per cent of patients develop local or regional recurrences and 10–15 per cent distal metastases[1]. Four clinical variables have been identified as having a poor prognosis including extremes of age, male gender, poorly differentiated histological features of the tumour and tumour stage. Age at the time of diagnosis is one of the most consistent prognostic facts as inpatients with papillary thyroid cancer. The risk of recurrence or death increases with age, particularly after the age of 40 years.

1 Perros, Boelaert, Colley (et al) for British Thyroid Association 'Guidelines for the management of thyroid cancer' (2014) 81 Suppl 1 Clin Endocrinol (Oxf) 1:1–122.

19.87 Fine needle aspiration cytology usually performed by ultrasound scan is a key investigation and the management of thyroid nodule. Follicular lesions have approximately a 10–20 per cent chance of malignancy and it is usually recommended that a thyroid lobectomy is the initial recommended surgery and subsequent completion thyroidectomy to be necessary if the histology proves malignant. It is recommended that all surgical decisions are reviewed within thyroid cancer multidisciplinary teams[1].

1 Perros, Boelaert, Colley (et al) for British Thyroid Association 'Guidelines for the management of thyroid cancer' (2014) 81 Suppl 1 Clin Endocrinol (Oxf) 1:1–122.

19.88 The mainstay of treatment for differential thyroid cancer is surgery. The rates of complications from thyroidectomy, particularly recurrent laryngeal nerve injury, hypoparathyroidism, and dysphagia, are lower in patients who undergo surgery by high-volume surgeons. It is recommended that all lymph nodes within the central compartment of the neck (level 6) which includes those in the pre and para-tracheal regions should be removed (level 6 node dissection). The cervical lymph nodes lying along the carotid cheek and internal jugular veins in level 2, 3 and 4 should be palpated. Any suspicious nodes should be sent for frozen section. A positive to these indicates the need for selective neck dissection (levels 2, 3, 4 and 5). Papillary thyroid cancer for most patients (especially those with tumours greater than 1cm in diameter, multifocal disease, extra thyroidal spread, familial disease and those with clinically involved nodes) requires a total thyroidectomy followed by radioiodine ablation and TSH suppression. In patients with clinically uninvolved nodes, total thyroidectomy would include node retrieval between the recurrent laryngeal nerves (level 6). The majority of patients with a tumour the size of more than 1cm diameter should have radioiodine remnant ablation therapy.

19.89 In the post treatment follow-up of papillary thyroid cancer, long-term serum TSH suppression with levothyroxine therapy reduces the risk of recurrence. Thyroglobulin is a specific and useful tumour marker. It is secreted by both normal and cancerous thyroid cells. In patients who have been treated with total thyroidectomy and radioiodine ablation of the remnant, detectable serum thyroglobulin is highly suggestive of residual or recurrent tumour. In patients who have not had a total thyroidectomy, the interpretation of serum thyroglobulin measurements is limited by the inability to differentiate between tumour and thyroid remnant. Thyroglobulin antibodies are measured to ensure that there is no assay interference which can lead to misinterpretation of thyroglobulin levels.

19.90 Early detection of recurrent disease can lead to cure and certainly long-term survival particularly if it is operable or takes up radioiodine. For recurrence in the thyroid bed or cervical lymph nodes, surgical re-exploration is a further method of management usually in combination with radioiodine therapy. Regular follow-up is necessary, particularly for detection of early recurrence, initiation of appropriate treatment, serum TSH suppression and if relevant, management of hypocalcaemia. Once the thyroid remnant has been ablated the frequency attendance is usually six monthly to annually thereafter. At clinic visits the patient history should be taken and a clinical examination should be performed. In addition assessment of the adequacy of serum TSH suppression and measurement of thyroglobulin as marked with tumour recurrence should also be measured[1].

1 Perros, Boelaert, Colley (et al) for British Thyroid Association 'Guidelines for the management of thyroid cancer' (2014) 81 Suppl 1 Clin Endocrinol (Oxf) 1:1–122.

DISEASES OF THE PARATHYROID GLANDS

19.91   The parathyroid glands lie in close approximation with, but function independently of, the thyroid gland. The parathyroid glands produce parathyroid hormone (PTH) which is one of the two major hormones modulating calcium and phosphate homeostasis; the other hormone is calcitriol (1,25-dihydroxyvitamin D). The regulation of serum ionised calcium is exclusively regulated through PTH, maintaining its concentration within a narrow range through stimulation of renal tubular calcium reabsorption and bone resorption. PTH also stimulates the conversion of 25-hydroxyvitamin D to calcitriol in renal tubular cells stimulating intestinal calcium absorption.

Hypoparathyroidism

19.92   Post-surgical hypoparathyroidism occurs as a result of parathyroid gland injury or resection during thyroid surgery and may be transient or permanent. Long-term supplementation with vitamin D or its analogues and oral calcium is the mainstay of management. The goal is correction of symptoms of hypocalcaemia and low normal albumin-corrected serum calcium[1].

1 Shoback 'Clinical practice. Hypoparathyroidism' (2008) 359 N Engl J Med 391–403.

19.93   Treatment with any of the vitamin D sterols (for example Alfacalcidol) carries the risk of vitamin D intoxication, presenting with hypercalcaemia, hypercalciuria, and hyperphosphataemia. Hypercalcaemia may occur with any vitamin D analogue but the timing of when hypercalcaemia emerges depends on the half-life of the analogue, ranging from days to several months. Thus ongoing monitoring for complications of therapy is required[1]. Symptomatic hypercalcaemia may manifest as gastrointestinal disturbance with constipation, dyspepsia, nausea, and vomiting; change in mental status ranging from fatigue to coma, soft tissue calcification or renal damage. Hypercalciuria is also a known effect of vitamin D therapy, due to the increased load of calcium filtered by the kidney in the setting of poor renal calcium reabsorption. Persistent hypercalciuria can occur even with normal or low normal serum calcium. Increased intestinal phosphate absorption occurs with vitamin D therapy and leads to hyperphosphataemia, especially in the face of decreased urinary phosphate excretion. There is an increased risk of precipitation of calcium-phosphate salts in soft tissues, such as the lens, basal ganglia, and kidney. Hyperphosphataemia can be treated by prescribing a low phosphate diet and by adding phosphate binders to maintain an acceptable calcium-phosphate product.

1 Bilezikian, Khan, Potts, Brandi, Clarke, Shoback, Jüppner, D'Amour, Fox, Rejnmark, Mosekilde, Rubin, Dempster, Gafni, Collins, Sliney, Sanders 'Hypoparathyroidism in the adult: epidemiology, diagnosis, pathophysiology, target-organ involvement, treatment, and challenges for future research' (2011) 26 J Bone Miner Res 2317–2337.

19.94   In patients with permanent hypoparathyroidism, serum calcium, phosphate, and creatinine measurements should be measured at least annually. Urinary calcium and creatinine levels can be measured to detect renal toxic effects of hypercalciuria. The goals of therapy are to control symptoms and to maintain a low normal to normal serum albumin corrected calcium (2.1–2.2mmol/l). Monitoring for cataract development should also be done annually. When concerned about vitamin D intoxication an elevated 25-hydroxyvitamin D level is an indicator of hypervitaminosis.

19.95   The following are recommendations for care in post-operative thyroid surgery patients[1]:

- monitoring of serum calcium should be supervised in the specialist clinic, with the assistance of the GP if appropriate;
- after total thyroidectomy, 30 per cent of patients will need calcium supplementation with or without Alfacalcidol. By three months, less than 10 per cent of patients will still require calcium supplementation;
- hypoparathyroidism is often transient and a predictor of this is an elevated (or upper normal range) serum parathyroid hormone (PTH) concentration at the time of the occurrence of hypocalcaemia. Thus, the majority of patients on calcitriol/Alfacalcidol/calcium supplements can have this treatment withdrawn. Supplements should be slowly and gradually reduced and serum calcium monitored every few months until withdrawn and eucalcaemia restored;
- the combined effects of hypocalcaemia and hypothyroidism are poorly tolerated and calcitriol/Alfacalcidol/calcium supplement withdrawal should take place during euthyroidism;
- if hypoparathyroidism is permanent, the lowest dose of supplements should be administered to maintain the serum calcium at the lower end of the normal range, while avoiding hypercalciuria. In stable cases annual measurement of serum calcium is recommended.

1 Perros, Boelaert, Colley (et al) for British Thyroid Association 'Guidelines for the management of thyroid cancer' (2014) 81 Suppl 1 Clin Endocrinol (Oxf) 1:1–122.

Hyperparathyroidism

19.96   The diagnosis of hyperparathyroidism is usually first suspected because of the finding of an elevated serum calcium concentration and an elevated PTH concentration or one that is inappropriately within the normal range given the patient's hypercalcaemia. Screening tests that include measurements of serum calcium currently identify at least 80 per cent of patients with primary hyperparathyroidism in the UK. These patients are usually asymptomatic and have mild and often intermittent hypercalcaemia. In most asymptomatic patients the mean serum calcium is usually between 2.75–2.85mmol/l.

19.97   The classical symptoms and signs of hyperparathyroidism reflect the combined effects of increased parathyroid hormone secretion and hypercalcaemia. These are known as 'bones, stones, abdominal moans and groans'. The abnormalities directly associated with hyperparathyroidism are nephrolithiasis and bone disease which are both due to prolonged parathyroid hormone excess. Symptoms attributable to hypercalcaemia include anorexia, nausea, constipation, polydipsia and polyuria. Symptoms in primary hyperparathyroidism are not necessarily related to serum calcium levels however they do seem to be more common in patients in whom hypercalcaemia develops rapidly. Nephrolithiasis remains the most common complication of hyperparathyroidism occurring in approximately 15–20 per cent of newly diagnosed patients. Vitamin D deficiency is common in patients with primary hyperparathyroidism and individuals with vitamin D deficiency and hyperparathyroidism have more clinically significant disease including larger adenomas, high concentrations of PTH, increased bone turnover and more frequent fractures.

19.98 Some patients with presumed asymptomatic hyperparathyroidism when carefully questioned have non-specific symptoms such as fatigue, weakness, anorexia, mild depression and mild cognitive or neuromuscular dysfunction. With time patients with hyperparathyroidism develop clinical manifestations including skeletal manifestation, nephrocalcinosis or kidney stones. Thus the differentiation between symptomatic and asymptomatic primary hyperparathyroidism is not always clear cut. Complaints of weakness and fatigue are common among patients with primary hyperparathyroidism, neurobehavioral symptoms have also been recognised and appear to be more prevalent in patients with hyperparathyroidism than the general population. These symptoms include lethargy, depressed mood, psychosis, decreased social interaction and cognitive dysfunction. It is not clear however if hyperparathyroidism plays a causal role and improvement after surgery is variable. The differences seen pre- and post-surgery are very small and are of uncertain clinical significance.

19.99 Patients with hyperparathyroidism may have decreased bone density, in particular at sites of cortical bone such as the forearm and the hip as compared to more cancellous sites such as the spine. The degree of bone loss is reflected by the severity of hyperparathyroidism and is useful for making recommendations for parathyroid surgery. Randomised trials have demonstrated increased bone mineral density following parathyroidectomy.

19.100 Patients with undiagnosed nephrocalcinosis or calcium kidney stones are regarded as having symptomatic disease regardless of the absence of symptoms. Thus these patients usually meet criteria for surgical intervention. The most important renal manifestations of primary hyperparathyroidism are nephrolithiasis, hypercalcuria, nephrocalcinosis and chronic renal insufficiency. Nephrolithiasis occurs in approximately 15–20 per cent of patients with primary hyperparathyroidism, conversely about 5 per cent of patients with nephrolithiasis have primary hyperparathyroidism.

19.101 Hyperparathyroidism may be associated with cardiovascular disease and in particular hypertension but the available data is observational and definite evidence for an improvement in cardiovascular function post-parathyroidectomy is lacking. Severe classical primary hyperparathyroidism is associated with an increased mortality, primarily due to cardiovascular disease. However the impact of milder hyperparathyroidism on cardiovascular mortality is uncertain. There is some suggestion that hyperparathyroidism may cause enduring damage to the cardiovascular system but the controversy remains as to whether this increased mortality is related to severity of disease as assessed by serum calcium levels.

19.102 Mortality data looking exclusively at patients with milder less symptomatic disease that is commonly seen today are limited. However a recently published study from Dundee has investigated mortality and disease-specific morbidities in untreated community-based patients with mild primary hyperparathyroidism in a ten-year retrospective population-based observational study from 1997 to 2006[1]. In total, there were 1,683 (69 per cent female) patients identified with mild primary hyperparathyroidism in Tayside. Patients were found to have an increased risk (approximately x 2.5) of all-cause mortality and cardiovascular mortality. Patients with mild primary hyperparathyroidism had a significantly increased risk of developing cardiovascular and cerebrovascular disease, renal dysfunction and fractures compared to the age- and sex-adjusted general population. The study therefore has suggested that mortality and morbidity were increased for patients with mild untreated primary hyperparathyroidism, which is similar to more severe primary hyperparathyroidism.

1 Yu, Donnan, Flynn, Murphy, Smith, Rudman, Leese 'Increased mortality and morbidity in mild primary hyperparathyroid patients. The Parathyroid Epidemiology and Audit Research Study (PEARS)' (2010) 73 Clin Endocrinol 30–34.

MULTIPLE ENDOCRINE NEOPLASIA

19.103 Tumours of the endocrine glands resulting in hyperfunctioning can occur in families and may be associated with other distinct endocrine tumours. Two main syndromes have been described.

19.104 Multiple endocrine neoplasia type 1 (MEN1) is an autosomal dominant predisposition to tumours of the parathyroid glands (which occur in nearly all patients by age 50 years), anterior pituitary, and pancreatic islet cells. Effective treatment is usually available for the hyperparathyroidism and pituitary disease in MEN1; as a result, the malignant potential of pancreatic endocrine tumors (PET) is now the primary life-threatening manifestation of MEN1. Functioning pancreatic islet cell or gastrointestinal endocrine cell tumors become clinically apparent in approximately one-third of patients with MEN1. The most common cause of symptomatic disease is the Zollinger-Ellison (gastrinoma) syndrome, leading to multiple peptic ulcers. Symptomatic insulinomas also occur with moderate frequency, while VIPomas and glucagonomas are rare. The prevalence of radiographically confirmed non-functioning tumours ranges from 30–80 per cent. Like hormonally active enteropancreatic tumours in MEN1, clinically 'nonfunctioning' PETs may be malignant and capable of causing liver metastases. Non-functioning PETs have been detected as early as ages 12–14 years in asymptomatic children with MEN1[1]. The best way to detect non-functioning tumours is unclear. A limited amount of data suggests that endoscopic ultrasound outperforms CT scanning in this setting. The extent to which additional surveillance for endocrine tumours, employing biochemical and/or radiographic methods, should be used can be debated since evidence for their efficacy in improving outcomes is not strong. Nevertheless, a widely cited consensus guideline document recommends routine annual measurement of serum calcium parathyroid hormone, gastrin, fasting glucose, insulin, insulin-like growth factor-1 (IGF-1), prolactin, and chromogranin-A, starting in childhood and continuing for life. Imaging tests (MRI of the pituitary and CT scan to evaluate for enteropancreatic tumours) are recommended every three to five years[1]. The long-term prognosis of patients with MEN1 is uncertain. Because effective treatment is available for hyperparathyroidism and pituitary disease in MEN1, the malignant potential of pancreatic endocrine tumours and thymic carcinoids are the primary life-threatening manifestations of MEN1. These tumours are often present at initial assessment and prevention of tumour spread by surgery should be balanced with potential operative mortality and morbidity.

1 Brandi, Gagel, Angeli (et al) 'Guidelines for diagnosis and therapy of MEN type 1 and type 2' (2001) 86 J Clin Endocrinol Metab 5658–5671.

19.105 Multiple endocrine neoplasia type 2 (MEN2) is subclassified into three distinct syndromes: MEN2A, MEN2B, and familial medullary thyroid cancer (FMTC). MEN2A is characterised by medullary thyroid cancer (MTC), phaeochromocytoma, and primary parathyroid hyperplasia. It is autosomal dominant and men and women are affected equally. Medullary thyroid cancer is a neuroendocrine tumour of the calcitonin producing C cells of the thyroid gland which accounts for approximately 3–5 per cent of thyroid cancers. The physiological role of calcitonin in humans is unknown. Multicentric C cell hyperplasia precedes the development of MTC, and 90 per cent of patients develop clinically apparent MTC, often early in life. The excellent prognosis for MTC diagnosed at its earliest stage underscores the importance of early diagnosis for sporadic and hereditary MTC[1].

1 Brandi, Gagel, Angeli (et al) 'Guidelines for diagnosis and therapy of MEN type 1 and type 2' (2001) 86 J Clin Endocrinol Metab 5658–5671.

19.106 Most cases of MTC (75 per cent) are sporadic, but as many as 25 per cent of all MTCs are considered to be familial. The clinical presentation and manifestations of MEN2-associated MTC are similar to those of sporadic MTC usually as a solitary thyroid nodule or cervical lymphadenopathy. In MEN2A and familial medullary thyroid cancer (FMTC), the peak incidence of index cases is in the third decade of life. Less common presentations specific to MEN2-associated MTC include recognition during a search initiated after an associated disease such as phaeochromocytoma or hyperparathyroidism becomes apparent, diarrhoea and flushing due to the secretion of other peptides by the tumour. The diagnosis of MTC is usually made based upon the cytological findings after fine needle aspiration biopsy of a thyroid nodule and serum basal and stimulated calcitonin levels[1].

1 Brandi, Gagel, Angeli (et al) 'Guidelines for diagnosis and therapy of MEN type 1 and type 2' (2001) 86 J Clin Endocrinol Metab 5658–5671.

19.107 Phaeochromocytoma is a tumour of the adrenal medulla which secretes excessive amounts of catecholamines (adrenaline and noradrenaline) which occurs in approximately 40 per cent of patients with MEN2. Uncontrolled catecholamine release results in sporadic or persistent hypertension, palpitations and sweating. Sporadic phaeochromocytomas are almost always unilateral whereas in contrast, those in MEN2A have been reported to be bilateral in approximately 30–100 per cent of patients. It is unusual for phaeochromocytoma to precede the development of MTC and be the initial manifestation of MEN2. In patients who have undergone regular screening, phaeochromocytomas have usually become evident about 10 years later than C cell hyperplasia or MTC. Thus, phaeochromocytomas in MEN2 are usually identified during screening or through heightened vigilance for symptoms in patients with known or suspected MEN2. In such patients, symptoms are similar to those in patients with sporadic phaeochromocytomas and may include attacks (paroxysms) of anxiety, headache, diaphoresis, palpitations or tachycardia. The biochemical diagnosis of phaeochromocytoma is confirmed, by measurement of plasma or urinary catecholamines. Biochemical screening for phaeochromocytoma should be performed yearly in MEN2 patients. As undiagnosed phaeochromocytoma could cause substantial morbidity or even death during thyroid or parathyroid surgery, it is important to consider this diagnosis as a component of possible MEN2A and, if present, to remove the tumour before removing the other endocrine tumours. Once the diagnosis of pheochromocytoma in MEN2A is established, the possibility of bilateral disease must be carefully evaluated[1].

1 Brandi, Gagel, Angeli (et al) 'Guidelines for diagnosis and therapy of MEN type 1 and type 2' (2001) 86 J Clin Endocrinol Metab 5658–5671.

PITUITARY DISEASE

19.108 The hypothalamus can be considered the coordinating centre of the endocrine system. It consolidates signals derived from the higher centres of the brain, autonomic function, environmental stimuli such as light and temperature, and peripheral endocrine feedback. In turn, the hypothalamus delivers precise signals to the pituitary gland which then releases hormones that influence most endocrine systems in the body. Specifically, the hypothalamic-pituitary axis directly affects the functions of the thyroid gland, the adrenal gland, and the gonads, as well as influencing growth, milk production, and water balance.

Hyperprolactinaemia

19.109 The pituitary contains lactotroph cells that produce prolactin, the hormone that stimulates lactation (formation of breast milk). Prolactinomas are benign (non-cancerous) tumours of the pituitary gland which develop when one of these normal cells develops a mutation that allows the cell to divide repeatedly, resulting in a large number of cells that produce an excessive amount of prolactin. They can cause symptoms, either when the high blood prolactin concentration interferes with the function of the ovaries or, less commonly, when the adenoma grows large enough to compress nearby structures in the head, such as the optic nerves. Most prolactinomas remain small, less than 1cm in diameter and are called microadenomas. A minority grow larger, occasionally to several cms, and are called macroadenomas. Prolactinomas occur in both men and women but are more commonly diagnosed in women who are less than 50 years than in older women or men. About 10 per cent produce growth hormone as well as prolactin.

19.110 Community studies suggest that hyperprolactinaemia (>600mU/l) is present in just over 1 per cent of women aged over 40 years. The clinical manifestations of hyperprolactinaemia are relatively few and usually easy to recognize. Once the presence of prolactin excess is identified, further evaluation to establish the underlying cause is usually straightforward.

Hyperprolactinaemia in premenopausal women causes hypogonadism, manifested by infertility, oligomenorrhoea (infrequent and irregular periods), or amenorrhoea (absence of periods), and less often by galactorrhoea[1].

1 Melmed, Casanueva, Hoffman, Kleinberg, Montori, Schlechte, Wass, Endocrine Society 'Diagnosis and treatment of hyperprolactinaemia: an Endocrine Society clinical practice guideline'(2011) 96 J Clin Endocrinol Metab 273–288.

19.111 Hyperprolactinaemia results in amenorrhoea due to inhibition of luteinizing hormone (LH) and follicle-stimulating hormone (FSH) secretion, via inhibition of the release of gonadotropin-releasing hormone (GnRH). As a result, serum gonadotropin concentrations are not supranormal, typical of other causes of secondary hypogonadism. The symptoms of hypogonadism due to hyperprolactinaemia in premenopausal women correlate with the magnitude of the hyperprolactinaemia. In most laboratories, a serum prolactin concentration above 500-600mU/l is considered abnormally high in women of reproductive age:

- a serum prolactin concentration greater than 2000mU/l is typically associated with overt hypogonadism, subnormal oestradiol secretion and its consequences, including amenorrhoea, hot flushes, and vaginal dryness;
- moderate degrees of hyperprolactinaemia (serum prolactin values 1000-2000mU/l) cause either amenorrhoea or oligomenorrhoea;
- mild degrees of hyperprolactinaemia (serum prolactin values 500-1000mU/l) may cause only insufficient progesterone secretion, and therefore, a short luteal phase of the menstrual cycle. Mild hyperprolactinaemia can cause infertility even when there is no abnormality of the menstrual cycle; these women account for about 20 per cent of those evaluated for infertility.

19.112 Women with amenorrhea secondary to hyperprolactinaemia have a lower spine and forearm bone mineral density compared with normal women or women with hyperprolactinaemia and normal menses. Restoration of menses following therapy results in an increase in bone density, although it may not return to normal. Adolescents, when compared to adults with prolactinoma, have lower bone density at the time of diagnosis and less improvement after two years of dopamine agonist therapy. Hyperprolactinaemia in premenopausal women can also cause galactorrhoea, but most premenopausal women who have hyperprolactinaemia do not have galactorrhoea.

19.113 The goals of treatment are to lower the level of prolactin in the blood to normal and to decrease the size of a large adenoma, especially if it is compressing surrounding structures. Not all prolactinomas require treatment. If it is large or causing symptoms, it should probably be treated, but if it is small and is not causing symptoms, it does not need to be treated. Prolactinomas can usually be treated successfully with medication alone. Medication lowers the prolactin level in the blood substantially, often to normal, and also usually reduces tumour size[1].

1 Melmed, Casanueva, Hoffman, Kleinberg, Montori, Schlechte, Wass, Endocrine Society 'Diagnosis and treatment of hyperprolactinaemia: an Endocrine Society clinical practice guideline'(2011) 96 J Clin Endocrinol Metab 273–288.

19.114 Dopamine agonists are very effective for decreasing prolactin levels and the size of most prolactinomas. Cabergoline, which appears to be the most effective dopamine agonist, lowers prolactin levels in about 90 per cent of people who have prolactinomas, often to a level that is normal. It also usually decreases the size of micro- and macroadenomas to normal. Prolactin levels usually fall within the first two to three weeks of treatment, but detectable decreases in adenoma size require more time, usually several weeks to months. When the adenoma affects vision, improvement in vision may begin within days of starting treatment. If the prolactin level decreases to normal or near normal levels, the effects of the elevated prolactin are reversed. In premenopausal women, ovarian function returns, oestrogen levels increase, menstrual periods return, and fertility returns.

19.115 Cabergoline is the first choice dopamine agonist due to its high efficacy and good tolerability profile including safety in pregnancy. Prolonged remission after discontinuation of Cabergoline may be observed if treatment has been given for at least two years, normal prolactin has been obtained with a low dose and tumour diameter has been reduced by at least 50 per cent. The major side effects are nausea, lightheadedness after standing, and mental fogginess. These side effects are most likely to occur when treatment first begins and when the dose is increased. They can be minimized by starting with a small dose, increasing the dose slowly if needed, using small doses more frequently, and taking the drug with food or at bedtime.

19.116 Neurosurgical treatment of prolactinomas is less effective than medical therapy and recurrence of hyperprolactinaemia is frequent. Besides classical indications such as drug intolerance, resistance or acute complications, indications also include young patients with a high likelihood of complete tumour resection and those who do not wish to take prolonged medical treatment, or patients who require high doses of Cabergoline, in whom surgical debulking may significantly improve post-operative hormonal control.

19.117 If the prolactin level remains normal and no adenoma is seen on MRI for two or more years, a trial period without medication can be considered. However, the high prolactin level often recurs after the medication is stopped. Monitoring of the prolactin level and, less frequently, the size of the pituitary, would continue during this time. If the prolactin levels begin to rise or the adenoma grows in size, restarting a dopamine agonist may be recommended. Women who have microadenomas usually do not have to continue taking dopamine agonists after menopause. The prolactin is usually measured a few months after treatment is stopped to be sure that it is not substantially higher than before treatment. This is usually done once per year for a few years and less often thereafter. Women who have macroadenomas should continue taking dopamine agonists after menopause to keep the size of the adenoma from increasing[1].

1 Melmed, Casanueva, Hoffman, Kleinberg, Montori, Schlechte, Wass, Endocrine Society 'Diagnosis and treatment of hyperprolactinaemia: an Endocrine Society clinical practice guideline'(2011) 96 J Clin Endocrinol Metab 273–288.

Acromegaly

19.118   Acromegaly is a rare clinical syndrome that results from excessive secretion of growth hormone (GH) with an annual incidence in six per million people. The average age at diagnosis is 40–45 years. The most common cause of acromegaly is a somatotroph (GH-secreting) adenoma of the anterior pituitary[1].

1 Melmed 'Acromegaly pathogenesis and treatment (2009) 119 J Clin Invest 3189–3202.

19.119   The clinical features of acromegaly are attributable to high serum concentrations of both GH and IGF-I, which is GH-dependent. The onset of acromegaly is insidious, and its progression is usually very slow. The average interval from the onset of symptoms until diagnosis is about 12 years[1], but determining the onset, which is usually done from old photographs, is very difficult. At diagnosis, about 75 per cent of patients have macroadenomas (tumour diameter 10 mm or greater), and some of the adenomas extend to the parasellar or suprasellar regions. Overall, approximately 60 per cent of patients eventually have headaches and 10 per cent have visual symptoms. Macroadenomas can also cause decreased secretion of other pituitary hormones, most commonly gonadotropins.

1 Colao, Ferone, Marzullo, Lombardi 'Systemic complications of acromegaly: epidemiology, pathogenesis, and management' (2004) 25 Endocr Rev 102–152.

19.120   Patients with acromegaly have peripheral soft tissue overgrowth and skin thickening. Characteristic findings are an enlarged jaw (macrognathia) and enlarged, swollen hands and feet, which result in increasing shoe and glove size and the need to enlarge rings. Joint symptoms are a common presenting feature of the disease as synovial tissue and cartilage enlarge, causing hypertrophic arthropathy of the knees, ankles, hips, spine, and other joints, and back pain is common. The overall frequency of sleep apnoea in patients with acromegaly is approximately 40–50 per cent. In most cases, craniofacial deformities, macroglossia, and enlargement of the soft tissues of the pharynx and larynx result in obstructive sleep apnoea. Predictive factors for the development of sleep apnoea include the severity of GH excess, duration of disease, obesity, older age, and male gender. Sleep apnoea symptoms gradually improve in some, but not all patients after correction of the underlying GH excess with transphenoidal surgery or medical therapy[1].

1 Melmed 'Acromegaly pathogenesis and treatment (2009) 119 J Clin Invest 3189–3202.

19.121   Patients with acromegaly appear to be at increased risk for colon polyps, colon cancer, and other tumours. Cardiovascular abnormalities include hypertension, left ventricular hypertrophy, and cardiomyopathy. Uncontrolled acromegaly is also associated with insulin resistance, overt diabetes in 10–15 per cent of cases, and impaired glucose tolerance in a further 50 per cent. The mortality rate of patients with acromegaly appears to be increased, especially if strict biochemical control is not achieved. Death is primarily from cardiovascular disease. Some studies have reported an average reduction in survival of as much as 10 years[1]. The overall weighted mean standard mortality ratio (SMR) has been calculated at 1.72, which represents a 72 per cent increase in mortality in acromegalic patients compared with the general population.

1 Melmed 'Acromegaly pathogenesis and treatment (2009) 119 J Clin Invest 3189–3202.

19.122 The clinical diagnosis of acromegaly is often delayed because of the slow progression of the signs of acromegaly over a period of many years. Both serum GH concentrations and IGF-I concentrations are increased in virtually all patients with acromegaly. Once a patient is suspected to have acromegaly, the next steps are biochemical testing to confirm the clinical diagnosis and imaging to determine the cause of the excess GH secretion. The main biochemical aim of treatment for acromegaly is to lower the serum IGF-1 concentration to within the reference range for the patient's age and gender and to lower the serum GH concentration to <1.0ng/mL. With normalisation of serum IGF-1 concentrations, the life expectancy of patients with acromegaly is similar to that of the general population. Therapy should also ameliorate symptoms, if any, due to the size of the somatotroph adenoma, but it should not cause hypopituitarism. Even if the serum IGF-1 returns to normal, bony abnormalities generally do not regress and joint symptoms persist.

19.123 Selective transsphenoidal surgical resection is the treatment of choice for patients with somatotroph adenomas that are small, large but still resectable, or large and cause visual impairment. Surgery may also be considered for large adenomas that are not entirely accessible surgically (eg those with cavernous sinus extension), with the goal of removing a sufficient mass of tissue to increase the likelihood that somatostatin analogue treatment will be effective postoperatively. When transsphenoidal surgery is performed by the most experienced pituitary neurosurgeons, GH secretion falls to normal in about 80–90 per cent of patients with microadenomas (less than 10 mm in diameter) and pituitary secretion of other hormones is preserved. The success rate is less than 50 per cent in patients with macroadenomas or higher preoperative serum GH concentrations.

19.124 Several medications are now available for treating acromegaly, including some that inhibit GH secretion and one that inhibits its action. Pharmacologic treatment is used when surgery alone has not reduced serum GH and IGF-1 to normal. Its role as primary therapy has not been clearly established. Somatostatin analogues are analogues of somatostatin (growth hormone-inhibitory hormone) that inhibit GH secretion. External beam radiation therapy is effective in reducing the size of somatotroph adenomas and decreasing GH and IGF-1 concentrations, often to normal, but because the decreases in GH and IGF-1 usually take years to occur, it is used mainly for patients whose disease is not controlled by surgery or medical therapy.

Cushing's syndrome

19.125 The symptoms and signs of Cushing's syndrome result directly from chronic exposure to excess glucocorticoid hormone. There is a large spectrum of manifestations from subclinical to overt syndrome, depending on duration and intensity of excess steroid production. Some manifestations such as obesity, hypertension, and glucose intolerance are common in individuals who do not have adrenal hyperfunction.

19.126 Iatrogenic Cushing's syndrome is the result of pharmacological doses of glucocorticoids for autoimmune disorders (including potent topical and inhaled preparations), such as vasculitis, systemic lupus erythematosus, and rheumatoid arthritis; for allergic disorders such as asthma; and to prevent transplant rejection. These patients have a relatively high frequency of serious glucocorticoid-induced side effects which can include long-term adrenal failure.

19.127 Pituitary adrenocorticotrophic hormone (ACTH)-dependent Cushing's syndrome (Cushing's disease) is five to six times more common than Cushing's syndrome caused by benign and malignant adrenal tumors combined and has a reported incidence of approximately 2 per million per year). Cushing's disease is most common in women aged 25 to 45 years. It is unusual in children, but still accounts for about one-third of cases of childhood Cushing's syndrome, occurring mostly after puberty. Asymptomatic non-secreting adrenal tumours are a common finding in the healthy population and rarely adrenal carcinoma and adenoma can cause Cushing's syndrome. About 1 per cent of patients with small-cell lung cancer have ectopic ACTH syndrome[1].

1 Dekkers, Horváth-Puhó, Jørgensen, Cannegieter, Ehrenstein, Vandenbroucke, Pereira, Sørensen 'Multisystem morbidity and mortality in Cushing's syndrome: a cohort study' (2013) 98 J Clin Endocrinol Metab 2277–2284.

19.128 The major symptoms and signs of Cushing's syndrome include supraclavicular fat pads, skin atrophy, wide purplish striae (stretch marks), and proximal muscle weakness. The relative severity of symptoms varies and is determined by the degree and duration of hypercortisolism. The most common feature of patients with Cushing's syndrome is progressive central (centripetal) obesity, usually involving the face, neck, trunk and abdomen. The extremities are usually spared and may be wasted. Menstrual irregularities are common in women with Cushing's syndrome. The major source of androgens in women is the adrenal glands and women with Cushing's syndrome often have signs of androgen excess such as hirsutism, scalp hair loss and acne. Bone loss, glucose intolerance and hypertension are also common. Symptoms of psychiatric disease occur in over 50 per cent of patients with Cushing's syndrome of any aetiology and may be the presenting symptom.

19.129 Once the biochemical diagnosis of hypercortisolism is established, its cause must be determined. Both laboratory and patient errors can cause misleading results. The aim of treatment is to reverse the clinical manifestations by reducing cortisol secretion to normal, remove any tumour and if possible avoid permanent hormone deficiency or dependence on any medications. Selective transsphenoidal surgical resection is the treatment of choice for patients with a pituitary adenoma. Among expert pituitary neurosurgeons, the cure rate approximates 70–80 per cent, but late recurrences reduce the permanent cure rate to approximately 60–70 per cent. Medical therapy, radiotherapy or bilateral adrenalectomy is available when surgery is delayed, unsuccessful or not possible[1].

1 Biller, Grossman, Stewart, Melmed, Bertagna, Bertherat, Buchfelder, Colao, Hermus, Hofland, Klibanski, Lacroix, Lindsay, Newell-Price, Nieman, Petersenn, Sonino, Stalla, Swearingen, Vance, Wass, Boscaro 'Treatment of adrenocorticotropin-dependent Cushing's syndrome: a consensus statement' (2008) 93 J Clin Endocrinol Metab 2454–2462.

Hypopituitarism

19.130   Damage to the anterior pituitary can occur suddenly or slowly, can be mild or severe, and can affect the secretion of one, several, or all of its hormones. As a result, the clinical presentation of anterior pituitary hormone deficiencies varies. Pituitary apoplexy presents acutely and can cause sudden impairment of ACTH secretion and symptoms of cortisol deficiency often on the background of an unknown pre-existing non-functioning pituitary tumour[1]. If hypopituitarism is due to a slowly enlarging sellar mass it may also have symptoms related to the mass, such as headache, visual loss, or double vision. Other insults, such as radiation therapy to the pituitary or hypothalamus, usually act slowly, causing symptoms many months or, more likely, years later. Classically the secretion of gonadotropins and growth hormone is more likely to be affected than ACTH and thyroid-stimulating hormone (TSH) although exceptions occur.

1 Rajasekaran, Vanderpump, Baldeweg, Drake, Reddy, Lanyon, Markey, Plant, Powell, Sinha, Wass 'UK guidelines for the management of pituitary apoplexy' (2011) 74 Clin Endocrinol (Oxf) 9–20.

19.131   Sheehan's syndrome refers to post-partum partial or complete hypopituitarism or pituitary failure due to pituitary necrosis occurring during severe hypotension or shock secondary to massive bleeding at or just after the delivery[1]. It is now a rare syndrome as a result of improved obstetric care, including treatment of haemodynamic complications with rapid blood transfusion or fluid replacement. The exact pathogenesis and natural history of Sheehan's syndrome are not well understood. The basic process is infarction of the pituitary, second to a rest of blood flow to the anterior lobe of the pituitary gland, and it may be due to vasospasm thrombosis or vascular compression. The pituitary gland is physiologically enlarged during pregnancy as a result of diffuse or nodular hyperplasia of the lactotrope cells stimulated by oestrogens produced by the placenta. Pituitary enlargement may result in compression of the superior hypophysial artery and thereby may cause a mild ischaemia. If sudden changes in the arterial pressure occur during delivery due to severe hypotension or shock after massive bleeding, it is believed to cause arterial spasm in small vessels and apoplexy.

1 Kovacs 'Sheehan's syndrome' (2003) 361 Lancet 520–522.

19.132   It has been suggested that the enlarged pituitary gland during pregnancy is more susceptible to ischaemic necrosis after post-partum bleeding massive enough to cause severe hypotension. On the other hand, Sheehan's syndrome may develop without any obvious post-partum bleeding although that is very rare. Other potential factors involved in the pathogenesis includes the size of the sella in which the pituitary sits at the base of the skull, or an association with disseminated intravascular coagulation (DIC) causing a hypercoagulable state making the pituitary gland more susceptible to ischaemia[1].

1 Tessnow, Wilson 'The changing face of Sheehan's syndrome' (2010) 340 American Journal of the Medical Sciences 402–406.

19.133   The spectrum of clinical presentation with Sheehan's syndrome is large and ranges from non-specific complaints such as weakness, fatigue and anaemia, to severe pituitary insufficiency resulting in coma and death. Most patients however have mild disease and go undiagnosed for a long time, presenting months to years after the last delivery complicated by severe vaginal bleeding with a history of failure of a post-partum lactation, failure to resume menses and the symptoms and biochemical picture characteristic biochemical findings of anterior pituitary failure.

19.134 Clinical manifestations of Sheehan's syndrome may change from one patient to another as in other types of hypopituitarism, hormonal deficiency varies from the loss of a single hormone to classic pan-hypopituitarism with loss of thyroid, adrenal, gonadotrophin, prolactin and GH[1]. The general principles of the treatment in hypopituitary patients are valid also in patients with Sheehan's syndrome. The aim of the treatment is to replace the deficient hormone or hormones. Treatment is important to correct the endocrine disturbance, but also to prevent or at least decrease the morbidity and mortality due to hypopituitarism. ACTH deficiency, which is the most likely to require emergency treatment, is treated with glucocorticoids, hypothyroidism is treated with levothyroxine, hypogonadism is treated with oestrogen hormone replacement therapy, and growth hormone replacement is required in growth hormone deficient patients. Hypopituitarism even if adequately replaced is associated with an increased long-term morbidity and mortality.

1 Tessnow, Wilson 'The changing face of Sheehan's syndrome' (2010) 340 American Journal of the Medical Sciences 402–406.

Diabetes insipidus

19.135 Polyuria is defined as the passing of a high volume of dilute urine exceeding three litres per day. Central diabetes insipidus is associated with deficient secretion of antidiuretic hormone (ADH) from the posterior pituitary. This condition is most often idiopathic (possibly due to autoimmune injury to the ADH-producing cells), or can be induced by trauma, pituitary surgery, or hypoxic or ischaemic encephalopathy.

19.136 A variety of conditions may result in the complaint of polyuria, including nephrogenic diabetes insipidus, psychogenic polydipsia, prostatic hypertrophy, or osmotic diuresis (including post-obstructive diuresis). The cause of polyuria is often suggested from the history and rarely by the plasma sodium concentration. Observing changes in fluid output and serum sodium levels during a water deprivation test and following the administration of the replacement hormone Desmopressin usually establishes the diagnosis.

19.137 In adults with diabetes insipidus and no cognitive impairment, true hypernatremia (plasma sodium concentration greater than 150mmol/L) should not occur because the initial loss of water stimulates thirst, resulting in an increase in intake to match the urinary losses. An exception to this general rule occurs when DI is due to a central lesion that also impairs thirst (adipsia). Adipsic diabetes insipidus is associated with significant morbidity including seizures and mortality. Withholding water (eg, for diagnostic or surgical procedures) or failure to provide sufficient fluids in adults with diabetes insipidus can result in severe dehydration. Thus, if oral intake has to be withheld, the patient should be hospitalised and hydrated intravenously, and the plasma sodium concentration closely monitored while intake is restricted.

ADDISON'S DISEASE

19.138 Cortisol is a steroid hormone secreted by the adrenal glands which is essential for life and regulates the blood pressure and the response to infections, stress, physical accidents, and surgery. The clinical presentation of cortisol insufficiency is variable, depending on whether the onset is acute, leading to an 'adrenal crisis', or chronic, with symptoms that are more insidious and vague. Addison's disease (primary adrenal cortical insufficiency or hypoadrenalism) is a rare disorder in which there is destruction of the adrenal cortex thus reducing the production of glucocorticoids, mineralocorticoids and androgens. The majority of cases are now due to autoimmune disease. Addison's disease is rare with an estimated incidence of about 6 cases per one million adults per year and may be associated with other autoimmune disorders including thyroid disease, type 1 diabetes and pernicious anaemia[1].

1 Orth and Kovacs 'Diseases of the Adrenal Cortex' in 'The Adrenal Cortex', Wilson, Foster, Kronenberg and Larsen (eds) Williams Textbook of Endocrinology (9th edn) pp 547–555.

19.139 Alternatively the cause of cortisol deficiency may be classified as secondary due to failure of the ACTH secreted from the pituitary gland which stimulates the adrenal cortex to produce cortisol. ACTH deficiency either isolated or combined with loss of other hormones produced by the pituitary due to pituitary failure is also rare. Prolonged administration of pharmacological doses of synthetic glucocorticoids (steroids) used to suppress an autoimmune response or disease is by far the most common cause of ACTH deficiency and consequent adrenal insufficiency. Patients who have in the past been treated with glucocorticoid therapy may rarely present with symptoms of glucocorticoid deficiency or hypotension, particularly during a critical illness or surgery. Patients with Addison's disease who are adequately treated can expect to work normally.

19.140 Clinical signs and symptoms do not become manifest until at least 90 per cent of the adrenal cortex is destroyed. The clinical presentation of adrenal insufficiency is variable depending on whether the onset is acute leading to adrenal crisis or chronic with symptoms that are more insidious and vague. The signs and symptoms depend on the rate and degree of loss of adrenal function and the presentation is often insidious in onset and may go undetected until an inter-current illness or stress precipitates a crisis. As a result the diagnosis of adrenal insufficiency depends upon a critical level of clinical suspicion and should be considered in any patient who presents with collapse and hypotension that doesn't respond to conventional fluid resuscitation.

19.141 Patients with adrenal insufficiency consistently have chronic malaise, lassitude, fatigueability, weakness, weight loss and anorexia. The weakness is generalised rather than being limited to particular muscle groups. Weight loss, which mostly results from anorexia but partly from dehydration, may not become evident until adrenal failure is advanced. Patients may exhibit extreme sensitivity to drugs such as narcotics, gastrointestinal complaints usually nausea and occasionally vomiting or abdominal pain or diarrhoea are common and correlate with severity of adrenal insufficiency. Vomiting and abdominal pain often herald an adrenal crisis. Cardiovascular symptoms include postural dizziness or syncope due to the combined effects of volume depletion and the loss of the mineralocorticoid effect of aldosterone. Clinical and laboratory features that suggest adrenal crisis in a patient with chronic primary adrenal insufficiency include:

- dehydration, hypertension or shock out of proportion to severity of current illness;
- nausea and vomiting with a history of weight loss and anorexia;
- abdominal pain mimicking an acute abdomen;
- unexplained hypoglycaemia;
- unexplained fever;
- investigations including hyponatraemia, hyperkalaemia, biochemical evidence of dehydration, hypercalcaemia or eosinophilia;
- other autoimmune endocrine deficiencies such as hypothyroidism or type 1 diabetes, family history of organ specific autoimmune endocrine diseases[1].

1 Orth and Kovacs 'Diseases of the Adrenal Cortex' in 'The Adrenal Cortex', Wilson, Foster, Kronenberg and Larsen (eds) Williams Textbook of Endocrinology (9th edn) pp 547–555.

19.142 Hyperpigmentation which is evident in most but not all patients with primary adrenal insufficiency is one of the characteristic findings. Patients are often aware of darkening of the skin caused by increased content of melanin in the skin which results from the melanocyte stimulating activity of the increased circulating ACTH levels from the pituitary gland.

19.143 Considering the diagnosis of adrenal failure in patients whose symptoms are vague and non-specific can be life-saving. Some patients never develop the full classical triad of hyperpigmentation, hypotension and hyponatraemia. The nature of the disease also means that patients who have struggled with sub-clinical symptoms for years as their adrenal function deteriorates suddenly become vulnerable to a crisis when they meet flu or another illness which they no longer have the adrenal reserves to combat. The clinical diagnosis of chronic adrenal insufficiency is often more difficult as the symptoms and signs are non-specific and the presentation is often insidious in onset and may go undetected until an inter-current illness or stress precipitates a crisis. As a result, the possible presence of adrenal insufficiency is sometimes overlooked while other possibilities are pursued. Healthcare workers often do not realise the urgency of treatment for acute adrenal crisis or fail to heed the requests of well informed patients for hydrocortisone.

19.144 Patients with adrenal insufficiency are at risk of developing life threatening adrenal crisis if steroids are reduced or stopped, or if glucocorticoid treatment is not increased during periods of increased stress (for example, illness, trauma, or surgery). Fatal but avoidable adrenal crisis is the second most common cause of death in patients with known Addison's disease, accounting for 15 per cent of deaths in patients with this disease.

Early treatment with parenteral hydrocortisone and intravenous rehydration with fluids are essential measures to avoid mortality[1].

1 Wass, Arlt 'How to avoid precipitating an acute adrenal crisis' (2012) 345 BMJ e6333.

OVARIAN FAILURE

19.145 The menopause occurs at an average age of 50.7 years. Menopause before the age of 40 years is most commonly taken to be the definition of premature ovarian failure (POF) and refers to the cessation of ovarian function at an earlier than expected age due to ovarian pathology. Chemotherapy or radiation therapy is a recognised cause of POF. The effect of radiotherapy is dependent on dose and age and on the radiation therapy field. POF is an important late effect of cytotoxic chemotherapy given for various malignant disease in young women and in particular, alkylation agents increase the risk of POF gravely particularly in women aged over 20 years.

19.146 The major medical issues for health surveillance in women with POF revolve around the quality of life and bone protection offered by hormone replacement therapy (HRT). Women also require emotional support to deal with the impact of the diagnosis on their health and relationships. Long-term follow-up is essential to monitor HRT and for health surveillance. Physiological replacement of ovarian steroid hormones for women under the age of 50 years is recommended. It must be accepted that there are a few long term risks/benefits data specifically for this young population.

19.147 The principle of HRT use in young women differs slightly from that in older women, with the main treatment goal being optimal quality of life and bone protection. Young women may require a higher oestrogen dose than that used in older age groups in order to optimise the quality of life and more closely match normal physiology in young women. Studies which have investigated the psychological well-being of women who have experienced menopause before the age of forty show high levels of depression, perceived stress, sexual difficulties and lower levels of self-esteem, and life satisfaction compared to the general population. The impact on fertility is deemed to be the single most distressing feature of the diagnosis regardless of whether the woman already had children or not[1].

1 Nelson 'Clinical Practice; Primary ovarian insufficiency' (2009) 360 New England Journal of Medicine 606–614.

19.148 The consequences of premature menopause can be divided into short and long term consequences. Short term consequences include vasomotor symptoms such as hot flushes, night sweats, palpitations and headaches, weight gain, dryness of the vagina and dyspareunia, urgency and stress incontinence. The psychological problems include irritability, anxiety, depression, forgetfulness, insomnia and poor concentration[1].

1 Panay, Kalu 'Management of premature ovarian failure' (2009) 23 Best Practice Research in Clinical Obstetrics and Gynaecology 129–140.

19.149 The terms hot flush, and vasomotor symptoms are often used to describe the same condition. Hot flushes occur in 75 per cent of cases and tend to be more severe than in the natural menopause and are the most common and distressing complaint. They are unpredictable in onset, may present with recurring periods of sudden explosive overwhelming uncomfortable sensations of intense heat of flushing that begins on the face or upper part of the neck and then to the upper chest. They may be associated with palpitations and feeling of anxiety and red blotching of the skin. Flushes last for two to five minutes, varying in frequency but some women experience episodes multiple times in the day. They decrease with the passage of time. Hot flushes have a detrimental effect on a woman's functional ability and quality of life. Sleep disturbance is seen in women with severe hot flushes presenting with cognitive or affective disorders resulting from sleep deprivation. Premature menopause may also present with atrophic vagina which reduces the vaginal secretion and the dryness of the vagina can cause dyspareunia, loss of libido, sexual dysfunction and other associated symptoms including headaches, skin atrophy and joint pains[1].

1 Neff 'The North American Menopause Society (NAMS) releases position statement on the treatment of vasomotor symptoms associated with menopause. Practice guideline' (2004) 70 American Family Physician 393–399.

19.150 Long term consequences of premature menopause include infertility, osteoporosis and an increased risk of premature death, cardiovascular disease and stroke. Osteoporosis is a skeletal disorder characterised by low bone mass and micro-architectural deterioration of bone tissue with consequent increase in fragility of bones and susceptibility risk of fracture. Women with premature menopause are at increased risk for low bone density, early onset osteoporosis and fractures. HRT is thus the cornerstone in prophylaxis of treatment of osteoporosis[1].

1 Nelson 'Clinical Practice; Primary ovarian insufficiency' (2009) 360 New England Journal of Medicine 606–614; Panay, Kalu 'Management of premature ovarian failure' (2009) 23 Best Practice Research in Clinical Obstetrics and Gynaecology 129–140.

19.151 Premature menopause is associated with an increased risk of ischaemic heart disease and angina and the risk increases with the earlier age of ovarian failure. It is also associated with an increased risk of cardiovascular mortality and total mortality. Oestrogen deficiency increases the risk of ischaemic heart disease and angina in the post-menopausal woman. Oestrogen is considered protective in the prevention of cardiovascular disease as it increases high density lipoprotein cholesterol (HDL-C) and reduces low density lipoprotein cholesterol (LDL-C) and triglycerides. There is some evidence that restoring normal oestrogen levels will reduce the later development of cardiovascular disease, osteoporosis and possibly dementia. It is good practice to recommend oestrogen replacement therapy for women with premature menopause[1].

1 Nelson 'Clinical Practice; Primary ovarian insufficiency' (2009) 360 New England Journal of Medicine 606–614; Panay, Kalu 'Management of premature ovarian failure' (2009) 23 Best Practice Research in Clinical Obstetrics and Gynaecology 129–140; Gallagher 'Effect of early menopause on bone mineral density and fractures' (2007) 14 Menopause 567–571.

19.152 There is limited epidemiological support for the hypothesis that oestrogen preserves overall cognitive function in non-demented women. However, in the Women's Health Initiative, both unopposed oestrogen and combined oestrogen and progestogen therapy had no global cognitive benefits in older non-demented postmenopausal women. Oestrogen deficiency after the menopause may contribute to the development of osteoarthritis but again the data are limited. In the early postmenopausal years, women who do not take oestrogen therapy typically gain fat mass and lose lean mass. Some studies suggest that postmenopausal hormone replacement therapy is associated with a decrease in central fat distribution. Although women typically gain weight during mid-life, it does not appear to be due to menopausal status or stage. The collagen content of the skin and bones is reduced by oestrogen deficiency. Decreased cutaneous collagen may lead to increased aging and wrinkling of the skin. Clinical data suggests that collagen changes may be minimised with oestrogen[1].

1 Nelson 'Clinical Practice; Primary ovarian insufficiency' (2009) 360 New England Journal of Medicine 606–614.

POLYCYSTIC OVARY SYNDROME

19.153 Polycystic ovary syndrome (PCOS) is an important cause of both ovulatory and menstrual irregularity and androgen excess in women. It is recognised as one of the most common endocrine/metabolic disorders of women and is estimated to occur in over 5 per cent of women. It is associated with obesity and insulin resistance and is thought to be a complex genetic trait, similar to cardiovascular disease, type 2 diabetes mellitus, and the metabolic syndrome, where multiple genetic variants and environmental factors interact to produce the disorder[1].

1 Rotterdam ESHRE/ASRM-Sponsored PCOS consensus workshop group Revised 2003 consensus on diagnostic criteria and long-term health risks related to polycystic ovary syndrome (PCOS) (2004) 19 Hum Reprod 41–47.

19.154 PCOS is characterised clinically by oligomenorrhea (infrequent and irregular periods) and hyperandrogenism (acne, hirsutism and male-pattern scalp hair loss), as well as the frequent presence of associated risk factors for cardiovascular disease, including obesity, glucose intolerance, dyslipidemia, and obstructive sleep apnoea. The typical polycystic appearance of the ovaries is seen on transvaginal ultrasound in the majority of women. However, this ultrasound appearance is non-specific as it may also be seen in normal women. Women with PCOS are also at increased risk for type 2 diabetes and there is some evidence that the presence of obesity, insulin resistance, impaired glucose tolerance (or type 2 diabetes), and dyslipidemia may predispose women with PCOS to coronary heart disease. The Rotterdam 2003 criteria[1] are now recognized, in which two out of three of the following are required to make the diagnosis of PCOS:

- oligo- or anovulation;
- clinical and/or biochemical signs of hyperandrogenism;
- polycystic ovaries (by ultrasound) defined as the presence of 12 or more follicles in at least one ovary and increased ovarian volume (>10mL).

1 Rotterdam ESHRE/ASRM-Sponsored PCOS consensus workshop group Revised 2003 consensus on diagnostic criteria and long-term health risks related to polycystic ovary syndrome (PCOS). (2014) 19 Hum Reprod 41–47.

19.155 There is no cure for PCOS so the overall goals of therapy include amelioration of hyperandrogenic symptoms (hirsutism, acne, scalp hair loss) with anti-androgen therapy, management of underlying metabolic abnormalities and reduction of risk factors for type 2 diabetes and cardiovascular disease by promoting lifestyle measures which improve insulin sensitivity such as diet and weight loss, correction of oligomennorhoea and prevention of endometrial hyperplasia and carcinoma, which may occur as a result of chronic anovulation and ovulation induction for those pursuing pregnancy[1].

1 Legro RS, Arslanian SA, Ehrmann DA, Hoeger KM, Murad MH, Pasquali R, Welt CK (2013). Diagnosis and treatment of polycystic ovary syndrome: an endocrine society clinical practice guideline. J Clin Endocrinol Metab 98:4565-4592.

HYPOGONADISM IN MEN

19.156   The sexually competent man must have desire for his sexual partner (libido) and a good blood supply to achieve penile tumescence and rigidity (erection) adequate for penetration and ejaculation. Impotence is defined as the inability to develop or sustain erection 75 per cent of the time. It is a common abnormality and may be due to psychological causes, medications, endocrine abnormalities, neurological, or vascular problems. Libido declines with testosterone deficiency, depression and in association with the use of prescription and recreational drugs[1].

1 McVary 'Clinical Practice. Erectile dysfunction' (2007) 357 New Engl J Med 2472–2481.

19.157   Psychological factors such as depression and performance anxiety are readily identifiable causes of impotence in men. Loss of libido and lack of interest in any sexual activity are common components of depressive illness and included in standard scales of depression. However, impotence is itself a depressing illness and many men, regardless of the aetiology of their impotence, will score high on these scales. Almost all of the antidepressant and many of the anti-hypertensive medications have been noted to have significant sexual dysfunction as side effects.

19.158   The testicular hormone testosterone plays an integral role in normal male sexual function and its deficiency results in impotence in men and sexual potency returns when testosterone levels are normalised. This effect is the result of testosterone acting through psychogenic channels to enhance libido and also being necessary for the sustaining of an erection by enhancing the action of an enzyme responsible for intra-penile blood supply. Other endocrine abnormalities including hyperprolactinaemia and thyroid dysfunction are also commonly associated with impotence. Restoration of normal endocrine function usually results in the return of erectile potency.

19.159   When testosterone deficiency first occurs after puberty has been completed, symptoms may include a decrease in energy and libido that occur within days to weeks. However, sexual hair, muscle mass, and bone mineral density do not fall to a readily detectable degree for several years. Men may also present with infertility.

19.160   Hypogonadism in a man refers to a decrease in testosterone production which can result from disease of the testes (primary hypogonadism) or disease of the pituitary or hypothalamus (secondary hypogonadism). The diagnosis of male hypogonadism is usually straightforward. Laboratory testing is based on measuring the serum testosterone and the pituitary hormones that control their production (LH and FSH). Testosterone is produced by the Leydig cells of the testes under stimulation of LH. Sperm are produced in the seminiferous tubules under stimulation principally by the high concentration of testosterone in the testes but also by FSH. Testosterone, in turn, inhibits both LH and FSH secretion. The diagnosis of hypogonadism can be confirmed by finding a low serum concentration of testosterone. In general, if the patient is hypogonadal and the LH and FSH concentrations are elevated, the cause of the hypogonadism is testicular damage, and if the LH and FSH are not elevated, the cause is pituitary or hypothalamic disease.

19.161   Trauma to the testes can be sufficiently severe to damage both seminiferous tubules and Leydig cells and result in primary hypogonadism. Secondary (or central) hypothyroidism is suspected if there is known hypothalamic or pituitary disease or there are associated other anterior and posterior pituitary hormone deficiencies. The presence of pituitary and hypothalamic conditions is best made by MRI studies. The patient diagnosed with secondary hypogonadism should also be evaluated for adrenal (eg the short synacthen test), thyroid and prolactin function and if indicated posterior pituitary and growth hormone function. When opiates are administered chronically for relief of chronic pain, they often cause pronounced secondary hypogonadism.

19.162   If hypogonadism is diagnosed then the following principles should guide testosterone therapy[1]. Testosterone can be replaced satisfactorily whether the testosterone deficiency is due to primary or secondary hypogonadism. The principal goal of testosterone therapy is to restore the serum testosterone concentration to the normal range. It is not yet known if restoring the normal circadian rhythm of testosterone is important. Native testosterone is absorbed well from the intestine, but it is metabolised so rapidly by the liver that it is virtually impossible to maintain a normal serum testosterone concentration in a hypogonadal man with oral testosterone. The solutions to this problem that have been developed over many years involve modifying the testosterone molecule, changing the method of testosterone delivery, or both.

1 Bhasin, Cunningham, Hayes (et al) 'Testosterone therapy in men with androgen deficiency syndromes: an Endocrine Society clinical practice guideline' (2010) 95 J Clin Endocrinol Metab 2536–2559.

19.163   An intramuscular formulation of another ester of testosterone, testosterone undecanoate is now commonly used for treatment of hypogonadism. When 1g dose is administered deep intramuscularly every three months, the serum testosterone concentration is usually maintained within the target reference range. Transdermal delivery of testosterone via body patches and gels are available. A potential advantage of transdermal administration is maintenance of relatively stable serum testosterone concentrations, resulting in maintenance of relatively stable energy, mood, and libido.

19.164   Patients who are treated with testosterone should be monitored to determine that normal serum testosterone concentrations are being achieved[1].

They should also be monitored for both desirable and undesirable effects. The timing of serum testosterone measurements varies with the preparation that is used. The serum testosterone should be measured midway between injections in men who are receiving testosterone enanthate, and the value should be mid-normal, eg 21–24nmol/L. The dose should be reduced if higher values are obtained. The serum testosterone can be measured at any time in men who are using any of the transdermal preparations, with the recognition that the peak values occur six to eight hours after application of the patch. The concentrations fluctuate when a gel is used, but not in a predictable way, so at least two measurements should be made at any dose of gel; the time of measurement does not appear to matter. The value should be well within the normal range (14–27nmol/L). If the patient has primary hypogonadism, normalisation of the serum LH concentration should also be used to judge the adequacy of the testosterone dose, no matter which testosterone preparation is used.

1 Bhasin, Cunningham, Hayes (et al) 'Testosterone therapy in men with androgen deficiency syndromes: an Endocrine Society clinical practice guideline' (2010) 95 J Clin Endocrinol Metab 2536–2559.

19.165
The desirable effects of testosterone administration include the development or maintenance of secondary sexual characteristics, and increases in libido, muscle strength, body composition, and bone density. Undesirable effects related directly to testosterone include acne, prostate disorders such as benign prostatic hyperplasia symptoms, sleep apnoea, and erythrocytosis (an increase in the number of red blood cells). Normalisation of the serum testosterone concentration should lead to maintenance of virilisation in those who already are. Men who become hypogonadal in adulthood and are still normally virilised but whose hypogonadism is manifested by a decrease in libido and energy should note a marked improvement in these symptoms. Although the time course of the effects of testosterone replacement is variable, failure of improvement when the serum testosterone concentration has been restored to normal suggests another cause of the symptoms.

19.166 Testosterone enanthate and the testosterone patch and gels have few side effects unrelated to the action of testosterone. Local skin irritation occasionally occurs with testosterone gels, but usually is not severe and does not necessitate discontinuation of therapy. Some men, especially those over the age of 50, experience an exacerbation of benign prostatic hyperplasia. A recent meta-analysis of 51 randomised trials of testosterone therapy in men designed to look at the primary endpoints of mortality, cardiovascular events and risk factors, prostate outcomes and erythrocytosis, no significant effects of testosterone were seen on the incidence of prostate cancer, need for prostate biopsy, increase in PSA, or change in lower urinary tract symptoms/score when compared to the placebo/non-intervention group[1]. Because prostate cancer is, at least to some degree, testosterone dependent, it seems theoretically likely that the risk of prostate cancer is less in hypogonadal men than eugonadal men and the risk increases to normal, but not above, when testosterone is replaced. However, no data are available to support or refute this assumption.

1 Fernández-Balsells, Murad, Lane (et al) 'Adverse effects of testosterone therapy in adult men: a systematic review and meta-analysis' (2010) 95 J Clin Endocrinol Metab 2560–2575.

19.167 It seems prudent to screen hypogonadal men for prostate cancer before beginning testosterone replacement and to monitor them for prostate cancer during treatment, just as one would monitor a eugonadal man[1]. There is no reason to think that men who rely on medication to maintain a normal serum testosterone concentration are more likely to develop these conditions than men who produce their own testosterone. Sleep apnoea may be worsened and symptoms such as excessive daytime sleepiness and witnessed apnoea during sleep. Erythrocytosis (an increase in the number of red blood cells) is a common adverse effect of testosterone administration, particularly with testosterone ester injections and periodic phlebotomy may be required.

1 Bhasin, Cunningham, Hayes (et al) 'Testosterone therapy in men with androgen deficiency syndromes: an Endocrine Society clinical practice guideline' (2010) 95 J Clin Endocrinol Metab 2536–2559.

19.168 When opiates are administered chronically, especially when they are administered continuously for relief of current pain, they often cause pronounced secondary hypogonadism. Opioid endocrinopathy can greatly affect patients causing reduced sexual function, decreased libido, infertility, mood disorders, osteoporosis and osteopenia. Although opioid endocrinopathy appears to be common, patients do not report their symptoms thus causing this adverse effect to go unnoticed without clinical monitoring, particularly in patients chronically taking the equivalent of more than 100mg of morphine daily. Diagnosing hypogonadism as opioid related can be challenging as other influences on endocrine function such as pathophysiology, co-morbidities, other drug therapies and patient age. Management options include discontinuing opioid therapy, reducing the opioid dose, switching to a different opioid and hormone supplementation. Studies suggest that administration of testosterone can induce a general improvement of the male chronic pain patients' quality of life and is an important clinical aspect of pain management[1].

1 Brennan 'The effects of opioid therapy on endocrine function' (2013) 126 American Journal of Medicine S12–18.

PRADER-WILLI SYNDROME

19.169 Prader-Willi syndrome (PWS) is the most common syndromic form of obesity, and is caused by the absence of expression of the paternally active genes on chromosome 15. The estimated incidence is around 1:30,000 with a population prevalence of approximately 1:50,000[1].

1 Goldstone, Holland, Hauffa (et al) 'Recommendations for the diagnosis and management of Prader Willi Syndrome (2008) 93 J Clin Endocrinol Metab 4183–4197.

19.170 Clinical manifestations of PWS include neonatal hypotonia as one of the hallmark features of this disorder leading to feeding difficulties. Genital hypoplasia including cryptorchidism and scrotal hypoplasia is a common clinical feature. In early childhood major motor milestones are delayed and children commonly manifest symptoms of hyperphagia with progressive development of obesity if access to food is unrestricted. Short stature is usually present during childhood and most patients fail to have a pubertal growth spurt as they are growth hormone deficient. Often secondary sexual characteristics are delayed or incomplete. Complications of obesity such as obstructive sleep apnoea and diabetes mellitus are common problems in adolescents and adults with PWS. A mild to moderate degree of cognitive impairment is a commonly associated characteristic although about 5 per cent of individuals with PWS will have intelligence quotients (IQs) in the low normal range.

19.171 Obesity results in insulin resistance which can manifest initially in impaired glucose tolerance and progress to type 2 diabetes mellitus. Type 2 diabetes has been reported in about 25 per cent of adults with PWS with a mean age of onset of 20 years. It is thus recommended that children and adolescents with PWS who have a body mass index more than the 95th centile should be screened for the development of type 2 diabetes by annual fasting blood glucose measurements.

19.172 Patients with PWS are known to have a high mortality rate. Obesity and its complications are factors contributing to increased mortality with death associated with obesity and its complications including cardiovascular problems, diabetes mellitus, sleep apnoea and hypertension. The cause of death in adults is circulatory or respiratory. The overall death rate in a PWS population is about 3 per cent a year comparing with an overall death rate of a population of England and Wales about 1 per cent per year and only about 0.13 per cent per year in those up to 55 years. There are no mortality data in PWS over the age of 50 years although it is estimated that the mean mortality rate is 7 per cent per year above 30 years. This is because of a failure to manage weight gain in later life and therefore prevent associated obesity related health problems. The specific medical disorders that account for a shortened life expectancy include type 2 diabetes (25 per cent), recurrent respiratory infections (50 per cent), high rates of fractures (29 per cent), leg ulceration (22 per cent of adults) and sleep disorders (20 per cent). It is hypothesised that a high pain threshold may result in the presence of some illnesses not being apparent. Cryptorchism (undescended or absent testes) is almost universal. Hypogonadism is therefore very common and contributes to the increased risk of osteoporosis and fractures.

CHAPTER 20

Neurology

Professor Martin M Brown

Professor Graham Venables

INTRODUCTION

20.1   The vulnerability of the nervous system to insults means that neurological impairments are frequently encountered in medico-legal practice. The brain is particularly liable to permanent damage even after transient insults. A cardiac arrest may be followed by recovery of cardiac function, but during the arrest blood flow and oxygen supply to the brain may be insufficient so that permanent brain damage results. Not infrequently, therefore, since the insult is via the cardiovascular or respiratory system the consequent neurological lesion is a result of a misadventure while the patient was under the care of a doctor other than a neurologist. Similarly, operations on the brain and spinal cord can easily result in brain or spinal cord damage from haemorrhage or the other complications of neurosurgery or orthopaedic spinal procedures. Such consequential damage is more frequent than that occurring from primary neurological disease. In addition, it should be noted that the symptoms of neurological disorders are often variable and provide considerable diagnostic difficulty to many clinicians. Patients with neurological symptoms commonly present to general practitioners or accident and emergency departments, leading to a risk of misdiagnosis, which can have serious consequences if they are not referred to a neurologist in good time. An analysis of claims involving the treatment of neurological disease recorded in the National Health Service (NHS) Litigation Authority Database, showed that diagnostic error and the consequences of procedures contributed to more than three quarters of claims against NHS Hospital Trusts (Table **20.1**)[1] and this number is likely to have risen in the last 10 years. This chapter concentrates on the clinical aspects of neurology disorders and practice relevant to these claims. Neurosurgical and paediatric neurological disorders are considered in more detail elsewhere.

The NHS Litigation Authority Annual Review 2013/14 showed that the number of claims arising from neurology comprised fewer than 2 per cent of clinical negligence claims received in 2013/14[2].

The value of claims arising from neurology by value was 2 per cent of clinical negligence claims received in 2013/14[3].

A retrospective analysis of successful neurology and neurosurgery claims over a 17-year period, occurring between 1995 and 2012, used the NHS Litigation Authority claims database. Four hundred and twenty-three claims were identified during the study period. 63.1 per cent of claims were due to negligence in neurosurgical care, whilst 36.9 per cent were due to negligence in neurological care. Payments were significantly higher in neurosurgery than in neurology cases. Diagnostic error was the most common cause of litigation. The disease categories with the highest numbers of successful litigation claims were spinal pathology, cerebrovascular disease including subarachnoid haemorrhage, intracranial tumours, hydrocephalus and neuropathy/neuromuscular disease[4].

Table 20.1 Neurological negligence claims in the NHS (559 cases analysed from 1995 to 2005).

Data extracted from McNeill, 2007[5]

The clinical error	Proportion
Diagnostic error (delayed or wrong diagnosis)	48 per cent
Improper performance of procedure (surgery or post-operative care)	28 per cent
Delayed performance of procedure (eg scan or transfer)	13 per cent
Inadequate informed consent (inadequate discussion of risks)	8 per cent
Drug error (failure to warn or recognise side effect)	7 per cent
The clinical problem	
Intervertebral disc disease	26 per cent
Central nervous system tumour	20 per cent
Central nervous system infection	11 per cent
Subarachnoid haemorrhage	8 per cent
Stroke	7 per cent
Epilepsy	7 per cent
Hydrocephalus	6 per cent
Subdural haematoma	3 per cent
Traumatic brain injury	2 per cent
Miscellaneous disorders (each <1 per cent)	10 per cent

1 McNeill 'Neurological negligence claims in the NHS from 1995 to 2005' (2007) 14 European Journal of Neurology 399–402.
2 NHS Litigation Authority Annual Review 2013/14, figure 16 at p 24.
3 NHS Litigation Authority Annual Review 2013/14, figure 17 at p 25.
4 NHS Litigation Authority Annual Review 2013/14, at p 47, citing 'A nationwide analysis of successful litigation claims in neurological practice' by Thomas Coysh and David P Breen, published in Journal of the Royal Society of Medicine, 2014.
5 McNeill 'Neurological negligence claims in the NHS from 1995 to 2005' (2007) 14 European Journal of Neurology 399–402.

20.2   The general practitioner (GP) is expected to refer almost all patients with serious neurological conditions to hospital for an opinion on diagnosis and management and an increasing number of claims are arising as a result of delays in referral (despite falling waiting times). The majority of medico-legal neurological cases involve hospital staff, except where the GP fails to recognise the importance of neurological symptoms, or makes a diagnosis of a benign neurological disorder rather than a more serious disorder. General practitioners may also be involved where there is a claim that they failed to adequately treat medical conditions, eg hypertension, that subsequently leads to stroke (see below). Since the last edition of this book, the number of neurologists has increased considerably and with it their role and geographical distribution. This has coincided with changes in the training curriculum for most non-neurological physicians with a reduction in their exposure to neurology. Many recently-appointed acute or general medical physicians have little or no training in this area, even though neurological disorders constitute 25 per cent of the acute medical intake in most district hospitals. Neurologists are therefore much more involved in both direct referrals from primary care and also the triage of acutely neurologically ill patients, than previously, and now see many of the patients previously managed by physicians alone. Despite this, armed with the membership of the Royal College of Physicians of the United Kingdom, indicating a level of knowledge of common neurological problems, the acute physician is still expected to manage the initial care of a patient with neurological disease. If in the judgment of the general physician more specialised help was required then the patient should be referred on to a neurologist. However, claims regularly arise because the physician has failed to seek neurological advice or has done so too late to influence the outcome. In this chapter, it is assumed that the patient is under the care of a neurologist or of a general physician who feels that further help from a neurologist is unnecessary.

20.3 In previous generations a large number of patients were managed by junior medical staff with little input from senior specialist staff. All acute admissions to hospital should be seen by a consultant within 24 hours of their admission and appropriate speciality advice sought. In an analysis of neurological malpractice claims in a North American centre, the authors considered that a failure of communication between the neurologist and the patient or other physicians (including the GP), contributed wholly or partly to 71 per cent of claims[1]. Inadequate supervision of junior staff was thought to have contributed in 25 per cent of the claims. The consultant has a responsibility to supervise junior staff closely and to impress upon them the importance of seeking help from more senior doctors whenever there is doubt about the diagnosis or management of a patient with neurological disease. Neurologists frequently receive referrals from other consultants, usually general physicians. The neurologist has a greater responsibility to ensure that his advice is correct in these circumstances, because the referring consultant has indicated his difficulty with the management of the particular patient. In these circumstances the neurologist should ensure that patients are fully investigated before transferring care back to the referring consultant. The consultant neurologist should ensure that he adequately supervises all junior staff and must be satisfied that the junior staff do not take responsibility for decisions for which the consultant should be responsible, and every patient should be discussed other than by trainees in their final year of training.

1 Glick, Cranberg, Hanscom, Sato 'Neurologic patient safety: An in-depth study of malpractice claims' (2005) 65 Neurology 1284–1286.

CONSENT

20.4 The details of the basis upon which consent is obtained are discussed elsewhere. Without doubt, lack of consent provides the basis for many civil actions. Historically a paternalistic approach has allowed the view that patients who are fully informed might refuse consent, but this view has been superseded by the need to respect patient autonomy for both diagnostic procedures and treatment of neurological conditions. Obtaining consent from patients with diseases of the brain and cranial nerves needs particular care because of issues around establishing competence. The Mental Capacity Act 2005 provides a basis for action when competence is impaired. For the medical practitioner the most important step is to ensure that consent is documented with the names of all concerned and any relevant witnesses. Whilst less relevant to neurological than neurosurgical practice, the House of Lords ruling in *Chester v Afshar*[1] has profound implications on consent for all medical practice.

1 *Chester v Afshar* [2004] UKHL 41, [2004] 1 AC 34.

HEAD INJURY

20.5   The management of the acute surgical aspects of head injury lies outside the scope of this chapter, but it is relevant to point out that good-quality initial management is important to avoid compounding brain damage from hypoxia (for example, from coma, impaired respiratory function). Few general physicians will encounter the effects of head injury but increasingly the management of the head injured patient will fall to the neurologist. Those treating patients with head injury should be aware of the National Institute for Health and Care Excellence (NICE) guidelines concerning the imaging and management of the head injured patient, and should take due note of the interplay between the organic and behavioural responses exhibited by patients with head injury. In particular clinicians should understand the hidden severity of head injury and its impact on daily life. Clinicians should also be aware of the potential for longer term consequences, including those due to the presence of chronic subdural haematoma and the impact of post traumatic epilepsy, dizziness, anosmia and substance abuse on activities of daily living.

CHRONIC NEUROLOGICAL CONDITIONS

20.6   Chronic neurological conditions which affect brain function and judgment can have medico-legal implications which occur independently of the conditions' immediate medical management. Areas that are affected include domestic law, for example, when a doctor may be asked to give an opinion in a divorce case concerning the difficulties the patient with a neurological disorder may have looking after a child without the help of a spouse. Issues around mental capacity not infrequently arise in people with long-term conditions such as multiple sclerosis, stroke or traumatic brain injury and the doctor may be asked whether the patient has capacity to manage their own affairs, consent to divorce or other legal proceedings, make a will or continue with their occupational or professional duties. Where the doctor is uncertain about the patient's capacity, or if the doctor's decision is likely to be challenged (eg by the patient, relatives, or in court), it may be helpful to ask a clinical psychologist to perform detailed psychometric testing as an objective measure of cognitive function. Doctors involved in this work should be able to demonstrate knowledge of the relevant law including the Human Rights Act 1998, the Mental Capacity Act 2005 and rulings such as *Masterman*[1]. Proper records should always be kept, not only to record the basis on which advice is given, but also to allow others to answer medico-legal queries and help the court to test a doctor's opinion.

1 *Masterman-Lister v Brutton & Co* [2002] EWCA Civ 1889, [2003] 3 All ER 162.

20.7 Much of the detail of the care of people with chronic or long-term neurological conditions has been defined in guidelines from NICE. These include guidelines for the management of people including those with multiple sclerosis, Parkinson's disease and epilepsy and also for imaging in people with brain and spinal trauma. Furthermore the 'National Service Frameworks for the Elderly and those with Long Term Neurological Conditions' and the National Strategy for Stroke lay down clear standards of care at both an organisational and clinical level. Clinicians involved in the care of people with these disorders should be familiar with these guidelines, since non-compliance will clearly leave the clinician at risk of being accused of breach of duty. Resource issues, eg restrictions on the use of certain, usually high-cost, drugs or access to specialised imaging, are a matter for those commissioning neurological services, but any unavailability, if clinically appropriate, should be clearly documented as a critical incident.

DRIVING

20.8 Neurological disorders frequently affect an individual's capacity to drive a motor vehicle from cognitive, visual or physical impairments or because of episodes of temporary loss of awareness. A doctor has a duty to inform a patient of the medical and medico-legal aspects of driving. On every driving licence there is an instruction, which on the modern licence reads:

'If you have a medical condition which has become worse since this licence/ counterpart was issued or you develop any new medical condition you must write and inform the Drivers Medical Branch, DVLA, Swansea SA99 1TU of the nature of your condition, as it may affect your fitness to drive'.

On the old UK driving licence, which is still in use, there is written:

'You are required by law to inform the DVLA Swansea SA99 1AT at once if you have any disability which is or may become likely to affect your fitness as a driver unless you do not expect it to last for more than three months'.

Another wording was:

'Drivers Medical Branch, Swansea SA99 1TU must be told at once if you now have any physical or mental disability or condition which affects your fitness as a driver or which might do so in the future (you need not tell the DVLA if the effect of the disability or condition is not expected to last more than three months) or you come to know in the future that you have such a disability or condition'.

All these forms of licence are currently in use. Although everyone is required to have signed their driving licence, many people have not read it or have forgotten what was written. The doctor has a duty to inform the patient that they should inform the Driver and Vehicle Licensing Agency (DVLA) about their medical condition, explaining that the statement they have signed is legally binding on them. The patient should also be advised to inform their insurance company of any serious condition that might affect their driving. Detailed information about current restrictions on driving in the UK can be obtained from https://www.gov.uk/browse/driving/disability-health-condition[1]. Where there is uncertainty about an individual's capacity to drive safely, they can be tested and receive advice at a Mobility Centre or Driving Assessment Centre.

1 For medical practitioners: At a glance guide to the current medical standards of fitness to drive, issued by Drivers Medical Group, DVLA, Swansea.

PROCEDURES IN NEUROLOGY

20.9 Modern imaging techniques dictate that most neurologists now request fewer invasive diagnostic procedures (investigative procedures that involve some degree of risk to the patient as a result of crossing skin into the body, eg catheter angiography) than in the past. The distinction between mildly invasive procedures and complex non-invasive procedures is not always clear. The medico-legal aspects of invasive neurodiagnostic tests are complex. Although more complex in the United States of America[1], the same principles apply here. Claims can arise if an invasive diagnostic procedure leads to complications without thorough previous investigation of the claimant, on the ground that the diagnosis could have been made by less invasive means, eg an MRI scan. It is therefore accepted that in general there should be close liaison between the neurologist and the neuroradiologist so that individual patients can be discussed, the most appropriate procedures performed, and the findings discussed in a multidisciplinary setting, eg involving experienced neurologists, neurosurgeons and neuroradiologists. Invasive procedures can also be therapeutic. Therapeutic procedures are performed because the procedure itself could help the patient and therefore the possible advantages can be judged against the potential risks. As the therapeutic procedures become more sophisticated, the neuroradiologist, who performs them, takes on increasing responsibility and ultimately it is the responsibility of the person who performs the procedure to obtain consent for that procedure, though this can be delegated to another trained individual. The neurologist, however, still has a duty to consider the advantages and disadvantages of the procedure and to discuss the situation with the patient and relatives where appropriate. Written material should also be available for all procedures.

1 Beresford 'Medicolegal aspects of neurodiagnostic tests' (1996) 14 Neurology Clinics 239–248.

20.10 Diagnostic procedures may confer no direct clinical benefit and therefore careful consideration of the risks is relatively more important. Any benefits to the patient are indirect and will only eventuate if the procedure reveals a disorder which can be treated subsequently. If no therapeutic procedure is contemplated then it is doubtful whether any high-risk diagnostic invasive procedure could be justified and, when deciding whether or not to do diagnostic invasive procedures, one should consider the later management of the condition including management if the result of the test was normal. The neurologist should consider whether the general condition of the patient warrants the discomfort and risks. Though modern imaging techniques are generally much safer than those previously undertaken, possible findings and subsequent treatments should be discussed with patients and carers and patient autonomy respected, provided sufficient information is given for the patient to make an informed decision.

20.11   Invasive diagnostic procedures are occasionally undertaken not because they could lead to treatment, but in order to confirm a diagnosis, give a prognosis and allow the patient or their carers to plan for the future more rationally. This may be particularly important in situations in which mental capacity might become impaired as the disease progresses.

20.12   Invasive diagnostic procedures in neurology are becoming safer, because techniques have improved, and less necessary, because non-invasive imaging has improved. Complications are likely to be less frequent in the future. Air encephalography and ventriculography are of historic interest only and have been replaced by computerised tomographic (CT) scanning and magnetic resonance imaging (MRI). Contrast myelography is now rarely performed and is usually undertaken in conjunction with CT imaging if there is a contraindication to the use of MRI. Medico-legal consequences of previously used contrast agents (eg Myodil) are still occasionally seen, though modern contrast materials are largely safe. Lumbar puncture to allow examination of the cerebrospinal fluid is frequently performed on patients with neurological disorders. Written consent should be obtained, since it is an invasive procedure, and the examination should routinely include the measurement of the cerebrospinal fluid pressure. Whilst initial discomfort, including low pressure headache, is not uncommon, long-term complications are rare[1].

1 Gelfand and Cook 'Streptococcal meningitis as a complication of diagnostic myelography: medicolegal aspects' (1996) 22 Clinical Infectious Diseases 130–132.

20.13   Screening with non-invasive technologies, including ultrasound and angiography utilising CT and MRI, has now become universal for patients with cerebrovascular disease, and this has reduced the need for invasive catheter angiography. Catheter angiography has become safer with the use of newer contrast materials and digital technologies, though contrast reactions can still occur and there remains a risk of causing stroke, eg in patients under investigation for high grade carotid stenosis. This risk of neurological sequelae in straightforward cases is around 1 in 500 patients, but it is higher if the patient's anatomy makes access to the site of interest difficult or the angiography is performed by an inexperienced radiologist.

20.14   Other imaging technologies such as single photon emission tomography (SPECT), functional MRI and positron emission tomography (PET) are specialist procedures which may assist in diagnosis or presurgical assessment, but are not universally available.

20.15   One of the few diagnostic tests regularly undertaken in the past by neurologists is the Tensilon test for myasthenia gravis in which a small dose of Tensilon® (edrophonium) is given. If the patient has myasthenia, the effects of the disease are temporarily reversed. Consent should be obtained for the procedure, which should only be undertaken in surroundings in which the cardiovascular complications (bradycardia or, rarely, cardiac arrest) can be managed safely. Nowadays, the diagnosis of myasthenia gravis is more commonly made using other investigations.

20.16 There are instances in which doctors have been accused of breach of duty by not arranging an investigation which is not easily available. It is the doctor's duty to decide if the investigation is indicated clinically, and if availability is in question the matter should be brought to the attention of the relevant manager. In the future it is more likely that a doctor will be accused of not having done a 'necessary' diagnostic procedure than that he will be accused of causing harm by performing an investigation – the reverse of what was happening in the past.

NEUROLOGICAL CONDITIONS

20.17 For most clinicians, be they neurologists or general physicians dealing with people with neurological diseases, patients do not come neatly packaged with a diagnosis. The remainder of this chapter is concerned with some of the difficulties encountered in practice with people with neurological presentations.

Coma

20.18 The neurologist will frequently be involved in the care of people in coma as a result of hypoxic ischaemic brain injury, metabolic disorder or traumatic brain injury and it is recommended that there should be a structured approach to recording their clinical status. From a medico-legal point of view the neurologist may be expected to offer a view about causation, condition and prognosis and should be familiar with neurological complications that are acquired in the context of critical care, including critical care neuropathy and myelopathy and the effects of drugs using a critical care setting. The neurologist may also be asked to confirm brain death or the presence of the vegetative state and should be familiar with the relevant up-to-date guidelines published by the Royal College of Physicians and NICE. There is increasing awareness not only of these conditions but also of minimally aware and locked in states, in which patients may have some cognitive abilities and in which they might be able to demonstrate sufficient capacity to make decisions for themselves. Attention is drawn to judgments about feeding[1].

1 *Bland v Airedale NHS Trust* [1993] AC 789, HL.

20.19 The prognosis for patients in coma of medical origin has been well described in a number of studies and those giving advice in this area should be familiar with them.

Behavioural and cognitive disorders

20.20 Behavioural disorders, eg disorientation, confusion, apathy and occasionally organic psychoses, are widely encountered in neurological practice as a consequence either of the disease or its treatment. The differential diagnosis of those presenting acutely is wide and their investigations should include simple measures to exclude metabolic disorders, eg hypoglycaemia, hypo- or hypercalcaemia, imaging to look for tumour, hydrocephalus or infections (including viral encephalitis), CSF examination and electroencephalography (to demonstrate subclinical status epilepticus). Less usual causes may include HIV infection, Creutzfeldt-Jakob disease, cerebral vasculitis and other autoimmune related inflammatory disorders, remote complications of previous infections, eg subacute sclerosing panencephalitis, and cancer. MRI is superior to CT in the diagnosis of many of these disorders and now is usually regarded as the modality of choice.

20.21   Drugs used in neurological practice can also affect behaviour. These include steroid-induced psychosis and alterations in mood induced by anti-epilepsy drugs including levetiracetam and topiramate. The reader is advised to consult the British National Formulary for the adverse effects of drugs and their interactions in specific cases. Excess alcohol and illicit drug use are common causes of behavioural disorders and impaired consciousness. Any patient in whom an alternative explanation is not immediately obvious should have a toxicology screen.

20.22   One of the most important and widely-missed causes of acute behavioural disturbance is Wernicke-Korsakoff syndrome, which results from a deficiency of vitamin B1 (thiamine). Patients usually have a history of alcohol abuse (which may be denied or not known about) with a confabulatory amnesia, a disorder of eye movement, ataxia and neuropathy. Treatment should be instituted immediately the condition is suspected before investigation, which is largely unhelpful in the condition, if impairments are to be reversed. Red cell transketolase levels may be low and imaging may show haemorrhage in the region of the mammillary bodies of the thalamus, but investigations are usually unhelpful. Delayed treatment invariably leads to persisting cognitive impairment.

20.23   All patients admitted to hospital with behavioural or cognitive disorders may present dangers to themselves, staff or other patients and require a risk assessment. Due account should be taken of their capacity to manage their own affairs, neurologists caring for them should be familiar with the relevant legislation including that concerning deprivation of liberty and will need to consider how to obtain appropriate advice on care from mental health services, including the legal mechanisms by which patients can be detained.

20.24   People with chronic behavioural or cognitive disorders present more frequently to mental health services but still require a formal diagnosis and risk assessment and present significant problems with regard to maintaining their own autonomy and capacity.

Falls and movement disorders

20.25   Patients may be subject to falls for a variety of reasons including epilepsy, disorders of cardiac and autonomic function, disorders of balance including cerebellar and vestibular function, disorders of postural control (eg Parkinson's disease) and the effects of prescribed drugs and alcohol. The neurologist needs to be aware of the large number of conditions that can cause falls and take a history and perform an examination that is appropriate. A drug history and collateral history from an observer is essential. The examination should include the measurement of lying and standing blood pressure and simple clinical tests of autonomic function. Investigations may include tests of autonomic function, prolonged electrocardiogram (ECG) recording as well as brain imaging, depending on what is found in the clinical assessment. Frequently care will involve other agencies including old age medicine and social services who may be required to make a risk assessment on the patient's suitability to remain at home. The clinician should be aware of the possible consequences of the fall, including traumatic brain injury and the development of subdural haematoma. A careful history from the patient and any witness is essential to narrow down the differential diagnosis. Investigations including ECG, electroencephalogram (EEG) and a brain scan may be required, but these are often normal.

20.26 Medico-legal consequences include those of missed or delayed diagnosis, especially when the cause is not neurological, eg they have a cardiac conduction disorder, or when the patient experiences the adverse effects of drugs, especially those affecting cognitive function or behaviour, about which they have not been warned.

Disorders of the senses

20.27 Disorders of the senses rarely cause medico-legal difficulties for neurologists. They may be required to comment on them in the course of the assessment of condition in head injury cases and should be aware of the early consequence of head injury in these areas and the prognosis for each of these symptoms.

20.28 Anosmia, paraosmia and parageusia are all seen after head injury and anosmia can be a consequence of drugs (penicillamine) or rarely compression of the olfactory tract by intracranial tumour (sub frontal meningioma).

20.29 Visual loss can occur acutely in optic neuritis and pituitary apoplexy or subacutely in compressive lesions of the optic chiasm and it is delayed diagnosis of these that causes most concern in medico-legal practice. A curious feature of visual loss resulting from any retro-orbital cause is that the patient may not be aware of the loss of visual field and they may present with other symptoms or a history of bumping into objects, which can lead to misdiagnosis. In extreme cases, a cortically blind patient may deny any difficulty with vision. All patients presenting with sudden visual loss should undergo an ophthalmic assessment and urgent imaging of the optic chiasm. Visual loss on one side of the visual field of both eyes (homonymous hemianopia) is caused by damage to the visual pathways on one side of the brain, most commonly as the result of a stroke. Atherosclerosis narrowing the carotid artery, which supplies the ophthalmic artery as well as the brain, can lead to unilateral visual loss or sudden unilateral blindness. Sudden visual loss is unusual in temporal arteritis in the absence of headache or other more classical symptoms but all patients should have ESR or CRP estimation and consideration of a temporal artery biopsy to exclude the diagnosis (see para **20.35**).

20.30 Disorders of eye movement including an acute painful third nerve palsy suggesting the presence of an unruptured posterior communicating artery aneurysm and that occurring in Wernicke's syndrome are described elsewhere in this chapter.

20.31 Disorders of balance and hearing can follow head injury and require formal assessment by a specialist in audiovestibular medicine. Acute balance or hearing loss is rarely a presenting feature of an acoustic neuroma, though all those with long-standing unilateral hearing loss should undergo imaging to exclude a lesion on the cerebellopontine angle.

Headache – acute/chronic

20.32 Headaches are very common and are rarely due to serious progressive disease, leading to complacency and the risk that the doctor may dismiss headaches as benign when they are actually a symptom of serious pathology. A careful medical, psychiatric and social history and neurological examination will make the management easier and reassure patients. The doctor's assessment is easier if abnormal physical signs are present and it is extremely rare for there to be significant structural disease of the nervous system in the absence of other neurological symptoms and physical signs. The length of the history of headaches of a similar nature is a helpful indicator and any patient who has been having similar headaches for several years without the development of any abnormal physical signs is unlikely to have serious progressive disease. Headaches of recent onset, or worsening, or those that have changed in character should be investigated more fully and given the availability of imaging, the threshold for requesting a brain scan should be low. There are four groups of patients who cause medico-legal concern: those with missed subarachnoid haemorrhage or meningitis; those with temporal arteritis; and those in whom there is a delayed diagnosis of a cerebral tumour.

Subarachnoid haemorrhage

20.33 The problem of missing a subarachnoid haemorrhage is unlikely to arise when it is of such severity that the patient has been admitted to hospital, because the history of a sudden severe generalised headache, as though the patient has been hit on the head, associated with neck stiffness on examination and sometimes vomiting, is characteristic. But if the initial haemorrhage is not severe or the patient did not seek immediate medical help and has some spontaneous improvement before he seeks help, the headache may not be prominent and the diagnosis is more difficult, especially if neck stiffness is absent or not examined. Whilst unusual, in mild cases the headache may diminish in an hour or two if the patient rests and therefore the cessation of a headache while a patient waits in an emergency department does not exclude a subarachnoid haemorrhage. Such headaches are known as 'sentinel' headaches, but commonly they are ignored by patients or doctors. Transient headache or neurological symptoms are not unusual and may be accompanied by nausea, visual disturbance due to a third nerve lesion, and transient motor or sensory symptoms. The commonest errors are attributing the symptoms to migraine or a viral infection. This can have serious consequences if the patient is discharged without further investigation because there is a high risk that the patient will bleed again with much more serious consequences. Whilst the authors do not advocate defensive medicine, a policy of investigating all patients who present with sudden onset headache with brain imaging by CT (with CT angiography if available) and CSF examination is of low morbidity and cost, and serves to exclude virtually all instances of subarachnoid haemorrhage. Occasionally, patients present with neurological symptoms without headache and diagnosis is then very difficult. It is important that lumbar puncture is performed more than 12 hours after onset, but within seven days or so, to be sure of detecting blood in the CSF. If the lumbar puncture is delayed, the CSF should be examined for the degradation products of blood (xanthochromia). A third of patients will succumb as a result of their initial subarachnoid haemorrhage and one third will rebleed within six to eight weeks of their initial presentation with a similar mortality rate if they are not treated appropriately. A high index of diagnostic suspicion is therefore required of all who see acute onset headache. Most subarachnoid haemorrhages are the result of bleeding from a ruptured cerebral aneurysm or arteriovenous malformation. It is therefore essential that all but the most moribund patients with subarachnoid haemorrhage are referred as an emergency to a neuroscience centre for further investigation (usually catheter based angiography) and treatment, eg coiling or clipping of the aneurysm.

Meningitis

20.34 Meningitis, when severe, is easy to diagnose, but in the early stages or in less virulent types it can be difficult. It is particularly hard to recognise in young children and babies. The cardinal symptoms and signs are vomiting, fever and neck stiffness and in meningococcal meningitis, a characteristic skin rash. It is not uncommon for a patient who presents with a mild headache to be reassured, and then to return hours or a day later with severe meningitis. The prognosis of bacterial meningitis is dependent on early treatment with antibiotics and therefore to miss early meningitis is serious. Untreated bacterial meningitis can be fatal or lead to permanent damage to the nervous system and special senses. Some types of viral meningitis are more benign. Therefore the doctor should consider meningitis even when the history is short. If he decides to do nothing, a careful follow-up is necessary. When in doubt, investigations are necessary and this will probably involve a lumbar puncture to look for organisms, so long as this is thought to be safe. Therefore, before doing a lumbar puncture the doctor should exclude raised intracranial pressure by CT or MR imaging. Tuberculous (TB) meningitis is more chronic and the symptoms less specific, and the diagnosis is therefore often delayed for some weeks. TB meningitis is slow to respond to treatment and resistant bacteria are common. Therefore, abnormal CSF should always be followed up with a second examination repeated until the CSF has returned to normal.

Temporal arteritis

20.35 Despite the well-recognised classical presentations of temporal arteritis (headache with scalp tenderness, jaw claudication) or polymyalgia rheumatica (stiffness and pain around the limb girdles) associated with elevated inflammatory markers, patients still fail to be diagnosed and lose vision as a consequence. All patients at risk of developing temporal arteritis, ie those with headache of recent onset above the age of 55, should have a blood test to measure the erythrocyte sedimentation rate (ESR) or c-reactive protein (CRP) level and, if there is a high index of suspicion, also undergo temporal artery biopsy. Early steroid treatment is essential to avoid loss of vision.

Brain tumour

20.36 The commonest medico-legal problem in this category results from delay in diagnosis; the subsequent management is rarely a problem. Early on brain tumour can be very difficult to diagnose and it may not be negligent to be unable to reach a diagnosis at the initial consultation. However, it is important to consider this diagnosis even if it is only a remote possibility, eg in the case of a patient with a single attack of epilepsy. Indications for considering brain imaging to exclude tumour include unexplained persistent headache of recent origin, focal neurological symptoms and new onset epilepsy. It would be unusual to fail to detect even a small tumour with MRI. Repeat scans may be necessary to decide if a lesion of uncertain pathology is growing, which would make a tumour more likely, but it is not easy to judge the best time for them. Tumours can sometimes be missed on CT and deterioration in the patient's condition is probably the most important indication to repeat previously normal CT imaging or to request an MRI, and it would be negligent not to investigate fully and more thoroughly any patient who was getting worse without a clear diagnosis.

20.37 Migraine, including thunderclap headache, causes a large proportion of severe headaches. Migraine headaches are characterised by unilateral or bilateral head pain of varying severity associated in severe attacks with nausea, vomiting and photophobia. In migraine with aura, the headache is preceded by focal neurological symptoms, typically a visual disturbance described as fortification spectra lasting 20–30 minutes. Occasionally, migraine aura occurs without headache and then the diagnosis can be difficult. Migraines tend to be recurrent and are not life-threatening but can cause severe disability. Individual migraine headaches very rarely last more than two or three days at the most and one of the commonest serious errors is to diagnose migraine in a patient who has more long-lasting headache. Because of the tendency of the headaches to recur over a long period of time it is important that a policy for the management is made and the medication monitored. If the drugs used cause unwanted effects they should, if possible, be avoided. Frequent use of analgesics can lead to persistent 'rebound' headaches and a vicious cycle of chronic analgesic abuse. Clinicians offering patients treatment with methysergide should be aware of the potential for pleural and retroperitoneal fibrosis and take the precautions set out in the British National Formulary. Simple reflex triggers for migraine should be elicited including those for benign sex headache, a cause of concern and one in which, at first presentation should arouse the suspicion of subarachnoid haemorrhage.

20.38 Patients with hydrocephalus and a ventricular shunt are at risk of developing blockage of the shunt leading to a rapid rise in the intracerebral pressure, causing blindness and other serious consequences. Any patient with a shunt who develops any new neurological symptoms, especially headache or drowsiness, should undergo urgent brain imaging and be referred to the unit normally looking after them or another specialist centre. Shunt infection should be suspected if the patient develops unexplained fever or chronic malaise.

SUDDEN LOSS OF CONSCIOUSNESS

20.39 The differential diagnosis of attacks in which consciousness or awareness is suddenly lost is extensive. The causes include: primarily neurological disease (eg epilepsy); cardiac disease (eg disorders of heart rhythm leading to brain hypoperfusion and a seizure); and much more rarely, hypoglycaemia from an insulin-secreting tumour of the pancreas. Non-epileptic attack disorder (pseudoseizures) accounts for up to a quarter of all attacks in which consciousness may appear to be lost and can cause considerable diagnostic uncertainty.

Epilepsy

20.40 The social and legal consequences of epilepsy are well known and, given the varied and sometimes non-specific phenomenology of seizures, it is surprising that the diagnosis does not lead to even more frequent medico-legal problems. Because of the varying manifestations of seizures, the neurologist needs to constantly consider the possibility that the symptoms which may suggest neurological disease could be evidence of cardiac, vascular, psychiatric or other disease. Similarly, the GP will need to consider the need to refer patients with suggestive symptoms to a neurologist.

Diagnosis

20.41 There is no difficulty in identifying a typical generalised convulsion, but the diagnosis of a single episode or a few episodes without obvious convulsive features can be difficult. Seizures need to be distinguished from other causes of loss of consciousness or changed awareness and from psychiatric disorders. Medico-legal practice abounds with claims of misdiagnosed epilepsy, many of which can be sustained because a systematic approach to diagnosis was not adopted. The clinician should first seek an accurate history not only from the patient but also any eye witness, including children, since the initial diagnosis rests on the clinical phenomenology of the attack. Once the description of the attack is clear, the clinician should consider whether there is a continuing tendency to seizures, ie does the patient have epilepsy. The neurologist cannot be expected to make a diagnosis if the evidence is inadequate but does have a duty to seek out the evidence and could be negligent if all the information which the patient can remember about the episode, including its immediate antecedents and subsequent situation, is not elicited. The doctor should never accept from the patient: 'I can remember nothing'. A careful history of what the patient remembers prior to the 'I can remember nothing' will often help to distinguish epilepsy from hysterical hyperventilation, syncope, or hypoglycaemia. If the patient's attacks continue, the patient should be told to write down what is remembered as soon as possible after the attack. After a generalised seizure, the patient may be amnesic for all of the ictus and sometimes for the post-ictal period of up to an hour or more, especially if they suffer from post-ictal confusion. It is important to take account of the fact that patients may not be aware of having had a seizure, especially when the seizure is the type known as a complex partial seizure (previously often referred to as temporal lobe epilepsy). It is therefore advisable to get a history from a witness if at all possible. It is important to stress to the patient that diagnosing an event which occurred in the past and which has left no obvious sequel depends to a major extent on the evidence that the patient produces. The doctor should explain that the doctor needs the help of the patient to discover that evidence. The neurologist could well be negligent if a diagnosis of epilepsy, which has important implications concerning driving and employment, is made without all clinical evidence, eg in people with micturition syncope, or without an ECG that could have revealed a cardiac arrhythmia.

20.42   Investigations for blackouts and other funny turns in themselves rarely confirm the phenomenology of the event, and may not be necessary if the cause is obvious from the history, eg syncope associated with an injection or other typical precipitant. However, investigations may provide supportive evidence for the diagnosis once a clinical description is available.

20.43   An ECG is essential in all patients who present with their first ever seizure looking for obvious rhythm or conduction abnormalities (including an abnormal PR or QT interval) and also left ventricular hypertrophy that could indicate the presence of hypertrophic obstructive cardiomyopathy.

20.44   The EEG is of limited value in the management of the patient with sudden loss of consciousness. An event captured during a recording may confirm or refute the diagnosis of both epileptic and non-epileptic attacks. However, minor non-specific lateralised or generalised changes with or without epileptiform features are of no diagnostic significance and should not be used to override clinical opinion about the event itself. A normal EEG during a major attack demonstrates that the attack during the EEG was not epileptic, but does not prove that all the previous attacks were not epileptic. Prolonged ambulatory EEGs with or without video monitoring may be helpful if the attacks are considered to be non-epileptic[1] or a patient is being considered for surgery in which case knowledge of the seizure source is essential. EEGs should normally be reported by a neurophysiologist, while the technical staff may provide a technical report describing the features of the recording, including any relevant observations concerning the patient's activity during the recording. Only those who can demonstrate appropriate training and competences should report EEGs.

1 Plesner, Munk-Andersen, Luhdorf 'Epileptic aphasia and dysphasia interpreted as endogenous depression' (1987) 76 Acta Neurologica Scandinavica 215–218.

20.45   An epileptic seizure is merely a symptom and not a diagnosis in itself. Brain imaging (the standard of care is now accepted to be MRI) is always required, other than in the idiopathic generalised epilepsies (ie those likely to be of genetic origin), to define any structural cause for the seizures. There remains a range of opinion about the frequency of follow up imaging should the initial scan be normal or a (radiologically) benign lesion be disclosed, but in most cases repeat brain imaging is only required if the patient's epilepsy increases in frequency or changes type without obvious explanation.

Management

20.46 The second commonest complaint by patients with epilepsy, after that of misdiagnosis, is that their epilepsy has been improperly managed. Side effects of the medications used to control epilepsy are also a common issue but rarely lead to medico-legal complaints, except in cases of fetal malformation or interaction with other medications. Unless there is significant structural abnormality within the brain, the vast majority of patients will respond to broad spectrum antiepilepsy drugs, but not all become symptom-free. No anti-epileptic treatment can be guaranteed to be 100 per cent successful and all have unwanted adverse effects. Compliance by the patient in taking his medication correctly may be poor and the neurologist has a duty not only to prescribe the treatment but also to monitor its effect and help the patient to achieve maximum benefit. Increasingly the monitoring of patients with epilepsy is undertaken by nurse practitioners with special expertise in epilepsy and it is the responsibility of the neurologist to ensure that practitioners providing this service are competent and are working to agreed protocols. Confusion may also arise when hospital doctors and the GP, independently and at different times, prescribe treatment; therefore arrangements about the transfer of care should be explicit and robust. All patients with epilepsy, unless in remission, should be under the care of an appropriately-trained specialist and followed up in accordance with NICE guidelines.

Anticonvulsant and other monitoring

20.47 Patients in whom seizures are well controlled and who are not experiencing adverse effects do not need routine monitoring other than that outlined in the British National Formulary and NICE guidelines. Patients whose seizures are not well controlled or who are experiencing adverse effects should be seen in a clinic that may be undertaken by a hospital or GP specialist who has appropriate competences to manage epilepsy.

Counselling

20.48 The management of the patient with epilepsy extends far beyond drug management and informing the patient of the diagnosis. Information should cover the following areas and be documented in the patient's notes.

Social and employment

20.49 Patients should be counselled about the stigmatisation associated with epilepsy and given advice about discrimination and the working environment when appropriate.

Prenatal counselling

20.50 Data from the Belfast Pregnancy register have confirmed the incidence of fetal malformations associated with the more commonly-used anti-epilepsy drugs. Sodium valproate and carbamazepine are the drugs most commonly associated with fetal malformation. Sodium valproate has also been shown to be associated with developmental delay in children born of mothers with epilepsy who were exposed to sodium valproate in utero. Lamotrigine is now accepted as being the drug of choice for most types of epilepsy in women of child-bearing years. Female patients should also be advised to take folic acid supplements if there is a possibility of their becoming pregnant. Clinicians and epilepsy specialist nurses should be aware of the potential risks of drug withdrawal, including the likelihood of seizure relapse and drug side effects when counselling patients considering changes to their medication. Any advice should be documented in detail rather than just noting that counselling had taken place and (with appropriate consent) patients' spouses/partners should be included in any discussion if drug changes are planned during pregnancy.

20.51 Some idiopathic epilepsy syndromes are under direct genetic control and in other patients genetically determined abnormalities of the brain are responsible for the seizures. Genetic counselling should be made available as recommended in the 'National Service Framework for Long Term Conditions'[1].

1 Longterm Conditions NSF Team. National Service Framework for Long Term Conditions. Department of Health, London, 2015.

Antiepilepsy drugs, interactions and contraceptives

20.52 Some anticonvulsant drugs, eg carbamazepine, increase the rate of metabolism of oestrogen and this can reduce the efficacy of the contraceptive pill. The patient should be advised about the increased risk of becoming pregnant while taking an oral contraceptive and told to get advice from the doctor supervising her contraceptive regime. This may mean taking a combined oral contraceptive containing a higher dose of oestrogen than present in the 'low dose' pill.

Other drugs have interactions with anticonvulsants and the doctor prescribing a drug should take a full drug history and check for possible drug interactions. Appendix 1 of the British National Formulary gives a list of those drugs of which the doctor should be aware. The possible unwanted effects of the drugs prescribed should be discussed with the patient and advice given about what to do if they occur.

Patients should be warned that drugs may cause drowsiness or decreased motor function which will necessitate extra care when doing things which could put them at risk.

With increasing travel, patients should also be made aware of possible interactions between antiepilepsy drugs, particularly sodium valproate, and certain antimalarial drugs, eg mefloquine. The latter may also worsen existing seizure disorders.

Driving and epilepsy

20.53   Patients who have had a seizure should not drive unless the DVLA, having considered the circumstances, grants a licence or allows a valid driving licence to continue. The medical rules published by the DVLA remain under review and the current restrictions can be accessed online[1]. EU harmonisation has not yet taken place and those driving within Europe should be made aware of this. The current wording adopted by the DVLA is:

'An applicant for a Group 1 licence who has suffered from epilepsy must satisfy the following conditions in order to obtain a licence: he shall have been free from any epileptic attack during the period of one year immediately preceding the date when the licence is granted; or (if not so free from attack) has had an epileptic attack whilst asleep more than three years before the date when the licence is granted and has had attacks only whilst asleep between the date of that attack and the date when the licence is granted, where the licensing authority is satisfied that the driving of a vehicle by him in accordance with the licence is not likely to be a source of danger to the public'.

A neurologist should be conversant with the current regulations, which are subject to amendment. The procedure for informing the DVLA should be followed even if the patient stops driving because the requirement to inform the DVLA is independent of whether the patient is actually driving. Should the medical practitioner be aware that the patient has not informed the DVLA and continues driving, the doctor continues to have a duty of confidentiality, but also has a duty to the patient to encourage and persuade them to comply with the law and document such advice both in the hospital notes and in writing to the general practitioner. The doctor can reinforce the advice by writing to the patient. There is no reason why a relative should not write to the DVLA telling them the patient has an illness that might affect driving. If one considers that the patient's behaviour is psychotic, a psychiatric referral is necessary. It has been argued by some that doctors have a duty to inform the authorities, especially when a PSV licence, train-driving or flying is concerned, but the correct action in individual cases can be difficult to decide. If doubt continues, the doctor could seek help from their medical defence society or employer. It is essential that the doctor reiterates the advice at every opportunity and records it each time. Only by doing this can the doctor justify their position if there is a subsequent accident with serious consequences.

1   https://www.gov.uk/government/organisations/driver-and-vehicle-licensing-agency.

WEAKNESS AND PARALYSIS

20.54   The neurologist will see a large number of patients with weakness or paralysis; many will have accompanying sensory symptoms, degrees of unsteadiness or sphincter disturbance. The causes of motor dysfunction are numerous and depend often on the site within the nervous system and time course over which damage has occurred. Within the central nervous system causes range from stroke, brain infections, tumour, degenerative brain or spinal disease and inflammatory disease. When the neuromuscular apparatus is affected the cause may lie within the muscles, the neuromuscular junction or the peripheral nervous system itself, ie a peripheral neuropathy or focal damage to individual peripheral nerves.

20.55   When the presentation suggests that the spinal cord is the site of the pathology, the differential diagnosis should always include compression of the spinal cord since it is usually the missed compressive pathology rather than any delay in diagnosing multiple sclerosis that leads to the legal claim.

20.56   The definitive investigation for people thought to have spinal cord disease is MRI, though myelography usually combined with CT scanning is still available for those who cannot tolerate MRI. Whilst in the past it might have been acceptable to delay making a diagnosis until such time as there were definite neurological impairments, attitudes have now changed because the available investigations have improved and therefore more evidence is available to confirm or cast doubt on the diagnosis of multiple sclerosis. Peripheral nerve and muscle disease requires expert investigation including electrophysiology studies and sometimes nerve or muscle biopsy.

Stroke

20.57   Until a few years ago, stroke received relatively little attention in the UK, despite the fact that it is the commonest cause of adult physical disability and the third commonest cause of mortality. Thus, patients with stroke were in the past routinely admitted under general physicians with little or no expertise in stroke care. Similarly, transient ischaemic attack (TIA) and minor stroke have in the past been managed by general practitioners without a referral to hospital. Much of this attitude to stroke reflected the belief that there was little that could be done to prevent or treat stroke. However, over the last few years, a number of clinical trials have convincingly shown the benefits of a range of stroke prevention measures, including treatment of hypertension, lowering of cholesterol with statin drugs, warfarin for atrial fibrillation, and antiplatelet agents eg aspirin, as well as adopting a healthy lifestyle. Similarly, trials have shown benefits of thrombolysis (clot-busting treatment) for acute ischaemic stroke in selected patients who can start treatment within 4.5 hours of onset, as well as benefits to all patients with stroke who are managed in an organised stroke unit including multidisciplinary medical, nursing and therapy input. Stroke has therefore become an area where it is accepted that all patients with suspected stroke should, at least initially, be managed by a team led by neurologists or physicians (often geriatricians) trained in stroke management ('stroke physicians').

20.58   The publication of the 'National Service Framework for the Elderly' in 2001, included a section on stroke, and has undoubtedly improved the provision of stroke units in the UK, but did nothing to improve the delivery of thrombolysis. The cost of stroke to the community, and the failure to deliver thrombolysis, was highlighted by a National Audit Office report to the government in 2005, and this stimulated the development of a National 'Stroke Strategy' by the Department of Health in 2007. The National 'Stroke Strategy' proposed clear guidelines for the management of stroke, which were echoed in NICE guidelines and in the National Clinical Guidelines for Stroke published by the Royal College of Physicians. One of the important issues addressed by the National 'Stroke Strategy' was the need for patients with acute stroke to reach hospital quickly and have the diagnosis established in time to receive thrombolysis. Similarly, patients with TIA need to be referred to hospital as an emergency, particularly those at high risk of recurrent stroke, for rapid investigation to exclude treatable causes of stroke recurrence, eg severe carotid stenosis which might require surgery or stenting to be urgently performed. Since then, all areas of the UK have set up improved acute stroke services and often daily TIA clinics. Stroke care in London was transformed in 2010 with the introduction of eight specialised hyperacute stroke units (HASUs). These serve a population of approximately 1 million in their respective segments of the city. The London Ambulance Service is mandated to take all patients with suspected stroke to one of the eight HASUs at any time of the day or night, bypassing the local accident and emergency department. The HASUs have been so successful in improving outcome and mortality from stroke, while saving costs, that it is likely the model will be followed in other large cities. In rural areas, because of the need to deliver thrombolysis as soon as possible, and the difficulty in transporting patients rapidly to a specialised centre, other methods of ensuring the patient gets appropriate input from a specialist service have been tried, including telemedicine. The publicity accompanying these changes, together with advertising campaigns sponsored by the Department of Health educating patients on the symptoms of stroke and the need to treat stroke as an emergency, has substantially increased the number of medico-legal claims, particularly those related to a delay in diagnosis and treatment or delivery of thrombolysis.

20.59   Intravenous thrombolysis is only suitable for about 15 per cent of all stroke patients and on average only between 1 in 2 and 1 in 20 benefit from thrombolysis in terms of improved outcome, depending mainly on when they are treated. However, all patients should benefit from being admitted to a specialised stroke unit, for example a HASU, for the first two or three days and then an acute stroke unit thereafter if they need continued rehabilitation. Nevertheless, it has to be accepted that the benefits in terms of better outcome are more difficult to quantify in an individual patient.

20.60   In addition to the changes in the provision of stroke services, there has also been a large investment in randomised trials of new treatments. One of the most promising is thrombus extraction for ischaemic stroke. This new technique is only suitable for patients with a thrombus occluding a major artery inside the skull and who can be treated within a few hours of onset. The technique involves threading a very small catheter up into the brain from the groin. The tube has a device on the end to extract the clot. The most promising devices are known as stent retrievers. Currently, this treatment is only available in a limited number of centres and has to be proven to work before it can be widely introduced. Other promising treatments for acute stroke undergoing investigation include hypothermia and stem cell transplants.

20.61   Any physician seeing a patient with stroke needs to be aware of the fact that stroke is not a diagnosis, but a syndrome of the sudden onset of focal neurological deficit, arbitrarily defined as persisting for more than 24 hours, that can be due to a variety of underlying vascular diseases. TIA is similarly defined but, by definition, the symptoms and signs last less than 24 hours, usually less than one hour. About 20 per cent of patients whose symptoms resolve within 24 hours have signs of acute cerebral infarction on MRI and many experts would therefore label such patients as having had a stroke rather than a TIA. However, in part because of the poor availability of MRI for stroke and TIA in many hospitals, this distinction has not been widely accepted in the UK. Nevertheless, all patients with TIA or stroke require investigations to establish the mechanisms of their symptoms and to determine whether there is significant brain damage. CT scan remains the mainstay of initial diagnosis and should be performed as soon as possible in all patients to distinguish between the two main pathologies causing stroke (intracerebral haemorrhage and cerebral infarction), and to exclude common stroke mimics such as a tumour or subdural haematoma, which may require surgery. Most hospitals have fairly easy access to CT and therefore the problems of missed diagnosis of a tumour or subdural haematoma mimicking stroke are no longer common. However, medico-legal issues more commonly arise when a CT scan is normal or misinterpreted. In such cases, an MRI scan should be requested, or the patient referred to a neurologist for a further opinion about the cause of their neurological symptoms. MRI is much more sensitive than CT to the changes of cerebral ischaemia, particularly when the problem affects the brainstem or cerebellum, causing symptoms such as dizziness, vertigo or unsteadiness, which may be misinterpreted by the unwary as having a benign cause related to the balance organs or alcohol toxicity, if the CT scan is normal. Some units routinely combine plain CT of the brain with CT angiography. This has the advantage that intracranial vessel occlusion, as well as disease narrowing or occluding the blood vessels supplying the brain from the heart upwards, can be readily and rapidly identified. The findings can assist diagnosis and also help to plan thrombolysis or invasive treatments, such as thrombus extraction.

20.62 Other investigations in stroke should be directed at elucidating the underlying cause. An ECG is required to exclude cardiac arrhythmias, particularly atrial fibrillation, that can lead to clots forming in the heart and embolising to the brain to cause stroke. Ideally, every patient should have echocardiography to exclude other causes of cardiac embolism, but the limited availability of echocardiography in the NHS means this test is not always performed, and important, but treatable, rare causes of stroke, such as an atrial myxoma or the effects of rheumatic heart disease, are missed. In younger patients, transoesophageal echocardiography is often performed to exclude a small patent foramen ovale (PFO). Although there is a lot of enthusiasm among cardiologists to close PFO in young patients with stroke, PFO is a common finding in normal young adults and the evidence that closure of PFO or anticoagulation is beneficial is controversial. The randomised trials that have been performed have failed to show much benefit from routinely closing PFO.

20.63 Imaging of the blood vessels supplying the brain, namely the carotid arteries if an ischaemic stroke is in the anterior part of the circulation, or the vertebral arteries if the stroke is in the posterior circulation, is important to exclude treatable narrowing, particularly atherosclerotic stenosis, and in younger patients, arterial dissection. Dissection is commonly associated with trauma, eg whiplash injury and therefore establishing the diagnosis can have implications for insurance claims. Routine blood tests are important to exclude common treatable conditions such as anaemia or diabetes, and rarer conditions such as polycythaemia or other abnormalities predisposing to hypercoagulability. Younger patients may also require tests to exclude treatable genetic causes of stroke, eg Fabry disease, but these would only usually be performed if there was a family history or other suggestive feature of the condition.

20.64   One of the commoner reasons for stroke to lead to a medico-legal claim is when the stroke has developed as a complication of some other procedure, eg catheter angiography, or a surgical procedure. Stroke is an accepted, but rare, complication of almost all forms of surgery, and can also complicate infections or care of patients who are very sick on intensive care units. It is often difficult to identify the mechanism by which stroke occurs in these situations. It can therefore be difficult to know whether the stroke was caused by the negligent performance of the procedure or would have occurred however well the procedure was performed. In such situations, the neurologist would rely very much on other experts to describe what was done in the procedure and whether there was evidence of anything untoward or out of the ordinary that might have injured an artery, if the procedure takes place in arteries supplying the brain, or that might have led to a general hypercoagulable state if the procedure was carried out outside the brain or blood vessels supplying the brain. A specific, but rare, complication of surgery, particularly orthopaedic operations on long bones, may need to be excluded, namely cerebral fat embolism. It is occasionally alleged that air embolism has caused stroke as a result of the inadvertent or inappropriate insertion or removal of catheters.

20.65   The commonest medico-legal issue in the treatment of acute stroke is the claim that thrombolysis should have been given or would have been given if the diagnosis had been made early enough. The indications for thrombolysis are limited and there are a number of strict contraindications. It has been shown that failure to observe these results in unacceptable rates of cerebral haemorrhage, which is the main side effect of thrombolysis. In experienced units, this complication still occurs in as many as 6 per cent of patients and can lead to the death of the patient. However, the trials showed that overall the mortality rate in patients receiving thrombolysis was not increased, implying that the treatment saves the same number of lives as the number lost from cerebral haemorrhage caused by the treatment, or alternatively, it only causes fatal cerebral haemorrhage in patients who would have died anyway. Nevertheless, it is important that thrombolysis is only given by a unit experienced in its use and by staff trained in stroke medicine and the selection of patients for thrombolysis. Analysis of the trials has shown that the benefit of thrombolysis rapidly declines over the course of time and by 4.5 hours after onset, there appears to be no significant improvement in outcome. Thus, the earlier the patient receives thrombolysis, the better. However, because of its hazards, the patient needs assessment in hospital by an expert stroke physician and requires a brain scan to exclude a cerebral haemorrhage, and other blood tests, before thrombolysis can be administered.

20.66   Allegations of mismanagement of stroke after the period in which thrombolysis could be given are less common. However, stroke may be complicated by the presence of pneumonia, cerebral oedema or pulmonary embolism, and occasionally medico-legal cases involve a claim that if these complications had been better managed, the patient's outcome would have been better. It is often difficult to substantiate such claims, mainly because the outcome of stroke is difficult to predict and extremely variable. Thus it is often difficult to know how the patient would have fared if the diagnosis had been made earlier, or the patient managed in a different manner.

20.67 Issues in the prevention of stroke more commonly lead to medico-legal issues than acute stroke treatment. Most cases in the past have involved the treatment of hypertension. The majority of patients with hypertension have no symptoms and the main reason for treating hypertension is to prevent stroke, as well as heart disease. Hypertension has often been present for many years before a patient has a stroke. There may therefore have been numerous opportunities for the patient's blood pressure to have been checked and treated in general practice. Most of these medico-legal allegations relate to the failure of GPs to adequately control the patient's hypertension before their stroke. The issue relates to the fact that the lower the patient's blood pressure, the less the chances of stroke occurring. A number of guidelines have been issued by organisations, including NICE and the British Hypertension Society, which set targets for treatment. However, such targets are often not achievable in practice, either because the patient develops side effects, not enough drugs are used, or commonly, because patient compliance is poor. The evidence also suggests that it may take a year or two to get the maximum benefit from antihypertensive treatment.

20.68 Increasing realisation by the public that stroke can be prevented after TIA or minor stroke has led to increasing number of claims related to delayed diagnosis or inadequate management of these patients. Studies in Oxford and in Paris have shown that the rate of recurrent stroke can be reduced dramatically by seeing a patient in a specialised TIA clinic within 24 hours of onset. It is not certain what measures are responsible for the benefit of rapid diagnosis and assessment, but it probably relates to a combination of the early prescription of antiplatelet agents, blood pressure lowering medications and statins to lower cholesterol, and perhaps also to other measures such as stopping smoking and relief of anxiety. General practitioners should therefore start patients on aspirin or an alternative antiplatelet agent immediately and refer the patient as an emergency to their local TIA clinic in order to prevent early stroke recurrence. Not all patients with a TIA have a high risk of recurrence and a number of scoring systems have been developed to identify those at highest risk. One in common use in the UK is known as the ABCD2 score[1] (Table 20.2). Patients with a high score of 4 or more should be seen either in hospital or in a rapid-access TIA clinic immediately and certainly within 24 hours. Patients with lower scores can be seen less urgently, but should be referred and seen within seven days of symptoms. However, these scores are not particularly reliable.

Table 20.2 Table used to calculate the ABCD^2 score from the history and clinical features of a transient ischaemic attack and the blood pressure at the time of examination of the patient. A score of 4 or more is considered indicative that the patient has a high risk of stroke in the next few days.

Age	60 years or older	1
	Less than 60 years	0
BP	Systolic ≥ 140 or diastolic ≥ 90	1
	Systolic < 140 and diastolic < 90	0
Clinical features	Unilateral weakness	2
	Speech disturbed without weakness	1
	Others	0
Duration	60 minutes or longer	2
	10–59 minutes	1
	< 10 minutes	0
Diabetes	Known diabetic	1
	Not known to be diabetic	0
Total ABCD^2 score (0 to 7)		

1 Johnston, Rothwell, Nguyen-Huynh, Giles, Elkins, Bernstein, Sidney 'Validation and refinement of scores to predict very early stroke risk after transient ischaemic attack' (2007) 369 Lancet 283–292.
2 Johnston, Nguyen-Huynh, Schwartz, Fuller, Josephson (et al). National Stroke Association guidelines for the management of transient ischaemic attacks (2006) 60 Ann Neurol 301–313.

20.69 Ideally all TIA and minor stroke patients should have an MRI when they attend the hospital or clinic because MRI is more sensitive to minor abnormalities than CT. However, in practice limited access to MRI means many patients only get CT. One particular condition that is associated with a high risk of stroke recurrence is severe carotid stenosis. All patients with appropriate symptoms in the carotid territory should therefore have some form of carotid imaging on the day they attend the hospital or TIA clinic to identify carotid stenosis. Randomised trials have shown that suitable patients with carotid stenosis benefit from carotid endarterectomy by an overall reduction in the risk of stroke even though the operation risks stroke or death at the time of surgery. Current NICE guidelines indicate that carotid surgery should be performed within 14 days of symptoms. However, it makes sense to operate as soon as possible, so long as the patient is stable, all the necessary investigations have been completed and there has been a discussion between the surgeon, stroke physican and radiologist to confirm the suitability of the patient and the stenosis for surgery. Stenting is an alternative to carotid endarterectomy which tends to be reserved for patients who are not suitable for surgery or for younger patients, because in older patients it carries a slightly higher risk of stroke at the time of the procedure than carotid endarterectomy.

20.70 Another common issue in stroke prevention is a failure to prescribe warfarin in patients with atrial fibrillation, or to adequately monitor the effect of warfarin in patients with atrial fibrillation by testing the international normalised ratio (INR) on regular blood tests. There is good evidence that warfarin prevents stroke in patients who have atrial fibrillation and other risk factors for stroke, but this evidence is often ignored by doctors, because warfarin is also known to be harmful and to cause cerebral haemorrhage and gastrointestinal haemorrhage in a significant proportion of patients, particularly those who are elderly. The balance of risk and benefit may therefore not be clear in individual patients, and it is important that all patients with atrial fibrillation are assessed for their risk factors, and a clear decision made as to whether warfarin or antiplatelet therapy alone is indicated to prevent thromboembolism. It is important to document that a discussion has been held with the patient and the risks and benefits described, and a decision made taking into account the patient's preferences and other circumstances. For example, a patient who falls regularly, or is unwilling to give up excess alcohol consumption, should not in most circumstances be given warfarin. New anticoagulants are being marketed as an alternative to warfarin for atrial fibrillation on the basis that they do not require monitoring and appear to have a lower risk of cerebral haemorrhage. At present the place of these anticoagulants is uncertain. Stroke physicians and neurologists prescribing anticoagulants will need to keep abreast of the latest NICE guidelines as well as policies in their own hospital.

20.71 Anticoagulation is also indicated in patients with cerebral venous thrombosis. This rare condition can present in a variety of ways, including with ischaemic, haemorrhagic infarction or frank cerebral haemorrhage. Trials have suggested that anticoagulation is safe in patients with haemorrhagic infarction, but when the haemorrhage is large, the decision whether to start anticoagulation or not is difficult.

20.72 It is often supposed that anticoagulants would be beneficial in other causes of ischaemic stroke, eg in patients with dissection and also in patients with progression or recurrence of stroke on antiplatelet agents. However, there is no evidence to support these suppositions and indeed the trials show that with the exception of patients with a cardiac source of embolus, anticoagulants are no better than aspirin at preventing stroke and have more dangerous side effects.

20.73 A list of medical issues encountered to date in the author's own series of patients with stroke is given in Table 20.3.

Table 20.3 Issues alleges to have caused or exacerbated stroke in the author's series of 152 adult cases assessed in 10 years between January 2004 and July 2014

Alleged problem	Per cent	Number of cases
Failure of diagnosis or treatment of medical condition	45 per cent	
Failure to diagnose and/or start treatment after stroke or TIA leading to recurrence[1]		37
Poor treatment of hypertension		10
Failure to treat other risk factors		1
Failure to diagnosis medical condition prior to presentation with stroke[2]		10

Failure to diagnose subarachnoid haemorrhage		6
Failure to anticoagulate dissection		3
Failure to anticoagulate atrial fibrillation		2
Inappropriate prescription or monitoring of drug therapy	10 per cent	
Failure to achieve adequate anticoagulation		11
Inappropriate prescription of OCP or HRT		3
Ovarian hyperstimulation syndrome		1
Invasive procedures	15 per cent	
Stroke post surgery[3]		16
Failure to recognise hypoxia after surgery		1
Stroke after inadvertent arterial catheterisation		4
Paradoxical air embolism during removal of venous catheter		1
Trauma	18 per cent	
Carotid or vertebral artery dissection after road traffic accident or other injury		9
Vertebral artery dissection associated with neck manipulation or other physical treatment		5
Stroke after accidental injury without alleged dissection		13
Failure to treat or poor care after diagnosis of stroke leading to death or exacerbating disability	10 per cent	
Failure to thrombolyse		9
Inadequate nursing care		3
Failure to provide adequate rehabilitation		1
Inadequate medical management post-stroke		2
Miscellaneous	3 per cent	
Two cases attributed to inadequate treatment of anaemia, one case attributed to transfusion of sickle cell disease, and one case attributed to stress at work		4

1 Includes two in whom the diagnosis of stroke was missed on CT.
2 Five with endocarditis, two polycythaemia, one leukaemia, one heart failure and one sepsis.
3 Includes two post-carotid endarterectomy and two post-cardiac surgery.

Multiple sclerosis

20.74   Following clinical assessment, investigations should include MRI and examination of the cerebrospinal fluid. Evoked potentials including visual, auditory and somatosensory evoked potentials may demonstrate delay in conduction times within specific pathways in the central nervous system and are of value in demonstrating disease at sites remote from those at which symptoms are occurring. Evoked potentials are less important now that MRI is used routinely. MRI scanning can show the lesions of demyelination within the brain and, to a lesser extent, the spinal cord. Multiple white matter lesions in a typical distribution on MRI, especially if they enhance following the injection of gadolinium, provides strong, but not unequivocal, evidence of multiple sclerosis. Repeating the MRI after a reasonable interval and assessing the changes may be helpful in cases of doubt and is required prior to the early introduction of the newer disease modifying therapies. Examination of the spinal fluid may show characteristic protein abnormalities, oligoclonal immunoglobulin bands, and an elevated white cell count, especially when the disease is active. The normality of investigations does not disprove multiple sclerosis or their presence prove that the patient's symptoms are due to multiple sclerosis. Multiple sclerosis is a relatively common condition and being chronic lasts for years and therefore it is possible for a patient to develop a second pathology.

20.75   Neurologists may be asked to give a view as to whether multiple sclerosis has been triggered by stress or proceeding trauma. Unfortunately, the cause of multiple sclerosis remains uncertain, and therefore patients may seek causes (or cure if they improve spontaneously) in recent events that are entirely coincidental. In the view of the writers there is little evidence epidemiologically to support the view that demyelinating disease is caused by stress or trauma, and neither would the evidence suggest that relapse is triggered by such events.

Spinal cord compression

20.76   Structural pathology around or within the spinal cord can cause paraplegia or tetraplegia. Most commonly this is due to degenerative disease of the spinal column ie spinal spondylosis and less usually to a spinal tumour or developmental abnormality causing external compression of the spinal cord. Intramedullary disease includes cavitation (syringomyelia), spinal tumour or, less commonly, arteriovenous abnormalities of the spinal cord; however, the latter usually cause symptoms through causing ischaemia of the spinal cord. Rarely, there may be an underlying infectious process whether tuberculous or pyogenic; diabetes is a risk factor for such infections. In medico-legal practice there is considerable debate as to the timing of investigations and when to refer for a surgical opinion and, if indicated, when to intervene surgically. A frequent allegation of breach of duty of care lies in delayed diagnosis. However, it is often more difficult to prove that the outcome in terms of any resulting neurological disability would have been better with earlier intervention, because, although it stands to reason that the early compression is relieved by surgery, there is little clinical evidence that supports early intervention. The more rapid the progression of symptoms, the more urgent the need for referral and consideration of surgery. However, pyogenic spinal epidural abscess is an indication for emergency surgical decompression. Sudden catastrophic onset of paraplegia implies either sudden vertebral collapse (eg from metastases in the spine) or an occlusion of one of the arteries (usually the anterior spinal artery) supplying the spinal cord. Such patients are unlikely to benefit from decompressive surgery. Spinal cord trauma is more often encountered by orthopaedic or general surgeons and displaced vertebral fractures are not uncommonly seen and missed in accident and emergency departments unless appropriate imaging is undertaken. This includes fractures of the odontoid peg and lower section of the spinal column and may lead to rapidly progressive disability especially if precautions to immobilise the neck are not taken in head injured patients. Non-traumatic pathology can progress slowly within the spinal canal with only minimal symptoms and perhaps no signs, until suddenly there is a rapid progression of the symptoms and signs with irreversible changes. A central disc prolapse may cause bladder symptoms and little else and delayed diagnosis is not infrequent. Whilst minor symptoms in the limbs, bowel or urinary systems can be due to spinal cord disease, it is impractical and unreasonable to investigate all minor symptoms which may present in the absence of abnormal clinical signs. However, advice to the patient and their GP should always include 'Come and see me again at once if the condition worsens or alters', to avoid a false sense of security. Bladder symptoms in the context of back pain should always be taken seriously and trigger urgent referral and imaging.

20.77 The investigations of suspected structural spinal cord disease are straightforward. Patients with pathology within the cervical spinal canal should undergo lateral flexion extension views of the cervical spine to confirm that there is no subluxation and then undergo MRI of the neck or, if they are unable to tolerate this, CT cervical myelography. Patients with lumbar spinal disease should undergo plain X-rays, bone scan and MRI. NICE has issued guidelines on imaging in head and cervical spine injury.

20.78 Disorders of the peripheral nervous system include peripheral neuropathies, myasthenia gravis and both congenital and acquired myopathies. These rarely lead to medico-legal claims except in the context of traumatic neuropathies and steroid-induced myopathy.

MEDICALLY UNEXPLAINED SYMPTOMS

20.79 There is no clear borderline between psychiatry and neurology and the neurologist may be referred patients who suffer from psychological or psychiatric disorders or other medically unexplained symptoms. Whilst neurological consultations and assessment are themselves psychotherapeutic and nothing further than reassurance needs to be done, there remain a large pool of patients in whom there is a psychodynamic explanation for their symptoms and the neurologist has as much a duty of care in this area as does any other clinician. In general terms the neurologist should be able to come to a conclusion about the origin of symptoms with a minimum of investigations and have sufficient insight to understand that symptoms may be medically unexplained or have their origin other than in classical neurological diseases.

However, more often the mechanism of medically unexplained illness is obscure. Sometimes it is obvious that the patient is malingering or seeking extra attention from their family or the medical practitioner, eg the patient with a gait disorder is seen to walk normally when they think they are not being watched. More commonly, there may be no obvious secondary gain in such patients, and a psychiatric opinion may reveal psychopathology, but often the psychiatrist will find no clear psychiatric illness. Nowhere is this more acute than in people with non-epileptic attack disorder where there may well be a history of childhood sexual abuse and it is incumbent on the investigating clinician to be aware of and identify this and then make the appropriate onward referral, either via the GP or directly to an appropriate expert. Patients should understand the reason for such a referral and give their consent to it to avoid misunderstanding, complaint or litigation. Patients who have 'functional' symptoms or signs mimicking organic disease of the nervous system are particularly challenging. They are often resistant to the suggestion that their symptoms are not caused by a physical illness.

20.80 Part of the neurological assessment of any patient should be an understanding of their mental state and its consequences, in particular their anxieties and any depressive features. There have been numerous instances in medico-legal practice where the contribution of depression in particular has been overlooked and the neurologist accused of breach of duty.

DRUG THERAPY

20.81 Since the last edition of this book there has been an outpouring of therapies for neurological diseases. In general, the clinician should keep abreast of these and be aware of the dose regimes, interactions and adverse effects, the majority of which are set out in the British National Formulary. There is ongoing debate as to when care involving these newer drugs can be transferred to the patient's GP and many areas will have their own advice about this. In general terms it is accepted that a clinician who advises the use of a medication has responsibility both to prescribe and monitor it, though shared care protocols may make transfer of this responsibility to primary care easier.

20.82 It is important to advise patients of the commoner side effects of drugs and also be aware that drugs prescribed by others may have a profound effect on the nervous system, these include psychotropic medications that may cause an extrapyramidal syndrome, and those that lower blood pressure, which may cause symptoms due to brain or spinal cord ischaemia. If the patient cannot be precise, the doctor may need to pursue the matter with other doctors and ask the patient to bring all medications at the next consultation.

CHAPTER 21

Oncology

Professor Martin Gore

Dr Michael Davidson

Dr Aisha Miah

INTRODUCTION

21.1   The speciality of oncology encompasses the screening, diagnosis and treatment of all human cancers. Cancer can present in any age group and arise from almost any tissue of the body, with treatments and outcomes that vary widely between different tumour types. Its management involves oncologists, who specialise in the delivery of anti-cancer medicines and radiotherapy, as well as many other specialist doctors, surgeons and allied healthcare professionals. This chapter gives an overview of the epidemiology, biological underpinnings and treatment of cancer, and how oncology services are instituted and delivered in the UK.

21.2   There has historically been a tendency in oncology to treat these many and varied human cancers as separate, if overlapping, disease processes, each with their own unique treatment pathways and outcomes. More recently, work has been done towards rationalising the study of cancer by outlining at a very fundamental level the hallmarks that a cell must possess to be defined as cancerous[1]. These basic properties of all cancer cells are that they:

- stimulate their own growth;
- are insensitive to inhibitory signals that might impair their growth;
- evade their own programmed cell death (apoptosis);
- have limitless replicative potential;
- stimulate the growth of their own blood vessels (angiogenesis); and
- invade local tissues and spread to distant sites (metastasis).

1 Hanahan, Weinberg 'The hallmarks of cancer' (2000) 100(1) Cell 57–70.

21.3   Thus cancer cells can be thought of as cells which have evaded the body's normal control mechanisms for growth, reproduction and spread. In order for a normal cell to undergo this change the genes which regulate these processes must be altered. Broadly, these genetic alterations can occur in two distinct ways. *Oncogenes* are genes which promote cell growth and reproduction, whilst *tumour suppressor genes* are those which inhibit cell division and survival. Malignant transformation can occur through the over-expression of existing oncogenes, the formation of new oncogenes, or by the disabling of tumour suppressor genes. It has been found that changes in many such genes are required to transform a normal cell into a cancer cell, known as the *multiple-hit hypothesis*. These genetic changes can come about through sporadic mutations arising from errors in the normal division of cells or through external factors which introduce errors into the process of cell replication. Such genetic errors are self-amplifying and compounding, as the original error will drive a cell to ever faster and more unstable division, increasing the likelihood of further genetic abnormalities and thus allowing the cell to escape the controls that limit normal growth and regulation.

21.4   Cancer is primarily an environmental disease, with the majority of cases attributable to external factors which cause or predispose to these harmful genetic mutations. Common environmental factors that contribute to cancer include tobacco, alcohol, diet, obesity, sunlight, and environmental and occupational pollutants. Traditional non-surgical management of cancer has involved the directly cytotoxic, or cell killing, modalities of chemotherapy and radiotherapy. As understanding of the more fundamental changes which drive cancers at a cellular level has improved, a newer generation of 'targeted' therapies has been developed, directed at specific genetically-altered pathways in individual cancers.

21.5   Greater understanding of the causes and biological underpinnings of cancer, and advances in diagnosis and treatment, have led to improvements in global survival rates, however the overall incidence of cancer continues to rise, a trend particularly marked in the developed world. Cancer is now the leading single-disease cause of death in the UK[1], responsible for more than one in four deaths, and survival rates here have traditionally lagged behind equivalent western European countries. The largest ever population-based study of European cancer survival recently showed that the UK and Ireland have lower than average survival rates for many cancers, particularly of the colon, ovary, kidney, stomach and lung[2]. The reasons for this are undoubtedly complex and multi-factorial, but are likely to be related to problems around delayed diagnosis and relative underuse and unequal access to modern effective treatments. Patient and lifestyle factors such as levels of smoking, alcohol consumption and poor diet were not accounted for in the above study, and almost certainly also contribute to the UK's relatively poor outcomes. There is a pronounced social gradient to cancer outcomes, with cancer mortality rates for the most deprived fifth of neighbourhoods in England over one and a half times the rate in the most affluent fifth[3].

1 Cancer Stats: Cancer statistics for the UK. Cancer Research UK. Available from: http://www.cancerresearchuk.org/cancer-info/cancerstats/.
2 De Angelis, Sant, Coleman, Francisci, Baili, Pierannunzio (et al) 'Cancer survival in Europe 1999-2007 by country and age: results of EUROCARE--5-a population-based study' (2014) 15(1) The Lancet Oncology 23–34.
3 Improving Outcomes: A Strategy for Cancer. Third Annual Report. Available from: https://http://www.gov.uk/government/uploads/system/uploads/attachment_data/file/264511/IOSC_3rd_Annual_Report_-_Proof_version_-_9_December_2013_v2.pdf.

STRUCTURE OF CANCER SERVICES IN THE UK

21.6   In the 1990s, following the Calman-Hine report[1], there was a move to reorganise cancer services in the UK based on geography and specialisation by cancer type and treatment modality. The NHS Cancer Plan followed in 2000 with the aim of eliminating inequalities of cancer care and the system we have today evolved. Multi-disciplinary teams are mandated and these consist of multi-professional specialists in a particular cancer type and treatment modality. Services are organised in a 'hub and spoke' manner, with cancer centres serving populations of approximately two million, treating patients with less common tumours and delivering more complex treatments. Cancer units are based in local Acute Trusts and are responsible for timely diagnosis and the treatment of those with common tumours.

1 A policy framework for commissioning cancer services: A report by the Expert Advisory Group on Cancer to the Chief Medical Officers of England and Wales (Department of Health and Welsh Office, 1995).

21.7   The Department of Health started a series of reviews of individual cancers in 1998 called 'Improving Outcomes Guidance'. These published reviews set out the requirements for the membership of the multi-disciplinary team and how patients should be treated. This function is now a responsibility of the National Institute for Health and Clinical Excellence, NICE.

21.8   The aim of the cancer services structure as described above is to reduce questionable practices and to drive up the quality of care by the implementation of evidence-based decisions. Multi-disciplinary meetings take place weekly in cancer centres and units. They are audited for attendance as well as the information gathered and the consensus opinions reached. The doctors and nurses who are looking after a particular patient will then discuss the team's view and any suggested treatment options.

21.9   Patients have 'the right to make choices about the services commissioned by NHS bodies and to information to support these choices'[1]. This is often interpreted as a 'right' to a second opinion. The issue of a patient's right to this is one that rests with the commissioners of healthcare rather than the providers of healthcare. The former are responsible for providing a process by which a second opinion can be obtained. Attendance at cancer services under the two-week waiting time rule, whereby any patient suspected of cancer must be seen and investigated within two weeks of the referral being received, is exempt from this second opinion 'right'.

1 The NHS Constitution for England 2013. Available from: http://www.nhs.uk/choiceintheNHS/ Rightsandpledges/NHSConstitution/Pages/Yourrightstochoice.aspx.

21.10   Internationally, it is recognised that cancer services are well organised in the UK and yet, as highlighted previously, cancer survival still lags behind that seen in other parts of western Europe. There is increasing attention being paid to whole pathway redesign because the fragmentation of diagnostic and treatment provision that sometimes occurs is seen to be a major issue in relation to poor patient experience and outcome.

SCREENING

21.11   Early diagnosis is key to improving cancer outcomes. If the disease can be identified at an early, localised stage, curative treatments are often much more likely to be successful. Therefore the aim of cancer screening is to detect a cancer after it has developed, but before it has manifested any physical symptoms. There are numerous requirements that must be met for this to be possible, and as a result relatively few tumour types are amenable to large-scale screening programmes. Mass screening should only be offered in those cancers where there is an effective early treatment available, and where intervening at an early stage has definite benefit in terms of improving outcome. The screening test being used must be safe, cost effective and easy to utilise on a large number of people, with a high chance of correctly identifying the cancer in those patients where it is present. Equally, there has to be a low chance of falsely identifying cancer in healthy patients.

21.12   In the UK there are currently three active cancer screening programmes. The largest and most well known is the NHS National Breast Cancer Screening programme which provides screening every three years for all women aged 50 and over. Currently, women aged between 50 and 70 are invited routinely and those over the age of 70 by request. The NHS

Cervical Screening programme offers all women aged between 25 and 49 cervical screening every three years, and women aged 50 to 64 screening every five years. This also incorporates testing for human papilloma virus (HPV), a common and treatable sexually transmitted virus that increases the risk of cervical cancer. The NHS Bowel Cancer Screening programme is one of the first national bowel screening programmes in the world and the first cancer screening programme in the UK for both men and women. Those aged 60 to 74 are sent a self-testing kit (faecal occult blood, or FOB, test) every two years. It is planned to expand FOB testing to the age of 55 by 2016. Certain cancers are inherited along genetic lines, and in specific cases such as a strong family history or an atypical development of one or more cancers at a young age, an individual will be referred for genetic testing and counselling. This is decided on a case-by-case basis by clinicians, and there are no population-based genetic screening programmes currently in use.

21.13 Although the above initiatives have impacted positively on overall outcomes, there are some frequently raised concerns about screening programmes. It is possible to have 'false-positive' screening results, whereby a screening test is suspicious for a malignancy but subsequent biopsy is non-cancerous. This has the potential to cause not only significant psychological distress, but exposes patients to risks associated with an invasive biopsy. With increasing refinement of screening tests this is relatively uncommon, with the latest figures from the NHS Breast Cancer Screening Programme from 2013–14 showing that of just over two million women screened 4.3 per cent were brought back for further biopsy, and of this group invasive cancer was identified in just under half[1]. A more widely-recognised problem is that of over-diagnosis, defined as a cancer identified by screening that would not otherwise have been detected or caused a significant problem during the patient's lifetime. In 2012 the Independent Breast Screening Review looked into the overall benefits and risks of the screening programme[2]. It concluded that breast screening in the UK saves 1,300 lives a year and should continue, but that there are on-going issues with over-diagnosis and over-treatment in a significant minority of patients, with over-diagnosis estimated in around 11 per cent of the cancers identified.

1 Breast Screening Programme, England. Statistics 2013–14. Health and Social Care Information Centre. Available from: http://www.hscic.gov.uk/catalogue/PUB16803/bre-scre-prog-eng-2013-14-rep.pdf.
2 The Benefits and Harms of Breast Cancer Screening: an independent review jointly commissioned by cancer research UK and the department of health, 2012.

DIAGNOSIS

21.14 Most cancers are not picked up through mass screening programmes, but through the manifestation of physical signs and symptoms. Given that almost all systems and organs of the body can be affected, the disease can present in equally varied ways. The majority of new cancer patients in the UK will initially present to their GP with a novel or persistent physical symptom. There are certain red flag signs and symptoms encompassing the main presenting features of the commonest cancers which, when seen by a GP, should prompt referral to a specialist. Examples of these include a persistent cough in a smoker raising the possibility of a lung cancer, or an alteration in bowel habit suggesting a gastro-intestinal cancer. NICE have published comprehensive guidance on red flag symptoms and what is expected of GPs when they are encountered[1]. Often a GP will carry out basic diagnostic tests, such as an X-ray or blood test, however if cancer is suspected these should not delay an urgent referral being made to the appropriate local hospital specialist.

1 Referral for suspected cancer NICE guideline CG27 (2005). Available from: http://guidance. nice.org.uk/CG27.

21.15   The current national target is that all patients referred with suspected cancer should have a maximum wait of two weeks before they are seen. The specialist referred to will depend upon the type of cancer suspected, with the referral going to a consultant physician or surgeon who specialises in that branch of medicine. So, for example, suspected lung cancer cases will go to a consultant respiratory physician, whilst suspected bowel and breast cancer cases will go to the local gastrointestinal or breast surgical team. Every area should have in place clear referral pathways, and often there are specialist clinics dedicated to seeing suspected cancer cases and ensuring diagnostic tests are performed in a timely manner. It is then the role of the specialist to perform appropriate investigations to confirm the diagnosis and establish the extent, or stage, of the cancer.

21.16   Fundamental to this is the obtaining of a specimen of cancer tissue for laboratory analysis. Not only will this confirm the diagnosis, but increasingly genetic abnormalities within certain cancers will be looked for at this point, often guiding future treatment options. The type of diagnostic test employed will be dictated by the type of cancer suspected, however it will often consist of an endoscopic test such as bronchoscopy to the airways of the lung or colonoscopy to the bowel, as these allow doctors to directly visualise the cancer as well as obtain specimens. Most cancers are then staged using variations of the tumour, node, metastases (TNM) staging system. Radiological imaging, usually with computed tomography (CT) scanning, will ascertain the size of the primary tumour, and evidence of spread to lymph nodes and surrounding structures in the body. Accurate staging is vital, as it has a profound impact upon the goals and outcomes of anti-cancer treatment.

21.17   Cancer patients should wait no more than 31 days from the decision to treat to the start of their first treatment, and there should be no more than a 62-day wait from any urgent GP referral to the commencement of treatment. This 62-day standard also includes all patients referred from NHS cancer screening programmes. The right to see a specialist within two weeks for a suspected cancer diagnosis, as well as to commence treatment within established time frames, has been formalised in the NHS Constitution[1], a document released by the Department of Health (DOH) in 2013 which sets out explicitly the obligations and rights of patients and staff within the NHS, many of which are legally enforceable. Waiting times are monitored by the NHS auditing committee and trusts face financial penalties if these are not met. Generally the NHS performs well, with 95.2 per cent of cancer referrals meeting the two-week wait target and 86.7 per cent of treatments meeting the 62-day target from GP referral to commencement of treatment[2].

1 TheNHSConstitutionforEngland2013.Availablefrom:http://www.nhs.uk/choiceintheNHS/
Rightsandpledges/NHSConstitution/Pages/Yourrightstochoice.aspx.
2 NHS England, Cancer Waiting Times 2014. Available from: http://www.england.nhs.uk/
statistics/statistical-work-areas/cancer-waiting-times/.

21.18   Because early detection and prompt treatment of cancer is so vital, perceived or actual delays in diagnosis of cancer or commencement of treatment make up a significant proportion of complaints with respect to oncology treatment. A common issue is that of multiple visits to a GP before a diagnosis of cancer is made or an appropriate referral undertaken. To put this into context, most GPs will see only around eight or nine new patients with cancer each year[1]. However, they see many more patients presenting with symptoms that could potentially be cancer, but are also the symptoms of many other diseases as well. Therefore it is often not a straightforward decision to refer patients to secondary care for further investigation. It has been suggested that part of the problem in delayed diagnosis may be the relatively prominent role that the GP plays in the UK healthcare system. In many other countries 'generalists' play a less central role in healthcare delivery, with those experiencing a health problem directly attending a specialist in that area with access to more advanced diagnostic tests, rather than requiring a GP to act as a gatekeeper for referral.

1 Improving Outcomes: a Strategy for Cancer 2011. Available from: https://http://www.gov.
uk/government/uploads/system/uploads/attachment_data/file/213785/dh_123394.pdf.

21.19   The Department of Health have recognised this problem, and in their 'Improving Outcomes: a Strategy for Cancer' 2011 guidance[1] mandated that GPs have access to specialised tests in patients for whom the two-week urgent referral pathway is not appropriate, but whose symptoms require further investigation. These include chest X-rays to aid in the diagnosis of lung cancer; ultrasound in ovarian and other abdomino-pelvic cancers; flexible-sigmoidoscopy and colonoscopy in bowel cancer; and magnetic resonance imaging (MRI) in brain cancer. It is hoped that measures such as this will improve and expedite cancer diagnosis in the UK, however delayed diagnosis remains a significant problem. In May 2013 the National Cancer Intelligence Network produced data looking at the proportion of cancer patients in the UK presenting via an emergency route, showing that 24 per cent of newly-diagnosed cancers first present to secondary care as an emergency, either through the emergency department or via unplanned hospital admissions[2]. It has been shown that emergency admissions for cancer present at a more advanced stage and have poorer overall survival than those diagnosed via screening or primary care[3].

1 Improving Outcomes: a Strategy for Cancer 2011. Available from: https://http://www.gov.
uk/government/uploads/system/uploads/attachment_data/file/213785/dh_123394.pdf.
2 Routes to Diagnosis: Exploring Emergency Presentations 2013. Available from: http://
www.ncin.org.uk/publications/data_briefings/routes_to_diagnosis_exploring_emergency_
presentations.
3 McPhail, Elliss-Brookes, Shelton, Ives, Greenslade, Vernon (et al) 'Emergency presentation of
cancer and short-term mortality' (2013) 109(8) British Journal of Cancer 2027–2034.

21.20   Perhaps the most important single generic issue in clinical negligence in the field of oncology concerns the issue of causation in negligently missed cancer or negligently delayed diagnosis cases. As mentioned, the burden of diagnosing new cancer cases in the UK primarily falls on GPs; however this issue also affects a wide range of specialist doctors and surgeons to whom patients are referred for their 'diagnostic work-up'. It is less of an issue for oncologists, as by the time a patient reaches them the diagnosis of cancer will already have been established.

21.21   Negligence is defined as a breach of duty causing injury, ie did the actions of the doctor result in a worse outcome for the patient (*not* was there a lost chance of a better outcome)? When considering negligence in the context of possible delays in cancer diagnosis there are two components which need to be considered: what happened historically and what would have happened but for the breach of duty. The 'worse outcome' in missed or delayed cancer diagnosis cases can be evaluated by addressing whether the delay had a negative impact upon either prognosis or morbidity. Thus it needs to be decided whether, on the balance of probabilities, the cancer would have been completely cured if it had been diagnosed at an earlier time-point, or, if not curable, did the delay then cause a reduction in life expectation? Also, if the delay led to the cancer being diagnosed at a more advanced time-point with a heavier symptom burden and requirement for more intensive treatments, what additional pain, suffering and loss of amenity was potentially caused?

21.22   Given the complex multi-disciplinary approach required for cancer diagnosis, delays in diagnosis are almost always present to a certain degree, and a sizable proportion of cancers are incurable at the time of diagnosis. Unless detected by screening or incidentally at an early stage, by the time cancers are advanced enough to cause significant symptoms the chance of cure will often be low due to local or metastatic spread rendering them unsuitable for radical curative treatments. Thus it is unusual for a delay in diagnosis to be responsible for rendering a curable cancer absolutely incurable. Although waiting times for referrals and diagnostic tests are understandably acutely felt by patients, the days to weeks that this takes will often be insignificant to the overall clinical outcome, as the cancer will have been growing undetected for many months or even years prior to this. It should be borne in mind that different cancers have different rates of growth and tendencies towards early or late metastatic spread, and robust proof of harm or lack thereof due to a delayed diagnosis is often difficult to define objectively. Loss of life expectation and physical or psychological distress due to delayed diagnosis can be equally difficult to quantify. If a delay has led to a cancer being diagnosed at a more advanced stage, a cure may never have been possible, but the patient may be more symptomatically deteriorated and less able to tolerate aggressive palliative or life-extending treatments. These evaluations will depend upon the individual circumstances of each case, and need to take into account a detailed analysis of the complete diagnostic process, as well as the type and stage of cancer at the time of eventual diagnosis.

21.23   Where there have been repeat visits to a medical practitioner with a persistent or evolving symptom, and there is documented evidence that the symptom has been overlooked or appropriate investigations have not been requested, then there is a more definite case to be made for negligence on the part of the clinician involved. As mentioned before, many cancer symptoms are insidious and shared with myriad other conditions. The NICE guidance on 'red flag' symptoms and cancer diagnostic pathways for GPs and other healthcare professionals has gone some way towards rationalising the process, and this gives objective clinical standards of care that should be met when looking at such cases of delayed or missed diagnosis.

TREATMENT DECISION MAKING

21.24   Once a definitive diagnosis has been made and the cancer has been adequately staged, a decision will be undertaken to commence treatment. The modalities of cancer treatment are varied and incorporate a wide range of medical, radiographic and surgical interventions. Broadly speaking, treatments can be split up into two main approaches, radical or palliative. Radical treatment is undertaken with the aim of removing all cancerous cells from the body – both what is visible on scanning and any residual microscopic disease – with the intent to cure the patient. Palliative treatment is intended to control the cancer and to slow down or arrest its natural progression when a radical approach is not possible. Generally radical treatment can only be offered in early stage cancers, before it has spread to surrounding tissues or organs of the body, whereas palliative treatment is offered for cancers at an advanced or metastatic stage.

21.25   The main forms of radical treatment are surgical resection or radical radiotherapy, often combined with synchronous chemotherapy. However some forms of blood and immune system cancers can be cured with chemotherapy alone. Radical treatments can be further sub-divided into neo-adjuvant or adjuvant. Neo-adjuvant treatment is the administration of treatment with chemotherapy and/or radiotherapy to shrink the cancer prior to definitive surgical resection. This is done both to improve surgical outcomes and decrease the chance of future relapse. Adjuvant treatment is the administration of chemotherapy and/or radiotherapy after surgical resection, again with the aim of decreasing the chance of future relapse. These approaches of adjunctive medical treatment combined with surgery are commonly used in bowel and breast cancers.

MULTI-DISCIPLINARY TEAMS

21.26   It is now standard practice for all new cancer cases in the UK to be discussed at a multi-disciplinary team (MDT) meeting specialising in that specific tumour type. NICE has issued guidance on the composition of MDTs for the major cancers, defining core and extended members and most MDTs as a minimum will include a surgeon, radiologist, pathologist, oncologist, and clinical nurse specialist. However many will also incorporate other healthcare professionals such as palliative care doctors and nurses, physiotherapists, occupational therapists, psychologists, dieticians, speech therapists and pharmacists. MDTs aim to ensure that all patients receive timely treatment and care from appropriately skilled professionals, incorporating the most up-to-date and evidence-based practice.

21.27   MDTs are complex and expensive to run and often pose a major logistical challenge to hospital trusts. There is little robust evidence to directly prove that the organisation and provision of cancer care through the MDT system has improved outcomes, as a directly comparative trial between MDT and non-MDT based systems would be extremely difficult to run. However, the benefit of multi-disciplinary team working is supported by a strong clinical consensus amongst healthcare professionals. In a large 2009 survey, at least 90 per cent of respondents agreed that effective MDT working resulted in improved clinical decision making and more coordinated and effective patient care[1]. As such it is now an expected standard of care that all new cancer cases will be discussed through a specialist MDT, and often a pre-existing case where a change of management is needed will be brought back to the MDT for further discussion. Making decisions in a team, however, does not absolve doctors of their individual responsibility for patient care, and ultimately it is at the discretion of the consultant looking after the patient to discuss the treatment plan with them and institute any MDT recommendations. As such, the MDT itself cannot be held collectively accountable for any errors or oversights. Rather, it is the individual, named, lead consultant at that time who remains responsible for the patient's overall care.

1 Multi-disciplinary team members' views about MDT working: results from a survey commissioned by the National Cancer Action Team. National Cancer Intelligence Network, wwwncinorguk/mdt (2009).

CONSENT

21.28   Frequently in oncology, patients will be asked to give their consent for complex, lengthy and potentially dangerous treatments. It is beholden on the clinician performing these treatments to provide adequate information in order to obtain informed consent. There is guidance issued by the General Medical Council (GMC) to all doctors on how consent for medical procedures should be taken[1]. This stresses a cooperative and open approach between patient and clinician to facilitate a discussion on what the treatment involves.

1 Consent guidance: patients and doctors making decisions together (2008). Available from: http://www.gmc-uk.org/guidance/ethical_guidance/consent_guidance_index.asp.

21.29   In oncology consent, information must be given regarding the incidence of common toxicities, as well as rarer and potentially serious delayed toxicities such as infertility and secondary cancers. Complaints around consent are generally to do with inadequate information regarding the treatment being offered and possible associated harms. Most institutions utilise standardised consent forms for common procedures and treatments. These outline the toxicities of a given treatment, whilst allowing for the clinician to augment with any additional information they feel necessary. Though consent forms cannot replace direct communication, they can enhance the consent process. They serve as a guide for clinicians during consent conversations to help ensure that all required information is covered, as well as providing a take-home reference for patients about the risks, benefits, and alternatives to their treatment plan. In addition a written consent form, signed by both patient and doctor, serves as an instant, standardised document that provides evidence that the doctor has engaged the patient in an appropriate discussion regarding their treatment.

TREATMENT MODALITIES: PHARMACOLOGICAL TREATMENT

Chemotherapy

21.30 For most people the treatment of cancer is associated with chemotherapy, and this remains the foundation of pharmacological therapy. Chemotherapy encompasses a wide range of chemical agents which are used either individually or in recognised combinations to exert a directly cytotoxic effect on dividing cancer cells. They do so by disrupting cell replication at various stages in its normal cycle. The history of utilising chemical agents to treat cancer is long and colourful, with the first and oldest class of chemotherapies, the alkylating agents, first being hypothesised from the observation of low blood cell counts in the victims of mustard gas attacks in the First World War. During the Second World War the German bombing of an Allied cargo ship containing a clandestine cargo of the same substance in Bari, Italy, caused widespread similar and devastating effects. Although the many casualties caused by the so-called 'Bari Harbour Incident' were widely covered up at the time, autopsies of victims taken by American medical staff led to the development of one of the earliest chemotherapy agents based on mustard, known as mustine. Common alkylating agents still in use today include chlorambucil, cyclophosphamide and the platinum-derived drugs carboplatin and cisplatin. The antimetabolite class of drugs includes methotrexate, 5-fluorouracil (5-FU) and gemcitabine. Antimicrotubule agents include vinblastine, vincristine, paclitaxel and docetaxel. Topoisomerase inhibitors include doxorubicin, etoposide and irinotecan. As different classes of chemotherapy exert their effect at different stages of the cell's reproductive cycle, often a combination of agents from different classes will be used together or in sequence to maximise the cytotoxic response.

21.31 The side effects of chemotherapies can be understood when considering that they work their therapeutic effect by preferentially targeting dividing cells. Thus it is the most rapidly-dividing cells of the body, such as bone marrow cells, hair follicles, and the cells lining the mouth, stomach, and intestine that are most affected. Chemotherapy related toxicities can occur during or immediately after administration, within hours or days, or chronically, from weeks to many years post treatment. The majority of chemotherapy regimes will cause myelosuppression and immunosuppression. Myelosuppression is the impairment of bone marrow function and subsequent decrease in blood cell lines, leading to deficiencies of red cells, white cells and platelets. A deficiency of active white cells – neutropaenia – can predispose to serious infection known as neutropaenic sepsis. This is a potentially fatal complication of chemotherapy delivery and all centres delivering treatment will have guidelines in place for its prevention, recognition and management. Nausea and vomiting are perhaps the most well-known and feared side effects of chemotherapy, however the development of less emetogenic chemotherapy drugs and more effective anti-emetic and supportive agents have meant that these symptoms can be controlled in the majority of cases. Hair loss (alopecia) is caused by chemotherapeutic agents attacking the dividing cells within the hair follicle. Again this is variable between different chemotherapies, with some causing only mild hair thinning and some causing total hair loss.

21.32 Some types of chemotherapy have the potential to cause infertility, and patients of reproductive age may choose to have fertility preservation prior to treatment, including cryopreservation of semen, eggs, or embryos. As well as this many chemotherapies are potentially teratogenic during early pregnancy, to the extent that abortion is usually recommended if conception takes place whilst on treatment. Second- and third-trimester exposure does not usually increase the teratogenic risk, however it may increase the risk of birth complications such as bleeding and infection. Further common side effects are gastrointestinal upset, mouth ulcers, rashes and fatigue. There are a wide range of rarer but very serious organ-specific complications such as cardiac, renal and liver impairment.

Targeted therapy

21.33 Whereas chemotherapies are indiscriminate in targeting both cancerous and non-cancerous cell alike, a newer generation of agents have been developed to target specific molecular pathways required by cancer cells for growth and survival. Unlike chemotherapy, only cancers expressing certain genetic abnormalities will be amenable to targeted agents, and it is now standard practice in many tumour types to screen for such clinically relevant genetic mutations at the time of diagnosis. Targeted agents are often utilised alongside more traditional chemotherapy regimes. The two commonest forms of targeted agent are tyrosine kinase inhibitors (TKIs) and monoclonal antibodies.

21.34 Tyrosine kinases are enzymes that are involved in the activation of many of the proteins involved in cell signalling pathways. TKIs have been developed to target and 'switch off' pathways integral to cancer development, such as those involved in growth, reproduction and blood supply. Unlike traditional chemotherapy, many of these TKIs have been developed for oral use. They display a different side effect profile to chemotherapy drugs with fatigue, gastrointestinal upset and rashes often being the most prominent toxicities. As they are not indiscriminately targeting dividing cells, problems with myelosuppression and hair loss are rarely encountered.

21.35 An antibody is a protein produced by the immune system to specifically target foreign or damaged components of cells, in order to identify and destroy them. Monoclonal antibodies are artificially produced antibodies which are created to be specific to a certain cell or surface protein expressed by a cell. They are used in cancer treatment to either directly block proteins involved in cell function, or to sensitise cells to treatment with chemotherapy and radiotherapy. They can be produced from the immune cells of mice (murine), humans (humanised), or a combination (chimeric). The use of humanised and chimeric monoclonal antibodies has gone some way to overcoming the difficulties with allergic reactions that were a common feature of early antibody treatment.

21.36 A novel therapeutic approach which has become more prevalent in recent years is that of harnessing the body's own innate immune system to target and destroy cancerous cells. These so called immunotherapeutic drugs are monoclonal antibodies which bind to and inhibit proteins which regulate immune response, resulting in an excess of immune cells which can target and kill cancer via the body's own cell killing pathways. There has been some success in this field, most notably in melanoma skin cancers. The attraction of this approach is that once the immune system recognises and targets malignant cells, durable anti-cancer responses can be seen. Drugs of this type are currently being trialled in a range of human cancers.

Delivery of systemic anti-cancer treatment

21.37 Although some chemotherapies and newer targeted agents can be given in oral form, most chemotherapy agents are delivered via the intravenous route. This can be done through a temporary cannula placed in the vein for the duration of the infusion, or a more permanent peripherally inserted central catheter (PICC). Central venous catheters and implantable ports are surgically placed devices, usually requiring a day case operation with general anaesthetic to insert and remove. These various modes of delivery have different indications and the choice will depend upon the duration and type of treatment, local availability and to some extent patient preference.

21.38 Before embarking on a course of systemic anti-cancer therapy it is up to the prescribing doctor to make a thorough assessment of the patient's fitness for the treatment being considered. This assessment will be in the form of a medical history and examination, particularly focused on any health problems which may impact on the safety and tolerability of chemotherapy. Dependent on the regime being used a baseline set of medical investigations will be performed. This almost always includes blood tests, and may include more advanced scans to assess a patient's cardiac and renal function. An overall general assessment of a patient's fitness, both prior to and during chemotherapy, is referred to as 'performance status'. The most commonly used scale in the UK to assess performance status is the Eastern Cooperative Oncology Group (ECOG) score, which consists of a simple six-point scale[1]:

- 0: Asymptomatic (fully active, able to carry on all pre-disease activities without restriction);
- 1: Symptomatic but completely ambulatory (restricted in physically strenuous activity but ambulatory and able to carry out work of a light or sedentary nature);
- 2: Symptomatic, <50 per cent in bed during the day (ambulatory and capable of all self care but unable to carry out any work activities. Up and about more than 50 per cent of waking hours);
- 3: Symptomatic, >50 per cent in bed, but not bedbound (capable of only limited self-care, confined to bed or chair 50 per cent or more of waking hours);
- 4: Bedbound (completely disabled. Cannot carry on any self-care. Totally confined to bed or chair);
- 5: Death.

1 Eastern Cooperative Oncology Group Performance Status Scale. Available from: http://www.ecog.org/general/perf_stat.html.

21.39 Other more detailed scoring systems are available, however they are not generally utilised in the day-to-day delivery of treatment. The concept of performance status is key to the safe delivery of systemic anti-cancer therapy. In general large oncology trials, and by extension the evidence base upon which chemotherapy is based, are restricted to those relatively fit patients with an ECOG performance status of zero or one. This becomes particularly relevant in the delivery of palliative courses of chemotherapy, where the aim of treatment is to control the cancer rather than cure. Often in this situation a person may be significantly incapacitated from their disease and in this case the administration of chemotherapy can do more harm than good, as side effects from the drug have the potential to outweigh any potential benefits in terms of anti-cancer effect. Performance status should always be clearly documented prior to embarking upon a course of chemotherapy and throughout treatment. Any deterioration in performance status may necessitate a decision to alter or even stop treatment altogether.

21.40 The aim of chemotherapy dosing is to deliver a dose which will have a sufficient anti-cancer effect, whilst not causing excessive toxicity to the patient. There are a number of ways that chemotherapy agents are dosed, the most commonly used being the body surface area (BSA), calculated by applying a standardised mathematical formula to a patient's height and weight. Recently there have been concerns highlighted over this method, as there are many other factors influencing drug metabolism which are not taken into account when using BSA such as gender, age, body habitus and organ function. However it is not practical to do complex and expensive direct measurements of drug levels in every patient receiving chemotherapy, and as such BSA will remain the mainstay of dose calculation for the majority of these drugs. Doses of some drugs are made using weight only, or a calculated or directly measured assessment of renal function. It is standard practice to document the height, weight and BSA prior to every cycle of chemotherapy, and any significant changes in these should prompt a dose alteration.

21.41 Once a patient is assessed and a chemotherapy course is decided upon the practicalities of delivery are arranged. Certain highly myelosuppressive or toxic regimes may require an elective admission into hospital to be given, however the vast majority of treatment is delivered on an outpatient basis in specially constituted wards or 'suites'. Patient safety is paramount in the delivery of chemotherapy and close monitoring is vital. Dependent on the regime, treatments are administered in weekly, two-weekly or three-weekly cycles. Prior to every cycle an assessment by an oncologist takes place. This involves identification and management of side effects and, importantly, assessment of fitness for further treatment via blood tests and evaluation of performance status. Checking of bloods prior to each cycle is a critical safety measure. As mentioned previously, suppression of blood counts is a very common side effect of many of these treatments and if white cells are found to be low this may well necessitate a dose reduction or delay. The development of granulocyte colony stimulating factor (gCSF), a drug which stimulates bone marrow production of white cells, has allowed for the safer delivery of more myelosuppressive chemotherapy regimes. Before any cycle of chemotherapy is given there should be a clear, documented assessment of side effects, patient fitness, and the results of any relevant blood tests and investigations. Treatment should only proceed if these criteria for safe delivery are met.

21.42 All units delivering chemotherapy should have provision for dealing with acute problems when they arise. Patients are provided with information prior to commencing chemotherapy on common side effects they might expect, as well as given education on signs and symptoms that should prompt the seeking of urgent medical assistance. It is good practice for a patient to be assigned a 'key worker', whom they can call with any queries or concerns. There are certain signs and symptoms which, if experienced, should prompt the patient to seek urgent medical attention. The most common is a high temperature or any symptoms of infection. If this occurs the patient should be advised to either attend their cancer unit for assessment or, if very unwell, dial 999 and be brought to their local emergency department. All emergency departments in the country have facilities to diagnose and treat infections in immunosuppressed oncology patients, and in this situation the prompt administration of antibiotics can save lives. As well as the recognition of potentially life-threatening adverse events, there are numerous problems encountered with chemotherapy, both physical and psychological, that, although not life threatening in themselves, can have a significant impact upon quality of life. Oncologists should be equipped with the skills to overcome or at least partially alleviate common toxicities, as the goal in modern oncological practice is to allow the patient to pursue his normal lifestyle and activities as much as possible whilst on chemotherapy.

Response assessment

21.43 It is crucial that any course of systemic anti-cancer therapy is seen to be having its desired effect in treating the cancer. Assessment of response is multifactorial and dependent on the overall aim of treatment. For adjuvant treatment given after surgery there is no objective measure of a successful outcome in the short term, as response is quantified through the absence of cancer relapse, which can often occur many months or years after the event. In this situation a set number of cycles of chemotherapy are given prior to the patient going onto regular follow up. For neo-adjuvant treatment given to a localised cancer before surgery, generally shorter courses of treatment are administered, consisting of between two and four cycles.

21.44 For palliative treatment the question of response assessment becomes more complex. Chemotherapy with palliative intent has two aims: to relieve the symptoms the patient is experiencing due to the cancer, and to provide a degree of control over the growth of cancer to prolong life. Ultimately chemotherapy agents will only control a cancer for a certain period of time before resistance develops. As and when this occurs treatment must be altered or discontinued altogether. Subjectively, response can be assessed by the clinician through quality of life measures such as performance status and cancer-related symptoms. Objective markers can be used, with some cancers secreting certain proteins or 'tumour markers' which can be picked up on blood tests and used as a proxy measure of disease activity.

21.45 The gold standard of response assessment is through radiographic imaging. Traditionally this was done through plain X-rays, however this has now been superseded by CT scanning. Normally after a set number of cycles a CT scan will be undertaken, either of the area of the body known to be affected or, more commonly, a full restaging scan incorporating the chest, abdomen and pelvis. The images will then be compared to previous scans in order to make an assessment of response to treatment. The most commonly used criteria of response is that of Response Evaluation Criteria In Solid Tumors (RECIST)[1], a set of standardised rules that define whether tumours improve (respond), stay the same (stabilise), or worsen (progress) during treatment. Originally published by an international collaboration between various global research organisations, the majority of clinical trials evaluating cancer treatments for response use the RECIST criteria. For a patient on treatment undergoing a scan, an outcome of stable disease, disease response, or progressive disease will be made. If the disease is stable or responding and the patient is fit and well enough to continue then further cycles of chemotherapy will be administered until the next restaging scan. If there is progressive disease then a change or discontinuation of treatment is necessary.

1 Eisenhauer, Therasse, Bogaerts, Schwartz, Sargent, Ford (et al) 'New response evaluation criteria in solid tumours: revised RECIST guideline (version 1.1)' (2009) 45(2) European Journal of Cancer 228–247.

Problems in chemotherapy administration

21.46   People are now living for longer than ever before with cancer, and the number of patients receiving systemic anti-cancer treatment has dramatically increased in recent years. In 2008, the National Confidential Enquiry into Patient Outcome and Death (NCEPOD) report, Systemic Anti-Cancer Therapy: For better, for worse?[1], looked into deaths within 30 days of those receiving systemic anti-cancer therapy and identified a number of problems in the quality and safety of patient care at both an organisational and clinical level within the NHS. The ensuing National Chemotherapy Advisory Group (NCAG) report, Chemotherapy Services in England: Ensuring Quality and Safety (2010) suggested a number of reforms to improve the delivery of chemotherapy[2]. These consist of practical measures on prescribing, preparing and administering drugs including the use of a regularly updated, easily accessible 'protocol book' outlining chemotherapy doses and alterations, and of pre-printed or electronic prescribing rather than older written prescriptions. With e-prescribing chemotherapy prescriptions are completed onto a standardised electronic proforma. This incorporates data such as patient height, weight and blood tests and will automatically flag up any inconsistent prescriptions or errors.

1 For Better, For Worse? A review of the care of patients who died within 30 days of receiving systemic anti-cancer therapy. National Confidential Enquiry into Patient Outcome and Death. Available from: http://www.ncepod.org.uk/2008report3/Downloads/SACT_report.pdf.
2 Chemotherapy Services in England: Ensuring quality and safety. National Chemotherapy Advisory Group 2008. Available from: http://webarchive.nationalarchives.gov.uk/20130107105354/http://www.dh.gov.uk/prod_consum_dh/groups/dh_digitalassets/documents/digitalasset/dh_104501.pdf.

21.47   The main safety issue in the delivery of chemotherapy is the provision of support and emergency care when patients become unwell. The NCAG report advises that prior to starting chemotherapy, patients should receive verbal and written information about treatment, toxicities, and who to contact with problems. They also recommend a 24-hour telephone advice service should be available for queries, manned by nurses experienced in dealing with chemotherapy toxicity. More serious problems may necessitate attendance at local emergency departments, and it is at this stage that poor provision of care may potentially be encountered. Often a patient will be attending a hospital other than the base hospital where they are undergoing chemotherapy. They will be assessed by staff who are not familiar with their oncology history or perhaps unaware of the side effects and toxicities associated with their particular treatment.

21.48 Fragmentation of care and poor communication between hospitals and healthcare trusts is a perennial problem within the NHS. IT systems and electronic records of scans, blood tests and clinical notes are generally only accessible within the hospital or trust where the patient has been receiving treatment. Once a cancer patient is admitted to a different hospital with an acute problem, this lack of information can be detrimental to care. In order to address these issues, a major and far-reaching recommendation from the NCAG report was the institution of acute oncology services (AOS) in every hospital. These are dedicated teams consisting of oncology doctors and nurses who are involved in the acute admission and on-going inpatient care of all cancer patients. It is recommended that any cancer patient admitted to hospital should be reviewed by the AOS within 24 hours, with the team also providing referral and treatment pathways for common oncological emergencies such as neutropenic sepsis and spinal cord compression.

TREATMENT MODALITIES: RADIOTHERAPY

21.49 Radiotherapy is the practice of medical treatment using ionising radiation. There are two ways of delivering radiotherapy: external beam radiotherapy and internal radiotherapy. External beam radiotherapy usually involves using a linear accelerator machine to focus high-energy radiation beams onto the target tissue. Internal radiotherapy is delivered from a radioactive source placed inside the body: a solid source placed close to a tumour (brachytherapy) or liquid or capsule (radioisotope therapy).

21.50 External beam radiotherapy delivers high-energy photons (as X-rays or gamma rays), electrons or, rarely, protons to the tumour with the aim of causing double and single stranded DNA breaks, resulting in cell death. The primary objective in treating a patient with radiotherapy is to enhance tumour cell kill but minimise toxicity to surrounding normal tissue. This is described as the *therapeutic index*. For certain cancers chemotherapy is delivered concomitantly with radiotherapy, as this has been seen to enhance radiotherapy effect (radio-sensitisation); this is advantageous in improving tumouricidal effect but can also increase toxicities.

21.51 Radiobiology is the study of the therapeutic effect of radiation, which, over the last 50 years has established effective therapeutic doses according to different histological diagnoses and provided evidence to determine the tolerance doses of normal tissue structures. By dividing total radiation dose into a number of treatments (fractionation), frequent – usually daily – small doses have been found to be most effective, as this interval between fractions allows for normal tissues to repair and recover, whereas cancer cells, which are no longer controlled by normal tissue growth factors or repair mechanisms, are less likely to recover.

21.52 The characteristics of photon beams, electron beams and radiation dose delivered will be considered and applied dependent on the site and size of the tumour, and whether it is in close proximity to critical normal tissue structures. The unit for radiation [energy] absorbed [per unit mass of tissue] is described as *gray*. Photon therapy treatment allows radiation to be delivered to deep-seated tumours, with the disadvantage being a gradual dose fall-off to the surrounding normal tissue structures. Consequently, this requires modulation of the photon beam to deliver radiation from different angles in an attempt to deliver a high dose to the cancer and as low a dose as possible to the neighbouring normal tissue structures. Electrons have properties which can allow high doses of radiation to be delivered to superficial tumours, with a steep dose gradient ensuring very low doses at depth.

21.53 Radiotherapy remains an essential component of cancer treatment, with approximately 50 per cent of cancer patients requiring radiotherapy at some point in their treatment pathway. It also forms part of the treatment of 40 per cent of patients who are cured of their cancer. As with chemotherapy, there are clear guidelines from evidence-based practice in the recommendation of radiotherapy in the neo-adjuvant and adjuvant setting where it is applicable in certain cancers. For both radical and palliative radiotherapy the Royal College of Radiologists has provided recommendations for the treatment of localised and metastatic disease and guidance on the total dose and number of treatments (fractions) for specific cancers[1]. All these guidelines are based on institutional experiences (retrospective reviews) and clinical trials[2]. The techniques for delivering radiation and the treatment platforms used are summarised below.

1 The Royal College of Radiologists Board of Faculty of Clinical Oncology, Radiotherapy Dose-Fractionation 2006. Available from: http://www.rcr.ac.uk/docs/oncology/pdf/Dose-Fractionation_Final.pdf.
2 Delaney, Jacob, Featherstone, Barton 'The role of radiotherapy in cancer treatment: estimating optimal utilization from a review of evidence-based clinical guidelines' (2005) 104(6) Cancer 1129–1137.

Conformal radiotherapy

21.54 Conformal radiotherapy is also called 3D conformal radiotherapy and is the most commonly used type of radiotherapy. A planning CT scanner is used to locate the cancer, and computer programmes then design photon beams to be shaped and arranged from different angles to plan the radiotherapy treatment area precisely in three dimensions: width, height and depth.

Intensity modulated radiotherapy

21.55 Intensity modulated radiotherapy (IMRT) varies the strength of the photon beams (modulates) to match the size, shape and position of the tumour. This is a form of highly conformal radiotherapy, aiming to maximise effectiveness and minimise damage to normal tissues.

Image guided radiotherapy

21.56 Image guided radiotherapy integrates additional imaging modalities, eg MRI, with a planning CT scan to aid in defining the cancer accurately. In addition, in certain clinical scenarios, on treatment imaging is performed to confirm the position of the tumour as seen on the original planning CT scan is identical during treatment delivery.

Stereotactic ablative body radiotherapy

21.57 Stereotactic ablative body radiotherapy (SABR), also known as stereotactic body radiotherapy (SBRT) or stereotactic radiosurgery (SRS), is a specialised form of radiotherapy to precisely target radiotherapy to certain cancers accurately. It can be delivered by linear accelerators but different machines, specially designed treatment machines, such as Cyberknife™ are commonly used. With SABR, many smaller, thin beams of radiation are directed from hundreds of different angles and image guidance allow accurate tracking of mobile tumours, eg lung cancers during respiration. Consequently, a much higher dose can be delivered over a shorter number of treatments.

Proton therapy

21.58 Proton therapy is an example of a particle therapy. The treatment is delivered from an entirely different machine. The advantage of proton treatment is that radiation delivery can be planned to release the maximum dose of radiation at a specified depth. A proton beam conforms to the shape and depth of a tumour. Proton therapy is recommended in specific clinical scenarios which have been listed by the UK NHS proton therapy panel. Currently, patients travel abroad to receive this treatment but it is anticipated that proton therapy will be available in the UK within the next five years[1].

1 NHS England: Guidance for the Referral of Patients Abroad for NHS Proton Treatment 2010. Available from: http://www.england.nhs.uk/wp-content/uploads/2014/04/ref-pats-abroad-guide.pdf.

Radiotherapy patient pathway

21.59 To provide an understanding of the issues raised during the treatment planning and delivery, an example of a treatment pathway is described below. The illustration adapted from NHS Radiotherapy Services England 2012 provides a summary[1].

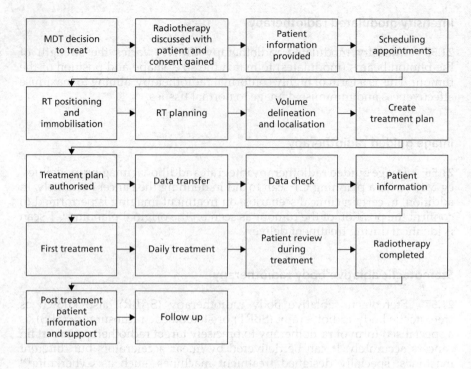

From MDT decision to treat to first treatment the access targets are:

- Patients should receive RT within 31 days of agreeing to treatment
- Patients needing radical RT should be treated within 28 days
- Patients needing palliative RT should be treated within 14 days
- Patients needing urgent RT should be treated within 48 hours.

1   Following diagnosis and completion of staging investigations, and clinical condition a multi-disciplinary team delivers a recommendation to discuss radiotherapy. A clinical oncologist, as part of the MDT gives the opinion as to whether radiotherapy for this patient is deliverable and confirms the intent of treatment. This is either radical treatment or palliative treatment, and whether treatment with concomitant chemotherapy is suitable.

2   The patient meets with the clinical oncologist to be informed of the proposed treatment plan and is assessed for fitness for treatment.

3   The clinical oncologist will then describe the rationale for the treatment, the expected outcome based on the current evidence where appropriate, the potential side effects that may occur and the incidence of developing the listed side effects. Side effects are divided into early side effects which are commonly temporary and occur during treatment and resolve within a few weeks following completion of treatment and late side effects which can start to manifest as early as three months after completion of treatment and continue to increase in incidence two to five years after treatment.

4   Once the patient has had an opportunity to understand the information, understood the intention of treatment, had an opportunity to ask any further questions, and has agreed to proceed with radiotherapy, the

patient provides informed consent, written information about their proposed treatment and commences the preparatory part of treatment. Pre- treatment investigations are completed and the patient proceeds to radiotherapy planning processing.

5   During radiotherapy planning, the disease site (gross tumour volume, GTV), the areas at risk of microscopic spread (clinical target volume, CTV) and the reproducibility of the patient's position (planning target volume, PTV) must all be considered. Immobilisation devices and diagnostic information are used to position the patient, scan the region of interest and construct the GTV, CTV and PTV alongside critical normal tissue structures (defined as organs at risk).

6   Therapeutic radiographers deliver the radiation treatment and medical physicists and dosimetrists formulate the optimal plan.

7   There are clear referenced protocols defining the treatment dose and the dose constraints that should be applied to critical normal tissue structures to deliver effective treatment but minimise the incidence of long-term side effects.

8   Once an optimal plan has been achieved, the plan is checked and accepted by the clinician, the plan is checked by the physicist. A final check is also performed by the therapeutic radiographers before delivery of treatment.

9   In individual circumstances, adaption to the proposed plan will need to be made according to the patient's circumstances, co-morbidities. For example a proposed dose may not be safely delivered to a particular part of the tumour because it will cause unacceptable damage to an adjacent uninvolved organ. This must be explained to the patient and documented clearly.

10   On treatment imaging is performed to verify treatment has been delivered correctly.

11   Radical treatments can be up to 30–35 treatments over 6.5–7 weeks, during which time the patient is also assessed and managed for acute toxicities. Supportive treatments are offered.

12   Palliative treatments can vary between 1–12 treatments. A hypofractionated (large dose per fraction) is delivered in an attempt to relieve symptoms.

13   A post-treatment review is commonly performed approximately 4–6 weeks after radiotherapy to confirm benefit and recovery of early toxicities.

14   Response can be measured clinically or radiologically.

15   Regular follow up is recommended to assess for any evidence of relapse but also to assess, record and manage late effects from radiotherapy.

1 Department of Health: Radiotherapy Services in England 2012. Available from: https://http://www.gov.uk/government/publications/radiotherapy-services-in-england-2012.

21.60   Treatment delivery and machine quality are checked regularly as required by law. The process is described as *quality assurance*, with clear national guidelines mandating frequent checks on the treatment machines and processes. A multi-professional quality assurance team for radiotherapy involves the clinicians, therapeutic radiographers, radiation protection officers and physicists who regularly meet to confirm all appropriate safety checks have been performed, protocol and treatment guidelines have been updated in line with current evidence and appropriate clinical training achieved.

21.61   The Ionising Radiation (Medical Exposure) Regulations 2000 (IR(ME)R)2000[1] are intended to protect the patient from the hazards associated with ionising radiation[2]. The guidance notes provide information for all disciplines to emphasise appropriate responsibility in the delivery of radiotherapy. Any major errors with radiotherapy delivery reported under IR(ME)R 2000 are conducted under criminal law. In collaboration between the professional bodies representing clinicians, therapeutic radiographers, radiotherapy physicists and national patient safety agency (NPSA), the British Institute of Radiology also provides key recommendations for delivery of safe radiotherapy[3]. This requires externally accredited quality management systems to monitor that radiotherapy is delivered as intended and in accordance with protocols, to maintain and continually improve the quality of the service and to investigate and learn from incidents.

1 SI 2000/1059.
2 Ionising Radiation (Medical Exposure) Regulations 2000 (IRMER) 2012. Available from: https://http://www.gov.uk/government/publications/the-ionising-radiation-medical-exposure-regulations-2000.
3 British Institute of Radiology: Towards Safer Radiotherapy 2010. Available from: https://http://www.rcr.ac.uk/docs/oncology/pdf/Towards_saferRT_final.pdf.

21.62   It should be highlighted that in the UK radiotherapy is generally safe. Between 2000 and 2006, 181 incidents affecting 338 patients were reported in the UK under IR(ME)R 2000. This equates to an incidence of approximately 40 per 100,000 courses of radiotherapy, of which 24 incidents were likely to have a clinically significant adverse outcome (= 3 per 100,000 course of radiotherapy)[1].

1 Ionising Radiation (Medical Exposure) Regulations 2000 (IRMER) 2012. Available from: https://http://www.gov.uk/government/publications/the-ionising-radiation-medical-exposure-regulations-2000.

21.63   The discipline of radiotherapy continues to strive to improve patient's outcomes. Over the last 30 years, patient experiences have been paramount in improving treatment delivery. RAGE (Radiotherapy Action Group Exposure) was founded in 1991 following publicity surrounding Lady Audrey Ironside's injuries as a result of long term disabling side-effects following radiotherapy treatment for breast cancer. These effects included oedema and rarely severely disabling brachial plexus neuropathy associated with radiation damage. RAGE raised public awareness to campaign for national standards in radiotherapy and seek supportive care and compensation for the injuries suffered. This landmark task force helped to set up national guidance for safer radiotherapy.

21.64   In addition, through the conducting of clinical trials and reporting on early and late toxicities and radiation doses to normal tissue structures, radiobiological analyses of dose-response relationships have provided tolerance doses and potential risk of reversible or permanent damage to specific organs. Data are now available on the risk of radiation-induced secondary cancers, particularly following radiotherapy for Hodgkin's lymphoma, with such patients routinely undergoing more intensive screening for breast cancer, and for radiation-induced sarcomas following breast radiotherapy. In 2010, an international panel of radiation therapy experts formed a committee to develop QUANTEC (quantitative analysis of normal tissue effects in the clinic). Following a review of the published literature this now provides references for tolerance doses for specific organs and general principles in dose-response analysis to guide clinicians in optimising radiotherapy treatments whilst minimising side effects[1].

1 Bentzen, Constine, Deasy, Eisbruch, Jackson, Marks (et al) 'Quantitative Analyses of Normal Tissue Effects in the Clinic (QUANTEC): an introduction to the scientific issues' (2010) 76(3 Supp) International Jnl of Radiation Oncology, Biology, Physics S3–9.

21.65 Side effects are commonly divided into early (occurring during radiotherapy and usually recovering within three months after completing radiotherapy) and late (developing as early as three months after completing radiotherapy to years later). Side effects described and listed as part of the consent process are dependent on the anatomical location of treatment, the treated volume and the total dose delivered. Expected early side effects include: mucositis, dry mouth, fatigue, erythema and desquamation for treatment of the head and neck region; erythema, dysphagia and mild lung inflammation in the thoracic region; nausea, diarrhoea, desquamation, urinary frequency and proctitis in the abdomino-pelvic region. The intensity (grade) and duration will vary according to total dose. Expected late effects are usually of low grade, however it is important to take consent on the risk of permanent tissue damage. Particularly expected late toxicities are fibrosis and lymphoedema, but generally they are of low grade. More critical late effects that require addressing and discussing in the consent process (again depending on the anatomical site and the treatment intent) include the anticipated very low risk of: neurological damage, kidney damage, bowel dysfunction, bowel perforation, gonadal dysfunction and the risk of a radiation-induced malignancy.

CLINICAL TRIALS

21.66 As the practice of oncology continues to evolve, the discipline strives to improve quality of care through evidence-based practice. This requires the development of clinical trials, from assessing novel therapies in terms of safety and potential benefit (Phase 1 trials) to testing new potentially effective treatments against the current standard of care (Phase 3 trials). In addition to determining objective outcomes with regard to disease control, parallel quality of life measures are often incorporated to help understand impact on lives and cancer survivorship.

21.67 Clinical trials and studies are regulated by local research committees within academic institutions, with peer review to confirm an appropriate scientific question is being asked, and by research ethics committees to confirm safety, appropriateness of the study from a participant's perspective, and good ethical conduct[1]. The Medicines and Healthcare Products Regulatory Agency (MHRA) are an additional body which regulates medicinal products and medical devices being tested within clinical trials before approval of the product for availability onto the market[2]. Clear operational guidelines and protocols are required to cover recruitment, treatment administration and follow-up of participants, with serious adverse events being reported to chief investigators of studies and independent data monitoring committees to advise on safety and continuation.

1 NHS Health Research Authority: National Research Ethics Service. Available from: http://www.nres.nhs.uk/.
2 Medicines and Healthcare Products Regulatory Agency. Available from: http://www.mhra.gov.uk/ - page=DynamicListMedicines.

21.68 An important consideration in oncology trials is that of clinical equipoise. A problematic and potentially ethically difficult situation arises in a clinical trial if it becomes clear that one treatment arm is significantly outperforming all others. Often once a predetermined statistical threshold of significant treatment effect is met, patients will be allowed to 'cross over' onto the more successful treatment arm. Experimental agents should not be offered to patients unless there is reason to believe they will be as, or more, efficacious than existing possible treatments. A caveat to this is a situation where there are no standard, proven lines of therapy left open for a patient. In this situation the patient may wish to be considered for an early Phase 1 trial of an untested agent.

SUPPORTIVE CARE IN ONCOLOGY

21.69 Cancer affects all aspects of a person's life, as well as having a profound impact upon those caring or being cared for by them. Over and above the physical signs and symptoms directly related to the disease and its treatment there are a range of broader problems encompassing employment, financial, family and spiritual issues that often need to be addressed. There are a number of allied healthcare specialists who work closely alongside the medical team to provide support for patients undergoing cancer treatment. Coordinating this complex delivery of care is often the role of the oncology clinical nurse specialist (CNS) and most larger centres will have multiple CNSs covering specific tumour groups within the hospital. It is the CNS's role to provide specialist information, medical and emotional support to patients and their carers from the time of diagnosis onwards. A CNS should be a point of contact by telephone when patients are away from the hospital, as well as providing continuity of care to oncology inpatients. There are also specialist physiotherapists, occupational therapists and dieticians trained in the support of oncology patients. The psychological burden of the disease and its treatment can be profound, and access to specialist psychological support should be available to those who require it. Spiritual support is provided via hospital chaplaincy services.

21.70 There are many groups throughout the country run by current and former cancer patients to provide support and disseminate information. Often these groups maintain an active presence on social media. The largest cancer support charity in the UK, and very much the 'public face' of cancer care, is Macmillan. This organisation has a multi-faceted role. Through their website they provide comprehensive and understandable information for patients and carers on all aspects of cancer treatment. They also directly employ cancer specialist nurses and doctors, as well as working in partnership with NHS providers in the building and running of cancer care facilities. Initially their role was primarily in the supportive and palliative field, however they have expanded over the years to cover every aspect of cancer care, including treatment, diagnostic, outpatient, information and support centres. They are also a source of financial advice and support for cancer patients, with specialist advisers on benefits, employment, insurance and wills.

CANCER FOLLOW-UP AND SURVIVORSHIP

21.71   As treatment for cancer improves, the number of people living with and beyond cancer increases, with over two million cancer survivors alive in the UK. Traditional after care for cancer consists of a formalised schedule of follow-up appointments and investigations, with the aim of identifying and treating recurrence. These involve a combination of medical check-up, physical examination and investigations such as blood tests, imaging and endoscopic procedures. The frequency and nature of follow-up care is dictated by type of cancer, treatment received, and the person's overall health, including possible treatment-related problems. Most centres will have documented follow up guidelines for common cancers. It is the responsibility of the treating consultant to oversee adequate follow-up of patients and such follow-up visits constitute a significant proportion of outpatient oncology work. Due to the complexity and variation in follow-up schedules, missed appointments, scans and patients being 'lost to follow-up' are a potential source of complaint and litigation in oncology. Again, the CNS role is important to act as a contact point and coordinate and oversee follow-up visits and appointments.

21.72   A follow-up solely focused on detecting and treating recurrence of cancer can overlook the considerable long-term impact the disease and its treatment can have on all aspects of a patient's life. There has been an increased focus on survivorship issues in recent years, going beyond the medical follow-up of cancer patients in an effort to look more holistically at the long-term impact of cancer and its treatment. In 2013 The National Cancer Survivorship Initiative (NCSI) published 'Living with and beyond cancer: Taking Action to Improve Outcomes'[1]. This emphasised a move away from a 'one-size fits all' approach to follow-up to more personalised care planning based on assessment of individual risks, needs and preferences, with the aim of enhancing overall quality of life post cancer treatment.

1 Living with and beyond cancer: taking action to improve outcomes. Department of Health. Available from: https://http://www.gov.uk/government/uploads/system/uploads/attachment_data/file/181054/9333-TSO-2900664-NCSI_Report_FINAL.pdf.

PALLIATIVE AND END-OF-LIFE CARE

21.73   Palliative care is a medical speciality dedicated to the relief of symptoms and alleviation of suffering caused by illness. Although traditionally associated with the care of the dying, it is increasingly recognised that palliative services play an important role at all stages of the cancer pathway, and there is often close integration of oncology and palliative care services in both the inpatient and outpatient setting. Any large oncology centre will have a team of palliative care doctors and specialist nurses. Often they will not be directly responsible for the care of the patient, but rather will advise on symptom control issues and provide psychological support to the patient and family. Outpatient palliative care services in the UK are organised around the hospice system. Around a quarter of a million patients are cared for by hospices in the UK each year, either in hospice or their own home via community palliative care services. Hospices provide terminal care for the dying, as well as admissions for symptom control and respite care. They deliver wide-ranging holistic and supportive care to patients and families, consisting not only of medical and nursing care for pain and symptomatic control, but also specialist occupational and physiotherapy, complementary therapies, spiritual support, practical and financial advice, and bereavement support for carers, families and friends.

21.74 The interaction between palliative care and oncology, and the transition from active oncological management to supportive care is crucial to the overall quality of care given to cancer patients. This change of focus needs to be handled sensitively by all involved, as often it can be difficult to accept for patients and their families. The key to this is through open communication from the time of diagnosis onwards, clearly expressing the goals and likely outcomes of any treatment course embarked upon. A particularly contentious issue over end-of-life care in recent years has been the use of the 'Liverpool Care Pathway for the dying patient' (LCP), developed by Liverpool University Hospital and Liverpool's Marie Curie Hospice in the late 1990s for the care of terminally ill cancer patients. The LCP was developed to aid members of the clinical team in matters relating to continuing medical treatment, discontinuation of non-essential medications and comfort measures during the last days and hours of a patient's life. A number of highly publicised complaints led to a high-profile media campaign against the pathway. In July 2013, an independent review into the LCP found problems in its use, advising that it should be phased out and replaced with 'individual end-of-life care plans' for dying patients[1]. The complaints and errors highlighted in the report were generally less to do with the LCP itself, and more around the decision-making and consent process when initiating patients on the pathway, as well as communication with patients and families around end-of-life issues such as withdrawal of medicines, intravenous fluids and artificial nutrition.

1 More care, less pathway: a review of the Liverpool Care Pathway. Available from: https://http://www.gov.uk/government/uploads/system/uploads/attachment_data/file/212450/Liverpool_Care_Pathway.pdf.

21.75 A further issue around end-of-life care receiving substantial media attention recently is that of 'do not attempt resuscitation' (DNAR) orders. These are formal documents in a patient's hospital record which stipulate that in the event of cardiac or respiratory arrest, cardiopulmonary resuscitation (CPR) and advanced cardiac life support should not be carried out. In patients with advanced cancer this is often an entirely appropriate decision. The success rate for CPR is low, with only around 15 per cent of all patients who receive CPR in hospital surviving[1]. In terminally ill cancer patients who are approaching the end of life this percentage is likely to be considerably lower, and CPR may in many cases be an undignified and futile endeavour. It was in an attempt to stop unnecessary CPR being performed in both the hospital and community that DNAR forms were introduced. As with any other medical intervention, a patient or their relative cannot demand resuscitation if the treating doctor believes it is not clinically indicated, and ultimately the decision to perform CPR is a clinical one. The issue of how much patients and their families should be consulted over DNAR decisions has been a somewhat ill-defined area. Traditionally it has been advocated as best practice that these decisions, where possible, should be discussed with the patient, however there has been no legal obligation to do so.

1 Zoch, Desbiens, DeStefano, Stueland, Layde 'Short- and long-term survival after cardiopulmonary resuscitation' (2000) 160(13) Archives of Internal Medicine 1969–1973.

21.76   In the recent case of an oncology patient who was admitted to hospital after a car accident, the Court of Appeal ruled that the medical team involved acted unlawfully by placing a DNAR decision in her notes without her knowledge, judging this to be a violation of the right to respect for her private life under Article 8 of the European Convention on Human Rights[1]. Thus there is now a legal obligation by the treating clinician to discuss all resuscitation decisions with the patient 'unless he or she thinks that the patient will be distressed by being consulted and that that distress might cause the patient harm'. This still leaves a degree of uncertainty around the placement of DNAR orders, as there is no guidance on how to define or quantify the distress or harm that may potentially be caused to a patient by discussions around resuscitation, and ultimately it remains a judgment by the treating doctor as to whether a DNAR conversation is appropriate. In light of this recent ruling, however, it is safe to say that there must be very valid and justifiable reasons for a patient and their family not to be consulted before a DNAR decision is made, and that all discussions should be clearly documented in the patient record.

1 *Tracey v Cambridge University Hospital NHS Foundation Trust* [2014] EWCA Civ 822, [2015] 1 All ER 450.

COMMUNICATION

21.77   One of the most important aspects of delivering high quality cancer care is communication between medical professionals, patients and their families. Good communication can improve the experience for patients and doctors alike, whereas poor communication can cause uncertainty and reduce compliance with treatments, as well as increase emotional burnout in healthcare professionals[1]. The GMC outlines in its guidance *Good Medical Practice* that effective communication with both colleagues and patients is one of the fundamental skills required of doctors[2]. The patient-centred model of communication is now commonly taught to all UK medical undergraduates, and emphasises shared decision-making and an appreciation of patient concerns and expectations as being of key importance in any clinical encounter. Some older patients may well favour a more traditional didactic rather than collaborative approach, and it is an understanding of such differences and a tailoring of approach to the individual situation that is a crucial skill in oncology. It is now appreciated that communication skills can be taught successfully, and during their training oncologists are encouraged to attend an 'advanced communication skills' course, consisting of lectures and workshops covering all aspects of effective communication in an oncology context.

1 Ong, Visser, Lammes, de Haes 'Doctor-patient communication and cancer patients' quality of life and satisfaction' (2000) 41(2) Patient Education and Counseling 145–156.
2 Good Medical Practice: The duties of a doctor registered with the General Medical Council. Available from: http://www.gmc-uk.org/static/documents/content/Good_medical_practice_-_English_0414.pdf.

OVERVIEW AND CONCLUSION

21.78   Recent concerns over dramatic failings in certain aspects of NHS care, most notably in the 2013 Mid Staffordshire Foundation Trust Report, have led to a renewed focus on the provision and maintenance of high standards within the NHS. A key component of this is openness and transparency in acknowledging and acting upon failings in care. Improving Outcomes: a Strategy for Cancer was published in 2011 with a view to providing a long-term strategic plan for cancer services in the UK by outlining reforms and improvements in early prevention, diagnosis, treatment and follow-up[1]. Subsequent annual updates have reported improvement in survival rates and positive overall progress in many outcome indicators[2], however there remain significant areas where provision of complex oncological care has the potential to fall short, generating complaint and legal action.

1 Improving Outcomes: a Strategy for Cancer 2011. Available from: https://http://www.gov.uk/government/uploads/system/uploads/attachment_data/file/213785/dh_123394.pdf.
2 Improving Outcomes: A Strategy for Cancer. Third Annual Report. Available from: https://http://www.gov.uk/government/uploads/system/uploads/attachment_data/file/264511/IOSC_3rd_Annual_Report_-_Proof_version_-_9_December_2013_v2.pdf.

21.79   It is now explicitly set out in the NHS constitution that a patient who complains regarding any aspect of their care has the right to have this acknowledged within three working days, and to have their complaint appropriately and comprehensively investigated in a timely manner[1]. Every hospital should have a clear procedure for complaints, and all NHS trusts have a Patient Advice and Liaison Service (PALS) to offer confidential advice, support and information on health-related matters, including complaints and legal action. If patients are not satisfied with how a complaint has been dealt with at a local level, they have the right to escalate their grievance to the Independent Parliamentary and Health Service Ombudsman.

1 The NHS Constitution for England 2013. Available from: http://www.nhs.uk/choiceintheNHS/Rightsandpledges/NHSConstitution/Pages/Yourrightstochoice.aspx.

21.80   In 2012–13 there were 93 successful clinical negligence claims against the NHS specific to oncology, paying out just over £4m in damages[1]. In terms of overall complaints to the NHS in general, the most common were regarding 'all aspects of clinical treatment,' with the next two most common being around 'attitudes of staff' and 'communication/information to patients'. These three areas accounted for over half of all complaints received[2]. Common reasons for oncology-specific complaints at a more local level often involve attitudes of staff and poor communication, as well as administrative and organisational issues such as delays in procedures, clinic appointments and patient transport. Complaints such as these are generally made more frequently than complaints about actual clinical care received. As always, effective communication is crucial in ensuring high standards of care. Appropriate systems should always be in place to minimise the potential for any clinical or organisational mistakes, but in the delivery of multi-faceted and complex oncological care, often incorporating terminal care and dying, it is inevitable that perceived or actual mistakes will sometimes occur. A transparent and collaborative approach between doctor, patient and family throughout the cancer treatment pathway is key to reducing errors and minimising harms.

1 NHS Litigation Authority Freedom of Infomation Request for clinical negligence claims coded under the specialty of oncology (2014).
2 Data on Written Complaints to the NHS 2012–13, Health and Social Care Information Centre. Available from: http://www.hscic.gov.uk/catalogue/PUB11490/data-writ-comp-nhs-2012-2013-rep.pdf.

CHAPTER 22

Psychiatry

Dr Laurence Mynors-Wallis

INTRODUCTION

22.1   In broad terms, psychiatry is no different from other specialities in medicine when considering clinical negligence. Psychiatrists are expected to undertake a thorough examination of their patients, request appropriate investigations, come to a conclusion with regard to diagnosis and treatment, monitor the effectiveness of the treatment and make necessary adjustments as required to the treatment plan. Psychiatry does differ in one important aspect of treatment and that is in the potential use of Mental Health Act legislation in order to compulsorily treat patients. This is an important additional responsibility which alters the balance between clinician and patient responsibility for treatment decisions.

22.2   Psychiatrists, like other doctors, are guided in their work by standards set by regulatory and professional bodies, including the Royal College of Psychiatrists, the General Medical Council and by the policies and procedures of the organisations in which they work. In the UK, the National Institute of Health and Care Excellence has set out guidance for the assessment and treatment of many common psychiatric disorders to inform practitioners with regard to evidence-based practice. It is expected that psychiatrists will be mindful of the relevant advice and guidance available and if they depart from it will set out a reasoned justification for doing so.

PSYCHIATRIC DISORDERS

22.3   Psychiatric disorders are common. It is broadly accepted that one in four individuals will experience a psychiatric disorder at some point in their lives. The majority of patients with the common mental disorders of anxiety and depression are seen and treated in primary care by their general practitioners without referral to psychiatrists. Psychiatrists in the UK focus their work on the more severe mental disorders, including psychotic disorders and the management of patients with the more severe common disorders that have not responded well to treatment.

22.4   In the past, psychiatric diagnoses were broadly categorised into neurotic and psychotic disorders. Neurotic disorders represent part of the spectrum of common emotions such as low mood and anxiety but in a severe and sometimes disabling form with symptoms occurring in situations in which individuals do not normally experience them. In psychotic disorders, eg schizophrenia, patients experience symptoms, for example, hearing voices or holding bizarre beliefs that are rarely experienced by most in the general population. There is, however, a significant overlap between neurotic and psychotic symptoms. For example, patients with depression can become so unwell that they hold delusional beliefs about guilt and poverty and similarly patients with psychotic disorders, such as schizophrenia, can be enormously troubled by symptoms of anxiety. Hence the distinction between psychotic and neurotic disorders is now rarely used in clinical practice, which favours a more precise diagnosis meeting the criteria set in one of the two classificatory systems.

22.5 The classification of psychiatric disorders is set out in two documents: the *International Classification of Diseases* in its 10th edition (ICD-10)[1] the 11th revision due to be published in 2015; and the *Diagnostic and Statistical Manual of Mental Disorders*, now in its 5th edition (DSM-5)[2]. These classification systems have many similarities but also important differences. The DSM-5 has been developed particularly for use in North America. It sets very clear criteria for diagnosis and can be particularly helpful in a medico-legal setting because of the precision and clarity of the diagnostic categories. The ICD-10 has been developed for use in the rest of the world and, reflecting this, the diagnostic categories are broader, which often gives it greater utility in clinical settings where there are many patients whose diagnosis does not fall neatly within the DSM classificatory system.

1 *The ICD-10 Classification of Mental and Behavioural Disorders* (1992).
2 *The Diagnostic and Statistical Manual of Mental Disorders* (5th edn, 2013).

22.6 In the UK, although the ICD-10 system is used within the Department of Health, it is acceptable clinically for practitioners to use either system.

22.7 There is a small group of doctors who question the value of diagnosis. The position of the vast majority of psychiatrists and the Royal College of Psychiatrists is clear: patients benefit from clarity about diagnosis because of the important implications with regard to understanding treatment and prognosis[1].

1 Craddock and Mynors-Wallis 'Psychiatric Diagnosis: impersonal, imperfect and important' (2014) 204 British Journal of Psychiatry 93–95.

22.8 The broad diagnostic categories found in both classifications are as follows:

(1)   organic disorders: dementia, delirium, mental disorders due to brain damage, dysfunction and physical disease;
(2)   mental and behavioural disorders due to drug and alcohol use;
(3)   schizophrenia and delusional disorders;
(4)   mood (affective disorders): depressive disorders and bipolar affective disorder (manic depression);
(5)   anxiety disorders;
(6)   obsessive compulsive and related disorders;
(7)   trauma and stress related disorders;
(8)   somatic symptom and related disorders;
(9)   behavioural disorders: eating disorders, sleep disorders, sexual dysfunction and behavioural disorders;
(10)   disorders with onset usually in childhood and adolescent: attention deficit hyperactivity disorder, conduct disorder, separation anxiety;
(11)   neurodevelopmental disorders including intellectual disability;
(12)   personality disorders.

ASSESSMENT

22.9 At the core of good psychiatric practice is a thorough clinical assessment of the patient. A thorough assessment allows the psychiatrist to make a diagnosis, formulation and treatment plan.

22.10   The standards for psychiatric assessment are set out clearly in the syllabus of the Royal College of Psychiatrists. What is expected is summarised in the first learning outcome for core psychiatric training[1] as follows:

'To be able to perform a specialist assessment of patients and document relevant history and examination on culturally diverse patients to include:

- presenting or main complaint;
- history of present illness;
- past medical and psychiatric history;
- systemic review;
- family history;
- social and cultural history;
- developmental history'.

1 Royal College of Psychiatrists *Competency Based Curriculum for Specialist Core Training in Psychiatry* (February 2010).

22.11   The first standard in *Good Psychiatric Practice*[1] emphasises this point.

'A psychiatrist must undertake competent assessments of patients with mental health problems and must:

(a) be competent in obtaining a full and relevant history that incorporates developmental, psychological, social, cultural and physical factors, and:

  (i) be able to gather this information in difficult or complicated situations
  (ii) in situations of urgency, prioritise what information is needed to achieve a safe and effective outcome for the patient
  (iii) seek and listen to the views and knowledge of the patient, their carers and family members and other professionals involved in the care of the patient

(b) have knowledge of:

  (i) human development and developmental psychopathology, and the influence of social factors and life experiences
  (ii) gender and age differences in the presentation and management of psychiatric disorders
  (iii) biological and organic factors present in many psychiatric disorders
  (iv) the impact of alcohol and substance misuse on physical and mental health

(c) be competent in undertaking a comprehensive mental state examination
(d) be competent in evaluating and documenting an assessment of clinical risk, considering harm to self, harm to others, harm from others, self-neglect and vulnerability
(e) be competent in determining the necessary physical examination and investigations required for a thorough assessment
(f) ensure that they are competent and trained, where appropriate, in the use of any assessment or rating tools used as part of the assessment'.

1 Royal College of Psychiatrists College Report CR154 (3rd edn, 2009).

22.12   *Good Psychiatric Practice* sets out standards of practice for psychiatrists and is aligned to the General Medical Council *Good Medical Practice* (2006), the standard for all medical practitioners. These standards of practice apply to members of the Royal College of Psychiatrists or other psychiatrists whatever their grade, whatever their clinical setting and whenever they are practising.

22.13 The Royal College of Psychiatrists has a standard, set out in *Safe Patients and High Quality Services; a Guide to Job Descriptions and Job Plans for Consultant Psychiatrists*[1] that in general adult and old age psychiatry approximately one hour should be set aside for completing such an assessment. On occasions, less time may be required for patients with relative straightforward conditions. At times, for those patients with more complex disorders and a long history, the assessment may be completed over several appointments. Following a careful history and examination further investigations may be required for example, blood tests, scans or more specialist diagnostic tools. In psychiatry, however, investigations are often of less value in determining management than in many branches of medicine. Investigation may require gaining information from other informants, such as family and friends.

1 Safe Patients and High Quality Services: a Guide to Job Descriptions and Job Plans for Consultant Psychiatrists, Royal College of Psychiatrists College Report 174 (November 2012).

22.14 Assessment requires, in modern psychiatric practice, an assessment of risk. Risk is often considered under three headings: risk to self (risk of self-harm or suicide); risk to others; and risk of self-neglect. The assessment of risk is an imprecise technique. Different categorisations are used, but commonly a judgment is made: low, moderate or high. The exact definitions of what is meant by such adjectives is far from clear. What is expected, however, is that the assessment sets out the psychiatrist's understanding of the risks involved and a resulting management plan, where possible, seeking to reduce the risks identified. The standard is clear in *Good Psychiatric Practice*:

'A psychiatrist must appropriately assess situations where the level of disturbance is severe and risk of adverse events, such as injury to self or others, or harm from others, may be high, and take appropriate clinical action'.

22.15 Although a psychiatrist is an expert in mental health, it is expected that part of the assessment will take account of the physical health of the patient. It is known that patients with mental health problems often have poor physical health outcomes and that the treatments provided may have significant adverse physical health side effects. The Royal College of Psychiatrists has set standards with regard to the physical health of patients with schizophrenia and published audit findings[1].

1 Report of the National Audit of Schizophrenia (2012).

22.16 A thorough assessment should lead to a formulation of the patient's problems that includes an appropriate differential diagnosis. The diagnosis should be made using an accepted classification system, either ICD-10 or DSM-5. The formulation allows for broader consideration of the patient to include problems and difficulties and aetiology.

22.17 Following assessment, diagnosis and formulation, a management plan must be drawn up. This should be done in collaboration with the patient and where appropriate carers and relatives. The management plan should incorporate interventions to address the key areas identified in the formulation including diagnoses, risks, physical disorders and relevant problems. Again, *Good Psychiatric Practice* has a clear standard for this:

'A psychiatrist must ensure that treatment is planned and delivered effectively, and must:

(a) formulate a care plan that relates to the patient's goals, symptoms, diagnosis, risk, outcome of investigations and psychosocial context; this should be carried out in conjunction with, and agreed with, the patient, unless this is not feasible;

(b) if the treatment proposed is outside existing clinical guidelines or the product license of medication, discuss and obtain the patient's agreement, and where appropriate, the agreement of carers and family members;

(c) involve detained patients in treatment decisions as much as possible, taking into account their mental health and the need to provide treatment in their best interests;

(d) recognise the importance of family and carers in the care of patients, share information and seek to fully involve them in the planning and implementation of care and treatment, having discussed this with and considered the views of the patient'.

TREATMENTS

22.18 Psychiatric interventions can be broadly classified into three categories:

(1) physical treatments, medication and electroconvulsive therapy (ECT);
(2) psychological treatments;
(3) social interventions, eg support with housing, advice about employment, help with finances.

Management should include arrangements for follow up and if no follow up is required, the reason for this should be stated.

22.19 All patients should have a care plan. For those on the Care Programme Approach (CPA) (see para **22.37**), clear guidance and formal documentation should be evident. For the many patients treated by an individual practitioner (often a doctor alone), the care plan should be set out in the letters that the psychiatrist writes to the patient's GP, often but not always copied to the patient.

Physical treatments

Electroconvulsive therapy (ECT)

22.20 ECT is largely restricted to patients with severe depressive disorders meeting the following criteria:

(1) psychomotor retardation resulting in significant difficulties with maintaining adequate food and fluid intake;
(2) severe psychotic depressive disorder not otherwise responding to treatment.

Other indications for ECT include a prolonged and severe manic episode which has not responded to drug treatment, and catatonia[1].

1 Guidance on the use of Electroconvulsive Therapy (April 2003), National Institute for Clinical Excellence Technology Appraisal 59.

22.21 The benefits of ECT treatment have been shown in several randomised controlled trials. It is recommended in a NICE Technology Appraisal[1]. It is important that clear standards for ECT delivery are adhered to, including informed consent, an explanation for the patient of side effects, and appropriate monitoring of efficacy. The Royal College of Psychiatrists has in place an accreditation scheme to which many of the organisations which deliver ECT subscribe and adhere to their standards[2].

1 Guidance on the use of electroconvulsive therapy Issued: April 2003 last modified: October 2009 NICE technology appraisal guidance 59.
2 ECTAS Standards (11th edn, 2013).

Medication

22.22 The main psychiatric drugs can be broadly grouped into the following categories:

(1) antidepressants;
(2) antipsychotics;
(3) anxiolytics;
(4) mood stabilisers;
(5) anti-dementia drugs;
(6) stimulants.

Antidepressants

22.23 Antidepressants are among the most widely prescribed drugs in medicine. They act on serotonin and noradrenergic pathways in the brain, though the detailed mechanism of action is poorly understood. The most widely-prescribed class of drugs is the specific serotonin reuptake inhibitors (SSRIs). These include fluoxetine, citalopram, paroxetine, sertraline and fluvoxamine. These drugs are relatively safe in overdosage and side effects are often better tolerated than the older generation of drugs.

22.24 Tricyclic antidepressants were the first class of antidepressants to be made available and have been used in the treatment of depression since the 1950s. This class of drugs is toxic if taken in overdosage and therefore caution and a risk/benefit assessment has to be used in patients who are a significant suicidal risk; side effects include sedation and dry mouth.

Monoamine oxidase inhibitors are a third group of antidepressants not widely used nowadays, largely reflecting the fact that they require patients to limit certain aspects of diet.

Other widely used antidepressants in the UK include venlafaxine, a specific serotonin and noradrenalin reuptake inhibitor, and mirtazapine which has a different mechanism of action from other antidepressants.

Antipsychotics

22.25 The use of antipsychotic drugs in the 1950s, starting with chlorpromazine, contributed to the significant reduction in the number of psychiatric beds needed for patients with severe mental illness. Current drugs are broadly grouped into two categories: the first generation antipsychotic drugs (including chlorpromazine, haloperidol, trifluoperazine, sulpiride, perphenazine) which are effective but are recognised as having significant side effects including sedation and both short- and long-term movement disorder side effects. The second generation antipsychotic drugs or atypical antipsychotics (risperidone, quetiapine, olanzapine, amisulpiride, aripiprazole) are equally but not more effective than the older drugs. The side effects of the atypical antipsychotics vary, but include weight gain, movement side effects and the risk of developing diabetes.

22.26   Antipsychotic drugs can be given in oral dispersible form to improve compliance and by depot injection.

Clozapine is an antipsychotic drug that is particularly effective for treatment resistant schizophrenia but needs careful monitoring through blood tests because of a potential side effect of lowering white cell counts in the blood.

22.27   Antipsychotic drugs should be used with caution in patients with cardiovascular disease. The British National Formulary recommends that in prescribing for the elderly, a balance of risk and benefit should be considered before prescribing antipsychotic drugs.

'In elderly patients with dementia, antipsychotic drugs are associated with a small increased risk of mortality and an increased risk of stroke or transient ischaemic attack ... It is recommended that:

- Antipsychotic drugs should not be used in elderly patients to treat mild to moderate psychotic symptoms.
- Initial dose of antipsychotic drugs in elderly patients should be reduced to half the adult dose or less taking into account factors such as the patient's weight, cormorbidity and concomitant medication.
- Treatment should be reviewed regularly'.

Antipsychotic drugs are sometimes prescribed alongside anticholinergic drugs such as procyclidine to avoid the Parkinsonian side effects of the antipsychotic.

Anxiolytics and hypnotics

22.28   Older anxiolytic and hypnotic drugs such as barbiturates and carbamates are now obsolete because of their lack of safety in overdose. The most widely-used drugs for anxiety are the antidepressant drugs. Benzodiazepine drugs continue to be widely prescribed both as anxiolytics and hypnotics. They are effective in reducing anxiety and aiding sleep but all have significant problems with tolerance and dependence. Tolerance is when over time an increasing dose of the medication is required to achieve the same effect. Dependence is when patients experience physical symptoms when trying to reduce and stop the medication. Benzodiazepines should only be prescribed for brief, time-limited episodes. The advice in the BNF[1] is clear:

'Anxiolytic Benzodiazepine treatment should be limited to the lowest possible dose for the shortest possible time:

(i)   Benzodiazepines are indicated for the short term relief (2–4 weeks only) of anxiety that is severe, disabling or causing the patient unacceptable distress, occurring alone or in association with insomnia or short term psychosomatic, organic or psychotic illness;

(ii) the use of Benzodiazepines to treat short term mild anxiety is inappropriate;

(iii) Benzodiazepines should be used to treat insomnia only when it is severe, disabling or causing the patient extreme distress'.

Other drugs used in the management of anxiety are buspirone and pregabalin.

1 BNF 66 (2013). BMJ and Pharmaceutical Press, London.

22.29   For the short-term relief of disturbed sleep, a new class of sedative drugs has been introduced: the 'Z Drugs' (zopiclone, zolpidem, and zaleplon).

Mood stabilisers

22.30   Mood stabilisers are drugs used to prevent or reduce the severity of relapses for patients with bipolar disorder. The first made available was lithium, which requires regular blood test monitoring. Other mood stabilisers include anticonvulsants, eg sodium valproate and carbamazepine. Antipsychotic drugs can also be used as mood stabilisers.

Stimulants

22.31   Stimulants are recognised as effective in treating attention deficit hyperactivity disorder (ADHD) in children and there are increasing requests for them to be prescribed in adults reflecting the fact that the disorder does not stop on an 18th birthday.

Drugs for dementia

22.32   Anticholinesterase inhibitor drugs and the glutamate receptor antagonist, memantine, are used in the treatment of dementia. In some patients, these drugs slow the progression of dementia but they do not reverse it and do not stop the inexorable decline of dementia. There is little evidence for their efficacy for types of dementia other than Alzheimer's disease.

Psychological treatments

22.33   Although there are different types of psychological treatments, there is considerable overlap between therapies described. There is also evidence that the relationship between the therapist and the patient can be more important in predicting recovery than the specific type of therapy offered. The main categories of therapy used in the UK are as follows:

(1)   **Cognitive behaviour therapy (CBT)**: CBT is the treatment for which there is the strongest evidence base, with controlled trials demonstrating its particular effectiveness in the treatment of depression and anxiety disorders. The content of the treatment has been set out in manuals. The treatment is time limited and usually offered for between 12 and 16 one-hour long sessions. The treatment is based on the concept that a problem is caused by the patient's perception (their cognitions about

what has happened) rather than by the event itself. Therapy aims to change the cognitions by talking and challenging the thoughts and by specific behavioural tasks. CBT can be delivered on an individual basis, in groups or as self-help via books and computer programmes;

(2) **Counselling**: Counselling is a more non-specific treatment than CBT with less evidence demonstrating its effectiveness. It can provide an opportunity for individuals to talk about their current experiences and difficulties with a professional. Therapists often attempt to link the past to current difficulties;

(3) **Psychodynamic psychotherapy**: This is the therapy espoused by Freud and Jung. There is much less evidence for its effectiveness as a treatment than CBT-based treatments and it is not now widely available in the UK. Treatment occurs over a period of at least 18 months;

(4) **Dialectical Behaviour Therapy (DBT)**: DBT was introduced in 1991 by Linehan and colleagues as a treatment for patients with borderline personality disorder. Patients are taught to both understand their emotional difficulties and, using both group and individual work, taught new skills to better manage emotional distress.

22.34   In England, psychological therapies are widely delivered through the Improving Access to Psychological Treatment (IAPT) Programme. IAPT offers a stepped-care treatment approach with often a telephone assessment, followed by signposting to self-help and support groups, stepping up to more complex treatment delivered by more experienced therapists as necessary.

Social interventions

22.35   Many psychiatric disorders are, if not caused by, certainly worsened by social problems. Also many patients with a severe mental disorder such as schizophrenia experience significant problems in management of their everyday lives. An important part of many psychiatric management plans, therefore, is the practical help and support given to patients with concerns such as housing, employment, benefits, daytime activities and social interactions. An important concept of modern psychiatry is that of recovery. Recovery does not mean simply the improvement and reduction of psychiatric symptoms, but an approach to enable patients with mental illness to lead fulfilled and rewarding lives.

Physical healthcare

22.36   As noted above, patients with a mental disorder have poor physical health outcomes compared with the general population. It is important that psychiatrists, as doctors, are alert to the physical health treatment requirements of their patients. Psychiatrists in inpatient units have a responsibility for ensuring that their patients receive appropriate physical health treatments. If they do not feel confident in the management of conditions diagnosed, they must make the appropriate referral to other specialists.

Care Programme Approach

22.37   In England and Wales, treatment within NHS services is provided within the framework of the Care Programme Approach (CPA). This is key national guidance[1] which should ensure patients with the most severe disorders get the treatments required. The CPA guidance[2] says that you should get help under CPA if you have:

- severe mental illness (including personality disorder);
- problems with looking after yourself including:
  - self-harm;
  - suicide attempts;
  - harming other people including breaking the law;
  - a history of becoming unwell and needing urgent help;
  - not wanting support or treatment;
  - vulnerability;
- severe distress at the moment or you have felt a lot of severe distress in the past;
- problems working with Mental Health Services or have done in the past;
- another non-physical condition alongside mental illness, for example learning disability, drug or alcohol misuse;
- services from a number of agencies such as housing, physical care, criminal justice or voluntary agencies;
- recently been detained under the Mental Health Act or are detained at the moment;
- recently been put in touch with Crisis/Home Treatment Team or getting their help at the moment;
- a need for a lot of help from carers or you provide a lot of care to someone yourself (children or adult);
- disadvantage or difficulties due to parenting responsibilities, physical health problems or disability, unsettled accommodation or housing issues, employment issues, mental illness significantly affecting your day to day life, ethnicity issues.

Local teams will follow guidance set their by organisations which may differ in detail but not in principle from what is set out above.

1 Care Programme Approach: Positive Practice Guidance (2008).
2 Care Programme Approach Factsheet Version 2 (2013). Rethink Mental Illness, www.rethink. org/resources/c/care-programme-approach-cpafactsheet.

22.38   Patients looked after within the framework of CPA should have a care coordinator (often a nurse) who should:

(1)   fully assess the patient's needs;
(2)   set out a care plan with the patient which shows how the needs will be met;
(3)   regularly review the care plan to check progress.

The care coordinator is the person who links together and coordinates all the people who may be providing an individual's care.

22.39   The care plan should fully involve the patient and, if appropriate, their carers and may include interventions looking at the following:

(1)   medication;

(2)   therapy;
(3)   help with money problems;
(4)   advice and support;
(5)   help with everyday living tasks including employment and training;
(6)   help with housing;
(7)   community care services.

The care plan should be reviewed on a regular basis as set out in local policies, usually every 6 or 12 months.

LEGAL ISSUES

22.40   Mental health legislation varies across the different countries of the UK. In England and Wales, the current legislation is the Mental Health Act 1983 which was amended in 2007. The Mental Capacity Act 2005 regulates decision making on behalf of incapable adults and was implemented in 2007.

In Scotland, the Mental Health (Care and Treatment) (Scotland) Act of 2003 replaced the previous Mental Health Act of Scotland 1984 in October 2005. The relevant capacity legislation is the Adults with Incapacity Act 2000, which was implemented between April 2001 and 2003.

In Northern Ireland, the care and treatment of patients with mental disorder is regulated by the Mental Health (Northern Ireland) Order of 1986, amended by the Mental Health (Amendment) (Northern Ireland) Order of 2004. There is currently no specific incapacity legislation.

22.41   All the Mental Health Act legislations allow medical practitioners to admit patients to hospital for assessment and treatment, detain patients who are already in hospital and, with the provision of Community Treatment Orders, authorise compulsory powers for patients in the community. Details of how the Acts are implemented differ in different countries within the UK but all have safeguards allowing for appeals by patients and their relatives. All require the use of least restrictive practices compatible with safe and effective care and all have relatively broad definitions of mental illness or mental disorder.

The Human Rights Act 1998 has been used in legal cases to determine whether satisfactory care was provided.

Consent to treatment

22.42   It is fundamental to the provision of medical care that treatment for patients should be with their consent. For consent to be valid, the patient must have capacity to make the medical treatment decisions and the consent must be informed, ie the patient has fully understood the details and implications of what is proposed, and they must be freely given, ie not under duress. General Medical Council *Good Medical Practice*[1] sets out clearly:

'You must be satisfied you have consent or other valid authority before you undertake any examination or investigation providing treatment or involve patients or volunteers in treatment or research'.

1 *Good Medical Practice* (2013). General Medical Council, London.

22.43   If a patient does not consent to treatment that the psychiatrist believes to be necessary, they must consider firstly whether compulsory treatment under Mental Health Act legislation applies or whether best interest treatment under capacity legislation applies.

Mental Capacity Act 2005 (England and Wales)

22.44   The Mental Capacity Act 2005 (applicable in England and Wales) is underpinned by a set of five key principles:

(1)   presumption of capacity: a person is presumed to have capacity unless it is established that he lacks capacity;

(2)   all practical steps are taken to allow autonomy: a person is not to be treated as unable to make a decision unless all practical steps to help him to do so have been taken without success;

(3)   allow unwise decisions: a person is not incapable merely because he makes an unwise decision;

(4)   best interests: an intervention under the Act on behalf of a person who lacks capacity must be in his best interests;

(5)   least restrictive option: any intervention under the Act on behalf of a person who lacks capacity should restrict, as little as possible, his basic rights and freedom.

22.45   There is a two-stage process for assessing incapacity:

(1)   a person lacks capacity if he is unable to make a decision for himself in relation to any matter because of permanent or temporary impairment of the functioning of the mind;

(2)   a person is unable to make a decision for himself if he is unable to:

—   understand the information relevant to the decision;

—   retain that information for a sufficient period to make a decision;

—   use or weigh that information as part of the process of making a decision;

—   communicate the decision.

THE TRAINING AND EXPERIENCE OF PSYCHIATRISTS

22.46   Psychiatrists are doctors who have undergone the same core training as doctors in any other speciality. This is often poorly understood by the general public, who can be confused, particularly about the distinction between a psychologist (who is not a medical practitioner) and a psychiatrist.

22.47   The training of psychiatrists matches in structure that of the training for doctors in other specialities. It is now the case that all doctors on graduating from medical school in the UK undertake two years of foundation training. In these posts the doctors are closely supervised by more senior doctors. The doctors usually rotate through posts every four months, in order to obtain wide experience across many fields of medicine. At present, doctors are registered with the General Medical Council at the completion of their first foundation year of training. At the time of writing this chapter, there is discussion of whether registration with the General Medical Council should occur immediately after graduating from medical school.

22.48 On completion of the foundation years, doctors enter more specialist training to equip them to become general practitioners or specialists within their chosen fields. The duration of training depends on which branch of medicine the doctors choose to enter. Some doctors choose to undertake further periods of general training (known as core specialist training) in which they continue to train in a variety of specialities before undertaking specialist training.

22.49 At the completion of the six years of specialist training and the demonstration that they have obtained the required skills and knowledge, psychiatrists obtain their certificate of completion of specialist training and are eligible to be on the General Medical Council Specialist Register in Psychiatry.

CLINICAL NEGLIGENCE: WHAT CAN GO WRONG

22.50 It should be clear from reading the chapter so far that there are several areas in which clinical negligence may occur, that is when the doctor who owed a duty of care to an individual, breached that duty by failing to provide the required standard of care, and that this resulted in foreseeable and reasonably avoidable injury or loss.

Assessment

22.51 There are two important aspects to the assessment:

(1) **Who does the assessment**: patients have a right to be assessed by somebody with suitable skills and knowledge. If an assessment has been done by a doctor in training, the question needs to be asked how experienced was the doctor, what training had they had and what was the level of supervision offered by a more experienced doctor? Psychiatrists specialise in different areas of practice relating to age, eg children, adults, older people, and specialism, eg forensic psychiatry, intellectual disability, neuropsychiatry etc. There is considerable overlap in training and experience, but all psychiatrists should be competent in their area of practice and if working outside their obvious specialisation they may be required to demonstrate their competency.

It is not always the case that assessments are done by doctors. If an assessment has not been done by a doctor, what training and experience did the practitioner have in undertaking the assessment? Were they operating within their competency and what were the local protocols guiding when advice and guidance from a doctor should be sought?

(2) **The quality of the assessment**: a judgment should be made as to whether the standard of assessment is satisfactory in the clinical context. It is acceptable for an assessment to concentrate on the clinical aspects that appear to be most relevant. It is important, however, that if there

are issues concerning risk, particularly to self and others, a detailed and thorough assessment is undertaken taking into account the history of what has happened in the past as well as the individual's current mental state and stated intentions. If necessary, information should be sought from informants and other sources before important decisions are made.

22.52 In the assessment of self-harm and risk of suicide, the NICE Quality Standard[1] is as follows:

'When assessing the risks of repetition of self-harm or risks of suicide, identify and agree with the person who self-harms the specific risks for them, taking into account:

- methods and frequency of current and past self-harm;
- current and past suicidal intent;
- depressive symptoms and their relationship to self-harm;
- any psychiatric illness and its relationship to self-harm;
- the personal and social context and any other specific factors preceding self-harm, such as specific unpleasant affective states or emotions and changes in relationships;
- specific risk factors and protective factors (social, psychological, pharmacological and motivational) that may increase or decrease the risks associated with self-harm;
- coping strategies that the person has used to either successfully limit or avert self-harm or to contain the impact of personal, social or other factors preceding episodes of self-harm;
- significant relationships that may either be supportive or represent a threat (such as abuse or neglect) and may lead to changes in the level of risk;
- immediate and longer-term risks.

Consider the possible presence of other coexisting risk-taking or destructive behaviours, such as engaging in unprotected sexual activity, exposure to unnecessary physical risks, drug misuse or engaging in harmful or hazardous drinking.

When assessing risk, consider asking the person who self-harms about whether they have access to family members', carers' or significant others' medications.

In the initial management of self-harm in children and young people, advise parents and carers of the need to remove all medications or, where possible, other means of self-harm available to the child or young person.

Be aware that all acts of self-harm in older people should be taken as evidence of suicidal intent until proven otherwise'.

1 Quality Standard 34; Self-harm. NICE (June 2013).

22.53 Guidance is provided on the use of risk assessment tools and scales:

'Do not use risk assessment tools and scales to predict future suicide or repetition of self-harm.

Do not use risk assessment tools and scales to determine who should and should not be offered treatment or who should be discharged.

Risk assessment tools may be considered to help structure risk assessments as long as they include the areas in the bullet list identified above'.

A thorough assessment of risk is an important foundation on which subsequent management decisions are built.

Diagnosis and formulation

22.54 The outcome of the assessment should be a formulation (a summary) of the patient's difficulties, including a judgment about risk, together with a diagnosis. It is to be expected that this judgment is informed by the assessment that has been undertaken and is in line with the relevant evidence base.

22.55 A key judgment that is required following many psychiatric assessments is the risk of self-harm and suicide. In making this judgment, clinicians draw on:

(1)   relevant past history;
(2)   current diagnosis;
(3)   stated intent;
(4)   recent behaviour, including drug and alcohol use.

22.56 There needs to be a justification for the level of risk determined, supported by the findings from the assessment. A relevant court case found concerns about diagnosis, risk assessment, supervision of junior staff and treatment.

22.57 In *Drake v Pontefract Health Authority, Wakefield and Pontefract Community Health NHS Trust*[1], the key issues were whether a failure to properly diagnose the plaintiff's depression and assess her risk of suicide was negligent and causative of plaintiff's injuries resulting from suicide attempt. The plaintiff attempted to commit suicide by jumping from a footbridge. Prior to doing so she had consumed a quantity of paracetamol tablets. As a result of her actions she sustained serious personal injury and became permanently disabled. At the time of the incident, the plaintiff was a patient at Pontefract General Infirmary. The conclusions of the judgment were as follows:

'(1)   the plaintiff attempted to commit suicide at a time when she was suffering from a psychiatric illness, namely agitated depression, which affected her judgment and mental state and which was responsible for the suicide attempt and consequential injuries;
(2)   the defendants' medical staff failed to diagnose this condition, failed to properly assess the risk of suicide and accordingly failed to give the plaintiff appropriate treatment and were thereby in breach of the duty of care they owed to the plaintiff;
(3)   Dr V was negligent in failing to diagnose the plaintiff's condition correctly, failing to properly assess the risk of suicide and in failing to give appropriate treatment;
(4)   Dr J was negligent in permitting Dr V to interview and treat the plaintiff following the referral of Dr P, without immediate supervision from either herself or an experienced doctor who specialised in psychiatry;
(5)   the treatment offered to the plaintiff following her assessment by Dr V was inappropriate. In particular … the continued prescribing of Fluanxol 1 mg per day failed to deal with or in any way address the plaintiff's illness which included a major depressive element which carried with it a serious risk of suicide;
(6)   had the plaintiff been given the appropriate antidepressant medication following her referral, on the balance of probabilities, she would not have attempted to commit suicide'.

1 [1998] Lloyd's Rep Med 425.

Management

22.58   There are several aspects of management of a patient with psychiatric problems that may be considered in a case of negligence:

(1)   the decision whether or not to admit to hospital including the decision about use of the Mental Health Act 1983;

(2)   the treatment whilst in hospital, including the levels of observation of the patient, the use of periods of leave and the decision to discharge;

(3)   the prescription of medication including choice of medication, dose and combinations used and monitoring;

(4)   whether treatment plans meet the requirements of the CPA process and relevant guidelines.

22.59   Of course, before a psychiatrist is involved in the care of a patient, the patient must be referred to them by the general practitioner. In *Mahmood v Siggins*[1] the patient had a history of bipolar illness and presented to his general practitioner. The finding of negligence was made because of the absence of sufficient examination of the claimant's mental state and as a result of that a failure to arrange appropriate treatment and follow up.

1   [1996] 7 Med LR 76, QBD.

Hospital admission

22.60   The use of a hospital bed for patients with psychiatric problems has decreased significantly over time, as has duration of admissions. This reflects the increasing use of crisis response and home treatment teams which have been established to provide intensive support to patients at home as an alternative to hospital admission. Hospital admission is now reserved for the most ill patients who cannot be safely managed at home, either because of the nature of their illness or because of the risk that they present to themselves or others. It will be the case that if a patient harms themselves or others following an assessment which has not led to a hospital admission, relatives will rightly question whether a hospital admission would have prevented the adverse incident. In order to answer this question, the quality of the assessment and whether the judgment following that assessment can be justified will be scrutinised.

22.61   It is likely to be difficult to prove that a decision not to admit to hospital was negligent because:

(1)   the expectation of commissioners and providers of services is that patients will be treated at home where possible;

(2)   the expectation that, in considering whether to use the Mental Health Act 1983, the least restrictive options are to be used;

(3)   the recognition that in-patient care rarely offers specific interventions that cannot be delivered in the community.

22.62   If a patient is known to be at significant risk to themselves or others and the decision is taken not to admit them to hospital or to use the Mental Health Act if necessary, the reasons should be set out in the clinical record. What would not be acceptable is the recording that the reason for not admitting a patient was made because of the lack of availability of beds, or that risks are identified which the treatment plan fails to adequately address.

Care in hospital

22.63 There is an expectation that following hospital admission, there will be a further and more intensive assessment and a review of the diagnosis and management plan. Most providers of inpatient care will have standards and protocols which staff are expected to follow.

Observations

22.64 A key decision following inpatient admission is the level of observation that patients are under. All inpatient units will have a clear policy to guide staff in this important area of practice. Observation levels vary from general observations, which mean that nurses should know which patients are on the ward but do not necessarily know their immediate whereabouts, through timed observations when patients are physically checked at timed intervals, usually between 15, 30 or 60 minutes, constant observations are when patients are kept within line of sight at all times and the most intensive or special observations when patients are within arm's length. The use of timed observations is controversial, although they continue to be widely used. Gournay and Bowers[1] offer a useful description of general and constant observation:

'General observation can be thought of as the observation and monitoring of the physical geography of the ward and as a component of constant review of safety in the light of opportunities the ward and its contents provide for harm to come to patients. The general observation should be an established part of ward routine and followed rigorously and regularly by nurses as part of their everyday practice to maintain the safety of patients. Constant observation should be used for patients who are considered to present a significant risk to self or others. An allocated member of staff should be constantly aware at all times of the precise whereabouts of the patient through visual observation or hearing'.

1 Gournay and Bowers 'Suicide and self-harm in psychiatric inpatient units: a study of nursing issues in 31 cases' (2000) Journal of Advance Nursing 32.

22.65 The only observations that can prevent an episode of suicide in hospital are when patients are kept within line of sight. At all other times, clinicians have to take a risk because there will be times when the patient is not in direct observation of nursing staff. It is accepted that a balance needs to be struck between keeping the patient safe by watching them and the often intrusive and unpleasant nature of being kept under close scrutiny. Nursing advice is to limit the use of timed observations in favour of using skilled nursing time to engage with the patient and build up a rapport and a relationship in order that the patient will let staff know how they are feeling and if they have suicidal thoughts.

22.66 In *Hunter-Blair v Worthing Priority Care NHS Trust Settlement*[1] Mr Hunter-Blair was diagnosed as schizophrenic when 19, and had since then periods of in-patient treatment. In January 1996 his condition deteriorated. After admissions to two other hospitals, he was transferred to the Homefield Hospital in the extra care area. At transfer, he was noted as being a paranoid schizophrenic with a history of absconding from hospital. It was noted he needed to be constantly observed. The nursing plan at Homefield recorded 'absconding risk'. On 10 October 1996 he attempted to leave the ward. On 11 October 1996, inexplicably, he was able to leave the unit unobserved and unhindered.

1 February 2000, Medical Litigation Cases 0944.

22.67 It was alleged by the claimant that the Homefield staff were in breach of their duty of care to him in allowing him to abscond. When he absconded, he made his way to a multi-storey car park and jumped off, in a presumed suicide attempt, breaking both ankles and injuring his back.

22.68 The claimant's psychiatric expert considered that 1:1 supervision should have been adopted. The psychiatric nursing expert did not consider that this was mandatory, even though the claimant was a high suicide risk but did say that five minute observations would be appropriate. The notes of the unit were not well kept and it was noted that Mr Hunter-Blair had not been monitored for the 35 minutes before he was noticed missing rather than the five minute observations recommended in the care plan. Eventually the defendants admitted 75 per cent liability.

Ligature audits

22.69 Patients have a right to expect that the ward environment will be safe and will have been checked for ligature points. There is a national never event: hanging from a non-collapsible curtain rail. There are many other potential ligature points in a hospital inpatient ward and it would be expected that hospital providers will have regularly reviewed and assessed the potential ligature points in the ward and done all that is sensible to remove them in order to provide a safe ward environment.

Leave and discharge from hospital

22.70 Leave, either accompanied or unaccompanied, is a stage at which patients may be at increased risk. Decisions about leave should be made by a multidisciplinary team and involve senior clinicians who have the experience to make the necessary judgments about when it is safe for the patient to leave the ward environment. Decisions about discharge should similarly be made in a multidisciplinary way. The decision should involve patients and their immediate family, where appropriate, together with staff from the community who will be responsible for monitoring the care of the patient following discharge.

22.71 It is recognised from the National Confidential Inquiry into Suicide and Homicide by people with mental illness[1] that the greatest risk of suicide following discharge from hospital is in the first two weeks after leaving hospital. There is a national expectation that all patients discharged from hospital receive a follow up within seven days of leaving hospital and for those at high risk of self-harm, within 48 hours. It is important that this follow-up review is not simply a tick-box exercise, but is a planned meeting with the patient at which they are able to talk about their experience since discharge, how they are feeling and a thorough and expert assessment is made of their current suicidal intent.

1 National Confidential Inquiry into Suicide and Homicide by People with Mental Illness (July 2013) www.bbmh.manchester.ac.uk/cmhr/research/centreforsuicideprevention.

22.72   Leave was considered in the case of *G v Central and North West London Mental Health NHS Trust*[1]. The key issues included:

- unescorted leave;
- informal in-patient leaving hospital grounds, getting on to train line and being hit by train;
- the claimant was permitted by medical staff to have periods of unescorted leave from the unit, provided that she remained on hospital premises;
- whether the defendant's decision to permit her to leave unit unaccompanied was negligent;
- whether the defendant's encouragement to the claimant to control herself and to take responsibility for her actions was an appropriate way of managing her very difficult behaviour.

1 (19 October 2007, unreported).

22.73   A claimant mental patient, who presented a mixed picture such that that medical staff gained the impression that she had a greater ability to control her behaviour than may in fact have been the case, failed to establish that the defendant's management was reasonable.

The conclusions of the judgment were as follows:

'Psychiatry – perhaps more than any other branch of medicine – is not an exact science. A doctor practising in this field has to make difficult decisions about the management and treatment of patients suffering from a range of mental illnesses and distress. Many of these decisions inevitably involve the assessment of risk, together with the balancing of any risk which may be present against the benefits of making progress with the patient's rehabilitation. The claimant's was such a case.

From the medical records I have seen and from the way in which she gave her evidence, I have formed the impression that Dr G is a capable, conscientious and careful doctor. It is clear from the records that she carried out regular reviews of the claimant's condition and that those reviews included discussions (often quite lengthy discussions) with the claimant and her husband, as well as with other members of her team. Her reviews were supplemented by reviews made at other times by junior doctors. During the period of the claimant's admission, Dr G made a number of adjustments to her medication in response to problems that were reported to her. These adjustments continued to be made right up to the time of the Ward Round immediately preceding the claimant's suicide attempt. She was, in my judgment, making every effort to respond to the claimant's needs throughout the period of her admission.

There is no doubt that Dr G had the risks associated with leave in mind and that she discussed them with the claimant and her husband. The medical records make this clear. I accept her evidence that she was seeking to balance those risks against the benefits to the claimant that a greater degree of freedom would bring'.

Medication

22.74   The prescription of medication must be done in adherence to the relevant prescribing standards. The prescription of most psychiatric drugs is relatively straightforward but in some cases special considerations apply.

Lithium

22.75   Lithium is a mood-stabilising drug used in the treatment of patients with bipolar affective disorder as a prophylactic. It is also used as an adjunct to antidepressant medication for patients with a treatment-resistant depressive disorder. Lithium is unusual in psychiatric practice as it is not the dose that is important but rather the concentration of drug in the bloodstream. Patients on lithium, therefore, require regular monitoring of their blood lithium levels and there is clear guidance as to the frequency at which this should occur. The reason for this is that lithium is a drug that has a narrow therapeutic window. If the concentration of the lithium in the blood is too low, it is not therapeutic; if it is too high, patients are at risk of lithium toxicity. Lithium can also have an adverse effect on thyroid and kidney function and hence blood tests looking at the activity of the thyroid gland and kidney need to be checked regularly. The National Patient Safety Agency[1] issued an alert setting out the following guidance:

'Some patients taking Lithium have been harmed because they have not had their dosage adjusted based on recommended regular blood tests. If patients are not informed of the known side effects or symptoms of toxicity, they cannot manage their Lithium therapy safely.

Regular blood tests are important. Clinically significant alterations in Lithium blood levels occur with commonly prescribed and over-the-counter medicines. The blood level of Lithium is dependent on kidney function and Lithium has the potential to interfere with kidney (renal) and thyroid functions.

All healthcare organisations in the NHS where Lithium therapy is initiated, prescribed, dispensed and monitored are asked to ensure that by 31 December 2010:

- patients prescribed Lithium are monitored in accordance with NICE guidance;
- there are reliable systems to ensure blood test results are communicated between laboratories and prescribers;
- at the start of Lithium therapy and throughout their treatment patients receive appropriate ongoing verbal and written information and a record book to track Lithium blood levels and relevant clinical tests*;
- prescribers and pharmacists check that blood tests are monitored regularly and that it is safe to issue a repeat prescription and/or dispense the prescribed Lithium;
- systems are in place to identify and deal with medicines that might adversely interact with Lithium therapy.

* The NPSA has developed a patient information booklet, Lithium alert card and record book for tracking blood tests.'

1 Patient Safety Alert (1 December 2009), National Patient Safety Agency.

22.76   Oyebode[1], in an article on clinical errors in medical negligence, notes that the combination of lithium and diuretics can result in elevated and toxic lithium levels. Most negligence claims regarding these drugs arise when a general practitioner prescribes a diuretic to a patient who is on lithium and no one adequately monitors lithium levels or acts on the results of monitoring. Lithium should also be used with caution in combination with non-steroidal anti-inflammatory drugs.

1 Oyebode 'Clinical errors and medical negligence' (2006) Advances in Psychiatric Treatment 12.

Sodium valproate

22.77   Sodium valproate is an anticonvulsant drug that is used as a mood stabiliser in the treatment of bipolar affective disorder. It is a psychiatric drug that has a particular adverse impact on the unborn fetus; the risk is greatest in the first three months of pregnancy. It is recommended that women should not be prescribed sodium alproate if they are intending to become pregnant and that the medication should be stopped if they do become pregnant, unless there is no safe alternative. It is important that if women of child-bearing age are prescribed sodium valproate, that they are aware of the risks and benefits of the medication and are using reliable contraception.

Clozapine

22.78   Clozapine is an antipsychotic drug recommended for use for treatment resistant schizophrenia. It is recommended that patients should have had a therapeutic trial of at least two antipsychotic drugs before starting clozapine. Clozapine is an effective antipsychotic drug but has a recognised, albeit small, risk of causing a serious reduction in the number of white cells in the blood. These are the cells that fight infection. This could be life threatening for the patient. In order to prevent such a catastrophic reaction, patients on clozapine require regular monitoring of their white cells. This is initially weekly and over time reduces to monthly. The prescription of clozapine can only occur in conjunction with the Clozaril Monitoring Service and there is a clear system established in the UK so that the clozapine cannot be prescribed until the blood tests taken indicate that it is safe to do so.

22.79   Clozapine has other important side effects and there are a small number of cases where people have died because of severe constipation resulting in a burst colon. Doctors should be aware of this and patients should be warned to let their doctor know if they are suffering constipation or abdominal pain as they may need treatment with laxative medication to avoid serious complications occurring.

Other antipsychotic drugs

22.80   Antipsychotic drugs vary in the nature and frequency of the side effects. There is an expectation, however, that all patients prescribed these drugs will be warned about the most serious side effects so that they can make an informed choice about the decisions made and that the side effects will be monitored appropriately. Key side effects for antipsychotic medication include:

(1)   movement side effects (particularly with older antipsychotics):

- antipsychotic induced Parkinsonism characterised by tremor, rigidity and bradykinesia (generally occurs within four weeks of treatment and is dose dependent);
- akathisia: a feeling of inner restlessness, subjective distress and objective component, for example pacing and inability to sit still;
- tardive dyskinesia: late onset involuntary repetitive, purposeless movements linked to the chronic use of antipsychotics, particularly in high dose. It is difficult to treat;

- acute dystonia: sustained and often painful muscle spasm usually occurring within one week of commencing or rapidly increasing the dose of antipsychotic;

(2) weight gain, particularly with olanzapine;

(3) diabetes (particularly the newer antipsychotics);

(4) sedation;

(5) hyperprolactinemia causing gynaecomastia, galactorrhea, erectile dysfunction, loss of libido;

(6) neuroleptic malignant syndrome: a rare, life threatening, idiosyncratic reaction to antipsychotic medication characterised by fever, muscular rigidity, altered mental state and autonomic dysfunction.

Psychiatrists must be able to justify the dose and duration of the prescription of antipsychotics and be clear with the patient about the risk and benefit profile.

Antidepressant medication

22.81 Although antidepressants are known to be an effective treatment for depression, it has been suggested that they can increase the risk of suicide, particularly in the first two weeks of prescription. Particularly with the SSRIs, an increase in agitation early on and the possible increase in energy and motivation before a patient's mood lifts may increase the risk of suicide. The extent and importance of these effects remain unclear, but both add to the importance of ensuring appropriate monitoring of patients at risk of suicide when starting antidepressant medication. Evidence suggests that young people who take SSRIs have increased suicidal thoughts (but not actual suicidal acts), therefore in the UK SSRIs are not licensed for people under 18, although specialists may use fluoxetine in some cases.

22.82 Serotonin syndrome is a rare but potentially fatal syndrome occurring in the context of initiating or dose increase of a serotonergic agent characterised by altered mental state, agitation, tremor, shivering, diarrhoea, hyperreflexia, myoclonus ataxia and hyperthermia.

Benzodiazepines

22.83 Benzodiazepines are an effective treatment for short-term sleep problems and anxiety. However, as noted above, they are addictive and they should be prescribed only for short-term, time-limited (less than four weeks) courses. Patients who have been incorrectly prescribed courses of benzodiazepines outside these criteria may become dependent on them and find it difficult to come off the medication. For the short-term relief of disturbed sleep, a new class of sedative drugs has been introduced: the 'Z Drugs' (zopiclone, zolpidem, and zaleplon). These were marketed as being less addictive than benzodiazepines but work in a similar way. There is not enough evidence to show that they are less likely to cause dependence than benzodiazepines. The advice for their use therefore is much the same as for benzodiazepines: only when psychological methods have failed, at the lowest possible dose and for short periods of time.

22.84   The *Benzodiazepine Litigation* was a product liability claim against the drug manufacturers rather than medical negligence claim. It involved thousands of claimants and cost over £40 million in legal aid. Not one penny was obtained in compensation; of interest is the judicial consideration of the toxicity of these drugs in the context of the underlying morbidity:

'There are very considerable problems on causation; these involve distinguishing between the effects of the drug and the underlying condition for which it was prescribed, the problems caused by previous addiction to benzodiazepine drugs other than those prescribed by the defendants, and distinguishing between symptoms due to the drugs or, in some cases, other drugs or excess alcohol, and the fact that many plaintiffs may suffer at least some withdrawal symptoms in any event. There is the difficult question of balancing the benefit of the drug against the undesirable consequences of taking it...'[1].

1   *AB v John Wyeth and Brother Ltd* [1994] 5 Med LR 149, per Stuart-Smith LJ at 153.

22.85   In a judgment of the Supreme Court of the Northern Territory of Australia[1], a psychiatrist was negligent in: (1) implementing and continuing a benzodiazepine drug regime in which the patient undertook 17 months of continuous alprazolam treatment; (2) failing to inform the patient of the true nature of the drugs which he was prescribing; (3) failing to inform her that they were psychologically and physiologically addictive; (4) failing to provide her with the opportunity to consider and choose a different approach. Negligence had caused the patient to become psychologically habituated to the drug and physiologically dependent upon the drug, which led to her suffering considerable difficulties in withdrawing from the benzodiazepines.

1   *D Pty Ltd Marinovich* [1999] NTSC 127, Medical Litigation Cases 0196.

22.86   Barbiturates are now rarely prescribed but the case below could have resulted from benzodiazepine prescribing. In *Fleming v Toltz*[1] psychiatry treatment by barbiturates was held to be negligent and caused the plaintiff (K) model's inability to work. The plaintiff was, in 1989, one of the top 10 models in Australia. In late 1989 she found a lump in her breast. An operation was performed under local anaesthetic. The breast became infected. On 21 February 1990 she suffered a severe anxiety attack. The deceased defendant, Dr F, admitted her to hospital. While K was in the hospital she was treated with a number of drugs including pentobarbitone or nembutal. By March 1990, plaintiff had become addicted to pentobarbitone. In October 1990 she was admitted to a detoxification unit. After her release from the detoxification unit, K continued to feel mentally unwell. She became overweight and later developed very high blood pressure. In late 1990, the plaintiff felt that she was unable to resume her career notwithstanding that she wished to do so. There was no doubt that Dr F was negligent in his treatment of K. The issue in the claim against the Executor of the Estate of Dr F was whether the plaintiff's inability to work in subsequent years could be fully attributed to Dr F's negligence.

1   (4 July 2000, unreported), New South Wales Supreme Court.

Dosage of medication

22.87   All medications should be prescribed in line with the dosages recommended in the BNF. Although medication can be prescribed outside the criteria set, this would be a decision that should only be taken by an experienced psychiatrist and in open discussion with the patient, weighing up potential benefits and problems. Patients should be aware that the medication is being prescribed outside the recommended dosage limits and give consent. The treatment should be considered as a therapeutic trial by the prescribing doctor and only continued if the benefits outweigh the potential risks. The Royal College of Psychiatrist's Guidance[1] has clear criteria for the prescribing of high-dose antipsychotic medication and recommends that it should occur only rarely.

1 Royal College of Psychiatrists. Consensus Statement on High Dose Antipsychotic Medication (2014).

22.88　There are two ways of calculating for patients who are on more than one dose of the same class of medication. The mechanism for calculating the total dose is either to convert the medication to chlorpromazine equivalents or to add up the percentages of the different medications involved, which should not be more than 100 per cent.

Non-medication treatment options

22.89　Psychiatric patients often benefit from a care plan that includes medication together with other options which, as noted above, could be psychological treatments and social interventions. There are NICE Guidelines for all the common mental disorders which set out treatments for which there is an evidence base. Although the implementation of NICE Guidelines are not mandatory, unlike Technology Assessments (for NHS providers), it is recognised good practice that the treatment set out in NICE Guidelines should be offered to patients as providing the best evidence-based treatment.

22.90　It is not the case that only treatments in such guidelines can be offered, as lack of evidence does not mean that there is no evidence for effectiveness. The role of a senior doctor is often to recommend treatments outside and beyond guidelines. This should be done, however, in full recognition of what is in the guidelines and a clear explanation written in the case notes as to why the action is being taken and how the patient's progress will be monitored.

Overall care

22.91　It can be the case that it is the overall failure of a care plan and the level of support provided that is seen as negligent as in the case of *Rafferty v Portsmouth Healthcare NHS Trust Hampshire County Council*[1].

In 1988 the claimant, then aged 20, was referred by her GP to the local NHS consultant psychiatrist for psychiatric treatment. From that date, the claimant was under the care of each of the defendants, sometimes as a patient under provision of the Mental Health Act, at other times voluntarily as a patient of the Trust. Her care was shared by a multi-disciplinary team, comprising of social services, who were providing counselling and other support, and the NHS Trust, who were providing her with psychiatric treatment.

There were several notable life events in the claimant's life during a number of years from 1988–1999. She was diagnosed with schizophrenia in November 1991. The claimant also misused alcohol from time to time in order to cope with her symptoms. During the period from 1994–1999 the claimant's alcohol misuse increased.

The defendants were made aware of this and yet failed to adjust her care plan and the level of support given to her was, in fact, reduced over a period of time. She attempted to take her own life on two occasions. These attempts failed.

On 16 May 1999 she jumped off a bridge and suffered serious fractures to both her legs in a further suicide attempt. The claimant suffered serious injuries as a result of which she had to have a below the knee amputation of one leg in May 2003. The case was settled for £100,000.

1 (30 July 2004, unreported).

Human rights legislation

22.92   There are two important cases clarifying the responsibility of providers under human rights legislation in offering care to patients.

Following *Savage v South Essex Partnership Foundation Trust and Mind*[1], there is a duty on health authorities under the European Convention on Human Rights, Article 2 to take all reasonable measures to prevent mental health patients from committing suicide. The background to the case was that a daughter of a deceased mental health inpatient claimed, as a result of her mother's death, that she had suffered distress, bereavement, loss and damage. The judgment under Article 2 proposes a general duty on public authorities to employ competent staff and to adopt systems of work which protect the lives of patients. If members of staff know, or are in a position to know, if a particular patient presented a real and immediate risk of suicide, there is an additional operational obligation to do all that could reasonably be expected to prevent such an eventuality. In *Osman v United Kingdom*[2] a real risk was defined as one that has been objectively verified, and an immediate risk is one that is present and continuing.

1 [2008] UKHL 74.
2 (1998) 29 EHRR 245.

22.93   Anna Savage's mother committed suicide on 5 July 2004 after absconding from a hospital run by South Essex Partnership NHS Foundation Trust whilst detained under the Mental Health Act 1983, s 3. Anna Savage started proceedings seeking a declaration and damages under the Human Rights Act 1998 on the basis that the Trust was a public authority and liable for a breach of her mother's right to life under Article 2 of the European Convention on Human Rights as well as her own right to family life under Article 8.

The trust asked the court initially to decide as a preliminary issue what on the facts alleged was the proper test in law in order to establish a breach of

Article 2. The judge accepted the trust's argument that it was necessary to at least establish gross negligence.

Anna Savage appealed to the Court of Appeal on grounds that the judge was wrong in law, and that where the deceased was compulsorily detained under the Mental Health Act 1983 the test was the same as where the deceased was detained in prison. In each case the deceased was not only in the care of the state but detained under compulsion. The test should be determined by the nature of the relationship between the deceased and the state and there was no relevant distinction between the two classes of case.

The Court of Appeal found that it was not necessary for Anna Savage to establish gross negligence, and found that the *Osman/Keenan* test applied, ie was there a real and immediate risk to life, and the question was therefore whether the authority had done all that was reasonably necessary to avert that risk. In this case the court found that the trust had failed to take measures to avoid the real and immediate risk that patient posed to herself. This failure was distinct from duties owed under the law of negligence. The additional duty arose owing to the patient's vulnerability and the hospital's overall control over her activities.

22.94 In the case of *Savage*, a clear distinction was drawn between voluntary and detained psychiatric patients, as control of a detained patient was seen as comparable as that with a patient. The distinction was removed in the case of *Rabone v Pennine Care NHS Foundation Trust*[1] as the court found the difference between the voluntary and detained patient was not substantial.

Melanie Rabone, aged 24, was admitted to hospital in April 2005. She had had a recent history of serious self-harm attempts. Immediately prior to her admission, she had tied a lamp flex around her neck. On admission, Melanie was advised that if she attempted to leave she would be assessed for detention under the Mental Health Act 1983. She was assessed as moderate to high suicide risk and she was placed on 15 minute observations. Melanie remained on 15 minute observations for eight days. She was then assessed in the presence of her mother by her consultant psychiatrist. She requested to return home for the weekend. Despite her mother raising concerns about the safety of this course, the consultant allowed her two days' leave. On the second day of this leave, she hanged herself.

After Ms Rabone's death experts agreed that the decision to send her on leave was negligent, and the family had previously accepted compensation for this negligent care. However, the parents argued that the NHS had additional duties under the Human Rights Act 1998 to protect the patient's life. Under the same law, they also sought additional compensation as victims. The newly formed UK Supreme Court, in its first medical case, agreed.

1 [2012] UKSC 2.

22.95 The Supreme Court made the following findings:

(1) non-detained mental health patients should be afforded the same degree of protection as detained mental health patients under the

ECHR, Article 2. Both the general obligation and operational obligation apply to both categories of patients;

(2)   physically unwell patients will not ordinarily attract the higher protection of the operational obligation;

(3)   the test for real and immediate risk is a risk which is more than remote or fanciful and which is present and continuing;

(4)   the parents were found to be victims within the meaning of the Convention;

(5)   notwithstanding the recovery of damages in the negligent claim, Mr and Mrs Rabone could recover damages for their own loss.

PSYCHIATRIC INJURY

22.96   When a physical injury is suffered, a degree of associated distress is implied and no separate award is made unless that distress amounts to an identifiable psychological illness. In practice, this requirement is met if the illness comes within the DSM-5 or ICD-10 definitions.

22.97   The law adopts a restrictive approach in awarding damages for negligently-inflicted psychiatric injury. In addition to a duty of care, the courts have laid down several conditions which must be satisfied by claimants in order to establish liability for negligently-inflicted psychiatric injury.

Psychiatric injury

22.98   First, there must be an actual psychiatric injury: *Behrens v Bertram Mills Circus Ltd*[1]. Emotions of grief or sorrow are not sufficient to amount to psychiatric injury: *Hinz v Berry*[2]. Nor are feelings of fear, panic or terror: *Hicks v Chief Constable of South Yorkshire Police*[3], *Reilly v Merseyside Regional Health Authority*[4]. It is established, in the case of psychiatric illness, that if there is more than one contributory factor (or trigger) causing or prolonging that illness the claimant can recover damages for the condition if the negligence of the defendant was a substantial or significant cause.

1 [1957] 2 QB 1.
2 [1970] 2 QB 40.
3 [1992] 2 All ER 65.
4 [1994] EWCA Civ 30.

Primary and secondary victims

22.99   In cases where the psychiatric injury is sustained as a result of injury or immediate fear of injury to another, the claimant is referred to as a 'secondary victim.' Recovery by secondary victims is subject to a number of policy restrictions[1].

1 Clinical Negligence Chapter 38. Gill and Bloom.

22.100 Primary victims are those who are involved 'mediately or immediately as a participant'[1]. This was later restricted to those in the zone of physical danger. See *Page v Smith*[2] and *White v Chief Constable of South Yorkshire*[3].

1 Per Lord Oliver in *Alcock v Chief Constable of South Yorkshire Police* [1992] 1 AC 310.
2 [1996] AC 155.
3 [1998] UKHL 45.

22.101 Secondary victims are those not within the physical zone of danger but witnesses of horrific events. *Alcock v Chief Constable of South Yorkshire Police*[1] arose out of the appeal to the House of Lords by victims of the Hillsborough Stadium disaster in 1989. Ninety five people were killed and over 400 physically injured. Scenes of the ground were broadcast live on television. Although the Chief Constable admitted liability and negligence in respect of the death from physical injuries, 16 actions brought by claimants who had suffered psychiatric injury alone were not upheld. In an eventual appeal to the House of Lords, it was established that secondary victims must demonstrate that the four *Alcock* criteria are present in order to establish liability:

(1) a close tie of love and affection. This will be presumed in parent and child and between spouses but must be proved in other relationships. In particular siblings are not normally considered to have a close tie of love and affection[2]. When dealing with the scope of relationships between primary and secondary victim of a defendant's negligence, Lords Ackner and Keith made it clear that it was the existence of a tie of love and affection that was important rather than a strict consideration of the blood relationship. They also made it clear that consideration should be given to the individual circumstances in each case. A claimant who had witnessed his two brothers being killed did not have his claim upheld, as he had not produced sufficient evidence of a close tie of love and affection with his brothers;

(2) witness the event with their own unaided senses: seeing the events on television is not sufficient;

(3) proximity to the event itself or its immediate aftermath. In *Alcock*, the relatives that had visited the makeshift mortuary to identify loved ones were held not to come within the immediate aftermath of the event. See also *Taylorson v Shieldness Produce Ltd*[3] and *McLoughlin v O'Brian*[4]. What constitutes immediate aftermath is decided on the particular facts of the case: *W v Essex County Council*[5].

In April 1998, the Court of Appeal considered the issue of proximity in the case of *Terence Tranmore v T E Scudder Ltd*[6]. This was a case in which the claimant's son was killed during the course of his employment when a building collapsed. Breach of duty was admitted. The claimant attended the building site as soon as he was informed of the accident, some two hours after the death of his son. The emergency services were present and the claimant remained there for some two hours before being told that his son was dead. The claimant developed a recognised psychiatric injury but failed to succeed, as it was held that he was not present at the scene of the accident, nor was he present in the immediate vicinity. He did not witness his son's death or suffering, nor was he a witness to his son being in a position of extreme danger. As two hours had passed between the collapse of the building and the claimant's attendance, the case did not have the immediacy required before the necessary proximity could be said to exist. It was held that this case was close to but just beyond the boundaries drawn by the decided cases[7].

(4)   psychiatric injury must be a result of a shocking event. Lord Ackner in
Alcock v Chief Constable of South Yorkshire Police stated:

> '"Shock", in the context of this cause of action, involves the sudden
> appreciation by sight or sound of a horrifying event, which violently agitates
> the mind. It has yet to include psychiatric illness caused by the accumulation
> over a period of time of more gradual assaults on the nervous system'.

This excludes those who suffer psychiatric injury as a result of the long
term process of providing care for a loved one who has suffered severe
injuries due to the defendant's negligence: *Sion v Hampstead Health
Authority*[8].

1 [1992] 1 AC 310.
2 *Alcock v Chief Constable of South Yorkshire Police* [1991] UKHL 5.
3 [1994] PIQR P329.
4 [1983] 1 AC 410.
5 [2000] 2 WLR 601.
6 [1998] EWCA Civ 733.
7 [1991] UKHL 5.
8 [1994] EWCA Civ 26.

Foreseeability

22.102   Primary victims only need to establish that physical harm was
foreseeable. There is no requirement that psychiatric injury was foreseeable
provided personal injury was foreseeable: *Page v Smith*[1].

1 [1996] AC 155.

22.103   As far as foreseeability of injury to a secondary victim is concerned,
Alcock v Chief Constable of South Yorkshire Police confirmed the principle
that it is necessary to show that the injury (psychiatric injury arising from
shock) was reasonably foreseeable. In that respect, the claimant must show
proximity to the accident both in time and space. Direct and immediate sight
or hearing of the accident is not required. It is reasonably foreseeable that
injury by shock can be caused not only through the sight and hearing of the
event but also of its immediate aftermath[1]. The injury itself must be induced
by the shock.

1 *Alcock v Chief Constable of South Yorkshire Police* [1992] 1 AC 310 per Lord Ackner.

22.104   An exception to this is in relation to work-related stress, where an
employer is under a duty not to cause psychiatric injury to an employee but
only where the injury is foreseeable: *Barber v Somerset County Council*[1] and
Sutherland v Hatton[2].

1 [2004] UKHL 13.
2 [2002] EWCA Civ 76.

OTHER MEDICAL PSYCHIATRIC LITIGATION CASES

Confidentiality

22.105   In a breach of confidentiality case[1] an expert forensic psychiatrist's
medico-legal report containing defamatory material was sent to the client's

general practitioner and consultant psychiatrist without her consent. Damages were awarded for mental stress resulting from the breach of duty of confidentiality.

1 *Cornelius v de Taranto* [2001] EWCA Civ 1511.

Work-related stress

22.106 In *Hartman v South Essex Mental Health & Community Care NHS Trust*[1] the judgment noted that liability for psychiatric injury caused by stress at work is in general no different in principle from liability for physical injury. But, as Buxton LJ put it in *Pratley v Surrey County Council*[2], having referred to *Overseas Tankship (UK) Ltd v Morts Dock & Engineering Co Ltd (The Wagon Mound)*[3]:

'It is not the act but the consequences on which tortious liability is founded. The defendant will be deemed liable for those consequences, not because he has caused them in the course of some careless or otherwise undesirable activity, but only if they were caused by his failure to take precautions against a foreseen or foreseeable and legally relevant danger'.

1 [2005] EWCA Civ 6.
2 [2003] EWCA Civ 1067, [2004] ICR 159 at para 32.
3 [1961] AC 388.

22.107 It is foreseeable injury flowing from the employer's breach of duty that gives rise to the liability. It does not follow that because a claimant suffers stress at work and that the employer is in some way in breach of duty in allowing that to occur that the claimant is able to establish a claim in negligence. As Simon Brown LJ put it in *Garrett v Camden London Borough Council*[1]:

'Many, alas, suffer breakdowns and depressive illnesses and a significant proportion could doubtless ascribe some at least of their problems to the strains and stresses of their work situation: be it simply overworking, the tension of difficult relationships, career prospect worries, fears or feelings of discrimination or harassment, to take just some examples. Unless, however, there was a real risk of breakdown which the claimant's employers ought reasonably to have foreseen and they ought properly to have averted there can be no liability'.

1 [2001] EWCA Civ 395 at para 63.

22.108 In *Hatton*, following detailed discussion in the preceding paragraphs Hale LJ, who gave the judgment of the court, helpfully set out sixteen propositions. They are useful signposts for judges faced with the sometimes complex facts of stress at work cases. They are:

(1) there are no special control mechanisms applying to claims for psychiatric (or physical) illness or injury arising from the stress of doing the work the employee is required to do. The ordinary principles of employer's liability apply;
(2) the threshold question is whether this kind of harm to this particular employee was reasonably foreseeable: this has two components: (a) an injury to health (as distinct from occupational stress), which (b) is attributable to stress at work (as distinct from other factors);
(3) foreseeability depends on what the employer knows or ought to know about the individual employee. Because of the nature of mental disorder,

it is harder to foresee than physical injury, but may be easier to foresee in a known individual than in the population at large. An employer is usually entitled to assume that the employee can withstand the normal pressures of the job unless he knows of some particular problem or vulnerability;

(4) the test is the same whatever the employment: there are no occupations which should be regarded as intrinsically dangerous to mental health;

(5) factors likely to be relevant in answering the threshold question include: (a) the nature and extent of the work done by the employee. Is the workload much more than is normal for the particular job? Is the work particularly intellectually or emotionally demanding for this employee? Are demands being made for this employee unreasonable when compared with the demands made of others in the same or comparable jobs? Or are there signs that others doing this job are suffering harmful levels of stress? Is there an abnormal level of sickness or absenteeism in the same job or the same department? (b) signs from the employee of impending harm to health. Has he a particular problem or vulnerability? Has he already suffered from mental illness attributable to stress at work? Have there recently been frequent or prolonged absences which are uncharacteristic of him? Is there reason to think that these are attributable to stress at work, for example because of complaints or warnings from him or others?

(6) the employer is generally entitled to take what he is told by his employee at face value, unless he has good reason to think to the contrary. He does not generally have to make searching enquiries of the employee or seek permission to make further inquiries of his medical advisers;

(7) to trigger a duty to take steps, the indications of impending harm to health arising from stress at work must be plain enough for any reasonable employer to realise that he should do something about it;

(8) the employer is only in breach of duty if he has failed to take the steps which are reasonable in the circumstances, bearing in mind the magnitude of the risk of harm occurring, the gravity of the harm which may occur, the costs and the practicability of preventing it, and the justifications for running the risk;

(9) the size and the scope of the employer's operation, its resources and the demands it faces are relevant in deciding what is reasonable; these include the interests of other employees and the need to treat them fairly, for example, in any redistribution of duties;

(10) an employer can only reasonably be expected to take steps which are likely to do some good: the court is likely to need expert evidence on this;

(11) an employer who offers a confidential advice service, with referral to appropriate counselling or treatment services, is unlikely to be found in breach of duty;

(12) if the only reasonable and effective step would have been to dismiss or demote the employee, the employer will not be in breach of duty in allowing a willing employee to continue in the job;

(13) in all cases, therefore, it is necessary to identify the steps which the employer both could and should have taken before finding him in breach of his duty of care;

(14) the claimant must show that that breach of duty has caused or materially contributed to the harm suffered. It is not enough to show that occupational stress has caused the harm;

(15) where the harm suffered has more than one cause, the employer should only pay for that proportion of the harm suffered which is attributable to his wrong doing, unless the harm is truly indivisible. It is for the defendant to raise the question of apportionment;

(16) the assessment of damages will take account of any pre-existing disorder or vulnerability and of the chance that the claimant would have succumbed to a stress related disorder in any event.'

22.109 In *Doherty v State of New South Wales*[1], a police officer in New South Wales Police Force Forensic Services Group sustained psychological injury in the course of work as a crime scene investigator and the employer's duty of care was not discharged by referral of the plaintiff to a psychologist and general practitioner. The specialist work of a crime scene investigator involved a high risk of psychological injury which a safe system of work was required to address. There was a causal connection between the psychological injury and breach of duty. The particulars of negligence alleged were as follows:

(1) failing to take any or any adequate care for the plaintiff in circumstances where the defendant knew or ought to have known that the plaintiff was vulnerable to psychological injury;

(2) failing to adequately monitor the plaintiff's coping with constant exposure to scenes of death;

(3) failing to provide a system whereby the plaintiff was adequately monitored and reviewed (whether by appropriate testing or diagnostic interviews or otherwise), and if necessary, referred for treatment, provided with leave and/or transferred to alternative duties so that the illness did not develop in a fully-fledged manner, or alternatively become chronic;

(4) failing to recognise the plaintiff's symptomatic behaviour and refer the plaintiff for appropriate treatment, if necessary, providing him with leave from his duties or other work unlikely to aggravate his then condition;

(5) failing to withdraw the plaintiff from further traumatic exposures;

(6) failing to act on indications of developing psychological illness;

(7) adopting a form of psychological testing which was either ineffective or inappropriate or not acted on;

(8) after the plaintiff's symptoms first became evident, returning the plaintiff to duties which were unsuitable and which caused the plaintiff's condition to become worse.

1 [2010] NSWSC 450.

22.110 In *Courtney v Our Lady's Hospital Ltd*[1] damages were awarded in Ireland for nervous shock following the death of the plaintiff's daughter. It was noted that the plaintiff had had a gross alteration of her personality and lifestyle and the complex of feelings that had dominated her life were very different from the content of a normal grief reaction and were to be attributed to the intense nervous shock suffered by the plaintiff quite understandably and foreseeably as a result of being present and witnessing the events that occurred. The events in question were the death of the plaintiff's 2½ year-old daughter from meningitis. The psychiatric illness suffered by the plaintiff was as a result of her being present and witnessing the shockingly traumatic sequence of events on the night that her daughter died, from the natural grief that would and indeed has resulted from the tragic death.

1 [2011] IEHC 226.

Death of child

22.111 In *Jones v Royal Devon & Exeter NHS Foundation Trust*[1] the claimant mother established that her capacity to work was adversely affected by her experiences arising out of the death of her neonatal daughter. The court accepted a diagnosis of a continuing adjustment disorder and awarded damages totalling over £200,000. The medical experts had initially disagreed with regard to the diagnosis and in particular the presence of post traumatic stress disorder. The judge recognised the difficulty in making a psychiatric diagnosis but accepted that a diagnosis of continuing adjustment disorder with complex symptomatology and requiring treatment had been in place following the death of her daughter. An important part of the case was the impact of the psychiatric symptoms on the claimant's ability to work.

1 [2008] EWHC 558 (QB), 101 BMLR 154.

Aircraft accidents

22.112 In the case of aircraft accidents there is additional legal precedent: *King v Bristow Helicopters, M v KLM Royal Dutch Airlines*[1]. A psychiatric condition developed by a passenger as a result of an accident on board an aircraft is not a 'bodily injury' within Article 17 of the Warsaw Convention 1929 as amended unless expert evidence establishes that the psychiatric condition has caused a physical symptom or was the expression of physical changes to the structures of the brain.

1 [2002] UKHL 7.

22.113 In *M v KLM* the alleged facts were that on 6 September 1998 the appellant was a passenger on a KLM flight. At the time, she was not yet 16 years of age and was travelling on her own. She was seated next to two men. After a meal, she fell asleep and woke to discover the hand of the man next to her caressing her left thigh from the hip to the knee. She got up, and told an air hostess what had happened and was moved to another seat. She was very distressed. On her return to England a doctor found that she was suffering from clinical depression amounting to a single episode of a major depressive illness. She does not allege that she suffered any physical illness. Her claim for mental injury under Article 17 was upheld in Bury County Court. On appeal by KLM the Court of Appeal held that what befell the appellant was an accident within Article 17 but that a mental injury falls outside Article 17. M appealed.

22.114 In *King v Bristow Helicopters Ltd* the alleged facts were that on 22 December 1993, Mr King was a passenger on board a helicopter, owned and operated by Bristow Helicopters Ltd. The helicopter took off from a floating platform in the North Sea in poor weather. The helicopter ascended and hovered for a short period, at which point its two engines failed. It descended and landed on the helideck. Smoke engulfed the helicopter; there was panic on board; and passengers feared that the helicopter was about to crash into the sea.

The door was opened and the passengers disembarked. Mr King developed post-traumatic stress disorder. As a result of the stress he suffered an onset of peptic ulcer disease. The Lord Ordinary, Lord Philip, allowed the claim to go to proof only in respect of the allegations concerning the peptic ulcer. The First Division of the Court of Session allowed the appeal and ordered that the entire claim should go to proof. Bristow Helicopters appealed.

22.115 It was held, by Lord Nicholls, Lord Mackay and Lord Hobhouse (Lord Steyn and Lord Hope concurring in the result but dissenting as to the construction of 'bodily injury') that the appeal by Bristow would be allowed and the appeal by M dismissed because a psychiatric condition developed by a passenger as a result of an accident on board an aircraft is not a 'bodily injury' within Article 17 of the Warsaw Convention 1929 as amended, unless expert evidence establishes that the psychiatric condition has caused a physical symptom or was the expression of physical changes to the structures of the brain.

Psychological effect of physical injury

22.116 In *Malvicini v Ealing Primary Care Trust*[1] the issues were:

(1) damages: personal injury: a nurse sustained a soft-tissue injury to her left upper arm and scapular region in a lifting accident
(2) development of seriously disabling condition, largely mediated by psychological factors;
(3) physical effects of injury largely dissipated: the remaining psychological effects seriously disabling;
(4) whether the disability was permanent;
(5) whether the claimant had Conversion disorder and symptoms suggestive of Persistent Somatoform Pain Disorder;
(6) defence expert opining that claimant might also have elements of malingering or exaggeration.

The claimant was awarded a total of £765,992 subject to 10 per cent deduction.

1 [2014] EWHC 378 (Admin), [2014] All ER (D) 85 (Mar).

22.117 This was a personal injury claim by the claimant, a qualified nurse, against her former employers, in respect of injuries she sustained in a lifting accident at her work in 2009. The defendant admitted that the accident had been caused by its negligence and/or statutory duty, but did not admit that the claimant had in fact been caused any injury.

22.118 The defendant's case was that the claimant had conversion disorder and symptoms suggestive of Persistent Somatoform Pain Disorder. A defence expert opined that the claimant might also have elements of malingering or exaggeration.

Duty of care

22.119 In *Pratt v The Scottish Ministers*[1] the pursuer, a prison officer, failed to prove that, but for the failure to refer him to a prison care team, he would not have developed the depressive condition from which he suffered. The claim arose out of an incident when the pursuer was employed as a prison officer. A fight broke out between two prisoners. The pursuer intervened. As he did so, one prisoner shook his head and a quantity of that prisoner's blood entered the pursuer's mouth. The pursuer believed that he might have swallowed some of that blood, that the prisoner was an intravenous drug user and therefore quite probably infected with hepatitis C, the HIV virus or AIDS. The pursuer became immediately fearful that he might contract one of those diseases and that he would die. In fact blood tests had negatived the presence of any infection. Nevertheless, it was contended for the pursuer that consequently he became clinically anxious and depressed with the result that he was unfit for work. He was granted ill-health retirement from the Scottish Prison Service (SPS) in January 2001.

It was averred for the pursuer that the SPS was under a duty of care to implement a system whereby the pursuer was provided with early counselling and support to help him deal with the trauma of the incident.

1 [2011] CSOH 86, 2011 SCLR 446.

CHAPTER 23

Litigation in clinical radiology

Professor Fergus Gleeson

IMAGING TECHNIQUES AND THE USE OF CONTRAST MEDIA

Introduction

23.1   Radiology departments (imaging departments or X-ray departments) undertake a large variety of diagnostic examinations and interventional radiological procedures. The diagnostic examinations may be on both symptomatic and asymptomatic patients, and may be performed as an initial examination or to monitor the patient's condition. Increasingly patients are imaged as a protective measure by doctors, so called defensive medicine. This has reduced the prevalence of suspected pathology detected on imaging, but increased the potential for detecting unsuspected coincidental disease. This has had a number of consequences; coincidental unsuspected disease is harder for the radiologist to identify, but if detected, particularly if malignant, may be at an earlier stage than when presenting clinically, and increase the possibility of cure.

Types of examinations

23.2   Radiographic and Computed Tomography (CT) images both depend on the fact that X-rays (a type of ionising radiation) are absorbed to a variable extent as they pass through the body. Conventional radiography, for example chest X-rays, produce an image in only one plane such as antero-posterior. Modern conventional radiographs can be manipulated on reporting workstations by changing their size, density and brilliance, but these manipulations have only a little effect on the ability to differentiate structures, both normal and abnormal when reporting.

CT differs from conventional radiography in that the image is obtained from multiple angles and the data are reconstructed by a computer to produce images in multiple planes and thicknesses.

Radionuclide imaging involves ionising radiation emitted from ingested or injected medical radio-isotopes, and may be categorised into Single Photon Emission Tomography (SPET) relying on the detection of gamma rays, and Positron Emission Tomography (PET) relying on the detection of photons caused by the annihilation radiation created when a positron collides with an electron.

Ultrasound (US) imaging relies on the detection of ultrasound waves reflected back onto a single transmission and receiving probe. The waves reflected are dependent upon both the tissue density causing the reflection and the differences in densities between the tissues.

Magnetic Resonance Imaging (MRI) relies upon the excitation of hydrogen atoms in a magnetic field, and the signal they generate when they realign themselves when the magnetic field changes.

Conventional radiography

23.3   As all the tissues along the path of the X-ray beam are projected on to a conventional radiograph, the tissues are superimposed upon each other.

Additionally, conventional radiographs have limited ability to differentiate tissues of different densities. This may prevent normal anatomical structures and pathological abnormalities from being identified. The presence of only two-dimensional information on, for instance, a CXR, may make localisation of abnormalities difficult and it may be necessary to take two views to gain information about the third dimension. These two views are usually at right angles to one another, eg the antero-posterior and lateral film. Sometimes two views at right angles are not appropriate and oblique views are substituted. Although the advent of improved access to CT, US and MRI is increasingly removing the use of multiple views, as these scans are performed in preference to calling the patient back to the X-ray department for a potentially unhelpful further conventional X-ray.

Portable X-rays

23.4 Portable X-ray machines are used to take films of patients in bed, on resuscitation trolleys, or in operating theatres. The positioning and radiation protection of these patients is inferior to examinations performed within the X-ray department. The images are often under- or over-exposed, resulting in examinations that are hard to interpret. The patients are also frequently slightly rotated, making some normal structures more pronounced than usual and others harder to see. Pathological abnormalities are very frequently more difficult to identify on portable X-rays. Consequently, portable films should only be requested when the patient cannot be moved safely or comfortably to the X-ray department.

Computed tomography (CT)

23.5 CT scanning is increasingly used in modern medicine, because of its significant advantages over other imaging techniques. The advent of multislice CT scanners enables multiple slices to be obtained simultaneously, providing increased patient coverage at much quicker speeds; it is now possible to scan the whole chest in four seconds. The section thickness has also reduced, with scanners able to produce section thicknesses of less than 0.5 mm. The use and indications for CT scanning have grown exponentially, and most modern hospitals are increasingly dependent upon CT.

23.6 The outstanding features of CT are:

(1) very small differences in X-ray absorption values can be visualised; compared to conventional radiography, the range of densities recorded is increased approximately ten-fold. This means that compared to conventional radiography, fat can be easily distinguished from other soft tissues, different fluid densities such as acute haemorrhage can be differentiated from CSF, and gradations of density within soft tissues can also be recognised such as normal liver parenchyma from tumour;

(2) the data obtained are three-dimensional; and

(3) scans may be performed very quickly, enabling patients that have been involved in major trauma, those with suspected vascular problems such as bleeding from vessels or blocked vessels and those with suspected cardiac disease to be scanned.

23.7 CT is performed in the axial plane, but since the data is three-dimensional it is possible to reconstruct images in other planes or as a three-dimensional image. Good quality reconstructions are now routinely obtained on reporting workstations, with axial, coronal and sagittal images as standard.

23.8 CT attenuation values are expressed on an arbitrary scale (Hounsfield units) with water density being zero, air density being minus 1,000 units and bone density being plus 1,000 units. The range and level of densities to be displayed can be selected by controls on the computer. The resulting images are displayed on a monitor known as a workstation. The basic image data, known as DICOM (Digital Imaging and Communications in Medicine) data, are stored electronically which allows retrospective image manipulation. The full data sets require large data stores, file servers, as a typical CT file is approximately 50–120 MB in size, dependent upon the area of body scanned and the section thickness. The workstations used to review the images are of varying standards. Dedicated workstations with extensive software programs that enable full image manipulations and calculations are present in radiology departments. Diagnostic reporting workstations will also be present in radiology departments; these reporting stations have less functionality than dedicated workstations, but the image spatial and contrast resolution is sufficient to allow formal reporting to be performed. Images may also be viewed on normal computer monitors elsewhere in the hospital, but the monitor quality is usually insufficient to allow formal image reporting.

23.9 If the images need to be viewed in another hospital or outside the hospital environment, the image data may be transferred electronically, in which case it should be encrypted prior to transfer, on CD or DVD. If the data is transferred as a hard copy file it should be password protected and may be stored as DICOM data which requires a DICOM reader to be loaded onto the viewing computer, or as already reconstructed non-DICOM data, which usually comes with viewing software already loaded onto the CD/DVD.

Magnetic resonance imaging (MRI)

23.10 MRI provides uniquely informative diagnostic information about neurological and musculoskeletal tissue, and is the investigation of choice for brain and spine disease, and bone and joint diseases. One of the advantages of MRI is that it involves no ionising radiation, and no adverse biological effects from standard diagnostic MRI have been demonstrated. It should not be used on pregnant women in the first trimester. Most MRI is performed at magnetic field strengths of 1.5 Tesla (T), but greater field strengths up to 3T are now in routine clinical use. The strong magnetic fields, however, mean that it is contraindicated in patients with cardiac pacemakers, intraocular metallic foreign bodies, and certain types of aneurysm clip. Before scans are performed, patients are routinely asked about prior medical device insertions and whether they may have been exposed to metal fragments. X-rays of the orbits should be routinely performed in metal workers.

23.11 MRI scanning uses multiple sequences in multiple planes and may be performed with or without intravenous contrast. The information provided is structural, as with CT scanning, but also provides detail of tissue composition, and MRI is particularly sensitive in the detection of oedema and inflammation.

The greatest use of MRI is in imaging the nervous and musculoskeletal systems, where it is, for the most part, the imaging technique of choice.

Ultrasound

23.12 In diagnostic ultrasound examinations, very high frequency sound is directed into the body from a transducer placed in contact with the skin or placed within the body. At the energies and doses currently used in diagnostic ultrasound, no harmful effects on any tissues have been demonstrated. As ultrasound has become more portable and cheaper it is increasingly used by non-radiologists, either sonographers or clinicians. Both groups require specified training and audit of their practice. Its increasing clinical use on wards, in out-patient departments and in emergency departments, has led to the Royal College of Radiologists (RCR) in conjunction with the relevant clinical specialist groups producing agreed training criteria[1].

1 Royal College of Radiologists *Ultrasound training recommendations for medical and surgical specialties* (2nd edn, 2012).

23.13 Fluid is a good conductor of sound, and ultrasound is, therefore, a particularly good imaging modality for diagnosing cysts, examining fluid-filled structures such as the bladder and biliary system, assessing pleural effusions and ascites, and demonstrating the foetus in its amniotic sac. Ultrasound can also be used to demonstrate solid tissue that has a different acoustic impedance from adjacent normal tissues, eg tumours and abscesses.

Doppler studies

23.14 Doppler studies are used to detect flow in blood vessels and in the heart. It is an extremely accurate technique for assessing arterial stenoses. Doppler is now used routinely to assess vascular disease in the carotid arteries and the lower limb vessels. It is also used routinely to assess both arterial and venous flow in renal transplants. Doppler echocardiography is able to demonstrate regurgitation through incompetent valves, and pressure gradients across valves can be calculated.

Contrast agents and their potential complications

23.15 Contrast agents are used to visualise structures or disease processes that would otherwise be invisible or difficult to see. Barium is widely used to outline the mucosal surface of the gastrointestinal tract for fluoroscopic procedures; all the other radio-opaque media for radiography and CT rely on iodine solutions to absorb X-rays. CT contrast media is commonly injected into peripherally-sited venous cannulae. It may be hand or pump injected. It may not be injected via a pump into a central venous catheter, as these have been shown to burst if subjected to the volume and pressure routinely used. The contrast medium is most commonly a non-ionic low or iso-osmolar contrast agent which is safe for the majority of patients. The most widely used MRI contrast agents are gadolinium compounds, again most commonly injected via a peripherally-sited cannula. Either pump or hand injection may be used. Ultrasound contrast agents are fundamentally different. They contain microscopic air bubbles that enhance the echoes received by the ultrasound probe.

23.16   Aside from atopic contrast reactions (see para **23.18**) the major concern relating to CT contrast media use is the worsening of renal function or the development of renal failure in patients with already impaired renal function. The RCR have produced guidelines on their use, and the steps that should be taken to lessen the chance of developing renal impairment following the administration of intravenous contrast.

23.17   Gadolinium contrast agents used in MRI are less likely to cause or worsen renal impairment, but their use in patients with known poor renal function has been associated with the development of a rare condition, nephrogenic systemic fibrosis (NSF), a fibrotic disease of the skin and internal organs resembling scleroderma. Different gadolinium contrast agents have different likelihoods of causing NSF.

23.18   Urticaria, bronchospasm, laryngeal oedema or hypotension develop very occasionally following intravenous injections of iodinated contrast media and, to a much lesser extent, gadolinium, which may be so severe as to be life threatening. The universal use of low osmolar iodinated contrast media (by far the commonest of which are the non-ionic agents) has dramatically reduced the incidence of adverse effects. Major contrast reactions using these agents are very rare, severe reactions being encountered in 0.04 per cent and life-threatening reactions or death in 0.004 per cent of individuals. The non-ionic, low osmolar agents are five to ten times safer than the older, high osmolar ionic[1]. Nevertheless, the RCR recommends[2] that appropriate steps be taken to reduce the risk of contrast reactions, particularly in individuals for whom an increased risk of an adverse event has been identified, such as: a previous contrast reaction; asthma; renal disease; diabetes mellitus or metformintherapy.

1 Katayama, Yamaguchi (et al) 'Adverse reactions to ionic and non-ionic contrast media' (1990) 175 Radiology 621–628.
2 Royal College of Radiologists *Standards for intravascular contrast agent administration to adult patients* (2nd edn, 2010).

23.19   The suggested steps are that a doctor should be immediately available in the department to deal with any severe reaction. If risk factors are identified, the decision about contrast agent administration should be taken only by the doctor (usually a radiologist) supervising the procedure[1]. Facilities for treatment of acute adverse reactions should be readily available and regularly checked. A patient should not be left alone or unsupervised in the first five minutes after injection of the contrast agent and it is advisable that the patient remains on the premises for at least 15 minutes after the injection. In patients at higher risk of a contrast media reaction the cannula should remain in place and the patient remain in the radiology department for at least 30 minutes after injection[2].

There is now thought to be no conclusive evidence that the use of prophylactic steroids is of benefit in preventing contrast media reactions[3].

1 Royal College of Radiologists *Standards for intravascular contrast agent administration to adult patients* (2nd edn, 2010).
2 Morcos, Thomsen (et al) 'Prevention of generalised reactions to contrast media: a consensus report and guidelines' (2001) 11 European Radiology 1720–1728; Morcos and Thomsen 'Adverse reactions to iodinated contrast media' (2001) 11 European Radiology 1267–1275.
3 Tramer, von Elm (et al) 'Pharmacological prevention of serious anaphylactic reactions due to iodinated contrast media: systematic review' (2006) 333 BMJ 675–678.

23.20   Large volume extravastion into the perivenous tissues is now becoming more common following the increasing use of infusion pumps injecting the relatively high flows needed for CT, and can cause tissue damage. It is important, therefore, to ensure proper placement of the cannula by checking free back-flow of blood before the pump is connected to the cannula. If significant extravasation occurs, the radiologists and radiographers in the CT unit should follow the department's Standard Operating Policy to ensure that the tissue damage that occurs is minimised.

Radionuclide imaging (nuclear medicine), including PET

23.21   The radioactive isotopes used in radionuclide imaging emit gamma rays. Gamma rays are electromagnetic radiation, similar to X-rays, produced by radioactive decay of the nucleus. This type of imaging is known as Single Photon Emission Computed Tomography (SPET), and is most commonly used to image the bones, kidneys and lungs.

23.22   The radioactive isotope is attached to a manufactured chemical agent (ligand) and then most commonly injected intravenously. The imaging may then be performed dynamically – in real time – and the movement of the radioactive tracer recorded. This enables perfusion imaging and excretion by the kidney to be visualised, or areas of infection such as bone or artificial joint infections to be visualised. Delayed imaging is more commonly performed than dynamic imaging. Delayed imaging may be performed at 20 minutes, for instance if the kidneys are being investigated, or at four hours if a bone scan is being performed to look for bone metastases.

23.23   Positron Emission Tomography (PET) scanning uses positron-emitting isotopes. PET scanners are now all linked to a CT scanner, and all examinations are performed as PET-CT scans. The CT scan component of the PET-CT scanner was initially a relatively poor-quality scanner, but now the CT scanners used are as good as high-quality stand-alone CT scanners. A cyclotron is needed to manufacture PET isotopes. As with SPET imaging, positron-emitting isotopes are joined to a chemical (ligand), which then become concentrated in different cells, or different parts of a cell in the human body. This enables PET-CT imaging to be used to investigate different biological processes, such as glucose or oxygen utilisation. The commonest PET isotope in clinical use is fluorine 18. It has a half-life of 110 minutes, so it is readily transported to different sites after it has been linked to a ligand.

23.24   The most commonly used tracer is 18F-fluorodeoxyglucose (18FDG). All cells use glucose to provide energy, and cancer cells upregulate their cell membranes to pull in more glucose than normal cells. This means they accumulate more 18FDG than non-cancer cells. Once inside the cell, 18FDG becomes trapped along the glucose pathway, as it is subtly different to glucose. Because there is increased 18FDG in cancer cells compared to its concentration in non-cancer cells, the cancer cells emit more positrons and are more easily seen than non-cancer cells. This is known as increased FDG avidity. It is this increased avidity that allows PET-CT to detect cancer. It has also been shown that the greater the avidity the more aggressive the tumour, and the worse the patient's prognosis. Unfortunately the relationship is not linear, and some tumour types, such as mucinous gastrointestinal tumours, are not particularly FDG avid.

23.25   Originally the difference between nuclear medicine imaging techniques and conventional imaging such as the CXR, CT and MRI was that nuclear medicine imaging depicted functional rather than anatomical information. For instance bone scans demonstrate areas of bone turnover with diseases such as prostate cancer and Paget's disease resulting in increased turnover demonstrated as areas of increased activity. Renograms demonstrate perfusion, function and excretion. This meant that the anatomical or structural information seen with nuclear medicine imaging was poor in comparison to conventional imaging, as the spatial resolution of the detectors in SPET and PET cameras is less than the detectors used in CT and MR scanners. This division of anatomical versus functional imaging is now less rigid, as conventional imaging by CT and MRI may now include functional imaging such as perfusion and tissue cellularity, and nuclear medicine imaging has become combined with CT as PET-CT and SPET-CT.

INTERVENTIONAL RADIOLOGY

23.26   Increasingly a variety of specialists, notably radiologists, cardiologists, urologists, gastroenterologists and vascular surgeons are now involved in carrying out various percutaneous techniques using imaging control. These techniques, which are usually performed under local anaesthesia, include obtaining biopsy samples, dilating vascular stenoses, occluding vessels or aneurysms and draining abscesses or other fluid collections.

These techniques are known collectively as interventional radiology (interventional cardiology when applied to the heart) or minimally invasive surgery when applied to the more complex procedures such as aortic aneurysm stenting.

23.27   As the procedures are now commonplace in hospitals, each department that performs them should have Standard Operating Policies in relation to performing the procedures and the pre-procedure requirements such as haematological parameters and lung function, their risks, and patient aftercare. There is also a requirement for the procedures to be performed by someone adequately trained and performing enough procedures annually to remain adequately skilled. All operators should audit their practice to ensure they remain within published guidelines for success and complication rates.

Percutaneous needle biopsy

23.28   Needle biopsy techniques are particularly useful for confirmation of suspected malignancy and for obtaining tissue for microscopy and culture, and in the investigation of other diseases such as hepatic fibrosis and cirrhosis. Under fluoroscopic, ultrasound, computed tomographic or rarely MR guidance, the tip of a specialised needle is passed to the desired site and a small amount of tissue is removed or cells aspirated. Most intrathoracic or intra-abdominal sites can be sampled. A narrow gauge needle can pass safely through vascular masses, loops of bowel and solid organs with only minimal risk of infection or bleeding. Apart from a small pneumothorax with intrathoracic biopsy, significant complications are uncommon. To obtain material for histological study a larger needle (14–18 gauge for soft tissues, 10–13 gauge for bone) is used. The larger needles require specific approaches to avoid damage to intervening structures and require stricter indications than fine needle aspiration. Specialised needles can be introduced via vascular catheters, eg trans-jugular liver biopsy for diffuse liver disease when percutaneous biopsy is regarded as unsafe.

Angioplasty and stent placement

23.29   A balloon catheter can be passed through an arterial occlusion or stenosis, usually using the femoral artery or vein to access the arterial or venous system respectively. The abnormal area can then be dilated by inflating the balloon. Angioplasty is employed widely in peripheral vascular disease, coronary artery stenosis, renal artery stenosis in patients with renal vascular hypertension and can even be used in carotid artery stenosis. Angioplasty using stents has become the most common form of angioplasty in the last decade. Stents are expandable metal mesh tube-like cylinders, sometimes embedded in plastic, which can be inserted through an artery or vein. The stents commonly contain chemicals that prevent blood clotting on their internal lumen and even prevent intimal tissue regrowth, both processes cause luminal narrowing and stent failure over time. Aortic stenting refers to a particular form of angioplasty, also known as minimally invasive repair of an aortic aneurysm, which involves positioning a large stent across the aneurysm, the stent having been introduced through a femoral arteriotomy. Because the procedure involves an arteriotomy it was initially performed in an operating theatre, but is increasingly performed in hybrid theatres, designed for vascular surgery and interventional radiology procedures.

Therapeutic embolisation

23.30   An artery can be occluded by introducing a variety of materials through a catheter placed selectively in a specific artery. Metal coils covered with thrombogenic filaments, gelatin foam, or cyanoacrylate glues that solidify on contact with blood, have all been used for therapeutic embolisation. This technique has been used primarily to control arterial bleeding predominantly following trauma or surgery. Embolisation to occlude aneurysms of the intracranial arteries and vessels feeding arteriovenous malformations (AVM), notably in the brain or lungs, is being increasingly undertaken and used to replace treatment by surgical placement of clips.

23.31 All embolisations are technically difficult and may be hazardous because of spill of the embolisation material away from its intended target site. This may result in tissue death – infarction – at sensitive sites elsewhere in the body. Cerebral aneurysm coils may cause cerebral infarcts, and liver embolisation may cause gastric or duodenal infarction.

23.32 If embolisations are to be performed, careful imaging is required prior to the procedure to check that there are no vascular anomalies that would result either in procedural failure or increase the risk of a complication.

Patients undergoing embolisation need to have the risks of the procedure explained to them, to ensure that proper valid consent is obtained. All operators should keep a detailed record of the numbers of procedures they perform and their success and complication rates. These should be made available to the patients and their families.

23.33 Inferior vena caval filters can be introduced percutaneously through the femoral vein. They are used in patients who are at risk of pulmonary embolism that cannot be managed satisfactorily with anticoagulation. The filters trap emboli originating from leg or pelvic vein thrombi. They can be placed temporarily or permanently.

Percutaneous drainage of abscesses and other localised fluid collections

23.34 Specially designed drainage catheters can be introduced percutaneously into abscesses or other fluid collections. The technique is suitable for many abdominal abscesses and for the drainage of pleural effusion and empyema. They are introduced under the control of whichever imaging modality is most convenient; the essential feature is that the operator must know the exact location of the abscess and must know that the route chosen for the catheter will be safe. Following a series of complications related to pleural fluid drainage, performed without image guidance, it is now mandated by the National Patient Safety Agency that all pleural fluid drainage procedures are performed under ultrasound guidance.

Biliary and urinary drainage

23.35 Internal drainage of the urinary system using double-J stents placed into an obstructed pelvicaliceal system with the distal end of the catheter in the bladder are usually placed by a urologist via a cystoscope. Alternatively, the double-J stents for long-term internal drainage catheters may be introduced percutaneously via the loin under ultrasound and fluoroscopic control. Short-term drainage (24–48 hours) can be achieved by percutaneous nephrostomy, which involves simply puncturing an obstructed kidney via a percutaneous approach under ultrasound control, and exchanging the needle for a small catheter which allows the urine to drain externally.

23.36 The last 10–15 years has seen an explosion of techniques designed to drain an obstructed biliary system. The methods used can be broadly divided into those in which the drainage tube is introduced endoscopically by a gastroenterologist, the most usual approach, and those in which it is introduced percutaneously, usually when the endoscopic route has failed. If the obstruction is due to stones, then endoscopic removal of the stones and sphincterotomy of the papilla of Vater is a frequently-chosen option. Non-operative stenting and drainage procedures are possible options for patients in whom curative surgery for an obstructing neoplasm is impossible. Patients may live for a considerable time with biliary stents in place. Usually the stent is introduced via endoscopy. If this approach is not successful, the stent can be placed over a guide wire that has been introduced through a cannula inserted percutaneously into a dilated bile duct within the liver. The guide wire can be manipulated through the narrowed section of the biliary tree into the duodenum via the common bile duct and a stent placed over the guide wire.

Transhepatic intrahepatic porto-systemic shunt (TIPS)

23.37   Patients who have portal hypertension with bleeding gastro-oesophageal varices may benefit from the creation of a connection between the portal and systemic venous system to lower the portal venous pressure. This communication may be conveniently performed percutaneously introducing a stent placed via the internal jugular vein which is passed through the heart into a hepatic vein and then pushed through into a portal vein.

Therapeutic ablation of tumours

23.38   Recently therapeutic techniques to ablate tumours have been developed, such as radiofrequency, microwave and cryoablation, and these have in some instances replaced tumour resection. They are particularly used in the lung, liver and kidney. The procedures are commonly performed under general anaesthesia.

23.39   Tumour embolisations may also now be performed to reduce tumour vascularity prior to resection and may even be used as a primary treatment for hepatic tumours, when radioactive spheres are injected into the tumours via microcatheters and cause tumour cell death by local radiation necrosis.

Careful follow up imaging is required to check that there has been no significant complication from the procedure and to monitor whether the tumour has reduced in size or is re-growing following treatment.

23.40   When radiologists perform vascular and interventional procedures they have shared responsibility for the post-procedure complications. When the patient returns to the ward, the nursing staff and the doctors on that ward must be aware of the management of the patient. It is the duty of the radiologists to see that instructions are given to the appropriate staff. The instructions, as previously discussed, should be pre-agreed and understood by all those involved in the procedure and the patient's aftercare.

RADIATION HAZARDS AND REGULATION OF RADIATION EXPOSURES

23.41 Complex radiological procedures, for example some CT studies, may involve a significant radiation dose. Radiation effects are commonly divided into stochastic and non-stochastic or deterministic effects. Stochastic effects of ionising radiation describe the probability of the effect occurring but not the severity of the effect, as a function of the dose the patient receives without the existence of a threshold required to cause the effect. This means that the greater the dose, the more likely the effect will occur, but it may occur at any radiation dose. Deterministic effects are dose dependent and have a threshold value below which there will be no effect. In the dose range relevant for diagnostic radiation exposures, inheritable damage and malignancy belong to stochastic radiation damage. The probability that damage will occur differs widely depending upon the tissue irradiated. Radiation is particularly harmful to dividing cells. Genetically adverse mutations may occur following radiation of the gonads, resulting in congenital malformations and a genetic risk to the population. Radiation to fetuses, at doses used for diagnostic examinations, is known to increase the frequency of leukaemia and other malignant neoplasms in the first ten years of life. Fetal exposure, in particular, should, therefore, be kept to the absolute minimum and preferably avoided. There is no known threshold for any of these harmful effects; hence there is no 'safe' radiation dose. Literature from the National Radiological Protection Board (NRPB), now known as the Radiation Protection Division of the Health Protection Agency (HPA), explains the typical effective radiation doses from diagnostic medical exposure and their risks, and provides comparative information for exposure to natural background radiation encountered when, for example, flying in an aeroplane[1].

1 Health Protection Agency *Risk of Solid Cancers following Radiation Exposure: Estimates for the UK Population* (2011).

23.42 Regulations were passed in 2000 governing the use of ionising radiation for medical imaging. The Ionising Radiation (Medical Exposure) Regulations 2000[1] are usually referred to by the acronym IRMER. The Department of Health has published guidance. The regulations and the enforcement agency responsible have undergone some changes.

1 SI 2000/1059.

23.43 The IRMER require health care employers to have written procedures in place for medical exposures including the safe and appropriate use of equipment in radiology and nuclear medicine; that persons undertaking medical exposure to ionising radiation are adequately trained; and that patients are not exposed to inappropriate doses of radiation. The relevant responsibilities are, in brief:

(1) *the employer* must ensure proper levels of training of referrers, practitioners and operators in their employ and keep a record of training and qualifications available for inspection. They must establish recommendations concerning referral criteria for medical exposures;

(2) *the referrer* is responsible for the provision of sufficient clinical information to enable justification of the medical exposure. The referrer has a particular responsibility to ensure the completeness and accuracy

of data relating to the patient's condition. Non-medical referrers (eg radiographers, chiropractors, osteopaths and physiotherapists) must be appropriately trained[1];

(3) *the practitioner* is defined as any health professional who is entitled to take responsibility for an individual medical exposure. Practitioners might include radiologists, radiographers, cardiologists, surgeons or others. The practitioner is responsible professionally and legally for the justification of each individual medical exposure. Therefore the practitioner requires extensive knowledge of the properties of radiation, radiation hazards and dosimetry, and any special situations where there are particular risks from ionising radiation;

(4) *the operator* is any person who carries out any practical aspect of the medical exposure. Where it is not practicable for the practitioner to justify an individual exposure the operator may authorise the exposure according to written guidelines approved and issued by the practitioner;

(5) *justification* of each imaging exposure includes consideration of the appropriateness of the request, the optimal imaging strategy, the immediate and the cumulative radiation effects, a factor of particular importance in exposures involving high radiation dose, such as barium enema, lumbar spine X-rays, CT and some radionuclide examinations, especially when there is a likelihood that repeated imaging will be required. The overall approach to dose reduction is the so-called ALARA principle ('as low as reasonably achievable'). If possible, alternative techniques such as ultrasound or MRI, which do not expose the patient to ionising radiations, should be considered.

1 Royal College of Radiologists 'Clinical imaging requests from non-medically qualified professionals', Joint recommendations from the Royal College of Nursing, Society and College of Radiographers, General Chiropractic Council, General Osteopathic Council, Chartered Society of Physiotherapy, NHS Alliance and Royal College of Radiologists (2006).

PICTURE ARCHIVING AND COMMUNICATION SYSTEMS (PACS)

23.44 All imaging is now digital and displayed on computer screens. The digital data is recorded, stored and transmitted, as per all other digital data. The storage and transmission of this data is via Picture Archiving and Communication System (PACS). As described earlier, the file sizes are large and the data is filed and transmitted in particular formats (as DICOM files). The data are visible as images on approved computers around the hospital, but should only be reported on high-quality monitors approved for diagnostic reporting. All rights to view images should be password protected.

23.45 Up until 2005 the radiological report was regarded as the permanent record, and the images and request information were regarded as transitory. In 'For the Record' (Department of Health 1999) the recommendations for storage referred to the report; the recommended length of time for retention of images was not specified since it was dependent on the policies of the local hospitals/organisations. The local decisions were based on a balance between the costs of additional film storage, versus the needs of the clinical service, and the potential costs of failed litigation due to the inability to produce the images.

23.46 In 2008, the guidelines published by the Royal College of Radiologists 'Retention and storage of images and radiological patient data' were updated. The original guidelines reflected the new advice by the Department of Health 'Records Management: NHS Code of Practice' (2006) Parts 1 and 2. With the increasing use of electronic records and electronic images, it is now considered that best practice should move towards retention of image data for the same duration as the report. The recommended times vary according to the particular jurisdiction, circumstances and type of examination. Examples of particular relevance to this chapter are that in England, Wales and Northern Ireland, general patient records should be kept for eight years after the conclusion of treatment; in Scotland they should be kept for six years after the date of the last entry or three years after death. Once litigation has been notified (or a formal complaint received) images should be stored until ten years after the file has been closed.

REPORTING RADIOLOGICAL EXAMINATIONS

23.47 There should be a system to ensure that either all examinations are reported by a radiologist or the responsibility for reporting, and potentially performing an examination, has been appropriately delegated to a suitably qualified individual. Some examinations may be performed and reported by radiographers or sonographers. Guidance on the requirements for non-medically qualified practitioners was published by the RCR in 2010 as 'Medical image interpretation by radiographers: Guidance for radiologists and healthcare providers'. All examinations reported by radiologists, radiographers and sonographers should be recorded on the radiology information system (RIS). Guidance on RIS is available from the RCR[1]. If the examination is not reported by a radiologist it is mandatory that there be a record of the interpretation in the notes. It is perfectly acceptable that fracture clinic films be reported by the orthopaedic surgeon seeing the patient and other specialists can report examinations within their expertise, for example, many chest physicians can interpret chest films on their patients. There should, however, be a full understanding of the medico-legal implications for the clinician and the hospital authorities. Whoever interprets a radiograph, depending on the circumstances, is responsible for the medico-legal consequences of that interpretation.

1 The guidance is available online only as a PDF: see http://www.rcr.ac.uk/docs/radiology/ pdf/IT_guidance_RISApr08.pdf.

23.48 Most hospitals have on-call radiologists, but very few provide a 24-hour reporting service for emergency department or other urgent films. This is particularly problematic for emergency departments where inexperienced doctors are often required to make the initial interpretation of the radiographs. A review[1] of the assessment of emergency radiographs by Senior House Officers (SHOs) compared with the assessment by a radiologist of senior registrar or consultant status showed that the error rate for emergency doctors for abnormalities with clinically significant consequences was 39 per cent. No improvement was found in the accuracy of the SHOs over the six-month tenure of the post. The paper, which was published in 1988, made the point that it is unrealistic to expect SHOs to acquire the complex skills of image interpretation through experience without formal training. It is true that many radiology departments give instruction on which films to request and teach the basic principles of interpretation to new emergency doctors, but there is no reason to believe that the situation is any different in 2014 than it was in 1988. Emergency films should, therefore, have priority for reporting by a radiologist within 24 hours of being taken.

1 Vincent, Driscoll, Audley and Grant 'Accuracy of detection of radiographic abnormalities by junior doctors' (1988) 5(2) Archives of Emergency Medicine 101–109.

23.49   Unfortunately, at the time of writing, a variable proportion of examinations go unreported for days, weeks or occasionally are not reported at all, despite the requirement that all films be reported (by a radiologist or other appropriately competent individual). There is still a shortage of clinical radiologists in 2014 and the workload is increasing. Radiologists spend a considerable amount of their time doing 'hands on' procedures in ultrasound, vascular and interventional radiology. CT scanning and magnetic resonance imaging frequently need to be directed by a radiologist at the time of the examination. As a result, plain film reporting often takes second place and reports may not reach the referring clinician for days. Any agreement to release unreported films should include that these films are returned to the department for reporting as soon as possible. The department of radiology should have a record of where unreported films have been sent. When a radiology department is not able to arrange reports on all examinations, the management should be made aware of the inability of the department to report all radiographs, or the inability to report films within a particular timescale, because the Hospital Trust may be held liable for operating an unsafe system. Outsourcing reporting companies now exist, and are able to link to hospital PACS and RIS and report the unreported examinations. Initially these companies reported plain films, but now report CT, MRI and NM examinations. Outsourced reporting is known as teleradiology. The RCR has published guidelines on teleradiology[1]. If teleradiology is used, hospitals, their medical directors and radiologists must ensure that the hospital uses teleradiologists who have medico-legal responsibility for their work and can be held to account in the UK. The RCR considers that such teleradiologists must be individually identifiable, licensed and revalidated by the GMC.

1 Royal College of Radiologists *Standards for the provision of teleradiology within the United Kingdom* (2010).

DELEGATION

23.50   Many tasks are delegated to non-medically qualified staff. Radiographers are trained to perform and report ultrasound, give intravenous contrast injections, do barium examinations and report certain types of plain X-ray films. Ultrasound examinations are the most frequent and widely-delegated of the complex tasks in medical imaging. Ultrasound examinations may be performed within a radiology department or in another specialist department, notably in an obstetric, cardiological or surgical department. The non-radiological departments carry their own medico-legal responsibility. When reports are issued by a radiographer or other paramedical staff, it is necessary that the name and status of the individual should appear on the report.

23.51   Delegation has legal implications and must be undertaken properly[1]. The delegator must be reasonably satisfied that the person to whom the task is referred is competent to undertake the task and, where practicable, the process should be defined in a protocol agreed by the referrer, the person to whom the task is referred and the respective employer(s). Also, the person who accepts the referral should assume responsibility for his actions. If this is so then the delegation is termed a 'proper delegation'. It is essential, therefore, that the delegator is aware of the need for the delegator to be contactable if a case proves to be more complex than expected and the delegatee should declare if he thinks that the task delegated is beyond his competence.

1   Royal College of Radiologists *Advice on delegation of tasks in departments of clinical radiology* (1996); GMC *Good Medical Practice* (2006).

INFORMED CONSENT

23.52   There are so many varied procedures performed in radiology departments that there is doubt when written consent should be obtained. In practice it is logistically impossible for radiologists to obtain written consent for every procedure such as barium examinations, intravenous urography, ultrasound, CT and MRI examinations etc, but it is necessary that an adequate explanation is given to the patient. This explanation should include the purpose of the procedure, the methods to be used, the alternatives, including the option not to have the procedure, and the potential complications. The Royal College of Radiologists website has information leaflets on a range of procedures[1].

1   www.rcr.ac.uk.

23.53   The GMC (2008) suggests[1] that written consent should be taken in cases where:

(1)   the treatment or procedure is complex and involves significant risk and/or side effects;
(2)   providing clinical care is not the primary purpose of the investigation or procedure, eg an pre-employment investigation;
(3)   there may be significant consequences for the patient's employment, social or personal life;
(4)   the treatment is part of a research programme or is an innovative treatment designed specifically for their benefit.

1   General Medical Council *Consent: patients and doctors making decisions together* (2008).

23.54   This advice should be based on what is in the best interest of the patient, with due acknowledgement of the risk and benefit involved, notably:

(1)   written consent is necessary for all complex investigations such as vascular and interventional procedures. Written consent, however, only means that there is evidence that consent may have been obtained. It often does not indicate the details of that consent. As with any form of consent, the patient must be fully informed. Implied consent refers to an action by the patient which infers that he agreed to intervention by the doctor. An example would be the patient presenting an arm for the intravenous injection of contrast;

(2)   there is often doubt about how much detail should be given to the patient, especially with regard to complications. The courts used to apply the 'prudent doctor' principle whereby the doctor weighed the risk of a complication against the risk of the patient declining necessary treatment. In recent years, however, there has seen a shift towards the 'prudent patient' model, prevalent in the USA. The emphasis of this model is on what the average 'prudent patient' would want to know about potential risks and treatment options. Some doctors are of the opinion that all the complications of a procedure should be listed and shown to the patient. The Patient Liaison Group of the Royal College of Radiologists has suggested that examinations or procedures having a known potential risk of complications of the order of greater than 1:2,000 should be brought to the attention of the patient when seeking consent[1]. There is, nevertheless, considerable uncertainty among radiologists regarding what patients should be told regarding the risks of intravenous contrast agents, given the exceedingly low incidence of major adverse reactions (death in considerably less than 1:10,000). The problem is that life-threatening vasovagal reactions (a profound slowing of the heart rate accompanied by a drop in blood pressure) are more frequent in patients who are very apprehensive than in more relaxed individuals. Thus, scaring patients by informing them of the possible adverse outcomes of the injection may put them at greater risk than from the direct effects of the contrast agent. The RCR, therefore, falls short of indicating that fully informed consent is mandatory, saying[2]:

> 'Patients should always be fully informed about any procedure and understand what it will involve. Appropriate patient information leaflets should be available in the department. The individual administering the contrast agent must ensure that the patient understands that it is to be given and agrees to proceed'.

1 Royal College of Radiologists *Standards for patient consent particular to radiology* (2010).
2 Royal College of Radiologists *Standards for intravascular contrast agent administration to adult patients* (2nd edn, 2010).

23.55   Consent should not be obtained after the patient has received pre-medication. It should be obtained before the procedure, allowing sufficient time for the patient to consider the procedure adequately and, if appropriate, to discuss it with relatives.

23.56   Informed consent should ideally be obtained by the radiologist performing the procedure. When this is not possible, it is essential that the individual to whom the task is delegated is fully conversant with all the issues that need to be covered, eg the details of the procedure, its complications, the alternatives, the reasons for the procedure and what it hopes to achieve. The final confirmation of informed consent at the time of the examination, however, remains the responsibility of the doctor involved in the procedure.

23.57   The law retains the right in any particular case to decide that a doctor should have informed the patient of certain risks if, in all the circumstances, the risks were sufficiently serious to persuade a court that a doctor should not properly keep them from a patient. Some patients do not wish to be told the complications of a procedure or indeed the details of any alternative procedure. If so, it is important that this should be recorded in the patient's notes. The RCR advises that in such circumstances another team member witnesses the patient's decision.

LITIGATION

23.58   Apart from a few, who work in free-standing small private practices and for teleradiology companies, almost all UK-based radiologists work in hospitals or out-patient facilities with a wide range of imaging equipment. As for all specialists, their medico-legal indemnity is provided through their employing health authority for their NHS responsibilities and through individual medical defence organisations for their private practice.

23.59   The league table for litigation costs has not changed over the past few decades and for hospital specialities in the UK it is still headed by obstetrics and gynaecology, followed by orthopaedics. In the UK, radiologists are still in a low position in this table but as imaging and interventional radiology become more central to patient care, more patients are initiating medico-legal claims against radiologists. When the interpretation of an imaging test is a factor in a claim, the doctor being sued may be the radiologist who formally reported the images, but the claim may be against the physician or surgeon who first saw the images. This applies particularly to emergency cases where no report was available at the time important clinical decisions were being made. Negligence claims involving medical imaging examinations can be subdivided into the following broad categories.

Failure to request imaging investigations when clinically indicated

23.60   Failure to request imaging investigations when clinically indicated is one of the commonest reasons for radiology claims against general practitioners. Hospital-based doctors have much easier access to imaging departments than general practitioners and a lower threshold for referral for imaging investigations.

Failure to see or to correctly interpret abnormalities

23.61   Radiologists fail to observe or correctly interpret abnormalities on a regular basis. Many studies have attempted to assess the error rate in standard practice. The results vary, but it is a reasonable approximation to say that in hospital practice, 1–3 per cent of radiologists' interpretations are erroneous. The great majority of these misinterpretations do not cause harm, either because they are corrected in good time by a subsequent observer or because the missed lesions/incorrect interpretations are not intrinsically of clinical importance. Even in cases of undoubted significant error there may be no effect on patient outcome (eg when a metastasis is missed in a patient who already has known metastases elsewhere in the body).

23.62   Errors are reduced by ensuring that individuals only undertake work that they have been trained to perform and ensuring that the working environment and the workloads are appropriate (Royal College of Radiologists 1999). However, even the best-trained radiologists working under ideal circumstances will occasionally overlook significant abnormalities or misinterpret findings because human error is inevitable.

23.63 The most frequent claims for radiological misses are for failure to diagnose a fracture or dislocation which subsequently causes chronic disability, or failure to diagnose a malignant tumour at a time when it was still potentially curable: failing to diagnose breast cancer on screening mammography and failing to diagnose an unsuspected lung cancer on a chest X-ray taken for other reasons are typical examples of cancers that are overlooked in day-to-day practice. A linking feature is that the conditions, be they trauma or cancer, are not diagnosed on clinical grounds alone and therefore the radiological miss has significant consequences for the patient.

23.64 The problem of missed lung cancers on chest radiography can serve as an example of the principles involved when thinking about such errors. Many factors contribute to a radiologist's failure to detect a lung cancer on a chest radiograph, including the size and shape of the tumour, lesion conspicuity, the quality of the image, the presence of other abnormalities on the image that distract the radiologist, and viewing time. Where the cancer in question is obvious, liability will be admitted, but many overlooked cancers are difficult to see. Several studies of missed lung cancer have been published[1]. They come to similar conclusions. The cancers are usually in an upper lobe, the mean diameter is 1.5–2.0 cm and almost all have ill-defined edges. Quekel and Kessels et al[2] surveyed chest radiographs of patients with non-small cell lung cancer in a typical community setting and found that the diagnosis was missed in 19 per cent of 259 patients whose lung cancer presented as a pulmonary nodule. There have also been reports of lung cancers overlooked at initial chest CT[3]: the mean diameter of overlooked tumours in one series of 14 patients was 1.2 cm and the maximum 2.0 cm[4]. Most cancers missed at CT are endobronchial in location or are situated in the perihilar region and confused with blood vessels.

1 Hayabuchi, Russell (et al) 'Problems in radiographic detection and diagnosis of lung cancer' (1989) 30 Acta Radiol 163–167; and Shah, Austin (et al) 'Missed non-small cell lung cancer: radiographic findings of potentially resectable lesions evident only in retrospect' (2003) 226 Radiology 235–241.
2 Quekel, Kessels (et al) 'Miss rate of lung cancer on the chest radiograph in clinical practice' (1999) 115 Chest 720–724.
3 Gurney 'Missed lung cancer at CT: imaging findings in nine patients' (1996) 199 Radiology 117–122.
4 White, Romney (et al) 'Primary carcinoma of the lung overlooked at CT: analysis of findings in 14 patients' (1996) 199 Radiology 109–115.

23.65 The dividing line between negligence and acceptable practice regarding radiological misses/misinterpretations is difficult to define. The usual basis on which claims are filed is that the interpretation of an image was erroneous. The defence will try to use the *Bolam* judgment[1] (see Chapter 1 for a discussion of *Bolam* and its modification by the House of Lords in *Bolitho*[2]). However, *Bolam* applies when there is evidence that there are alternative approaches to a particular problem, and the defending doctor can demonstrate that his practice was 'in accordance with a practice accepted as proper by a responsible body of medical men, skilled in that particular art'. *Bolam* does not address the issue of errors. The erroneous interpretation of an image was a central issue in *Penny v East Kent Health Authority*[3], a case in which an abnormal cervical smear was wrongly interpreted as normal. The Court of Appeal upheld the judge's original decision that the technicians looking at the slides through the microscope were exercising skill and judgment in determining what report they should make and in that respect the *Bolam* test was generally applicable and the appropriate standard to apply. However, the judge also said:

'… I find the *Bolam* principle ill-fitting to the facts of Mrs Penny's case. In *Bolam* and the cases which followed, the court was concerned with an aspect of professional conduct of which some members of the profession, but not others, disapproved. In other words in those cases the defendants' experts sought to justify as an *acceptable* professional practice what the defendant did or did not do. Here the position is different. All the experts agree that the cytoscreener was wrong. No question of *acceptable* practice was involved …'[4].

1 *Bolam v Friern Hospital Management Committee* [1957] 2 All ER 118.
2 *Bolitho v City and Hackney Health Authority* [1993] 4 Med LR 381.
3 *Penny v East Kent Health Authority* [2000] Lloyd's Rep Med 41, CA.
4 *Penny v East Kent Health Authority* [2000] Lloyd's Rep Med 41, CA.

23.66   The Court of Appeal supported this statement, commenting 'this was not a case where there were two acceptable standards of professional conduct involved'. The Court of Appeal stated, in their review of the relevant law pertaining to the case, that there were three questions which the judge had to answer:

(1)   What was to be seen in the slides (on the balance of probabilities)?
(2)   At the relevant time could a screener exercising reasonable care fail to see what was on the slide?
(3)   Could a reasonably competent screener, aware of what a screener exercising reasonable care would observe on the slide, treat the slide as negative?

This case, while not a radiological case, illustrates the modified *Bolam*[1] approach likely to be used in a court decision in a case where a significant treatable abnormality has been overlooked on an imaging test.

1 *Bolam v Friern Hospital Management Committee* [1957] 2 All ER 118.

23.67   Radiological experts often regard the failure to see a subtle (but definite) abnormality as an excusable error, since, as discussed previously, such errors are not all that infrequent. However, the Court of Appeal in the case of the cytology screening error discussed above found the question posed by the judge 'whether the cytoscreeners conduct though wrong, was excusable' difficult to understand. The *Bolam* judgment, therefore, should not be interpreted as saying that since good radiologists sometimes fail to observe a similar lesion, it was acceptable practice to have missed the lesion in question. It is worth noting, however, that the legal case occasionally hinges as much on the technical adequacy of the radiographs and appropriate communication of the findings, as on the issue of film interpretation.

23.68   The most serious missed traumatic lesions are fractures of the spine, particularly of the cervical spine because of the real risk of resulting paraplegia. A common problem is the poor quality of the radiographs, particularly the failure to show the lower cervical vertebrae. It can be a challenging task for a radiographer to lower the shoulders sufficiently to obtain good quality lateral views of the lower cervical spine in immobile or large patients. Emergency doctors are often reluctant to ask for repeat views when these are required. Many of the mistakes occur due to the inexperience of the emergency doctor and failure to ask for radiological advice at the time of first viewing the radiographs. CT scanning, which can be performed with relatively little movement of the patient, allows for reconstructions in any desired plane and provides much more informative images than plain radiographs, and should be undertaken whenever clinically indicated. The most frequent claims are for failing to diagnose fractures of the scaphoid bone, and dislocations of the carpal and tarsal bones. Scaphoid fractures, in particular, may be missed because of a failure to ask for scaphoid views. If a scaphoid fracture is suspected and not seen, the emergency doctor must ask for a repeat radiograph in 10–14 days' time.

Failure to consider alternative diagnoses

23.69 An abnormality may be observed and correctly described, but the report may fail to give the appropriate alternative interpretations (ie an adequate list of differential diagnoses). This problem is best avoided by proper training and expertise.

Ambiguous or misleading phraseology

23.70 Ambiguous or misleading phraseology in radiological reports is a relatively common, but easily avoidable, cause of medical litigation. Radiologists often see signs that are likely to represent unimportant incidental findings, but which could be highly significant, eg the early stage of a cancer. Phraseology, such as a chest X-ray report of abnormal pulmonary shadowing stating 'probable old tuberculosis, but a significant lesion cannot be excluded' may well lead to no action on the part of the referring general practitioner and a subsequent claim for a missed lung cancer. Another common example in cases of missed lung cancer, is a report that describes a pulmonary nodule as 'an ill-defined rounded shadow', which is ignored by the referring clinician because the patient has clinical features of a chest infection and the X-ray finding is thought to represent pneumonia. If a cancer is suspected by a radiologist, it is vital that the report spells this out, with an indication of the likelihood of cancer. The phraseology used in all cases should be unambiguous, indicating exactly what has been observed and the likelihood of the finding being significant disease.

Failure to adequately communicate significant findings

23.71 The issue of the communication of reports has been highlighted as a significant problem in UK radiology departments[1]. It has become clear that on occasion, although an examination may have been adequately reported, the report has not been acted upon. This may result in patients not being appropriately referred, for instance if a lung cancer is diagnosed on a pre-operative CXR and the doctor requesting the CXR fails to act upon the report by referring the patient to a chest physician. This may occur for a variety of reasons, including the report not being read.

1 National Patient Safety Agency *Safer practice notice 16. Early identification of failure to act on radiology imaging reports* (2007).

23.72   It is incumbent on trusts, departments and individuals to ensure that the designated pathways between radiology departments and referrers are designed to minimise the risk of serious harm to patients by significant imaging findings being overlooked, even though they have been correctly reported. The RCR has published guidance on the communication of results[1].

1 *Standards for the communication of critical, urgent and unexpected significant radiological findings* (2012).

Acceptance of technically inadequate examinations

23.73   It is the responsibility of the reporting radiologist or delegated clinician to ensure that the examinations he reports or reviews are technically fit for purpose, and if they fall below the necessary standard to ensure that a repeat examination is performed if necessary.

CHECKLIST

23.74
- Specialists in clinical radiology supervise and report all imaging techiques involving ionising radiations as well as ultrasound and magnetic resonance imaging. Interventional radiology is an increasing component of daily work;
- when medical specialists in other clinical disciplines perform clinical radiological tasks, formal protocols should be in place to ensure that the individuals are appropriately trained, that responsibilities are clearly defined and that there is a report of each patient-related activity in the patient's medical records;
- there are known hazards from the use of ionising radiation for diagnostic purposes and radiation exposures are, therefore, regulated under the Ionising Radiation (Medical Exposure) Regulations 2000;
- tasks are often delegated to non-medically qualified staff, notably to radiographers. Such delegation should be 'proper' and the medico-legal responsibility for tasks should be clear;
- the formality of informed consent for clinical radiological procedures depends on the complexity and risks of the procedure. Implied consent is frequent for standard intravenous contrast injections;
- the common causes of litigation related to clinical radiology are failure to request imaging investigations when clinically indicated, failure to see or to correctly interpret abnormalities, failure to consider alternative diagnoses, using ambiguous or misleading phraseology, and acceptance of technically inadequate examinations;
- it should be appreciated that the *Bolam* principle applies when there is evidence that there are alternative approaches to a particular problem, and the defending doctor can demonstrate that his 'practice was in accordance with a practice accepted as proper by a responsible body of

medical opinion, skilled in that specialty'. The *Bolam* judgment should not be interpreted as saying that since good radiologists sometimes fail to observe a similar lesion, it was acceptable practice to have missed the lesion in question.

BIBLIOGRAPHY

Department of Health 'For the record: managing records in NHS Trusts and Health Authorities' (1999)

Department of Health *Records Management: NHS Code of Practice* (2006) Parts 1 and 2

General Medical Council *Good Medical Practice* (2006)

General Medical Council *Consent: patients and doctors making decisions together.* 2008.

Gurney JW 'Missed lung cancer at CT: imaging findings in nine patients' (1996) 199 Radiology 117–122

Hayabuchi N, Russell WJ et al 'Problems in radiographic detection and diagnosis of lung cancer' (1989) 30 Acta Radiol 163–167

Health Protection Agency *Risk of Solid Cancers following Radiation Exposure: Estimates for the UK Population* (2011)

Katayama H, Yamaguchi K, et al 'Adverse reactions to ionic and non-ionic contrast media' (1990) 175 Radiology 621–628

Morcos SK, Thomsen HS, et al 'Prevention of generalised reactions to contrast media: a consensus report and guidelines' (2001) 11 European Radiology 1720–1728

Morcos SK, Thomsen HS 'Adverse reactions to iodinated contrast media' (2001) 11 European Radiology 1267–1275

National Patient Safety Agency *Safer practice notice 16. Early identification of failure to act on radiology imaging reports* (2007)

National Radiation Protection Board *X-Rays How safe are they?* (2001)

Quekel LG, Kessels AG et al 'Miss rate of lung cancer on the chest radiograph in clinical practice' (1999) 115 Chest 720–724

Royal College of Radiologists. Information leaflets www.rcr.ac.uk

Royal College of Radiologists 'Advice on delegation of tasks in departments of clinical radiology' (1996)

Royal College of Radiologists/College of Radiographers 'Interprofessional roles and responsibilities in a radiology service' (1998)

Royal College of Radiologists 'Making the best use of clinical radiology' (2012)

Royal College of Radiologists 'Workload and manpower in clinical radiology' (1999)

Royal College of Radiologists 'Standards for patient consent particular to radiology' (2010)

Royal College of Radiologists 'Standards for intravascular contrast agent administration to adult patients' (2nd edn, 2010)

Royal College of Radiologists 'Clinical imaging requests from non-medically qualified professionals', Joint recommendations from the Royal College of Nursing, Society and College of Radiographers, General Chiropractic Council, General Osteopathic Council, Chartered Society of Physiotherapy, NHS Alliance and Royal College of Radiologists (2006)

Royal College of Radiologists 'Retention and storage of images and radiological patient data' (2006)

Shah PK, Austin JH, et al 'Missed non-small cell lung cancer: radiographic findings of potentially resectable lesions evident only in retrospect' (2003) 226 Radiology 235–241

Tramer MR, von Elm E, et al 'Pharmacological prevention of serious anaphylactic reactions due to iodinated contrast media: systematic review' (2006) 333 Br Med J 675–678

Vincent C F, Driscoll P A et al 'Accuracy of detection of radiographic abnormalities by junior doctors' (1988) 5 Archives of Emergency Medicine 101–109

White CS, Romney BM et al 'Primary carcinoma of the lung overlooked at CT: analysis of findings in 14 patients' (1996) 199 Radiology 109–115

CHAPTER 24

Ophthalmology

Mr Ian A Pearce

INTRODUCTION

24.1   Vision depends on the eye and the visual pathways of the brain. The eye is concerned with the processing and focusing of light rays onto the retina which are then converted into electrical signals. The optic nerve transmits these electrical neural signals to the brain where they are further processed and visual images are perceived.

24.2   Disorders of the visual system can involve either the eye, optic nerve or brain individually or altogether and can be isolated or part of a syndrome of systemic disease.

24.3   Ophthalmology is a branch of medicine dealing with the diagnosis, treatment and prevention of diseases of the eye and visual system. An ophthalmologist is a fully trained and qualified doctor who specialises in the treatment of the eye and visual pathway, is regulated by the General Medical Council (GMC) and receives referrals of patients from many sources including GPs, optometrists and casualty doctors. In contrast, optometrists are non-medically qualified healthcare professionals trained to examine eyes, detect visual disorders, prescribe spectacles/contact lenses and can prescribe a limited number of anti–allergic and antibiotic medications. They are regulated by the General Optical Council (GOC) and can obtain further qualifications allowing for further enhanced roles of medication prescribing, routine screening of diabetic retinopathy and shared care management of glaucoma. In the UK, the terms optometrist and optician are often used interchangeably. However, in other regions of the world the term optician is restricted to less highly-trained technicians who dispense spectacles/contact lenses and are not directly involved in diagnosing ophthalmic conditions.

24.4   Ophthalmology integrates with many other branches of medicine and healthcare. In particular, there is a large crossover between ophthalmologists and neurologists. Where a patient has visual functioning adversely affected by diseases of the optic nerve, other cranial nerves or visual pathway in the brain rather than solely affecting the eye, then the personnel involved in the investigation and management of the patient will vary from region to region dependent on local expertise. In some areas such a patient may be managed by a neuro-ophthalmologist (an ophthalmologist trained specifically in this neurology of the visual pathway and ocular movement) whilst in other areas a neurologist specialising in ocular problems may manage the same patient.

PROVISION OF OPHTHALMIC CARE

24.5   Patients with ophthalmic problems come into contact with numerous practitioners with varying levels of skill and experience including GPs, optometrists, accident and emergency doctors and ophthalmologists.

24.6   Many patients will come first into contact with their GP for ophthalmic problems. Many GPs will not routinely perform a basic ocular examination in such cases such as measuring visual acuity or direct ophthalmoscopy (fundoscopy), although these skills are still expected of reasonably competent GPs. They should be able to take a history sufficient to determine whether it is reasonable for them to manage the patient, referral to optometrist for further investigation or whether referral to the Hospital Eye Service (HES) is required and the urgency of such a referral.

24.7   Many screening programmes have been established nationally to detect diabetic eye disease, glaucoma and visual problems in children. GPs should be aware of the need for diabetics to undergo regular screening for diabetic retinopathy in locally quality assured diabetic retinopathy screening programmes. They should also be aware of the importance of glaucoma screening by optometrists and opticians of the General Ophthalmic Service (GOS), particularly in individuals over age 40 with a family history of glaucoma for whom free NHS eye tests are available, and the importance of referral of children with possible squint for ophthalmic or orthoptic assessment.

24.8   Ophthalmic problems, alternatively, may present to the GOS, either directly or via a GP. Optometrists and opticians are trained to take a history, assess vision fully including visual field tests, and to carry out an ocular examination. Thus they can provide helpful advice to GPs on the necessity and urgency of referral to the HES, usually by means of the GOS 18 Form, as well as being able to make direct referral in an emergency, such as for acute angle closure glaucoma, bacterial keratitis, penetrating injury, suspected retinal detachment or marked papilloedema. However, they cannot provide a definitive ophthalmological opinion and GPs may still be responsible for determining whether a patient should be referred and how quickly. There are an increasing number of direct referral schemes from GOS to HES for a range of suspected pathologies including cataract, glaucoma, age-related macular degeneration and retinal vein occlusion.

24.9   Many optometrists will routinely perform visual field assessment and ocular photography on patients. These records are archived, generally electronically, and can provide an important record of the patient's presenting signs and of prior visual function.

24.10   In some areas, the increasing demand of managing patients with glaucoma has led to long-term follow-up within a shared care agreement between ophthalmologists and optometrists. Clear governance is essential in such schemes to identify who is primarily responsible for the patient's care in such cases.

24.11   The emphasis in the NHS on reducing waiting times for treatment of new patients has resulted in reduced priority being given to provision of appointments for follow-up patients, who consequently may have their appointments deferred. There is the potential for claims because follow-up patients are not reviewed at appropriate intervals or even lost to follow-up. This is particularly problematic for the areas of glaucoma and diabetic retinopathy which require prolonged follow up and have the potential for irreversible visual loss.

24.12   There is wide variation in facilities for care of patients presenting to hospitals with ophthalmic emergencies. Some hospitals have been able to provide round the clock walk-in ophthalmic casualties, all patients being seen initially by an on-call ophthalmologist. At the other extreme, emergency staff consult on-call ophthalmic staff based at another hospital, sometimes many miles away, for advice on emergency treatment and the need for ophthalmic assessment. Reduction in working hours of trainee ophthalmologists has made it increasingly difficult for hospitals to provide on-call ophthalmic cover. In some cases adjacent units have centralised on-call services and in others out-of-hours cover has been discontinued with no identifiable emergency care. This can result in patients having to travel to larger departments outside of their locality with consequential delays in treatment. Overall, there continue to be difficulties ensuring universal nationwide adequate care of patients with ophthalmic problems requiring emergency care.

MEASURING VISUAL FUNCTION

24.13   There are several aspects to normal visual functioning which include near and distance visual acuity, peripheral visual field, binocular single vision, stereopsis (depth perception), colour vision and contract sensitivity which can be individually or collectively affected by substandard ophthalmic care.

24.14   Many individuals have refractive errors when the eye cannot clearly focus the images from the outside world onto the back of the eye resulting in blurred vision. The common refractive errors are myopia (short-sightedness), hyperopia (long-sightedness), astigmatism (resulting from an irregularly curved cornea) and presbyopia (where the ageing eye loses ability to change its focus from distance to near for reading). The degree of refractive error is measured in dioptres.

24.15   Distance visual acuity is commonly measured and defined in terms of Snellen acuity. When using a standard letter chart the 'Snellen fraction' describes the smallest size of letter the patient can identify correctly. The fraction compares the patient's result to the result expected from the 'normal' visual system.

For example, 6/6 means that at six meters test distance the patient could correctly identify a letter that a 'normal' sighted person should see at six meters, ie 'normal' vision. In contrast, 6/60 means that the patient could only see at six meters what a 'normal' sighted person should see at 60 meters. In this case the patient's sight is approximately ten times poorer than 'normal' or requires detail to be brought ten times closer before it is seen.

24.16   Distance visual acuity can be described in terms of unaided acuity (ie without the addition of glasses or contact lenses to correct for any refractive error that the patient may have) or refracted visual acuity. This latter definition refers to the fact that visual acuity is measured with appropriate correction of a patient's refractive error.

24.17   If the patient does not have the appropriate glasses or contact lenses available when measuring acuity an approximation of the correct refracted visual acuity can be achieved by measuring the acuity whilst the patient looks through a small aperture (so called pinhole acuity which blocks out peripheral light rays which are most affected by refractive error). Although this pinhole acuity can be helpful in clinical practice to distinguish between simple refractive error and other causes of visual blurring it can be misleading and does not necessarily reflect the true fully refracted corrected visual acuity.

24.18   There are some important threshold levels for distance acuity. For a standard UK Group 1 driving licence not only does an individual have to see a standard vehicle registration mark (post 1-9-2001) at 20 metres but also be able to read 6/12 (with glasses/contact lenses) with both eyes open. A level of 6/60 with both eyes open is considered suitable to be registered as sight impaired (partially sighted) whilst 3/60 is considered severely sight impaired (blind).

24.19   Visual field loss can be secondary to numerous causes including ocular diseases such as glaucoma or retinal detachment, neuro-ophthalmic diseases such as cerebro-vascular accidents or pituitary tumours or iatrogenic causes such as retinal laser photocoagulation or systemic medications.

24.20   Visual field measurements are commonly performed with automated visual field analysers which can document absolute and progressive visual field loss. These automated systems perform reliability measurements during the test and it is important to discard test results that have high levels of fixation loss or high false negative/false positive results. In addition, it is not uncommon for visual field assessments generated with these analysers to give fluctuating sequential results. However, repeatable visual defects with low test error are considered significant.

24.21   If visual field loss is thought to be potentially affecting driving ability then a binocular Estermann field is performed. The DVLA define the minimum field for safe driving to be 120° along the horizontal meridian and 20° above and below the horizontal meridian.

24.22   A further aspect of visual functioning which if abnormal can be significantly debilitating is binocular single vision. If this is adversely affected patients experience double vision (diplopia). Diplopia can be extinguished immediately by occlusion of one eye (occlusive contact lens or patch) but with only monocular vision then stereopsis (depth perception) is lost. The extent of double vision can be documented by specialist techniques which can measure the size of area in which a patient can achieve binocular single vision.

24.23 Despite complete loss of vision in one eye many activities of daily living can be adequately performed unless there is pre-existing poor vision or reduced visual field in the fellow eye. However, if a patient's occupation or hobbies requires binocular vision and good stereopsis then reduced acuity in just one eye can significantly interfere with their performance. In addition, patients are often extremely anxious about protecting their remaining vision and will avoid particular activities and roles they previously enjoyed if they perceive any potential risk of ocular trauma with those activities.

24.24 Loss of vision in both eyes can have a profound effect on activities of daily living, loss of independence, restriction of mobility and frequently inability to earn a living. Consequently medico-legal cases involving poor vision in both eyes can give rise to large settlements.

OPHTHALMIC CLAIMS

24.25 Ophthalmology is a high volume speciality with an ever-increasing rise in patient expectations. Outpatient attendances in the NHS are 6.8 million annually, which is only second behind orthopaedics. In addition, cataract operations are one of the most common surgical procedures worldwide with over 330,000 performed each year in the UK.

24.26 Data from The Medical Defence Union (MDU) shows that ophthalmology, in the independent sector, ranks in the mid-range of specialities in terms of likelihood of being sued. Ophthalmic members face a claim on average once every 15 years with approximately one third of claims resulting in a settlement. Much of the work in the ophthalmic independent sector involves cataract surgery and laser refractive surgery which respectively account for 39 per cent and 34 per cent of cases resulting in compensation. The rapid rise in demand for refractive surgery to reduce dependence on spectacles, along with growing patient expectations, has led to an increase in claims and consequential increased MDU subscription rates for ophthalmologists undertaking such work.

24.27 The case mix of patients and surgery differs between the independent sector and the NHS, with laser refractive surgery not routinely offered in the NHS. Data from the NHS Litigation Authority show that there were 1,253 ophthalmology-related claims in the 15 years between 1995 and 2009. Of these, 963 were closed in that period with 67 per cent resulting in settlement payments totalling £32.1 million with a mean payment per claim of £33,000. Cataract surgery dominates once more, accounting for 34 per cent of all claims, whilst neuro-ophthalmology and paediatric ophthalmology had the highest mean payment per claim of £126,000 and £112,000 respectively.

24.28 This chapter describes the varied ways in which visual function can be adversely affected, the gateways for provision of ophthalmic care and the common diagnoses/treatments that lead to medico-legal claims.

CATARACT SURGERY

24.29   In the UK, over 330,000 cataract operations are performed annually, the vast majority by the technique of small incision phaco-emulsification with insertion of intraocular lens under local anaesthesia as a day case.

Cataract surgery is generally safe and produces excellent results. Subjective benefit occurs in 84–95 per cent of patients, pre-operative ocular co-morbidity being the most important predictor of poor outcome.

24.30   As a consequence of the high volume of surgery undertaken, the highest proportion of ophthalmic claims, both in the independent sector and the NHS, relate to cataract surgery. The most common settled claims are due to inadequate consent process for serious or frequently occurring complications, sub standard management of complications, errors in intraocular lens choice, wrong intraocular lens insertion and globe perforation during local anaesthesia.

The Royal College of Ophthalmologists have produced comprehensive guidelines for cataract surgery covering all aspects of care (RCOPHTH Cataract Surgery Guidelines September 2010).

Consent

24.31   A robust, comprehensive and comprehensible informed consent process explaining the treatment, alternatives, risks and benefits is essential in all surgical procedures. The RCOPHTH Cataract Surgery Guidelines provide example patient information and consent forms for routine cataract surgery.

The frequency of complications for cataract surgery by an experienced surgeon is less than 5 per cent.

24.32   In the majority of cases, the desired outcome after cataract surgery is good unaided vision for distance, although spectacles or contact lenses may be worn to achieve best distance vision, and reading glasses for near vision. This emmetropic post-operative refraction is the generally accepted standard by using monofocal intraocular lens (IOL) implants. There are, however, several options according to the patient's individual circumstances which may require a different post-operative refractive outcome such as a particular myopic (short-sighted) or hyperopic (long-sighted) spectacle prescription. Examples of these include balancing the refractive outcome with the fellow eye or if a particular focusing distance is predominantly required for work/ hobbies. The desired outcome should be agreed with the patient.

24.33   As the human eye ages the ability to adjust focus rapidly from distant to near targets reduces and fails at approximately 40–50 years and reading glasses are required (presbyopia). In patients who have cataract surgery at an earlier age to the development of this phenomenon then premature presbyopia is induced by the use of a monofocal IOL implant and thus must be specifically discussed in the consent process.

24.34 The use of bifocal, multifocal or accommodative IOLs is increasingly being promoted in the independent sector to further reduce dependence on any spectacle correction post-operatively and may become the standard of care in the NHS over the next decade. However, there are conflicting outcome results in the literature of the most appropriate intraocular lens design.

24.35 Improved depth of focus and near visual function is achieved with these IOLs when compared with the monofocal standard, but many patients will not achieve complete freedom from spectacles and post-operative glare and haloes can be problematic. Patient satisfaction is likely to be highest if these bespoke IOLs are reserved for patients who express a desire for spectacle independence but who are realistic about the likelihood of achieving this aim. This has led to the National Institute for Health and Care Excellence (NICE) to issue interventional procedures guidance for these types of IOLs advising special arrangements for consent (IPG209 and IPG264).

24.36 An alternative to multifocal IOLs to achieve spectacle independence is monovision. Monovision is achieved by leaving the dominant eye emmetropic and the non-dominant eye slightly myopic with focus for near targets.

It is a potential option particularly when the patient has been shown to tolerate monovision in previous contact lens wear. However, detailed and appropriate consent is essential as up to 40 per cent of patients cannot tolerate unaided monovision and thus subsequent interventions, ranging from spectacle wear to IOL exchange surgery, may be required post-operatively.

24.37 Although there are patients with mild cataract, particularly those still driving, in whom the risks of cataract surgery are justified, the presence of cataract does not by itself necessitate surgery. There are many individuals with cataract whose vision is adequate for their needs and in whom even the relatively small risks of routine cataract surgery are not justified.

24.38 Patients with co-existing ocular disease may have limited potential for visual improvement with cataract surgery. For example, patients with cataract may also have retinal disease related to ageing (age-related macular degeneration) and it may be very difficult to predict the visual outcome from cataract surgery. Such patients need to be made aware of this potential guarded prognosis for surgery and clear documentation regarding this is essential.

24.39 Although cataract surgery is regularly performed to a high standard, a varied collection of intra-operative and post-operative complications do occur ranging from mild periocular bruising due to the local anaesthetic to sight threatening infection and expulsive choroidal haemorrhage. The use of patient information sheets are helpful to outline the commonly-occurring and serious complications. However, it is imperative to stress the potential for visual loss with surgery as such a consequence often leads to claims.

24.40 The RCOPHTH Cataract Surgery Guideline example patient information sheet states that 'There is virtually no risk to the other eye.' However, sympathetic ophthalmitis can rarely occur with a risk of less than

0.01 per cent risk of loss of vision in the fellow eye. This risk is not routinely discussed with patients due to its very rare occurrence but must be explained if the patient specifically asks if there is any risk at all to the fellow eye.

24.41   Cataract surgery rarely needs to be performed as an emergency except if the cataract has swollen and is causing sight threatening inflammation or raised intraocular pressure.

24.42   The process of consent effectively starts during the initial consultation at which a diagnosis of cataract is made and the option of surgery is first mentioned. Printed information is used by most NHS ophthalmic units. On the day of surgery the procedure can be deferred if there is any concern that the patient is not sufficiently informed to provide consent.

24.43   Usually cataracts are bilateral and patients benefit from surgery on both eyes. Patients who have undergone successful surgery on one eye are particularly likely to believe that cataract surgery is free of any risk and they need to be advised that lack of complications at the time of surgery on the first eye does not mean that surgery on the second eye will necessarily be uncomplicated.

24.44   Bilateral cataract surgery at one sitting (Simultaneous Bilateral Cataract Extraction) is advocated by some surgeons and may be requested by patients. The primary objection is the unlikely but possible risk of serious post-operative complications occurring in both eyes, which needs to be made clear to the patient.

Management of complications

24.45   Complications can be broadly divided into those that rarely require further surgery and usually do not lead to poor visual outcome and those that usually require further surgery and have the potential to lead to poor visual outcome, even to the extent of complete loss of vision in the operated eye. An example of the former is posterior capsule tear without vitreous loss whilst examples of the latter are posterior capsule tear with displacement of lens fragments into the vitreous cavity, intraocular (choroidal) haemorrhage and post-operative infection (endophthalmitis).

24.46   Generally complications are not due to an unacceptable standard of care, as long as they are recognised and dealt with appropriately. Exceptions include when they arise from surgery performed under unsuitable conditions, for instance inadequate anaesthesia resulting in patient movement, from surgery performed by an insufficiently experienced or inadequately supervised surgeon, or from use of equipment known to be faulty.

Posterior capsule tear

24.47   Posterior capsule tear is the most common operative complication occurring during cataract surgery (2–4 per cent) and is the stimulus to many medico-legal claims. In the majority of cases it is not due to an unacceptable standard of care.

24.48 There is a large variation in the consequences of posterior capsule tear. A posterior capsule (PC) tear towards the end of the procedure that is appropriately managed usually results in no adverse consequences. If the vitreous gel prolapses forward when the PC tears then an anterior vitrectomy is performed to remove this prolapsing vitreous. A PC tear associated with vitreous loss has a much higher incidence of post-operative complications and potential visual loss due to chronic cystoid macular oedema (CMO), IOL instability, persistent inflammation, raised intraocular pressure (IOP) and retinal tear/detachment. Although PC tear is a recognised complication and not commonly associated with unacceptable standard of care, it is imperative that it is correctly identified and appropriate follow up and management of the potential post-operative complications is arranged. In addition, certain pre-operative risk factors such as the presence of pseudoexfoliation syndrome or previous vitrectomy surgery increase the risk of PC tear, and as such must be recognised and anticipated prior to cataract surgery.

24.49 A PC tear can result in displacement of either the whole cataractous lens or fragments of the lens into the posterior compartment (vitreous) of the eye. Attempts to retrieve the lens fragments from the anterior vitreous intraoperatively can result in retinal tears which proceed to retinal detachment. The retained lens material can result in severe inflammation, corneal oedema, raised IOP and cystoid macular oedema. Post-operatively, delay in managing these sequelae appropriately can lead to an irrecoverable poor visual outcome. Urgent referral to a specialist in vitreoretinal surgery is necessary to retrieve the retained lens material which is often performed within the first seven days of the original complicated cataract surgery.

Intraocular (choroidal) haemorrhage

24.50 Intraocular (choroidal) haemorrhage is rare, occurring in about 0.1 per cent of cases intraoperatively. Predisposing factors are marked myopia and uncontrolled severe systemic hypertension. It is rarely due to an unacceptable standard of care but it would be difficult to defend a claim if it occurred during surgery in a patient with uncontrolled severe systemic hypertension. Attempts to drain the haemorrhage are often futile and large choroidal haemorrhages have a very poor visual prognosis.

Post-operative infection (endophthalmitis)

24.51 The risk of post-operative bacterial infection (endophthalmitis) after routine cataract surgery is approximately 0.1 per cent and can have devastating results. In most cases there are no obvious predisposing factors. It is more likely after complicated surgery and if there is ocular surface infection or heavy bacterial colonisation preoperatively.

24.52 Prophylactic antibiotic therapy, usually at the end of surgery by periocular or intraocular injection and post-operatively by topical therapy is universally used. A prospective study by the European Society of Cataract and Refractive Surgeons (ESCRS) showed a significant decreased risk of endophthalmitis with the use of intraocular ocular injection of the antibiotic cefuroxime at the end of surgery compared with antibiotic drops. The ESCRS

2007 guidelines recommend injecting 1mg cefuroxime in 0.1ml saline (0.9 per cent) into the anterior segment of the eye at the end of surgery whilst acknowledging that this is an unlicensed use of cefuroxime given at the surgeon's discretion.

24.53 The RCOPHTH Cataract Surgery Guidelines do not mandate the use of intraocular cefuroxime unless locally audited results show a higher than average rate of endophthalmitis.

24.54 The severity of intraocular inflammation and the visual outcome depend upon the virulence of the infecting organism as well as the speed of recognition of the infection and the urgency/efficacy of treatment.

24.55 Acute infective endophthalmitis occurs between one day and two weeks post-operatively. Well recognised clues to endophthalmitis are pain, deteriorating vision, increasing redness of the eye and lid swelling. Since review during the early post-operative period is no longer routine, it is very important that patients are advised to seek immediate assistance if any of these symptoms develop and that there are clearly defined routes of communication, such as a dedicated telephone number, to facilitate emergency ophthalmic review.

24.56 As soon as infective endophthalmitis is considered likely, intraocular fluid, preferably from the vitreous, should be obtained for microbiological studies and antibiotics administered by intraocular injection, also preferably into the vitreous. The ESCRS guidelines recommend performing this within one hour. Although no specific guidance is available from the RCOPHTH as to timing it is widely accepted that unnecessary delay in giving appropriate intravitreal antibiotics is unacceptable. All units providing cataract surgery should have immediate access to intravitreal antibiotics and skilled personnel able to deliver them. Barriers in out of hours access of care for such an ophthalmic emergency or transfer of emergency patients from one hospital to another can result in unacceptable delays with severe consequences.

In some cases vitreo-retinal surgery (vitrectomy) may be beneficial but the timing and indications for such intervention is controversial.

24.57 Particularly after complicated cataract surgery, it may be difficult to differentiate endophthalmitis from severe post-operative non-infective inflammation. In such circumstances it may be appropriate to treat as non-infective inflammation with increased topical steroid drops but close monitoring at 8–12 hourly intervals is necessary. If there is further deterioration then immediate management as infective endophthalmitis should be instigated. The ESCRS guidelines recognise that there is often widespread use of a trial of topical steroid drops in post-operative inflammation but state that in uncomplicated phacoemulsification surgery with significant post-operative inflammation the patient should have an immediate vitreous biopsy and intravitreal antibiotics with no delay, and a trial of steroid drops should not be performed.

24.58 Endophthalmitis has a poor visual prognosis, with the possibility of complete loss of vision and even removal of the eye.

The development of endophthalmitis is rarely due to an unacceptable standard of care, unless surgery has been performed in the presence of ocular surface infection or without appropriate treatment to minimise heavy bacterial colonisation. Unacceptable standard of care is much more likely to occur as a failure to recognise the possibility of endophthalmitis or to institute timely appropriate investigation and treatment.

Incorrect intraocular lens (IOL) power

24.59   Errors with regard to IOL power can be either due to inaccuracies in calculating the power of IOL required for a particular refractive outcome or secondary to the incorrect IOL being chosen in the operating theatre.

24.60   Both wrong site surgery and wrong IOL implant (where the implanted IOL differs from the planned IOL) are considered by the Department of Health to be unacceptable and eminently preventable and are thus termed never events.

24.61   In 2009 the National Patient Safety Agency (NPSA) issued an alert requiring that an adapted version of the World Health Organisation (WHO) surgical checklist is completed for every patient undergoing a surgical procedure in England and Wales. An adapted checklist has been developed between the NPSA and RCOPHTH for cataract surgery which includes specific checklist items referring to planned refractive outcome, IOL model/ type/power, availability of IOL and alternative IOLs if needed.

24.62   Choice of power of intraocular lens to achieve the desired refractive outcome is guided by preoperative biometry measurements. The basic parameters are length of the globe (axial length), steepness of curvature of the anterior corneal surface (K readings), and a constant for the particular model of intraocular lens, which are then entered into various mathematical formulae. Different formulae are available and recommendations for the most appropriate formula to use in a particular scenario are available in the RCOPHTH Cataract Surgery Guidelines. Even then the surgeon has to make a judgment based upon general and personal experience about which power is most likely to produce the desired outcome. Thus, choice of intraocular lens is not an exact process.

24.63   There are two principal methods of measuring axial length: A-scan ultrasound; and laser interferometry (optical biometry). The latter tends to produce more accurate results but is not always able to be performed, particularly if there is a dense cataract. Which method is used has a small influence on the choice of intraocular lens power. For difficult cases, such as very short-sighted eyes, B-scan ultrasound is helpful to most accurately determine axial length.

24.64   Corneal curvature is measured by keratometry, for which there are various instruments, or corneal topography in difficult cases.

24.65   To maximise the reliability of biometry, several readings are obtained for both axial length and corneal curvature and it is standard practice to take measurements from both eyes for comparison. Differences between the eyes in terms of axial length or corneal curvature or measurements outside of acceptable parameters should alert the ophthalmologist to potential inaccuracies in the biometry.

24.66 With the routine use of optical biometry, when possible, modern IOL calculation formulae and optimisation of IOL constants then ophthalmologists should be able to achieve a refractive outcome within +/- 1Dioptre of the target in 85 per cent of cases (dioptre is a physical property of a lens rather than a physiological measure of vision).

24.67 Previous corneal refractive surgery alters the relationship between the anterior and posterior corneal curvature and presents particular problems in determining the appropriate power of IOLs. The patient needs to be advised of these problems both prior to refractive and cataract surgery.

24.68 It is thus important to determine whether prior refractive surgery has been performed, which may not be easy to detect on clinical examination, and to utilise available advice on appropriate adjustments to IOL power calculations. Even with the available methods for adjusting IOL power calculations there is still an element of unpredictability of outcome which needs to be stressed to the patient. It may be necessary to refer the patient to an ophthalmologist with expertise in refractive surgery.

24.69 When an undesirable and unplanned post-operative refractive outcome occurs the incident is commonly termed a 'refractive surprise'. Although the errors outlined above can cause such an outcome it may occur despite all reasonable care and reflects the lack of precision inherent in biometry.

24.70 Various options are available for managing an undesirable refractive outcome, including contact lens/spectacle correction, corrective laser refractive surgery, cataract surgery on the fellow eye with an appropriately adjusted refractive outcome or in occasional cases IOL exchange. This latter option can be technically challenging and PC tear and displacement of the IOL into the posterior segment of the eye are more prevalent in this repeat surgery. YAG laser capsulotomy is commonly performed post cataract surgery to improve vision if any post-operative thickening of the posterior capsule (lens bag) occurs. If IOL exchange is being contemplated then it is important to avoid YAG laser capsulotomy prior to exchange as this further increases the risk of intraoperative complications noted above.

Local anaesthesia

24.71 Local anaesthesia (LA) by periocular injection or topical administration, has become the standard technique for cataract surgery. General anaesthesia is used sparingly in selected cases. The assessment as to the most appropriate anaesthesia depends on psychological aspects of the patient and surgeon, the particular features of the globe and orbit, and the anticipated difficulty of the surgery.

24.72 Minor complications such as conjunctival swelling or haemorrhage are not uncommon (4.3 per cent) during LA but serious life or sight-threatening complications such as bradycardia or haemorrhage behind the eye are rare (0.06 per cent).

24.73 Sharp needle LA (peribulbar/retrobulbar) techniques have a 2.5 times higher risk of serious ocular and systemic complications than blunt needle techniques such as sub-Tenon's or topical LA techniques, and are generally only recommended when the anaesthetist and surgeon consider it absolutely necessary. However, it is accepted that the choice is often one of surgeon preference and practice within each hospital.

24.74 A rare but serious complication of periocular injection is perforation of the globe. The risk is generally accepted to be reduced for sub-Tenon's LA compared to sharp needle techniques. Absolute distinction between peribulbar and retrobulbar injection cannot always be made, but complications of both are reduced by using a short (25–31 mm) needle. Sharp needle LA is generally avoided in larger eyes with axial length greater than 26mm.

24.75 Globe perforation does not necessarily constitute an unacceptable standard of care, assuming that the injection was administered in a competent manner and the perforation is recognised as soon as reasonably possible and managed appropriately. Reports of severe pain or flashing lights during anaesthetic injection, a soft eye during surgery, and the presence of intraocular haemorrhage during or after surgery are all suggestive of globe perforation and should alert the ophthalmologist/anaesthetist. Early vitreo-retinal opinion is important in determining further management.

24.76 Anaesthesia using just anaesthetic eye drops (topical anaesthesia), occasionally augmented with intraoperative anaesthesia in the anterior chamber (intracameral), is advocated by some surgeons in routine cataract surgery. Although topical anaesthesia avoids the risk of globe perforation, it is not appropriate for every patient or every surgeon. Good patient cooperation and minimal anxiety are prerequisites for this mode of LA.

24.77 The main disadvantage of topical anaesthesia is the increased surgical difficulty as the eye is not paralysed and can move around during surgery, and the possible need to augment the anaesthesia in the event of intra-operative complications.

REFRACTIVE SURGERY

24.78 Refractive surgery encompasses a variety of techniques designed to reduce refractive (focusing) error of the eye and reduce spectacle or contact lens dependence. It can be used to manage defects such as short-sight (myopia), long-sight (hyperopia), astigmatism (uneven focusing power) and increasingly to reduce the need for reading glasses in middle-age (presbyopia).

24.79 The vast majority of refractive surgery is performed in the independent sector with a growing number of high street optometry chains offering the service alongside their traditional practice. There has been a significant growth of this type of surgery in the UK in the past 15 years and presently greater than a third of all ophthalmic medico-legal claims managed by the MDU involve issues pertaining to this form of surgery.

24.80 Technically, any ophthalmic surgeon can offer refractive surgery but both NICE (IPG164, 2006) and the Royal College of Ophthalmologists (Standards For Laser Refractive Surgery, 2011) have issued guidance on the appropriate experience and qualifications of surgeons performing laser refractive surgery, the consent process, clinical governance, advertising and post-operative management of patients.

Techniques

24.81 The most commonly used techniques for refractive surgery reshape the mid-portion (stroma) of the cornea with an excimer laser, programmed according to the required change in refraction. The varied laser techniques differ according to how access is achieved to the stroma. The majority of patients have both eyes treated at the same sitting under topical anaesthesia.

24.82 In photorefractive keratectomy (PRK) the surface cells of the cornea are removed and then a laser is applied directly to the surface. The laser removes microscopic portions of tissue from the cornea, altering its shape.

It can take up to three months for the eyesight to become stable and the disrupted corneal surface can cause post-operative pain particularly in the first 24–48 hours.

24.83 LASIK (laser assisted in situ keratomileusis) is a technique introduced in the 1990s and has revolutionised laser eye surgery. It has rapidly become the most popular technique with more than 100,000 patients a year now having this procedure performed. It uses a cutting instrument called a microkeratome to cut a flap in the surface of the cornea. The flap is folded back so that the laser can be used to remove some of the cornea and then folded back into its original position. The procedure is performed under local anaesthetic and recovery is rapid, within a few hours. Patients suffer less pain after the operation than with PRK.

24.84 LASEK (laser assisted epithelial keratomileusis) involves chemically removing the top layer of the cornea to create a flap before the laser reshapes the corneal stroma. It is used when the cornea is too thin for LASIK treatment.

Recovery time is longer than for LASIK but it may be safer if the cornea is thin or the patient play sports where there is a risk of injury to the face.

24.85 These varied techniques of laser refractive surgery are most suitable for selected patients with refractive error ranging from +4.0 dioptres of hyperopia to -9.0 dioptres of myopia. For more extreme refractive errors and, in particular, for the management of presbyopia then intraocular surgery in the form of clear lens extraction is being increasingly marketed. In essence, clear lens extraction is identical to cataract surgery in which the normal (non-cataractous lens) is removed with insertion of a single vision, multifocal or accommodative intraocular lens.

24.86 Other, less common, surgical procedures are also performed including insertion of an intraocular lens without lens extraction (phakic intraocular lens or piggy-back lens), intrastromal corneal ring segments (INTACS), radial keratotomy (RK), and conductive keratoplasty (CK).

Consent

24.87 In 2003 the MDU reported that the number of laser eye surgery negligence claims reported by its members had increased by 166 per cent over a period of six years, and that on average the cost of litigation against laser eye surgeons was triple that of ophthalmic surgeons not carrying out laser eye work. It was noted that 'while some of the claims are as a result of faulty surgical technique, an underlying feature in many more cases is patients' unrealistic expectations about what can or cannot be achieved'.

24.88 It is thus incumbent upon the surgeon not only to advise patients preoperatively about their treatment options and potential complications but also to identify and moderate any unrealistic expectations. The risks of refractive surgery should be weighed against the advantages and disadvantages of wearing glasses or contact lenses.

24.89 The best results for laser refractive surgery are achieved in patients with mild to moderate myopia whilst higher degrees of refractive error and hyperopia are not always as successful and may require clear lens extraction surgery. In addition, the benefits of refractive surgery with spectacle independence can be limited to the short-term either due to regression of the initial post-operative correction or the natural development of presbyopia such that they will again need spectacles, at least for reading, once they reach age 50.

24.90 The usually high quality of vision with spectacles and contact lenses for mild or moderate myopia, means that any optical aberrations after treatment are likely to be poorly tolerated. The patient who develops difficulty with driving at night about which they were not warned is likely to seek redress, especially if their ability to work is compromised, in which case the necessary settlement is likely to be large.

24.91 Laser corneal refractive surgery has important consequences on the subsequent management of cataract, in terms of IOL calculation and glaucoma, with difficulties in accurately measuring intraocular pressure, and must be discussed with patients prior to consideration of refractive surgery.

24.92 Most patients who decide to proceed with laser corneal refractive surgery will not obtain the full or even significant benefit until both eyes have been treated. Thus there is a strong impetus to either treat the fellow eye after only a short period of time or at the same sitting. Such arrangements may result in much greater consequence from any post-operative complications and this must be made clear in any consent process.

Outcomes and complications

24.93   Laser corneal refractive surgery is a rapidly evolving procedure and the most appropriate technique varies dependent on individual patient characteristics. Data on long-term outcomes, especially for the newer treatment modalities, are limited.

24.94   At 3–12 months after treatment, approximately 77 per cent of eyes achieve within 0.5 dioptres of the desired refractive outcome and approximately 91 per cent within 1.0 dioptre with the most commonly performed LASIK technique.

24.95   Serious complications resulting in reduced acuity are estimated to occur in less than 5 per cent of cases. Refractive outcomes are more predictable for myopia than for hyperopia. Outcomes are often less successful and less predictable with a higher incidence of complications in eyes with higher degrees of refractive error.

24.96   Complications of laser corneal refractive surgery include under-correction or over-correction, optical aberrations, ocular surface discomfort, corneal ectasia, flap complications, corneal infection or inflammation, including diffuse lamellar keratitis (DLK), corneal scarring, and reduction in best corrected vision.

24.97   Under-correction or over-correction may result from incorrect programming of the excimer laser but more commonly reflect the inherent unpredictability of outcome. It has been estimated that 5–15 per cent of patients undergoing LASIK require repeat treatment (enhancement), being more common with higher preoperative refractive error.

24.98   Optical aberrations post-operatively such as glare, haloes, and starbursts can be annoying and disconcerting for patients. They can be particularly troublesome with night driving and are more common in PRK than with LASIK. Development of Wavefront-Guided LASIK, in which a more sophisticated analysis of the optical properties of the eye determines the parameters of the laser treatment, has reduced the risks of these problems to less than 2 per cent.

These optical aberrations are more likely in patients with large pupils or large refractive errors.

24.99   Temporary or persistent ocular surface discomfort is more likely after PRK and LASEK than after LASIK. In addition, some patients experience dryness in the eye for the first couple of months after surgery because the nerves at the front of the eye promoting tear production and blinking have to re-grow. Lubricating eye drops may be needed for up to a year or longer term.

24.100   Corneal ectasia is a serious complication where severe thinning leads to a bulging forward of the central cornea which can lead to poor vision. It is mostly, if not entirely, limited to LASIK surgery although many cases can be avoided by careful preoperative assessment to detect underlying corneal disease, particularly keratoconus, and to avoid treatment of eyes with thin corneas.

24.101   Flap complications where the epithelial flap surface does not correctly sit post-operatively on the corneal stroma can occur after LASIK and LASEK in up to 4 per cent of cases. This can lead to ingrowth of epithelial cells into the cornea requiring further corrective surgery.

24.102   Infection of the cornea has been reported following LASIK in up to 0.16 per cent of eyes. The results show that it happens at about the same level as in people who wear contact lenses. If appropriately identified early and managed then the outcome can still be good. Diffuse lamellar keratitis (DLK) with inflammation within the layers of the cornea can lead to corneal scarring if not appropriately managed.

24.103   If the complications outlined above are not correctly identified or managed they can lead to permanent corneal scarring and visual loss. Management of these cases can be prolonged, require repeat surgery and rarely transplantation of the cornea.

DELAYED DIAGNOSIS OR TREATMENT

24.104   There are a number of conditions in which recognition of the correct diagnosis or institution of the correct treatment is commonly delayed. Such events tend to occur in general practice or in A & E departments. They are less likely to occur in ophthalmic units, but if they do there is a much greater likelihood that they are due to an unacceptable standard of care. In some cases this delay can result in significant permanent reduced visual function.

Acute red eye

24.105   Acute red eye is a very common entity and in the vast majority of cases is due to relatively benign disease, usually bacterial, viral or allergic conjunctivitis. These conditions present commonly to GPs with often bilateral redness, discharge and foreign body sensation. They are rarely accompanied by significant reduced acuity. However, patients presenting with more acute pain and loss of vision can be due to less common but serious conditions, such as acute angle closure glaucoma, acute uveitis, bacterial keratitis or herpetic keratitis, in which delay in diagnosis may result in severe permanent visual impairment.

24.106   An appropriate history to ascertain the nature, severity and onset of the red eye and associated pain is essential. Any past ocular history such as previous uveitis (inflammation in the eye), contact lens wear, herpetic eye disease or recent trauma should be identified. Basic visual acuity testing, which should be available in all GP surgeries or A&E departments, should be expected. Examination of pupillary movements and assessment of the corneal surface with fluorescein stain are simple tests that can be performed rapidly with a penlight torch and blue light filter.

24.107 Patients who present with atypical moderate or severe pain particularly if associated with marked impairment of vision should alert the physician that urgent ophthalmic or at least optician assessment may be required.

24.108 Acute angle closure glaucoma should always be considered in the differential diagnosis and typically presents with initially unilateral ocular pain severe enough to induce vomiting, with significant visual blurring, a hazy corneal reflex and mid dilated fixed pupil. Without urgent treatment to relieve the rapidly rising IOP, permanent visual loss can occur within 24 hours.

24.109 Bacterial or herpetic keratitis occurs typically with unilateral acute red eye, reduced visual acuity, focal grey infiltrates on the cornea and corneal epithelial staining with fluorescein stain when seen with blue light illumination. Permanent corneal scarring and associated reduced acuity can follow unless appropriate antimicrobial eye drops/ointment are given in the first few days. It would be routine for an ophthalmologist to perform conjunctival swabs and/or corneal scrapes on initial presentation to correctly identify the suspected microbial organism and any particular resistance to antimicrobial agents. Delay in identifying the organism this way could delay use of the most appropriate medication and thus lead to further corneal scarring.

24.110 Acute uveitis presents with either unilateral or bilateral red eye, marked photophobia and reduced acuity. The most typical presentation is inflammation of the anterior segment of the eye (iritis) with small poorly reacting pupils and moderate blurring. This diagnosis should be suspected if the acute red eye is not improving after a week or if there are recurrent frequent episodes. Delay in diagnosis over a few weeks can lead to the iris being stuck down to underlying the lens which can compromise later potential cataract surgery and to chronic visual loss due to untreated macular oedema.

Sharp penetrating ocular trauma

24.111 A steady stream of claims results from failure to diagnose perforating wounds of the eye. The patient's history is often that 'something has gone into my eye'. An appropriate history is important to identify what the patient was doing at the time, as certain activities are commonly associated with such injuries such as hammering, chiselling, high-speed drilling, grinding, or cutting.

24.112 It is essential that visual acuity is measured but in many cases if the lens or central cornea is unaffected then the acuity can be normal in the initial presentation. In many cases gross examination of the eye is unremarkable. The absence of a corneal foreign body may be interpreted as evidence that a foreign body has 'bounced out' or a sub-conjunctival haemorrhage may be ignored without consideration of the possibility of an underlying penetrating wound.

24.113 If there is a suggestive history but no visible foreign body the possibility of a perforating injury must be considered. Thorough ophthalmic examination is essential paying particular attention for any shallowing of the anterior chamber, fluorescein staining of the cornea which may identify a leak of fluid from the eye, mis-shapen pupil and conjunctival haemorrhage which may mask an underlying wound. It is important to fully dilate the pupil to assess the posterior segment of the eye and often an X-ray of the eye and orbit are ordered immediately to identify any radio-opaque foreign body.

24.114 Many small penetrating injuries can have self-sealing wounds and good spontaneous outcome if there is no retained foreign body. However, if an unidentified wound continues to leak then the eye can become soft, inflamed and potentially infected with irrecoverable visual loss.

24.115 Failure to identify a retained intraocular foreign body can lead to acute visual loss if accompanied by severe inflammation or infection. In addition, retained iron foreign bodies can have long-term slowly developing toxic effects on the eye with gradual visual loss. A rare occurrence with ocular trauma is sympathetic ophthalmia in which injury to one eye can lead to severe inflammation in the fellow eye. If this occurs, long-term management with systemic immunosuppression is often required to control the inflammation.

24.116 Although most claims are for total or near complete loss of vision in one eye only, settlements are often increased because of special damages for time off work related to the injury and its subsequent treatment, and because patients suffering penetrating ocular injuries commonly have occupations or hobbies requiring good binocular vision.

24.117 The introduction of seat belt regulations dramatically reduced the incidence of severe facial and eye injuries from windscreen breakages but similar injuries still occur, usually from assaults with broken glasses or bottles in public houses. The eye injury is easily missed because a deep wound in either lid, but particularly the upper one, rapidly results in marked swelling so that it becomes difficult to examine the globe.

24.118 Before undertaking repair of facial lacerations, especially those of the lids, the eyes must be examined. If there is any suspicion of an ocular injury or the eye cannot be visualised, ophthalmic examination, possibly requiring general anaesthesia, is essential.

Blunt ocular trauma

24.119 Severe blunt trauma to the eye from kicks or punches can lead to bleeding within the eye, behind the eye or globe rupture. As lid bruising and swelling, limiting ocular examination, occur rapidly following such trauma it is essential for the eye to be examined as soon as possible. Unless the eye can be adequately visualised and visual acuity tested then examination under general anaesthesia may be necessary.

24.120 Bleeding within the eye can cause a rapid rise in sight-threatening IOP and may require urgent management. Any bleeding within the eye would require specialist ophthalmic examination and possible vitreoretinal surgical intervention. If the intraocular haemorrhage is present in a soft eye the possibility of a globe rupture should be considered. The rupture often occurs underneath the ocular muscle insertions, and can be difficult to identify without examination under general anaesthesia

24.121 Bleeding behind the eye (retrobulbar haemorrhage) can be difficult to diagnose with gross lid swelling but severe proptosis (bulging globe) of the eye, severe loss of vision, inability to move the eye and fixed pupil movements should alert the examining physician to the possibility of sight-threatening retrobulbar haemorrhage which needs emergency surgery to cut the eyelid and release pressure within the orbit.

Retinal detachment

24.122 A steady flow of claims are brought often because the delay in the diagnosis and referral of retinal detachment has compromised the outcome of subsequent treatment. Further delay in management of the retinal detachment once identified or complications arising from surgery are also a cause for some claims.

24.123 It is extremely unlikely that a GP or emergency doctor will identify a retinal detachment by ophthalmoscopy (fundoscopy). Even optometrists with benefit of pupil dilation find it difficult. However, once again sufficient clues to the need for urgent ophthalmic referral are available in the history.

24.124 Acute retinal detachment may present as sudden painless monocular loss of vision. The characteristic history is sudden onset of floaters with flashes, then a curtain ascending across the field of vision leading to sudden loss of central vision. Spontaneous retinal detachment is more common in myopes and patients with previous cataract surgery.

24.125 If possible, it is preferable for patients to be referred for ophthalmic assessment when retinal detachment has not extended to involve the central retina ('macula on' retinal detachment), or even better when there is a retinal tear without any retinal detachment, because treatment outcomes are correspondingly better. Thus it is recommended that any patient with recent sudden onset of floaters and flashes, particularly a myope, should be referred urgently for ophthalmic assessment. This will mean that many patients with the benign entity of posterior vitreous detachment, which causes similar symptoms, will need to be referred for patients with retinal tears to be identified but the additional work is justified. Any patient with a history of a curtain rapidly ascending across the field of vision requires emergency ophthalmic referral as this is a highly suggestive symptom of retinal detachment.

24.126 Visualisation of retinal detachment may be impaired by intraocular haemorrhage or cataract, but ready access to B-scan ultrasound in most ophthalmic units circumvents this problem.

24.127 Diagnosis of chronic retinal detachment in children may be particularly difficult. Trauma is usually the underlying cause but it may have occurred some time before and the relevant history may not be forthcoming. There may be only shallow detachment and the detached retina is usually atrophic making it difficult to visualise. A diagnosis of amblyopia may be made in error.

24.128 Treatment of retinal detachment increasingly is performed only by ophthalmologists specialising in vitreo-retinal surgery. Poor outcome of surgery performed by ophthalmologists not specifically trained in vitreo-retinal surgery is increasingly difficult to defend.

24.129 If a 'macular on' retinal detachment is identified, emergency surgery is justified as the centre of the vision is still unaffected and thus the potential for relatively normal post-operative vision is likely. The exact timing of this emergency surgery is controversial with many surgeons advocating surgery within 24 hours, whilst others suggest that a delay of up to 72 hours does not compromise the outcome. In a survey of vitreoretinal surgeons within the UK, failure to schedule surgery over a weekend admission and reattach the retina prior to spontaneous macula detachment, was considered by a majority of the respondents to fall below an acceptable standard of care. If a delay of greater than 24 hours is anticipated then it is important that the patient is advised to rest in bed posturing so that fluid moves away from the macula and that any further deterioration is reported immediately.

24.130 Once the macular becomes detached ('macular off') then it is generally accepted that surgery can be scheduled on the next available urgent list, often within one week. For every week delay after this first week it is estimated a line of potential visual gain is lost from the final post-operative outcome.

24.131 There are several surgical approaches to retinal detachment surgery, each with their own particular set of complications which require appropriate informed consent. A particular issue that needs specific advice is when intraocular gas is injected into the eye as part of the surgery. When nitrous oxide is used for general anaesthesia it can cause the intraocular gas bubble to expand and thus this form of anaesthetic should be avoided during the present surgery and in any subsequent post-operative general anaesthesia until the gas bubble dissolves (up to three months). Failure to inform the patient and the anaesthetist can result in catastrophic rise in IOP and visual loss. In addition, patients must avoid air travel until the bubble dissolves. Generally it is common practice to give patients post-operative warning cards re-iterating these issues to prevent such sight-threatening events.

Age-related macular degeneration (AMD)

24.132 AMD is a condition that affects the central part of vision (macula) of an increasing number of people over the age of 50 years. Many are due to 'dry' AMD, where gradual deterioration of the macula occurs with gradual loss of central vision. However, 'wet' AMD, where exudation from leaking blood vessels under the retina occurs, can lead to rapid, permanent and significant visual loss. At present there is no treatment that can reliably halt the slow decline in dry AMD. In contrast, regular repeated injections in to the eye of vascular epithelial growth factor (VEGF) inhibitors can stabilise visual loss in the more severe wet AMD in up to 95 per cent of cases and improve acuity in up to 40 per cent of cases.

24.133   Critical to success in the use of anti-VEGF intravitreal injections is their use in the early stages of wet AMD development and when fluid recurs in the eye.

24.134   An increasing number of claims are occurring due to the delay in recognising and urgently referring patients from GPs and optometrists to HES. Further claims can occur due to delay in the HES seeing and treating the patients in a timely manner.

24.135   Patients over the age of 50 years presenting with recent onset of rapid deterioration of vision particularly if associated with distortion of images centrally should alert the GP or optometrist to the possibility of AMD. It would be reasonable for GPs to arrange urgent optometric assessment in the first instance if there is doubt about the need for hospital referral.

24.136   RCOPHTH Guidelines on the management of AMD recommend that once wet AMD is suspected then referral to the HES be within one week and if wet AMD is confirmed by the HES then treatment be started within one week. This two-week window of opportunity, and the need for repeated injections over many years, has put enormous pressure on ophthalmic units to provide consistent and timely treatment. Delay of initial treatment of greater than four weeks is likely to lead to successful claims if there is evidence of visual loss within this period from referral to treatment.

24.137   Due to the high numbers of intravitreal injections being delivered for AMD and other retinal disorders each year there is an increasing total number of adverse events such as infective endophthalmitis and wrong site surgery. The same principles of adhering to published national or local protocols and appropriate informed consent that relate to other forms of ocular surgery apply.

Diabetic retinopathy

24.138   Diabetic retinopathy (DR) is the major cause of visual loss in working-age patients. DR is generally asymptomatic in early disease but visual loss can occur due to progression to proliferative diabetic retinopathy (PDR) or more commonly the development of diabetic macular oedema (DMO). PDR leads to severe visual loss due to haemorrhage into the vitreous cavity from new vessels and / or progressive fibrosis leading to tractional retinal detachment. DMO occurs as a result of retinal vessel leakage and accumulation of fluid within the layers of the macula. Although significant reductions in visual acuity (VA) may be reversible in the short term, prolonged oedema can cause irreversible damage, resulting in permanent visual loss. The benefits of retinal laser photocoagulation in diabetic retinopathy, particularly pan-retinal photocoagulation (PRP) for proliferative disease, are well established. Recently, developments in management of DMO with intravitreal VEGF inhibitors have revolutionised care and have been recommended by NICE.

24.139 Claims with regard to DR generally occur due to delay in diagnosis, delay in treatment or adverse events that had not been adequately discussed prior to treatment.

24.140 Quality assured national screening programmes exist throughout the UK for identifying potential cases of DR, PDR and DMO annually. The increased availability of screening should minimise the risk of delayed diagnosis as long as patients are appropriately referred by GPs, diabetologists, or nurse specialists.

24.141 Once PDR is recognised it is recommended that laser PRP is delivered within two weeks. Failure to deliver within this time period has an increased risk of vitreous haemorrhage occurring which would then delay the delivery of laser and may require vitreoretinal surgery to remove the blood and perform adequate laser. Subsequently further laser may be required but precise timing for delivery is not mandated but is generally accepted to be delivered within weeks not months.

24.142 In PDR, the rapidity of disease progression may quickly result in severe bilateral disease with very poor visual outcome despite complete vitreo-retinal surgery. Large settlements are usually necessary in such cases.

24.143 If DMO is suspected either through a screening programme or by GP/optometrist then referral to the HES for confirmation and possible management is recommended. The timing of this referral and subsequent treatment is not as critical as in PDR as the rate of visual loss is much slower. If DMO is confirmed it is important that a detailed discussion of the possible risks and benefits of all the available treatments (laser, VEGF inhibitor injections, steroid injections and surgery) are discussed.

24.144 Due to the demands of an increasing diabetes epidemic and more patients being identified through screening programmes, it is imperative that follow up of existing DR patients in the NHS is not compromised. Patients who have their follow up appointments delayed are particularly at risk of permanent visual loss and many units have introduced failsafe systems to reduce this risk.

The delivery of treatment for DR is generally of a high standard, with few claims being due to poor laser technique or surgery.

24.145 The consent process, particularly for laser PRP, must be adequate and specifically refer to the risk of reduced driving visual field with repeated PRP laser treatments. Likewise, the rare but potentially devastating consequences of intravitreal VEGF inhibitors in the form of post-injection infective endophthalmitis must be stressed.

24.146 Previously intravitreal VEGF inhibitors were mainly given to patients older than 50 years with AMD. However, as DR affects a younger population it is imperative that the injections are avoided in patients who are pregnant, as there is potential risk to the fetus. Direct identification of potential pregnancy through questioning or urine testing and appropriate consent are mandatory in these circumstances.

Chronic glaucoma

24.147   Chronic open angle glaucoma (COAG) is the most common form of glaucoma, characterised by raised IOP, optic nerve head damage and consequential visual field loss. Ocular hypertension (OHT) is a frequent precursor to COAG but may only have raised IOP without any subsequent damage. As COAG is not symptomatic until there is advanced visual loss, effective treatment relies upon identification of pre-symptomatic disease, which is largely dependent upon the GOS. The clues to diagnosis are increased intraocular pressure, optic disc changes and visual field abnormalities, all of which can now be assessed in the GOS.

24.148   Annual screening of individuals over the age of 40 years who are first degree relatives of patients with open angle glaucoma has been available annually for many years in the GOS.

24.149   Clear guidance has been developed by NICE for the diagnosis and management of COAG and OHT (NICE CG85 2009). Importantly, the guidance gives recommendations for when patients should be followed up, with varying scenarios of IOP and optic nerve head/visual field progression. Although there is some disagreement within the ophthalmic community with regard to the thresholds for referral from GOS to HES, the guidance on the topic provides a framework for duty of care in glaucoma.

24.150   There continue to be a small number of patients in whom the need for hospital referral is not recognised, despite several GOS assessments, or the diagnosis is not made during hospital assessments, in either case usually because the necessary tests have not been performed or abnormal results not acted upon.

24.151   Once visual field is genuinely lost there is no prospect for recovery. As glaucoma is generally a bilateral disease the impact of visual field loss can affect the ability to hold a group 1 UK driving licence.

24.152   Failure to measure IOP in patients on long-term topical steroid therapy or following periocular or intraocular steroid injection is likely to represent an unacceptable standard of care.

24.153   Despite increased knowledge of the natural history of untreated glaucoma, determining likely outcome with earlier treatment continues to be difficult due to the often slow progression of field loss.

Giant cell (temporal) arteritis

24.154   Giant cell arteritis (GCA) is uncommon but it has the potential to render a patient completely blind in both eyes within a few days.

24.155 Early recognition, referral and treatment are essential and GCA should be regarded as a medical emergency. However, it is subject to wide variations in clinical practice, as it is often managed in primary or in secondary care by GPs, rheumatologists, non-rheumatologists and ophthalmologists. The British Society of Rheumatologists have issued guidance to encourage the prompt diagnosis and urgent management of GCA, with emphasis on the prevention of visual loss.

24.156 GCA is a systemic disease characterised by inflammation of medium-sized arteries. It virtually never occurs under the age of 50 and is more common in women. Frequently there is systemic malaise and weight loss. Characteristic features are headache, scalp tenderness with difficulty combing the hair or pain on resting the head on a pillow, pain in the jaw muscles on chewing (jaw claudication), and inflammation of the superficial temporal arteries of the scalp (temporal arteritis). GCA should be considered in any older patient with new onset severe headache. There may be pain and weakness in the muscles of the shoulder and pelvic girdles (polymyalgia rheumatica), resulting in difficulty lifting the arms above the head or getting out of a chair or bath.

24.157 Visual loss is usually sudden and severe, due to infarction of the optic nerve (ischaemic optic neuropathy) or retina (central retinal artery occlusion). Giant cell arteritis must be excluded in any older patient presenting with either entity, although other diagnoses are more common.

24.158 Erythrocyte sedimentation rate (ESR) and C-reactive protein (CRP) are usually markedly elevated but they may be normal. Temporal artery biopsy (TAB) is the cornerstone of diagnosis and often remains positive for two to six weeks after the commencement of treatment. A regular link with a local dedicated surgical unit experienced in TAB to support urgent referrals is recommended. However, TAB may be negative in some patients with GCA, due to the presence of skip lesions or to sub-optimal biopsy. Therefore, patients with negative biopsies should be managed as having GCA if there is a typical clinical and laboratory picture and response to steroids, typical findings on ultrasound, or visual symptoms.

24.159 Visual loss occurs early in the course of disease and, once established, rarely improves. Early treatment with high-dose steroids is imperative to prevent further visual loss.

24.160 The symptoms of GCA should respond rapidly to high-dose steroid treatment, followed by resolution of the inflammatory response. Failure to do so should raise the question of an alternative diagnosis. Steroid-related complications (eg weight gain, fractures, diabetes, hypertension, cataracts and bruising) are also common hence the importance of monitoring and titrating the dose down as soon as it is safe to do so. Bone protection (weekly bisphosphonate and calcium or vitamin D supplementation) should be co-prescribed with steroid therapy to reduce risk of osteoporosis with the prolonged steroid treatment.

Generally long-term management of systemic steroid therapy, particularly in difficult cases, is undertaken by a rheumatologist.

24.161 Determining likely outcome with earlier treatment is relatively straightforward when patients have lost vision following a protracted period of failure, usually by a GP, to investigate symptoms suggestive of giant cell arteritis, or when vision is lost in the fellow eye when a GP or hospital doctor, especially an ophthalmologist, has failed adequately to exclude the diagnosis or if necessary presumptively treated with systemic steroids. The latter situation is a particular risk when patients with sudden visual loss are being assessed by emergency staff in consultation with an on-call ophthalmologist at a distant hospital. Often the advice is for the patient to be assessed by the ophthalmic team the following day, by which time visual loss may have progressed to severe visual loss or even complete blindness in both eyes with the likely need for a large settlement, tempered only by the relatively short life expectancy and probable absence of employment considerations in an older female patient.

Visual loss due to intracranial mass

24.162 The highest settled claims in ophthalmology are in cases of missed/ late diagnosis of intracranial tumours. Their recognition, particularly in early presentation, are littered with potential pitfalls.

24.163 Gradual painless deterioration of vision is most commonly due to cataract, for which delay in diagnosis very rarely results in significant long-term harm because visual outcome after surgery is not affected. However, it may be due to an intracranial mass, such as pituitary tumour, meningioma, craniopharyngioma, or aneurysm, in which case delay in diagnosis has important consequences not only for visual outcome but also for the patient's general health and survival.

24.164 Crucial clinical clues that should prompt investigation for an intracranial mass are impairment of colour vision, abnormalities of pupil reactions, visual field defects (particularly bi-temporal hemianopia), optic disc changes and abnormalities of eye movements. Occasionally there are non-visual clues, such as headache, facial pain or numbness, other neurological abnormalities, or hormonal (endocrine) dysfunction. The history of the visual loss is usually not sufficiently specific to suggest an intracranial mass. However, the absence of any ocular cause to account for the degree of visual loss should alert the GP, optometrist or ophthalmologist to the possibility of intracranial pathology.

24.165 Optometrists, particularly those performing visual field tests, should be in a strong position to assist in the early detection of patients with visual loss due to an intracranial mass, if only by documentation of the clinical findings for transmission to and interpretation by an ophthalmologist.

24.166 The primary responsibility for recognition of the need for prompt investigation lies with the ophthalmologist. The essential step is to arrange appropriate imaging studies, and to ensure that they have been performed and any abnormality promptly acted upon.

24.167 Although MRI is likely to be most informative, in the first instance CT is usually adequate and more readily available. It is crucial that the radiology request clearly states why imaging is being requested so that the correct imaging parameters are used and the radiologist knows on which areas to focus. It is often preferable to request imaging of both head and orbits. Retrospective review of cases in which intracranial mass has been missed often highlights the benefit of contrast enhancement. Although the ophthalmologist may request contrast enhanced imaging, the responsibility for deciding whether contrast should be administered should lie with the radiologist.

24.168 Traditionally, ophthalmologists have referred such patients to neurologists for further management, possibly without themselves requesting any imaging studies. This practice is still acceptable but it increases the risk of delay in diagnosis.

24.169 There are still cases in which ophthalmologists fail to consider the possibility of an intracranial mass as the cause of deteriorating vision, particularly in older patients who almost always have cataracts to which the impairment may be ascribed. The unacceptable standard of care is usually due to a failure to examine the visual fields or ascribing the combination of visual field loss and optic atrophy to ischaemic optic neuropathy or low tension glaucoma.

24.170 In children diagnosis of intracranial mass presenting with visual loss, characteristically craniopharyngioma, is often delayed because the visual loss is not apparent to the family until very severe and clinical assessment is difficult. In many cases the disease has progressed to cause raised intracranial pressure (hydrocephalus), severe endocrine disturbance or growth disturbance, and the severe visual impairment only becomes apparent during further assessment.

24.171 Cases in which diagnosis of intracranial mass has been delayed may not be defensible. When vision in both eyes is impaired, settlement costs can be high. Determining the likely improvement in visual outcome with earlier diagnosis and treatment can be extremely difficult. Also there may be extensive discussion about apportionment of responsibility between different practitioners.

Visual loss due to raised intracranial pressure

24.172 There are many causes of raised intracranial pressure, most of which lie within the province of neurosurgery and neurology. An entity of particular ophthalmological importance is idiopathic ('benign') intracranial hypertension (IIH) because the optic nerve damage due to raised intracranial pressure may result in permanent impairment of vision. Increasingly cases with poor visual outcome, allegedly due to delay in diagnosis or inadequate treatment, have resulted in medico-legal claims.

24.173 IIH usually occurs in obese young women. It is characterised by raised intracranial pressure in the absence of intracranial or intraspinal mass, cerebral venous sinus occlusion or other neurological disease. A very similar entity can occur in association with various drugs, notably tetracycline, retinoids, and hormonal contraceptives, respiratory disease especially obstructive sleep apnoea syndrome, and various endocrine disorders.

24.174 The typical symptoms of IIH are headache, nausea and vomiting, transient or permanent visual loss, and double vision. The crucial clinical sign is optic disc swelling (papilloedema). There may be visual field defects, reduced visual acuities and poor colour vision. Usually neurological examination is otherwise normal apart from sixth cranial nerve palsies.

24.175 There is a wide range of disease severity in IIH. Mild cases may be identified incidentally by detection of optic disc swelling at a routine GOS assessment. Severe cases may present as an emergency with severe headache and fulminant bilateral visual loss.

24.176 It is generally accepted that GPs are not able reliably to detect papilloedema. Often they refer patients with headache for assessment by optometrists, who should be able to advise whether the optic discs are swollen. Fluctuating visual obscurations should alert the GP that urgent examination by either an optometrist or ophthalmologist is required.

Emergency department and generalists should be able to detect papilloedema.

24.177 GPs, emergency department doctors and generalists may ascribe recent onset persistent headache associated with nausea, vomiting and visual disturbance in a young woman to migraine, even when there is no past history of the condition. Due to absence of specific confirmatory tests migraine is generally considered a diagnosis of exclusion when other pathologies (particularly raised intracranial pressure) have been excluded by history, examination and investigation.

24.178 Neurologists and ophthalmologists should be sufficiently experienced to detect papilloedema, which gives them a significant advantage because its identification immediately should result in a decision to proceed with urgent or emergency investigations, including neurological imaging.

24.179 Once the possibility of raised intracranial pressure has been recognised, the primary concern is to exclude an intracranial mass that may require emergency or urgent neurosurgical intervention or other life-threatening intracranial disease. General medical doctors are capable of organising imaging and making the necessary referral if an abnormality is detected. They may not have the experience to know precisely what should be done if the imaging studies are normal. They may be able to undertake lumbar puncture but may fail to undertake the vital measurement of cerebrospinal fluid (CSF) pressure. They may not have any knowledge of idiopathic intracranial hypertension, the necessity of excluding cerebral venous sinus occlusion, the importance of stopping any medications that may be causative, or the crucial importance of monitoring vision. In patients referred by them to the on-call general medical team, even ophthalmologists may fail to ensure that the last is done.

24.180 Urgency of treatment in idiopathic intracranial hypertension is predominantly determined by the severity and rapidity of progression of visual impairment, emphasising the importance of regular ophthalmic assessment. In most cases medical treatment to reduce intracranial pressure, usually with acetazolamide, and weight loss are sufficient. If medical treatment is not adequate, it may be necessary to perform urgent surgery, usually a CSF shunt procedure by a neurosurgeon but sometimes optic nerve sheath fenestration if a suitably skilled ophthalmologist is available.

Given these complexities, determining whether the standard of care has been acceptable is often difficult.

24.181 Determining likely outcome with earlier treatment may be even more difficult, not least because there is so little published evidence on the influence of various treatment modalities, especially in cases presenting with severe bilateral visual loss.

24.182 Cerebral venous sinus occlusion can present in a very similar manner. Management is made much more difficult by the need for anticoagulant therapy that interferes with performance of lumbar puncture or any surgical procedure. There is even less published information on the influence of treatment on visual outcome.

Orbital cellulitis

24.183 Inflammation of the soft tissue around the eyelids is common with allergic or infective conjunctivitis. However, the orbital septum usually prevents the spread of infection backwards in to the orbit. Preseptal cellulitis is generally non sight threatening and can be managed with oral antibiotics and out patient follow up. However, swelling of the eyelids if accompanied by visual loss, limited eye movements or proptosis of the eye should alert the GP or ophthalmologist to the possibility of the much more serious condition of orbital cellulitis. Orbital cellulitis is usually secondary to acute (paranasal) sinusitis in children but may be secondary to orbital trauma at any age. It can rapidly result in severe impairment of vision, usually due to optic nerve compression, and rapidly progress if untreated to meningitis or death. It should be considered as a medical emergency with prompt treatment with intravenous antibiotics as an in-patient. Paranasal sinus washout or emergency drainage of orbital abscess, identified by CT or MRI, may be required.

24.184 Management of children with orbital cellulitis requires close cooperation between paediatricians, ophthalmologists, and ENT surgeons. Usually treatment is primarily under the care of paediatricians but regular ophthalmic review (potentially every 12 hours) and easy access to ENT services are essential.

24.185 Unacceptable care usually results from failure to recognise the severity of the condition at the outset, either by GPs or hospital staff, or failure to recognise progression of disease requiring surgical intervention.

24.186 Although ophthalmic assessment is difficult because of marked swelling of the lids and the child's cooperation it is essential to assess vision, or at least pupillary responses, eye movement and assess for proptosis of the globe. If the globe cannot be examined by retracting the eyelids it is essential to consider urgent CT or MRI imaging of the orbit to exclude orbital abscess which may require surgical drainage.

Amblyopia

24.187 During the first two to three years of life, the neuroretina develops rapidly in response to visual stimuli. This continues, albeit more slowly, until the age of seven or eight, after which the neuroretinal map is complete and set. If this normal development is disturbed amblyopia (lazy eye) can become established. However, if the sensory input is restored, the development can run its normal course again – rapidly in the first two or three years, and more slowly until seven or eight years old. So, the importance of amblyopia is that if it is detected early and managed appropriately, vision can be restored. After this critical development period, no further treatment will help, as the development process has stopped.

24.188 Amblyopia is relatively common, affecting 1 child in 50. There are several well-recognised forms of amblyopia including strabismus amblyopia (where an untreated squint leads to poor vision), refractive amblyopia (where an uncorrected refractive error leads to poor image quality) and deprivation amblyopia (where opacity in the eye leads to poor acuity development). Delay in the diagnosis and treatment of these varied presentations can have long term irreversible effects on acuity predominantly in one eye.

Any child with a suspected deviation of the eye should be sent for an early examination by an orthoptist, in the community or in an ophthalmic department, or by an ophthalmologist.

24.189 Within the UK, vision screening of children was developed as part of the child health surveillance programmes established during the 1960s and 1970s. The appropriateness of such programmes was called into question following a systematic review of their effectiveness. In 2003, the Health For All Children Report recommended changes in the way children are monitored and referred for suspected amblyopia and strabismus, and the Child Health Promotion Programme (CHPP) recommended all children be screened for visual impairment between four and five years of age by an orthoptist-led service. This recommendation has been adopted regionally in the UK, although not universally. Any unexplained poor acuity picked up by such screening needs investigation by an orthoptist and/or an ophthalmologist.

24.190 The major consequence of delayed diagnosis of amblyopia is that the associated reduced vision in the affected eye is diagnosed too late for effective treatment. This is generally after the age of eight. Although debate continues as to the most effective treatment and regime for amblyopia, it is imperative to correct the refractive error, or media opacity, in the affected eye and to provide some form of occlusion therapy to the unaffected eye. This occlusive therapy is by either by patching or by the use of atropine eye drops.

Careful follow up with these treatments is required to assess compliance and prevent too much occlusion to the unaffected eye which could ultimately lead to development of amblyopia in that eye.

INCORRECT TREATMENT

Topical steroids

24.191 Topical steroids have an essential role in the treatment of many ocular diseases, including ocular surface inflammation, intraocular inflammation (uveitis) and to prevent/control post-operative inflammation but they can be associated with several sight-threatening complications.

24.192 With high-profile adverse events occurring without regular monitoring, the tendency for GPs to initiate treatment with topical steroids has diminished.

24.193 A history of herpetic keratitis or contact lens wear, which predisposes to bacterial keratitis, is a particular contraindication to topical steroid therapy, as inappropriate use can lead to permanent corneal scarring and even globe perforation.

24.194 Topical steroid therapy may result in elevation of IOP leading to glaucoma. This can occur as early as with six weeks of use but is more commonly a problem with therapy lasting several months. Long-term topical steroids may be associated with development of cataracts.

24.195 Topical steroid therapy should be instituted only by an ophthalmologist and in general any patient on long-term topical steroid therapy should be under regular ophthalmic review, in part to emphasise to the patient the risks of the treatment.

24.196 GPs should not provide repeat prescriptions for topical steroid therapy except at the specific request of an ophthalmologist. They need to receive clear guidance on the strength, frequency and duration of therapy and to ensure that treatment is not continued inappropriately. They should not assume that the patient is still under hospital management.

24.197 Difficulties may arise in patients previously treated with topical steroids by an ophthalmologist, for example for uveitis, in whom symptoms recur and it is easier to request a prescription for topical steroids from the GP than await assessment in an ophthalmic unit. GPs need to resist the temptation to accede to the request, even if referral to the ophthalmic unit is being made. There is significant risk that the patient will not attend any hospital appointment because their symptoms will have been relieved by the steroid therapy. The only exception is a patient for whom an ophthalmologist has specifically recommended starting treatment straight away if symptoms recur, but the GP should insist upon written guidance from the ophthalmologist, who also should have made provision with the patient for early review.

24.198   Glaucoma due to topical steroid therapy may become apparent only when there is severe visual loss, the patient having become functionally blind, and treatment can only be expected to prevent further deterioration. It can be very difficult to determine whether the GP or HES should bear the burden of responsibility. In many cases the hospital is brought into a claim originally brought against the GP. It is also extremely difficult to determine when vision could have been salvaged and what difference delay in diagnosis has made to the visual outcome.

Eyelid tumours

24.199   Eyelid tumours are common. Usually they present no problem in diagnosis, basal cell carcinoma being the most common. However, a small number masquerade as infective lesions and are diagnosed as a meibomian cyst or chronic blepharitis.

24.200   If a supposed inflammatory lesion does not resolve within a reasonable period or does not respond to local medication, a neoplastic process should be suspected. A biopsy, either excisional or incisional, should be sent for histological study and additional treatment offered as necessary.

Dermolipoma

24.201   Dermolipoma is uncommon but its unsightly appearance may lead to request for removal.

Surgical removal is fraught with hazard unless a partial removal of the lesion near the cornea is undertaken. Radical removal involves deep dissection in the orbit with the risk of damage to the extra-ocular muscles (causing squint and/or ptosis), or injury to the lacrimal gland or ducts (causing a severe dry eye). Such surgery should be performed only by those with appropriate training.

Retinal laser photocoagulation

24.202   Retinal laser photocoagulation is widely used in the treatment of diabetic retinopathy and other retinal diseases. Successful claims are generally due to sub-standard care with poor levels of training or supervision or poor technique with either excessive laser or laser spots placed inappropriately at the fovea.

24.203   Laser burns to the fovea, the most sensitive area of the central retina, result in permanent impairment of central vision. Such cases are difficult to defend, particularly when they have occurred during pan-retinal photocoagulation to the peripheral retina, the laser operator having 'got lost' and strayed into the macular area. Settlements may be large, especially if vision in the fellow eye is already poor. When macular laser is performed there is an increased risk of burns to the fovea and thus meticulous technique and appropriate consent process identifying this specific risk is essential.

24.204 If panretinal PRP is planned, particularly if bilateral, it is imperative to counsel the patient as to the potential risk to peripheral visual field loss. Although the extent of this varies from patient to patient and with the numbers of PRP burns placed it can be significant enough to impact on the driving field with subsequent irreversible loss of driving licence. In most pathologies the PRP is indicated to prevent further visual loss but in specific cases there may be alternative therapies that could be considered with potentially less impact on the driving field which need to be explored in the consent process.

IATROGENIC DISEASE

24.205 Various surgical procedures by non-ophthalmologists may result in ocular, optic nerve or orbital damage. Eyelid surgery by plastic surgeons may be complicated by orbital haemorrhage possibly resulting in visual loss due to optic nerve compression. ENT surgery on the paranasal sinuses, particularly endoscopic surgery, or maxillo-facial procedures may be complicated by orbital haemorrhage or direct injury to the optic nerve or extra-ocular muscles. Dental surgery may result in corneal injuries.

24.206 During any general anaesthetic, there is risk of corneal abrasion either by direct trauma or more commonly by not taping the eyelids shut.

Cervical sympathectomy may be complicated by Horner's syndrome.

24.207 Successful defence in all such cases is likely to depend upon whether appropriate precautions to avoid the complication were taken and whether the patient was appropriately warned. Determining the likely outcome in the absence of such complications is usually straightforward.

Perioperative visual loss

24.208 Non-ocular surgery, most notably spine surgery in the prone position and cardiac bypass surgery, is occasionally associated with permanent, commonly bilateral, visual loss.

The cause is usually ischaemic optic neuropathy, to which many factors probably contribute, including blood loss, haemodilution, systemic hypotension that may be intentional, venous congestion and increased intraocular pressure due to prone positioning, the effects of anaesthetic agents on optic nerve perfusion, prolonged surgery, and pre-operative factors predisposing to vascular disease, including systemic hypertension and diabetes. In such cases, it may be very difficult to determine whether there has been any lack of care. Early post-operative transfusion to correct anaemia or haemodilution, as well as reversal of systemic hypotension may be beneficial. Spontaneous partial recovery of vision occurs in many cases.

24.209 Less commonly, visual loss is due to central retinal artery occlusion in which case direct pressure on the globe during prone positioning is also implicated. Whatever precautions are said to have been taken to avoid pressure on the globe during prone positioning, the only completely reliable method is for the patient's head to be suspended in Mayfield tongs.

Drug-induced visual loss

24.210 Visual impairment is a recognised adverse effect of a number of drugs. The effect may be idiosyncratic and thus unpredictable. For some drugs there is a clear dose relationship, relating either to daily or cumulative dose.

24.211 Recommendations for screening have been developed for a small number of drugs but a more important measure is warning the patient of the risk of visual impairment, the importance of seeking medical advice if any subjective visual impairment occurs, and if necessary the need to discontinue treatment. The patient should be provided with easy access to either the prescribing physician or an ophthalmologist. The GP needs to be informed that the patient is taking a drug that may affect vision.

24.212 A baseline ophthalmic assessment is often recommended but it is rarely useful except in patients with pre-existing visual impairment, to document visual function for future comparison, and to exclude ocular disease that is a contraindication to treatment with the particular drug or may interfere with detection of adverse effects.

24.213 Chloroquine causes a well-recognised retinopathy, for which the major predictive factor is cumulative dose. Most of the reported patients received more than 300g for the treatment of rheumatoid arthritis or lupus erythematosus, for which conditions hydroxychloroquine is now preferred. It is unusual for retinopathy to occur with appropriate prescribing for malaria prophylaxis but it may occur in patients who self-medicate excessively.

24.214 Hydroxychloroquine is much less likely to cause retinopathy than chloroquine. With the standard dose of 200 mg twice a day, retinopathy is very unlikely until after five or more years of continuous therapy unless there is impaired renal or liver function. The Royal College of Ophthalmologists' guidelines recommend assessment of vision by the rheumatologist or dermatologist prescribing hydroxychloroquine prior to treatment and annually thereafter. Any identified abnormality in visual functioning at baseline or follow up should be referred to an ophthalmologist for further investigation.

24.215 Ethambutol, important in the treatment of drug-resistant tuberculosis, continues to be the cause of several claims. The resulting optic neuropathy is partly dose-related and occurs in about 1 per cent of cases on the standard maintenance dose (15 mg per kg per day) and in about 5 per cent of cases on the higher induction dose (30 mg per kg per day), but is more likely if renal function is impaired. The optic neuropathy usually does not develop until after three months of treatment, by which time induction therapy should have been completed. There is no reliable screening test to detect toxicity prior to onset of symptoms. Discontinuation of ethambutol almost always results in recovery of vision but this may be delayed for many months.

24.216 Amiodarone, important in the treatment of cardiac arrhythmia, may cause optic neuropathy, although it may be difficult distinguishing it from coincidental ischaemic optic neuropathy. Whether the amiodarone should be discontinued requires discussion with the patient's cardiologist because the underlying cardiac arrhythmia may be fatal. All patients on amiodarone develop corneal deposits that gradually resolve on discontinuation of treatment. They do not affect vision but do indicate whether the patient is compliant with therapy.

24.217 Vigabatrin is an anti-epileptic drug which can be associated with visual field constriction that is often not apparent to the patient until severe. The field defect is commonly bilateral and nasal. It is presumably due to an idiosyncratic reaction because there does not appear to be a correlation with daily or cumulative dose. Its use in patients with pre-existing visual field defects is contraindicated.

24.218 The Royal College of Ophthalmologists recommend that a baseline visual field should be obtained before starting treatment. Perimetry should then be repeated every six months for five years. It can then be extended to annually in patients who have no defect detected. In a proportion of patients including children this is not possible, in which case visual electrodiagnostic studies can provide helpful information.

24.219 If visual field constriction is detected, or if adequate testing is not possible, a decision needs to be made by the patient's neurologist in consultation with the patient, and if necessary with the patient's parents or carers, whether treatment should be continued.

In most cases the visual field defect does not reverse on cessation of the drug.

24.220 Phosphodiesterase inhibitors, such as sildenafil (Viagra), have been associated with ischaemic optic neuropathy. Whether this is a causal or coincidental relationship remains unclear, but in many cases there does appear to be a convincing temporal relationship between ingestion of the drug and onset of visual loss. Although relatively small optic discs may increase the risk of visual loss, screening is not appropriate. At present, the appropriate advice is that patients should be warned of the risk of visual loss, especially if they have suffered visual loss previously in association with use of phosphodiesterase inhibitors.

CHECKLIST

24.221
- Poor vision in both eyes has a severe impact on everyday activities and results in large value claims.
- General practitioners should be able to take a history to determine whether hospital referral is required and how quickly.
- Optometrists and opticians can provide helpful advice to GPs on the necessity and urgency of hospital referral.

- Local difficulties ensuring adequate provision of emergency ophthalmic care can lead to delay in diagnosis and management of sight threatening conditions.
- Cataract and refractive surgery account for almost two thirds of ophthalmic cases resulting in compensation.
- Many claims relating to refractive surgery result from patients' unrealistic expectations.
- Many claims relating to cataract surgery result from complications not due to an unacceptable standard of care.
- Reducing medico-legal claims relating to cataract and refractive surgery depends upon a rigorous process for obtaining consent.

BIBLIOGRAPHY

RCOPHTH Cataract Surgery Guidelines. September 2010

NICE IPG209 Implantation of accommodating intraocular lenses for cataract. February 2007

NICE IPG264 Implantation of multifocal (non-accommodative) intraocular lenses during cataract surgery. June 2008

ESCRS Guidelines on prevention, investigation and management of post-operative endophthalmitis. August 2007

NICE IPG164 Photorefractive (laser) surgery for the correction of refractive errors. March 2006

RCOPHTH Standards for Laser Refractive Surgery. July 2011

RCOPHTH Management of Acute Retinal Detachment. June 2010

RCOPHTH Age-Related Macular Degeneration: Guidelines for Management. September 2013

RCOPHTH Diabetic Retinopathy Guidelines. December 2012

NICE CG265 Glaucoma: Diagnosis and management of chronic open angle glaucoma and ocular hypertension. April 2009

BSR and BHPR guidelines for the management of giant cell arteritis. (2010) 49 Rheumatology 1594–1597

RCOPHTH Hydroxychloroquine and Ocular Toxicity Recommendations on Screening. October 2009

RCOPHTH The Ocular Side-Effects of Vigabatrin (Sabril) Information and Guidance for Screening. March 2008

CHAPTER 25

General surgery

Mr James R H Scurr

INTRODUCTION

25.1   Since the first edition of this book there have been a large number of changes in the field of general surgery.

25.2   Laparoscopic surgery is now widespread and robotic surgery is being increasingly used. From a medico-legal perspective we have gained considerable experience also. It is not the complicated new procedures which regularly give rise to claims, but the common operation that is performed daily and where a good outcome is expected.

25.3   With increasing specialisation the definition of general surgery continues to evolve. One way of identifying general surgery is as those aspects of surgery which remain after specialists have taken their areas of expertise. Yet another way is to define general surgeons as those who are prepared to act in the front line: 'emergency surgeons'. They cope with the problems of patients admitted as emergencies with surgical conditions, dealing with initial assessment, resuscitation and early investigations. Some patients will then be transferred to the care of a specialist surgeon. The areas of surgery undertaken by a general surgeon will vary, with some surgeons developing a special interest within general surgery. This is important for some very complex operations performed relatively infrequently, for example, pancreatectomy, which are better done by surgeons with an interest, in a specialist centre. The results of surgery by specialists within the spheres of general surgery are clearly better, with lower morbidity and lower mortality.

25.4   It should be understood that the term general surgeon covers a vast spectrum of individuals of different interests, experience and skills. Much depends on the type of hospital in which the surgeon works. In a district general hospital the number of general surgeons maybe in single figures. While each surgeon develops an area of particular interest, none can afford to become too specialised because of the extra workload outside the speciality that he would leave for his colleagues. In teaching hospitals there are usually a larger number of surgeons and a greater degree of specialisation is feasible. The mistakes of a teaching hospital surgeon with a special experience in the field concerned must be viewed in a more critical light than the same mistake by his opposite number in a district general hospital. On the other hand, was it reasonable for the latter to embark on a very complicated case, or should they have referred the patient to the more specialised surgeon in the teaching hospital? Ongoing advances and new techniques can lead to some surgical procedures becoming redundant (eg the majority of peptic ulcer surgery).

25.5   The way surgeons are trained has changed dramatically in the last decade. There is a seamless progression from junior doctor to consultant, which has decreased the experience of the trainees and shortened their overall training. Whilst aspects of training have improved (eg the use of simulation), the overall experience of newly-appointed consultants has declined. It remains the consultant's responsibility to delegate cases and to assist junior staff and to make sure the standard of treatment provided conforms to that which will be considered acceptable by his colleagues.

25.6 Every doctor must remain responsible for his own actions, but any consultant who permits a trainee surgeon to perform an elective operation for which he is manifestly inadequately trained is at least irresponsible, although it is not right to comment here on his legal liability for negligence.

25.7 Emergency surgery, or unplanned admissions, are different from planned, routine or elective surgery. In the last 15 years there has been a move from a situation where relatively junior doctors in training would start emergency surgical procedures normally done by more senior surgeons to a situation where more senior surgeons are now resident or immediately available. The overall level of supervision has increased. The majority of surgical procedures, even when carried out as an emergency, are performed under the direct supervision of a senior surgeon. When there is an immediate threat to life, any attempt to save the patient would be considered good medical practice. Where there is no threat to life, time allows for appropriate assistance to be summoned. In most emergency situations there is time to take an adequate history, arrange appropriate investigations and prepare the patient properly, with an emphasis on appropriate preoperative resuscitation; only then comes the surgical treatment, performed by a surgeon competent to do this. Appropriate investigations are those which can be done without delaying the patient's management, and which add significantly to, or may alter the course of, treatment. Adequate resuscitation means placing the patient in a stable cardiovascular state so as to enable them to withstand an anaesthetic. This is done by the administration of fluids that have been lost from the circulating system by haemorrhage, exudation from damaged or inflamed tissues (occurs in burns or peritonitis), and the loss of salts and water (excessive vomiting or diarrhoea causing dehydration). Administrating an anaesthetic to a 'shocked' patient has been shown to be one of the commonest causes of death in patients admitted as a surgical emergency[1]. There are now strong recommendations that surgery should not be carried out after midnight unless it is truly a life or limb-threatening situation.

1 National Confidential Enquiry into Patient Outcome and Death (NCEPOD). Peri-operative Care: Knowing the Risk (2011) http://www.ncepod.org.uk/2011poc.htm.

25.8 Although more emergency surgery is now carried out by consultant surgeons, it remains an important part of the training programme. The surgical trainee must learn to manage patients in the emergency situation, and involvement in this aspect of surgical treatment remains important. The level of supervision, however, has improved in accordance with Royal College recommendations. Differing on-call arrangements mean that some emergency patients will have to be transferred to a centre with appropriate expertise.

GENERAL PRINCIPLES

25.9 With elective surgery there are general principles which affect all operations. Three areas can be identified:

(1) the investigation and diagnosis;
(2) informed consent; and
(3) complications which are common to all surgical procedures.

INVESTIGATIONS AND DIAGNOSIS

25.10   Investigations and diagnosis of a medical condition relate to the specific nature of the problem. In some situations it is not possible to make a diagnosis other than by surgical means, ie an exploratory operation or a biopsy. For the majority of surgical problems one can, having taken an adequate history and examined the patient, arrive at a working diagnosis. This diagnosis is then confirmed or refuted by appropriate investigations. Over-investigating a patient may delay their treatment and is expensive, but would not in itself constitute negligence, unless inappropriate in an urgent situation. To perform an investigation, and then either not wait for the answer, or fail to look at the answer, would represent negligence if it resulted in an error. The ready availability of ultrasound, CT scans (computed tomography) and MRI scans (magnetic resonance imaging) have inevitably led to increased patient demand. These investigations should only be used when appropriate, and form part of the overall clinical assessment. All these investigations have limitations, and particular care is required in their interpretation. Although the procedures themselves are not harmful, care should be taken not to place too much reliance on negative investigations in the face of a deteriorating clinical situation.

25.11   It is not intended to imply that the result of every investigation must be accepted by the surgeon at face value. Any single investigation is just an item of evidence which the surgeon has to evaluate in the light of many other items of evidence. A chemical investigation occasionally gives a wrong answer, and a radiological one is unable to distinguish between normal or abnormal tissues. Fear of litigation can lead to defensive reporting of radiological scans (see Chapter 23 on radiology), eg 'I cannot on the basis of this mammogram exclude the possibility of carcinoma,' rather than 'there is no evidence of carcinoma'. This sort of reporting does not make the surgeon's job any easier.

25.12   Before proceeding with any surgical procedure the indications for the operation must exist and adequate steps must be taken to investigate the patient properly, both in terms of the surgical procedure and in terms of assessing the patient's fitness to undergo the surgical procedure. Generalised abdominal pain is a common general surgical presentation. Whilst a laparoscopy may be the most appropriate investigation, both to make the diagnosis of, and then treat a patient with, appendicitis, other patients with vague upper abdominal pain, possibly related to gallstones or to a peptic ulcer, will require further investigations first. The extent of these investigations, again, will vary depending on the presenting symptoms, but should never be less than the specific investigations designed to refine the working diagnosis to the stage at which definitive treatment can be undertaken. All elective patients should have a formal full preoperative assessment.

INFORMED CONSENT

(See also Chapter 11 dealing with consent.)

25.13   Before embarking on any surgical procedure, the aims of the operation and the expected chances of success or failure should be fully explained to the patient. It is not adequate just to explain the procedure to the patient in medical terminology. It is important to explain to the patient, in terms which he can readily understand, exactly what the purpose of the operation is, what it involves, what the outcome will be and whether there are any specific complications. In addition, the implications of not having the procedure should be explained, as should any alternative treatment options which may be non-surgical. For laparoscopic operations it is important that patients understand that the procedure may have to be converted to an open procedure if it can not be technically or safely performed 'keyhole'. The development of a complication such as uncontrollable major bleeding would also require conversion to a laparotomy. Following any skin incision, numbness may result in the area surrounding the wound. This is unavoidable, but may cause patients distress if they have not been warned in advance. All surgical procedures are associated with some bleeding, and wound haematomas (collections of blood deep to the skin in the operation site) may occur. A patient properly prepared is more likely to accept these problems than a patient who has been given inadequate preoperative information.

25.14 An assessment of mortality risk should be made explicit to the patient and recorded clearly on the consent form and in the medical records[1]. Surgical procedures with a predicted mortality of ≥10 per cent should be conducted under the direct supervision of a consultant surgeon and a consultant anaesthetist, and then admitted to critical care post operatively[2].

1 National Confidential Enquiry into Patient Outcome and Death (NCEPOD). Peri-operative Care: Knowing the Risk (2011) http://www.ncepod.org.uk/2011poc.htm; The Royal College of Surgeons of England. The Higher Risk General Surgical Patient Towards Improved Care for a Forgotten Group http://www.rcseng.ac.uk/publications/docs/higher-risk-surgical-patient.
2 The Royal College of Surgeons of England. The Higher Risk General Surgical Patient Towards Improved Care for a Forgotten Group http://www.rcseng.ac.uk/publications/docs/higher-risk-surgical-patient.

25.15 The use of surgical devices and implants 'off-label' is not uncommon. This is when a clinician uses a device for an indication that has not been included in the instructions for use ('IFU')[1]. However, off-label use and/or device modification by a surgeon prior to use may render them personally liable if harm is caused to the patient[2]. The benefits and risks of such use is an essential part of the informed consent process.

1 Association of Surgeons of Great Britain and Ireland (ASGBI). The collective management of risk from surgical devices and implants. 2013. ASGBI, Available from: http://www.asgbi.org.uk/en/publications/consensus_statements.cfm.
2 Lennard, Coutinho and Campbel 'The surgeon and medical devices: adverse incident reporting and off-label use' (2013) 95(5) Ann R Coll Surg Engl 309–310.

COMPLICATIONS OF ALL SURGICAL OPERATIONS

25.16 Complications following surgery can be divided into two groups: those specifically related to the operation itself, and those related to any operation. Specific complications are discussed later. Sometimes, following a surgical procedure, there is a recognised associated condition which may occur in all patients, or may occur selectively. For example operations on varicose veins may result in small areas of numbness or altered sensation. These changes can be temporary or permanent, giving rise to minimal symptoms but, on occasion, quite severe and disabling complications. Although these problems are not caused by negligence, the patient who has received proper consent and understands tolerates this outcome better. Emergency surgery is associated with a significant (5–10 fold) increase in mortality and a similar increase in morbidity when compared to the procedure performed electively[1].

1 Association of Surgeons of Great Britain and Ireland (ASGBI). Patient Safety: A Consensus Statement. 2010. ASGBI, available from: http://www.asgbi.org.uk/en/publications/consensus_statements.cfm.

GENERAL COMPLICATIONS ASSOCIATED WITH ANY SURGICAL OPERATION

Wound infection, wound haematoma

25.17   One cannot cut tissues without dividing blood vessels, causing bleeding; one cannot cut the skin or the mucosa lining the alimentary tract without incurring the risk that micro-organisms from the environment gain access to the tissues. Following surgical procedures wound infection and wound haematomas (collections of shed blood) are quite common. The development of a haematoma or a wound infection does not itself constitute negligence, unless it can be shown that some predisposing condition was present which was not recognised, and which clearly should have been recognised in the preoperative period, or that there was a relevant problem during the operation, or in the immediate post-operative period, which was similarly unrecognised or ignored. Some surgical procedures, eg operations on the gastrointestinal tract, carry a significantly greater wound infection rate unless appropriate precautions are taken. These precautions include the use of prophylactic antibiotics. Operating on the large bowel without prophylactic antibiotics in a patient who subsequently developed a wound infection could be considered negligent. Failure to prepare the skin adequately or to sterilise the instruments could also be considered negligent. Skin preparation involves removing hair (with electric clippers) and painting the skin with an antiseptic solution. The skin is never sterile and the possibility of an infection always remains. The most common source of infection in a wound is from the patient themselves; their own organisms being transferred from the nasal sinuses, or other parts of the respiratory tract, or from their skin, into the wounds at the time of the operation. No wound can be considered immune from the possibility of a surgical site infection (SSI), but incisions made into uncontaminated tissues in good operating theatres have only a 1–3 per cent chance of showing any infection[1]. It is generally agreed that there is no indication for using prophylactic antibiotics in 'clean' cases, ie where gut or other infected body cavities are not being breached, and where there is no pre-existing infection in the tissues. However, if prostheses are being inserted it is very important to use prophylactic antibiotics, because foreign materials strongly predispose to infection, and once infection occurs, it cannot be controlled until the foreign material has been removed. There are situations, particularly in the presence of devitalised tissue which also encourages growth of micro-organisms, where failure to use prophylactic antibiotics might be considered negligent. An above-knee amputation for ischaemic disease is an example where prophylactic antibiotics are required.

1 Public Health England. National percentiles of SSI rates by surgical category. http://www.hpa.org.uk/webw/HPAweb&HPAwebStandard/HPAweb_C/1195733800109.

25.18 Wounds can become infected in the post-operative period and the signs of infection may manifest themselves from the second post-operative day onwards. Surgical incisions should be covered with an appropriate dressing at the end of the operation. Some complex wounds may be 'left open' to heal by secondary intention and require specialised wound and nursing care. If a wound that has been sutured becomes infected then the sutures may have to be removed early to reopen the wound and drain the infection/pus. Suture material can be absorbable or non-absorbable. Non absorbable stitches and staples do need to be removed from the skin once they have allowed the necessary healing to occur. A retained suture can lead to an abscess or a stitch sinus. Sutures impregnated with antimicrobial activity are commercially available but their role in the prevention of SSI has yet to be defined.

Bleeding

25.19 Bleeding occurs during all surgical procedures (primary haemorrhage). The bleeding stops as a result of vessel contraction and the formation of haemostatic plugs formed from the body's own clotting system. Abnormalities in the clotting system should be recognised preoperatively from a history of excessive bleeding tendencies, and appropriate investigations undertaken. Patients with a history of excessive bruising or bleeding at a previous surgical procedure clearly require preoperative investigations. The minimum investigations required include a full blood count, platelet count and blood clotting studies. Additional investigations may be indicated to exclude haemophilia and other genetic or acquired clotting deficiencies. Thrombophilia is a genetic or acquired pre-disposition to clotting, affecting up to 10 per cent of the population and accounting for clotting problems in young patients with no other risk factors. Inherited thrombophilia conditions include Factor V Leiden, antithrombin deficiency, protein C and protein S deficiencies. Some patients may be undergoing long-term treatment with anticoagulants (blood thinning agents), but still require surgical procedures. It may be appropriate to reverse the anticoagulation before the operation, or to take steps to counter the anticoagulant during the surgical procedure. It is important to have available adequate supplies of blood and of the relevant clotting factors if appropriate. To embark upon a surgical procedure unaware of the coagulation problem, despite a definite history, and, therefore, without adequate blood stores readily available for replacing losses, would constitute negligence.

25.20 Bleeding following a surgical procedure may occur when a clot from a previously sealed vessel is displaced by high blood pressure or a ligature has slipped. This is known as a reactionary haemorrhage. Often this will result in a self-limiting haematoma. Failure to identify that a patient is having a significant, or an on-going, post-operative bleed and not to take the appropriate action would represent negligent care. In patients where bleeding is more likely to occur post operatively, some surgeons will use drains. Trapped blood initially solidifies by clotting, forming a haematoma, and then subsequently liquefies. It may become infected, leading to local or sometimes generalised sepsis. The formation of a haematoma, assuming adequate steps have been take to prevent it, cannot be considered negligent. Failure to diagnose and treat a haematoma appropriately could constitute negligence. A small haematoma or extensive bruising around a wound will resolve with no treatment. An extensive haematoma may require formal drainage and, if it becomes infected, it will undoubtedly require drainage. This should be undertaken as soon as the diagnosis is made. Secondary haemorrhage is caused by the wound bed becoming infected and thus causing a delayed bleed.

25.21 In an effort to reduce peri-operative blood loss when the operation involves a territory with a particularly abundant blood supply, eg the face and the neck, the surgeon often asks the anaesthetist to administer drugs that lower the blood pressure during the operation. When the procedure is completed, and before the surgeon closes the wound, it is important that the surgeon asks the anaesthetist to raise the blood pressure back to normal; in the absence of this precaution a later rise in blood pressure might precipitate bleeding (a reactionary haemorrhage) from imperfectly-sealed blood vessels. Evidence that this precaution was not taken might well be considered negligence. In operations where significant blood loss is expected (eg vascular surgery) then the use of a blood cell salvage machine is used to allow autologous blood transfusion by recovering lost blood and re-infusing it into the patient.

Wound dehiscence/incisional hernia

25.22 Following the repair of any surgical wound there is a chance that it will fail to heal and the tissues will part or 'break down'. In some patients it is known that there is likely to be impaired healing, and it may be necessary to take special precautions in suturing the wound. These precautions may include additional sutures, and the leaving of the skin sutures in place for a longer period of time. True abdominal wound dehiscence is now relatively uncommon because there have been improvements in surgical technique and suture materials. When a wound does break down it is often the result of complicating sepsis. It is important to recognise wound dehiscence and to take appropriate action. Sometimes a minor dehiscence will occur which is not immediately apparent, and this phenomenon is probably responsible for the development of an incisional hernia, a weakness in the wound, occurring at a later date. The development of an incisional hernia may require further surgery to correct it. It is not in itself evidence of negligence. If the predisposing factor was a wound infection, the surgeon would only have been negligent if it could be shown that he did not take adequate precautions, either in terms of preparing the patient, or in terms of obtaining adequate sterility during the surgical procedure. If the predisposing factor were a wound haematoma, that, similarly, would only constitute negligence if it could be shown that the surgeon knowingly operated on a patient with an increased risk without initially seeking his consent or explaining the increased risk to him, or taking adequate precautions to prevent bleeding after the wound has been closed. A wound dehiscence occurring without any obvious predisposing causes is much more difficult to predict, and usually only occurs in a patient who is slow to heal. Surgeons tend to remove sutures as early as possible, because this is the way to obtain the best cosmetic result. Occasionally this may result in superficial wound breakdown, the net result being a slightly wider and uglier scar. This can be revised by excising the scar and re-suturing and would not constitute negligence.

25.23 Failure to recognise the development of an incisional hernia and to give advice or explanation may prove negligent. An incisional hernia is associated with the same complications as any other hernia, including potential bowel strangulation and intestinal obstruction. Having recognised the presence of an incisional hernia, appropriate treatment should be instituted. This may involve fitting the patient with a support or suggesting surgical repair. As with any hernia, following the repair of an incisional hernia there is a small chance that it will recur. The patient should be warned that there is no guarantee of success when it comes to repairing hernias.

Deep vein thrombosis/pulmonary embolism

25.24 Clinically significant venous thrombosis occurs within the deep veins (DVT). Thrombosis involves blood clotting, ie setting. A thrombus is a laminated clot involving platelets, fibrin and red cells. Blood remains fluid within the circulation because of a balance between factors causing it to clot and factors causing the clot to dissolve. Many things are known to upset this balance, and upsetting the balance can lead to excessive bleeding or excessive clotting.

25.25 The deep veins are those veins in the centre of the limbs and the pelvis; they are surrounded by muscles and lie deep to a non-elastic sleeve of fascia extending up the limb.

25.26 An embolus is an intravascular mass (solid, liquid, or gas) which travels within the circulation and goes on to cause a blockage. The commonest type of embolus is a thrombus that has formed within the deep veins that then breaks off and travels centrally, becoming trapped in the lungs (a pulmonary embolus). This can occur in any patient, both medical and surgical.

25.27 The risks of deep vein thrombosis are now clearly recognised. Up to 30 per cent of patients over the age of 40 years undergoing major surgical procedures will develop a deep vein thrombosis unless adequate prophylaxis is given. This data comes from studies carried out in the 1970s and 1980s using I125-labelled fibrinogen. This test has been replaced by venous duplex ultrasound imaging. The incidence of clinical deep vein thrombosis, ie thrombosis which is apparent on clinical examination alone, is considerably lower than this. The incidence of two serious complications, namely the post-thrombotic limb (swollen, pigmented or ulcerated) and pulmonary embolism (PE), are more difficult to quantify. NICE have recommended that all hospitalised patients should undergo venous thromboembolism (VTE) risk assessment on admission. Those at risk must be provided with appropriate thromboprophylaxis to reduce their risk of developing a deep vein thrombosis and its possible sequelae. Certain patients are recognised to be at increased risk, and these included patients over the age of 40 undergoing major surgical procedures, those with underlying malignant disease, a past history of venous thromboembolic disease and/ or obesity. Prophylactic modalities which have been shown to be effective include: peri-operative administration of subcutaneous low molecular weight heparin (LMWH), the wearing of graduated compression elastic stockings and the use of intermittent pneumatic compression devices[1]. If this prophylaxis is not employed and the patient develops a significant complication, namely, a pulmonary embolism, or a post-thrombotic limb, even many years later, the doctors could be considered negligent for failing to take steps to reduce these risks[2]. Most hospitals have local protocols both with regard to assessing the risk and to providing prophylaxis. If a hospital has a protocol in place and does not follow it, then it is very difficult for them to defend against these types of claims.

1 National Institute for Health and Care Excellence (NICE). Venous thromboembolism: reducing the risk: Reducing the risk of venous thromboembolism (deep vein thrombosis and pulmonary embolism) in patients admitted to hospital. http://publications.nice.org.uk/ venous-thromboembolism-reducing-the-risk-cg92.
2 Scurr and Scurr 'Is failure to provide thromboprophylaxis negligent?' (2007) 22(4) Phlebology 186–191.

25.28 Even with adequate VTE prophylaxis early diagnosis of deep vein thrombosis is important. Therapeutic doses of heparin (can be administered by either an intravenous route or a subcutaneous route for LMWH) should be started on clinical suspicion and continued if a venous duplex ultrasound scan confirms the diagnosis. Failure to consider the diagnosis, make it and provide reasonable treatment constitutes negligence.

25.29 Patient safety initiatives have now been implemented widely, with the World Health Organization (WHO) Surgical Safety Checklist to help prevent errors in the operating theatre being the best example[1]. This system is used to ensure surgery occurs on the correct patient and on the correct site/side. It also ensures that the team takes responsibility for ensuring that they are prepared for blood loss, avoids known allergies, prevent surgical site infections, provides appropriate venous thromboprophylaxis and avoids retained swabs or instruments. The process also aims to improve team working and communication.

1 Association of Surgeons of Great Britain and Ireland (ASGBI). Patient Safety: A Consensus Statement. 2010. ASGBI, available from: http://www.asgbi.org.uk/en/publications/ consensus_statements.cfm; World Health Organization (WHO). Safe Surgery Saves Lives. http://www.who.int/patientsafety/safesurgery/en/.

Post-operative chest conditions

25.30 Following any major surgical procedure, particularly those procedures associated with an abdominal incision, partial collapse of the lungs (pulmonary atelectasis) is extremely common. The condition may manifest itself by a slight rise in temperature on the first post-operative day. This is not associated with any infective process and is entirely a mechanical problem with a number of the alveoli (air sacs) collapsing. These may become secondarily infected to produce a productive cough. This is a common post-operative condition, and responds very well to chest physiotherapy, supplemented by antibiotics if infection becomes established. This complication does not constitute evidence of negligence. It might, however, be considered negligent to operate on a patient with a pre-existing chest infection without taking steps to reduce the risks to the patient. In a patient with acute respiratory disease an elective operation should be postponed, whereas an emergency procedure may have to proceed. Patients with chronic respiratory problems, for example, a productive cough, or undergoing an operation in which the risk of a 'post-operative chest' are increased (eg abdominal surgery) should be fully assessed before the operation and, if appropriate, given antibiotics and physiotherapy. Failure to recognise these risks and to attempt to correct them could be considered negligent.

Fluid balance

25.31 Patients undergoing major surgical procedures suffer considerable disturbances in their fluid and electrolyte balance. These disturbances may be brought about by blood loss, by excessive exudates, as for example in burns patients or in patients with pancreatitis or peritonitis, or by excessive water and electrolyte loss, as may occur from the gastrointestinal tract in the form of diarrhoea or vomiting. Additionally, in the post-operative period, fluid collects in the gut and is therefore essentially lost to the body. All patients require adequate fluid replacements, and the ideal fluid to replace the losses is the same as the fluid being lost. Patients losing blood should receive blood transfusions; patients losing water and electrolytes into the gut, or with excessive vomiting and diarrhoea, should receive crystalloid solutions to balance their fluid and electrolyte losses. The amount of fluid required is enough to replace any excess loss. Too little fluid leads to fluid depletion and the patient becomes dry and the urine output falls. Excessive fluid replacement overloads the patient, producing symptoms of cardiac failure. In patients losing or gaining considerable quantities of fluid, care must be taken to monitor their electrolyte balance and add additional electrolytes to the solution as and when required. Clearly, it is important to monitor the patient carefully in the post-operative period to assess that enough, but not too much, in the way of fluid replacement is being given. Daily fluid requirements will vary and are the maintenance fluid requirement (calculated by body weight) plus the volume required to replace measurable/estimated losses. On occasions these losses can be very considerable (eg a burns patient) and the volumes required to replace them equally considerable, totalling several litres within a 24-hour period. Negligence in this field includes failure to chart intake and output, errors in such charting, and gross errors in the decisions about the volumes and natures of the liquids given. NCEPOD reported in 2011 that the 30 day mortality in those patients in whom their advisers considered there to have been inadequate pre-operative fluid management was 20.5 per cent compared to 4.7 per cent mortality in those with adequate pre-operative fluid therapy[1].

1 National Confidential Enquiry into Patient Outcome and Death (NCEPOD). Peri-operative Care: Knowing the Risk (2011) http://www.ncepod.org.uk/2011poc.htm.

POST-OPERATIVE MONITORING

25.32 Following any surgical procedure it is necessary to perform repeated observations on the patient. The purpose is to check for abnormalities in the pulse, blood pressure, respiration, temperature and conscious level. The frequency of these observations will be determined by the nature of the operation and the patient's general condition. Observations are usually recorded quarter-hourly, half-hourly, hourly or four-hourly. Quarter-hourly observations, involving the blood pressure, pulse, respiration and temperature, imply that the patient is being observed almost continually. After major operations, observations including the central venous pressure, the intra-arterial blood pressure via an arterial line, and urine output may also be recorded on critical care units. NCEPOD reported that 8.3 per cent of high-risk patients who should have gone to a higher care level area post-operatively did not do so[1]. Following a general anaesthetic for a routine general surgical procedure, these observations would initially be on a quarter-hourly basis. If the blood pressure, pulse, temperature and respiration remain stable, then the frequency of the observations is reduced. Once the patient is fully alert, then the frequency can be reduced further. Failure to monitor a patient post-operatively is a frequent claim in medical negligence cases. The frequency of monitoring clearly depends on the clinical situation and the recordings on the chart represent the frequency with which the nurse has gone back to see the patient. Trends in measurements are more important than single observations and a declining blood pressure with a rising pulse indicates bleeding in a post-operative patient (see para **25.20**). Negligence in this field may be a failure to carry out monitoring of a nature and at a frequency required by the patient's condition, or it may be a failure to respond appropriately to the evidence produced by the monitoring. For example, in the case of a patient with a falling blood pressure and a rising pulse rate, if, despite this evidence, the frequency of post-operative monitoring is decreased still further, then this is likely to constitute negligence.

1 National Confidential Enquiry into Patient Outcome and Death (NCEPOD). Peri-operative Care: Knowing the Risk (2011) http://www.ncepod.org.uk/2011poc.htm.

SPECIFIC OPERATIONS

Principles

25.33   In any individual operation, certain anatomical structures are known to be at risk. The basic principles are that all anatomical structures should be preserved, or if damaged, then repaired, unless the disease process necessitates their removal. Should the surgeon anticipate that it may be necessary to destroy an anatomical feature, prior consent must be obtained. The likely consequences of the damage, with regard particularly to function as well as to form, must be explained.

25.34   During the course of a surgical procedure, surrounding structures that are not usually part of the field of that particular operation may be injured. For example, operating on a patient who has had a previous abdominal operation, or in whom, for other reasons, there are adhesions present, may necessitate dividing adhesions to neighbouring loops of bowel. In the course of this dissection, it may not be possible to avoid damaging the bowel. This in itself does not constitute negligence, but failure to recognise a hole in the bowel following such mobilisation, clearly is. The hole must be repaired, or the damaged segment resected, and continuity of the bowel restored by anastomosis. Injuries may also have delayed consequences that are not recognised or considered at the time of the initial operation. For example, the blood supply to the bowel may be injured but the ischaemic area only goes on to perforate in the post-operative period. Failure and/or delay in this situation, to diagnose and manage a perforation, could end up being harder to defend than the injury that caused it. Removal of the spleen at the time of upper abdominal surgery is sometimes necessary. This may be due to damage inflicted on the spleen during the surgical procedure, and such damage again usually due to adhesions, may be unavoidable. Recognising damage to the spleen and taking the appropriate action of repair, or excision, of the organ is not negligent. Failure to recognise the injury may result in severe post-operative bleeding when the haematoma ruptures. In a correctly-observed patient, the signs of shock will be detected early, a laparotomy undertaken and splenectomy performed. Failure to observe the patient in the post-operative period may result in these early complications being missed, and this is negligent. The patient should be told about the splenectomy because of the increased risk of infection. Some would argue that such patients need to be placed on long-term antibiotic therapy.

25.35   In the case of the spleen, it is not unusual for the surgeon to miss an injury during the operation. This is because the damage may have been produced by tension on ligaments or adhesions at some considerable distance from the spleen. A little bleeding occurs to form a subcapsular haematoma, and it is only when this ruptures that a problem occurs.

Laparoscopic surgical procedures

25.36   Laparoscopic surgical procedures are widely performed. Many surgical procedures originally performed by an open procedure are now routinely carried out using the laparoscope. The majority of cholecystectomies are now carried out laparoscopically. Anti-reflux procedures for hiatus hernias, obesity surgery, and many colorectal operations are also carried out using laparoscopic techniques. Laparoscopic vascular surgery for aortic aneurysms is now also technically possible. Surgical robots have been introduced and the number of procedures currently being carried out robotically continues to increase.

25.37   Many procedures including appendicectomy and repair of hernias can be carried out using an open procedure or a laparoscopic procedure. All surgeons carrying out laparoscopic procedures should be properly trained in both the procedure and with dealing with any potential complications. The benefits of laparoscopy include minimal tissue damage and a more rapid recovery. The disadvantages of laparoscopic surgery include damage to local structures, which may or may not be recognised at the time of surgery, and prolongation of the operative procedure. Early recognition of complications and appropriate management is essential[1].

1 Association of Surgeons of Great Britain and Ireland (ASGBI). Patient Safety: A Consensus Statement. 2010. ASGBI, Available from: http://www.asgbi.org.uk/en/publications/consensus_statements.cfm.

Inguinal hernia

25.38 Repair of an inguinal hernia is one of the most common general surgical procedures, often being undertaken by surgeons in training. The hernia may be repaired electively, or as an emergency if the contents become strangulated, ie if the neck of the hernia becomes so tight that drainage of blood from the contents of the hernia sac is impeded. Strangulated hernias may contain gut, and hernias remain a common cause of intestinal obstruction; early diagnosis and adequate treatment are clearly essential. If a hernia becomes strangulated, the contents are starting to die. Immediate surgical treatment is required, often with resection of the contents, which in itself may necessitate removing a portion of bowel. With dead contents the chances of local infection occurring increases considerably. Undue delay in repairing a hernia which has become strangulated increases the chances of having to resect the bowel, and the liability to wound infection. The diagnosis of strangulated inguinal hernia is a clinical one and the patient should be taken to theatre straight away, delaying only long enough for adequate resuscitation. Undue delay could constitute negligence.

25.39 The open repair of an inguinal hernia involves making an incision in the groin. During the making of this incision, cutaneous nerves will be divided and an area of numbness following this operation is not unusual. When these nerves regenerate, an area of oversensitivity may occur, and with time this too will settle. Damage to deeper nerves and other structures during the course of a hernia repair may occur (see para **25.46**). During the course of the repair of the hernia, it is necessary to mobilise the vessels supplying the testicle. Sometimes damage to these vessels will result in atrophy of the testicles, with subsequent disappearance. This might be interpreted as negligence, depending on whether there was evidence of a particularly difficult operative field (see paras **25.43–25.45**).

25.40 The inguinal canal – the point of weakness in the abdominal wall through which an inguinal hernia emerges – is a channel which carries the spermatic cord in the male. This consists of the vas deferens (the duct along which sperm travels, after manufacture in the testis) along with the nerves and blood vessels supplying the testis. The analogous structures in the female have no important function and can be divided; the inguinal canal can then be closed and a reasonably secure repair achieved. In male patients in whom it is thought likely that repair will be difficult, because of the size or of repeated recurrence, it may be deemed advisable to ask the patient beforehand for permission to remove the testis and cord, increasing the chances of achieving a permanent repair.

Laparoscopic repair of inguinal hernia

25.41 Laparoscopic repair of inguinal hernias has become increasingly common since the first edition of this book. The principle of the surgical repair remains the same, namely reduction of the hernia and the insertion of a mesh which forms the scaffolding on which the body will lay down fibrous tissues to complete the repair. All of the major complications (eg testicular injury and nerve injury) that can occur with open repair can also occur with laparoscopic repair. In addition, there are some complications specific to laparoscopy. The British Hernia Society with the Association of Surgeons of Great Britain and Ireland reviewed the current evidence in 2013 for open versus laparoscopic repair for unilateral primary inguinal hernias, and have made recommendations for the laparoscopic management of recurrent and bilateral groin hernias[1]. The benefits of laparoscopic hernia repair have been reported to include a more rapid recovery.

1 Association of Surgeons of Great Britain and Ireland. Groin hernia Guidelines (in partnership with British Hernia Society). 2013. ASGBI, available from: http://www.asgbi.org.uk/en/publications/issues_in_professional_practice.cfm.

25.42   Infections and haematomas following hernia repairs can occur. Meticulous haemostasis is important to prevent haematoma formation, which may increase the risk of an infection developing. Infection following a hernia repair may not settle, unless any non-absorbable suture material used for the repair, such as nylon or polypropylene mesh, is removed. Both infection and haematomas are recognised complications and are, in themselves, not a sign of negligence. Failure to recognise these complications and provide appropriate treatment, or else delay in treatment, may constitute negligence. The use of antibiotic prophylaxis is controversial. A recent Cochrane meta-analysis of randomised clinical trials reported that there was no clear evidence that routine administration of antibiotic prophylaxis for elective inguinal hernia repair reduces infection rates[1].

1 Association of Surgeons of Great Britain and Ireland. Groin hernia Guidelines (in partnership with British Hernia Society). 2013. ASGBI, available from: http://www.asgbi.org.uk/en/publications/issues_in_professional_practice.cfm.

25.43   Ischaemic orchitis and testicular atrophy are common reasons for medico-legal claims following inguinal hernia surgery[1]. However, they are recognised complications of hernia surgery. Not all patients with ischaemic orchitis will go on to develop testicular atrophy. Rough handling of the cord and delivery of the testicle into the inguinal canal can damage the blood supply to the testicle. In order to prevent ischaemic orchitis, dissection of a sac below the pubic tubercle should not be performed. Excessive dissection and the use of diathermy around the cord, especially when trying to remove a lipoma of the cord, can lead to thrombosis of the spermatic vessels causing these testicular complications. Care must also be taken to prevent making the internal or external rings too 'tight' so that they may affect the blood supply to the testicle.

1 Scurr JRH, Scurr JH. 100 consecutive claims of alleged negligence in elective open inguinal hernia repair in the UK Clinical Risk 2006; 12: 221–225; Alkhaffaf B, Decadt B. Litigation following groin hernia repair in England. Hernia. 2010; 14(2):181-6.

25.44   Atrophy of one testicle does not diminish testosterone levels or affect fertility. However, if the other testicle is already damaged or lost then this will have serious implications, as it did in several of the cases reported by Scurr et al[1]. Serious consideration should be given to whether it is reasonable to repair bilateral inguinal hernias in men of reproductive age at the same time.

1 Scurr and Scurr '100 consecutive claims of alleged negligence in elective open inguinal hernia repair in the UK' (2006) 12 Clinical Risk 221–225.

25.45   Thirteen of the sixteen claims following recurrent inguinal hernia repair in a reported series involved ischaemic orchitis/testicular atrophy[1].

The risk of ischaemic orchitis/testicular atrophy and the possible need for orchidectomy as a complication of recurrent inguinal hernia repair was often not consented for and therefore difficult to defend. In recurrent inguinal hernia surgery the patient must be consented for the possibility of testicular loss/orchidectomy.

1 Scurr and Scurr '100 consecutive claims of alleged negligence in elective open inguinal hernia repair in the UK' (2006) 12 Clinical Risk 221–225.

25.46　Nerve injury is the other major cause of medico-legal claims following inguinal hernia surgery. Injury can result in anaesthesia, hyperesthesia and chronic pain. These are difficult claims to handle, as pain is subjective. Chronic pain following hernia surgery is common. The ilioinguinal, genitofemoral and ilio-hypogatric nerves can all be involved. Protection of these nerves during surgery is essential. If, during a difficult dissection, the nerves are severely traumatised then division of the nerve leading to an area of local anaesthesia may be preferable to the hyperaesthesia which commonly occurs with local trauma. The genital branch of the genitofemoral nerve must be preserved in women, as it is the sensory nerve to the labia majora.

25.47　Most patients will report some numbness below and medial to the incision post-operatively. Patients should be consented for possible sensory loss. All the claims related to sensory loss previously reported were eventually discontinued[1].

1 Scurr and Scurr '100 consecutive claims of alleged negligence in elective open inguinal hernia repair in the UK' (2006) 12 Clinical Risk 221–225.

25.48　Injury to the bladder and bowel can have serious consequences. In sliding hernias, bladder or bowel can make up part of the wall of the hernial sac. Careful dissection is required to avoid visceral injury. Small bowel is often found in large inguinoscrotal hernias and must be reduced back into the abdomen with care, especially when incarcerated.

25.49　All types of hernia repair described and performed are associated with certain recurrence rates, which will vary between surgeons. It is impossible to guarantee freedom from recurrence and it does not imply negligence.

25.50　Preoperatively, it is important to examine the testicles and spermatic cords and document any abnormality. A history of previous inguinal or scrotal surgery (eg vasectomy) is also important, as this will increase the risk of ischaemic orchitis/testicular atrophy. Informed consent must include: bleeding/bruising, infection, recurrence, sensory loss, chronic pain and the risk of testicular atrophy. For recurrent hernia repairs the risk of orchidectomy must also be included. The side of the hernia must be confirmed preoperatively and marked by the operating surgeon.

25.51　Cases have been difficult to defend when the operation note does not describe the repair performed. It is important to record the type of hernia, whether it is direct or indirect, and the presence or absence of a lipoma. The size, contents and management of the sac, along with measures to protect the nerves and cord, should also be noted. The testicle should not be delivered from the scrotum and extensive dissection of sac below the pubic tubercle should not be performed. The type of repair and the nature of the prosthetic material should also be recorded.

25.52 Although the author has been able to provide some details of the sums involved in settling hernia cases[1] they do not record the true cost of these claims, which also includes legal costs paid to solicitors, experts, barristers and court fees. Very few of these cases were associated with large amounts for special damages, a clear indication that even in cases where a claim succeeded the claimant was probably able to continue working. The NHS Litigation Authority settled 209 groin hernia claims between 1995 and 2009, having to pay out over £7.35 million[2].

1 Scurr and Scurr '100 consecutive claims of alleged negligence in elective open inguinal hernia repair in the UK' (2006) 12 Clinical Risk 221–225.
2 Alkhaffaf and Decadt 'Litigation following groin hernia repair in England' (2010) 14(2) Hernia 181–186.

Stomach and duodenum

25.53 Elective operations on the stomach and duodenum for peptic ulcer disease are rarely performed now with modern medical therapy. Operations for the complications of peptic ulcer diseases, including bleeding and perforation, are still carried out. It is rare to see patients presenting with advanced peptic ulcer disease resulting in gastric outlet obstruction requiring surgery.

25.54 When a patient does present with a perforated duodenal ulcer, a certain amount of intra-peritoneal soiling occurs, and antibiotics should be administered. Any operation involving an abdominal incision in the presence of peritoneal soiling is associated with an increased risk of infection and subsequent incisional hernia formation.

25.55 Operations for carcinoma of the stomach may be palliative or curative. Palliative procedures involve bypassing the stomach in order to allow swallowing to continue or debulking the tumour. Curative operations tend to be extensive and involve the removal of surrounding structures, including the omentum, the spleen and surrounding lymph nodes. Although these operations are undertaken (because the patient has no other hope of a cure), the five-year survival rate is extremely low; these cancers have an aggressive nature and are rarely controlled by an operation. These operations may be complicated by failure to heal, breakdown of the anastomosis and alteration in digestion. The patient will notice when the majority of the stomach has been removed that they feel full, and may also have an alteration in bowel habit. These are recognised problems associated with surgery on the stomach and duodenum and should be explained to the patient beforehand.

The acute abdomen

25.56 Appendicitis, perforated peptic ulcer, gallstone complications, complications of diverticular disease (perforation, infection or abscess), intestinal obstruction and strangulated hernias form the majority of general surgical emergencies. Presenting symptoms include pain, (colicky, persistent, generalised or localised), nausea, vomiting, abdominal distension and absolute constipation. Some diseases, which do not require surgical intervention, can also produce abdominal symptoms which mirror those of the acute surgical abdomen.

25.57 General practitioners and emergency department physicians will regularly be faced with having to assess patients with acute abdominal pain. Analysis of claims from primary care have reported cases that have followed a 'failure to recognise the seriousness of the symptoms and signs, causing misdiagnosis and a failure to admit the patient for formal surgical evaluation. In secondary care, unnecessary delay in surgery resulting in avoidable sequelae has been reported to be a common cause for a complaint or claim'[1]. NCEPOD reported 20 per cent of non-elective patients received delayed surgery and one in five non-elective high-risk patients were delayed going to theatre[2].

1 Kavanagh 'The acute abdomen – assessment, diagnosis and pitfalls' (2004) 12(1) Casebook 11–17 (www.mps.org.uk).
2 National Confidential Enquiry into Patient Outcome and Death (NCEPOD). Peri-operative Care: Knowing the Risk (2011) http://www.ncepod.org.uk/2011poc.htm.

25.58 The acute abdomen presents a difficult diagnostic challenge[1]. The list of possible diagnoses is enormous, and the crucial decision is whether to operate on the patient, or whether to treat them conservatively (non operatively with antibiotics for example). This decision will be based on clinical experience, the availability of any additional investigations, and knowledge of the past history of the patient. The availability of CT scanning 24 hours a day means that it is increasingly used in the assessment of the acute abdomen. The two common errors are failure to operate when the indications are clearly present and operating when it turns out to have been unnecessary. The latter can usually be justified. Obviously, opening an abdomen or looking inside it with a laparoscope and finding nothing wrong can be a relatively safe procedure, and assuming that there was a clinical indication for performing the laparoscopy/laparotomy, this would be considered good clinical practice. Failure to operate in the presence of a clear indication may, however, be negligent. Young girls seen early in an attack of acute appendicitis which is not operated on may go on to develop a ruptured appendix and pelvic sepsis and consequently may experience fertility problems due to obstruction of the fallopian tubes by post-inflammatory adhesions. Failure to make the diagnosis of appendicitis in the face of suggestive symptoms and signs, and failure to operate in this situation, is negligent. The appropriate treatment for most cases of appendicitis, especially in a young, fit healthy adult, is an appendicectomy (open or laparoscopic). There may be indications for treating patients conservatively even in the presence of obvious perforation, but the mortality in this group is high. Conservative management can really only be justified if the patient's chances of surviving a surgical procedure are even less than their chances with conservative treatment.

1 Poston 'The Acute Abdomen: Assessment, Diagnosis and Pitfalls' (2005) 11(4) AvMA Medical & Legal Journal 159–165.

25.59 An ultrasound scan is often requested in women to help exclude a gynaecological cause for their lower abdominal pain, such as an ovarian cyst, inflammation of the fallopian tubes, or a tubo-ovarian abscess. A pregnancy test in women of child-bearing age is essential to exclude the possibility of an ectopic pregnancy. It may only be on laparoscopy that a gynaecological cause is identified and the appendix is seen to be normal. The involvement of a gynaecologist in the assessment and/or management of a woman with an acute abdomen is often required. The assessment and management of a pregnant woman with an acute abdomen can pose significant challenges for the clinical teams involved.

25.60 Most medico-legal claims following appendicitis have related to delayed diagnosis and delayed treatment[1]. As many cases of acute appendicitis are preceded by a prodromal illness such as acute tonsillitis, or gastro-enteritis, it is often quite difficult to define when the appendicitis actually started and when the patient should have been referred to the hospital. The use of antibiotics in this period can mask the signs and symptoms, making the ultimate diagnosis more difficult. The easiest time to make the diagnosis of acute appendicitis is when the patient first presents with centralised abdominal pain. The most difficult time to make the diagnosis is one week to ten days into the illness, when a confusing variety of symptoms may have appeared.

1 Mosedale, Nepogodiev, Fitzgerald, Bhangu 'Causes and costs of a decade of litigation following emergency appendectomy in England' (2013) 37(8) World J Surg 1851–1858.

25.61 Other medico-legal cases have involved failure to remove the appendix, failure to remove the whole appendix (particularly following laparoscopic removal), incorporation of the small bowel in the wound closure, and other wound problems such as infection, herniation (incisional or port site hernias) and damage to fertility[1].

1 Mosedale T, Nepogodiev D, Fitzgerald JEF, Bhangu A. Causes and Costs of a Decade of Litigation Following Emergency Appendectomy in England. World J Surg 2013; 37(8): 1851-1858.

25.62 The assessment of children with acute abdominal pain will often be requested by the paediatricians and an emergency surgeon on call for general surgery in a district general hospital would be expected to perform this. Very young children and those with complex intra abdominal conditions and/or co-existing medical conditions should be discussed with, and transferred to the care of, the regional paediatric surgical unit. Pain from testicular torsion can be referred to the abdomen and failure to examine the testicles in a young boy or adult and miss a testicular torsion would not be defensible (see Chapter 34 on urology).

25.63 Following a gastrointestinal perforation an erect chest X-ray may reveal air beneath the diaphragm. However, increasingly CT scans are being requested to confirm the diagnosis and plan treatment. Intra-abdominal collections of infected fluid (abscesses) can sometimes be drained effectively by radiological guidance, avoiding the need for a major laparotomy. This treatment may resolve the whole situation or just allow the stabilisation of the patient's condition prior to optimising them for a definitive surgical procedure (eg a bowel resection) as a more planned procedure by a specialist.

25.64   When the first edition of this book was written one of the most common causes of intestinal obstruction was still a strangulated hernia. Most patients now receive treatment for their hernia (see para **25.38**) long before the hernia strangulates, but a strangulated hernia remains an important surgical emergency. Most cases of intestinal obstruction seen today relate to intra-abdominal adhesions causing small bowel obstruction and tumours that cause large bowel obstruction.

Adhesions

25.65   Adhesions can be congenital, but much more commonly occur following previous intra-abdominal operations. Either kind of adhesions can result in bands which, in themselves, can cause intestinal obstruction. We still do not fully understand why some patients form numerous adhesions and others none at all. A number of factors which increase the chances of adhesion formation are known. Ischaemic pieces of tissue left within the abdominal cavity may precipitate adhesion formation. The use of starch or starch-containing gloves is also a further known precipitating cause of adhesions. Whilst nobody can prevent adhesion formation, excessive adhesion formation might make one think of some specific cause, such as starch on gloves. The operative division of adhesions is almost always followed by the formation of further adhesions. Historically the use of a glove powder containing starch would be likely to be considered negligent if problems with adhesions subsequently arose.

25.66   Following any intra-abdominal surgical procedure adhesions will develop. They may remain symptomless for up to 20 years before presenting with the signs and symptoms of intestinal obstruction. Whilst many cases of adhesional obstruction will resolve by the administration of intravenous fluids and nasogastric aspiration ('suck and drip') some patients will require further surgery. The risk of potential complications secondary to adhesions should be considered in all patients who have undergone abdominal surgery for trauma or extensive surgery as a result of a complication arising during the course of any intra-abdominal procedure[1]. The majority of clinical negligence cases concerned with intestinal obstruction have related to the development of adhesions following a previous major surgical procedure, and the allegation that those adhesions should never have occurred.

1 Ellis 'Medicolegal consequences of adhesions' (2004) 65(6) Hospital Medicine 348–350.

25.67   Relatively few claims relate to the failure to make the diagnosis of intestinal obstruction or the failure to provide appropriate treatment. Most cases of intestinal obstruction have fairly clear-cut presentations and in general their management is fairly straightforward. A tumour of the large bowel (colon cancer) remains a common condition that may present with intestinal obstruction. This may lead to claims of delayed or misdiagnosis of the cancer, but relatively few cases arise as a direct result of technical complications arising from the actual surgery.

25.68   Following the resection of an abnormal segment of bowel the two ends may be joined together (anastomosed) to restore continuity of the bowel. The alternative is to bring the end(s) out as a stoma (eg a colostomy) on the abdominal wall. A leak from an anastomosis can lead to significant morbidity (ie sepsis, need for further surgery, risk of tumour recurrence) and increase the mortality risk. There are many predisposing factors for a leak and it does not imply negligence. Early recognition of this complication and appropriate management is essential[1].

1 Association of Surgeons of Great Britain and Ireland (ASGBI). Patient Safety: A Consensus Statement. 2010. ASGBI, available from: http://www.asgbi.org.uk/en/publications/consensus_statements.cfm.

Radiation enteritis

25.69 Radiotherapy is widely used in the treatment of malignant disease. In the past it has been used for a number of other conditions, and so in very elderly patients radiation changes may be seen despite an absence of a history of malignant disease. Radiation enteritis and radiation strictures occur as a result of the bowel receiving too much radiation. Occasionally, loops of bowel are firmly adherent within the pelvis, and pelvic irradiation may then result in slight overdose to these loops of bowel. (In the normal way loops of bowel are mobile so that no one loop gets a repeated dose in several treatments.) This is an unpreventable complication and does not constitute negligence. Excessive doses of radiation to the lower abdomen or ill-planned radiotherapy may result in extensive radiation enteritis or stricture formation, sometimes with necrosis and tissue destruction.

Vascular surgery

25.70 Vascular surgery is no longer a subspeciality of general surgery (see Chapter 26 on vascular surgery). However, the majority of current consultant vascular surgeons have been trained and have practised as general surgeons for many years. Reconfiguration of vascular services in the UK is taking place such that many vascular surgeons will no longer be part of the general surgery emergency on-call team in a district general hospital. General/emergency surgeons requiring help will therefore need to call in a vascular surgeon for help or transfer the patient to a vascular centre for on going care.

25.71 When the first edition of this book was written, the general surgeon at that time may well have performed an operation that involved a vascular reconstruction and a bowel resection. Today it is likely that the vascular surgeon would perform the arterial reconstruction and then their colleague the gastrointestinal surgeon would come to perform the bowel resection and the anastomosis of the two bowel ends, if appropriate.

25.72 There is still a requirement for vascular surgical trainees to undertake a period of gastrointestinal/general surgery training. This is to ensure that they have experience of, and are competent to manage, other emergency intra-abdominal conditions that have traditionally come under general surgery. Likewise, current and future general surgical trainees are still required to have experience of vascular surgery to allow them to control major haemorrhage or injured blood vessels while the help of an experienced vascular surgeon is obtained.

Varicose vein surgery

25.73 The majority of operations performed on the veins are for varicose veins and traditionally consists of destruction of the veins by surgery with ligation and/ or avulsion. Modern endovenous techniques are now also available (see Chapter 26 on vascular surgery).

25.74 The treatment of varicose veins is extremely common and was traditionally a general surgical operation. Venous intervention has been associated with a large number of medico-legal claims in the past. It was a common misconception that most claims were against junior surgeons working unsupervised or that the majority of claims arose in the private sector. Many were actually against consultant general surgeons with no specific venous or vascular interest[1]. Now that vascular surgery has become a separate speciality, the non-specialist 'general surgeon' should no longer be performing varicose vein treatments.

1 Scurr and Scurr 'Varicose veins: a review of 200 consecutive medicolegal claims' (2005) 11(6) Clinical Risk 225–230.

Inadvertent damage to intra-abdominal structures

25.75 During intra-abdominal surgery a number of structures may be injured, including the spleen, the bile duct, the ureter, and the bowel. Damage to the spleen may necessitate splenectomy. The injury to the spleen may be produced as a result of direct damage, or due to traction on structures attached to the spleen. Removal of the spleen in older patients is less serious than in children, in whom it is associated with an increased incidence of pneumococcal infections. Following splenectomy, whether elective or inadvertent, vaccination is indicated along with antibiotic prophylaxis to reduce the risks of subsequent infections.

25.76 Damage to the bile duct may occur during cholecystectomy whether performed open or laparoscopically. The majority of bile duct injuries occur as the result of surgical error with failure to identify the structures adequately being the commonest cause. Careful operative dissection should avoid direct injury to the bile duct. It is crucially important to be confident that the structures have been correctly identified as there are many anatomical variants. Occasionally, stricture formation may occur in the bile duct as a result of local ischaemic changes. Extensive mobilisation of the bile duct is not indicated routinely. Exploration of a narrow bile duct and excessive mobilisation are two factors known to increase the chances of stricture formation. If an injury to the bile duct does take place, prompt recognition and appropriate treatment or referral to a surgeon competent to do this is the best line of management. The majority of cholecystectomies are now performed by laparoscopy.

25.77 The ureter may be injured or divided in the pelvis during pelvic surgical procedures (eg hysterectomy, colectomy), and careful attempts at identifying the ureters and preserving them should be undertaken. Occasionally it is necessary to divide the ureter for pelvic clearances, particularly in colorectal or pelvic cancer, and under these circumstances it may be necessary to exteriorise the ureter or to re-implant it. A deliberate decision to resect the ureter does not constitute negligence. Damage to the ureter, and failure to recognise this, clearly does (see Chapter 34 on urology and Chapter 36 on obstetrics and gynaecology).

25.78 Major damage to named arteries and veins can be life or limb[1] threatening, often requiring major reconstruction and resulting in significant morbidity. These should not occur in the elective setting with careful surgical technique by experienced surgeons with an understanding of the relevant anatomy.

1 Scurr, Scurr and Scurr 'Medico-legal claims following amputations in the UK and Ireland' (2012) 80(3) Med Leg Jnl 105–109.

25.79 Bleeding from a major injury to an artery and/or vein during an elective surgical operation or identified following trauma is likely to require the presence of a vascular surgeon to repair the injury. All surgeons (whether upper or lower gastrointestinal surgeons or gynaecologists) operating in the abdomen should have the skills to be able to control major bleeding while help is summoned.

25.80 The potential to injure the bowel and/or major blood vessels within the abdomen is a recognised complication of laparoscopic surgery. The major blood vessels actually lie at the back of the abdomen within the retro-peritoneum. However, in a thin woman these structures may actually lie only a short distance from the anterior abdominal wall and may therefore be easily damaged by a laparoscopic port insertion. A patient with known or unknown extensive intra-abdominal adhesions may make creating the pneumo-peritoneum for laparoscopy high risk for a bowel injury.

Retained objects

25.81 Leaving a foreign object unintentionally in the peritoneal cavity is a failure to follow basic surgical principles and represents negligence. Such objects range from retractors and surgical instruments through to needles and swabs[1]. Sometimes it is necessary to leave a pack within the abdominal cavity temporarily, and subsequently remove it. The intentional retention of pack is not negligent. Retention of instruments and foreign bodies within the abdominal cavity excites a reaction which invariably involves additional adhesion formation and requires recurrent surgical procedures to deal with the problem caused by such adhesions. To prevent instruments and swabs being left inside, the nurses will count the swabs and instruments at the beginning of the procedure and at the end of the procedure. Swabs are counted in fives and it is important that the total number of swabs counted in and out are the same, to avoid one rare but previously seen complication where five swabs were left inside the abdomen and the swab count therefore appeared correct.

1 Hariharan, Lobo 'Retained surgical sponges, needles and instruments' (2013) 95(2) Ann R Coll Surg Engl 87–92.

Trauma and emergency surgery

25.82   The emergency general surgeon makes up a vital part of the trauma team. Initial assessment and resuscitation will take place in the accident and emergency department. Most major trauma in the UK will now be direct to designated trauma centres with experienced teams of surgeons able to perform 'damage limitation' surgery or a resuscitative laparotomy for haemorrhage control. These surgeons would be expected to be able to control bleeding in the chest, abdomen and pelvis along with any extremity trauma. The help of specialist cardiothoracic, vascular, neurosurgical surgeons being available to be called on request for further ongoing management. The orthopaedic surgeon (see Chapter 32) and anaesthetist are also essential members of this multidisciplinary team from the start. Interventional radiologists are increasingly playing a role in haemorrhage control using endovascular techniques (see Chapter 26 on vascular surgery).

25.83   Complications following elective surgery occurring out of hours or presenting as an emergency can be technically very challenging, as these life-threatening events may be managed by surgeons from an entirely different sub-speciality[1].

1 Association of Surgeons of Great Britain and Ireland (ASGBI). Emergency General Surgery. 2012. ASGBI, Available from: http://www.asgbi.org.uk/en/publications/issues_in_ professional_practice.cfm.

25.84   Many groups have called for, and some units within the UK have already implemented, sub-speciality on-call rotas (eg separate upper and lower gastrointestinal surgeons on call).

OPERATIONS ENDANGERING NERVES

(See also Chapter 31 on otorhinolaryngology.)

25.85   The chapter on otorhinolaryngology (Chapter 31) includes a section on the head and neck, written from the viewpoint, mainly, of the surgeon who specialises in this field. However, not every district general hospital in the UK will have a specialist head and neck surgeon, and while complicated problems arising in this field are relatively uncommon and can be transferred to the care of the nearest specialist, the general surgeon may have to provide a service to deal with a number of minor and intermediate procedures necessitating an operation in this territory, for example the excision of a lymph node for histological examination.

25.86   It is remarkable how many important anatomical structures in the neck are damaged during minor operations. They are usually nerves, and the one most at risk seems to be the accessory nerve; destruction of this nerve leads to a dropped shoulder on the same side with consequent complaints of weakening and pain in the shoulder region. The anatomy of the accessory nerve is very well described and even the most junior surgeon would be expected to avoid cutting it.

25.87 Endocrine surgery remains a subspeciality of general surgery and important nerves are at risk during thyroid and parathyroid surgery because of their intimate anatomical relationship to the structures that are being excised.

25.88 The recurrent laryngeal and superior laryngeal nerves on each side must be clearly identified and safeguarded. Injury to one (causing a weak hoarse voice) or both recurrent laryngeal nerves has been a common cause of medicolegal claims following thyroidectomy. Injury to both recurrent laryngeal nerves is extremely rare, but is a serious problem that may require a tracheostomy for airway obstruction.

25.89 Patients undergoing thyroid surgery must be warned about the risks of nerve damage, hypocalcaemia, possible keloid scar formation and the potential need for long-term thyroxine replacement.

DAY SURGERY

25.90 Day surgery is a surgical event completed in one day, the patient arriving in the unit and being discharged later in the day. Some operations are carried out using full general anaesthesia, others using local anaesthesia or sedation. Patient preference and economic considerations have made day surgery extremely attractive.

25.91 It is important that all patients undergoing day surgery are properly assessed. The patients have to be assessed regarding the suitability of the surgery and their fitness to undergo local or general anaesthesia. There is a wide range of procedures suitable for day case surgery, ranging from simple lumps and bumps through to hernias and even laparoscopic procedures. Patients that require more than a few hours of post-operative observations would not be suitable for day case surgery. Many skin lesions can be removed under local anaesthetic and this may even be performed in primary care by a suitably trained general practitioner or by a dermatologist or plastic surgeon, particularly if the lesion is suspected to be a skin cancer.

25.92 When assessing a patient for suitability, age, home circumstances and co-existing medical illnesses should be considered. A number of medical conditions are contraindications to day case surgery.

25.93 As with all surgical patients, a venous thromboembolism risk assessment should be carried out prior to undergoing day case surgery. Although most procedures will be of short duration, many patients will still have risk factors for venous thromboembolism and appropriate prophylaxis should be provided.

25.94 Before discharging a patient from the surgical day unit, the patient must be assessed to check they have fully recovered from the anaesthesia, that they are aware of the surgical procedure that they have undergone and informed about any potential problems that might arise and how to deal with them. A contact telephone number should be provided and suitable arrangements made to follow the patient up. Written instruction sheets should be provided to the patient containing this additional information. The patient should be given a copy of the discharge letter that will be sent to their GP indicating the treatment provided.

25.95 Day surgery is extremely effective and very efficient. It is important that all patients are properly assessed, the surgery carried out by experienced surgeons with a full working knowledge of day surgical procedures and that the patients are adequately followed up. Currently up to 70 per cent of elective surgical procedures in the UK are carried out on a day case basis.

ACKNOWLEDGEMENTS

This chapter has been adapted and updated from the versions in previous editions by Mr John H Scurr FRCS. John's over 20 years of experience as an expert witness and an analysis of his database of over 5000 claims, that he has given an opinion on, have formed the basis of this chapter.

BIBLIOGRAPHY

Ellis, Calne, Watson *Lecture Notes: General Surgery* (12th edn, 2011).
Ellis, Mahadevan *Clinical Anatomy: Applied Anatomy for Students and Junior Doctors* (12th edn, 2010).
Novell, Baker, Goddard (eds) *Kirk's General Surgical Operations* (6th edn, 2013).
Paterson-Brown (ed) *Core Topics in General & Emergency Surgery: A Companion to Specialist Surgical Practice* (5th edn, 2013).
Williams, Bulstrode, O'Connell (eds) *Bailey & Love's Short Practice of Surgery* (26th edn, 2013).

CHAPTER 26

Vascular surgery

Professor Cliff Shearman

BACKGROUND

26.1   Vascular surgeons treat people with disorders of the arteries, veins and lymphatics. Broadly these conditions can be divided into those affecting the lower limb, the carotid artery, dilatation or aneurysms of arteries (anywhere in the body outside the brain but most especially the aorta) and

901

venous disorders. Atherosclerosis, the deposition of fatty material within the blood vessel wall, is a common cause of vascular disease, but other conditions such as thrombosis, inflammation and trauma can also be involved.

26.2   Many patients with vascular disease do not need interventional treatment, but benefit from advice about lifestyle and medication to reduce their risk of future cardiovascular events such as stroke and heart attack. This aspect of treatment is often suggested by vascular surgeons, but is most commonly initiated by general practitioners in the community. There are very few angiologists (physicians who specialise in the medical treatment of vascular disease) in the UK, unlike many other European countries, and vascular surgeons need to be aware of the non-surgical treatment of vascular disease as well.

26.3   Interventional treatments range from open surgery such as bypass, endarterectomy (direct removal of the atherosclerosis) or repair of an aneurysm, to endovascular therapies (treatment delivered within the lumen of the blood vessel) such as angioplasty with or without stenting. A stent is a metallic mesh placed inside a vessel which holds the blood vessel open. Vascular surgeons tend to work in multi-disciplinary teams including interventional radiologists, anaesthetists, diabetic specialists, nurse specialists and rehabilitation experts[1]. One of the most challenging aspects of providing surgical services is that approximately 40 per cent of patients need emergency or urgent treatment and this often involves complex interventions.

1 The provision of vascular services document for patients with vascular disease 2012: The Vascular Society of Great Britain and Ireland: www.vascularsociety.org.uk.

The vascular speciality

26.4   Until 2012 vascular surgery was a sub-speciality of general surgery. Many surgeons who undertook vascular surgery also practised general surgery and many units only had 2–3 vascular surgeons, resulting in periods when no one with vascular expertise was available to treat patients. Training was in general and vascular surgery, with trainee surgeons at specialist registrar level spending six years acquiring general and vascular training before becoming consultant surgeons.

26.5   In 2008 the publication of results of aortic surgery across Europe showed that the UK had the highest mortality rates (7.5 per cent) following elective abdominal aortic aneurysm repairs. Coming at a time when screening for abdominal aortic aneurysms (which to give benefit relies on low mortality rates from planned surgery) was being introduced in England, this catalysed major changes to improve the quality of vascular services. The outcome of these changes has been to develop larger vascular units with a minimum of six vascular surgeons and interventional radiologists to provide 24-hour services seven days a week. In many areas small units have moved into neighbouring larger sites while in others a network has been developed with a single centre or hub for all major interventional work but other services still provided in the local site. This has resulted in consolidation of personnel and facilities.

26.6   Specialist vascular teams have lower mortality rates and superior clinical outcomes for aortic surgery, carotid surgery and lower limb bypass. This is particularly true of emergency and urgent situations and the National Enquiry into Perioperative Deaths (CEPOD) identified the benefits of specialist vascular teams treating patients with vascular disease[1].

1 National Confidential Enquiry into Perioperative Deaths (NCEPOD). Abdominal aortic aneurysm: a service in need of surgery (London 2005): www.ncepod.org.uk/2005aaa.htm.

26.7   It was also clearly shown that units which had higher volumes of cases had better results. It is hard to quantify a minimum number, but initially it was suggested that no unit should continue to conduct aortic surgery if it was doing less than 33 cases per year and this recommended number is likely to increase. These arguments also pertain to other aspects of vascular surgery such as carotid surgery and lower limb bypass to prevent amputation. Larger volume units also have the advantage of being able to support larger clinical teams to ensure around the clock availability. Most of these changes have come about based on recommendations from the specialist society, the Vascular Society of Great Britain and Ireland. The development of National Specialist Commissioning for vascular surgery has led to the development of minimum criteria which must be met by any unit in England and Wales providing vascular services. These criteria include case volume, personnel numbers and availability of facilities, and came into effect in April 2014.

26.8   The techniques available to treat vascular disease have markedly changed. Increasingly patients can be offered endovascular treatments. These are most commonly delivered by interventional radiologists working with the vascular teams. Arteries can be dilated (angioplasty), stented open with expanding metal stents or grafts placed inside the artery using radiological imaging. These procedures are less invasive than conventional open surgical procedures, but require different skill sets than those usually held by conventionally trained surgeons. Although often appealing to patients due to their less invasive nature and quicker recovery times, endovascular treatments may have implications such as long-term follow up or specific complications which need to be conveyed to the patient.

26.9   Voluntary reporting of results to the National Vascular Database (now National Vascular Registry) set up by the Vascular Society of Great Britain and Ireland has been possible for a number of years. However, outcome reporting by unit[1] has expanded year on year and it became mandatory for all vascular surgeons to report their outcomes for carotid and aortic surgery in 2013[2]. These data are published annually and are in the public domain. In 2014 the registry also includes lower limb bypass surgery and amputations. Individual surgeons' results are displayed in a way that shows whether they are performing within an expected range. This is more problematic to determine when case numbers are low, but there are mechanisms in place to identify surgeons whose performance falls outside the expected range and to alert their employing institution so that action can be taken.

1 Outcomes after elective repair of infra-renal abdominal aortic aneurysm. A report from the Vascular Society 2012: www.vascularsociety.org.uk.
2 National Vascular Registry. 2013 report on surgical outcomes. Consultant level statistics: www.rcseng.ac.uk/surgeons/research/surgical-research/docs/national-vascular-registry-report-on-surgical-outcomes.

26.10   With increased awareness of outcomes in the public domain, the need to get better results and more complex treatments, it became apparent that there was no longer a role for the general surgeon undertaking occasional vascular surgery (or, for that matter, vascular surgeons undertaking occasional general surgical procedures). Also, in order that the vascular surgeons of the future could gain the skills and knowledge required during the training time available they needed to focus entirely on vascular surgery. To this end, on 16 March 2012 vascular surgery became a separate surgical speciality and a new training programme based on a vascular surgery curriculum and examination was approved by the General Medical Council in October 2012. The first group of trainees took up post in 2013 and will complete their six-year training programme in 2019. They will focus entirely on gaining the skills and knowledge to deliver vascular services.

Current situation of vascular surgery

26.11   The above changes are still evolving but have already had considerable benefit. The mortality rate for elective aortic surgery has fallen to 1.8 per cent[1]. At this time all surgeons undertaking vascular surgery interventions should be part of a multi-disciplinary team involving interventional radiologists, anaesthetists, nurse specialists with strong links to other specialities such as diabetes, stroke medicine and cardiology. Some units will be closely aligned with renal units and provide vascular access (fistulae) for dialysis. These teams must be big enough to provide continuous around the clock services, or if not must be part of a network, such that all patients have access to specialist care at all times. The individual surgeons should be entering their data on the National Vascular Registry for index procedures including carotid surgery, aortic surgery, lower limb bypass and major amputation. Patients for elective surgery should be discussed at a multi-disciplinary meeting to ensure all potential options of treatment are considered and outcomes regularly reviewed. The numbers of cases undertaken by the unit must meet NHS England National Specialist Commissioning Specifications[2].

1 Waton, Johal, Groene, Cromwell, Mitchell, Loftus *Outcomes after elective repair of infra-renal abdominal aortic aneurysm* Royal College of Surgeons of England (November 2013).
2 2013/14 NHS Standard Contract for specialised vascular services (adults): www.england.nhs. uk/wp-content/uploads/2013/06/a04-spec-vascu-adult.pdf.

26.12   At present nearly all practising vascular surgeons in the UK were trained in general surgery with vascular surgery as a sub-speciality interest. For all the reasons outlined above increasingly few practise general surgery as well as vascular surgery and this is likely to disappear completely over the next few years. By 2019 many newly-appointed vascular surgeons will be appointed who have trained only in vascular surgery.

Impact of changes on patients and services

26.13   Any patient who needs vascular surgery should have access to a vascular unit in a timely fashion. That unit should be equipped and staffed to offer any aspect of vascular treatment the patient may require, except for extremely rare conditions which may require transfer to a specialist unit, eg paediatric vascular conditions. The outcome results of the unit and the individual members of team should be available on the National Vascular Registry.

26.14   For patients requiring elective interventions who do not live in close proximity to a vascular unit this may involve an outpatient consultation at their local hospital with a member of the vascular team who has travelled to the clinic. If they require complex intervention, however, they will need to go to the main vascular unit for this, although may receive any rehabilitation care and follow-up appointments at their local hospital. Patients who require emergency surgery may have to travel to a vascular unit, but arrangements should be in place at their local hospital to ensure that this can be carried out. It is no longer acceptable for a hospital which does not have vascular services on site not to have robust arrangements in place with their local vascular unit. These arrangements must include arrangements with the ambulance service for transfer of patients with urgent conditions such as ruptured aneurysms or lower limb vascular trauma. The increasing use of helicopter transfer has made this easier in many parts of the country and modelling of vascular services has indicated that there are few places in the UK where this cannot be achieved within an hour. However, it is important to recognise that only a small proportion of patients will need such urgent transfer and for the majority transfer within 2–3 hours is acceptable and should be achievable with prospective planning.

GENERAL ASPECTS OF VASCULAR SURGERY

Terminology

26.15   The consequence of arterial disease is generally to reduce blood supply to an organ or structure which is termed ischaemia.

Chronic ischaemia

26.16   There is considerable confusion about the terminology relating to ischaemia. In many patients the arterial disease progresses over a period of time: this is termed chronic ischaemia. Initially the patient may have no symptoms, but the earliest manifestation is pain in the leg on walking, intermittent claudication. In the majority of patients with intermittent claudication the limb will not deteriorate and is not at imminent risk.

26.17   If, however, the condition worsens then the patient experiences pain at rest, often at night, the skin breaks down and the gangrene may develop. At this stage there is a real risk that without intervention the leg will be lost. The term critical ischaemia is used to describe this situation. Attempts have been made to characterise critical limb ischaemia using objective criteria. The persistence of nocturnal rest pain for longer than two weeks with or without tissue loss and an absolute ankle blood pressure of 50mmHg have been suggested by the Trans-Atlantic Inter-Society Consensus Document on the management of peripheral arterial disease (TASC II)[1]. While this is helpful in developing consistency when reporting results between units, it has less value for the individual patient. The need to amputate a limb may be brought about by a numbers of factors other than lack of blood supply, including worsening infection or poorly-controlled pain. Conversely, some patients with correctly diagnosed CLI who do not receive intervention do not lose their leg.

1 Trans-Atlantic Inter-Society Consensus for the Management of Peripheral Arterial Disease (TASC II). Norgren, Hiatt, Dormandy, Nehler, Harris, Fowkes on behalf of the TASC II Working Group. (2007) 45(1) J Vascular Surgry supplement S.

26.18 The term Critical Limb Ischaemia (CLI) is commonly used. Many clinicians will use the term to describe a leg that they feel is at risk of being lost rather than using the strict definition of CLI outlined above. Thus the term can be very subjective.

Acute ischaemia

26.19 Sudden blockage of an artery, for example in the leg, will result in a sudden decrease in limb perfusion causing a potential threat to limb. This can occur by a blood clot travelling from another part of the body such as the heart (embolus), blockage of a diseased artery or bypass graft and trauma to the artery. Unlike chronic ischaemia the limb has no time to adapt to the situation and depending on which artery and at what level it is blocked the limb can be put at immediate risk. If a large proximal artery such as the femoral artery in the leg is blocked it is likely that unless blood supply is restored within hours the limb will be irreversibly damaged and require amputation at a later date. The time window to restore circulation is often given as six hours, although in reality it will vary from situation to situation depending on the severity of ischaemia that has resulted. However the time frame is short and immediate investigation and action is generally necessary. In some patients with acute limb ischaemia the blockage occurs peripherally or clot passes downstream so there may be some initial improvement in symptoms. However, urgent referral and investigation is still required to identify the underlying cause and take measures to prevent further episodes.

26.20 Some patients with established peripheral arterial disease will suffer a sudden deterioration in their condition. This is commonly due to ulceration or rupture of an atherosclerotic narrowing (plaque). The blood clot forms on the surface which either blocks or further narrows the artery. This situation is termed acute on chronic ischaemia and has become the most common presentation of acute limb ischaemia.

26.21 It is important to recognise that acute and chronic ischaemia are entirely different clinical situations. Most importantly, suspicion of acute ischaemia is an emergency situation and needs immediate referral to a vascular unit

Diagnosis of arterial disease

26.22 Narrowing or blockage of the arteries is the commonest reason a patient seeks advice from a vascular surgeon. Although a number of conditions can cause this situation to develop, the large majority of patients are affected by atherosclerosis, a very common condition affecting the western world. Atherosclerosis is an inflammatory condition associated with cigarette smoking, high blood pressure, elevated cholesterol and diabetes. It is more common in men and tends to manifest itself in middle age and the elderly. Atherosclerosis can affect arteries anywhere in the body, but if affecting the lower limb vessels is termed peripheral artery disease (PAD). Initially PAD causes no symptoms and the subject is unaware of it, but as the condition worsens they may develop pain in their leg on walking, intermittent claudication. If the condition continues to deteriorate they will start to get pain at rest and tissue breakdown leading to ulceration and gangrene.

26.23   In a large epidemiological study it was found that approximately one third of men and women over 55 years of age had PAD although most were asymptomatic. Four per cent of this population had symptoms of intermittent claudication, but remained stable over five years with only 2–3 per cent deteriorating. PAD is then very common and many patients who are admitted for treatment of other conditions affecting the leg will have asymptomatic arterial disease. This should be identified before surgical intervention, as undiagnosed PAD may increase the risk particularly if a tourniquet is to be used. Failure to ascertain that the circulation is normal before an elective lower limb procedure is usually negligent. Pre-operative identification of PAD allows reassessment of the indications for the primary treatment, the adoption of other treatment strategies or the opportunity to correct the underlying arterial disease.

26.24   The diagnosis of PAD is straightforward and is based on a clinical history of symptoms such as intermittent claudication or rest pain, absence of pulses in the limb on palpation and the measurement of the ankle brachial pressure index (ABPI). Measurement of ABPI is a simple clinical test that is performed with a standard blood pressure cuff placed around the ankle and a portable Doppler ultrasound probe. The highest ankle blood pressure recorded is compared to the highest pressure measure in the arms and expressed as a ratio. A normal ABPI is between 0.9 and 1.2. Arterial disease will result in a lower ABPI proportional to the severity of the disease. The National Institute for Health and Care Excellence (NICE) guidelines recommend that this should be carried out in any patient in whom PAD is suspected. Measurement of ABPI is a basic skill taught to medical students[1]. ABPI is also commonly measured by nurses prior to the use of compression garments and dressing and for the assessment of patients with diabetes.

1 Lower limb peripheral arterial disease. Diagnosis and management. NICE Clinical Guideline 147. Methods, evidence and recommendations (August 2012).

26.25   Patients present with leg pain for a number of reasons and it can be difficult to determine a cause for the symptoms. Any suspicion of PAD should lead to the documentation of a clinical history, vascular examination of the leg (documenting pulse palpation) and the recording of an ankle pressure. Given a patient with undiagnosed leg pain, a reasonable doctor would record that they had excluded PAD by the methods outlined above.

26.26   Measurement of ABPI is still not widely adopted despite the NICE guidelines. Pulse palpation, even by an expert, is difficult especially in patients with swollen limbs or ulcers and the false assumption that a pulse is present is a common problem and often leading to delay in referral and treatment. Doppler ultrasound is often incorrectly used. The test relies on the detection of the flow of blood in the arteries. It does not quantify this and even in limbs with very poor blood supply a signal may be detected. An expert may be able to distinguish differences in the nature of the signal (triphasic which is normal, biphasic which is common in adults and monophasic which suggests a reduced blood flow) but this is of no value to the non-specialist and should not be relied upon. The measurement of pressure is a more reliable indicator of the state of the circulation and less operator dependent.

26.27 Based on the above, any doctor should reasonably be expected to be able to diagnose peripheral arterial disease based on history, clinical examination and measurement of ABPI. If there remains any doubt, referral to a specialist should be made.

Investigation of arterial disease

26.28 In patients in whom intervention is contemplated more detail imaging of the vascular system is undertaken. Duplex ultrasound is the first line investigation. It is non-invasive, safe and inexpensive. It can visualise the blood vessels but also gives functional information about the severity of a narrowing in arteries. It is very operator dependent and units undertaking it need to have quality assurance processes in place to ensure reliability. In some patients this is the only investigation required to plan treatment.

26.29 More detailed information can be obtained from computerised tomography (CT) angiograms which give detailed images of the blood vessels. However, the dose of X-ray radiation is large and if the scans are repeated regularly may increase the cancer risk of the patient. Of more direct relevance, the contrast agent used to enhance the blood vessels can cause damage to the kidneys. This is particularly important in patients who already have impaired renal function. Patients undergoing CT angiography should have their renal function checked prior to this investigation. With the development of trauma and stroke centres, CT scanning is usually available around the clock and images of the blood vessels can be obtained within minutes.

26.30 Magnetic resonance (MR) angiography is becoming the preferred investigation to image the blood vessels. It is relatively non-invasive. Systemic interstitial fibrosis is a rare but potentially fatal complication associated with the gadolinium contrast used and, again, is more likely to occur in patients with impaired renal function.

26.31 Standard angiography, where the artery is punctured and a catheter or tube inserted into the vessel to obtain images of the blood vessels, is much less frequently done. It is invasive and can cause bruising, bleeding and pain at the puncture site and again the contrast agents used may damage the kidneys. Apart from situations where very detailed pictures of the distal blood vessels are required it has been largely superseded by MR and CT angiography as a diagnostic tool.

26.32   Hydration of the patient, if necessary with intravenous fluid, can reduce the effect of the contrast agents used and failure to recognise renal impairment before any form of contrast examination is negligent.

Failure to diagnose

26.33   A common reason for litigation in vascular surgery is failure to diagnose a condition which then continues to deteriorate to the point where even appropriate treatment results in a poor outcome[1]. This may be failure to recognise the clinical condition completely, such as acute limb ischaemia, or lack of appreciation of the urgency of the situation such as in a diabetic foot infection. These problems often arise in primary care where it may be felt that the clinician would not have the specialist knowledge or skills to make the diagnosis. However, there is often lack of evidence in the records that an appropriate examination of the vascular system was carried out which makes it very hard to defend. There are also clear guidelines for the management of patients in whom these conditions are suspected which suggest prompt referral to a specialist unit.

1 Markides, Subar, Al-Khaffar 'Litigation claims in vascular surgery in the United Kingdom's NHS' (2008) 136 Eur J Vasc Endovasc Surgery 452–457.

26.34   Vascular specialists are at risk of causing inappropriate delay which subsequently results in a poor outcome. This most commonly involves co-ordinating the investigation and treatment of the patient in what can be a busy and pressurised environment. It is important that the patient is seen by a competent vascular surgeon to determine the urgency of the situation. Increasingly this will mean the consultant vascular surgeon.

26.35   In emergency situations it is usually possible to get basic investigations about the patient's condition and more specifically about the presenting complaint, often necessitating imaging their blood vessels with an angiogram. This enables appropriate, targeted treatment which is safer. In most emergency situations with rapid access to CT scanners it is possible to get this information in a timely fashion, but on occasion if the patient's condition is rapidly deteriorating or there is delay in getting investigations a decision needs to be made to proceed directly to surgical intervention. This can be a very difficult decision as the risks of intervention are generally higher. This decision should only be made in the presence of the consultant vascular surgeon responsible for the patient. The rationale for the action should be clearly recorded.

26.36   The same argument applies to delay in getting a patient to the operating theatre. Emergency operating theatres usually work continuously 24 hours day and it may require negotiation with other clinical teams and the theatre staff to get a patient to theatre urgently. Most hospitals can, in difficult situations, open extra operating facilities, but this will usually need the presence of the senior doctor responsible for the patient. Again problems of this nature should be clearly documented by the vascular surgeon. However, what is generally not acceptable is to book an emergency patient onto the operating list and then fail to try to ensure that the patient gets to theatre in an appropriate time. If the responsible surgeon cannot get the patient to theatre, despite all their efforts, this should be reported to the senior management team at the time.

26.37 Many patients with vascular surgical problems require urgent treatment rather than immediate emergency intervention. Usually this means the patient is appropriately investigated, their condition optimised, and they have treatment on the next available elective operating session. This can significantly improve results for patients such as those requiring amputation of a leg who are often elderly and frail and suffer a high risk of dying within 30 days of surgery. It has been clearly demonstrated that by carrying out their amputation urgently rather than as an emergency mortality rates can be significantly lowered.

26.38 This is a difficult area for decision making, particularly when patients arrive at hospital during the night. Although facilities to treat the patient should be available 24 hours a day, at night the teams are often running on minimum numbers. The consultant vascular surgeon will not usually be on a shift and so will have been working during the day and may have to work the next day, so their performance may be less than optimal. Also the vascular surgeon, who will often be the only vascular trained member of the out-of-hours team, has to continue to provide an emergency service, so committing to undertake a procedure must be balanced against the risk of not being able to respond to other emergencies.

26.39 A diabetic foot infection which needs surgery may be safer carried out at 8am rather than 3am and likewise a patient with tenderness over an abdominal aortic aneurysm, which has been shown to be intact on a CT scan, may have a safer operation during the day when all the vascular team are present. However, if there is a deterioration in their condition overnight they may suffer a worse outcome or even death because of the delay.

26.40 There are many situations where a reasonable vascular surgeon would not carry out emergency surgery in the middle of the night and the risk to the patient of waiting until the day time would be minimal. However, there are some high-risk situations, in particular patients with symptomatic abdominal aortic aneurysms or acute ischaemia of the leg, in which experts subsequently reviewing a case would find it hard to understand why intervention was not undertaken sooner. In these situations, while it might be reasonable to wait until normal working hours to perform surgery, the rationale for this needs to be clearly documented and shared with the patients and their family. It is very hard to defend a decision to delay an intervention without evidence of sound clinical reasoning behind it.

Failure to record decisions

26.41 Many decisions in vascular surgery are made based on a balance of risk. The risk of repairing an abdominal aortic aneurysm compared with the risk of it rupturing in the patient's lifetime or the clinical impression that a patient's leg is not salvable and amputation should be carried out are decisions that have major consequences for the patient . It is often impossible in these situations to find any record of how the decision was made and who was responsible for it. This is improving in elective surgery, where currently all patients should be discussed by a multi-disciplinary team and a clear record made of the recommendation. However, in emergency or urgent situations this is not possible. For example, the patient who suffers acute limb ischaemia presents late and treatment gives a poor result may at some stage be offered an amputation. A clear record of why this decision was made and that it was discussed with the patient would make many cases much easier to defend. It is also apparent that claimants often brings cases because they did not have a clear explanation of a treatment that might have been quite appropriate at the time, but was not clearly explained to them.

26.42   The same applies to operation records, which vary enormously in their content and format. Considering that concerns regarding intra-operative performance make up 50 per cent of claims against vascular surgeons, it is surprising that more care in completing the record is not taken. In many vascular operations the original operative plan has to be changed due to findings at surgery. Again a clear explanation in the notes about why a procedure was done in a certain way will make clear to any subsequent reader the logic of what was done. The recording of normal findings, particularly at the end of a procedure, eg the colon was pink and the ureters intact after an iliac artery aneurysm repair indicate that the operating surgeon was aware of the possible complications of a procedure and checked that they had not occurred. While the occurrence of subsequent ischaemia of the colon (a potential complication of aortic surgery) may not be held to be a result of negligence, failure to consider it as a diagnosis in an ill patient may be. The essential components of an operation note are outlined in *Good Surgical Practice*[1].

1 *Good Surgical Practice* Royal College of Surgeons of England (2008).

Communication

26.43   It is apparent in many investigations of complaints and adverse outcomes that communication with the patient and his family has been poor. Many surgeons find it difficult to talk to patients in whom an adverse outcome has occurred and give them clear and honest explanations of what has happened. Although this cannot excuse negligence, it is important that the outcome for the patient is the best that can be achieved and that they have a clear picture of the prognosis. It is often wise to involve another colleague in the management of the patient and to discuss the case with the relevant defence organisation as soon as possible.

Guidelines

26.44   There are a number of guidelines relating to vascular surgery. NICE has published guidelines on the management of PAD, the diabetic foot, venous disease and the treatment of patients who have suffered a stroke including the role of carotid endarterectomy. The Trans-Atlantic Intersociety Consensus for the Management of Peripheral Arterial Disease (TASC II) document examined the available evidence for management of vascular disease up to 2007. The Scottish Intercollegiate Guideline Network (SIGN) has produced similar guidelines for most vascular conditions in Scotland.

26.45 Many of the initial guidelines were produced by speciality associations or patient groups and as such could only be considered as recommendations. However, with the development of national bodies such as NICE and SIGN and the increasing expectation that surgical practice should be evidence-based, the situation is changing. The guidelines are usually developed by panels of experts, patients and health care analysts who examine the current evidence in detail and base their recommendations on this. Although there are often areas where evidence is lacking, it is hard for an individual clinician to make a strong argument for not adhering to the consensus views of such a panel. Many commissioners of health care now demand that providers such as hospitals meet the NICE guidelines and the quality standards which have been produced based on these. While guidelines cannot be applied to every patient, it is wise to ensure that if the management of the patient deviates from what is thought to be best practice in the guideline, explanations are recorded, stating why this decision has been made.

SPECIFIC VASCULAR CONDITIONS

Medical management of vascular disease

26.46 Patients with atherosclerotic arterial disease have a significantly increased risk of suffering from future cardiovascular events such as heart attack and stroke. In particular patients with PAD have a four-fold increased risk of dying for cardiovascular disease compared to people without PAD. Smoking cessation, cholesterol lowering drugs such as statins and control of high blood pressure reduce these risks significantly. Advising the patient to take an antiplatelet drug such as aspirin or clopidogrel further reduces the risks of cardiovascular death. Although vascular surgeons are not expected to be expert in the individual aspects of the medical management of their patients, they are expected to ensure that the patients have had the correct advice and appropriate treatment, particularly as this information has been available for a number of years and is widely known. Not to advise a patient about the benefits of this therapy or to ensure that they have been offered the correct treatment could significantly increase their risk of a heart attack and stroke and be held to be negligent.

Aortic aneurysm surgery

Elective treatment of abdominal aortic aneurysms

26.47 Aneurysms are focal, pathological dilatations of a blood vessel. Abdominal aortic aneurysms (AAA) are the commonest peripheral artery aneurysm and affect up to 4 per cent of men over the age of 65, although not all of these men will need treatment. Aneurysms occur less frequently in women. The main risk to the patient from an aneurysm is the risk of rupture which is commonly fatal with approximately 10,000 deaths annually in England and Wales. Some patients do survive a rupture to reach hospital but even then the chance of surviving an emergency repair is around 60 per cent.

26.48   The NHS Abdominal Aortic Aneurysm Screening Programme was initiated in 2008 and offers all men an ultrasound scan to detect AAA on their 65th birthday. The aim is to reduce deaths from ruptured AAAs by offering elective surgical treatment.

26.49   Most patients with AAAs then have no symptoms and many have only a small risk of rupture. Surgical repair of an aneurysm is a major operation which carries risk of significant complications, including death. Patients need to be counselled very carefully about the benefits and risks of treatment.

26.50   The strongest predictor of the risk of rupture is the diameter of the aneurysm. There is good evidence that the risk of rupture between 4.0–5.5 cms is no more 1 per cent per year. It is generally hard then to justify intervention for an AAA less than 5.5 cms unless the patient has had symptoms thought to be associated with the aneurysm, such as pain. Most of the data used to determine the risk of rupture has come from studies comprising largely of men and it is unclear whether it is reasonable to extrapolate this to women who tend to have smaller blood vessels. Some surgeons will argue that treatment should be offered to women with smaller aneurysms but if this is the case it should be clearly documented. For larger aneurysms the evidence for the annual risk of rupture is less strong but is probably 9.4 per cent for aneurysms between 5.5–6.0 cms, 10.2 per cent between 6.0–6.9 cms and 32.5 per cent for aneurysms over 7 cms[1].

1 Nordon, Hinchliffe, Loftus, Thompson 'Pathophysiology and epidemiolgy of abdominal aortic aneurysms' (2011) 8 Nat Rev Cardiology 92–100.

26.51   Until the last decade most AAAs were repaired by open surgery, replacing the dilated segment of artery with a man-made graft. The risk of death from treatment depends on the patient's co-morbidity, especially heart disease, and needs to be carefully assessed but based on the National Vascular Registry was 3.8 per cent in 2013. The morphology of the aneurysm, where it begins in relation to the renal and visceral arteries, and previous abdominal surgery all affect the mortality risk. Other potential complications which must be considered with the patient include bleeding requiring further surgery, renal failure requiring dialysis, problems with the distal circulation supplying the limbs which can result in amputation and impotence due to damage to the pelvic nerves. Around 15 per cent of patients suffer a transient reduction in blood supply to the left colon after aortic surgery. This may simply be associated with a slower recovery, but in some results in death of part of the colon requiring further surgery and perhaps the need for a colostomy. Arteries from the aorta supply the spinal cord and if they are involved in the aneurysm the spinal cord may be damaged due to lack of blood supply. These arteries tend to be concentrated around the thoracic aorta, but in a very small proportion of people a dominant vessel arises from the abdominal aorta. In these individuals repair of an aneurysm can result in paralysis of the lower limbs and bladder. Although occurring in less than 1 per cent of cases, as the outcome is devastating the risk should be communicated to the patient.

26.52   As can be seen from the above, the balance of risk in either treating the AAA or leaving it can be very close in some patients. Often the decision as to whether to proceed or not is based on the patient's attitude to surgery and their feeling about leaving an aneurysm. The rationale for the decision to operate and the risks and benefits suggested to the patient should be recorded.

26.53   More recently it has become possible to repair AAAs by placing a covered stent inside the aorta by passing it from the femoral artery using radiological imaging. Endovascular aneurysm repair (EVAR) is less invasive, is associated with a lower mortality risk (0.8 per cent) and faster recovery. This makes it more attractive to patients. Not all patients are suitable for EVAR due to the anatomy of their aneurysm and if the graft fails to seal in the aorta (endoleak) the aneurysm will not be excluded and the AAA is still at risk of rupture. Also the long-term durability of EVAR is unknown and patients are currently followed up for their lifetime with regular scans. Following EVAR, around 20 per cent of patients will require further intervention due to endoleaks or graft migration.

Again when suggesting an EVAR to a patient it is essential to record that the need for follow up and the potential need for further intervention have been discussed and recorded.

Ruptured abdominal aortic aneurysms

26.54   A particularly difficult dilemma for a vascular surgeon occurs in patients who have suffered a rupture of their AAA and are still alive at the time of arrival in hospital. Some patients experience severe abdominal pain passing through to their back at the time of aneurysm rupture but the bleeding is temporarily contained by the surrounding structures. It is important to ensure that, in any patient with a sudden onset of such pain, an aneurysm is excluded before other diagnoses are considered as if further bleeding occurs there is a high chance of death. This is usually done with ultrasound scanning or CT scanning, as clinical examination alone is unreliable to exclude an aneurysm.

26.55   If the patient has been otherwise fit and well, is conscious and has a recordable blood pressure generally emergency repair should proceed. However, many of these patients are elderly and frail with significant other medical conditions and have had a poor quality of life in the months prior to the rupture. When the patient is able to communicate, then it is vital to ascertain their wishes, but many will be in an obtunded state and unable to express their wishes. A number of factors have been shown to reduce significantly the chance of survival of emergency surgery. Loss of consciousness, impaired renal function, low haemoglobin, changes on the ECG recording of the heart suggesting ischaemia and age over 76 years are associated with a poor outcome. If three of these factors are present the mortality is 100 per cent. However, in many patients there may be a slim chance of survival with surgery but a prolonged recovery time and risk of significant complications such as non-recoverable renal failure make the prospect very unattractive. Faced with a patient in whom not intervening will result in certain death but surgery has a very small chance of success can be challenging. Whenever possible the situation must be discussed with family members and the reason for the decision reached should be recorded. Failure to undertake surgery could be considered to have contributed to the death of the patient.

26.56 Some patients with ruptured AAA will need to be transferred to a vascular unit. As outlined above, there should be clear guidelines in place for this and there should be no undue delays. It is likely that there will be some patients who succumb during transit, but studies of centralisation of services have shown that generally the overall survival rate will improve due to better outcomes from a more experienced team.

Carotid artery surgery

26.57 Carotid endarterectomy (CEA) is an operation to remove atherosclerosis form the carotid artery. It has been shown to be of benefit in reducing the risk of stroke in patients who have suffered a transient ischaemic attack (TIA; a focal neurological deficit recovering with 24 hours) or non-devastating stoke in the area of the brain above a diseased carotid artery. The operation only benefits those patients who have a degree of atherosclerosis in excess of 50 per cent (measured using the North American Symptomatic Endarterectomy Trial criteria or 70 per cent by the European Carotid Surgery Trial) and who have received normal medical therapy.

26.58 To be of maximum advantage the operation should be undertaken as soon as possible following the neurological event. The current national target is within 14 days with an ambition to reach 48 hours. Many units do not currently achieve this and the national median time for symptom to surgery is 15 days (interquartile range 8–40 days)[1]. Some patients may suffer a stroke during the time waiting for surgery. At present the majority of patients do not receive surgery within 14 days of their neurological event, but this is improving. It is likely in the near future that units which are unable to provide surgery within the target time frame will be held responsible for a stroke occurring during the wait.

1 UK carotid endarterectomy audit. Round 4 public report (August 2012). Carotid Intervention Audit (CIA) Steering Group. Royal College of Physicians Clinical Standards Department: www.vascularsociety.org.uk/wp-content/uploads/2012/11/UK-Carotid-Endarterectomy-Audit-Round-4-Public-Report.pdf.

26.59 CEA carries a risk of causing stroke and this must be discussed with the patient. Also there are a number of cranial nerves which appear in the operative field and these are at risk of non-function after surgery. This is usually temporary but can be permanent. Hoarseness, weakness of the tongue and numbness on the angle of the jaw are relatively common and must be discussed. Any surgeon undertaking carotid surgery should be submitting their data to the National Vascular Registry so they can assure the patient that their performance is within an acceptable range and that their unit is performing in line with other units in terms of access times to surgery. There is no benefit in operating on patients whose carotid artery has totally occluded and in fact it is dangerous to do so. If, for any reason, the CEA is delayed then up-to-date imaging must be obtained to ensure that the artery is still patent.

26.60 There have been considerable advances in endovascular treatment of carotid artery disease by stenting to avoid the morbidity of surgery. There are a number of studies examining this at present in a few centres worldwide and it should only be undertaken in these centres as part of a study.

26.61 Some patients will be found to have atheroma in their carotid artery that has not caused any clinical event. These are termed asymptomatic. The benefit of CEA in these patients is small and the current stroke guidelines suggest that they should only be offered intervention if they are part of a trial to evaluate the outcomes.

Lower limb

26.62 Missed acute limb ischaemia is a significant cause of amputation. In any patient the sudden onset of severe leg pain in a patient should make the clinician consider acute limb ischaemia. Some patients such as those with atrial fibrillation (an irregular heartbeat) or known peripheral arterial disease are at increased risk, but if pulses in the legs cannot be confidently felt, or the ABPI is low or un-recordable, acute limb ischaemia should be suspected and the patient transferred immediately to a vascular unit for assessment[1].

1 Shearman and Shearman 'Diagnosis of acute limb ischaemia – why is it missed so often?' in Greenhalgh (ed) *Controversies in Vascular and Endovascular Disease 2013* (Biba) pp 350–357.

26.63 Acute limb ischaemia can occur after lower limb surgery. Popliteal artery injury occurs infrequently after knee replacement surgery (incidence of 0.017 per cent) either due to transection or blunt injury during instrumentation, but diagnosis of the problem is often delayed[1]. Prior to lower limb surgery the circulation should be checked and the presence of pulses recorded. After surgery the pulses should be checked again and if absent a vascular surgical opinion should be sought. The window of opportunity to repair the artery and restore circulation is a matter of hours and delay will result in limb loss. Failure to recognise acute limb ischaemia in patients after surgery is negligent and will add to delay and result in a poor outcome.

1 Bernhoff, Rudstrom, Gedeburg, Bjorck 'Popliteal artery injury during knee replacement. A population based nationwide study' (2013) 95B Bone Joint J 1645–1649.

Compartment syndrome

26.64 If the pressure rises in a contained area within the body it will reduce blood flow to the tissues in that compartment. If the pressure is high it may cause complete ischaemia, resulting in death of the tissues if the pressure is not released.

26.65 After the circulation has been re-established in a leg the muscles swell. The muscles are contained within in-elastic fascial compartments and this can cause a marked increase in the compartment pressure to the extent that it can impair blood flow. This causes damage to the nerves and muscles in the compartment which will become irreversible if unrelieved.

26.66   The patient may experience pain out of keeping with clinical situation, have a tense area over the front of leg and pain on passive dorsiflexion of the foot. Careful examination may reveal patchy areas of reduced sensation on the foot. It is possible to monitor compartment pressures, but any surgeon who considers that compartment syndrome is a real possibly due to the severity or duration of acute limb ischaemia should release the four fascial compartments of the leg and if necessary (although much less commonly) the thigh as soon as possible. In a limb salvage situation the worst consequence of fasciotomies will be scarring of the leg. Failure to carry out fasciotomies may result in loss of the leg despite having restored adequate circulation. Failure to undertake fasciotomies on restoring circulation to a severely ischaemic limb is negligent.

26.67   Complete release of the fascial compartments must be established. It is sometimes possible to leave some compartments intact if they are soft, but in an emergency situation it is usually better to release all four. The surgeon must ensure that no bands of fascia are left which may constrict the muscle and cause them to die which will result in limb loss. Failure to do this is negligent.

26.68   Fasciotomies are often slow to heal and may require skin grafting. Often the patient will have residual nerve dysfunction with weakness and numbness or muscle damage. It is important to document the presence of any deficit before fasciotomies and to warn the patient that even with fasciotomies the limb function may not return to normal due to the period of ischaemia. During fasciotomies the common peroneal nerve is at risk of injury around the neck of the fibula. The surgeon should take care when releasing the lateral compartment around this area and document that they did so. Injury of the common peroneal nerve will result in foot drop and numbness on the foot and is negligent.

Amputation

26.69   When the tissues of the foot and leg are not viable, there is no possibility of re-vascularising a severely ischaemic limb, or there is extensive life-threatening infection in the leg not controlled by antibiotics, amputation should be considered. Major amputation of a limb is above the ankle joint. Amputations below this level are termed minor although may have significant impact on the patient. Around 15,000 amputations are undertaken annually in England and Wales and the majority are for complications of diabetes and PAD. The mortality rate for amputation is high (16.8 per cent) most commonly due to the general poor health of patients needing surgery[1]. It is important that the patient's general health is optimised prior to surgery and the procedure undertaken by an experienced anaesthetist and surgeon. However, the long-term survival of a patient after amputation is poor and over 50 per cent will be dead within five years. This has to be taken into account when estimating costs of care needed after leaving hospital.

1 Moxey, Hofman, Hinchliffe (et al) 'Epidemiological study of lower limb amputation in England between 2003 and 2008' (2010) 97 Br J Surg 1348–1353.

26.70   It is rare for patients to make claims about the conduct of an amputation itself despite there being considerable variation in the quality of the surgery which can affect the prospects of gaining mobility with prosthesis. Deep vein thrombosis is common after amputation and prophylactic measures must be used to reduce this risk.

26.71   There are considerable advantages in below knee amputations in gaining mobility with a prosthetic limb and it is usual to try and achieve this. However, the more distal the amputation the more problematic will be healing and around 20 per cent of below knee amputations fail to heal primarily and will need further intervention. There are no good tests of the ability of an amputation stump to heal and the level of amputation is usually determined by clinical assessment. Generally failure to heal is not an indication of negligence.

26.72   Short stumps making the fitting of prosthesis impossible, persistent pain either locally or perceived in the leg (phantom pain) and failure to heal are common problems. There are a number of techniques to perform below knee amputation but there is no evidence that any is superior.

26.73   The impact of amputation on the patient in terms of their lifestyle and ability to work is significant and greatly affects the damages if a negligent act has caused their amputation. In assessing this it must be considered that following amputation for arterial disease the life expectancy of a person is significantly reduced. There is also a risk that even if the negligent act had not occurred, the patient's arterial disease could have deteriorated and ultimately resulted in amputation at some stage in the future.

Venous operations

26.74   Operations for varicose veins are common, with over 50,000 procedures a year being undertaken in the UK, and regularly cause patients to make complaints due to the failure to warn them of the potential complications of nerve injury, scarring, recurrence and deep vein thrombosis. The most common indication for varicose vein surgery is to relieve symptoms such as aching and discomfort and to improve appearance. The patient must be warned about the potential risks of the intervention and this should be documented.

26.75   Nerve injury may occur if a simple varicose vein is being avulsed (phelebectomy) and usually results in a small patch of sensory loss, but can cause permanent pain. It can be impossible to avoid this even if the operation is performed with due care, but warning a patient of this possibility prior to treatment often means that is accepted by the patient. Also small venous flares sometimes develop at phlebectomy sites and the patient should be warned about this.

26.76   If a major nerve is injured this can result not only in sensory problems but loss of power, which can be debilitating. The common peroneal nerve where it passes around the neck of the fibula in the leg is at risk from phlebectomy or open surgery in the popliteal fossa. The saphenous and sural nerves (both sensory) are closely associated with the long and short saphenous veins respectively and also at risk. It is hard to defend injury to the named nerves as it is well recognised and the surgeon should be fully aware of the risk and avoid it. Sometimes even in what seems to have been a straightforward procedure the nerve is noted to be non-functional after surgery. This may be due to pressure on the nerve or direct injury and the help of a peripheral nerve expert should be sought, who will usually expose the nerve to make sure it is in continuity and not compressed. If a nerve injury is suspected then expert help should be sought as early as possible. If the nerve has been injured it may take up to 24 months to assess the level of recovery that may be achieved.

26.77 Increasingly varicose veins are treated using endovenous techniques or foam injection sclerotherapy. Endovenous techniques rely on using laser or radiofrequency devices to cause thermal damage to the main truncal veins from inside, resulting in obliteration of the vein. Removal of the associated visible varicose veins is then performed as before by phlebectomy. The immediate advantage of these treatments is that they are less painful and recovery is quicker. It is possible to undertake them as an outpatient or office-based procedure under local anaesthetic. This has a number of advantages including early mobilisation which reduces the risk of deep vein thrombosis and if peripheral nerves are picked during phlebectomy the patient is often aware of an unpleasant sensation and the surgeon can stop before serious injury occurs. This is particularly true of the common peroneal nerve. Burn injuries to the skin have been reported when the veins are very superficial or the patient thin. This should be uncommon and can be avoided by using adequate amounts of fluid to surround the vein.

26.78 NICE recommended that endovenous techniques should be the first line interventional treatment offered to patients having varicose veins treated. However these procedures are relatively new and although the results over 10 years seem to be as good as conventional surgery, the patient should be made aware that sometimes treated veins may re-open or re-cannalise after treatment.

26.79 Liquid injection sclerotherapy has been used for many years and can be useful for smaller varicose veins and in particular the small reticular or spider veins. This is usually a cosmetic procedure and patients may be disappointed as it is often not possible to treat all the veins; staining of the skin can occur in up to 10 per cent of cases. Blistering may also occur which, if marked, can leave scarring. It is essential to document that the patient has been warned about this and many surgeons will ask consent to photograph the area before and after treatment, which can be very useful if there is a dispute about the cosmetic outcome.

26.80 Standard injection therapy is rarely effective in large trunk veins such as the long or short saphenous vein. However, ultrasound controlled foam injection sclerotherapy can be used in this situation and is very appealing as it can be undertaken as an outpatient procedure and is relatively painless. Foam is made by mixing air with the sclerosant which causes an intense inflammatory response in the vein. This sometimes has the appearance clinically of a thrombophlebitis. Although the surgeon does a number of things to control the placement of the foam by observing its injection using duplex ultrasound and compressing the junctions of the truncal vein, foam commonly enters the deep veins. In most individuals this causes no harm, but in a few it may enter the arterial circulation through previously abnormal communications between the right and left side of the heart. If this occurs, damage to the eye and the brain can occur which has been reported to result in transient or permanent blindness or stroke. The numbers of cases reported is very small and usually associated with large volumes of sclerosant. NICE approved the use of ultrasound-guided foam injection sclerotherapy in April 2009 but patients must be followed up. Although it appears that the risk of this is very small, it must be discussed with the patient, and this discussion should be documented, because of the serious consequences to the patient.

Venous thromboembolism (VTE)

26.81   Deep vein thrombosis (DVT) is a serious condition which can occur spontaneously, but more commonly follows surgery, trauma or any illness that causes immobility. The immediate risk is of propagation of the clot in the legs or pelvis resulting in parts breaking off and passing to the lung, a pulmonary embolus (PE). This can be fatal or result in significant damage to the lung in the longer term, causing breathlessness. Initial treatment is to prescribe anticoagulants which will reduce the chance of further clot forming. In the majority of patients consideration should be given to using an inferior venal cava filter (IVC) in patients at high risk of PE who cannot receive anticoagulation, eg following trauma or who have had further PEs despite adequate anticoagulation. In the UK the use of IVC filters is quite low and the decision is usually made by a surgeon or radiologist with experience in this area.

26.82   In the majority of patients the thrombus is broken down over the first few months and the veins recanalise. This usually results in a reduction of leg swelling and pain. However, the valves which are an integral part of the venous system are frequently damaged and become incompetent. This results in increased pressure on the veins of the leg when the patient is standing or walking. This can cause aching, swelling, varicose veins and in a few patients ulceration which is known as post-thrombotic leg syndrome. These symptoms may not become apparent for several years but it has been identified that up to 30 per cent of patients will develop them. The symptoms can be reduced by wearing a compression stocking. After a DVT patients are at approximately 30 per cent increased risk of developing further DVTs in the future[1].

1 Prandoni, Lensing, Cogo (et al) 'The long term clinical course of acute deep vein thrombosis' (1996) 125 Ann Int Med 1–7.

26.83   Most recently NICE has recommended that patients with extensive DVTs involving the iliac veins should be considered for thrombolytic therapy to try to dissolve the clot rapidly in an attempt to reduce the long-term complications of DVT[1].

1 Venous thromboembolic diseases: the management of venous thromboembolic diseases and the role of thrombophilia testing National Institute for health and clinical excellence. Clinical guideline 144 (June 2012).

26.84   Failure to prevent a DVT or to diagnose if it occurs can have serious consequences. It is a high-profile condition which the NHS in England has campaigned to reduce, as many are preventable.

26.85   All hospitals should carry out an assessment of a patient's risk of developing venous thromboembolic (VTE) complications within 24 hours of admission and take appropriate prophylactic measures to reduce that risk. Failure to do this would be negligent. Some patients are at extremely high risk of VTE due to comorbidities such as obesity or cancers, but generally the prophylactic measures will reduce the risk of DVT by greater than 50 per cent, so on the balance of probabilities will prevent DVT.

26.86   Many patients will seek advice about leg pain and swelling. In patients at high risk, for example following trauma or immobility, it is essential to have a high index of suspicion for the diagnosis of DVT. Clinical examination is not reliable and cannot be relied upon as so many hospitals have rapid access or walk in clinics which screen patients using a questionnaire and a D-dimer blood test. If the score is elevated, a duplex ultrasound scan is performed, which is the best test to diagnose a DVT. If the scan cannot be performed immediately then anticoagulation is commenced until a DVT is excluded. DVT is a common condition; diagnosis is generally straightforward and based on screening and duplex ultrasound, so failure to consider the diagnosis, particularly in a high-risk patient, is difficulty to defend. Unnecessary delay in making a diagnosis, resulting in failure to commence anticoagulation, will usually be held to have caused a preventable PE or caused more damage to the venous system, resulting in a greater chance of post-thrombotic leg syndrome.

Complications affecting the foot in diabetes

26.87   The prevalence of diabetes is escalating and there are over three million people living with diabetes in the UK. The feet of people with diabetes are particularly vulnerable for a number of reasons. Diabetes, especially if longstanding, is associated with damage to the nerves, peripheral neuropathy. This results in drying and cracking of the skin and changes in shape of the foot, making it more prone to injury and reduced sensation. This means that the patient is unaware of any injurious event such as ill-fitting shoes. People with diabetes are also four times more likely to develop peripheral arterial disease, and so if they develop a wound on the foot it is less likely to heal due to lack of blood supply. Finally, people with diabetes are more prone to infection and the clinical signs of this such as temperature may be obtunded. Infection can rapidly spread, causing irreversible damage to the foot[1].

1   Cheer, Shearman, Jude 'Managing complications of the diabetic foot' (2009) 339 Br Med J 1307.

26.88   At any time 2–3 per cent of people with diabetes will have a foot ulcer and over 25 per cent of these will lead to a minor amputation (below the ankle) or major amputation. Diabetes associated with PAD is currently the commonest cause of major amputation in the UK. It is suggested that 85 per cent of these amputations could be avoided by timely intervention to prevent foot ulceration or by treating it promptly if it occurs.

26.89   The commonest cause for litigation in this area is concern over delayed referral. There are clear guidelines to describe the care that people with diabetes should get regarding their feet, including when to refer to a specialist foot care team. Despite this, a large number of patients continue to be treated by non-specialist teams and only referred when they become very unwell. Even after admission to hospital, emergency treatment is often delayed as there appears to be no appreciation of the seriousness and urgency of the situation. The 2011 NICE guidelines outline that any patient admitted to hospital with a diabetic foot problem or found to have one while in hospital should be seen within 24 hours by a member of a multi-disciplinary foot care team, who will have the experience to determine management of the foot complication[1].

1 Diabetic foot problems. Inpatient management of diabetic foot problems. March 2011 NICE clinical guideline 119: www.nice.org.uk/guidance/CG119.

26.90   Initial treatment is control of the diabetes, antibiotics (usually intravenously) and surgery to remove dead tissue and drain infection. This should be done by a surgeon experienced in this field. It is common to have to re-inspect the wounds after 1–2 days to ensure all the infected tissue has been removed. Further assessment of the circulation is then undertaken and if the circulation is poor either surgery or angioplasty undertaken to improve it.

26.91   Diabetic foot complications can be difficult to treat, but delay in referral appears to be the biggest issue. There is considerable geographical variation in the amputation rates for people with diabetes suggesting a variation in service provision and there are still many areas which do not have a diabetic foot care team.

Thoracic outlet syndrome (TOS)

26.92   The subclavian artery, vein and brachial plexus pass over the first vertebra at the base of the neck. These structures may be compressed in this area causing neurological symptoms such as pain, numbness or weakness, arterial damage resulting in emboli into the arm and hand or obstruction of the vein. These problems may be caused by repetitive use of the arm in an individual who is susceptible by having a narrow thoracic outlet or a cervical rib, but can follow trauma which may be relatively minor such as falling on an outstretched arm.

26.93   Although the thoracic outlet may be examined using MR scanning and the structures interrogated using duplex ultrasound and nerve conduction studies there is no definitive diagnostic test and the diagnosis is made based on clinical signs. Management of thoracic outlet syndrome has tended to be carried out by vascular surgeons but it is a highly specialised area. Treatment is by physiotherapy and in some patients by decompressing the area by removing a cervical rib or band.

26.94   The subclavian vein is the most anterior structure in the thoracic outlet and is at risk of compression between the first rib and clavicle. Body builders who increase the muscle bulk of their neck muscles by exercise are prone to this condition. Initially the vein becomes thickened and may thrombose due to the repeated trauma (Paget Schroetter Syndrome). This results in a sudden onset of arm swelling and pain. Early diagnosis allows thrombolysis of the vein and decompression of the thoracic outlet.

26.95   About 75 per cent of patients who have surgery gain some benefit. However, recurrence of symptoms may occur and the operation is associated with a number of complications including damage to the vascular structures and nerves, which the patient must be warned about[1].

1 Thompson 'Thoracic outlet syndrome' in Parvin, Earnshaw (eds) *Rare Vascular Disorders* (2005) pp 123–130.

Endoscopic thoracic sympathectomy

26.96   Cutting the sympathetic nerves that supply the upper limb can have benefit in patients with excessive sweating of the hand, palmar hyperhidrosis[1]. However sympathectomy has also been used (without evidence) for a wide range of indications such as facial flushing. There are a number of potential complications, most notably compensatory truncal sweating, pain, bleeding, persistent pneumothorax and recurrence. A number of patient web sites have been set up which make claims that the operation has ruined the lives of many patients. Botulinus toxin has replaced sympathectomy in many patients with hyperhidrosis. However there is still an indication for sympathectomy in a few people with marked symptoms.

1 Cerfolio, Campos, Bryant (et al) 'The Society of Thoracic Surgeons expert consensus for the surgical treatment of hyperhidrosis' (2011) 91 Ann Thoracic Surg 1642–1648.

Pain management

Dr Tim W Johnson

INTRODUCTION

27.1 Chronic pain has relevance to clinical negligence in three areas: pain caused by the consequences of clinical practice in a wide range of medical specialities; problems (including further pain) caused by the negligent application of pain management techniques in the pain clinic; and the avoidable non-relief of chronic pain.

27.2 Chronic pain is a complex phenomenon. This chapter will attempt to explain some of the most relevant concepts and terms, in particular the discordance between the extent of injury and the severity of any resulting pain. The definitions of clinical terms used are taken from the taxonomy developed by the International Association for the Study of Pain (IASP)[1].

1 IASP (2012) International Association for the Study of Pain, Taxonomy. from www.iasp-pain. org/Education/Content.aspx?ItemNumber=1698.

THE SPECIALITY OF PAIN MANAGEMENT

Origins of the speciality

27.3 Pain management has grown out of the speciality of anaesthesia over the last 50 years. Anaesthetists originally demonstrated interest and competence in administering strong analgesic medications such as morphine, and nerve block injections to patients with what was at the time described as intractable pain. Anaesthetists are still the core clinicians in most pain clinics although some other specialties are increasingly becoming involved. These medical specialties include rheumatology, psychiatry and neurology. Other medical clinicians such as specialist surgeons, gynaecologists and physicians may be involved in highly specialised clinics to tackle complex pain problems such as urogenital/pelvic pain, cardiac/chest pain and facial/trigeminal neuralgia pain. Pain clinics also need to have psychology, physiotherapy, nursing and occupational therapy staff in order to make them truly multidisciplinary.

Routes of referral

27.4 Patients are most commonly sent to pain clinics by their GPs. The referral should provide background information, including details of previous investigations and consultations, as well as a full medication history. The pattern of previous presentation with pain symptoms is very informative. An alternative route for referrals is from other medical or surgical specialties in cases where pain cannot be controlled by interventions within that particular speciality, eg a patient with chronic spinal pain who has not been helped by, or is deemed unsuitable for surgery.

27.5 Pain management services are now widely available through the NHS, although provision is variable between areas: this is being addressed by current reorganisations (2014). The intention is to provide universal access to pain management services that will be arranged in three tiers: integrated within primary care (general practice) offering initial assessment and access to generic treatments (advice, basic medications and exercise therapy); in specialist pain clinics operating in local general hospitals and providing a wide range of assessments and interventions (sophisticated medication, injections and rehabilitation); and specialised pain services operating regionally and providing the most comprehensive services for relatively rare or very complex pain problems which might include complex regional pain syndrome or urogenital pain. Within these three levels, clinics will vary from individual practitioners working independently to large multidisciplinary teams staffing pain management programmes.

DEFINITION AND PURPOSE OF PAIN

27.6 The IASP definition of pain is:

'an unpleasant sensory and emotional experience associated with actual or potential tissue damage, or described in terms of such damage'.

This definition allows for all pain conditions to be included. Using the example of burning pain, it can include the pain of touching a hot surface as well as the pain of burnt skin and the burning pain of diabetic neuropathy even though they have very different origins and significance. The term 'experience' implies a state of consciousness and this will involve an integration of all inputs to and processes within the nervous system. Thus, it is not surprising that mood, distraction or fear will condition the experience of pain in many different ways. This definition also allows phantom limb pain to be included even though the site of pain has been physically amputated – this is because the central nervous system has retained the full capacity to experience pain related to the missing part.

27.7 The fundamental purpose of pain is to provide a protective alarm mechanism for the body. Blistered heels cause limping and prevent further more serious damage to vulnerable tissues when wearing new shoes. Patients born without normal sensation or who have lost sensation, eg in diabetic peripheral neuropathy, can develop devastating tissue damage and ulceration if precautions are not taken.

27.8 The avoidance of pain provides an incentive to restrict activity and allow time for proper healing to occur. Animals (and humans) who are injured tend to lie low and become reclusive until their pain is settled and healing occurs; their irritability and depressed mood are part of the normal sequence of protective mechanisms to restrict activity. This irritability and low mood can become an important component of a chronic pain syndrome if pain does not resolve with healing or if healing is delayed. Thus, it is quite normal for patients with disabling pain to develop depression several months after injury and it usually coincides and is potentiated by disappointment at failed initial treatments and a despondency that pain is never going to settle.

27.9 Pain behaviour is the result of the experience of pain. There are many manifestations. Examples include: limping; use of a walking aid; avoiding social contact; taking medication; endorsing pain symptoms on a questionnaire; and crying. It usually acts as a powerful social cue and solicits high levels of sympathy and social support. This support and understanding may become exhausted if the pain continues and there is exclusion from normal activity. Social and personal relationships suffer and there is further deterioration including anxiety, clinical depression and high levels of disability, all of which will exacerbate the experience of pain.

This is the world of chronic pain.

SOME CLASSIFICATIONS OF PAIN

Acute versus chronic pain

27.10 There is no universally agreed distinction. Usually a period of three or six months is used as the cut-off between acute pain symptoms and chronic pain. Alternatively, chronic pain is considered to be 'pain beyond healing'. Chronic pain syndrome is not precisely defined but is usually taken to mean pain that has persisted for more than a few months, together with psychological and social consequences that interact with and exacerbate each other.

Nociceptive versus neuropathic pain

27.11 Nociception describes the process by which the body's sensory systems take on board and react to a noxious stimulus. Nociceptive pain involves a normal nervous system reacting to the abnormal stimulus of tissue damage, which then generates the experience of pain.

27.12 Neuropathic pain results from pain being generated from within the nervous system without external stimulus or tissue damage. This can be caused by physical damage to the nerves, eg chemotherapy induced neuropathy or nerve compression, or from the more subtle aberrations of nerve function and sensitivity which are seen in fibromyalgia.

Neuropathic pain can be thought of as 'nerves behaving badly', a term that patients often appreciate because it allows both physically- and psychologically-related nerve dysfunction to be considered as one entity.

Anatomical source of pain

27.13   **Visceral** pain is used to describe pain originating from the inside organs (mainly within the chest, abdominal and pelvic cavities). The day-to-day function of these organs is usually undetectable (the nociceptors are 'silent') but when primed, triggered and 'switched on' they all have the capacity to generate high levels of very distressing pain. Examples are irritable bowel syndrome and chronic pancreatitis.

Pain within the bones, muscles, joints and connecting structures such as ligaments and tendons is usually referred to as musculoskeletal.

27.14   In pain somatisation, psychological distress is thought to become manifest as physical symptoms (in this case pain) within the body: an everyday example of somatisation is butterflies in the stomach associated with anxiety. Painful examples of somatic symptoms seen in patients with some complex chronic pains include headache, and facial, chest and abdominal pains. Somatic pain is no less real than the acute pain caused by tissue damage: they both generate genuine pain experience. Atypical is another term used to describe pain symptoms that cannot be related specifically to tissue damage. Recent research using sophisticated brain scanning demonstrates substantial neurophysiological change within the relevant nerve pathways in such cases and this reinforces the belief that such pains are genuine and have an organic basis. Simple descriptive terms are now often used to describe pain syndromes. Examples are low back pain and chronic pelvic pain.

Cancer versus non-cancer pain

27.15   Cancer pain is caused by a complex combination of abnormalities within the body including irritation, compression and destruction of tissues, extensive surgery and psychological adaptation to treatment, changes in lifestyle and a life threatening disease. Cancer pain can be classified as both acute and chronic, and nociceptive and neuropathic.

Coding of chronic pain problems

27.16   Chronic pain can be seen to be an extremely complex phenomenon. It usually cuts across medical specialties and may defy classification systems such as ICD 10 and DSM 4 or 5.

In terms of resulting pain, suffering and loss of amenity, there is more variation within individual pain conditions than between them and so, from a clinical point of view, precise coding has little relevance.

ASSESSMENT OF PAIN

27.17   A patient's pain is best understood and assessed by considering a wide range of data. The clinical history is probably the most useful means of assessing the patient's experience of chronic pain and it is the only truly valid perspective, but it is clearly subjective and reporting of it is also subject to observer bias. The clinical history should include all elements of previous pain problems and responses to pain, as well as current fears and concerns about the pain. Understanding and expectations of the pain are critical in determining reaction to and progress with pain. A detailed examination of all of the medical, employment and benefit records will allow triangulation of important facts and provide information regarding previous response to injury and pain which can predict future responses. Consistency across all sources of data is usually fundamental to validating the patient's reports of pain.

27.18 The findings (clinical signs) from physical examination must be interpreted very carefully because patients with chronic pain can be expected to be more sensitive and reactive to many standard clinical tests. Allodynia (pain due to a stimulus that does not normally provoke pain) or hyperalgesia (increased pain from a stimulus that normally provokes pain) are often seen in neuropathic pain, eg post-stroke pain or with traumatic peripheral neuropathy. Neuropathic chronic pain symptoms tend to be more diffuse than those originating from simple nerve injury and are often seen to spread regionally or into a whole limb or the whole side of the body. Such signs and sensitivities could be misinterpreted as over-reaction and this will be particularly so in the context of a clinical examination for medico-legal purposes. The clinical signs of Waddell[1] were originally formulated to highlight the need for detailed psychological assessment rather than straightforward spinal surgery in patients with spinal pain who are distressed. The signs are not intended to detect exaggeration or fabrication. The term functional overlay has often been used to describe 'non-organic' reactions to painful injury that are better understood from a complete examination of the psychological and social context in which the pain is experienced.

1 Waddell, McCulloch (et al) 'Nonorganic physical signs in low-back pain' (1980) 5(2) Spine 117–125.

27.19 Elements of exaggeration of pain presentation are sometimes seen in even the most genuine claimants during medico legal examination. This may be due to a desire to convince regarding the genuine nature symptoms rather than to deceive. There is a natural tendency to describe symptoms at their worst or most distressing, as these have the greatest impact on the patient. Malingering or overt fabrication of pain-related problems is usually apparent from gross inconsistencies when all sources of information are taken into account.

INVESTIGATION OF PAIN

27.20 There are no direct means of assessing the experience of pain. The measures that are used do not diagnose or validate pain absolutely, but they may indicate trends.

The pain diagram is a simple means of the patient recording symptoms graphically. Analysis of the distribution, density and type of marking can inform diagnosis, eg chronic widespread pain will involve all the body, whereas cervical radiculopathy will probably radiate down one arm. Pain scales for adults can use numerical rating (eg 0–10) or visual analogue scales to record the level of pain symptoms; children can be encouraged to choose a face from a series ranging from smiling to tearful. More sophisticated scales and well-validated tools such as the McGill Pain Questionnaire involve the subject selecting from ranges of pain adjectives that have been given numerical values and which are then added up to give a total score. Some questionnaires have been formulated to assess the multi-dimensional nature of chronic pain; they include components to assess psychological wellbeing and physical function (eg Brief Pain Inventory). There are well-established psychometric tools that can be used to specifically measure psychological distress – anxiety and depression, and other constructs such as self-efficacy and catastrophisation. There are many methods of assessing physical function including questionnaires and timed walk over a fixed distance.

MECHANISMS OF PAIN

Pain pathways

27.21 Pain facilitation (wind up) by peripheral and central nerve sensitisation occurs in both acute and chronic pain and accounts for the very wide range of responses to any noxious stimulus (Wolfe 2011)[1]. Intrinsic pain inhibition mechanisms also exist within the brain and spinal cord and normally operate to dampen down pain sensitivity; the effects of stress may act against this inhibition. Overall, pain experience will result from the combined mechanisms of pain generation and the balance between facilitation and inhibition. Inadequate inhibition of pain may account for some chronic pain states such as fibromyalgia.

1 Woolf 'Central sensitization: implications for the diagnosis and treatment of pain' (2011) 152 (3 Supp) Pain S2–15.

27.22 Deafferentation describes loss of normal nerve input to the central nervous system. The nervous system needs to be subject to everyday stimuli in order to maintain normal function and sensitivity; without this input, pain may develop, eg after nerve section or amputation. Preventing deafferentation pain is the rationale for avoiding limb amputation or organ excision for pain conditions unless it is absolutely necessary, eg cancer. Unfortunately amputation, particularly for chronic neuropathic pain conditions, has been found to be unhelpful and the pain can be made much worse.

27.23 The variability of the sensitivity of the nervous system can be described as neuroplasticity. It is accounted for by physical changes within individual and groups of nerve fibres within the brain and spinal cord including the sprouting of nerve terminals creating new synaptic connections to other nerves (crosstalk). It is accompanied by many neurochemical changes. This physical and chemical remodelling and 'rewiring' of nerves provides a physiological basis for understanding the permanent changes in neuronal sensitivity seen in chronic pain conditions.

27.24 The higher cerebral functions of mind and mood are controlled by many complex chemical systems. One important neuropeptide is serotonin

(5-hydroxytryptamine), the concentration of which is abnormally low in states of mood depression; however, at high concentrations it has an analgesic effect. Hence, the use of medications such as amitriptyline, a tricyclic antidepressant which raises the level of serotonin in the CNS – it has a dual use in chronic pain, for treating both depression and heightened nerve sensitivity.

The biopsychosocial model of pain

27.25   The biopsychosocial model is one of the best ways of understanding the complexity of chronic pain as being dictated by biological, psychological and social variables. Variability within these factors and interplay between them explains the disconnection between the type and degree of physical injury and the severity of any resulting pain.

Biological factors

27.26   Genetically determined variations in enzymes that break down stress hormones (eg adrenaline) can be seen to be associated with differences in pain response to acute pain, eg after shoulder surgery[1]. Similarly, differences in steroid metabolism, again genetically determined, have also been found to alter the responses to acute trauma including psychologically distressing physical trauma[2]. Some clinical syndromes that have a genetic basis, eg benign joint hypermobility syndrome (double jointedness), have been found to have associations with a number of pain conditions and sensitivities including low back pain and symphysis pubis dysfunction in pregnancy[3]. These three examples represent only a small fraction of the possible genetic variations that will alter pain predisposition and sensitivity.

There are many other biological factors that will affect pain and pain sensitivity in the body: ageing or degenerative change, overuse or disuse, scarring or contractures and physical damage to the components of the peripheral nervous system.

1 George, Wallace (et al) 'Evidence for a biopsychosocial influence on shoulder pain: pain catastrophizing and catechol-O-methyltransferase (COMT) diplotype predict clinical pain ratings' (2008) 136(1-2) Pain 53–61.
2 Bortsov, Smith (et al) 'Polymorphisms in the glucocorticoid receptor co-chaperone FKBP5 predict persistent musculoskeletal pain after traumatic stress exposure' (2013) 154(8) Pain 1419–1426.
3 Ross and Grahame 'Joint hypermobility syndrome' (2011) 342 BMJ 275–277.

Psychological factors

27.27   Fear is one of the major psychological determinants of developing chronic pain: see Figure 1[1]. Vulnerable individuals with a painful injury experience heightened pain and rather than progressing to recovery by way of re-exposure to the vicissitudes of daily life, they enter a cycle of further increasing pain sensitivity mediated by anxiety, avoidance and hypervigilance. Reinforcing factors such as unemployment and financial difficulty may prevail in the social environment. Subjects who think catastrophically (rumination, helplessness and symptom magnification) will be particularly vulnerable.

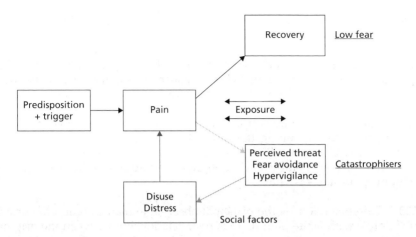

1 Turk and Wilson (2010). 'Fear of pain as a prognostic factor in chronic pain: conceptual models, assessment, and treatment implications' (2010) 14(2) Curr Pain Headache Rep 88–95.

27.28 Anger has been found to mediate the relationship between perceived injustice and the development of chronic pain[1]. Therefore, it is not surprisingly that in unresolved cases of clinical negligence where there is pain combined with understandable anger, the intensity of the pain is substantially increased. On this basis there may be some prospect for reduction in levels of pain intrusion following a just settlement of proceedings. However, anger will not necessarily diminish and other mechanisms of pain generation will persist after settlement of litigation.

1 Scott, Trost (et al) 'Anger differentially mediates the relationship between perceived injustice and chronic pain outcomes' (2013) 154(9) Pain 1691–1698.

27.29 The idea that pain can be psychological in origin is used to explain pain somatisation. Psychological distress, perhaps as a result of traumatic life experiences, is thought to generate the physical symptoms of pain. Such symptoms may have an important defensive function in protecting the subject from re-exposure to a difficult situation or in maintaining a more acceptable environment. This is the realm of clinical psychology and psychiatry. A definition of persistent pain somatisation disorder is provided by ICD 10 (F45.4):

'The predominant complaint is of persistent, severe, and distressing pain, which cannot be explained fully by a physiological process or a physical disorder, and which occurs in association with emotional conflict or psychosocial problems that are sufficient to allow the conclusion that they are the main causative influences. The result is usually a marked increase in support and attention, either personal or medical'.

27.30 Iatrogenic pain: doctors and other medical practitioners can be responsible for increasing or perpetuating distress associated with pain by dismissing pain complaints or not believing the sufferer. The conflicting opinions that arise are confusing to patients. There may be a tendency for expectant treatment ('maybe it will settle') rather than for expedited pain management. Delays in understanding the pain and providing effective management cause avoidable additional distress and promote loss of function and role.

27.31　Referrals between clinicians can establish or perpetuate errors that attribute pain to specific events, whereas constitutional factors may be more responsible. This misattribution may be inadvertent or deliberate.

27.32　Failure to provide appropriate rehabilitation (eg recommending exercises without explaining the rationale for increasing levels of pain by physical activity) can result in more pain and a negative attitude towards further attempts at therapy. Early definitive and authoritative management of chronic pain states is vital.

27.33　Pain behaviour is the principal observable manifestation of chronic pain. Unlike with acute pain there is poor relationship between the original injury and the symptoms that develop. Figure 2 illustrates the tenuous relationship between tissue injury and pain behaviour via the processes of nociception, pain and suffering. Of particular note is the influence of pain context. For example, injuries tolerated voluntarily by sportsmen, eg boxers, may be no different to those inflicted during the process of torture, but factors such as isolation, fear and loss of personal control dictate very different effects and consequences of the injuries.

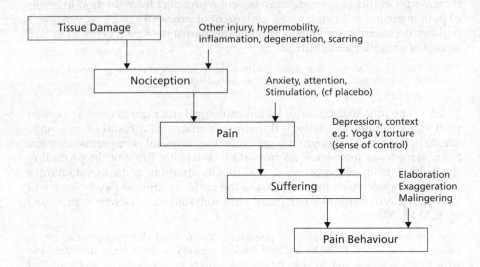

(Acknowledgement: Loeser)

Social factors

27.34　Pain behaviour is a powerful social cue. Chronic pain symptoms and their physical consequences can often disrupt social and personal relationships. Loss of role as a partner, employee or parent is distressing and difficult to regain. There are often major financial consequences due to loss of income from employment and the need for substantial care and dependence on others. Socio-economic factors, including litigation, may have a role in the development and progress of pain symptoms after injury in motor vehicle accidents[1]; it is unlikely that similar data could be derived from clinical negligence cases because of the relatively low incidence, divergence and extreme complexity of presentation.

1 McLean (et al) 'Incidence and predictors of neck and widespread pain after motor vehicle collision among US litigants and nonlitigants' (2014) 155 Pain 309–321.

27.35 This complexity and the profound interaction between biological, psychological and social factors can be understood by reference to Figure 3, derived from the work of Diatchenko[1]. As the number of interacting factors increases, so does the burden of pain and the probability that pain will become intermittent, intrusive and finally persistent and severe. For some patients the burden of and focus upon pain becomes so great that it takes over the whole of life.

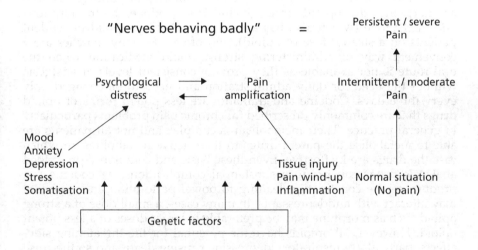

1 Diatchenko (et al) 'Idiopathic pain disorders – pathways of vulnerability' (2006) 123(3) Pain 226–230.

PAIN TREATMENT: GENERAL APPROACHES

27.36 It is very unlikely that any single treatment will provide complete relief for any chronic pain state. Usually a multidisciplinary approach with medical, psychological and physical therapies will be most appropriate. Even so, outcomes generally are poor in absolute terms so that many patients with established chronic pain, once they have accepted their condition and are prepared to adopt a coping approach rather than pursue a complete cure, may be satisfied with 30–50 per cent pain relief.

Medications

27.37   Some medications used in the treatment of chronic pain are unlicensed for this purpose because there are insufficient studies available to confirm fully the efficacy and safety, eg amitriptyline. However, it is widely accepted that a range of unlicensed medications can be used in appropriate circumstances and there is helpful guidance available[1].

1 Use of medicines outside of their UK marketing authorisation in pain management and palliative medicine (British Pain Society, 2012), available at www.britishpainsociety.org/book_useofmeds_professional.pdf.

Opioids

27.38   These are the morphine type of painkillers that are used for acute pain, eg post-operative pain or post-traumatic pain and extensively for cancer pain management. Generally opioids have little use in managing chronic pain, particularly if it is neuropathic in origin. Nevertheless, reasonable benefit has been reported in a minority of patients. As well as morphine, the opioid group includes oxycodone, hydromorphone and methadone (which also has a use in maintaining opioid dependent patients on a steady dose of opioid), and others. Fentanyl patches are a convenient way of administering strong opioid medication when the oral route is not available as they provide consistent levels of analgesia without the need for daily administration and need to be changed only every three days. Codeine and tramadol are less potent forms of opioid drugs that are commonly prescribed for chronic pain problems particularly in general practice. Their metabolism is complex and not all patients are able to metabolise the parent drugs to their active metabolites, in which case the drugs are ineffective. Even these basic and commonly-prescribed analgesic drugs can produce substantial complications, eg codeine can produce severe constipation leading to bowel perforation and tramadol may interact with antidepressants. In many cases, a small dose of a strong opioid such as morphine may be preferable to larger doses of a less potent opioid. However, all opioids have the potential for life-threatening side-effects, particularly respiratory depression causing death and so their use must be understood and closely supervised.

27.39   For morphine and similar drugs both modified release (usually taken every 12 hours) and short-acting immediate release preparations are available. The aim is to provide reasonable steady-state analgesia with additional doses readily available for breakthrough pain. The process of adjusting the dose to clinical need is referred to as titration. It is essential to issue warnings regarding side effects such as sedation which may affect driving, and to prescribe laxatives to prevent constipation, which is frequent and if unrecognised can lead to severe bowel dysfunction or even perforation.

27.40   Addiction to opioids as a result of therapeutic use for chronic pain is uncommon in patients without existing substance-dependence behaviours. Pseudo-addiction is a term used to describe prominent opioid seeking behaviours in patients who have justifiable benefit from opioids but fear that their prescriptions will be withdrawn or that they are being disbelieved. Withdrawal effects from opioids are rarely dangerous but can be very distressing and disruptive; they are usually avoided by gradual reductions in the doses of medication over weeks or even months (the body has its own intrinsic opioid hormones that are suppressed by external opioids and these need to be allowed time to recover). A high level of inter-professional communication is required for the proper supervision of long-term opioid management and referral to specialist pain clinics is advisable for prolonged high dose opioid therapy. Nationally agreed recommendations on many aspects of opioid prescribing in chronic pain are available[1].

1 Opioids for persistent pain: Good Practice (British Pain Society, 2010), available at www. britishpainsociety.org/book_opioid_main.pdf.

Non-steroidal anti-inflammatory drugs (NSAIDs)

27.41 This group of medications includes ibuprofen and diclofenac. Their use is mainly for inflammatory type acute pain, although benefit in some chronic non-inflammatory painful conditions is seen. They can cause gastric ulceration, renal impairment and coagulopathy and there is some evidence that they may predispose towards cardiac or vascular events (heart attack or stroke) so the treatment benefit needs to be weighed against the relative risks of side effects and complications – a careful history taken before prescribing is important. Paracetamol does not reduce tissue inflammation but is usually included in this group because it provides analgesia within the central nervous system (CNS) by a similar mechanism of prostaglandin synthesis inhibition. It is less likely to cause complications and is commonly used in conjunction with other analgesics because it is generally well tolerated.

Anticonvulsants

27.42 Some of the medications that were originally developed to treat epilepsy have found a role in managing neuropathic pain (pain caused by a lesion or disease of the somatosensory nervous system-peripheral or central). Gabapentin and pregabalin are the two agents most frequently used; they are generally safe and well tolerated. Another anticonvulsant, carbamazepine, is used specifically for treating trigeminal neuralgia; it often has more significant side-effects and complications than the gabapentinoids.

Antidepressants

27.43 The ability for tricyclic antidepressants to increase the levels of serotonin within the CNS has an important analgesic effect in patients with chronic neuropathic pain. However, amitriptyline and several similar medications in this group can be very dangerous in overdose and this may need to be considered in vulnerable individuals who are at risk of self-harm. Side effects including dry mouth, constipation and urinary retention are often an obstacle to their use. They have an advantage in that they can be used to treat the depression of mood as a result of pain along with neuropathic pain itself. More effective antidepressant medications and the supervision of a psychiatrist may be required for severe depression symptoms.

Topical treatments

27.44 Capsaicin is extracted from the chilli pepper and can be formulated as a cream or a patch to be applied to the skin. It is known to attenuate the function of the peripheral C nerve fibres that are involved in nociception so it is often tried where there is local damage to the peripheral nervous system, eg on sensitive surgical wounds. However, it is very irritant. Other approaches are to use local anaesthetic creams or patches (lidocaine); these may reduce the sensitivity of skin where there is allodynia or hyperaesthesia. Massage from applying a cream or the physical cushioning effect of a soft patch may be either helpful or a nuisance.

Other drug treatments

27.45 There are reports of substantial benefit with neuropathic pain from the use of cannabis, particularly in multiple sclerosis and pharmaceutical preparations of this drug do have established value in treating nausea and vomiting particularly in terminal illness. Its use as an analgesic is less certain because of its cognitive side-effects. Ketamine, a powerful anaesthetic drug with hallucinogenic properties and established illicit use, has been advocated for the treatment of neuropathic pain. However, side effects are frequent and can be distressing and there are concerns about long-term effects on the bladder so its use is not widespread outside of cancer pain management.

Injections

27.46 These can be temporary, using a local anaesthetic such as bupivacaine to produce a nerve block. The intention is that by switching off the nerves supplying a painful area for a short period of time there will be a resetting of sensitivity levels which results in a more prolonged settlement of chronic pain symptoms. Substantial long-term benefits are unusual and the need for repetition can create a reliance on this type of treatment that is unhelpful. There may be a substantial placebo effect (as with all chronic pain treatments). Physical damage as a result of unrecognised weakness or numbness is possible following a nerve block and this should be carefully guarded against by warning the patient. There is a risk of physical damage to the nerve being blocked from improper insertion of the injection needle. This is covered in detail in the Anaesthesia chapter in this book (see para **28.72**). Steroids can be added to the local anaesthetic mixtures used for injections. This is widely practised and may improve the benefit, although the scientific evidence to support its use is scant. There are risks of osteoporosis, infection and upsetting control of diabetes from the use of regular high doses of steroids.

27.47 Neurolytic injections where nerves are deliberately damaged by the injection of toxic substances (glycerol, phenol or alcohol) can be useful in a number of pain states. These techniques are used much less than in previous decades because of their relatively poor outcome and progressive improvement in drug therapy and psychological understanding of chronic pain. The main roles for this type of technique are in cancer pain, spasticity from nerve injury and in a minority of chronic neuropathies including trigeminal neuralgia. Nerves can also be destroyed by using heat energy delivered by a needle placed close to a nerve (radio frequency lesioning). This technique can even be applied to the spinal-cord (cordotomy) but there are obviously major risks to be considered as well as potential benefits and it is largely restricted to terminal illnesses.

Neurostimulation

27.48 There are a number of techniques in regular use that involve stimulation of peripheral tissues or nerves in order to reduce pain. Acupuncture and TENS (transcutaneous electrical nerve stimulation) are low technology examples that can have useful sustained benefits in some patients with chronic pain. More invasively, electrical stimulation can be applied directly to the spinal cord or areas of the brain using implanted electrodes (spinal-cord or deep brain stimulation). This involves more risk. Spinal cord stimulation has been endorsed as a treatment for neuropathic pain[1] and is approved by NICE.

1 Spinal cord stimulation for the management of pain (British Pain Society/Society of British Neurological Surgeons, 2009), available at www.britishpainsociety.org/book_scs_main.pdf.

Psychological therapies

27.49 Most patients with significant chronic pain will have psychological distress as a normal component of the condition. It is incorrect and unhelpful to consider chronic pain in a dualistic way, as either physical or psychological; it is almost always both.

Treatments used include cognitive behavioural therapy (CBT), hypnotherapy, mindfulness, and acceptance and commitment therapy (ACT). It is important that these are implemented as part of a multidisciplinary strategy together with medical and physical therapies rather than as stand-alone treatments.

Physical therapy

27.50 There are a number of mantras that are used in managing chronic pain, all of which have a grounding in a commonsense approach of reducing sensitivity by regaining function. These include 'use it or lose it', 'a strong painful body is better than a weak painful body' and 'no pain, no gain'. Pain is often taken as a reason for inactivity, which tends to cause more pain sensitivity. Therefore, robust supervision of physical therapy is required, that includes exploration and understanding of the patient's concerns.

Pain management programmes

27.51 Here, a range of clinicians work closely together to maximise function, minimise symptoms, recognise and understand the obstacles to coping with the pain and challenge and correct misunderstandings or apprehensions concerning the pain. For chronic pain problems that are distressing and disabling, prolonged treatment over many months including as an inpatient may be necessary. The intention of such programmes is to restore function despite the pain rather than specifically to relieve pain. The requirements for programmes have been defined and usually include occupational and vocational rehabilitation[1].

1 Guidance for Pain Management Programmes for adults (British Pain Society, 2013), available at www.britishpainsociety.org/pub_professional.htm#pmp2013.

PAIN CONDITIONS CAUSED BY MEDICAL TREATMENT

27.52 Almost every medical or surgical treatment or misapplication of treatment has the potential to generate complications resulting in chronic pain. The following are the most frequent chronic pain problems that are seen in association with allegations of clinical negligence.

Post-surgical pain

27.53 Surgery as a form of legitimate trauma is responsible for many chronic pain conditions. The risk of developing chronic post-operative pain is often advisably included during the consent procedure for even straightforward and routine surgical interventions. It is clear from the genetic studies already reviewed that some patients are more prone to develop troublesome post-operative pain than others and a history of developing pain after previous surgical interventions is a poor prognostic sign. Most post-surgical pain conditions do settle, but this settlement is rarely complete. In cases of post-surgical pain, further surgical procedures to explore the wound or to remove metalwork or scar tissue because of pain should be resisted unless there is a clear nociceptive cause for the pain (eg infection or impingement on a vital structure) as there is a substantial risk of making things much worse rather than better. Repeated surgery on the same part of the body, eg repeating a procedure that has been done incompletely or incorrectly, will have a much higher risk of precipitating chronic pain than a procedure done once and correctly. Post-surgical pain has been extensively reviewed by Macrae[1].

1 Macrae 'Chronic post-surgical pain: 10 years on' (2008) 101(1) British Jrnl Anaesth 77–86.

Peripheral neuropathy

27.54 This may be associated with radiation, chemical or drug toxicity, metabolic problems (most commonly diabetes), or following peripheral nerve trauma. Peripheral nerves are generally unforgiving structures and even minor insults may result in permanent symptoms including allodynia, hyperalgesia and dysaesthesia (an unpleasant abnormal sensation, whether spontaneous or evoked) in the affected territory. A wide range of chemotherapy drug treatments often together with therapeutic radiation for treating cancer problems are a well-recognised source of damage to the nerves. There is obviously the possibility of these treatments being used inappropriately with severe chronic neuropathic pain consequences. Direct trauma to nerves can result from pressure effects following compartment syndrome or incompletely decompressed nerve compression syndromes, eg carpal tunnel syndrome, or from positioning or instrumentation during surgery. These nerve lesions are often partial and the territory of the nerve becomes hypersensitive.

Amputation and phantom pains

27.55   More complete damage to nerves from deliberate or inadvertent nerve section or complete amputation may result in a phantom pain or phantom sensation. This is most often seen in limbs where painful distortions of the sensed amputated limb are felt, but it can affect internal organs such as the bowel or bladder. For example, tenesmus is the very distressing symptom of still needing urgent bowel evacuation following total excision of the rectum. In cases of limb amputation, exquisite sensitivity can develop at the stump from neuroma formation at the divided nerve end; this may be helped by the nerve end being buried deep in muscle tissue to protect it from physical pressure effects.

Complex regional pain syndrome (CRPS)

27.56   This is one of the most severe consequences of peripheral nerve injury (CRPS type 2) but it also occurs spontaneously with often only minor damage to non-nerve tissues (CRPS type 1). The syndrome involves an exaggerated response of peripheral inflammatory mechanisms including pain generation that becomes more enhanced rather than settling during the tissue healing process. Severe painful sensitivity develops with swelling, vascular changes and trophic changes (including abnormal growth or wasting of muscle, bone, hair, nails and skin).

Table 1 – Budapest diagnostic criteria for CRPS

A–D must apply:

A: Continuing pain which is disproportionate to inciting event
B: One sign in two or more categories
C: One symptom in three or more categories
D: No other diagnosis can better explain the signs and symptoms

Category specifications

Sensory	Allodynia – touch, temperature or pressure or hyperalgesia Hyperalgesia – to pinprick
Vasomotor	Temperature and colour – changes or asymmetry
Sudomotor/oedema	Sweating or swelling – changes or asymmetry
Motor/trophic	Reduced movement, weakness or trophic changes

27.57   Revised criteria for the diagnosis of CRPS have been published in 2010[1]: see Table 1. These do not specify clearly the extent of abnormality required for inclusion and they have an improved but still relatively low diagnostic specificity (0.68) and have been considered to be over inclusive[2]. However, there is no doubt that CRPS in its substantive forms is extremely distressing and has a devastating effect on physical function. With proper early management, the essence of which is adequate analgesia and vigorous physical rehabilitation – exercise and exposure to stimuli – the symptoms and signs may be seen to settle often to a considerable degree leaving a modified post-acute form of the condition. CRPS symptoms and signs often spread regionally within the limb affected but can also spread contralaterally to the opposite limb, or ipsilaterally to affect the whole of the same side of the body[3]. Factors thought to predict poor prognosis are: coldness of the limb, occurrence of the condition following an injury other than a fracture, a pre-existing pain condition, young age and the lack of psychological distress[4].

1 Harden, Bruehl (et al) 'Validation of proposed diagnostic criteria (the Budapest Criteria) for Complex Regional Pain Syndrome' (2010) 150(2) Pain 268–274.
2 Bass 'Complex regional pain syndrome medicalises limb pain' (2014) 348 BMJ g2631.
3 van Rijn, Marinus (et al) 'Spreading of complex regional pain syndrome: not a random process' (2011) 118(9) J Neural Transm 1301–1309.
4 Borchers and Gershwin 'Complex regional pain syndrome: a comprehensive and critical review' (2014) 13(3) Autoimmun Rev 242–265.

FIBROMYALGIA (CHRONIC WIDESPREAD PAIN)

27.58   This is a long-term pain condition with symptoms affecting many parts of the body and it is strongly associated with fatigue, and sleep and mood disturbance. There is thought to be ineffective damping of nervous system sensitivity. The condition can occur in any patient group but is most frequently seen in middle-aged women. It is not a degenerative or progressive condition and once recognised and managed appropriately as a chronic pain problem it tends to be accepted and tolerated with necessary restriction or modification of activity: there are no effective treatments. When originally described, the diagnosis depended on a range of symptoms (disseminated pain, fatigue, sleep and mood disturbance) and also the findings of tenderness to palpation (4 kg/cm^2) at 11 out of 18 specified points in the body – the fibromyalgia points[1]. More recent criteria permit diagnosis to be made on the basis only of: widespread pain for greater than three months accompanied by sleep disturbance and fatigue, with other conditions excluded[2]: see Table 2.

Table 2: Diagnostic criteria for fibromyalgia (2014)

All must apply:

A: Widespread pain for at least three months
B: Sleep disturbance
C: Fatigue
D: Other conditions excluded eg myopathy, hypothyroidism, inflammation

1 Wolfe, Smythe (et al) 'The American Rheumatology 1990 Criteria for the Classification of Fibromyalgia: Report of the Multicenter Criteria Committee' (1990) 33(2) Annals Rheum 160–172.
2 Rahman, Underwood (et al) 'Fibromyalgia' (2014) 348 BMJ g1224.

Tender points are optional; they are not necessary for diagnosis

27.59 Tender points have become an optional consideration. Many patients who develop troublesome chronic widespread pain following clinical negligence will already have a past medical history suggesting a tendency to pain sensitivity reactions in any case. Conditions associated with the sensitivity of fibromyalgia include: irritable bowel syndrome (IBS), Raynaud's phenomenon, headache, migraine, paraesthesias, subjective oedema, sexual dysfunction, anxiety, panic disorder, cold intolerance, restless leg syndrome and temporomandibular joint dysfunction. There is no easy way of determining whether the patient would have developed a recrudescence or advancement of their pre-existing conditions in any case.

CLINICAL NEGLIGENCE PROBLEMS GENERATED BY PAIN MANAGEMENT PRACTICE

Supervision of medications

27.60 Prescribing potent and potentially very toxic drugs requires a high level of shared knowledge, agreement and communication between clinician and patient; this is particularly so with opioids. Confusion often arises between modified (delayed, long-acting) release preparations of morphine such as MST, and the immediate release forms (Sevredol (tablets) and Oramorph (liquid)) and toxicity could result. Fentanyl patches can be as small as postage stamps yet contain a lethal dose of medication intended for delivery over three days. If patches are used inappropriately, for example by exposure to external heat or doubling up on the dosage, the results could be fatal. It is advisable for discussions between clinicians and patients to be supported by written materials that include clear guidelines on proper medication use, side-effects and complications.

Complications of injection treatments

27.61 Whenever injections are used in pain clinics there is potential for needle trauma particularly to nerves which are usually the target. Other risks include the injection of the wrong drug (systemic toxicity, nerve damage or arachnoiditis), introduction of infection (for example, into the spine: epidural abscess or meningitis), or bleeding which could cause a haematoma and pressure on nerves resulting in permanent damage. There are clear guidelines available to guide practitioners[1]. Recommendations for clinical practice include obtaining fully informed consent and the use of appropriate X-ray screening in more than one plane when injections are made into structures close to vulnerable nerves and vessels, eg around the spinal cord. Some pain treatments involve the application of electrical energy by the use of electrodes applied to the body and with these come the risk of electrical burns if they are inappropriately applied or excessive current is used.

1 BPS/RCoA. (2011). Recommendations for good practice in the use of epidural injection for the management of pain of spinal origin in adults. from www.britishpainsociety.org/booklet_rcoa_epidural.pdf.

Missed diagnosis, inadequate treatment of pain

27.62   Patients are usually referred to pain clinics for symptom control having had investigations in other departments or from the GP to exclude underlying severe pathology, such as prolapsed intervertebral disc or cancer in a patient presenting with spinal pain. A system of red flags alerts is in use to prompt questioning and reduce the risk of missed or incorrect diagnosis. For example, night-time back pain might indicate spinal metastases, and loss of sphincter control could indicate impending cauda equina syndrome: both of these require immediate active investigation and specific management rather than just symptom control. It is expected that competent clinicians working in the field of pain medicine will recognise and pursue causes for pain where appropriate.

Given that the treatment of chronic pain generally does not produce high levels of pain relief, it may be difficult to criticise individual chronic pain management approaches and strategies that prove to be ineffective. However there are some responsibilities inherent in caring for patients with chronic pain and protecting them from harm. For example, many patients presenting to pain clinics are highly distressed and the risk of deliberate self harm should be considered. Also inappropriate opioid drug regimes, even if commenced elsewhere, should be tackled perhaps by liaison with drug rehabilitation services.

Clinical practice is increasingly driven by guidelines, eg NICE[1]. Recommendations exist already for spinal cord stimulation, low back pain and osteoarthritis. The guidelines are intended to guide rational and equitable use of resources. However, they could also potentially be seen as providing a yardstick against which clinical practice is judged.

1 NICE. Guidelines. from http://guidance.nice.org.uk.

MEDICO LEGAL CONSIDERATIONS WITH CHRONIC PAIN CASES

Specific diagnosis of pain conditions versus outcome

27.63   It should be apparent that the impact and consequences of an injury in terms of chronic pain depend on many factors other than the nature and extent of the inciting injury. A specific medical diagnosis may satisfy a particular legal test but may make little difference to clinical management, eg in a patient with limb injury and neuropathic pain symptoms, the diagnosis of CRPS may provide a greater financial settlement over neuropathic pain. However, the medical management and clinical outcome do not necessarily differ.

Medical literature concerning chronic pain conditions is of limited value

27.64   There are many scientific studies of pain conditions but few of these will take into account the complexities and interactions of chronic pain problems that are generated by specific injury in particular patients. Results from individual studies may be misleading and they should be interpreted very carefully.

Consistency of evidence is critical

27.65 Consistency of evidence: history, physical examination and any other information is critical in determining the credibility of claims for compensation in cases involving chronic pain symptoms; all of the evidence must be very carefully assessed in context. In many patients who develop chronic pain after clinical negligence there will be elements of vulnerability or predisposition to developing chronic pain in any case: the effects of the clinical negligence can often be seen as an additional or trigger factor that precipitates or accelerates symptoms. It is usually the case that injury-related pain symptoms are more intrusive than pain symptoms generated by constitutional mechanisms.

Pain trajectory

27.66 The pain trajectory is a useful means of considering the likely non-injury course and progression of pain symptoms against what has actually happened. It is also useful to illustrate prognosis. Figure 4 demonstrates the course of a pain reaction after a simple acute injury.

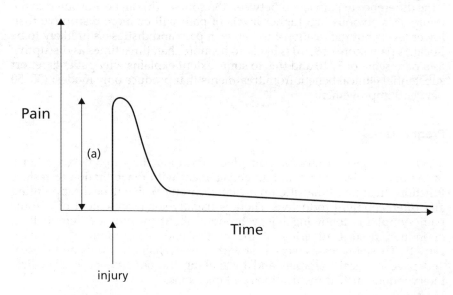

27.67 In a normal subject there is a modest rise in pain (a), with prompt and fairly complete resolution. Figure 6 demonstrates a pre-existing pain condition at a relatively low level but this predicts a greater absolute rise in pain (b), up to a higher level (c) with less prompt and less complete recovery (d). A further injury from this higher level will produce near maximal pain response (e) with even slower and less complete recovery (f).

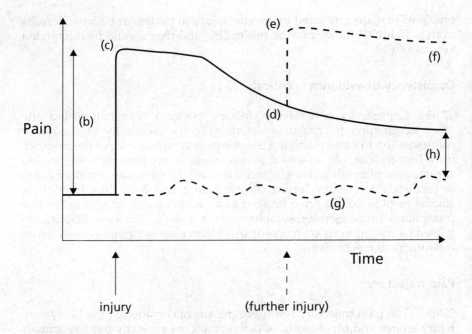

27.68 An estimate of what would have been the time course of pain symptoms absent the injury (g) allows an estimate of the effects of the injury – the difference in pain levels between the courses (h) can be attributed to the injury. It is obvious that higher levels of pain will be more disruptive than lower levels but the relationship between pain and distress is unlikely to be linear. A pain score of 9/10 is likely to be more than three times as disruptive as a pain score of 3/10 and this to some extent explains why patients report substantial clinical benefit from treatments that produce only modest (30–50 per cent) improvement.

Prognosis

27.69 Tolerance of chronic pain depends upon the subject's acceptance of the pain as permanent and an engagement with rehabilitation to restore function. Treatments that attempt to 'cure' chronic pain will be disappointing and often counter-productive. There is usually some settlement of chronic pain symptoms following injury brought about by physical remodelling of injured tissues, rewiring of the nerves and reprogramming of brain activity. These processes work best with active rehabilitation using physical and psychological therapies and by making the best use of any medical interventions such as medications and injections.

27.70 Litigation in cases of chronic pain that are a consequence of clinical negligence offers the claimant the prospect of financial remedy, improved resources for rehabilitation and closure but it is usually a stressful and challenging process to go through. It can have an adverse affect on the chronic pain condition by reiterating the history of events, delaying treatment and reinforcing the sense of loss. Therefore, prompt settlement of cases is clinically advantageous.

CHAPTER 28

Anaesthesia

Justin Turner

Dr Abdul Ghaaliq Lalkhen

SUMMARY

INTRODUCTION: SCOPE OF ANAESTHESIA

28.1   Anaesthetists form the largest single hospital medical speciality and whilst the perioperative anaesthetic management of the surgical patient is the core of the speciality's work and the content of this chapter, many anaesthetists have a much wider scope of practice, which may include:

- the preoperative preparation of surgical patients;
- the resuscitation and stabilisation of patients in the Emergency Department;
- pain relief in labour and obstetric anaesthesia;
- intensive care medicine;
- transport of acutely ill and injured patients;
- pre-hospital emergency care;
- pain medicine which includes the relief of post-operative pain, the management of acute pain teams and chronic and cancer pain management;
- the provision of sedation and anaesthesia for patients undergoing various procedures outside the operating theatre[1].

1 Royal College of Anaesthetists, 2014.

28.2   The word 'anaesthesia' means without the capacity for sensation or feeling. The purpose of an anaesthetic is to enable the patient to have a surgical procedure without experiencing pain and at the same time provide relaxation to the muscles sufficient to allow the surgeon to perform a successful operation whilst maintaining the vital functions of the body as close to normal as possible (homeostatsis). The effects of an anaesthetic should be transient and there should be no long-term consequence.

28.3   Surgery can be performed under general anaesthesia where the patient is rendered unconscious by medication in a controlled and reversible manner or regional anaesthesia where only one part of the body is anaesthetised by using local anaesthetic to prevent transmission of nerve signals thus providing numbness and loss of muscle power.

28.4   There are surgical procedures where it is possible to use either of the techniques above and for other procedures a combination of general and regional anaesthesia may be advantageous.

ANAESTHESIA AND THE LEGAL PROCESS

28.5 Medicolegal cases arising from untoward incidents during anaesthesia form a significant proportion of claims handled by Trusts, health authorities and medical defence organisations in both the NHS and the private sector. An analysis of claims of the National Health Service Litigation Authority (NHLSA) by Cook et al[1] found that one in 40 claims are related to anaesthesia and anaesthetists are among the specialists who have faced charges of involuntary manslaughter related to their clinical practice[2].

1 Cook, Bland, Mihai and Scott 'Litigation related to anaesthesia: an analysis of claims against the NHS in England 1995–2007' (2009) 64(7) Anaesthesia 706–718.
2 Ferner and McDowell 'Doctors charged with manslaughter in the course of medical practice, 1795–2005: a literature review' (2006) 99(6) Jnl Royal Society of Medicine 309–314.

28.6 The Medical Protection Society opened 300 files in 2011 relating to anaesthetists: 12 per cent were due to negligence claims, 10 per cent disciplinary and GMC issues, 16 per cent were complaints about patient care, 13 per cent coroner's' inquests and 26 per cent adverse events[1].

1 Adams, Bell and Bodenham 'Quality and outcomes in anaesthesia: lessons from litigation' (2012) 109(1) British Journal of Anaesthesia 110–122.

ASSESSING THE STANDARDS OF ANAESTHETIC PRACTICE

28.7 Assessment of the standards of care in anaesthesia can be performed against professional standards. Guidance on the conduct, evidence and quality of care for all doctors is provided by the General Medical Council as well as the National Institute for Health and Care Excellence (NICE), the Care Quality Commission and the Medicines and Healthcare products Regulatory Agency (MHRA).

28.8 Guidance specific to the provision of anaesthetic care is provided by two main organisations: the Royal College of Anaesthetists (RCOA) and the Association of Anaesthetists of Great Britain and Ireland (AAGBI). The RCOA is the professional body responsible for the speciality of anaesthesia throughout the UK. Its principal responsibility is to ensure the quality of patient care through the maintenance of standards in anaesthesia, pain medicine and intensive care. The College's activities include:

- setting standards of clinical care;
- establishing the standards for the training of anaesthetists and those practising critical care and/or acute and chronic pain medicine;
- setting and running examinations;
- continued medical education of all practising anaesthetists.

28.9 The AAGBI provides advice on clinical management of specific clinical problems faced by the anaesthetist. Both organisations provide guidance documents for the individual anaesthetist and anaesthetic departments. These documents also provide a professional standard to which specific patient care can be compared.

28.10   The courts can be assisted by an expert witness when assessing the standard of anaesthetic care. Anaesthesia, as with many other specialities of medicine, has increasingly divided into subspecialities. Some anaesthetic areas of practice are generic, such as airway management, whilst other areas, for example anaesthetic management for a caesarean section (which is the domain of the obstetric anaesthetist), require greater practical knowledge of this subspeciality of anaesthesia. An expert involved in routine patient care in that subspeciality may be better placed to provide the required expert opinion.

OVERVIEW OF POTENTIAL HARM DURING ANAESTHETIC CARE

28.11   The commonest type of injury that may result in a medico-legal claim against an anaesthetist is dental damage. The injury tends to be minor and the cost of repair small[1]. These claims are often dealt with at a Hospital Trust level without insurer involvement.

1 Aitkenhead 'Injuries associated with anaesthesia. A global perspective' (2005) 95(1) British Journal of Anaesthesia 95–109.

28.12   Serious permanent injury related to anaesthesia is rare. The most common serious injuries sustained are neurological injury including brain injury and death[1].

1 Cook, Bland, Mihai and Scott 'Litigation related to anaesthesia: an analysis of claims against the NHS in England 1995–2007' (2009) 64(7) Anaesthesia 706–718; Hove, Nielsen and Christoffersen 'Patient injuries in response to anaesthetic procedures: cases evaluated by the Danish Patient Insurance Association' (2006) 50(5) Acta Anaesthesiologica Scandinavica 530–535; Staender (et al) 'A Swiss anesthesiology closed claims analysis: report of events in the years 1987–2008' (2011) 28(2) European Journal of Anesthesiology 85–91.

28.13   Psychological injury related to anaesthesia is most commonly associated with failure of the anaesthetic technique leading to awareness during a general anaesthetic, and pain when using a regional anaesthetic.

CONSENT

28.14   Consent in anaesthetics is unusual because anaesthesia facilitates the patient having their surgery and is not therefore therapeutic.

28.15   The patient will have seen a surgeon who will assess the need for surgery and discuss the associated risks and benefits of the proposed procedure within their expertise and in accordance with their speciality.

28.16   Many patients will meet an anaesthetist for the first time on the day of surgery and may therefore have less time to consider the benefits and risk of the available anaesthetic options. It is considered poor practice, however, for the first meeting with the anaesthetic team to be in the anaesthetic room, and it is unacceptable to provide new information to patients undergoing elective surgery in the anaesthetic room[1].

1 Bogod 'Consent for Anaesthesia Revised Edition' (2006), AAGBI.

28.17   It is not currently necessary to have a separate consent for the procedure and the anaesthetic but it is necessary to have all discussion of anaesthetic technique and associated risk recorded in the patient's notes[1].

1 Bogod 'Consent for Anaesthesia Revised Edition' (2006), AAGBI.

Issues surrounding consent

Emergency surgery

28.18   Surgery is performed when the benefits of immediate surgery outweigh the risks. Preoperative assessment should be to the same standard as surgery for elective care. It is unlikely in the case of emergency surgery that patients will reject surgery based on anaesthetic risk. Whilst it is possible that patient preference may influence the choice of anaesthetic, this is less likely for the majority of emergency surgery due to the clinical constraints of the situation. Expert opinion would be required to comment on a discussion of anaesthetic risk and benefit compared to risks to the patient of not proceeding with surgery.

Elective anaesthesia

28.19   Patients undergoing elective surgery would be expected to attend a preoperative assessment which is usually nurse-led[1]. This is an opportunity to provide information about anaesthesia in general and if appropriate specific for the procedure. It is expected that information on serious risk is provided in a written format[2]. Patients should have the opportunity to see their anaesthetist on the day of surgery to discuss any questions they have and to discuss the plans for their anaesthetic. The discussions should be documented.

1 Royal College of Anaesthetists Structure, Organisation and Regulations (2014), available at: www.rcoa.ac.uk/about-the-college/structure-organisation-and-regulations.
2 Association of Anaesthetists of Great Britain and Ireland *Recommendations for Standards of Monitoring during Anaesthesia and Recovery* (revised edition, 2007).

Elective anaesthesia in a higher-risk patient

28.20   Increasingly it is recognised that for elective surgery in patients with significant co-morbidities and a greater than 1 in 100 risk of dying, it is appropriate for them to be seen in a preoperative clinic by an anaesthetist[1]. This allows a discussion about the relative risk and benefit of the anaesthetic technique to take place. The risks of complications from proceeding with surgery in the face of medical comorbidity can also be discussed from an anaesthetic perspective.

1 Royal College of Anaesthetists Structure, Organisation and Regulations (2014), available at: www.rcoa.ac.uk/about-the-college/structure-organisation-and-regulations.

28.21   Failure to provide this level of information preoperatively may represent a failure to provide sufficient information to the patient about the predictable risks of anaesthesia and surgery for that individual.

STANDARDS OF MONITORING

28.22 There is on-going development of a wide range of instruments capable of monitoring physiological change in response to surgery and anaesthesia as well as the delivery of the anaesthetic.

The development of improved alarms for ventilators has led to reductions in the number and severity of injuries caused by disconnection from the ventilator and ventilator failures[1].

1 Mehta, Eisenkraft, Posner and Domino 'Patient injuries from anesthesia gas delivery equipment: a closed claims update' (2013) 119(4) Anesthesiology 788–795.

28.23 The use of monitors may vary based on several factors including ignorance of the technology, unwillingness to change on the part of the anaesthetist or the hospital, the availability of equipment and the ease of use.

These factors led to the development of standards of monitoring by the AAGBI[1].

1 Association of Anaesthetists of Great Britain and Ireland *Recommendations for Standards of Monitoring during Anaesthesia and Recovery* (revised edition, 2007).

28.24 The drawing up of standards for minimum monitoring introduces the question of whether a practitioner who falls below the standards is negligent. The standard published by the AAGBI is widely accepted in the UK and there is an expectation that anaesthetic services meet the set standards of monitoring[1]. Claims of negligence would be difficult to defend if the standard was not observed.

1 Royal College of Anaesthetists Structure, Organisation and Regulations (2014), available at: www.rcoa.ac.uk/about-the-college/structure-organisation-and-regulations.

28.25 Currently the minimum levels of monitoring during surgery include:

(1) the continued presence and vigilance of the anaesthetist;
(2) pulse oximetry;
(3) electrocardiography;
(4) eon-invasive blood pressure monitoring;
(5) airway gas monitor for oxygen, carbon dioxide and anaesthetic gases;
(6) airway pressure monitoring.

28.26 The use of monitoring is dependent on the clinical case. Invasive blood pressure monitoring is now commonly used in the perioperative period because it enables continuous blood pressure monitoring as well as blood gas analysis in the sick patient.

ANAESTHETIC TRAINING

28.27 The training programme for anaesthetists consists of basic (two years), intermediate (two years), higher level (two years) and advanced (one year) training. Trainees are supervised to varying degrees depending on their experience and ability.

28.28   Anaesthetists of varying experience often work alone without direct supervision as a result of the number of clinical areas (emergency departments, wards, critical care etc) in which anaesthetists are needed. The political agenda is the provision of care by specialist doctors and it is beginning to be generally accepted that out-of-hours care, which was traditionally delivered by trainees, should now be delivered directly by specialist doctors including consultants, particularly in complex cases. The question of responsibility is important from a medico-legal point of view. All qualified doctors are personally responsible for their own individual clinical actions and they are expected to seek advice about problems outside their experience. The employer is expected to provide this senior assistance as the need arises and it is therefore incumbent on a department of anaesthetics to arrange its cover in such a way that there is immediate availability of senior help. All anaesthetists should only be asked to undertake what is within their own declared range of responsibility; they should have access at all times to senior help (for example a named consultant responsible for a trainee undertaking a solo list); and they should realise that they act on their own if they do not seek advice on matters outside their experience. No lowering of professional standards can be made if delegation of duties was appropriate and advice was readily available.

FAILURE TO ACHIEVE THE GOALS OF A GA TECHNIQUE: AWARENESS

28.29   General anaesthesia is usually maintained by the continuous administration of an anaesthetic vapour (which is inhaled) or a continuous infusion of an intravenous drug, usually propofol. Pain relief may be administered in the form of a potent opiate which may be given intravenously as a continuous infusion or more often as a bolus injection with both techniques. A muscle relaxant can be used to provide paralysis in order to enable optimal conditions for airway management and surgery.

Awareness

28.30   Awareness is defined as the explicit recall of events during general anaesthesia. The purpose of a general anaesthetic is to render the patient unconscious for the duration of their surgery. If a patient has clear recall of their surgery then there has been a failure in the standard of their care.

28.31   The interpretation of the alleged episode as awareness must be made with caution. Dreaming is not uncommon during anaesthesia but the content of a dream does not relate to any actual events taking place at the time.

28.32   Awareness under general anaesthesia must be differentiated from patients undergoing a procedure with sedation. Due to the hypnotic properties of the drugs used, many patients having sedation may have no memory of surgery. Sedation is administered to relax the patient during surgery, the primary goal being that verbal contact with the patient is still maintained. Memory of being in the operating theatre is therefore to be expected and this cannot be classified as awareness. There may be issues of consent if the patient did not want to be awake[1]. If the patient has pain during a procedure under sedation and this is not then acted upon, then the standard of care maybe below that which is accepted.

1 Kent, Mashour (et al) 'Psychological impact of unexpected explicit recall of events occurring during surgery performed under sedation, regional anaesthesia, and general anaesthesia: data from the Anesthesia Awareness Registry' (2013) 110(3) British Journal of Anaesthesia 381–387.

28.33 Awareness under general anaesthesia is relatively uncommon and research estimates vary, with the largest study based on a national audit in the UK quoting a risk of 1 in 15,400[1].

1 Pandit, Cook, Jonker and O'Sullivan 'A national survey of anaesthetists (NAP5 Baseline) to estimate an annual incidence of accidental awareness during general anaesthesia in the UK' (2013) 68(4) Anaesthesia 343–353.

28.34 Awareness can be divided into that which occurs during the dynamic phases of anaesthesia which are induction and emergence (awakening) at the end of surgery (less likely to be associated with pain and distress), and the other being during surgery with a greater risk of pain and distress[1].

1 Pandit, Cook, Jonker and O'Sullivan 'A national survey of anaesthetists (NAP5 Baseline) to estimate an annual incidence of accidental awareness during general anaesthesia in the UK' (2013) 68(4) Anaesthesia 343–353.

28.35 If sufficient time is allowed for the induction of anaesthesia and appropriate medication is administered, then it should be possible to avoid awareness at induction. Consideration would, however, have to be given to the urgency of the clinical situation and the stability of the patient because lower doses of induction agent and a slight risk of awareness may be preferable to larger drops in blood pressure in an unstable patient. The expert witness would have to consider the appropriateness of the drugs used and the dosage given in assessing whether these were within normal dose limits for the specific patient. The order in which drugs are given is of importance, because if the muscle relaxant has been given before a hypnotic anaesthetic drug then this represents error (the patient would be paralysed but still awake).

28.36 Awareness during the dynamic phase of emergence refers to the recall of events after surgery has finished but the patient is not fully awake, for example recall of an airway device still in place or being moved back to a bed. At this stage the anaesthetic has been ceased and full recovery is expected within minutes. As the anaesthetic agents have been stopped and their effects will wear off, it could be reasonably argued that recall was a rare but unavoidable event. If, however, the claimant remembered a part of the end of the surgical procedure which they should have no recall of, such as the stitches being inserted to the skin, this would not be acceptable.

28.37 Awareness during surgery can include the sensation of pain, being paralysed and therefore unable to move. These experiences are more likely to cause distress and psychological problems, for example post-traumatic stress disorder (PTSD), and also result in litigation[1].

1 Pandit, Cook, Jonker and O'Sullivan 'A national survey of anaesthetists (NAP5 Baseline) to estimate an annual incidence of accidental awareness during general anaesthesia in the UK' (2013) 68(4) Anaesthesia 343–353.

28.38   The symptoms of PTSD in awareness can be divided into three groups[1]:

(1)   experiencing/recalling the events either as flashbacks or nightmares;
(2)   physiological hyperarousal such as anxiety or irritability;
(3)   avoidance, such as avoidance of hospitals or doctors.

1 Ghoneim 'The trauma of awareness: history, clinical features, risk factors, and cost' (2010) 110(3) Anesthesia and Analgesia 666–667.

Causes of awareness

28.39   Awareness during surgery results from a failure to provide sufficient anaesthetic drugs to maintain an unconscious state.

The choice of drugs used for an anaesthetic may be dictated by the operation and certain drugs are associated with a greater risk of awareness. The use of a muscle relaxant is associated with a greater risk of awareness as is the use of continuous infusion of intravenous anaesthetic rather than an anaesthetic vapour. Electing to run a 'light' or low dose anaesthetic may be acceptable during haemodynamic instability (for example emergency surgery) but this would not be reasonable for the majority of cases and may result in awareness[1].

1 Ghoneim, Block, Haffarnan and Mathews 'Awareness during anesthesia: risk factors, causes and sequelae: a review of reported cases in the literature' (2009) 108(2) Anesthesia and Analgesia 527–535.

Equipment failure may lead to insufficient drug delivery

28.40   Minimum standards of monitoring require continuous monitoring of anaesthetic vapour[1]. Awareness with inhalational anaesthesia may be due to failure to turn the anaesthetic vaporiser on, or an empty vaporiser, or a leak in the circuit[2].

1 Association of Anaesthetists of Great Britain and Ireland *Recommendations for Standards of Monitoring during Anaesthesia and Recovery* (revised edition, 2007).
2 Mehta, Eisenkraft, Posner and Domino 'Patient injuries from anesthesia gas delivery equipment: a closed claims update' (2013) 119(4) Anesthesiology 788–795.

28.41   Intravenous anaesthesia is associated with a greater risk of awareness. It is not possible to monitor the actual delivered dose in a way that is similar to inhalational agents, and drug delivery is based on mathematical models drawing on weight, height and age. Disconnections of the intravenous line are possible resulting in no anaesthetic being delivered and it is advised that the cannula site is regularly checked to minimise this risk[1].

1 Anderson, Bythell (et al) 'Checking Anaesthetic Equipment 2012' (2012) 67(6) Anaesthesia 660–668.

Monitoring to prevent awareness

28.42   The anaesthetist may observe clinical signs as an indicator of awareness: a raised heart rate, raised blood pressure, sweating and lacrimation are all associated with increased arousal and awareness.

28.43 Minimum standards of monitoring for inhalational anaesthetic require continuous monitoring of anaesthetic vapour concentration[1], which differs for each agent; however a minimum alveolar concentration (MAC) is defined for each gas. A recorded MAC above 0.5 to 0.8 would be expected to prevent awareness[2].

1 Association of Anaesthetists of Great Britain and Ireland *Recommendations for Standards of Monitoring during Anaesthesia and Recovery* (London, The Association of Anaesthetists of Great Britain and Ireland, revised edition, 2007).
2 Mashour (et al) 'Prevention of intraoperative awareness with explicit recall in an unselected surgical population: a randomized comparative effectiveness trial' (2012) 117(4) Anesthesiology 717–725; Avidan (et al) 'Prevention of intraoperative awareness in a high-risk surgical population' (2011) 365(7) New England Journal of Medicine 591–600.

28.44 Brain function, in the form of electrical activity, can be monitored using an electroencephalogram (EEG). EEG activity is used as a marker of depth of anaesthesia. A common system currently used is Bispectral Index (BIS – an EEG monitor) which in total intravenous anaesthetic can reduce the risk of awareness. This is not the case in patients receiving inhaled anaesthesia, where close monitoring of the anaesthetic vapour concentration is as effective[1]. Routine use of awareness monitors is currently not part of day-to-day practice in the UK[2]. NICE[3] stated that in patients receiving a total intravenous anaesthetic the use of awareness monitoring is cost effective. Awareness in this group of patients, in the absence of an awareness EEG monitor, would be difficult to defend.

1 Avidan (et al) 'Prevention of intraoperative awareness in a high-risk surgical population' (2011) 365(7) New England Journal of Medicine 591–600.
2 Pandit, Cook, Jonker and O'Sullivan 'A national survey of anaesthetists (NAP5 Baseline) to estimate an annual incidence of accidental awareness during general anaesthesia in the UK' (2013) 68(4) Anaesthesia 343–353.
3 *NICE Diagnostics Guidance: Depth of anaesthesia monitors – Bispectral index (BIS), E-Entropy and Narcotrend Compact M* (2012).

Investigation of awareness

28.45 A report of awareness should be reviewed by a senior anaesthetist and a record of the patient's experience of awareness should be made. It may be possible to corroborate specific details they recall. An explanation of the cause of the awareness should be given. It is good practice to offer to meet the patient again if they have further questions. In view of the risk of distress and PTSD, consideration should be given to offering psychological support to the patient. Failure to offer support following a case of awareness would not be acceptable.

FAILURE TO MANAGE THE AIRWAY INCLUDING INAPPROPRIATE TECHNIQUE OR DEVIATION FROM GUIDELINES

28.46 General anaesthesia leads to a loss of control of the airway for the patient, the risk being that the airway can become obstructed, which can rapidly lead to hypoxia: the consequence of profound hypoxia is brain damage or death.

The other area of risk to a patient undergoing general anaesthesia is aspiration. The patient will have no airway reflexes to protect them from aspirating fluid, which can either be regurgitated stomach contents or blood. Aspiration then leads to a chemical inflammation of the lungs (pneumonitis) which in severe cases can lead to prolonged intensive care admission or death.

It is a core skill, therefore, for the anaesthetist to be able to control and protect the airway.

28.47   Maintenance of a patent's airway is obtained by the use of airway devices of which the most common forms are:

- a face mask held in place by the anaesthetist;
- a laryngeal mask (LMA) which is positioned in the upper airway above the vocal cords (supraglottic). The LMA causes less airway irritation than an endotracheal tube and is the most common form of airway device used during anaesthesia but does not protect against aspiration of stomach contents[1];
- an endotracheal tube is passed through the vocal cords into the trachea which allows greater control of the airway with protection against aspiration. It is, however, more irritating to the airway and usually requires a muscle relaxant to be administered as part of the anaesthetic.

1 Cook (et al) on behalf of the Fourth National Audit Project 2011, 'Major complications of airway management in the UK: results of the Fourth National Audit Project of the Royal College of Anaesthetists and the Difficult Airway Society. Part 1: Anaesthesia' (2011) 106(5) British Journal of Anaesthesia 617–631.

28.48   The 4th National Audit of the Royal College of Anaesthetists[1] was a prospective audit of all major airway complications in the UK with the aim of determining the incidence of major airway problems. The Audit found that common themes that contributed to serious airway complications were:

- poor airway assessment;
- poor planning;
- failure to plan for failure to secure the airway;
- repeated attempts at a technique which had already failed;
- use of a supraglottic device in an inappropriate clinical setting.

1 Cook (et al) on behalf of the Fourth National Audit Project 2011, 'Major complications of airway management in the UK: results of the Fourth National Audit Project of the Royal College of Anaesthetists and the Difficult Airway Society. Part 1: Anaesthesia' (2011) 106(5) British Journal of Anaesthesia 617–631.

Airway assessment

28.49   Assessment of the airway is one goal of the preoperative visit. There is no specific test that allows the anaesthetist to predict accurately in all patients the risk of airway difficulties[1]. There are, however, many factors that can be taken into account which guide the anaesthetist's choices in airway management.

1 Shiga, Wajima, Inoue and Sakamoto 'Predicting difficult intubation in apparently normal patients: a meta-analysis of bedside screening test performance' (2005) 103(2) Anesthesiology 429–437.

28.50   Patient factors include obesity, which is the commonest contributing factor to problems in airway management, impacting on all parts of airway management during the hospital stay. Elective surgery patients with a Body Mass Index greater than 40 should have a review by an anaesthetist[1].

Other patient factors that can be assessed include gastroesophageal reflux, dentition, mouth opening, and neck size

1 Cook (et al) on behalf of the Fourth National Audit Project 2011, 'Major complications of airway management in the UK: results of the Fourth National Audit Project of the Royal College of Anaesthetists and the Difficult Airway Society. Part 1: Anaesthesia' (2011) 106(5) British Journal of Anaesthesia 617–631.

28.51   If the patient has had previous anaesthetics there is the opportunity to review those records including the airway management at that time, but this may not be practical for emergency surgery. If there have been significant difficulties in airway management previously both the patient and their GP should have been informed of the risks with regard to the patient's airway. It would be difficult to defend the failure to provide clinically important information that would inform the choice for both the patient and anaesthetist. Advice on the information to be provided is available from The Difficult Airway Society.

28.52   Surgical pathology affecting the airway represents a group with significant risk in the perioperative period and should be thoroughly assessed prior to surgery.

28.53   The most appropriate method of protecting the airway is judged on a combination of factors including patient factors (obesity, history of reflux, when the patient last ate, pregnancy) and surgical factors (type of operation, patient position, duration of the surgery).

28.54   The choices an anaesthetist can consider to protect the airway are:

- avoidance of a general anaesthetic by using a regional technique. This has become the preferred option for women undergoing caesarean section;
- an 'awake intubation' refers to the technique whereby local anaesthetic is used to numb the upper airway and the patient is intubated whilst still awake and able to control their own breathing. This is used when there is concern that control of the airway may present a significant challenge;
- rapid sequence induction refers to a technique whereby pressure is applied to the cricoid cartilage to help prevent regurgitation on induction and therefore aims to minimise the risk of aspiration prior to intubation;
- routine intubation which is performed for most patients requiring intubation;
- insertion of a laryngeal mask;
- use of a facemask which is practical only for procedures of short duration.

28.55   It may be impossible to secure the airway in some patients due to gross abnormalities, for example, of the upper airway due to tumours. This group of patients may need an awake tracheostomy where a surgical incision is made in the trachea usually by an ear, nose and throat surgeon.

Medico-legal claims against the anaesthetist with respect to airway management arise as a result of failure to choose an appropriate technique, damage caused by the technique employed or failure to maintain an adequate airway:

- dental damage;
- failure to intubate and failure to ventilate leading to hypoxia and organ damage;
- no rapid sequence induction despite indications leading to aspiration.

DENTAL DAMAGE

28.56 Damage and displacement of teeth accounts for a large number of claims against anaesthetists and in most cases is preventable.

The teeth at greatest risk are the upper incisors and canines. Teeth with caps or crowns and those in poor condition are particularly at risk. The consensus expert opinion is that to damage teeth is generally below an acceptable level of practice.

The commonest cause of damage is due to the laryngoscope blade and teeth can be chipped, broken or dislodged. Any oral airway device can also cause dental damage.

28.57 Assessment of dentition and dental work should be recorded preoperatively and a discussion of dental risk recorded.

28.58 There would be a defence for causing dental damage in an emergency where there is an urgent need to obtain a protected airway to allow oxygenation and prevent more serious injury. This would not be the case in any planned procedure.

28.59 A plastic protector (gum guard) can be placed over the teeth to give added protection during intubation (the process where a laryngoscope is used to allow the vocal cords to be visualised so that the endotracheal tube can be placed correctly). Dental damage is often caused when the upper teeth become an inadvertent fulcrum for the laryngoscope blade. In patients who have had significant dental work, dental damage can also occur at the point of emergence from anaesthesia. This is caused by biting on the oral airway. Dental damage at this point can be avoided by the use of a soft bite block, extubation during deep anaesthesia or use of a nasal airway.

28.60 There is no defence for not noticing dental damage and if a tooth or crown is lost then it must be located and retrieved, if necessary, with a bronchoscope. Teeth are difficult to see on a chest radiograph so an apparently clear film does not exclude the presence of a tooth.

If a tooth has been displaced then a dental opinion should be obtained and consideration should be given to whether re-implantation is possible.

28.61 Due to the frequency of dental damage and the relatively low cost of the claims, many hospital anaesthetic and legal departments will have a policy for dealing with the patient with dental damage. A patient suffering dental damage during an anaesthetic should be given advice on how to remedy the problem.

Failure to intubate or failure to ventilate

28.62   The inability to intubate the trachea and ventilate the lungs of a patient can lead rapidly to hypoxia and serious harm in the form of organ damage. Allowing the patient to breathe a high concentration of oxygen (100 per cent) prior to starting the anaesthetic will allow a greater length of time to secure the airway before harm can occur.

28.63   Assessment of the airway prior to the induction of anaesthesia may enable difficulties in airway management to be anticipated in some but not all patients. It is important in these cases to choose the most appropriate technique for airway management and also to have back up plans prepared in case the initial plan is unsuccessful.

28.64   The best practice in all patients where intubation fails is to follow a set algorithm for airway management. If it is also impossible to ventilate the patient a rescue 'can't intubate, can't ventilate' algorithm needs to be followed[1]. It would be difficult to defend a case in which these or similar guidelines were not followed.

1 Henderson 'Difficult Airway Society guidelines for management of the unanticipated difficult intubation' (2004) 59(7) Anaesthesia 675–694.

28.65   The 4th National Audit Project by the Royal College of Anaesthetists found that in cases of difficult intubation the course of action followed was repeated attempts at the procedure which had already failed. The consequence of this strategy is airway swelling and the loss of the ability to ventilate. Repeated attempts with a failed technique would not be an acceptable standard of care.

28.66   Airway difficulties can also occur during extubation which are often minor but can lead to hypoxic brain injury or death. It is important therefore that a structured plan is also put in place for extubation[1].

1 Popat 'Difficult Airway Society guidelines for the management of tracheal extubation' (2012) 67(3) Anaesthesia 318–340.

No rapid sequence despite indications leading to aspiration

28.67   Aspiration is the commonest cause of death due to anaesthesia. Whilst aspiration can occur in low-risk patients, the majority occur in patients with known risk factors for regurgitation and aspiration[1].

1 Cook (et al) on behalf of the Fourth National Audit Project 2011, 'Major complications of airway management in the UK: results of the Fourth National Audit Project of the Royal College of Anaesthetists and the Difficult Airway Society. Part 1: Anaesthesia' (2011) 106(5) British Journal of Anaesthesia 617–631; Kluger and Short 'Aspiration during anaesthesia: a review of 133 cases from the Australian Anaesthetic Incident Monitoring Study (AIMS)' (1999) 54(1) Anaesthesia 19–26.

28.68   It is important to consider the choice of airway device, the use of rapid sequence induction and the conduct of extubation in patients with known risk factors for aspiration.

28.69   The use of an endotracheal tube with a cuff provides the greatest protection against aspiration and should therefore be the airway of choice for the patient at risk of aspiration. The laryngeal mask airway offers protection from upper airway secretions and some devices have a suction port to aspirate stomach contents. The laryngeal mask airway does not allow the same degree of protection as an endotracheal tube. The use of this device in a patient with known risk factors for aspiration would not be considered the safest option and would be subject to significant criticism.

28.70   Rapid sequence induction is used in patients with a high risk of aspiration at induction; the definition of who is at high risk would be a matter of opinion. Rapid sequence induction includes the use of cricoid pressure, this is pressure on the cricoid cartilage to produce an occlusion of the oesophagus and prevent regurgitation. The use of cricoid pressure can cause worsening of the view for intubation and so make intubation potentially more difficult; this has led to debate as to whether to continue this practice[1]. NAP 4 suggests that cricoid pressure should still be used and would be considered best practice for patients with significant risk of aspiration.

1 El-Orbany and Connolly 'Rapid sequence induction and intubation: current controversy' (2010) 110(5) Anesthesia and Analgesia 1318–1325.

28.71   Aspiration of gastric content or blood from surgery can also occur at extubation. The plan for extubation should make provision for minimising the possibility of aspiration in patients at risk. The patient should be awake and able to protect their own airway prior to extubation; suction should be used to clear any secretions in the upper airway and consideration should be given as to whether the stomach should be emptied using a nasogastric tube.

COMPLICATIONS OF REGIONAL TECHNIQUES USED TO FACILITATE ANAESTHESIA SUBSEQUENT TO DEVIATION FROM CURRENT STANDARDS

28.72   Regional anaesthesia refers to the process of anaesthetising an area of the body by blocking nerve transmission. Local anaesthetics act by blocking the electrical channels which facilitate nerve transmission.

The types of block that can be used include:

- an epidural where local anaesthetic is infused via a catheter (small plastic tube) which is placed in the epidural space (between the dura and the surrounding vertebrae). The infusion allows prolonged usage during labour or after surgery;
- a spinal block is where local anaesthetic is injected into the cerebrospinal fluid that surrounds the spinal cord. This is a single injection which is often faster onset than an epidural. It is commonly used for surgery of the lower limb and caesarean section;

- epidural and spinal blocks are combined in the term central neuraxial blockade;
- peripheral nerve blockade is where a group of nerves such as the brachial plexus which supply the arm or a single nerve, such as the ulnar nerve which supplies part of the hand, are targeted and local anaesthetic injected around the nerve.

28.73   Medico-legal claims may arise from patients experiencing pain during surgery despite having had a regional anaesthetic or from complications of regional anaesthesia subsequent to deviations from current standards.

28.74   General advantages to a regional technique compared with general anaesthesia may include: improved patient satisfaction and less post-operative cognitive dysfunction (especially in the elderly), less immunosuppression and a decreased incidence of nausea and vomiting as well as being an alternative for patients who are too ill to tolerate general anaesthesia. Additional benefits of central neuraxial blockade (CNB) include: decreased blood loss; improved mobility following major knee surgery; reduced incidence of deep vein thrombosis and superior pain control in the immediate post-operative period.

Pain during a procedure under a regional technique

28.75   Pain during a procedure under a regional technique is similar to awareness in an inappropriately managed general anaesthetic. Inadequate analgesia after a regional block should receive immediate attention, which might include giving additional local anaesthetic, performing a new block, or conversion to general anaesthesia. All local anaesthetic blocks have a risk of failure and this should be explained as part of the consent process. If a recognised technique has been used, the failure of a block can be defended. Failure to follow a recognised series of strategies to provide a pain-free procedure in the face of a clear lack of efficacy of the regional technique is unacceptable.

An example of the above situation is that of an epidural block used for labour analgesia and which is then used as the anaesthetic technique to perform a caesarean section.

28.76   Prior to a shift on the labour ward all running epidurals should be assessed in terms of their effectiveness. Action should be taken early to rectify unsatisfactory epidurals. An epidural at high risk of failure is one that has required unscheduled additions of local anaesthetic[1]. If the patient needs a caesarean section the epidural should be topped up (local anaesthetic added) in the labour room prior to moving to theatre. Prior to surgery starting the anaesthetist must ensure and document that the patient cannot feel cold and light touch from T4 (around the nipple line) and T5 to down to S5 (the perianal area) with a good motor block[2].

If the epidural block is inadequate and surgery can be safely delayed, a spinal block can be performed. If surgery cannot be delayed the patient has to have a general anaesthetic.

1 Halpern, Soliman, Yee, Angle and Loscovich 'Conversion of epidural labour analgesia to anaesthesia for Caesarean section: a prospective study of the incidence and determinants of failure' (2009) 102(2) British Journal of Anaesthesia 240–243.
2 Russell 'A comparison of cold, pinprick and touch for assessing the level of spinal block at caesarean section', (2004) 13(3) International Journal of Obstetric Anesthesia 146–152.

28.77   If the patient experiences pain during surgery the anaesthetist has to ask about the nature of the pain. Discomfort, pulling or pressure is not necessarily indicative of an inadequate anaesthetic but a sharp pain is and surgery should be stopped. The patient may be given an inhaled analgesic (entonox) and/or further local anaesthetic added to the epidural. If the patient still continues to experience pain a general anaesthetic should be offered (guidelines are available through the Obstetric Anaesthetists Association).

28.78   Similar principles apply to a peripheral nerve block where, for example, a hand or leg is anaesthetised. The block is checked prior to surgery starting using light touch or cold and the degree of anaesthesia recorded. If the patient experiences pain during surgery a documented stepwise approach should be followed to render the patient pain free.

Complications

28.79   The decision to perform a regional technique is based on a risk benefit assessment of the individual patient and the planned surgery. Deviations from the recommendations of practice guidelines may be acceptable based on the judgment of the responsible anaesthetist. According to the American Society of Regional Anaesthetists (2013) the aim of practice guidelines are to summarise evidence-based reviews and consensus statements and are designed to encourage safe and quality patient care. Following these guidelines, however, does not guarantee a specific outcome and they evolve as a result of new scientific evidence. The issues highlighted below represent important areas of practice and potential injury.

28.80   A national patient safety initiative called Stop Before You Block under the auspices of the RCOA is aimed at reducing the incidence of inadvertent wrong-sided nerve block during regional anaesthesia[1].

1 Adyanthaya, SS & Patil, V 2014, 'Never events: an anaesthetic perspective', *Continuing Education in Anaesthesia, Critical Care & Pain*, pp 55.

Limiting nerve injury in central neuraxial blockade (CNB)

28.81   Spinal cord injury is a significant concern in CNB (4.2 per 100,000 according to NAP 3). The spinal cord may be damaged as a result of compression by a blood clot and CNB is generally contraindicated in patients who have bleeding disorders or who are anti-coagulated. The prevention of deep vein thrombosis following surgery is a major cause of perioperative morbidity and mortality and patients are often given anticoagulants before or after surgery. Policies regarding the timing of administration of these drugs have to be agreed locally to facilitate safe CNB.

An epidural abscess compressing the spinal cord may develop where needle placement is made during an untreated active infection or where an improper aseptic technique is used.

28.82 Optimum aseptic technique for CNB requires the use of barrier precautions, which include: hand washing with surgical scrub solution; the wearing of a cap, mask, sterile gown and gloves; and the use of a large sterile drape. It is recognised that any substance which kills bacteria is potentially harmful to nerves, and chlorhexidine was implicated in a case of arachnoiditis following CNB as a result of contamination of the equipment with this substance. The anaesthetist must therefore be meticulous in taking measures to prevent chlorhexidine from reaching the cerebrospinal fluid, including keeping it away from the drugs and equipment to be used and allowing the solution to dry before the skin is palpated or punctured[1].

1 Cook, Bland, Mihai and Scott 'Litigation related to anaesthesia: an analysis of claims against the NHS in England 1995–2007' (2009) 64(7) Anaesthesia 706–718; AAGBI Draft Guidelines 2014; Checketts 'Wash & go – but with what? Skin antiseptic solutions for central neuraxial block' (2012) 67(8) Anaesthesia 819–822.

28.83 CNB should be performed in adult patients who are awake and can report pain during the procedure, even though there is an inconsistent relationship between reported pain and nerve injury. CNB in the presence of general anaesthesia or heavy sedation should be avoided where possible. If, however, due to patient choice or clinical factors this is not possible, the potential for increased risk should be discussed with the patient.

28.84 In the paediatric population the benefit of ensuring a cooperative and immobile patient may outweigh the risk of performing CNB under general anaesthesia or heavy sedation.

The needle can damage the spinal cord directly during a spinal block and this can happen if the needle is inserted at a level above which the spinal cord terminates and so is considered unsafe. Unrecognised lateral needle placement may damage a peripheral nerve and abnormal position of the spinal cord in patients with challenging anatomy may result in nerve injury[1].

1 Neal (et al) 'ASRA practice advisory on neurologic complications in regional anesthesia and pain medicine' (2008) 33(5) Regional Anesthesia and Pain Medicine 404–415.

28.85 CNB should be avoided in patients with known tumours in the epidural space close to the planned site of epidural insertion and caution exercised in patients who have pre-existing extradural pathology in terms of whether CNB is in the patient's best interest.

28.86 Policies regarding post-operative monitoring of patients who have had CNB are mandatory to identify complications and magnetic resonance imaging (MRI) is the diagnostic modality of choice for suspected epidural haematomas or abscesses. Diagnosis of a compressive lesion demands immediate neurosurgical consultation for consideration of decompression[1].

1 Neal (et al) 'ASRA practice advisory on neurologic complications in regional anesthesia and pain medicine' (2008) 33(5) Regional Anesthesia and Pain Medicine 404–415.

28.87   Late development of neurological symptoms is a rare complication of epidural anaesthesia. The Royal College of Anaesthetists recommends provision of patient information on risk of developing neurological problems following an epidural.

Limiting injury in peripheral nerve blocks (PNB)

28.88   Peripheral nerve injury is an infrequent complication of regional anaesthesia. It is therefore extremely difficult to obtain reliable and consistent data about its incidence. There are no animal or human data to support the superiority of one nerve localisation technique – paraesthesia (the nerve is contacted and the patient reports a sensation), nerve stimulation (electrical stimulation of the nerve produces movement confirming the correct nerve to be blocked), ultrasound – over another with regard to reducing the likelihood of nerve injury[1]. This is largely because the incidence of injury is so low that it would be impractical from a research point of view to conduct comparative studies[2].

1 Jeng, Torrillo and Rosenblatt 'Complications of peripheral nerve blocks' (2010) 105 (Supp 1) British Journal of Anaesthesia 97–107.
2 Neal (et al) 'ASRA practice advisory on neurologic complications in regional anesthesia and pain medicine' (2008) 33(5) Regional Anesthesia and Pain Medicine 404–415.

28.89   There are no data to support the concept that peripheral nerve stimulation or ultrasound guidance, and/or injection pressure monitoring reduce the risk of peripheral nerve injury in patients under general anaesthesia or heavy sedation. Because general anaesthesia or heavy sedation removes all opportunity for adults to communicate symptoms of potential nerve injury, peripheral nerve block should not be routinely performed in most adults during general anaesthesia or heavy sedation[1]. However, the risk-to-benefit ratio of performing peripheral nerve block under these conditions may improve in select patient populations (dementia, developmental delay and in children and infants when unintended movement could compromise vital structures).

1 Neal (et al) 'ASRA practice advisory on neurologic complications in regional anesthesia and pain medicine' (2008) 33(5) Regional Anesthesia and Pain Medicine 404–415.

28.90   There are no human data to recommend one local anaesthetic or additive over another with regards to reducing the likelihood of neurotoxicity[1]. Systemic local anaesthetic toxicity can be treated according to recognised algorithms and failure to follow recommendations is unacceptable[2].

1 Neal (et al) 'ASRA practice advisory on neurologic complications in regional anesthesia and pain medicine' (2008) 33(5) Regional Anesthesia and Pain Medicine 404–415.
2 The Association of Anaesthetists of Great Britain and Ireland: AAGBI Safety Guideline: Management of Severe Local Anaesthetic Toxicity (2010).

28.91   Patients with diseased or previously injured nerves (eg diabetes mellitus, severe peripheral vascular disease, or chemotherapy) may theoretically be at increased risk for block-related nerve injury. It may be reasonable to avoid more potent local anaesthetics, and also reduce local anaesthetic dose and/or concentration, and avoid, or limit, vasoconstrictive additives in these patients There have been cases which have described worsening of neurological deficits after regional anaesthetic techniques in patients with multiple sclerosis or previous exposure to chemotherapy and it may be prudent to avoid CNB in these patients[1].

1 Neal (et al) 'ASRA practice advisory on neurologic complications in regional anesthesia and pain medicine' (2008) 33(5) Regional Anesthesia and Pain Medicine 404–415.

28.92 An abnormally painful response to injection of local anaesthetic during a PNB (implying a potential breach of the nerve lining) should precipitate immediate cessation of injection and consideration may be given to aborting the PNB[1].

1 Jeng, Torrillo and Rosenblatt 'Complications of peripheral nerve blocks' (2010) 105 (Supp 1) British Journal of Anaesthesia 97–107.

28.93 If there is complete absence of nerve function beyond the duration of the expected action of the local anaesthetic the opinion of a neurologist should be sought and the need for electrophysiological studies and/or radiologic imaging evaluated. Consideration should be given to bilateral examination and early studies to establish baseline, pre-existing lesions, and prognosis. Nerve lesions that fail to resolve two to five months after initial neurological evaluation should prompt consideration of neurosurgical consultation.

INVASIVE MONITORING: SUBSEQUENT TO DEVIATION FROM CURRENT STANDARDS

28.94 Central venous cannulation allows monitoring of venous pressure and allows the administration of inotropic drugs to the circulation in the critically ill and those undergoing major surgery.

28.95 Venous access is via the jugular, subclavian or femoral vein, all of which can be identified using ultrasound. Ultrasound devices suitable for venous access are required for all anaesthetic departments[1].

1 Royal College of Anaesthetists Structure, organisation and Regulations (2014), available at: www.rcoa.ac.uk/about-the-college/structure-organisation-and-regulations.

28.96 The original analysis that formed the basis for NICE Guidance 49 (2002) suggested that ultrasound guidance would avoid 90 arterial punctures (typically the carotid) for every 1,000 patients treated. In view of this, it would be difficult to defend a medico-legal claim if ultrasound was not used and significant injury occurred.

28.97 Fearnley, Bell and Bodenham[1] go further, noting that, despite studies which have added further support to these recommendations, the transition to routine ultrasound guidance for central venous cannulation has been slow and incomplete. They argue that the evidence base is now so compelling for the use of ultrasound during central venous catheter insertion by the jugular route that arterial puncture and its consequent complications are indefensible and potentially criminal. The issue according to the authors is less a matter of financial compensation and more one of disregard for patient safety which merits the attention of the GMC, or criminal charges if the outcome of the complication is death. This view is challenged by Clutton-Brock[2], who questions the validity of their conclusions and the role of clinical guidelines.

1 Fearnley, Bell and Bodenham 'Status of national guidelines in dictating individual clinical practice and defining negligence' (2012) 108(4) British Journal of Anaesthesia 557–561.
2 Clutton-Brock 'Status of national guidelines in dictating individual clinical practice and defining negligence: letter 1' (2012) 109(2) British Journal of Anaesthesia 284; author reply is at 285–287.

28.98 The operator and other attending staff would be assessed on all elements of the procedure including the following:

- performance in: patient assessment; choice of technique; consent; the initial vessel puncture; guidewire; dilator; and catheter insertion sequence;
- timely recognition of the problem at the time of insertion, or later on X-ray verification of position, or on use of the device;
- correct early management of the misplaced device, which would include some or all of the following: resuscitation; leaving the devices in situ to slow any bleeding; chest drain insertion; and emergency referral for surgical or interventional radiology repair.

COMPLICATIONS OF POSITIONING

28.99 Optimal positioning of a patient for the proposed surgical procedure is a recognised anaesthetic and surgical responsibility, as is the avoidance of any neural, vascular, ophthalmic, skin, or other tissue or organ injury in association with that positioning.

Soft tissue injury including compartment syndrome

28.100 Compartment syndrome is a condition in which increased pressure within a closed compartment compromises the circulation and function of the tissues within that space. The most common cause of compartment syndrome is trauma, usually after a fracture. Compartment syndrome also occurs in the context of positioning for prolonged surgical procedures, particularly when the patient is in the lithotomy position for more than four hours. It is recognised after urological, colorectal, and gynaecological procedures[1].

1 Mar, Barrington and McGuirk 'Acute compartment syndrome of the lower limb and the effect of postoperative analgesia on diagnosis' (2009) 102(1) British Journal of Anaesthesia 3–11.

28.101 Acute compartment syndrome requires prompt diagnosis and management. Delays in treatment can result in significant disability including neurological deficit, muscle necrosis, amputation, and death.

28.102 The anaesthetist has a role in the prevention and recognition of compartment syndrome in the perioperative period. Recognition of this potential problem, with the legs intermittently being brought back into the horizontal position from the lithotomy position, the avoidance of compression stocking and maintaining normotensive anaesthesia, fall within the anaesthetist's duty of care. Post-operatively recognising that disproportionate leg pain may be due to compartment syndrome and frequent assessment of patients that have had CNB may avoid the consequences of untreated compartment syndrome. A systematic review by Mar, Barrington and McGuirk[1] did not provide convincing evidence that patient controlled analgesia, opioids or regional analgesia delayed the diagnosis of compartment syndrome. Whatever the mode of analgesia used, a high index of clinical suspicion, on-going assessment of patients, and compartment pressure measurement are essential for early diagnosis.

1 Mar, Barrington and McGuirk 'Acute compartment syndrome of the lower limb and the effect of postoperative analgesia on diagnosis' (2009) 102(1) British Journal of Anaesthesia 3–11.

Neurological injury due to patient positioning

28.103 Perioperative peripheral nerve injuries (PPNIs) result in significant patient morbidity and are a leading cause of anaesthesia-related litigation. The term most often used in the literature is PPNIs or anaesthesia-related nerve injury when specific anaesthetic factors such as regional anaesthesia are implicated. The term 'surgical positioning palsies' imply that the PPNI is due to intraoperative malpositioning of the patient which is often deemed to be the responsibility of the anaesthetist.

28.104 A PPNI refers to symptoms and signs of nerve injury in the post-operative period related to a peripheral nerve[1]. Muscle weakness, pain, and abnormal sensations in the affected nerve territory indicate that a nerve injury has occurred. Tests of nerve conduction including electromyography and electrophysiological data may further confirm the diagnosis. Upper limb nerve injuries occur more commonly than lower limb injuries (60:40). Ulnar nerve injuries are more likely to have a motor component, whilst lower limb PPNI are predominantly sensory. Analysis of the closed claims database reveals that a PPNI with a motor deficit (muscle weakness) was more likely to result in a medico-legal claim.

1 Cheney, Domino, Caplan and Posner 'Nerve injury associated with anesthesia: a closed claims analysis' (1999) 90(4) Anesthesiology 1062.

28.105 Poor positioning of the patient during surgery and insufficient padding of vulnerable areas which is considered the responsibility of the anaesthetist in most claims of negligence may be the cause of PPNIs. The issue of causation may be muddied because diseases affecting the blood supply of nerves like hypertension, tobacco use and diabetes mellitus are associated with the development of PPNI and the presence of these conditions which compromise the health of nerves may explain why some patients develop nerve injury despite adequate positioning precautions. The exact cause of PPNI is further complicated by the fact that merely being in hospital for a long time is associated with PPNI, and because the signs of PPNI may only appear 48 hours after surgery doubt can be cast on the exact cause of the injury. There is also a body of evidence and opinion which suggests that some nerves, such as the ulnar nerve, may be at greater risk regardless of intraoperative management.

28.106 Factors associated with PPNI include the type of surgery, with neurosurgery, cardiac surgery, general surgery and orthopaedic surgery being associated with a higher incidence of PPNI[1].

Extremes of body mass, male gender (associated with ulnar nerve neuropathy), arthritis and alcohol dependence are also factors which are important predisposing factors for PPNI.

1 Welch (et al) 'Perioperative peripheral nerve injuries: a retrospective study of 380,680 cases during a 10-year period at a single institution' (2009) 111(3) Anesthesiology 490.

28.107 Peripheral nerves may be injured directly by the needle during an attempt to perform a peripheral nerve block. General and epidural anesthesia are associated with a higher incidence of PPNI compared to techniques where the patient was able to change their position intraoperatively.

Malnutrition, hypovolaemia, dehydration, hypotension, hypoxia, electrolyte disturbance[1] and hypothermia have also been associated with PPNI[2].

1 Sawyer (et al) *Peripheral Nerve Injuries Associated with Anaesthesia* (2000).
2 Stephens and Appleby 'Polyneuropathy following induced hypothermia' (1955) 80 Trans-American Neurol Ass 102–104.

28.108 There are no studies which definitively indicate how to prevent PPNI and precautions are taken by understanding the anatomy of nerves and how they may be put at risk during surgery. The American Society of Anesthesiologists (ASA) has produced a practice advisory for the prevention of perioperative PPNI[1]. Their recommendations are largely based on empiric knowledge and consensus opinion.

1 Practice advisory for the prevention of perioperative peripheral neuropathies: An updated report by the American Society of Anesthesiologists task force on prevention of perioperative peripheral neuropathies (2011) 114(4) Anesthesiology 741.

28.109 Documentation of the intraoperative measures taken to prevent PPNI is essential given that adequate positioning does not guarantee that the patient will not develop a nerve injury. Documentation has been highlighted as an area of poor practice. Documentation should include the overall position of the patient and the position of the arms and legs as well as specific padding around the elbows (protecting the ulnar nerve) and fibular head (protecting the peroneal nerve). Specific positioning precautions taken because of risk factors for PPNI identified before surgery should be documented as well. The authors' practice is to record the above on a drawing made on the anaesthetic record, indicating the position of all limbs and the padding applied to vulnerable areas. Post-operative assessment in the post anaesthetic care unit of nerve function should be documented and early recognition and treatment of PPNI may be facilitated.

Medicolegal implications of PPNI

28.110 The liability for PPNIs generally, however, tends to fall to the anaesthetist – particularly in cases of upper limb PPNIs (usually the ulnar nerve). Lower limb PPNIs are more difficult in terms of liability, since all members of the theatre staff are involved in positioning the patient.

28.111 The 1990 closed claims analysis[1] showed that of the 1,541 claims related to anaesthesia, 227 (15 per cent) were for anesthesia-related nerve injury. Ulnar neuropathy 34 per cent (77 cases) was the most frequent nerve injury, brachial plexus injury accounted for 23 per cent (53 cases) and the lumbosacral nerve roots accounted for 16 per cent of cases. A series of case reports from the Medical Protection Society in the UK showed a similar distribution.

1 Kroll, Caplan, Posner, Ward & Cheney 'Nerve injury associated with anesthesia' (1990) 73 Anesthesiology 202–207.

28.112 Whilst nerve damage is a significant source of anesthesia-related claims, the exact mechanism of the injury is often unclear. The closed claims analysis by Cheney in 1999 showed that in 30 out of 113 claims of ulnar nerve injury, padding was specifically mentioned as having been applied and whilst anaesthesia care was deemed appropriate in 73 per cent of cases payment was made in 38 per cent of claims for nerve injury and in 47 per cent of ulnar nerve injury claims. The temporal relationship between the injury and the operation results in the conclusion that something must have been done wrong during the perioperative period. It is clear from the closed claims analysis that whilst the meticulous documentation of measures employed to prevent PPNIs will assist in refuting the claim, this may not be sufficient to avoid liability.

Ophthalmic injury

28.113 Perioperative eye injuries account for 2 per cent of claims against anaesthetists and occur at a frequency of less than 0.1 per cent during general anaesthetics.

The most common injury is corneal abrasions which are extremely painful. They may result from direct trauma from carelessly applied face masks, laryngoscopes during airway instrumentation, surgical drapes or objects dangling from the neck of the anaesthetist like identification badges on lanyards or stethoscopes.

28.114 The anaesthetised patient is unable to completely close their eyes due to relaxation of the muscles which normally serve this function. Corneal damage may be caused by exposure keratopathy as a result. Tear production is also reduced during general anaesthesia, rendering the eye more susceptible to abrasion[1].

1 White 'Care of the eye during anaesthesia' (2004) 5(9) Anaesthesia & Intensive Care Medicine 302–303.

28.115 Chemical injury to the cornea may occur with antiseptic agents which inadvertently run into the eye. The only antiseptic skin preparation which is non-toxic to the eye is 10 per cent povidine-iodine which should always be the choice for facial surgery.

28.116 Strategies to protect the eye from abrasion begin with vigilance by the anaesthetist. The practice in the authors' institution is to use an aqueous gel applied to the cornea and the eyes are then taped shut. During head and neck procedures with the risk of antiseptic solution passing into the eyes a protective foam mask is applied over the eyes and the edges taped to create a sealed shield. Skin sensitivity to adhesive tape may be an issue which can result in damage to the eyelid as well as other areas where adhesives are used (wound and cannula dressings).

28.117 Post-operative visual loss (POVL) is a much rarer complication of anaesthesia, with perioperative ischaemic optic neuropathy (PION) occurring, overall, in 1/60 000–1/125 000 anaesthetics[1]. Cardiac and spine surgery are the most frequent specialities resulting in POVL, the former due to haemodynamic changes affecting oxygen delivery to the eye, and the latter due to increased pressure which reduces oxygen delivery. Diabetes, hypertension, smoking and polycythaemia are also factors associated with increased risk of POVL[1].

1 Roth 'Perioperative visual loss: what do we know, what can we do?' (2009) 103 (Supp 1) British Journal of Anaesthesia 31–40.

28.118 Horseshoe headrests used in the prone position have been implicated in nearly all cases of POVL due to direct pressure. The authors' practice during major spine surgery in the prone position is to use the 'proneview' head rest which is a cut out support with a mirror on the base. The anaesthetist can therefore see the position of the eyes at all times, ensuring that the orbits are not compressed. An urgent review by an ophthalmologist must be arranged for patients complaining of post-operative visual disturbance.

FAILURE TO ENSURE PHYSIOLOGICAL STABILITY

28.119 The role of the anaesthetist is to maintain and support the normal physiological processes necessary to sustain life (homeostasis) in an anaesthetised patient despite the derangements caused by anaesthetic drugs and any derangement (for example bleeding) caused by the surgery itself. In order to achieve homeostasis the anaesthetist must provide case-appropriate monitoring and take steps to avoid hypotension, hypoxia, hypovolaemia, anaemia, hypothermia, biochemical derangements, and abnormalities of coagulation.

Ventilation, oxygenation and oxygen delivery

28.120 Hypoxic brain damage associated with anaesthesia can arise for a variety of reasons. The commonest cause of failure of oxygen supply to brain tissue is a fall in oxygen concentration in the lungs with consequent inability to oxygenate the blood. Delivery of an abnormally low oxygen tension to the breathing system or blockage of the airway may be the cause of low lung oxygen tension. The reasons for failure to deliver oxygen to the patient's lungs may range from failure of the hospital's central oxygen supply to the operating theatre, an empty oxygen cylinder on an anaesthetic machine or problems with the anaesthetic machine and breathing tubes. Continuous monitoring of the inspired oxygen concentration with a calibrated and alarmed oxygen monitor is mandatory[1]. Failure of artificial ventilation will result in hypoxia; the ventilator may cease to function or may become disconnected from the patient. Both of these have formed the basis of a number of actions for substantial damages. A disconnection alarm and/or capnograph are essential in every case.

1 Association of Anaesthetists of Great Britain and Ireland *Recommendations for Standards of Monitoring during Anaesthesia and Recovery* (London, The Association of Anaesthetists of Great Britain and Ireland, revised edition, 2007).

28.121 The anaesthetist has to ensure that his equipment is functioning correctly throughout the anaesthetic and would be liable if he allowed the ventilator to become disconnected from the patient.

28.122 An anaesthetist would be expected to take the following precautions to avoid accidents resulting in cerebral hypoxia.

A preoperative routine check must be made of the anaesthetic machine and equipment at the start of the operating list according to accepted checklists[1] and a level of monitoring acceptable to national guidelines employed[2]. Although most untoward incidents which give rise to claims of negligence occur during the maintenance of anaesthesia, the induction of anaesthesia is often accompanied by major and potentially hazardous physiological changes, and it is essential that these are detected by observation of the full range of minimum monitoring equipment, which should be attached to the patient and in working order before the induction of anaesthesia.

1 *Checklist for Anaesthetic Apparatus – 3* (2004) AAGBI.
2 Recommendations for Standards of Monitoring During Anaesthesia and Recovery (AAGBI, 2000).

28.123 An anaesthetist should at all times be in close contact with the patient and in a position to maintain continuous observation of the patient and the monitoring equipment.

Hypotension, hypovolaemia and anaemia

28.124 Failure of oxygen delivery to the brain may also result from failure of the circulatory system due to an inability of the heart to pump an adequate volume of blood to the tissues, or as a result of an absolute or relative lack of blood. There are numerous reasons for this in anaesthetic practice, mainly associated with myocardial depression by drugs or circulatory failure due to hypovolaemia (blood loss). Cerebral hypoxia may occur in a patient if the available blood is distributed to a wider area due to dilation of blood vessels which can occur if the blood pressure is deliberately lowered or with a central neuraxial block.

Hypothermia, coagulation status and biochemistry

28.125 The anaesthetist is responsible for maintaining the patient's body temperature. Hypothermia is associated with an increased risk of surgical site infection and also impairs the ability of blood to clot.

The anaesthetist is also responsible for maintaining a haemoglobin level which facilitates carrying adequate amounts of oxygen to the brain, kidneys and heart and ensuring that the patient has sufficient ability to mount a clotting response to the surgical insult.

Regular assessment of the electrolyte status of the patient and correction of abnormalities falls to the anaesthetist in order to prevent problems with the contraction of the heart and the clotting process.

DRUG-RELATED COMPLICATIONS

Anaphylaxis

28.126 Anaphylaxis is defined by the European Academy of Allergy and Clinical Immunology (EAACI) nomenclature committee as a severe, life threatening, generalised or systemic hypersensitivity reaction.

It is estimated that there are 500 severe anaphylactic reactions during anaesthesia each year. Permanent disability or death may be avoidable through early recognition and optimal management.

Death and disability are caused by cardiovascular collapse and hypoxia secondary to bronchospasm (similar to severe asthma) and airway obstruction due to swelling.

28.127 Drugs associated with a greater risk of anaphylaxis used commonly during anaesthetics include muscle relaxants and antibiotics. Latex and chlorhexidine (a commonly used antiseptic) are other common perioperative causes of anaphylaxis[1].

1 Harper (et al) 'Suspected anaphylactic reactions associated with anaesthesia' (2009) 64(2) Anaesthesia 199–211.

28.128 Preoperative assessment should include a review of previous drug intolerances and any history of anaphylaxis. Both the patient and the patient record should be consulted. It is indefensible to administer a drug to a patient if they are known to have had a previous severe reaction to that drug.

The presentation of anaphylaxis is variable and features include low blood pressure, bronchospasm, tachycardia, flushing or a rash and swelling. Many of the features can be caused by other anaesthetic problems, however anaphylaxis should always be considered.

28.129 If a diagnosis of anaphylaxis is suspected it should be managed in keeping with the Association of Anaesthetists Safety Drill (2009) which should be readily available in the anaesthetic room. Failure to follow the drill or have access to the drill would be open to significant criticism.

28.130 Following a case of suspected anaphylaxis it is important that the patient and the GP are informed about the incident. The medical record should include all the possible agents. The patient should also be referred to a specialist unit for further investigation and it is the responsibility of the anaesthetist involved to make the referral[1].

1 Harper (et al) 'Suspected anaphylactic reactions associated with anaesthesia' (2009) 64(2) Anaesthesia 199–211.

Malignant hyperpyrexia

28.131 Malignant hyperpyrexia is a rare but life threatening complication of anaesthesia. It occurs in patients with a genetic predisposition when exposed to specific triggers. The drugs that act to trigger malignant hyperpyrexia are suxamethonium (a muscle relaxant) and inhaled anaesthetic agents[1].

1 Schneiderbanger 'Management of malignant hyperthermia: diagnosis and treatment' (2014) 10 Ther Clin Risk Manag 355–362.

28.132 The trigger agents cause uncontrolled muscle contraction which results in an increased metabolic rate. The increased metabolic rate causes increased carbon dioxide production and an increasing temperature.

The complications of malignant hyperpyrexia can include coma, cardiac arrest, disseminated intravascular coagulation and renal failure.

The early signs of malignant hyperpyrexia include a raised heart rate, increasing end tidal carbon dioxide, muscle rigidity and a rising temperature.

28.133 Raised heart rate is also a sign of light anaesthesia and so may initially be treated by increasing the anaesthetic agent which effectively exacerbates the problem. This would be a reasonable first step in a patient with tachycardia; however a tachycardia that persists combined with a rising end tidal carbon dioxide should alert the anaesthetist to the possibility of malignant hyperpyrexia. Minimising delay in diagnosis and treatment may lead to a reduction in the complications caused by malignant hyperpyrexia[1].

1 Larach (et al) 'Clinical presentation, treatment, and complications of malignant hyperthermia in North America from 1987 to 2006' (2010) 110(2) Anesthesia and Analgesia 498–507.

28.134 Once malignant hyperpyrexia is suspected, treatment should be initiated immediately. It is recommended that the treatment of such a rare but life-threatening complication utilise an algorithm to facilitate management[1]. It would be difficult to defend the management of a patient that did not follow such a treatment plan. An algorithm should also be readily available in the theatre environment to prevent a delay in treatment.

1 Glahn, Ellis, Halsall, Muller, Snoeck, Urwyler, Wappler and European Malignant Hyperthermia Group 2010 'Recognizing and managing a malignant hyperthermia crisis: guidelines from the European Malignant Hyperthermia Group' (2011) 105(4) British Journal of Anaesthesia 417–420.

28.135 Following a case of malignant hyperpyrexia the patient should be referred to a specialist unit for further investigation and this would be the responsibility of the anaesthetist. The GP and the patient should be informed of the risk for future anaesthetics and due to the genetic risk factors the patient should be counselled that family members may be affected and so may also need investigation.

Suxamethonium apnoea

28.136 Suxamethonium is a muscle relaxant drug which is used by anaesthetists in emergency situations where rapid control of the airway is required.

'Suxamethonium apnoea' is a rare, genetically inherited condition. When suxamethonium is used, the muscles are profoundly relaxed and the patient is unable to breathe for themselves. The effect usually lasts for three to four minutes. In patients who have suxamethonium apnoea however, the effect is prolonged for anything up to four hours.

All anaesthetists should be aware of the condition, and in the unlikely event that a patient develops it after being given suxamethonium, breathing is assisted by means of a mechanical ventilator until the drug wears off. The patient is usually sedated during this time because of the risks of awareness. However, there should be no long-lasting effects and recovery is complete.

If someone in the patient's family is known to be affected then screening for the condition should take place.

FAILURE TO ENSURE ADEQUATE POST-OPERATIVE CARE

28.137 An anaesthetist's responsibilities extend into the post-operative period and a comprehensive handover and clear instructions for care to the recovery nurse in the post anaesthetic care unit (PACU) or safe transfer to a critical care environment if required would be considered basic duties. Guidelines for immediate post-anaesthesia recovery have been published by the AAGBI[1] and govern the conduct of individual anaesthetists and the protocols implemented in trusts.

1 Booth (et al) 'Immediate post-anaesthesia recovery 2013' (2013) 68(3) Anaesthesia 288–297.

Recovery room problems/handover

28.138 A high standard of monitoring should be maintained until the patient is fully recovered from anaesthesia and if the PACU is not immediately adjacent to theatre, mobile monitoring must be used. The anaesthetist is responsible for ensuring that this transfer is accomplished safely. Clinical observations must be supplemented by the appropriate monitoring devices according to national published guidelines[1].

1 Booth (et al) 'Immediate post-anaesthesia recovery 2013' (2013) 68(3) Anaesthesia 288–297.

28.139 All patients must be observed on a one-to-one basis by an anaesthetist or registered PACU practitioner until they have regained control of their airway, have stable cardiovascular and respiratory systems and are awake and able to communicate. The removal of tracheal tubes is the responsibility of the anaesthetist[1].

1 Booth, H, Clyburn, P, Harrop-Griffiths, W, Hosie, H, Kilvington, B, MacMahon, M, Smedley, P & Verma, R 2013, 'Immediate post-anaesthesia recovery 2013', Anaesthesia, vol 68, no 3, pp 288–297.

28.140 Agreed, written criteria for discharge of patients from the PACU to the ward should be in place in all units and an effective emergency call system must be in place in every PACU and tested regularly,

28.141 The patient, prior to discharge from the PACU should be fully conscious, able to maintain a clear airway and have protective airway reflexes. Breathing and oxygenation should be satisfactory and the

975

cardiovascular system stable, with no unexplained cardiac irregularity or persistent bleeding. Pain and post-operative nausea and vomiting should be adequately controlled, and suitable analgesic and anti-emetic regimens prescribed. Temperature should be within acceptable limits and oxygen therapy should be prescribed if appropriate. Intravenous cannula should be patent and flushed if necessary to ensure removal of any residual anaesthetic drugs and intravenous fluids should be prescribed if appropriate[1].

1 Booth, H, Clyburn, P, Harrop-Griffiths, W, Hosie, H, Kilvington, B, MacMahon, M, Smedley, P & Verma, R 2013, 'Immediate post-anaesthesia recovery 2013', Anaesthesia, vol 68, no 3, pp 288–297.

Acute pain

28.142 Effective pain management is fundamental to the quality of care received by patients and as part of enhanced recovery programmes. The overall incidence of severe pain after surgery reported in the literature is 11 per cent. Effective pain management in the perioperative period affects morbidity and duration of hospital stay and helps to ensure the best outcome for the patient, preventing unnecessary distress and the development of chronic pain.

28.143 Patients should not be returned to the ward until control of post-operative pain is satisfactory. Rapid and flexible pain control in the PACU is facilitated by specific protocols for the management of post-operative pain.

28.144 All PACU staff should be specifically trained in the management of patients with patient-controlled analgesia, epidurals, spinals and peripheral nerve blockade. Patient-controlled analgesia consists of an electronically controlled infusion pump containing an opiate. The patient has a hand-held controller with a button, which, when pressed delivers a pre-set amount of drug. The patient can therefore manage their own pain relief. The PCA device has a timed lockout period which limits the number of times that the patient can give themselves a dose of opiate. Patients with PCAs are monitored on a regular basis in order to check for signs of opioid toxicity.

28.145 Precise instructions and the recognition and management of their side-effects should be incorporated into protocols, including reversal of opioid toxicity with naloxone. Naloxone is used to reverse opiate toxicity. A balance must be achieved in the use of naloxone to allow reversal of excessive respiratory but not analgesia. It would be considered poor practice to fully reverse the effects of opiates and leave the patient in pain. Intravenous opioids should not be administered by nurses unless there is the immediate availability of an anaesthetist. Syringes should be clearly labelled with the name of the drug they contain.

No patient should return to the ward in uncontrolled pain, where problems will escalate. This may be defined as a pain score of four or more on a visual analogue scale (VAS).

28.146 Acute pain services are usually managed by anaesthetists with an interest in this subspeciality. When these services are functioning optimally they will be able to demonstrate that there are local treatment protocols available. These include definitions of the observations required, maintenance of equipment, appropriate documentation for charting observations, and completion of documentation (leads to improved pain control) competency of staff, patient information, and evidence of reporting, analysing and preventing adverse incidents.

28.147 These are all requirements of the Clinical Negligence Scheme for Trusts and incorporate good medical practice. The above indicators are clearly outlined in the RCOA's compendium of audit recipes which are designed to make explicit the standards which define good practice.

SUMMARY AND CONCLUSION

28.148 Anaesthetists primarily act to facilitate surgery and provide effective post-operative analgesia. Challenges may arise from the complexity of the surgical procedure and/or the patient's altered physiology and ability to recover from the surgical process. The individual anaesthetist therefore has to tailor the anaesthetic care to the individual patient, balancing between prescriptive algorithms and practice advisories and professional judgment. Defined thresholds of acceptable professional practice, however, protect clinicians against complaints and civil action.

BIBLIOGRAPHY

Adams, Bell and Bodenham 'Quality and outcomes in anaesthesia: lessons from litigation' (2012) 109(1) British Journal of Anaesthesia 110–122

Adyanthaya and Patil 'Never events: an anaesthetic perspective' (2014) Continuing Education in Anaesthesia, Critical Care & Pain 55

Aitkenhead 'Injuries associated with anaesthesia. A global perspective' (2005) 95(1) British Journal of Anaesthesia 95–109

'Practice advisory for the prevention of perioperative peripheral neuropathies: An updated report by the American Society of Anesthesiologists task force on prevention of perioperative peripheral neuropathies' (2011) 114(4) Anesthesiology 741, doi:10.1097/ALN.0b013e3181fcbff3

Anderson, Bythell, Gemmell, Jones, McIvor, Pattinson, Sim and Walker 'Checking Anaesthetic Equipment 2012' (2012) 67(6) Anaesthesia 660–668

Malignant Hyperthermia Crisis (2011) AAGBI

Checklist for Anaesthetic Apparatus – 3 (2004) AAGBI

Recommendations for Standards of Monitoring during Anaesthesia and Recovery (2007) AAGBI

Avidan, Jacobson, Glick, Burnside, Zhang, Villafranca, Karl, Kamal, Torres and O'Connor 'Prevention of intraoperative awareness in a high-risk surgical population' (2011) 365(7) New England Journal of Medicine 591–600

Bogod 'Consent for Anaesthesia Revised Edition' (2006) AAGBI

Booth, Clyburn, Harrop-Griffiths, Hosie, Kilvington, MacMahon, Smedley and Verma 'Immediate post-anaesthesia recovery 2013' (2013) 68(3) Anaesthesia 288–297

Checketts 'Wash & go – but with what? Skin antiseptic solutions for central neuraxial block' (2012) 67(8) Anaesthesia 819–822.

Cheney, Domino, Caplan and Posner 'Nerve injury associated with anesthesia: a closed claims analysis' (1999) 90(4) Anesthesiology 1062.

Clutton-Brock 'Status of national guidelines in dictating individual clinical practice and defining negligence: letter 1' (2012) 109(2) British Journal of Anaesthesia 284; author reply 285–287.

Cook, Bland, Mihai and Scott 'Litigation related to anaesthesia: an analysis of claims against the NHS in England 1995–2007' (2009) 64(7) Anaesthesia 706–718.

Cook, Counsell, Wildsmith and Royal College of Anaesthetists Third National Audit Project 2009, 'Major complications of central neuraxial block: report on the Third National Audit Project of the Royal College of Anaesthetists' (2009) 102(2) British Journal of Anaesthesia 179–190.

Cook, Woodall, Frerk and on behalf of the Fourth National Audit Project 2011 'Major complications of airway management in the UK: results of the Fourth National Audit Project of the Royal College of Anaesthetists and the Difficult Airway Society. Part 1: Anaesthesia' (2011) 106(5) British Journal of Anaesthesia 617–631.

El-Orbany and Connolly 'Rapid sequence induction and intubation: current controversy' (2010) 110(5) Anesthesia and Analgesia 1318–1325.

Fearnley, Bell and Bodenham 'Status of national guidelines in dictating individual clinical practice and defining negligence' (2012) 108(4) British Journal of Anaesthesia 557–561.

Ferner and McDowell 'Doctors charged with manslaughter in the course of medical practice, 1795–2005: a literature review' (2006) 99(6) Journal of the Royal Society of Medicine 309–314.

Ghoneim 'The trauma of awareness: history, clinical features, risk factors, and cost' (2010) 110(3) Anesthesia and Analgesia 666–667.

Ghoneim, Block, Haffarnan and Mathews 'Awareness during anesthesia: risk factors, causes and sequelae: a review of reported cases in the literature' (2009) 108(2) Anesthesia and Analgesia 527–535.

Glahn, Ellis, Halsall, Muller, Snoeck, Urwyler, Wappler and European Malignant Hyperthermia Group 2010 'Recognizing and managing a malignant hyperthermia crisis: guidelines from the European Malignant Hyperthermia Group' (2011) 105(4) British Journal of Anaesthesia 417–420.

Halpern, Soliman, Yee, Angle and Loscovich 'Conversion of epidural labour analgesia to anaesthesia for Caesarean section: a prospective study of the incidence and determinants of failure' (2009) 102(2) British Journal of Anaesthesia 240–243.

Harper, Dixon, Dugue, Edgar, Fay, Gooi, Herriot, Hopkins, Hunter and Mirakian 'Suspected anaphylactic reactions associated with anaesthesia' (2009) 64(2) Anaesthesia 199–211.

Hove, Nielsen and Christoffersen 'Patient injuries in response to anaesthetic procedures: cases evaluated by the Danish Patient Insurance Association' (2006) 50(5) Acta Anaesthesiologica Scandinavica 530–535.

Jeng, Torrillo and Rosenblatt 'Complications of peripheral nerve blocks' (2010) 105 (Supp 1) British Journal of Anaesthesia 97–107.

Kent, Mashour, Metzger, Posner and Domino 'Psychological impact of unexpected explicit recall of events occurring during surgery performed under sedation, regional anaesthesia, and general anaesthesia: data from the Anesthesia Awareness Registry' (2013) 110(3) British Journal of Anaesthesia 381–387.

Kluger and Short 'Aspiration during anaesthesia: a review of 133 cases from the Australian Anaesthetic Incident Monitoring Study (AIMS)' (1999) 54(1) *Anaesthesia* 19–26.

Larach, Gronert, Allen, Brandom and Lehman 'Clinical presentation, treatment, and complications of malignant hyperthermia in North America from 1987 to 2006' (2010) 110(2) Anesthesia and Analgesia 498–507.

Mar, Barrington and McGuirk 'Acute compartment syndrome of the lower limb and the effect of postoperative analgesia on diagnosis' (2009) 102(1) British Journal of Anaesthesia 3–11.

Mashour, Shanks, Tremper, Kheterpal, Turner, Ramachandran, Picton, Schueller, Morris, Vandervest, Lin and Avidan 'Prevention of intraoperative awareness with explicit recall in an unselected surgical population: a randomized comparative effectiveness trial' (2012) 117(4) Anesthesiology 717–725.

Mehta, Eisenkraft, Posner and Domino 'Patient injuries from anesthesia gas delivery equipment: a closed claims update' (2013) 119(4) Anesthesiology 788–795.

Mitchell, Dravid, Patel, Swampillai and Higgs 'Difficult Airway Society Guidelines for the management of tracheal extubation' (2012) 67(3) Anaesthesia 318–340.

NICE Diagnostics Guidance: Depth of anaesthesia monitors – Bispectral index (BIS), E-Entropy and Narcotrend Compact M National Institute for Health and Clinical Excellence, London.

Neal, Bernards, Hadzic, Hebl, Hogan, Horlocker, Lee, Rathmell, Sorenson and Suresh 'ASRA practice advisory on neurologic complications in regional anesthesia and pain medicine' (2008) 33(5) Regional Anesthesia and Pain Medicine 404–415.

Pandit, Cook, Jonker and O'Sullivan 'A national survey of anaesthetists (NAP5 Baseline) to estimate an annual incidence of accidental awareness during general anaesthesia in the UK' (2013) 68(4) Anaesthesia 343–353.

Postoperative Visual Loss Study Group 'Risk factors associated with ischemic optic neuropathy after spinal fusion surgery' (2012) 116(1) Anesthesiology 15–24.

Roth 'Perioperative visual loss: what do we know, what can we do?' (2009) 103 (Supp 1) British Journal of Anaesthesia 31–40.

Royal College of Anaesthetists 2014. Structure, organisation and Regulations [online] Available at: http://www.rcoa.ac.uk/about-the-college/structure-organisation-and-regulations [Accessed on 18 June 2014].

Royal College of Anaesthetists 2010. Curriculum for Anaesthetic Training. [online] Available at: http://www.rcoa.ac.uk/careers-training/training-anaesthesia/the-training-curriculum/CCT2010 [Accessed on 18 June 2014]

Russell 'A comparison of cold, pinprick and touch for assessing the level of spinal block at caesarean section' (2004) 13(3) International Journal of Obstetric Anesthesia 146–152.

Sawyer, Richmond, Hickey and Jarrratt *Peripheral nerve injuries associated with anaesthesia* (2000).

Shiga, Wajima, Inoue and Sakamoto 'Predicting difficult intubation in apparently normal patients: a meta-analysis of bedside screening test performance' (2005) 103(2) Anesthesiology 429–437.

Simms and Terry 'Well leg compartment syndrome after pelvic and perineal surgery in the lithotomy position' (2005) 81(958) Postgraduate Medical Journal 534–536.

Staender, Schaer, Clergue, Gerber, Pasch, Skarvan and Meister 'A Swiss anesthesiology closed claims analysis: report of events in the years 1987–2008' (2011) 28(2) European Journal of Anesthesiology 85–91.

Stephens and Appleby 'Polyneuropathy following induced hypothermia' (1955) 80 Trans Am Neurol Ass 102–104.

Welch, Brummett, Welch, Tremper, Shanks, Guglani and Mashour 'Perioperative peripheral nerve injuries: a retrospective study of 380,680 cases during a 10-year period at a single institution' (2009) 111(3) Anesthesiology 490.

White 'Care of the eye during anaesthesia' (2004) 5(9) Anaesthesia & Intensive Care Medicine 302–303.

CHAPTER 29

Neurosurgery

Mr Martin J Gillies

Mr Richard S C Kerr

INTRODUCTION

29.1 The nervous system is the principal means with which we negotiate the outside world. Injury to the nervous system (brain, spinal cord and nerves) therefore may result not simply in physical impairments, but social and economic impairments too. Legal proceedings arising from complaints in the management of nervous system disorders may focus upon the deleterious effect of medical errors on claimants' economic or social capacities, not simply on physical harm. The role of medicine in many disorders of the nervous system concerns prevention of secondary injury: despite the sophistication of modern medicine, damage to the nervous system caused by a primary event (for example head injury, spontaneous bleed, acutely prolapsed disc) is often irreversible and may set a spiral of deterioration in motion that may be beyond the abilities of physicians to halt.

29.2 The scope of this chapter is to describe current management strategies of nervous system disorders in which a neurosurgeon would be reasonably expected to play a lead role, although not necessarily an exclusive role. Within the UK health system, neurosurgery is a 'tertiary service', meaning a patient may have been managed by another hospital-based specialist, or even pre-hospital specialist, prior to transfer to the care of a neurosurgeon. Neurosurgeons may therefore become involved in complaints arising from problems with delayed diagnosis or timely transfer to neurosurgical care, in addition to surgical and post-surgical care.

29.3 The skull is a rigid structure, whereas the brain consists of soft tissue; the intracranial contents may expand in a variety of diverse pathological situations as trauma, bleeding, tumours, infection, hydrocephalus and metabolic disturbance causing increased intracranial pressure. The tissues of the central nervous system are sensitive to hypoxia and intolerant of compression. There may be a limited opportunity in time to deal with compromised tissue, whatever the pathological process. Such considerations influence the reasoning underlying the decision-making of the neurosurgeon. Managing this problem in a variety of different clinical contexts is a major challenge for the neurosurgeon.

HEAD INJURY

29.4 Head injury is the most common cause of death and disability in people under 40 years of age in the UK. 1.4 million people each year attend emergency departments in England and Wales because of recent head injury, of which around 200,000 are admitted to hospital. Approximately

33–50 per cent are children aged under 15. The vast majority do not have significant impairment of conscious level and recover spontaneously without any specific specialist intervention. Neurosurgeons are typically involved in the management of moderate to severe head injury, which account for approximately 5 per cent of head injuries. Head injury severity is defined by the patient's post-resuscitation Glasgow Coma Scale (GCS) score. The GCS is the universally accepted measure of conscious level in current clinical practice. Three features are independently observed: eye opening; motor (movement) response; and verbal response to verbal or painful stimuli. Observations made are easily reproducible between individuals and can be accurately compared when made by different observers. Clinically GCS is a 15-point scale. The GCS has a range of 3 points (worst) to 15 (normal). The range of eye opening score is 1 (none) to a maximum of 4 (spontaneous); the verbal score is 1 (none) to a maximum of 5 (orientated in time and place); and the motor score from 1 (none) to a maximum of 6 (obeys one step commands). These three individual components should be recorded (E, V, M) as well as the total. Coma is defined as the inability to obey commands, speak or open the eyes to pain and corresponds to a GCS of less than 9 in most cases. Mild head injury is defined as post-resuscitation GCS greater than 12, moderate as a GCS of 9–12, severe as GCS less than 9. The children's coma scale (for age less than four years, ie pre-verbal children) is similar to adult GCS except for the verbal response. The verbal responses range from:

- 5: smiles orientated to sound, follow objects, interacts;
- 4: crying, consolable, interaction inappropriate;
- 3: inconsistently consolable, interaction moaning;
- 2: inconsolable, interaction restless; and
- 1: no verbal response.

29.5   Grading GCS/head injury severity may be confounded by a host of factors including, for example, concomitant injury or medical conditions affecting breathing, circulation, blood chemistry, drug or alcohol use. Injury severity is a major determinant of survival of head injury and, for the clinician, the conscious level is the best empirical measure of impaired cerebral function after closed head injury. Conversely, injury severity does not correlate well to risk of morbidity (symptoms) after head injury; even clinically mild head injury can result in significant social and economic impairment.

29.6   When clinicians make judgments upon the optimal management of head injured patients, the pace and development of the pathology from the moment of onset (ictus) is of paramount importance. This evidence is determined by clinical, radiological and surgical facts. The history of the injury is important in the evaluation of the head injury and is usually obtained from eye witnesses of the accident and from the family or friends of the injured person. Important information can be obtained from ambulance personnel. Previous medical history before the injury may be relevant. The sequence of events after the ictus may distinguish between primary brain damage, which may be irreversible, and secondary injury, which may be preventable with surgical or medical intervention.

Further reading:
Teasdale and Jennett (1974) ii Lancet 81–84
www.nice.org.uk CG176
Valadka, Andrews (eds) *Neurotrauma: evidence-based answers to common questions* (2005)

29.7 Over the past 10 years, care of head injured patients has evolved substantially. NICE have issued three guidelines (2003 CG4, 2007 CG56 and 2014 CG176) over the past two decades updating earlier guidance on the management of head injury. The main changes have been the replacement of skull X-rays with head computed tomography (CT) scans as the main modality of investigation of head injury, and the establishment of regional trauma networks. The new guidance is based largely on evidence collated in the USA and Canada by the Brain Trauma Foundation. Although NICE offers detailed guidelines to assist hospitals in the management of head injured patients, the expectation is that referring hospital trusts develop local protocols for the management of head injury in conjunction with specialist services such as neurosurgery.

29.8 Currently, patients suffering moderate to severe head injuries are taken directly from the scene of injury to the regional trauma centre within the trauma network of district general hospitals. This centre has a neuroscience unit, and may not be the closest hospital to the scene of injury with emergency department or ITU facilities. At the scene of injury, attending health care professionals, often including specialist doctors, make an assessment of the severity of the patient's injuries using nationally-agreed triage tools and deliver emergency treatment as indicated. This often includes intubation (placing a tube in the airway to prevent asphyxiation) in the case of head-injured patients. Head injuries are frequently associated with spinal injuries, therefore attending medical professionals will normally institute measures to prevent secondary injury to the spinal cord at the scene, known as spinal immobilisation or spinal precautions. The patient is then transferred to the regional trauma centre to continue investigation and management of their injuries by physicians with a special interest in trauma. Doctors at specialist registrar grade and above who work regularly with trauma patients will normally be expected to have attended an advanced trauma life support (ATLS) course and maintain valid certification in ATLS. After resuscitation (stabilisation of the airway, respiratory and circulatory functions) patients will normally undergo detailed CT scans to diagnose internal injuries to the brain, spine, chest, abdomen and pelvis. Neurosurgeons frequently become involved at this point when a CT head or spine scan identifies an abnormality, if not already in attendance as part of the trauma team. Regional trauma centres endeavour to meet specific time targets within this management sequence to avoid additional harm to patients resulting from delays in correct management of the patient's injuries.

29.9 Minor head injuries may present to health services in different ways, for example to GPs, local emergency departments or other hospital-based specialists (eg paediatricians or general medical doctors). Specialists involved in the care of children must be alert to the possibility of non-accidental injury (assault) in children presenting with any type of head injury. NICE offers guidelines to aid clinicians in the diagnosis of non-accidental injury (CG89).

The decisions these doctors must make is whether: (1) to perform a CT scan of the head (with or without cervical spine imaging); (2) to admit or discharge the patient; and (3) to refer to neurosurgery or not.

Requesting a CT scan

29.10 NICE guidelines stipulate certain features in the patient's medical history which indicate that a scan is necessary (patients over 15 years of age). A CT head scan should be performed within one hour if the following are identified:

- GCS less than 13 on initial assessment;
- GCS less than 15 two hours after injury on assessment in the emergency department;
- suspected open or depressed skull fracture;
- sign of basal skull fracture;
- post-traumatic seizure;
- focal neurological deficit;
- more than one episode of vomiting since the head injury.

29.11 Additionally, patients on anticoagulants (blood thinners), such as warfarin, should have a CT within eight hours if none of the above are present but if one of the following risk factors is present:

- age greater than 65 years;
- a history of bleeding or clotting disorder;
- dangerous mechanism of injury (for example, a pedestrian or cyclist struck by a motor vehicle, an occupant ejected from a motor vehicle or a fall from height of greater than a metre or five stairs);
- more than 30 minutes' retrograde amnesia of events immediately before the head injury.

29.12 A provisional radiology report should be available within one hour of the scan. If none of the above risk factors are present and the patient has not suffered change of conscious level or amnesia since the head injury, a scan need not be performed.

29.13 In the case of children, additional guidance is offered. Risk factors indicating a CT scan within one hour of identification are:

- suspicion of non-accidental injury;
- post-traumatic seizure, but no history of epilepsy;
- on initial assessment GCS less than 14 or, for children less than one year old, GCS (paediatric) less than 15;
- at two hours after the injury GCS less than 15;
- suspected open or depressed skull injury or tense fontanelle;
- any sign of basal skull fracture (haemotympanum, 'panda' eyes, cerebrospinal fluid leakage from the ear or nose, bruising of the region behind the ears (Battle's sign);
- focal neurological deficit;
- for children less than one year old, presence of bruise, swelling or laceration of more than 5cm on the head.

29.14 If none of the above is present, but if more than one of the following are present, a scan is indicated within one hour:

- witnessed loss of consciousness for more than five minutes;
- abnormal drowsiness;
- three or more discrete episodes of vomiting;
- dangerous mechanism of injury (high-speed road traffic accident either as a pedestrian, cyclist or vehicle occupant, fall from height of greater than three metres, high speed injury from an object;
- amnesia (anterograde or retrograde) lasting longer than five minutes (assessment not possible in pre-verbal children and unlikely in any child aged less than five years).

If the patient is on warfarin, a scan is indicated within eight hours if none of the above factors are present.

If one factor is present from the latter list, observation for four hours is recommended, CT scan being indicated if there is a deterioration in conscious levels, or further vomiting within that period.

If no risk factor is identified and the patient is not on warfarin, the clinician may at his discretion institute observation or discharge as appears appropriate, without performing a scan.

29.15 Risk factors that indicate a CT scan of the neck should be performed are:

- GCS less than 13 on initial assessment;
- intubation;
- a definitive diagnosis of cervical spine injury is required urgently (eg before surgery);
- other body areas are being scanned for head injury or multi-region trauma;
- the patient is alert and stable, there is a suspicion of cervical spine injury and any of the following are present: age over 65; dangerous mechanism of injury (fall from higher than one metre or five stairs, axial load to head [eg diving], high speed motor vehicle collision, rollover motor accident, ejection from a motor vehicle, accident involving motorised recreational vehicles, bicycle collision); focal peripheral neurological deficit or paraethesia in the upper or lower limbs.

29.16 In patients with normal conscious level, the minimum recommended cervical spinal imaging modality is plain spinal radiography (lateral, AP and PEG views); abnormalities on these indicate the need for further investigation with CT and/or MRI as appropriate. Patients continue to undergo cervical spinal immobilisation until such time the spine can be cleared of injury clinically and/or radiologically. CT cervical spine scans are currently used to identify spinal fractures, therefore the cervical spine is cleared (cervical spinal immobilisation is discontinued) in obtunded patients if no fracture is detected on CT scan. The sensitivity of CT scan for clinically significant injury is 99 per cent, depending on the experience of the reporting radiologist. However, even in the best hands CT scans can potentially miss 1 per cent of cervical spine injuries that require operative intervention. In cases judged to have a high risk of cervical injury with no fracture identified on CT cervical spine scan, cervical spinal immobilisation often continues until a MRI of the cervical spine is available and in some circumstances until the patient is clinically assessable (when they have recovered to normal conscious level). There are risks of prolonged cervical spine immobilisation (eg pressure sores, delayed mobilisation, etc), including airway obstruction but these have to be balanced against the considerable risk of major disability (tetraplegia) resulting from secondary spinal cord injury caused by mobilisation of an unstable injury of the cervical spine. NICE guidance on the management of spinal injuries is in progress, but not currently published (expected 2016). Suspected injuries to other regions of the spine (thoracic, lumbar) are dealt with in a similar fashion: immobilisation until clinical and/or radiological assessment then instigation of appropriate treatment, including bracing, operative fixation, and bed rest.

Further reading:
National Institute for Health and Clinical Excellence (2014) CG 176 *Head injury: triage, assessment, investigation and early management of head injury in children, young people and adults* Manchester: NICE. Available from www. nice.org.uk/CG176 Reproduced with permission.
(2010) 68(1) J Trauma 109–113
(2010) 35(18) Spine (Phila Pa 1976) 1721–1728.
Spinal immobilisation for trauma patients, Editorial Group: Cochrane Injuries Group Published Online: 23 APR 2001 DOI: 10.1002/14651858.CD002803

Admitting the patient

29.17 The following findings indicate admission to hospital:
- patients with new, 'clinically significant' abnormalities on imaging. Neuroscience units are expected to offer guidance to referring hospital trusts as to what constitutes 'clinically significant';
- patients in whom GCS has not returned to 15 after imaging, regardless of the imaging results;
- when a patient has indications for CT scanning but this cannot be done within the appropriate period, either because CT is not available or because the patient is not sufficiently cooperative to allow scanning (caveat the combative patient, see below);
- continuing worrying signs (for example, persistent vomiting, severe headaches) of concern to the clinician;
- other sources of concern to the clinician (for example, drug or alcohol intoxication, other injuries, shock, suspected non-accidental injury, meningism, cerebrospinal fluid leak).

29.18 Patients with minor head injury may require hospital admission, but may not be appropriate for transfer to neurosurgery (see below). The patient is admitted under the care of a team led by a consultant trained in the non-operative management of head injury during their higher specialist training to a ward with medical staff trained in the correct method of neurological observation appropriate to the patient's age. In most UK hospitals this will be the trauma and orthopaedic team in the case of adults, or paediatric team in the case of children aged under 16 years.

Observation of admitted patients

29.19 For patients admitted for head injury observation the minimum acceptable documented neurological observations are: GCS; pupil size and reactivity; limb movements; respiratory rate; heart rate; blood pressure; temperature; blood oxygen saturation. Observation of infants and young children (aged under five years) should only be performed by units with staff experienced in the observation of infants and young children with a head injury.

29.20 Patients with minor head injury are observed at least half-hourly until GCS 15 is achieved, the frequency being reduced after two hours if the patient remains GCS 15. The total period of observation in most areas will be 24–48 hours, but this is at the discretion of the admitting physician, normally based on locally-agreed protocols within the regional trauma network, and dependent on the clinical status of the patient. For example, patients who remain symptomatic after 48 hours or who do not have adequate social resources may require longer admission.

29.21 If the patient after achieving GCS 15 deteriorates subsequently at any time, the frequency of observation should be increased to half-hourly and in most cases repeat assessment by a doctor is warranted. The following features generally indicate an urgent repeat CT head scan. Most neurosurgeons would recommend a low threshold for repeat head scan, especially in patients who have never achieved GCS 15 during the observation period:

- development of agitation or abnormal behaviour (caveat the intoxicated patient);
- a sustained (that is, for at least 30 minutes) drop of 1 point in GCS score (greater weight should be given to a drop of 1 point in the motor response score of the GCS);
- any drop of 3 or more points in the eye-opening or verbal response scores of the GCS, or 1 or more points in the motor response score;
- development of severe or increasing headache or persisting vomiting;
- new or evolving neurological symptoms or signs such as pupil inequality or asymmetry of limb or facial movements.

29.22 Prior to CT scan, the attending physician should consider if intubation of the deteriorating patient is indicated and if there is a non-neurological cause for deterioration. If the patient is fitting, has a GCS of less than 9, has a drop of more than 2 points in GCS within the first two hours after initial assessment, or has developed airway, respiratory or cardiovascular instability, then in most circumstances the patient will merit intubation and stabilisation prior to transfer to the scan room.

29.23 In the case of a patient who has had a normal CT scan but who has not achieved a GCS equal to 15 after 24 hours' observation, a further CT scan or MRI should be considered, again, in addition to other potential non-neurological explanations for failure to recover to normal consciousness. Common non-neurological causes for impaired conscious level include abnormal blood sugars, derangement of salt levels in the blood, liver or kidney problems, infection, respiratory failure (hypoxia), shock (low blood pressure), excessive blood loss, heart problems, intoxication with drugs (including those prescribed by doctors) and alcohol excess. Elderly patients are particularly prone to impaired consciousness from these factors.

Discharge

29.24 In patients who do not merit a CT head or cervical spine scan who achieve GCS 15 at the initial assessment and do not have any other reason for admission (eg another significant injury, medical illness, alcohol or drug intoxication, etc), the attending physician may discharge the patient without admission. Similarly, if the patient has a normal CT head scan and/or normal cervical spine imaging, has no other reason for admission, remains GCS 15 from initial assessment onwards, and whom the physician assesses to have a low probability of clinically significant head injury, he may be discharged without observation.

29.25 Discharged patients should have adequate adult supervision for at least 24 hours after discharge, unless the head injury is judged to have a negligible risk of deterioration. The patient and their companion(s) should receive verbal and written advice concerning symptoms to monitor for and what to do if the patient deteriorates. Written advice should be age appropriate and include the following details:

- details of the nature and severity of the injury;
- risk factors that mean patients need to return to the emergency department;
- a specification that a responsible adult should stay with the patient for the first 24 hours after their injury;
- details about the recovery process, including the fact that some patients may appear to make a quick recovery but later experience difficulties or complications;
- contact details of community and hospital services in case of delayed complications;
- information about return to everyday activities, including school, work, sports and driving;
- details of support organisations.

29.26 Patients with minor head injury admitted for observation with abnormal CT scans will normally be advised to avoid contact sports for six weeks post injury[1]. This is to avoid the risk of second impact syndrome, a rare condition described in young adults where two clinically minor head injuries in succession cause disproportionately severe brain swelling, with the associated risk of mortality. Return to other activities, especially work, will depend on the patient's symptoms. Patients may suffer with post-concussive symptoms for a considerable time after minor head injury that may impair return to normal activities. Approximately 50 per cent of patients will continue to suffer with neurological symptoms three months after head injury, impairing their ability to work.

1 'Consensus Statement on Concussion in Sport, The 4th International Conference on Concussion in Sport Held in Zurich November 2012' (2013) 47(5) Br J Sports Med 250–258.

29.27 In most regions, services are available for patients suffering persisting problems after head injury, including neuropsychologists and neurological rehabilitation. However, the nervous system has limited abilities to recover from injury, therefore a proportion of patients will suffer permanent impairment despite optimum treatment.

CONSULTING WITH NEUROSURGERY

29.28   NICE offers guidance to non-neurosurgeons concerning findings on initial assessment that should prompt referral to neurosurgery. Neurosurgery services are expected to develop local guidance to feeding hospitals including what counts as 'surgically significant', therefore the following list is not meant to be exhaustive:

- new 'surgically significant' findings on CT head or spine scans;
- persisting coma (GCS less than or equal to 8) after initial resuscitation;
- unexplained confusion which persists for more than four hours;
- deterioration in GCS score after admission (greater attention should be paid to motor response in deterioration);
- progressive focal neurological signs;
- a seizure without full recovery;
- definite or suspected penetrating injury;
- a cerebrospinal fluid leak.

Transfer from hospital to a neuroscience unit

29.29   Guidelines on the transfer of patients with head injuries are composed by the regional trauma network[1], consisting of the referring hospital trusts, the neuroscience unit and the local ambulance service, and recognise that:

- transfer to a neuroscience unit would benefit all patients with serious head injuries (GCS 8 or less) irrespective of the need for neurosurgery;
- if transfer of those who do not require neurosurgery is not possible, ongoing liaison with the neuroscience unit over clinical management is essential.

1 https://www.braintrauma.org.

29.30   The neuroscience unit receiving the patient should have the capability to manage all manner of associated injuries the patient may have suffered. This entails round the clock availability of a multitude of resources, including anaesthetic support, radiological investigation availability, emergency theatres staffed and equipped to perform orthopaedic, general surgical, ENT, plastic, maxillo-facial, and neurosurgical procedures. The patient is admitted to the neuroscience unit under a single named neurosurgery consultant who takes primary responsibility for the patient's care, although several named speciality consultants may be involved.

29.31   Patients with head injuries requiring emergency transfer to a neuroscience unit are accompanied by a doctor with appropriate training and experience in the transfer of patients with acute brain injury, normally but not exclusively a specialist registrar or consultant anaesthetist and appropriately trained dedicated assistant. In the case of the transfer of children, the doctor should have the appropriate training to deal with the unique challenges associated with the transfer of children.

29.32   Although transfer to a neuroscience unit is often urgent, patients should be adequately resuscitated (stabilisation of respiratory and cardiovascular status) prior to transfer. In the case of moderate to severe brain injury this stage will often include intubation of the patient. Failure to adequately resuscitate or intubate the patient where necessary prior to transfer may cause avoidable secondary brain injury, worsening the outcome for the patient.

Further reading:
Trauma: Who cares? A report of the National Confidential Enquiry into Patient Outcome and Death (2007)
Carmont 'The Advanced Trauma Life Support course: a history of its development and review of related literature' (2005) 81(952) Postgraduate Medical Journal 87–91

SPECIFIC NEUROSURGICAL ENTITIES

29.33 Intracranial bleeding (haemorrhage) is a frequent complication of head injury and is readily identified by CT scan, upon which blood is usually bright white compared to the grey of the brain. Several anatomical patterns of intracranial bleed are described, which may be present individually or in combination. To understand the distinct patterns of intracranial bleeding resulting from head injury, a brief description of the anatomy of the brain within the skull is necessary. The brain is invested in three layers of tissue, named the dura mater, arachnoid mater and pia mater, collectively the meninges. The innermost layer, the pia mater, tightly adheres to the brain, while the outermost layer the dura mater conforms to the shape of the cavity of the skull in which the brain is located, the calvarium. The calvarial cavity and the brain are not the same shape, therefore a space forms between the middle layer (arachnoid mater) and the innermost layer (pia mater) which is named the subarachnoid space. The subarachnoid space surrounds the whole brain, albeit with different dimensions in different locations, and is filled with cerebrospinal fluid. Arteries (blood vessels containing oxygenated blood) enter the cranial cavity via apertures in the skull and pierce the dura mater attached to the inner surface of the skull to enter the cavity. Major arteries supplying the brain substance are located in the subarachnoid space on the undersurface of the brain (circle of Willis) in which they divide into small divisions and enter the brain substance via the pia mater. In the brain substance vessels are small (arterioles and capillaries). Veins form within the brain substance and coalesce on the brain surface. Major veins lie within the subarachnoid space complementing the arteries. Veins then leave the cavity by piercing the arachnoid mater and dura mater to enter large venous vessels (sinuses) located within the dura mater. The brain sits within the calvarial cavity of the skull but is not rigidly attached to the skull directly, allowing movement of the brain to a limited extent independent of the skull. Therefore blood vessels – given they traverse the subarachnoid space – are at risk of injury when the head is subjected to trauma. The common forms of bleeding are extradural haematoma, subdural haematoma and intraparenchymal bleeding.

Extradural haematomas

29.34 Extradural (also known as epidural) haematomas result from bleeding from vessels lying between the dura mater and the skull. Bleeding causes the dura to be stripped away from the inner table of the skull, causing a clot to form in the epidural space. In health this space is not present. They are typically caused by a skull fracture especially in the temporal region where the middle meningeal artery is at risk of injury. Often the underlying brain is not injured by the initial event causing the haematoma, but becomes secondarily injured as the expanding haematoma causes compression of the underlying brain. The injury may be clinically minor without obvious signs of external trauma. Classically patients lose consciousness at the scene but rapidly recover to GCS 15 before a subsequent, potentially terminal decline as the brain becomes compressed. A proportion of patients suffer no loss of consciousness at the time of injury, or conversely fail to recover from an initial loss of consciousness.

29.35   Extradural haematomas associated with mass effect radiologically or clinically are considered a surgical emergency (except in rare circumstances that will not be considered here). This is because if the extradural haematoma is identified and surgically evacuated rapidly after the time of injury, patients generally have a good chance of an excellent neurological outcome, whereas increasing delay is associated with increasing risk of death and major disability. Patients who present already unconscious tend to have a worse outcome than awake patients: the severity of the associated head injury at presentation is a major determinant of outcome.

Further reading:

Bullock, Chesnut, Ghajar, Gordon, Hartl, Newell, Servadei, Walters, Wilberger, Surgical Management of Traumatic Brain Injury Author Group 'Surgical management of acute epidural hematomas' (2006) 58(3 Suppl) Neurosurgery S7–15; discussion Si–iv. Review

Leitgeb, Mauritz, Brazinova, Majdan, Wilbacher 'Outcome after severe brain trauma associated with epidural hematoma' (2013) 133(2) Arch Orthop Trauma Surg 199–207. doi: 10.1007/s00402-012-1652-y. Epub 16 November 2012

Subdural haematoma

29.36   Subdural haematoma refers to bleeding in the potential space between the dura mater and arachnoid mater, the two outermost layers of the lining of the brain. The space is not present in health, rather bleeding strips the arachnoid layer away from the dura, allowing blood to collect between the layers, exerting pressure on the underlying brain. Bleeding can result from injury to veins or arteries as they cross from the brain to the dura mater lining the skull. A particular class of vein, the bridging veins, are believed to have a particular role in the generation of subdural haematomas. The bridging veins originate from the cerebral hemispheres, cross the subarachnoid space to enter the venous sinuses (vessels) within the dura mater which drain blood from the brain back to the heart. Since the brain can move independently of the skull to an extent and since the veins are rigidly attached at the pia and as they enter the dura mater, the veins are at risk of avulsion or tearing injury during head injury, classically acceleration-deceleration injuries or rotational injuries since the brain and skull will move independently to an extent. Injury to these veins tends to occur where they are attached to the dura, hence blood collects between the dura and arachnoid mater. Two forms of subdural bleeding are common in neurosurgical practice: acute and chronic. Acute subdural refers to fresh bleeding in the subdural space resulting in the formation of a solid blood clot. Acute subdurals are frequently associated with injury to the underlying brain (cerebral contusion). Chronic subdurals are believed to be the result of small amounts of blood collecting in the subdural space which becomes expanded over time (days to weeks) as the blood degrades and draws water in from the circulation by osmosis. Both forms will be considered below.

Acute subdural haematoma

29.37 In younger patients, acute subdual haematoma in most cases is associated with a high energy impact, therefore acute subdural haematomas are more frequently associated with underlying primary brain injury and patients are more likely to present in coma than in extradural haematomas. The mortality rate and risk of long-term disability after injury are therefore correspondingly higher than with extradural haematomas. Thin acute subdural haematomas (less than 10mm maximum thickness not associated with significant midline shift) may be managed non-operatively by a period of medically-induced coma directed by intracranial pressure monitoring. Acute subdural haematomas greater than 10mm with more than 5mm mildline shift will tend to be managed operatively by craniotomy. In many cases the underlying brain will be swollen, therefore the panel of skull cut to allow evacuation of the clot may not be replaced, to allow decompression of the swollen brain. The panel of bone is replaced with an artificial bone substitute electively weeks to months later in a procedure named craniolplasty. Several factors are associated with greater chance of death or severe disability from the injury: age greater than 60 years; dilated pupil at presentation and GCS motor score less than 4 at presentation.

Further reading:
Bullock, Chesnut, Ghajar, Gordon, Hartl, Newell, Servadei, Walters, Wilberger, Surgical Management of Traumatic Brain Injury Author Group 'Surgical management of acute epidural hematomas' (2006) 58(3 Suppl) Neurosurgery S16–24; discussion Si–iv. Review
Choi, Muizelaar, Barnes, Marmarou, Brooks, Young 'Prediction tree for severely head-injured patients' (1991) 75(2) J Neurosurg 251–255

Acute and chronic subdural haematomas in the elderly

29.38 In the elderly population, especially those on warfarin, acute subdural haematomas may occur with low energy impacts or even spontaneously, and may not be associated with significant primary brain injury (ie brain injury caused by the impact). Instead the brain becomes secondarily injured by compression by the haematoma. Elderly patients are at increased risk of morbidity and mortality from surgery (including general anaesthesia) compared to younger patients and are unlikely to return to functional independence if they require emergency intubation for a neurological condition: increased age is an independent risk factor for poor outcome of emergency neurointensive therapy. Nonetheless, a subset of elderly patients benefit from neurosurgery. GCS and premorbid functional status are the best guides to identify this subset. Patients who present with acute subdural haematomas with a GCS 13–15 will normally be managed conservatively: warfarin is reversed with an antidote (Vitamin K or prothrombin complex) and the patient admitted for observation (often in a district general hospital). If the patient recovers without deficit, they may be discharged with outpatient follow-up by the admitting team. If during the period of observation (or after discharge) they become more symptomatic with weakness or severe head ache and vomiting, the patient may be offered neurosurgery if the haematoma has liquefied sufficiently to allow the fluid to be evacuated via burr holes (chronic subdural haematoma). Burr hole evacuation is a relatively safe procedure in the elderly and can be done under local anaesthesia in cooperative (or comatose) patients with high general anaesthetic risk. In many cases, elderly patients may not present at the acute subdural phase but some time afterwards (weeks to months) as the acute subdural liquefies, expands and becomes a chronic subdural haematoma. Elderly patients who present with acute subdural haematomas and GCS less than 9 are poor candidates for neurosurgery and are highly unlikely to survive to discharge from institutional care with or without optimum treatment. Burr hole evacuation is not an option in this group because an acute haematoma is a solid entity and cannot be removed through burr holes. A craniotomy would be required.

29.39 The group of elderly patients who present with a GCS between 9 and 12 often pose a clinical dilemma to clinicians and there may be heterogeneity of opinion on the best course of action amongst individual clinicians about individual patients. In determining the best course of action, clinicians will take account of factors such as the size of the haematoma, the patient's premorbid condition, associated medical conditions, next of kin views and any advanced wishes the patient may have expressed. Elderly patients with acute subdural haematomas greater than 10mm in size with more than 5mm of shift may have a better outcome with acute surgery (mini craniotomy) than patients managed without surgery in the initial phase, but an 80-year-old patient who is fit and active living in their own home without carers is a different prospect from an 80-year-old patient admitted from a nursing home with advanced dementia.

Further reading:
Stocchetti, Paternò, Citerio, Beretta, Colombo 'Traumatic brain injury in an aging population' (2012) 29(6) Neurotrauma 1119–1125. doi: 10.1089/neu.2011.1995. Epub 2 April 2012

Restarting warfarin in elderly patients after subdural haematomas

29.40 Once an acute (or more commonly chronic) subdural haematoma has been dealt with, clinicians are faced with the decision as to whether to restart warfarin or not. A heterogeneity of opinions may be expressed by neurosurgeons on this question but incontrovertible evidence on the issue is difficult to find. A prospective study on this question found a low risk of re-bleed after evacuation of chronic subdural haematoma if warfarin was started more than three days after surgery[1]. However, the decision to restart warfarin entails a weighing up of risks and benefits of the treatment.

For example a common dilemma faced by clinicians is balancing the risk of serious intracranial bleeding with future falls in patients with uncontrolled atrial fibrillation with the benefit derived from preventing strokes. The best advice is to seek advice from the clinician prescribing the warfarin as they may be the best placed to assess the risk/benefit ratio in an individual.

1 Panczykowski and Okonkwo (2011) 114 J Neurosurg 47–52.

Intraparenchymal traumatic haemorrhage and diffuse head injury

29.41   Many moderate to severely head injured patients will have neither an extradural nor an acute subdural haematoma, and the role of surgery in these patients is the subject of ongoing clinical study (eg STITCH trials). Clinical factors associated with poor outcome in moderate to severe diffuse head injury include age greater than 60 years, dilated pupil at presentation, GCS motor score less than 4, prolonged period of hypoxia, hypercapnia and/or hypotension. CT head scan features associated with poor outcome include loss of grey/white differentiation, effacement (compression) of the fluid spaces in the brain (ventricles and basal cisterns) and midline shift (swelling in a hemisphere causing the hemisphere to cross the midline of the skull) (Marshall CT score). The presence of significant petechial haemorrhage (small puncta of bleeding in the brain substance) in the absence of other findings is also significant predictor of outcome (Adams score). Isolated subarachnoid haemorrhage due to trauma is a common finding and may be found on CT scans of patients with clinically minor head injury who make a full recovery. However the presence of subarachnoid haemorrhage in the basal cisterns without other signs of trauma and a poor or unwitnessed history of trauma should prompt a clinician to consider the possibility of aneurysmal subarachnoid haemorrhage (see below).

29.42   Patients with diffuse head injury are often managed non-operatively, at least initially. A neurosurgeon or appropriately-trained anaesthetist insert an intracranial pressure monitor and use a variety of pharmacological agents to reduce intracranial pressure for a period of time afterwards until the patient's pressure stabilises or it becomes apparent that further treatment is warranted or judged futile. Most UK neurosurgeons would advocate medical management with the aim of keeping intracranial pressure below 20mmHg, but alternative strategies include sedation of the patient and use of serial CT head scans with clinical examination to determine the nature and timing of medical or surgical interventions without measuring intracranial pressure.

29.43   Operative interventions available to aid the control of intracranial pressure include insertion of an external ventricular drain, evacuation of haemorrhagic contusions/intraparenchymal haematomas, and decompressive craniectomy (removal of a large panel of bone). The evidence base for these surgical interventions is equivocal, therefore the opinions of neurosurgeons on what constitutes optimal management in diffuse brain injury may be heterogenous and vary from case to case. Nonetheless, patients with moderate to severe head injury as a group benefit from management within a neuroscience unit.

Further reading:

Gregson, Rowan, Mitchell, Unterberg, McColl, Chambers, McNamee, Mendelow 'Surgical trial in traumatic intracerebral hemorrhage (STITCH(Trauma)): study protocol for a randomized controlled trial' (2012) 367(26) N Engl J Med 2471–2481. doi: 10.1056/NEJMoa1207363. Epub 12 December 2012

Chesnut, Temkin, Carney, Dikmen, Rondina, Videtta, Petroni, Lujan, Pridgeon, Barber, Machamer, Chaddock, Celix, Cherner, Hendrix, Global Neurotrauma Research Group 'A trial of intracranial-pressure monitoring in traumatic brain injury'

Prophylactic heparin in head injury

29.44   Thromboembolism (pulmonary embolus, blood clot in the lung or deep vein thrombosis, blood clot in the legs) is a major cause of death in hospital, and in a significant proportion of cases may be preventable (NICE guidelines CG92). Factors that predispose to pulmonary embolus include conditions to which a moderately to severely head injured patient may be subjected, for example prolonged immobility, orthopaedic injuries, etc. The NHS had made great strides in trying to reduce the incidence of pulmonary embolus by the routine use of prophylactic fractionated heparin (a 'blood thinner'). However, fractionated heparin is associated with an increased risk of bleeding that may cause avoidable harm to neurosurgery patients. This risk is exacerbated if the patient suffers heparin-induced thrombocytopenia (HIT syndrome). This refers to the reduction in circulating platelets that form a major constituent of blood clots caused by heparin, which makes it more difficult for blood to clot if bleeding occurs. Evidence on the relative risks and benefits of prophylactic fractionated heparin on neurosurgery patients is equivocal (compare the two references below). Most studies seem to suggest that starting pharmacological prophylaxis is relatively safe 36 hours after injury. However, in practice within this period operative procedures may be required. Therefore a patient started on prophylactic fractionated heparin may be exposed to greater risk of haemorrhage during procedures than non-heparinised patients. An unfractionated form of heparin exists which can be reversed rapidly with an antidote; however this form needs to be infused continuously and can cause unpredictable derangements of clotting which may expose the patient to greater risk of haemorrhage than the fractionated form. Neurosurgeons do use this form of heparin if the patient has a requirement to be continuously anticoagulated for a pre-existing medical condition, for example in patients with artificial heart valves, accepting the increased risk of haemorrhage. Neurosurgeons may choose not to give prophylactic heparin, instead mechanical prophylaxis may be used to decrease the risk of thromboembolism. If HIT syndrome has developed, heparin prophylaxis is contraindicated and mechanical prophylaxis is the only option. Mechanical prophylaxis refers to elasticated stockings and mechanical calf compression devices. Mechanical prophylaxis decreases the risk of pulmonary embolus compared to no prophylaxis. Its performance compared to prophylactic heparin is not known.

Further reading:
www.nice.org.uk/guidance/cg92

Lin, Davis, Wong 'Evaluation of heparin prophylaxis protocol on deep venous thrombosis and pulmonary embolism in traumatic brain injury' (2013) 79(10) Am Surg 1050–1053

Farooqui, Hiser, Barnes, Litofsky 'Safety and efficacy of early thromboembolism chemoprophylaxis after intracranial hemorrhage from traumatic brain injury' (2013) 119(6) J Neurosurg 1576–1582. doi: 10.3171/2013.8.JNS13424. Epub 20 September 2013

Praeger, Westbrook, Nichol, Wijemunige, Davies, Lyon, Wills, Bailey, Rosenfeld, Cooper 'Deep vein thrombosis and pulmonary embolus in patients with traumatic brain injury: a prospective observational study' (2012) 14(1) Crit Care Resusc 10–13

Post traumatic infection

29.45   Infection and cerebrospinal fluid leakage (rhinorrhoea and otorrhoea) commonly complicate head injury. Traumatic scalp wounds need to be treated seriously because an underlying fracture or penetration of the skull by a sharp object may lead to dangerous intracranial infection, eg meningitis or abscess formation. Scalp wounds should be thoroughly cleaned, the traumatised edges removed and careful interrupted sutures inserted. General anaesthetic should be avoided if at all possible in dealing with these or other peripheral injuries while the patient's level of consciousness is being observed. With its profuse blood supply the scalp heals well but where indicated, prophylactic antibiotic cover should be used, for example visibly contaminated wounds or wounds caused by animals, etc. The treatment of compound depressed fractures of the skull consists of excision of the wound, location and removal of in-driven fragments of bone, foreign bodies and hair, evacuation of non-viable brain and haematoma, dural repair and replacement of the larger bone fragments after decontamination. Conversely, closed skull fractures with no or minimal depression of the skull fragments may be dealt with non-operatively.

Further reading:

Bullock, Chesnut, Ghajar, Gordon, Hartl, Newell, Servadei, Walters, Wilberger, Surgical Management of Traumatic Brain Injury Author Group 'Surgical management of depressed cranial fractures' (2006) 58(3 Suppl) Neurosurgery S56–60; discussion Si–iv

29.46   Infection may complicate the management of a severely head injured patient. It is an important cause of secondary deterioration and is usually associated with a fracture of the vault or skull base, or recent emergency neurosurgery. Fractures of the anterior fossa involving the air sinuses may allow leakage of cerebrospinal fluid (CSF) down the nose, and/or the entry of free air into the cranial cavity[1]. Occasionally fractures of the middle fossa involving the temporal bone lead to rhinorrhoea, but more commonly they result in otorrhoea. Usually the leak occurs within a few days of the injury and most neurosurgeons do not operate to repair if it stops, as it usually does, in a few days or a week. Persistent rhinorrhoea (normally more than two weeks) must be dealt with surgically to prevent meningitis[2]. Nonetheless, giving prophylactic antibiotics to patients with base of skull fracture with CSF leak does not prevent meningitis. Indeed prophylactic antibiotics acting on the central nervous system may predispose to the development of drug-resistant organisms amongst the patient's nasal flora[3], therefore in the absence of symptoms of nervous system infection, antibiotics are not indicated for base of skull fracture with or without CSF leak. Rarely, rhinorrhoea can occur or persist for considerable periods of time after injury and may declare itself some years after the injury by the occurrence of meningitis or brain abscess. In these rare cases, meningitis is treated with appropriate antibiotics, any brain abscess by drainage and antibiotics and repair of the CSF fistula (the conduit from the brain CSF spaces to the outside) as soon as possible. A neurosurgeon may anticipate the need for repair if there is radiological evidence suggesting that spontaneous dural repair is unlikely to take place (eg a skull base fracture involving the paranasal sinuses and wide separation of bony edges)[4]. These repairs can be technically challenging, and may require a multi-disciplinary team approach, with maxillo-facial or ear nose and throat surgeons. CSF leaks can recur or persist post operatively. While the patient is in hospital the occurrence of a cerebrospinal fluid leak is usually recognised and dealt with, but if the onset is delayed it is likely to be missed unless the patient specifically complains of it. A previous history of head injury or skull base surgery should alert a doctor to the possibility of a CSF leak.

1 Briggs (1974) 61 Br J Surg 307–312.
2 Abuabara 'Cerebrospinal fluid rhinorrhoea: diagnosis and management' (2007) 12(5) Med Oral Patol Oral Cir Bucal E397–400.
3 The Cochrane Collaboration *Antibiotic prophylaxis for preventing meningitis in patients with basilar skull fractures (Review)* (2011).
4 Reilly and Simpson *Craniomaxillofacial Trauma* (1995) p 367.

Outcome measures

29.47 While there are many scales to measure outcome following severe head injury the most commonly used is the Glasgow Outcome Scale. It has five categories:

1 good recovery;
2 moderate disability;
3 severe disability;
4 vegetative state;
5 dead.

29.48 There has been much debate about when to assess outcome but the evidence would suggest that most recovery occurs within the first six months to a year. A small percentage (2–5 per cent) will survive in the persistent vegetative state (PVS). This state was defined in 1972 and classification of patients as being in this state should be confined to those who fulfil the criteria of their description. They are patients who show no awareness of self or the environment, but have characteristic physical features of sleep/wake rhythms, periods of eye opening and abnormal motor responses in all four limbs. Basic cardio-respiratory function is retained without artificial support. If the PVS is diagnosed earlier than three months after the injury, errors of diagnosis can occur. The prolonged survival of some of these patients can raise serious ethical and legal questions, which are generally beyond the scope of the neurosurgery speciality.

Further reading:
Jennett B and Bond M (1975) i Lancet 480–484
Jennett B and Plum F (1972) i Lancet 734–737
Sommer, Norup, Poulsen, Morgensen 'Cognitive activity limitations one year post-trauma in patients admitted to sub-acute rehabilitation after severe traumatic brain injury' (2013) 45(8) J Rehabil Med 778–784. doi: 10.2340/16501977-1208
Katz, Polyak, Coughlan, Nichols, Roche 'Natural history of recovery from brain injury after prolonged disorders of consciousness: outcome of patients admitted to inpatient rehabilitation with 1-4 year follow-up' (2009) 177 Prog Brain Res 73–88. doi: 10.1016/S0079-6123(09)17707-5

29.49 The concept of brain death, like PVS, is a result of modern intensive care, particularly artificial cardiorespiratory support. The diagnosis of brain death and therefore the point at which artificial supportive measures can legitimately be discontinued is important both in human terms, to avoid unnecessarily prolonged grief, and legally, particularly when the patient is being considered as a source of organ donation. The criteria for the diagnosis of brain death were published by the royal colleges in 1976 (BMJ) and have been reaffirmed subsequently, most recently in 2008[1]. The most recent code of practice concerns the diagnosis of death, to demonstrate that the diagnosis of death is a separate consideration to the issues surrounding organ donation. Briefly, brain death is the irreversible loss of the capacity for consciousness combined with the irreversible loss of the capacity to breathe. A patient meeting the criteria for brain death may show some neurological activity and continue to have signs of function in other organ systems. PVS is not brain death, as these patients have the capacity to breathe unaided, although they may have irreversibly lost the capacity for consciousness. The criteria used to diagnose brain death are:

- the patient's condition is due to irreversible brain damage of known aetiology, or, in some cases, all reversible causes of the patient's condition have been ruled out by investigation and the passage of sufficient time. If diagnostic uncertainty is present, brainstem testing should not take place;
- exclusion of potentially reversible causes of coma:

    — no evidence that the patient's condition is due to depressant drugs;
    — the patient's condition is not due to hypothermia (core temp higher than 34°C);
    — exclusion of potentially reversible metabolic or endocrine disturbances;
    — exclusion of reversible or confounding causes of respiratory depression (apnoea).

1 http://www.aomrc.org.uk/doc_view/42-a-code-of-practice-for-the-diagnosis-and-confirmation-of-death (2008 guidance).

29.50 If these conditions are met, the patient's brainstem reflexes are tested. Brain death is diagnosed if the above pre-conditions are met and the following found on examination:

(1)   the pupils are fixed in diameter and do not respond to sharp changes in the intensity of incident light;

(2)   there is no corneal reflex;

(3)   the vestibulo-occular reflexes are absent. These are absent when no eye movement occurs during or after injection of at least 50ml of ice cold water into each external auditory meatus in turn over one minute, clear access to the tympanic membrane having been established by direct inspection with an otoscope and the head positioned at 30 degrees to the horizontal. This test may be contraindicated on one or other side by local or spinal trauma;

(4)   no motor responses within the cranial nerve distribution can be elicited by adequate stimulation of any somatic area;

(5)   there is no gag reflex or reflex response to bronchial stimulation by a suction catheter passed down the trachea or spatula applied to the back of the throat;

(6)   no respiratory movements occur over five minutes when the patient is disconnected from the mechanical ventilator for long enough to ensure that the arterial CO2 tension rises above the threshold for stimulating respiration, ie PCO2 must normally reach at least 6.0 kPa and be 0.5kPa higher by the end of the five minutes, whilst PO2 and BP remain within normal limits (apnoea test).

29.51   Testing is conducted by two doctors who have been fully GMC registered for at least five years. At least one of the two must be a consultant. The doctors must not have or be perceived to have any conflict of interest with the patient or their family, nor be members of the transplant team. The doctors act together whilst testing and must perform the tests on two occasions The doctors reverse roles between each occasion: doctor A observes doctor B performing the tests and vice versa. The interval between testing depends on the patient's clinical condition. If the diagnosis of death is made on the first round of testing, the second round can be performed shortly afterwards, once it has been confirmed that the patient's blood chemistry has returned to baseline parameters after the first apnoea test. Death is confirmed by the second round of tests, but the legal time of death is the time at the end of the first round of tests.

29.52   If patients show signs of brainstem function, the diagnosis of brain death cannot be made. However, the presence of residual brainstem functions in patients likely to have suffered brain damage resulting in irreversible loss of the capacity for consciousness do not prevent the withdrawal of treatment, if treatment is reasonably judged to be futile.

29.53   Additional tests (eg electroencephalography, CT scans, etc) are not required to make the diagnosis of brain death in the UK, but ancillary tests such as these can be used to facilitate testing, especially to reduce diagnostic uncertainty or exclude confounding factors as the cause of loss of brainstem reflexes/apnoea. In cases where uncertainty continues despite testing and specialist opinion, the passage of time often clarifies matters: brainstem death is associated with the eventual cessation of cardiac activity despite intensive therapy support, although the period between brainstem death and cessation of cardiac activity may vary from hours to months.

INTRACRANIAL TUMOURS

29.54   Intracranial tumours include primary tumours arising from the intracranial structures and secondary tumours which have spread from tumours arising in other parts of the body. The basis of diagnosis of cerebral tumours depends on the history and clinical examination indicating the need for further investigation. Further investigation consists of timely imaging of the brain. MRI head scan with contrast is the investigation of choice, although a CT head scan may be adequate to confirm the presence of a tumour. In many cases imaging of the chest, abdomen and pelvis will be indicated before a suitable management plan for an individual patient can be determined. Brain tumours of all types may present with epilepsy, raised intracranial pressure or focal neurological abnormalities, either in isolation or combination. A history of progression of such symptoms should lead to early further investigation. Avoidance of diagnostic delay is particularly important when dealing with benign and therefore potentially curable tumours, in whom the incidence of post-operative complications and overall survival may be related to the size of the tumour and the ease with which it can be removed surgically. In certain circumstances, undue delay in diagnosis may be associated with an opportunity cost to the patient in terms of which treatment options are available to them. For example, slow growing benign tumours of the cerebellopontine angle (CPA) may be amenable to a form of radiotherapy (eg gamma knife therapy) if detected when they are below a certain size, avoiding the need for complex surgery. Surgery in the CPA is associated with a significant risk of cranial nerve problems that can result in substantial disability. The risk of disabling cranial nerve injury is less with gamma knife therapy whilst offering comparable outcomes to surgery in terms of long-term survival and prevention of symptom progression (see below), at the cost of potential risks associated with radiation exposure.

Gliomas

29.55   Gliomas are tumours of brain tissue and account for nearly half of all primary cerebral tumours in adults. They vary widely in their degree of malignancy from the low grade well-differentiated astrocytomas (WHO grade 2, less commonly in adults WHO grade 1), which may present with a history of epilepsy of many years duration, to the glioblastomas (WHO grade 4) which may have a history as short as a few weeks. Although surgical resection of these tumours is rarely curative, surgery is still the mainstay of treatment of gliomas. Surgery is necessary to provide a histological diagnosis, and may be used to lower the intracranial pressure by reducing tumour bulk, before adjuvant treatment, such as radiotherapy and/or chemotherapy is commenced. If diagnosis by biopsy is not made, despite the increasing accuracy of imaging techniques, the presence of a curable lesion such as a meningioma or a brain abscess may be missed. It is essential that patients and their relatives are given sufficient information before operation, regarding the prognosis of the tumour and possible complications of surgery, to enable them to make a balanced decision on informed consent, given the non-curative nature of surgery for malignant gliomas.

29.56   The delayed diagnosis of low grade glioma (LGG) in adults (WHO grade 2 astrocytomas or oligodendrogliomas) may give rise to a complaint that earlier diagnosis might have improved the long-term outlook of the patient. An important observation is that the natural history of a well differentiated glioma in the individual patient or a population of patients is unknown (see Cochrane review on role of biopsy compared to excision of LGG). A significant proportion of patients with a low grade glioma will develop a malignant (WHO grade 4) glioma within 10 years. The quality of life of these patients is usually high until transformation of the tumour to a higher grade occurs. Pre-operative factors are important prognostic indicators. Positive prognostic factors include:

- age less than 40 years;
- tumours not crossing the midline;
- not involving the ventricles;
- confined to one lobe;
- measuring less than 6 cms (maximum diameter); and
- patients with epilepsy but without neurological deficits.

29.57   Several studies demonstrate the influence of tumour genetics on survival, eg IDH 1- 2- mutations, and MGMT methylation status amongst others. The major problem is that there is no prospective randomised study that has analysed the impact of the extent of tumour resection on malignant recurrence risk and survival rates. Retrospective studies of outcome related to extent of resection based on MRI findings suggest that total or subtotal resection (greater than 90 per cent) is associated with better long-term survival than resections of less than 90 per cent or biopsy alone (although see Cochrane review[1]).

1 Veeravagu, Jiang, Ludwig, Chang, BlackL, Patil, Cochrane Database Syst Review 'Biopsy versus resection for the management of low-grade gliomas' (2013) 30; 4:CD009319. doi: 10.1002/14651858.CD009319.pub2.

29.58   The aim of modern surgery is therefore gross total resection on MRI, or supratotal resection (resection beyond the margins of the tumour visible on FLAIR sequence MRI). Surgeons have a range of techniques available to maximise resection whilst avoiding injury to 'eloquent' parts of the brain (areas of the brain associated with speech or complex executive functions). These techniques include:

- preoperative functional MRI to identify important speech areas;
- awake craniotomy with intraoperative cortical mapping of eloquent areas;
- 5-ALA labelling to distinguish tumour from normal brain;
- image-guidance techniques.

29.59   Over the past two decades a variety of image-guidance systems have become available to surgeons to facilitate intracranial procedures, including glioma surgery. Their use is ubiquitous in UK neurosurgery departments. These systems, based on cold war stealth fighter-bomber guidance technology, allow surgeons to use a pre-operative scan to make an on-screen virtual image of an individual patient's brain. During an operation, a guidance wand is used to manipulate the on-screen image such that the surgeon can use the image to aid identification of structures in the vicinity of the tip of the guidance wand. This can aid identification of the tumour margins, allowing maximal resection or help prevent inadvertent injury to essential structures. Although the use of guidance systems has become ubiquitous, the question of whether their use is mandatory or not in glioma surgery is moot. A recent Cochrane review of the subject did not yield evidence that guidance techniques, nor any of the other techniques described above, improved patient outcome in glioma surgery[1].

1 Barone, Lawrie, Hart 'Image guided surgery for the resection of brain tumours' Cochrane Database Syst Rev. (2014) Jan 28;1:CD009685. doi: 10.1002/14651858.CD009685.pub2.

29.60 There is also considerable debate as to whether radiotherapy (traditional external beam radiation therapy or focus therapy) and/ or chemotherapy are beneficial in reducing the incidence of recurrence or increasing the time of the occurrence of transformation of benign cells into more malignant cells. Trials are in progress to attempt to answer these questions. The literature points to a mean survival of patients with these WHO grade 2 gliomas of between 40–60 per cent at five years from the diagnosis with falling to between 25–40 per cent at ten years.

Further reading:
Pignatti, van den Brent, Curran (et al) 'Prognostic factors for survival in adult patients with cerebral low-grade glioma' (2002) 20 J Clin Oncol 2076–2084. (2013) 15(8) Neuro Oncol 1102–1110. doi: 10.1093/neuonc/not080. Epub 27 June 2013
Duffau 'A new philosophy in surgery for diffuse low-grade glioma (DLGG): oncological and functional outcomes' (2013) 59(1) Neurochirurgie 2–8. doi: 10.1016/j.neuchi.2012.11.001. Epub 12 February 2013. Review
Hardesty, Sanai 'The value of glioma extent of resection in the modern neurosurgical era' (2012) 18(3) Front Neurol 140. doi: 10.3389/fneur.2012.00140. eCollection 2012

29.61 The diagnosis of patients with malignant gliomas (WHO grade 3 or 4) is seldom delayed owing to the rapidly progressive history[1]. High grade astrocytomas, however, which may present with a long history of uncomplicated epilepsy, can pose a diagnostic dilemma and the eventual diagnosis may be delayed. When considering whether the delay has caused harm however, this delay may be of little importance, as early diagnosis of these tumours may have little influence on the treatment or long-term outlook (see above). In order to avoid problems with informed consent, patients and their relatives must be made fully aware of the results and possible complications following surgery to the gliomas.

1 Yang, Han 'Preface. Modern management of high grade glioma, Part I' (2012) 23(2) Neurosurg Clin N Am xiii. doi: 10.1016/j.nec.2012.02.003. Epub 24 February 2012; Yang, Han 'Modern management of high grade glioma, Part II' (2012) 23(3) Neurosurg Clin N Am xiii–xiv. doi: 10.1016/j.nec.2012.05.004. Epub 30 May 2012

29.62 The common surgical complications of tumour surgery (whether benign or malignant) include:

- death;
- neurological deterioration from intracranial bleeding; or
- brain injury associated with surgery;

- acute brain oedema;
- wound infection;
- seizures.

29.63 Gliomas are termed intra-axial tumours, as they arise from within the brain substance. The next most commonly occurring primary brain tumours are extra-axial tumours, as they arise out with the brain substance, but rather from elements on the inside of the skull. These tumours cause their effect by local pressure on surrounding structures and by increasing the volume of the intracranial contents and thereby the intracranial pressure. These tumours are often histologically benign and include the meningiomas, schwannomas – commonly vestibular, pituitary and suprasellar tumours. As these tumours are usually benign, the history may be long and insidious, so that by the time the diagnosis is made the tumour may have reached considerable size and caused irreparable damage to surrounding neurological structures. In such cases the results of surgery, both in terms of operative mortality and recovery of neurological deficits may be disappointing and lead to questions of diagnostic delay being raised by the patient or surviving relative.

Meningiomas

29.64 Meningiomas represent the next most common group of intracranial tumours after gliomas. Usually histologically benign (WHO grade I), they can at times show a more aggressive clinical course (WHO II) and rarely are frankly malignant (WHO III). The diagnosis is made by appropriate imaging techniques (CT or MRI) and treatment is by surgical removal, although gamma knife therapy or conservative management with interval head scanning may be more appropriate in certain circumstances. Surgery exposes the patients to a variety of complications which can be grouped according to those which are general to all neurosurgery and those which are specific to the site of origin of the meningioma.

29.65 General complications include:

- death;
- neurological deterioration from intracranial bleeding; or
- brain injury associated with surgery;
- acute brain oedema;
- wound infection;
- raised intracranial pressure post-operatively, which may be due to oedema or venous infarction;
- seizures are a common feature of meningiomas with a preoperative incidence of approximately 15 per cent.

29.66 While there is a tendency for seizure frequency to decrease post-operatively, a significant number of patients with no pre-operative history will develop post-operative epilepsy. Epileptic seizures have a significant impact on patients since seizures place restrictions on driving and professional activities, however the role of prophylactic anti-epileptic medication after meningioma surgery is not proven and a subject of debate in the literature.

29.67 Although meningiomas are usually histologically benign, there is a definite mortality rate, the actual figure depending on the histological type (WHO grade) and the degree of surgical resection (Simpson grading): Complete resection of a benign lesion has a better prognosis than partial resection of a malignant meningioma. Meningiomas arising in the anterior cranial fossa and the cerebellopontine angle have a particular incidence of post-operative complication derived specifically from the site of origin of the lesions. A common symptom of tumours arising in the anterior cranial fossa (olfactory groove, suprasellar and spheno-orbital regions) is visual dysfunction which may present as monocular visual deterioration, bi-temporal field loss or central scotomas. The post-operative outcome is closely related to the degree of preoperative visual loss, the duration of the symptom and the size of the tumour, emphasising yet again the deleterious effects of delayed diagnosis on outcome. Anosmia occurs frequently as a result of damage to the olfactory nerve, which may be the result of direct pressure from the tumour or unavoidable traction related to the surgical approach. The close anatomical relationship of medially placed tumours (sphenoid wing, clinoidal process) to the arteries of Circle of Willis puts at risk the major branches of the internal carotid artery during the surgical removal of tumours in this site, making total removal unlikely and the recurrence rate high. Meningiomas arising within the posterior fossa form another group of this type of tumour which can carry significant post-operative complications, for example facial weakness, sensory disturbance of the face and balance problems.

29.68 Slow growing meningiomas, especially those in the cerebellopontine angle, less than 3cm in size with minimal symptoms may be treated with gamma knife therapy. Although the treatment does not remove the tumour, it may prevent further growth of the tumour therefore preventing neurological deterioration and maximising life expectancy. Long term outcomes have been published from several centres that suggest gamma knife therapy is as effective as surgery in terms of progression free survival (ie preventing increasing growth of the tumour) and overall survival with fewer side effects in terms of cranial nerve injury than surgery. Delayed diagnosis of a growing tumour that grows beyond the 3cm limit for gamma knife therapy may therefore impose an opportunity cost on the patient.

Further reading:

Ambekar, Sharma, Madhugiri, Nanda 'Trends in intracranial meningioma surgery and outcome: a Nationwide Inpatient Sample database analysis from 2001 to 2010' (2013) 114(3) J Neurooncol 299–307. doi: 10.1007/s11060-013-1183-6. Epub 13 July 2013

Chaichana, Pendleton, Zaidi, Olivi, Weingart, Gallia, Lim, Brem, Quiñones-Hinojosa 'Seizure control for patients undergoing meningioma surgery' (2013) 79(3–4) World Neurosurg 515–524. doi: 10.1016/j.wneu.2012.02.051. Epub 30 March 2012

Hasseleid, Meling, Rønning, Scheie, Helseth 'Surgery for convexity meningioma: Simpson Grade I resection as the goal: clinical article' (2012) 117(6) J Neurosurg 999–1006. doi: 10.3171/2012.9.JNS12294. Epub 12 October 2012

(2011) 114(5) J Neurosurg 1399–1409. doi: 10.3171/2010.11.JNS101193.

Sughrue, Rutkowski, Chen, Shangari, Kane, Parsa, Berger, McDermott 'Modern surgical outcomes following surgery for sphenoid wing meningiomas' (2013) 119(1) J Neurosurg 86–93. doi: 10.3171/2012.12.JNS11539. Epub 22 February 2013.

Kane, Sughrue, Rutkowski, Berger, McDermott, Parsa 'Clinical and surgical considerations for cerebellopontine angle meningiomas' (2011) 18(6) J Clin Neurosci 755–759. doi: 10.1016/j.jocn.2010.09.023. Epub 19 April 2011

Sughrue, Rutkowski, Shangari, Chang, Parsa, Berger, McDermott 'Risk factors for the development of serious medical complications after resection of meningiomas' (2011) 114(3) J Neurosurg 697–704. doi: 10.3171/2010.6.JNS091974. Epub 23 July 2010

Sughrue, Rutkowski, Chang, Shangari, Kane, McDermott, Berger, Parsa 'Postoperative seizures following the resection of convexity meningiomas: are prophylactic anticonvulsants indicated?' (2011) 114(3) J Neurosurg 705–709. doi: 10.3171/2010.5.JNS091972. Epub 25 June 2010

Wang, Li, Zhu, Yang, Wang, Gong, Liu 'Surgical management and evaluation of prognostic factors influencing postoperative visual outcome of suprasellar meningiomas' (2011) 75(2) World Neurosurg 294–302. doi: 10.1016/j.wneu.2010.08.021

Pepper, Hecht, Gebarski, Lin, Sullivan, Marentette 'Olfactory groove meningioma: discussion of clinical presentation and surgical outcomes following excision via the subcranial approach' (2011) 121(11) Laryngoscope 2282–2289. doi: 10.1002/lary.22174. Epub 12 October 2011

Vestibular schwannoma

29.69 Vestibular schwannoma (historically called acoustic neuroma) is a tumour that arises from the superior vestibular division of the 8th cranial nerve. These tumours arise in the cerebellopontine angle and are in close proximity to the facial nerve, brainstem and cerebellum so that operative removal carries a risk of facial palsy, deafness, limb weakness and disturbance of balance. The majority of patients present with gradual progressive hearing loss in one ear although a small number will present with sudden hearing loss. Many patients experience tinnitus in one ear. It is rare for patients to have normal hearing at presentation. Less common presentations include facial numbness or pain with the involvement of the trigeminal nerve and incoordination from cerebellar compression and ear ache. Facial weakness is uncommon. The diagnosis of vestibular schwannoma should be considered in any patient complaining of:

- unilateral or asymmetrical auditory symptoms (either hearing loss or tinnitus) whether of progressive or sudden onset;
- impaired facial sensation;
- patients with imbalance which cannot otherwise be explained.

29.70 Investigations should include:

- audiology (pure tone audiometry);
- speech discrimination (auditory brainstem responses);
- CT and MRI imaging.

29.71 The management of these patients is best undertaken by a dedicated multi-disciplinary team working in specialist centres, especially if patients have neurofibromatosis type 2. Neurofibromatosis type 2 is a rare genetic condition which predisposes the sufferer to developing bilateral vestibular schwannomas and meningiomas.

29.72 There are three management options for vestibular schwannoma patients;

- interval scanning;
- micro-surgical removal of the vestibular schwannoma;
- stereotactic radio-surgery/stereotactic fractionated radiotherapy.

29.73 Consent needs to be full and patients should be presented with the full range of management options available to them. The option of no intervention with interval scanning should be considered, at least in the short term, in patients with a small vestibular schwannoma and good hearing. Older patients and patients in poor medical condition may be managed in this way, although it is by no means certain that vestibular schwannoma will grow less aggressively in old patients. Small tumours (less than 3cms diameter) may be considered for either micro-surgery or stereotactic radio-surgery; tumours greater than 3cms are only treatable with surgery. Post-operative facial nerve function is dependent on the size of the tumour: Pre-operative size of tumour is the only significant predicator of post-operative facial nerve function that has been identified in large case series. Stereotactic radio-surgery and fractionated stereotactic radiotherapy may be delivered by a gamma knife or a linear accelerator (LINAC). Outcome studies report excellent rates of hearing and facial nerve preservation and comparable outcomes to surgery in terms of progression free survival. However, there is the rare complication of malignant transformation following stereotactic radio-surgery, or of radiation damage to surrounding areas.

Further reading:
(2013) 60 Suppl 1 Neurosurgery 120–125. doi: 10.1227/01. neu.0000430307.78949.4e
(2013) 73(1) Neurosurgery 48–56; discussion 56–57. doi: 10.1227/01. neu.0000429862.50018.b9
Mackeith, Kerr, Milford 'Trends in acoustic neuroma management: a 20-year review of the oxford skull base clinic' (2013) 74(4) J Neurol Surg B Skull Base 194–200. doi: 10.1055/s-0033-1342919. Epub 1 April 2013
Gurgel, Dogru, Amdur, Monfared 'Facial nerve outcomes after surgery for large vestibular schwannomas: do surgical approach and extent of resection matter?' (2012) 33(3) Neurosurg Focus E16. doi: 10.3171/2012.7.FOCUS12199
Bloch, Sughrue, Kaur, Kane, Rutkowski, Kaur, Yang, Pitts, Parsa 'Factors associated with preservation of facial nerve function after surgical resection of vestibular schwannoma' (2011) 102(2) J Neurooncol 281–286. doi: 10.1007/s11060-010-0315-5. Epub 6 August 2010
Hasegawa, Kida, Kato, Iizuka, Kuramitsu, Yamamoto 'Long-term safety and efficacy of stereotactic radiosurgery for vestibular schwannomas: evaluation of 440 patients more than 10 years after treatment with Gamma Knife surgery' (2013) 118(3) J Neurosurg 557–565. doi: 10.3171/2012.10. JNS12523. Epub 9 November 2012

29.74 Tumours of the pituitary gland and suprasellar region above the pituitary gland frequently present problems both pre- and post-operatively similar to those seen with suprasellar meningiomas. Because of their proximity to the visual apparatus and the carotid arteries visual loss is the main indication for surgery to pituitary and suprasellar tumours such as craniopharyngiomas. Visual loss is classically bitemporal hemianopia although in practice any pattern of visual field loss is seen. Visual acuity is normally preserved within the remaining visual field but not always. Surgery to pituitary tumours is, in the vast majority of cases, through the nose via the transphenoidal route (microscopic or endoscopic) and in the large series the mortality rate ranges between 0.2–1 per cent and the occurrence of meningitis 2 per cent. The competent medical and surgical management of these patients usually requires close cooperation between the neurosurgeon with a sub-speciality interest and the endocrinologist.

29.75 Craniopharyngiomas are often more challenging than pituitary tumours. Craniopharyngiomas are tumours which arise in the region above the pituitary gland. They have solid and cystic components and are often locally advanced by the time they come to medical attention since they tend to grow slowly over time. Complete surgical resection is often not possible, although if feasible complete removal is the optimum treatment. Complete resection is often not feasible as the craniopharyngioma often invades or is firmly attached to major blood vessels and essential brain structures such as the hypothalamus. The aim of surgery in most cases is decompression of adjacent structures, especially visual apparatus. Decompression may be achieved by direct removal of craniopharyngioma bulk via a craniotomy or transphenoidal approach or by decompressing cystic parts of the tumour. As with pituitary tumours, endocrine management is essential as compression of the pituitary gland immediately beneath the craniopharyngioma may result in a range of hormonal disturbances that require medical management.

Further reading:

Gao, Zhong, Wang, Xu, Guo, Dai, Zheng, Wang, Luo, Jiang 'Endoscopic versus microscopic transsphenoidal pituitary adenoma surgery: a meta-analysis' (2014) 12 World J Surg Oncol 94. doi: 10.1186/1477-7819-12-94

Murad, Fernández-Balsells, Barwise, Gallegos-Orozco, Paul, Lane, Lampropulos, Natividad, Perestelo-Pérez, Ponce de León-Lovatón, Albuquerque, Carey, Erwin, Montori 'Outcomes of surgical treatment for nonfunctioning pituitary adenomas: a systematic review and meta-analysis' (2010) 73(6) Clin Endocrinol (Oxf) 777–791. doi: 10.1111/j.1365-2265.2010.03875.x. Review

Cerebral metastases

29.76 Cerebral metastases are the most common intracranial tumours and are much more common than primary brain tumours in the general population. The main symptoms are similar to other brain tumours, namely headache and vomiting, seizures or focal neurological signs. The diagnosis is made by imaging the brain with the best test being contrast enhanced MRI scanning, although the diagnosis may be made by contrast enhanced CT scanning. Many cancer patients will have regular follow-up after treatment, therefore metastases may be detected on routine screening in the absence of any symptoms in some patients. The diagnosis is made on the clinical history and the presence of multiple lesions. However, problems arise with single metastases which need to be distinguished from benign or malignant primary brain tumours, abscesses, cerebral infarction and haemorrhage. Brain metastases have a poor prognosis with untreated patients having a median survival of a few weeks or months. Several methods of treatment are available for patients with intracranial metastases. Corticosteroids, radiotherapy and surgical therapy all have an established place in treatment, with surgery plus radiotherapy the preferred choice in patients who are fit enough to contemplate surgery. Chemotherapy may also be useful in treating brain metastases in some patients with chemo-sensitive tumours. Focused radiotherapy has been shown to be effective, though it does depend on tumour size. Each patient needs to be carefully assessed to determine the optimum treatment which will include the extent of the systemic disease, the patient's neurological state, current quality of life and the number and sites of the metastases. The decision regarding the appropriate therapy will involve multiple disciplines. There needs to be team work and coordination if the patient is to be satisfactorily treated.

Further reading:
Aragon-Ching and Zujewski (2007) 13(6) Clin Cancer Res 1644–1647; Chang, Robins, Mehta (2007) 5(1) Clin Adv Hematol Oncol 54–64
Yamamoto (2007) 20 Prog Neurol Surg 106–128

Hydrocephalus

29.77 Hydrocephalus refers to a build-up in cerebrospinal fluid (CSF) volume within the brain and may be caused by too much CSF production (rare), obstruction to flow of fluid from the site of production within the interior of the brain to the site of reabsorption in the subarachnoid space over the brain surface by a tumour or other space occupying lesion, or reduced reabsorption. Hydrocephalus is very much the domain of neurosurgery and may be treated by drainage procedures (eg external ventricular drain and ventriculoperitoneal shunt) or removing the cause of obstruction to flow (eg removing a tumour or colloid cyst, etc). Hydrocephalus is usually associated with raised pressure resulting in headache, vomiting, visual symptoms (including reduced vision or blindness if present for a long period) and reduced conscious level. Normal and low pressure hydrocephalus entities are described in the literature in which headache, vomiting and reduced conscious levels are not normally a feature, but may be associated with other symptoms such as cognitive impairment, incontinence and gait (walking) disturbance. Idiopathic Intracranial Hypertension, although not strictly a hydrocephalus entity, presents with similar symptoms to high pressure hydrocephalus, especially headache and visual loss, and is often treated with ventriculoperitoneal shunt.

Further reading:
Rigamonti *Adult Hydrocephalus* (2014)
Paranathala, Sitsapesan, Green, Cadoux-Hudson, Pereira 'Idiopathic normal pressure hydrocephalus: an important differential diagnosis' (2013) 74(10) Br J Hosp Med (Lond) 564–570

Wakerley, Tan, Ting 'Idiopathic intracranial hypertension' (2014) 20 Cephalalgia pii: 0333102414534329

29.78 Hydrocephalus, both congenital and acquired, is effectively treated by the insertion of a valved shunt system. This provides an alternative route for cerebrospinal fluid drainage, and usually a ventriculo-peritoneal system is employed (tube from brain to abdomen). On occasions other sites, such as the ventriculo atrial (heart) or ventriculo pleural (chest) shunts are used. Endoscopic third ventriculostomy is an alternative procedure used frequently in paediatric neurosurgical practice, especially if hydrocephalus is caused by aqueductal stenosis. Aqueductal stenosis refers to narrowing of the narrowest part of the ventricular system most commonly caused by intraventricular bleeding and infection at the time of birth. The procedure involves inserting a camera (endoscope) into the ventricular system through a burr hole and making a hole in the thin membrane at the floor of the ventricular system, allowing brain fluid (CSF) to bypass the obstructed aqueduct. Although endoscopic third ventriculostomy is more likely to fail to treat hydrocephalus than a shunt, if the procedure is successful it avoids the life-long problems associated with shunts[1]. It is good practice to include requirement for shunt as a specific risk of the procedure during the consent process.

1 (2014) 13(3) J Neurosurg Pediatr 295–300. doi: 10.3171/2013.11.PEDS13138. Epub 3 January 2014.

29.79 As with intracranial tumours, complaints regarding patients with hydrocephalus largely revolve around delay in diagnosis and treatment, both of the underlying condition and of complications arising following the shunt insertion or ventriculoscopic surgery. The diagnosis can usually be made on clinical grounds and confirmed by further investigation, in the form of ultrasound, CT or MRI scanning. Common complications which follow shunt insertion are blockage of the system, which will cause recurrence of the hydrocephalus and the symptoms related to it, and infection which may cause meningitis and potentially catastrophic brain damage. Both these complications must be detected and treated early if irreparable brain damage and death are to be avoided. There are long-term complications of hydrocephalus management and these have been reviewed by Sgouras et al[1]. One particular area of concern is that of visual complications: these complications need to be recognised and acted on, for delay can result in permanent blindness. Shunt revision procedures are often necessary during patients' lives but routine revision procedures are not common practice in the absence of symptoms or evidence of shunt dysfunction.

1 Sgouras S, Malluci C, Walsh AR et al (1995) 23(3) Pediatr Neurosurg 127–132; de Robaupierre, Rillet, Vernet (et al) (2007) Childs Nerv Syst (17 Jan) (E Pub).

CONGENITAL ABNORMALITIES

29.80 Neurosurgery, in common with many surgical disciplines, is, increasingly, becoming divided into sub-specialities. The growth of paediatric neurosurgery as a separate discipline has removed the treatment of many congenital abnormalities from the every-day experience of the general neurosurgeon. The treatment of non syndromic craniosynostosis and syndromal craniosynostosis (eg Crouzon's and Apert's Syndromes) are undertaken in regional specialist paediatric cranio-facial units and treatment should not be undertaken outside these designated units. In designated units, there is close cooperation between neurosurgeons, plastic and ENT surgeons, supported by nurses with a specialist interest in the disorders. In these units the risks of surgical treatment are well recognised and are conveyed to the parents. The treatment of spinal dysraphism is the province of the paediatric neurosurgeon and paediatric spinal orthopaedics[1]. The Chiari malformation (type 1) with associated syringomyelia, while often congenital in origin, often presents in adult life, where its management is part of general neurosurgical expertise. However some more complex cases will require additional expertise.

1 Leland Albright, Pollack and Adelson *Principles and Practice of Pediatric Neurosurgery* (3rd end, 2014).

Spinal dysrhaphism

29.81 Babies born with open neural tube defects at the head end (anencephaly, hydro-anencephaly, occipital encephalocele associated with Chiari 3 malformation) have given rise to a number of cases involving complex ethical questions concerning continuing treatment. General agreement concerning the complex ethical problems has not yet been reached, but it is essential that the parents are closely involved with any decision making. This is particularly important because of the involvement of several surgical and medical disciplines in the management of the child from the first day of the baby's life. If treatment is agreed to be in the patient's best interests, skin defects associated with open neural tube defects (encephalocele) are repaired to reduce the risk of meningitis posed by delicacy of the membranes separating neural tissue from the outside world. Hydrocephalus occurs in these children and needs to be recognised and treated early, normally with a ventriculoperitoneal shunt (ETV is not normally an option).

29.82 Spina bifida aperta is a form of open neural tube defect affecting the bottom end of the spinal cord. The outcomes are much better than defects at the head end: many children with open spina bifida will have normal or near normal intelligence and have a high degree of independence, not withstanding wheelchair use. As with encephalocele, the open neural tube defect (myelomenigocele and related entities) needs to be repaired to avoid the risk of meningitis, and most patients will require a shunt within a few months of birth for hydrocephalus. The decision to treat is normally not controversial, as many children with this form of neural tube defect will have a good quality of life with the right support. Multiple specialties in addition to neurosurgery will normally be involved in the patient's care to maximise the patient's health and independence during childhood and beyond[1].

1 Bowman, McLone, Grant, Tomita, Ito 'Spina bifida outcome: a 25-year prospective study' (2001) 34(3) Pediatr Neurosurg 114–120.

29.83 More subtle forms of neural tube defect exist that may be asymptomatic, or be associated with relatively mild neurological deficits. Although the forms are multiple, they are termed spina bifida occulta, so called because the skin is intact over the defect. Patients with known spina bifida occulta and progressive neurological deficits should be investigated with MRI and the diagnosis of tethered cord syndrome should be considered. Indeed, any child with progressive lower limb symptoms should be investigated for tethered cord syndrome as the child may have a form of spina bifida occulta that has no external manifestations, and be hitherto undiagnosed at the time of presentation. Tethered cord syndrome refers to progressive neural dysfunction caused by stretching of neural tissue fixed to an occult neural tube defect as the patient grows. Various surgical procedures are described in this syndrome depending on the specific anatomical form of the neural tube defect. As a general rule surgery is effective in dealing with pain and bladder dysfunction caused by the tethered cord but may not reverse neurological deficits associated with the syndrome. Detethering surgery carries a small risk of worsening neurological status.

29.84 Problems with spinal dysraphism and congenital neurosurgical disorders in general are becoming less frequent with the advent of effective antenatal screening, folic acid supplementation in pregnancy, and more liberal abortion laws. However the importance of diagnosis and fully informed discussion with the parents and relatives explaining the condition, the complications, treatment and long-term outcome cannot be over-emphasised.

Syringomyelia

29.85 Progressive syringomyelia, causing increasing spinal cord dysfunction, is frequently associated with Chiari 1 malformations[1], historically known as Arnold-Chiari malformation. The first line treatment of this condition is posterior fossa and upper cervical cord decompression by means of a craniectomy and C1 laminectomy (foramen magnum decompression). If the patient has hydrocephalus, a ventriculo-peritoneal shunt is inserted prior to contemplating foramen magnum decompression. It should be noted that hydrocephalus may occur after foramen magnum decompression in approximately 10 per cent of cases, and patients should be informed of this pre-operatively, as treatment involves a second surgical procedure, namely insertion of a ventriculo-peritoneal shunt. The early institution of foramen magnum decompression results in the progression of syringomyelia being arrested in the majority of cases and in some patients improvement in neurological dysfunction occurs. If a foramen magnum decompression fails to halt progression of a syrinx, second line treatment by means of the insertion of a syringopleural shunt may be offered. The investigation of choice in patients with suspected Chiari 1 malformation is MRI scan, the development of which has led to earlier diagnosis and treatment before significantly disabling neurological problems have arisen.

1 Klekamp 'Surgical treatment of Chiari 1 malformation – analysis of intraoperative findings, complications, and outcome for 371 foramen magnum decompressions' (2012) 71(2) Neurosurgery 365–80; discussion 380. doi: 10.1227/NEU.0b013e31825c3426.

Subarachnoid haemorrhage

29.86 The incidence of subarachnoid haemorrhage ('SAH') in the UK is approximately 8 per 100,000 of population. Approximately 75–80 per cent of spontaneous SAH is due to ruptured intracranial aneurysm and a further 4–5 per cent of cases are due to arteriovenous malformations that have bled. Roughly 10–15 per cent of patients die before reaching medical care and the overall mortality rate is 45 per cent (range 32–67 per cent). One of the major causes of morbidity and mortality is rebleeding. The maximum frequency of rebleeding is in the first day (4 per cent on day 1) then 1.5 per cent daily for 13 days. Around 15–20 per cent of patients rebleed within 14 days, 50 per cent will rebleed within six months. Thereafter the risk is 3 per cent per year. The other major cause of morbidity and mortality in those patients reaching neurosurgical care is symptomatic vasospasm producing delayed ischaemic neurological deficits. This pathology occurs in around 40 per cent of patients who suffer an SAH and 40 per cent of those are at risk of dying or suffering a major neurological deficit. In an analysis of major published studies a mean death rate of 30.6 per cent in patients with vasospasm was demonstrated. Hydrocephalus is another major complication of aneurysmal subarachnoid haemorrhage. This may be treated temporarily by external ventricular drain, lumbar puncture, or permanently with ventriculoperitoneal shunt. Other complications of subarachnoid haemorrhage include cerebral salt wasting (hyponatraemia, low sodium in the blood), seizures, myocardial stunning resulting in hypotension or cardiac dysrhythmias and pulmonary oedema (fluid in the lungs).

Further reading:
Hop, Rinkel, Algra (et al) (1997) 28 Stroke 660–664
Sangha, Natalwala, Mann, Uppal, Mummadi, Haque, Aziz, Potluri 'Co-morbidities and Mortality associated with Intracranial Bleeds and Ischaemic Stroke' (2014) 4 Int J Neurosci 1–21
Lovelock, Rinkel, Rothwell 'Time trends in outcome of subarachnoid hemorrhage: Population-based study and systematic review' (2010) 74(19) Neurology 1494–1501. doi: 10.1212/WNL.0b013e3181dd42b3. Epub 7 April 2010.

29.87 The effect of delayed diagnosis following an aneurysmal SAH has been well documented in the literature for many years[1]. The consequence of such a delay is that the patient could suffer a rebleed with increased morbidity and mortality. It has been shown that as a direct result of delay significantly more patients died or were severely disabled than those whose haemorrhage was diagnosed without delay.

1 Neil-Dwyer and Lang (1997) 31 J RC Physicians (London) 49–52.

29.88 The majority of patients who suffer an SAH complain of a sudden headache which is quite unlike any headache they have previously experienced. Only 2 per cent of patients deny headache having suffered an SAH, while 40 per cent of patients may have no confirmatory signs such as neck stiffness. It is the history of headache with its mode of onset, severity and persistence which is the single most certain way of making a diagnosis of subarachnoid haemorrhage.

29.89 The investigations which will confirm the diagnosis are CT scanning and lumbar puncture. CT examination within 48 hours of an SAH will detect blood in more than 95 per cent of cases. However by the third and fourth day that percentage will have dropped to 70 per cent and by the fifth day will be less than 50 per cent. If the CT scan is regarded as normal, and there is a suspicion of the possibility of the patient having suffered an SAH, then a lumbar puncture must be carried out. The classical findings of a lumbar puncture carried out after 12 hours of a SAH are of uniformly bloodstained cerebrospinal fluid (CSF), xanthochromia and possibly a raised CSF pressure. Spectrophotometry is used to detect xanthochromia in the CSF of SAH patients. By the fifth day after the haemorrhage the CSF is likely to be yellowish in colour due to breakdown products of the haemoglobin and by day 10 there will be an increase in the number of white blood cells with the yellow tingeing (xanthochromia) disappearing by the end of the third week. The only abnormality following the third week for about a further week is a raised protein level but the CSF will be clear[1]. Patients with confirmed spontaneous SAH or suspected SAH in patients with equivocal results are investigated with angiography. This involves CT angiography (a contrast CT head scan) followed by digital subtraction angiography (formal angiogram). The time between performing CT angiography and digital subtraction angiography will depend on the clinical history, and results of the initial CT scan.

1 Perry, Sivilotti, Stiell (et al) (2006) 37 Stroke 2467–2472.

29.90 Patients who are diagnosed as having had a subarachnoid haemorrhage are referred to a neurosurgical unit. A recent observational study of neurosurgical units in the UK has shown that 33 per cent of patients were treated within two days of the haemorrhage, a further 39 per cent between days three and seven and 10 per cent between days eight to ten[1]. Patients who were diagnosed as a subarachnoid haemorrhage should be started on oral nimodipine (a calcium antagonist) as this has been shown to reduce the incidence of poor outcomes[2].

1 NCEPOD Subarachnoid Haemorrhage: Managing the Flow (2013).
2 Pickard, Murray, Illingworth (et al) (1989) 298 Br Med J 636–642.

29.91 The grade of the patient prior to treatment is a prognostic indicator. The most used grading system is the World Federation of Neurological Societies (WFNS) grading scale. This has five levels. The best level is a patient who is conscious, orientated with no neurological deficits (grade 1) and the worst level is a patient who is unconscious with or without neurological deficits (grade 5).

29.92 There are two major methods of treating aneurysms surgically or endovascularly (introducing coils into the aneurysms). In 2002 in the International Subarachnoid Aneurysm Trial of neurosurgical clipping versus endovascular coiling in terms of survival free of disability at one year the patients did significantly better with endovascular coiling[1]. However in an observational prospective study between 2001–2002 involving all the neurosurgical units in the UK there was no significant difference in the outcome with regard to neurosurgical clipping or endovascular coiling[2]. In this extensive survey, favourable outcome (good recovery – moderate disability) was obtained in 62 per cent of patients with an unfavourable outcome in 38 per cent. The most important determinant of outcome was the grade of the patient at surgery with WFNS grade 1 and 2 patients having the best outcomes. Importantly it is essential that patients and their relatives are fully aware of the treatment options, the results and likely outcome not only in terms of morbidity and mortality but also psychosocially. There is evidence to show that after a successful outcome over 50 per cent of patients are depressed; 7 per cent lost their jobs as a result of the haemorrhage; more than half (54 per cent) were off work six or more months; and one in five were off for more than one year[3].

1 Molyneux, Kerr, Stratton, Sandercock, Clarke, Shrimpton, Holman, International Subarachnoid Aneurysm Trial (ISAT) Collaborative Group 'International Subarachnoid Aneurysm Trial (ISAT) of neurosurgical clipping versus endovascular coiling in 2143 patients with ruptured intracranial aneurysms: a randomised trial' (2002) 360(9342) Lancet 1267–1274.
2 Royal College of Surgeons of England National Study of Subarachnoid Haemorrhage (2006).
3 Pritchard, Foulkes, Lang (et al) (2001) 15 Br J Neurosurg 456–463; Al-Tamimi, Ahmad, May, Bholah, Callear, Goddard, Quinn, Ross 'A comparison of the outcome of aneurysmal subarachnoid haemorrhage before and after the introduction of an endovascular service' (2010) 17(11) J Clin Neurosci 1391–1394. doi: 10.1016/j.jocn.2010.03.024.

STEREOTACTIC SURGERY

29.93 Stereotactic surgery refers to a method of three-dimensional placement of surgical instruments within the brain, combining a three-dimensional Cartesian coordinate system and a three-dimensional positioning instrument which is firmly attached to the head. Gamma knife therapy, described above, involves similar techniques. In the late 1950s and the 1960s stereotactic surgery was used to produce accurately situated lesions in the thalamus to treat the tremor of Parkinson's disease. The availability of the drug L-dopa after 1968 resulted in a substantial drop in the number of such procedures performed and until the advent of CT scanning in the 1970s, stereotactic surgery became almost extinct in most centres. CT and MRI scanning provides a precise three-dimensional database which can easily be incorporated into a stereotactic system and this has led to a re-emergence of interest in stereotactic surgery for a range of purposes, such as biopsy of deep-seated tumours and accurate placement of deep brain stimulation systems in the treatment of movement disorders. Patients must be made aware that when used to treat movement disorders the placement of electrodes carries some risks. Risks include:

- lead insertion associated haemorrhage;
- stroke;
- errors in lead placement;
- an inherent risk that surgery may not offer much improvement;
- infection.

29.94 It is likely that both ethical and medico-legal issues will become increasingly important in the future of stereotactic surgery, with the possible development of stem cell transplants and other technologies for an increasing range of degenerative conditions. In general, the surgery is performed in specialised units by neurosurgeons who have a large experience in this highly specialised type of surgery.

Further reading:
Esselink, de Bie, de Haan (et al) (2006) 148 Acta Neurochir (Wien) 1247–1255

Pereira, Green, Nandi, Aziz 'Deep brain stimulation: indications and evidence' (2007) 4(5) Expert Rev Med Devices 591–603

CNS INFECTION

29.95 CNS infection covers a range of entities including meningitis, cerebral abscess, subdural empyema and spinal epidural abscess. CNS infection treatment has been revolutionised by the introduction of effective antibiosis, and many historic clinic-pathological entities common in the earlier part of the twentieth century are rarely encountered in clinical practice[1].

1 Chalif, Gillies, Magdum, Aziz, Pereira 'Everything to gain: Sir Hugh Cairns' treatment of central nervous system infection at Oxford and abroad' (2013) 72(2) Neurosurgery 135–142; discussion 142. doi: 10.1227/NEU.0b013e31827b9fae.

Cerebral abscess

29.96 Diagnosing a cerebral abscess can be difficult because the presenting symptoms tend to be non-specific. It tends to occur more commonly in males, with general symptoms of raised intracranial pressure in which the commonest features are headache, vomiting and nausea. Pyrexia is usually present but meningeal irritation is less common. CT and MRI scanning have been responsible for reducing mortality in this condition. Nonetheless, no imaging modality can specifically diagnose an abscess, since the imaging characteristics of abscesses on CT and MRI are similar to those of metastatic and glial tumours. The major factor in determining outcome is the patient's level of consciousness pre-operatively. There are two surgical methods of treating abscesses, namely excision and aspiration. The mainstay of treatment is antibiotic therapy: appropriate, aggressive, intravenous antibiotic therapy has been a major factor in reducing the morbidity and mortality of this condition. There are now studies since the advent of CT scanning which have mortality rates from 0–10 per cent with the two major factors contributing to mortality being delayed diagnosis and the poor clinical state of the patients at the time of surgery[1]. Lumbar puncture is contra-indicated in these patients with raised intracranial pressure, so a CT scan prior to this procedure is essential.

1 Sharma, Mohandas, Cooke 'Intracranial abscesses: changes in epidemiology and management over five decades in Merseyside' (2009) 37(1) Infection 39–43. doi: 10.1007/s15010-008-7359-x. Epub 12 January 2009.

Subdural empyema

29.97 Subdural empyema is less common than cerebral abscess. It affects males more than females and the common age at presentation is between 10–20 years old. Infection commonly results from direct extension mainly from the paranasal sinus and the mastoids and occasionally from compound skull fractures. The common presenting features are sinusitis, pyrexia, headache, neurological deficits, seizures, neck stiffness and less commonly swelling over the forehead and vomiting. The main investigation is a CT scan but this may fail to demonstrate the pathology particularly if contrast is not given and if the scan quality is poor. MRI scanning may give more information than CT scanning but this investigation is not widely available out of normal working hours in the UK for this type of urgent case, and pus and blood cannot be distinguished confidently on MRI. Although a lumbar puncture is contra-indicated in many patients the clinical picture resembles meningitis and as a result a lumbar puncture is often performed. However if there is a clinical suspicion of this pathology a lumbar puncture should not be carried out in patients with a meningitic picture and neurological signs. The most significant determinants of a good outcome are

- early diagnosis;
- aggressive removal of the source of infection;
- draining of the subdural pus;
- treatment of the infection with the appropriate antibiotic and surgical therapy, eg draining dental abscesses, draining skin boils etc.

29.98   The two important principles with surgery are to achieve adequate decompression of the brain and complete evacuation of the pus collection. The outcome will depend on the level of consciousness as the time of surgery. In patients with GCS 8–15 at the time of surgery 85 per cent had a good outcome and 5 per cent a poor outcome while in the group of patients GCS 3–7 59 per cent had a good outcome and 12.5 per cent a poor outcome[1].

Further reading:
Hall, Truwit 'The surgical management of infections involving the cerebrum' (2008) 62(Suppl 2) Neurosurgery 519–530; discussion 530-1. doi: 10.1227/01. neu.0000316255.36726.5b. Review
Kombogiorgas, Seth, Athwal, Modha, Singh 'Suppurative intracranial complications of sinusitis in adolescence. Single institute experience and review of literature' (2007) 21(6) Br J Neurosurg 603–609. Review

1 Nathoo, Nadin, Gouws (et al) (2001) 49 Neurosurgery 872–878.

Spinal epidural abscess

29.99   Spinal epidural abscess is a rare condition and because of its infrequent occurrence the diagnosis is often delayed. Other spinal elements may also be involved, eg intervertebral disc (discitis), bone (osteomyelitis) and facet joints (pyogenic facet arthropathy). The major features are usually back pain, fever, tenderness over the spine with pyrexia, sweats and rigor being common. Classically four stages are described: backache, which may be present for some time; root pain; limb weakness with bowel and bladder symptoms; and paralysis. The major predisposing factors include: diabetes mellitus; patients who are immuno-compromised; IV drug abusers; and elderly patients with no other identifiable risk factor. MRI imaging is the study of choice for diagnosis and it can differentiate from other conditions such as transverse myelitis and spinal cord infarction. Treatment of pyogenic epidural abscess is potentially a neurosurgical emergency because patients may neurologically deteriorate rapidly and unpredictably. The aims of treatment are to establish a bacteriological diagnosis, prevent or reverse neurological deficits by surgical decompression and removal of pus, relieve pain, establish spinal stability if necessary with spinal fixation and eradicate the infection and prevent a relapse. The appropriate choice of antibiotics is guided by local antibiotic policies and culture results when available. The final neurological outcome depends on the speed of diagnosis and treatment, location of the abscess and the severity of the neurological deficit before surgery (if surgery is indicated). There is general agreement in the literature that patients with deficits persisting more than 36 hours have essentially no chance of recovery. An alternative approach to open surgery in patients with back and radicular pain without significant neurological deficit is to treat medically with intravenous antibiotics effective against microbacteriological pathogens identified from blood cultures or pus removed from the extradural space by percutaneous CT-guided aspiration. There is great importance placed on these patients being monitored meticulously, particularly their neurological state, temperature and laboratory values of C-reactive protein and WBC.

Further reading:
Sorensen (2003) 17 Br J Neurosurg 513–518
Hadjipavlou, Mader, Necessary, Muffoletto 'Hematogenous pyogenic spinal infections and their surgical management' (2000) 25(13) Spine (Phila Pa 1976) 1668–1679

SPINAL TUMOURS

29.100 Spinal epidural metastases occur in a significant proportion of cancer patients at some time and are by far the most common spinal tumour. 80 per cent of these metastases arise from primary tumours whose sites are lung, breast, GI tract, prostate, melanoma and lymphoma. Pain is the first symptom in 95 per cent of patients with spinal epidural metastases and this may be focal, radicular or referred. The key features of the back pain are persistence at rest and present at night. When the spinal cord becomes involved this leads to parasthaesiae, leg weakness and urinary and bladder symptoms. The definitive investigation is MRI scanning which can detect multiple lesions which may or may not cause bony destruction and will demonstrate paraspinal pathology. Although treatment for spinal epidural metastases has not been shown to prolong survival the aim of treatment is pain control, preservation of spinal stability, maintenance of sphincter control and mobility[1]. The main treatment decision will be whether to perform open surgery with post-operative radiotherapy or perform radiotherapy alone. The main prognostic factors are whether the patient has signs of leg weakness and bladder disturbance; paraplegia and urinary incontinence are poor prognostic features.

1 http://guidance.nice.org.uk/CG75.

29.101 Adult spinal cord tumours account for about 15 per cent of central nervous system neoplasms with 60 per cent of the cases being extramedullary (outside the substance of the spinal cord) and the remainder intramedullary (within the substance of the spinal cord)[1]. Extramedullary tumours are slow growing so that symptoms are variable and depend on tumour location. The clinical features of early cord compression are symptoms and signs of motor pathway involvement, mild spastic paraparesis (weakness). Bladder symptoms are of particular importance as they point to impeding spinal cord failure. Sensory symptoms tend to occur later than motor symptoms and tend to indicate a later stage in the deterioration of cord function. Upper cervical and foramen magnum tumours would seem to present with neck pain, distal arm weakness. Mid-cervical tumours may present with hemi-cord syndrome with dissociated sensory loss. Thoracic tumours present with signs of stiffness and then distal weakness with gait ataxia. Bowel and bladder function is not usually impaired until late in the clinical course. Ependymomas of the filum terminale can present with back pain followed by pain radiating into both legs. The key feature is that these symptoms and signs develop over a long period of time and this often leads to diagnostic errors. The definitive investigation is MRI scanning with Gadolinium enhancement being important particularly for the detection of small tumours. The use of the correct imaging techniques and interpretation as well as a recognition of the likely area of the pathology are important requisites if an appropriate demonstration and description of the pathology is to be obtained. The treatment for extramedullary tumours is surgery. It is important that the patient is fully informed of the benefits and risks of surgery and the results of damage to the spinal cord. The only additional treatment in aggressive filum ependymomas that recur is radiotherapy. The response of spinal cord ependymomas to radiation therapy is unpredictable and because radiation therapy markedly increases the morbidity of future surgery, that may be necessary, a cautious approach is advisable. Intramedullary tumours are in 80 per cent of cases primary glial tumours and these include astrocytomas, ependymomas, and the less common glial neoplasms such as oligodendrogliomas and sub-ependymomas. Metastases involving the spinal cord occur in less than five per cent of intramedullary spinal cord tumours. Intramedullary tumours can be difficult to diagnose as early symptoms are usually non-specific and may only progress very slowly. The symptom duration before diagnosis is often two to three years. Pain is the most common symptom but patients may have sensory and motor disturbances. An important differential diagnosis is demyelinating disease, eg multiple sclerosis (MS). If MS is suspected this needs to be investigated fully with appropriate neurological assessments, MRI scanning and, if necessary, examination of the cerebrospinal fluid for oligoclonal bands. MRI scanning is the definitive investigation and contrast enhancement is necessary to define the lesion and although it can distinguish between various tumour histology it is no substitute to traditional histological diagnoses.

1 Waters, Peran, Ciacci 'Malignancies of the spinal cord' (2012) 760 Adv Exp Med Biol 101–113. Review.

29.102 The aim of surgery is to diagnose the tumour and to determine whether there is a clear interface between the tumour and the spinal cord. It has become clear that radical removal alone cannot routinely be seen as definitive treatment and the surgical priority should be long-term tumour control with preservation of neurological function. Gross total removal is appropriate provided the patient remains intact. Intramedullary tumours are approached by standard laminectomy procedures with the patient in the prone position. Some surgeons use intraoperative monitoring in these cases, with somatosensory evoked potentials and direct motor evoked potentials being routinely employed. However, it would appear that only rarely do they influence surgical decisions or techniques and are not used routinely in the UK. In low grade astrocytomas where there is a plane between tumour and the spinal cord an attempt at total excision may be made. For high grade astrocytomas or for low grade astrocytomas without a plane of separation biopsy alone or biopsy with limited excision is the preferred option. For aggressive astrocytomas post-operative radiotherapy is usually recommended.

29.103 It is difficult to determine the prognosis of these tumours as there are no well-designed studies giving long term functional results following microsurgery. It would appear that better results occur in cases with minimal neurological deficits post-operatively. In the case of astrocytomas complete removal is rarely possible and long term functional results are poorer than with ependymomas. In astrocytomas there is a 50 per cent recurrence rate within four to five years[1].

1 Bansal, Ailawadhi, Suri, Kale, Sarat Chandra, Singh, Kumar, Sharma, Mahapatra, Sharma, Sarkar, Bithal, Dash, Gaikwad, Mishra 'Ten years' experience in the management of spinal intramedullary tumors in a single institution' (2013) 20(2) J Clin Neurosci 292–308. doi: 10.1016/j.jocn.2012.01.056. Epub 28 December 2012.

DEGENERATIVE SPINAL CONDITIONS

Prolapsed intervertebral disc

29.104 Most lumbar disc protrusions occur at the lower two intervertebral spaces at L4–5 and L5–S1, with L3–4, L2–3 and L1–2 much less common. The herniated lumbar disc usually spares the nerve root exiting at that interspace and impinges on the nerve root exiting the neural foramen one level down (eg an L5–S1 disc protrusion usually causes S1 radiculopathy). Prolapsed lumbar discs are usually laterally placed but a smaller number are centrally placed lesions and are of great importance as they can produce cauda equina compression, paraplegia and loss of sphincter function. The clinical syndrome associated with lumbar disc prolapse consists of two components occurring either separately or in combination; back or spinal pain, probably arising from a torn annulus, and radicular pain, owing to nerve compression. In a large number of patients there is a paucity of neurological signs with the findings of limited lumbar movement and tension signs (eg sciatica). In some patients loss of the ankle reflex if the S1 root is involved and sensory loss in the appropriate dermatome may be found, in a few patients weakness of ankle dorsiflexion and even rarer a foot drop may be present. The majority of disc lesions producing this clinical picture respond to conservative measures such as:

- bed rest;
- exercises;
- a course of anti-inflammatory drugs; and
- spinal manipulation.

29.105 Spinal manipulation is being practised increasingly both by medically qualified personnel and specialists in complementary techniques such as osteopathy and chiropractic treatment. Caution is necessary when performing spinal manipulation, particularly when performed under general anaesthetic, as this may occasionally be followed by acute cauda equina compression with disastrous complications[1]. Surgery should be considered when conservative measures have failed; the main indications for operative intervention include repeated attacks of severe sciatica, an acute attack which fails to respond to conservative measures, or progressive neurological problems. Conversely, surgery is almost always absolutely indicated in patients presenting with acute cauda equina syndrome (see below). Operation should be reserved for patients with unequivocal clinical evidence of nerve root compression corroborated by appropriate imaging (MRI/CT scanning). Back pain associated with degenerative spinal conditions in itself is not normally an indication for spinal surgery.

1 Phillips and Lauryssen *The Lumbar Intervertebral Disc* (2009).

29.106 The key areas that need to be discussed and recorded in the notes when obtaining consent from a patient are:

- the results of the definitive investigations;
- an explanation of how the surgery will be carried out;
- the probable outcome and the likely benefits of the surgery;
- probable complications – temporary complications and the therapeutic steps to correct them (pain, infection) – permanent results and complications;
- other risks that are foreseeable and reasonable alternatives to the proposed procedure.

29.107 If a complication or unexpected outcome occurs, an explanation should be given to the patient and if appropriate an apology made. While post-operative surgical complications are unusual the list of possible complications is extensive:

- infection;
- superficial wound infection;
- deep infection;
- increased motor deficit (some transient);
- tearing of the dura leading CSF fistula;
- pseudo-meningocoele;
- recurrent herniated lumbar disc.

29.108 There are the uncommon complications of a cauda equina syndrome, injuries to structures anterior to the vertebral bodies, great vessels (aorta, the common iliac artery and veins), ureters, bowel and sympathetic trunk. Rare infections include meningitis, discitis, spinal epidural abscess, post-operative arachnoiditis, thrombo-phlebitis and deep vein thrombosis with a risk of pulmonary embolus, and requirement for further surgery (eg spinal stabilisation, removal of recurrent discs, repair of pseudomeningocele). If spinal fixation is required in addition to decompression, additional risks include metal-work infection, metal fatigue, malposition of screws and non-fusion of the spine requiring repeat fixation surgery.

29.109 A potential error in the surgical approach for prolapsed lumbar intervertebral disc is to wrongly identify the disc level. This may occur because of obesity and lumbo-sacral anomaly. Errors of identification can be prevented by the use of pre-operative X-ray markers in order to accurately establish the correct surgical level or to screen the patient on the table and inserting a needle to accurately identify the appropriate disc space. Another possible error is for the surgeon to explore the wrong side at the correct level. The problem is compounded by the operation being finished without finding the disc and without reference to the notes or the imaging.

29.110 The surgical technique employed to treat a laterally-placed prolapsed lumbar disc will vary according to the training and preference of the operating surgeon and will range from the classical hemi-laminectomy to the micro-discectomy, including endoscopic techniques, all of which can be equally successful if preceded by adequate thought and planning. A successful outcome is achieved in a large proportion of cases of suitably selected patients, although there is a recognised recurrence rate (5–10 per cent) after initial success, which may be due to recurrent disc material at the site of previous surgery, a new disc prolapse at a different spinal level, or the development of adhesions at the site of the original operation[1]. Long term, most patients continue to benefit from surgery, but there is a risk of no improvement or worsened symptoms despite adequate surgery, termed failed back surgery syndrome.

1 (2014) 39(1) Spine (Phila Pa 1976) 3–16.

Lumbar stenosis

29.111 Lumbar spinal stenosis has become more of a problem in our increasing elderly population. Lumbar stenosis may be caused by degeneration in a number of spinal elements including facet joints (facet joint arthropathy), ligamentum flavum hypertrophy, spondylolisthesis (degeneration of intervertebral joints) and pars interarticularis defects. The latter two features are more common in younger men, especially those who have suffered repetitive spinal trauma during competitive sport. The symptoms are usually low back, radicular pain, problems of micturition, weakness of the legs and neurogenic claudication (neurological symptoms present during exercise but not at rest). The latter symptom can be distinguished from intermittent vascular claudication by a careful assessment of the patient's complaint[1]. However both conditions may coexist in elderly patients and very careful imaging with the involvement of a vascular surgeon may be necessary. Operations may be undertaken with a poor outcome because the other condition was present. It is essential that the patient is informed of the complexity of the problem. While this pathology is found commonly on routine radiological investigation, particularly with modern imaging, surgery in the form of wide decompression without spinal fixation should be reserved for those patients with clear evidence of nerve root or cauda equina compression both clinically and by suitable imaging techniques. In more elderly patients the post-operative complication of a dural tear with subsequent CSF fistula is commoner than in the younger population with soft disc prolapse. The leak can usually be recognised and treated by dural suture during the operation but nevertheless as it can lead to prolonged hospitalisation and delayed rehabilitation. Patients undergoing wide decompressive laminectomy for lumbar stenosis should be warned of its possible occurrence. Younger patients, especially those with significant spondylolisthesis and pars defects may require spinal fixation in addition to decompression with associated risks described above. The other area of concern is the need for multiple operations in this condition. Re-operating can be very difficult as the normal anatomical structures and planes are altered and the risk of damage to the dura and nerve roots is greater. Under those circumstances the surgeon needs to inform the patient of the increased risks with re-operation. In addition the surgeon needs to be very clear that further operations are in the best interest of the patient.

1 Issack, Cunningham, Pumberger, Hughes, Cammisa 'Degenerative lumbar spinal stenosis: evaluation and management' (2012) 20(8) J Am Acad Orthop Surg 527–535. doi: 10.5435/ JAAOS-20-08-527. Review.

Cauda equina

29.112 Cauda equina syndrome occurs when a large midline disc herniation presses several roots of the cauda equina. It may rarely be a complication of lumbar surgery or anaesthetic procedures if a sizeable epidural blood clot forms and causes pressure on nerve roots. The commonest levels in the lumbar region are L4–5 and L5–S1. Symptoms are commonly back pain radiating into both legs, a sensation of numbness in the buttocks (saddle anaesthesia), perineum and sometimes down the back of both thighs and both bowel and bladder symptoms. There is loss of bladder control which can result in total urinary retention, loss of bladder sensation and the desire to micturate leading to bladder distension and overflow incontinence. Anorectal continence is also lost. Cauda equina syndrome may be termed complete if power, sensation and sphincter control in combination are lost, or incomplete if not. Symptoms of this nature should prompt urgent investigation by the attending doctor, in the form of a lumbar MRI scan. The syndrome tends to develop acutely or atypically slowly, the prognosis being worse in the acute onset groups of patients. While initially the debate centred on the need to carry out a decompression within hours, recent studies have shown no difference in surgical outcome comparing intervention at less than 24 hours of the onset of symptoms with those patients decompressed between 24 and 48 hours. However there does seem to be a better outcome for those who are treated within 48 hours compared to those who have been treated later than 48 hours after onset of the cauda equina syndrome. In practice, most surgeons will tend to operate on next available daytime list from time of diagnosis.

29.113 Owing to the significant disability associated with complete cauda equina syndrome (leg weakness, incontinence, sexual dysfunction), delays in diagnosis and/or appropriate management of cauda equina syndrome may result in a significant disability of a physical or socioeconomic nature.

Further reading:
Shapiro (2000) 25 Spine 348–352; Ahn, Ahn, Buchowski (et al) (2000) 25 Spine 1515–1522; Chang, Nakagawa, Mizuno (2000) 53 Surg Neurol 100–105 (2011) 25(4) British Journal of Neurosurgery 503–508

Cervical surgery

29.114 Degenerative spinal disease commonly affects the cervical spine. Degenerative changes (cervical stenosis) are observed commonly on radiological images of the cervical spine, and can result in a spectrum of signs and symptoms, ranging from asymptomatic to quadriparesis. Patients commonly present to neurosurgery with neck pain, radicular arm pain (shooting pains in the arm) with or without associated hand weakness, and/or cervical myelopathy. Cervical myelopathy refers to spinal cord dysfunction caused by compression resulting in difficulties with walking, frequent falls and anti-gravity movements such as climbing stairs. On examination stiff legs and exaggerated reflexes are often present, although sensation and strength are often preserved. Surgery may be offered to patients who have persistent radicular pain, or who have signs of spinal cord injury secondary to compression (T2 signal change on MRI), whether the patients have clinical signs of myelopathy or not. Clinical signs often do not correlate with radiological severity of stenosis. Therefore patients with asymptomatic or minimally symptomatic stenosis but severe radiological stenosis may be offered surgery prophylactically to prevent a 'stinger injury'. A stinger injury is severe spinal cord injury (including tetraplegia) caused by a relatively minor neck injury in the context of a cervical stenosis. The overall risk of a stinger injury in the general population is low, but is a particular consideration in patients who are professional or keen amateur athletes. Surgery may be offered to allow continued participation in sport (after an appropriate rest interval), since standard advice would be to discontinue competitive sport in untreated cervical stenosis.

29.115 The commonly performed procedures for cervical stenosis are anterior cervical decompression and fusion or disc replacement (ACDF), or cervical laminectomy with or without fixation. Anterior cervical decompression involves removing the disc and associated osteophytes (degenerative changes) via the front of the neck, whereas cervical laminectomy involves making an incision at the back of the neck and removing posterior degenerative elements. The aim of both types of surgery is to decompress the spinal cord and exiting nerve roots. Wrong level surgery is a risk in cervical spine surgery, as it is in lumbar surgery, therefore intraoperative lateral radiography is normally used in practice to check the correct level(s) has(ve) been approached and operated upon.

29.116 The risks of ACDF are legion, many of which can cause death or severe disability, although the risk of severe permanent complications is low numerically. Many of the following complications require further surgery or treatment. Specific risks of ACDF include

- infection;
- CSF leak;
- recurrent symptoms/failure to improve;
- adjacent segment disease (instability);
- laryngeal nerve injury (voice symptoms);
- Horner's syndrome (sympathetic nervous system injury);
- airway obstruction;
- stroke related to manipulation of the carotid vessels in the neck;
- injury to the wind pipe or oesophagus;
- neurological injury resulting in limb weakness, loss of sensation, double incontinence, loss of sexual function;
- in the worst cases tetraplegia.

29.117 It is particularly important to warn patients of the specific risks of ACDF since definitive evidence that operative treatment is superior to non-operative treatment in the long term is lacking. The benefit of surgery is a more rapid improvement, even instantaneous, in symptoms compared to non-operative treatment, with the stated aim of surgery being to prevent symptom progression. Progressive myelopathy from cervical stenosis is a severely disabling condition.

29.118 Cervical laminectomy carries fewer types of risk, and is the procedure of choice for elderly patients or those with extensive degenerative disease. ACDF is the procedure of choice for younger patients (generally less than 65) with disease limited to one or two spinal levels.

Further reading:
Surgery for cervical radiculopathy or myelopathy, Editorial Group: Cochrane Back Group DOI: 10.1002/14651858.CD001466.pub3
(2013) 13(11) Spine J 1650–1658. doi: 10.1016/j.spinee.2013.06.020. Epub 14 September 2013
(2003) 22(3) Clin Sports Med 483–492. Review
(1998) 43(2) Neurosurgery 268–273; discussion 273–274.

CHAPTER 30

Spinal surgery

Professor Adrian T H Casey

INTRODUCTION

30.1   The spine consists of the spinal cord (and nerve roots) and the spinal column. Spinal surgery is thus concerned with nervous tissue and skeletal structures and the deranged anatomical relationship between these tissues in pathological conditions. Accordingly, the speciality of spinal surgery comprises both orthopaedic surgery and neurosurgery. Spinal surgery is a rapidly developing field, with specialists being trained in either orthopaedics or neurosurgery. It is a speciality coming of age and it is likely that in the near future it will be recognised in its own right. In the meantime there is some variation in practice between the two disciplines.

30.2 The functional anatomy of the spine reflects our evolution as segmental organisms. The spinal column is a semi-rigid tube made up of differing but repeated units: the bony vertebrae and intervertebral discs. The spinal cord is contained within the spinal canal, from which motor and sensory nerve roots emerge at their respective level from the spinal column; there is both segmental organisation and longitudinal organisation; the column is longer than the cord, which ends at about the level of the first lumbar vertebra. Below the first lumbar vertebra is the sheaf of nerve roots, the cauda equina. The spine thus consists of highly organised nervous tissue contained within a limited space. These nervous tissues (like the brain within the skull) are highly sensitive to compression within the spinal canal. The nerve roots are susceptible to entrapment as they emerge from the spinal column, especially at cervical and lumbar-sacral levels. A lesion of the spinal cord, whether partial or complete, may be associated with disturbance of motor and sensory function below the level of the lesion; there may be a clinical sensory level of the trunk which correlates with a pathological lesion of the cord at thoracic level. A lesion of a nerve root, a radiculopathy, may be associated with sensory disturbance of a dermatome, or motor disturbance in a root value distribution. A lesion of the neural tissues of the spine must be considered in a spatial context; whether it is a cord lesion or root lesion it must be considered in a temporal context if it involves compression, since there may be only a limited opportunity to avoid or reverse damage by decompression.

30.3 In the UK intradural procedures are the exclusive province of neurosurgeons and scoliosis is nearly the exclusive province of orthopaedists. In the USA, many neurosurgeons also deal with scoliosis, whilst in Japan a select group of orthopaedic surgeons also deal with intradural tumours including intramedually microsurgical procedures. Some operations are commonplace, eg lumbar spine decompression; others are quite rare (syndromic conditions, spinal cord tumours, syringomyelia, tethered cord, spinal cord herniation), whilst others are complex, eg correction of scoliosis and demand rigorous training and experience in a dedicated spinal unit. These surgeries should not be performed by the occasional surgeon.

30.4 Spinal surgery varies from the simple lumbar discectomy for slipped disc to complex correction of deformity or delicate excision of intramedullary tumours. All spinal surgery carries risk of nerve or spinal cord damage resulting in paralysis. In terms of medical litigation it is an expensive speciality to practise. Complications may not be frequent but when they occur they often do not recover and usually do not affect survival. Paralysis will affect the quality of life and compromise employment status, despite disability discrimination laws. Therefore financial settlements will often be substantial.

DIAGNOSIS

30.5   Patients first presenting to a spinal surgeon will be referred by a GP or another hospital specialist. Correct diagnosis and subsequent successful management is based on this initial doctor/patient interaction. This will often be based on a detailed history of the patient's complaints, and aggravating and relieving factors and associated symptoms such as neural dysfunction or bladder and bowel disturbance.

30.6   This will be supplemented by a neurological and musculoskeletal examination. Recognised pitfalls exist with the examination often being curtailed due to pressure of time in a busy clinic, ill-tempered patients because they have been in pain for so long, or even patients exaggerating symptoms for compensation claims. Inebriated trauma patients who cannot cooperate with a detailed neurological examination or give a coherent history are a significant problem in the casualty setting.

30.7   For elective outpatients visits, The Society of British Neurological Surgeons (SBNS) have issued guidance on the time period recommended for a new appointment (30 minutes) with 15 minutes for a follow-up visit. Spinal orthopaedic societies hold similar views.

30.8   Back pain patients not uncommonly have psychological issues. It is sometimes difficult to assess these patients, where functional overlay may be significant. Waddell et al in 1980 developed a standardised assessment of behavioural responses to examination[1]. The signs were associated with other clinical measures of illness behaviour and distress, and are not simply a feature of medico-legal presentations. Despite clear caveats about the interpretation of the signs, they have been misinterpreted and misused both clinically and medico-legally. Behavioural responses to examination provide useful clinical information, but need to be interpreted with care and understanding. Isolated signs should not be over-interpreted. Multiple signs suggest that the patient does not have a straightforward physical problem, but that psychological factors also need to be considered. Some patients may require both physical management of their physical pathology and more careful management of the psychosocial and behavioural aspects of their illness. Behavioural signs should be understood as responses affected by fear in the context of recovery from injury and the development of chronic incapacity. They offer only a psychological 'yellow-flag' and not a complete psychological assessment. Behavioural signs are not on their own a test of credibility or faking.

1 Waddell, Somerville (et al) 'Objective clinical evaluation of physical impairment in chronic low back pain' (1992) 17(6) Spine 617–628.

30.9   The diagnosis or management plan for a spinal patient can be made based on history and examination in a significant number of cases, particularly in general practice. However, for the vast majority of hospital-referred patients diagnosis and management is aided by radiological studies. These typically include X-rays of the presumed pathological area of the spine. Often these will be complemented by magnetic resonance imaging (MRI) or computed tomography (CT) scan. MRI is very good for demonstrating anatomy and pathology of nerves, discs, muscles or revealing tumours. A CT scan shows superiority in demonstrating bony anatomy but involves a significant radiation dosage.

30.10 Guidelines for the use of these studies are not rigid compared to recommendations for CT scan following head injury. Areas of developing consensus include cervical spine clearance in trauma including the unconscious patients[1] and back pain RCGP[2].

1 Barba, Taggert (et al) 'A new cervical spine clearance protocol using computed tomography' (2001) 51(4) Jnl Trauma 652–656; discussion 656–657.
2 ME B *The Management of Back Pain in General Practice* (1995) RCGP clinical series. London: Royal College of General Practitioners.

30.11 The radiology department should report the studies in a timely fashion. Most surgeons will prefer to see the actual study rather than rely on the radiologist's report unless the scan is reported as completely normal. Levels of thoracic pathology should be ideally counted from L5/S1 as well as from the top C2. The pathology and the lumbosacral junction should be included on one film. Pitfalls of missing an intradural tumour near the conus T12–L1 or a low sacral tumour by the study not including the thoracolumbar and lumbosacral region are well recognised and seem to occur very rarely now.

PREOPERATIVE CONSENT

30.12 Informed consent in spinal surgery is a thorny issue. Few surgeries are completely curative, and many come with a long list of potential complications. All patients undergoing spinal surgery expose themselves to some risk of nerve or spinal cord injury. It is beholden on the clinician to explain this risk in a sympathetic and realistic fashion. Usually there are treatment options and the risk of surgery should be balanced against the risks of conservative non-operative treatment.

30.13 Mainly painful spinal conditions may be self-limiting and surgery is not always required. The natural history of sciatica is usually favourable. Traditionally patients are told that 70 per cent are better spontaneously within two to three months. The classic and oft-quoted Weber study[1] examines this. Two hundred and eighty patients with herniated lumbar discs, verified by radiculography, were divided into three groups. One group consisted of 126 patients with uncertain indication for surgical treatment, who had their therapy decided by randomisation which permitted comparison between the results of surgical and conservative treatment. Another group comprising 67 patients had symptoms and signs that beyond doubt, required surgical therapy. The third group of 87 patients was treated conservatively because there was no indication for operative intervention. Follow-up examinations in the first group were performed after one, four, and ten years.

1 Weber 'Lumbar disc herniation. A prospective study of prognostic factors including a controlled trial. Part I' (1978) 28(3–4) Jnl Oslo City Hosp 33–61; Weber 'Lumber disc herniation. A prospective study of prognostic factors including a controlled trial. Part II' (1978) 28(7–8) Jnl Oslo City Hosp 89–113; Weber 'Lumbar disc herniation. A controlled, prospective study with ten years of observation' (1983) 8(2) Spine 131–140.

30.14   The controlled trial showed a statistically significant better result in the surgically-treated group at the one-year follow-up examination. After four years the operated patients still showed better results, but the difference was no longer statistically significant. Only minor changes took place during the last six years of observation.

30.15   A major multi-centre trial shows that for those patients who did have surgery the recovery was faster, more predictable and more reliable. However there were difficulties in randomisation in both groups with cross-over from both treatment groups (surgical and non-operative)[1].

1 Weinstein, Lurie (et al) 'Surgical vs non-operative treatment for lumbar disk herniation: the Spine Patient Outcomes Research Trial (SPORT) observational cohort' (2006) 296(20) Jama 2451–2459; Weinstein, Tosteson (et al) 'Surgical vs non-operative treatment for lumbar disk herniation: the Spine Patient Outcomes Research Trial (SPORT): a randomized trial' (2006) 296(20) Jama 2441–2450.

30.16   Some patients claim not to understand what is meant by nerve or spinal cord damage and the long-term implications regarding paralysis and bladder and bowel dysfunction. For high-risk cases this should be spelt out. It is arguable how precise the consenting surgeon should be when the risk is a mere fraction of a per cent[1]. Neurological complications are more readily accepted when the disease is known to be progressive, or a disease which itself will ultimately cause paralysis, eg tumour, or spinal trauma. For patients with simple degenerative lumbar disc disease this complication would be unpalatable for many.

1 *Sidaway v Board of Governors of the Bethlem Royal Hospital and the Maudsley Hospital* [1985] AC 871.

30.17   It is usually emphasised to the patient that all spinal surgery is major surgery and carries specific risks, eg nerve or spinal cord damage, csf fistula, but also carries general risks common to most major surgery, namely infection (including chest, urinary, and wound), bleeding, thrombosis (DVT/PE), and a small risk from the anaesthetic. Realistic expectations following the surgery should also be imparted to the patient, eg 70 per cent of patients have significant pain relief or improvement in neurological symptoms. It is important to comment on whether the operation will help axial neck or back pain or radicular symptoms. Sometimes an operation may be performed in which the patient has very unrealistic expectations. This is often true for surgery for back pain. The use of printed information sheets or internet patient information material is becoming more commonplace and makes this process more consistent.

WRONG-SITE SURGERY

30.18   It is every patient's nightmare to have surgery performed on the wrong site. It is also the surgeon's nightmare to operate on the wrong level. Reasons for this may be related to poor practice. Most hospitals have guidelines in place to prevent errors, but reports of medical disasters related to wrong side surgery are still not infrequent. The spine causes problems where counting levels is also an issue. Problems arise when anatomy is not conventional, eg segmentation anomalies, or when there are technical difficulties obtaining good quality preoperative studies, eg X-ray penetration to visualise the cervico thoracic junction where the view is obscured by the shoulders. These X-rays in large patients are often referred to as 'cloud-a-grams', Parallax errors can also arise if radiographer and/or surgeon do not pay attention.

30.19   Several factors are repeatedly found to be involved in cases of wrong-site surgery. General anaesthesia is almost always involved. The surgeon is often not in the operating room during the preoperative preparation or during induction of anaesthesia. If present, the surgeon is often rushed or in a hurry. Finally, prone or lateral positioning of the patient after induction of anaesthesia is disorienting to the surgeon, and can lead to site misidentification at the time of incision.

30.20   In response to the unique challenges of reducing wrong-site surgery in the spine, the North American Spine Society (NASS) introduced and recommended implementation of its SMaX program in 2001. SMaX stands for: Sign your surgical site, Mark the intended level of intervention intraoperatively and X-ray the marked site to confirm during the procedure the correct level of surgery. To aid in accomplishing this improvement in patient safety, NASS proposed a checklist of six items for the surgical team to complete:

(1)   involve the patient in confirming the operative site either through informed consent or during the actual marking. The surgeon is encouraged to personally obtain the consent and the consent/operative permit should clearly state the site and side of proposed surgery and be shared with the patient, surgeon, anaesthetist assistant or scrub nurse and circulating nurse;

(2)   the surgeon should sign his name to the operative site with a marking pen when the patient is awake and aware in the operating room. Each member of the operative team should verify the correct operative site prior to anaesthesia;

(3)   verify the correct patient is in the operating room and that the medical record and X-rays present are for that patient;

(4)   each of the following should be checked against the signed site:
    (a)   medical record;
    (b)   imaging studies marked left and right to prevent being placed on the view box backwards;
    (c)   informed consent;
    (d)   OR/anaesthesia record;

(5)   consider having the surgical assistant or scrub nurse always stand opposite the side where the primary surgeon stands;

(6)   consider or suggest an intraoperative X-ray during the procedure, after exposure using markers that do not move to confirm the vertebral level to be operated. The X-ray should contain as much regional anatomy as possible with a marker as close to the intended disc space as possible: it is optimal to have both the surgeon and a radiologist read this film during the procedure and agree on the correctness of the level.

These measures have been adopted by the North American Spine Society but similar, less formalised, versions are used by most spine surgeons in the UK. Most spine surgeons would use an image intensifier to localise skin incision preoperatively and again operative level during the procedure. Only in difficult cases would a radiologist be requested during surgery. Most hospitals would use a generic WHO surgical checklist prior to commencing surgery[1].

1 www.who.int/patientsafety/safesurgery/checklist/en/.

30.21   Thoracic disc surgery is an area where the risks of wrong level are quite high and the mistake might not be realised until quite late, after extensive bony work. Preoperative X-rays should check for lumbosacral anomalies and an anterior posterior study should determine the number of ribs. It is usually regarded as essential to count the levels from the lumbosacral junction on the preoperative MRI and repeat this using the image intensifier in theatres. Counting from C2 on the MRI and then lumbosacral junction is risky if the patient has a lumbosacral anomaly. It is unreliable to count intraoperatively from C2; the chances of miscounting through the shoulders will be significant. Alternative methods include counting the ribs from the inside of the chest where rib one should not be palpable.

PATIENT POSITIONING

30.22   Many spinal operations last in excess of two hours. Care must be given to protect vulnerable areas. These include the ulnar nerve in the supine position, the radial nerve in the lateral position (protected by an axillary jelly roll), and the common peroneal nerve just below the knee again in the lateral position.

30.23   Peri-operative care is the responsibility of the whole team but is usually supervised by the anaesthetist and will usually include invasive blood pressure monitoring, pulse oximetry, continuous ECG, and end tidal CO2. For cases where a significant blood loss is anticipated (eg vascular tumour) urinary output is monitored following urinary catheterisation. Heating blankets are commonly employed to avoid hypothermia. Maintenance of normothermia is associated with a decreased infection rate[1]. Preoperative antibiotics are usually given to decrease the infection rate. This is probably more important in instrumented spinal cases. There is no consensus on drug and dosage.

1 Buggy 'Can anaesthetic management influence surgical-wound healing?' (2000) 356(9227) Lancet 355–357.

30.24   Steroids were once very popular for many spinal neurosurgical cases, especially acute traumatic spinal cord injury. The evidence from the NASCIS study is increasingly questioned[1]. Likewise its use for cervical myelopathy is regarded less favourably now, with concerns about complications from its use. For intradural tumours it is still believed to be important to reduce oedema.

1 Hurlbert 'Methylprednisolone for acute spinal cord injury: an inappropriate standard of care' (2000) 93(1 Suppl) Jnl Neurosurg 1–7.

SPINAL CORD MONITORING

30.25 Spinal cord monitoring in the form of somatosensory evoked potentials (SSEP) is used in high-risk cases. The argument for its use is strong when the insult can be removed. It is therefore popular for spinal deformity cases, where corrective forces applied by pedicle screw rod constructs can be removed if the spinal cord signals drop. Typically if they drop in amplitude by 50 per cent this is regarded as a significant event. Their use has probably supplanted the use of the wake-up test. There is no literature to defend its use in decreasing the risk of paralysis. There are invariably false positives, false negatives do occur but are rare.[1] If signals are reduced during surgery, reversible causes of cord dysfunction include poor perfusion related to low blood pressure or cord deformation following instrumented correction.

1 May, Jones (et al) 'Somatosensory evoked potential monitoring in cervical surgery: identification of pre- and intraoperative risk factors associated with neurological deterioration' (1996) 85(4) Jnl Neurosurg 566–573.

30.26 Spinal cord monitoring is not regarded as appropriate for simple spinal cases, eg lumbar laminectomy or microdiscectomy. Many would argue that it is essential for intramedullary spinal cord tumours, eg ependymoma. However, spinal electrical signals are frequently lost once the dorsal columns are explored during the microsurgical dissection. Motor evoked potentials (MEP) may overcome this problem, but the technique is demanding for neurophysiologist and anaesthetists.

POST-OPERATIVE CARE

30.27 This should ensure adequate pain relief following the procedure. If high-dose opiates are used, respiratory observations are desirable. These will be combined with standard neurovascular and wound observations. Following major surgery high-dependency or intensive care is desirable. Steroids used for certain tumours should be reduced judiciously to avoid a cushingoid state developing. Attention should be given to deep vein thrombosis prevention, including potential use of TED stockings, flowtrons boots and heparin. The spine presents some potentially conflicting issues with the use of anticoagulants. A post-operative bleeding tendency could have disastrous consequences (ie haematoma causing paralysis). This is certainly the case for intradural pathology. The risks following a simple discectomy, lumbar or cervical, are quite small either way. There is no consensus. Patients who will have prolonged incumbency or have other risk factors such as previous DVT, carcinoma or paraplegia should be seriously considered for DVT prophylaxis.

30.28 It is beyond the scope of this chapter to summarise the large field of spinal surgery. More in-depth analysis can be found in the selected bibliography at the end of this chapter. However a brief synopsis with emphasis on potential complications is given below, followed by comment on selected conditions.

COMMON OPERATIONS

Anterior cervical discectomy/cervical corpectomy

30.29   This operation is indicated for nerve root compression (radiculopathy) or spinal cord compression (myelopathy). The neural structures are decompressed using microsurgical techniques. The compression is caused by a slipped disc or bony spur (osteophyte). For those patients with radiculopathy causing arm pain (brachalgia) the response from surgery is very good with 85–90 per cent of patients having a good recovery. For those with spinal cord compression the results are less good. Despite technically successful surgery only 60 per cent of patients improve and often the improvement is modest. If the patient's neurological decline (trouble walking or numb clumsy hands) is arrested, the surgery is regarded as successful. Not infrequently patients' symptoms of numbness in their hands (due to cervical myelopathy) is erroneously diagnosed as carpal tunnel syndrome. They may end up having unnecessary carpal tunnel decompression and their diagnosis of cervical spondylotic myelopathy is delayed.

30.30   Once the bony spur and disc are removed the spine is reconstructed with a bone graft or interbody fusion cage. For two level cases or corpectomies, where the discs and intervening vertebral body are excised, it is commonplace to instrument the region with an anterior locking plate to prevent the reconstruction from failing. The bone graft, cage or plate with screws may dislodge, partially (protrusion) or completely (extrusion). This can cause dysphagia (swallowing problems) or the backed out screws may even perforate the oesophagus, with serious complications (infection/ mediastinatis).

30.31   Specific complications of the surgery can be neurological, vascular or from damage to structures in the neck, eg oesophagus pharynx or thoracic duct. Iatrogenic damage to the spinal cord or nerve root is very rare. The most common symptomatic nerve damage is to the recurrent or superior laryngeal nerve (< 1 per cent). The latter cause either a hoarse voice or affect the timbre of the voice. Usually this recovers spontaneously. If persistent, it can be injected by an ear nose and throat surgeon with good symptomatic recovery. Damage is not thought to be by careless laceration but represents damage caused by retraction by the surgeon against the endotracheal tube placed by the anaesthetist. Some authorities recommend periodic release of the deep cervical retractors to avoid this problem.

30.32   If bilateral recurrent laryngeal damage occurs, stridor will result. Tracheostomy may be required. Bilateral damage typically occurs following trauma or revision surgery when the second/revision surgery is performed on the contra lateral side.

30.33   Less common nerves damaged include the sympathetic chain causing a Horner's syndrome (ptosis and meiosis), marginal mandibular nerve causing unilateral drooping of the angle of the mouth and hypoglossal nerve causing weakness of the tongue. Neuropraxia to the superficial cervical plexus results commonly in skin numbness for a few weeks, but is rarely permanent. Neuropraxia to the oesophageal plexus causes dysphagia.

Very rarely an iatrogenic oesophageal laceration occurs. If this is recognised it should be repaired and feeding via a nasogastric tube for five to seven days instituted. Unrecognised fatal mediastinitis can occur.

30.34 Finally vascular injury can occur. Damage to the external jugular vein in the form of a small laceration is of no concern provided it is coagulated or ligated. Delayed bleeding in the post-operative period can result in airway compromise and death from respiratory obstruction. Reports of dyspnoea from the patient should be taken seriously and interpreted as imminent airway obstruction. Likewise if the wound is noted to be swelling or bleeding in the first few hours after surgery this should also be taken as a warning. Most surgeons place a wound drain to decrease the chance of this happening, but this does not give complete protection. Complication rates for this common operation have been reported extensively in the literature by many authors[1].

1 Flynn 'Neurologic complications of anterior cervical interbody fusion' (1982) 7(6) Spine 536–539; Flynn 'Neurologic complications of anterior cervical discectomy in Louisiana' (1984) 136(7) Jnl LA State Med Soc 6–8.

Posterior cervical decompression with or without instrumentation

30.35 The anatomy of the posterior approach is more straightforward. This is probably the most common method to decompress the nerve roots, spinal cord, or stabilise the spine. Cervical foramenotomy is a keyhole microsurgical procedure to decompress the nerve and sometimes to remove a herniated disc. There is a small risk of iatrogenic nerve injury causing weakness or numbness in that nerve's territory, but this is very rare. Spinal fluid leak is also a possibility: guidelines for this complication are given at para **30.42**. Finally, if too much facet is removed, the spine could be rendered unstable causing pain, deformity or further neurological damage.

30.36 To decompress the spinal cord requires a large exposure and more bony resection. This involves a hemilaminectomy or laminectomy. Complications are similar in nature to those of foramenotomy. Kyphotic deformity is a more common risk. It is associated with young age, tumours, neurological loss, neurofibromatosis and radiotherapy. If these risk factors are judged to be significant, consideration should be given to stabilising the spine with bone graft and spinal instrumentation.

30.37 Spinal fixation in this region is most commonly performed using a screw rod system. Screws are inserted into the lateral masses or pedicles and then connected by a titanium rod. Historically this technique was preceded by various wiring procedure (sublaminar). These were associated with a small chance of spinal cord damage when passing the wire under the lamina, inadvertently traumatising the spinal cord. Screw techniques offer more rigid fixation and an improved spinal cord safety margin. However, such techniques come with a small risk of iatrogenic nerve root injury or vertebral artery injury. The reported rate of iatrogenic injury in expert hands is very small. There are two main techniques: Magerl and Roy Camille[1]. They will be commonly used for traumatic injuries, eg unilateral or bilateral facet dislocation, fracture dislocations or atlantoaxial subluxation seen in rheumatoid arthritis. Posterior lateral mass or pedicle screws will also be used following tumour excisions which destabilise the spine.

1 Omeis, DeMattia (et al) 'History of instrumentation for stabilization of the subaxial cervical spine' (2004) 16(1) Neurosurg Focus E10.

30.38 A compromise technique used in degenerative or mild cases which seems to work well is that of laminoplasty. This has also been used extensively in the paediatric population to prevent kyphotic deformity. The Japanese have also popularised its use in ossification of the posterior longitudinal ligament (OPLL). This is a rare condition in the Caucasian population, being more common in Orientals, Arabic and Asian races. In the UK, with its multi-ethnic population, OPLL in its early stages is occasionally misinterpreted as simple disc disease. There are several laminoplasty techniques but all serve to stabilise the spine, decrease the chance of kyphotic deformity and post laminectomy membrane without removing all movement (cf rigid fixation of lateral mass screws)[1].

1 O'Brien, Peterson (et al) 'A novel technique for laminoplasty augmentation of spinal canal area using titanium miniplate stabilization. A computerized morphometric analysis' (1996) 21(4) Spine 474–483; discussion 484.

THORACIC DISCECTOMY

30.39 This is a rare procedure. It is associated historically with significant complications. It is now widely accepted that the herniated thoracic discs should be excised by an anterolateral approach (thoracotomy) in the vast majority of cases. There are a few small series of cases approached via a laminectomy, sometimes with intradural division of the dentate ligament to facilitate cord rotation. In selected hands this procedure has been performed successfully. However the general, current, consensus of opinion is that this technique is not appropriate, providing poor visualisation of the anteriorially-placed pathology and is associated with a high rate of neurological problems. Costotransversectomy (or extracavitory approach), which is a compromise between the two approaches has a good record but again cannot provide direct visualisation of the pathology. Problems with accurate localisation of the operative levels have been already described at para **30.18**ff. Finally, new techniques have been developed to minimise wound size and perhaps post-thoracotomy pain by using mini-thoracotomy procedures or endoscopically guided procedures (video assisted thoracic surgery – VATS).

LUMBAR DISCECTOMY

30.40 This is probably the most commonplace spinal surgical procedure. It can be performed as an open procedure for disc prolapse. Nowadays it is usually performed using the operating microscope to improve visualisation (magnification and illumination).The results of open or microscopic techniques appear to be very similar in the literature.

30.41 Keyhole procedures which use endoscopic instruments are being refined. Most endoscopes only offer 2-D visualisation compared to 3-D provided by the modern neurosurgical microscope. Use of lasers is still not widely accepted as offering any advantage. Coblation is another method of trimming the disc. Again there is no consensus that this represents a genuine step forward. Introduced in 2000, DISC nucleoplasty uses a unique plasma technology called Coblation® to remove tissue from the centre of the disc. During the procedure, the DISC Nucleoplasty SpineWand is introduced through a needle and placed into the centre of the disc, where a series of channels are created to remove tissue from the nucleus. Tissue removal from the nucleus acts to decompress the disc and relieve the pressure exerted by the disc on the nearby nerve root. As pressure is relieved, pain is reported to be reduced, consistent with the clinical results of earlier percutaneous discectomy procedures. Long-term results are awaited.

30.42 Risks of conventional lumbar disc surgery have been reported by many authors. However the best quality evidence comes from the recent Spine Patent Outcomes Research Trial (SPORT) studies[1]. Specific complication include a small risk of nerve injury causing numbness, weakness and pain. Major damage from bleeding or inappropriate packing of haemostatic agents can also damage more than one nerve root, causing incontinence by compressing the cauda equina (see para **30.46**). There are also risks of inadvertently tearing the dura. This will cause a leak of spinal fluid (CSF). This is usually, but not always, recognised at the time of surgery. Repair is effected by direct suturing. This can be supplemented by fibrin glue or patching with artificial dura. A dural tear is a recognised complication and would not be regarded as negligent.

1 Weinstein, Lurie (et al) 'Surgical vs non-operative treatment for lumbar disk herniation: the Spine Patient Outcomes Research Trial (SPORT) observational cohort' (2006) 296(20) Jama 2451–2459; Weinstein, Tosteson (et al) 'Surgical vs non-operative treatment for lumbar disk herniation: the Spine Patient Outcomes Research Trial (SPORT): a randomized trial' (2006) 296(20) Jama 2441–2450.

30.43 Infection can also occur. Superficial infection is not usually a serious problem; deep infection causing discitis can be a formidable problem. Delays in diagnosis can occur, causing osteomyelitis, epidural abscess, and late complications of deformity and instability. Deep infection should be managed aggressively including prolonged antibiotics until inflammatory markers normalise. Antibiotics should be selected on the basis of cultures. Biopsy and or debridement of the disc can be helpful. Assessment by X-rays and MRI will help judge potential development of osteomyelitis or epidural infected collections.

LUMBAR LAMINECTOMY

30.44 The risks of this procedure are similar to discectomy. If too much bone is removed, the facet joints in particular are damaged and instability will occur (spondylolisthesis). There is a continuum of the procedures to decompress the lumbar spine from microdiscectomy to fenestration to laminotomy, including hemi-laminectomy.

30.45 Lumbar laminectomy is a commonplace procedure, usually used for degenerative disc disease especially for lumbar canal stenosis. This latter condition presents with the symptoms of claudication. A typical history is that a patient can walk a certain distance eg 200m before he experiences numbness, heaviness, pain, cramps or pins and needles in his legs. He typically rests for five to eight minutes and can then proceed. The history is very similar to vascular claudication secondary to narrowing of the leg vessels. The vascular type is more common and is seen in smokers and diabetics. Misdiagnosis does occasionally occur. The age groups are similar and smoking and degeneration of the spine are common. Inevitably there will be some patients who overlap. Radiological studies, MRI for the spine and selected vascular studies (angiogram/doppler studies) will usually clarify the situation.

CAUDA EQUINA SYNDROME

30.46 This is a common area of medical negligence. It typically results from a large central disc herniation. This acutely compresses the cauda equina, the nerves that control bladder, bowel and sexual functions. These nerves also control lower leg function. Typically a patient presents with back pain, weakness of their legs and trouble passing urine. Red flag features include saddle anaesthesia, perineal numbness and sphincter disturbance. Partial presentations may be misinterpreted as a severe exacerbation of simple sciatica. Urinary retention may not initially be noticed by the patient or if the patient is in severe pain, the pain may be erroneously ascribed as the cause of retention. Patients with sciatica should be questioned about bladder function and sensation in their ano-genital region.

30.47 Surgical treatment is urgent in most surgeons' views, but there is not complete uniformity of opinion[1]. Surgical decompression within 24–48 hours probably maximises neurological and bladder recovery[2]. There is huge forensic interest in the time limits of decompression for reversibility, partial reversibility and irreversibility, and whether there are any qualitative markers (such as sphincter disturbance) for irreversibility.

1 Shapiro 'Cauda equina syndrome secondary to lumbar disc herniation' (1993) 32(5) Neurosurgery 743–746; discussion 746–747; Shapiro 'Medical realities of cauda equina syndrome secondary to lumbar disc herniation' (2000) 25(3) Spine 348–351; discussion 352; Gleave and MacFarlane 'Prognosis for recovery of bladder function following lumbar central disc prolapse' (1990) 4(3) British Jnl Neurosurg 205–209; Gleave and Macfarlane 'Cauda equina syndrome: what is the relationship between timing of surgery and outcome?' (2002) 16(4) British Jnl Neurosurg 325–328.
2 Shapiro 'Cauda equina syndrome secondary to lumbar disc herniation' (1993) 32(5) Neurosurgery 743–746; discussion 746–747; Shapiro 'Medical realities of cauda equina syndrome secondary to lumbar disc herniation' (2000) 25(3) Spine 348–351; discussion 352.

CORD COMPRESSION

30.48 Cord compression can arise from a number of different pathologies (tumour, disc prolapse, infection, trauma) arising from different structures (vertebra, meninges, cord). Clinical presentation is usually slowly progressive but may be acute. There may be sensory, motor or sphincter disturbance; there may be involvement of the nerve roots at the level of the compression. If the compression is high there may be long tract signs below the level of the compression. There may be a sensory level on the trunk, depending on the level of the compression. An acute cord compression is potentially catastrophic and requires rapid assessment and decompression. A possible pitfall is a falsely localising level; the early clinical sensory level determines the imaging investigation but there is subsequently found to be missed pathology causing a compression at higher level: the clinical pathological correlation may be inexact in the early stages of acute compression.

INTRADURAL PROCEDURES

Tumours

30.49 Intradural surgery refers to surgery within or inside the dura. This is the membrane or sheath that covers the spinal cord and nerves. This surgery is relatively uncommon and it is usually for tumours. The most common tumours are benign (neurofibroma or meningioma). The former arise from the nerve roots. The nerve root needs to be sectioned to remove the tumour. Numbness in the area of that nerve will result, eg top of foot for L5 nerve. Weakness is very rare. For some reason the tumour seems to arise from sensory rather than motor branch of the nerve. If the tumour is large and compresses the spinal cord, weakness will ensue and may not improve completely after surgical excision. This is a spinal cord phenomenon rather than an effect of nerve damage.

30.50 Meningiomas are fairly common spinal tumours. Their growth is slow and delays in diagnosis are frequent, particularly if they occur at the foramen magnum. They are more common in women than men. Spinal fluid leaks are a problem after this surgery. The tumour arises from the meninges dura. For young patients it is desirable to remove this affected dura, to decrease the chance of recurrence. For older people electrical coagulation is thought to be a reasonable compromise. Cadaveric dura was used to repair the dura in the 1980s. There were several well-documented cases of transmission of Creutzfeldt-Jakob Disease.

30.51 Ependymomas have a variable spectrum of biological behaviour (benign to malignant). If removed completely a cure can be effected. Cauda equina ependymomas represent the easier surgical prospect with a favourable histology (myxopapillary sub type). Spinal cord tumours are more challenging and should be operated on by spine or tumour neurosurgeons, rather than the occasional surgeon. The surgical results in specialised centres are significantly superior to historical figures. Even in good hands most patients are worse after surgery for intramedullary tumours (within the substance of the spinal cord). Neurological recovery will usually occur over three to six months provided there has been no vascular damage. Surgical results may be improved by the use of spinal cord monitoring (sensory and motor evoked potentials).

30.52 Spinal fixation is occasionally required to prevent post-operative deformity: kyphosis or scoliosis. The major risk factors for this appear to be young age, neurological disability and radiotherapy. Neurofibromatosis (NF), a genetic condition which predisposes to multiple neurofibromas, is also an independent risk factor. It is argued that failure to stabilise the spine in a child with NF is negligent. For those with NF genetic counselling should be offered at an appropriate age, along with long-term surveillance for the development of other tumours. This is also the case with haemangioblastomas. These are usually small hypervascular tumours occurring in individuals with Von Hippel-Lindau syndrome. Von Hippel-Lindau disease (VHL) is a rare, genetic multi-system disorder characterised by the abnormal growth of tumours in certain parts of the body (angiomatosis). The tumours of the central nervous system (CNS) are benign and are comprised of a nest of blood vessels and are called hemangioblastomas (or angiomas in the eye). Hemangioblastomas may develop in the brain, the retina of the eyes, and other areas of the nervous system. Other types of tumours develop in the adrenal glands, the kidneys, or the pancreas. Symptoms of VHL vary among patients and depend on the size and location of the tumours. Symptoms may include headaches, problems with balance and walking, dizziness, weakness of the limbs, vision problems, and high blood pressure. Cysts (fluid-filled sacs) and/or tumours (benign or cancerous) may develop around the hemangioblastomas and cause the symptoms listed above. Individuals with VHL are also at a higher risk than normal for certain types of cancer, especially kidney cancer. It is this last fact which is so important and is occasionally forgotten.

Syringomyelia

30.53 Intradural surgery is also performed for spina bifida and syringomyelia. Syringomyelia is the term used to describe a cystic cavity within the substance of the spinal cord. It usually occurs in association with cerebellar ectopia (Chiari malformation). In this condition the base of the brain (cerebellar tonsils) herniate outside the skull and cause a degree of compression of the spinal cord. More importantly the cerebellar tonsils interfere with normal cerebrospinal fluid flow (CSF). The CSF is driven into the spinal cord dissecting a cavity over a long period (years). The cavity causes spinal cord dysfunction. This is usually a congenital condition rather than acquired. Further details on this condition are available in the selected bibliography. This disease is relatively uncommon and delays in treatment and misdiagnosis do occur. A rare but classic presentation is with severely arthritic joints (Charcot neuropathic joints). Most rheumatologists and orthopaedic surgeons will never see this presentation in their whole career. In the MRI era these problems are far less common. Surgery involves enlarging the opening of the base of the skull and dural covering: foramen magnum decompression. This is straightforward surgery but is dogged by potential problems, including csf leak, hydrocephalus, and occasionally meningitis. Many patients suffer from quite bad headaches for a few weeks. Deaths can rarely occur from hydrocephalus which occurs in the first three to six weeks.

30.54 Syringomyelia, also occurs in a small number of patients (2–6 per cent) following spinal trauma. It usually occurs several years later with a secondary deterioration in neurological function. This is usually picked up without diagnostic delay. Its importance lies in the fact that it is unpredictable. Its potential occurrence should be factored into any court settlement following major spinal cord injury.

COMMON CONDITIONS

Congenital

30.55 Spina bifida is mainly the province of paediatric neurosurgeons. Spinal dysraphism is the term used to cover the broad spectrum of anatomical, congenital anomalies. The severe open defects are evident at birth and closed. There are some rare disorders as well. Some of these are termed occult dysraphic states. There may be clues to their presence. Some of these clues or stigmata of the occult dysraphic state are birth marks over the lower spine, eg cutaneous haemangioma, sacral dimple, fatty lump (lipoma) or hairy patch over the base of the spine. Evaluation requires MRI. Abnormalities seen include lipomyelomeningocoele, tethered low-lying spinal cord by fatty filum terminale or even split spinal cord (diastematomyelia). These patients invariably have foot abnormalities – asymmetry or pes cavus – and develop bladder and bowel dysfunction. In the antenatal period blood tests for spina bifida are performed routinely. Pre-conception folic acid supplements are recommended. The attending paediatrician and midwife are trained to inspect newborns for stigmata of spinal dysraphism. If picked up at or shortly after birth most authorities recommend prophylactic untethering. Failure to diagnose may compromise neurological function for later life.

Developmental

30.56 Developmental disorders of the lower back are caused by abnormalities in the formation and growth of the skeleton. Scoliosis is one example of a developmental disorder that can be caused by several different congenital abnormalities of the spinal column, and that also occurs during periods of accelerated growth, like puberty. Many of these conditions need to be followed closely during development so that they can be treated accordingly. Although the treatment for many of these conditions is conservative, surgery may be required to keep some disorders from worsening, and in order to prevent long-term disability and or deformity. A small percentage of scoliosis cases have an underlying cause, eg tumour, syrinx, tethered cord or cerebellar ectopia (Chiari malformation).

30.57 Congenital scoliosis is defined as a curvature of the spine that is the result of malformations of the vertebral elements. Most of this development happens during the third to sixth week in utero (after conception). In spite of the opportunities for error, congenital malformations are relatively rare. Congenital scoliosis is categorised into three groups: failures of formation; failures of segmentation; and combinations of these defects. The most common failure of formation is called a hemivertebra. Hemivertebra produce a growth imbalance in the spine and, therefore, result in the spine growing crooked. Failures of segmentation include block vertebra and unilateral bars, which produce a growth tether of the spine. Finally, when these occur in combination, such as a hemivertebra on one side and a bar on the other, the scoliosis can progress in very rapid manner. Idiopathic scoliosis is the most common form of scoliosis possibly affecting up to one per cent of the population. It is usually diagnosed at the time of an adolescent growth spurt. In order for a physician to diagnose and treat idiopathic scoliosis, he or she must first rule out all other causes of scoliosis. Most idiopathic curves present in adolescence are painless, gradual, have a typical curve pattern (for example, a right thoracic curve), and the neurological exam is normal. Idiopathic scoliosis is much more common in females.

Trauma

30.58 The diagnosis of an unstable spinal injury and its subsequent management can be difficult. A missed spine injury can have devastating long-term consequences. In major trauma, spinal column injury must therefore be presumed until it is excluded.

30.59 Some studies of spinal trauma have recorded a missed injury rate as high as 33 per cent. Delayed or missed diagnosis is usually attributed to failure to suspect an injury to the cervical spine, or to inadequate cervical spine radiology and incorrect interpretation of radiographs. An appropriate procedure for the evaluation of the potentially unstable spine must be robust and easy to implement, with a high sensitivity, given the potential importance of such injuries. It must also address the main issues raised by the modalities available for diagnosis.

30.60 For spinal trauma, the main concerns are which patients can be cleared by clinical examination alone, how many plain X-rays are necessary and when additional imaging using CT or MRI should be used. An assessment for ligamentous injury in the absence of a fracture is also important, especially in unconscious patients who are unable to complain of neck pain or tenderness.

30.61 While it is tempting to focus on the cervical spine, it is important to assess and clear the entire spinal column. The thoracolumbar spine, whilst more protected, is at risk in major trauma and must be assessed both clinically and radiologically. Additionally, five per cent of spinal injuries have a second, possibly non-adjacent, fracture elsewhere in the spine.

30.62 The unconscious patient with a head injury presents particular challenges. There is an emerging consensus that the cervical spine should be cleared by contiguous multi-slice CT concentrating on the cranio-cervical junction and cervico-thoracic junctions. Plain X-rays may miss 50 per cent of junction injuries. It would be regarded as negligent not to pursue clearance of cervical spine by CT scan if C7/T1 is not visualised.

30.63 At the cranio cervical junction common injuries include dens fractures, hangman fracture and Jefferson fractures. The odontoid peg C2 fracture is probably the most frequently missed. This risks paralysis and even death in the short term. In the long run progressive tetraparesis may also occur[1]. The evidence base of cervical spine injury has been nicely reviewed by a working party nominated by the congress of neurosurgeons[2].

1 Crockard, Heilman (et al) 'Progressive myelopathy secondary to odontoid fractures: clinical, radiological, and surgical features' (1993) 78(4) Jnl Neurosurg 579–586.
2 Hadley, Walters (et al) 'Guidelines for the management of acute cervical spine and spinal cord injuries' (2002) 49 Clin Neurosurg 407–498.

30.64 Spinal cord injuries are not always associated with bony injuries. In elderly people with a narrow spinal canal hyper-extension injuries can damage the spinal cord without obvious bony injury. High velocity injuries in children typically affect the upper cervical spine. In the absence of bony injuries evident on X-rays the term SCIWORA has been used (spinal cord injury without radiological abnormality). Awareness of this is important for those dealing with spinal injury.

30.65 Spinal injury without bony or neurological injury is usually referred to as whiplash. The word is in common parlance. This is a controversial area. It behoves the treating team to exclude treatable causes such as missed fractures, instability or disc disease. This area is complex. The authors refer the reader to the monograph by the Quebec task force and the oft-cited Lancet article where issues of real injury versus compensation culture are analysed in detail[1].

1 Freeman, Croft (et al) '"Whiplash associated disorders: redefining whiplash and its management" by the Quebec Task Force. A critical evaluation' (1998) 23(9) Spine 1043–1049; Conlin, Bhogal (et al) 'Treatment of whiplash-associated disorders – part I: Non-invasive interventions' (2005) 10(1) Pain Res Manag 21–32; Conlin, Bhogal (et al) 'Treatment of whiplash-associated disorders – part II: Medical and surgical interventions' (2005) 10(1) Pain Res Manag 33–40; Schrader, Obelieniene (et al) 'Natural evolution of late whiplash syndrome outside the medicolegal context' (1996) 347(9010) Lancet 1207–1211.

30.66 Stability of spinal injury is usually assessed by the Denis 3 column theory. However there are competing 2 column theories and more recently the AO classification. All these classifications facilitate rational treatment and comparison of management results. More detailed reviews can be found in specialist textbooks.

Inflammatory

30.67 Rheumatoid arthritis affects the cervical spine causing instability and, in about 15 per cent, neurological problems. Typically it affects the atlanto axial junction C1/C2. When the spine is unstable surgical fixation is usually recommended. For those patients with rheumatoid arthritis who need major joint reconstruction (hip or knee), X-rays in flexion and extension are recommended prior to general anaesthesia. Anecdotal reports of spinal cord injury after general anaesthesia abound, where X-rays were not performed or not interpreted correctly.

Infective

30.68 Infection in the spine may be bacterial, mycobacterial (tuberculosis – TB), fungal or viral. The most common types of non-surgical infection are probably TB. In the UK this is a re-emerging problem in immigrants from the Indian subcontinent and Africa, particularly Somalia. There are associations with HIV. In the author's practice several cases of missed TB have been seen, with ensuing paralysis in immigrants who cannot speak English and verbalise their symptoms. Back pain in the presence of fever and night sweats is a red-flag symptom. TB most commonly affects the thoracic spine which is also a 'red flag' symptom[1].

1 See para **30.71** below on RCGP guidelines for red flags in back pain.

30.69 Bacterial infection is less common. It occurs in the context usually of immunosuppression by other disease processes, eg renal failure, steroid medication, diabetes, septicaemia. In certain cases it is iatrogenic and a potential source of litigation if due diligence has not been observed. After spinal surgery it can occur causing discitis, osteomyelitis or if the CSF is infected, meningitis. Prompt aggressive treatment is required to prevent disaster. Infection after surgery is inevitable in a certain percentage of patients. It will be multi-factorial. Provided the surgical team have followed high standards of cleaning, theatre and ward hygiene there will be no negligence. Some surgeries carry very low risk of infection, eg anterior cervical discectomy (0.2 per cent). Some carry much higher, eg posterior spinal instrumented fusion, particularly occipito-cervcial fixation (10 per cent). Guidelines have been issued for the use of prophylactic antibiotics[1]. Most surgical groups would favour the use of either one dose or three post-operative doses. Antibiotics can cause problems eg pseudomembranous colitis and development of resistance eg MRSA. There is a fine balance to be maintained.

1 'Antimicrobial prophylaxis in neurosurgery and after head injury. Infection in Neurosurgery Working Party of the British Society for Antimicrobial Chemotherapy' (1994) 344(8936) Lancet 1547–1551.

30.70 In the presence of deep infection wound wash out is usually recommended, as is surgical exploration and evacuation when there is epidural infection which may cause paralysis.

BACK PAIN

30.71

'The Royal College of General Practitioners Clinical Guidelines for the Management of Acute Low Back Pain (ME 1995)

Red flags for possible serious spinal pathology: consider prompt referral (less than 4 weeks)
- Presentation under age 20 or onset over 55;
- Non-mechanical pain;
- Thoracic pain;
- Past history – carcinoma, steroids, HIV;
- Unwell, weight loss;
- Widespread neurological symptoms or signs;
- Structural deformity cauda equina syndrome: immediate referral;
- Sphincter disturbance;
- Gait disturbance;
- Saddle anaesthesia.'

Neoplastic

30.72 Tumours may be primary or secondary. Primary bone tumours are rare and the treatment should be coordinated by a multi-disciplinary team. This is usually performed in a regional bone tumour unit or neurosurgery unit. Chemotherapy and radiotherapy are often required. Their treatment is outside the scope of this chapter and the reader is referred to specialist texts.

30.73 Tumours of the neuroaxis are also relatively rare. Their diagnosis and management is discussed in the intradural surgical section at para **30.49** above.

30.74 Secondary spread of tumours is common. Cancer spreading to the spine is the most common spine tumour diagnosis. Breast, bronchus, kidney, prostate and less commonly thyroid are the most frequent cancer types. Malignant melanoma and multiple myeloma can also cause pathological spinal fractures and cord compression. Cancers and tumours of the spine and spinal cord are relatively rare. The most common symptom that patients with a spinal tumour have is pain. Because back pain is very common, it is also not a specific symptom of any one disease or medical condition. Therefore, the challenge is to determine how to evaluate back pain with the goal of specifically excluding a tumour as the cause of the pain. Luckily, most back pain is not due to a tumour. However, if a cancer were discovered after a long period of 'conservative' management of back pain, most patients would feel that their problem should have been investigated more thoroughly in the beginning. What is the best way to resolve this conflict? There is no easy answer to this question, but the use of 'red flag' labelling may help. Over 80 per cent of spine tumours will present with pain. Pain symptoms that may suggest that a tumour or a cancer is responsible for the pain include pain that continues to get worse despite treatment, and that may be associated with other symptoms such as fatigue or weight loss. The pain may be worse at night, and not necessarily be related to level of activity. When associated with neurological symptoms such as loss of bowel and bladder control or pain running down the legs, further evaluation is clearly warranted.

30.75 Treatment is multi-modality, involving surgery, radiotherapy and chemotherapy depending on the tumour type. Patients with spinal pain in the context of cancer should be evaluated by CT or MRI. Plain X-rays are inadequate. More than 40 per cent of bone must be eroded before it can be detected on plain radiographs.

30.76 Delays in diagnosis are common, and anecdotally diagnosis and neurological decline always seem to occur on a Friday night. Although there are common incidents of mismanagement and delayed recognition of spinal metastasis, cases coming to court are probably rare because once cancer has spread to the spine the majority of patients die within three to six months. Surgery can very rarely affect survival. The benefits of surgery are palliative to decrease pain and to allow the patient a better quality of life by not having been paralysed in the last few months or last year of their life. Survival is more influenced by tumour type and response to drugs, chemotherapy and radiotherapy. A recent randomised trial has demonstrated that surgery plus radiotherapy is superior to radiotherapy alone.

Degenerative

30.77 Degenerative conditions of the spine represent the largest volume of work for health professionals. There are many people looking after patients, eg GPs, physiotherapists, osteopaths, chiropractors, rheumatologists, neurologists, pain specialists, orthopaedic and spinal neurosurgeons. These conditions affect the lumbar spine the most, presumably due to increased weight and forces. The thoracic spine is rarely affected.

30.78 The cervical spine, when affected by degenerative disc disease, results in pain, nerve entrapment causing pain and potentially sensory and motor symptoms. Pain in the arm is referred to as brachalgia and is often the result of a laterally placed disc compressing a nerve root (cervical spondylotic radiculopathy). When there is a central disc herniation it presses on the spinal cord causing various degrees of paralysis. This is called cervical spondylotic myelopathy. Typically this presents with numb clumsy hands. Occasionally this is misdiagnosed as carpal tunnel syndrome. The diagnosis is only made when the patient fails to improve after carpal tunnel decompression. Some of these patients have manipulations of their neck by osteopaths, chiropractors or even physiotherapists. Paraesthesia (pins and needles) affecting the hands should be regarded as a contraindication. Occasionally this is forgotten with tetraparesis ensuing.

30.79 Patients with cervical spondylosis may of course be the victims of road traffic accidents. It will always be very difficult to gauge how much of a patient's symptoms were due to a pre-existing condition and how much due to their trauma. Some medico-legal specialists seem to have developed a sixth sense and seem to be able to judge this. Boden has analysed the MRI scans of a cohort of non-spinal patients having scans of their larynx and found that degenerative disc disease and spondylosis are quite common in an asymptomatic population[1].

1 Boden, McCowin (et al) 'Abnormal magnetic-resonance scans of the cervical spine in asymptomatic subjects. A prospective investigation' (1990) 72(8) Jnl Bone Joint Surg Am 1178–1184.

30.80 Degeneration affects the lumbar spine in different ways. Slipped discs cause sciatica. Usually this responds well to non-operative measures. Spontaneous resolution is the rule not the exception. Surgery is indicated for those individuals with neurological compromise or severe pain for two to three months. The most common disc herniation is in a postero lateral direction. This will compress the traversing nerve root. Occasionally the disc herniation is very laterally placed and will compress the traversing nerve root. Far lateral discs are occasionally not noticed by radiologists or surgeons. Wrong level surgery can occur in the presence of degenerative disc disease at two levels.

30.81 Central disc herniation, if modest, may just cause back pain. If the disc herniation is large it will compress the cauda equina risking bladder and bowel function. This is a surgical emergency (see above). Fortunately it is rare. Compensation is often sought for delays in diagnosis, or tardy treatment. If degeneration is severe, instability can occur.

30.82 Spondylolisthesis is the term given when two vertebra slip relative to each. The most common cause is degeneration and failure of the facet joints. Spondylolithesis can also occur as a congenital condition associated with spina bifida. It can also occur in athletes (fast bowlers, swimmers) or dancers. This represents a fatigue fracture of a part of bone between the facet joints (pars interarticularis). A missed diagnosis in a professional athlete or dancer may be an expensive mistake.

30.83 A spondylolisthesis is graded according to the amount that one vertebral body has slipped forward on another (I–V). A grade I slip means that the upper vertebra has slipped forward less than 25 per cent of the total width of the vertebral body, a grade II slip is between 25 and 50 per cent, a grade III slip between 50 and 75 per cent, a grade IV slip is more than 75 per cent, and in the case of a grade V slip, the upper vertebral body has slid all the way forward off the front of the lower vertebral body. This is a special situation that is called a spondyloptosis. Grades III and IV present major technical challenges. Neurological complications and instrumentation failure do occur and can be significant. There is controversy on how safe it is to reduce the deformity. This work should only be performed in large specialist units.

30.84 Finally, severe degeneration in a small number of individuals may cause a curvature of their spine: degenerative scoliosis. This presents a major surgical challenge. If surgery is embarked upon it is major surgery on an elderly individual. There are some surgical triumphs, but also a fair share of surgical disasters. This is work that should only be performed by specialist spine surgeons working in a spinal deformity service.

Vascular

30.85 Vascular disorders of the spine are uncommon clinical problems. A haemangioma is a benign tumour that can involve the body of the vertebra. This tumour is often found in the lower thoracic or upper lumbar spine, usually involving only a single vertebra. Interestingly, not all haemangiomas produce symptoms such as pain. Haemangiomas typically occur during mid-life, affecting females more often than males. The most common symptom associated with a haemangioma is pain. This is typically the result of a large haemangioma involving the entire vertebral body. Haemangiomas may be discovered as part of an evaluation for back pain. They have a very characteristic appearance on regular X-rays, referred to as 'honeycombing'. There may also be a varying degree of collapse and loss of vertebral height with extensive involvement. When the collapse is severe, impingement on the spinal cord or neural elements will produce severe pain and loss of function in the legs, bowel or bladder. There are a number of treatment options for vertebral haemangioma, ranging from observation to radiation to surgical resection. Treatment decisions are based upon the severity of symptoms or neurologic compromise.

30.86 Spinal cord vascular malformations (arterial and venous) represent a heterogeneous group of blood vessel disorders that affect the spinal cord parenchyma either directly or indirectly. This group consists of spinal arteriovenous malformations (AVMs), dural arteriovenous fistulas (AVF), spinal haemangiomas, cavernous angiomas, and aneurysms. AVMs and AVFs are rare disorders that may cause neurologic deterioration. An accurate diagnosis is important because these lesions may represent a reversible cause of myelopathy. Improvements in spinal cord imaging, such as MRI and angiography, have provided further insight into the anatomy and pathophysiology of these lesions. In addition, less invasive treatment options, such as neuroendovascular surgical approaches, are presently being further explored.

30.87 All the intradural intramedullary AVMs are very rare and outside the scope of this chapter. AVFs are also quite rare, typically occurring in patients over 40. Symptoms increase over an extended period of months to years and include progressive weakness of the legs and concurrent bowel or bladder difficulties. Typically, pain is located in the distal posterior thoracic region over the spine, without a significant radicular component. Activity or a change in position may exacerbate symptoms in the thoracic or lumbar region and can result in thoracic spinal cord venous congestion and lower-extremity weakness. Their importance in a medico-legal context is that these lesions can be mistakenly diagnosed as spinal stenosis and neurogenic claudication. The typical history of a patient with spinal claudication does not usually include lower-extremity weakness, but it can include a significant pain component similar to that of a spinal dural AVF. For those patients who do not improve neurologically following adequate decompressive surgery for spinal stenosis, the surgeon should consider the presence of a dural fistula.

CONCLUSION

30.88 The preceding paragraphs have dealt with the common operations and conditions. Spinal surgery is a large field with common and not so common conditions. Technically it is a demanding speciality. There appears to be an emerging consensus that certain conditions are best treated in specialised centres, where diagnostic and surgical skills can be concentrated and can evolve to improve patients' treatments. Degenerative disc disease managed by physiotherapy, selected injections, discectomy and simple decompressions is regarded as the province of all spine surgeons whether they are from neurosurgical (still involved in cranial work) or orthopaedic (still involved in trauma and general orthopaedics) backgrounds.

30.89 Certain areas are regarded as complex and these would include deformity (scoliosis) and spinal intradural procedures (tumours/syringomyelia). This area has been called complex spine surgery and includes most forms of instrumentation or surgery on uncommon conditions, eg thoracic disc, spinal cord hernia, rheumatoid cervical spine, intramedullary spinal cord tumours. These are performed in regional units by nominated or specially-trained spine surgeons. Poor surgical results in these surgeries when performed by occasional spine surgeons is likely to attract criticism in this era of sub-speciality specialisation. This is potentially a form of clinical negligence not always recognised by the legal fraternity.

More importantly, it is imperative that expert medico-legal opinion is obtained from doctors who are genuine specialists in the spinal field. Cranial neurosurgeons and general orthopaedic and trauma surgeons are not deemed by their peer group to be experts in complex spinal surgery. Opinions on instrumented spine, deformity or tumours should be sought from those individuals with significant, contemporary or recent surgical experience in these areas[1].

1 Casey 'The ugly face of medical negligence: where has justice gone?' (2014) 2 European Spine Journal.

BIBLIOGRAPHY

Antimicrobial prophylaxis in neurosurgery and after head injury. Infection in Neurosurgery Working Party of the British Society for Antimicrobial Chemotherapy' (1994) 344(8936) Lancet 1547–1551.

Barba, Taggert (et al) 'A new cervical spine clearance protocol using computed tomography' (2001) 51(4) Jnl Trauma 652–656; discussion 656–657.

Boden, McCowin (et al) 'Abnormal magnetic-resonance scans of the cervical spine in asymptomatic subjects. A prospective investigation' (1990) 72(8) J Bone Joint Surg Am 1178–1184.

Buggy 'Can anaesthetic management influence surgical-wound healing?' (2000) 356(9227) Lancet 355–357.

Casey 'The ugly face of medical negligence: where has justice gone?' (2014) 2 European Spine Journal.

Conlin, Bhogal (et al) 'Treatment of whiplash-associated disorders – part I: Non-invasive interventions' (2005) 10(1) Pain Res Manag 21–32.

Conlin, Bhogal (et al) 'Treatment of whiplash-associated disorders – part II: Medical and surgical interventions' (2005) 10(1) Pain Res Manag 33–40.

Crockard, Heilman (et al) 'Progressive myelopathy secondary to odontoid fractures: clinical, radiological, and surgical features' (1993) 78(4) Jnl Neurosurg 579–586.

Flynn 'Neurologic complications of anterior cervical interbody fusion' (1982) 7(6) Spine 536–539.

Flynn 'Neurologic complications of anterior cervical discectomy in Louisiana' (1984) 136(7) J La State Med Soc 6–8.

Freeman, Croft (et al) '"Whiplash associated disorders: redefining whiplash and its management" by the Quebec Task Force. A critical evaluation' (1998) 23(9) Spine 1043–1049.

Gleave and MacFarlane 'Prognosis for recovery of bladder function following lumbar central disc prolapse' (1990) 4(3) Br J Neurosurg 205–209.

Gleave and Macfarlane 'Cauda equina syndrome: what is the relationship between timing of surgery and outcome?' (2002) 16(4) Br J Neurosurg 325–328.

Hadley, Walters (et al) 'Guidelines for the management of acute cervical spine and spinal cord injuries' (2002) 49 Clin Neurosurg 407–498.

Hurlbert 'Methylprednisolone for acute spinal cord injury: an inappropriate standard of care' (2000) 93(1 Suppl) Jnl Neurosurg 1–7.

May, Jones (et al) 'Somatosensory evoked potential monitoring in cervical surgery: identification of pre- and intraoperative risk factors associated with neurological deterioration' (1996) 85(4) Jnl Neurosurg 566–573.

ME B *The Management of Back Pain in General Practice* (1995) RCGP clinical series. London: Royal College of General Practitioners.

Menezes, Sonntag *Principles of Spinal Surgery* (1996).

O'Brien, Peterson (et al) 'A novel technique for laminoplasty augmentation of spinal canal area using titanium miniplate stabilization. A computerized morphometric analysis' (1996) 21(4) Spine 474–483; discussion 484.

Omeis, DeMattia (et al) 'History of instrumentation for stabilization of the subaxial cervical spine' (2004) 16(1) Neurosurg Focus E10.

Samuels 'A lawyer, thinking of the neuro fraternity, reflects upon recent judicial decisions' (2004) 18(2) Br J Neurosurg 119–123.

Schrader, Obelieniene (et al) 'Natural evolution of late whiplash syndrome outside the medicolegal context' (1996) 347(9010) Lancet 1207–1211.

Shapiro 'Cauda equina syndrome secondary to lumbar disc herniation' (1993) 32(5) Neurosurgery 743–746; discussion 746–747.

Shapiro 'Medical realities of cauda equina syndrome secondary to lumbar disc herniation' (2000) 25(3) Spine 348–351; discussion 352.

Waddell, Somerville (et al) 'Objective clinical evaluation of physical impairment in chronic low back pain' (1992) 17(6) Spine 617–628.

Weber 'Lumbar disc herniation. A prospective study of prognostic factors including a controlled trial. Part I' (1978) 28(3–4) Jnl Oslo City Hosp 33–61.

Weber 'Lumbar disc herniation. A prospective study of prognostic factors including a controlled trial. Part II' (1978) 28(7–8) Jnl Oslo City Hosp 89–113.

Weber 'Lumbar disc herniation. A controlled, prospective study with ten years of observation' (1983) 8(2) Spine 131–140.

Weinstein, Lurie (et al) 'Surgical vs non-operative treatment for lumbar disk herniation: the Spine Patient Outcomes Research Trial (SPORT) observational cohort' (2006) 296(20) Jama 2451–2459.

Weinstein, Tosteson (et al) 'Surgical vs non-operative treatment for lumbar disk herniation: the Spine Patient Outcomes Research Trial (SPORT): a randomized trial' (2006) 296(20) Jama 2441–2450.

CHAPTER 31

Otorhinolaryngology

Professor Tony Cheesman

SCOPE OF PRACTICE

31.1   The speciality of otorhinolaryngology (often shortened to otolaryngology or ENT) historically developed to manage conditions involving the upper air and food passages. The logical link for these distinct anatomical areas was that pathology in one area often influenced function in the other two areas. Chronic sinusitis, as an example, commonly presents with both ear and throat problems. With the simplified surgery available in those days an ENT surgeon would be competent to practise in all areas of the speciality.

With the improving health of the nation, inflammatory disease in these areas has declined dramatically, consequently changing the scope of the speciality.

31.2   Over the last three decades the scope of otolaryngology practice has increased dramatically. This has resulted from improvements in both the training of ENT surgeons and in the general technological advances of medicine. In particular, advances in anaesthesia and imaging have enabled ENT surgeons to manage previously non-treatable conditions.

31.3   Currently the speciality is concerned with the management of disease of ear, nose and throat including all aspects of cancer of the head and neck. It deals with patients of all ages; in terms of paediatric practice, ENT makes the biggest surgical contribution. Much of ENT practice is now non-surgical; some 80 per cent of patients seen in the outpatient department are treated medically.

31.4   The specialist association for otolaryngology is The British Association of Otorhinolaryngologists-Head and Neck Surgeons. It forms a joint organisation with the British Academic Conference in Otorhinolaryngology called ENT UK. Its website (www.entuk.co.uk) contains a vast amount of literature regarding the speciality for both doctors and patients.

31.5   ENT UK has published a series of position papers setting out the consensus view of the management of various aspects of the speciality. Effectively these papers provide management guidelines.

31.6   The standards of medical care in the UK are determined by the General Medical Council and set out in its Good Medical Practice guidance. The standards of surgical practice are set out in the booklet *Good Surgical Practice* published by the Royal College of Surgeons of England (September 2014) in collaboration with the various surgical colleges and the surgical specialist associations. It requires doctors to undergo continuing professional development and this is checked by an annual appraisal and a five-yearly revalidation.

31.7   An important proviso in medico-legal terms is the statement in *Good Surgical Practice* that 'when providing elective care for patients with non-urgent conditions any procedure should lay within the limits of competence of a given surgeon and within the range of their routine practice'. It emphasises that referral to another specialist or unit is important to ensure that the required resources and skills are available.

31.8   This principle is particularly important in otolaryngology with its commonly practised sub-specialties of otology, rhinology, laryngology and head and neck surgical oncology. Furthermore in each of the sub-specialties there is increasingly super-specialisation. With such a wide range of pathologies, different operative techniques and equipment, it is now very difficult for any surgeon to be competent in all aspects of otolaryngology. This super-specialisation is well recognised in the NHS, with all ENT departments having different consultants with special interests in one of the above sub-specialties. All consultants are fully competent for routine outpatient practice and on-call duties. When they encounter a patient requiring more specialised care they will make an internal referral to one of their colleagues. For the rarer cases requiring super-specialist care, often delivered in conjunction with related specialties (such as neurosurgery), well-established regional referral pathways exist.

31.9   Such clear distinctions of specialist skills are not so well established in private practice. Patients seeking private care should rely upon the appropriate informed referrals of their GPs. The selection of specialists from the internet may not always be in the patient's best interest.

EDUCATION AND TRAINING

31.10   Trainees in otolaryngology now cover a very wide spectrum of pathology and are required to be competent in many different surgical skills. The wide syllabus for otolaryngology training can be found on the Intercollegiate Surgical Curriculum website (www.iscp.ac.uk).

31.11   During the first two foundation years of postgraduate training doctors are encouraged to choose a future career pathway. Hopefully many would have been exposed to a three-month period in otolaryngology practice, or alternatively have developed an interest during their undergraduate studies.

31.12   If they do not have exposure to ENT in their foundation years it is unlikely that they will be accepted for higher surgical training in otolaryngology. This experience then needs to be sought in one of the post-foundation training programmes. During this early period trainees are required to collect points for length of ENT exposure, research contributions and higher degrees. The performance of at least two audits is considered essential.

31.13   Entry into higher surgical training is by competition on a nationwide basis, and training posts are allocated by the selection committee depending on each applicant's performance. The better performers are given greater choice of where they are sent for training.

31.14   Higher surgical training programmes involve the rotation through different consultants and departments to ensure that trainees have exposure to all aspects of the speciality. Both regional and national teaching courses are available and trainees are expected to attend several them.

31.15   After six years of training trainees sit the Intercollegiate Specialty Board examination leading to Certificate of Completion of Training (CCT) certification in otolaryngology. The CCT is awarded by the Joint Committee on Surgical Training to candidates on completion of their training who have fulfilled the following requirements:

- are fully registered GMC and have a licence to practise.
- have undertaken six years higher surgical training in a UK or Ireland training programme;
- have successfully passed the Intercollegiate Specialty Board examination;
- have gained all the required competencies for the speciality of otolaryngology[1].

Although the CCT certificate enables them to enter consultant practice, most trainees will seek a further two years of super-specialisation.

1 See www.jcst.org.

31.16   The standard of training has been greatly enhanced over the last decade with the wider use of television attached to either the endoscopes or operating microscope. This enables trainees to see in detail operations that previously were only seen by the operating surgeon. It also allows detailed supervision of the trainees during their initial surgical procedures.

FREQUENCY OF MEDICO-LEGAL PROBLEMS IN OTOLARYNGOLOGY

31.17   There are no accurate figures for the frequency of litigation in otolaryngology practice. The relatively high incidence in United States and Australia is probably a reflection on their legal systems. Several studies of complication rates for rhinological surgery suggest many potential cases fail to reach the courts.

31.18   According to the NHSLA database, there has been a dramatic increase in the number of cases involved in ENT litigation. In 1996 there were two claims and in 2013 there were 107 claims. On average 50 per cent of claims were successful.

Matthew[1] made an analysis of the claims related to otology and tonsillectomy practice over a period of 15 years:

- there were 40 claims related to tonsillectomy (7.7 per cent total claims in otolaryngology). 94 per cent of claims were successful with payment of damages;
- there were 137 claims in otology (26 per cent of total claims in otolaryngology). 84 per cent of these claims were successful with payment of damages.

Over this 15-year period there were 1,359 claims in otolaryngology; 55 per cent of them were successful. Claims in otolaryngology represent 4 per cent of the claims related to the whole of surgery.

1 Mathew, Asimacopoulos, Walker, Gutierrez, Valentine, Pitkin 'Analysis of clinical negligence claims following tonsillectomy in England 1995 to 2010' (2012) 121(5) Ann Otol Rhinol Laryngol 337–340; Mathew Asimacopoulos, Valentine 'Toward safer practice in otology: a report on 15 years of clinical negligence claims' (2011) 121(10) Laryngoscope 2214–2219. doi: 10.1002/lary.22136. Epub 6 September 2011.

Informed consent in otorhinolaryngology

31.19   The GMC's guidance on informed consent is clear.

- the person providing the treatment is responsible for ensuring valid informed consent has been obtained;
- this task may be delegated to a junior member of the team provided:
  — they are suitably trained and qualified;
  — they have sufficient knowledge of the proposed treatment and understand the risks involved.

In ENT practice this presents some difficulties because of the wide range of radically different procedures performed in each of the different subspecialties.

31.20   Several surveys into the consent process in ENT departments in the UK have shown an improving situation. Puwanarajah[1] found that there was an increase in the seniority of junior doctors responsible for obtaining consent pre-operatively. They also found that 65 per cent of ENT departments provided information sheets related to the treatment.

1 Puwanarajah, McDonald 'Changes in surgical consent practices for common otolaryngology procedures: impact of Modernising Medical Careers' (2010) 124(8) J Laryngol Otol 899–904.

31.21   Information sheets regarding the most common ENT operations are now widely available. Most departments will have their own leaflets or have available those produced by ENT UK. In the private sector most of the private insurers have such details on their websites. Although these sheets contain useful information they are often lacking in significant detail of the potential complications of any particular procedure.

Any general search on the internet needs to be made with caution, as not all sites give reliable information, and frankly many are merely advertisements for a particular supplier.

31.22   The consent process for surgical procedures differs between NHS and private practice. In private practice the surgeon controls the complete consent process from the outpatient department to the pre-operative review. In the NHS the pre-operative consent is generally taken by a junior member of the medical staff.

31.23   In both cases the consent process starts with the outpatient consultation, when the doctor listing the patient for surgery must explain the particular medical problem, the proposed treatment and its likely success;

this should include alternative non-surgical treatments. They should also inform the patient of the result of failing to undergo treatment.

If the surgical procedure is complex with a significant outcome it is common practice to review the patient on a subsequent visit to ensure that they understand what is proposed.

31.24   While many surgeons are requesting patients to sign a consent form at this stage, other surgeons feel that this places undue pressure on the patient to proceed. A copy of the consent form plus any information sheets should be given to the patient. There are several studies that indicate the patient's recall of these consent discussions is often poor, even when supplied with handouts; consequently the pre-operative consent must be equally detailed and another consent form signed.

Details to be included on consent form

31.25   There remains considerable discussion as to how much detail should be given regarding potential complications. Most surgeons will list the common complications or normal sequelae of the given procedure. They will also mention significant complications even if they occur only rarely. However increasingly in the United States and Australia the listing of complications has become more rigid and patients are generally given a printed list of complications in the order of frequency or severity.

31.26   In the UK most consent forms require the surgeon to enter the surgical procedure, listing the potential benefits and also complications. The detail included is left to the discretion of the surgeon and his assessment as to how much detail the patient would wish to know. Prior to *Sidaway*[1], complications with an incidence rarer than 1 per cent were deemed as unimportant and were often not discussed. Many experienced surgeons are reticent to include all complications as they feel it could possibly infer that they were not very competent.

1 *Sidaway v Board of Governors of the Bethlem Royal Hospital and the Maudsley Hospital* [1985] AC 871.

31.27   The complication rate for any procedure depends on several factors:

- the experience and competence of the surgeon are probably most important;
- the extent of the pathology and its inherent cause of many complications;
- anatomical variations often lead to complications and adequate imaging is essential to define these variations pre-operatively;
- trainee surgeons require careful supervision to minimise complications.

31.28   The North American and Australian practice of using standard lists of all known complications as a check list during consent is to be recommended. Careful wording will indicate that these are a standard requirement and not a reflection on any particular surgeon's practice. In discussing the list with the patient the surgeon is able to indicate the likely occurrence of a given complication occurring in their hands.

(A specimen consent form appropriate for nasal surgery is set out at para **31.138**).

COMMON OTORHINOLARYNGOLOGY PROCEDURES AND THEIR COMPLICATIONS

Tonsillectomy and adenotonsillectomy

31.29 In the 1950s adenotonsillectomy was the commonest operation performed in the UK. Indeed, adenotonsillectomy was synonymous with ear nose and throat surgery. The frequency of the procedure has declined dramatically – a reduction of some 90 per cent since infections and the indications for both adenoidectomy and tonsillectomy are now better understood and the operations are now only offered to patients likely to benefit.

31.30 In general practice and paediatrics there is a general feeling that still too many tonsillectomies are being performed. Consequently GPs tend to dissuade their patients from referral. As a result the ENT speciality is now concerned that too few tonsillectomies are being performed, as evidenced by the increased admissions for quinsy and the medical treatment of severe tonsillitis. The speciality's view is covered in ENT UK's position paper on the Indications for Tonsillectomy (2009).

31.31 Although tonsillectomy is not a difficult operation it uses different techniques from those used in routine surgery. Because the surgeon is working down the narrow tunnel created by the oral cavity, instruments need to be held in a different way. Similarly the ligation of bleeding points needs to be done in a specific way. Learning these techniques improves the ability of the surgeon in other fields of ENT surgery. Conversely some surgeons have recommended alternative techniques for the removal of tonsils, such as laser resection and co-ablation surgery. These have not received universal acceptance and tend to have a higher incidence of bleeding as a complication.

31.32 Most tonsillectomies are performed by junior staff in the NHS. It is important that they are trained adequately and then supervised until the consultant is confident of their ability to operate separately.

Complications

31.33 Complications are as follows:

- post-operative pain is the most common complaint following tonsillectomy and it is important that adequate analgesia is given and continued as long as necessary;
- the gag used to open the mouth during surgery has a potential to damage any loose teeth. Dentition should be assessed pre-operatively. If the operation is prolonged the maximal opening of the mouth puts a strain on the temporo-mandibular joint and temporary dysfunction may occur;

- bleeding during surgery is the most common complication and although only 100 ml is lost on average, this is a significant percentage of a small child's blood volume. Accordingly trainees are taught the importance of estimating the blood volume from a child's weight;
- bleeding may also occur some hours after the operation if a ligature comes loose. This is termed reactionary haemorrhage and requires the patient to be returned to theatre for further control of the bleeding point. In this situation with excessive bleeding, blood is often inhaled and it is important to consider whether a bronchoscopy should be performed to clear the bronchi;
- bleeding may also occur several days later due to infection of the tonsillar bed. This late bleeding often requires readmission and treatment with antibiotics;
- if the tonsil is very fibrosed, such as results from a previous quinsy, it may be difficult to separate the faucial pillars from the tonsil and this can cause damage and scarring of the soft palate, occasionally leading to rhinolalia. This particular complication is potentially serious for a professional voice user and in such a case appropriate consent and a skilled surgeon are necessary;
- similarly the pharyngeal wall deep to the tonsil can be breached and the dissection continued into the neck leading to damage of the glossopharyngeal nerve.

Rigid endoscopy of the upper air and food passages

31.34   Despite the widespread use of diagnostic flexible endoscopy for the oesophagus and bronchial tree, there is still a need for the use of rigid endoscopes, particularly for the removal of foreign bodies. Such endoscopy is an important part of ENT practice. During training junior surgeons are taught these techniques on both models and animal cadavers.

31.35   Lasers are being increasingly used during endoscopic surgery of the larynx and pharynx. Careful safety arrangements are essential and ENT UK has a paper listing the essential requirements for a unit using laser surgery.

Complications

31.36   The main general complication from rigid endoscopy is damage to the teeth. This complication is also a potential problem for anaesthetists. Detailed assessment of the dentition pre-operatively is essential and patients should be warned of the potential dangers of dislodgement, particularly if they have dental bridges. There is also a danger that the enamel may be chipped.

31.37   To prevent these injuries protection of the teeth is essential and although silastic dental splints prevent chipping of the teeth, they do not prevent dislodgement of teeth or bridges. To minimise this particular damage rigid splints are essential to spread the load over the whole of the anterior arch.

RHINOLOGY

31.38   The ENT subspeciality of rhinology covers:

● anatomical nasal obstruction and cosmetic deformities of the nasal pyramid;
● infection and inflammation of the paranasal sinuses;
● tumours of the nose and paranasal sinuses.

The nose, paranasal sinuses and the middle ear cleft are all part of the upper respiratory tract. It is lined with a respiratory epithelium with mucus glands and cilia.

The mucus is moved by cilia action towards the nasopharynx. There are well-defined cilia pathways. This flow of mucus driven by the cilia is one of the primary defence mechanisms of the upper respiratory tract.

Normal cilia movement depends on good aeration of the paranasal sinuses and middle ear cleft.

31.39   The upper respiratory tract is the most common site of infection in the body, the common cold being the most frequent. The acute inflammatory response to the virus causes severe congestion of the mucosa blocking the ostia and fluid exudate collects in the cavities. This inflammation blocks mucus spread and often a bacterial infection will result, acute sinusitis. Treatment with antibiotics may well resolve the infection but they do not restore sinuses to normal function. This requires return of normal cilia function to restore the mucus blanket.

31.40   Chronic inflammation may develop with a further change in the mucosa and often gram-negative and anaerobic bacteria flourish. With chronic infections surgical drainage is often necessary and, in addition, in the upper respiratory tract restoration of normal aeration by enlarging the natural ostia.

31.41   Another potent cause for the development of chronic inflammation is atopic or allergic rhinitis, which causes a similar acute inflammation. Surgery for chronic sinus infections in atopic patients remains essential for drainage and aeration, but the surgery will not eradicate the allergic condition. Accordingly it is important that patients are clearly informed that the surgery is to resolve the infection and that their allergy will need to be managed medically. The condition is increasingly being managed by medical rhinologists generally with an immunological background.

Epistaxis

31.42   The commonest nasal problem is epistaxis and this is managed both by general practitioners and ENT surgeons. It occurs in two forms; the most frequent is intermittent minor bleeding which arises from Little's area of the nasal septum. The primary problem is drying of the nasal mucosa with crust formation and the removal of the crusts, often by nasal picking, causes bleeding. The most effective treatment is to prevent drying of the mucosa by the routine application of grease such as Vaseline, or Naseptin if the crusts are obviously infected. A persistent bleeding point needs to be cauterised under local anaesthetic, and if silver nitrate is used care must be taken to ensure that area of cauterisation does not expand beyond the bleeding point. Excessive cauterisation can cause septal perforation and a skin burn.

31.43   Profuse nasal bleeding often lasting for 30 minutes or more is due to a rupture of one of the branches of the sphenopalatine artery in the back of the nose. It is more common in the elderly as a result of atherosclerosis and hypertension. Immediate management often requires nasal packing, which is a particularly skilled procedure requiring excellent anaesthesia of the nasal mucosa. To overcome this problem many practitioners use inflatable balloons or compressed foam packs as these are more easily inserted into the nasal cavity. Correction of any hypertension is equally important.

Ligation of the sphenopalatine artery is now performed endoscopically at the back of the nose.

Intra-arterial embolisation by radiologists is also effective in stopping these bleeds, but it needs to be done by an experienced interventional radiologist because of the small risk of inter-communication with branches of the internal carotid circulation.

Functional endoscopic sinus surgery (FESS)

31.44   The major advance in nasal surgery has been the development of functional endoscopic sinus surgery (FESS) for the treatment of chronic sinus infections. This intranasal surgery depends on the use of solid Hopkin rod endoscopes which enable excellent visualisation of the nasal cavities. Concomitant use of a sucker is essential to remove the usual bleeding common in nasal surgery, as this can obscure the endoscopic view. Such bleeding is reduced by the use of vasoconstrictor nasal sprays given immediately prior to the surgery.

31.45   The apparent excellent view down the endoscope can mislead the surgeon, particularly trainee surgeons, into thinking they know exactly where they are in the nasal cavities. To minimise this problem it is mandatory that all patients undergoing FESS should have a comprehensive CT examination of the paranasal sinuses. Using both coronal and axial views much of the anatomy and its variations can be learnt prior to surgery. Most FESS surgeons are highly skilled in the reading of CT images. Increasingly the more advanced FESS procedures are being done with image guidance. This relates the position of the endoscope and instruments in real time to a CT image, ensuring accurate anatomical location. At the present time this equipment is not widely available in the UK, but increasingly in the USA is becoming considered mandatory for sinus surgery.

31.46   The standard technique of operating with the endoscopic image displayed on a television requires a good image on the screen. If there are problems with the television equipment the surgeon should suspend or modify the procedure to ensure good anatomical location within the nasal sinuses is preserved.

Complications of sinus surgery

31.47   Traditionally the major complications of sinus surgery were excessive bleeding and failure to resolve the pathology adequately. With the advent of endoscopic surgery there has been an increased potential for additional, and often very significant, complications[1]:

- damage to the orbital periosteum and orbital contents, including the optic nerve leading to diplopia or loss of vision;
- untra-orbital haemorrhage is a serious ophthalmological complication and immediate surgical decompression of the orbit is essential to preserve vision. There are several ENT surgical procedures to decompress the orbit and these should be performed promptly by the operating rhinologist. Calling for ophthalmological help would cause unacceptable delay.

1 See Lund, Wright, Yiotakis 'Complications and medicolegal aspects of endoscopic sinus surgery' (1997) 90(8) R Soc Med 422–428.

31.48   The above complications have become regrettably more common since the advent of the micro-debrider in sinus surgery. Although the debrider can speed the surgery and in skilled hands produce more accurate removal of tissue, it remains a potentially dangerous instrument in inexperienced hands. A defendant in such a case would need to demonstrate proper training and frequent experience with the debrider. Potential problems include:

- damage to the lacrimal duct leading to epiphora;
- breaching of the floor of the anterior fossa leading to CSF leakage, pneumocephalus and possible meningitis;
- damage to the olfactory nerves giving anosmia;
- damage to intracranial blood vessels leading to stroke and possible death.

31.49   Fortunately, surveys of endoscopic sinus surgery in the UK have shown a low frequency with such complications; Harkness[1], with a national audit, found the complication rate for major complications using FESS was 1.4 per cent. This reflects the high standards of teaching such surgery and most rhinological surgeons will have attended specialised practical courses in this field of surgery, often cadaver based. The use of television to display the endoscopic view enables close supervision of a trainee during their initial surgical procedures. This has led to a shortening of the surgical learning curve and a decreased incidence of complication.

1 Harkness, Brown, Fowler, Topham 'A national audit of sinus surgery. Results of the Royal College of Surgeons of England comparative audit of ENT surgery' (1997) 22(2) Clin Otolaryngol Allied Sci 147–151.

Advanced endoscopic sinus surgery

31.50   Many rhinologists have expanded the scope of endoscopic surgery. It is increasingly used for benign tumours of the nasal cavities and paranasal sinuses. Highly specialised rhinologists have further developed the technique to manage malignant tumours extending up to and including the skull base. The trans-nasal endoscopic route is now the standard procedure for the closure of cerebral-spinal fluid leaks from the anterior fossa. It is also used for some conditions of the orbit, in particular blockage of the lacrimal duct.

31.51 Many rhinologists when performing these extended procedures often work in conjunction with other specialties, such as neurosurgery and ophthalmology. However some highly specialised rhinologists are so experienced in this type of surgery that they are competent enough to do the surgery single-handed. (These surgeons often retain very close working relationships with the other specialties with whom they will often discuss such cases at a Skull Base MDT meeting).

31.52 This wide range of skills can present medico-legal problems in determining whether any particular surgeon is operating within his level of competence. It is certainly true to say those routine rhinologists skilled in FESS for sinus infections do not have the surgical skills to perform the more advanced procedures. The defence of any action against them would require them to demonstrate their surgical expertise listing any specialised courses they have attended and also to give some indication of their routine workload.

Surgery for nasal obstruction

31.53 Persistent nasal obstruction is a particularly aggravating symptom often made worse by periods of nasal congestion from an underlying atopic rhinitis. Common causes of obstruction are a deviated septum or enlarged inferior turbinates.

Septal surgery

31.54 The major complications of septal surgery are:

- excessive removal of the septal cartilage particularly anteriorly which leads to collapse of the cartilaginous nasal bridge giving a cosmetic defect, the saddle deformity. This may not be obvious immediately following the surgery;
- a septal haematoma may occur post-operatively and this is noted by the development of bilateral nasal obstruction. If it develops it should be drained at a further procedure. If it is left it may become infected with the potential for serious cavernous sinus thrombosis. It may also lead to a saddle deformity of the nasal bridge;
- with complex nasal spurs, damage to the nasal mucosa may result in a perforation of the septum. This results in epistaxis, crusting and occasionally a whistling sound during respiration. If it is a problem surgical repair is possible;
- perhaps the most annoying complication is re-deviation of the septum following apparently successful surgery. This occurs because of the propensity of bent cartilage to rebend again. There are many techniques to reduce occurrence of this complication.

Turbinate surgery

31.55 Hypertrophy of the inferior turbinates is a common cause of nasal obstruction. It may be an anatomical variation, but also occurs from the overuse of vasoconstrictor nose drops, rhinitis medicamentosa. It is also a common feature of chronic sinus infection.

31.56 Surgeons use a variety of techniques to reduce the bulk of the turbinates and a common complication of this surgery is post-operative haemorrhage.

Excessive resection of the inferior turbinates may lead to an excessively dry nose or atrophic rhinitis with crusting and frequent epistaxis. Such an occurrence must be considered inappropriate surgery.

Septo-rhinoplasty and cosmetic rhinoplasty

31.57 A deformed nasal bridge gives not only a cosmetic defect but also nasal obstruction. For the last three decades ENT surgeons have been responsible for the surgical correction of combined septal and nasal pyramid deformities. This septo-rhinoplasty requires a thorough understanding of the nasal anatomy. It is often performed, not only to improve cosmetic appearance, but to improve nasal function. It has long been taught to ENT trainees and is considered a standard ENT procedure. Inevitably this has led to ENT surgeons widely performing cosmetic rhinoplasty and indeed, increasingly, they are undertaking other facial cosmetic procedures. Such surgeons have generally sought additional specialised training and many have additional cosmetic qualifications such as Fellowship of the European Academy of Facial Plastic Surgery.

31.58 The major complication of this surgery is a failure to produce the desired result for the patient. Most surgeons find that 10 per cent of their cases end with a less than desirable result due to unpredictable healing and scarring. Accordingly they advise their patient beforehand of the possible need for revision surgery.

31.59 Careful explanation of the potential benefits from cosmetic surgery is essential following discussions with the patient. Ideally standardised photographs need to be taken and the discussion repeated on a subsequent second visit to ensure patient fully understands the pros and cons of this type of surgery.

Management of nasal tumours

31.60 Traditionally the management of nasal tumours, both benign and malignant, has been performed by oncologically trained ENT surgeons in conjunction with medical oncological colleagues. This is considered essential because knowledge of the natural history of the large number of different tumours that occur within the nose and paranasal sinuses is essential for the selection of the correct treatment protocol.

31.61   The development of craniofacial resections to encompass tumours breaching the anterior skull base led to a significant improvement in cure rates. This procedure was initially performed by external approaches often in conjunction with a neurosurgical colleague but increasingly is now being performed by solely endoscopic techniques. The exact role of endoscopic surgery with malignant tumours has still not been finally defined, and the standard external craniofacial resection remains the gold standard.

31.62   The widespread use of FESS has led to many routine ENT surgeons encountering a tumour during a routine nasal procedure. Many then proceed to remove it endoscopically. When the histology becomes available and they realise that they are dealing with a malignancy they often try to retrieve the situation by referring the patient straight to radiotherapy. Sadly this approach results in frequent recurrences after one to two years and the opportunity for curative management is lost. All non-oncologically trained ENT surgeons on encountering abnormal tissue during a nasal procedure should merely biopsy the area. If a malignancy is found, the case should be referred onto an appropriate oncologically trained ENT surgeon.

OTOLOGICAL MANAGEMENT AND PROCEDURES

31.63   The ENT subspeciality of otology covers disease involving the middle ear cleft, the otolabyrinth and tumours of the VII and VIII cranial nerves. With the decrease in inflammatory disease in this anatomical area, the result of the increased health of the nation, otological surgeons are increasingly performing more neuro-otological procedures. These are related to the function and pathology of the inner ear and its intracranial connections.

31.64   The middle ear cleft, like the paranasal sinuses, is part of the upper respiratory tract and prone to its common infections. The acute inflammation of the middle ear cleft, generally due to a virus, results in otalgia and deafness. An associated red tympanic membrane results in the diagnosis of acute suppurative otitis media by many GPs, due to the difficulties in interpreting the appearances of the tympanic membrane. However in most cases the problem is merely tubal obstruction requiring decongestant therapy. Failure to re-aerate the middle ear and clear it of its inflammatory exudate leads to secretory otitis media with long-term deafness.

31.65   Secretory otitis media is a big problem in children and their loss of hearing has significant effects on early learning. Its traditional management with the insertion of grommets and adenoidectomy led this procedure to be the most commonly-performed operation in the NHS. This has resulted in disagreement between paediatricians and otolaryngologists. The current consensus is that insertion of grommets should be delayed for three months to allow the ear adequate time to re-aerate. Sadly, many commissioning authorities still regard grommet insertion as an unnecessary procedure. There is general agreement that grommets should not be inserted before the child has reached the age of three.

31.66   There is disagreement amongst ENT surgeons as to whether the insertion of grommets should be accompanied by adenoidectomy (and tonsillectomy if indicated). The recurrence rate of secretory otitis media and the need for repeat grommet insertion is lower if adenoidectomy is performed as a primary procedure. Indeed many surgeons recommend antral lavage as well because of the frequency of muco-purulent disease involving the antra in the patients with secretory otitis media. See ENTUK's Position Paper on OME (Glue Ear) Adenoid and Grommet (2009).

Sequelae and complications of grommet surgery

31.67   The main complications of grommet surgery are:

* the need to reinsert them as a result of the recurrence of the secretory otitis media. The rest of the upper respiratory tract needs to be examined to exclude infection elsewhere and if adenoidectomy has not been performed then it is generally beneficial;
* with the need to reinsert grommets frequently many surgeons prefer to use long-term grommets, but these are prone to more scarring of the drum and middle ear;
* scarring of the drum and tympanosclerosis are not uncommon;
* a bigger problem is thinning of the drum and gross retraction leading to adhesive otitis media and possible cholesteatoma formation in later years.

Chronic suppurative otitis media

31.68   Acute otitis media often results in drum rupture; this clears the exudate from the middle ear and in most cases the drum will heal spontaneously. Persistence of a perforation leads to chronic suppurative otitis media with intermittent infections and a conductive deafness. This is termed tubo-tympanic otitis media. The bacteria involved in each infection tend to be gram-negative, and conservative nonsurgical management requires the use of aminoglycoside antibiotic drops. The patient also needs to prevent water entering the ear.

Aminoglycoside antibiotics are known to be ototoxic (see below).

31.69   If the recurrent infections are troublesome or the deafness is significant consideration can be given to repairing the drum with a myringoplasty. If the initial infection was significant and resulted in damage to the ossicular chain its continuity can be restored by ossiculoplasty.

31.70   A more serious type of chronic suppurative otitis media is termed attico-antral otitis media. This condition is typified by a marginal perforation of the tympanic membrane with the ingrowth of squamous epithelium into the middle ear and the formation of cholesteatoma. Cholesteatoma is essentially a result of the spread of squamous epithelium into the normally mucosal-lined middle ear cleft. Cholesteatoma can also arise *de-novo* in the middle ear in the absence of an obvious perforation; this is commonly termed congenital cholesteatoma. The viable squamous epithelium continues to desquamate with a build-up of a collection of dead epithelial cells. This collection of dead epithelial cells is known as the cholesteatoma and its surrounding viable sac secretes osteo-lytic enzymes, which erode the bones of the middle ear cleft:

- erosion of the ossicles results in conductive deafness;
- erosion of the inner ear bone leads to permanent deafness and vertigo;
- erosion of the bone covering the facial nerve leads to facial palsy;
- erosion of the cortical bone separating middle ear cleft from the dura of both the middle and posterior fossae can result in intracranial infection ranging from meningitis to cerebral abscess. The associated infection can cause thrombosis and thrombophlebitis of the sigmoid sinus.

31.71 Fortunately the incidence of cholesteatoma has decreased dramatically and its complications are now relatively rare in the UK. However, the known complications of cholesteatoma require it to be actively managed. This requires complete removal of the squamous epithelium from the middle ear cleft. In the past this was achieved by some form of opening of the mastoid cavity which exteriorised the squamous epithelium to an enlarged external auditory meatus. This allowed the desquamation to proceed without complication, although often it required the patient to attend the ENT clinic for regular cleaning of the mastoid cavity to remove the squamous debris. This remains necessary for the rest of the patient's life.

31.72 To reduce this lifetime burden many otologists have sought to perform closed mastoidectomy procedures. Whilst these abolish the need for regular cleaning of mastoid cavities, they run the risk of leaving residual cholesteatoma hidden in the middle ear cleft. To resolve this problem, surgeons often perform a second-stage procedure after one to two years to ensure there is no residual cholesteatoma. They often defer ossicular reconstruction to the second stage of the operation. This ensures the patient presents for the second operation and often the hearing results are better. An alternative approach to routine second-stage surgery is modern imaging which can detect a recurrence in the closed cavity. The role of closed versus open mastoidectomy remains under discussion, but it is generally agreed that closed techniques are best performed by surgeons with considerable expertise in this type of surgery.

Importance of specialist assessment

31.73 It is sometimes difficult for a general practitioner to assess an ear with chronic otitis media. A cholesteatoma sac is often hidden behind a flake of wax and an accurate diagnosis requires cleaning of the ear under microscopic control. In view of the seriousness of missing a case of cholesteatoma, it is probably mandatory that all cases are referred for otological opinion.

Ototoxic ear drops

31.74 The infective bacteria in chronic otitis media are generally of the gram-negative variety and the appropriate ear drops generally contain amino-glycoside antibiotics. These are known to be ototoxic and the National Formulary recommends that they should not be used in the presence of a perforation. However, the Formulary acknowledges that they are frequently used by ENT surgeons. There is an alternative antibiotic drop containing topical quinolones, which is used in ophthalmology. However, it is not licensed for use in the ear. Not all otologists agree to its value even though its spectrum of activity is suitable for ear infections and it is not ototoxic.

31.75   ENT UK has produced a position paper regarding the use of ototoxic ear drops. This recommends:

- ototoxic ear drops should only be used in the presence of an active infection;
- they should only be used for two weeks;
- the patient must be warned of the risks of using them and to cease their use if their hearing deteriorates;
- a base-line audiogram should be performed before use.

Their use would be considered acceptable practice if the above guidelines were followed.

OTOLOGICAL PROCEDURES

Myringoplasty and ossiculoplasty

31.76   A common procedure is myringoplasty for the repair of tympanic membrane perforations. If there are disruptions to the ossicular chain these can be corrected at the same time with an ossiculoplasty.

Myringoplasty is recommended for troublesome tubo-tympanic otitis media.

31.77   However the specific objectives of the operation must be discussed with the patient, including the chances of success. Generally repair of the drum is successful in preventing recurrent infections in better than 80 per cent of cases. The success in improving hearing is not as good and depends upon the particular ossicular problem. Success rates range from 50–70 per cent. It is also important to realise that unless the improvement in hearing can achieve an air conduction threshold comparable to that of the other ear, the patient will not appreciate the improvement obtained.

31.78   Ossiculoplasty tends to be more frequently performed by specialised otologically trained ENT surgeons. The success rate depends on the degree of damage to the ossicles.

31.79   With every surgical procedure on the middle ear there is a small risk of damage to the inner ear, irrespective of the skill of the surgeon. The average incidence of damage to the inner ear from middle ear surgery is approximately 5 per cent and it is very important that this is explained to the patient during the consent procedure.

Stapedectomy

31.80   Stapedectomy operations are performed for fixation of the stapes footplate following otosclerosis. In the early days of stapedectomy most ENT surgeons performed several stapedectomies each week until the backlog of cases was treated.

31.81   Today, otosclerosis is uncommon and not many stapedectomies need to be performed. It is a particularly skilled operation and is best left in the hands of an experienced otologist who performs the operation regularly. Even in the best hands sensorineural deafness occurs in some 4 per cent of cases, resulting in complete deafness and often disabling tinnitus.

Accordingly many surgeons require their patients to have a trial of a hearing aid to see whether this will resolve their problems without the need for surgery.

31.82   Because of the risks of the surgery it should only be performed in cases of bilateral deafness and in the UK it is recommended that only one ear is operated on. Patients also need to be advised that there is a long-term decline in hearing in some cases.

Complications of ear surgery

31.83   The main complications of ear surgery are:

- post-operative infection. In the presence of an existing infection most surgeons will cover the operation with antibiotics;
- significant bleeding may occur if the sigmoid sinus is damaged;
- failure to close the perforation;
- failure to clear the cholesteatoma;
- failure to improve the hearing to a useful level;
- damage to the chorda tympani nerve. This nerve runs through the middle ear just deep to the tympanic membrane and it is very vulnerable to surgery. Damage to the nerve results in loss of taste sensation to the anterior two thirds of the tongue. The patient may not notice this or possibly complain of a temporary metallic taste in the mouth. However if the patient relies on normal taste for their work or social enjoyment its loss can be very significant, hence it is important to warn the patient during the consent procedure;
- increased deafness, tinnitus and vertigo may result from damage to the inner ear. Even with excellent surgical technique the inner ear is vulnerable in 5 per cent of cases. Again it is important to discuss this during the consent procedure, particularly when the other ear has poor hearing;
- damage to the dura separating the middle ear cleft from the intracranial cavity may lead to CSF leakage or intracranial infection which can be severe and even fatal;
- damage to the facial nerve which may be temporary or permanent.

Management of facial palsy

31.84   The facial nerve is a major concern to the ENT surgeon in three different areas. It is probably most at risk in the cerebellopontine angle and internal auditory meatus. It then enters its bony canal to pass through the temporal bone where it is at risk from middle ear and mastoid surgery. It leaves the temporal bone at the stylomastoid foramen to pass through the parotid gland to supply the muscles of the face. The main trunk of the facial nerve contains secretor-motor fibres to the salivary and lacrimal glands, and special sensory fibres for taste to the anterior two thirds of the tongue. These different fibres are used for topo-diagnosis of a facial palsy.

31.85   Facial nerve monitoring by measuring action potentials in the facial musculature is essential for surgery in the cerebellopontine angle and parotid gland. In these areas touching the facial nerve causes facial nerve monitor to be activated and its different responses are of considerable value to the surgeon. Most surgeons would consider facial nerve monitoring mandatory for surgery in the cerebellopontine angle and parotid gland.

31.86   The use of the facial nerve monitor for mastoid surgery remains controversial. In those cases where facial nerve decompression is necessary, again most surgeons would consider its use as mandatory. However for routine mastoid surgery, although it is used by many surgeons, the consensus view in the UK is that it cannot be relied upon to prevent damage to the facial nerve during routine mastoid drilling. Drilling in the region of the facial canal does not routinely activate the monitor and there are many cases documented where a facial palsy has resulted from drilling into facial canal without a warning from the monitor. Consequently many surgeons feel that the use of the monitor gives a false sense of security to the surgeon. It is considered better to rely on using facial nerve landmarks to protect the course of the nerve.

31.87   At the end of every middle ear and mastoid procedure it is mandatory that the surgeon checks the patient for the presence of a facial palsy. If some facial weakness is noted then the ear should be re-explored, preferably by an experienced otologist. The objective of the operation is to explore the course of the nerve and to ascertain whether it has been injured. Immediate repair and/or local bony decompression can be very valuable. Subsequent electro-diagnostic tests should be performed to predict the outcome of the injury.

Detailed explanation and apology to the patient and relatives is important both for the patient and the surgeon.

Neuro-otological surgery

31.88   This super-specialised branch of otology entails surgery to the inner ear or its connections to the brain. Most ENT surgeons undertaking this type of surgery will have undergone specialist training. They frequently work in collaboration with neurosurgeons.

Cochlear implantation

31.89   This technique is used in patients with sensorineural deafness where the cochlear nerve is preserved. Sound is received by an external hearing aid and impulses are transmitted through the skin to a receiver lying in a surgical depression in the temporal bone. Wires pass from the receiver to an electrode surgically placed in the basal turn of the cochlea. These transmit electrical impulses, derived from the sound, to the nerve endings in the cochlea.

31.90 Young patients rapidly learn to hear these impulses as speech and implantation is customarily done at age 2–3 years. Reasonably good results are obtained in adults with late onset deafness. The detailed work up of these patients in the Audiology Department prior to surgical implantation is often able to predict the potential benefits of an implant. Potential complications from the surgery are similar to mastoid surgery, but fortunately rare.

Surgical management of vertigo

31.91 Most cases of vertigo can be treated satisfactorily by medical means supported by vestibular rehabilitation from physiotherapists. Failure to respond to medical treatment which leaves the patient with persistent problems causing a poor quality of life may be amenable to surgical treatment.

31.92 Various surgical procedures are used to help vertiginous patients. Some, such as the saccus decompression procedure, are thought to modify inner ear function. However this operation is subject to considerable controversy.

31.93 More successful procedures are those designed to block transmission of abnormal labyrinthine sensations to the brain. Ideally they should only modify labyrinthine function and preferably leave the cochlea intact. Each particular procedure has its own risks and they must be carefully explained to the patient.

31.94 The commonest such procedure is the installation of the ototoxic drug gentamicin into the middle ear, so that it is adsorbed into the labyrinth via the round window membrane. This results in decreased labyrinthine function in that ear. Although several separate installations may be necessary, it is often successful in helping patients with Meniere's syndrome. However this procedure also has a 30 per cent chance of giving increased hearing loss.

Other procedures to achieve the same result are surgical labyrinthectomy and vestibular nerve section.

All of these procedures require a very detailed description of the surgical approach, the chance of success and possibility of complication.

Management of vestibular schwannomas

31.95 The traditional use of the term acoustic neuroma is incorrect as they are benign tumours of the vestibular nerve sheath and should be referred to as vestibular schwannomas. As they increase in size they cause pressure on the immediately adjacent cochlear nerve and facial nerve.

31.96 Fortunately with the advent of MRI scanning these tumours are now being detected when they are still of a small size. Most ENT surgeons agree that it is important to investigate any unilateral otological symptom with MRI scanning to exclude a vestibular schwannoma. The sensitivity of the referral process may be disputed, but all ENT surgeons agree that it is mandatory for a unilateral sensorineural deafness, in particular when of sudden onset.

31.97 The management of these tumours is controversial because of the advent of focused radiotherapy and its success in preventing further growth of the tumour. There is still surgical concern as to the side-effects and long-term results of radiation to this tumour.

31.98 The most significant advance in management over the last decade has been the realisation that many of these tumours do not continue to grow after presentation. Consequently most surgeons will monitor small vestibular schwannomas with repeat MRI scans at increasing intervals. If no growth is seen, most surgeons are happy to continue monitoring their patient.

Sadly many radiotherapists often commence treatment without a monitoring period and there is concern that such an approach may give a false success rate from radiation therapy.

31.99 The exact indications for surgery are still debatable but larger tumours with active growth into the cerebellopontine angle are generally recommended for surgical resection. Surgery is generally done by a joint team consisting of a neurosurgeon and neuro-otological surgeon, as such a team tends to get better results particularly related to facial nerve function. All such cases should be discussed in a skull base multi-disciplinary team (MDT).

HEAD AND NECK ONCOLOGY

31.100 The surgical management of head and neck oncology has long been an important part of otolaryngological practice. The speciality has worked closely with its medical oncology colleagues. With the current interest in reconstruction, surgical oncology is becoming increasingly a multi-disciplinary activity. Close cooperation with both plastic and maxillo-facial surgeons maybe beneficial to the patient.

31.101 Although there is no formal subspeciality of head and neck surgical oncology, the Joint Committee on Surgical Training is currently working to formulate advanced training programs in head and neck surgical oncology.

31.102 Each unit practising head and neck oncology surgery will have a MDT. This committee represents all diagnostic, therapeutic and rehabilitative specialties. Ideally all new cases should be referred for discussion by the MDT. Equally follow-up reviews during treatment are important to keep all members of the team informed of the progress of the patient. One disadvantage of MDT practice is that the patient is not directly represented and their views must be given by the presenting consultant.

31.103 The MDT is an advisory group and, as such, has no clinical responsibility in itself. The presenting clinician remains clinically responsible for the patient, unless there is a formal referral to another consultant, who would naturally take responsibility for the patient under their direct clinical control.

31.104   As the MDT is such a disparate body, it would not be unusual for a highly-experienced clinician, having listened to the general advice of the MDT, to decide to treat the patient with a different protocol, based on their experience and the views of the patient. Such a disagreement would be recorded in the MDT minutes and continued review by the MDT would monitor the progress of that patient.

31.105   Medico-legal problems regarding the complex management of head and neck oncological patients are not very common. With widespread interdisciplinary consultation the patient is generally well informed regarding the treatment options and possible consequences of any particular form of treatment. However, there are often medico-legal concerns regarding the clinical pathway prior to establishing a definitive diagnosis and commencement of therapeutic management.

31.106   Many head and neck cancers present early with noticeable changes in voice and swallowing; these symptoms are well-known to suggest a possible malignancy and generally result in early referral.

31.107   General practitioners all have detailed guidelines from NICE and SIGN detailing dangerous alerting symptoms. Similarly most ENT departments have urgent referral clinics, which can result in the patient being diagnosed and treatment organised within a two-week period.

31.108   A common question concerns causation in negligent delay referral/ diagnosis of oropharyngeal cancers and tumours of the sinuses. Negligence is a breach of duty causing injury: the causal issue is whether there is a worse outcome (not whether there is a lost chance of a better outcome). There are two limbs to this inquiry: (1) what happened historically? and (2) what would have happened but for the breach of duty? The 'worse outcome' in missed cancer diagnosis cases generally consists of a number of components which can be considered in the response to a number of inquiries:

(1)   on the balance of probabilities would the cancer have been completely cured?
(2)   on the balance of probabilities, has the cancer caused a reduction in life expectation ('lost years'), if not curable? (reduced life expectation);
(3)   on the balance of probabilities, what additional pain and suffering and loss of amenity was caused by the negligent delay in diagnosis? (worse symptoms from more advanced cancer and more extensive treatment).

Even if the cancer would not have been cured there may be modest claims for lost years and incremental pain suffering and loss of amenity.

Presentation with a neck lump

31.109   However, some primary tumour sites in the head and neck do not produce obvious symptoms and patients present with cervical lymphadenopathy. Sadly the management of 'lumps in the neck' can fall below the acceptable standard. Such patients presenting to an ENT urgent referral clinic will have a detailed history and examination of the known primary sites for tumours of the head and neck. This will include endoscopic inspection of the upper air and food passages supplemented by imaging where indicated.

31.110 Careful palpation of the neck should be performed to assess the site and number of enlarged nodes. Many clinics will also have ultrasound scanning immediately available and the ability to perform a fine-needle aspirate (FNA) of neck lumps. Cytological examination of fine needle aspirates requires an experienced cytopathologist and often the diagnosis is not completely clear. In such a situation, repeat FNA is indicated. This is best done by the cytopathologist themselves to enable them to do repeat aspirates until they are happy with a diagnosis or not.

31.111 Even if a working diagnosis can be established at this first clinical presentation, it is essential that the patient is scheduled for a direct examination under anaesthetic to assess the extent of the primary tumour and to biopsy it. Histological confirmation of the tumour type is essential to classify the tumour and ensure the correct treatment protocol.

Unknown primary

31.112 If FNA suggests a malignant tumour and no obvious primary site is found detailed imaging, preferably with both CT and MRI scans, should be performed prior to any surgical biopsies (tissue changes following a biopsy will confuse the imaging assessment). Should imaging fail to demonstrate a primary tumour, usually the next step is to perform blind biopsies under general anaesthesia of the usual primary sites in the head.

Failure to demonstrate a primary site for an unknown cervical malignancy is a complex clinical problem generally requiring surgical or radiotherapy treatment.

31.113 One of the most common errors in the management of cervical lymphadenopathy is to proceed initially to open resection of the node for histological examination. The histological diagnosis obtained is rarely better than that achieved by FNA. The problem with open resection is its potential to spread tumour further in the neck, and compromise long-term cure.

31.114 If it is clinically indicated to remove a neck lump for histological examination this should be done with frozen section histology. If the frozen section indicates a malignancy it is important to immediately proceed to a formal neck dissection of the nodes on that side of the neck.

Accessory nerve paralysis

31.115 Enlarged lymph nodes in the posterior triangle of the neck are relatively common. Their pathological nature should be established by FNA to exclude malignancy. If they are of inflammatory nature and causing a cosmetic defect it is reasonable to consider surgical resection. Such a procedure places the accessory nerve at risk because of its small size and course across posterior triangle.

31.116   Accessory nerve paralysis is a serious problem leading to very significant dysfunction of the shoulder joint, as well as the cosmetic defect from a drooping shoulder.

31.117   Prior to such a procedure the patient should be fully informed of the potential risk. To minimise damage to the nerve at surgery, wide exposure and monitoring of the nerve function are essential.

Thyroidectomy

31.118   Thyroidectomy used to be a common operation for the management of thyrotoxicosis. Successful medical management of thyrotoxicosis means that thyroidectomy is now generally performed for thyroid tumours and multi-nodular goitres.

31.119   These cases are often worked up in a joint endocrine clinic and any thyroid nodules are assessed with imaging. An ultrasound study is generally done first and there are considerable advantages in performing an FNA under radiological control at the same time. The diagnosis of the FNA depends on an experienced cytopathologist. If they are unsure regarding the diagnosis, a repeat FNA will often help in confirming a preoperative pathological diagnosis.

31.120   It is well known that the final histological diagnosis of thyroid tumours often requires formal histological diagnosis with the post-operative specimen. Sometimes this change in diagnosis requires further surgery to remove more of the gland and the patient should be made aware of this possibility. However, it is important to have a reasonably secure pre-operative diagnosis to advise the patient appropriately and to select the probable extent of the thyroid surgery.

Potential surgical problems

31.121   The main complications of thyroid surgery are:

* post-operative haematoma. If this occurs it must be evacuated to prevent airway problems;
* if large amounts of thyroid tissue need to be resected, such as with a bilateral subtotal thyroidectomy, there is a post-operative risk that the patient will be hypothyroid with possible disturbances of calcium metabolism. Repeat thyroid function tests and calcium estimations need to be done in the post-operative period to ascertain whether long-term replacement therapy will be necessary. Most thyroid surgeons will accept post-operative hypocalcaemia as a possible sequela of thyroid surgery;
* the traditional low placed thyroid scar invariably caused unsightly scarring and most surgeons now will use a transverse incision, placed in a pre-existing skin crease. There is currently a fashion for endoscopic removal of thyroid neoplasms, which obviates the need for a neck incision, but such procedures inevitably have a limited exposure of the gland and its surrounding anatomy;

- from an ENT perspective, the most significant problem with thyroid surgery is vocal fold paralysis as a result of damage to the recurrent laryngeal nerves;
- a unilateral recurrent laryngeal nerve palsy involving the abductor muscles of the larynx will leave the vocal fold paralysed in a median position. This results in virtually normal speech and it may not be apparent unless endoscopic examination of the vocal folds is performed. This should be done pre-operatively with every thyroidectomy to establish the status of the vocal fold movements. If one fold is found to be paralysed then especial care must be made to protect the opposite recurrent laryngeal nerve. If this is not done the patient may end with bilateral vocal fold palsies. In this situation the vocal folds are both in the midline giving both respiratory stridor and poor voice;
- recurrent laryngeal palsies will often cause some swallowing problems initially, but swallowing generally returns to normal;
- to prevent recurrent laryngeal injury at the time of thyroid surgery it is mandatory to anatomically identify both recurrent laryngeal nerves to ensure their preservation. (It has been argued that such identification runs the possibility of causing iatrogenic injury to the nerve, however most experienced thyroid surgeons do not accept this argument.) More recently, monitoring of the recurrent laryngeal nerves with an electrode around the endotracheal tube at the glottis has been advocated as a means of reducing the frequency of recurrent palsies. Sadly many clinical studies have failed to demonstrate a conclusive advantage to monitoring. With more experience in placing the electrodes there is every hope that monitoring will have a role to play in the future. Most thyroid surgeons will accept post-operative vocal fold palsy as a possible sequela of thyroid surgery provided that a pre-operative assessment of vocal fold movement was performed to exclude existing pathology;
- superior laryngeal nerve palsy. The superior laryngeal nerve is very close to the upper pole of the thyroid gland and is endangered when the superior thyroid artery is ligated. It interferes with the pitch of speech and is consequently important to professional voice users. In such cases careful anatomical location is essential at surgery.

Anterior spinal fixation

31.122 Anterior spinal fixation with the application of metal plates to the anterior surfaces of the cervical vertebrae requires extensive exposure of the anterior neck structures and both the vagus and accessory nerves are prone to injury. Ideally a pre-operative assessment of vocal fold movements should be performed to exclude any existing paralysis. The patient should be warned regarding voice and swallowing problems and about the possibility of shoulder drop.

Occasionally these metal plates erode into the pharynx or oesophagus, long-term surgical repair becomes necessary.

Salivary gland surgery

Submandibular gland

31.123 The usual indication for surgery of the submandibular gland is duct obstruction due to calculi forming in the gland. Such cases present with intermittent swelling of the gland during salivation and occasionally with an infection. Not all calculi are radiopaque, so the best pre-operative examination is an ultrasound study.

31.124 Alternatively, sialography of the duct may show the stones. If ultrasound shows a tumour within the gland an immediate FNA is indicated because of the high incidence of malignancy in submandibular tumours.

31.125 Occasionally a submandibular calculus is located in the submandibular duct as it passes across the floor of the mouth. This is easily palpable, but it is essential that an ultrasound examination is performed to exclude other calculi.

31.126 If a single calculus in the duct is the problem then it can be removed relatively easily by marsupialising the duct in the floor of the mouth. There are two potential problems:

- the submandibular duct crosses the lingual nerve at its posterior extent;
- an intraoral calculus may be displaced back into the submandibular gland. To prevent this happening most surgeons will temporarily occlude the duct with a suture at the posterior end of its oral course.

31.127 Multiple calculi in the submandibular gland and recurrent bacterial infections are indications for submandibular gland resection via the neck. The gland is also removed as an integral part of a block dissection of the cervical lymph nodes for a malignancy.

31.128 There are several potential problems from submandibular resection:

- the submandibular branch of the facial nerve dips some 2 cm below the lower border of the mandible and it is vulnerable to the usual incision for submandibular resection. Some surgeons place the incision more inferiorly and others immediately develop the exploration deep to the platysma muscle to avoid damage to the mandibular branch of the facial nerve;
- the two other nerves vulnerable in this operation are the lingual and hypoglossal nerves. They are immediately deep to the gland and must be positively identified anatomically. This may be difficult with an acutely infected gland.

Tumours of the submandibular gland are not very common but when present are generally of malignant pathology.

Parotid gland

31.129 Calculi are uncommon in the parotid gland and inflammations are generally treated conservatively.

31.130 The usual indication for parotid resection is the occurrence of a parotid tumour. There are many different types of parotid tumour with a whole spectrum of malignancy. 70 per cent of parotid tumours are benign and 70 per cent are located in the superficial lobe of the parotid gland.

31.131 The usual first step in managing parotid lumps is an ultrasound examination and this should be accompanied by a radiologically-controlled FNA at the same time. It will also indicate whether there is any associated cervical lymphadenopathy.

31.132 A pre-operative histological diagnosis of tumour type is very useful in advising the patient and in planning an appropriate operation. However, FNA cytology of parotid tumours can be difficult to interpret and if the cytologist is not confident with the diagnosis a repeat FNA should be performed. MRI imaging is also useful to define the anatomy of the gland and the location of the tumour within it.

31.133 The major potential problem in parotid gland surgery is the facial nerve passing through the gland; dividing it into deep and superficial lobes. It is also the key to successful surgery. This depends on accurately identifying the nerve where it leaves the stylo-mastoid foramen and then by following it forward through the gland the tumour can be removed surrounded by a cuff of the resected lobe.

31.134 Old-fashioned enucleation of parotid tumours is to be condemned as it invariably leaves remnants of the tumour capsule in the tumour bed. The surgeon should always aim to resect the tumour with cuff of normal parotid gland surrounding it, thus ensuring its complete removal. Tumours present in the deep lobe often end up being enucleated from the parotid bed and in such cases consideration should be given to post-operative radiotherapy.

31.135 If the tumour is known to be of a malignant nature and it is found in contact with the facial nerve most surgeons recommend resecting that particular branch of the facial nerve to ensure cure. The decision as to whether to perform an immediate facial nerve graft is debatable and depends upon the experience of the surgeon.

31.136 Most experienced parotid surgeons would expect zero injury to the facial nerve. The mandibular branch of the facial nerve is most at risk from the open repair of mandibular fractures but this is a well-known risk and with appropriate technique can be avoided as with submandibular resection. Perhaps a maxillofacial opinion should be sought.

USEFUL WEBSITES

31.137

www.entconsent.co.uk
This site was constructed to give patients undergoing ear, nose and throat surgery access to accurate information about the operation they are to undergo; contains useful guidelines for consent.

www.entuk.org
The website of the British Association of Otorhinolaryngologists. An excellent source of publications for both patients and professionals; produces Management Guidelines and Position Papers.

www.medscape.com
Medscape is an American online magazine of news and updates; has useful review articles by good authors that are useful for legal practioners as well as professionals.

www.nccn.org
The website of the National Comprehensive Cancer Network; publishes clinical practice guidelines in oncology/head and neck cancers. Produced for North American practice, but are very clear and applicable to UK practice.

www.sign.ac.uk
Scottish Intercollegiate Guidelines Network (SIGN); produces Guidelines for Scottish Practice. Not completely accepted in rest of UK.

www.nice.org.uk
National Institute for Health Care and Excellence; issued service guidance on improving outcomes in head and neck cancers.

APPENDIX: DRAFT STANDARD CONSENT FORM FOR NASAL SURGERY

Everywhere Hospital

Standard Consent Form

31.138 This form is designed to facilitate the consent process prior to nasal surgery.

The advantages of the proposed operation will have been explained to you in the Outpatient Department. The normal outcomes and any possible complications should have been explained at the same time. However experience tells us that many patients only remember the advantages and tend to forget possible complications. Accordingly this form is designed to remind the patient of the normal outcomes of this particular surgery and importantly all of the possible complications. Including all complications is important to ensure the patient is fully informed. However the majority of the complications are by nature very rare and in going through the list the doctor obtaining consent will indicate the possible significant complications.

Although the doctor obtaining this consent may not be doing the operation he is fully aware of the nature of the procedure and its particular complications.

Whilst in the Outpatient Department you should also have been informed about:

1   Any alternative nonsurgical treatment.
2   The advantages and disadvantages of an alternative surgical procedure.
3   The outcome of refusing any treatment.

It is important that you understand and are happy with this information. Please ask for clarification if in doubt. You are also entitled to include any comments you may wish.

List of outcomes and complications for nasal surgery

Common complications of any surgical procedure:

- Anaesthetic complications (these will be covered by the anaesthetist).
- Increased bleeding from the nose. This may require nasal packing.
- Infection in the operative site. This may need antibiotics occasionally.

Common normal immediate results of this type of surgery:

- Temporary increased nasal obstruction.
- Increased nasal secretions from the nose and into the throat.
- Bloodstained secretions.
- Need for postoperative cleaning of the nasal cavity.

Known complications occurring as a result of nasal surgery:

- Septal perforation.
- Adhesion formation
- Septal haematoma which may lead to significant infection.
- Redeviation of septum
- Recurrence of sinus problems
- Excessive drying and crusting of the nose.
- Damage to adjacent structures.
  - Bruising of cheek.
  - Loss of sensation to the lower cheek.
  - Loss of sensation to teeth and palate.
  - Disturbance of vision rarely blindness.
  - Disturbance of smell and taste.
  - Damage to tear duct.
  - Damage to lining of brain cavity leading to a leakage of brain fluid.
  - Meningitis and brain injury.
- Tissues may be removed for further examination.
- Follow up medication may be necessary.

CHAPTER 32

Orthopaedics

Peter Reilly

Michael Fertleman

INTRODUCTION

32.1   This chapter concerns orthopaedic and trauma surgery. In the UK training system, this speciality relates to problems of the musculoskeletal system. Trauma historically has referred to broken/fractured bones and their treatment, and elective surgery has referred mainly to planned admissions. The distinction is a little artificial, as many planned procedures relate to the sequelae of trauma, for example ligament reconstructions and the removal of metalwork. Furthermore, the distinction between elective orthopaedic surgery and sports medicine surgery may at times be imprecise.

TRAUMA

32.2   A fracture is defined as a breach in the cortex (outer layer) of the bone. These injuries are common and form a severity spectrum related to the

1083

amount of energy transferred, the loading pattern, the mechanism of injury and the underlying state of the bone.

32.3   Many classification systems are applied to fractures to aid communication, guide treatment and facilitate research. The AO classification is widely used[1]. Numerous individual fractures may have there own classification systems, which reflects the difficulties in designing a universally applicable system.

Descriptive terms related to fractures are frequently more intuitive, the more commonly used are explained below.

1 https://aotrauma.aofoundation.org/Structure/education/self-directed-learning/reference-materials/classifications/Pages/ao-ota-classification.aspx.

32.4   A fracture may be closed (where the skin is intact) or open (where the skin over the zone of injury is breached). Articular fractures involve the joint; extra-articular do not. Simple fractures typically have two parts (simple wedge fractures may have three parts), complex fractures have more than two parts; the term 'comminuted' implies multiple fragments.

Relating to the angulation of fractures in the diaphysis (shaft) of bones, an angle of less than 30° is described as transverse, and an angle of greater than or equal to 30° is termed oblique. In addition, the term 'spiral' is used where the angle is less than 30° and where the fracture was caused by a rotational (twisting) force.

32.5   Bones in children behave differently when loaded compared to adults, resulting in a number of paediatric fractures. Greenstick fractures are incomplete, with the bone cortex and periosteum (covering) remaining intact on one side; these are typically caused by angulation forces. Axial loading of immature bone can cause a buckle (torus) fracture, these are again incomplete. Plastic deformation may also occur in skeletally immature bone, where forces bend the bone to the point it cannot spontaneously return to its normal shape, yet no fracture is visible on the radiograph. An important concept in the management of paediatric fractures is remodelling, a limited ability to regain normal alignment after a displaced fracture. This is influenced by multiple factors, including the age of the child, the plane and degree of displacement, and the position relative to the growth plate.

32.6   Abnormal bone may fracture more easily than normal bone. The term pathological fracture is frequently applied to bone altered by a neoplasm (primary or secondary tumour), but could equally refer to non-tumour situations such as osteoporosis.

32.7   Some fractures should always be treated operatively; some may be treated operatively, and a significant number do not require any form of surgical intervention. The body heals the injury over a period of time and a good clinical outcome is obtained.

32.8   It is important to consider potential problems with the treatment of fractures. In keeping with the majority of medical events, the first stage in the treatment of an acute injury is appropriate resuscitation of the patient. A patient may have polytrauma, with injury to multiple bones or associated head, chest and abdominal injuries. However, the majority sustain trauma to a single bone or limb.

32.9   Having resuscitated the patient appropriately, the next step is adequate history taking. This will allow an assessment of the patient's energy transfer, pain and past medical history. Trauma frequently involves patients with impaired consciousness due to the injury, drugs or alcohol. This should be borne in mind, as a complete assessment can only be made when those factors are not affecting the patient. Likewise, a common cause of an injury being missed is a 'distracting injury'; for example a patient with an open tibial fracture may be treated well for this injury, but have a co-existing finger fracture, which is not identified until later and which ultimately causes long-term problems.

32.10   In general fractures are painful. The level of pain is increased when the area is loaded, for example during palpation by an examining doctor or when bearing weight. There may be an obvious deformity or limb asymmetry. Fractures often, but not always, have soft tissue signs such as bruising or swelling associated with them. These signs may be subtle; the magnitude of response is related to the force transfer, anatomical location of the injury and limb dependency.

32.11   During the initial assessment of a fracture, it is important to examine the neurovascular status of the limb, which should be carefully documented in the notes. Trauma patients are vulnerable to compartment syndrome. This is a situation where in a confined body space (fascial compartment) the pressure rises due to swelling, reducing with the blood flow, establishing a vicious circle where, as the tissue becomes less well supplied with oxygen, swelling increases, further raising the pressure in the compartment. The cardinal signs of compartment syndrome are pain disproportionate to the injury and increased pain on passive muscle stretching. It is known that loss of sensation and pulse are also features of compartment syndrome but unfortunately these are late signs and may indicate that significant damage has already been done. There are methods of measuring the compartment pressure to ensure that it is not raised. However, a high index of clinical suspicion should be maintained and if in doubt, a senior opinion sought or the compartment decompressed.

32.12   X-rays and CT scans expose the patient to ionising radiation, therefore there must be a good indication before such radiological investigations are undertaken. The indication may be related to the mechanism of injury, the patient's symptoms or clinical signs. In some circumstances there are strong guidelines, such as the Ottawa ankle rules[1]. The majority of the time the ordering of imaging is guided by the level of clinical suspicion.

1 Stiell, McKnight, Greenberg (et al) 'Implementation of the Ottawa Ankle Rules' (1994) 271 JAMA 827–832.

32.13   Inadequate imaging may also cause problems in the treatment of trauma. This may be due to the pressure of multiple injuries leading to pain in the patient and limiting the X-ray views obtained. The recent trend towards early CT scanning, which is a rapid source of useful information, should minimise problems related to the inadequate visualisation of injuries on plain x-rays. This particularly relates to injuries to the axial skeleton, spine and pelvis.

32.14   The general principle guiding fracture treatment is that the body is trying to heal. In cases where a good outcome is thought likely from the fracture it may be sufficient to protect the injured area, for example with a splint, plaster, walking boot or the use of crutches.

An important adjunct to any treatment strategy is appropriate rehabilitation.

32.15   If a less favourable outcome is thought to be likely, due to soft tissue injury or fracture angulation/displacement, then intervention would be considered. The process of returning a fracture configuration to a more anatomical position is called reduction. It may be possible to achieve a satisfactory position 'closed' (without breaching the skin) through manipulation or traction. An 'open' reduction is when a surgical approach to the fracture is used to facilitate reduction.

32.16   When an acceptable reduction is achieved, a method of maintaining the position is required. Techniques commonly used with closed reduction are casting and percutaneous wiring. In some cases, particularly paediatric, traction (a system of weights and pulleys) may be used both to reduce the fracture and maintain the reduction. Internal fixation is discussed in more detail below. It is important to note that intramedullary nailing is most frequently used with closed reduction. A common orthopaedic abbreviation is ORIF (open reduction and internal fixation). The majority of the time this procedure involves a surgical approach to the fracture, restoration of anatomy and stabilisation with a plate[1].

1 A more detailed yet clear description of fracture management can be found in *Apley's System of Orthopaedics and Fractures* (9th edn).

METHODS OF FRACTURE FIXATION

32.17   In broad terms, fracture fixation may be internal or external. Internal fixation includes a number of techniques. These include plating with screw fixation, which is termed 'extramedullary', as the plate is sited on the outside of the bone. Another method of internal fixation is 'intramedullary', which involves passing a rod through the bone to provide stability and maintain the position. Intramedullary fixation may take the form of simple wires, or may be locked with screws passing through the bone and the rod, to provide further stability.

32.18   External fixation is a method of providing stability and maintaining length/alignment of the bone where a device sits outside the skin and is attached to the bone through wires or pins. These external fixators may be simple, with a single bar, or more complex with a frame.

The 'missed' fracture

32.19   The 'missed' fracture is a common medico-legal orthopaedic problem and may arise for a number of reasons. Specific case examples are dealt with in more detail below, but in general delay in diagnosis and treatment can lead to a suboptimal outcome for the patient.

32.20   The adverse consequences of a missed fracture may be due to the delay itself, ie pain, suffering, loss of amenity during the period before accurate diagnosis, and longer recovery time due to late treatment. In some patients the effects of delay are not purely temporal and lead to a worse outcome. Examples include cases where there is further displacement due to load bearing, neurological problems, bone death (avascular necrosis), non-union, mal-union and arthritis.

32.21   Why are fractures missed? As might be expected, there are many factors. Broadly speaking, either the area was not appropriately imaged or the imaging was not correctly understood. As mentioned above, X-rays must be clinically indicated. On some occasion they are simply not obtained, when in retrospect they would have been appropriate. In some situations other imaging modalities which would have been superior to X-ray, such as CT and MRI, were not utilised.

32.22   There are occasions where the treating clinician did not diagnose or appreciate the injury visible on the imaging. This may be due to a lack of time, knowledge or experience; if in doubt discussion with a more appropriate clinician is considered the next step. A failsafe mechanism is the reporting of imaging by radiologists; they have greater experience in the field but the disadvantage of only limited clinical information.

32.23   No bony injury, 'NBI', is a frequently-used medical abbreviation. It does not reliably exclude a fracture, as on occasion subtle non-bone signs such as an effusion (fluid in a joint) or soft tissue swelling are the only features of a bone injury.

Delayed treatment for fractures, a frequent cause for complaint

32.24   In some cases delayed treatment may be due to the need to physiologically optimise a patient due to pre-existing illness (see below) or polytrauma. Often delays are simply due to logistical problems, such as lack of theatre time, equipment or appropriately-trained staff.

32.25   Further problems with trauma are incorrect decision making and inadequate provision of care following the correct decision-making process. These can lead to problems either with the fracture itself or the fixation, and may result in multiple operations.

32.26   In some cases the sequelae of the injury itself, such as pain, stiffness and an inability to perform activities of daily living, can lead to complaint from a patient. These may occur despite good medical treatment and merely reflect the severity of the initial problem.

Trauma case example demonstrating wider medical issues and variety of surgical treatments; fractured neck of femur

32.27   Since the last edition of this work, there has been further recognition of the importance of careful management of medical complications around the time of orthopaedic surgery[1]. The most intense focus is with the frailest patients admitted to the orthopaedic department, invariably as an emergency. The most likely reason for admission in the frail elderly is a broken hip (fractured neck of femur). Hospitals providing a service for hip fracture patients will now employ orthopaedic surgeons and a physician/geriatrician to co-manage the patient whilst in hospital for treatment of the fracture[2].

1 British Orthopaedic Association Standards for Trauma, Standard 1 (Version 2, January 2012).
2 The management of hip fracture in adults, NICE, Clinical Guideline 124 (June 2011).

32.28   Fractured neck of femur is a diagnosis associated with a significant mortality rate: up to 10 per cent within 30 days, and around one third within a year. The consequences of a fracture, aside from mortality, can be a considerable burden in morbidity. Following discharge from hospital, patients are in need of a period of rehabilitation, and a proportion never fully regain functional independence. A significant number of these patients are transferred, after a period of rehabilitation, to long-term institutional care.

32.29   Therefore, from a medico-legal perspective, the underlying circumstances of the fracture become very relevant. An orthogeriatrician, specialising in the management of elderly patients undergoing orthopaedic surgery, will be interested in the circumstances, and not just the consequences, of the fall. Often patients have pre-existing cognitive impairment and are unable to recall the circumstances of the fall when a history is taken in hospital, particularly as the patient may be in pain and may have also been given morphine-based analgesia. The full facts surrounding the fall may take some time to emerge, until a collateral history can be acquired from relatives and carers after the patient has been admitted to hospital.

32.30   Of particular interest in the 10 per cent of broken hip patients referred to the coroner, are any issues of neglect from an institution looking after the patient around the time of the fall. Most institutions, be they hospitals, residential or nursing care facilities, have policies in place to reduce the risk of falls. Most institutions require their patients to undergo regular assessment of their falls risk so that preventative measures can be put in place.

32.31   Most patients suffering from a fractured neck of femur fall from a standing position in what is described as a low energy fracture. The reason for a fall resulting in a low energy fracture is due mostly to underlying metabolic bone disease. In elderly patients the most common by far would be osteoporosis, a disease whose rate of progress can be modified by medication. Therefore in order to prevent subsequent fractures from occurring, when patients suffer a low energy fracture, osteoporosis assessments should occur either in hospital or via the general practitioner with appropriate medication commenced in order to reduce the risk of further fracture in the event of another fall.

32.32   As well as having an accurate assessment of the circumstances of the fall causing the admission, a health care practitioner undertaking a falls assessment will be interested in the circumstances of any previous falls, and identify any strategies or treatments to lower the incidence of falls occurring. Such assessments could involve cessation of medications that may contribute to dizziness on standing, modification of medications causing salt imbalance, an assessment for underlying cardiac disease, and appropriate referrals for optimising vision and hearing.

32.33   It is well known that patients admitted to hospital for treatment of fractured neck of femur may suffer deterioration of cognitive function[1]. This is particularly found in patients with pre-existing dementia or mild cognitive impairment. The deterioration can present as an acute delirium, which may be hypo- or hyper-active and is associated with a high mortality. Recent studies have suggested that the presence of acute delirium is associated with long-term cognitive impairment.

1 Delirium Diagnosis Prevention and Management, NICE, Clinical Guideline 103 (July 2010).

32.34   The role of a physician/geriatrician in the care of patients around the time of orthopaedic surgery is to aid in the management of pre-operative optimisation to ensure the lowest chance of perioperative morbidity and mortality. Common complications which may result in a delay in surgery taking place include infection of the chest or urine leading to septicaemia, recent infarction of the brain (stroke) or myocardium (heart attack), the presence of heart failure leading to fluid overload, anaemia leading to the need for blood transfusion, and electrolyte imbalance. Each of these complications can exacerbate delirium, and prompt treatment can facilitate a return to a non-delirious state.

32.35   Whilst a patient is waiting for surgery to take place, in addition to any treatment for an underlying reason that might delay surgery, treatment is also given, if appropriate, to ensure adequate hydration through intravenous fluids, as well as treatment to prevent deep vein thrombosis and pulmonary embolism. The standard treatment for DVT/PE for hospital inpatients in the UK is subcutaneous heparin, which should be given to all patients admitted with a fractured neck of femur unless they happen to be on another anticoagulant, or unless there is some other contraindication which would be identified through the completion of a standard venous thrombo-embolism risk assessment.

32.36   Patients who remain in hospital under the care of an orthopaedic team are often immobile and are therefore at risk of developing pressure ulcers. Such ulcers occur at points of pressure, which include the heels, the sacrum and sites where plaster of Paris casts are used:

'An avoidable pressure ulcer can develop when the provider did not do one or more of the following:

— evaluate the individual's clinical condition and pressure ulcer risk factors;
— define and implement interventions consistent with individual needs, individual goals, and recognized standards of practice;
— monitor and evaluate the impact of the interventions;
— or revise the interventions as appropriate'[1].

Therefore the development in any institution of a pressure ulcer is often a source of medico-legal dispute. Whilst patients remain immobile in hospitals, assessment of pressure risk should be routine with the provision of interventions where needed, such as pressure-relieving cushions and mattresses and the regular turning of bedbound patients.

1 Black, Edsberg (et al) 'Pressure ulcers: avoidable or unavoidable? Results of the National Pressure Ulcer Advisory Panel Consensus Conference' (2011) 57(2) Ostomy Wound Management 24–37.

32.37 The exact timing of surgery can be difficult, as it is well-established that the longer a patient waits for surgery to a broken hip, the greater the chance of complication. The decision to operate is usually taken at a morning trauma meeting, and the exact timing of the operation is usually at the discretion of the surgeon, the anaesthetist and possibly the physician/geriatrician.

32.38 A fracture of the proximal femur may be considered intracapsular (inside the joint) or extracapsular (outside the joint). This distinction is important, since intracapsular fractures are much more likely to have the blood supply to the head of the femur disrupted and consequently result in avascular necrosis (bone death). Intracapsular fractures may be displaced (moved from the anatomical position) or undisplaced (maintaining the anatomical position). In general, displaced intracapsular fractures are treated with arthroplasty (the replacement of the damaged bone with a metal prosthesis). The majority of these are replacements of the femoral component only (hemiarthroplasty), but in the more active and younger patient a total hip replacement can be considered. The latter tends to give a better functional outcome but also carries a higher risk of complications, particularly related to dislocations.

32.39 A major consideration in the treatment of an intracapsular fracture with hemiarthroplasty is the use of cement. Historically, uncemented prostheses such as the Austin Moore were used, particularly in frailer patients. Evidence now suggests that these prostheses, although giving a faster operation time with short-term gains, lead to a large amount of long-term problems, particularly related to pain. A number of patients go on to require re-doing (revision) to another type of prosthesis with revision surgery associated with a high complication rate. Consequently national guidance suggests that surgeons not use uncemented prostheses for fracture neck of femur. Unfortunately, the use of cement in a small minority of patients leads to a cement reaction, which makes them extremely unwell and can be fatal. Death due to cement reaction can be very emotive for the next of kin and it provides an example of a situation where guidance on a national level for the greater good can lead to individual tragedy.

32.40   In patients who are unlikely to walk in the future because of pre-existing disease, a displaced intra-capsular fracture may be managed in the same way as an undisplaced fracture, with screw fixation. The expectation varies related to the sub-group: in the frailest patients, surgery is purely a palliative measure, giving some stability to the fracture to give pain relief and thereby facilitate nursing care. In the undisplaced group, screw fixation is a less invasive technique with a good functional outcome, but a significant minority will go on to develop avascular necrosis (bone death secondary to loss of blood supply), even with appropriate treatment. The loss of blood flow to the femoral head causes collapse leading to pain and loss of function; the reaction of the patient to the resultant hip replacement often depends on the initial discussion of the treatment rationale and careful management of their expectations.

32.41   Extracapsular fractures are less likely to result in avascular necrosis. Their treatment is dependent on the exact configuration and the surgeon's preference. The majority are treated either with an extramedullary device, dynamic hip screw (DHS) or intermedullary nailing. There are theoretical advantages related to greater stability with the last of these techniques.

The diagrams demonstrate the fracture of the proximal femur and the various treatments available.

Hip joint

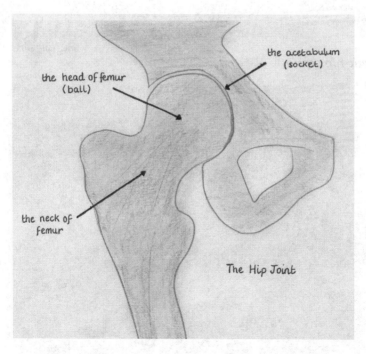

the acetabulum (socket)

the head of femur (ball)

the neck of femur

The Hip Joint

Intramedullary nail with screws

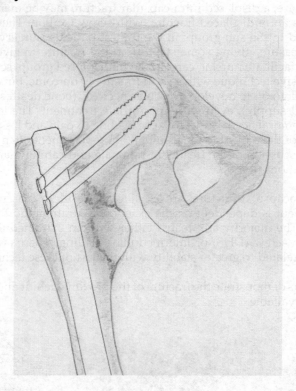

Dynamic hip screw

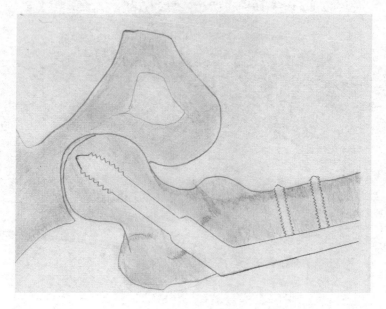

Total hip replacement

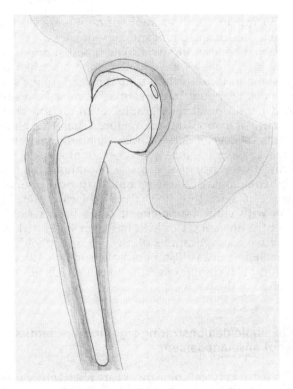

Hemiarthroplasty

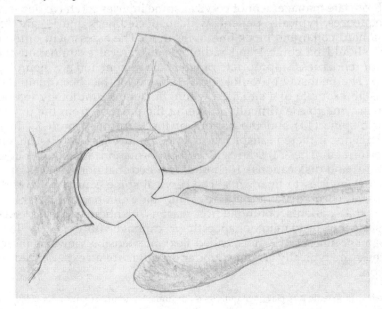

Trauma case example demonstrating difficulty in diagnosis

32.42 Scaphoid fracture is an example of an injury which is difficult to diagnose and may result in significant consequences for the patient. The scaphoid is a carpal bone in the wrist. The blood supply to the scaphoid is atypical. The artery passes beyond the bone and then doubles back, entering the distal pole (part furthest from the heart) of the scaphoid before passing proximally. Scaphoid fractures may occur as a result of a fall on an outstretched hand. Initial radiographs, even an appropriate scaphoid series, do not always demonstrate a fracture. Therefore patients with the appropriate signs such as tenderness in the anatomical snuffbox should be treated as if they have a fracture. However, immobilisation is frequently overused, owing to the fear that a missed scaphoid fracture may cause death of the proximal pole of the scaphoid. Historically, serial X-rays have been used to see if a fracture line is radiologically developing. These, in combination with clinical assessment, have been used to establish a diagnosis. Recently, fine-cut CT or MRI has been suggested as a more cost-effective alternative. Complications of missing a scaphoid fracture which does not heal include a SNAC (Scaphoid Non-union Advanced Collapse). The treatment for this is complex and the condition can adversely affect the long-term function of the hand.

Trauma case example demonstrating significant potential consequences of mismanagement

32.43 Injuries to the cervical spine (neck) are relatively common, and may have significant impact on the patient from a neurological perspective. It is likely that the majority of the damage is done at the index event. However, inappropriate management of cervical spine injuries can have devastating consequences. Typically, patients with suspected neck injuries are treated with a hard collar and block immobilisation. The assessment of the neck injury should be clinical and radiological. Clinical examination should look for tenderness, appropriate range of movement and any neurological deficit. The mainstay of radiological examination has been plain X-rays. This is an example of a situation where inadequate radiology frequently occurs, owing to the difficulty in seeing the junction from the top of the thoracic spine (T1) and the bottom of the cervical spine (C7). In most departments, if there is suspicion of a neck injury then a CT scan should be performed. The CT scan will give information about bony injuries (fractures and dislocations). It should be noted that normal CT scans will not show injuries to ligaments. The cervical spine cannot be considered adequately cleared if the patient cannot be examined thoroughly. This means that patients obtunded for reasons mentioned earlier, such as drugs, alcohol, head injury or anaesthetic, cannot be fully cleared[1]. In some cases, a specific set of X-rays, called flexion extension views, is indicated and these are typically arranged under the advice of an experienced spinal surgeon.

1 British Orthopaedic Association Standards for Trauma, Standard 2 (November 2008).

ELECTIVE ORTHOPAEDIC SURGERY

32.44   Elective surgery can also be termed orthopaedic as opposed to trauma surgery. As mentioned in the introduction, this may also involve the sequelae of trauma as well as the repair of ligaments and tendons, which have been damaged in an injury. Another main thrust of elective orthopaedics relates to the treatment of arthritis with joint replacement.

Arthroscopy

32.45   A significant proportion of elective orthopaedics relates to arthroscopic (keyhole) surgery. This involves the placement of a camera into the joint. The purpose of an arthroscopy may be diagnostic, an information-gathering exercise, or therapeutic to treat a problem.

32.46   The complication rate of diagnostic arthroscopy is low. Therapeutic arthroscopy is more problematic. In particular, the surgical techniques frequently have a significant learning curve. This has a number of implications, relating not only to the training of surgeons but also to the introduction of novel techniques which may be relatively complex, untested and of little proven benefit to patients. The pressure on surgeons to be able to perform the latest operation is in part related to financial pressure, the technical ability of the surgeon, efforts of the implant manufacturers and patient expectation.

32.47   The complications of therapeutic arthroscopy are the general complications of any procedure, ie infection and bleeding. A tourniquet is often used in lower limb arthroscopy as a method of reducing the blood flow to the area, and consequently, the bleeding. Problems have occurred related to tourniquets on many occasions. In particular, these can be due to inadequate padding under the tourniquet, excessive tourniquet inflation pressure, prolonged tourniquet times and fluids tracking under a tourniquet which can potentially cause a burn.

32.48   Some frequently performed arthroscopic therapeutic procedures, such as anterior cruciate ligament reconstruction and shoulder stabilisations, require implants to be inserted into the joint. These may break, become loose inside the joint, or cause problems due to abrasion when they become prominent and penetrate the joint surface. The trend in arthroscopic implants has moved away from metal implantations in joints towards polymers, dissolving polymers and more recently, bone-substituting polymers. In common with many vogues in orthopaedics, this progression confers theoretical benefit but, as yet, an insufficient evidence base.

32.49   Two commonly performed arthroscopic procedures are anterior cruciate ligament reconstruction in the knee and stabilisation of the shoulder (also called a Bankart or labral repair). The anterior cruciate reconstruction is performed in patients who have ruptured the ligament and are feeling symptoms of instability as a result. The objective of the surgery is to use a graft material as a ligament substitute, to provide stability to the knee with the graft material anchored to the femur above and the tibia below.

Historically, synthetic grafts have been tried, but as yet these have not proven as satisfactory as taking grafts from the patient. The common donor sites are the patellar tendon, which attaches the kneecap to the tibia and the hamstrings. The popularity of different grafts/fixation techniques waxes and wanes over time. Again, complications related to ACL reconstruction are not uncommon. They include ongoing feelings of instability, problems with the fixation device and graft failure. The general complications outlined above may occur.

32.50 The shoulder is the most commonly unstable joint in the body, dislocation of which occurs when the joint surfaces move to a non-articular position. Subluxation may be considered a partial dislocation. The majority of patients experience a single episode, but some patients have ongoing feelings of instability in the shoulder, which may result in an inability to perform activities of everyday life or a favoured sport. These individuals may be considered for surgical intervention. This is a good example of a situation where the specific surgical treatment offered varies according to a number of factors, including severity of the injury (degree of damage to the soft tissues, socket and the ball) as well as the expectation of the patient. The most common cause of recurrent shoulder instability is damage to the labrum at the front of the socket, frequently called a Bankart lesion. Arthroscopic surgery involving a soft tissue repair is commonly performed, with success rates of approaching 90 per cent. The success rate of open Bankart repair is slightly higher; the difference is particularly marked in sub-groups such as contact athletes. In more severely damaged shoulders, it may be necessary to move bone either from another part of the same patient or, in extreme cases, from a femoral head donor into the site of a bony defect. The most common subtype of bone moving operation is called a Laterjet procedure; this has been performed open for many years and has a high success rate. Pioneered in France, over the last 10 years, the technique has evolved into an arthroscopic method and has resulted in a large number of complications, particularly neurological, relating to a steep learning curve. This again begs the question about appropriate decision making, maximum potential benefit with minimum risk and consent. As with all operations, it is important for the patient to understand the surgery, risk of complications, influence of surgeon experience and motivation to use a technique with a limited track record.

Arthroplasty

32.51 Arthroplasty is predominantly related to the treatment of osteoarthritis. However, as mentioned earlier, arthroplasty may be used in relation to certain fractures.

32.52 An excision arthroplasty takes the form of removal of bone. This is an acceptable treatment in certain areas of the body, for example it is still used in the wrist and the joint between the collarbone and the shoulder blade. Excision arthroplasty is now considered only a salvage procedure in the hip where it is sometimes termed a Girdlestone manoeuvre. In joints which are weight bearing, it tends to give a poor functional result.

32.53 A hemiarthroplasty is a replacement of half a joint. This is most frequently used in the hip after a fracture and in the shoulder joint for the treatment of arthritis. A total replacement involves working on both sides of the joint, removing the diseased cartilage and inserting new bearing surfaces. The majority of total joint replacements are performed as a planned procedure for arthritis.

32.54 The knee joint can be a little confusing as it is possible to perform a total replacement of a single compartment of the joint. This is termed a unicompartmental replacement. The knee has three separate articulating areas; the medial aspect of the femoral tibial articulation, the lateral aspect of the femoral tibial articulation and the patellofemoral joint.

32.55 Total hip replacement is a procedure which is well established, has high success rates and good patient satisfaction levels. Even related to the established hip arthroplasty techniques, there are problems; in particular these relate to the longevity of the prosthesis. The bearing surfaces may wear out or the components may become loose. If symptomatic, this may lead to a revision procedure where all or part of the original prosthetic joint is removed and replaced. Revision procedures are more complex and therefore carry a higher risk to the patient.

32.56 The desire to reduce the revision rate and also to make revision surgery less complex through preservation of bone stock has led to a number of changes in the nature of hip arthroplasty. An example of the former is the desire to change the load-bearing surfaces. Traditional hip arthroplasties had a metal ball pressing on a polyethylene socket; both components were cemented to the bone. The hard metal ball caused wearing of the socket and the release of particles, which may be responsible for loosening of the prosthesis from the cement which secures it to the bone. The desire to improve this led to a vogue for metal-on-metal hip replacement. The wear debris from metal-on-metal was felt to be too small to stimulate the chemical reaction responsible for loosening. It is well documented that despite this theoretical benefit, the problems related to the metal ion release far outweighed the gains and has resulted in a huge revision burden being created as well as class action against the manufacturers. This is a further example of a desire to bring change without appropriate research, where pushing surgeons towards using novel techniques has resulted in a deleterious outcome for a significant sub-group of patients.

32.57 Resurfacing hip replacements are designed to remove less of the femur bone. The driver for this is preservation of bone stock in younger patients, in whom revision surgery is likely to be necessary. The increased bone stock would make a revision procedure less technically demanding. Unfortunately, there have been problems relating to this, in particular the femoral prosthesis may act as a stress riser (a point in the bone structure where the focal stress exceeds the mean stress for that structure and subsequently fractures may occur).

32.58 Joint replacements in general have a risk of infection, dislocation, nerve injury, revision and periprosthetic fracture. The correct placement of a prosthetic implant is important in terms of its functionality and durability. The specific joints have a tolerance or acceptable range for implant insertion. The desire to improve implant positioning has led to the development of a number of aids, such as computer assisted positioning and robotic surgery. The benefit of these is as yet unproven.

CHAPTER 33

Plastic surgery

Timothy E E Goodacre

INTRODUCTION

33.1   Plastic surgery is the surgery of restoration of form and function for conditions ranging from congenital deformity, traumatic injury, and cancer management, to conditions where quality of life can be enhanced by a range of surgical techniques. The speciality is defined by technique rather than anatomical site, and has very blurred boundaries, which can present difficulties in the public mind when the definition is used loosely and almost exclusively as synonymous with cosmetic surgery by the mass media.

33.2   Plastic surgical techniques originate from the use of tissue manipulation and repair, which have a long history (the earliest being recorded in ancient Sanskrit texts for nasal reconstruction). The mainstay of general surgical repair is the sutured wound, but in many circumstances, tissue loss or damage requires repair using skin and other tissues imported from elsewhere. Freely transferred (grafted) or vascularised (flap transfer) tissue is used in a vast array of forms and methods, a diversity of reconstruction that is sometimes referred to as the 'reconstructive toolbox'.

33.3   The huge diversity of techniques mean that the discipline of plastic surgery as a whole is not quickly learnt, and is as dependent upon a mindset of good judgment and versatility in adapting techniques to given situations as to the individual surgeon's technical ability. However, specific techniques can be taught rapidly, and when confined to well-defined areas of practice can be safely adopted. It is, though, uncommon for conditions to present uniformly such that 'one size fits all', and as in the example of breast reconstruction following mastectomy, practitioner versatility with all forms of reconstruction invariably presents a patient with the best options for choice and outcome.

33.4   A further effect of the sheer range of techniques is that even well-trained practitioners may have relatively little specific experience of each method: even within a busy practice, fewer operations of a given type might be performed than in other, more clearly-defined, specialities.

Spectrum of practice

Congenital deformity

33.5   Plastic surgeons manage a wide range of congenital deformities, including common head and neck conditions such as cleft lip and palate, craniofacial anomalies, limb anomalies in the hands and feet, radial club hand, urogenital anomalies such as hypospadias, and numerous skin conditions such as pigmented naevi and vascular malformations.

Cancer

33.6   Alongside the primary management of skin cancer, soft tissue sarcoma, and cancer of the head and neck, plastic surgeons manage the more complex deficiencies of tissue that arise following oncological destruction of tissue by advanced disease or as a consequence of major treatment by surgery or radiotherapy.

Traumatic tissue damage and loss

33.7   As well as burn injury, plastic surgeons manage traumatic tissue loss by restoration or repair. This might involve microsurgical re-anastomosis, or tissue grafting or flap reconstruction. Dramatically increasing versatility in microsurgical flap reconstruction has pushed the standards of repair much higher than previously, with a resultant decrease in amputation rates and better functional restoration.

Post infective conditions

33.8   Great advances have been made in the past decade in the management of chronic infected conditions (especially involving bone) that were previously intractable. This area is one in which the combined work of plastic surgeons with other disciplines in multi-disciplinary teams is exemplified, and will undoubtedly improve further.

Aesthetic reconstruction

33.9   Conditions which benefit from aesthetic improvement are not confined to the conventionally understood term 'cosmetic surgery'. The restoration of facial movement in those afflicted by facial palsy using sophisticated multi-staged microsurgical techniques is but one example of the use of the 'toolbox' to address conditions which improve quality of life.

33.10   Cosmetic surgery as a term embraces a wide range of techniques that are used to bring body shape and size into the 'norms' for society, but that can also be extended into the beautification of already 'normal' bodies. The specific problems thrown up by this field of surgery and its unique concerns are addressed at para **33.25** ff.

Problem solving

33.11   The wide variety of reconstructive methods used by plastic surgeons to address tissue manipulation render it a valuable resource to manage diverse medical problems. It is therefore a regular part of practice to be referred 'problem cases' from primary, secondary and tertiary sources to determine whether a plastic surgical solution can be offered. This aspect of practice has grown exponentially in recent years, as the value of such techniques has become more widely understood across medical and surgical specialties. Such cases are frequently complex, with multiple pathologies and previous therapeutic attempts, and carry a greater risk of failure than simple primary pathological conditions.

33.12   It is inevitable that, where a technique proves invaluable on a regular basis, there is a move towards that technique being adopted by the 'parent specialty' of the condition concerned. Thus the complex reconstruction of major head and neck cancer resection defects by plastic surgically developed composite free tissue transfers has now been widely adopted by maxillofacial surgeons.

33.13   As a problem solving specialty, plastic surgery continues to innovate and attempt novel treatments that regularly drift into more orthodox practice. Currently, composite vascularised allografts (transplants such as limbs and facial tissue) are being established, as well as fat transfer techniques, tissue engineered substitute use, and bioengineered products.

33.14   The extent of such problem solving and willingness to adopt exploratory methods to seek effective management of very difficult conditions renders the specialty vulnerable to litigation. Truly informed consent in such circumstances can be difficult, if not impossible, and time-honoured values such as trust and respect play a significant part in successful management of such conditions with reconstructive techniques.

ORGANISATION OF THE SPECIALITY

NHS provision

33.15   The provision of plastic surgery within NHS facilities has been the subject of considerable change in the past two decades. In the pre-NHS era and shortly afterwards, a major discrepancy between available consultant expertise and patient demand led to an effective rationing by default, with conditions of lower priority entering lengthy waiting lists, frequently only managed in due course by the junior cadres of surgeon, despite the relative seniority and skills such surgeons possessed at that time. Little surgery of a truly 'cosmetic only' nature has ever been performed on a regular basis within the NHS, although some congenital conditions which leave the sufferer outside the norms of society to a considerable extent (such as total absence of breasts, massive breast asymmetry, prominent ears at 90 degrees to head and so forth) were managed in 'reasonable' fashion.

33.16   Since the removal of waiting lists almost totally in the mid-1990s, the pressure on services has increased at the same time as some exceedingly expensive new medical therapies became widely available (the biologic treatments for cancer and autoimmunity). The inevitable need to reduce expenditure led to the targeting of an array of body-image related conditions for removal of funding. This approach has now been universally adopted, and in many circumstances sufferers from diverse body tissue related anomalies have been left to live with their conditions unless they can afford privately funded care (which a significant majority cannot).

Current NHS services

33.17   The NHS has seen a huge increase in consultant staff numbers within plastic surgery since 1990. This has accompanied sub-specialisation, with the areas of congenital deformity (cleft lip and palate, craniofacial disorders, congenital hand and limb anomalies, and urogenital conditions) being managed by single speciality experts. Likewise, cancer reconstruction has largely been diverted to specialists with expertise in head and neck, breast, sarcoma, or skin cancer. Traumatic conditions have been increasingly referred to tertiary plastic surgical units for primary and secondary management, undoubtedly reflecting reduced tolerance by the general public for inferior or sub-standard results from wound repair management in general, non-specialist facilities.

33.18   General practitioners have become less willing to manage smaller cutaneous lesions on an elective or urgent basis, in part without doubt due to the increased pressure brought to bear following ligation for poor scarring and inadvertent iatrogenic damage. The associated pressure on tertiary referral centres, along with the growth of complex time-consuming techniques of reconstruction, is severe and has resulted in the national speciality body (BAPRAS) increasing its recommended staffing number per head of population from 1 to 100,000 to 1 to 80,000.

Litigation

33.19   Despite the aforementioned spectrum of practice and widespread use of novel and complex surgical techniques, litigation within reconstructive practice in the NHS is not a subject of major concern. This may in part be due to the exceptionally high standard that has been set and maintained (despite considerable pressure to modify it) by the UK wide InterCollegiate Examination Board for the exit examination that all UK trained specialists are required to pass before entering the GMC Specialist register. That requirement does not pertain to surgeons trained elsewhere in the EU, or indeed beyond. The impact of the introduction of such externally trained surgeons will usually be mollified by their practice within a tightly-knit NHS framework where isolated independent practice is usually impossible other than for short periods of time.

Private practice

33.20   Plastic surgery in independent private practice consists, for the majority of practitioners, of a mix of 'pure' cosmetic surgery (plastic surgeons prefer the term 'aesthetic surgery') alongside skin conditions and a lower volume of the same conditions that are seen in NHS reconstructive practice.

33.21   The majority of NHS plastic surgeons will undertake a certain amount of aesthetic practice. Having trained in all such procedures throughout the body, they will feel able to perform breast surgery, nasal and eyelid surgery for example, whereas the general breast, or ENT surgeon, would perhaps not feel so multiply accomplished. They will, indeed have been thoroughly examined in the theoretical aspect of such procedures in their exit (FRCS(Plast)) examination. However, many will not have performed the procedures often in practice, since NHS management has relied increasingly on consultant-delivered care in recent years, along with a dilution of training opportunities following the purchasing changes described previously.

33.22   This reduction in expertise in the newly-appointed consultant is a source of anxiety amongst the profession, and solutions are being sought, including mentored training pathways, end-of-training additional 'fellowships', MSc courses and so forth. The matter has been referred by the Department of Health to the Royal College of Surgeons, which has set up a working party to report to the Secretary of State in 2015.

33.23   Low levels of expertise in early practice years leads to an inevitable increase in litigious events relating to poor practice and outcomes from that group of consultants. It is interesting to note that anecdotal evidence suggests that this is also probably mirrored by an upturn in such adverse outcomes from surgeons in their last year of surgical practice.

AESTHETIC PRACTICE

33.24   Aesthetic procedures are performed in both publicly-funded and private sectors, although the vast majority in this century are now managed in the latter due to funding constraints.

Such procedures differ from 'medically indicated' interventions in that they rarely involve 'pathological' tissue and, akin to patients undergoing vaccination or contraceptive interventions, do not involve managing 'disease'. This affects the assessment of the consent process.

33.25   In managing cases of alleged negligence, there needs to be a clear distinction between 'medical' and 'aesthetic' problems, since if an adverse outcome is due to a medical failure (such as a wound infection that might similarly occur in therapeutic surgery) the same criteria will apply in case assessment.

33.26   'Aesthetic' problems, however, can occur either when there is a clear failure in surgical technique (incorrect implant placement or incision planning), or when aesthetic expectations are not met despite satisfactory medical management of the procedure. This latter category of complaint can be the most difficult to pursue unless the failure is obviously unsatisfactory to a lay person, as it is this standard of observation which would be the norm in a court.

33.27   For this matter, the legal framework is guided by *Thake v Maurice*[1]:

(1)   these are private operations, therefore there are contract terms;
(2)   these procedures are indicated by aesthetic considerations.

Whilst there could be a 'warranty' to achieve a result, it would be exceptionally uncommon for a surgeon to provide such a warranty, which would have to be express. It is, however, not infrequent for some commercial provider groups now to offer some form of aesthetic satisfaction guarantee, which is justified within their business plan as financially manageable. However, for all surgeons operating on a private (non NHS) basis, there is an implied warranty to use reasonable skill. In practice the 'warranty' argument does not arise and the standard in contract is the same as the standard to be expected in tort.

1 [1986] QB 644.

Aesthetic breast surgery

33.28   Procedures to change the shape and size of the breast are some of the most common in cosmetic surgery. They very occasionally involve minors, when severe macromastia (enlargement of breasts) or gross asymmetry related to Poland's syndrome (a malformation of chest wall development) is present, or in males when significant non-pubertal gynaecomastia develops. As with all cases involving minors, informed consent involves parental support, within the background of *Gillick* competence[1], which can present additional difficulties when 'non-medical' treatments are involved.

1 For more detail on consent, see Chapter 12.

Breast augmentation

33.29   Breast enlargement is usually accomplished using a prosthetic device inserted through an incision below the breast or in the axilla. It can be placed in a plane just beneath the existing breast tissue (subglandular) or beneath the pectoral muscle (partially sub-muscular, sometimes termed 'bi-planar'). Various rationales are offered for each approach, with assorted 'scientific' or otherwise arguments to support, especially relating to masking the implant contour outline, reduction in impact of internal scar contracture, and long term outcome. There is no consensus view on the optimal method of placement, which may depend on the considerable number of variables associated with any given technique and surgical performance.

33.30   Devices used are predominantly silicone filled in countries that approve their use (almost all developed nations, with the US re-introducing gradually), with saline-filled devices being the other main option. The outer coating shell is usually textured to reduce contracture, with one device on the market using a form of coating that incorporates into the surrounding scar (capsule) with the objective of generating still less contracture (Silimed™).

33.31   The majority of breast augmentation cases undertaken by consultants with NHS practice (ie not those whose only practice has been commercial) are for three consumer types:

- the young woman with little/no breast tissue who wishes to have a body contour within the norms for her peer group;
- the older woman who either wishes to correct breast volume loss with ageing, or has developed breast drooping ('ptosis') and who does not want the scarring associated with an uplift procedure ('mastopexy') and wants to restore cleavage volume;
- patients with significant breast asymmetry.

Other requests come more from fashion demands and media-fuelled motivation, generating a cohort of patients who are arguably more price sensitive and frequently seek surgery from purely commercial providers.

Adverse outcomes from breast augmentation

33.32   The perception of this procedure as simple and readily available belies the technical difficulty that can pertain to certain aspects. The exact size and appearance of the breast following surgery can never be precisely determined despite numerous published methods with that intent. Concerns with unacceptable sizing or shaping are common amongst litigants. Elements of asymmetry (especially in inframammary crease positioning) are common, as with all plastic surgical procedures that involve a procedure undertaken bilaterally. The limits of 'acceptable asymmetry' are indeterminate, and are influenced by pre-operative counselling, although 'significant' asymmetry (however that might be determined) would always be unacceptable other than in cases of pre-existing asymmetry that are notoriously difficult to correct.

33.33   Post-operative numbness of the nipples, as well as some surrounding breast skin, is a complication that cannot always be avoided, and does not indicate negligent practice so long as proper consent was obtained. Infection of the implant can be catastrophic, and is rare. It is more common with larger augmentations, as well as repeat procedures.

33.34   All breast implants will develop a layer of scar tissue around the foreign material (which is the normal physiological response from the body). Such scar tissue can contract naturally (again, a normal physiological response that does not indicate 'rejection' or any other adverse phenomenon) and lead to palpable hardness of the breast that in more advanced stages can become painful as well as socially unacceptable in appearance. Such contracture is commonly described by Baker's grades 1 to IV (best to worst)[1]. Contracture does not indicate negligent treatment, and is an inevitable consequence to some extent or other.

1 See US Food and Drugs Administration 'Breast Implant Complications Booklet'.

33.35   Breasts with little natural tissue cover around the implant will have some palpable margins, which can wrinkle or 'ripple', and give rise to concern. Prolonged implant malformation with crease lines can lead to failure of the shell integrity with associated gel leak. The incidence of implant failure from elastomer shell breakdown is uncertain, but has been shown after the 2011/12 PIP implant crisis to be far higher than previously understood, and may be in the region of 15–20 per cent for many well manufactured devices at 10 years.

33.36   All breast implants will leak some of the filler through the elastomer shell, regardless of the material used to manufacture the latter. Implant 'bleed' will be manifest on ultrasound or MR scanning, and should be distinguished from true gel leak from shell rupture. Most gel which has 'bled' or even leaked from a rupture will be contained within the confines of a mature scar capsule. However, gel can migrate beyond the capsule in some cases, and then be transmitted to the regional lymph glands where palpable masses may be felt. Such 'silicone granulomas' are thought to be entirely harmless, although they frequently cause great concern to patients and generate adverse media attention to silicone as a filler.

Mastopexy

33.37   Surgery to uplift a ptotic ('droopy') breast involves a range of procedures, which are used depending upon the degree of abnormal hang as well as patient preference following consultation. The most common techniques are similar to breast reduction whilst avoiding the removal of tissue other than excess skin. Almost all methods involve a circumferential incision around the nipple, thereby inevitably placing nipple sensitivity and function at risk. Small uplifts can be confined to this circumareolar technique, but must have a supportive (usually permanent) 'purse string' suture placed around the nipple to prevent unacceptable scar stretching.

33.38   Most uplifts will, however, require the addition of a vertical scar beneath the nipple extending to the inframammary crease. Even larger uplifts still will add lateral and medial extensions to this vertical scar (generating an 'anchor-shaped' scar pattern) to avoid 'dog ear' production from excess cutaneous tissue).

33.39 Mastopexy is a difficult procedure, especially in delivering satisfactory symmetry and a lasting result. Mature patients who want to restore a more youthful breast shape frequently ask to combine it with augmentation. This combined procedure is notorious amongst experienced cosmetic surgeons as being highly likely to generate some aspect of post-operative discontent, and detailed and careful preliminary counselling is essential in such cases.

Breast reduction

33.40 Breast reduction is a frequently-requested procedure, and in many cases has a major functional component in the presenting symptoms. Back and neck pain, shoulder 'grooving', and inframammary intertrigo (skin inflammation and fungal infection) are common and well managed by the procedure. Less substantial breast size can still generate requests for reduction, but the 'balance' of beneficial outcome weighed against adverse sequelae can become less favourable in such cases. Again, careful counselling and good judgment are required when managing such patients.

33.41 Breast reduction is one cosmetic procedure that can be requested at a young age, not infrequently by those under the age of 18 when gigantomastia is present. In such circumstances, the usual constraints of consent are essential, but school age is not a barrier to some (rare) patients whose school years can be significantly blighted by this condition.

33.42 The main adverse effects of breast reduction are the scarring, potential loss of nipple sensation and function, and loss of ability to breast feed. Other than some scar formation, none of these are invariable, but are dependent upon the technique used, degree of pre-morbid deformity, and nature of the breast tissue itself (there being great variability in degree of fibrosis and parenchymal pliability and cystic change). Asymmetry can again be a problem, residual 'dog ears' at the scar extremities, and over-resection is a potentially serious and unacceptable outcome.

33.43 Litigation is less common following this procedure, possibly because of the functional improvement that often ensues regardless of the perfection of cosmetic outcome.

Rhinoplasty

33.44 Surgery to the external nose is usually sought from plastic surgeons for aesthetic reasons, but may be accompanied by functional concerns, especially when following trauma to the face. Rhinoplasty is always a difficult procedure, frequently underestimated by less experienced practitioners. Litigation is common and adverse outcomes highly contentious due to the prominence of the nose in overall appearance as well as susceptibility to sequential detailed photographic recording.

33.45 Rhinoplasty can be performed using 'closed' access (with no externally visible scars) or 'open' using a small incision in the columella portion of the nasal skin. Experienced surgeons may use either approach, the choice in each individual case depending on judgment regarding the need for access to component parts. Some scarring within the nostril cavity is inevitable.

33.46 During the procedure, elements of the bony 'hump' can be resected or adjusted, usually requiring fracturing of the remaining elements to reposition the architecture of the bridge line. The nasal tip can be refashioned to narrow or make more pointed, reduced in length or breadth, and asymmetries corrected. The number of manoeuvres that can be incorporated into a rhinoplasty is enormous, and the procedure is as much an art and craft as a science. The considerable variability in outcome will relate as much to individual surgical ability and patient variability as the adoption of one or other previously defined 'technique'.

33.47 Adverse outcomes may result from failure to address the predominant concerns of the patient, the residual impact of injured structures with bony or cartilaginous irregularities, functional problems due to nasal obstruction, and asymmetry. These are sufficiently common that some advice sheets[1] suggest that it would be expected for up to 10 per cent of patients to require further surgical correction within a year of the primary procedure. Commercial arrangements to account for such concerns vary between providers, and can be a source of discontent between patient and surgeon.

1 Available from The British Association of Plastic Reconstructive and Aesthetic Surgeons (BAPRAS) and The British Association of Aesthetic Plastic Surgeons (BAAPS).

33.48 Since the outcome of any rhinoplasty will almost inevitably have some imperfections, however minor, there are a small number of patients for whom anything short of perfection will be unacceptable. Amongst this group will be those with degrees of body dysmorphic disorder, whose psychological well-being is permanently disordered due to perceived (but usually not discernable) disfigurement. Nasal appearance is high on the list of body areas which feature in such cases, and therefore claimants in the field of rhinoplasty will have some with this underlying well-acknowledged psychological condition.

Abdominoplasty

33.49 This procedure to reduce abdominal excess tissue is usually sought to correct the sequelae of childbirth, as well as weight loss. It is not a procedure primarily for weight loss: the potential for adverse outcomes following surgery are increased with higher levels of body mass index. The spectrum of abdominoplasty ranges from the 'mini-abdominoplasty', which removes a 'melon slice' of tissue from the lower third of the abdomen, through conventional abdominoplasty, to the major tissue removing operations following massive weight loss and bariatric procedures. These latter procedures generate significant scars and are performed in a variety of ways. It is helpful if they are presented as 'work in progress' to patients, and expectations of highly finessed outcomes dispelled from the outset.

33.50 Conventional abdominoplasty involves removal of as much superficial tissue from above the abdominal musculature as can be achieved (within the constraints of viable tissue tension on closure), with re-draping of the remaining undermined skin from above the wound downwards towards the waist. The umbilicus is mobilized on its 'stalk', and then repositioned in the correct site through a new position in the re-draped and tightened remaining abdominal skin. If a separation of the rectus muscle bundles (the so-called 'six-pack' muscles of the abdominal wall) is diagnosed either pre-operatively or intra-operatively, it is a normal part of this procedure to correct this divarication by the insertion of a permanent suture between the bundles. This manoeuvre will usually improve the underlying muscle layer contour and enhance outcomes. It is, however, not mandatory.

33.51 Conventional abdominoplasty usually aims to mobilise the remaining skin layer sufficiently to leave a simple (albeit long) scar across the lower waist line, the only other being a small circumferential umbilical scar. However, in a patient with relatively little skin excess, it might not be possible to advance the upper skin far enough to remove the need to close the tissues with an additional vertical scar element running in the midline above the waistline scar.

33.52 Adverse outcomes from abdominoplasty include the development of collections of serous fluid in the large closed space that is left following redraping of the skin flap. Drains may be used initially, as well as quilting of the tissue layers together, but such seroma formation can persist for several months and be difficult to eradicate. The abdominal wall will be numb (often permanently) after this operation, and asymmetry might be evident. Lateral 'dog ears' of tissue where the excision has ended are common and may require secondary excision.

33.53 The more serious complications include dehiscence (parting) of the repaired skin layers, with ensuing infection and possible tissue loss. This will inevitably cause worse scarring, and usually requires protracted wound management, which can be distressing for patients embarking on the procedure for quality of life. More serious still is the loss of tissue due to necrosis from either closure under excess tension (leading to vascular compromise) or severe infection. In severe cases, such tissue necrosis can require eventual skin grafting, leaving a seriously compromised appearance.

Prominent ear correction

33.54 This procedure to set back or refashion prominent or malformed ears is common, especially for children whose parents wish to prevent or alleviate teasing due to appearance. Responsible surgeons adopt one of two main methods. The older technique involves 'de-gloving' part of the ear (pinna) cartilage from a posterior incision, and reshaping the framework by scoring the cartilage as well as inserting sutures (skin then re-draped over the newly-formed construct). Newer techniques aim to avoid potential risks of de-gloving (which include necrosis of the skin, infection and haematoma) by using a more closed insertion of permanent suture material from the newly formed ear folds into the posterior ear region. These so-called 'concho-mastoid sutures' are at risk of failure and full relapse of the deformity, reported to be in the region of 5–10 per cent and which then require repeat surgery. However, this method is less problematic than anterior scoring and best evidence is yet to confirm the preferred method for this deformity.

33.55   More unusual and complex ear anomalies are the domain of highly-specialised ear reconstruction surgeons, and there is a strong move towards the centralisation of all such cases into centres of expertise.

PROCEDURES FOR CONDITIONS OF AGEING

Cosmetic eyelid correction (blepharoplasty)

33.56   Eyelid surgery is common, and can be requested to correct excess upper lid folds, lower eyelid bags, and the overall appearance of ageing. It can be undertaken under general or local anaesthesia, and involves the removal of excess skin and muscle from the upper lid, correction of fat herniation from the orbital cavity, and various procedures to the lower lid to correct convex 'bags' as well as elevate fat to rejuvenate the appearance. It does not correct all wrinkling of the skin, which is a condition better addressed by topical treatments or botulinum toxin paralysis of the surrounding musculature. The exceptionally prominent nature of the eyes in human visual appearance renders this form of surgery most prone to failure from the consumer perspective when residual asymmetry (common) or untoward side effects are present. Preoperative counselling to detect pre-existing conditions is essential, and recent eye testing of great value. Common post-operative conditions include swelling and bruising of the lids and cheeks, prolonged chemosis (jelly-like swelling) of the conjunctivae of the eyes, persistent dry eye, ectropion (out-rolling of the lower lid), 'scleral show' (visible whites of the eyes below the pupil – a condition normal in a small percentage of patients, but unacceptable as a post-operative state), and epiphora (excess tearing of the lids). The eyes may appear excessively sunken after excess fat bag removal, but more conservative removal of tissue (especially in the upper lid) may leave residual tissues that reduce the impact of the rejuvenation.

33.57   The most serious adverse consequence of blepharoplasty remains loss of sight in one or other eye, following intra-orbital haemorrhage or haematoma. This condition is so rare that many surgeons never warned patients of the risk, until *Chester v Afshar*[1] modified much practice.

1 [2004] UKHL 41, [2005] 1 AC 134.

Facelift (rhytidectomy)

33.58   Patients seek a facelift to rejuvenate the face generally, especially when significant jowls or midfacial lines (nasolabial folds) have developed, or skin and fat accumulated under a dropped chin (the so called 'turkey gobbler' deformity). Smoking (which in itself can lead to premature ageing and thinning of the skin, so generating disproportionate referrals from this group) is a well-established additional risk factor for skin necrosis and poor wound healing. Patients in the younger age group (below 50) often seek correction for more minor and early signs of ageing, and the balance of risk against benefit is consequently less favourable for a beneficial outcome.

33.59   The operation varies, from simple skin lifting and trimming, to much more involved dissection of the deeper layers of muscle and 'SMAS' layer (the superficial musculoaponeurotic system) which can either be tightened or dissected in a separate plane. The deeper planes – including a plane that runs very much more deeply beneath all the facial muscles just above the facial skeleton – run the risk of damage to the important facial nerve and its fine branches. The majority of facelifts in the UK are undertaken under general anaesthetic.

33.60   Post-operative complications which the patient should be informed about include the extent and quality of the scars which would lie above, in front and in many cases behind the ears – in some cases an incision is made in the skin crease underneath the chin. Haematoma (blood clot) beneath the skin and skin necrosis adjacent to the ear may lead to increased scarring. There is always a loss of sensation to the cheek skin and possibly the ears which may be permanent. Damage to the greater auricular nerve can result in permanent loss of sensation to the ear and to a painful neuroma in the neck. The most important complications, however, are damage to the branches of the facial nerve, in particular the frontal branch to the forehead or the marginal mandibular nerve to the corner of the mouth. Some areas of alopecia of the scalp hairline (especially behind the ear) is common, and men should be advised that part of the beard area of the cheeks will be transposed behind the ear.

Brow lift

33.61   As part of the ageing process the eyebrows droop (develop 'ptosis'). This results in excess skin in the upper lid, frown lines around the base of the nose and forehead creases. Correction of brow ptosis is often done in conjunction with eyelid or facelift surgery. Formerly the operation involved an incision from ear to ear across the top of the scalp (in the position of an Alice hair band). This open procedure is associated with many sensory changes in the scalp and has now been superseded by an endoscopic approach where small incisions are made in the hair-bearing area of the scalp and an endoscope inserted through one portal and an elevating dissector through another portal, allowing the nerves of the forehead to be preserved. Various methods of fixation are used to retain the brows in their new position including bone fixation and external screws.

33.62   Post-operative complications include bruising and swelling, small areas of baldness around the scalp incisions, and temporary loss of sensation in the forehead and scalp. Permanent loss of sensation indicates damage to the supra-orbital nerves and to the smaller supra-trochlear nerves in the middle of the forehead and can result in painful neuromata. The most serious complication is damage to the frontal branch of the facial nerve, causing paralysis to the frontalis muscle with the long-term result being a low paralysed eyebrow.

Liposuction

33.63 Liposuction is a surgical technique to remove fat. Different words are used for the same surgical procedure: liposuction, assisted lipectomy, liposculpture, ultrasonic assisted liposuction. It is the most commonly performed surgical procedure in the United States.

33.64 Patients seek liposuction for two main reasons. Some seek simply to lose weight, for which this surgical procedure is poorly suited. More appropriate conditions are those with abnormally sited or difficult to eradicate fatty excess areas, such as thigh 'saddlebags', flank excess (especially following abdominoplasty), and buttock and thigh excess in otherwise reasonably balanced figures.

33.65 Liposuction depends upon the skin contracting down after the removal of fat and therefore patients with poor skin tone, including so-called cellulite, will not be fully restored to juvenile skin tension, and must have expectations appropriately guarded. Sometimes liposuction is undertaken with more formal skin excision such as in an abdominal reduction or occasionally with a facelift or breast reduction.

33.66 Surgery is undertaken either in very small, limited procedures under local anaesthetic or more often under day-case general anaesthesia. If more than three litres of fat are removed, patients should be admitted for overnight stay in order to be adequately resuscitated and monitored. Patients in whom more than five litres of fat are removed may require a blood transfusion. In very obese patients uneven or unequal removal of fat may result. Very occasionally if liposuction is undertaken too superficially subcutaneous scarring may become visible. In some notable, but very rare, cases where too much fat has been removed, death has occurred from inadequate post-operative care and resuscitation.

33.67 This area is an example of other medical practitioners becoming involved in cosmetic surgical procedures. General practitioners and dermatologists are increasingly undertaking liposuction under local anaesthetic as a so-called office procedure.

Lasers

33.68 Laser is an acronym for Light Amplification Simulated Emission Radiation. Lasers were invented in 1960 and have now become widely used in many fields of medicine. The modern laser clinic will have multiple lasers, each producing a different wavelength of light. Different pigments will absorb the different wavelengths and become ablated. Therefore the type of laser being used will depend upon what lesion is being treated. The most common are:

- a tunable dye laser used to thrombose vascular lesions. These would include spider neavi, port wine stains, telangectasias. Usually this treatment is undertaken on an outpatient basis except in children where general anaesthetic is required for co-operation. The patient should be warned that multiple treatments are required to ablate the port wine stain and that telangectasias may recur. If too much energy is used permanent white scarring will result;

- carbon dioxide lasers have recently been introduced. They burn in a very accurate, controlled way the superficial layers of the skin which results in the improvement of facial wrinkles and acne scars and the rejuvenation of sun-damaged skin. This is a painful procedure and therefore local anaesthesia or more commonly a day-case general anaesthetic is required. A burn is produced and therefore intensive post-operative care of the skin is required either with Vaseline or with biological dressings. The patient must be informed of the post-treatment pigmentation changes in the skin. Initially for four or five months there will be redness of the skin which will resolve, as for any burn, and then the treated area will become either hypopigmented and pale, or, in darker-skinned people, hyperpigmented and darker. If too much energy is used in the laser beam, or the wound becomes infected, then instead of producing a partial thickness burn the injury can become full thickness with the development of obvious scarring in the treated area.

  Lasers are also used for the removal of hair and the removal of tattoos. Due to the multiple pigmentation of tattoos several different lasers are required. If the area is overtreated, permanent scarring of the skin can result and usually multiple treatment courses are required;

- intense pulsed light machines (IPL) are amongst the latest generation of lasers. They are non-ablative and are used in skin regeneration as well as for vascular and hair removal.

Cosmetic labial and vaginal surgery

33.69 The reported demand for surgical alteration of female external genitalia has increased substantially over the past decade in many western countries. Prior to this vogue, there has always been a small demand from women either suffering from posttraumatic labial fullness (for example after the resolution of a haematoma in this thin labial tissues), or more commonly those on the extreme side of development with psychological or emotional disturbance as a consequence. Some women have also conventionally sought such surgical reduction when fullness of the labia minora following childbirth causes chafing and soreness, particularly on exercise.

33.70 Surgery involves careful planning of the skin and subcutaneous tissue fullness, ensuring that the clitoral tissue is not affected, or the area 'unhooded' leading to unpleasant sensory changes and the potential for permanent distressing urinary flow diversion. Scars need to be planned such that post surgical dyspareunia (painful intercourse) is avoided.

33.71 Adverse effects of such surgery include hypersensitive scars, dyspareunia, urinary discomfort, and poor appearance. The frankly irreversible effect of surgical modification of this area has led to compensation claims, with few experts available operating in this field with the ability to offer sound opinion on prognosis and outcome. There is also a highly-charged socio-political environment surrounding such procedures, with well-known protagonists against all operations who present a strong case including published literature.

33.72 Vaginal rejuvenative surgery is less commonly sought, but again is believed to be on the increase. It can be seen as in some ways a restorative technique for the consequences of childbirth, but the field is rife with novel techniques including thermal techniques (both heat and cold) for soft tissue tightening. The inability to determine measurable outcome in any meaningful sense renders the area vulnerable to litigation, with the absence of acknowledged standards within the main body of responsible practitioners a major concern.

STANDARDS OF PRACTICE

33.73 The standard of practice for plastic surgeons has changed significantly in recent years, with much higher public profiles of individuals following the GMC relaxation of previously stringent demands on the avoidance of advertising. This change in the past two decades has seen the establishment of commercial practices with aggressive marketing and promotion of cosmetic interventions amongst a certain group of plastic surgeons with aesthetic interests. Not all aesthetic surgeons with a rigorous background of comprehensive training have adopted such a path, but the influence of commercial business practice alongside clear socio-economic changes in western (and other) societies has modified the landscape for surgery, almost certainly irrevocably.

33.74 In response to these changes, national specialty bodies such as BAPRAS have revised their Code of Practice to attempt to define the standards to which best practice should adhere. BAAPS has a similar code, which is more closely worded, to serve as a guide to membership of a more limited closed association. The Royal College of Surgeons of England has published a guide to cosmetic surgical practice in general, although much of this relates to institutional provision rather than individual surgical endeavour. Following the 2012 White Paper report by Sir Bruce Keogh[1], generated in the wake of the PIP Implant scandal, the RCS of England has been charged with setting new standards for cosmetic surgical training, practice, and outcome evaluation. These three areas have working parties due to report at some point in 2015, which is awaited with great interest.

1 Poly Implant Prothèse (PIP) breast implants: final report of the Expert Group: Department of Health (June 2012). In June 2015 the General Medical Council published draft guidance for doctors who offer cosmetic interventions, and launched a public consultation on the draft guidance, Consultation on cosmetic interventions guidance. This project forms part of the Government's response to Sir Bruce Keogh's review of cosmetic interventions. The draft guidance draws together principles from existing GMC guidance that are relevant to cosmetic practice and introduces new principles that our group of expert advisers considered were necessary to address specific concerns about cosmetic interventions.

33.75 There is currently activity within the EU to attempt to harmonise standards within aesthetic surgical practice, led by the European Committee for Standardisation (CEN) 'mirror groups' (in the UK this is the British Standards Institute), but progress has been mired by widely differing practices throughout the EU, and it is unlikely that any robust and workable framework for surgical practice will emerge from this forum in the foreseeable future.

CAUSATION

33.76   In the field of aesthetic and cosmetic interventions, causation matters are usually less complex. Since those seeking such surgical intervention are on the whole without other underlying medically significant conditions, adverse outcomes can usually be attributed to the procedure itself unless other misadventure was incurred. This clarity does then mean that a high degree of responsibility for determining the presence or otherwise of any pre-existing morbid conditions falls on the aesthetic practitioner. The shared nature of this responsibility with the patient's general practitioner is a matter that can arise in some complex cases.

Urological surgery

Mr John Reynard

THE SPECIALITY OF UROLOGY: DEMOGRAPHICS, TRAINING, SUB-SPECIALISATION

34.1   Urology is the speciality which encompasses the medical and surgical management of disease of the urinary and (male) genital systems. There is some overlap with the speciality of urogynaecology, which covers incontinence and pelvic organ prolapse disease in women. Whether the urological expert is qualified, or the urogynaecology expert is better placed, to comment on these areas of practice will depend on his area of sub-specialist interest. Paediatric urology, a range of urological conditions unique to neonates and children, is beyond the scope of this chapter.

34.2   For a surgical speciality covering so much pathology and one which is rapidly evolving, this chapter can give only a flavour for those areas of urological practice that lend themselves to litigation. It focuses on those common areas of litigation relating to urological conditions[1]. The urological expert witness need not be long in practice to recognise that there are recurring themes in urological litigation and it is on these areas that this chapter will focus.

1 Notley, Reynard, Badenoch *Urology and the Law – Lessons from Litigation* (2007).

The changing face of urological practice and training

34.3   In the UK the British Association of Urological Surgeons (BAUS), based in the Royal College of Surgeons in Lincoln's Inn Fields, is the main professional body overseeing training in and the management of the profession of urology. Founded in 1948, its aim is as relevant today as it was then, namely 'to promote a high standard in the practice of urology'[1].

1 www.baus.org.uk.

34.4   There are 1,380 urologists on the specialist register of the GMC[1], comprising consultant urologists and associate specialists. BAUS reports that the last 12 years has seen a 70 per cent expansion in the consultant urological workforce, from 514 in 2000 to 875 in 2012 (not all are members of BAUS and not all GMC registered urologists are consultants, hence the disparity between GMC and BAUS 'urologist' numbers)[2]. This expansion in consultant numbers has coincided with a 28 per cent increase for in-patient work, and a 32 per cent increase in the overall outpatient workload in the last eight years. Of consultant urologists, 98 per cent practise within the NHS, with 76 per cent doing private practice as well, 22 per cent doing solely NHS work and 2 per cent as sole private practitioners.

The average UK urology department comprises a median of six whole-time equivalent consultants (WTEs), with the largest department employing 20 consultants.

1 www.gmc-uk.org/doctors/register/search_stats.asp, as at November 2014.
2 Burgess and Joyce *Workforce Report for BAUS and The SAC in Urology* (BAUS, September 2012), in Finch, Payne, Joyce, Burgess 'Defining working patterns for UK consultant urologists: results of a national census' (2013) 6 Journal of Clinical Urology 414–421.

Training

34.5   Following completion of the two Foundation Years and two further years of core training in surgery, the prospective urologist will apply for a five-year post in higher surgical urological surgical training (ST3–7: surgical trainee in years 3 through to 7, the first two years being as a core trainee in the surgical specialities in general). The syllabus for urological training as at 2015 can be found on the GMC website[1].

1 www.gmc-uk.org/Urology_Curriculum_Final_14_03_08.pdf_30533657.pdf.

34.6   The Joint Committee on Surgical Training Guidelines for the award of a Certificate of Completion of Training in Urology requires that a trainee must have undertaken five years of higher surgical training in a recognised training unit, have successfully passed the Intercollegiate Speciality Board Examination and pass their final ARCP (Annual Review of Competence Progression)[1].

1 www.jcst.org/quality-assurance/documents/cct-guidelines/urology-cct-guidelines.

34.7   The urology section of the last edition of this book expressed concerns that reduction in duration of the working week of the surgical trainee would lead to inadequate surgical exposure and training, by limiting the previously long hours spent in the operating theatre, acquiring surgical skills so that 'the newer trainees are unlikely to attain the expertise of earlier generations'[1].

1 *Clinical Negligence* (4th edn, 2008), Ch 43.

34.8   Modern surgical training time is less than in former years (now averaging nine years post-qualification as a doctor, as for example against the 11 years it used to take to attain consultant status post-qualification) and those hours spent training have been limited by the European Working Time Directive (to 48 hours per week versus 80–90 hours per week which was common for previous generations).

34.9   It has probably always been the case that newly-appointed consultants would seek the advice and support of more senior consultants, both in elective and emergency work; the senior consultant effectively mentoring the more junior consultant during the first few years of the latter's consultant career. This too will go some considerable way to offsetting the disadvantage of shortened surgical training. Conversely, with increasing sub-specialisation it is no longer unusual for the older consultant to call upon the services of the younger consultant where sub-specialist skills dictate.

Sub-specialisation and departmental organisation

34.10   This is the era of sub-specialisation in all fields of surgery. In previous decades, it was not uncommon for surgeons to cover the full range of urological diagnosis and treatment. Sub-specialisation was in its relative infancy. Now Oxford alone has 12 consultant urologists, most providing a general service (for the management of haematuria, lower urinary tract symptoms, scrotal pathology), but also each with a sub-specialist interest.

34.11   So the sub-specialist urologist usually also contributes to the general urology service of his department, this activity accounting for 70 per cent of most urologists' direct clinical care time, 30 per cent being spent on a sub-specialist field[1]. Only 4 per cent of consultant urologists report a practice with no sub-speciality interest.

1 Burgess and Joyce *Workforce Report for BAUS and The SAC in Urology* (BAUS, September 2012), in Finch, Payne, Joyce, Burgess 'Defining working patterns for UK consultant urologists: results of a national census' (2013) 6 Journal of Clinical Urology 414–421.

34.12   Smaller district hospitals, which may only employ three or four urologists, may be unable to provide the full range of specialist urology services and the trend, particularly with urological cancer, is towards amalgamation of services with other nearby hospital Trusts or of the development of a hub and spoke model, where services are centralised in large teaching hospitals which provide effectively a visiting specialist service to adjacent satellite hospitals. None of this sits easily with the concept of each Trust being independent of (or in competition with) its neighbours.

34.13   Sub-specialisation has the distinct advantage of bringing with it better outcomes (practice makes perfect). However, it also brings with it the disadvantage of deskilling of the sub-specialist surgeon. This is seen most notably in the management of obstructing ureteric stones (not all urologists can confidently ureteroscope the upper ureteric stone), the management of complications following reconstructive surgery (such as managing problems related to artificial urinary sphincters) and in the management of major renal trauma or serious renal infection where, in both situations, open exploration of the kidney may be required for control of bleeding or infection. Surgeons who do not sub-specialise in open renal surgery may well have to call on the services of those who do, and since the sub-specialist renal surgeon cannot always be on-call, this can create logistical problems in organising an emergency urology service.

The urology ward

34.14   As with all surgical specialities, urological nursing requires specialised training. Patients are best managed in an environment providing nurses skilled in the subtleties and nuances of urological care. Unfortunately patients cannot always be managed on specialist urology wards where beds are limited in number (through financial restraints). In a well-publicised whistle-blowing case, a hospital Trust saw fit, on financial grounds, to dismantle a specialist urology ward built up over many years, to the detriment of patient care[1]. Lawyers representing patients who allege sub-standard treatment should consider the potential impact that nursing on a non-specialist ward may have had on the outcome.

1 *Niekrash v South London Healthcare NHS Trust* [2012] UKEAT 0252.

The ageing population and urological surgery

34.15 As with all surgical specialities, it is now routine for the urologist to manage and operate on patients in their late 80s and 90s, but nothing is 'routine' in such individuals who often have a host of co-morbidity, issues of cognitive function, and who are nowhere near as physically robust as younger people. The risks of managing such patients should not be under-estimated, either by the urological surgeon or expert witness or by lawyers and barristers where allegations of sub-standard management are made.

UROLOGICAL STANDARDS OF CARE

34.16 The expert urologist will be well aware of the standard textbooks that outline the practice of urology (such as *Campbell-Walsh Urology*[1], regarded by many as the bible for urology) and of Guidelines from the American Urological Association[2] and European Association of Urology[3] that can be used as an evidence base for determining what the standard of urological care is. These are carefully constructed, well researched, voluminous, evidence based documents. The EAU updates its guidelines annually, the AUA less frequently so. NICE also publishes a host of guidelines relating to techniques and treatments for urological conditions.

1 Wein, Kavoussi, Novick, Partin, Peters *Campbell-Walsh Urology* (10th edn, 2012).
2 AUA: https://www.auanet.org.
3 EAU: www.uroweb.org.

34.17 No guideline is absolutely comprehensive and there are irritating (sometimes glaring) omissions. So, for example, for such a common procedure as urethral catheterisation, neither the AUA or the EAU give any guidance on whether antibiotic prophylaxis should be administered and so the expert is left trying to make an educated guess as to what standard practice is, when for example, reporting on breach of duty in a patient who becomes septic after urethral catheterisation. This is frustrating for experts and those instructing them.

CONSENT FOR UROLOGICAL TREATMENT

34.18 All urologists in UK practice will be aware of the BAUS procedure specific consent forms, first published in 2003 and revised in 2013, but it is surprising how frequently they are not used and how inadequate the process of consent can be. They now number 97 and they provide a comprehensive standard of what a responsible body of urologists think patients should be informed of. Because of their questionable readability[1], it is the urologist's duty to help the patient, face-to-face, to interpret the jargon used within each information leaflet (handing the patient a BAUS consent form as the only attempt to inform is not adequate consent).

1 Graham, Reynard and Turney 'Consent information leaflets – readable or unreadable?' *Journal of Clinical Urology* 2051415814555947, first published on 2 December 2014 as doi:10.1177/2051415814555947.

HAEMATURIA

The significance of haematuria

34.19   Haematuria is the presence of blood in the urine. Its causes are legion, but it is of relevance from a medico-legal perspective principally because the failure to recognise that it may be due to renal or bladder cancer, and less frequently kidney stones, can lead to delays in diagnosis of these serious conditions. Needless loss of life and loss of renal function may follow and greater morbidity may occur from the requirement for more complex treatment arising as a consequence of delayed diagnosis. Alleged delayed diagnosis of renal or bladder cancer in a patient presenting with haematuria is a frequent source of a request for an expert urology opinion.

34.20   Haematuria may be a patient-reported symptom, a sign (reported as a finding by someone else) or an investigation result (the presence on dipstick testing of blood in the urine).

Because it may indicate the presence of serious underlying pathology, it is a finding that urologists do and GPs should take seriously since while a few red blood cells can be found in the urine of normal people (explaining why no abnormality is found in approximately 70–90 per cent of 'patients' with microscopic or dipstick haematuria[1], despite full conventional urological investigation), about 5–10 per cent of individuals with non-visible haematuria and about 20–25 per cent with blood visible in their urine have an underlying urological cancer.

1 Khadra, Pickard, Charlton (et al) 'A prospective analysis of 1930 patients with hematuria to evaluate current diagnostic practice' (2000) 163 J Urol 524–527; Edwards, Dickinson, Natale (et al) 'A prospective analysis of the diagnostic yield resulting from the attendance of 4020 patients at a protocol-driven haematuria clinic' (2006) 97 BJU Int 301–305.

Changing haematuria terminology

34.21   The terminology used to describe haematuria has changed within the last six years[1]. Haematuria are now categorised as: (a) 'visible' haematuria (VH; formerly macroscopic, frank or gross haematuria) where the patient or doctor has seen blood in the urine or describes the urine as red or pink; or (b) 'non-visible' haematuria (NVH; formerly microscopic or dipstick haematuria). Non-visible haematuria is either symptomatic (s-NVH, ie lower urinary tract symptoms such as frequency, urgency, urethral pain on voiding, suprapubic pain) or asymptomatic (a-NVH).

1 The Joint Consensus Statement on the Initial Assessment of Haematuria - The Renal Association and British Association of Urological Surgeons (July 2008) http://www.baus. org.uk/Resources/BAUS/Documents/PDF%20Documents/BAUS%20in%20general/ haematuria_consensus_guidelines_July_2008.pdf.

34.22 The sensitivity of urine dipstick testing of a freshly voided urine sample is now so accurate at detecting haematuria that routine confirmatory microscopy is no longer considered necessary: if someone is dipstick positive for blood, they are managed as if they had microscopic haematuria. This overcomes the problem of urine samples that genuinely contain blood, but which when sent from the community by the GP to a hospital lab, undergo red cell blood lysis in transit so that by the time the sample reaches the lab the red blood cells have lysed and cannot be detected (thus giving a falsely negative result).

34.23 Dipstick haematuria is considered to be significant if 1+ or more. 'Trace' haematuria is considered negative. No distinction is made between haemolysed and non-haemolysed dipstick-positive urine; as long as 1+ or more of blood is detected, it is considered significant haematuria.

34.24 Significant haematuria is defined as:

- any single episode of VH;
- any single episode of s-NVH (in absence of urinary tract infection (UTI) or other transient causes);
- persistent a-NVH, defined as two out of three dipsticks positive for NVH (in the absence of UTI or other transient causes).

Can a single episode of haematuria be ignored?

34.25 A failure to urgently refer (under a two-week wait cancer referral) any patient with even a single episode of VH, who is later diagnosed with advanced urological cancer, is a frequent request for an opinion from an expert urologist. Some GPs (and patients) wrongly presume that a single episode cannot be serious, and that urological referral may be deferred until the VH recurs. Many symptoms reported to GPs are self-limiting and not indicative of serious disease and so watching and waiting is reasonable in many instances, but haematuria is not such a symptom. Renal or bladder cancers bleed only intermittently, in their early (curable) phase of growth and the intermittent nature of haematuria should not be taken as an indication that urological referral need not be made.

34.26 Where urinary tract infection (UTI) is thought to be the cause of VH or NVH, the UTI should be treated and repeat dipstick testing done to confirm the absence of haematuria. UTI is most easily excluded by a negative dipstick result for both leucocytes and nitrites. If the dipstick is positive for haematuria with a negative dipstick result for both leucocytes and nitrites, the haematuria should be investigated further.

When is urological referral warranted?

34.27 The rules are clear and are based on joint guidelines published by BAUS and the Renal Association[1]. Urological referral is warranted in:

- all patients with VH;
- all patients with s-NVH;
- a-NVH in patients aged 40 or more;
- persistent a-NVH (defined as two out of three positives for NVH).

In agreement with BAUS and the Renal Association, NICE cancer referral guidelines state[2] that patients should be referred using a suspected cancer pathway referral (for an appointment within two weeks) for bladder or renal cancer if they are:

- aged 45 and over and have unexplained visible haematuria without urinary tract infection; or
- have visible haematuria that persists or recurs after successful treatment of urinary tract infection; or
- are aged 60 and over and have unexplained non-visible haematuria and either dysuria or a raised white cell count on urine testing.

NICE also recommends consideration be given to non-urgent referral for bladder or renal cancer in people aged 60 and over with recurrent or persistent unexplained urinary tract infection.

So, both BAUS and the Renal Association and NICE cancer referral guidelines emphasise that UTI, especially if recurrent or persistent, can be the first presentation of significant genito-urinary pathology (eg stones or bladder cancer) and that such cases warrant an urgent referral.

1 The Joint Consensus Statement on the Initial Assessment of Haematuria – The Renal Association and British Association of Urological Surgeons (July 2008).
2 National Institute for Health and Clinical Excellence (2015) *NG13 Suspected cancer: recognition and referral*. Reproduced with permission.

34.28 For the patient under 40 with a-NVH, if eGFR is >60mL/min, BP <140/90, and there is no proteinuria (PCR[1] <50mg/mmol or ACR <30mg/mmol), then while the a-NVH persists, it is recommended that the patient has an annual eGFR, BP check, and proteinuria check. If VH or s-NVH develops, referral to urology for a cystoscopy and imaging is indicated. If eGFR is <60mL/min, BP >140/90, or there is proteinuria (PCR >50mg/mmol or ACR >30mg/ mmol), nephrological referral is indicated. A significant proportion of patients with a-NVH have glomerular disease despite having normal blood pressure, a normal serum creatinine, and no proteinuria (though most do not develop progressive renal disease and those that do usually develop proteinuria and hypertension as impending signs of deteriorating renal function)[2].

1 Protein assessment on a single urine sample. Protein:creatinine ratio (PCR) or albumin:creatinine ratio (ACR). Significant proteinuria is a PCR >50mg/mmol or an ACR >30mg/mmol.
2 Topham, Harper, Furness (et al) 'Glomerular disease as a cause of isolated microscopic haematuria' (1994) 87 Q J Med 329–335; Tomson, Porter 'Asymptomatic microscopic or dipstick haematuria on adults: which investigations for which patients? A review of the evidence' (2002) 90 Br J Urol 185–198.

Urological investigation of haematuria

34.29 The principle of investigation is to image the urethra and bladder by direct telescopic ('cystoscopic') inspection and the ureters, renal pelvis and renal collecting system and parenchyma ('meat') of the kidneys by a variable combination of renal ultrasonography and CT urography (CTU). The advent of high resolution renal and ureteric CT scanning has relegated the intravenous urogram (IVU) to the history books. It is difficult to imagine a situation where an IVU would be requested.

34.30   Diagnostic cystoscopy is nowadays carried out using a flexible cystoscope, unless radiological investigation shows a bladder cancer, in which case it makes more sense (in that it saves time) to proceed to rigid cystoscopy and resection or biopsy of the tumour (transurethral resection of bladder tumour (TURBT)) under anaesthetic.

What type of CT scan is best?

34.31   Multidetector CT urography (MDCTU) involves administration of intravenous contrast followed by the rapid acquisition of images of the kidneys, ureters and bladder. Overlapping thin sections are reconstructed in multiple planes (so-called multiplanar reformatting) so providing high spatial resolution of lesions in multiple planes. In theory it could obviate the need for all other investigations, even cystoscopy, but at the cost of a higher radiation dose (a 3-phase MDCTU has a radiation dose of 20–25mSV compared with 5–10mSV from a 7-film IVU). MDCTU has a 93 per cent sensitivity and 99 per cent specificity for diagnosing bladder tumours in those with VH[1] and equivalent diagnostic accuracy to retrograde ureterography (retrograde administration of contrast via a catheter inserted in the lower ureter to outline the ureter and renal collecting system). However, for all patients with haematuria (VH and NVH) it detects (its sensitivity) only 65 per cent of all urological tumours. In 98 per cent of cases it accurately defines cancer as cancer (specificity) only rarely defining a benign lesion as a cancer (2 per cent false positive rate)[2]. For all types of haematuria (VH and NVH) it misses 40 per cent of bladder tumours (because many such tumours are too small to be radiologically visible).

1 Cowan, Turney, Taylor (et al) 'Multidetector computed tomography urography for diagnosing upper urinary tract urothelial tumours' (2007) 99 BJU Int 1363–1370.
2 Sudakoff, Dunn, Guralnick (et al) 'Multidetector computed tomography urography as the primary imaging modality for detecting urinary tract neoplasms in patients with asymptomatic hematuria' (2008) 179 J Urol 862–867.

34.32   So, the role of MDCTU in the investigation of haematuria remains controversial. Targeting MDCTU at those at higher risk of urological cancer (aged less than 40, smokers, occupational exposure to benzenes and aromatic amines) may represent the best use of this expensive, high radiation resource. But watch this space as CT imaging becomes evermore sophisticated.

Should patients with a-NVH undergo cystoscopy?

34.33   The American Urological Association (AUA)'s *Best Practice Policy on Asymptomatic Microscopic Hematuria*[1] recommends cystoscopy in all high-risk patients (high risk for development of TCC) with microscopic haematuria (the AUA still uses the term 'microscopic' haematuria): so for example smokers, those with occupational exposure to chemicals or dyes (all of which cause bladder cancer).

1 http://www.auanet.org/education/guidelines/asymptomatic-microhematuria.cfm.

34.34 For the low-risk patient with a-NVH the AUA recommends that 'it may be appropriate to defer cystoscopy', but if so urine should be sent for cytology and it concludes 'the decision as to when to proceed with cystoscopy in low-risk patients with persistent microscopic haematuria must be made on an individual basis after a careful discussion between the patient and physician'.

34.35 Deferring cystoscopy may be deemed reasonable if patients are informed that there is a possibility, albeit low, of finding a bladder cancer. The decision therefore become theirs, based on the information necessary to allow them to make an informed choice.

Further investigation after a normal cystoscopy and CTU?

34.36 If no cause for VH or NVH is found, some recommend proceeding to retrograde ureterography or ureteroscopic examination of the ureters and renal pelvis, quoting studies that show ureteric or renal transitional carcinoma being found in a small proportion of patients. Such investigations are themselves not free from potential harm and their diagnostic yield is low, so other urologists argue that further testing is not required, quoting the absence of development of overt urological cancer with prolonged (two to four year) follow-up[1].

1 Mishriki 'Diagnosis of urologic malignancies in patients with asymptomatic dipstick haematuria: prospective study with 13 year's follow-up' (2008) 71 Urology 13–163.

34.37 Very few patients with persistent dipstick or microscopic haematuria, in the absence of visible haematuria, will have additional significant urological or nephrological pathology (such as IgA nephropathy) identified[1].

1 Grossfeld 'Evaluation of asymptomatic microscopic hematuria in adults: the American Urological Association Best Practice Policy-Part II: patient evaluation, cytology, voided markers, imaging, cystoscopy, nephrology evaluation and follow-up' (2001) 57 Urology 604–610.

34.38 The AUA's *Best Practice Policy on Asymptomatic Microscopic Hematuria* advises repeat urinalysis, urine cytology, and BP measurement at 6, 12, 24, and 36 months, with repeat imaging and cystoscopy where dipstick or microscopic haematuria persists.

PROSTATE CANCER

34.39 An allegation of failure to diagnose prostate cancer when at an early, curable stage is a frequent request for an expert urological opinion.

The diagnostic problem facing the GP is that men with lower urinary tract symptoms and prostate cancer reside within an ocean of similar men with benign prostatic hyperplasia (BPH, which causes benign enlargement of the prostate) and are not easy to detect and the clinical examination of the prostate and the tests (serum prostate specific antigen, PSA) have diagnostic inaccuracies. The PSA blood test lacks specificity (so a positive – elevated – PSA may be falsely positive, ie due to a non-cancerous cause) and sensitivity (so a PSA within the 'normal' range, even adjusted for age, may be a false negative, a cancer being present when the normal test results suggests it is not).

34.40   A digital rectal examination (DRE) and PSA should be done after counselling with regard to the implications: (a) false negatives and false positives occur with both; (b) if a man is a candidate for prostate cancer treatment (he should, as a general rule of thumb, have a life expectancy of 15 years in order to benefit – from 'added years' – from aggressive prostate cancer therapy; this criterion is a reflection of the slow growth rate of prostate cancer in many men); and (c) if he wishes to know whether or not he has prostate cancer.

34.41   GPs should consider the possibility of prostate cancer not only in men with lower urinary tract symptoms (LUTS), but also in those with erectile dysfunction, haematuria, lower back pain, bone pain or weight loss. Urgent referral (a two week cancer referral) is required, according to NICE[1] if their prostate feels malignant on digital rectal examination.

NICE also suggests that consideration should be given to doing a PSA test and digital rectal examination to assess for prostate cancer in men with:

- any lower urinary tract symptoms, such as nocturia, urinary frequency, hesitancy, urgency or retention; or
- erectile dysfunction; or
- visible haematuria.

NICE also recommends specialist referral 'using a suspected cancer pathway referral (for an appointment within two weeks) for prostate cancer if their PSA levels are above the age specific reference range'.

1 National Institute for Health and Clinical Excellence (2015) *NG13 Suspected cancer: recognition and referral*. Reproduced with permission.

34.42   The process of diagnosis requires a TRUS biopsy (transrectal ultrasound guided biopsy). An ultrasound probe inserted into the rectum images the prostate and through the probe a biopsy needle is directed into suspicious looking areas of the prostate. This is not without risk, for the needle passes through the rectum which is teeming with bacteria into the prostate, as it samples cores of prostatic tissue. Septicaemia (blood poisoning) occurs in 2 per cent of men. Each hospital will have its own antibiotic prophylaxis policy for TRUS biopsy, based on the bacterial flora of the local population, but even with appropriate antibiotic prophylaxis septicaemia may still develop. In rare cases this may be fatal.

34.43   Further risks include rectal haemorrhage severe enough to require hospitalisation in 1 per cent risk and urinary retention in approximately 2 per cent of men. Nothing can prevent these unpleasant side effects. The BAUS consent form for TRUS biopsy mentions all of these side effects, but in the occasional case there has been a failure to warn[1].

1 http://www.baus.org.uk/Resources/BAUS/Documents/PDF%20Documents/Patient%20 information/TRUSP.pdf.

34.44   TRUS prostatic biopsy may fail to detect a prostate cancer, for it cannot sample every bit of the prostate, so a man with negative biopsies cannot be absolutely reassured that he is free of cancer. The whole unpleasant process may need repeating.

34.45 Once diagnosed, a host of options are available for discussion. Precisely what option a man chooses depends on his age, the predicted aggressiveness of his cancer (only 3 per cent of men die of prostate cancer, but many men in their 70s and beyond have it but die of other causes) and his perception of the risks of each option.

34.46 If he opts for radical prostatectomy, damage to the rectum leading to a rectourethral fistula is a 'rare' (according to BAUS less than 1 in 50 chance – is that rare?) but devastating complication[1]. Rectal damage can occur in the very best of hands and it is not *prima facie* evidence of negligence. If the injury is recognised at the time of radical prostatectomy, repair of the rectum should probably be undertaken by a colorectal surgeon and consideration given to a temporary diverting colostomy. Where no such colostomy is fashioned, and the rectal repair breaks down leading to a rectourethral fistula, the advice of a colorectal expert will clearly be required to determine whether management fell below standard.

1 http://www.baus.org.uk/Resources/BAUS/Documents/PDF%20Documents/Patient%20 information/Prostatectomy_cancer_retropubic.pdf.

VASECTOMY

34.47 Significant bleeding leading to a haematoma requiring further surgery occurs with a frequency of 1 in 10 to 1 in 50, so it cannot be described as rare. It is usually impossible from the operation note to be able to conclude that the operation was carried out negligently (no surgeon deliberately leaves a bleeding vessel unchecked and would certainly not record the fact that he had done so).

34.48 However, a patient may not have been warned of this eventuality and inadequate consent may thus form the foundation for a successful case. More important in terms of frequency, and far more disabling (for in rare cases it may impact on ability to work, and so may have a very significant impact on quantum), is the occurrence of chronic testicular pain, which occurs in 10–30 per cent of men post-vasectomy. Again, consent is crucial and there are certainly men who have declined vasectomy once warned of this potential risk.

34.49 Even in this day and age, when it is so well-known that vasectomy does not guarantee sterility, it is still possible to come across the odd case where no such warning has been given. The patient and his partner must be advised that sufficient specimens of semen must be produced after the operation (and that alternative contraception must be continued) until they have been shown to contain no motile spermatozoa on two consecutive specimens. Viable spermatozoa reside in the seminal vesicles, downstream of the site of division of the sperm transmitting tube, the vas, and these are the source of persistent fertility. So-called early failure of the procedure occurs 1 in 250–500, due to early recanalisation of the vas and late failure occurs in 1 in 4,000 men, due to the same process of rejoining of the ends of the vas ends, after initial negative sperm counts, resulting in pregnancy years later. A failure to warn of any of these risks is regarded as negligent.

LITIGATION IN STONE DISEASE

34.50   Litigation tends to arise as a consequence of complications of treatment and the failure to offer less or indeed non-invasive options.

There are, in broad terms, five options for managing stones: active surveillance (watching and waiting); extracorporeal shock wave lithotripsy (ESWL); ureteroscopic and flexible ureterorenoscopic ablation (using laser lithotripsy or pneumatic lithotripsy); percutaneous nephrolithotomy and open stone surgery. Which option is 'best' is determined by stone location, stone size (stone 'burden') and of course the patient's preferences based on their perception of outcomes and risks.

34.51   As with so much urological surgery, the trend in the last 15–20 years has been away from open surgery and towards telescopic surgery, because recovery times are shorter, morbidity less and stone clearance equivalent or near equivalent.

34.52   For stones that have migrated from the kidney into the ureter, 68 per cent of small ones (< 5 mm) will pass spontaneously (and usually within six weeks) whereas 47 per cent of those 5 mm or greater in maximum dimension will do so[1]. There is no one correct approach, to managing such stones. To a considerable degree local facilities will dictate the options that the urologist will discuss with the patient, for not all centres have ready access to an emergency lithotripsy service. Some patients prefer to watch and wait, accepting that further episodes of pain may occur and that ultimately intervention may be required if the stone fails to pass in a reasonable time frame. Others (perhaps with work commitments) prefer ESWL or ureteroscopy and are willing to accept the potential risks associated with such treatments. The urologist's role is to offer the choices and outline the risks and outcomes of each option.

1 Preminger (et al) 'Guideline for the management of ureteral calculi' (2007) 52 Eur Urol 1610–1631; Parekattil, Kumar, Hegarty (et al) 'External validation of outcome prediction model for ureteral/renal calculi' (2006) 175 J Urol 575.

34.53   A major source of litigation related to stone disease is the injudicious use of stone baskets used to extract fragments of stone from the ureter (or from the kidney using a flexible ureteroscope). The complex of stone and basket may become stuck in the ureter, if too large a fragment is removed. The ureter is a delicate and therefore unforgiving organ and the inexperienced surgeon may (negligently so) pull too hard and either tear a hole in the side of the ureter, or worse still, avulse the whole ureter. This is a very serious injury indeed and complex reconstructive surgery or even loss of the kidney often follow. Such cases are difficult to defend.

34.54   Options for symptomatic small renal stones (those causing loin pain) include watchful waiting (if the episodes of pain are infrequent), ESWL and flexible ureterorenoscopic laser lithotripsy As a general rule large stones (>1cm or thereabouts in diameter) require treatment, since they are less likely to follow an indolent course, but patient factors such as advanced age, co-morbidity, etc may dictate a watch and wait approach.

34.55 If followed over five years, approximately 70–80 per cent of small asymptomatic renal stones (<1cm in size) remain so and for this reason, especially for the older patient, with co-morbidity, the option of long-term watchful waiting is an appealing one which patients should be offered. Some younger patients may also prefer to watch and wait, if offered the choice.

34.56 While ESWL does not require an anaesthetic and is done as a day case procedure, and is therefore generally considered a benign, complication-free procedure, very occasionally severe complications can occur. The BAUS consent form for ESWL[1] outlines 'Severe infection requiring intravenous antibiotics (less than 1 per cent) and sometimes drainage of the kidney by a small drain placed through the back into the kidney'. Septicaemia after ESWL is very unusual, but it is a serious condition, and the BAUS standard is to warn patients of its possible occurrence.

1 http://www.baus.org.uk/Resources/BAUS/Documents/PDF%20Documents/Patient%20 information/ESWL.pdf.

34.57 Very occasionally cases of very severe bleeding following ESWL occur, though these are rare, due to the shock waves rupturing a branch of a renal artery. The consequences can be devastating. Such an occurrence is probably unavoidable, but such cases serve as a reminder the urologist should emphasise that ESWL is not a benign, complication-free option (though BAUS does not indicate that patients should be warned of such a risk). After all, if the shock waves are powerful enough to fragment a hard stone within the kidney, it should come as no surprise (to urologist or patient) that collateral damage can occur.

34.58 The American Urological Association Antibiotic Prophylaxis Guidelines of 2008[1] and the European Association of Urology Guidelines on Urological Infections of 2013[2] provide conflicting advice on whether antibiotic prophylaxis should be administered before ESWL. The EAU says:

'No standard prophylaxis is recommended. However, prophylaxis is recommended in cases of internal stent … due to the increased bacterial burden (eg indwelling catheter, nephrostomy tube, or infectious stones)'.

The AUA Guidelines state that prophylaxis is indicated in all patients, this recommendation being based on a meta-analysis of eight RCTs which:

'demonstrated a benefit of therapy in significantly reducing the incidence of postoperative bacteriuria from a median of 5.7 per cent to 2.1 per cent, even with preoperative urine showing no growth'[3].

1 http://www.auanet.org/education/guidelines/antimicrobial-prophylaxis.cfm.
2 http://www.uroweb.org/gls/pdf/18_Urological%20infections_LR.pdf.
3 Pearle, Roehrborn 'Antimicrobial prophylaxis prior to shock wave lithotripsy in patients with sterile urine before treatment: a meta-analysis and cost-effectiveness analysis' (1997) 49 Urology 679–686.

34.59 Ureteric stones in pregnancy present a very significant challenge. The term 'ureteric stones' is used, but in fact many pregnant women with loin pain who are *presumed* to have stones do not. The range of diagnostic tests able to be performed on pregnant women is limited (CT scanning) because of concerns over irradiating the fetus, and so a presumptive diagnosis (based on imperfect imaging and symptoms) must often be made. Ultrasound scanning is useless at identifying ureteric stones and most women have dilated ureters in later pregnancy (due to the muscle-relaxing effects of progesterone and the obstructive effect of the enlarging fetus compressing the ureter) so the presence of so-called hydroureteronephrosis (a dilated ureter and renal collecting system) which in the non-pregnant individual often implies distal obstruction from a stone, is of no diagnostic value in late pregnancy. Specialists are left then with the unsatisfactory situation of having to make the diagnosis based on symptoms alone (which get it wrong 50 per cent of the time) and of having to consider invasive treatment, with its very significant potential risks, where there may be no stone.

34.60 In such a situation one often feels damned if one does intervene and damned if one doesn't intervene in the pregnant woman with a suspected ureteric stone. Not to intervene with ureteroscopy, J stenting or insertion of a nephrostomy for an obstructing ureteric stone risks premature labour and so the birth of an infant at risk of severe sequelae (eg hypoxic brain damage). However, intervening with ureteroscopy (and to a lesser extent with J stenting) also risks inducing premature labour. So the stakes are high and, as a consequence, managing a pregnant woman with loin pain is never something a urologist will approach other than with anxiety. It is to be realised that dogmatic recommendations in both a clinical and medico-legal context should be avoided.

34.61 No one option (nephrostomy, J stent or ureteroscopy) can be regarded as the 'correct' option and this is why in *Campbell-Walsh Urology* it is concluded that[1]:

'When treatment is selected it should be recognized that there is some controversy regarding the most appropriate method of intervention'.

1 Matlaga, Lingeman 'Surgical Management of Upper Urinary Tract Calculi' in *Campbell-Walsh Urology* (10th edn, 2012) p 1381.

34.62 The EAU Guidelines summarise management of the pregnant woman with loin pain as follows[1]:

'If intervention becomes necessary, placement of a ureteral stent or a percutaneous nephrostomy tube are readily available primary options ... Ureteroscopy is a reasonable alternative to avoid long-term stenting/drainage ... Conservative management should be the first-line treatment for all non-complicated cases of urolithiasis in pregnancy (except those that have clinical indications for intervention)'.

1 (2013), p 55 at http://www.uroweb.org/gls/pdf/21_Urolithiasis_LRV2.pdf.

URETERIC INJURIES DURING PELVIC OR ABDOMINAL SURGERY

34.63 The determination of whether or not a ureteric injury represents sub-standard surgical technique is a matter for the gynaecology or obstetric expert (in the context of ureteric injury during hysterectomy or Caesarean section) or colorectal expert (in the context of ureteric injury during colectomy). The urology expert is usually called upon to determine the causative effects of such an injury, in terms of loss of renal function, requirement for additional intervention and long term symptoms and what the outcome would have been had the diagnosis been made intra-operatively or earlier in the post-operative period.

34.64 In the case of ureteric injury at hysterectomy, if this has caused obstruction alone, the cardinal symptom will be loin pain. Where a hole has been made in the ureter, urine will leak out from the ureter and find its way through the healing suture line (not yet watertight) used to close the vagina (off the top of which the uterus has been removed). A so-called uretero-vaginal fistula develops. Urine leaking from a hole in the ureter often causes a degree of peri-ureteric oedema and the interruption to the integrity of the ureter often interferes with the transmission of peristaltic waves down the ureter which propel urine formed in the kidney into the bladder. Obstruction (and pain) may therefore co-exist with a uretero-vaginal fistula (and a vaginal urine leak).

34.65 In the case of a ureteric injury at the time of colectomy, excessive fluid output from a drain or once this is removed the development of a collection of urine (a urinoma) in the pelvis (manifesting as a fever or ileus – temporary cessation of intestinal activity with abdominal distension and vomiting) leads to the diagnosis, though it may take several days for the penny to drop.

34.66 As a general rule the best time to repair a ureteric injury is at the time of the surgery that caused it. Patients are spared unpleasant symptoms (pain, vaginal urine leak, pelvic urine collections) and the need for additional investigations and procedures and simpler options (J stenting alone or direct repair of a ureteric injury) often suffice. Delay often adds to the complexity of surgery required to fix the problem.

34.67 While in some patients a period of stenting may suffice to allow ureteric healing, most will require formal ureteric re-implantation into the bladder following diagnosis of a ureteric injury diagnosed post-operatively. The blood supply of the lower ureter, the usual site of injury, is relatively tenuous and a direct ureteric repair may, through lack of blood supply either stenose or break down and leak urine. Re-implantation into the bladder, with its excellent blood supply, allows healing without stricture formation or urine leaks.

34.68 Studies documenting the outcomes of patients managed with J stent insertion are few and far between and describe outcomes in very small numbers of patients. In Ustunsoz's paper[1] 5 of 9 patients (56 per cent) with ureteric disruption or fistulas (leakage of urine from a partial ureteric disruption) were successfully managed by J stenting alone and 13 of 15 patients (87 per cent) with ureteric obstruction were successfully managed by J stenting alone. Of those four patients with a partial ureteric injury (where there was still a degree of continuity between the proximal and distal ureters), all were successfully managed with J stenting alone, even when the diagnosis was delayed by 11 to 49 days. Of those three patients with a complete ureteric injury (where there was no continuity between the proximal and distal ureters), all three required ureteric re-implantation.

1 Ustunsoz (et al) 'Percutaneous management of ureteral injuries that are diagnosed late after Cesarean Section' (2008) 9 Korean J Radiol 348–353.

34.69   So, it seems that the essential factor in determining success of J stenting was not delay in diagnosis, but whether the ureteric injury was partial or complete. If there is a partial ureteric injury then it is often possible to insert a stent, either via a retrograde approach (from the ureter as it enters the bladder) or an antegrade approach (through the kidney from above, by placement of a nephrostomy into the kidney and then a stent via this route, where the retrograde approach has failed). If there is complete ureteric injury we usually fail to pass a stent and even where we are successful, the ureter will usually heal with stricture formation such that a ureteric re-implantation will ultimately be required.

34.70   In Ku's series[1] 30 patients with ureteric injuries post-obstetric or gynaecological surgery were reviewed. Thirteen were managed with re-implantation and 17 endoscopically by stent placement. Eleven of the 17 required no additional treatment and six required re-implantation. So, overall 11/30 (37 per cent) avoided the need for re-implantation. Those patients who were successfully managed with nephrostomy and/or stent placement were diagnosed between 2 to 235 days post-injury (median 42 days), so again it would appear (if one can draw any conclusions from such small numbers) that delay in diagnosis is not the critical factor in determining ability to stent or not, but rather whether an injury is partial or complete.

1 Ku (et al) 'Minimally invasive management of ureteral injuries recognized late after obstetric and gynaecologic surgery' (2003) 34 Injury Int J Care Injured 480–483.

LOWER URINARY TRACT SYMPTOMS (LUTS)

34.71   It is all too easy for the GP to assume that any patient with LUTS has benign prostatic obstruction (if male), an overactive bladder or a simple urinary tract infection.

34.72   Serious pathology presenting with LUTS includes bladder or (in men) prostate cancer, neurological disease (spinal tumours) or other pelvic pathology (pelvic tumours). Additional symptoms are usually present but must be sought by taking a careful history. Has there been blood in the urine, bladder (lower abdominal) pain, pain in the perineum, buttocks or radiating down the legs, erectile or ejaculatory disturbances or odd tingling sensations in the distribution of the pelvic nerves (sacral nerve S2, 3 and 4). Examination of the prostate (does it feel malignant), a focused neurological examination (assessing perineal and lower limb sensation) and testing for haematuria are critical.

TESTICULAR PAIN

34.73   Testicular (scrotal) pain may arise from pathology within the scrotum or from that outwith the testis, the pain being perceived to arise in the scrotum, but in fact being referred from other organs. This phenomenon reflects the embryological origin of the testes from just below the kidneys, whence they descend into the scrotum, bringing with them their blood, lymphatic and nerve supply, the latter thus being derived from exactly the same anatomical level as the kidney, specifically the first lumbar nerves. Thus pain arising from the kidneys may be perceived to arise within the testes and pain arising from the testes may be perceived to arise within the kidneys.

34.74 The two most important causes of testis pain that may lead to litigation are testis torsion and more uncommonly ureteric stones, the issue principally being one of delayed diagnosis leading to loss of the twisted testis or additional pain and morbidity from delayed diagnosis of an obstructing ureteric stone. Approximately 10 per cent of testicular cancers present with pain as well as rapid enlargement of the testis. Very occasionally in such cases infection of the testis and its associated drainage tubules, the epididymis (an epididymo-orchitis) is erroneously diagnosed, leading to a delay in diagnosis of testis cancer.

34.75 The pathophysiology of testis torsion is based on anatomical abnormalities in the testis of some boys and men that allows the testicle to twist on the pedicle through which its blood supply is derived. The venous outflow of blood from the testicle is initially obstructed, thereby impairing inflow of fresh oxygenated blood, and ischaemia develops which, if unrelieved, will lead to infarction.

34.76 Prompt surgical exploration allows detorsion of the testis and re-establishment of blood flow to the testis, thereby allowing the testis to be saved, the testis then being 'fixed' within the scrotum by three sutures such that it can never again become torted. Delayed diagnosis leads to death of the testicle, which must therefore be removed. Since the opposite side may have exactly the same anatomical abnormality, that side too must be fixed.

34.77 Urological lore states that a testis must be detorted within six hours from the symptom onset if the testis is to be saved. This derives from Hellner's 1933 experimental study in dogs[1]. If, through some unnecessary delay a GP, emergency department doctor or more rarely a urologist (since few urologists tend to make this mistake) fails to establish the diagnosis and arrange prompt surgical exploration, then that doctor may be deemed to have been negligent. The delay usually arises as a consequence of an incorrect diagnosis of epididymo-orchitis and the patient is discharged on antibiotics, only to return several days later with ongoing pain. In those cases of suspected testis torsion where an epididymo-orchitis is identified at exploration, usually no harm follows.

1 Hadway, Reynard 'The six-hour rule for testis fixation in testicular torsion: is it history?' (2013) 6 Journal of Clinical Urology 84–88.

34.78 Of course, if for whatever reason the patient delays their attendance, then much of these six hours may be consumed by factors outside the control of the doctor or hospital. It is asking too much of any hospital to arrange review by a surgeon, transfer to an operating theatre and detorsion within one hour, for a patient who arrives at hospital five hours after the onset of pain indicative of torsion. However, where a patient arrives within one hour after the onset of pain, there would have to be some very good excuse why detorsion should not be possible within the next five hours, for it is usually possible for a surgeon to see a patient within one or two hours of their arrival and for a theatre to be made ready and the patient to be anaesthetised in the following one to two hours.

Somewhere in between will be a grey area where breach of duty may be less easily proven.

34.79   Most hospitals run a single emergency operating theatre and if that theatre and theatre team are occupied, a delay in surgery to detort the testis may follow. The correct approach in such a situation is for the admitting urologist to request that a second emergency operating theatre be opened. This is expensive, requiring as it does additional on-call staff to be called in from home and so in these times of austerity there is a reluctance to do so. The requesting surgeon often faces resistance, but they must persevere by explaining the requirement for a second theatre to be opened. Not to do so would be regarded as sub-standard. Written documentation summarising the details of the request, eg 'I have a patient with suspected testicular torsion – you need to open a second theatre', will provide the urological surgeon with a robust defence.

34.80   The problem with the six hour rule from a pathophysiological perspective is that while torsion relieved within six hours of onset of pain will allow 98 per cent of testes to be salvaged (so reaffirming that exploration within six hours is legally safe), almost 90 per cent still remain viable with delays of seven to 12 hours to detorsion. Only beyond 12 hours does the salvage rate really drop off, with only 25 per cent of testes remaining viable after 12–16 hours of torsion[1].

1 Hadway, Reynard 'The six-hour rule for testis fixation in testicular torsion: is it history?' (2013) 6 Journal of Clinical Urology 84–88.

34.81   What of delays in detorsion of six to eight hours? Should the six-hour rule be religiously applied, based as it is on experimental data in dogs, as the benchmark against which delays in exploration are deemed to be negligent or not, when clinical data suggests relatively high salvage rates in humans with slightly longer delays? It is not possible to give a simple answer, save to say that as long as the doctors (GP, emergency department or urologist) have made reasonable efforts to minimise delays once a patient comes under their care, in the ways outlined above, and allowing for uncontrollable delays prior to the patient seeking medical advice, many experts would not necessarily be critical where the delay extended beyond six hours. Each case will, obviously, be judged on its merits.

INJURIES TO THE BLADDER: BLADDER PERFORATION AND DISTENSION INJURIES

34.82   Every urologist will, from time to time, perforate a bladder during a transurethral resection of a bladder tumour or bladder biopsy. The bladder is relatively thin, especially in elderly women. During attempts to adequately resect a bladder tumour (adequate meaning to provide a deep enough biopsy that the extent of invasion of the tumour into the bladder muscle can be assessed) a hole may be created in the bladder. This may not represent negligence, nor necessarily does failing to immediately (intra-operatively) recognise it.

34.83   Where the urologist may legitimately be criticised is in failing to recognise such an injury post-operatively. Lower abdominal pain, poor urine output, abdominal distension and abdominal tenderness are the signs that the urologist should look for. Failing to do so in the context of any procedure where a hole may be made in the bladder and where the patient is unwell post-operatively, would generally be regarded as negligent.

34.84   With any combination of those symptoms where a catheter has not been left in place after the primary procedure, one should be inserted and a cystogram should be done. This involves direct instillation of radiological contrast fluid into the bladder, *under pressure*, with radiological screening to determine if leakage of contrast occurs. If the leak of contrast is confined to the tissues immediately around the bladder (a so-called extraperitoneal perforation) all that is required is a period of several weeks of catheter drainage, for spontaneous healing to occur. If, however, loops of bowel are outlined by the contrast, the perforation is intraperitoneal. The safe approach is laparotomy to repair the hole in the bladder, but as importantly if not more so, to allow careful examination of the bowel, a loop of which adjacent to the bladder may also have been perforated.

34.85   Sometimes there will be gross abdominal distension in a case of extraperitoneal perforation, by way of transudation of fluid which has accumulated in the extraperitoneal space around the bladder into the intraperitoneal cavity. This may compromise respiration by effectively splinting the diaphragm, or lead to concern that there may be an intraperitoneal perforation. In such cases a laparotomy will allow drainage of the fluid and confirmation that there is no intraperitoneal perforation or bowel injury.

The impact of gynaecological or obstetric bladder perforation (development of a VVF) has already been discussed.

34.86   A surprisingly frequent source of litigation arises as a consequence of distension injuries to the bladder. Deliberate distension of the bladder has been used for the management of symptoms of bladder overactivity (and indeed BAUS still publishes a consent form detailing its risks, effectively endorsing this as a treatment option). This is regarded by some as a somewhat antiquated treatment for bladder overactivity in the era of bladder botulinum toxin injections. The scenarios include overdistension of the bladder in the post-partum period, especially in the context of a forceps delivery and regional (epidural) anaesthesia, and following other surgical procedures where inadequate (sub-standard) monitoring of urine output belies incomplete bladder emptying with increasing distension of the bladder.

ADULT CIRCUMCISION

34.87   For such a 'simple' operation, circumcision is a source of a disproportionate amount of problems for patients and surgeons alike. One only has to read the BAUS consent form to appreciate the list of risks and poor outcomes that may follow[1]:

Common (greater than 1 in 10):

• swelling of the penis lasting several days.

Occasional (between 1 in 10 and 1 in 50):

• bleeding of the wound occasionally needing a further procedure;
• infection of the incision requiring further treatment and/or casualty visit;
• permanent altered or reduced sensation in the head of the penis;
• persistence of the absorbable stitches after 3–4 weeks, requiring removal.

Rare (less than 1 in 50):

• scar tenderness;
• failure to be completely satisfied with the cosmetic result;
• occasional need for removal of excessive skin at a later date;
• permission for biopsy of abnormal area on the head of the penis if malignancy is a concern.

1 http://www.baus.org.uk/Resources/BAUS/Documents/PDF%20Documents/Patient%20 information/Circumcision.pdf.

34.88 Poor cosmetic outcomes after circumcision are hardly surprising when one considers that circumcision is indicated for so-called balanitis xerotica obliterans (BXO), an inflammatory condition that may literally plaster the foreskin to the glans of the penis, obstructing the flow of urine (a so-called phimosis, which is the reason why circumcision must be undertaken).

34.89 As noted in the BAUS consent form, significant bleeding leading to a haematoma requiring further surgery occurs from time to time. As with vasectomy it is usually impossible from the operation note to be able to conclude that the operation was carried out negligently. As with vasectomy no surgeon deliberately leaves a bleeding vessel unchecked. Small vessels may go into spasm and bleeding may only declare itself some hours after the operation.

34.90 A surprising number of men report permanent altered or reduced sensation in the head of the penis after circumcision[1]. Some regard this as a benefit (they last longer during sex), whereas others are disappointed by the reduction in sensation.

1 Bronselaer, Schober, Meyer-Bahlburg, T'Sjoen, Vlietinck, Hoebeke 'Male circumcision decreases penile sensitivity as measured in a large cohort' (2013) 111 BJU International 820–827; Fink, Carson, DeVellis 'Adult circumcision outcomes study: effect on erectile function, penile sensitivity, sexual activity and satisfaction' (2002) 167 J Urol 2113–2116.

34.91 As with so many procedures, the process of warning a patient that circumcision is not the simple procedure that it might appear on face value to be and that it has certain important potential implications, could offset the risk of litigation that often follows unexpected post-operative developments.

BLADDER CARCINOMA

34.92   GP delays in referral of patients with haematuria is a common request for an expert urology opinion regarding the impact such delays have had on the need for more aggressive treatment than would otherwise have been required, or on prognosis.

34.93   The dominant form of bladder cancer is transitional cell carcinoma and at presentation this can be broadly categorised into superficial and muscle invasive variants. Muscle invasive bladder cancer requires radical radiotherapy (many suffer long-term side effects and cure is not always effected) or radical cystoprostatectomy (profoundly life changing, as many require diversion of their urine into a stoma – an ileal conduit – and most men are impotent).

34.94   While many patients with superficial bladder cancer experience recurrent superficial tumours throughout their lives, some superficial tumours may advance to invade the muscle of the bladder and hence to require radiotherapy or cystoprostatectomy.

34.95   The instillation of BCG (a deactivated form of the TB bacillus) into the bladder stimulates an immune reaction, which not only kills the TB bacteria, but also kills bladder cancer cells. This is so-called intravesical immunotherapy. Its use is recommended by the EAU and AUA in tumours at high risk of recurrence or progression to more advanced disease. However, if through a delay in referral of a patient with haematuria their bladder cancer is not diagnosed while still in its superficial phase, this delay may cause a lost opportunity for administration of BCG immunotherapy. The tumour may advance to invade the bladder muscle and hence the opportunity for preservation of the bladder (and of sexual function) will be lost.

34.96   Whether BCG genuinely reduces the requirement for cystoprostatectomy remains controversial. The European Association of Urology Guidelines (2007) state '… controversy existed until recently as to whether BCG could delay or prevent progression to muscle-invasive disease'. This statement was based on a meta-analysis carried out by the EORTC (European Organisation for Research and Treatment of Cancer) by Sylvester[1] which showed that 260 of 2,658 patients on BCG (9.8 per cent) had progression compared to 304 of 2,205 patients in the control groups in which no BCG was administered (13.8 per cent), a reduction of 27 per cent in the odds of progression on BCG. Thus, in relative terms BCG reduces the risk of progression by just over one quarter, but in absolute terms (and the bottom line is absolute risk reduction, whatever clinical trial you are appraising) BCG results in a 4 per cent difference in progression rate between those who receive BCG and those who do not. Many would argue that statistically significant though that might be, it is hardly an impressive reduction in risk.

1 Sylvester, van der Meijden, Lamm 'Intravesical bacillus Calmette-Guerin reduces the risk of progression in patients with superficial bladder cancer: a meta-analysis of the published results of randomized clinical trials' (2002) 168(5) J Urol 1964–1970.

34.97   To complicate the issue yet further, conversely a later meta-analysis of trials by Böhle[1] reported no benefit of BCG over conventional intravesical chemotherapy, 7.7 per cent of patients in the BCG group progressing to muscle invasive disease compared with 9.4 per cent in the mitomcyin C group (mitomycin is a chemotherapeutic drug which when instilled into the bladder kills cancer cells), a difference which did not reach statistical significance.

1 Böhle, Bock 'Intravesical bacillus Calmette-Guerin versus mitomycin C in superficial bladder cancer: formal meta-analysis of comparative studies on tumor progression' (2004) 63(4) Urology 682–687.

34.98   In answer to the question 'What is the effect on recurrence and progression of TURBT combined with an induction course of intravesical BCG versus TURBT combined with an induction course of intravesical BCG and maintenance BCG therapy?' the AUA 'Guideline for the Management of Non-muscle Invasive Bladder Cancer (Stages Ta, T1, and Tis): 2007 Update'[1] concluded:

'… the literature and the current meta-analysis support the use of an induction course of intravesical BCG combined with maintenance BCG therapy as compared to an induction course of BCG alone to decrease recurrence and *possibly* progression in patients with higher-risk non-muscle invasive bladder tumors'. [author's emphasis]

1 AUA Guideline for the Management of Non-muscle Invasive Bladder Cancer (Stages Ta, T1, and Tis): 2007 Update. Hall MC 2007 https://www.auanet.org/education/guidelines/bladder-cancer.cfm.

34.99   Perhaps most importantly, Jones and Larchian writing in the 10th Edition of *Campbell-Walsh Urology*[1], state that the 'apparent advantage [of BCG in reducing progression] is temporary in many cases'. Many patients, whether they receive BCG or not, are destined to lose their bladders.

1 Jones, Larchian 'Non-muscle invasive bladder cancer (Ta, T1 and CIS)' in *Campbell-Walsh Urology* (10th edn, 2012) p 2344.

34.100   Cookson and colleagues from the world-renowned Memorial Sloan-Kettering Cancer Center, New York[1] studied the long-term outcome of patients with high risk superficial bladder cancer treated with aggressive transurethral resection alone or combined with intravesical BCG (the majority – 76 per cent – receiving BCG). At 15 years follow-up in a group of 86 patients, 76 per cent of whom received BCG therapy, 32 of 86 (37 per cent) were alive, 29 of 86 (34 per cent) had died of bladder cancer and only 23 of 86 (27 per cent) had an intact functioning bladder.

1 Cookson, Herr, Zhang (et al) 'Natural history of high risk superficial bladder cancer' (1997) 158 J Urol 62–67.

34.101   So, whether progression to muscle invasive disease (and so loss of the bladder) is caused by delays in referral of patients presenting to their GPs with haematuria, because of the lost opportunity to treat aggressive superficial bladder cancer with BCG, is not a simple question to answer.

RECONSTRUCTIVE UROLOGY

34.102   Following hysterectomy, and occasionally Caesarean section, an injury to the bladder may occur (and in the case of hysterectomy the urethra also), especially where previous surgery has led to obliteration of the normal tissue plane between the vagina and bladder (the bladder and vagina literally become stuck together by scar tissue and dissection of the uterus during hysterectomy or incision of the uterus during Caesarean section can lead to inadvertent bladder injury).

34.103 If recognised at the time of surgery, the bladder should be repaired. If the injury is not recognised at the time of surgery, or where the repair breaks down, urine may leak from the bladder and find its way through the vaginal closure (post-hysterectomy) or uterine closure (post-caesarean section). A fistulous communication between the two organs develops (a fistula being a communication between two epithelial lined organs). A VVF (vesico-vaginal fistula) may also occur as a consequence of incorrect placement of sutures through the back wall of the bladder during closure of the vaginal cuff at the time of hysterectomy or following the application of diathermy to the bladder. Tissue necrosis may occur around the sutures or at the site of diathermy, leading to development of a fistula between the bladder and the vagina.

34.104 Such fistulas will, generally speaking, never close (other than in a few cases diagnosed early and where the urine is diverted away from the fistula by placement of a catheter) and the woman is left in a constant state of urinary incontinence - a most miserable condition. The patient will often sue.

34.105 The medico-legal issues are whether the initial bladder injury have occurred in the first place. Did poor surgical technique cause the VVF (a question for the expert obstetrician or gynaecologist)? Who should repair the bladder if an injury is identified at the time of the initial operation (obstetrician, gynaecologist or urologist)? Was the technique used of an appropriate standard? And if a VVF develops, where should it be repaired and by whom? (by a gynaecologist or urologist?; in a general hospital or regional referral centre?).

34.106 Whether it is acceptable for an obstetrician or gynaecologist to repair an intra-operative bladder injury depends on their experience. The experienced obstetrician and gynaecologist may have successfully repaired more bladders than the newly-appointed (inexperienced) consultant urologist and may be able to prove as much (with audit data).

34.107 A carefully documented operative note will assist the defence. It should detail the use of a continuous suture technique, placement of omentum between the bladder and vagina (a well-vascularised pedicle of tissue which optimises the chances of healing) and placement of a drain (to allow free drainage of fluid that – inevitably – leaks from the bladder while it is healing), thereby discouraging localised infection which is a contributory factor that may lead to breakdown of the repair.

34.108 When identified early after the operation that caused it, a VVF may heal with catheter drainage alone. Hilton[1] reported that 7 per cent of urogenital fistulae closed without the need for surgery with catheter drainage alone. Bazi[2] concluded:

'Among all factors possibly affecting success of bladder drainage as an exclusive therapy for the VVF, the interval period between the causative insult and initiation of drainage seems to be the most significant ... When the catheter was inserted less than 3 weeks following the initial insult, 22 (39 per cent) of 57 women had spontaneous VVF closure. In contrast, when the catheter was inserted more than 6 weeks after the insult, only 1 (3 per cent) of 32 VVF spontaneously healed'.

So, delays in diagnosis can impact on the chance of requiring complex surgery.

1 Hilton 'Vesico-vaginal fistula: new perspectives' (2001) Oct 13(5) Curr Opin Obstet Gynecol 513–520.
2 Bazi 'Spontaneous closure of vesicovaginal fistulas after bladder drainage alone: review of the evidence' (2007) 18(3) Int Urogynecol J Pelvic Floor Dysfunct 329–333.

34.109 For an established VVF, the move is away from repair by the occasional fistula surgeon towards that done by the sub-specialist with experience in such surgery. Such services are increasingly being concentrated in regional centres, a move led by Specialised Services Commissioning. The 'Complex Gynaecological Services CRG (Clinical Reference Groups) service specifications state 'The arguments for centralisation of services for fistula management are overwhelming and data indicates that probably only three centres are required in England to manage lower urinary fistulae'[1].

1 http://www.england.nhs.uk/wp-content/uploads/2013/06/e10-comp-gynae-urin-fistulae.pdf.

34.110 The rationale of Specialised Services Commissioning is 'to bring equity and excellence to the provision of specialised care and treatment. This is achieved through a commissioning process which is ... outcome based'[1].

1 http://www.england.nhs.uk/ourwork/commissioning/spec-services.

34.111 In the case of VVF repair, this recommendation is based on the view that 'Maintenance of skill requires the regular and consistent involvement in the management of a range of gynaecological and urological conditions, and a minimum of three and optimally ten cases of lower urinary tract fistula per year'[1]. The experience of surgeons and their outcomes show a clear advantage to the woman operated on by the experienced surgeon. In a recent review 281 teams performed just a single VVF repair, only ten consultant teams performed a mean of >3 per year, 1 in 9 women required re-operation after surgical repair of a urogenital fistula, and those units undertaking >30 procedures over 10 years had a significantly lower re-operation rate (7.4 per cent) than those undertaking lower numbers (13.2 per cent).

1 Cromwell, Hilton 'Retrospective cohort study on patterns of care and outcomes of surgical treatment for lower urinary-genital tract fistula among English National Health Service hospitals between 2000 and 2009' (2013) 111 BJU Int E257–262.

34.112 So, who should repair a VVF and where it should be repaired are questions in evolution at the time of writing this chapter, but the writing is on the wall for the occasional surgeon[1]. Many urologists and gynaecologists are already referring VVFs and other complex gynaecological fistula work to specialist centres. In cases of failed primary VVF repair, the barrister should ask why such a referral was not made, how the surgeon's outcomes compared with those from the specialist centres and therefore if it was reasonable for that surgeon to have attempted the repair.

1 Hilton, Cromwell 'The risk of vesicovaginal and urethrovaginal fistula after hysterectomy performed in the English National Health Service – a retrospective cohort study examining patterns of care between 2000 and 2008' (2012) 119 BJOG 1447–1454.

RENAL CELL CARCINOMA (RCC)

34.113   There is increasing interest in drug treatments for metastatic RCC (that which has spread to lymph nodes or more distant sites), but such treatment 'buys' just a few additional months of life in some individuals and at the cost of not insignificant side effects. The mainstay of treatment, aimed at cure where there is no overt spread of the cancer outside the kidney, remains surgery in the form of so-called radical nephrectomy. This may take the form of radical or partial nephrectomy, ie surgical removal of the kidney or that part of the kidney containing the tumour.

34.114   Once removed, pathological examination of the tumour, combined with pre-operative radiological imaging, allows staging of the cancer, according to the TNM system of cancer staging. Cancer stage is crucial in determining prognosis.

Renal cancer staging (TNM system)

34.115

Stage	
T1	Tumour <7cm in greatest dimension T1a <4cm T1b >4cm
T2	Tumour >7cm
T3	T3a Tumour extends into major veins or directly invades adrenal gland or perinephric tissues but not beyond Gerota's fascia T3b Tumour extends into renal vein or vena cava below diaphragm T3c Tumour extends into vena cava above diaphragm
T4	Tumour invades beyond Gerota's fascia
N0	No regional nodes
N1	Metastasis in a single regional lymph node
N2	Metastasis in more than one regional lymph node
M0	No distant metastasis
M1	Distant metastasis

As a generalisation, patients with T1 tumours (< 7cm in greatest dimension) do well; those with T2 tumours (tumour > 7cm) do well, but less so than T1 tumours; whereas those with T3 (extending into major veins or invading the adrenal gland or perinephric tissues) and T4 tumours (invades beyond Gerota's fascia) have a significantly poorer prognosis, many dying of metastatic RCC within five years.

34.116 The management of RCC has witnessed a significant evolution in the last 5–10 years or so. The principal changes are:

(1) a move away from radical nephrectomy (removing the whole kidney) towards partial nephrectomy, the rationale being to preserve as much renal function as possible, thereby limiting the impact of loss of renal function on the development of cardiovascular disease (impaired renal function is an independent risk factor for cardiovascular disease);

(2) a move towards a more conservative approach for small renal masses, with biopsy in selected cases and observation ('active surveillance') rather than immediate nephrectomy, the rationale being that many small RCCs will follow an indolent course (with a minimum two year follow-up of 178 renal masses, presumed to RCCs on their radiological appearance, 12 per cent grew to greater than 4cm and 1.1 per cent metastasised[1]);

(3) a move towards a laparoscopic as opposed to open surgical approach.

There are areas of controversy in the management of RCC, where experts may have conflicting opinions.

1 Jewett, Mattar, Basiuk (et al) 'Active surveillance of small renal masses: progression patterns of early stage renal cancer' (2011) 60 Eur Urol 39–44.

Which operation should a patient get? Partial versus radical nephrectomy

34.117 The line between when a partial as opposed to radical nephrectomy is indicated is a fine one and will be determined by the skill and confidence of the surgeon that he can perform this complex surgery and their outcomes in terms of cure and morbidity. Some surgeons are especially skilled in doing partial nephrectomy, but the standard of care is determined by the average surgeon and the expert witness must be mindful of this. So, while in the most recent edition of the *Oxford Handbook of Urology*[1] it is stated 'Robotic assisted or laparoscopic partial nephrectomy is becoming the standard approach in centres with expertise for small peripheral RCC', this 'standard' approach in centres of expertise does not equate to the standard of care across the UK. Whether all patients should be managed in *specialised* centres capable of offering laparoscopic partial nephrectomy, is an area of potential controversy. The move (not yet achieved) towards centralisation of urological cancer services in hospitals employing a number of renal cancer surgeons capable of offering all options, will accelerate the move towards laparoscopic partial nephrectomy becoming the standard approach.

1 'Renal Cell Carcinoma (Localized): Surgical Treatment' in Reynard, Brewster, Biers *Oxford Handbook of Urology* (2013) p 254.

Should patients be offered alternatives to surgery?

34.118 The role of less invasive options (such as cryotherapy (literally freezing the tumour with a probe) or radiofrequency ablation (destroying the tumour by a heating effect)), and whether they can achieve equivalent outcomes in terms of cure with genuinely lower morbidity and who (the less fit patient or maybe all patients?) should be offered such approaches, remain areas of research. Until these questions have been answered, patients should only be offered such options within the context of a clinical trial.

Loss of a kidney for benign disease

34.119 Not all small (indeed not all large) renal masses are cancers. Of 2,935 solid renal tumours treated over a 30 year period, 12.8 per cent were benign and 87.2 per cent were malignant[1]. For those tumours <1 cm in diameter, 46.3 per cent were benign. Of the 250 tumours <2 cm in diameter 30 per cent were benign. So, as tumour size increases, there is a significantly greater probability of malignant as opposed to benign pathology (and of a high-grade as opposed to low-grade RCC).

1 Frank, Blute, Cheville, Lohse, Weaver, Zincke 'Solid renal tumors: an analysis of pathological features related to tumor size' (2003) 170 J Urol 2217–2220.

34.120 So, removing all renal masses either by partial or radical nephrectomy risks overtreatment and potential morbidity in those where subsequent histology demonstrates a benign lesion. Conversely, assuming that a tumour is benign because it is small, risks leaving a ticking time bomb in the patient, that may metastasize even while still small.

34.121 Of all the areas of controversy in management of suspected RCC, in litigation terms this is perhaps the most significant one, for removing a kidney for a benign lesion is now said to be the commonest source of litigation after nephrectomy[1].

1 Osman, Collins 'Urological litigation in the UK National Health Service (NHS): an analysis of 14 years of successful claims' (2011) 108 BJU Int 162–165.

34.122 Biopsy has not formed part of the traditional diagnostic work-up in suspected renal cancer, principally because of sampling error concerns, ie will the biopsy hit the malignant part of the tumour and obtain an adequate sample to allow the pathologist to determine, with certainty, that the mass is benign or malignant (even in centres of excellence biopsy is non-diagnostic in 33 per cent of cases[1]). A benign biopsy does not exclude the possibility of cancer cells elsewhere in the mass. Occasionally a biopsy may assist in the choice of treatment, where for example imaging suggests the possibility of bilateral renal cancer.

1 Jewett, Mattar, Basiuk (et al) 'Active surveillance of small renal masses: progression patterns of early stage renal cancer' (2011) 60 Eur Urol 39–44.

34.123 The traditional indication for renal biopsy has been to determine if a renal tumour is: (a) metastatic (where nephrectomy would not be appropriate) or a primary tumour (where nephrectomy would potentially be appropriate); or (b) where a lymphoma is suspected (based on radiological appearances) where systemic chemotherapy, and not nephrectomy, is the appropriate approach to therapy. The advent of ablative therapies (radiofrequency ablation or cryotherapy) has widened the indication for renal biopsy, though more for defining treatment success or failure in the setting of research studies.

Delays in diagnosis of RCC and causation

34.124 Delays in diagnosis of RCC not surprisingly leads to litigation in a proportion of cases and a question that is often posed to the urologist expert is, what was the stage at first presentation, and therefore in causation terms what impact has any delay in diagnosis had on survival (was the prospect of cure lost) or morbidity (was a radical nephrectomy required where a partial nephrectomy may have been possible with earlier diagnosis)?

34.125 While our understanding of tumour biology (growth characteristics, metastatic potential) is improving, partly based on recent observational studies of small renal masses, accurate prediction of the stage months or years previously is difficult. The problem, of course, is that the rate of growth and the risk of metastasis of RCCs is not uniform from tumour to tumour. The best current evidence (and this may change as data accumulates) suggests a growth rate for T1a lesion (starting at <4cm in size) in the order of 0.2 to 0.4 cm per year[1].

1 Chawla (et al) 'The Natural History of Observed Enhancing Renal Masses: Meta-Analysis and Review of the World Literature' (2006) 175 J Urol 425–431; Mason, Abdolell, Trottier (et al) 'Growth kinetics of renal masses: analysis of a prospective cohort of patients undergoing active surveillance' (2011) 59 Eur Urol 863–867; Rosales, Haramis, Moreno (et al) 'Active surveillance for renal cortical neoplasms' (2010) 183 J Urol 1698–1702; Youssif (et al) 'Active surveillance for selected patients with renal masses: updated results with long-term follow-up' (2007) 110 Cancer 1010–1014.

34.126 Prediction of tumour stage some years earlier can also be determined by the metastatic potential of small RCCs (T1a). A number of studies with average follow-up of 30–48 months reported *de novo* development of metastatic RCC in 1–6 per cent of individuals[1]. One can extrapolate that a patient with presenting metastatic disease at a certain point in time, very probably did not have a T1a RCC 3–4 years earlier, but rather was likely to have had more advanced disease. Determining other stages of disease at certain points in time is more difficult.

1 Chawla (et al) 'The Natural History of Observed Enhancing Renal Masses: Meta-Analysis and Review of the World Literature' (2006) 175 J Urol 425–431; Mason, Abdolell, Trottier (et al) 'Growth kinetics of renal masses: analysis of a prospective cohort of patients undergoing active surveillance' (2011) 59 Eur Urol 863–867; Rosales, Haramis, Moreno (et al) 'Active surveillance for renal cortical neoplasms' (2010) 183 J Urol 1698–1702; Youssif (et al) 'Active surveillance for selected patients with renal masses: updated results with long-term follow-up' (2007) 110 Cancer 1010–1014.

34.127 Nowadays more than 50 per cent of renal cell carcinomas (RCCs) present incidentally; diagnosed on a scan done for some other unrelated reason. The classic triad of haematuria, flank pain and a flank mass is an increasingly less frequent mode of presentation. Whether a patient was symptomatic or not at presentation can also provide a predictor of stage at that point in time. Not surprisingly patients with symptoms of RCC (visible blood in the urine, kidney pain) are more likely to have more advanced disease than are those undergoing a scan for non-urological symptoms and where the tumour is incidentally diagnosed – so-called incidentalomas.

34.128 So, Tsui[1] found that 54 per cent of patients with symptomatic renal cell carcinoma had T4 lesions. In Patard's study[2] of those with local symptoms such as haematuria, 47.2 per cent had T3 tumours and 4.4 per cent had T4 tumours. In Lee's study[3] 48 per cent of symptomatic RCCs (including haematuria) were T1/2 tumour stage and 52 per cent were T3/4 tumour stage. Finally in Hsu's study[4] only 39 per cent of the symptomatic renal cell cancers (eg haematuria) were stage T1 and 2 whereas 61 per cent were stage 3 and 4. So, patients with symptomatic renal cancer are more likely than not to have had advanced (T3 or T4) disease at presentation.

1 Tsui, Shvarts, Smith, Figlin, Dekernion, Belldegrun 'Renal cell carcinoma: prognostic significance of incidentally detected tumors' (2000) 163 J Urol 426–430.
2 Patard, Leray, Rodriguez, Rioux-Leclercq, Guille, Lobel 'Correlation between symptom graduation, tumor characteristics and survival in renal cell carcinoma' (2003) 44 European Urology 226–232.
3 Lee, Katz, Fearn, Russo 'Mode of presentation of renal cell carcinoma provides prognostic information' (2002) 7 Urologic Oncology 135–140.
4 Hsu, Chan, Siegelman 'Small renal cell carcinomas: correlation of size with tumor stage, nuclear grade and histologic subtype' (2004) 182 AJR 551–557.

34.129 In terms of survival, 40–70 per cent of patients with T3a tumours will survive five years, 30–50 per cent with T3b tumours, 20–40 per cent with T3c tumours and 0–20 per cent with T4 tumours[1].

1 Campbell, Lane 'Neoplasms of the upper urinary tract' in *Campbell-Walsh Urology* (10th edn, 2012), Chapter 49 Malignant Renal Tumours p 1444.

34.130 It is generally fair to say that delays in diagnosis, while not necessarily impacting on survival, probably do increase the morbidity of subsequent treatment. A patient may, through delays in diagnosis, move from being a candidate for partial nephrectomy to requiring radical nephrectomy and other complex treatment. The loss of renal function may well have an impact on cardiovascular morbidity.

RENAL AND URETERIC TRANSITIONAL CELL CARCINOMA

34.131 Occasionally haematuria or loin pain are caused by a transitional cell carcinoma of the ureter or renal pelvis (upper tract TCC).

34.132 CT urography reveals a so-called filling defect: an area of the ureter or renal pelvis that fails to fill with radio-contrast material, since this area is composed of a solid mass. Ureteroscopic (in the ureter) or flexible ureterorenoscopic (in the renal pelvis) biopsy of the mass allows a pathological diagnosis (failing to do so risks excising the kidney and ureter for a benign lesion but whether biopsy is necessary in all cases remains an area of debate). Arranging such a procedure takes time and requires a readily available surgeon skilled in the technique of ureterorenoscopic biopsy.

34.133 Pathological analysis of the biopsy specimen also takes time, and this is made more difficult by the small dimensions of ureteroscopes that necessarily limits the size of the biopsy specimens. The specimen may be so small that the pathologist may be unable to determine whether the lesion is a transitional cell carcinoma or benign. The whole process may need to be repeated in an attempt to obtain larger or more biopsies. Add to this the interval from diagnosis to treatment by nephroureterectomy, excision of the whole kidney and ureter, and it is easy to see that the time scale to definitive treatment may be prolonged, even with entirely appropriate care.

34.134   All of this for a type of cancer where the thin lining of the renal pelvis and ureter shortens the distance that the cancer must travel to move from being superficial to muscle invasive or to invade the tissues outside the ureter or renal pelvis and where therefore the lengthy and complex diagnostic process may allow the cancer to move from being curable to incurable.

34.135   Once an upper tract TCC has advanced into the periureteric or perirenal fat (a T3 cancer), fewer than 50 per cent of patients survive beyond five years.

34.136   From a medico-legal perspective, unnecessary delays in this pathway may represent a breach of duty or have causative effect on prognosis, but proving that a delay was avoidable may be difficult.

UROSEPSIS

34.137   The *Bradford* case[1] concerned a fatality due to 'gross medical negligence' aggravated by subsequent alteration of the medical records. It has highlighted the devastating consequences of failing to recognise or adequately treat the patient with urosepsis, especially in the context of the obstructed kidney. It is fair to say *Bradford* has focused the minds of urologists in a way that probably no other case has.

1 *R v Garg* [2012] EWCA Crim 2520.

34.138   Bacteraemia (the presence of pathogenic organisms in the blood) can progress to septicaemia or sepsis, the clinical syndrome caused by bacterial infection of the blood (confirmed by positive blood cultures for a specific organism).   Patients with septicaemia develop a systemic inflammatory response syndrome (SIRS), the systemic response to the infection. SIRS is defined by at least two of the following:

(1)   fever (>38°C) or hypothermia (<36°C);
(2)   tachycardia (>90 beats/min in patients not on B-blockers);
(3)   tachypnoea (respiration >20 breaths/min or $PaCO2$ <4.3kPa or a requirement for mechanical ventilation);
(4)   white cell count >12 000 cells/mm^3, <4000 cells/mm^3, or >10 per cent immature (band) forms.

34.139   Severe sepsis (septic shock) is the state of organ dysfunction caused by hypoperfusion. The patient becomes hypotensive (hypotension in septic shock is defined as a sustained systolic blood pressure (BP) <90mmHg, or a drop in systolic pressure of >40mmHg for >1 hour, when the patient is normovolaemic, and other causes have been excluded or treated). Hypoperfusion manifests itself as lactic acidosis, oliguria (a low urine output) and often an altered mental state.

34.140   In the hospital setting, the most common causes of urosepsis are the presence or manipulation of indwelling urinary catheters, urinary tract surgery (especially endoscopic surgery such as TURP, ureteroscopy and percutaneous nephrolithotomy - PCNL), and urinary tract obstruction in the presence of infected urine (particularly that due to stones obstructing the ureter).

34.141 The principles of management include early recognition, resuscitation, localisation of the source of sepsis, early and appropriate (type and dose) antibiotic administration (usually nowadays directed following advice form a microbiologist), and removal of the primary source of sepsis.

34.142 Early recognition is based on an appreciation that the pyrexial, shivering, tachycardic, tachypnoea and confused patient may be septic. A focused history, based on the scenarios described above in which urosepsis may arise, will raise suspicions and direct investigations and treatment.

34.143 Investigations are directed at identifying a systemic inflammatory response syndrome which once diagnosed should lead to urinary tract imaging which is designed to identify sources of obstruction (predominantly the infected obstructed ureteric stone). Given one radiological investigation there is no substitute for the CT-KUB which will detect the hydronephrosis that usually accompanies an obstructing ureteric stone (termed pyonephrosis where the urine is infected) and the stone itself.

34.144 Intravenous fluids are administered along with empirical antibiotic therapy (adjusted later when cultures are available). The patient with septic shock who fails to respond to a fluid challenge on the ward within 1–2 hours with improvement in their blood pressure and improvement in organ perfusion (resolving confusion and improved urine output) should be transferred to ITU for intensive treatment.

34.145 Where there is obstruction, eg a ureteric stone, identified on CT scanning, nephrostomy or J stent drainage of the kidney is carried out urgently. The trend is towards doing so irrespective of the time of day or night, since delay in decompressing the obstructed kidney can prove fatal.

RECURRENT URINARY TRACT INFECTIONS

34.146 Recurrent urinary tract infection is defined as more than two infections in six months or three within a year. Most cases of recurrent UTIs are due to re-infection (infection by different bacteria). In cases of bacterial persistence (infection by the same organism) a focus of infection should be sought within the urinary tract, eg a renal stone. Reasonable imaging studies include a plain abdominal X-ray or renal ultrasound scan.

34.147 In the absence of an underlying cause such as a stone, while a cure cannot be effected, strategies directed at suppressing bacterial growth can provide long term symptomatic relief. One such strategy is the use of low dose antibiotics, low dose being defined as 25 per cent of the usual treatment dose.

34.148 Nitrofurantoin is a commonly prescribed antibiotic for recurrent urinary tract infections. Significant side effects from its use have been reported which include a spectrum of lung disease presenting as acute, sub-acute and chronic interstitial lung disease.

34.149 The acute reactions are thought to represent a hypersensitive pneumonitis and often resolve after withdrawal of the drug. In the chronic form, nitrofurantoin has been reported to cause diffuse interstitial pneumonitis and bronchiolitis obliterans[1]. Shortness of breath and a cough are common symptoms.

1 Cameron, Kolbe, Wilsher, Lambie 'Bronchiolitis obliterans organising pneumonia associated with the use of Nitrofurantoin' (2000) 55 Thorax 249–251.

34.150 From 1963 to 2010 the Medicines and Healthcare products Regulatory Authority (MHRA) was notified of 2,595 adverse drug reactions and 26 fatalities related to nitrofurantoin use; 392 of these were respiratory-related and 11 of these fatal[1].

1 Weir, Daly 'Lung toxicity and Nitrofurantoin: the tip of the iceberg?' (2013) 106 Q J Med 271–272.

34.151 Early recognition of nitrofurantoin-induced lung toxicity (based on the development of breathlessness or a cough) and cessation of nitrofurantoin is essential. About half of the patients become asymptomatic within 24 hours and 88 per cent within 72 hours[1]. Recovery from chronic reactions may take months[2] and in some cases permanent pulmonary damage can occur[3].

1 Holmberg, Boman, Bottiger, Eriksson, Spross, Wessling 'Adverse reactions to nitrofurantoin. Analysis of 921 reports' (1980) 69 Am J Med 733–738
2 Mendez, Nadrous, Hartman, Ryu 'Chronic nitrofurantoin-induced lung disease' (2005) 80 Mayo Clin Proc 1298–1302; Sheehan, Wells, Milne, Hansell' Nitrofurantoin induced lung disease: two cases demonstrating resolution of apparently irreversible CT abnormalities' (2000) 24 J Comput Assist Tomogr 259–261.
3 Sheehan, Wells, Milne, Hansell' Nitrofurantoin induced lung disease: two cases demonstrating resolution of apparently irreversible CT abnormalities' (2000) 24 J Comput Assist Tomogr 259–261.

What advice should doctors give to patients prior to prescribing nitrofurantoin?

34.152 In the British National Formulary, a bible of pharmaceutical prescribing used in the UK, advice from March 2007 onwards[1] under 'Cautions' for use in prescribing nitrofurantoin included 'pulmonary disease; on long-term therapy monitor liver function and monitor for pulmonary symptoms especially in the elderly (discontinue if deterioration in lung function)'. It would be difficult for a doctor to defend a failure to warn a patient of the existence of this side-effect on the one hand and of the warning symptoms (breathlessness and a cough) that should lead a patient on long-term nitrofurantoin to seek medical advice.

1 *British National Formulary* (53rd edn), p 316.

GLOSSARY OF TERMS AND ABBREVIATIONS

34.153

ARCP: Annual Review of Competence Progression
AUA: American Urological Association
BAUS: British Association of Urological Surgeons

BCG: Bacille Calmette Geurin (a deactivated form of the TB bacillus used in the treatment of bladder cancer

BPH: benign prostatic hyperplasia

CRG: Clinical Reference Groups (in the context of Specialised Services Commissioning)

CTU: Computerised tomographic urography

DRE: digital rectal examination

EAU: European Association of Urology

LUTS: lower urinary tract symptoms

PCNL: Percutaneous nephrolithotomy

PSA: prostate specific antigen

ST3: Surgical trainee, year 3

TCC: Transitional cell carcinoma

TRUS: Transrectal ultrasound

Ureteroscope: A telescopic instrument for inspecting the ureter and for treating ureteric stones and tumours

Ureter: The tube connecting the kidney to the bladder and through which urine is transported from the one to the other

VVF: Vesico-vaginal fistula

CHAPTER 35

Dental surgery

Dr David Corless-Smith

Dr Christopher Dean

INTRODUCTION

35.1   Dentistry, often regarded as a speciality of medicine, is a profession quite separate from medicine and surgery, having its own qualification and dedicated regulation. The distinctive characteristics of the organisation and regulation of dental practice generate a number of special features in professional negligence claims against dentists (quite apart from the unique nature of clinical dental surgery). These aspects of the landscape of dental practice which impact upon dental negligence claims, together with an examination of the terrain of clinical dental surgery, focusing particularly on the standards of care expected from, and common errors made by, dentists, form the subject matter of this chapter.

REGULATION OF DENTAL PROFESSIONALS

35.2   The Dentists Act 1984 provides the statutory authority to practise dentistry, with s 38 of the Act making it a criminal offence for any person who is not a registered dentist or a registered dental care professional to practise dentistry[1]. Dental care professionals include dental nurses, dental technicians, dental therapists, dental hygienists, orthodontic therapists and clinical dental technicians.

1 There is no corresponding statutory prohibition in respect of the provision of medical services, ie it is not a criminal offence for a person other than a registered doctor or any other health care professional to provide medical treatment (except optical care).

35.3   Dentists and dental care professionals are regulated by the General Dental Council (GDC), a body first established by the Dentists Act 1956. The function of the GDC is to protect patients and to promote public confidence in dental professionals through the promotion of high standards of education and professional performance, and assessing the fitness to practise of dental professionals[1]. The GDC achieves its supervision of the dental profession by maintaining a register of all qualified dentists and other dental care professionals, issuing guidance on the standards of dental practice and conduct expected from dental professionals[2], and by exercising a disciplinary function through its fitness to practise procedures. A dental professional may be adjudged as being unfit to practise by reason of misconduct, poor health or deficient professional performance. In the event of a determination of impairment to practise, the sanctions which may be imposed include erasure from the register, suspension from the register for up to 12 months, the imposition of conditions relating to the dental professional's practice for a period of up to 36 months, or a reprimand.

1 Dentists Act 1984, s 1(2): 'It shall be the general concern of the Council to promote high standards of dental education at all its stages and high standards of professional conduct among dentists'.
2 The latest incarnation of the GDC's guidance on ethical standards is 'Standards for the Dental Team' issued in September 2013.

35.4   In common with other healthcare regulators, the GDC has been the subject of considerable criticism in recent years in relation to whether it is adequately achieving its public role of protecting patients against underperforming dental practitioners. The GDC's fitness to practise procedures have been described by the Council for Healthcare Regulatory Excellence, and its successor the Professional Standards Authority for Health and Social Care, as unfit for purpose due to poor decision making and the slow speed of disposal of complaints. Despite the implementation of a number of reforms to its disciplinary processes aimed at earlier disposal, patients are still waiting years for the resolution of their complaints. Another significant lacuna in the protection afforded to dental patients is the GDC's laissez-faire system of enforcement of professional indemnity for the dental profession[1].

1 See para **35.46** ff on dental professional indemnity cover.

COMPLAINTS AGAINST DENTAL PROFESSIONALS

35.5 Complaints against dental professionals are dealt with initially at practice level (so-called 'local resolution'). The GDC sets out detailed guidance as to how dental professionals are expected to deal with complaints[1]. If a complaint is not resolved directly with the practice, the procedure for pursuing a complaint against a dental professional depends on whether the complaint relates to the provision of NHS or private treatment. Complaints concerning NHS dental services follow the same procedure as complaints about NHS medical care[2]. The NHS complaints procedure follows three stages, namely local resolution, independent review by the Health Services Commission and finally referral by the Healthcare Commission to the Health Service Ombudsman[3].

1 Standards for the Dental Team Principle Five: Have a clear and effective complaints procedure.
2 The complaints procedure forms part of the NHS dental contract and any failure to comply would amount to a breach of the dentists' terms of service with the PCT.
3 See Chapter 2 for further details of the NHS complaints procedure.

35.6 If local resolution of a complaint concerning private treatment is not achieved the patient can refer the complaint to the Dental Complaints Service (DCS), a non-statutory body funded by the GDC. The DCS in the first instance repeats an attempt to mediate an informal resolution to the complaint. If this fails, a complaints panel is convened which will make one of a number of recommendations including a full or partial refund of fees paid; a contribution from the dental professional towards remedial treatment up to the cost of the original treatment; an apology from the dental professional, recommendations as to future practice, or no action. The recommendations are simply that, and the DCS has no powers of enforcement.

GENERAL DENTAL PRACTICE

35.7 The dental profession (in distinction to the medical profession) is predominantly a general practice profession. Most dentists in the UK (circa 25,000 of some 39,000 registered dentists) practise in general dental practice, so-called 'high street' dentistry. The majority of general dental practitioners provide treatment under the provisions of the NHS (around 62 per cent) either exclusively or in conjunction with private practice.

35.8 General dental practices are broadly of two types: they are either owned and operated by individual dentists, or by corporate bodies. There are in addition a small number of community dental clinics which provide general dental care operated and managed by NHS Trusts. Dentists may own a practice as a sole trader or in partnership or via a company (or limited liability partnership). Whether providing NHS or private dental services, individual practice owners (so called 'practice principals') are independent practitioners[1].

1 NHS dental practices are not owned by the NHS and dentists providing NHS dental services are not NHS employees. See below for a discussion of NHS dentistry.

35.9   A minority of dentists practise in a legal partnership, in which the business of the practice is jointly owned and the profits and expenses of the practice are shared[1]. The vast majority of joint practice owners – despite styling themselves as partners – are in fact independent practitioners but operating a practice expense-sharing arrangement. This is the standard business structure for dentists practising out of the same premises and involves joint employment of staff, joint management, joint ownership or rental of premises and equipment and joint liability for common practice expenses. Such a contractual arrangement allows each dentist to retain ownership of, and earnings from, their individual dental practice subject to their respective contribution to the outgoings of the practice[2].

1 The profit shares of the individual partners are usually calculated by a formula which reflects their own personal working contributions.
2 As each party practises on their own account with no sharing of individual profits, the essential element of a legal partnership viz carrying on a common business is absent. See the Partnership Act 1890, s 1. However some expense-sharing arrangements may amount to a legal partnership despite the principal dentists not sharing their own profits if the profits generated by associates within the practice are shared.

35.10   Increasingly dental practices are owned and managed by companies: so-called 'dental bodies corporate'. These are a unique class of company authorised pursuant to the Dentists Act 1984, s 43[1] to carry on the business of dentistry in the UK. In practice, these companies fall into two camps: (i) the incorporatisation of a single practice by the practice owner for reasons of business efficiency; and (ii) corporate dental chains which comprise multiple practices owned by a single corporate body with common branding and management.

1 Section 43 imposes conditions concerning board membership, namely the majority of directors must be registered dentists or dental care professionals, and the provision of names and addresses of all dentists and dental care professionals working within the body corporate (whether or not practising as such) to the GDC. The presumed objective of these requirements is to bring the business activities of the dental corporates within the purview of the dental regulator. There is, however, no similar restriction on shareholdings in a dental body corporate.

35.11   Non-practice owning dentists working in general practice do so either as assistant or associate dentists. Assistant dentists are employed by the practice owner whether sole principal, expense-sharing joint principals, partnership, limited liability partnership or body corporate.

35.12   Associate dentists are unique to general dental practice and the employment status of associate dentists is equivocal. The essence of the working arrangement between practice owner and associate dentist is that the associate contracts to provide dental services to patients of the practice and is remunerated accordingly. The traditional method of payment of an associate is by allocation of a proportion (measured as a specific agreed percentage) of treatment income to the associate, the practice owner retaining the balance of the treatment income[1]. Invariably the practice owner provides all the dental equipment and materials and the services of chair-side assistance from a dental nurse. The associate shares the administrative support of the practice staff and the practice owner will determine the associate's days and hours of working and holiday entitlement.

1 Assistant dentists may be paid on this percentage of treatment income basis or by way of hourly rate or salary.

35.13 The working arrangement between an associate dentist and practice owner appears for all practical purposes to be identical to that existing between an assistant dentist and practice owner. The distinguishing feature between the two contractual arrangements is that an associate contract[1] will prescribe that the associate dentist is to be regarded as self-employed. This presumptive employment status is relevant to, but not determinative of, the issue of a practice principal's vicarious liability for the services provided by an associate dentist, as discussed below.

1 Most practice owners utilise standard contracts approved by the British Dental Association and Dental Practitioners Association which affirm the self-employed status of the associate.

SPECIALIST DENTAL PRACTICE

35.14 The other sectors of dental practice are the hospital dental services, salaried primary care services (formerly the community dental services), specialist practices and academic dentistry.

35.15 Despite the numerical predominance of general practitioners within the dental profession, no fewer than 13 specialties of dental practice are recognised[1]. These are:

(1) oral surgery (also known as oral and maxillofacial surgery): diagnosis and treatment of pathology of the jaw and mouth requiring surgical intervention;

(2) orthodontics: diagnosis, prevention and correction of irregularities of the teeth, bite and jaw relationships;

(3) paediatric dentistry: concerned with the oral health care of children;

(4) endodontics: concerned with the cause, diagnosis, prevention and treatment of diseases and injuries of the tooth root and dental pulp;

(5) periodontics: concerned with the diagnosis, treatment and prevention of diseases and disorders (infections and inflammatory) of the gums and other structures around the teeth;

(6) prosthodontics: concerned with the replacement of missing teeth and the associated soft and hard tissues by prostheses (bridges, dentures) which may be fixed or removable, or may be supported and retained by implants;

(7) restorative dentistry: the restoration of diseased, injured, or abnormal teeth to normal function. This pan-speciality includes all aspects of endodontics, periodontics and prosthodontics;

(8) special care dentistry: concerned with the improvement of the oral health of individuals and groups in society who have a physical, sensory, intellectual, mental, medical, emotional or social impairment or disability;

(9)   dental public health: a non-clinical speciality involving the prevention of oral diseases, and the promotion of oral health to the population rather than the individual. It involves the assessment of dental health needs and ensuring dental services meet those needs;

(10)   oral medicine: concerned with the oral health care of patients with chronic recurrent and medically-related disorders of the mouth and with their diagnosis and non-surgical management;

(11)   oral microbiology: the diagnosis and assessment of facial infection. This is a clinical speciality undertaken by laboratory-based personnel who provide reports and advice based on interpretation of microbiological samples;

(12)   oral and maxillofacial pathology: laboratory investigation of diseases of the oral cavity, jaws and salivary glands from tissue samples. This is a clinical speciality undertaken by laboratory-based personnel;

(13)   dental and maxillofacial radiology: involves all aspects of medical imaging which provide information about anatomy, function and diseased states of the teeth and jaws.

Hospital dentists are, in the main, specialists in oral surgery, orthodontics or restorative dentistry. Practitioners of the other aforementioned specialties tend to practise in dental hospitals or academic university dental departments.

1 The General Dental Council recognises the sub-specialities and maintains specialist registers in relation to each speciality.

NHS DENTISTRY

35.16   NHS dental services are provided in primary care, community and hospital settings. NHS dentists provide general dental services to the NHS on an independent contractor basis. The NHS dental contract regulates the relationship between the dentist and the NHS and the methodology of, and remuneration for, the provision of dental services. NHS dental contracts have undergone a series of radical transformations in respect of their underlying philosophy of treatment provision as successive governments have struggled to remedy fundamental shortcomings in the provision of NHS dental treatment[1]. When NHS dentistry started in 1948 the general state of dental health was poor and dentists were paid for individual items of treatment encouraging high productivity but with no account being taken of the quality of treatment or of the prevention of dental disease. This instilled in NHS dentistry a 'drill and fill' treadmill ethos exacerbated by a succession of fee reductions for items of treatment.

1 Multiple government-commissioned reports into NHS dentistry have been published in the last 20 years, including: Improving NHS Dentistry (July 1994); Modernising NHS Dentistry: Implementing the NHS Plan (September 2000); Access to NHS Dentistry Select Committee on Health Report (March 2001); NHS Dentistry: Options for Change (August 2002); The Economics of Dental Care (June 2004); Framework Proposals for primary dental services in England from 2005 (March 2004); NHS Dentistry: Delivering Change (July 2004) etc.

35.17   In October 1990 an NHS contract was implemented which saw a shift away from self-contained episodes of treatment towards continuing care. Dentists received a capitation fee for each patient they agreed to care for over a two-year period, renewable at any time by agreement between the patient and dentist. For the first time patients registered with their dentist and this incentivised dentists to undertake preventative rather than simply restorative work. In addition combining private and NHS treatment was permitted.

35.18   In April 2006 another new NHS dental contract came into service. The focus of concern of this contract was to improve access to NHS dentistry, as significant numbers of dentists had ceased to provide NHS dentistry because of disenchantment over remuneration and the persistence of the 'treadmill' ethos causing widespread non-availability of NHS dental services. Under the new contract, Primary Care Trusts (PCTs) were made responsible for commissioning NHS dental services directly from dentists to ensure local access to NHS dental treatment. The aspiration was to provide a more uniform distribution of availability of NHS dentistry as PCTs would now decide which practices would provide NHS dental services and encourage dentists to set up practices in areas of limited availability[1]. In April 2013, following the abolition of PCTs, this function was transferred to NHS England, a single national commissioning body operating through 27 area teams, while in Wales the role is performed by seven Health Boards.

1 Under the 1990 NHS dental contract all dentists were entitled to provide NHS dentistry, whereas under the 2006 contract dentists must bid for, and negotiate with NHS England/ Welsh Health Board, the right to provide NHS treatment.

35.19   Under the extant 2006 contract, care is delivered to patients as discrete courses of treatment[1] which are categorised into four bands according to the volume and complexity of work to be done. Each band is allocated a specific number of Units of Dental Activity (UDA), reflecting the putative time to be taken to complete a course of treatment within that band. The patient will pay a single charge according to the band to which their treatment plan is assigned. The banded courses of treatment are as follows:

- Band 1: clinical examination, radiographs, scaling and polishing, and preventative dental work such as oral health advice = 1 UDA;
- Band 2: routine treatment such as restorations, root canal treatment, periodontal treatment, surgical procedures including extractions and adding teeth to dentures = 3 UDAs;
- Band 3: complex treatment such as crown and bridgework, dentures and orthodontics = 12 UDAs;
- Band 4: urgent treatment including examination, radiographs, tooth dressings, recementing crowns, extraction of 1 or 2 teeth and a single restoration = 1.2 UDAs.

1 A course of treatment is defined as 'an examination of a patient, an assessment of his oral health, and the planning any treatment to be provided to that patient as a result of that examination and assessment and the provision of any planned treatment (including any treatment planned at a time other than the time of the initial examination)': the National Health Service (General Dental Services Contracts) Regulations 2005, reg 1(2).

35.20   Dentists will contract with their local PCT to provide a set number of UDAs over a 12-month period for an agreed contract value. The contract is renewable year on year and both the agreed workload 'UDAs' and contract budget can be varied by negotiation. Contracts may be agreed at practice level or with individual dentists. Practice owners usually prefer to enter into practice-based contracts rather than allowing associate dentists to negotiate their own contract with NHS England (or the Welsh Health Board) in order to retain control of the practice income.

35.21   There are a number of inherent flaws in the UDA system of remuneration as currently arranged. Whilst the 1990 contract attempted to encourage the concepts of continuing care and regular attendance through the medium of registration of patients with an individual dentist, the 2006 contract focuses on self-contained courses of treatment. Thus there is no continuing clinical relationship between dentist and patient in between courses of treatment and the dentist is under no obligation to treat a patient again following completion of an individual course of treatment.

35.22   Furthermore, the dentist determines the objectives of the course of treatment in terms of the level of oral health to be achieved. An individual treatment plan can be very limited in the extent of the dental care to be provided[1]. In fact minimal intervention[2], together with a phased approach to treatment planning[3], is the prevailing treatment philosophy and this can be a justification for splitting up the necessary treatment into a number of courses of treatment, with each individual course attracting its own UDA quota and patient charge. Indeed there is a financial incentive for the dentist to carry out the minimum amount of treatment to qualify for a particular banded course of treatment with its attendant UDA value. In this way the maximum yield of UDAs may be achieved for the minimum amount of clinical activity. This is possible because the bands of courses of treatment each encompass a wide range of treatments with differing levels of complexity and chair-side time to complete the work.

1 There is no obligation to achieve 'dental fitness' at the conclusion of a course of treatment as under the 1990 dental contract.
2 See Framework proposals for primary dental services in England from 2005.
3 See Bain *Treatment Planning in General Dental Practice – A Problem-based Approach* (2003).

35.23   This behaviour which may be described as 'UDA gaming' has a tendency to steer into a treatment philosophy known as 'supervised neglect' whereby a patient regularly attends the dentist and treatment is provided to remedy symptoms or gross pathology with no emphasis on the prevention of dental disease. Supervised neglect is an extreme distortion of minimal intervention and exposes a dentist to an allegation of failing to diagnose timeously and treat a developing dental disease such as caries or periodontal disease.

35.24   Another casualty of UDA gaming is a patient's informed consent. A dentist may be tempted to offer only that treatment option which can be speedily completed rather than advising the patient of all available treatment options, lest the patient should opt for a more time-consuming treatment within the same band (thereby yielding an equivalent UDA for the quicker treatment option). Alternatively a dentist may canvas all treatment options but manipulate the patient choice of treatment by misrepresenting the relative risks and benefits of the available options. A paradigm example of such manipulation, which vitiates the patient's consent to the treatment provided, is that of a dentist recommending the extraction of a tooth and either failing to offer the alternative option of root canal treatment altogether, or exaggerating the risk of failure of such treatment, or misrepresenting the availability of such treatment under an NHS course of treatment and offering the treatment on a privately paying basis only[1].

1 Tooth extraction and root canal treatment are both Band 2 treatment attracting three UDAs but root canal therapy is a significantly more time-consuming procedure.

THE BASIS OF DENTAL PRACTITIONER LIABILITY

35.25   The manner in which dental services are delivered in terms of the organization of dental practices, the employment relationships between practitioners, and the nature of dentistry itself with its particular emphasis on the supply of materials in the course of providing treatment to the patient creates a number of specific and unique features regarding the legal liability of dentists to their patients.

35.26   There are essentially three types of action which a patient may bring against a dentist: breach of contract; negligence; and product liability[1].

1 An action in battery can be brought if the dentist has not obtained the patient's consent for the treatment (ie the patient is ignorant of the nature of the procedure) but this is rare.

Contract

35.27   There is no contractual relationship between a dentist and a patient being treated under the NHS. The basis for this view of the jurisprudence underlying the dentist-patient relationship in the NHS setting is derived from case law[1] analysing the nature of the pharmacist-patient and GP-patient relationship which held that NHS treatment was provided pursuant to a statutory duty and that there was no contract between a patient and the NHS healthcare provider. The statutory duty to treat the patient (in the context of NHS care provision) was considered antithetical to a legal relationship based on bargaining between healthcare practitioner and patient. Furthermore, the indirect[2] and direct payments[3] made by a patient in the receipt of NHS treatment do not constitute sufficient consideration for the formation of a contract. A dentist provides NHS dental services to patients pursuant to a statutory arrangement[4] with NHS England or the relevant Health Board in Wales, renewed annually, in which the dentist agrees to provide a prescribed quota of dental treatment[5].

1 *Pfizer Corpn v Ministry of Health* [1965] AC 512, HL, which held that the supply of a prescription medicine was not made pursuant to a contract despite the prescription charge, and *Reynolds v Health First Medical Group* [2000] Lloyd's Rep Med 240, which held that a GP's services were provided pursuant to statute.
2 A GP's capitation payment for each registered patient in *Reynolds*.
3 NHS prescription charge in *Pfizer*. Cf NHS dental charges.
4 The National Health Service (General Dental Services Contracts) Regulations 2005, SI 2005/3361 and the National Health Service (Personal Dental Services Agreements) Regulations 2005, SI 2005/3373.
5 Whilst this statutory arrangement is styled as either a general dental services contract or a personal dental services agreement, the relevant regulations in fn 4 above expressly state that these are not legally enforceable contracts.

35.28   Where a dentist is providing private dental treatment and the patient is the paying party, then a contractual relationship between the dentist and patient will be present. Whilst the scope of treatment provided under a privately paying contract[1] will be specific to the express terms of the contract, terms relating to the quality of the treatment are implied into the contract by law. A term will be implied into the contract that reasonable skill and care will be adopted[2]. The standard of care to be achieved is the same as the duty to exercise reasonable care and skill in the tort of negligence[3]. Thus the law does not distinguish between the standard of care to be provided to patients treated privately and under the NHS. The law will not, however, imply a guarantee that the treatment will be successful regardless of any representation made by the dentist to that effect[4].

1 Payment may be made by the patient directly, via a payment plan scheme such as Denplan or by an insurance company.
2 See *Thake v Maurice* [1986] 1 All ER 497 and *Eyre v Measday* [1986] 1 All ER 488. The Court of Appeal held in both cases that a surgeon contracted to carry out an operation was subject to a duty implied by law to carry out the operation with reasonable skill and care. See also the Supply of Goods and Services Act 1982, s 13: 'In a contract for the supply of a service where the supplier is acting in the course of a business, there is an implied term that the supplier will carry out the service with reasonable care and skill'. A business includes a profession (s 18(1)).
3 A private patient can thus bring a 'negligence' claim in contract or tort although in practice nothing turns on which cause of action is pleaded.
4 See *Thake v Maurice* [1986] 1 All ER 497, in which such representations of likely success were found to be mere therapeutic reassurances. However, the provision of elective cosmetic dentistry, which is more akin to a business transaction than the provision of healthcare, may see the courts less reluctant to imply such a warranty of success.

35.29   A substantial proportion of dental treatment involves the restoration of teeth or the replacement of missing teeth with prostheses. Some restorations are fabricated directly from dental materials in the mouth by the dentist, for example dental amalgam and composite restorations. Other restorations and prostheses, for example crowns and bridges and dentures, are manufactured by a combination of clinical procedures carried out by the dentist and fabrication of the restoration or prosthesis by a dental technician in a dental laboratory. Thus the provision of restorations and prostheses can be characterised as either a contract of sale or a contract for work and materials, depending on the view a court takes as to the predominant element of the contract: the supply of the restorations which amounts to a sale of goods or the provision of services, namely the process of production of the restorations[1]. The designation of the contract is largely academic, as virtually identical warranties as to the quality and fitness for purpose of the goods supplied are implied into both types of contract[2]. Where goods are sold in the course of a business there is an implied term that the goods supplied under the contract are of satisfactory quality and fit for their purpose[3]. The duty to supply goods of satisfactory quality is strict and it is no defence that reasonable care was taken[4]. Thus a dentist may potentially be liable for the provision of restorations or prostheses that are not of satisfactory quality or fit for their intended purpose even if reasonable care has been exercised in their fabrication. However such 'strict' liability has two significant limitations. First, it applies only to goods supplied under a contract and is therefore not relevant to NHS dental treatment. Second, the quality of a restoration or prosthesis very much depends on the skill and care of the dentist during the clinical stages of the manufacture of the restoration or prosthesis, not least in the exercise of judgment as to whether to fit (or supply) a restoration which is clearly of unsatisfactory quality. As such, a restoration or prosthesis is unlikely to be held to be of unsatisfactory quality without an element of attendant negligence on the part of the dentist, save for those provided under private contract where the description of the restoration and the price are such as to raise the threshold of 'satisfactory quality'.

1 Contracts in which the sale of goods is the predominant element are categorised as contracts of sale and governed by the Sale of Goods Act whilst contracts in which goods are supplied as part of the provision of a service are known as contracts for work and materials (also called contracts for mixed goods and services) and are regulated by the Supply of Goods and Services Act 1982.
2 See *Samuels v Davis* [1943] KB 526 in which the Court of Appeal implied a warranty of reasonable fitness for purpose into a contract to make dentures and said 'it is a matter of legal indifference whether the contract was one for the sale of goods or one of service to do work and supply materials'.
3 See the Sale of Goods Act 1979, s 14(2) and Supply of Goods and Services Act 1982, s 4(2). The Sale of Goods Act 1979, s 14(2A) and the Supply of Goods and Services Act 1982, s 4(2A) both set out identical tests of satisfactory quality, viz goods are of satisfactory quality if they meet the standard that a reasonable person would regard as satisfactory, taking account of any description of the goods, the price (if relevant) and all the other relevant circumstances. Section 14(2B) of the 1979 Act additionally offers a non-exhaustive list of aspects of the quality of goods to be considered in assessing whether the goods are of satisfactory quality namely fitness for all the purposes for which goods of the kind in question are commonly supplied; appearance and finish; freedom from minor defects; safety, and durability.
4 See *Grant v Australian Knitting Mills Ltd* [1936] AC 85. There is thus a clear distinction in contracts for works and materials between the warranties in respect of the quality of goods supplied and those in respect of the standard of services supplied.

Negligence

35.30   Most dental treatment is carried out in general practice and, in turn, general dental practice is the highest risk area in terms of claims experience. The most common basis of a claim against a dentist is in negligence and the putative defendant is usually the individual practitioner who provided the treatment to the patient. However, in view of the set-up of general dental practice described above, practitioners other than the treating dentist may also be liable in negligence to the patient depending on the status of the respective dentists within the practice.

35.31   A practice principal may be liable for the negligence of assistant and associate dentists either by way of vicarious liability or pursuant to the imposition of a personal non-delegable duty of care owed directly to patients of the dental practice to deliver dental care of a reasonable standard.

35.32   A practice owner's vicarious liability for the negligence of an assistant dentist arises out of the existence of an employer-employee relationship and is unequivocal. The question as to whether a practice principal is vicariously liable for the negligence of an associate dentist was, until recently, uncertain as it depended upon a determination of the employment status of the associate dentist which is far from clear cut. The manner in which an associate dentist provides dental services within a dental practice is indistinguishable from that of an assistant dentist and the distinction between a contract of service and a contract for services was indefinable and there was no sensible reason why a practice principal's vicarious liability should rest on this particular issue. The test for the requisite relationship to establish vicarious liability is now whether the relationship is akin to employment[1]. Thus the tests for vicarious liability and the employee-employer relationship are not entirely congruent.

1 See *E v English Province of Our Lady of Charity* [2012] EWCA Civ 938, [2013] QB 722, in which the Court of Appeal revised the two-stage test of vicarious liability: (i) a relationship akin to employment sufficiently close to be fair and just to impose vicarious liability; and (ii) a connection between the relationship of the tortfeasor and the party to whom vicarious liability attaches and the tortious act. This new two-stage test was approved by the Supreme Court in *Catholic Child Welfare Society v Various Claimants (FC)* [2012] UKSC 56, [2013] 2 AC 1.

35.33 The current test of the employee-employer relationship is multi-factorial and involves identifying and weighing (often conflicting) factors in the working arrangement to ascertain whether the work is carried out under a contract of service or a contract for services[1].

1 *Ready Mixed Concrete (South East) Ltd v Minister of Pensions and National Insurance* [1968] 2 QB 497, [1968] 1 All ER 433.

35.34 Whilst no one factor is determinative, the level of control that a practice owner exerts over the manner in which an associate dentist works is significant. Typical features of an associate dentist's contract which would point towards employed status include the practice owner dictating the hours worked and number of days taken as holiday leave, providing dental instruments and materials and the services of a dental nurse and administrative staff[1]. Factors supporting self-employed status include the parties' intention as to the employment status of the associate[2]; National Insurance and PAYE contributions are not deducted from the associate dentist's pay[3], associate dentists are required to obtain their own professional indemnity cover, and whether the associate has the right to delegate the performance of their services in their absence through illness or holiday. This so-called 'right of substitution' of a locum is viewed by the courts as particularly decisive because it is inconsistent with an obligation to perform services personally and the court will scrutinise whether the right can be freely exercised by the associate, or was never intended to be exercised and is in reality a device to disguise employee status.

1 Where a practice principal has a practice-based NHS contract this will impose obligations on the principal as contract provider to ensure that any dentist providers in the practice (including associates) are compliant with conditions stipulated under the contract relating to quality assurance. This additional level of control on the part of the practice principal over the associate's clinical activity – both quantum and quality – is indicative of an employer-employee relationship. Likewise, registration of a dental practice with the Care Quality Commission imposes on the practice principal a very high level of control over all staff – including clinical staff – to enforce quality assurance outcomes relating to patient safety.
2 See Chapter 2 for further details of the NHS complaints procedure. The label that the parties use to describe the working relationship – invariably self-employed – is subservient to the practical reality of the relationship.
3 Her Majesty's Revenue and Customs has been content historically to treat associate dentists as self-employed.

35.35 The test for the imposition of vicarious liability is likewise multifactorial and focuses upon whether the tortfeasor is in business on his own account, or is operating within the business of the principal[1]. An associate dentist does not carry on his own practice but provides dental services to patients of the practice principal (for the benefit of the practice principal) and the practice principal retains control over which patients the associate dentist treats. It is submitted that under the new test a practice principal will invariably be held to be vicariously liable for negligent treatment provided by an associate dentist[2].

1 In *E v English Province of Our Lady of Charity* [2012] EWCA Civ 938, [2013] QB 722 the Court of Appeal adopted a multiple test, viz: (i) control test: the level of managerial control over the activity of the tortfeasor; (ii) organisation test: how central the activity of the tortfeasor was to the organisation of the employer; (iii) integration test: whether the tortfeasor was integrated into the employer's organisation; and (iv) entrepreneur test: whether the tortfeasor was in business on his own account.

2 See *Whetstone v Medical Protection Society* [2014] EWHC 1024 in which Seymour J held that a practice principal was vicariously liable for the negligence of a self-employed associate dentist.

35.36   A question arises as to whether a practice principal may be directly liable for the negligence of an assistant or associate dentist. Such direct liability to a patient may come about by the imposition of a non-delegable duty owed to a patient by a practice principal in respect of the standard of care provided by an associate dentist or via the practice principal's direct duty to provide a safe system of delivery of care for patients of the practice.

35.37   There is authority for the proposition that a health care institution has a direct primary liability to patients in respect of negligence on the part of clinical staff regardless of their employment relationship with the institution[1]. The principle underpinning the imposition of such a non-delegable duty is that the health care provider assumes responsibility for the care of patients who are particularly dependent upon the observance of a proper standard of care, and liability to the patient should not turn on whether the clinician providing the treatment was an employee or independent contractor. The relationship between a practice principal and associate dentist is closely analogous to that of any other health care institution and clinicians engaged to provide medical care within the institution. Patients attend a dental practice to receive dental care and they are unconcerned with (and have no control over) the employment status of the treating dentist.

1 *Cassidy v Ministry of Health* [1951] 2 KB 343 per Denning LJ, 'the hospital authorities accepted the plaintiff as a patient for treatment and it was their duty to treat him with reasonable care. They selected, employed and paid all the surgeons and nurses who looked after him. He has no say in their selection at all. If those surgeons did not treat him with proper care and skill then the hospital authorities must answer for it, for it means that they themselves did not perform their duty to him. I decline to enter into the question whether any of the surgeons were employed only under a contract for services as distinct from a contract of service ... But the liability of the hospital authorities should not and does not depend on nice considerations of that sort. The plaintiff knew nothing of the terms on which they employed their staff: all he knew was that he was treated in the hospital by people whom the hospital authorities appointed and the hospital authorities must be answerable for the way in which he was treated'. This obiter dicta was expressly approved in *Woodland v Essex County Council* [2013] UKSC 66 in which the Supreme Court set out the following criteria for the imposition of a non-delegable duty of care: (i) the claimant is especially dependent on the defendant for protection against the risk of injury, for example a patient or child; (ii) there is a pre-existing relationship between the claimant and defendant which places the claimant in the custody or care of the defendant which gives rise to a positive duty to protect the claimant from harm; (iii) the claimant has no control over whether the defendant performs his duty personally or delegates the performance; (iv) the defendant has delegated some function which is an integral part of that positive duty; (v) the delegate has been negligent in the performance of the very function of that duty delegated to him by the defendant.

35.38   The second type of direct non-delegable duty on a practice principal is that to provide a safe system of care delivery to patients of the practice.

This organisational duty encompasses the appointment and supervision of competent staff, the provision of proper facilities and equipment and the establishment of safe systems of implementing care to patients. In contrast to the non-delegable duty described above, this duty is not necessarily contingent upon the negligence of an individual clinician providing care to a patient (although there may be such concomitant negligence). Examples of such organisational breaches on the part of the practice principal may include employing an incompetent associate dentist, failing to ensure that an associate has professional indemnity cover, failing to supervise an inexperienced dentist in the performance of a particular procedure[1], failing to implement procedures to protect patients from cross-infection, and failing to instigate systems to minimise errors in communications and administration such as the booking of appointments and referrals to professional colleagues.

1 Inexperience is irrelevant to setting the standard of care to be achieved: see *Wilsher v Essex AHA* [1987] QB 730, CA.

35.39 A practice principal will be jointly and severally liable for the negligence of any partners[1] and vicariously liable for the negligence of any dental care professionals[2] or administrative staff working under a contract of employment.

1 Partnership Act 1890, s 12.
2 Some dental care professionals, such as dental hygienists and therapists, are frequently engaged on a self-employed basis. However such contractual arrangements are likely to be considered by the courts in reality to be contracts of employment as the level of control exerted by a practice principal over the work of a dental care professional is near complete and includes prescription of their clinical activity.

35.40 The relevance of the above account concerning the joint liability of practice principals is that not infrequently there may be considerable practical difficulties for a patient in pursuing a claim against the individual dentist who provided treatment. The dentist may no longer be practising at the relevant dental practice and their whereabouts unknown. A particular demographic feature of general dental practice is the employment of foreign-trained dentists[1] who practise in the UK for a number of years and then return to their country of origin. Thus a patient contemplating pursuing a claim against such an absent dentist may face insurmountable obstacles in locating the putative defendant. Alternatively, the treating dentist may not have professional indemnity cover[2]. In such circumstances establishing liability against the practice principal provides a substitute defendant.

1 Some 30 per cent of registered dentists in the UK are foreign trained: FOIA request to General Dental Council 2012.
2 See para **35.46** ff on dental professional indemnity cover.

35.41 Another issue of joint liability prevalent in claims against dentists is the allocation of individual responsibility where several dentists have provided care to the patient. A further demographic characteristic of general dental practice is the mobility of junior dentists between practices. A patient will not infrequently have a course of treatment (even in relation to an individual tooth) delivered by a number of dentists. In such circumstances the respective apportionment of liability between the treating dentists can be problematic.

35.42 Two examples will illustrate the difficulties of apportionment. D1 provides root canal treatment to a tooth and D2 subsequently provides a crown restoration to the tooth. The tooth develops an abscess and is extracted. Both the root canal treatment and crown are of a negligent standard and have contributed to the development of the abscess. D1 and D2 are represented by different defence organisations and make separate offers to settle. In the absence of co-operation between the defence organisations in jointly settling the claim and apportioning liability between D1 and D2[1], the claimant must assess the sufficiency of the respective offers and judge independently whether to settle or pursue the claim against D1 and/or D2.

1 Where two or more tortfeasors are liable for the same damage (here the avoidable loss of the tooth) they are entitled to claim a contribution from each other under the Civil Liability (Contribution) Act 1978. The dental defence organisations frequently decline to jointly deal with and settle a claim against their respective members which alleges common injury or loss.

35.43 In the second scenario D1, D2 and D3 provide successive periods of care for the claimant over a 10-year period, during which the claimant suffers bone loss associated with six teeth, four of which are extracted and two which have a reduced prognosis. D1, D2 and D3 have failed to diagnose and properly treat the claimant's periodontal disease which has allegedly caused the bone loss. They are individually responsible for the bone loss accruing during their successive periods of care. D1 and D2 deny liability. D2 makes an offer but alleges contributory negligence on the basis that the claimant has not attended regularly and has failed to adopt a satisfactory oral hygiene regime despite receiving professional instruction from D2. The apportionment between D1, D2 and D3 in respect of their liability for their individual contributions to the bone loss and tooth loss is fraught with both evidential[1] and practical[2] difficulties.

1 Periodontal bone loss is episodic not linear and individual apportionment between defendants may be impossible.
2 Settlement against one defendant may fully compensate the claimant and preclude pursuing a claim against another concurrent tortfeasor. Alternatively, settlement against some of the defendants may incompletely compensate the claimant for the damage caused but it is not cost-effective to pursue the claim against defendants resisting liability. See *Jameson v Central Electricity Generating Board* [2000] 1 AC 455 and *Heaton v Axa Equity & Law Assurance Society plc* [2002] UKHL 15, [2002] 2 AC 329.

Product liability

35.44 Product liability refers to the liability of manufacturers and suppliers of products for injury and losses caused by the defective condition of the product[1]. Such claims may be brought in contract, negligence or under the Consumer Protection Act (CPA) 1987. The CPA 1987 sought to impose strict liability for defective products[2] on manufacturers and suppliers where the product causes physical injury[3] including death or property damage. It might be supposed that in view of the high frequency of materials handling and provision of restorations and prostheses by dentists in their practice that they may be particularly vulnerable to such claims compared to medical practitioners.

1 The focus of product liability claims is the safety of the product (as opposed to its quality) and the damage caused to users of the product rather than to the product itself.
2 CPA 1987, s 3.
3 CPA 1987, s 5.

35.45 In practice this appears not to be so, because injuries caused to patients by exposure to drugs or other medical products are more usually attributable to negligent conduct on the part of the dentist rather than an inherent defect in the product itself. An example would be accidental injection of bleach whilst disinfecting a root canal into the jaw bone causing widespread bone necrosis. Liability would fall to the dentist for a failure to exercise reasonable care in the handling of an inherently hazardous substance rather than in his capacity as supplier of an allegedly defective product. A more borderline example would be the breakage of a needle during the administration of local anaesthetic, resulting in the needle tracking into a tissue space. The cause of the needle fracture may be due to a manufacturing defect in the needle or negligent technique on the part of the dentist. In any event, either cause attaches liability to the dentist for the resultant injury, although if a manufacturing defect is proven, the dentist (whilst liable as a supplier) could claim an indemnity from the needle manufacturer. A significant limitation of a claim brought under the CPA 1987 is that there is no liability for damage to the product itself[1]. Thus a claim in respect of the provision of defective restorations or prostheses brought under the 1987 Act would not recover the cost of replacement restorations/prostheses.

1 CPA 1987, s 5(2) provides 'A person shall not be liable… in respect of any defect in a product for the loss of or any damage to the product itself'.

DENTAL PROFESSIONAL INDEMNITY COVER

35.46 Further to a 2011 European Union Directive[1], the Health Care and Associated Professions (Indemnity Arrangements) Order 2014[2] amended, inter alia, the Dentists Act 1984 to create for the first time a statutory requirement for registered dentists, practising as dental practitioners, to have in force a professional indemnity arrangement providing appropriate cover for such practice[3].

1 Directive 2011/24/EU on the application of patients' rights in cross-border healthcare.
2 SI 2014/1887, effective 17 July 2014. The Order marked the partial and late, by eight months, transposition into domestic law of the requirements of EU Directive concerned with protecting the rights of EU citizens who are provided with healthcare in EU countries other than their domicile.
3 Dentists Act 1984, s 26A(1) as substituted by the Health Care and Associated Professions (Indemnity Arrangements) Order 2014, Article 4. Prior to the very recent implementation of this legal requirement for dental professionals to have professional indemnity cover as a condition of practice, the GDC expected dentists and dental care professionals to hold 'appropriate insurance or indemnity' as a matter of professional obligation. See GDC 'Standards for the Dental Team' Standard 1.8. However the GDC did not enforce the possession of indemnity cover, relying instead upon an individual dental professional complying with their professional ethical standards.

35.47 The effect of Article 3 of the Health Care and Associated Professions (Indemnity Arrangements) Order 2014, which amended the Dentists Act 1984, s 18(2), is to compel dentists to provide documentary evidence of their indemnity arrangements to the GDC when seeking registration. An indemnity arrangement is defined as either a policy of insurance, or in the alternative as, 'an arrangement made for the purposes of indemnifying a person' or a combination of the two[1]. It may be argued that such open drafting allows the

GDC to continue to recognise membership of a dental defence organisation[2], professional indemnity insurance[3] and NHS indemnity as all amounting to sufficient indemnity cover for dentists. Nevertheless, the disappointing lack of clarity of the Order, in particular in its risible definition of one variation of satisfactory indemnity arrangement being 'an arrangement made for the purposes of indemnity', makes it likely that some registrants will continue to argue, as they have done repeatedly in the past, that a 'self-funded' indemnity arrangement, ie reliance upon the dentist's own funds to pay dental negligence claims, amounts to a sufficient indemnity arrangement, to the obvious detriment of affected patients.

1 Dentists Act 1984, s 26A(2) as substituted by the Health Care and Associated Professions (Indemnity Arrangements) Order 2014, Article 4.
2 There are three such dental defence organisations in the UK, viz: Dental Protection, Dental Defence Union and Medical and Dental Defence Union of Scotland. The defence organisations provide occurrence-based liability indemnity covering claims relating to treatment provided during the currency of the dentist's membership regardless of when the claim is notified. Presently the defence organisations do not provide indemnity for a practice principal's vicarious and direct liability for treatment provided at the practice by other dental professionals. This is a significant lacuna in indemnity cover.
3 Commercial insurance is offered on a claims-made basis which covers claims notified and relating to treatment provided during the currency of insurance cover. 'Run-off' cover is taken out to provide cover relating to claims notified after the expiry of the policy but concerning treatment provided during the cover period of the policy.

35.48 The Health Care and Associated Professions (Indemnity Arrangements) Order 2014 substituted the Dentists Act 1984, s 26A, entitled 'Indemnity arrangements'. Section 26A(4) empowers the GDC to make rules regarding the information to be supplied regarding indemnity which will be required of three groups: would-be registrants; existing registrants who wish to be retained on the register; and those seeking restoration to the register. The new s 26A also allows the GDC to make rules which will empower the registrar to seek indemnity information at a stage of the registrar's choosing and sets out the potential sanctions of erasure or non-registration for non-compliance, plus the possibility of a breach being treated as a matter of misconduct[1].

1 Dentists Act 1984, s 26A(8) and (9) as substituted by the Health Care and Associated Professions (Indemnity Arrangements) Order 2014, Article 4.

35.49 While the recent amendment of the Dentists Act 1984 appears to mark a welcome step in the improvement of dental patient protection through statutory regulation of professional indemnity cover for the dental profession, unfortunately there remains no obligation on the part of an individual dental professional to divulge details of professional indemnity cover to a patient or to identify the indemnity provider, nor is there any requirement for the GDC to make the detail of indemnity arrangements of registered dentists a matter of public record.

35.50 The current position regarding the availability of information concerning a dentist's indemnity status remains that there is no procedural mechanism for a patient seeking disclosure of details of a dentist's professional indemnity provider in the event that such disclosure is not forthcoming voluntarily[1]. Neither the GDC nor the dental defence organisations will currently provide any information to a patient regarding the identity of a dentist's indemnity cover provider[2] and there is no evidence to suggest that there will be any improvement in this lack of transparency regarding indemnity under the amended statutory regime.

1 European Directive 2011/24/EU on the application of patient's rights in cross border healthcare, Article 4, para 2(b) requires that healthcare providers should provide relevant information to help individual patients to make an informed choice and imposes an express requirement that healthcare providers should provide clear information to patients before treatment on 'their insurance cover or other means of personal or collective protection with regard to professional liability'.
2 The GDC and dental defence organisations both erroneously cite the Data Protection Act 1998 as the basis for non-disclosure of the identity of a dentist's indemnity provider.

35.51 Where the dental treatment complained of has been provided under the NHS, the NHS contract provider (the practice principal that holds the practice-based contract with NHS England or the Welsh Health Board) has an obligation under the terms of the NHS contract to ensure that any dentists providing treatment under the NHS contract (known as contract performers) have appropriate indemnity cover and to provide details of the indemnity cover provider to NHS England (or Welsh Health Board). Where a claim is anticipated against an absent contract performer, details of the performer's indemnity provider can be sought from either the practice principal, NHS England or the Welsh Health Board[1].

1 Such requests for disclosure of indemnity provider details will rarely result in voluntary disclosure and should be made under the auspices of a Freedom of Information Act request.

35.52 The concatenation of the historical failure on the part of the GDC to instigate a system of enforcement of professional indemnity cover for the dental profession, and the absence of provision of information to patients concerning professional indemnity cover, and the high levels of mobility between practices of junior dentists, and the short periods of practice in the UK by foreign-trained dentists has produced an unacceptably high incidence of dental patients unable to pursue meritorious claims because either the dentist's whereabouts, or the identity of their indemnity provider, or both, is unknown. The 2014 statutory changes are, in the judgment of the authors, unlikely to eliminate this significant mischief.

DENTAL RECORDS AND DISCLOSURE

35.53 Dental professionals are required to 'make and keep contemporaneous, complete and accurate records'[1] of care provided to a patient. Dental clinical records comprise handwritten or computerised clinical notes, radiographs (either digital or films), investigation reports, laboratory prescriptions, study models, photographs and correspondence. Information recorded should include the patient's presenting complaint, medical history, previous dental history, findings of extra-oral and intra-oral examinations including soft-tissue, periodontal and tooth examination. Tooth examination must include full dental charting detailing teeth present, current restorations, the presence of caries, tooth wear and tooth mobility, details of endodontically treated teeth, occlusal relationship and abnormalities, examination of any prostheses, special investigations (including radiographs and tooth vitality testing), diagnosis (including differential diagnoses), advice regarding available treatment options and their comparative benefits and risks and cost, agreed treatment plan, and full details of treatment carried out including drugs prescribed and materials used[2].

1 GDC *Standards for the Dental Team*, Standard 4.1.
2 Dental record keeping tends to err towards brevity and is usually largely comprised of abbreviations.

35.54   Requests for disclosure of dental records should be made to the practice at which the patient was treated and be directed to the practice principal in their capacity as 'data controller'[1]. Not infrequently the putative defendant may no longer be working at the practice, and upon notification of the potential claim will often request disclosure of any paper records directly to themselves. Patient representatives should be aware that it is physical possession of the clinical records that confers data controller status and should direct any application for disclosure of the patient's records accordingly. It is not uncommon for disclosure of dental records to be incomplete, with missing record cards or radiographs or study models, which materialise only upon threat of an application to the court for an order to compel full disclosure.

1 Applications for disclosure of dental records may be made pursuant to a data subject access request under Data Protection Act 1998, s 7 or pursuant to a pre-action disclosure application under County Courts Act 1984, s 52 and CPR 31.16. The former jurisdiction obviates the need to prove that the respondent is likely to become a defendant and can be used against a practice principal delaying disclosure of a patient's records but who is not a putative defendant to a claim.

35.55   Dental records, unlike GP records, do not transfer between dental practitioners when a patient registers for dental care elsewhere. Where a patient has received treatment from a number of dentists at different practices, individual disclosure requests for the patient's records must be made to each practice. The law does not prescribe a minimum period of retention for dental records generally although dentists providing NHS dental treatment in general practice are required under their NHS contract with NHS England/Welsh Health Board to retain their records for a minimum of two years after the course of treatment has completed[1]. This is clearly an inadequate retention period as claims for dental negligence can arise many years after treatment and dental defence organisations uniformly advise their members that dental records should be retained for a minimum period of 11 years on the basis of the 10-year long-stop limitation period for claims brought under the Consumer Protection Act 1987[2].

1 NHS General Dental Services Regulations 1992, SI 1992/661, Sch 1, Pt IV, para 25(2).
2 This appears to be rather incautious advice on two counts: first, claimants bringing a clinical negligence claim alleging personal injury have the benefit of a three-year limitation period commencing from their date of knowledge with no long-stop period; and second, claims against dentists brought under the Consumer Protection Act 1987 are very rare.

35.56   Lastly an issue may arise as to the ownership of dental records[1]. In the case of general dental practitioner notes, the FP25 record and radiographs are probably the property of the NHS. Computer records are the property of the practice principal. In the case of private dental records ownership lies with the individual treating dentist or practice principal. The ownership of private patients' radiographs is not clear. One view is that the patient has paid for the radiograph as an individual item of treatment and in so doing acquires ownership of the film. An alternative view is that the patient is paying for the dentist's interpretation of the X-ray image and not the film itself.

1 This question may arise where original records and radiographs come into the possession of the patient and the practice principal, or putative defendant, then assert ownership rights over the original records. In view of the patient's right of access to copies of records and radiographs this is probably of little practical importance.

STANDARD OF CARE REQUIRED OF DENTAL PROFESSIONAL

35.57 The standard of care expected of a dental professional is the same as that required of a doctor or any other clinician, namely to exercise the care and skill of a reasonable professional. Negligence is a failure to reach that standard, and a patient must adduce evidence that the dentist has failed to act in accordance with responsible professional practice[1]. A specialist is required to achieve the standard of care of a reasonably competent specialist. However, it is the task undertaken rather than the status of the practitioner which determines the standard of care required. A general dental practitioner will carry out many procedures which are specialist in nature, such as the surgical extraction of a wisdom tooth, complex endodontic treatment of a molar tooth or extensive crown and bridgework, and in doing so must achieve the competency of the relevant specialist[2].

1 'A doctor [sic dentist] is not guilty of negligence if he acted in accordance with a practice accepted as proper by a responsible body of medical [sic dental] men skilled in that particular art' *Bolam v Friern Hospital Management Committee* [1957] 2 All ER 118 at 122. Evidence of common professional practice is not conclusive as to the requisite standard of care. The court will subject the professional practice to a cost-benefit analysis and judge whether such practice is fair, just, reasonable or responsible. See *Bolitho v City and Hackney Health Authority* [1997] 4 All ER 771, 'the judge, before accepting a body of opinion as being responsible, reasonable or respectable. will need to be satisfied that, in forming their view, the experts have directed their minds to the question of comparative risk and benefits and have reached a defensible conclusion on the matter'.
2 In agreeing to undertake specialist treatment a general practitioner is professing to be competent to perform the task with reasonable skill and care. In a claim against a general practitioner relating to specialist treatment expert evidence as to acceptable practice can be adduced from either a relevant specialist or a general practitioner.

35.58 The circumstances which can give rise to a claim for negligence against a dentist range across the entire practice of dentistry although common errors include:

(1) failure to diagnose the presence of dental disease, most commonly dental caries and periodontal disease;
(2) misdiagnosis of dental condition;
(3) failure to treat or delay in providing treatment;
(4) failure to plan treatment appropriately;
(5) failure to refer or delay in referral for specialist treatment;
(6) failure to carry out special investigations such as appropriate radiography;
(7) provision of treatment of an unsatisfactory standard;
(8) provision of unnecessary treatment;
(9) iatrogenic mishaps such as incorrect tooth extraction, injuries caused by dental instruments, inhalation or ingestion of dental instruments;

(10) failure to advise of treatment alternatives and the respective risks and benefits;
(11) failure to give appropriate preoperative warnings;
(12) failure to give appropriate post-operative advice.

These errors of investigation, diagnosis, advice and treatment will be explored further in the subsequent sections surveying the standard of care expected in each clinical speciality of dentistry.

CONSENT TO DENTAL TREATMENT

35.59   Obtaining a patient's consent for treatment has particular significance in dental practice. The reason for this is that there is often a genuine choice for the patient in terms of available treatment options in relation to a particular clinical condition. A fractured or decayed tooth can be treated with a range of restorations and a missing tooth can be replaced with a variety of prostheses. Elective treatment for cosmetic reasons will yield an even greater choice of options. Each treatment option will carry its own advantages and disadvantages in terms of aesthetics, functionality, longevity, tooth damage and cost and it is for the patient to choose their preferred option. The dentist must not manipulate the patient's choice by providing inaccurate or misleading advice.

35.60   The GDC sets the professional standard of disclosure of information required to obtain valid consent of a patient as follows:

'You must obtain valid consent before starting treatment explaining all the relevant options and costs. You should find out what your patients want to know as well as what you think they need to know. Things that a patient might want to know include: options for treatment, the risks and the potential benefits; why you think a particular treatment is necessary and appropriate for them; the consequences, risks and benefits of the treatment you propose; the likely prognosis; your recommended option; the cost of the proposed treatment; what might happen if the proposed treatment is not carried out; and whether the treatment is guaranteed, how long it is guaranteed for and any exclusions that apply.

You must check and document that patients have understood the information you have given.

You must make sure that patients understand the decisions they are being asked to make. You must provide patients with sufficient information and give them a reasonable amount of time to consider that information in order to make a decision.

You must tailor the way you obtain consent to each patient's needs. You should help them to make informed decisions about their care by giving them information in a format they can easily understand'[1].

Thus dentists are under a specific professional obligation to provide intelligible information to patients concerning all available treatment options (including no treatment) and their comparative risks, benefits, prognoses and costs and to ensure that the patient has in fact understood the information.

1 GDC *Standards for the Dental Team*, Principle Three: Obtain valid consent.

35.61 The GDC Standards do not provide guidance about the risks (in terms of their likelihood of materialisation and severity of consequence) of which a patient must be informed. The law[1] has adopted a standard of information disclosure fastened to the expectations of a reasonable patient, namely 'significant risk[s] which would affect the judgment of a reasonable patient'. The effect of the *Bolam* test of liability is that the GDC's professional standard is tantamount to the legal standard for information disclosure to patients in dental practice.

1 *Pearce v United Bristol Healthcare NHS Trust* [1999] PIQR 53, CA. This 'reasonable patient' standard of information disclosure was approved by the House of Lords in *Chester v Afshar* [2005] 1 AC 134. See also *Montgomery v Lanarkshire Health Board* [2015] UKSC 11.

35.62 A claim alleging a patient's lack of 'informed consent' to the treatment provided by a dentist will concern either a failure to offer an alternative treatment option or a failure to warn of a risk inherent in the procedure. In the former scenario the patient must establish that the dentist did not advise the patient of alternative available treatment options and if so advised the patient would have opted for another treatment option. In the latter situation the patient must prove that the dentist did not warn of a particular risk associated with the procedure undertaken (and that risk has materialised) and the patient, if advised of the risk in question, would either have declined to undergo the treatment or would alternatively have postponed the actual procedure carried out (in order to seek further advice) and consequently would not have had the actual procedure on the day it was undertaken[1].

1 *Chester v Afshar* modified the test of causation in consent claims such that the claimant no longer has to prove that she would never have undergone the procedure had she been properly advised, simply that she would not have undergone the treatment on that day. Without such modification of the usual causation rule a patient's right to make an informed choice would likely not be vindicated. See also *Montgomery v Lanarkshire Health Board* [2015] UKSC 11.

35.63 Where a dentist deliberately misleads a patient as to the clinical necessity for a procedure, the patient's consent is vitiated and the dentist is liable in battery[1]. Thus, for example, if a dentist falsely represents to a patient that a course of cosmetic treatment is indicated for therapeutic reasons and no such clinical indication exists, then upon engaging in the treatment, the dentist would be vulnerable to a claim in battery[2].

1 See *Appleton v Garrett* [1997] 8 Med LR 75 where a dentist provided unnecessary dental treatment for profit. The basis for liability in battery is that the patient was unaware of the true nature and quality of the treatment, ie that it was not therapeutic but wholly unnecessary.
2 Such a misrepresentation must be made in bad faith in order to secure the patient's 'consent' to treatment which confers no clinical benefit. Such cases of gross overtreatment for profit are not unheard of.

STANDARDS OF CARE AND COMMON CLAIMS IN CLINICAL DENTISTRY

Dental examination

35.64 There is a requirement to take a full social, medical and dental history before first examination of a new dental patient. The examination should comprise extra-oral and intra-oral assessment, including screening for dental caries and periodontal disease, requiring exposure of radiographs.

Radiographic examination

35.65 The relevant guidelines regarding radiographic examination recommend patient specific X-ray films are exposed for new patients including posterior bitewings and selected periapical views[1].

1 Pendelbury, Horner, Eaton (eds) *Selection Criteria for Dental Radiography* (2004).

35.66 Comprehensive assessment allows coherent diagnosis of the presence of pathology and appropriate treatment planning. Full recording of the outcome of the assessment, the diagnosis and treatment planning is essential.

Dental recall interval

35.67 Frequency of re-examination for adults is no longer automatically every six months but is determined by clinical need. It is for the attending clinician to determine the specific oral disease profile of the patient, taking into account dental history and evidence of active dental caries and periodontal disease. The decision regarding recall interval is made at the conclusion of the course of treatment which follows the first examination. The assessment of oral disease status must be communicated to the patient, with a recommendation as to recall frequency, which must be recorded.

35.68 The recall frequency range for routine dental examinations recommended by the National Institute for Health and Care Excellence (NICE) is between 3 and 12 months if the patient is under 18 years of age, and between 3 and 24 months if the patient is an adult[1].

1 Dental recall – Recall interval between routine dental examinations (NICE, CG19 2004).

Repeat dental radiography

35.69 Repeat radiographic examination depends upon risk of dental disease. The Faculty of General Dental Practitioners provides definitive guidance[1]:

(1) patients identified as high caries risk should have posterior bitewing radiographs exposed at six-month intervals or until no new or progressing carious lesions are evident;

(2) moderate caries risk patients should have bitewing films exposed at 1-year intervals;

(3) low caries risk patients should have bitewing films exposed at 2-year intervals;

(4) patients with periodontal disease should have selected radiographic views exposed for areas where disease is identified clinically.

1 Selection Criteria for Dental Radiography (2013).

35.70 Common errors in dental examinations include a failure to diagnose the presence of dental caries due to inadequate visual inspection or failure to take appropriate screening radiographs or inadequately interpreting radiographs and missing the presence of caries.

Restorative dentistry

Crown and bridgework

35.71   Crowns are routinely provided to protect teeth that are heavily broken down or root treated, or to restore implants. In some cases crowns are also prescribed to improve the appearance of severely discoloured teeth, or correct the shape and/or position of teeth.

35.72   Fixed bridgework may be provided in the form of a traditional fixed bridge with crowns, known as retainers, placed on supporting teeth on either side of the missing tooth or teeth, or as a resin-bonded bridge (Maryland Bridge) where the support is bonded to the adjacent supporting tooth, or as a traditional cantilever bridge with a single retainer on a supporting tooth at one side of the gap only.

Assessment, diagnosis and treatment planning

35.73   A full assessment must be undertaken before crown or bridge placement, including detailed examination of the teeth in question, and appropriate testing including vitality testing and exposure of radiographs.

35.74   The careful clinician will consider the tooth shape and anatomy, the amount of residual tooth structure, the status of any pre-existing restoration, the status of the dental pulp and the bone surrounding the tooth, the presence of any associated pathology, the occlusion and overall prognosis of the tooth, before planning crown or bridge provision.

Risks associated with crowns and bridges

35.75   Crown and bridge provision is not appropriate in the presence of active decay and/or gum disease, and must be provided on teeth which are free of pathology. It should be noted that crowns are rarely the best option to improve the shape/aesthetics/position of otherwise healthy teeth: there are far more conservative methods of restoration that should be considered first[1].

1 Alternative methods of improving appearance which conserve tooth structure include orthodontic treatment, bleaching, or direct composite veneers.

35.76   Approximately 20 per cent of prepared teeth will lose vitality following crown or bridge provision[1]. Accordingly patients must be advised of the specific risk of nerve death associated with crown or non-adhesive bridge provision prior to agreeing to undergo the treatment.

1 Saunders and Saunders 'Prevalence of periradicular periodontitis associated with crowned teeth in an adult Scottish subpopulation' (1998) 185 British Dental Journal 137–140.

35.77   A large scale study indicates that approximately 50 per cent of all crowns will require re-intervention at 12 years[1]. Accordingly, a crown and traditional bridgework replacement cycle of 12 years may be considered.

1 Lucarotti and Burke 'Analysis of an administrative database of indirect restorations over 11 years' (2009) 37(1) J Dent 4–11.

Common defects with crowns and bridges

35.78   The following are common defects:

(1)   unacceptable aesthetics, whether inappropriate size or shape or shade selection or inappropriate angulation compared to neighbouring teeth. Extensive occlusal adjustment of the crown after cementation can result in unsatisfactory aesthetics;

(2)   defective marginal fit: this may be a deficiency between the margin of the restoration and the prepared tooth or alternatively a positive ledge, both defects precipitating plaque accumulation and development of caries. Deficiencies and ledges should be less than 5mm and capable of being polished to be acceptable; and

(3)   problems with the occlusion: if the occlusal surface of the restoration does not fit the occlusal relationship of the jaws a premature contact can occur causing inflammation and pain in the restored tooth and muscles of mastication and temporo-mandibular joint[1].

1 Maglad, Wassell, Barclay, Walls 'Risk management in clinical practice. Part 3. Crowns and bridges' (2010) 209 British Dentistry Journal 115–122.

Cosmetic dental treatment

Tooth whitening

35.79   This common procedure does not produce permanent change and involves the application of bleaching compounds to the exterior of teeth, with or without light activation. Short duration tooth sensitivity after whitening is a common side effect. Dentists engaging in tooth whitening must protect the patients' soft tissue so as to avoid contact between the soft tissues and the bleaching agents, and consequent chemical damage.

35.80   Existing restorations cannot be whitened, and therefore, heavily restored teeth may not be suitable for the whitening procedure. Patients who are at high risk of sensitivity or those with active decay and/or gum disease should not have their teeth whitened.

Adhesive restorations

35.81   Commonly referred to as white fillings, unlike traditional amalgam restorations, these adhesive restorations do not contain mercury. Ensuring adhesion of the white filling to the tooth structure involves the controlled use of acid gel, which with restoration contraction on setting can result in thermal hypersensitivity after placement.

35.82   Occasionally teeth will become non-vital after white fillings are placed, but there is no evidence that this happens more frequently after adhesive restorations than after any other type of filling material. However, it is generally accepted that white fillings are not ideal for large or deep cavities because of the difficulty of ensuring moisture control during the filling process, and of achieving satisfactory light curing of the filling material at the depth of the restoration with resultant restorative failure.

Porcelain veneers

35.83 Porcelain veneers are thin facings of porcelain which are glued onto the front of natural teeth after removal of up to 2mm of surface enamel, amounting to the loss of up to 30 per cent of a tooth's total structure by volume. Infrequently veneer provision can result in the loss of vitality of the veneered teeth, with an increased incidence when the tooth is over-prepared. A large scale recent study has shown a half life for porcelain veneers of approximately 10 years[1].

1 Burke and Lucarott 'Ten year outcome of porcelain laminate veneers placed within the general dental services in England and Wales' (2009) 37 J Dent 31–38.

35.84 Factors which increase the risk of veneer failure include bonding onto pre-existing composite restorations, placement by an inexperienced operator and using veneers to restore worn or fractured teeth where a combination of parafunction, large areas of exposed dentine and insufficient tooth tissue exist[1]. Porcelain veneers are not suitable to correct tooth crowding and cannot mask deep discolouration. Common defects of veneers include unsatisfactory aesthetics relating to shade, size and shape and decementation caused by inadequate bonding technique or occlusal interferences or fracturing due to occlusal trauma.

1 Walls, Steele and Wassell 'Crowns and other extra-coronal restorations: Porcelain laminate veneers' (2002) 193 British Dentistry Journal 73–82.

Smile makeovers

35.85 The term 'smile makeover' is used by its proponents to describe a basket of treatments intended to change a patient's smile and hence facial appearance for the better. As an elective procedure the informational requirement on the practitioner proposing a smile makeover to a patient is high, including treatment option information, detailed risk advice, and clear advice regarding the future reparative cycle of any treatment provided and the cost of any proposed treatment options.

35.86 A smile makeover does not improve the health of the teeth, nor does it address any dental disease. In fact, many treatments sold to patients by dentists to 'improve' patients' smiles weaken the teeth involved, diminish their long-term prognosis, and attract high quantum when litigated.

Endodontics

35.87 Endodontics is the study and treatment of pathology involving the dental pulp. Often referred to colloquially as 'the nerve', dental pulp tissue provides sensory innervation, nutrient supply and infection resistance to the tooth. The dental pulp is located within the hollow space of the crown of a tooth, and within the lumen of a tooth's root complex, and communicates with blood vessels, and nerves, etc in the bone surrounding the tooth via a small opening, known as a foramen, at, or close to, the end of each tooth root. The end of the root of a tooth is known as the root apex.

When healthy, dental pulp tissue has a soft gelatinous consistency and is non-mineralised. It consists of blood and lymphatic vessels, nervous tissue and connective tissue.

When is endodontic treatment required?

35.88   There are a number of clinical situations in which dental pulp tissue can become irreversibly damaged, whether by dental caries, trauma to the relevant tooth, or other factors such as chemical irritation or excessive heat. The effect of the damage is to render the pulp tissue non-vital and hence unable to protect the tooth from microbial infection.

35.89   A loss of tooth vitality in the absence of endodontic treatment presents a significant risk of subsequent dental infection with associated clinical signs and symptoms. Localised dental infection may then extend into the surrounding bone, with an increase in the severity of signs and symptoms and an associated risk to general health.

35.90   There are also a number of dental procedures in which elective devitalisation of vital pulp tissue may be considered, including the provision of space for post placement to support a crown, where pulp vitality is doubted prior to restoration, or when a proposed procedure would itself compromise pulp vitality. Accordingly, in those circumstances endodontic treatment may be provided as an alternative to the maintenance of a healthy, vital dental pulp.

35.91   The objective of endodontic treatment, whether to non-vital teeth or vital teeth, is to disinfect the tooth space previously occupied by pulp tissue, and then to seal the space to prevent contamination or re-contamination by microorganisms. If infection is associated with loss of vitality, then endodontic treatment to the relevant tooth will include drainage of the infected material prior to disinfection.

Types of endodontic treatment

35.92   Endodontic treatment may be divided broadly into two categories: conventional root canal treatment (RCT) also known as orthograde endodontic treatment, or in the alternative, surgical endodontic treatment.

Endodontic success rates

35.93   The limited available scientific evidence indicates higher success rates for conventional root canal treatment compared with surgical endodontics[1]. The weighted average success rates are as follows:

RCT of uninfected teeth: 93 per cent
RCT of infected teeth: 77 per cent
Surgical endodontic treatment of infected teeth: 63 per cent

1 Friedman 'Treatment outcome and prognosis of endodontic therapy' in Ørstavik and Pitt Ford *Essential Endodontology* (1998).

35.94   By reason of the superior success rates and reduced morbidity of conventional root canal treatment, it is accepted that conventional root canal treatment should, subject to features peculiar to the tooth and patient in question, always be the approach adopted in providing endodontic treatment[1].

1 Carrotte 'Endodontic problems' (2005) 198 British Dentistry Journal 127–133.

Practitioner competence

35.95   It is a given that all general dental practitioners should be able to recognise and treat commonplace dental pulp tissue pathology and provide conventional root canal treatment[1].

1 'Quality guidelines for endodontic treatment: consensus report of the European Society of Endodontology' (2006) 39 International Endodontic Journal 921–930.

Contraindications to root canal treatment

35.96   Root canal treatment is not appropriate for teeth which cannot be made functional, nor for teeth which cannot be restored after endodontic treatment, nor for those which have insufficient periodontal support.

Contraindications to surgical endodontics

35.97   Surgical treatment is not appropriate where non-surgical conventional root canal treatment with a reasonable prospect of success could be undertaken. Local anatomy or patient medical health may make surgery a poor treatment option. Surgical endodontics should not be provided when teeth are not restorable, or when there is poor periodontal support. Operator skill and experience is an important consideration in determining whether or not a referral should be made if surgical endodontics is in contemplation.

Assessment, diagnosis and treatment planning

35.98   When assessing the endodontic status of a tooth it is essential that good diagnostic quality radiographs are exposed, allowing an assessment of the presence or absence of pathology within the tooth and the surrounding bone. Radiographs should be compared with historical films, if available, to provide a longitudinal guide to changes in radiographic appearance. All radiographs must be reported with relevant clinical details recorded within the patient's clinical record.

35.99   The vitality status of the pulp tissue is measured with an electronic pulp tester which allows for quantitative readings to be obtained. Other clinical tests should be undertaken and all relevant clinical signs and test outcomes should be recorded.

35.100   In reaching a diagnosis of the cause of the patient's symptoms, attention must be paid to the clinical history and presenting symptoms in conjunction with clinical signs and the results of clinical testing. The differential diagnoses must be coherent, and derived logically from the outcome of the assessment.

35.101 Treatment planning should address the diagnosis and consider the different options for endodontic treatment. Due consideration should be given to related factors, including the restorability of the tooth in question.

Consent to endodontic treatment

35.102 Treatment option information and reasons for the recommendation of the proposed course of endodontic treatment must be provided. The relevant risk information including the success rate of each option is essential to enable the patient to make an autonomous choice to undergo treatment. Where appropriate, the option of referral to a specialist endodontist should be offered as an alternative.

Root canal treatment guidelines[1]

35.103 The following guidelines should be followed:

- preoperative radiograph must be exposed and analysed which shows at least the full root of the tooth and 2–3mm of bone around each root apex, known as the periapical area;
- local anaesthesia given as appropriate;
- dental caries must be removed from the tooth and restorability of the tooth confirmed;
- tooth isolated by application of rubber dam;
- access cavity through crown into pulp chamber created, pulp tissue within pulp chamber removed and root canal openings identified;
- root canals must be instrumented to the terminus of their lumen, commonly where the root canal ends at the apical constriction of the root. This distance is referred to as the working length. The working length for each root canal is established either by use of an electronic device in conjunction with confirmatory radiograph or by radiography alone. Working lengths should be recorded;
- shaping and cleaning of the root canal lumen to the appropriate lengths must be carried out;
- irrigation of the root canal complex is carried out during the instrumentation phase. It is common to use disinfectants such as sodium hypochlorite or chlorhexidine. Great care is required in the use of such disinfectants including their delivery using a Luer-Lok device to avoid needle dislodging, use of a side venting needle, and low pressure irrigant delivery[2];
- filling, or obturation, of the root canal complex takes place using a plastic material, commonly gutta-percha, in conjunction with root canal sealer cement. The quality of the root canal filling must be verified after placement by taking a radiograph of the root apices. The post-operative radiograph should show that the prepared root canal is filled completely. No space between the root canal filling and the canal wall should be seen. There should be no canal space visible beyond the end-point of the root canal filling, which will usually be located between 0.5mm and 2mm from the radiographic end of the root. This type of root filling is also known as an orthograde root filling;
- the treated tooth should be restored immediately so that bacterial re-contamination is prevented.

1 'Quality guidelines for endodontic treatment: consensus report of the European Society of Endodontology' (2006) 39 International Endodontic Journal 921–930.
2 Spencer, Ike, Brennan 'Review: the use of sodium hypochlorite in endodontics – potential complications and their management' (2007) 202 British Dentistry Journal 555–559.

35.104 Common errors in conventional endodontic treatment include under-filling of the canal system which predisposes the tooth to reinfection of the canal system and periapical area, or over-filling the canal beyond the apex, which can cause inflammation or infection of the periapical area. Extrusion of toxic irrigant or sealant material beyond the apex of the canal into the periapical area can cause widespread bone necrosis or even nerve paraesthesia if introduced into the mandibular canal. Appropriate post-operative radiographs are clinically essential in order to check the outcome of root canal obturation, and are essential evidence in determining breach of duty.

35.105 Another common mishap is a root perforation. This is caused by either over-zealous instrumentation of the root canal or misalignment during preparation of the post hole prior to fitting a post-retained crown and invariably amounts to negligent technique. Lastly, inhalation or ingestion of an endodontic instrument is indefensible.

35.106 Root canal treated posterior teeth are at higher risk of catastrophic failure than non-root treated teeth and therefore it is generally accepted that heavily restored posterior teeth should be protected after completion of root canal treatment by restoration with a crown or inlay which covers the cusps of the teeth and thereby significantly reduces the risk of vertical tooth fracture[1].

1 Smith and Schuman 'Restoration of endodontically treated teeth: a guide for the restorative dentist' (1997) 28 Quintessence Int 457–462.

35.107 An endodontic instrument can fracture within the root canal complex during normal use and the retained fragment may prevent the successful conclusion of treatment. Such a fracture is not evidence of faulty technique provided that the instruments, expressly designed to be single use only, were used in accordance with manufacturers' instructions.

35.108 When an instrument fracture occurs, the patient must be informed immediately of the fracture. Appropriate radiographs must be exposed and, if necessary, a referral made to a specialist endodontist to assess with a view to removal of the retained fragment or obturation around the lodged instrument.

35.109 Where multiple instrument fractures occur, and in particular when such fractures go unnoticed and unreported, it is reasonable to infer that the multiple fractures occurred due to defective technique on the part of the operator amounting to breach of duty.

Surgical endodontic guidelines[1]

35.110 The following guidelines should be followed:

- preoperative radiograph must be exposed and analysed which shows at least the full root of the tooth and 2–3mm of bone around each root apex, known as the periapical area;

- local anaesthesia achieved;
- appropriate surgical flap raised, and reflected;
- bone overlying the apical area of the relevant tooth must be removed using an appropriate rotating instrument with copious irrigant cooling;
- the relevant procedure is then performed. This may include: periradicular curettage (ie the removal of diseased tissue from the bone surrounding the tooth); biopsy (ie the surgical removal of a tissue specimen for examination); root-end resection (ie the removal of a section of root which could not be disinfected, commonly the apical section), and root end preparation and filling. This procedure involves preparation of a 3mm deep cavity within the resected root end and the placement of a root-end filling, also known as a retrograde root filling. The material commonly used for a root-end filling is mineral trioxide aggregate (MTA). Amalgam is not an acceptable root-end filling material;
- a radiograph to assess the quality of the root-end filling must be exposed and analysed before flap closure;
- surgical flap is closed.

1 Guidelines for Surgical Endodontics. Version 2. Faculty of Dental Surgery of the Royal College of Surgeons of England. 2012.

35.111 Common errors in surgical endodontic treatment include a failure to remove diseased tissue associated with the root-end, whether in whole or in part, failure to resect the end of the root or otherwise prepare the root-end to accommodate a retrograde root-end filling, and incomplete/inadequate root-end filling. Appropriate post-operative radiographs are required clinically in order to check treatment outcome, and are essential in the determination of failures amounting to breach in surgical endodontic treatment.

Periodontal disease management

35.112 Periodontal disease is a localised infection of the supporting structures of teeth comprising the connective tissue attachment between tooth root and bone, known as the periodontal ligament, and the alveolar bone itself. The infection is caused by the presence of bacteria. The relevant bacteria form an adherent mass or biofilm known as dental plaque, which covers all exposed tooth surfaces. Plaque cannot be rinsed off, but can be removed by brushing, flossing and professional intervention.

Chronic periodontitis

35.113 The most common form of periodontal disease is chronic periodontitis, a long-standing inflammatory condition caused by the presence of plaque, but mediated by features which are specific to the patient. This is a common disease, with the NHS reporting that 45 per cent of all dentate adults in England, Wales and NI demonstrate evidence of chronic periodontal disease[1].

1 The NHS Information Centre for health and social care. Disease and related disorders – a report from the Adult Dental Health Survey. 2009.

35.114 Untreated active chronic periodontal disease results in the progressive loss of bone support to the teeth. Bone support loss is associated with the development of periodontal pocketing around the affected teeth. These periodontal pockets form under the gum as periodontal ligament is lost and as the supporting bone is resorbed, and are a marker for the presence and progression of disease. The severity of bone loss is related to the pocket depth, with a depth measurement of 4–6mm being considered moderate, and over 6mm being regarded as deep[1].

1 Palmer and Floyd *A Clinical Guide to Periodontology* (2nd edn, 2003).

35.115 Other indicators of active chronic periodontal disease may include bleeding on probing, tooth mobility, the presence of pus, and the appearance of the soft tissues including either recession or swelling.

35.116 In most cases the deterioration caused by untreated chronic periodontitis is slow to moderate, but episodes of more rapid tissue destruction can occur. Risk factors for chronic periodontitis include smoking, systemic disease, stress and genetics.

Aggressive periodontitis

35.117 The rare but rapidly progressing form of periodontal disease known as aggressive periodontitis is also important due to the severity and rate of bone loss with which it is associated. The extent of destruction caused by aggressive periodontitis is disproportionately greater than would be indicated by the, often minimal, amount of plaque present.

35.118 Aggressive periodontitis may be subdivided into two forms: generally aggressive periodontitis (GAP) and locally aggressive periodontitis (LAP). Distinguished in part by the extent of the disease within the mouth, the two forms also afflict different age groups with GAP affecting adult patients under the age of 30, while LAP is a disease which starts in adolescence.

Screening for periodontal disease

35.119 The periodontal status of all dental patients should be determined at the first examination appointment with a general dental practitioner, and thereafter every year. The basic periodontal examination (BPE) is commonly used for routine screening for periodontal disease, allowing an assessment to be made of those patients who demonstrate evidence of periodontal disease requiring more detailed analysis.

35.120 The BPE screen divides the mouth into six sections, and in each sextant the support structure of each tooth is probed using a specialised instrument. The maximum depth measurements of any periodontal pockets in each sextant are noted and the relevant BPE code allocated to each sextant is determined on a scale of 0–4 according to pocket depths.

35.121 A common mistake made by dentists is to confuse the pocket depth readings in mm with the BPE code. There is no such correlation and an error of this type renders the screening valueless.

35.122 All patients with a BPE code in any sextant of 3 or more require a full periodontal charting to be undertaken which records (measured in mm) six pocket depths per tooth and as a general rule, radiographs should also be taken to assess bone levels in these patients[1]. Such patients will commonly require intensive treatment for periodontal disease.

1 The British Society of Periodontology. Basic Periodontal Examination. 2011.

Diagnosis of periodontal disease

35.123 In reaching a diagnosis of periodontal disease, attention must be paid to relevant clinical history and presenting symptoms in conjunction with analysis of dental radiographs and the results of detailed periodontal pocket charting. The relevant disease type must be recorded within the clinical notes and the diagnosis and prognosis and treatment requirements communicated to the patient.

Treatment of chronic periodontitis

35.124 Treatment comprises two phases: first, initial treatment, the aim of which is to arrest the progression of the disease by controlling plaque and eliminating other contributory factors including if applicable, providing oral hygiene advice and smoking cessation advice; and second, corrective treatment. Corrective treatment techniques include the removal of mineralised deposits, a process known as 'scaling', root debridement, various types of periodontal surgery and the use of antibiotics.

Treatment of aggressive periodontitis

35.125 Once identified, these conditions require intensive management, often by a specialist. Treatment includes achieving adequate plaque control in affected pockets, professional instrumentation of affected areas to disrupt the relevant bacterial population and anti-bacterial medication.

Maintenance phase

35.126 Maintenance therapy at intervals of three months is required for patients who have undergone periodontal treatment. These maintenance appointments allow for monitoring and limited treatment of isolated areas of active disease, and are required in the long term in order to maintain the therapeutic benefit of periodontal disease treatment.

Monitoring of patients after treatment

35.127 In order to determine the success of treatment, pocket depths are re-recorded, radiographs re-taken and bleeding and other indices used. The British Society of Periodontology advises that the BPE screen cannot be used to assess the response to periodontal therapy because it provides no information about change in individual sites, and instead comprehensive probing depths measured in mm must be recorded at six sites per individual tooth in order to assess the response to treatment[1].

1 The British Society of Periodontology. Basic Periodontal Examination. 2011.

35.128   Patients who have undergone initial therapy for periodontal disease and who are in the maintenance phase of care, should have full probing depths throughout the entire dentition recorded at least annually[1].

1 The British Society of Periodontology. Basic Periodontal Examination. 2011.

Referral for specialist periodontal care

35.129   General dental practitioners should consider carefully at the diagnostic stage of periodontal disease management whether or not the patient would be better served by early referral to a specialist periodontologist, rather than having treatment provided by a general dental practitioner or dental hygienist. This is particularly relevant when the periodontal disease diagnosis is of severe or widespread disease or disease has been diagnosed as being of an aggressive type.

35.130   If deterioration of the post-treatment periodontal condition, or disease progression, is noted during the maintenance phase, then it is essential that this is recorded, that the patient is informed of the re-infection, and that a timely referral is made to a specialist.

Periodontal mismanagement claims

35.131   General dental practitioners and dental hygienists provide partnership care of patients with periodontal disease, often over many years, and accordingly liability may be shared between multiple clinicians. Determining breach of duty even in multi-defendant periodontal claims can be relatively straightforward, but causation can be problematic with indemnifiers routinely defending such claims on that basis. Expert periodontal advice is essential to determine causation.

Minor oral surgery

Dental extractions

35.132   Comprehensive assessment, diagnosis and treatment planning are essential preconditions to successful dental extractions. Assessment of teeth will include the exposure of radiographs allowing an assessment of the presence or absence of pathology associated with the teeth, the morphology of the roots and the relationship of the teeth to the relevant surrounding anatomical features.

35.133   All radiographs must be reported with relevant clinical details recorded within the patient's clinical record. Exceptionally, when a tooth is significantly mobile and there is no risk posed to surrounding anatomy by extraction, radiographs may not be required as part of the assessment process.

35.134   Once a coherent, logical diagnosis is established, treatment planning should address the diagnosis and consider the different treatment options. A full medical history is essential when the extraction of a tooth is in contemplation. Due consideration should be given to available options to preserve the tooth. Predicting the likelihood of tooth fracture and making an appropriate choice of extraction approach, whether conventional using forceps, or surgical involving the raising of surgical flaps and elective bone removal, forms an important part of the assessment process.

35.135 Obtaining valid consent to a proposed extraction requires communication of risks of the procedure, coupled with appropriate alternative treatment options and the advantages and disadvantages of each. The risks associated with extractions vary dependent upon the particular characteristics of the tooth and the patient in question. Dental practitioners must provide accurate and specific risk information to patients, and document the same.

Tooth fracture during extraction

35.136 Notwithstanding careful preoperative assessment and appropriate choice of extraction modality, it is nevertheless relatively common for teeth to fracture during attempted extraction, resulting in incomplete delivery of the tooth. The cause of fracture may be multi-factorial and establishing breach in terms of technical execution of the extraction by the clinician is often problematic.

35.137 However, once tooth fracture has occurred, the attending clinician must identify that incomplete extraction has been achieved and advise the patient accordingly. Then, by careful examination of the extracted elements and the bony socket, along with exposure of appropriate radiographs, the clinician must determine whether or not retrieval is within his skill and expertise, and undertake the same, or in the alternative make a referral to a relevant specialist.

35.138 If there is no pathology associated with a retained root fragment, and if the retained fragment is small in size, eg less than or equal to 1/3 original root length, and its retention would not interfere with future treatment provision, it may be appropriate to leave the root in situ.

Fracture of the mandible

35.139 Fracture of the mandible, whether intra- or post-operative is a very rare but recognised complication of the extraction of lower teeth, specifically third molars, with a reported incidence of 0.0033 per cent to 0.0049 per cent[1]. It is not routinely necessary for clinicians to warn patients that jaw fracture is a risk associated with the extraction of mandibular third molar teeth, save for in circumstances where the risk of the same is elevated. Such circumstances include; extractions in elderly patients, in the presence of gross pathology such as large cysts involving the loss of bone volume, or where there is ankylosis involving the third molar in question, that is the fusion of the tooth to the surrounding alveolar bone. There is also some evidence that the depth of impaction relative to the adjacent molar teeth, the extent to which the impacted tooth is covered by the ascending ramus of the mandible, and the angulation of the impacted tooth are all relevant factors which increase the risk of mandibular fracture.

1 Ethunandan, Shanahan and Patel 'Iatrogenic mandibular fractures following removal of impacted third molars: an analysis of 130 cases' (2012) 212 BDJ 179–184.

35.140 The prudent clinician must therefore carefully analyse the impacted third molar before advising the patient, and provide relevant warnings regarding the risk of jaw fracture to patients, particularly the elderly, when considering the removal of mandibular third molars which are deeply buried, and/or horizontally impacted, and where the extraction is proposed in the presence of gross pathology which has reduced bone volume in the area. Appropriate referral to an oral and maxillofacial department is indicated for 'high risk' patients.

35.141 Intra-operative fractures may be related to poor technique, including improper instrumentation, excessive use of force, and excessive bone removal. However establishing poor technique can be highly problematic in the context of a claim in negligence, particularly when there has been inadequate imaging prior to the extraction in question.

35.142 Mandibular fractures are more common in the post-operative phase than intra-operatively and the risks of the same may be reduced by appropriate advice to maintain a soft diet for four weeks post-operatively, and by avoidance of contact sports or trauma for four weeks post-operatively.

Collateral damage during extraction: uncontrolled/inappropriate application of force

35.143 All dental extractions, whether performed using conventional forceps or by means of a surgical approach, should be carried out using the controlled application of appropriate forces, properly directed. Surrounding anatomy including soft tissues and adjacent teeth should be protected, as appropriate, by the use of retractors and other instruments.

35.144 Save in unusual circumstances, for example if a dental patient makes a gross sudden movement of the head during an extraction attempt, any collateral damage whether to hard or soft tissues is actionable. Quantum of such claims can vary from minor soft tissue damage which does not require repair, and where clinical signs and symptoms are of short duration, which is of low value, while, the inadvertent avulsion of teeth adjacent to the designated tooth for example, will attract higher quantum. When damage has occurred to the skin of the face during dental treatment it is important to consider the aesthetic impact of scarring and any future surgical revision of the same when calculating the quantum of the claim.

Collateral damage during extraction: planning failure

35.145 The anatomy surrounding a tooth to be extracted must be assessed preoperatively and important structures including nerve bundles, blood vessels, air sinuses and so on, must be located and avoided by careful planning of the extraction approach. In some limited circumstances, eg where maxillary air sinuses are enlarged and the roots of the maxillary teeth are intimately involved with the floor of the maxillary sinus, the involvement of the relevant structure with the tooth in question may significantly raise the risk of collateral damage upon dental extraction. In such circumstances full specific risk information must be provided to the patient in advance of agreement to the procedure.

Incorrect tooth extraction

35.146 On occasion clinicians extract healthy teeth without clinical or therapeutic rationale for the same, and claims ensue based on consent. Circumstances where this occurs most commonly include shared care during orthodontic treatment when a treating orthodontist provides a written prescription for the extractions of teeth in order to create space within the dental arches for tooth movement, and the extractions are then carried out by the client's general dental practitioner. If incorrect tooth notation is recorded by the orthodontist in the prescription, it is accepted that tortious liability attaches to the relevant orthodontist, but it is also considered that the duty of care of the attending general dental practitioner extends to being satisfied that the proposed extractions are reasonable within the context of the proposed orthodontic treatment, and a clinician who fails to discharge this duty may also be joined in the claim as appropriate.

35.147 Claims for incorrect tooth extraction also arise with shared care in general practice when diagnosis of dental pathology necessitating a dental extraction is made by one clinician but the extraction is then carried out later by another, relying upon the sometimes-illegible earlier diagnosis. More generally, healthy teeth may be removed following inadequate assessment, diagnosis and treatment planning, typically in the absence of diagnostic quality radiographs. In these circumstances, the first indication that the patient may have that the wrong tooth has been extracted is on the day following the extraction, when the symptoms of dental pain resume unabated after the effects of the local anaesthetic have worn off.

Impacted third molar extractions

35.148 Historically, the extraction of impacted third molars, also referred to as wisdom teeth, was undertaken prophylactically in order to avoid the non-specific risk of future pathology in the region of the third molars.

However following the publication by the National Institute for Health and Care Excellence (NICE) of Guidance on the Extraction of Wisdom Teeth in 2000 this practice is deemed inappropriate[1].

1 Guidance on the Extraction of Wisdom Teeth (NICE, 2000), para 1.3 TA1.

35.149 NICE advises that extraction of impacted wisdom teeth should be limited to patients with evidence of pathology, including dental caries, infection, tumour and so on. A single episode of inflammation around an impacted wisdom tooth, a condition known as pericoronitis, is deemed by NICE to be insufficient grounds for extraction of the tooth[1]. The Guidelines state:

'The practice of prophylactic removal of pathology-free impacted third molars should be discontinued in the NHS'. (paragraph 1.1)

'Surgical removal of impacted third molars should be limited to patients with evidence of pathology'. (paragraph 1.3)

1 Guidance on the Extraction of Wisdom Teeth, para 1.4.

35.150 The exposure of appropriate radiographs preoperatively in relation to impacted third molars is mandatory, see above. In particular the surgical removal of lower third molars endangers two important sensory nerves, the lingual and the inferior alveolar nerves, and the location of the inferior alveolar nerve and its relationship to the impacted third molar in question must be determined as part of the assessment process. Damage to the lingual nerve can result in loss of sensation to the tongue with evidence that up to 2 per cent of all patients undergoing removal of lower third molars experience permanent impairment following surgery[1]. Damage to the inferior alveolar nerve can result in sensory disturbance to the soft tissue of the face including the lip, with permanent impairment noted in up to 2.2 per cent of extraction cases[2].

1 Loescher, Smith, Robinson 'Nerve Damage and Third Molar Removal' (2003) 30 Dent Update 375–380.
2 (2003) 30 Dent Update 375–380.

35.151 Not all nerve damage is actionable. As set out above, it is accepted that there is a risk of nerve damage during the extraction of an impacted third molar which may occur despite appropriate preoperative assessment and treatment planning, and notwithstanding that the extraction is executed to the appropriate standard.

35.152 Accordingly the likelihood of temporary and/or permanent nerve impairment forms an essential part of the risk profile of surgical extraction of impacted wisdom teeth about which patients should be warned before they consent to undergo the procedure. The assessing clinician must also consider and advise the patient of whether or not the risk of nerve impairment would be reduced if the extraction were to be carried out within a specialist unit, and, if relevant, should offer the option of referral to the patient. In particular any evidence on radiographic assessment that the relevant impacted third molar is in close conjunction with, or overlaying, the inferior alveolar nerve bundle, should prompt the reasonable general dental practitioner to consider referral of the patient to a specialist unit for further assessment and treatment in relation to the impacted tooth. Additionally, as with the extraction of non-impacted teeth, patients must be provided with information regarding applicable alternative treatment approaches. A failure to advise the patient in terms above, providing specific risk and treatment option information, prior to the surgical extraction will leave the clinician at risk of a claim in consent in the event that the patient sustains nerve damage during the extraction.

35.153 When it occurs, the extent of nerve injury after the extraction of impacted third molars ranges from neuropraxia where no anatomical break in the nerve bundle occurs and recovery is likely within weeks, to neurotmesis or complete anatomical disruption of the nerve bundle with no possibility of recovery. The extent of the injury not only goes to quantum but if physical discontinuity of the nerve bundle can be demonstrated, may also increase the likelihood of a successful claim in breach in relation to technical execution of the extraction.

Coronectomy

35.154 Since 2005, coronectomy, that is the removal of the crown only of an impacted wisdom tooth, has been described as an alternative to extraction on the basis that this procedure significantly reduces the risk of damage to the inferior alveolar nerve compared to removal of the entire tooth. Save for teeth with active infection, mobile teeth or profoundly horizontally impacted lower wisdom teeth, coronectomy is now routinely offered as an alternative treatment option to surgical extraction[1].

1 Ahmed, el Wafae, Bouchra 'Coronectomy of third molar: a reduced risk technique for inferior alveolar nerve damage' (2011) 38 Dent Update 267–276.

Third molar extraction claims

35.155 Claims for the avoidable injury to either the inferior dental nerve or the lingual nerve following extraction of a lower wisdom tooth are common. The basis of the claim may include a lack of clinical indication for the extraction, a failure to obtain the patient's informed consent through incomplete or misleading risk information concerning permanent nerve injury, a failure to offer the option of coronectomy or negligent surgical technique.

Orthodontic extractions

35.156 Teeth are commonly removed in order to create space for the orthodontic movement of teeth. It is the treating orthodontist's responsibility to draft an accurate prescription correctly identifying the notation of teeth for extraction but additionally the extracting clinician must ensure that the orthodontist's instructions are logically consistent with the orthodontic diagnosis and proposed orthodontic treatment.

Maxillary tuberosity fracture

35.157 Assessment of upper posterior teeth for extraction must include an analysis of the risk of fracture of the maxillary tuberosity, and communication of the risk to the patient. If the risk of fracture is elevated, a referral to a specialist unit may be indicated where the risks of the procedure may be reduced and repair may be effected in a timely fashion. It is therefore essential that radiographs of upper posterior teeth are exposed and analysed before treatment planning, and appropriate steps taken thereafter[1].

1 Bell 'Oro-antral fistulae and fractured tuberosities' (2011) 211 British Dentistry Journal 119–123.

Oro-antral communication

35.158 The creation of an oro-antral communication (OAC) also known as a oro-antral fistula (OAF) between the oral cavity and the overlying sinuses within the facial bones can occur when an upper tooth is extracted. Careful preoperative assessment will alert the clinician to the risk of such a complication and may enable selection of the appropriate extraction technique or operator to avoid such a complication.

35.159   The creation of an OAC is not of itself evidence of breach of duty. However, when an OAC occurs the attending clinician must assess and diagnose the complication, and then manage it appropriately whether by repair or referral. If a defective tooth removal technique has been used, then, coincident with the creation of an OAC, fragments of tooth root may be displaced into the connected sinus. Such displacement is regarded as amounting to breach of duty. Prompt removal or referral is essential in such cases to avoid chronic sinus pathology.

Treatment of dentoalveolar infection

35.160   The majority of dental infections are relatively mild and can be managed by local therapy alone. It is accepted that drainage of infected material whether by tooth extraction, surgical incision or via an opened root canal is the most important factor in treatment of acute dental infection[1]. Antibiotics should only be used, after drainage has been achieved, when there is evidence of a spreading infection, and a need to prevent the onset of serious consequences[2].

1 Peterson 'Principles of management and presentation of odontogenic infections' in Peterson (ed) *Contemporary Oral and Maxillofacial Surgery* (3rd edn, 1998) pp 392–417.
2 Kuriyama, Absi, Williams and Lewis 'An outcome audit of the treatment of acute dentoalveolar infection: impact of penicillin resistance' 198 British Dental Journal 759–763.

Oral medicine

Oral cancer

35.161   This pathology accounts for approximately 2 per cent of all malignant tumours in patients in the UK, with more than 6,700 new cases diagnosed in 2011. Patients with advanced oral cancer have a poor prognosis, but if diagnosed early the prognosis is good[1].

Accordingly, it is essential that dental professionals identify potential signs and symptoms of oral cancer when examining patients, and then act by referring the patient urgently if appropriate. The NICE referral guidelines for suspected cancer provide essential guidance[2]. Patients should be examined for potential malignancy at every dental examination[3].

1 Cancer Research UK. UK oral cancer statistics. 2014. http://info.cancerresearchuk.org/cancerstats/types/oral (accessed December 2014).
2 National Institute for Health and Care Excellence. C27 Referral for suspected cancer: NICE guideline. London: NICE, 2005.
3 Cancer Research UK. Mouth Cancer referral guidelines for dentists. 2005. http://publications.cancerresearchuk.org/downloads/product/dentist1.pdf (accessed December 2014).

35.162   Claims brought against dental professionals in relation to a failure of timely diagnosis or failure to provide a timely referral in respect of oral cancer are commonly defended on causation grounds, namely that the delay in treatment has had no significant impact on the treatment provided or prognosis and survival rate of the patient.

Referral guidelines

35.163 A patient who presents with symptoms suggestive of head and neck cancer should be referred to an appropriate specialist.

Any patient with persistent symptoms or signs related to the oral cavity, where no definitive diagnosis of a benign lesion can be made, should be referred or followed up until the symptoms and signs disappear. If the symptoms and signs have not disappeared after six weeks, an urgent referral should be made.

35.164 If a patient presents with unexplained red and white patches of the oral mucosa that are painful, or swollen, or bleeding, unexplained ulceration of the oral mucosa or a mass persisting for more than three weeks, or unexplained tooth mobility, then an urgent referral should be made.

35.165 Patients with an unexplained lump in the neck which has recently appeared or a lump which has not been diagnosed before that has changed over a period of three to six weeks, or with an unexplained persistent swelling in the parotid or submandibular gland, should be referred urgently.

35.166 If patients present with an unexplained persistent sore, or painful, throat, or with unilateral unexplained pain in the head and neck area for more than four weeks, associated with otalgia (ear ache) but with normal otoscopy, an urgent referral should be made.

35.167 With the exception of persistent hoarseness, for which an urgent referral for a chest X-ray should be made in the primary care setting[1], investigations for head and neck cancer in primary care are not recommended as they can delay referral[2].

1 C27 Referral for suspected cancer: NICE guideline (NICE, 2005) 1.11.7.
2 C27 Referral for suspected cancer: NICE guideline 1.11.12.

Dental implants

35.168 Fully part of mainstream UK dentistry since the mid 1990s, dental implants provide a highly effective solution to the problem of replacement of missing teeth. From a patient's perspective, dental implants function like natural teeth, allowing recreation of normal speech and chewing, and achieving a natural aesthetic, while avoiding damage to healthy teeth. Dental implants have the additional benefit of maintaining the underlying bone, are unaffected by dental caries and demonstrate high long-term survival rates. Where appropriate, therapy involving the use of dental implants is now the remedial treatment of choice for tooth replacement.

35.169 Dental implants are constructed of titanium and rely on the concept of osseointegration, ie the establishment of a direct functional and structural union between the titanium of the implant and the bone of the jaw into which the dental implant is placed.

35.170 A dental implant consists of a titanium screw or cylinder of between 8mm and 16mm in length, which is inserted into a prepared bony socket in the bone of the jaw. Once integrated with the bone, the dental implant then acts as a replacement 'root' ripe for restoration.

35.171   After placement, a dental implant is commonly restored with an additional attachment called an abutment which is fitted to the top of the implant, often by means of a screw, although some systems provide a one-piece combined implant and abutment. Whereas the implant is buried within bone, the abutment itself projects through the gum overlying the implant and its supporting bone, into the oral cavity, and acts as the connector between the integrated implant within the bone and the supported restoration superstructure.

35.172   The restoration superstructure on the abutment may take the form of a single crown, the retainer of a bridge, or the implant may be connected to a removable prosthesis such as a multi-tooth denture. Securing the overlying restoration superstructure to the abutment may be achieved by the use of a screw, allowing for retrieval of the restoration if necessary, or by cementing the restoration permanently into position. When implants are used to support removable prostheses, the abutments will take the form of connectors which allow patients to remove the prostheses with ease.

Success rates of dental implants

35.173   According to the Association of Dental Implantology, survival rates for dental implants have been reported to be in excess of 90 per cent after 15 years[1]. There is, however, a difference in success rates between implants placed in the upper jaw or maxilla at 85–90 per cent compared with 95 per cent success for implants placed in the lower jaw or mandible[2].

1 *A dentist's guide to implantology* (2012).
2 Palmer 'Risk management in clinical practice. Part 9. Dental implants' (2010) 209 British Dentistry Journal 499–506.

35.174   Although success rates for dental implants in both jaws are high, it should be noted that when dental implants fail the resulting loss of hard and soft tissue can present significant difficulties for remediation.

Practitioner competence

35.175   Dental implantology is not a recognised dental speciality within the UK. However, the dental regulator, the General Dental Council, stipulates that dentists who place dental implants should comply with the Faculty of General Dental Practice's Training Standards in Implant Dentistry[1].

1 Training Standards in Implant Dentistry (2012).

35.176   The Faculty distinguishes between simple and complex dental implant treatment. Complex dental implant treatment is defined as involving any of the following factors: treatment where the end result could not be easily visualised; a patient who is medically compromised; implant surgery which would involve bone grafting, or a requirement to alter soft tissue position, or amendment of bite relationships; the presence of factors increasing the risk of failure; or if it was anticipated that the implants would be loaded early. Simple dental implant treatment involves none of the stated features of complexity.

35.177 The Standards state that while replacement of missing teeth involving the straightforward placement and restoration of implants may be carried out by a general dentist who has completed a relevant course of training and mentoring and who has acquired detailed skill and knowledge, complex implant treatment demands a high level of skill and experience, and is likely to require a team approach comprised of separate surgical and restorative teams, with the surgical standard required being equivalent to that of a dentist seeking a specialist surgical qualification[1].

A failure to adhere to the Faculty's Standards of training and experience by a practitioner providing dental implant treatment is prima facie evidence of a breach of duty.

1 Training Standards in Implant Dentistry (2012).

Contraindications to dental implants

35.178 Dental implant treatment is not appropriate when a patient has undergone radiotherapy to the jaws or neighbouring structures, nor when there is untreated oral pathology, including in particular untreated periodontal disease or dental infection.

35.179 Children should not be provided with dental implants, save for temporary use in orthodontic treatment, until the facial skeleton has finished growing, which usually occurs about 18 years of age.

35.180 Dental implants for patients undergoing intravenous bisphosphonate therapy (but not oral therapy) are regarded as inappropriate because of the risk of osteonecrosis, ie the localised death of the jaw bone following the surgical phase of implant treatment. Patients with significantly suppressed immune systems, for example those who have undergone organ transplantation, are also unsuitable for dental implant provision because of the risk of infection.

Relative contraindications to dental implants

35.181 Uncontrolled diabetes is considered to be a relative contraindication to dental implant provision with an increased risk of treatment failure.

Smoking is not an absolute contraindication to implant provision, but the habit increases the risk of implant failure on a dose-dependent basis and it is accepted that patients should be warned of this association[1].

1 Palmer 'Risk management in clinical practice. Part 9. Dental implants' (2010) 209 Br Dent J 499–506.

35.182 The imposition of excessive grinding or clenching forces upon implants in patients with parafunctional habits can result in occlusal overloading of dental implants. In susceptible individuals this is a significant factor in implant failure, and must be identified in advance of dental implant placement.

Assessment, diagnosis and treatment planning

35.183 This is a complex area of dental implant treatment. A detailed history and examination must be undertaken. All relevant systemic and local features identified. A series of special investigations must be performed, particularly in connection with complex dental implant treatment[1].

1 A Dentist's guide to Implantology (2012).

35.184 These investigations include:

- clinical photographs;
- study models;
- bite relationships recorded using an articulated facebow;
- a wax model of the final restored appearance;
- construction of a stent based on the proposed restoration which will show up on a CT scan;
- digital imaging of the patient, preferably cone beam CT (CBCT);
- digital 3-D image analysis.

35.185 Straightforward dental implant treatment will require, at least, radiographic examination of the patient, consideration of occlusal relationships, study models, a wax model of the final restored appearance, and detailed radiographic analysis.

In all cases, the quality, density and volume of bone in the site under consideration, adjacent anatomical structures and any bony pathology must be fully considered.

35.186 Planning to determine suitability of dental implant treatment must be 'top down'. In other words, detailed planning of dental implant treatment must start with determining the feasibility of the proposed dental implant restorative superstructure. If there is insufficient bone to support an implant upon which to rest the final restoration, then either bone augmentation will be required or alternatives to dental implants must be considered.

35.187 Treatment planning of dental implant treatment will require a determination of the location, depth, angulation, number, size and spacing of the proposed implants, and details of the temporary and permanent restorations. This will allow a detailed financial costing to be prepared.

Consent to dental implant treatment

35.188 All the relevant available treatment options to replace missing teeth must be communicated to the patient with reasons for recommendation of dental implant treatment, and the advantages and disadvantages of each treatment option. The prognosis for dental implant treatment must be explained.

35.189 The patient must be advised of relevant risk factors for treatment failure associated with dental implant treatment. For example, a warning must be given of the association between a smoking habit and an increased failure rate of dental implant treatment. Generic and specific risks relevant to the contemplated surgical procedure must be communicated to the client.

Dental implant placement

35.190 In most cases dental implant treatment has three phases; initial surgical placement, exposure of the implant with abutment placement, and restoration. Four phases may be required in the event that bone augmentation is required before surgical placement of the dental implant, whether block grafting, ridge expansion, sinus elevation or distraction osteogenesis.

35.191 The practice of placing 'immediate' implants reduces the treatment phases required to two, with implants and abutments placed immediately, often directly upon extraction of teeth, and the permanent restoration provided at a second visit. Such immediate dental implant placement is classified as complex.

35.192 The wide range of dental implant procedures and systems precludes consideration here of all but the essential elements of dental implant placement.

- construction of a surgical stent or guide, the function of which is to ensure that the dental implants are placed in the correct location, and at the correct angulation;
- surgical exposure of the jaw bone is undertaken using an aseptic surgical technique, at which stage it is essential for the clinician to re-evaluate the sufficiency of bone for dental implant placement by direct examination of the bone;
- creation of an implant socket of appropriate depth and diameter using appropriate rotating drill in conjunction with a surgical stent or guide, and appropriate cooling of bone site;
- insertion of a dental implant to appropriate depth, secured by means of application of specific measured torque;
- sealing of coronal portion of dental implant with cover screw or healing abutment;
- radiographic assessment of location, angulation and depth of dental implants;
- surgical closure;
- subsequent removal of cover screw or healing abutment and replacement with screw-retained abutment;
- restoration of dental implant by securing the restorative superstructure to the abutment whether by cementation, the use of screw-retention through the restoration into the abutment, or the use of other components in connection with removable restorative superstructures.

Peri-implantitis

35.193 Failures of the restorations placed upon dental implants share many features of failures of the same restorations placed on natural teeth. However, specific to dental implant restorative superstructure is the connection between poor design and execution of the superstructure and the development of peri-implantitis or localised inflammation of the tissues around an implant, resulting in the loss of supporting bone. In particular, poor fit of the restorative superstructure to the abutment or its defective design can result in plaque accumulation which leads to peri-implantitis. If not monitored and untreated, the progressive bone loss which occurs in peri-implantitis will lead to dental implant mobility and loss.

35.194 Dental implant claims concern deficiencies in assessment and treatment planning and consent and surgical technique. Errors include: (i) inadequate assessment of sufficiency of bone quality and quantity to house implant fixtures; (ii) insufficient number of implants to support superstructure; (iii) inappropriate site location of implant fixture; (iv) poor design of abutment-superstructure connection; and (v) unsatisfactory aesthetics of superstructure

Orthodontics

35.195 Orthodontics is the dental speciality concerned with facial and dental development, and the identification and treatment of dental anomalies. Although a recognised specialist area of dental practice, simple orthodontic treatment may be carried out in general dental practice without the requirement for specialist training.

Orthodontic diagnosis

35.196 All general dental practitioners have a responsibility to identify the existence of orthodontic malocclusions, and either provide the appropriate orthodontic treatment or refer for specialist consideration in a timely fashion.

Un-erupted teeth

35.197 General dental practitioners have a particular role in the diagnosis and timely treatment or referral of missing or un-erupted teeth. In particular, maxillary canine teeth have a relatively high incidence of failure to erupt, known as impaction, affecting 1.5 per cent of the population[1]. Clinicians must be aware of the key dates of eruption in relation to these teeth, with the majority of maxillary canines palpable by ages 10 to 11, and non-eruption deemed late in girls at approximately age 12.3 years and in boys at age 13.1 years[2].

1 Husain, Burden, McSherry *Management of the palatally ectopic maxillary canine* (The Royal College of Surgeons of England, Faculty of Dental Surgery, 2010).
2 Husain, Burden, McSherry, Morris and Allen 'National clinical guidelines for management of the palatally ectopic maxillary canine' (2012) 213 British Dentistry Journal 171–176.

35.198 Careful practitioners should be suspicious of problems with maxillary canine eruption if the canines are not palpable by age 10–11 years or if palpation suggests unilateral eruption only. Once these indicators are present, a comprehensive assessment of the malocclusion must take place with accurate localisation of the canines and appropriate orthodontic diagnosis and treatment planning, in most cases by a specialist orthodontist in conjunction with surgical input[1].

1 Husain, Burden, McSherry, Morris and Allen 'National clinical guidelines for management of the palatally ectopic maxillary canine' (2012) 213 British Dentistry Journal 171–176.

35.199   Case reports show that timely interceptive measures can correct the path of eruption of the permanent teeth[1], while delay may result in resorption of the roots of adjacent teeth, and/or cystic change and may then necessitate surgical intervention to expose and guide unerupted teeth to their putative position in the dental arch.

1 Ericson, Kurol 'Early treatment of palatally erupting maxillary canines by extraction of the primary canine' (1988) 10 European Journal of Orthodontics 283–295.

Orthodontic treatment planning and execution

35.200   Detailed orthodontic assessment and treatment planning is essential to successful treatment. Treatment may be by means of fixed or removable appliances which may require space creation through tooth extraction or the application of extra-oral traction. In children with developing facial skeletons, functional appliances may be of assistance.

Adult orthodontics

35.201   One of the recent forms of simple orthodontics for adults commonly offered by general dental practitioners is treatment using aligner systems. Following assessment and diagnosis, a computer generated sequence of plastic mouthguards or aligners is constructed and worn by the patient on a sequential basis. Each of the aligners is incrementally different in shape from its predecessor so that upon conclusion of wear of the entire sequence of aligners, the teeth have been moved into the desired positions, and the original malocclusion has been corrected.

35.202   Careful pre-operative assessment is essential as aligner treatment is not suitable for cases of severe malocclusion including patients with significant crowding or spacing, skeletal discrepancies or severe tooth rotation. Some practitioners attempt to remedy these limitations of aligner orthodontics by completing the correction of the misaligned teeth with placement of crowns and veneers. This is indefensible.

Assessment of the standard of orthodontic care

35.203   Assessment of the standard of orthodontic treatment planning and execution in litigated claims is often complex and advice should be sought from specialist expert orthodontists.

Paediatric dentistry

35.204   Claims involving allegations of dental negligence in connection with children often concern failure to diagnose and treat dental disease in a timely fashion, and failure, commonly in the hospital setting, to provide care of the appropriate standard when children's permanent teeth are avulsed by trauma.

Treatment of avulsed permanent teeth

35.205   The relevant 2013 guidelines for the treatment of avulsed permanent teeth in children indicate that teeth which have been out of the mouth and kept dry before re-implantation, for less than 30 minutes, or teeth which have been stored in an appropriate fluid for less than 90 minutes, may show successful replantation.

35.206   The guidance advises that the decision to replant is almost always the correct decision unless other injuries are severe and warrant preferential emergency treatment, or where the medical history indicates that the patient would be put at risk by replantation of a tooth, or where the avulsed tooth is very immature with a short root and wide open apex[1].

1   Day, Gregg *Treatment of avulsed permanent teeth in children* (UK National Clinical Guidelines in Paediatric Dentistry, 2013).

CONCLUSION

35.207   The number of negligence claims against dentists has increased dramatically over the last 10 years to the extent that the claims experience of the dental profession in the UK exceeds that of any other country, and marks dentistry as one of the most high-risk clinical disciplines. There are a number of factors at play which may explain this rise in dental claims.

35.208   First, there is little doubt that the provision of dental services – involving, as it does, direct payment by the patient for those services – closely resembles a commercial transaction (including the sale of goods). This engenders in the patient a more consumerist attitude towards the provision of dental care in the event that the outcome of treatment is less than satisfactory. The cost of correcting unsatisfactory treatment often significantly exceeds the cost of the original treatment and therefore there may be a financial imperative for the patient to pursue a claim against the treating dentist.

35.209   Another significant factor in precipitating a claim is the issue of patient consent to treatment. Most dental conditions allow a number of alternative treatments and it is for the patient to elect their choice. Many dentists are still rooted in a paternalistic 'dentist knows best' treatment philosophy and simply offer their own preferred dental solution, depriving the patient of appropriate choice. When the dentist's choice of treatment fails and a patient belatedly discovers the other treatment options, a claim quickly ensues. Furthermore, there are financial incentives within the current NHS dental contract for dentists to offer the patient only more simple (and cheaper) treatments rather than alternative (more expensive) treatment options. This 'gaming' of the NHS contract by dentists improves their short-term financial position at the expense of an increased risk of claims.

35.210   Yet another reason for the rise in dental negligence litigation is the popularity of cosmetic dentistry. With the decline of dental disease, dentists are increasingly 'selling' cosmetic dentistry to patients. This treatment is entirely elective and invariably carries high expectations as to the aesthetic outcome. When these patient expectations are not met (and these treatments demand an especially high level of expertise) a claim for the cost of corrective treatment is almost inevitable.

35.211   There are also factors outside the control of the dental profession which impact on the incidence of dental claims, most notably the existence of firms of solicitors specialising in claims against dentists and their increasing willingness to assume the financial risk of pursuing such claims. Before the advent of conditional fee funding, the cost of pursuing a claim against a dentist operated as a bar to legal action in all but the most high value claims. Conditional fee funding then provided access to justice for all, but the tide is once again turning against dental patients. The so-called 'Jackson reforms'[1] with their laudable aim of reducing the cost of litigation will particularly impact upon dental negligence claims, which feature an unfortunate combination of high investigation cost, complexity and modest claim value. It is inevitable that lower quantum dental claims will once again become uneconomic to advance, and in the future, only those patients who have been severely injured by their dentists will enjoy access to justice.

1 Review of Civil Litigation Costs: Final Report (2010), by Lord Justice Jackson.

CHAPTER 36

Obstetrics and gynaecology

Leroy Edozien*

INTRODUCTION

36.1   Both numerically and in terms of value, clinical negligence claims in obstetrics and gynaecology continue to dwarf those encountered in any other speciality. By the end of March 2011, more than 13,000 obstetrics and gynaecology claims, with a total estimated value in excess of £5.2 billion,

---

* I gratefully acknowledge the erudite contribution of Mr Roger Clements who wrote this chapter in earlier editions of the book.

had been notified to the NHS Litigation Authority (NHSLA) under the Clinical Negligence Scheme for Trusts since it started in 1995[1]. Obstetrics and gynaecology accounts for approximately 20 per cent of all claims notified to the NHSLA and approximately 50 per cent of the total value. Obstetric claims outnumber gynaecology by at least 4:1. The majority of obstetric claims are brought on behalf of the baby, most alleging brain damage. In almost all, the mother will have a subsidiary claim. In the minority of cases the claim arises out of physical injury or death of the mother. Surgical accidents account for most claims in gynaecology.

1 *Ten Years of Maternity Claims. An Analysis of NHS Litigation Authority Data* (NHSLA, 2012).

36.2 Most women consulting an obstetrician or gynaecologist are essentially healthy and seek care for the oversight and correction of their physiological functions during childbearing and the control of their fertility. Such matters are widely discussed in the media and as a consequence a well-informed generation have high expectations of their medical attendants and are more likely to complain of their treatment when they feel it has not fulfilled their expectations. These expectations are sometimes reinforced by doctors who themselves promote undue dependency on their skills by premature and over-enthusiastic public presentation of the results of research work. Further, childbearing and associated hazards such as miscarriage, ectopic pregnancy, unwanted pregnancies and the desire to limit the number of children, affect practically every woman and her partner.

36.3 Litigation in obstetrics and gynaecology illustrates, perhaps better than any other speciality, the aphorism that the less the original pathology the more likely that patient is to sue when something goes wrong.

36.4 The obstetrician is especially vulnerable, being concerned not with the health and welfare of one person, but of two (or more). He has, as part of his duty of care, the management of birth. Jeffcoate[1] observed

'In these days of high death and injury rate from traffic accidents, it still remains true that the most dangerous journey made by any individual is through the four inches of the birth canal'.

Half a century later, this statement is still true; there is a greater chance that a baby will die during the post-natal period than during the whole of the next 50 years of its life. Eight out of every one thousand babies born in the UK will die around the time of birth whilst a larger, but not precisely known, number will suffer some permanent damage and at least 20 of them will require special skills and assistance at the time of birth. Negligent care in pregnancy could damage an individual for the whole of their life.

1 Jeffcoate 'Prolonged Labour' (1961) ii Lancet 67.

36.5 Much of obstetric care occurs out of hours. In the past, consultant timetables were arranged, almost exclusively, so that the consultant was present in the unit only during daytime, and it was common for the consultant to be running an antenatal or gynaecology clinic while 'covering' the labour ward. After 'office hours', the consultant on duty was at home. Although available for on-call duties, the most senior and experienced member of the team was not routinely present when most deliveries happened. This began to change with the publication of Minimum Standards. First, consultants' labour ward sessions became 'dedicated' sessions, meaning that they were not rostered to do any other clinical activity at the same time, and had to be physically present on the unit. The next step was the appointment of 'resident' consultants, who had to undertake night duties on the labour ward. Despite these recommendations, most obstetric units in the UK do not have consultant presence after hours. In autumn 2014, St Mary's Hospital, Manchester became the first unit to have round-the-clock consultant presence every day of the week (168-hour consultant presence).

36.6   Two professions are involved: obstetrics and midwifery. The obstetrician deals with a large number of women, most of whom are normal, in circumstances which demand special vigilance and attention to detail just because an unexpected complication could arise suddenly. He shares ante-natal and intra-partum care with midwives as well as with training grade doctors. Delegation of care is more problematic in obstetrics than in most other clinical specialities. In labour and at the time of delivery, the obstetrician relies on the skills of midwives who are recognised as independent practitioners, able to make diagnoses, exercise clinical judgment and prescribe treatment. Responsibility is shared more diffusely. In most maternity units all labouring women are notionally under the care of a consultant obstetrician, but during labour they are under the supervision of the duty consultant.

36.7   'Changing Childbirth'[1] recommended (2.4) that midwives should have direct access to maternity unit beds and independently manage women who choose to book with them. Some mothers were to be cared for by midwives throughout pregnancy and labour. Access to an obstetrician would only occur when there was specific referral in the event of an abnormality. Others, whilst notionally under the care of a consultant obstetrician, would be looked after by midwives throughout. A third group would be identified early in the pregnancy as requiring consultant input and those mothers would be looked after by midwives, under the direct and immediate supervision of a doctor. The spirit of patient-centred care underlying 'Changing Childbirth' has been widely accepted in the last decade, but implementation of the recommendations has been patchy. Generally, women are categorised as 'low risk' or 'high risk' based on risk assessment at booking. Low risk women are assigned to 'midwifery-led care' and only see an obstetrician if problems develop later in pregnancy.

1 Department of Health *Changing Childbirth: Report of The Expert Maternity Group: Survey of Good Communications Practice in Maternity Services* (1993) HMSO.

36.8   The delivery of maternity care has been influenced not so much by 'Changing Childbirth' as by service reconfigurations and workforce pressures. The Working Time Regulations[1] (still more commonly referred to as the European Working Time Directive, EWTD) have led to a reduction in training grade doctors' average working hours. One problem in redesigning maternity services is that they cannot be considered in isolation, given the close links with gynaecology and neonatology. Most obstetricians also have a commitment to gynaecology, and this has implications for the duty rota.

Neonatologists have to be present for some deliveries and be readily available for others. In birth units where a neonatologist is not available, appropriate arrangements for transfer of ill babies must be in place. Neonatal services have had to be reconfigured not only to comply with the Regulations but also in response to the need for optimised care (exemplified in a national survey which showed that the care of premature babies could be improved)[2]. Many obstetric units have been closed or merged to form larger units in order to comply with the Regulations and to be in a position to provide better quality care. These developments have facilitated midwifery-led care and extended roles for midwives. Even when a woman is under a named obstetrician, it is often the case that most or all of her care is provided by a midwife.

1 SI 1998/1833.
2 *Confidential Enquiry into Stillbirths and Deaths in Infancy.* Project 27/28: 'An enquiry into quality of care and its effect on the survival of babies born at 27–28 weeks' (2003), CESDI.

36.9   A woman has the choice to give birth:

(1)   in an obstetric delivery suite (where her care would usually be provided entirely by midwives if there are no risk factors or complication);
(2)   in a midwifery-led unit which is functionally and sometimes geographically integrated with an obstetric unit;
(3)   at a stand-alone midwifery-led unit;
(4)   at home.

36.10   With training grade doctors delegation is implicit. The consultant inevitably assumes responsibility for the actions of trainees under his direct supervision and his duties in this regard may be summarised:

(1)   to satisfy themselves that the person to whom they delegate a particular task or responsibility is competent to carry it out safely and properly, having directly observed the abilities and skills of their trainee. Generally, it would be wrong to assume by reference to their past anecdotal experience, the recommendation of others, or the mere possession of paper qualifications that the person concerned is either sufficiently skilled or competent to carry out the duty assigned (this was affirmed in *Greenhorn v South Glasgow University Hospitals NHS Trust*[1]);
(2)   to provide guidance for their nurses, midwives and training grade doctors;
(3)   to leave explicit instructions in individual cases to warn of foreseeable difficulties, to call for advice, and to ask for more experienced skill;
(4)   to ensure that nurses and midwives know that they can obtain consultant advice direct and to override the position of training grade doctors;
(5)   to be ready to attend in person, or know that there is a named deputy of equivalent rank experience who can be called in their stead, whenever complications demanding their presence arise.

1 2008 CSOH 128.

36.11   Death and handicap cause feelings of guilt and grief in almost all of those who are associated with the event, including the professional attendants, even when no mistakes are made. The grief is often smothered and the feeling of guilt reduced by trying to forget the mistake as soon as possible, leading to avoidance of the parents. Such behaviour leads to further suspicion and resentment and may provoke the need to investigate matters by recourse to litigation. When things go wrong communications frequently break down. Mistakes in judgment will often be accepted if freely admitted, frankly explained and sincere regrets expressed in a timely way. Frequently, such opportunities to provide information are denied, avoided, hurried or given with bad grace and/or the matter of concern to the patient or parents is avoided.

36.12   Obstetricians, like other health professionals, are obliged to be honest and open with patients when things go wrong. Obstetricians are also obliged to participate in the reporting and investigation of patient safety incidents, and to facilitate learning from these incidents.

36.13   Contemporary practice in obstetrics and gynaecology must be evidence supported. A series of guidelines has been published by the Royal College of Obstetricians and Gynaecologists (RCOG), and some of those that are of considerable significance in the context of litigation are listed at the end of this chapter.

36.14   Obstetrics was described in the mid-1980s as the least scientific of all medical specialities. Since then obstetrics has travelled far along the road to evidence-based medicine. Paradoxically, some have blamed a commitment to evidence-based medicine for an excess of medical intervention in pregnancy care, while others have said there would be less intervention if the evidence were followed. What is important to appreciate is that evidence is only one factor in the determination of optimal care for a particular woman. The woman's own circumstances (medical, psychosocial, cultural, etc) and preferences have to be taken into consideration. The evidence should be presented and her choice should be respected.

36.15   The gynaecologist deals with few patients who are seriously ill. The majority seek advice about fertility, the control of family size or the correction of menstrual problems. Since none of these conditions is perceived as an illness, adverse outcome is more than usually difficult to accept.

OBSTETRICS

36.16   The causes of complaint are summarised in Table **36.1**. The three most frequent categories of claim were those relating to management of labour (14.05 per cent), Caesarean section (13.24 per cent) and cerebral palsy (10.65 per cent)[1]. Cerebral palsy and management of labour, along with cardiotocograph (CTG) interpretation accounted for 70 per cent of the total value of all the maternity claims.

Table 36.1 Obstetric causes for complaint

(a)	Injuries to the baby
	Cerebral palsy
	Stillbirth and early neonatal death
	Brachial plexus injury (Erb's and Klumpke's paralysis of the arm)
	Facial scars and other soft tissue injuries
	Fractures of the skull and limbs
	Failure to prevent Rhesus sensitisation.
(b)	Wrongful abortion; termination of an otherwise viable pregnancy
(c)	Wrongful birth of a handicapped child, because of failure to detect and/or prevent an inborn abnormality, eg neural tube defect, rubella syndrome, Down syndrome, haemoglobinopathy.
(d)	Maternal injuries
	Scars of the perineum and vagina causing difficult sexual intercourse
	Loss of urinary control–stress incontinence, ureteric and vesico-vaginal fistula
	Faecal incontinence and recto-vaginal fistula
	Rupture of the uterus
	Failure to remove vaginal or abdominal swabs
	Anaesthetic awareness and/or failure adequately to relieve pain
	Loss of future childbearing capacity from infection or the need for hysterectomy
	Death or permanent brain damage due to eclampsia, anaesthesia, undetected and/or uncontrolled haemorrhage.

1 *Ten Years of Maternity Claims. An Analysis of NHS Litigation Authority Data* (NHSLA, 2012).

36.17 Brain damage or 'cerebral palsy', thought to have arisen from injury around the time of birth, is the most costly injury if liability is admitted or found by the courts. Because of the large sums of money involved, such cases are usually vigorously defended.

36.18 Between 1 per cent and 2 per cent of babies are born with some defect or handicap, varying from a slight blemish, such as an extra digit, to conditions causing total life-long dependence because of physical and mental handicap. The term 'cerebral palsy' is applied to a group of babies whose motor function is both delayed and deviant. The abnormality affects both posture and movement, is non-progressive and is usually acquired at a time of rapid brain development. It may be associated with other neurological impairment such as mental retardation. It is not a diagnosis, nor does it imply an aetiology. Cerebral palsy affects 1–4 per thousand of the population; in most cases no satisfactory causative explanation can be found. Known causes are traditionally divided into prenatal, perinatal and postnatal. Prenatal causes include inherited (genetic or chromosomal) defects, preterm delivery and intra-uterine infection. The majority of other associated conditions have as their common theme a shortage of oxygen to the baby's brain.

36.19   Hypoxia means a relative deficiency in the oxygen supply to the baby, whilst anoxia means that it is completely cut off. Asphyxia is an older term and refers to a total obstruction of the exchange of respiratory gases, including the elimination of carbon dioxide. The organ responsible for the supply of oxygen to the baby is the placenta, via the umbilical cord. Any deficiency in the function of the placenta or obstruction to the umbilical cord will impair gas exchange. In acute conditions it is the reduction in the oxygen supply that is the crucial factor. In some chronic conditions affecting placental function the supply of nutrients to the fetus may also be reduced so that its growth and development are impaired, in addition to the exchange of respiratory gases.

36.20   The hypoxic associations with cerebral palsy[1] include the chronic pre-partum hypoxia often associated with maternal disease (such as hypertension and diabetes) and intrauterine growth restriction (IUGR); acute pre-partum hypoxia may be caused by placental separation (abruptio placentae) or intracranial haemorrhage; acute intra-partum hypoxia may be associated with obstruction of the flow of blood through the umbilical cord (through prolapse or entanglement) with placental abruption or the entrapment of the baby in the birth canal at a time when the umbilical cord is no longer functional and the baby cannot breathe (as in delayed breech delivery or shoulder dystocia). Post-partum hypoxia may arise in a previously normal child and be caused by aspiration of meconium, depression of the neonatal respiratory centre by narcotic analgesics or by inadequate resuscitation of the baby at birth. Most often post-partum hypoxia is a continuation of a situation that began in utero.

1 (1996) 2 Clinical Risk 2.

36.21   Cerebral palsy occurs in different forms. In the mature infant, severe oxygen deprivation may later be associated with the spastic quadriplegia form of cerebral palsy; there may or may not be involuntary muscular activity of the dyskinetic or athetoid type. The athetoid type of cerebral palsy is characteristic, but not exclusively, of damage to the basal ganglia of the brain whereas spastic diplegia is typical of severe prematurity. Damage to the basal ganglia is caused by kernicterus, the deposition of bile pigments released into the blood stream as a consequence of the abnormal break down of red blood cells in babies suffering from severe haemolytic disease. Nevertheless the identification of a specific type does not usually allow the unequivocal identification of a cause. It is now generally accepted that only in one in ten instances can cerebral palsy be attributed to events around the time of birth. In most cases claims are made on the basis of the balance of probability concerning the cause, usually with the positive exclusion of other non-negligent causes. The proof of causation must depend upon experts' opinions from paediatricians, as must evidence concerning the present condition and prognosis for the child.

36.22   The obstetrician nevertheless has the right to express an opinion and will probably be expected to do so in respect of the cause of cerebral palsy when he is of the opinion that the management of pregnancy and labour was not of an acceptable standard. The essential requirements necessary to link peri-partum events with cerebral palsy were spelled out by Freeman and Nelson[1] in the form of four questions which must be answered in the affirmative:

(1) Was there evidence of marked and prolonged intrapartum asphyxia?
(2) Did the infant, as a newborn, exhibit signs of moderate or severe hypoxic-ischaemic encephalopathy during the newborn period, with evidence also of asphyxial injury to other organ systems?
(3) Is the child's neurologic condition one which intra-partum asphyxia could explain?
(4) Has the work up been sufficient to rule out other conditions?

1 Freeman and Nelson 'Intrapartum asphyxia and cerebral palsy' (1998) 82(2) Paediatrics 240–249.

36.23 The causes, diagnoses, types and prognosis of cerebral palsy are dealt with elsewhere. Table **36.2** summarises some of the errors of management associated with brain damage and cerebral palsy.

Table 36.2 Errors of medical management associated with cerebral palsy

Antenatal
Failure to detect or to take account of:
– high-risk factors
– appropriate notes to draw attention to the need for special care
– fetal abnormality
– intra-uterine infection, eg rubella, toxoplasmosis, herpes
– abnormalities by making regular and appropriate clinical observations and ordering other special investigations (including ultrasound scans) throughout pregnancy and as often as the situation demands
– intra-uterine growth retardation
– symptoms and signs of impending eclampsia
– twins
– abnormal and/or unstable presentations
– cephalo-pelvic disproportion caused by a contracted pelvis and/or a large baby especially in a breech position
– risk of placental abruption
– placenta praevia
– the need to monitor fetal well-being
– premature labour.
Labour
Failure to detect or to take account of:
– the need to monitor properly the dosage of oxytocin and fetal and maternal well-being, when it is used intravenously for the induction and acceleration of labour
– malpresentation
– disproportion
– umbilical cord complications, eg entanglement, presentation, prolapse and ruptured vasa praevia
– changes in the fetal heart rate

– the need to take an adequate fetal blood sample, if facilities are available, when it is indicated and to repeat the examination as indicted by the circumstances
– dysfunctional labour and the secondary arrest of labour
– the need to avoid difficult vaginal delivery especially in the presence of fetal distress
– the need to conduct an adequate trial of labour
– previous injury to the uterus (trial of scar)
– the need to conduct a proper trial of forceps
– the need to use the vacuum extractor properly
– the need to have adequate experience and expertise to carry out Caesarean section when difficulties could be anticipated
– the need to conduct delivery in an appropriate environment
– the need to have the necessary paediatric and anaesthetic assistance available.
Postnatal
Failure to detect or to take account of:
– the need to reverse the effect of narcotic drugs given to the mother
– the need to have the necessary paediatric assistance available
– the need to intubate and provide proper respiratory support for the baby
– the appropriate surroundings and expertise required and necessary for the further care of the baby.

36.24 Other physical, and usually less severe, injuries to the baby range from paralysis of an arm to a scar on the face, buttocks or limb of a baby inflicted by the incision for Caesarean section.

36.25 Stillbirth is numerically an important cause of litigation but such actions are relatively more frequently settled out of court, since the amount of compensation is low and persuades the defendant health authority or Trust to settle more readily.

36.26 The commonest reason for a woman to seek compensation on her own behalf because of injury during childbirth is for disability that limits sexual intercourse, resulting from damage to the perineum and vagina, usually because of an episiotomy and/or tear and/or its improper repair. Less often control of bladder and bowel function is lost because of more extensive damage to the sphincters and to the supports of these organs. Injury during childbirth may also have psychological or psychiatric sequelae, giving rise to litigation. The majority of these cases settle out of court.

36.27 The more serious, but less common, causes of complaint by the mother include the loss of future childbearing capacity as the result of puerperal infection that occludes the fallopian tubes and of the need to carry out hysterectomy for uterine rupture and/or to control bleeding, damage to the bladder or ureters, the failure to remove swabs from the vagina or abdominal cavity, and failure to relieve pain adequately in a variety of procedures such as Caesarean section, forceps delivery, breech delivery, twin delivery and manual removal of the placenta.

36.28   Analgesia and anaesthesia used to relieve pain in labour and during operative deliveries may be associated with accidents that are a cause for complaint. They range from the comparatively trivial effects of inexpertly given injections, through awareness during Caesarean section, to total physical and mental handicap and sometimes death as the result of failed intubation, airway obstruction, the administration of wrong anaesthetic gases or total spinal anaesthesia from an epidural block.

36.29   Maternal deaths are uncommon: 10 per 100,000 women giving birth in 2009–12. A proportion of them occur suddenly and unexpectedly in circumstances that sometimes give rise to litigation, such as during anaesthesia, as a result of uncontrollable haemorrhage or as a result of eclampsia.

36.30   Maternal deaths are the subject of an inquiry not only by the coroner but also by the Department of Health. For more than 50 years there was a Confidential Enquiry into Maternal Deaths (CEMD) and from 1993 there was a similar inquiry for babies, the Confidential Enquiry into Stillbirths and Deaths in Infancy (CESDI). In April 2003 CEMD and CESDI were amalgamated to form the Confidential Enquiry into Maternal and Child Health (CEMACH)[1]. In July 2009 CEMACH became an independent charity with the new name Centre for Maternal and Child Enquiries (CMACE).

1 Centre for Maternal and Child Enquiries (CMACE). *Saving Mothers' Lives: reviewing maternal deaths to make motherhood safer: 2006–08. The Eighth Report on Confidential Enquiries into Maternal Deaths in the United Kingdom* (2011) 118(Suppl 1) BJOG 1–203.

36.31   The national programme of work investigating maternal deaths, stillbirths and infant deaths, including the CEMD, is now called the Maternal, Newborn and Infant Clinical Outcome Review Programme (MNI-CORP), and is run by MBRRACE-UK (Mothers and Babies: Reducing Risk through Audit and Confidential Enquiries across the UK). The MBRRACE-UK system applies to England, Wales and Scotland; modified arrangements are in place for Northern Ireland.

36.32   The maternal death rate in London rose from 9.1 per 100,000 maternities in 2005–6 to 21.6 per 100,000 in 2010–11[1]. This was higher than the maternal mortality rate in the rest of the UK. In 2010, a review by CMACE into the deaths of 42 mothers in London over 18 months found that three out of every four cases might have been avoided with better care.

Failure to escalate concerns to senior colleagues and failure to record 'routine' observations have also been implicated in maternal deaths in the UK[2].

1 Bewley, Helleur 'Rising maternal deaths in London, UK' (2012) 379 Lancet 1198 doi:10.1016/ S0140-6736(12)60511-X.
2 Knight, Kenyon, Brocklehurst, Neilson, Shakespeare, Kurinczuk (eds) on behalf of MBRRACE-UK. *Saving Lives, Improving Mothers' Care – Lessons learned to inform future maternity care from the UK and Ireland Confidential Enquiries into Maternal Deaths and Morbidity 2009–12* (National Perinatal Epidemiology Unit, University of Oxford, 2014).

36.33   Adverse outcome of labour is often followed by the break-up of parents' relationships. Where the woman has received soft tissue injuries to the vagina, making intercourse painful, or has to endure a period of faecal or urinary incontinence, a period of rehabilitation and readjustment may prove too long and too difficult both for her and for her partner. The damage to her self-esteem may be such that the relationship never recovers. Even without physical injury, it is common for women who have had bad experiences in labour or who have given birth to a handicapped child to lose interest in sexual relations, even to develop an aversion to sexual activity. Mothers of handicapped children frequently divert all of their physical and emotional energies into caring for the handicapped child to the exclusion of their partner. The partner, who is usually the baby's father, may have been present at the delivery, powerless to intervene, and may himself suffer severe psychological sequelae. Often his perception of his own exclusion from the special relationship between the mother and handicapped child may lead to estrangement.

36.34   Other important areas giving rise to claims for compensation are those associated with the increasing ability to diagnose and treat some abnormalities in the fetus. Successful claims have been brought for failure to detect congenital or inherent defects relating to the wrongful birth of a handicapped child, and also in cases where an apparently healthy baby has been aborted on medical advice, because tests had, in the event wrongly, suggested that it would be born with a serious handicap or could not survive.

ANTE-NATAL CARE

36.35   Care of the woman and her baby before labour includes the identification of risk and the development of strategies to deal with the risk. A pregnancy is regarded as high risk if, in the opinion of the midwife or obstetrician, there is a likelihood of an adverse outcome to the woman or her baby greater than the incidence of that outcome in the general pregnant population. The art of good ante-natal care is to identify this small number of women amongst the vast majority who are perceived to be of normal or low risk.

36.36   As well as a system of continuous risk assessment, ante-natal care includes education and the management of intercurrent illness and social or psychosocial difficulties. It also provides an opportunity for the pregnant woman to get to know those who will care for her in labour. The aims of ante-natal care can be summarised:

(1)   the amelioration of the discomforts and minor complaints of pregnancy;
(2)   provision of advice, education, support and appropriate reassurance for the woman and her family;
(3)   provision of a screening programme as a basis for continuous risk assessment;
(4)   specific and appropriate response to risk factors in mother and baby, as they emerge during the screening process.

36.37   Ante-natal care is about preventive medicine, aimed to detect and, as far as possible, to prevent abnormalities in mother and fetus. It also looks forward to labour and provides an opportunity, where abnormalities can be foreseen, for the consultant to formulate a plan for the management of labour which can be executed even in his absence.

36.38   The most difficult decisions in obstetrics often need to be made on the labour ward, in circumstances of some urgency. Nearly 70 per cent of emergency workload in the labour ward occurs *outside* the hours of nine to five, when consultants are rarely on the premises and management is left to midwives and training grade doctors[1]. The need for more consultant time in the labour ward cannot be over-emphasised.

1 O'Donoghue, Sheridan, O'Sullivan, Greene, Higgins 'Timing of birth related to obstetric practice and neonatal outcome' (2008) 101 Irish Medical Journal 205–207; Pasupathy, Wood, Pell, Fleming, Smith 'Time of birth and risk of neonatal death at term: retrospective cohort study' (2010) 341 BMJ c3498.

36.39   In 1999 the RCOG and the Royal College of Midwives (RCM) jointly produced the document *Towards Safer Childbirth* which recommended minimum levels of staffing for labour wards. The document was updated by both colleges together with the Royal College of Paediatrics and Child Health and the Royal College of Anaesthetists in 2007 and it was recommended that 'a consultant obstetrician or equivalent should be present for 40 hours during the working week in all units with over 2,500 births a year, and units with more than 6,000 births a year should provide 60 hours consultant presence'[1].

1 Royal College of Obstetricians and Gynaecologists, Royal College of Midwives, Royal College of Anaesthetists, Royal College of Paediatrics and Child Health. *Safer childbirth: minimum standards for the organisation and delivery of care in labour* (2007), available at: http://www.rcog.org.uk/womens-health/clinical-guidance/safer-childbirth-minimum-standards-organisation-and-delivery-care-la.

36.40   In 2011 the RCOG reported that despite an 8 per cent rise in the number of consultants in the specialty between 2007 and 2009, the presence of consultants on the labour ward was 'woefully short' of the recommendations made in multi-professional standards. It called for 24-hour, seven days a week consultant presence on labour wards 'to meet the needs caused by the growing complexity of the case mix, the increase in operative birth rates, and the reduction in trainee numbers, hours, and experience'[1].

1 *High Quality Women's Health Care: A proposal for change* (RCOG, July 2011), available at https://www.rcog.org.uk/en/guidelines-research-services/guidelines/high-quality-womens-health-care/.

36.41   The RCOG medical workforce census 2012/13 showed that consultants were present on the labour ward 59.15 hours per week on average, with four units providing over 98 hours consultant presence per week. The census looked at the times of day that consultants were present on the labour ward. The majority have consultants present in the morning (197 units) and afternoon (198 units) with 124 units having consultants present at the weekend, 121 units in the evening but only 35 overnight. St Mary's Hospital, Manchester, is the first maternity unit in the UK to have 24/7 consultant presence.

36.42   As consultants (and, in particular, the consultant under whom the woman is booked) are usually not available on site out of hours, the decisions made in the ante-natal clinic are of the greatest importance in determining patterns of care in labour.

The booking visit

36.43　It is no longer universal practice for patients to attend the hospital clinic for booking. The booking visit, often conducted in the patient's home or in the GP's surgery, remains the only occasion on which a full medical history is taken and recorded. It used to be the case that every new obstetric patient had a full physical examination. That is no longer the case, but women newly arrived in the UK have a chest auscultation to exclude a heart murmur. The booking visit remains an important opportunity for triage, as it is usually the moment when the pattern for care in pregnancy is laid down.

36.44　Even with the patient booking in consultant units, a system of shared ante-natal care is commonly provided so that even in high-risk cases the patient is seen partly by the hospital ante-natal clinic and partly by her family doctor and midwives. To facilitate this system the woman has 'hand-held' maternity records which she carries until the end of the pregnancy. A short glossary of common terms and abbreviations should be provided to aid the patient's understanding of the entries made by the doctors and midwives.

36.45　At the booking visit a series of routine blood tests are normally taken. Whilst some of the tests are innocuous (haemoglobin, blood group, Rhesus antibodies etc) others may have potentially serious repercussions for the woman and her baby, and a valid consent should be obtained. It is routine practice to screen for previous exposure to rubella and, when indicated, for cytomegalovirus and toxoplasma. Whilst these require a little explanation it may be more difficult to explain to a woman the significance of positive testing for hepatitis B and syphilis. Whilst there is universal acceptance that no HIV tests should be requested without counselling as to the potential of either a negative or a positive result, tests for other serious infections may not be mentioned. Hepatitis B is particularly important in this regard. Whilst the identification of hepatitis B is of considerable benefit to the baby and to the woman's family, the repercussions for the woman herself (particularly if she is also a healthcare professional) may be catastrophic. As with HIV, explanation of the consequences of both negative and positive results must be given beforehand and the woman's consent properly obtained.

36.46　The booking visit provides an opportunity to assess the woman's history and the risk factors already present. Perinatal mortality and morbidity are affected statistically more often in certain groups of women who can be identified in advance, because they show one or more of these risk factors. For example, *Why Mothers Die* found a higher risk of maternal death in women from minority ethnic groups, women who were socially disadvantaged, poor attenders, and women with pre-existing medical conditions including psychiatric illness. There may be an accumulation of further risks as complications arise during pregnancy and labour. It is against such a known background of risks that obstetricians and midwives have to modify their management of the woman and particularly increase their vigilance. It may be necessary to alter the care arrangements and even the place of delivery as risks are identified. Women with serious underlying pre-existing medical or mental health conditions should be immediately referred to appropriate specialist centres. Lack of appropriate referral of potentially high-risk women was a key finding in the confidential enquiry into maternal deaths[1].

1 Draycott, Lewis, Stephens, Centre for Maternal and Child Enquiries (CMACE) 'Saving Mothers' Lives: reviewing maternal deaths to make motherhood safer 2006–2008. Executive Summary' (2011) 118 (Suppl 1) BJOG e12–e21 DOI: 10.1111/j.1471-0528.2011.02895.x.

36.47 Ethnicity and country of origin are also important because of the occurrence of certain inherited anaemias (haemoglobinopathies) in African and Afro-Caribbean women and in women from the Mediterranean littoral. Where abnormal haemoglobin is detected it is essential to offer screening to the father of the baby; successful litigation has followed the failure properly to assess the risk to the fetus of an inherited defect of haemoglobin.

Screening for fetal abnormality

36.48 Increasingly, errors in counselling or screening for fetal abnormality are emerging as causes for litigation. Any woman with a previous history (or family history) of a child born with a congenital abnormality should be referred for genetic counselling, preferably *before* the pregnancy begins. For the remainder, certain universal screening tests are now available. Adequate counselling is essential *before* screening tests are undertaken.

36.49 Apart from the haemoglobinopathies, the first widely employed test was screening for maternal serum alpha fetoprotein (MSAFP). Although its function is unknown, alpha fetoprotein is normally produced by the fetal liver; it is not produced by healthy adults. It was discovered in 1956 and by the early 1970s there were reports of raised levels of this protein in maternal serum in babies with neural tube defects (spina bifida and anencephaly). In these conditions (and in others such as exomphalos and gastroschisis) where the integument of the baby is compromised, this (normal) protein leaks into the maternal circulation. Its detection may alert the obstetrician to the fetal abnormality. The protein will also leak from a dead fetus or in circumstances where the maternal-placental barrier is breached, for instance where there has been an episode of bleeding in early pregnancy. The demonstration of raised MSAFP is a useful screening technique for fetal abnormalities, particularly those affecting the spinal cord. Even when no specific abnormality can be demonstrated, a raised MSAFP is statistically associated with a poor outcome for the pregnancy.

36.50 From the late 1970s MSAFP was in general use in the UK as a screening test for spina bifida and anencephaly (neural tube defects, NTD). Initially women with raised MSAFP were further investigated by amniocentesis (sampling of the amniotic fluid) to confirm that there was an excessive leak of alpha fetoprotein in the amniotic fluid. This test, however, is not diagnostic and has been replaced by careful ultrasound examination to NTD (the precise reason for the leak). MSAFP is no longer used routinely for the sole purpose of screening for NTD.

Down syndrome

36.51   Down syndrome (trisomy 21) is a chromosomal abnormality associated with reduplication of the 21st chromosome, confirmed only by sampling cells from the baby. After about 16 weeks, cells can be obtained by amniocentesis; the amniotic fluid contains cells from fetal skin which can then be grown in culture and examined whilst they are dividing, to determine the chromosomal content. The risk of miscarriage of a (probably) normal fetus is about 1:200 amniocenteses. Cells are grown from the sample then subjected to chromosomal analysis, and it could take 2–4 weeks to obtain a result. However, some conditions such as Down syndrome can be identified within a couple of days using the fluorescence in-situ hybridisation (FISH) technique. Amniocentesis before 16 weeks' gestation carries a higher risk of miscarriage and of fetal talipes.

36.52   A sample of fetal cells can also be obtained by a needle biopsy of the placenta, a chorion villus sample (CVS), but this test carries a higher risk of about one miscarriage in 50–100. The information from CVS is usually available more quickly than from amniocentesis and it can be performed as early as 11 weeks. Thus, if the result is abnormal, the pregnancy can be terminated at an earlier gestation. A careful balance has therefore to be struck in deciding which invasive test to perform, the earlier quicker test having the higher miscarriage rate.

36.53   There is reluctance to use invasive tests unless the chance of finding an abnormal result is sufficiently high to justify taking the risk of procedure-related miscarriage. Risk factors for Down syndrome have emerged over the past two decades. Although one form of the condition occurs sporadically throughout the population, the association with maternal age has long been established. The risk rises from 1:1,500 in teenage to 1:28 by the age of 45. Other chromosomal abnormalities also increase with age. The overall incidence of chromosomal abnormalities is 1 in 12 at the age of 45. This has led to the 'screening' of mothers by amniocentesis on the grounds of maternal age alone. Some departments traditionally offered screening over the age of 35 (overall risk of 1 in 250), others to later age groups up to 38 (overall risk 1 in 111). However, only 40 per cent of Down syndrome babies are detected by this means because of the relatively few babies born to women in the older age groups.

36.54   Anecdotal reporting in the late 1970s of unusually low levels of MSAFP (in Down syndrome) led to the development of a screening method involving both age and MSAFP. This in turn led to the search for other markers for Down syndrome; an association with raised levels of human chorionic gonadotrophin (hCG) and reduced levels of serum oestriol then led to the practice of offering a 'triple test' to all mothers. Serum screening for Down syndrome by this technique relies on the use of maternal age and three principal markers – serum AFP, serum unconjugated oestriol (uE3) and serum hCG – to determine the risk of Down syndrome. These variables, together with gestation, are fed into a computer programme which produces a risk assessment. Some hospitals offered the less sophisticated 'double test', dropping the oestriol element of the triple test, others offered quadruple test which utilises the three markers plus inhibin. In pregnancies with Down syndrome, inhibin levels tend to be raised. The 'quad test' picks up 7 of every 10 affected babies.

36.55   The current practice in the NHS is to offer one of two tests, depending on the gestational age. A combined test uses the results of maternal demographic details, an ultrasound scan (performed between 11 weeks, 2 days and 14 weeks, 1 day of pregnancy) and a blood test (done between 10 weeks and 14 weeks 1 day) to calculate the risk of the baby having Down syndrome. The scan ('nuchal translucency scan') measures the thickness of the pocket of fluid at the back of the baby's neck. The blood sample is tested for free beta-hCG and placenta-associated plasma protein A (PAPP-A). If the pregnancy has progressed beyond the age limit for the combined test (14 weeks 1 day), then a quad test is offered.

36.56   The concept of an integrated test has been patented but not found wide application. The mother has a blood test in the first trimester to measure the amount of pregnancy-associated plasma protein-A (PAPP-A), and an ultrasound scan to measure crown rump length (measurement of the fetus from the top of the head to the bottom of the buttocks) and nuchal translucency (measurement of a skin fold at the back of the baby's neck); then between 15–22 weeks she has the quadruple test, and all the results are combined to give a single risk estimate. This has more complicated logistics than the combined test, and the composite risk is not known until the second trimester.

36.57   Women are described as screen positive if their risk lies above a specified cut-off level, or screen negative if it does not. The cut-off level is somewhat arbitrary and, at least in the NHS, depends on the resources available for the next step in investigation, the amniocentesis. Where cost is not a factor the threshold for further intervention should be determined by the patient, with proper counselling. This system is capable of identifying more than 60 per cent of Down syndrome in the population since it includes women of all ages; it also reduces the need for older women to be subjected to amniocentesis if their computer-estimated risk is low. The earliest time at which biochemical screening for Down syndrome can be undertaken is 15 weeks and since the test takes about a week to turn round this allows amniocentesis to be performed between 16 and 17 weeks to women above the cut-off level. The search continues for other markers of Down syndrome to avoid unnecessary amniocentesis.

36.58   The most recent advance in screening for Down syndrome is non-invasive prenatal testing (NIPT), which is a test for the baby's DNA fragments (known as cell-free fetal DNA) in a sample of blood taken from the mother. It is reported to detect at least 98 out of 100 of all babies with trisomy. Cell free fetal DNA comprises approximately 3–13 per cent of the total cell free DNA circulating in maternal blood. It is cleared from the maternal circulation within the first hour after birth, so the test is specific to the index pregnancy. The test is done at a gestational age not less than 10 weeks (before this time there is not enough cell-free fetal DNA in the maternal circulation). As maternal blood also contains cell-free *maternal* DNA, NIPT could give a false positive result. False positives may also be due to abnormal cell lines that are of placental origin but not representative of the baby's constitution. A confirmatory CVS or amniocentesis is, therefore, required for NIPT positive cases. False negative results could occur if the test is done too early or if the mother has a high body mass index. These limitations should be discussed with the woman/couple before the test is done.

A pilot study is in progress and, based on its findings (due to be reported in 2015), the UK National Screening Committee (UK NSC) will decide whether NIPT should be introduced as part of the NHS Fetal Anomaly Screening Programme.

36.59   It is essential that before embarking on a screening programme the parents are fully informed of the significance of an 'abnormal' result. It should not be assumed that just because the test is positive the woman will necessarily elect for CVS or amniocentesis; many do not. Neither should it be assumed that if following invasive testing a chromosomal abnormality is demonstrated, the woman will necessarily choose abortion. For some women abortion is not an option but they are greatly helped in dealing with their handicapped baby by the opportunity for counselling and support during the ante-natal period.

36.60   Each maternity unit should have a formalised, robust system to ensure that all tests are reported on and the results relayed to the appropriate persons. In many units there is a dedicated midwife whose role is to facilitate or deliver counselling as well as collating and coordinating results of screening tests.

1 NHS Litigation Authority *Clinical Negligence Scheme for Trusts Maternity Clinical Risk Management Standards* (April 2006).

Ultrasound

36.61   Ultrasound of the baby in the uterus has been almost universally available throughout the UK since the 1980s. By its use pregnancy can be dated with accuracy, the placental site can be determined, the number of babies present ascertained and a search for fetal abnormalities made. Early ultrasound is vital in confirmation of the dating of the pregnancy. There is ample evidence from ultrasound studies in IVF pregnancies (ie where the exact length of pregnancy at the time of the scan is known) that the commonly-used ultrasound dating formulae are accurate, and many units now date pregnancies solely on the basis of early pregnancy scan measurements. The usual measurement made to estimate fetal size at this gestation is the biparietal diameter of the fetal skull (BPD). This measurement is then plotted on the appropriate chart so that in later pregnancy the progress of the baby may be compared with the standard curves (Figure **36.1** at the end of this chapter).

36.62   The association between nuchal oedema in the first trimester and certain chromosomal abnormalities has become evident with high resolution ultrasound. Late in the first trimester, a thin collection of fluid can be identified at the back of the neck of normal fetuses (nuchal translucency).

36.63   Nuchal translucency (NT) should not normally exceed 3 mm. A measurement equal to or greater than 3.5 mm is associated with increased risk of cardiac, chromosomal and other anomalies. Between 65 and 85 per cent of trisomic fetuses will have a large nuchal thickness. The NT test is capable of detecting eight of every ten babies with Down syndrome. It is important to emphasise that this does not mean the screen-positive baby has an 80 per cent chance of having Down syndrome.

36.64   It is routine practice to offer a detailed ultrasound examination of the baby between 18 weeks 0 day and 20 weeks 6 days. At this stage there is optimal visualisation of the fetal skull, brain, face, spine, heart, lungs, kidneys, bladder, gut, abdominal wall and limbs. This is the optimum time for diagnosing abnormalities of the nervous system but it is essential that the training of the doctor or ultrasonographer is adequate to recognise the important markers, such as ventricular dilatation, in cases where the defect may be small and difficult to visualise.

There are national quality standards for prenatal screening and diagnostic services in the UK[1], and for obtaining consent[2].

1 Donna Kirwan and the NHS Fetal Anomaly Screening Programme (NHS FASP) in collaboration with the Royal College of Obstetricians and Gynaecologists (RCOG), British Maternal and Fetal Medicine Society (BMFMS) and the Society and College of Radiographers (SCoR). 18+0 to 20+6 Weeks Fetal Anomaly Scan National Standards and Guidance for England. (NHS FASP, 2010).
2 National Health Service Fetal Anomaly Screening Programme (NHS FASP) Consent Standards Review Group. Consent Standards and Guidance (NHS FASP, July 2011).

Subsequent ante-natal visits

36.65   Whether with the hospital ante-natal clinic, community midwife or GP visits are conducted at traditional intervals at which it was customary to conduct an abdominal examination of the mother, examine her urine and record her weight and blood pressure. Most hospitals have ceased to record weight on the basis that it is too crude an indicator to be helpful. These 'standard' observations are aimed at the detection of the commoner complications of pregnancy:

(1)   pre-eclampsia (hypertension);
(2)   anaemia;
(3)   abnormal/unstable lie of the baby or malpresentation;
(4)   abnormalities of fetal growth;
(5)   diabetes (glycosuria).

36.66   Pregnancy-induced hypertension (PIH) is the term used to describe the *temporary* hypertension of pregnancy. If there is proteinuria (the presence of protein in the maternal urine) in addition to hypertension, the term pre-eclampsia is used. The cause of the condition is unknown. Confusion occurs because women already suffering from chronic hypertension may have superimposed pre-eclampsia in the later weeks of pregnancy. These conditions may restrict the growth of the baby or result in preterm delivery. The blood pressure may be so high as to threaten the mother either with the development of fits (eclampsia) or stroke. A blood pressure of 140/90 in a previously normotensive patient, or a significant deterioration in previous hypertension calls for hospital care. In the past many women with pre-eclampsia were admitted into an obstetric ward for rest and observation.

In the 1990s maternity day assessment units emerged as efficient and cost-effective alternatives to inpatient care for many obstetric conditions including pre-eclampsia. In mild cases of pregnancy-induced hypertension, the woman may be looked after in the community, with visits from the community midwife. The condition of both the pre-eclamptic mother and her baby are intensively monitored, and in severe cases admission into the antenatal ward is indicated. Women with pre-eclampsia and a systolic blood pressure of 150–160 mmHg or more require immediate antihypertensive treatment. The confidential enquiries into maternal deaths found that the single most serious failing in the clinical care provided for mothers with pre-eclampsia was the inadequate treatment of their systolic hypertension. If rest and antihypertensive medication do not improve the hypertension, or if there is concern for the baby's condition, the only treatment available is delivery.

36.67 National quality standards[1] require that pregnant women at increased risk of pre-eclampsia at the booking appointment should be offered a prescription of 75 mg of aspirin to take daily from 12 weeks until birth. Women at high risk include those with any of the following: hypertensive disease during a previous pregnancy; chronic kidney disease; autoimmune disease such as systemic lupus erythematosis or antiphospholipid syndrome; type 1 or type 2 diabetes; chronic hypertension.

1 NICE Quality Standards Hypertension in pregnancy [QS35] (July 2013).

36.68 Also, women with hypertension in pregnancy should have a blood pressure target set below 150/100 mmHg or, if they also have target organ damage, below 140/90 mmHg. Women who have had hypertension in pregnancy should have a plan for ongoing antihypertensive management included in their postnatal care plan, which is communicated to their GP when they are transferred to community care after the birth.

36.69 The hypertensive complications of pregnancy present no problem if the pregnancy is near term but the development of hypertension at an earlier gestational age requires a careful risk benefit analysis of continuing the pregnancy or alternatively delivering a premature baby.

36.70 Anaemia may be prevented or corrected by the administration of iron and folic acid; some prescribe routine dietary supplements; others prescribe selectively. The aim is to keep the haemoglobin concentration above 11 grams per decilitre at first contact and 10.5 g/dl at 28 weeks. If it falls below 10 g/dl a panel of haematological investigations (red cell folate, serum ferritin) should be performed to assess iron stores and find the cause of anaemia.

36.71 **Abnormal presentation and unstable lie**: the commonest form of abnormal presentation is breech, which accounts for about 3 per cent of presentations at term. Breech presentations are classified as frank (both hips are flexed and both knees are extended so that the feet are adjacent to the fetal head), complete (both hips and both knees are flexed, but feet not below the fetal buttocks) and incomplete (one or both hips are not completely flexed). With incomplete breech, the presenting part may be one or both feet (footling breech) or, rarely, one or both knees (kneeling breech). Until the beginning of this century, the majority of breech presenting babies were delivered vaginally. In 2000, Hannah and colleagues completed a clinical trial involving 2,088 term fetuses in breech presentation at 121 institutions in 26 countries[1]. The subjects were randomly allocated to a planned (elective) Caesarean delivery group or a planned vaginal birth group. This trial concluded that, at least for perinatal mortality and serious neonatal morbidity by six weeks of life, elective Caesarean section (CS) was safer for the fetus and of similar safety to the mother when compared with intention to deliver vaginally. Since the publication of this work, it has become standard practice to recommend elective CS for breech presentation at term. There is no robust evidence regarding the optimal mode of delivery for the preterm breech baby.

1 Hannah, Hannah, Hewson (et al) 'Planned caesarean section versus planned vaginal birth for breech presentation at term: a randomised multicentre trial' (2000) 21 356(9239) Lancet 1375–1383 (Term Breech Trial Collaborative Group).

36.72 To reduce the incidence of CS, external cephalic version (ECV), hitherto a useful but neglected option, became more popular. ECV entails abdominal manipulation aimed at turning the baby from breech to cephalic presentation. It is standard practice to administer a tocolytic (drug that relaxes the uterus) before this manipulation, and the operator would usually be a consultant or a registrar trained in this procedure. On average the success rate of ECV with a trained operator is about 50 per cent. Spontaneous reversion to breech presentation after successful ECV occurs in less than 5 per cent. It is generally safe, with relatively few case reports of placental abruption, uterine rupture and fetomaternal haemorrhage. All rhesus negative women undergoing ECV must have prophylaxis against rhesus isoimmunisation (resulting from fetomaternal haemorrhage).

By lowering the incidence of breech presentation ECV reduces the CS rate. The RCOG recommends that ECV should be offered from 36 weeks in nulliparous women and from 37 weeks in multiparous women. ECV before 36 weeks of gestation is not associated with a significant reduction in noncephalic births or Caesarean section.

36.73 Unfortunately, the emergence of CS and ECV as the dominant approaches to the management of breech presentation at term has resulted in vastly reduced opportunities for obstetricians and midwives to acquire skills in breech vaginal delivery (other than at simulation training). This has safety implications, as some women will not be willing to have ECV and CS, and others will present so late in labour, with the breech on the perineum, that CS is not a practical option. There remains the second twin presenting as a breech; this twin will usually be delivered vaginally.

36.74 The policy of CS for all term breeches has diminished the skill base of the doctors in training so that when they are, as is inevitable, confronted by an unplanned breech delivery, they often do not have the required experience and technique to perform it safely. This risk may be mitigated by regular simulation training; both low-tech and high fidelity mannikins are available.

36.75 The options for a breech presentation at or near term are ECV, elective CS, and breech vaginal delivery. A proper decision in the ante-natal clinic, following discussion with a consultant or suitably experienced doctor, is essential. If a woman with no previous vaginal birth of a normal-sized baby at term has declined the options of ECV (or has had an unsuccessful ECV attempt) and elective CS, the prospects of a safe vaginal breech delivery should be assessed. A proper ante-natal assessment should include:

(1)   ultrasound assessment for fetal weight (babies weighing more than 3.5 kgs do badly when delivered vaginally as a breech) and attitude (the hyperextended neck may be a hazard at delivery);

(2)   an assessment of the mother's pelvis. Traditionally, radiological (in modern practice, MR rather than X-ray or CT) pelvimetry was performed, but studies suggest that it does not improve neonatal outcome; also there are no robust studies that have determined the threshold of pelvic measurements that predict safe vaginal breech delivery (in other words, the cut-off measurements are arbitrary);

(3)   exclusion of footling or kneeling breech presentation;

(4)   the exclusion of all other pregnancy complications (eg placenta praevia, interfering fibroids and concerns about fetal wellbeing).

There should also be assurance that a doctor experienced in the conduct of breech vaginal delivery will be present at delivery.

A previous CS is regarded as a contraindication to breech vaginal delivery but there is, in fact, no robust evidence about the safety or otherwise of vaginal breech birth in a woman with one previous CS.

36.76   Transverse, oblique and unstable lie: when the baby's spine is parallel with the maternal spine, the lie is described as longitudinal. Either the head or the breech may be the presenting part. Otherwise, the lie of the baby may be transverse or oblique. The lie changes frequently in early pregnancy but a variable presentation (unstable lie) is uncommon and dangerous in the last month. In such circumstances, if the woman goes into labour when the lie is not longitudinal there is an increased likelihood that the umbilical cord will prolapse when, as is likely to occur early, the membranes rupture. A further danger is that the woman, particularly if she is multiparous, will go into strong labour with a transverse lie; labour will then become obstructed and there is a real danger that the uterus may rupture. For these reasons, it is customary to admit the woman to hospital for observation from 36 weeks onwards and for immediate treatment if either complication should occur. The condition is commoner in women with a lax uterus and abdominal wall because of repeated childbearing, and those with an excess of amniotic fluid. It may be due to an obstructing cause – such as placenta praevia, contracted pelvis, pelvic tumours such as uterine fibroids and ovarian cysts – in which case the baby should be delivered by planned CS.

36.77   Multiple pregnancy is usually diagnosed by ultrasound. Occasionally twins are discovered on an early pregnancy scan but on later examinations only one baby is found because the second twin has died. The situation requires no intervention; there is usually no sign of the dead twin at the time of delivery. Special problems arise when, as the result of ante-natal screening, one twin is found to be abnormal. The parents are then faced with difficult decisions. Although the abnormal twin may selectively be 'reduced', the procedure requires considerable skill and inevitably puts the normal twin at risk. The Abortion Act 1967 (as amended by the Human Fertilisation and Embryology Act 1990) allows the obstetrician to reduce the number of fetuses in a multiple pregnancy, provided that grounds for abortion exist. There is no difficulty in interpreting the law if the fetus to be reduced is severely abnormal. However if all of the fetuses are apparently normal, the reduction is legal either because triplets or higher multiple pregnancies result in a greater risk to maternal health than twin or single pregnancies, or if there would be a significant stress to mental health if all the fetuses were lost as a consequence of pre-term labour. Most higher order multiple pregnancies result from assisted reproduction. National guidance limiting the number of embryos transferred in IVF treatment has helped to reduce this number.

36.78   The majority of twins arise from multiple ovulation and are simply siblings sharing a womb. A small minority occur because the original fertilised ovum divides to produce two identical (monozygotic) individuals. Such twins usually share the outer membrane (chorion) and are described as monochorionic. Very occasionally they may share the inner membrane (monoamniotic). Their circulations may be intimately connected so that blood may flow from one twin to the other, leading to the dangerous circumstance of twin-to-twin transfusion syndrome (TTTS). If a significant transfusion occurs, the major problem is for the recipient twin who develops an overloaded circulation, hypertension, heart failure and gross oedema. The recipient twin tends to be surrounded by an excess of amniotic fluid (polyhydramnios). The donor twin becomes anaemic and growth restricted whilst its amniotic sac shows a depletion in amniotic fluid (oligohydramnios). Thus ultrasound scan shows gross polyhydramnios in one sac with a recipient twin who has a large bladder, and an oligohydramniotic sac with a smaller donor twin who has an empty bladder and appears stuck against the wall of the uterus. When one twin dies before the other there is a risk of disseminated intravascular coagulation occurring in the surviving fetus with consequent severe damage. To have the best chance of saving the babies, TTTS has to be diagnosed early. For this reason, monochorionic twins should be monitored at two week intervals (or more frequently, as indicated) for the earliest signs of TTTS.

36.79   Fetal growth can only be monitored effectively by ultrasound. Attention has been focused mainly on the baby with intrauterine growth restriction (IUGR) – also known as fetal growth restriction (FGR) – but the fetus of excessive weight (macrosomia) may also be at increased risk. At both ends of the scale clinical observation is notoriously unreliable. Growth charts (Figure **36.1** at the end of this chapter) can be used to demonstrate an abnormal pattern of weight gain and to draw attention to a fetus at risk. There are two patterns of IUGR which have different significance and prognosis.

36.80   In symmetrical IUGR all parameters of fetal growth are below expectation. In late pregnancy the biparietal diameter is an unreliable guide to fetal growth because of individual variations in the shape of the head, but both head circumference and abdominal circumference will show similar patterns of delayed growth. The most common explanation for symmetrical IUGR is that the baby is genetically small. Then there is no increased risk. In other circumstances the baby of average genetic potential may be globally retarded either because of some early pregnancy insult or because of a severe inherited abnormality. In these rare cases of symmetrical growth restriction, further investigations are indicated.

36.81 Asymmetric IUGR is the problem which more commonly confronts the obstetrician. The growth of the baby's soft tissues is selectively reduced because the baby's nutrients are restricted. This is commonly attributed to placental insufficiency. The baby is effectively starved; body fat is reduced, as is the size of the liver, so that its abdominal circumference lags behind its head circumference. Even in severe malnutrition the blood supply to the brain is conserved so that the baby's head continues to grow. This head-sparing effect can only be demonstrated by comparing abdominal and head circumference. When there are grounds for suspecting chronic malnourishment of the baby, a combination of ultrasound measurements should be made including BPD, head circumference, abdominal circumference and femur length. A relative diminution in amniotic fluid volume is also usual with IUGR.

36.82 Every district general hospital should have the ability to carry out such examinations. More sophisticated ultrasound assessments are also possible: Doppler scan and production of a 'biophysical profile' of the baby (which includes not only measurements of its size and amniotic fluid volume but its movements and breathing activities in utero). Doppler blood flow studies of the placental, umbilical and fetal vessels are available in district general hospitals and can provide vital information about fetal wellbeing.

36.83 All women should be assessed at booking and those with risk factors for fetal growth restriction should be offered increased surveillance (serial ultrasound measurement of fetal size and umbilical artery Doppler scan).

36.84 All women except those with high body mass index or polyhydramnios should have serial measurement of symphysis-fundal height (SFH) at each antenatal appointment from 24 weeks of pregnancy, to monitor fetal growth. If the SFH suggests that the baby is small for gestational age, ultrasound measurement of fetal size and umbilical artery Doppler scan is offered.

36.85 Where a fetus is demonstrably malnourished and particularly where there is Doppler evidence of reduced placental and umbilical blood flows, a decision must be made concerning the time and mode of delivery. An already malnourished baby is unlikely to withstand the rigours of labour without becoming still more distressed, or to remain much longer in the uterus without the risk of intrauterine death or permanent damage. These are matters of fine clinical judgment but there is general acceptance that when IUGR is established the baby should be delivered with as little further stress as possible and this often (but not always) means by planned (elective) Caesarean section. The timing of delivery, the most finely balanced decision, will depend on the maturity of the pregnancy but generally, babies born after 36 weeks are at no disadvantage, babies born between 32 and 36 weeks may require special care but the majority will survive without handicap; babies born before 32 weeks may require neonatal intensive care including ventilation with a relatively high frequency of morbidity and mortality.

36.86 Fetal movement is a good indicator of fetal wellbeing: about half of women with a stillbirth perceived reduce fetal movement before fetal death. Unfortunately, failure of mother and/or health professionals to respond appropriately to reduced perception of fetal movement is a common antecedent of stillbirths. It is no longer fashionable, nor is it evidence-based, to ask women to keep special charts to record movements but the observation by the mother that movements are diminished should be the trigger for inquiry into risk of fetal growth restriction. A history should be taken to explore risk factors such as smoking, previous presentation with reduced movement, hypertension and other medical conditions. Fetal growth and wellbeing should be assessed by ultrasound and, if the gestational age is 28 weeks and over, a cardiotocograph should be recorded.

36.87 Cephalo-pelvic disproportion (CPD) means that the baby's head is too big to pass safely through the maternal pelvis. In an absolute sense the baby may be too big or the pelvis too small. More commonly it is the attitude of the baby which determines success or failure. The fetal head is normally completely flexed so that the chin rests on the chest. In this attitude the smallest diameter of the head presents to negotiate its passage through the bony pelvis (see Figure **36.2** at the end of this chapter). If the head becomes deflexed a wider diameter is presented to the pelvis; there is then relative disproportion. Deflexion of the fetal head is common when the back of the fetal head (the occiput) is directed towards the maternal spine instead of to the pubis (the occipito-posterior position).

36.88 During the ante-natal period the obstetrician may be put on notice that disproportion is likely by:

(1)   previous history of difficult delivery;
(2)   mother of small stature (less than 5 feet or 1.52 metres);
(3)   an exceptionally large baby;
(4)   failure of the head to engage in the pelvis in the last month of a first pregnancy.

36.89 Engagement of the fetal head is a critical concept for the understanding of labour. The fetal head (see Figure **36.3** at the end of this chapter) is not a sphere but an ovoid. The well-flexed head presents its narrowest diameters to the maternal pelvis; its broadest point is always the distance between the two parietal eminences (BPD). The narrowest straight of the maternal pelvis is the entrance or inlet. Once the BPD has passed the inlet, disproportion is unlikely to occur. All of this can be detected by abdominal examination of the pregnant woman to determine whether the biparietal diameter of the fetal head is still *palpable* in the abdomen. If it is, the fetal head is *not* engaged. Engagement implies that this widest diameter has passed the narrow strait and is no longer accessible to examination. To make the examination easier, the fetal head is notionally divided into fifths (see Figure **36.4** at the end of this chapter). If three-fifths of the head are palpable in the abdomen the head is not engaged; two-fifths or less of the head palpable indicates engagement. The progress of the descent of the head becomes of vital importance in labour.

36.90 In a first pregnancy it is usual for the head to be engaged before the onset of labour. Engagement usually occurs sometime in the last three weeks of the pregnancy. If it does not, it behoves the obstetrician to question whether there may be some obstruction or disproportion preventing engagement.

36.91 If CPD is suspected, digital examination of the shape and size of the bony pelvic cavity through the vagina (clinical pelvimetry) may provide a rough guide to its shape and dimensions. Clinical pelvimetry is not a skill that contemporary training grade doctors are familiar with and its reliability is questionable, so it has largely been abandoned. Measurement of the pelvic diameters by X-ray or MRI (radiological pelvimetry) does provide accurate information but correlates poorly with the outcome of labour. It is not possible to forecast the diameter of the fetal head that will have to pass through the pelvis, for this depends on the degree of flexion; this in turn depends on the efficiency of the uterus and can only be tested by labour. In circumstances of clinical doubt, the consultant would determine upon a trial of labour in appropriate cases.

36.92 Consultant decisions and the laying down of a proper plan for the conduct of labour are essential, not only in suspected cephalo-pelvic disproportion but in certain other potentially dangerous circumstances summarised in Table **36.3**. Adverse outcomes and litigation have often resulted from the failure to lay down a plan for intrapartum care in at-risk cases, and this failure was underscored in the MBRRACE-UK report 2014 (see para **36.32** above).

Table 36.3 Some circumstances in which personal involvement by a consultant is essential if errors in labour management are to be avoided

1	Breech labour
2	Suspected cephalopelvic disproportion
	trial of labour
3	Previous Caesarean section
	trial of vaginal birth
	particularly the potentially dangerous use of Syntocinon (oxytocin) with a previous scar
4	Twin delivery
	particularly where the second baby presents as a breech or transverse
5.	Diabetic pregnancy
6	Major haemoglobinopathy

36.93 Serious maternal disease, coincident with the pregnancy, needs special ante-natal provision. Diabetic patients should be managed in co-operation with a diabetic physician and major haemoglobinopathies with a consultant haematologist. Similar arrangements should be in place for women with cardiac conditions, epilepsy, mental ill-health and other medical diagnoses. Ideally the woman should be seen in a joint (multi-disciplinary) clinic.

36.94 Preterm labour (before 37 weeks) may occasionally occur as the result of serious maternal disease. There are a variety of other causes and often the explanation is lacking. Drugs are available (tocolytics) to inhibit uterine activity and provided only that the membranes are intact and the cervix less than 4 cm dilated, they can usually be used to delay labour by at least a few hours. There is no consensus that, of themselves, they convey any benefit to the fetus. However, since the early 1970s there has been increasing evidence that steroid hormones (glucocorticoids) given to the mother between 24 hours and seven days *before* pre-term delivery has considerable benefit for the baby. There is now overwhelming evidence of the efficacy and safety of the use of corticosteroids in the acceleration of lung maturity, a 40 per cent reduction in neonatal mortality and a reduction in intraventricular haemorrhage of even greater magnitude. All women threatened with preterm labour between 24 and 34 weeks gestation should be treated with antenatal corticosteroids.

36.95   Severe visual impairment often follows extreme prematurity; retinopathy of prematurity is a sequel to increased levels of oxygen in the blood of premature babies. Much litigation has resulted from this association[1].

1 (1997) 3 Clinical Risk 2 (March).

36.96   Prelabour rupture of the membranes (PROM) is loosely defined as spontaneous rupture of membranes, *not* followed within a few hours by the spontaneous onset of labour. If it is clear from the history and inspection of the woman's sanitary pad that the membranes have ruptured, a speculum examination for the purpose of confirming the diagnosis is not required. If not, then a sterile speculum examination should be performed. The RCOG and NICE recommend that women with PROM at term (37 completed weeks) should be offered a choice of immediate induction of labour or expectant management (but expectant management should not exceed 96 hours following membrane rupture)[1]. One case of chorioamnionitis (infection of the fetal membranes) will be avoided for every 50 women undergoing immediate induction but clinical trials show no difference in neonatal infection rates between immediate induction and expectant management.

1 NICE Guidelines. Induction of labour CG70 (July 2008).

36.97   Before 37 weeks (preterm PROM) the decision to wait or to intervene is more complex. The dangers of preterm delivery must be weighed against the risk of intrauterine infection which occasionally follows prolonged membrane rupture. Swabs should be taken from the vagina; the most serious infection is that caused by Group B streptococci. Women with preterm PROM should be given a 10-day course of antibiotic; co-amoxiclav is not recommended for women with preterm PROM because of concerns about necrotising enterocolitis.

Group B streptococcus

36.98   Group B streptococcus (GBS) is an opportunistic pathogen carried in the vagina or rectum of 10–30 per cent of women. It can be transmitted to the baby during labour, potentially causing early-onset group B streptococcus (EOGBS). Approximately 1 in 10 of affected babies will die, and the health and social care costs for surviving infants are high. This is largely preventable by administering intravenous antibiotics ('intrapartum antibiotic prophylaxis') to the woman during labour. It has been estimated that if a woman has a positive GBS swab in the current pregnancy, intrapartum antibiotic prophylaxis (IAP) reduces the risk of early-onset GBS disease (EOGBS) from

1 in 434 to 1 in 2170, and the risk of consequent mortality is reduced from 1 in 4,000 to 1 in 20,000.

36.99 GBS-specific IAP (intravenous benzylpenicillin, or clindamycin for women allergic to benzylpenicillin) should be offered where any of the following applies, as they are all associated with a relatively high incidence of EOGBS:

* previous baby with invasive GBS infection;
* GBS bacteriuria in the current pregnancy;
* vaginal swab positive for GBS in current pregnancy;
* pyrexia (temperature higher than 38°C) in labour (broad-spectrum antibiotics to include GBS cover);
* chorioamnionitis (broad-spectrum antibiotics to include GBS cover).

If a woman known to carry GBS experiences spontaneous rupture of the fetal membranes at term, labour should be induced and IAP should be commenced. IAP is not necessary if the woman is having an elective Caesarean section with intact membranes.

36.100 In the USA and Canada, pregnant women are routinely screened for carriage of GBS but in the UK neither the National Screening Committee nor the RCOG recommends routine antenatal screening. The reluctance to recommend screening in the UK appears to be based primarily on financial and logistic considerations, with the RCOG holding its position (which is based on expert opinion, in the absence of more robust evidence) 'until it is clear that antenatal screening for GBS carriage does more good than harm and that the benefits are cost-effective'. An opposing school of thought holds that, given the impact of IAP on rates of EOGBS, it is illogical not to screen for women who will benefit from it.

36.101 The RCOG guideline also states that 'current evidence does not support screening for GBS or the administration of IAP to women in whom GBS carriage was detected in a previous pregnancy'[1]. This author argues, however, that each woman who has had a positive GBS culture in a previous pregnancy should be given the opportunity to make an informed choice regarding testing in the current pregnancy. Carriage of GBS can be temporary or persistent; about half of women with GBS carriage in a previous pregnancy will be carriers in the current pregnancy.

1 Royal College of Obstetricians and Gynaecologists. The Prevention of Early-onset Neonatal Group B Streptococcal Disease. Green-top Guideline No 36 (2nd edn, July 2012); Turrentine, Ramirez 'Recurrence of group B streptococci colonization in subsequent pregnancy' (2008) 112 Obstet Gynecol 259–264. doi: 10.1097/AOG.0b013e31817f5cb9.

36.102 Ante-partum haemorrhage is defined as bleeding from the genital tract after the 24th week of pregnancy. It may be due to an abnormally situated placenta (placenta praevia) or to a premature separation of the placenta (abruptio placentae or accidental haemorrhage). In either case immediate admission to hospital and further investigations are required.

36.103 Placenta praevia may threaten the life of both mother and baby. The placenta lies low in the uterus, in its lower segment, and may cover all or part of the cervix so as the cervix dilates the placenta separates giving rise to fresh painless bleeding. The bleeding may first occur early in the pregnancy and recur intermittently in greater or lesser amounts. The diagnosis is confirmed by ultrasound. If the amount of bleeding permits, conservative management is continued until the baby is mature, at which time it may be delivered safely by Caesarean section. Occasionally catastrophic haemorrhage may demand earlier delivery with the risk to the baby of prematurity. A consultant obstetrician should be present at the CS, as there could be heavy intra-operative bleeding. In cases of placenta praevia and previous CS, there is a high risk of the placenta being adherent to the CS scar (*placenta accreta*), often necessitating a hysterectomy. This should be anticipated and discussed with the woman in advance, and her consent obtained for hysterectomy in the event of uncontrollable bleeding. Prophylactic use of a balloon to occlude the internal iliac arteries, with or without arterial embolization occlusion, may be used to reduce blood loss at Caesarean section in cases of *placenta accreta*, but complications such as thromboembolism and vascular injury have been reported, and the risks of this intervention should be discussed with the woman when it is offered.

36.104 Placental abruption presents a much more immediate threat to the baby, as well as to the mother. It may be unheralded and catastrophic, with total separation of the placenta and massive concealed intra-uterine bleeding, causing the death of the baby before it can be delivered. Alternatively the process of placental separation may be more gradual and partial so that the baby can be extracted from the uterus alive, but nevertheless only to survive with hypoxic brain damage. Placental abruption can also cause serious maternal complications including disseminated intravascular coagulation (leading to uncontrollable haemorrhage), renal failure and sometimes death. In lesser degrees the process may begin with repeated painful revealed losses of blood, often in association with hypertension, and with ultrasound evidence of retroplacental bleeding. In such cases, it may be possible to deliver the baby before catastrophe strikes. The balance has to be nicely judged on the clinical picture and the maturity of the pregnancy. When signs of major placental abruption occur with a mature live baby, the situation is one of the greatest urgency. If the baby is to be salvaged, delivery must be achieved within minutes of the diagnosis.

36.105 Ante-natal admission may thus be required for a variety of conditions, most commonly:

(1)   hypertension;
(2)   ante-partum haemorrhage;
(3)   fetal (intrauterine) growth restriction (IUGR).

36.106 These conditions often require prolonged inpatient care and mothers are constantly frustrated by the need to remain in hospital for long periods when nothing is apparently done. Whilst care in the community is now much more frequently offered in hypertension and in IUGR, hospital still remains the only place of safety for patients with a significant risk of haemorrhage. Constant counselling, explanation and reassurance are essential to obtain the woman's agreement to a hospital stay, particularly for the mother who has small children at home.

INDUCTION OF LABOUR

36.107 Where the continuation of the pregnancy poses a threat to mother or baby, labour may be induced. Fashions change; in the 1960s and 1970s there were high induction rates, mostly for social indications; these are no longer considered acceptable. The main controversy centres on prolonged pregnancy. The rationale for delivery at or soon after term is that perinatal mortality and morbidity increase significantly after the completion of the 42nd week of pregnancy, attributed to placental ageing and insufficiency. Some obstetricians set an arbitrary time limit when they induce labour if it does not occur spontaneously. This varies from 41 to 42 weeks and often with sub-variables, such as maternal age, twins or a breech presentation. There used to be a minority view that pregnancy may be allowed to continue indefinitely in the absence of other complications provided only that the condition of the fetus is carefully monitored, but it is now universal practice to induce labour by 42 weeks unless the woman declines this. The RCOG and NICE recommend that women with uncomplicated pregnancies should be offered induction of labour beyond 41 weeks and that women who decline induction of labour should be offered increased antenatal monitoring from 42 weeks, consisting of a twice weekly CTG and ultrasound estimation of maximum amniotic pool depth[1]. Inextricably interwoven with this indication is pressure often brought on the obstetrician by the woman and her family to induce labour either because of understandable social reasons or simply because she is fed up and uncomfortable.

1 Royal College of Obstetricians and Gynaecologists. *Induction of labour*. London; RCOG Press 2001; National Institute for Health and Care Excellence. Induction of labour. NICE guidelines [CG70] July 2008

36.108 The second commonest indication for induction of labour is hypertension. Most obstetricians will induce labour if pre-eclampsia occurs at term. If the pregnancy is less than 34 weeks and maternal condition allows, the management is conservative. In severe pre-eclampsia delivery may be necessary irrespective of gestational age in the interests of maternal wellbeing.

36.109 IUGR is an indication for induction of labour, sometimes linked to hypertension or repeated small antepartum haemorrhage of undetermined origin. Other less common indications include established intrauterine death, twin pregnancy, Rhesus incompatibility, maternal diabetes and fetal abnormality.

36.110 There is wide agreement for the preferred method of induction of labour. If there is no immediate urgency, the sweeping of membranes (digital separation of the membranes through the partially dilated cervix) is often sufficient. Membrane sweeping is associated with a reduction in the length of time to spontaneous labour, reduces the incidence of prolonged pregnancy and reduces the need for the use of formal methods of induction of labour. It does not increase infection rates in mother or baby.

36.111 If the cervix is tightly closed (unfavourable) the intra-vaginal administration of prostaglandin (either by a pessary or gel) is often sufficient to provoke uterine contractions or at least to dilate the cervix sufficiently to allow the artificial rupture of the membranes. The treatment may be repeated after a few hours if labour is not established. A period of CTG monitoring is essential before and after each application of prostaglandin.

36.112 Artificial rupture of the membranes (ARM) is an effective method of induction, but only if appropriately timed; premature ARM, when the cervix is unfavourable, only increases the risk of 'failed induction' and recourse to Caesarean section. Once the membranes are ruptured and if labour is not well established it may be augmented by giving intravenous oxytocin (Syntocinon) according to the regime recommended by the RCOG and endorsed by NICE[1].

1 Royal College of Obstetricans and Gynaecologists. *Induction of labour* (2001); NICE Guidelines Induction of labour CG70 (July 2008).

36.113 The complications of induction include:

(1)   failure to achieve the desired objective;
(2)   intrauterine infection;
(3)   prolapse of the umbilical cord;
(4)   haemorrhage from an unsuspected placenta praevia or vasa praevia.

36.114 Vasa praevia is a rare condition in which the insertion of the cord into the placenta is abnormal (see Figure **36.5** at the end of this chapter). If there is a succenturiate lobe or a vellamentous insertion of the placenta the unsupported vessels may overlie the cervix. If one of those vessels is torn as the membranes rupture, haemorrhage may result. Unlike other forms of ante-partum or intra-partum haemorrhage it is the baby who bleeds in this condition. There will be bright red vaginal bleeding; the baby's heart rate will be increased, sometimes with a characteristic (sinusoidal) CTG pattern. Unless the diagnosis is made quickly the baby may be exsanguinated before delivery. Bedside tests are available for the detection of fetal blood, rapidly distinguishing it from maternal blood.

INTRA-PARTUM CARE

36.115 Admission of the mother in labour provides another critical opportunity for the reassessment of risk. Her ante-natal record should be reviewed and the consultant decisions for labour appropriately implemented. If new risk factors have emerged, a senior doctor must immediately be informed and see the patient.

36.116 The mother's own views on the conduct of her labour should be recorded and, if there are no contraindications, implemented. Many women greatly benefit from the support of their partner during labour and are increasingly requesting management which involves the minimum of interference and the maximum of independence for the mother. Hospitals increasingly seek to provide a 'home from home' environment in which the mother may have some of the advantages associated with home delivery, but within a hospital where emergency help is available should things go wrong.

36.117   Water baths are now commonplace. In the great majority of women with no special risk factors there seems no reason to resist the request for the management of the first or even the second stage of labour in a water bath. Both the Royal College of Obstetricians and Gynaecologists and the Royal College of Midwives support labouring in water for healthy women with uncomplicated pregnancies. The evidence to support underwater birth is less clear but complications are rare if good practice guidelines are followed in relation to eligibility criteria and infection control[1].

1   Royal College of Obstetricians and Gynaecologists/Royal College of Midwives Joint statement No1 'Immersion in water during labour and birth' (April 2006).

36.118   The use of electronic fetal monitoring (EFM), particularly in low risk pregnancies, has been controversial. To the protagonists, the proposition that listening to the baby some of the time is just as effective as listening to the baby all of the time runs contrary to common sense. To the antagonists, EFM has not been shown to reduce perinatal mortality and cerebral palsy. The RCOG and NICE have weighed in with guidelines for EFM[1]. The guidelines state that a woman who is healthy and has had an otherwise uncomplicated pregnancy should be offered intermittent auscultation in labour to monitor fetal wellbeing, and that continuous electronic fetal monitoring should be offered and recommended for high-risk pregnancies where there is an increased risk of perinatal death, cerebral palsy or neonatal encephalopathy. EFM should be used where oxytocin is being used for induction or augmentation of labour. It must be emphasised that if intermittent monitoring is to be used, it must be done properly. In the active stages of labour, intermittent auscultation should occur after a contraction, for a minimum of 60 seconds, and at least every 15 minutes in the first stage and every five minutes in the second stage. If such monitoring reveals abnormalities or if new risk factors emerge during labour, the need for EFM should be reassessed. It is important to emphasise that variability cannot be detected by the unaided ear.

1   Royal College of Obstetricians and Gynaecologists *Induction of Labour. The Use of Electronic Fetal Monitoring. The Use and Interpretation of Cardiotocography in Intrapartum Fetal Surveillance* (2001); NICE *Intrapartum care: Care of healthy women and their babies during childbirth* (2007).

36.119   It has traditionally been assumed that for all patients there is a distinct advantage in recording a brief CTG trace immediately upon admission. With the reassurance of a normal admission trace, appropriate patients may then be managed by intermittent auscultation. The guidelines do not recommend this practice, because current evidence does not support the use of the admission cardiotocography (CTG) in low-risk pregnancy. However, many obstetricians and midwives have experienced the situation where an admission trace reveals fetal distress in a hitherto low-risk pregnancy, so the practice of recording an admission CTG has continued in many units.

36.120   The CTG (see Figure **36.6** at the end of this chapter) produces two recordings. The upper channel (the cardiograph) represents the fetal heart; the lower (the tocograph) records contractions of the uterus. The cardiograph may be recorded by an ultrasound signal through the mother's abdominal wall or by an electrode attached to the baby's scalp (fetal scalp electrode). The tocograph is produced by an external tocodynamometer.

36.121 Modern machines electronically date and time the recording (provided that the clock is properly set). The record should be identified by writing on the name and registration number of the woman and by the date and time, if it is not automatically recorded. Doctors and midwives may also annotate the document with important events of the labour. The recording produced is often crucial to expert consideration of the standards of care in labour. They do not fit comfortably into record holders and are more often lost or damaged than any other part of the clinical record. They are often supplied, in the context of litigation, in unsuitable A4 fragments, impossible to interpret. A full and continuous copy must be properly assessed; such copies can be made by feeding the original through an old-fashioned domestic fax machine; professional copies can be made by the Times Drawing Office[1]. Interpretation of CTGs is a complex subject about which experts frequently differ. The use of a standard format to interpret and respond to fetal heart rate patterns facilitates safety in clinical practice and clarity in medico-legal communication.

1 15 Maddox Street, London W1S 2QQ; tel 0207 629 5661.

36.122 Some authors attempt to distinguish between patterns suggestive of stress (a healthy fetus using compensatory mechanisms in response to hypoxia or other stresses) and fetal distress, implying a degree of fetal compromise. In practice, although fetal distress is a term which defies definition, it is used to describe all circumstances in which the baby's response is *potentially* indicative of stress. This includes not only a wide spectrum of abnormalities on the CTG but also the passage of meconium in the amniotic fluid.

36.123 It is recognised from clinical negligence claims and from the confidential enquiries into stillbirths and neonatal deaths that there are problems with interpretation of CTGs. All pregnancies, regardless of risk category, need effective monitoring: only 1 in 5 of claims for CTG interpretation involves a high-risk pregnancy. Appropriate formal and informal training of all staff in the interpretation of CTGs is a key requirement for safe obstetric and midwifery practice[1]. To facilitate interpretation, a uniform approach is desirable, and the pneumonic DR C BRAVADO provides one[2]. Define the background Risk; Contractions (tocograph); Baseline (fetal heart) Rate; Accelerations; Variability; Decelerations; Overall assessment and plan.

1 Ugwumadu 'Understanding cardiotocographic patterns associated with intrapartum fetal hypoxia and neurologic injury' (2013) 27 Best Pract Res Clin Obstet Gynaecol 509–536. doi: 10.1016/j.bpobgyn.2013.04.002.
2 American Academy of Family Physicians *Advanced Life Support in Obstetrics* (ALSO) Course Syllabus.

36.124 The four features used to assess a CTG are baseline fetal heart rate, baseline variability (fluctuations in the fetal heart rate, usually more than two cycles per minute), fetal heart rate accelerations and decelerations. Fetal heart rate accelerations are a sign that the baby is healthy. The baseline rate, variability and decelerations are categorised as normal/reassuring, non-reassuring and abnormal as shown in Table **36.4**.

Table 36.4 Categorisation of fetal heart rate (FHR) features

	Feature		
	Baseline (beats/ minute)	**Baseline variability (beats/ minute)**	**Decelerations**
Normal/ reassuring	100–160	5 or more	None or early
Non-reassuring	161–180	Less than 5 for 30–90 minutes	Variable decelerations: • dropping from baseline by 60 beats/minute or less **and** taking 60 seconds or less to recover • present for over 90 minutes • occurring with over 50 per cent of contractions. **OR** Variable decelerations: • dropping from baseline by more than 60 beats/minute **or** taking over 60 seconds to recover • present for up to 30 minutes • occurring with over 50 per cent of contractions. **OR** Late decelerations: • present for up to 30 minutes • occurring with over 50 per cent of contractions.
Abnormal	Above 180 **or** below 100	Less than 5 for over 90 minutes	Non-reassuring variable decelerations (see row above): • still observed 30 minutes after starting conservative measures • occurring with over 50 per cent of contractions. **OR** Late decelerations: • present for over 30 minutes • do not improve with conservative measures • occurring with over 50 per cent of contractions. **OR** Bradycardia or a single prolonged deceleration lasting 3 minutes or more.

36.125   On the basis of this categorisation, a CTG should be classified as normal, non-reassuring or abnormal[1]. A CTG is

- normal if all three features fall into the reassuring category;
- non-reassuring if there is one non-reassuring feature but the other features are two normal/ reassuring;
- abnormal if there is one abnormal feature or two non-reassuring features.

1 Intrapartum care: care of healthy women and their babies during childbirth (NICE, December 2014).

36.126   A CTG showing bradycardia or a single prolonged deceleration with baseline below 100 beats/minute, persisting for three minutes or more warrants urgent intervention (see Table **36.5**).

Table 36.5 Management based on interpretation of cardiotocograph traces

Category	Definition	Interpretation	Management
CTG is normal/ reassuring	All 3 features are normal/ reassuring	Normal CTG, no non-reassuring or abnormal features, healthy fetus	• Continue CTG and normal care. • If CTG was started because of concerns arising from intermittent auscultation, remove CTG after 20 minutes if there are no non-reassuring or abnormal features and no ongoing risk factors.
CTG is non-reassuring and suggests need for conservative measures	1 non-reassuring feature **AND** 2 normal/ reassuring features	Combination of features that may be associated with increased risk of fetal acidosis; if accelerations are present, acidosis is unlikely	• Think about possible underlying causes. • If the baseline fetal heart rate is over 160 beats/minute, check the woman's temperature and pulse. If either are raised, offer fluids and paracetamol. • Start 1 or more conservative measures: — encourage the woman to mobilise or adopt a left-lateral position, and in particular to avoid being supine — offer oral or intravenous fluids — reduce contraction frequency by stopping oxytocin if being used and/or offering tocolysis. • Inform coordinating midwife and obstetrician.

Category	Definition	Interpretation	Management
CTG is abnormal and indicates need for conservative measures AND further testing	1 abnormal feature **OR** 2 non-reassuring features	Combination of features that is more likely to be associated with fetal acidosis	• Think about possible underlying causes. • If the baseline fetal heart rate is over 180 beats/minute, check the woman's temperature and pulse. If either are raised, offer fluids and paracetamol. • Start 1 or more conservative measures (see 'CTG is non-reassuring…' row for details). • Inform coordinating midwife and obstetrician. • Offer to take an FBS (for lactate or pH) after implementing conservative measures, or expedite birth if an FBS cannot be obtained and no accelerations are seen as a result of scalp stimulation. • Take action sooner than 30 minutes if late decelerations are accompanied by tachycardia and/or reduced baseline variability. • Inform the consultant obstetrician if any FBS result is abnormal. • Discuss with the consultant obstetrician if an FBS cannot be obtained or a third FBS is thought to be needed.
CTG is abnormal and indicates **need for urgent intervention**	Bradycardia or a single prolonged deceleration with baseline below 100 beats/minute, persisting for 3 minutes or more*	An abnormal feature that is very likely to be associated with current fetal acidosis or imminent rapid development of fetal acidosis	• Start 1 or more conservative measures (see 'CTG is non-reassuring…' row for details). • Inform coordinating midwife. • Urgently seek obstetric help. • Make preparations for urgent birth. • Expedite birth if persists for 9 minutes. • If heart rate recovers before 9 minutes, reassess decision to expedite birth in discussion with the woman.

Abbreviations: CTG, cardiotocography; FBS, fetal blood sample.
* A stable baseline value of 90–99 beats/minute with normal baseline variability (having confirmed that this is not the maternal heart rate) may be a normal variation; obtain a senior obstetric opinion if uncertain.

36.127   A sinusoidal pattern, sometimes seen with fetal anaemia, oscillates smoothly 2–5 times per minute with an amplitude of 5–10 bpm. A sinusoidal pattern is not always pathological: sometimes healthy fetuses manifest this pattern.

36.128   Accelerations (see Figure **36.6** at the end of this chapter) from a normal baseline are the hallmark of fetal health. Decelerations are generally ominous and are classified:

(1)   early: when they are coincident with and make a mirror image of the uterine contraction, and do not exceed 40 beats per minute;
(2)   late: when there is a significant lag time (see Figure **36.6**) between the peak of the contraction and the nadir of the deceleration;
(3)   variable: when there is no fixed relationship between contraction and deceleration and/or the deceleration exceeds 40 beats per minute.

36.129   Various reports, such as the CESDI, have identified poor interpretation of CTGs or failure to respond appropriately to CTG abnormalities as the most common factor in adverse outcomes resulting from substandard intrapartum care.

36.130   Not every abnormality of the CTG requires immediate delivery. Unless the tracing is diagnostic, further information about the baby is desirable if unnecessary operative intervention is to be avoided. Such information can be obtained by examination of the amniotic fluid (is it meconium- or blood-stained?) and by carrying out blood gas analysis of a fetal blood sample taken by puncturing the baby's scalp through the dilating cervix to suck up a capillary sample of blood. Such an analysis gives evidence of the state of exchange of respiratory gases (oxygen and carbon dioxide) and whether or not the baby is suffering from impairment of this exchange and showing acidosis. With prolonged hypoxia, carbon dioxide accumulates to give a respiratory acidosis. In a continued deficiency of oxygen, anaerobic metabolism results in a metabolic acidosis, reflected in the pH. A pH ≥ 7.25 is normal and a pH ≤ 7.20 indicates acidosis and warrants immediate delivery of the baby. If the pH is between 7.21 and 7.24 a repeat sample should be obtained within 30 minutes if CTG abnormalities persist, or delivery should be considered if this result shows a substantial fall since the last sample. A normal FBS should not be an excuse for complacency: the sample is only relevant at the time it is taken and, if CTG abnormalities persist, a further blood sample should be taken to reassess the baby's condition – or the baby delivered.

36.131   Fetal blood sampling (FBS) is available in practically all obstetric units in the UK. In contemporary practice the use of EFM without facilities for FBS counts as sub-standard care.

36.132   The RCOG/NICE guidelines state that units employing EFM should have ready access to fetal blood sampling facilities. It is also recommended that where delivery is contemplated because of an abnormal fetal heart-rate pattern, in cases of suspected fetal acidosis, fetal blood sampling should be undertaken in the absence of technical difficulties or contraindications. Contraindications to fetal blood sampling include maternal infection (eg

HIV, hepatitis viruses and herpes simplex virus), fetal bleeding disorders (eg haemophilia) and prematurity (<34 weeks). Where there is clear evidence of acute fetal compromise (eg prolonged deceleration greater than three minutes), fetal blood sampling should not be undertaken and the baby should be delivered urgently. Fetal blood sampling has on occasion featured in litigation either because (when it was available) it was not used, or the sample was improperly taken, or contaminated so as to give an abnormal result, or misinterpreted or wrongly relied upon. Intrapartum stillbirths have also occurred because staff spent critical time doing an FBS when the baby should have been delivered on account of bradycardia.

36.133 Progress in labour is recorded on a partogram (see Figure **36.7** at the end of this chapter). Strictly only the central part of the figure is a partograph, consisting of two plotted lines of progress. The remainder of the chart records additional information such as the quality of the uterine contractions, intravenous fluids, urinalysis, pulse, blood pressure etc. Criteria of progress are cervical dilatation and descent of the presenting part. Cervical dilatation is measured in centimetres; there are ten points on the scale because ten centimetres equals full dilatation. Progress of labour can thus be compared with the average pattern of both first (primigravid) and subsequent (multipara) labours (Figure **36.8**). Descent of the head is also plotted on the partogram, in terms of the fifths palpable (Figure **36.4**). It is important to emphasise that the recording of head level is by abdominal examination, whilst the assessment of cervical dilatation requires a vaginal examination. The station of the head may also be determined on vaginal examination, by referring the leading part of the fetal head to the maternal ischial spines. Not infrequently, descent is *wrongly* charted by reference to station only and not head level (Figure **36.9**). The requirements for the documentation of vaginal examination in labour are set out clearly in the standard textbooks of midwifery but scant attention is made to proper documentation of certain critical facts such as moulding, caput and the position of the fetal head. The examiner may also determine the position of the fetal head by reference to the skull sutures and fontanelles (Figure **36.3**) and their position with reference to the mother's pelvis.

36.134 Moulding describes the overlapping of the separate and mobile bones of the fetal skull (see Figure **36.3**) as the result of uterine activity compressing the head into the pelvis changing its shape so that it may be accommodated.

36.135 Caput succedaneum is the soft tissue swelling which forms, also as the result of pressure, further distorting the shape of the head. The examiner who relies entirely on vaginal findings for head descent may be seriously misled (Figure **36.9**). What is important in assessing descent of the fetal head is not how low the leading soft part is, but how low the bony presenting part is.

36.136 Trial of labour is a term originally used to describe the management of labour in the presence of suspected borderline cephao-pelvic disproportion (CPD). It is a term of art and its management was described in all the standard textbooks. Given the suspicion of disproportion, the labour is conducted under the direct supervision of a senior doctor so that if the suspicion is confirmed, labour may be terminated safely by Caesarean section. In 21st century obstetric practice, such trials are unfashionable and the term trial of labour is often used in a different context such as trial of vaginal delivery after a previous CS.

36.137 Slow progress in primigravid labours is often due to poor uterine action; this may be a response to CPD. The proposition that effective uterine action is the key to normal delivery underpins the package of interventions known as active management of labour[1]. Active management includes strict diagnostic criteria for labour, early amniotomy (artificial rupture of the membranes, ARM), early infusion of the intravenous hormone, oxytocin (Syntocinon), and continuous professional support. Enthusiasm for the package as originally conceived in Dublin has waned due to lack of evidence of benefit in reducing CS rates, but elements of it, particularly ARM and Syntocinon infusion, are commonly used to speed up labour. The improved uterine action increases head flexion, promotes moulding and restores the progress of labour to normal (1 cm dilatation of the cervix per hour). If acceleration or augmentation of the labour with oxytocin fails to achieve normal progress, the attempt at vaginal delivery is deemed to have failed and the baby delivered by CS.

1 O'Driscoll, Meagher, Robson *Active Management of Labour* (4th edn, 2003).

36.138 When Syntocinon is employed, electronic fetal monitoring is mandatory. Much litigation arises from the abuse of Syntocinon. The drug makes uterine contractions more powerful and thus more effective. However, if the fetus is already stressed by the effect of contractions, Syntocinon will make that distress worse. It is axiomatic that Syntocinon must never be used in the presence of fetal distress, and must be discontinued if fetal distress occurs.

36.139 The length of labour is often a matter of dispute. Labour is said to be in the *active* phase when the cervix is more than 3 cm dilated. Until then the woman is said to be in the *latent* phase of labour, a phase which may without harm last for many hours (see Figure **36.8** at the end of this chapter). Sometimes a woman may be conscious of uterine contractions over a period of several days or even one or two weeks at a time when the cervix is not dilating, a period of *false* labour.

36.140 Generally, women who have had a previous vaginal delivery do not suffer uterine inertia; they react to disproportion by an increase in uterine activity. If the obstruction is not relieved the uterus may rupture. It follows that acceleration of labour with oxytocin in a multiparous patient must be undertaken with much greater caution than in the nullipara. Her uterus may be more sensitive to oxytocin; the baby she is carrying may be much larger than any she has previously borne.

36.141 The term trial of scar is sometimes used to describe the management of labour in the presence of a scar on the uterus, usually from previous CS. This is a misnomer: the scar is not on trial; indeed if there are any doubts about the integrity of the scar, a CS should be performed. The more appropriate term is trial of vaginal delivery. Provided there is no contraindication to CS, most obstetricians will allow a trial of vaginal delivery under strict supervision. A scar represents a weakness in the uterus which is susceptible to rupture. The use of oxytocic drugs such as prostaglandin and oxytocin in such labour is controversial and those who permit it must be scrupulous in their monitoring of the labour.

36.142 It is essential that before embarking upon a trial of vaginal delivery after a prior CS the woman is given adequate information to allow her to make a proper decision; she should be told of the true incidence of rupture (based on the experience of the unit in which she is booked) and the possible consequences should rupture occur.

36.143 Rupture of the uterus is rare but often results in fetal death, frequently causes grave maternal injury and occasionally maternal death. While a previous CS scar is the commonest antecedent, the intact multiparous uterus may also be ruptured by the injudicious use of oxytocin. Rarely an intact uterus may rupture spontaneously. The occurrence may be dramatic and obvious with severe internal haemorrhage or, particularly in the case of a ruptured scar, may be silent and only discovered after delivery. Warning signs are unreliable but there is often a rise in maternal pulse rate and there may be fetal distress before rupture. The sudden loss of the fetal heart, the abrupt cessation of uterine contractions and the appearance of blood in the urine are all suggestive that the uterus has already ruptured.

36.144 Breech labour demands constant risk assessment. A planned breech vaginal delivery is now a rarity, and most breech deliveries will be either preterm or undiagnosed term breech. The discovery of an unfavourable presentation, such as a footling, at the beginning of labour should lead to CS. Great care must be taken when the membranes rupture because there is an increased risk of prolapse of the umbilical cord. The membranes should not be ruptured when the breech is high or in an unfavourable position. The labour demands careful monitoring. Slow progress in spite of careful ante-natal selection may be an indication that the baby is bigger than anticipated, and a warning of problems to come. The use of oxytocin in breech labour is controversial.

Twin labour demands the monitoring of both fetal hearts, effectively only possible with EFM.

36.145 Umbilical cord complications are frequently unpredictable, may be undetected and cause death of the infant or cerebral palsy. Cord entanglements are common and usually of no consequence. They may be associated with signs of fetal distress of mild degree, especially late in the first stage of labour. The commonest problem is a cord round the neck; the baby is not strangled by the cord but if it is tight the blood flow may be restricted causing hypoxia. Similarly, there may be a true knot in the cord which may be unnoticed by all concerned including the baby until the placenta is delivered. This is because the pulsating blood flow through the cord usually prevents the knot from being drawn tight.

36.146 If a loop of umbilical cord lies beside or below the presenting part of the baby – particularly likely with preterm babies, when the lie is unstable or transverse, breech presentation and twins – and is detected by its synchronous pulsation with the baby's heart on vaginal examination when the membranes are still intact, this is called presentation of the cord. The baby is in no immediate danger. However, the baby should be delivered as quickly as possible by CS, because the membranes may rupture at any time, converting cord presentation into cord prolapse, a serious threat to the baby. The fetal circulation may be occluded by the compression of the cord between the presenting part and the maternal pelvis during uterine contractions. The blood flow through the cord may also be impaired because its blood vessels go into spasm following the drop in temperature between the mother's body and the outside air. Spasm of the cord vessels will also be encountered when the cord is handled. The treatment for this condition is delivery of the baby as soon as possible by CS, if the cervix is not fully dilated. Whilst preparations are being made for this, every precaution is taken to relieve the umbilical cord from compression, by digital elevation of the presenting part through the vagina. If the cervix is fully dilated, forceps delivery is usually the quickest option.

36.147 Epidural analgesia is frequently employed as an alternative to systemic pain relief and has its own special problems, requiring scrupulous supervision and monitoring. Whilst midwives may be trained to give subsequent 'top-up' doses, the siting of the block and its subsequent supervision should be in the hands of an obstetric anaesthetist. In the event of CS or other operative delivery, the block may be continued, with suitable adjustment, to provide pain relief at delivery.

36.148 The second stage of labour begins from full dilatation of the cervix, ending with the delivery of the baby. It consists of two sections: the passive phase (prior to pushing); and the active phase (which commences with pushing). Midwives and obstetricians commonly wait for some descent to occur and/or for the woman to feel an urge to push, before encouraging maternal down-bearing effort. The baby is at much greater risk once maternal expulsive efforts begin and a much higher standard of monitoring is required.

36.149 Classical teaching about the length of the second stage of labour has been complicated by the introduction and uptake of epidural analgesia. With an effective block the mother, even with the cervix fully dilated, may have no desire to push. In those circumstances the second stage may be treated as an extension of the first and requires no different management. However, once maternal effort begins, broad time limits are applied to the duration of pushing. Provided progress is being maintained (as judged by the descent of the head) and provided that there is no fetal distress it is reasonable to allow a nullipara to push for about 45 minutes; after this time she will become exhausted and careful consideration should be given to operative delivery. Traditionally a limit of 30 minutes is applied to multiparous women but, as with nullipara, fetal wellbeing is more important than the clock. The CTG in the second stage of labour is notoriously difficult to assess and frequently a subject of controversy between experts.

OPERATIVE DELIVERY

36.150 Forceps delivery is a common source of litigation. The baby may suffer internal head injuries, surface marks and bruises, facial nerve injury or superficial bleeding around one or both of the baby's eyes (subconjunctival haemorrhage). Most of these are temporary and require no specific treatment but others are permanent and/or need surgical treatment. The more severe injuries are usually associated with poor technique. The common errors are:

(1)   attempting vaginal delivery when:

    (a)   mechanical warning signs are ignored or misinterpreted;
    (b)   basic rules are disregarded;
    (c)   fetal compromise is already present;
    (d)   head position or head level are wrongly assessed or not assessed at all;

(2)   delivery is undertaken by doctors too junior or inexperienced;
(3)   repeated attempts at delivery;
(4)   delay in the decision-delivery interval.

36.151   Trial of forceps may be undertaken if there is doubt in the mind of the operator concerning the outcome. Such trial is only permissible if the cervix if fully dilated, the head engaged and no more than one fifth palpable and the pelvis adequate. It should be closely supervised by an experienced obstetrician, in an operating theatre with full preparations for immediate CS should it fail. There is no place for a trial of forceps if the baby is already showing signs of distress. The procedure frequently involves rotation of the baby from an occipito-posterior or occipito-transverse position with the specially designed Kjelland's forceps or with a vacuum device. Such an operation requires considerable skill and judgment, only acquired by extensive experience. The baby delivered by forceps may have bruises or marks on the face or head, and vacuum extraction of the baby may cause lacerations to the scalp. These injuries mostly disappear soon after birth but in some cases they are permanent. Liability will be determined on the facts of the particular case. When forceps are correctly applied, the blades should straddle the side of the head, so marks running over the baby's nose (for example) indicate that the baby's position had been misjudged by the operator. If the head has not been appropriately rotated, more force is required to effect delivery, and the delivery is traumatic.

36.152   The ventouse (vacuum-assisted delivery) is an alternative to forceps and in some UK centres has superseded forceps as the more popular instrument. Largely due to its ease of application, ventouse is often employed by the less experienced obstetrician whose skill is insufficient for anything other than a very simple forceps delivery. The operation involves applying a suction cup to the baby's head and creating a vacuum so as to draw soft tissue into the cup, creating a purchase for traction to be applied. The older cups were made of metal but the modern instrument has a plastic cup which more readily falls off if excess traction is applied. Nevertheless the injudicious, and particularly repeated, use of the instrument may result in both maternal and fetal damage particularly when applied to the mal-rotated head. A moderate swelling of the scalp ('chignon') is expected where the vacuum was applied but more severe injuries (in the worst cases, a bald patch) are usually due to traction applied in the wrong direction or in breach of the basic rules which require attempted vacuum delivery to be abandoned if there is no descent within a limit of three pulls and no more than 15 minutes of vacuum traction.

The ventouse takes longer in its execution and may be inappropriate in circumstances of fetal distress. Ensuring safe practice in operative vaginal delivery calls for training, team work and compliance with basic rules[1].

1 Edozien 'Towards safe practice in instrumental vaginal delivery' (2007) 21 Best Pract Res Clin Obstet Gynaecol 639–655.

36.153 Shoulder dystocia is arguably the most frightening of all obstetric emergencies. It may follow spontaneous delivery of the head but is more commonly seen after forceps or ventouse delivery. The chin fails to clear the perineum (this is the 'turtle sign'). Unless the baby's shoulders can be released within a very few minutes, disaster will surely follow. Excessive traction with lateral flexion of the neck may produce injury to the nerve roots in the neck (brachial plexus) leaving the baby with a paralysed arm (Erb's or Klumpke's paralysis); worse, the baby may suffer asphyxia because the chest cannot be expanded. If the baby is known to be large (heavier than 4 kg), if the mother is diabetic or has gained excessive weight, the pregnancy is prolonged, the labour has been dysfunctional and operative delivery necessary from the mid-pelvis, the problem can (and should) be anticipated. The UK Supreme Court ruled that a diabetic woman with a big baby should have been warned antenatally of the risk of shoulder dystocia, even if such a warning would induce a request for a planned Caesarean delivery[1]. In general, however, it is accepted that shoulder dystocia is largely unpreventable.

1 *Montgomery v Lanarkshire Health Board (Scotland)* [2015] UKSC 11.

36.154 Until the mid-1990s obstetric and midwifery textbooks presented a somewhat confused picture about the management of shoulder dystocia. A consensus has appeared in the last five years. It is essential that all doctors and midwives should be familiar with a shoulder dystocia drill[1]. The patient is placed in the McRoberts position (extreme hip flexion) and suprapubic pressure applied to the anterior shoulder, so as to dip it beneath the maternal symphysis. These simple manoeuvres will relieve the majority of shoulder dystocia. If not the shoulders must be rotated, within the pelvis ('internal manoeuvres'); alternatively the posterior arm must be delivered first. These manoeuvres require a generous episiotomy to allow the operator's hand into the pelvis.

1 Royal College of Obstetricians and Gynaecologists Shoulder Dystocia Green-top Guideline No 42 (2nd edn, March 2012).

36.155 Breech delivery gives rise to few problems provided only that there has been good intra-partum monitoring to eliminate, by CS, those babies that are either too large or insufficiently robust. The common problems in the second stage of breech delivery are:

(1) incorrect diagnosis of full dilation (leading to premature pushing and entrapment of the head);
(2) failure to appreciate the significance of delay in the descent of the baby;
(3) difficult delivery of the after-coming head.

36.156 Operative vaginal delivery is occasionally followed by intracranial haemorrhage in the baby; there is a much stronger association with breech delivery; the strongest association of all is with preterm delivery[1]. A paediatrician should always be present at an operative delivery or where fetal distress suggests the need for skilled resuscitation.

1 (1998) Clinical Risk 4:3 (May).

36.157 Twin delivery demands the presence of a senior obstetrician, an anaesthetist, two midwives and at least one paediatrician. Provided that the presentation of the first twin is cephalic, labour may proceed normally until after the first baby is born. It is the delivery of the second baby which poses hazards. Rarely its presence may have been missed. It is common practice to give an oxytocic drug to promote uterine retraction following the birth of the child. If this is done in the case of the first twin, the uterus contracts tightly around the second baby, seriously impairing its oxygen supply. Cerebral palsy caused by such an insult has been the subject of large settlements. Even without such an accident, the second twin is at increased risk. The placenta may be compromised by the events of the first delivery, there is a greater likelihood of prolapse of the umbilical cord and an increased incidence of malpresentation. In practice the presentation of the second twin cannot be determined until after the first baby is delivered, for it frequently changes. The obstetrician should immediately determine the lie of the second twin. Every effort should be made to preserve the membranes intact until the lie is longitudinal; correction by external version is usually easy, provided that the membranes are intact. Should the membranes rupture with an abnormal lie, swift intervention will be necessary to save the second twin.

36.158 Caesarean section is now classified as elective (planned for a time to suit the patient and maternity team), scheduled (needing early delivery but no maternal or fetal compromise), urgent (maternal or fetal compromise which is not immediately life-threatening) or emergency (immediate threat to life of woman or fetus). It may be carried out under epidural or spinal analgesic block or general anaesthesia. The vast majority of cases are performed under regional analgesia, which carries significantly lower risk. With general anaesthesia a fine balance has to be struck between keeping it as light as possible in the interests of the baby and yet eliminating maternal awareness. If the mother is not actually unconscious she cannot object, because she will have been totally paralysed in order to achieve relaxation of the abdominal muscles. Several claims have been settled on the finding that the woman was aware during a CS, because the anaesthetic was inadequate.

36.159 Almost without exception the type of operation used today is a lower segment Caesarean (LSCS) through a transverse suprapubic incision. Very rarely the upper segment (classical) approach may be chosen to overcome a particular problem such as transverse lie with a prolapsed arm or uterine fibroids which totally obscure the lower uterine segment. A classical CS may also be necessary at very early gestations (eg 26 weeks), when a lower segment has not formed.

36.160 The most frequent complaint concerning CS is that it is performed too late. There is now an agreed *classification of urgency of caesarean section*:

(1)   immediate threat to the life of the woman or fetus;
(2)   maternal or fetal compromise which is not immediately life-threatening;
(3)   no maternal or fetal compromise but needs early delivery;

(4)   delivery timed to suit woman or staff.

There has been debate on what constitutes an appropriate interval between decision and delivery, but it is generally accepted that in category 1 cases the decision-delivery interval should not exceed 30 minutes. In conditions of extreme emergency (such as prolapsed cord) it should be possible in most units to deliver the baby within 15 minutes.

36.161 The commonest complications of CS are:

(1)   tear resulting from difficulty in delivering a head from deep in the pelvis;
(2)   haemorrhage;
(3)   damage to the bladder (which lies immediately in front of the lower segment).

Occasionally the baby is injured by the surgeon's knife as it incises the uterus. Except in conditions of extreme emergency such injuries are difficult to defend, as there are surgical techniques for avoiding scalpel injuries to the baby. The longer and the deeper the injury, the more likely it is that the injury could have been avoided had due care been exercised. Even a short laceration could, after a number of years, produce a disproportionate scar and the parents should be warned to expect this.

36.162 Hysterectomy is sometimes necessary in order to control haemorrhage at Caesarean section, particularly in the context of a ruptured uterus. Rarely surgery in such difficult circumstances may be associated with injury to the ureter or bowel.

36.163 Labour ward organisation is critical to safe practice. Nowhere is communication between the various levels of staff more important. The chain of command is often difficult. The judgment of the senior midwife is often superior to that of the inexperienced training grade doctor. In every labour ward the coordinating midwife should have the authority to directly contact the consultant if she feels that decisions are not being taken appropriately or that the doctor is unable to cope. Labour ward protocols dealing with emergencies such as haemorrhage, ruptured uterus, prolapsed cord and shoulder dystocia are required for risk management purposes.

Care after delivery

36.164 The third stage of labour may be complicated post-partum haemorrhage (arbitrarily defined as more than 500 ml) with or without difficulty in delivering the placenta. The (almost) universal practice of administering oxytocic drugs during the second stage of labour has greatly reduced the incidence of haemorrhage, but it still presents as an occasional life-threatening emergency. The causes include:

(1)   failure of the uterus to contract;
(2)   retained fragments of placenta or membranes;
(3)   laceration of the cervix or vagina (often by instrumental delivery);
(4)   unsuspected rupture of the uterus.

Every unit must have a clearly defined protocol for the management of this emergency, for swift intervention is essential. Senior staff are unlikely to be immediately available out of hours and junior medical staff and midwives should be in no doubt as to the proper management. Uncross-matched O negative blood should be available on the labour ward for use in dire emergencies.

36.165 Episiotomies and vaginal tears are common subjects for complaint. It is important to recognise the extent of a tear and classify it accordingly:

- first degree: injury to perineal skin only;
- second degree: injury to perineum involving perineal muscles but not involving the anal sphincter;
- third degree: injury to perineum involving the anal sphincter complex: 3a: less than 50 per cent of external anal sphincter (EAS) thickness torn; 3b: more than 50 per cent of EAS thickness torn; 3c: both EAS and internal anal sphincter (IAS) torn;
- fourth degree: injury to perineum involving the anal sphincter complex (EAS and IAS) and anal epithelium.

36.166 Failure to recognise a third degree tear (involving the anal sphincter) will result in loss of continence of faeces or flatus. Other complications suffered by claimants include rectovaginal fistula and psychiatric injury. Timely recognition and effective repair by a senior doctor with appropriate anaesthesia usually gives excellent results. Allegations of negligence may relate to failure to consider a Caesarean section or perform or extend the episiotomy, failure to recognise the true extent of the injury, failure to repair the tear or to repair it adequately. Claims are commonly settled when the injury is missed or incompletely repaired.

36.167 Although the unintended retention of swabs or instruments in a body cavity has been classified as a 'never event' (patient safety incident that should never occur if appropriate preventative measures are in place), it still happens. Surprisingly it is still not universal practice to count swabs before and after the repair of the perineum; a retained swab, discovered many days or weeks after delivery, will result in an indefensible action. Damages may be compounded by the breakdown of the perineal repair, resulting from the associated infection.

36.168 Whether a woman has had a spontaneous or operative delivery, she needs close monitoring immediately following delivery, and her condition should be stable before she is returned to the postnatal ward. Mortalities and near-misses have occurred as a result of failure to monitor a woman following delivery. Women with conditions such as pre-eclampsia are particularly at risk of post-delivery complications. The Maternity Early Warnings Score (MEWS) – a composite of physiological readings and clinical observations – facilitates effective assessment and speedy response to the needs of acutely ill, critically ill and recovering women. Another common failing in postnatal care is the omission of thromboembolism prophylaxis. All women should have their risk of venous thromboembolism assessed continually.

36.169 Claims arising from secondary post-partum haemorrhage (any excessive blood loss after the first 24 hours) associated with small pieces of retained placenta and membrane are common. They are seldom successful since it is, in practice, very difficult to be certain that the placenta has been completely delivered.

Stillbirth

36.170 A baby is stillborn when delivered without signs of life after 24 weeks of pregnancy. The commonest causes are congenital defects, placental abruption, maternal hypertension and diabetes, intra-uterine and intra-partum hypoxia.

36.171 Intra-uterine death of the baby usually leads sooner rather than later to the onset of labour and delivery. Sometimes the birth of the baby may be delayed for many days or even weeks after it has died. When such delay occurs, post-mortem changes may be so advanced that the skin peels off (maceration), the skull collapses and vital internal organs liquefy, especially the brain. This process may render post-mortem examination unhelpful as to the cause. Even with a fresh stillbirth there may be little evidence as to why it happened except for the ante-mortem changes of asphyxia. Evidence as to cause may have to be sought from chromosome analysis of parents and, if possible, of the baby's tissues. Examination of the mother may reveal evidence of possible causes, such as hypertension, diabetes, thrombophilia, auto-immune disease, and unsuspected infection. More often than not, no cause is found.

36.172 The group of stillbirths that cause particular frustration to both medical attendants and the parents occur suddenly in otherwise apparently normal mature infants, often without any preceding evidence of serious abnormality. It is because of this that many obstetricians apply working rules and say, for example, that all women with diastolic blood pressure of 90 or more should have labour induced, and similarly in women whose pregnancy is prolonged past the due date by an arbitrary number of days. Despite such rules, which can be associated with their own problems, babies nevertheless do die suddenly and unexpectedly in utero. It is from this group of women that complaints about the standard of care arise, particularly if communication between the medical staff and the parents was not of the best before and after the event. Obstetricians cannot complain that parents litigate in such circumstances when they have made little attempt to share such information as they have concerning the cause of death.

36.173 The mother who has suffered bereavement or whose baby is seriously ill in the first few days of life requires special attention in the puerperium. Explanations as to why the baby died or is unwell may need to be repeated many times, as such news is poorly absorbed in circumstances of great distress. Where errors have occurred during pregnancy and delivery there should be a clear policy of honest explanation, given by the most senior obstetrician, supported by a consultant paediatrician. Sharing with the patient the realisation of error, admitting that it occurred and facing the responsibility for it requires considerable courage. When parents perceive that there is something covered up, they are more likely to become hostile; information imparted thereafter may not be believed.

36.174 Support and explanation to the parents in such circumstances is a basic requirement of good practice. Failure to provide adequate counselling may exacerbate damages suffered (and subsequently claimed for) by the parents. It is becoming the norm for maternity units to have dedicated bereavement midwives.

Care of the critically ill woman

36.175 For every maternal death there are nine women who develop severe maternal morbidity. Critically ill women may be cared for on a high dependency room in the labour ward that is equipped with the appropriate monitoring equipment or, depending on severity, in a critical care unit. Conditions that warrant high dependency or critical care include massive haemorrhage (>2,500ml loss), severe pre-eclampsia, eclampsia, sepsis, thromboembolism, amniotic fluid embolism, diabetic keto-acidosis, and failure of liver, kidney, heart or respiratory function. Obstetricians and midwives must be alert to recognise, and respond appropriately to, deterioration in maternal condition. Unfortunately, delay or failure in recognition of a deteriorating condition remains a recurring cause of maternal death. The Maternity Early Warning Score (MEWS), comprising observations of respiratory rate, heart rate, blood pressure, temperature, oxygen saturation, consciousness level and urine output, is designed to facilitate not only recognition of deterioration but also appropriate response[1]. Standards of care for the critically ill woman have been prescribed in national guidance[2].

1 Isaacs, Wee, Bick, Beake, Sheppard, Thomas, Hundley, Smith, van Teijlingen, Thomas 'Members of the Modified Obstetric Early Warning Systems (MObs) Research Group. A national survey of obstetric early warning systems in the United Kingdom: five years on' (2014) 69 Anaesthesia 687–692. doi: 10.1111/anae.12708. Epub 7 May 2014.
2 Royal College of Anaesthetists & Royal College of Obstetricians and Gynaecologists. Providing equity of critical and maternity care for the critically ill pregnant or recently pregnant woman (July 2011); Association of Anaesthetists of Great Britain & Ireland & Obstetric Anaesthetists' Association. OAA / AAGBI Guidelines for Obstetric Anaesthetic Services (June 2013).

36.176 **Severe pre-eclampsia** affects multiple systems. It is diagnosed when any of the following is present:

- persistent headaches;
- visual disturbances;
- epigastric or right upper quadrant pain and/or elevated liver function tests;
- pulmonary oedema (fluid in the lungs);
- systolic blood pressure >160 mmHg or diastolic blood pressure >110 mmHg on two occasions at least two hours apart;
- proteinuria: >5 g in a 24hr collection;
- oliguria (reduced production of urine): <500 ml in 24hr;
- elevated serum creatinine;
- low platelet count (thrombocytopenia) and/or deranged blood clotting test;
- reduced amniotic fluid volume (pligohydramnios);
- placental abruption.

36.177 The key interventions are delivery of the baby, control of hypertension, maintenance of fluid balance and prevention of seizures. An infusion of magnesium sulphate reduces the likelihood of seizures occurring in a woman with severe pre-eclampsia.

36.178 In cases complicated by the HELLP syndrome (Haemolysis, Elevated Liver enzyme levels and Low Platelet count), morbidity and mortality rates could be high due to disseminated bleeding and multi-organ involvement.

36.179 Amniotic fluid embolism is a rare but serious condition which has clinical features similar to an anaphylactic shock. The clinical features include sweating, breathlessness, loss of consciousness, bleeding, hypoxia. Unfortunately approximately 1 in 4 of affected women will die within one hour of presentation. The cause of amniotic fluid embolism is not known but it is thought to be due to egress of amniotic fluid into the maternal circulation.

36.180 Peripartum cardiomyopathy is diagnosed if the following are present:

- heart failure in the last month of pregnancy or within five months of delivery;
- absence of any other identifiable cause for heart failure;
- absence of heart disease prior to last month of pregnancy;
- echocardiographic evidence of reduced function in the left ventricle.

Consent in obstetrics

36.181 Save only in the circumstances of elective CS, meaningful consent cannot be obtained from a mother in advance for operative intervention in labour. The indications for such intervention arise during the course of labour and cannot always be foreseen. Clearly, whenever possible, foreseeable complications should be discussed with the patient so that she is prepared for the decisions which may have to be taken. More commonly the occurrence of fetal distress or slow progress or haemorrhage overtakes both the obstetrician and the patient unexpectedly and there is little time for explanation. The relationship of trust built up between the obstetric team and the labouring woman should create an atmosphere in which consent can be obtained, notwithstanding these difficulties.

36.182 Several cases have been before the courts where obstetricians sought declarations that CS would not be unlawful although conducted against the mother's refusal. In no such case has a court ever refused such a declaration. Indeed, it is difficult to envisage circumstances in which a judge would take the 'inhumane' option of allowing mother or baby (or both) to die. Whilst the Court of Appeal[1] has reiterated the previously established principles:

(1) the competent woman's absolute right to refuse treatment at all times;
(2) the absence of fetal rights before birth;

the courts nevertheless, tend to find extenuating circumstances which allows these principles to be overturned. Such intervention by the courts makes the relationship between the obstetrician and the labouring woman no easier; the obstetrician may well wonder in the light of the Court of Appeal judgment[2] whether such a declaration in the event will protect him or her from a subsequent civil action[3].

1 *Re MB (adult: medical treatment)* [1997] 2 FCR 541 AC, 38 BMLR 175–194.
2 *St George's Healthcare NHS Trust v S; R v Collins, ex p S* [1999] Fam 26, [1998] 3 WLR 96, CA.
3 Lord Justice Thorpe 'Consent for Caesarean section Part I – Development of the law' (1999) 5(5) Clinical Risk 173–176; Lord Justice Thorpe 'Consent for Caesarean section Part II – Autonomy, capacity, best interests, reasonable force and procedural guidelines' (1999) 5(5) Clinical Risk 900. An unborn child is not a person: *CP (a child) v First-tier Tribunal (Criminal Injuries Compensation) (British Pregnancy Advisory Service/Birthrights and another intervening)* [2014] EWCA Civ 1554.

36.183   Where the woman has mental health problems and lacks capacity to make decisions about her treatment, guidance on the process that should be followed by trusts wishing to deliver the baby by court-authorised Caesarean section has been provided by Mr Justice Keehan in *NHS Trust v FG*[1].

1 [2014] EWCOP 30.

36.184   More commonly the obstetrician is faced with a dire emergency and little time to explain to his willing patient precisely why she needs to have surgical intervention. The presentation of a consent form to a distressed, exhausted and often narcotised patient is, in these circumstances, unhelpful. The consent form has limited place in obstetric practice, save only for elective procedures and those done in circumstances of no urgency. It is pointless to ask a patient to sign a form which she has no time or inclination to read.

36.185   It is not generally accepted practice to obtain written consent for some obstetric procedures which nevertheless may carry with them profound consequences, such as ante-natal blood tests, screening tests including HIV antibody testing, induction of labour, artificial rupture of membranes, the acceleration of labour, the conduct of labour as a 'trial of scar', the use of forceps, breech delivery and emergency delivery of the second twin under general anaesthesia. There should be no problem so long as the woman is properly informed and implicitly gives her consent. In some units written consent is not usually obtained for amniocentesis or chorionic villous biopsy, procedures that primarily affect the baby.

36.186   The solution is not the profusion of yet more consent forms; rather the problem can be dealt with by providing written information to reinforce oral explanations and for the woman's future reference. For example, a brief oral and written explanation of ante-natal blood tests and ultrasound examination given at the first visit to the ante-natal clinic provides information, saves time for the staff and may prompt the mother to ask further questions if she needs answers. Similarly, those contemplating the use of epidural analgesia or seeking sterilisation after delivery can be given a written summary of the issues involved.

GYNAECOLOGY

36.187 The main causes of complaint are summarised in Table **36.6**.

Table 36.6 Causes for complaint in gynaecology

(a)	Failure of sterilisation sometimes leading to abortion or wrongful birth
(b)	Complications of abortion, including:
	– failure and sometimes wrongful birth
	– perforation of the uterus and/or damage to other organs
	– loss of future childbearing capacity due to infection or the need for hysterectomy
(c)	Contraception
	– failure to prevent pregnancy
	– oral contraception and cardio-vascular accidents including death
	– the side-effects of injectable steroidal contraceptives
	– perforation of the uterus and infection following the introduction of intra-uterine contraceptive devices
(d)	Failure to interpret or act appropriately upon cervical cytology
(e)	Missed diagnosis
	– ectopic pregnancy
	– cancer
	– pregnancy (operating on a woman without first excluding a pregnancy)
(f)	Gynaecological surgery (including diagnostic and operative laparoscopy)
	– defective consent
	– posterior abdominal wall vessel injury at laparoscopy
	– failure to detect internal haemorrhage
	– injury to the gastro-intestinal tract
	– injury to the bladder and/or ureters
	– delay in the diagnosis of pregnancy, ectopic pregnancy and genital cancer
	– unnecessary hysterectomy or other operation
	– failure to remove swabs and other artefacts

36.188 Data from the NHS Litigation Authority show that intraoperative problems account for 27.6 per cent of claims in gynaecology. Other causes of claims include failure or delay in diagnosis (16 per cent), failure to recognise complication (8.5 per cent), delayed treatment (6 per cent), lack of consent (5.7 per cent), and failed sterilisation (5.7 per cent).

Sterilisation

36.189 Female sterilisation used to be responsible for more litigation than any other single surgical procedure, either because of defective consent or because the operation was unsuccessful. Gynaecologists have since plugged the consent loophole.

36.190 Laparoscopic methods involve either diathermy coagulation of part of the tube or the application of silastic (Falope) rings or clips (Hulka-Clemens or Filshie). When clips are applied it is particularly important for the operator to ensure that the clip is applied to the appropriate part of the fallopian tube where it is narrow (the isthmus) so that the clip may completely occlude the lumen; application of clips to the wider ampulla is more likely to leave a channel open. In an endeavour to reduce the failure rate some surgeons apply two clips to each uterine tube. Diathermic coagulation has been abandoned by the majority of gynaecologists not only because of the higher failure rate, but also because of the inherent risk of causing serious damage to neighbouring organs, even if the tubes are coagulated with the safer bipolar (rather than unipolar) diathermy.

36.191 Surgical mistakes are more likely to occur with the closed laparoscopic methods than when the abdomen is open at laparotomy, particularly if the surgeon is inexperienced and unsupervised. Instead of coagulating, or applying rings or clips to the tubes, the neighbouring round ligaments are mistaken for them. A new development in permanent contraception is the insertion of a coil in each fallopian tube, via the vagina and cervix. The coil (Essure) consists of metal and polyester fibres which induce scar tissue formation, and subsequent occlusion of the tube. Three months after insertion, a hysterosalpingogram is performed to confirm occlusion. During this interval, an alternative form of contraception should be used.

36.192 Whatever method of sterilisation is employed, a properly performed operation may still fail in its purpose. There are two principal mechanisms; the two halves of the divided fallopian tube may come together and rejoin ('recanalisation'); or a tuboperitoneal fistula may form in the proximal segment. When natural regeneration of the uterine tube occurs, macroscopic inspection may show no evidence of previous surgery, although the tube will usually be thinner at the point of healing. On microscopic examination the join will usually be evident to the pathologist for whilst the inner and outer epithelium of the tube renews itself, the muscle in between is incapable of regeneration and heals by the formation of scar tissue (collagen). Fistula formation is particularly likely following diathermy coagulation of the tubes.

36.193 An advantage of sterilisation carried out at open operation is that the portion of the tube removed may be subjected to histological examination. Following the failure of the sterilisation a second operation takes on a particular forensic significance. The operator has an opportunity and duty to inspect carefully the site of previous surgery and to send the entire fallopian tube en bloc to the pathologist with a specific request to search for the reason for failure. Such total salpingectomy can be performed laparoscopically.

36.194 Failure rates for female sterilisations were historically quoted in the range of three to five per thousand women. Those figures are no longer tenable following the United States Collaborative Review of Sterilization Working Group Report[1] which showed a cumulative ten year probability of pregnancy after clip sterilisation some ten times higher than this, with 36.5

pregnancies per thousand procedures. The cumulative risk of pregnancy was highest amongst women sterilised at a young age with bipolar coagulation (54.3 per thousand) and clip application (52.1 per thousand). If these figures are repeated in other studies it will no longer be true to say that sterilisation is the most effective method of birth control, for figures quoted for the Mirena intrauterine system are at least as good for the prevention of pregnancy.

1 Peterson, Xia, Hughes, Wilcox, Tylor and Trussell 'The risk of pregnancy after tubal sterilization: findings from the US collaborative review of sterilization' (1996) 174 American Journal of Obstetrics and Gynaecology 1161–1170; *Obstetrical and Gynaecological Survey* vol 51, no 12, Supplement.

36.195   Failure of sterilisation may be due to negligence (tube not completely occluded or clip applied to wrong structure or wrong part of the tube) or could be considered non-negligent (a properly occluded tube that has 'recanalised' naturally over time). A study of 131 failed sterilisations suggested that early failure increased the probability that the failure mechanism was likely to be negligent rather than non-negligent (median failure intervals: 7.0 versus 12.0 months)[1].

1 Varma, Gupta 'Failed sterilisation: evidence-based review and medico-legal ramifications' (2004) 111 BJOG 1322–1332; Varma, Gupta 'Predicting negligence in female sterilization failure using time interval to sterilization failure: analysis of 131 cases' (2007) 22 Human Reproduction 2437–2443.

36.196   Controversy still surrounds the performance of sterilisation during pregnancy, either at the time of CS, in the puerperium or in combination with abortion. Some reported series have shown higher failure rates at this time, but there is no agreement. The US study referred to above found the lowest incidence of pregnancy following post-partum partial salpingectomy (7.5 per thousand). Whilst planned CS may be an opportune moment to perform simultaneous sterilisation, consent for sterilisation cannot properly be obtained in the context of an emergency operation. Where a decision for sterilisation is combined with a request for the termination of a pregnancy there is undoubtedly a much higher incidence of regret. There is also a significant increase in morbidity and mortality, which led the authors of a 1982–1984 report on *Confidential Enquiries into Maternal Deaths* to express reservations about the combined procedure.

36.197   Consent for sterilisation places peculiar responsibilities upon the surgeon. It has been accepted for over 25 years that women seeking sterilisation should be warned that the operation should be regarded as irreversible. It should not be contemplated or undertaken therefore, unless childbearing is complete. This warning is given almost without exception. However, emphasis upon the irreversibility of sterilisation has led many women in the past to believe that this also means it cannot fail. But failure of sterilisation is a relatively common experience, and in no way related to the concept of irreversibility. Since the early 1980s expert opinion has generally been to the effect that warnings of failure were not only appropriate but necessary. Since that time many hospitals have developed special written forms of consent for sterilisation, spelling out the appropriate risks (Figure **36.10**), a practice endorsed by the Department of Health.

36.198 Apart from the failure rate, it is now routine to inform the woman of the risk of ectopic pregnancy, the complications of laparoscopy and the possibility of menstrual cycle disturbance. The woman is given an explanation of all the alternative methods available to her, including vasectomy for her partner. All women undergoing laparoscopic tubal occlusion should, as part of the consent process, be informed that the Mirena coil offers long-term, equally effective but reversible contraception, without the risks of laparoscopy. It is conceivable that sterilisation claims based on consent may reemerge with rising awareness that the Mirena coil offers an equally effective and safer alternative to laparoscopic tubal ligation. A woman who suffers injury to a viscus at laparoscopy could reasonably claim that had she been made aware of the Mirena coil she would not have opted for surgical contraception. Another alternative to laparoscopic sterilisation is hysteroscopic sterilisation, an operation performed without a general anaesthetic, in an outpatient setting, with a device ('Essure') inserted into each fallopian tube. The device (the inserts are made from polyester fibers, nickel-titanium and stainless steel and solder) causes tissue to grow around it, blocking the tube in about three months, during which time the woman must continue to use alternative contraception. The risks include fainting during insertion, perforation and expulsion. A test of tubal patency (hysterosalpingogram) is done after three months. The manufacturers claim a failure rate lower than that of laparoscopic sterilisation, but the true failure rate will emerge after wider use of the device over many years.

Other common gynaecological causes for complaint

36.199 Abortion is defined as the expulsion of products of conception before 24 weeks of pregnancy. In medical terms there is no difference between abortion and miscarriage, but in the lay mind the word abortion carries with it a suggestion that it follows a deliberate act, either criminal or therapeutic. Natural or spontaneous abortion is described in several stages of threatened, inevitable, incomplete and complete. The meaning of these terms is literal.

36.200 Medically-induced abortion should be carried out under the terms and regulations of the Abortion Act 1967 (as amended by the Human Fertilisation and Embryology Act 1990). The techniques used to achieve it vary in accordance with the duration of pregnancy and with the expertise of the surgeon. The medical errors occurring in connection with the operation include:

(1) failure to terminate the pregnancy;
(2) damage to the uterus by perforation leading to haemorrhage;
(3) damage to neighbouring organs, particularly the bowel and bladder.

36.201 Minimal access surgery has enjoyed a massive expansion but not always with happy results. The special problems of laparoscopic surgery and gynaecology[1] and hysteroscopic surgery[2] are described elsewhere. Almost every operation previously conducted by gynaecologists can now be performed by (or with the assistance of) minimal access surgery. In the late 1980s, as these skills rapidly developed, gynaecologists with no particular training or expertise took on laparoscopic procedures well beyond their capabilities, with disastrous results and much litigation. With the introduction of clinical governance, guidelines and training, this problem has been contained. Still, cases are encountered where a surgeon has undertaken surgery that is beyond his competence.

1 Donnez, Jadoul, Squifflet, Donnez 'A series of 3190 laparoscopic hysterectomies for benign disease from 1990 to 2006: evaluation of complications compared with vaginal and abdominal procedures' (2009) 116(4) BJOG 492–500. doi: 10.1111/j.1471-0528.2008.01966.x.
2 O'Connor and Magos 'Minimal access surgery: avoiding complications at hysteroscopic surgery' (1995) 1(6) Clinical Risk 207–211.

36.202 Diagnostic laparoscopy involves the passage, blind, of the Veress needle into the peritoneal cavity, in order to create a pneumoperitoneum. The procedure in skilled hands is simple; it is the second most common of all gynaecological operations. It is essential for safe practice that guidelines are followed and that trainees are properly supervised[1]. The risk of bowel or vascular injury is approximately 1 in 1,000. Significant numbers of claims have been brought (and settled) for the occasional fatal complication of posterior abdominal wall vessel injury (Figure **36.11** at the end of this chapter). This particular injury can only occur if the operator directs the Veress needle or trocar backwards to the posterior abdominal wall. Head down tilt before the needle is inserted will tend to increase the risk[2]. The resulting injury to the aorta and its main branches or to the inferior vena cava and its major tributaries produces an immediately life-threatening crisis. Several deaths have been reported. With proper care this type of injury to fixed structures within the abdominal cavity whose anatomy and surface markings are well known is *always* avoidable. The bowel, however, is ubiquitous within the abdomen and even in skilled hands, the occasional bowel injury may not be avoidable. Provided the injury is recognised and the bowel repaired, long term sequelae are uncommon. The use of a Visiport optical trocar helps to reduce the risk of a trocar-induced bowel injury.

1 la Chapelle, Bemelman, Rademaker, van Barneveld, Jansen, on behalf of the Dutch Multidisciplinary Guideline Development Group Minimally Invasive Surgery 'A multidisciplinary evidence-based guideline for minimally invasive surgery: Part 1: entry techniques and the pneumoperitoneum' (2012) 9(3) Gynecol Surg 271–282.
2 Clements 'Minimal access surgery: major vessel injury' (1995) 1(3) Clinical Risk 112–115.

36.203 General surgeons use an open entry technique instead of the closed (Veress needle) technique favoured by gynaecologists. Although it would intuitively appear to be a safer option, the open technique has not been shown in studies to have lower bowel injury rates than the closed technique[1].

1 Royal College of Obstetricians and Gynaecologists. Preventing entry-related gynaecological laparoscopic injuries. Green top guideline No 49 (2008).

Hysterectomy

36.204 With the emergence of Mirena coil and endometrial ablation as effective and less invasive treatment options for heavy menstrual bleeding, fewer hysterectomies are being performed in the UK than was the case in the past. The operation is still performed for cancer, large uterine fibroids, endometriosis and heavy menstrual bleeding that has not responded to other measures.

36.205 Hysterectomy may be performed through a choice of routes: open abdominal, vaginal and laparoscopic. When the laparoscopic route is chosen, the operation may be a laparoscopic total hysterectomy (the entire womb is removed and the whole of the operation is performed laparoscopically) or a laparoscopically-assisted vaginal hysterectomy (a part of the operation is done laparoscopically and the remainder is performed vaginally). The abdominal route has higher morbidity and requires longer hospital stay than the other routes. The laparoscopic route has the advantage of shorter stay and quicker recovery, but is more expensive and requires appropriate surgical skills over and above the skills for open surgery. The vaginal route is inexpensive, has lower morbidity rates and relatively short hospital stay but the size of the uterus may exclude this option. In practice, it is the skill of the attending surgeon rather than clinical assessment that is the main determinant of the route of hysterectomy in cases of benign pathology.

36.206 Regardless of the routine chosen, there is the option to remove only the body of the uterus, conserving the cervix (sub-total hysterectomy), but other than in cases where there is technical difficulty in performing a total hysterectomy, this option carries no notable advantage and is seldom used. Where a sub-total is performed, the woman must be advised to continue having cervical smear screening while eligible for it.

36.207 The ovaries should be assessed when hysterectomy for benign uterine pathology is considered. The question of whether to remove or conserve normal ovaries in a perimenopausal or postmenopausal woman should be discussed with the woman, and the decision should be documented. The rationale for removing normal ovaries is prevention of ovarian cancer, but it is for the woman to make an informed choice whether to have this organ removed.

36.208 Hysterectomy may result in damage to surrounding structures particularly when, as in endometriosis or cancer, the anatomy is grossly distorted. The structures most at risk are the rectum, the bladder and the ureter. Several successful actions have been brought for damage to the ureter whose intimate relations with the gynaecological organs are, or should be, well known to the gynaecologist. In conditions of normal anatomy there is seldom an excuse for damage to the ureter. In circumstances of difficult surgery the damage may not be avoidable but should *always* be recognised: 'the venial sin is injury to the ureter, but the mortal sin is the failure of recognition'[1].

1 Higgins 'Ureteral injuries' (1962) 182(3) Journal of the American Medical Association 225.

Cervical screening

36.209 Each year about 2,300 women are diagnosed with cervical cancer in England (in 2010, there were 2,305 new cases). Fortunately, the readily-accessible location of the cervix and the existence of a pre-invasive phase of the disease have afforded an opportunity for cervical cancer to be prevented by means of a screening programme. Cervical screening does not test for cancer but for abnormalities which, if left untreated, could lead to cervical cancer. The NHS Cervical Screening Programme, which was set up in 1988, screens over three million women in England each year at a cost of £175 million. In 2010/11 the coverage of eligible women was 78.6 per cent.

36.210 All women between the ages of 25 and 64 are eligible for a free cervical screening test, and this is done at different intervals depending on age: three yearly between 25–49 and five yearly in the age group 50–64. Women age 65 and above are only screened if they have not had a test since age 50 or have had recent abnormal tests.

36.211 The sample of cells is obtained from the neck of the womb with a spatula or brush. The traditional technique was to smear this sample on to a slide, which was sent to a laboratory for examination under a microscope, but this technique has been superseded by liquid based cytology (LBC). With LBC the sample is not smeared on to a slide. Rather, the head of the brush is broken off into a pot containing preservative fluid, or rinsed directly into the preservative fluid. The sample is spun to remove mucus, pus or other debris, and a slide is prepared for examination.

36.212 The smear is reported as negative (normal), borderline, or dyskaryotic (abnormal). A borderline result means that minor cell changes were seen, but will probably go back to normal on their own and the screening test is repeated, usually in six months. Dyskaryosis is graded as mild, moderate or severe, and examination of the cervix under magnification (colposcopy) is usually the next step. Testing for human papilloma virus (HPV), a sexually transmissible virus associated with increased risk of cervical cancer, has been incorporated in the NHS Cervical Screening Programme. If a screening test shows borderline changes or low-grade dyskaryosis, the sample is tested for HPV. If HPV is found the woman is invited to go for colposcopy. If no HPV is found, she goes back to regular screening every 3–5 years depending on her age.

36.213 Sometimes the screening test is reported as 'inadequate' or 'unsatisfactory'. This means the sample was inadequate and the test needs to be repeated. The screening test is not perfect, and there are false positives and false negatives. Even a genuinely negative test result does not preclude the possibility of a cancer developing before the next test is due.

36.214 At colposcopy, biopsies may be taken from areas identified by special stains as possibly abnormal. The biopsies are examined under the microscope (histology) and reported as normal or showing cervical intraepithelial neoplasia (CIN) or, much less commonly, cancer. CIN is not cervical cancer but an early warning stage and is graded as CIN 1 (mild), CIN 2 (moderate) and CIN 3 (severe). In some cases the biopsy shows cancer but with the cancerous cells all contained within the lining of the cervix (carcinoma in situ). In many cases of CIN 1, cells return to normal spontaneously.

36.215 Abnormal cells may be treated by means of loop excision of the transformation zone (LETZ, utilising a loop of wire heated by an electric current), or by using a laser beam. Sometimes a cone of tissue encompassing the area(s) of abnormality is removed (cone biopsy).

36.216 Things can go wrong – and litigation may ensue – at various stages in the journey from screening to treatment. Many of the women who develop cervical cancer have never been screened and GPs are in a position to identify and reach eligible women who have not had a test. A screener may wrongly interpret the findings on a slide as negative whereas there are abnormalities that require further testing, and cytology laboratories must have quality assurance measures in place to reduce the likelihood of this error. In cases of equivocally abnormal cytology, communication between laboratory and clinician must be unequivocal, so that the next step in the woman's care is not missed or delayed. Often, continued surveillance is needed, either on account of borderline results or to ascertain that treatment has been successful, and procedures have to be in place (and be followed) to ensure that a woman at risk is not lost to follow up. Given the success of the national screening programme, the cardinal risk factor for cervical cancer is failing to go, or to be invited, for screening tests as and when due.

Urinary incontinence

36.217 The bladder is usually emptied by voluntarily contracting the muscles of the bladder wall (detrusor muscles). In some women the detrusor muscles involuntarily contract too often ('overactive bladder'), and the woman has urgent and frequent need to pass urine, and leaks urine (urge incontinence). The cause of an overactive bladder is often not known; in some cases it is due to infection or to neurological disorders. The condition is usually treated with drugs rather than surgery.

36.218 A pressure mechanism involving the urethra retains urine in the bladder but in some situations where the pelvic floor muscles are weak, this pressure is readily overcome by pressure inside the bladder, and urine leaks involuntarily. This is known as stress incontinence. In this condition, any activity that raises bladder pressure (such as laughing or sneezing) causes urine to leak out of the urethra. The underlying weakness may be caused by damage during childbirth or at hysterectomy, or by diseases that affect the central nervous system or connective tissue. Stress incontinence is also precipitated by raised intra-abdominal pressure due to pregnancy or obesity. It is usually treated by pelvic floor physiotherapy and surgery.

36.219 The traditional surgical treatment of stress incontinence is colposuspension which was historically done by open surgery and more recently by laparoscopy. The bladder neck is lifted and sutured to a fixed point in the pelvis. This has largely been superseded by a less invasive approach in which a plastic tape, made of non-absorbable polypropylene mesh, is inserted through a vaginal incision such that the middle part of the tape supports the urethra. Depending on where the two ends of the tape are threaded through, the operation is called a transobturator tape procedure (TOT, threaded through the inner thigh) or tension-free vaginal tape procedure (TVT, threaded behind the pubic bone, through to the abdomen). There is a risk of the bladder being perforated by the instrument used to thread the tape, so a cystoscopy (camera inspection of the bladder cavity) is performed to exclude this complication. There is also a risk of urinary retention, which may warrant removal of the tape. Erosion of the tape through the vagina may also occur. Approximately 9 in 10 women will be happy with the outcome of a tape procedure.

Benign ovarian cysts

36.220 With more widespread and frequent use of ultrasound scan, benign ovarian cysts are more readily diagnosed. Often they are found incidentally in the course of investigating problems not directly related to the ovary. Some of these are 'functional' cysts; they come and go, and require no intervention. The cyst may be a 'dermoid' (in technical terms, mature cystic teratoma), the components of which may include any of: hair, fat, bone, nails, teeth, cartilage, sebum, blood, and thyroid or other tissue. Benign ovarian cysts less than 5 cm are usually managed conservatively, especially in the young woman.

36.221 Ovarian cysts may undergo torsion (twisting on their pedicle), presenting as pain. This requires urgent surgical treatment, to avoid gangrene and necrosis resulting from compromised blood supply.

36.222 A risk of malignancy index (RMI) should be used to triage the postmenopausal woman who has an ovarian cyst. The RMI is a composite score that takes account of the ultrasound scan features of the cyst, the women's menopausal status, and the serum level of the analyte Ca125. A woman assessed as medium or high risk on this score should be managed by a suitably trained and experienced surgeon.

Labiaplasty

36.223 There is increasing demand for labial reduction surgery ('labiaplasty'). This is driven by consumer awareness, television programmes and popular magazines. Although many women request this solely for cosmetic reasons, some women have redundant labial skin that causes problems with clothing, sexual intercourse or activities such as running or horse-riding. If it is performed for cosmetic reasons, the operation should be done by a surgeon trained in cosmetic/plastic procedures. Where a gynaecologist has to excise redundant labial skin, it should be made clear that this is not done for cosmetic reasons, that there is no guarantee regarding symmetry or other cosmetic outcomes and that scar tissue may form. In cases where there is no functional impairment attributable to redundant skin, the woman may feel reassured simply by the gynaecologist confirming that her anatomy is a variant of normal and requires no correction. The gynaecologist should explore the possibility of underlying psychological issues when a woman requests labial surgery.

Consent for gynaecological procedures

36.224 The general principles for consent to surgery are explained in **Chapter 11**. Gynaecological surgery not only involves issues common to all form of surgery, namely the risks of the procedure itself, but also those relating to future childbearing capacity and sexual enjoyment.

36.225 For the consent to be real, the woman must have a clear understanding of what is intended, the possible alternatives to the procedure and the common sequelae. The patient's signature on a form does not provide evidence that she has been properly counselled. The evidence for this must be derived from her recollection, which usually is a matter of credibility between her and the doctor concerned. Correspondence between the surgeon and the GP may provide evidence that proper information was or was not given. The surgeon may note the details of his discussion with the woman in advising her and obtaining her consent. If the advice is given in a true spirit of providing her with information adequate to make her choice, it is unlikely that a well-informed woman will complain that she was not properly advised. Consent is a matter of trust between the patient and the doctor; proper fulfilment of that trust should be the most important factor in reducing complaints leading to litigation, rather than a form of words agreed to by signature of the woman in terms which are non-specific, not easily understood and designed for the defence of the doctor.

36.226 For elective procedures it is appropriate to obtain consent in the out-patient department, when the woman has a real opportunity to decline or to choose an alternative treatment. Once admitted, patients seldom exercise their right to leave hospital without surgery.

36.227 The Department of Health has issued guidelines[1] and model consent forms which have been adopted across England and Wales.

1 Department of Health *Reference guide to consent for examination or treatment* (2001).

36.228 A form of consent should fairly provide protection in the form of documentation for both the patient and the doctor. It should not require either a bespoke specification of the procedure to be carried out, or a detailed catalogue of the possible complications. It should only need to record the understanding of the woman of the intentions of the surgeon in general terms. The fine detail should depend on the circumstances of the particular woman and should be a matter of trust. Such mutual trust cannot be fostered, if the task of obtaining consent is delegated to a trainee with little experience either of human relationships or the operation concerned. The duty of obtaining real consent for the operation, rather than a signature to a form of words, must be the duty of the surgeon who is to carry out the operation.

36.229 The form of consent (see Figure **36.10** at the end of this chapter) usually contains a form of words to deal with alternative and additional procedures which 'would only be carried out if it is *necessary* in my best interest and can be justified by medical reasons'. The word necessary here carries its ordinary English meaning of 'that cannot be dispensed with or done without, requisite, essential or needful'. It does not cover procedures which the surgeon may believe to be expedient, such as the removal of ovaries at the time of hysterectomy (without specific consent).

36.230 Doctors exhibit paradoxical attitudes in respect of obtaining written consent to procedures concerning birth control. Some doctors, especially those who specialise in family planning, but not usually consultant gynaecologists or GPs, require written consent before they insert an intra-uterine contraceptive device (IUCD), but not before they prescribe an oral contraceptive pill. Nevertheless, it is accepted practice that women should be informed of certain risks and warning symptoms of complications associated with the use of steroidal contraceptives and IUCDs. Infection is the most common complication of IUCDs but this is mostly due to sexual transmission and there is no increased risk in monogamous couples. Poor technique at insertion may result in uterine perforation or embedding of the device in the uterine musculature. If a woman cannot feel the thread of the device, this could mean that: (a) the thread has retracted, usually an indication that it was cut too short; or (b) the coil has translocated through a perforation; or (c) the coil has been expelled. At insertion, these risks should be discussed, and the projected date of expiry/removal should be stated, so that the device is not forgotten in the uterus.

36.231 Women who wish to use oral contraceptives should be warned of the symptoms that may herald thrombo-embolic complications, such as headaches, visual disturbance, chest pain and pain in the legs. This warning and additional information, including a list of contraindications to the use of oral contraceptives, is also provided in information leaflets inserted into the packet by the manufacturers.

36.232 Women who are given long-term injectable steroidal contraceptives, such as Depo-Provera, are usually warned of the incidence of menstrual disturbance, but less often of the possible delay in return of fertility and of other side effects, which may be unpleasant.

36.233 Written consent is usually obtained for surgical termination of pregnancy under general anaesthesia. It should also be obtained when pregnancy is terminated, for fetal abnormality or for social reasons, by 'medical means' in a conscious woman. The practice differs widely in the amount and quality of the information given to a woman who is to have her pregnancy terminated. Two issues have been contested.

36.234 First, whether or not there is a duty to warn that despite carrying out an operation to terminate a pregnancy, it may nevertheless continue. This problem most often arises with attempts to terminate pregnancy early, before nine weeks. The possibility of this happening is about 1 in 1,000; such accidents usually also involve allegations of delay in diagnosing continuation of the pregnancy so that a further attempt to terminate the pregnancy is no longer possible or acceptable to the woman. Second, complaints have been made in respect of failure to warn (as distinct from its actual occurrence) that during the course of an abortion damage may be done to the uterus and/or other intra-abdominal organs, or that the operation may be complicated by pelvic infection.

36.235 The signature of a Jehovah's Witness that she does not wish to have a blood transfusion under any circumstances is usually sought (see Figure **36.12** at the end of this chapter) whereas the risk inherent in blood transfusion is not acknowledged by obtaining consent from a patient who *is* to receive a transfusion.

COMMON RECURRING THEMES

36.236 There are three powerful occurring themes. First, most successful litigants have suffered not from one single error of management but a whole cascade of deficiencies. This is particularly true in obstetric injury to the fetus where errors in the ante-natal clinic, lack of consultant supervision and poor preparation for labour are exacerbated by poor systems of control in the labour ward, sub-standard management, often by poorly supervised trainees, leading to critical errors in the interpretation of vaginal examinations and CTG traces, culminating in a disastrous operative delivery of an already compromised baby. The proximal cause of the error is often a trainee unsupervised and out of his depth; the remote and more important causes are with senior staff who have neglected their responsibilities. To address this, the RCOG published the advisory document *Responsibility of Consultant On-call*[1]. Matters are often made much worse by negative attitudes on the part of obstetric and midwifery staff, particularly *after* the accident has occurred.

1 Royal College of Obstetricians and Gynaecologists. Responsibility of Consultant On-call (Good Practice No 8). March 2009.

36.237 The second theme is delay. Delay is ubiquitous in obstetric malpractice. Care of the obstetric patient is all about the timely recognition of abnormalities and swift intervention. Delay in recognition of fetal distress and dysfunctional labour commonly ends in disaster. Even when problems are recognised, delay in implementation may exacerbate them. The same theme runs through gynaecology, with delay in responding to the abnormal cervical smear, delay in recognising the ectopic pregnancy and post-operative delay in recognising complications resulting from surgical error.

36.238 The third theme is communication. Good communication is the key to avoiding litigation. Whilst good practice may provide a reasonable defence to litigation, good communication will often obviate it. The great majority of plaintiffs complain that no one told them why the accident occurred. Often, an innocent explanation is available but not given; that explanation surfaces only during the litigation process. Even when the explanation is not innocent, the adult patient may refrain from litigation if given an early and frank explanation of the accident.

CHECKLIST

36.239
- Approximately 20 per cent of all claims and approximately 50 per cent of all payments by the NHS Litigation Authority relate to claims arising out of birth.
- Cerebral palsy is the commonest condition leading to litigation. Because of the large sums of money involved, such cases are usually vigorously defended and often come to trial.
- Only in one in ten instances can cerebral palsy be attributed to events around the time of birth.
- Intraoperative problems account for 27.6 per cent of claims in gynaecology.

- Lack of consultant presence on the delivery suite after hours, the Working Time Regulations as applied to training grade doctors, and a shortage of midwives have combined to create a workforce crisis which compromises patient safety and enhances the prospect of increased claims.
- Injury during childbirth may also have physical, psychological or psychiatric sequelae for the mother, giving rise to litigation. The majority of these cases settle out of court.
- There has been a proliferation of clinical practice guidelines in obstetrics (less so for gynaecology). This means that for most commonly occurring conditions, the acceptable standards of practice are quite well established.
- Consent remains a significant issue in malpractice claims in both obstetrics and gynaecology.

APPENDIX

Figure 36.1   Ultrasound measurements of fetal growth

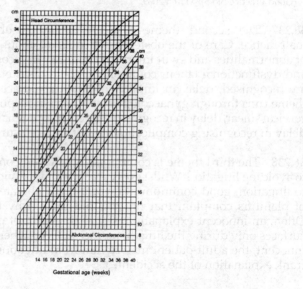

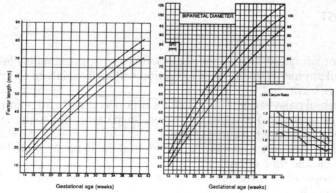

Figure 36.2   Deflexion attitudes

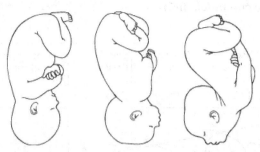

In (a) the child is in the military attitude of early deflexion often associated with the occipito-posterior position; in (b) there is more deflexion amounting almost to brow presentation; in (c) extension is complete and the face presents.

Reproduced from *Obstetrics and Gynaecology for Postgraduates* (2nd edn), Churchill Livingstone.

Figure 36.3   The fetal head

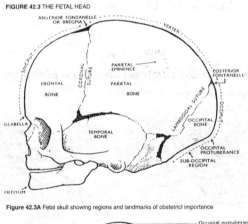

FIGURE 42.3 THE FETAL HEAD

Figure 42.3A Fetal skull showing regions and landmarks of obstetricl importance

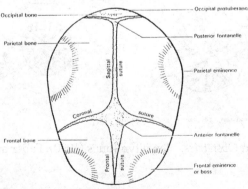

Figure 42.3B View of fetal head from above (head partly flexed).

Reproduced from *Myles' Textbook for midwives*, Churchill Livingstone, 1993.

Reproduced from Myles' *Textbook for Midwives*, (1989), Churchill Livingstone

1263

Figure 36.4   Progressive descent of the head, assessed in fifths still palpable above the pelvic brim

FIGURE 42.4 PROGRESSIVE DESCENT OF THE HEAD, ASSESSED IN FIFTHS STILL PALPABLE ABOVE THE PELVIC (AFTER CRICHTION, MODIFIED BY LASBREY)

Completely above	Sinciput +++ Occiput ++	Sinciput ++ Occiput +	Sinciput + Occiput just felt	Sinciput + Occiput not felt	No part of head palpable
5/5	4/5	3/5	2/5	1/5	0/5

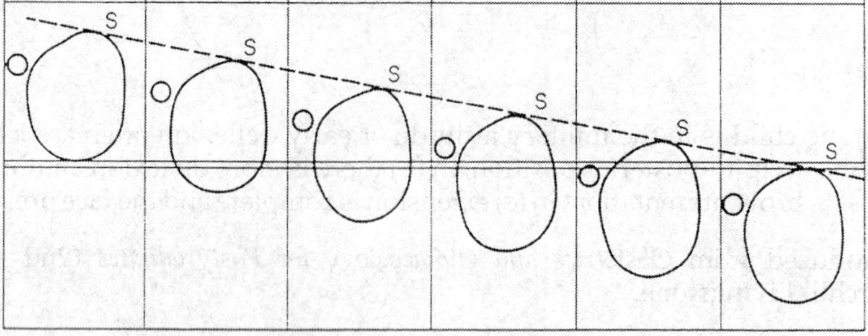

Reproduced from *Munro Kerr's Operative Obstetrics*, Baillière Tindall, 1982.

Reproduced from Munro Kerr's *Operative Obstetrics* (1982), Baillière Tindall

Figure 36.5   The four most common abnormal placental forms

FIGURE 42.5 THE FOUR MOST COMMON ABNORMAL PLACENTAL FORMS

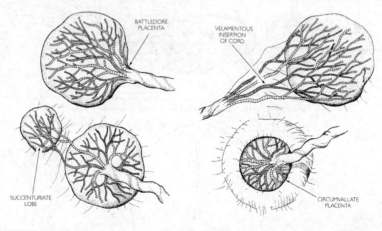

BATTLEDORE PLACENTA

VELAMENTOUS INSERTION OF CORD

SUCCENTURIATE LOBE

CIRCUMVALLATE PLACENTA

Reproduced from Obstetrics, Llewellyn Jones, Faber and Faber, 1994.

Reproduced from *Obstetrics*, Llewellyn Jones (1990), Faber and Faber

Figure 36.6   Cardiotocograph

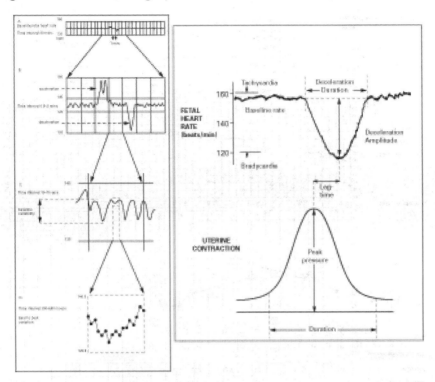

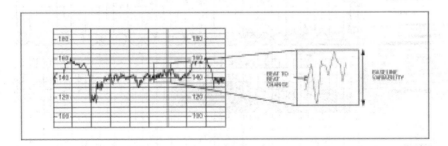

Reproduced from *Sonicaid Handbook*.

Figure 36.7   Progress in labour recorded on a partogram

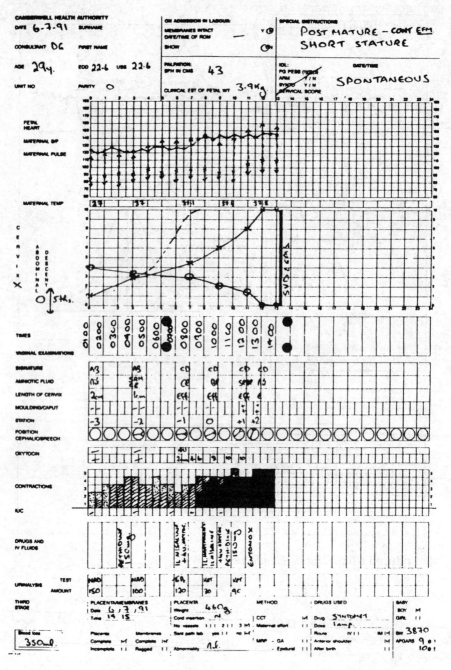

Reproduced from *Fetal Monitoring in Practice*, Gibb and Arulkumaran (Butterworth Heinemann, 1992).

Figure 36.8 Progress of labour compared with first (primigravid) and subsequent (multipara) labours

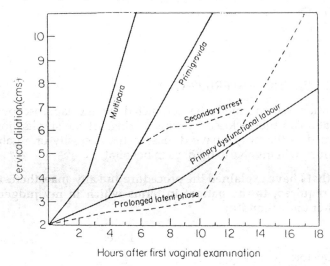

Reproduced from *Dewhurst's Integrated Obstetrics and Gynaecology for Postgraduates* (Blackwell, 1986).

Figure 36.9 Station of head and moulding and caput (a) destroying reliability of assessing head level by station (b)

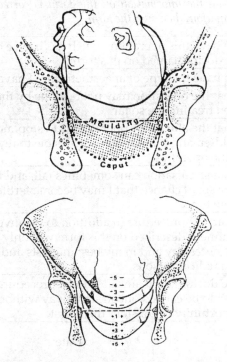

Reproduced with permission of the *South African Medical Journal*.

Figure 36.10   Consent form for sterilisation

NORTH MIDDLESEX HOSPITAL NHS TRUST
CONSENT FORM for sterilisation
PATIENT'S SURNAME:
OTHER NAMES:
DATE OF BIRTH:
Unit No:
TYPE OF OPERATION: STERILISATION

This operation will normally be conducted by the laparoscopy method and the Fallopian tubes closed by clips or rings. If the sterilisation cannot be performed in this way I have discussed the necessity of an abdominal incision which will involve extra days in hospital.

I confirm that I have explained the procedure and any anaesthetic (general/ regional) required, to the patient in terms which in my judgement are suited to her understanding.

Signature: Date:

Name of Doctor:

PATIENT

1. Please read this form carefully.

2. If there is anything that you do not understand about the explanation, or if you want more information, you should ask the doctor.

3. Please check that all the information on this form is correct. If it is, and you understand the explanation, then sign the form.

I agree	* to have this operation, which has been explained to me by the doctor named on this form.
	* to have the type of anaesthetic that I have been told about.
I understand	* that the operation may not be done by the doctor who has been treating me so far.
	* that the aim of the operation is to stop me having any children and it might not be possible to reverse the effects of the operation.
	* that sterilisation can sometimes fail, and that there is a very small chance that I may become fertile again after some time.
	* that any procedure in addition to the investigation or treatment described on this form will only be carried out if it is necessary and in my best interests and can be justified for medical reasons.
I have told	*the doctor about any additional procedures I would *not* wish to be carried out straightaway without my having the opportunity to consider them first.

Signature: Date:

Address:

Figure 36.11   Needle inserted at 45° angle (a) with patient flat, (b) tilting the patient can result in injury to major vessel

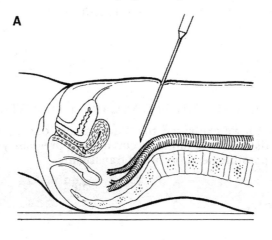

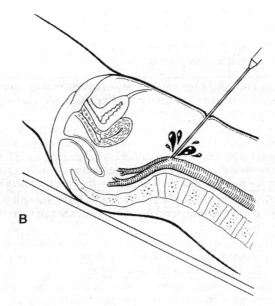

Reproduced from *Clinical Risk* (1995) 1:3 (RSM Press Ltd).

Figure 36.12 **Consent form for treatment of a patient who refuses a blood transfusion**

NORTH MIDDLESEX HOSPITAL NHS TRUST

CONSENT FORM for treatment by a patient who refuses a blood transfusion

PATIENT'S SURNAME:

OTHER NAMES:

DATE OF BIRTH:

Unit No:

TYPE OF TREATMENT: ANTE-NATAL CARE and DELIVERY

I confirm that I have explained the plan for care during pregnancy and some of the risks which might occur during pregnancy and delivery, including the possible need for blood transfusion.

Signature: Date:

Name of Doctor:

PATIENT

1. Please read this form very carefully.

2. If there is anything that you do not understand about the explanation, or if you want more information, you should ask the doctor.

3. Please check that all the information on this form is correct. If it is, and you understand the explanation, then sign the form.

I agree	* to ante-natal care and delivery of my baby at the north middlesex hospital on the strict understanding that under no circumstances would i accept blood transfusion.
I understand	* that the care may not be provided by the doctor who has been treating me so far, but I direct that this express exclusion of the transfusion of blood is binding on all practitioners treating me, including surgeons, anaesthetists, midwives, operating theatre technicians and nurses and on the staff of any other hospital in which my treatment is undertaken.
	* that any procedure not described on this form will only be carried out if it is necessary and in my best interests and can be justified for medical reasons.
	* that during my pregnancy and delivery it may be considered necessary to give me a blood transfusion so as to prevent injury to my health or even to preserve my life.
I have told	* the doctor that I expressly withhold my consent to and forbid the administration to me of a blood transfusion in any circumstances or for any reason whatsoever and I accordingly absolve the surgeon, the hospital and every member of the medical staff concerned from all responsibility, and from any liability to me, or to my estate, or to my dependants, for any damage or injury which may be caused to me, or to my estate, or to my dependants, in any way arising out of or connected with my refusal to consent to blood transfusion.
	* the doctor about any additional procedures I would *not* wish to be carried out straightaway without my having the opportunity to consider them first.

Signature: Date:

Address:

CHAPTER 37

Challenges in paediatric surgery

Mr Robert A Wheeler

ORGANISATION AND SCOPE OF THE SPECIALITY

37.1   Children's surgery is provided for in both district general hospitals (DGH), and tertiary centres. In the former, children are looked after jointly by paediatricians (physicians treating children) and adult general surgeons and urologists who provide the surgical operation, and contribute to the post-operative treatment of the child.

37.2   In this setting, much of the nation's 'general surgery of childhood', relating to surgery for hernias, undescended testes, circumcisions (euphemistically described as 'groinery') is performed. Increasingly, anxious to avoid inconvenience for families who might otherwise need to travel long distances, surgeons from tertiary centres travel to some of the 8–12 district hospitals in their region to provide some of this elective day case surgery. These surgeons also have 'peripheral' outpatient clinics booked at these hospitals, often combined on the same day as the theatre list. In this way, disruption to the family both for consultation and (if necessary) operation is minimised. Nevertheless, peripheral operating does have the disadvantage that if the patient suffers complications, perhaps some bleeding on the first post-operative night, it is possible that they will have to make a long journey to the specialist centre for a remedy.

37.3   A further potential disadvantage is a reduction in the familiarity and skills of local DGH surgeons and anaesthetists. If they deal with fewer elective day cases, they may be less prepared to deal with even the straightforward emergency surgery, such as appendicitis and torsion of the spermatic cord which they have traditionally dealt with. This risk has eventuated, and tertiary services are now under increasing pressure to accept paediatric surgical emergencies from their region that would formerly have been treated locally. Furthermore, there are children whose delayed presentation for surgery may have caused harm that could otherwise have been avoided.

37.4   Tertiary centres for children's surgery are ubiquitously located in university hospitals, and provide specialised surgery. Paediatric and neonatal surgery in these centres usually comprises upper and lower gastrointestinal surgery, urology, oncology and thoracic surgery. All have dedicated paediatric anaesthesia, and most have neonatal and paediatric intensive care. Depending on the size of the centre, they will be co-located with paediatric orthopaedics, ENT, cardiothoracic, neurosurgery and plastics. If the tertiary hospital also treats adults, rather than being restricted only to children, there will in addition be the panoply of adult specialities which will allow the paediatric surgeons' versatility of treatments primarily designed for adults but which are sometimes useful for children, including bariatric surgery, and other advanced techniques of minimally invasive surgery.

37.5   Children's surgery comprises the surgical care of neonates (up to 44 weeks' post conceptual age); infants (44 weeks post conception to 1–2 years), and children up to their 16th birthday. Neonatal surgery is thus distinguished from paediatric surgery merely by the age of the patient. There is variation within each of the four countries in the UK over the upper age limit: in some hospitals children's surgeons see only children below the age of six; others choose a cut-off of 12 years. However, the move to uniformity, with a transfer to adult care at 16 years, seems inevitable. In all cases, it is adult general surgeons and urologists who take on the care of the children once they leave the ambit of paediatric surgery. Outside London, few children are treated privately.

ROUTE OF REFERRAL TO SERVICES

37.6 Tertiary paediatric surgical centres take referrals of babies and children from their local district general hospitals, as well as providing a secondary service (as the local 'district' hospital) from the general practitioners in their own city. Children's surgery is supported and complicated by the provision of intensive care beds, both neonatal and paediatric. When either service is full, babies or older children will be refused local admission, and then distributed amongst the national network of hospitals with intensive care beds for these age groups. It is not unheard of for a child refused admission in Yorkshire to be transferred to the south coast of England, or visa versa. Such transfers may be by road or air, but whilst the inherent delays in treatment are rarely identified as causing harm to the patient, parents are almost always perplexed by the need for such distant transfers, and often harbour dissatisfaction with the treatment their child has received. Following treatment, older children will return to their homes, but neonatal surgical patients are often sent to 'convalesce' (in terms of proving that they can gain weight and grow) back in their local hospital. It is not infrequent for confusion to arise as a result of this transfer, whereby differences in reasonable practice between the secondary and tertiary neonatal units are misconstrued by parents as clinical errors, and what prove to be fruitless complaints emerge.

LAW AND INFORMED CONSENT

37.7 General consent law relating to children sometimes fails fully to confront the nuances of daily surgical practical. For instance, it is commonplace to encounter a child who is herself a parent, and the question is raised as to whether her parental responsibility is sufficient to allow her to provide valid consent for the treatment of her child. At an even more fundamental level, it is rarely appreciated that only a small minority of parents who attend hospital for their children's surgery recognise that the possession of parental responsibility is of legal importance when providing consent.

Equally, whilst daily fare to lawyers, very few surgeons (and fewer parents) are aware that both parents must consent to ritual circumcision[1].

1 See 'The law and ethics of male circumcision: Guidance for doctors' (June 2006, BMA).

37.8 When considering competent children, whether on the basis of *Gillick*[1] or statute, there is widespread misunderstanding amongst surgeons of the child's ability to defend their decision to refuse treatment. Plainly, English courts have opposed the wishes of any child seeking to refuse life-saving treatment. The apparent incongruity of accepting the competent child's consent, but rejecting the same child's refusal has led to the rhythmically satisfying (but clearly erroneous) chant beloved of children's doctors; 'yes to yes but no to no'. Such a mantra has caused great confusion in practice, since self evidently, competent children refuse (non-life saving) treatment on a daily basis throughout the NHS, leaving both staff and parents unsure as to whether it is lawful to accept this refusal, and in the latter group, angry at what they perceive to be deliberate dereliction of duty on behalf of the clinicians. In reality, these staff are balancing the risks and benefits of forcing not-entirely-necessary treatments on unwilling and at time belligerent children, and correctly concluding that the child's welfare is best served by desistance.

1 *Gillick v West Norfolk and Wisbech Area Health Authority* [1986] AC 112.

DIFFICULTIES, CHALLENGES, CAUSATION

Introduction

37.9   Children's surgery is an unusual speciality. Unlike adult surgical disciplines, where subspecialisation has resulted in organ- or system-specific specialists (breast, thyroid, or vascular surgery), paediatric surgeons, with some exceptions, remain as generalists. Although we are thus prone to litigation arising from almost every anatomical region, the vast majority of complaints are founded upon incidents relating to the commonest treatments and conditions. This chapter explores some of the questions, assumptions and pitfalls encompassed in diverse areas of paediatric surgery, arising frequently in expert practice.

'Drips' (intravenous infusions)

37.10   The illnesses in childhood that merit admission to hospital almost invariably necessitate an intravenous infusion. This is delivered through a plastic cannula inserted into a vein, through skin that has usually been numbed with a topical anaesthetic cream. Although parents often assume that the cannula is always sited in the hand or arm, finding a vein in these sites may be difficult. It may prove impossible in children covered with a generous layer of subcutaneous fat. The feet may be tried and in the case of babies, the scalp. Use of the scalp necessitates shaving a patch of skin, often leading to profound parental distress. The child may also be distressed, as it is not uncommon for 4–6 separate 'stabs' to be needed before a vein is finally found and entered successfully. Sometimes, veins can be successfully punctured, only for it then to be impossible to thread the cannula into the vein. The needle is then removed, and a substantial bruise appears. The end result is a terrified, fighting, bruised child, a horrified parent who is doing their best to provide comfort and a junior doctor faced with a patient who still needs a drip. Such a distressing story is regrettably commonplace. It reflects the difficulty of the task and does not, in itself, suggest an unreasonable approach to establishing venous access. The correct approach is then to call for senior help, but one can see how dissatisfaction begins.

37.11   Once the cannula is correctly sited, it needs to be fixed securely to the patient, who may then devote hours to its removal. Fixing usually involves a splint (to reduce limb mobility), padding (to protect the skin from the splint), sticky tape and bandages. Skin damage due to imperfect padding or unduly tight dressings is not uncommon, but should be avoidable. The dressing needs to be taken down with sufficient regularity to ensure that the infusion has not caused local inflammation around the point of entry to the skin, or extending over the skin covering the vein. These observations should be recorded in the notes.

37.12   Cannula insertion is a common enough procedure to make a hospital protocol mandatory, and it should be established that a written version existed. This should be reviewed for the guidance given concerning the use of anaesthetic creams, appropriate padding and robust fixation.

37.13   If inflammation does occur, it is described as 'tissuing' of the vein and is an absolute indication for prompt removal of the cannula. If it is not removed, irreversible tissue damage may occur. It is important to review whether the entry site was checked meticulously, and that early signs of inflammation were acted upon.

37.14   Despite proper care, drips still tissue. Damage to the vein may occur if excessively concentrated fluids are infused though limb cannulas; substantial local swelling and pain results, and if the fluid leaks out into the surrounding tissues, the loss of tissue may be so severe as to require tendon repair and skin grafting. This is particularly common with high strength (20 per cent+) glucose solutions and fluids containing blistering agents such as calcium. The drug charts, fluid charts and nursing notes should be scrutinised to ascertain if the fluids were infused via an appropriate route.

37.15   For these reasons, frequent inspections of the site must be made and the dressings taken down sufficiently to allow the staff to see the point of entry of the cannula into the skin. Any redness at this site should alert them to a possible problem; other indicators are pains in the limb during fluid administration, or increasing difficulty in injecting into the cannula. If tissuing does occur, a prompt response should be made to reduce the swelling. There are various methods for ameliorating the tissue damage that may occur, and failing to consider or implement these would constitute a lapse below the reasonable standard.

Long-term central venous access

37.16   There is an increasing demand for children to have prolonged venous access, notably for oncology treatment, long-term intravenous nutrition, the management of cystic fibrosis and of immunopathies. Problems relating to the insertion and maintenance of long-term central venous catheters (CVC) are often the subject of litigation, since insertion and maintenance are inherently troublesome.

37.17   Long-term CVCs in children are almost invariably inserted during a general anaesthetic, and may be placed by a surgeon, an anaesthetist or increasingly, an interventional radiologist in the case of percutaneous insertions. The catheter may be inserted using an 'open' technique, where an incision is made in the neck and the internal or external jugular vein is dissected, controlled and cannulated under direct vision. Alternatively, a percutaneous ('closed') technique can be used, where the vein is punctured directly through the skin, without a significant incision and with no dissection. This approach is generally applied to the internal jugular and subclavian veins, although it can be applied to any detectable vein of sufficient size.

37.18   Both open and percutaneous approaches have their advocates, risks and advantages, and the disclosure for consent should reflect these variants. The open approach enables the vein to be identified with confidence, and haemostasis to be achieved with certainty. However, it also involves greater post-operative discomfort and inevitably more scarring. The vein, having been handled, is less likely to be available for subsequent catheterisation should the first CVC have to be removed. The percutaneous approach involves a minimal wound, less post-operative discomfort and limitation, and allows multiple opportunities to recatheterise the same vein should subsequent CVC placement become necessary. However, by definition, the needle's passage percutaneously into the vein may be performed blindly, and may damage contiguous structures. This may lead to arterial or venous bleeding, damage to major nerves, and air leaks resulting in pneumothorax. Intercostal drainage or thoracotomy to repair the damage may be required. The occurrence of these complications does not speak for itself, in terms of reflecting substandard care; all major series of percutaneous CVC placement report these complications.

37.19   These dangers may be ameliorated by the use of ultrasound guidance. In children who are receiving a CVC via an internal jugular puncture, NICE guidance makes the use of an ultrasound probe mandatory. This guidance is ignored by some hospital Trusts, who would appear to accept the risk of litigation rather than provide the necessary funds for equipment and training that would be necessitated by adherence to the guidance. It also has to be recognised that 'blind' puncture of these great vessels has been the stock-in-trade for anaesthetists and some surgeons for many years, providing the support of a reasonable body of practitioners for the practice. Whether this would pass scrutiny on the basis of logic and good sense is another matter. What is not in doubt is that the dangers flowing from either approach should be disclosed, since a reasonable parent would wish to consider the possibility of these complications occurring to their child, before providing consent.

37.20   There is debate as to the optimum site for the tip of the CVC. If placed in the superior vena cava (SVC, the final common venous channel draining the whole of the head, neck and upper limbs), the CVC tip is held in the centre of the blood stream by the stable laminar flow, and is unlikely to move sufficiently to cause damage to the walls of the vessel. For this reason, perforation of the vessel or the heart is unlikely. However, laminar flow precludes optimum mixing of the infused fluids with the blood. Imperfect mixing can result in blood clot formation, so thrombosis of the superior vena cava is more likely with the CVC tip in this site. If the tip is placed in the right atrium, the reverse situation pertains. The atrium is a site of turbulent flow, so there is excellent mixing, and a low incidence of thrombosis. On the other hand, the CVC tip is not held in the centre of the atrial cavity by the stream of blood, and is rather more likely to penetrate the atrial wall. Both thrombosis and perforation can have fatal consequences. Both sites have their proponents within children's surgery, the North Americans tending to favour the SVC; the Europeans the right atrium, and the UK surgeons remain undecided. Some surgeons adopt a compromise, placing the tip at the junction between the two, at the site where the SVC enters the atrium, and record this on the intraoperative X-ray, which is a mandatory investigation.

37.21 In reality, the CVC tip can be demonstrated to move into and out of the heart by several centimetres as the child moves the head and limbs in relation to the trunk, making the entire discussion somewhat academic. Thus whilst failure to check the site of the CVC with an X-ray falls below the reasonable standard, there is less certainty as to the standard for the site of its tip.

37.22 Regrettably, there are inherent complications of having a CVC in situ. The catheters can fall out, block, become infected and break. Various innovative surgeons have adopted techniques to minimise these complications, since most of the latter result in CVC removal, and necessitate subsequent reinsertion. However, in a recent survey, 25 per cent of all long-term CVCs placed for oncology treatment in children had to be replaced within six weeks of insertion. This can be both dangerous and distressing for the child, and leads to much understandable dissatisfaction from the parents. These inherent dangers of long-term venous access are not risks that a reasonable parent could be expected to anticipate, and should be spelled out during the consent process.

Lumps and bumps in the head, neck and upper limbs

37.23 Children often present for surgical review with swellings, either within or beneath the skin. Difficulty may arise if the parents are falsely reassured that the swellings will resolve spontaneously, since many will not; and if they are excised incompletely, since many will recur. Furthermore, if the lump proves to be a lymph node, and is indicative of systemic disease, an opportunity for timely treatment may be missed.

37.24 Dermoid cysts form during development, when cells destined for the dermis layer become buried (sequestered) beneath the junction of advancing (joining) plates of tissue. These islands of cells are thus placed beneath the developing dermis, but grow inexorably, and form a lump. By definition they lie beneath the lines of fusion, and they often lie in the midline, since this is where the lateral masses of an embryo fuse. The commonest visible site is at the front of the neck, where the swelling can enlarge, become infected and be confused with a thyroglossal cyst. The correct approach is completely to excise the dermoid cyst through a skin crease incision, although if the child presents with an infected cyst, the infection should be eradicated before an operation is attempted.

37.25 If there is any doubt that the lesion is, in reality, a thyroglossal cyst, it is vital to perform an ultrasound examination of the thyroid gland before surgery. Because in patients with a thyroglossal cyst, rarely, all of the thyroid tissue is contained within the cyst, and the ultrasound will reveal an absent thyroid gland. If this is found, serious consideration will be needed before the 'cyst' is excised.

37.26 Furthermore, if the anterior neck cyst proves to be a thyroglossal remnant, not only the cyst, but also the accompanying thyroglossal tract, will have to be excised. This involves resection of the body of the hyoid bone, through which the tract traverses. Without these measures, the symptoms relating to the thyroglossal remnants will recur, and will be more difficult fully to excise at a second operation. Failure clinically to distinguish between thyroglossal and midline cervical dermoid cysts falls well within the acceptable standard. Inadvertent removal of the whole thyroid gland for the want of an ultrasound does not. In normal circumstances, it would not be acceptable to permit recurrence of a thyroglossal remnant by failing to remove the hyoid bone. But excision of the whole thyroglossal tract can be very challenging, and provided the main surgical steps had been taken, a recurrence does not speak for itself, and may well fall within the normal standard expected.

37.27 The most well-known location of a dermoid cyst in childhood is at the external angle of the orbit, located within or close to the lateral part of the developing eyebrow. This is the external angular dermoid. The swelling is often not obvious until the end of infancy, but once noted, is most unlikely to resolve spontaneously. If left alone, the cyst can enlarge greatly, and occasionally become infected. However, the greatest danger is of internal expansion. The cyst is characteristically bound down to the outer layer ('table') of the skull by the periosteal membrane that covers the bone, and its expansion can lead to erosion through the bone. This may lead to compression of the underlying dura mater that surrounds the brain. For this reason, and to minimise the scarring that is inevitable from the excisional surgery, early removal is necessary, and represents the appropriate standard of care.

37.28 The dermoid will recur if its wall is incompletely excised. Excision can be difficult, and it is not uncommon to hear of a dermoid being ruptured during removal. The material that is spilt is the sebaceous material that the cyst contains, and its spillage has no consequence. This is not inconsistent with a reasonable standard of care. However, under normal circumstances, the reasonable surgeon will be able fully to excise the wall of the cyst. It is clearly vital that risks of recurrence should form part of the disclosure for consent. In circumstances when the surgery proved difficult, perhaps with copious bleeding (which is not unusual), there is little that the reasonable surgeon can do to ensure complete removal of the wall, particularly if the cyst fragments. But the parents must be instructed to be watchful and report recurrence. This warning should be repeated at the post-operative review, by which time the histology should be available, which will confirm the completeness (or otherwise) of excision.

37.29 Unusually located 'dermoids' may prove to be misdiagnoses, with significant consequences. For instance, mid-line swellings around the bridge of the nose or the forehead may prove to be connected to the frontal sinuses, or contain brain. For this reason, such lesions should be referred to maxillofacial or neurosurgeons, since general surgeons would normally be ill equipped to deal with the surgery, or its potential complications.

37.30 Another lesion lying under the skin of the upper limbs, neck and face (and frequently causing diagnostic and therapeutic confusion) is the pilomatrixoma, sometimes called the 'benign calcifying epithelioma of Malherbe'. This is a group of cells destined to become part of the epithelial layer, but 'left behind ' during development, buried beneath the skin. The body's reaction to this lesion is to treat it as a foreign material, and calcification occurs, particularly if the lesion ruptures. The end result is a rather alarming hard and craggy lesion, often attached to the skin, that nevertheless remains mobile in the subcutaneous tissues, and has distinct edges and surfaces, feeling rather like a piece of bone in a bizarre location. If left alone, these grow, and frequently ulcerate through the skin, causing significant and unnecessary distress.

37.31   The treatment is excisional surgery, but the lesions will recur if the mass is incompletely excised. Since the lesion is pale, yellow and hard, it is easily visible and usually straightforward to remove, along with any skin to which it is adherent. However, large pilomatrixomas can be friable and break during removal, and every fragment must be removed if recurrence is to be avoided. Thus recurrence does not necessarily imply a substandard procedure, but if the surgical field was reported as ideal, recurrence will be hard to explain. Metachronous pilomatrixomas are unusual but occur, particularly where a genetic diagnosis underlies their formation; the second lesion in such patients is often mistaken for a recurrence, until the case is more carefully considered.

37.32   Enlarged lymph nodes in a child's neck are commonplace, and rarely indicate sinister disease. The 'necklace' distribution of normal cervical lymph nodes represents a line of defence against microbes that enter the mouth, nose and ears, and frequently become enlarged during both local and systemic viral and bacterial illnesses. Lymph nodes that become enlarged for a prolonged time, more than a few weeks, need careful consideration, since they may represent the development of lymphoproliferative disease. This becomes more likely if the nodes become hard, irregular or progressively bigger.

37.33   In these circumstances, the history should ascertain whether there are symptoms and signs of systemic disease, such as weight loss, unexplained pyrexia or persistent malaise. Any of these should prompt investigation, including a blood count, film and chest X-ray, together with a paediatric referral. An ultrasound scan to determine the nodal architecture, and possible presence of pus, may be relevant.

37.34   There is no rigid rule as to when a lymph node biopsy becomes mandatory, although some authors suggest that histology should be obtained from any single node that persists for more than three months. If the decision not to operate is taken, it should be supported by valid reasoning, negative findings in the history and investigations, and informed parental agreement to expectant management. Surgeons who steadfastly refuse to perform a biopsy because they disregard the importance of 'simply reassuring mother' are disproportionately (highly) represented in the group that subsequently become the focus of complaints. Their behaviour often falls below the reasonable standard of care, since the surgeon has a duty to care for both the child and the family, and should give proper weight to the interests of both.

37.35   Inevitably, cases emerge where, in retrospect, a sinister lymph node should have been biopsied weeks or sometimes months before the biopsy finally took place. The notes reveal obvious markers, such as systemic features, that should have led to the procedure. But due to the indolence of some lymphoproliferative illnesses in childhood, often no damage can be attributed to the delay in diagnosis, to the surprise and disappointment of the claimants.

Pyloric stenosis

37.36 This is a relatively common disease of infants in the first six weeks of life. The pylorus is the muscular ring at the exit of the stomach, and it can become thickened ('hypertrophied') and bulky, preventing the drainage of stomach contents towards the duodenum. These babies present with vomiting, their mothers characteristically reporting a forceful or 'projectile' vomit that can cross the room. Invariably, the vomit is of milk. If there is any suggestion that the vomit contains bile (and is therefore green), this implies continuity between the stomach and duodenum. In this case, the diagnosis of pyloric stenosis should be abandoned, and the alternative, life-threatening diagnosis of midgut malrotation should be considered, and excluded as an emergency.

37.37 The baby with pyloric stenosis is characteristically hungry and losing weight. The diagnosis should be confirmed either by clinical tests or ultrasonography, and surgery planned. However, babies with pyloric stenosis have often been vomiting for many days before diagnosis, and have become severely depleted in fluid and electrolytes. Resuscitation is therefore of paramount importance, and full fluid and electrolyte restoration may take several days to achieve. It is imperative that surgery is delayed until the blood electrolytes have returned to normal levels; crucially the sodium, potassium and bicarbonate must all be normal before anaesthesia is administered. The bicarbonate, particularly, is important, and must be less than or equal to 25mmols per litre, otherwise the baby may suffer post-operative apnoeas. Although the delay between diagnosis and surgery can cause parental anxiety and frustration, it is crucial if post-operative deaths are to be avoided.

37.38 The surgery (pyloromyotomy, Ramstedt's procedure) can be performed through a right upper quadrant or periumbilical incision; some surgeons prefer a laparoscopic approach. The procedure involves identifying the thickened pylorus, and incising the muscle so that the muscular ring is interrupted, and this allows the underlying pyloric lining (mucosa) to bulge through. This has the effect of widening the pyloric canal, and the obstruction is thus removed.

37.39 Although the essence of the procedure is to leave the mucosa intact, this is sometimes difficult, and experienced surgeons occasionally breach the mucosa and enter the gastric lumen. This falls well within the standard of care, since the surgery can be technically difficult, particularly in very small babies. However, the cardinal rule is that the integrity of the mucosa should be tested following the pyloromyotomy, to ensure that no leak is evident. This is done either by milking gastric contents through the pylorus, or asking the anaesthetist to inflate the stomach with air; in either circumstance, the surgeon examines the incised pylorus carefully, to ensure there is no leak.

If one is found, the mucosal breach can easily be closed with an absorbable suture, and the baby is then kept nil-by-mouth for 24 hours before feeds are re-introduced. In the absence of a leak, feeds are usually recommenced within a few hours of returning to the ward, although surgeons are united in their insistence on adhering to widely varied regimes of feeding babies after pyloromyotomy.

37.40   The most frequent complications after pyloromyotomy are wound infection and incisional hernia; there is debate as to whether these are more frequently associated with the para umbilical approach. For this reason, it is important that there was a demonstrable discussion about the benefits and disadvantages of the varied approaches as part of the disclosure for consent. An incomplete pyloromyotomy, that fails to lead to a resolution of the vomiting, is uncommon, and falls below the reasonable standard of care in normal circumstances. This should not be confused with a period of post-operative vomiting, which is very common, but resolves spontaneously within 7–10 days after surgery.

Intussusception

37.41   This is a surgical emergency affecting infants. It is caused by a section of bowel (the 'intussusceptum') becoming inverted into the segment of bowel directly downstream; with the theoretical result that the intussuscepted bowel could emerge through the anus. On occasion, the section that inverts does so because a lymphoid mass, polyp or diverticulum on its surface acts as the 'lead point' of the inversion process. Children with intussusception present with severe colicky pain, pallor, an abdominal mass and the signs of gut obstruction. Additionally, blood stained mucus may be passed per rectum, immortalised as 'redcurrant jelly stool'.

37.42   These signs flow from the underlying pathology. The inversion of the intussuscepted bowel may cause its blood supply to be compromised; and ischaemia may ensue. The presence of the intussusceptum obstructs the bowel lumen, causing gut obstruction. The net effect of these processes is the formation of a mass of devitalised and obstructed bowel. If it is not reduced, bacterial translocation can occur, causing septicaemia, collapse, multi-system failure and death.

37.43   If diagnosed promptly, the child, after resuscitation and antibiotics, should have the diagnosis confirmed with ultrasound. Providing that the child is well enough, the intussusception can be cured by the use of an air enema (pneumatic reduction), administered under radiological control. This forces the intussusceptum back to its normal position, and restores bowel patency.

37.44   For those children who are diagnosed late, are in a grave clinical condition or who have evidence of gut perforation, air reduction is contraindicated. In this situation, following fluid resuscitation, an emergency laparotomy should be performed. It may be possible to reduce the bowel by pulling the intussusceptum out of the recipient segment; or bowel resection may be required. Even if reduction is possible, the intussusceptum may be necrotic, and gut resection may be required. Recurrence of intussusception is well recognised, may follow either air or open reduction, and its risk must be made clear to the parents during the initial admission.

37.45   Intussusception is a disease with one per cent mortality. Children die usually because of late diagnosis, or inadequate fluid resuscitation. There is a larger group of children who do not die, but suffer long-term neurological and co-morbidity because of their collapse for want of resuscitation, antibiotics and prompt appropriate treatment. This is a sufficiently common condition to allow an expectation that any hospital accepting emergencies will either be able to provide definitive treatment for an infant with suspected intussusception, or will recognise the necessity for resuscitation and early transfer to an appropriate facility.

Acute appendicitis

37.46   The appendix often becomes inflamed in childhood. The illness may progress to appendiceal suppuration and eventual perforation, spilling gut contents into the abdominal cavity, resulting in peritonitis and abscess formation. Spreading infection may affect adjacent organs and inflammatory cells may appear in the urine, although there is no urinary infection as such. The timescale for the progression of the disease varies from hours to days. In infants and toddlers, in whom the disease is rather less common, the progression may be alarmingly fast and bowel perforation can occur within a few hours of the onset of illness.

37.47   A well-known condition, the diagnosis of appendicitis is frequently suggested by a general practitioner or relative before the patient reaches hospital. On arrival, the parents have a clear expectation that the next logical step is surgery. However, just because the disease is common, it must not be assumed that its diagnosis is always easy. Appendicitis is a famous mimic, presenting with the clinical signs of other diseases, which are 'appropriately' treated for a few days before the true diagnosis becomes clear. Therefore, a claim by parents that the time to diagnosis was excessive should be treated with caution.

37.48   The surgeon needs to confirm the diagnosis before surgery is undertaken, because appendicitis is only one of many causes of abdominal pain in childhood; in many of these there is no requirement for surgery. Usually, the diagnosis can be confirmed on physical examination, although it is most important that the urine should be checked for infection. This is because urinary infection may present with abdominal pain. In a small child, this may be clinically indistinguishable from appendicitis. A chest infection may also present with a similar pain and needs to be excluded. It is important to note whether the chest examination was documented; was a mid-stream urine sample (MSU) taken? To compound the problem, early pneumonia in young children may manifest only as rapid breathing, without further physical signs, and may not be evident on chest radiography. Children with appendicitis may also present with rapid breathing; and abdominal pain can be present with both diagnoses. Furthermore, if the inflamed appendix is adherent to the dome of the bladder, bacteria may cross from the appendix into the bladder, giving a positive urine test and leading the physician to believe that a urinary infection is the cause of the abdominal pain.

37.49 An ultrasound examination of the abdomen may visualise an inflamed appendix. The ultrasound examination is variably reliable because it is operator-dependent. Whilst a positive ultrasound diagnosis would normally precipitate surgery, few radiologists will confidently exclude the diagnosis. The reasonable surgeon should not discount highly suggestive persistent clinical features consistent with appendicitis on the basis of a negative ultrasound.

37.50 The patient's evaluation therefore takes time if there is real doubt over the diagnosis. Observation is of value; faced with a child who is unwell, but who has yet to develop convincing signs which merit surgical intervention, a common approach is to wait and see, possibly for a day or two. The notes should demonstrate that the process of observation was an active one. Monitoring should be regular and frequent, with clear recordings of the vital signs; any changes in condition should prompt appropriate investigations, or the eventual conclusion that surgery is required. Once the decision to operate has been made, most surgeons would administer, as a minimum, a single dose of antibiotics. This may be given whilst the child is waiting to go to theatre, or during the induction of anaesthesia, and should be documented. If the appendix proves to be grossly abnormal, or the infection has spread within the abdomen, a longer course of antibiotics would be usual. These would initially be administered intravenously, and then orally when the child is able to eat and drink.

37.51 It is also considered mandatory to administer adequate pain relief once the diagnosis is made. The use of pre-diagnosis pain relief may be controversial, some surgeons wishing to avoid 'masking the symptoms' whilst making up their minds. Although many specialist paediatric surgeons would disapprove, it appears to be widespread practice amongst adult surgeons in district hospitals to withhold pain relief before the diagnosis is made, and may be regarded as reasonable.

Adhesion advice

37.52 It is self-evident to surgeons that abdominal pathology and surgery can lead to adhesions; and the adhesions, in their turn, can lead to complications. But it is incorrect to assume that the parents will possess this knowledge. It is therefore important to ensure that parents are adequately warned of this possibility, before leaving hospital. This advice should be reiterated in the follow-up outpatient visit, since adhesion obstruction, if neglected, can result in morbidity and death in small children. The following advice to parents represents a template for the standard of information that should be disclosed.

37.53 Any patient who has had abdominal surgery can be prone to adhesion obstruction. Adhesions are caused by the original disease or the trauma of surgery, but they may manifest many years later. The bowel may be kinked or obstructed by an adhesive band and thus upstream dilatation of the bowel occurs. If the obstruction does not resolve spontaneously, green (bile-stained) vomiting commences. In childhood, the management of adhesion obstruction is surgical and thus requires an urgent referral to a paediatric surgeon.

Hernias in the umbilical region

37.54   The umbilical hernia represents a congenital hernia at the site of attachment of the umbilical cord. Being a circular scar, and bearing in mind that scars contract with time, it can be predicted that the umbilical hernia defect will get smaller given time. The majority of umbilical hernias close in the first year of life. The vast majority of umbilical hernias will close by the age of seven years, although undoubtedly a very few will persist and require surgery following that date. Umbilical hernias are not usually associated with significant symptoms, although pain is sometimes reported. Very rarely, obstruction of an umbilical hernia has been recorded.

37.55   The usual approach is therefore conservative and expectant. However, if faced with a child who starts school with a protruding umbilicus and gets teased, this may be an indication for surgery. It seems unreasonable to leave an obviously protrudent hernia as a focus of teasing when the relatively simple day case procedure would solve the problem. There is considerable discordance amongst surgeons as to the appropriate age for surgery. Few would agree to operate within the first year of life, but there is then a broad spread of opinion as to the optimum time for intervention. The surgery itself is not usually problematic, although parents sometimes (rightly) complain if the scar is placed in a site away from the umbilicus. Under normal circumstances, it should be possible to hide the scar within the umbilicus itself, or at its superior or inferior rim.

37.56   A common clinical mistake is to assume that all swellings at the infant umbilicus are umbilical hernias. In contrast to the circular central umbilical defect, the transverse slit defect of a supraumbilical hernia is located near the superior margin of the umbilicus. But both of these hernias emerge into the umbilical cavity, causing diagnostic confusion. They can be distinguished by diligent examination, and need to be; the supraumbilical hernia will not resolve spontaneously, is prone to cause pain, and should be repaired. These hernias are repaired as a day case procedure, and both can recur if the suture gives way, although this is relatively uncommon.

37.57   The epigastric hernia is located in the midline between the umbilicus and the xiphoid process. It is notable because the hernial defect is characteristically tiny, 1–2 mm in diameter. Through this hole emerges extraperitoneal fat, the resultant swelling being the size of a pea. These lumps of fat can occasionally twist, become deprived of their blood supply, and undergo (painful) ischaemic necrosis. For this reason, repair is generally advised.

37.58   The key to the procedure is accurate marking of the hernia whilst the child is awake immediately before surgery. If this is not done, it may be impossible to find the defect, since the pea-sized fat-containing sac, which is diaphanous, will have emerged into the subcutaneous tissue and will be surrounded by fat of an identical colour and consistency. Only if the incision is accurately marked will dissection bring the surgeon down directly onto the tiny defect, which can be identified and closed. Otherwise, it will be impossible to locate the defect, and despite extensive dissection, the procedure will have to be abandoned, and repeated. This difficulty is sufficiently well known to render the failure to mark the site of the bulge accurately preoperatively as indicative of substandard care.

Hernias and hydrocoeles

37.59 The vast majority of children's hernias and hydrocoeles are congenital, insofar as they are caused by an abdominal structure (typically bowel, omentum or bladder) passing in to the processus vaginalis, which has remained patent (at the deep ring) after birth.

37.60 During development, the testis forms on the posterior abdominal wall, and descends down towards the groin. On reaching the inguinal region, it passes medially between the anterior abdominal wall muscles, entering these at the deep inguinal ring. The testis then passes medially through the inguinal canal, and then emerges from those muscular layers at the superficial inguinal ring from where it descends into the scrotum. As the testis enters the deep inguinal ring during its downward journey, it becomes associated with the peritoneal lining of the abdominal cavity. During its passage through the inguinal canal, it effectively 'drags' the adherent peritoneum, thus creating a tube of peritoneum (the processus vaginalis) that extends from the deep ring, along the inguinal canal, through the superficial ring and into the scrotum. In most children, the tissue forming the processus becomes reabsorbed at or soon after birth, the peritoneal tube becoming indiscernible.

37.61 For children in whom the reabsorption takes a few months or years, the processus remains patent during this time. Usually, this patent tube is narrow, preventing the entry of solid abdominal structures, but allowing peritoneal fluid to pass into the groin, and down into the scrotum, contained by the processus. The collections of fluid that present in this way are described as a hydrocoele; either scrotal, or of the cord, the latter describing hydrocoeles limited to the inguinal region. Hydrocoeles are normally self-limiting, since once the processus fuses and is reabsorbed, the continuity with the peritoneum is lost, and the hydrocoele fluid dissipates.

37.62 For this reason, paediatric surgeons will not operate on hydrocoeles during infancy. Few hydrocoeles cause symptoms, although occasionally the swelling becomes so tense that it can cause pain, an indication for surgery. There is a theoretical risk that a tense hydrocoele extending into the groin (ie up into the inguinal canal) could exert sufficient pressure on the testicular vessels to exceed the testicular venous pressure, leading to pressure atrophy of the testis. Physical examination of the patient clearly needs to include an opinion as to whether the pressure within the hydrocoele could pose a threat to the testicular circulation. Furthermore, the parents should be warned that during the expectant treatment of a hydrocoele, any new symptoms suggestive of increasing pressure should lead to a prompt surgical review.

However, a balance should be struck between the benefit derived from operating on a hydrocoele that is likely to resolve spontaneously, and the potential damage that may be caused to the spermatic cord during the procedure. It is important that the disclosure for consent for hydrocoele surgery reflects this.

37.63 Another potential pitfall is to mistake a hernia for a hydrocoele. Herniation of abdominal organs through the open processus can occur if the diameter of the processus at the deep ring is sufficiently wide to allow the organ to enter. Small bowel, omentum, bladder and ovary are all sufficiently mobile in children to enter the deep ring. On entering the deep ring, the organ, eg the small bowel becomes the 'contents' of the hernial sac, the latter constituted by the processus. The sac may extend only into the groin, described as an 'incomplete' hernia, or may extend down to the scrotal base, the 'complete' form. Invariably, a hernia will necessitate surgical repair, since the natural history is that it will persist, enlarge, and potentially be complicated by incarceration, leading to obstruction or strangulation. Any attempt to manage children's hernias non-operatively would normally be inconsistent with a reasonable standard of care.

37.64 If the bowel contained within the hernial sac gets stuck within the sac and cannot return to the peritoneal cavity, it is incarcerated. Other than being impossible to reduce into the abdomen, and causing a persistent bulge in the groin, incarceration may have few consequences. However, the incarcerated bowel (or other sac content) is not in a normal anatomical position, and is prone to suffer from a reduced blood supply. Under certain circumstances, this may lead to pain, tenderness and obvious inflammatory changes; the signs of strangulation. Because the bowel loop is herniating into the groin, the bowel tube becomes kinked, preventing free passage of bowel contents, and the upstream bowel becomes distended; gut obstruction thus supervenes.

37.65 These complications require prompt surgical attention. A child with a complicated hernia should be referred as an emergency to a centre capable of dealing with it. The emergency treatment involves resuscitation of the child, followed by a manual reduction of the hernia, usually after appropriate pain relief. Successful manual reduction will push the contents back into the abdominal cavity leaving the sac empty, although it will remain inflamed for a few days. This inflammation, or the associated swelling, will make re-herniation less likely, since the processus is temporarily blocked by the thickness of its own walls, and the bowel will find it more difficult to enter at the deep ring.

There is no place for 'gallows traction', a suspensory technique that is now recognised as entirely inappropriate, ineffective and unsafe.

37.66 If manual reduction fails, emergency surgical reduction should be performed. Failure to operate may lead to loss of the hernial contents, and perforation if bowel is involved. Furthermore, if the hernia is not reduced, the continued pressure it applies on the testicular vessels may lead to ischaemic damage to the testis, potentially with testicular loss. Assuming successful reduction of the hernia is achieved, surgery will be deferred for 48 hours to allow the inevitable oedema within the inguinal canal to resolve. This resolution makes damage to the testicular vessels and vas less likely; but this remains a recognised complication that in some circumstances would be consistent with the reasonable standard of care.

37.67 It can be seen that the purpose of the physical examination of a child with a groin swelling is to differentiate between a hernia and a hydrocoele, since only the former is likely to require surgery. In theory, distinguishing between the two pathologies is straightforward, since the examiner should be able to feel the solid structures within the hernial sac. If the swelling is palpable in the scrotum, there should be a continuous swelling between the deep ring and the distal part of the swelling, since in infants (unlike adults), the abdominal wall of the groin will not be sufficiently thick to hide the inguinal swelling from the examining hand. The traditional surgical description of an inguinal hernia is of a swelling that the hand cannot 'get above'. Additionally, it should be possible manually to 'reduce' the solid contents, causing the swelling completely to disappear. On the contrary, hydrocoeles are usually confined to the scrotum, with no palpable mass within the groin. The narrow processus is not palpable in the groin, so no groin swelling is perceptible, and the examining hand can 'get above' the hydrocoele.

37.68 Surgery on inguinal hernias or hydrocoeles in boys involves identifying the vas and vessels as they course down the inguinal canal, towards the testis. Once identified, these structures must be avoided, since damage may result in blockage or division of the vas; or ischaemia to and potentially loss of the testis. In children who have had no previous groin surgery, and where there has been no history of hernia incarceration, loss of the testis due to vascular damage at the time of surgery might indicate a procedure that had been performed below the expected standard of care. However, in infants less than 3 kg, or children in whom a previous groin dissection had been performed, it has to be recognised that even a diligent surgeon taking every precaution may damage the vessels with resultant loss of the testis. Similarly, in children who present with an incarcerated hernia, such swelling may have resulted from the incarceration that the tissue planes will have been obscured, rendering the avoidance of damage impossible.

Inguinal hernias in girls

37.69 The ovary is a common content of inguinal hernias in girls. If not treated when signs of strangulation are present, the ovary may be lost due to ischaemia, so strangulated hernias in girls should be treated with the same degree of urgency as in boys. Frequently, a sliding form of hernia is encountered, with the fallopian tube being fused to the side of the hernial sac. Failure to separate these structures during the herniotomy may lead to subsequent tethering of the fallopian tube. Damage to the fallopian tube should be avoidable in normal circumstances. But when a fallopian tube is found tethered near the deep ring years later, a distinction needs to be drawn between a simple adhesion causing the tethering, and an obvious inadvertent inclusion of the fallopian tube in the ligature used to close the processus at the deep ring. The latter is likely to fall below the reasonable standard, whilst adhesion formation can follow the most diligent surgery.

Undescended testes

37.70   The testes should be present in the scrotum at full term. During the routine neonatal, six-week and infant examinations, the presence of the testes should be documented, and prompt referral to a surgeon made if either is imperfectly descended. The consequences of imperfect descent are that the testis may not grow satisfactorily, and that its function may be impaired. Over a 20-year period, testes that were originally undescended are at an increased risk of malignancy. This is one of the main reasons for moving the testis to the scrotum (orchidopexy), so that the testis can be regularly examined by the patient to ensure that there are no painful, irregular or abnormal areas. Orchidopexy does not reduce the risk of malignancy. If the undescended testis is allowed to remain in the abdomen, it is inaccessible to the examining fingers, so that should a malignancy develop, the patient will be unaware of this until the tumour has reached an advanced stage, when curative treatment will be less likely.

37.71   It is recognised that in some boys, where the testis has been confidently located in the scrotum by an experienced doctor in the first few years of life, subsequent examinations reveal an undescended testis. This is the 'ascending testis syndrome', but it can only be diagnosed if the earlier examination findings are clearly documented. If they are not, the clear implication is that the testis has always been imperfectly descended; a missed diagnosis. The undescended testis will neither grow nor function satisfactorily if it remains outside the scrotum. There is debate as to when irreversible damage occurs, but it seems likely that testes moved after the age of four years will have undergone permanent degeneration. However, it is unknown as to whether this has any effect on overall function of the individual, given the presence of a normally descended contralateral testis.

37.72   Orchidopexy carries some hazards, mainly because it is the adherence of the blood vessels to the invariably associated hernial sac that needs to be divided before the testis can be moved into the scrotum. The dissection of the vessels off the sac may damage the vessels (or the vas) and lead to testicular atrophy in 5 per cent of patients. This risk may be increased in small children yet the data indicate that postponing the surgery until the child is bigger may result in degenerative changes. As a compromise, many paediatric surgeons perform the surgery in the second year of life.

37.73   The retractile testis is defined as one that can be brought down to the base of the scrotum, ie into the most inferior site of the scrotal sac; and will remain temporarily at that site without being held in place by the examining fingers. If the testis can so be placed, it follows that the spermatic cord is long enough to allow the scrotal location. Many males are able to 'drag' the testis upward away from its scrotal position and into the groin. They achieve this by recruiting the cremasteric reflex. The cremaster muscle is inserted into the spermatic cord; when the muscle contracts, it foreshortens the spermatic cord, resulting in testicular ascent. This largely involuntary muscle can be utilised in a deliberate way; sumo wrestlers learn to bring their testes into the abdominal cavity, using the same manoeuvre. Small boys, perhaps in a less deliberate way, drag their testes out of the scrotum when anxious; so it is very common to review a child who is reported to have 'undescended testes'; but who in reality, with persistence, can be shown to be normal.

37.74   It is perfectly acceptable, if in doubt, to perform an examination under anaesthesia in these circumstances. The retractile testes will be effortlessly brought to the scrotal basis, remain there without assistance, and requires no treatment. The diagnostic clue is the scrotum, which is well developed in the (retractile) boy whose scrotum is usually occupied, when not being subjected to medical examination. But the undescended testis is associated with a poorly developed scrotum, and a testis that, if it can be brought into the scrotum at all, will 'ping' back into its original site when released by the examining fingers.

Torsion of the testes, its appendages, and differential diagnosis

37.75   It is evident that children's surgeons take a different approach to the acute scrotum, in some specific areas of practice (to be read in conjunction with and in contrast to **Chapter 34**).

37.76   In children with thin scrotal skin, it may be possible to palpate a painful and tender torted epididymal appendage, located at the superior pole. It is also sometimes possible to see the twisted and infarcted appendage at the site; the 'blue dot sign'. Only in these circumstances can a confident differentiation between a torted testicular appendage, and a torted testis be made. If the diagnosis of a torted appendage can be made, then the patient and his parents can be given the options of non-operative care, with adequate analgesia, or excisional surgery. Although the former avoids surgery and a scar, the recovery time is usually prolonged over several days, and most families opt for surgery.

37.77   In the absence of these positive clinical signs of an alternative pathology, no clinical or ultrasound examinations can confidently exclude testicular torsion. Doppler studies are intermittently advocated, but paediatric radiologists have good reason to avoid reaching firm conclusions on the basis of such examinations, since they are neither sensitive nor specific enough to be certain. For this reason, all children in whom testicular torsion cannot be excluded should have an emergency scrotal exploration. To omit this is to fall below the reasonably expected standard.

37.78   Neonatal torsion is a separate entity. Newborn boys sometimes present with a swollen scrotum at birth, occupied by an enlarged, woody, non-tender testis. There is some debate amongst children's surgeons as to whether immediate surgery is justified, since the great majority of these testes are found to have long-standing infarction, implying an antenatal torsion. This hypothesis is supported by the fact that the neonatal testis has not yet taken up the investment of the processus vaginalis that will later form its anterior and postero-lateral coverings, and is rather confusingly described as undergoing 'extravaginal torsion'. (This description refers to the relationship of the testis to its coverings, rather than its recent proximity to the birth canal.) The condition thus stands apart from the generality of testicular torsion in older children, and those who choose not to operate will find ample data to justify their decision as logical, and capable of withstanding critical scrutiny.

37.79 Idiopathic scrotal oedema is an important differential diagnosis in children with a 'hot' scrotum. In this condition, the scrotal skin becomes red, oedematous and looks inflamed, although it is often non-tender. The induration is often remarkable, with scrotal skin of 1 cm thickness not being unusual. The oedema is not confined to the scrotum and often extends to the penile shaft, the groins, the contralateral hemi-scrotum and the perineum. There are generally sufficient diagnostic elements to make a confident diagnosis, avoiding surgery. The prognosis is good, but the condition may recur, and is often temporally associated with a viral infection. Idiopathic scrotal oedema is well documented, appearing in major textbooks of surgery. From the perspective of a paediatric surgeon, to operate upon a boy who exhibits only the characteristic signs of this condition would fall below the reasonable standard of care. However, if any signs inconsistent with idiopathic scrotal oedema are present, such as testicular tenderness (or diagnostic uncertainty), the reverse would be true.

Male circumcision

37.80 Although this operation has become controversial, it is still common. Many babies are circumcised for religious reasons; a few die each year as the result of haemorrhage following surgery outside hospital. But it must be recognised that bleeding and infection are also relatively common complications of circumcision within hospital, and the relative rates of complications from the entirety of the two groups is unknown. Circumcision of the healthy foreskin is also widely requested for boys by their parents who regard the circumcised penis as normal, and the uncircumcised state as unhealthy. This attitude is prevalent amongst circumcised fathers. Whether the recent observation that circumcised men are less likely to get infected with HIV during vaginal intercourse, in comparison with the non-circumcised cohort, will influence the indications for paediatric circumcision remains to be seen.

37.81 'Adult' surgeons working in district general hospitals inevitably see adults requiring circumcision, and tend to provide such surgery to any boys who present with a prepuce that is too narrow to allow emergence of the glans. This restriction of movement, and the consequent inability of the boy to pull his prepuce back over the glans are called 'phimosis'. The phimosis is usually physiological; by puberty, it will resolve, as the highly-specialised preputial skin stretches and increases in diameter sufficiently to fall back across the glans. Alternatively, and unusually in this age group, the phimosis may be caused by scarring. This will usually be the result of BXO (see para **37.86** below), or rarely, due to repeated infection.

37.82 If a child suffers repeated episodes of preputial infection that results in a thickened inelastic white ring of pathological, scarred, phimosis then the situation merits circumcision. Provided that there is no clinical sign of scarring, and the prepuce is supple, healthy and potentially elastic, there is powerful evidence to conclude that the boy will not require surgery. Parents are advised against retracting the prepuce in the bath. This is because, with the best will in the world, if his parents retract his prepuce they will stop the moment the child complains of pain. But if the boy himself retracts it he will stop the moment before it hurts. The time difference between these two moments may result in very minor tearing of the prepuce, which may result in scarring.

37.83 Paediatric surgeons tend to limit the surgery to children with preputial disease. Nevertheless, the most determined parents will obtain a circumcision at any cost, which might include sub-optimal anaesthesia and surgery; most of us will capitulate and perform the surgery. However, since the majority of paediatric circumcisions are still performed in district hospitals, it must be acknowledged that two reasonable standards indications for circumcision in children may exist. The indication for surgery should therefore be considered. Did the benefits justify the risks? Were the parents made aware of this balance, and the differences between the specialist and generalist approaches, before they agreed to the surgery?

37.84 Ritual or 'religious' circumcision also needs consideration, since surgeons are advised that of the entire panoply of surgery, this procedure, along with sterilisation, is singled out as requiring consent from both parents.

37.85 Consent includes the alternatives to treatment, so it should be mentioned that uncircumcision is advocated in the USA, where men in their mid twenties are now litigating against those who facilitated their circumcision; they claim a resultant diminution of sexual satisfaction. Consent should also acknowledge the risks of bleeding and infection post-operatively, together with the recognition that the post-operative penis often becomes swollen, bruised, battered and inflamed for several weeks after the surgery. This can be most alarming if the parents and child are not forewarned.

37.86 A small number of children have an unarguable indication for circumcision, balanitis xerotica obliterans (BXO). This is a scarring condition of the foreskin, histologically akin to its female equivalent, lichen sclerosis et atrophicus, and is progressive. It represents the main 'medical' indication for circumcision, because it can result in complete obstruction to urinary flow if left untreated. Even after the circumcision is performed, it is mandatory to follow the children in out patients for a prolonged period because the disease sometimes involves the underlying meatus, giving narrowing and outflow obstruction. An arrangement for outpatient review of a clinical diagnosis of BXO (or if subsequent histology confirms the disease in an asymptomatic patient) is necessary to conform to the reasonable standard of care. The anxiety about missing this diagnosis stems from the loss of opportunity for follow up to identify the urinary diagnosis early. This is now considered so important that all excised foreskins, even if clinically normal, are sent for histological analysis.

37.87 The foreskin also has a major role to play in reconstructive penile surgery, particularly for hypospadias. If a child is born with an anatomical abnormality of the penis, circumcision is contraindicated; otherwise valuable skin will be wasted. Circumcision is relatively straightforward, although damage to the underlying glans occasionally occurs due to faulty technique.

A common complaint is that too little or too much skin is removed. The former may result in 'baggy' skin; the latter in excessively tight skin. It should be recognised that the post-operative appearance of the circumcised penis can be horrifying in the early stages. Once the inflammation is settled, parents may still be dissatisfied with the result. However, there is such wide variation in the circumcised appearance throughout the UK that an expert will be wary of pronouncing a 'bad' result in all but extreme cases. This does not apply to excessively tight skin or glanular damage, which would both be regarded as avoidable. Excessively tight shaft skin is of far greater functional importance, because it may result in painful erections.

37.88 The use of unipolar diathermy (an electrocoagulation technique to stop bleeding) is absolutely contraindicated, because of the danger of inadvertently coagulating the main vessels in the penis. If penile damage occurred during the surgery, the use of unipolar diathermy would usually indicate a fall below the reasonable standard. The use of post-operative dressings is very variable, although if they are used, removal often causes both pain and bleeding and can be most traumatic for both child and parents.

37.89 Another complication of circumcision is meatal stenosis, probably caused by damage to the blood supply of the external urinary meatus. Although particularly noted after surgery for BXO, meatal stenosis can occur after any circumcision. Its presence does not necessarily indicate a lapse in the standard of care, but failure to warn the parents of its clinical features does. The signs and symptoms of meatal stenosis include the passage of an increasingly fine urinary stream, which may be associated with straining. The micturition time becomes prolonged and there may be associated spraying. Should the stenosis remain undiagnosed, incomplete bladder emptying and subsequent urinary tract infection may be a result. Meatal stenosis is usually remedied by simple dilatation under anaesthesia and thus it is important that it should be referred back early.

Hypospadias

37.90 The condition of hypospadias usually encompasses three main abnormalities. First, the meatus (distal opening) of the urethra is placed in an abnormal site on the underneath (ventrum) of the penis, rather than at the penile tip. The consequence of this is that the urinary stream may be fragmented into a spray, and will tend to pass directly downward. Thus a small boy may well pass urine on to his feet, or the feet of the person standing next to him when he is trying to aim for the wall. This obviously gives significant social difficulties as well as the practical difficulties in passing the entire urinary stream accurately into a lavatory bowl.

37.91 Second, there is a substantial flap of dorsal skin, instead of the ring of skin that constitutes the normal foreskin (prepuce). If this is left untreated, the skin will hang rather like a flag off the end of the penis and may cause significant embarrassment. In some children with hypospadias, there is the additional abnormality of 'scrotal engulfment', where the root of the penis appears to be rather low, set between the upper parts of the right and left side of the scrotum. If this is not recognised pre-operatively, the eventual result may be poor, with persistent tethering of the ventral skin.

37.92   Third, because of such tight ventral skin, boys with untreated hypospadias may suffer bent erections. This may clearly give them difficulty with coitus later on.

37.93   In boys with hypospadias, it is crucial that the testes are examined. If one or both are absent, an intersex state may be present. In this situation, it is mandatory to check the sex chromosomes, to ensure that the patient is a genetic male, and not a masculinised girl. Failure to recognise this situation may lead to the patient's death, or at the very least, completely inappropriate surgery.

37.94   Hypospadias surgery is usually performed between 12–18 months of age. The surgery involves creating a neo-urethra between the congenital hypospadiac meatus and a new position at the apex of the glans. At the same time, the glans is formed into a conical shape with the meatus placed centrally. The preputial skin is re-arranged so that the substantial dorsal component is brought round to the ventrum. This transfer of skin enables any ventral tightness to be abolished and for any scrotal engulfment to drop back into the correct site. The net result of moving more skin ventrally is to abolish any tendency to bent erections.

37.95   This surgery is not without complications. The main difficulty is that the newly-fashioned urethra may leak at some site along its length and a fistula may become established. The meatus of the neo-urethra may also become tight and meatal dilatation is occasionally necessary in the first few post-operative years. The substantial transfer of skin to the ventrum may also be associated with skin flap failure and this again may need further surgery to ensure adequate skin cover. The overall burden of complications in hypospadias approaches 10 per cent; apart from early meatal dilatation, secondary operation is almost invariably delayed to allow the swelling from the first operation to resolve. In practical terms this means that any re-operation occurs at least six months after the first attempt at correction. With such a high baseline complication rate (compared with other surgical procedures), it can be seen that even in ideal surgical circumstances, an imperfect outcome does not necessarily speak for itself, when considering liability of the surgeon.

37.96   In the first post-operative week a urethral stent is left in situ and this will either drip into the nappy (in infants) or be drained into a urinary bag in older children. The stent is removed after one week. Until the tube is removed prophylactic antibiotics, antispasmodics and aperients are given. The penis is grossly swollen for several weeks after surgery and it is not until the end of about two months that the residual swelling and bruising has resolved. Given all these potential difficulties, most children end up with a normal appearance and normal urinary function. Hypospadias surgery has improved dramatically over the past ten years, with the advent of procedures based on a better understanding of the anatomical defect, and a more standardised approach to post-operative care. Many children operated on in the 1980s and early 1990s had serious complications, and hypospadias surgery exemplifies the rule that standards should be viewed in the context of their era.

Neonatal gut obstruction

37.97   This is a topic that merits a chapter of its own, since it is caused by a wide variety of pathologies, for which there are diverse treatments, each with pitfalls that may have devastating consequences. However, they have a common theme, and a single imperative rule. If a newborn baby presents with the vomiting of a green coloured fluid, this is almost always indicative of serious surgical pathology, and invariably requires emergency referral to a neonatal surgeon.

37.98   All doctors are taught this fundamental rule during their training, although not all may learn it, and there are, sadly, some who do not act upon it. Bile is made in the liver, stored in the gallbladder and excreted into the duodenum. When it emerges from the papilla into the duodenum, it is a golden yellow colour. If, due to obstruction downstream of the duodenal papilla, the bile cannot flow distally, it will accumulate in the duodenum, and reflux back into the stomach. The acids and pepsin in the stomach act on the yellow bile and turn it green. If the obstruction is not relieved, the baby will vomit green fluid.

37.99   The vomiting itself is unlikely to kill the baby, but the cause of the obstruction may. In particular, babies may suffer a condition called mid-gut malrotation, where the bowel is imperfectly fixed to the back wall of the abdomen. The result is that the bowel is very mobile, and this configuration allows the bowel to twist, sometimes up to 760 degrees. This is a 'volvulus'. The bowel involved in the volvulus is characteristically the midgut, extending from the latter part of the duodenum, including the entire small bowel, and often the ascending colon. This has the immediate effect of blocking the bowel, just below the duodenal papilla, and causing the obstruction.

37.100   The crucial effect, however, is vascular. The corkscrew configuration of the volvulus compresses and kinks the blood vessels to the entire midgut, shutting off the blood supply and causing acute ischaemia. This bowel has a rapid cell turn over, is highly metabolically active and requires a generous blood supply for oxygen and cellular nourishment. Ischaemia can therefore result in bowel death within in a few hours. The consequence of a missed mid gut volvulus is thus death, due to infarction of the twisted segment and subsequent translocation of the gut bacteria causing septicaemia and multi-systems failure.

37.101   If the diagnosis and treatment is too late to save the gut, the baby may still survive if appropriate surgery can be performed in time. This will involve excision of the dead bowel segment. If the entire mid gut is removed, the child will be left with no capacity to absorb enteral nutrition. The only option that remains will be to feed the child parenterally with intravenous nutrition, in the hope that the baby can survive long enough for a small bowel transplant. Although there is now a measurable short-term success rate for this therapy, the life-long consequences of bowel transplantation are unknown. In the meantime, many babies die of their parental nutrition, since prolonged intravenous feeding causes hepatic failure, and this is exacerbated by the inevitable CVC infections that will occur during the time the child is awaiting transplantation.

37.102 For this reason, if no other, all doctors should be aware of the dangers of midgut volvulus, and the paramount importance of its cardinal sign: green vomiting. Other causes of gut obstruction in newborns include Hirschsprung's disease, meconium ileus, gut atresia, inguinal hernias and duplication cysts; but due to the timescale of its natural history, it is midgut volvulus that must be recognised beyond all others.

STANDARDS OF PRACTICE

37.103 Standard setting in this speciality is still in its infancy. Since we deal with all aspects of the general surgery of children, most procedures are low volume, making generalised standard setting difficult. The mortality rates are minuscule and morbidity, such as wound infection, bleeding and venous thromboembolism, rare. The commonest setting for perioperative death (usually a powerful measure of performance, and thus amenable to standard setting) is in neonatal surgery, where the co-morbidities of prematurity and congenital malformation provide too many variables to allow operator- or system-dependent errors to be identified that could be remedied by setting clinical standards.

CHECKLIST

37.104

- Any neonate vomiting green fluid may be gravely ill and requires emergency management.
- Hypospadias surgery, although commonly performed, is sufficiently difficult for some of the post-operative complications to be regarded as unavoidable.
- All foreskins excised during circumcision should be subjected to histological analysis, for fear of missing balanitis xerotica obliterans.
- Idiopathic scrotal oedema is a recognisable diagnosis, and does not merit scrotal exploration.
- Neonatal testicular torsion is managed differently from torsion in other age groups.
- Boys in whom testicular torsion cannot be excluded must invariably have the scrotum explored.
- The conservative management of undescended testis in two year olds is inappropriate.
- 'Gallows traction' is an inappropriate, ineffective and unsafe treatment for obstructed infant hernias.
- Umbilical hernias rarely require treatment, unless the child is being teased.
- Parents need to be made aware of the signs and dangers of adhesion obstruction.

–   Appendicitis can be difficult to diagnose in children.
–   Intussusception is a fatal disease if missed, but can be easily diagnosed if appropriately investigated.
–   Babies with pyloric stenosis may die of post-operative apnoeas if not fully resuscitated preoperatively.
–   There is no rigid rule as to when the biopsy of persistent lymphadenopathy becomes mandatory.

CHAPTER 38

Neonatology

Professor A Michael Weindling

Professor John S Wyatt

THE SCOPE OF THE SPECIALITY

38.1   Newborn babies are not just small adults. They present particular challenges because of immaturity: the human may be delivered and survive after only slightly less than 60 per cent of gestation. It is the only species where life can be supported while the individual still has important organs (eg the lungs, heart, kidneys, gastrointestinal tract, and skin) that may not be mature enough to function without special help. Some diseases uniquely affect premature individuals, eg respiratory distress syndrome due to surfactant deficiency and bronchopulmonary dysplasia (diseases of the lungs), necrotising enterocolitis (a disease of the bowel), periventricular haemorrhage and periventricular leukomalacia (diseases of the brain), and retinopathy of prematurity (a disease of the eye).

38.2   Neonatology is the term given to the hospital-based speciality where care is given to newborn babies. It is at the interface of fetal medicine and obstetric practice and general paediatrics, and this is reflected by a continuum, whereby an adverse event before birth might lead to clinical manifestations after birth and disabilities in later childhood. Neonatologists have the expertise to assess and treat newborns' particular medical problems and use equipment that is designed specifically for the tiniest patients.

38.3   The newborn baby is cared for by the specialist paediatrician and a team of specialist nurses, who are responsible for care from the moment of birth. Until then, the care of the unborn baby is the responsibility of the obstetrician and midwife; they may discuss the best approach to care of an unborn baby with a paediatrician if the problems are complex (eg extreme prematurity or multiple congenital abnormalities), but remain responsible for the care of the mother and her unborn baby. The neonatal paediatrician, or neonatologist, looks after the infant from delivery until discharge from hospital. Many also have follow-up clinics, but if any further specialist services are required (eg physiotherapy, cardiology, neurology), they are provided by other hospital-based specialists.

What a neonatologist does

38.4   If a problem is identified before birth, the obstetrician may consult with a neonatologist during the pregnancy. A neonatal paediatrician should therefore have an understanding of the complexities of antenatal care, while not actually being responsible for its delivery. Most newborn babies (over 90 per cent) are healthy and do not require specialist care. However, if a baby is premature, or has a serious illness, injury, or birth defect identified before delivery, a neonatologist may be present at delivery and is responsible for the baby's subsequent care.

38.5   It is axiomatic that care should be provided by a person who is competent to provide that care. Thus a consultant, or a medically-qualified trainee (formerly known as a senior house officer or registrar, now known as a speciality trainee (ST)), or a specialist nurse (a neonatal nurse or an advanced neonatal nurse practitioner (ANNP)) who attends a delivery to resuscitate a baby should all have the same set of skills, ie skills appropriate for the effective resuscitation of the newborn baby.

38.6   Every newborn baby will be examined during the hours after birth and details of this examination are discussed below. Neonatal paediatricians are responsible for this examination being properly carried out. However, most of their time is spent caring for babies born very prematurely (from around 23 weeks of gestation) and for those born close to term but in a poor condition, usually because of hypoxic ischaemia ('hypoxia' means shortage of oxygen and 'ischaemia' means a reduced blood supply). Usually the latter leads to the former, as, for example, when the umbilical cord which carries blood providing oxygen and nutrients from the placenta to the baby, becomes obstructed. Sometimes these babies are referred to as having been 'asphyxiated', a term which originally meant pulseless, but which more recently has been used to describe a baby who is born with cardiorespiratory depression. This is discussed in more detail below.

38.7   In summary, neonatologists provide the following services:

- care for the newly born baby delivered by Caesarean section or other operative means (eg forceps or ventouse suction) that require specialist medical intervention in the delivery room because of issues relating to the health of the mother or unborn baby;
- the diagnosis and treatment of newborns with conditions such as breathing disorders, infections, and birth defects;
- the coordination of care and the medical management of babies born prematurely, critically ill, or in need of surgery (although the surgery should be performed by a specialist paediatric surgeon);
- ensuring that critically ill newborn babies receive proper nutrition to promote appropriate growth.

The training

38.8   A neonatologist has trained as a general paediatrician. In the UK, this means a period of postgraduate training of about ten years after qualification. A consultant neonatologist would be expected to be skilled in the care of sick newborn infants, ie in their resuscitation and in their ongoing care. Resuscitation and subsequent care will be administered by a team of junior doctors (who are all trainees) and specialist nurses under the leadership of the consultant neonatologist.

38.9   In a smaller district general hospital (DGH) providing fewer than about 2,000 deliveries a year, the care of the newborn will be led by a general paediatrician, usually one with a special interest in the care of the newborn. But in a larger DGH (some have more than 5,000 births a year, and some more than 8,000), care of the newborn will be by a team of consultant neonatologists, junior doctors and specialist nurses.

The relationship with other specialists

38.10   The neonatologist provides medical expertise and coordinates the deployment of other specialists: radiologists, paediatric surgeons and neurosurgeons, paediatric cardiologists, pathologists (biochemists, microbiologists, haematologists). It would represent a failure of care if a neonatologist did not make a referral to the appropriate specialist.

The scope of the speciality and its risks

38.11   Neonatologists are responsible for the care of infants who have often been born in a poor condition (because of preceding intrauterine adverse events) or who are vulnerable because of their extreme prematurity before structural and functional maturity has been achieved. This vulnerability means that the small patient is often exposed to a wide range of invasive treatments and procedures, most of which carry inherent risks of complications. Parental expectations, fuelled by good news stories in the news media, are high, and when things do not go well explanations that focus on 'unavoidability' often will not suffice, especially when the result is a disabled child. The forensic study of the course and quality of the care to which the baby was subjected involves the careful examination of the medical record and establishment of a clear line of causation. To complicate matters, a baby that was born in a very poor condition because of prenatal or intrapartum adversity, will be subjected to the full deployment of intensive care procedures, all of which are potentially hazardous.

The two key sources of information in this forensic examination are the medical records, which should include the maternal record so that a clear understanding of events leading up to the birth of the baby may be obtained, and any autopsy report.

THE NEONATAL MEDICAL RECORD

The clinical record

38.12   Medical experts and lawyers rely on the clinical records when they reconstruct events, and should be aware of some of the pitfalls in interpreting entries in the records. The records are important in establishing an accurate chronology, as even parents' memories may be flawed given the passage of time and the very disturbing events that they are trying to remember. However, lawyers and the assisting experts should be aware that even if entries in the records include a time in the left-hand margin, it is often unclear whether this reflects the true time of occurrence or the time the note was written. Consideration of the nursing records and charts may provide additional useful information.

38.13   Sometimes the records repeat a list of problems at the time (eg respiratory distress, oedema, anaemia etc); the house officer may simply copy this list from one day to the next, and it becomes difficult to know which medical problems are old and which are new. In these circumstances more information can be obtained by reviewing the intensive care charts which the nurses complete and which generally provide hourly information on cardiorespiratory vital signs.

38.14   Laboratory investigation forms are an additional source of information about the timing of events as they sometimes include the time a specimen was received in the laboratory. Allowance needs to be made for delays in the specimen reaching the laboratory. Chest X-rays remain the most common imaging investigation on neonatal units and the films generally include a date and time stamp.

38.15 Although the intentional alteration of medical records in order to deceive is extremely rare, overwriting of numbers due to error is common and the result may be indecipherable, especially when photocopied records are examined.

The perinatal autopsy

38.16 A properly carried out perinatal autopsy is an important source of information that allows for a good understanding of the cause of a stillbirth or neonatal death. The rate of neonatal autopsies has declined, and this may be because the doctor asking for consent is not convinced about the usefulness of this investigation. Although these days parents may decline an autopsy for religious reasons or because they feel the baby 'has been through enough', the results of an autopsy have been shown to change a diagnosis or provide important additional information in 22–76 per cent of cases. If confirmation of clinical findings is also considered, then perinatal autopsy has been shown to have value in up to 100 per cent of cases[1]. Porter and Keeling[2] found that autopsy examination showed clinically important information that had not been recognised during life in 66 cases (44 per cent of cases in their series). Histological examination of tissues was essential for making or confirming the pathological diagnosis in 20 per cent of all perinatal deaths. A study in Scotland showed that parents who consented to autopsy gave many reasons for agreeing, but the principal one was to obtain answers to their questions, with a desire to help others being the second most common motivation[3].

1 Gordijn, Erwich, Khong 'Value of perinatal autopsy: critique' (2002) 5 Pediatr Dev Pathol 480–488.
2 Porter and Keeling 'Value of perinatal necropsy examination' (1987) 40(2) J Clin Pathol 180–184.
3 McHaffie, Fowlie, Hume, Laing, Lloyd, Lyon 'Consent to autopsy for neonates' (2001) 85(1) Arch Dis Child Fetal Neonatal F4–F7.

38.17 The perinatal autopsy must be carried out in a rigorous manner by a competent pathologist, ie one who has been properly trained and who follows a standardised approach, such as that described by the Society of Obstetricians and Gynaecology of Canada[1]. The pathologist's approach to the autopsy must be systematic. The autopsy of a fetus or newborn baby differs critically from one that is performed on an adult in that anatomical normality cannot be assumed, and normal as well as abnormal findings need to be described and photographed. Organs and the baby need to be measured or weighed to investigate for intrauterine growth restriction and a genetic abnormality. The autopsy report should include a clinical summary and a clinico-pathologic discussion, ie a narrative relating the pathological findings to the clinical course. Published guidelines are available[2].

1 Désilets, Oligny 'Fetal and perinatal autopsy in prenatally diagnosed fetal abnormalities with normal karyotype' (2011) JOGC 1047.
2 Hutchins, Berman, Moore, Hanzlick, The Autopsy Committee of the College of American Pathologists 'Practice guidelines for autopsy pathology: autopsy reporting' (1999) 123 Arch Pathol Lab Med 1085–1092.

38.18 A careful general external examination is of particular importance if permission for an autopsy is declined. Ideally, it should be performed and documented by an experienced clinician and the presence or absence of major fetal external malformation should be recorded.

38.19 At autopsy, all major organs must be weighed and organ maturity and structure assessed. Histological examination must look for changes that could indicate a storage disease or an intrauterine infection (TORCH: toxoplasmosis, other infections, rubella, cytomegalovirus, herpes simplex virus).

38.20 Skin biopsy for fibroblast cultures may allow future genetic studies, and this is particularly important these days as modern genetic techniques become more sensitive and accurate. This can be done with appropriate parental consent even if consent for a full autopsy is withheld. If appropriate samples of muscle and from the central nervous system are taken, a neuropathologist may subsequently be able to provide a diagnosis. Myopathies (inherited disorders of muscle) should be suspected if a fetus shows stigmata of in utero dyskinesia such as multiple contractures in association with polyhydramnios.

38.21 The placental examination is useful in establishing whether there was intrauterine infection, which may have precipitated premature labour. Macroscopic examination is divided into portions of the placenta: umbilical cord, extraplacental membranes, and the placental disc (fetal surface, maternal surface, and the cut surface). Careful examination may distinguish between amniotic fluid infection, which may cause both fetal and maternal inflammation, and blood-born placental infection. In a multiple pregnancy, examination of the dividing membranes separating the fetuses is required to establish chorionicity. When a twin-to-twin transfusion is suspected, injection studies of the fetal vessels may demonstrate abnormal vascular communications.

Standard X-rays done post-mortem may reveal unsuspected fractures or a pneumothorax (see below). Some advocate the use of radiography in every fetal or perinatal death.

38.22 Microbiological culture should also be performed and toxicological investigations should be considered, especially if the death is unexpected. Fluid (blood, cerebrospinal fluid) and tissues (spleen or lung) can be used for bacterial or viral cultures. Increasingly, morphologic studies aided by molecular techniques may assist in the identification of pathogenic organisms. When indicated, blood, urine, bile, and liver can be submitted to the appropriate toxicology laboratory.

38.23 All babies with congenital malformations should have cytogenetic analyses performed if these were not done antenatally. A frozen tissue sample (liver, placenta) provides a source of DNA, RNA, proteins and molecules that can be used in a variety of ways. Targeted molecular testing can later be performed if autopsy findings suggest a specific genetic syndrome. Newer approaches include microarrays and whole genome sequencing array; the possible contribution of these new molecular tools in providing a diagnosis that may explain a child's neurodevelopmental delay must form part of the thought processes of the legal team. The opinion of a medical geneticist may be vital.

STANDARDS OF CARE IN THE DELIVERY ROOM AND RESUSCITATION

Resuscitation and birth asphyxia

38.24   Most newborn babies cry and breathe spontaneously within several seconds of being born, but around 10 per cent require some sort of intervention and about one per cent need extensive resuscitation. All newborn infants must have their vital signs carefully assessed at birth. Assessment is generally made by recording the Apgar score (see the table in para **38.25** below). Virginia Apgar, an American obstetric anaesthetist working in New York, published her proposal for a score to assess the health of newly born babies in 1953. At that time there was great variation in resuscitation practices, which were not based on any detailed evaluation of the newborn infant. The Apgar score is generally used. It is based on an infant's condition in the minutes after birth. It comprises five signs (heart rate, respiratory effort, skin colour, muscle tone, and reflex activity). Zero, one or two points are awarded for each sign when the baby is one, five and ten minutes old. In practice the staff do not calculate the score to decide whether an infant needs resuscitation, and the need for resuscitation is driven primarily by whether or not the infant breathes promptly after birth and the heart rate.

38.25   The advantage of the Apgar score is that it is universally recorded. Its disadvantage is that staff attending a resuscitation do not pause to consider the score at one, five and ten minutes after birth, but sit down after the hurly-burly of the resuscitation and try to remember what the baby's condition was like at those times. Thus, the Apgar score is rather impressionistic. From a medico-legal viewpoint, it is therefore not worth debating whether a score of eight is substantially better than a score of, say, six. However, it is true to say that a baby with a score of seven and above is in a reasonably good condition, while one with a score of zero or one is barely alive, a score of one indicating that the only sign of life is a slowly beating heart.

Score/Sign	0	1	2
Heart rate	Undetectable	<100/min	>100 /min
Respiratory effort	Poor	Gasping	Normal
Skin colour	White	Blue (cyanosed)	Pink
Muscle tone	Absent, floppy	Diminished (hypotonic)	Normal
Reflex activity	Absent	Poor	Normal

38.26   The condition of a baby at the time of delivery is important when considering causation of later neurodisability. A baby who is close to death at the moment of delivery must have been placed in that state by preceding events, ie events during labour or earlier. Other features of the baby's subsequent condition will add further weight to the contention that the poor condition at birth was caused by hypoxic ischaemia. In this context long-hand documentation of an infant's heart rate, colour, and respiratory activity, noting the times at which the signs improve, provide an even clearer picture.

38.27 A baby who is not breathing is described as apnoeic. A baby who does not breathe after delivery is described as having primary or terminal apnoea. The difference is important. A baby in primary apnoea will not breathe and will be blue with normal muscle tone, heart rate and reflex responses, ie with an Apgar score of 5–7. By contrast, a baby who is in terminal apnoea will have a slowing heart rate, and will be unresponsive, floppy and pale (the condition used to be called asphyxia pallida, while primary apnoea was known as asphyxia livida).

38.28 When a baby's condition at birth is mildly depressed, this may be caused by drugs given to the mother (sedatives or anaesthetic agents), or, more commonly, by a mild degree of hypoxia sustained during labour. With each uterine contraction the placental vascular bed is compressed and oxygen transfer across the placenta is transiently impaired. At birth, the infant is slow to breathe but the heart rate is usually >100/minute, and the skin appears cyanosed rather than pale. The provision of positive pressure ventilation with a bag and mask usually provokes a few gasps followed by regular breathing, and then the infant becomes pink, the gasping respirations occurring before oxygen delivery to the body. This relatively common degree of depression, primary apnoea, is harmless.

An infant who has suffered severe fetal hypoxia will generally have a heart rate <100/minute, appears pale and has no spontaneous breathing or may be gasping (see below).

38.29 Infants who are severely depressed at birth require prompt positive pressure ventilation, and the most effective way of giving this is through an endotracheal tube following intubation. The endotracheal tube is normally connected to a bagging device. Positive pressure ventilation can also be given through an infant-sized facemask, and this is what normally happens as a short-term measure prior to intubation. Whichever method is used, the operator must check to ensure that there is symmetrical movement of the chest wall and that breath sounds can be heard equally on both sides of the chest by auscultation. This should be documented.

38.30 The Apgar score must be interpreted with care; it is a sensitive measure of well-being but not specific: a high score excludes significant birth hypoxia but a low score does not confirm it. A baby who is born in a depressed state because of hypoxia must have been hypoxic before birth. The timing and duration of an hypoxic ischaemia injury and whether delivery should have been expedited is often a matter of legal interest. In addition to the condition of a baby at birth, other indicators of fetal hypoxic ischaemia are: (a) those that occur before birth, ie loss of fetal movements, an abnormal CTG, a low fetal pH as measured by a fetal scalp blood sample, a low umbilical cord arterial pH; and (b) postnatal indicators that occur after birth, ie an hypoxic ischaemia encephalopathy (HIE), acidosis (due to the accumulation of lactic acid because of anaerobic respiration), and markers of organ injury (eg a rise in blood creatinine concentration due to renal damage).

Failure to respond to resuscitation

38.31 Even the most experienced paediatrician will find it difficult to intubate an infant from time to time, and more than one attempt may be needed. The important thing is for the clinician to recognise that the tube is in the wrong place and to take appropriate action. Between attempts, the infant should be supported by ventilation through a facemask. Infants with a heart rate <40/minute require external cardiac massage.

38.32 If there is difficulty in intubating, or the endotracheal tube is blocked or misplaced (either by being obstructed by a plug of mucus or a blood clot, misplacement in the oesophagus or by being inserted too far into the trachea and entering one of the bronchi, usually on the right side), the operator needs to recognise this by observing for chest wall movements and auscultating both sides of the chest, and take appropriate action. Between attempts at intubation it is important that ventilation is given through a facemask. Repeated attempts at intubation while allowing the infant progressively to deteriorate is inexcusable. Getting an airway established is critical for proper resuscitation. The mantra that is taught is A-B-C-D: Airway, Breathing, Circulation, Drugs. These days (from around 2010 onwards) the expectation is that the resuscitation team should be competent at advanced resuscitation (ie intubation and cardiovascular support) and should include at least one member who has a neonatal life support (NLS) certificate. The use of drugs during resuscitation is of secondary importance to the provision of effective positive pressure ventilation and cardiac massage where indicated. There is no reliable evidence to suggest that the use of adrenaline given through the endotracheal tube or subcutaneously is helpful, although it is commonly administered to infants who have severe bradycardia.

38.33 An attendant who has the appropriate skills to assess the need for resuscitation and to provide it must be present at all deliveries. When there is a perceived risk that resuscitation might be required the attendant will normally be a member of the paediatric team who has appropriate skills in advanced resuscitation. Local policies differ with respect to the indications for requesting the attendance of a paediatrician but will normally include very preterm births, Caesarean sections, instrumental deliveries carried out because of actual or impending fetal distress, and the antenatal diagnosis of certain congenital abnormalities.

38.34 Infants who have suffered a very severe episode of near-total fetal hypoxia may be moribund or effectively stillborn with an absent heart beat and their vital signs may not improve in spite of skilled attempts at resuscitation. However, the majority of infants with birth asphyxia do not fall into this category and if they do not respond adequately to resuscitation it may be due to problems with the resuscitation technique or failure to recognise an additional disorder.

38.35 A tension pneumothorax (qv) sustained during resuscitation generally presents as respiratory distress but in some cases where there is considerable postnatal hypoxaemia, respiratory drive may remain depressed and a pneumothorax may be overlooked. Auscultation of the chest, ie listening for symmetry of breath sounds when positive pressure ventilation is given, is important. If the diagnosis is suspected, transillumination of the chest may be helpful and if there is any doubt 'needling' of chest can be done pending an urgent chest X-ray.

38.36 Congenital abnormalities involving the lungs are often identified by antenatal ultrasound imaging, but may present unexpectedly postnatally. These disorders are generally large space-occupying lesions within the thorax and one of the most common is congenital diaphragmatic hernia. As with a large pneumothorax the diagnosis can be suspected by auscultation of the lungs, listening for asymmetry of breath sounds and by noting whether the apex beat is displaced. Loss of the normal abdominal protuberance resulting in a scaphoid abdomen may be observed, reflecting displacement of bowel mass into the thorax. An urgent chest X-ray secures the diagnosis.

38.37 Haemorrhagic shock is easily overlooked at resuscitation when pallor may be attributed to circulatory impairment due to severe preceding fetal hypoxia. One clue to the diagnosis of haemorrhage is that a tachycardia, rather than bradycardia, is present. The baby looks very pale and the peripheral circulation will be shut down. The most usual cause is feto-maternal haemorrhage where the fetus has lost blood into the maternal circulation through placental vessels where the fetal and maternal circulations are in very close proximity (which is how gases (oxygen and carbon dioxide) and nutrients pass between fetus and mother). Treatment is by urgent blood transfusion.

Hypothermia

38.38 Newborn infants, especially those who are preterm or underweight, rapidly lose heat after birth. A baby who is sick because of cardiovascular collapse (which includes those who have been exposed to severe hypoxic ischaemia) will have poor circulation because of myocardial dysfunction and peripheral circulatory shutdown, and will also be cold. However, allowing an infant to become hypothermic can aggravate or even precipitate circulatory and metabolic problems. The delivery room should feel comfortably warm and infants should be dried immediately after birth and covered with clothing or blankets. The use of carefully graduated and controlled hypothermia as a neuroprotective intervention in term infants at risk of hypoxic-ischaemic brain injury is discussed below.

Hypoxic-ischaemic brain injury

38.39 The fetal and neonatal brain depends on a constant supply of oxygen and glucose to maintain cellular integrity and function. The placenta provides oxygen and glucose to the fetus, transported in the blood flow of the umbilical vein. During labour, flow in the umbilical vein diminishes during uterine contractions and hence oxygen delivery can only occur in the intervals between uterine contractions. If uterine contractions exceed five in 10 minutes there is an increasing risk of progressive fetal hypoxia. Syntocinon increases the frequency, duration and force of uterine contractions and hence its use during labour always carries a risk of causing or exacerbating fetal hypoxia.

38.40 During the second stage of labour, maternal pushing and breath-holding, coupled with descent of the fetal head through the birth canal leading to an increased risk of mechanical compression of the umbilical cord, are often associated with a deterioration in fetal oxygenation.

38.41 The healthy fetus has adaptive mechanisms to resist the effects of fetal hypoxia. Circulatory changes ensure that cerebral and heart muscle blood flow is maintained at the expense of the other organs. In the presence of sufficient oxygen, respiration is described as aerobic and glycogen stores in muscle and liver are broken down to glucose to maintain cerebral and cardiac function. Anaerobic metabolism (metabolism in the absence of oxygen) leads to the further breakdown of glucose to lactic acid, releasing energy to maintain cellular function at the expense of increasing acidosis. It is only when these adaptive mechanisms are overwhelmed that permanent brain cellular injury results.

Terminology

38.42 At a cellular level hypoxia (shortage of oxygen) and ischaemia (shortage of blood supply) are inextricably inter-linked. Ischaemia leads to tissue hypoxia. Hypoxia causes circulatory failure which leads to ischaemia. Hence the preferred term by academics and clinicians for brain injury that results from this mechanism is hypoxic-ischaemic brain injury. The older term 'asphyxia' is still frequently employed. However this term is fundamentally ambiguous, because it may refer either to the clinical state of cardiorespiratory depression seen in newborn babies or to the underlying physiological process of hypoxic ischaemia. Hence the description of a baby as 'asphyxiated' at birth is semantically and forensically unclear.

Two patterns of brain injury

38.43 In infants born around term gestation (37–42 weeks) who sustain permanent brain injury due to a damaging episode of severe hypoxic ischaemia, two distinct pathological patterns of injury have been detected. They are usually referred to as: (a) 'acute profound' or 'acute near-total' injury; and (b) 'chronic partial' or 'prolonged partial' injury.

Acute profound pattern

38.44 Tissue damage is symmetrical and concentrated in the deep grey matter of the brain, including the basal ganglia and the thalami. The hippocampi may also be damaged. In addition a localised region of the cortex and sub-cortical white matter, adjacent to the lateral sulcus (the peri-rolandic or peri-sylvian region), is frequently involved.

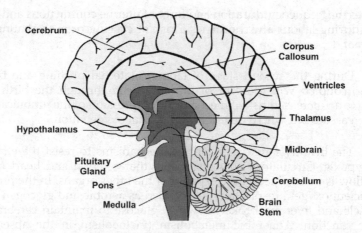

The brain in sagittal section. From http://i.livescience.com/ images/i/000/039/849/original/shutterstock_83941303.jpg?1367880927.

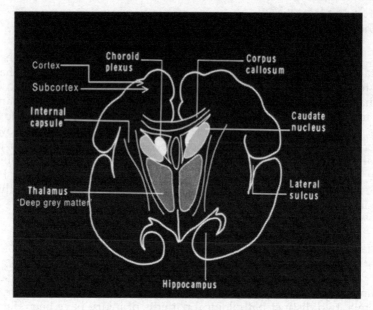

The brain in coronal section (author's own image)

38.45 These regions are known to have a high metabolic rate in the mature fetal brain close to term and hence they are thought to be most vulnerable to a profound and sudden drop in blood and oxygen supply. In the more minor forms of injury the remainder of the brain tissue is spared and relatively normal cerebral development and head growth after birth is common. Children who sustain this form of injury usually develop a characteristic form of cerebral palsy, known as dyskinetic or athetoid cerebral palsy. This is associated with involuntary movements and motor incoordination. Problems of swallowing and articulation are also common. Cognitive function may be normal depending on the degree to which the cerebral cortex and white matter are spared.

38.46 In the most severe forms of acute profound injury, widespread infarction (tissue death) occurs throughout the cerebral hemispheres, leading to encephalomalacia and subsequent failure of head growth or microcephaly. These children are likely to be profoundly disabled with severe four limb cerebral palsy, global developmental delay, epilepsy and sensory impairment, leading to a very high level of dependence and care requirements.

38.47 This form of injury is particularly associated with an acute catastrophic event during labour leading to a total or near-total interruption in oxygen and blood supply (sometimes described as a 'sentinel' event). Uterine rupture, massive placental abruption and cord prolapse are all recognised causes. Shoulder dystocia (qv), leading to a prolonged interval between the delivery of the head and that of the body, is also a recognised cause of acute profound injury. Cranial MRI studies of term infants who have sustained a sentinel event prior to delivery have confirmed the preponderance of central grey matter injury in this population[1].

1 Okereafor (et al) 'Patterns of brain injury in neonates exposed to perinatal sentinel events' (2008) 121(5) Paediatrics 906–914.

38.48 Infants delivered following a sentinel event show a characteristic pattern of severe cardiorespiratory depression. The heart rate is slow (less than 100 bpm) and in the most severe cases there is no detectable heart rate. There is no respiratory effort and the colour is severely cyanosed or pale. There is profound hypotonia and lack of response to stimulation.

38.49 Following the initiation of effective ventilation of the lungs there is characteristically a rapid rise in the heart rate to greater than 100 bpm, followed by an improvement in the colour. However there is frequently a further delay of several minutes or longer before regular respirations commence (when the respiratory centre in the brain stem is adequately perfused), and hypotonia and unresponsiveness may persist for minutes or hours. The delay in the initiation of respiration and neurological responsiveness reflects to some extent the severity of the preceding insult. This pattern of response is of considerable forensic importance in providing confirmatory evidence that the infant was exposed to severe hypoxic ischaemia immediately prior to delivery.

38.50 Various animal studies have attempted to reproduce the acute profound pattern of brain injury. Reference is often made to the classic experiments of Myers undertaken in fetal monkeys more than 40 years ago. Following complete occlusion of the umbilical cord, bradycardia (slowing of the heart), gasping respirations and metabolic acidosis occurred within minutes. Myers reported that limited thalamic injury was seen after 10–13 minutes and more widespread thalamic damage after 16–18 minutes. When the period of umbilical occlusion was prolonged beyond 20 minutes very severe brain injury and death were common. Other experiments on a range of animal models have demonstrated similar findings. Of particular interest was the finding in one series of studies in fetal monkeys that preceding exposure to a period of non-damaging partial hypoxic ischaemia was associated with a reduction in the duration of a superimposed acute profound insult required to cause permanent brain injury in some animals[1].

1 Rennie and Rosenbloom 'How long have we got to get the baby out?' (2011) 13 Obstetrician and Gynaecologist 169–174; Myers 'Two patterns of perinatal brain damage and their conditions of occurrence' (1972) 112 Am J Obstet Gynecol 246–276; Myers 'Four patterns of perinatal brain damage and their conditions of occurrence in primates' (1975) 10 Adv Neurol 223–234.

38.51   However it is important to recognise that it is not possible to translate precise timings in highly controlled animal experiments to human infants. The monkeys were uniformly healthy, receiving general anaesthesia throughout the insult and during resuscitation, and were exposed to precise and constant levels of hypoxic ischaemia. There are also significant differences in the anatomical development and maturational level of the brain between term fetal monkeys and human infants.

38.52   In clinical experience a high degree of variability in outcome is observed. There are a number of biological reasons for this: (a) it is likely that genetic variation within the population will influence the susceptibility of the brain to hypoxic-ischaemic injury; (b) there are likely to be individual differences in the degree to which the circulation to the brain is maintained in the presence of severe hypoxia-ischaemia; (c) there are likely to be individual differences in the degree to which anaerobic metabolism is successful in providing an alternative energy source to maintain cellular integrity during severe hypoxia-ischaemia.

38.53   Nonetheless it has become widely accepted that in term human infants a period of between about 10 and 30 minutes of total or near-total interruption in blood and oxygen delivery is sufficient to induce permanent brain injury of the acute profound pattern. It is logical to assume that insult durations towards the lower limit will tend to result in localised injury to the central grey matter without generalised hemispheric damage, whereas insults of durations approaching the upper limit will tend to cause generalised injury and very severe disability or death. The timescale to cause this profound acute pattern of hypoxic-ischaemic damage may be slightly more drawn out, but generally less than an hour.

38.54   In the unusual case of shoulder dystocia it is known that severe injury or death may result despite a relatively short interval of less than 10 minutes between delivery of the head and delivery of the body. There are a number of features of shoulder dystocia that may exacerbate the speed at which injury occurs following delivery of the head but prior to delivery of the body. These include mechanical compression of the vessels in the neck and increased hydrostatic pressure in the thorax relative to the head, impeding venous return from the brain.

38.55   Clinicians use blood gasses as a guide to a patient's condition and for treatment. The units may be mm Hg (millimetres of mercury) or kPa (kilopascals) and the conversion factor is 7.5, ie 1 kPa is 7.5 mm Hg. The most reliable measurement is from an arterial sample, but capillary and venous samples are also used. The normal arterial oxygen concentration (pO_2) is 60-85 mm Hg (8.0–11.3 kPa), and the normal carbon dioxide (CO_2) concentration in the blood (pCO_2) is 35-45 mm Hg (4.6–6.0 kPa). A measure referred to as the base excess is normally zero, and the more negative it is, the larger is the contribution to the acidosis by poor tissue perfusion; if tissue perfusion is poor (eg due to too little blood or heart failure), the baby is sometimes described as being shocked. Carbon dioxide converts to an acid and, as its concentration increases, the baby becomes increasingly acidotic, ie the number of hydrogen ions increases. The degree of acidosis is indicated by the pH, and because it is the negative logarithmic value of the hydrogen ion concentration, a lower value indicates more hydrogen ions. Acidosis is described as being respiratory if the predominant contribution is from CO_2, and metabolic if the predominant component is as a consequence of poor tissue perfusion. Cell function is most efficient when there is neither an acidosis or alkalosis. The pH value, which is normally above 7.32, falls as a result of acidosis; a pH below 7.00 indicates that a patient is close to death.

38.56   Blood samples taken from the umbilical vessels following a sentinel event frequently show a marked metabolic acidosis with pH less than 7.0 and base deficit greater than 20 mmol/L. However in cases involving abrupt and complete mechanical compression of the umbilical cord, the blood gas readings are likely to reflect the acid-base balance of the fetal circulation at the time that the cord compression commenced and hence may give paradoxically normal values. In these cases blood sampling from the neonatal circulation within the first hour of life will nearly always show a marked metabolic acidosis persisting from the time of delivery.

38.57   In cases where there has been severe but incomplete cord compression immediately prior to delivery it is common to find a significant discrepancy in the pH values obtained from the umbilical artery and vein, with a pH difference frequently greater than 0.15 pH units[1].

1 Armstrong and Stenson 'Use of umbilical cord blood gas analysis in the assessment of the newborn' (2007) 92 Archives of Diseases in Childhood (Fetal and Neonatal) F430–434.

Chronic partial pattern

38.58   Following a prolonged period (more than an hour and usually lasting several hours) of moderate or intermittent hypoxic ischaemia the regional pattern of brain damage is quite different, with injury concentrated in the cortical and subcortical regions in the arterial watershed zones between the distributions of the anterior, middle and posterior cerebral arteries.

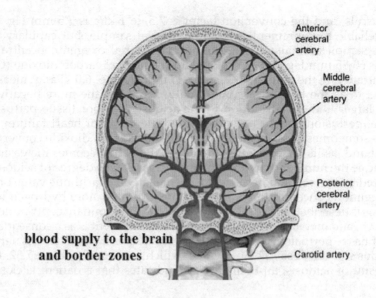

Anterior cerebral artery

Middle cerebral artery

Posterior cerebral artery

blood supply to the brain and border zones

Carotid artery

From http://1q3nfm4evj5z1sgm624e93ka.wpengine.netdna-cdn.com/
wp-content/uploads/2014/11/blood-supply-in-brain-watershed-zones.jpg

38.59   The injury is usually bilateral and symmetrical. Ulegyria, a characteristic pattern of cortical injury with damage concentrated in the depths of the sulci, is common.

38.60   The injury may range in severity from highly localised changes in watershed zones, with sparing of the remainder of the cerebral hemispheres, to generalised infarction and encephalomalacia.

38.61   The anatomical localisation of the injury is thought to represent the brain regions (watershed zones) most distant from the major arterial supplies and hence vulnerable to ischaemia because of a prolonged period of systemic hypotension and reduced cerebral blood flow.

38.62   Infants who sustain this form of injury characteristically develop symmetrical cerebral palsy of a predominantly spastic nature. Cognitive and cortical visual impairment is common and microcephaly is frequently seen because of reduced head growth over the months and years following delivery. Individuals who have purely cognitive deficits without cerebral palsy or motor impairments are unusual but they are being increasingly recognised. In these cases MRI imaging shows a localised pattern of injury within circulatory watershed zones that does not involve the motor areas.

38.63   The prolonged partial pattern of injury is commonly seen in infants who have been exposed to a long period of hypoxic ischaemia secondary to placental failure or partial abruption, intermittent cord compression, uterine hyperstimulation. It is also seen in cases where placental function has been impaired due to severe maternal illness leading to maternal hypotension. It may also occur postnatally if infants are exposed to a prolonged episode of hypotension and circulatory impairment.

38.64   Animal models of this form of injury have employed induced anaesthesia induced maternal hypotension. In one study in monkeys 2–4 hours of maternal hypotension induced diffuse brain injury similar to the chronic partial pattern observed in human term infants. Partial umbilical cord occlusion for 60 minutes or longer has produced similar injury, primarily involving the cerebral white matter. In animal models these prolonged insults are usually accompanied by a progressive decrease in blood pH to below 7.0 and an increase in base deficit to 20 mmol/L or more.

38.65   The problems in translating timings of insults from animal models into clinical practice discussed above apply just as strongly to the chronic partial form of injury. Nonetheless it has become widely accepted that in term human infants a period of at least 60 minutes of moderate partial hypoxic ischaemia is usually required before injury of the prolonged partial form will commence. In reality many infants appear to sustain damage over prolonged or intermittent insults which occur over many hours or even days. In the clinical situation with a high degree of variability between infants and in the precise nature of the insult, there does not appear to be any consistent relationship between the duration of the likely insult and the severity of the resulting brain injury.

38.66   There is ongoing clinical and scientific controversy over the likely time period over which the actual cellular injury occurs during a chronic partial insult. According to one view the prolonged period of hypoxic ischaemia causes progressive depletion of fetal reserves but circulatory collapse leading to the watershed zone injury only occurs at the end of this prolonged process and the damaging period may be as short as 20–30 minutes. According to the alternative view, an initial period of at least 60 minutes of partial hypoxic ischaemia is required to deplete the fetal reserves but following this the cellular injury accumulates progressively with time.

38.67   This controversy is obviously highly relevant to any attempt to determine the likely outcome if the prolonged partial insult had been terminated by early delivery. According to the first view, delivery after prolonged hypoxia but prior to the terminal circulatory collapse is likely to lead to a normal outcome. According to the latter view, brain injury will accumulate in an approximately linear fashion with time and hence early delivery may only lead to partial reduction in the severity of the injury.

38.68   Umbilical cord blood samples usually show a marked metabolic acidosis with little difference between venous and arterial values. However, it is important to recognise that clinical and medico-legal experience shows that severe metabolic acidosis is by no means always present in blood samples taken from the umbilical vessels, even though all the other evidence points to a prolonged partial form of injury during labour.

38.69   Several large prospective epidemiological studies compared umbilical cord pH values with evidence of brain injury. Ruth and Raivio reported a series of infants 'who had an adverse outcome with perinatal asphyxia as a possible or the most credible cause'. 93 per cent of these infants had an umbilical cord pH of >7.15[1]. Dennis and colleagues performed long-term follow-up on infants with various combinations of Apgar scores and cord pH values. Infants with low Apgar scores but normal pH values were at the greatest risk. Infants with low Apgar scores who did have evidence of umbilical cord acidosis had substantially better outcomes[2]. Retrospective studies have also indicated that a significant number of infants thought to have suffered intrapartum asphyxia did not have severe acidaemia at delivery[3]. Consideration of clinical events is important in understanding the likely course of events and their significance in an individual case.

1 Ruth and Raivio 'Perinatal brain damage: predictive value of metabolic acidosis and the Apgar score' (1988) 297 BMJ 24–27.
2 Dennis, Johnson, Mutch, Yudkin, Johnson 'Acid–base status at birth and neurodevelopmental outcome at four and one-half years' (1989) 161 Am J Obstet Gynecol 213–220.
3 Hermansen 'The acidosis paradox' (2003) 45 Dev Med & Child Neurol 353–356.

38.70 There are a number of plausible reasons for what has been termed the 'acidosis paradox'. First, as discussed above measurements taken from the umbilical vessels may not accurately reflect the fetal condition, eg if blood flow in the cord has been impeded or has ceased prior to delivery. Second, technical difficulties in obtaining reliable measurements from umbilical samples are relatively common and third, lack of glycogen stores (for example in the presence of chronic fetal growth restriction) is likely to lead to reduced generation of lactic acid in the presence of fetal hypoxic ischaemia.

Combination injuries

38.71 On occasion cranial MRI shows a regional pattern that suggests a combination of prolonged partial and acute profound patterns of injury. On theoretical grounds it is much more likely that these combination injuries are the result of a prolonged partial insult occurring over at least 60 minutes followed by superimposition of a terminal circulatory collapse which is itself reversed by resuscitation following delivery. The alternative sequence (acute profound followed by prolonged partial injury) must be extremely rare and requires an exceedingly unusual combination of events.

Fetal 'autoresuscitation'

38.72 The term 'autoresuscitation' refers to the relatively unusual circumstance in which a fetus who is exposed to a brain-damaging hypoxic-ischaemic insult recovers spontaneously, leading to cessation of the brain damaging process at some time prior to delivery. This phenomenon is generally recognised in two clinical scenarios. The first is in the context of uterine hyperstimulation due to inappropriate use of intravenous oxytocin infusions (Syntocinon). Excessively rapid and forceful uterine contractions are known to be associated with impaired placental function and progressive fetal hypoxia and acidosis. This is nearly always associated with 'pathological' CTG appearances and permanent brain injury (nearly always of the prolonged partial type) may be induced. If the oxytocin infusion is turned off, or at least significantly reduced, uterine hyperstimulation may cease, placental function recovers and fetal oxygen delivery is restored. The fetus may then be delivered in relatively good condition despite the presence of permanent brain injury.

38.73   A second clinical scenario is of severe maternal illness or injury close to the time of delivery, causing severe maternal hypotension or hypoxia. This may be associated with impaired placental function and damaging fetal hypoxic ischaemia. If the mother is resuscitated and her condition is treated effectively, placental function may improve leading to cessation of the damaging insult. Again the fetus may be delivered in relatively good condition despite the presence of permanent brain injury.

38.74   The nature and rate of physiological recovery during 'autoresuscitation', including the likely resolution of metabolic acidosis, is a matter of debate and discussion, and there is a dearth of relevant scientific evidence.

THE FIRST EXAMINATION

38.75   A midwife normally examines the newborn baby briefly in the delivery room to ensure that the infant is well and has no obvious abnormalities. In addition, it is important that a more detailed examination is carried out, generally by a paediatrician, but by any professional with appropriate training. With the expansion of midwifery-led maternity units and a policy of encouraging home births, appropriately trained (ie competent) midwives increasingly carry out these examinations. Traditionally a further examination was made shortly before discharge from the maternity unit. This has become an optional requirement because of the increasing tendency for the early discharge home of mothers who have had a normal birth without obstetric complications. The onus then falls on the community midwife and the GP to provide continuing surveillance, and if there are concerns about feeding or jaundice this must be communicated before the discharge.

38.76   The routine examination, done in the parents' presence, normally has a reassuring purpose. The examination must be properly recorded.

In the following paragraphs the importance of selected features of the routine examination will be highlighted.

Head circumference

38.77   The head circumference should be measured and documented, as it is a reflection of intrauterine brain growth. In infants who are light for dates due to intra-uterine growth restriction, head size (brain growth) is often spared. However, when growth restriction starts early in pregnancy or is very severe the head size may be proportionately small. A small head relative to birth weight may reflect an underlying developmental abnormality of the brain. An abnormally large head at birth may be a familial feature, but dilated cerebral ventricles (hydrocephalus) should be ruled out by a cranial ultrasound brain scan.

38.78   When it is alleged that a child's cerebral palsy was caused by birth asphyxia (hypoxic-ischaemic encephalopathy) one of the considerations is the rate of growth of the brain in early infancy. In severe damage acquired by any means (eg infection or hypoxic-ischaemic encephalopathy), the rate of brain growth often becomes impaired, culminating in a relatively small head by the age of six months or so. It is helpful in these circumstances to know what the head circumference was at birth as a baseline.

Facial dysmorphism

38.79 The impression that an infant has an unusual facial appearance should be supported by a carefully appraisal of the individual features documenting in what way each feature is unusual. Often when this is attempted the overall appearance may simply turn out to be part of the wide variation of normal facial appearances. If there is facial dysmorphism then it might form part of a syndrome associated with other congenital malformations and so it is especially important to examine the infant carefully with this in mind.

Birth trauma

38.80 True trauma, ie physical injury causing damage, is uncommon in clinical practice, but it is a cause for complaint and litigation.

Congenital heart disease

38.81 'Congenital' strictly means 'born with', but is generally used to refer to anatomical abnormalities that are developmental rather than acquired. In the context of medico-legal practice, it is important that such abnormalities should be recognised in a timely fashion and that appropriate action is then taken.

38.82 Most heart murmurs heard within six hours of birth in an otherwise healthy neonate are transient and not associated with congenital structural heart disease. However, congenital heart disease may present with signs that do not include a heart murmur, and a normal examination during the first few days of life does not guarantee that the infant's heart is structurally normal. The following signs may be present: subtle cyanosis especially of the lips and tongue (subtle cyanosis means the colour of raspberry yoghurt compared to strawberry yoghurt), pallor indicative of a poor cardiac output, mild respiratory distress, an apex beat felt best on the right side of the chest instead of the left (dextrocardia), absent or weak femoral pulses, and a palpable delay in the femoral pulse compared to the brachial. Any suspicion of congenital heart disease should lead to a chest X-ray and echocardiogram being carried out promptly, and an awareness of the possible co-existence of other congenital malformations.

Eyes

38.83 The eyes should be examined for a red reflex – the reflection of light from the retina. Its absence in one or both eyes may indicate congenital cataracts.

Palate

38.84 The palate should be carefully inspected for a cleft. A submucous cleft in the soft palate posteriorly can easily be overlooked. If the palate appears high-arched, or grooved it is important to palpate for a submucous cleft as well as simple inspection by eye.

Genitalia

38.85 Careful examination of the genitalia is necessary and the features to be noted in male infants are a malpositioned urethral opening (hypospadias), the degree of development of the scrotum, and whether both testes can be palpated. If the urethra is misplaced, or the scrotum is underdeveloped, and neither testes can be confidently palpated, advice from a paediatric endocrinologist must be sought and chromosome analysis carried out to determine the sex karyotype. If one or both testes are undescended and everything else looks fine then paediatric follow-up is all that is required in order to recognise testes that have not fully descended by one year so that surgery can be planned, and this is normally carried out before the age of five years.

38.86 In the female obvious signs of virilisation are easily recognised. However, the features may be subtle and include a large clitoris (common in preterm females), and partial fusion of the labioscrotal folds to resemble a scrotum. If there is any suspicion of ambiguous genitalia it is essential to be honest with parents and acknowledge uncertainty rather than offer an immediate opinion. It is important to involve a multi-disciplinary team which may include an endocrinologist, paediatric surgeon, geneticist and paediatrician so that effective counselling can be given based on a plan of investigations and the possible treatments that might be offered.

Anorectal abnormalities

38.87 The anus should be inspected for patency and position. There is an association of anal abnormalities with malformations of the large bowel and urogenital abnormalities.

Spinal abnormalities

38.88 Midline abnormalities at the bottom of the spine include dimples, hairy patches, or birthmarks. These may indicate an underlying abnormality of the vertebral column or spinal cord and lower limb function (muscle tone, movements, reflexes and sensation) and anal tone should be noted. A sacro-coccygeal pit or dimple is common and harmless. However, a pit that is above the second sacral segment may be a dermal sinus which communicates with the lining of the spinal cord and poses a risk of infection and meningitis. A neurosurgical opinion should be obtained.

Hips

38.89 The hip joints should be carefully examined for stability and dislocation, now referred to as congenital developmental dysplasia. One or both hips may be affected. Risk factors include a family history of the disorder, congenital postural deformities, female gender, breech delivery, oligohydramnios, and being the first-born. The examination is based on the methods described by Barlow (1962) and Ortalani (1937) and is well described in textbooks. Briefly, each hip joint is examined in turn with the infant lying supine and the hip flexed to 90 degrees. It is well known that a normal clinical examination in the first few days of life does not in itself rule out the possibility of the infant presenting in late infancy or early childhood with features of a congenitally dislocated hip. Some hips appear stable at first but subsequently become unstable or dislocated. The examination should be carefully documented in the medical records. Instead of relying on a tick in a box it is good practice to make a brief comment such as 'Both hips examined – Barlow/Ortalani – both stable'. Clinical examination is supplemented in many maternity units by ultrasound abnormal or not reassuring; there should be a relevant hospital guideline.

38.90 If the hip is unstable or overtly dislocated the opinion of an orthopaedic surgeon should be promptly sought so that those infants who will benefit from early splinting can be recognised. The problem with simply advising the use of a double napkin to keep the hips abducted and giving an appointment for the paediatric clinic in six weeks or so is that the patient may get lost to follow up, or may be seen by an inexperienced paediatrician who might overlook continuing instability of the joint.

38.91 Fortunately, current practice does not rely on a single screening examination soon after birth. Guidance is set out in the Department of Health publication 'Screening for the Detection of Dislocation of the Hip' (1986) recently reviewed by Shorter et al[1], which advises further examinations at 6 weeks, 6–9 months, and 15–21 months. After six weeks the Ortalani and Barlow methods no longer apply and instead the focus should be on the 'classical signs' of dislocation, which include limited abduction of the hip, leg shortening, asymmetrical posture of the hips at rest, and flattening of the buttock on the affected side when the infant is laid prone.

1 Shorter, Hong, Osborn 'Screening programmes for developmental dysplasia of the hip in newborn infants' (2011) 9 Cochrane Database of Systematic Reviews Art No CD004595. DOI: 10.1002/14651858.CD004595.pub2.

Spina bifida

38.92 Spina bifida is a developmental abnormality where during very early embryonic development there is incomplete fusion of the neural tube, which forms the spinal cord. Usually the lower back is affected, but the lesion may be higher, even in the neck at the base of the brain. There is often an associated abnormality of the brain (an Arnold-Chiari malformation) where drainage of cerebrospinal fluid is impaired and the baby develops hydrocephaly.

38.93 The opening may be covered by skin and not immediately obvious on visual inspection (spina bifida occulta); sometimes there is only a dimple or a tuft of hair that overlies the spinal abnormality; individuals affected in this way (the estimated incidence in the general population is 10–20 per cent) may be symptom-free. If the opening in the centre of the back is sufficiently large, the spinal cord may be visible or may protrude through the gap (known as a myelomeningocoele or meningomyelocoele). The effects are weakness or paralysis of the legs, incontinence of bladder and bowel, and there is associated hydrocephaly in about 90 per cent of cases and diminished cognition.

Medico-legal issues

38.94   First, the incidence of the condition has fallen markedly from around 3 cases per 100 births in the 1970s in the UK to about 0.15 per 1,000 live births in 1998. This is partly due to a better diet including folate supplementation, which reduced the incidence of spina bifida by about 70 per cent in the 1970s, and to screening by antenatal ultrasound during early pregnancy and abortion of fetuses found to have spina bifida. Some anticonvulsants, notably phenytoin, may interfere with folate metabolism. Thus there may have been failure to give advice or to screen effectively. Second, a failure to provide appropriate counselling if a fetus is found to have spina bifida. Prenatal fetal surgery is not practised in the UK. Third, appropriate postnatal surgical intervention both for the spinal lesion and for associated hydrocephaly. Fourth, failure to involve a multidisciplinary team.

Cranial synostosis (craniosynostosis)

38.95   As the baby's head passes down the birth canal during the birth process, the bones that make up the skull slide over each other. They are able to do this because they are joined by fibrous tissue, known as sutures. The resulting temporary deformation of the skull shape is known as moulding, which makes it possible for the head and the brain to change shape without being damaged. The bones that make up the skull then grow together by calcification of the sutures and this process is complete when an infant is about 15 months old.

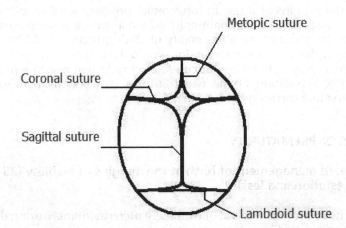

'The sutures' by Estrellita Uijl and Rob Swenker, Own work. Licensed under CC BY 3.0 via Wikimedia Commons at http://commons.wikimedia.org/wiki/File:The_sutures.jpg#/media/File:The_sutures.jpg

38.96   Craniosynostosis occurs when one or more sutures fuse prematurely. Its incidence is about 1:2,500 births. Several genetic mutations have been identified as causes of premature craniosynostosis. Biomechanical forces also play a part, and the advice to lay babies on their backs to sleep to diminish the risk of cot death has resulted in some presenting with heads that appear flattened at the back.

38.97   Since skull growth cannot occur perpendicular to the fused suture, the skull grows parallel to the line of fusion, giving rise to an abnormally shaped skull and sometimes facial features. Most common is premature fusion of the sagittal suture; this is in the centre of the skull passing between front and back and its premature fusion results in the head having an abnormally elongated shape from front to back (scaphocephaly, keel-like; or dolichocephaly, meaning elongated). The second most common line of premature fusion is along the coronal suture, which passes across the skull at the front, resulting in a flattened facial appearance. Unilateral coronal synostosis results in anterior plagiocephaly with skewing of the facial features. Trigonocephaly, premature fusion of the metopic suture, results in a narrow forehead and ridging of the suture line; the overall shape of the head when viewed from the top is triangular. Premature fusion of the lambdoid suture is most rare.

38.98   Turricephaly (tower-like or steeple head, sometimes called oxycephaly or acrocephaly) is due to premature fusion of two suture lines, the coronal and lamdoid, and results in an abnormally conical or pointed shape of the head.

Medico-legal issues

38.99   Since head growth is consequent on brain growth – a small head is a sign of a small brain (microcephaly) – the premature fusion of all the skull bones will impair brain growth. The condition, known as 'clover leaf skull', is fortunately very rare, but separation of the sutures needs to be done in a timely fashion to avoid a rise in intracranial pressure leading to impaired mental development. More commonly, only one suture fuses prematurely. It may be claimed that the abnormality of skull growth should have been recognised earlier and that intervention would have improved appearances. In practice, it may initially be difficult to be certain that a suture has fused prematurely. Separation of the fused sutures is a serious neurosurgical intervention that carries considerable risk.

DISEASES OF PREMATURITY

Labour ward management of birth at the margins of viability (25 weeks' gestation and less)

38.100   The improved survival of extremely preterm infants during the past 20 years has resulted in care being initiated for those who are considered to be at the margins of viability (25 weeks' gestation and less). Many will die in the delivery room in spite of attempts at resuscitation and stabilisation there. Those who survive to be admitted to the neonatal intensive care unit will experience months of intensive care and uncertainty. For those who survive to be discharged home, there is a substantial risk of developing disabilities in the form of learning impairment, visual problems, hearing deficits, and cerebral palsy (see below).

38.101 There are various sources of data for outcomes for infants born at the margins of viability and there is agreement that for each week of gestation from 22 to 25 weeks there is a significant and measurable improvement in survival rates. As a broad guide the proportion of live-born babies at different gestational ages who survive to be discharged home, and their disability rates are shown in Table 38.1.

TABLE 38.1 SURVIVAL[1] AND DISABILITY[2] RATES OF PRETERM INFANTS BORN AT THE MARGIN OF VIABILITY

	Gestational age [weeks]			
	22	23	24	25
Survival to discharge	<10 per cent	15–25 per cent	30–40 per cent	55–65 per cent
Disability among Survivors	*	64 per cent	50 per cent	40 per cent

1 Survival data reflect the 'best estimate' of survival after live birth based on the literature.
2 From Marlow N, Wolke D, Bracewell MA, Samara M 'Neurologic and developmental disability at six years of age after extremely preterm birth' (2005) New England Journal of Medicine 352: 9–19. This study, known as the EPICure study, identified all births in the UK and Republic of Ireland from 20 to 25 weeks gestation during a 10-month period in 1995. The infants were followed up to the age of six years and the disability rates refer to children with moderate and severe disabilities expressed as a proportion of surviving infants.
* Insufficient data.

38.102 Given the relatively high mortality rates and the substantial risks of long-term disability among survivors there is often uncertainty about the level of immediate care that these infants should be offered in the delivery room.

38.103 Poor management in the delivery room of babies born at the margins of viability often results in complaints. However, there are potential medico-legal implications when such a baby survives following confusion in the delivery room, and subsequently has a poor outcome. It may be alleged that in spite of the known risk of disability among survivors, uncertainty around the resuscitation led to a significant delay in supporting the infant such that the risk of disability was substantially increased.

38.104 In most cases of threatened delivery at the margins of viability there is time to discuss the situation with parents before the birth and to come to some agreement about how the infant will be managed. Information given by the obstetrician and paediatrician should not conflict and joint counselling is important. Parents need time to reflect on the information they receive. Parents want to know about the chances of their baby surviving and what the future holds. Counselling needs to be done with caution because the figures depend on which denominator is used. For example, some studies that report higher survival rates express survival as a percentage of neonates admitted to the neonatal intensive care unit, ignoring those extremely preterm babies who die in the delivery room. Counselling should ideally be done by the most senior paediatrician available.

38.105 Delivery should be attended by the most senior paediatrician available because decisions about whether or not to resuscitate will depend on the baby's condition during the minutes before delivery, for example the fetal heart rate, and at delivery. Whatever prior decisions have been made it is essential that the infant is examined for signs of life and vigour, and that the opportunity is taken to consider whether the appearance of the baby is consistent with the supposed gestational age. Surprises are not uncommon and it may be necessary to reverse a prior decision not to give continuing life support, pending further discussion with the parents. If the gestational age has been misjudged and the baby appears more vigorous than had been expected it is better that this is discovered by the paediatrician than by the parents who are preparing for their baby's death. It is especially important that there should be no doubt about classifying a newborn baby as live- or still-born. The distinction is quite clear: the baby must be classified as live-born even if death subsequently occurs shortly after birth if there is a sign of life, defined by the World Health Organisation as a detected heart beat, movement, or respiration, after the cord has been cut. For parents, the emotional accompaniments of birth are huge and it is a time of heightened sensitivity. Any confusion and uncertainty among the staff is readily recognised, and raised urgent voices are often interpreted as panic. It is especially important that all attendants are seen to manage births at the margins of viability with confidence, and this is more likely to occur if an experienced paediatrician is present. There are legal implications: a live birth fatality may be subject to an inquest, but a still birth is not.

Managing the dying baby

38.106 A decision to withhold resuscitation or ongoing support for the infant should be made in conjunction with the parents and led by the most senior paediatrician available, the consultant if possible. A strategy for the redirection of care from intensive to palliative care should be drawn up and recorded.

38.107 The baby is likely to be in a poor condition, with a slow heart rate, pallor, weak respiration, and a paucity of movement. Parents should be warned that, even when mechanical ventilation is stopped, as the baby is alive there may well be visible breathing activity and occasional limb movements. Although it is uncommon for the condition of such babies to improve spontaneously it does sometimes happen to the extent that a decision to withhold intensive care is subsequently reversed.

38.108 The Nuffield Council on Bioethics in their report 'Critical Care Decisions in Fetal and Neonatal Medicine: Ethical Issues' (2006) attempted to clarify decisions around the provision of intensive care for babies born at the margins of viability. It endorsed the notion that an experienced paediatrician should be present at the delivery and that there should be a confirmatory assessment of the gestational age and condition of the baby. The report stated that at 25 completed weeks of gestation and above it should be the normal practice for resuscitation and intensive care to be instituted unless there is a severe abnormality incompatible with any significant period of survival. At 24 completed weeks of gestation, normal practice should be the initiation of intensive care and support from birth unless the parents and clinicians agree that in the light of the baby's condition it is not appropriate. At 23 completed weeks of gestation precedence should be given to the wishes of the parents regarding resuscitation and intensive care. However, when the condition of the baby indicates that survival will be limited or that there will be a substantial burden placed on the baby by intensive care there is no obligation on doctors to proceed with treatments. These considerations should be discussed with parents and it is reasonable to offer full care in the short term until a decision is reached. At 22 completed weeks of gestation, standard practice should be not to provide resuscitation and intensive support unless requested by the parents after informed discussion with an experienced paediatrician. Below 22 completed weeks of gestation no baby should be resuscitated unless this forms part of a clinical research study that has been assessed and approved by a research ethics committee and with informed parental consent.

Respiratory distress syndrome (RDS)

38.109 A syndrome is a collection of signs and symptoms. However, for neonates, the term RDS is used widely to describe a single disease entity that is caused by functional and structural immaturity of the lungs due to a deficiency of a lipoprotein known as surfactant, which facilitates expansion of the lungs on inspiration and helps maintain a normal lung volume on expiration. Synonyms are idiopathic respiratory distress syndrome (IRDS, although the cause is well known), surfactant-deficient respiratory distress syndrome (SDRDS), and hyaline membrane disease (HMD).

38.110 RDS is the most common potentially serious disorder of preterm neonates. It presents within a few hours of birth with signs of respiratory distress: tachypnoea, ie a raised respiratory rate (>60 per minute), retraction of the rib cage on inspiration, and grunting on expiration, cyanosis and a raised heart rate. There are other causes of respiratory distress and so all infants with one or more of these signs must have a chest X-ray. The classical chest X-ray appearance of RDS is a diffuse ground glass appearance of the lung fields reflecting atelectasis (collapse of terminal air spaces), with a superimposed 'air bronchogram' which is due to air in the bronchial tree being highlighted against the more opaque appearance of atelectasis. The appearances normally have a symmetrical distribution.

38.111 The incidence of RDS increases with the degree of prematurity, affecting around 60 per cent of babies at less than 28 weeks' gestation, 30 per cent at 28–34 weeks, and <5 per cent in those born at more than 34 weeks' gestation. The natural course of the disease is variable, but without intervention, the signs generally get worse over the days after birth, reaching peak severity at around 3–4 days, and then subside over the ensuing week.

There was a dramatic improvement in survival in 1993, when artificial surfactant given through an endotracheal tube became widely available. This occurred at around the same time as the general use of antenatal steroids. Ventilatory support should be given as required according to the results of blood gas monitoring.

Medico-legal issues associated with RDS

38.112 The medico-legal implications surrounding RDS are complex. For example, during the course of the disorder acute deterioration is common, and cardio-respiratory instability may be causally implicated in brain haemorrhage and brain ischaemia in preterm neonates and these complications may culminate in later neurodevelopmental disability. It may be alleged that the care fell short of a reasonable standard because appropriate treatment was not given to reduce the risk of RDS occurring, or that the management of the disorder itself was inadequate.

Failure to prevent RDS by neglecting to treat the mother in preterm labour with glucocorticoids

38.113 The administration of betamethasone or dexamethasone to mothers in preterm labour or threatened preterm labour is associated with a reduced incidence of RDS, less need for respiratory support, a lower neonatal mortality, less haemorrhagic and ischaemic brain lesions, a reduced incidence of necrotising enterocolitis, and less systemic infection in the first 48 hours of life. The recommended dose regimen varies but a typical example is two 12 mg doses 24 hours apart. Maximum benefit is seen when delivery occurs between 24 hours and 7 days after commencement of the course, but some benefit is observed when interval between the dose to delivery is somewhat less than 24 hours.

38.114 Whereas previously there was uncertainty about the risk-benefit balance in certain pregnancies the conclusions based on a large systematic review of the literature[1] is summarised as follows:

'A single course of antenatal corticosteroids should be considered routine for preterm delivery with few exceptions. Further information is required concerning optimal dose to delivery interval, optimal corticosteroid to use, effects in multiple pregnancies, and to confirm the long-term effects into adulthood'.

1 Roberts & Dalziel 2006 'Antenatal corticosteroids for accelerating fetal lung maturation for women at risk of preterm birth' (2006) 19(3) Cochrane Database Syst Rev CD004454.

Failure to give surfactant treatment for preterm infants with RDS or those at risk

38.115 A solution of surfactant, synthetic or derived from animals, given down the endotracheal tube in intubated neonates with RDS significantly reduces neonatal mortality, the combined risk of chronic lung disease and death, and the incidence of pneumothorax. More than one dose may be given. It is a safe treatment provided care is taken during the procedure, which entails temporary disconnection from the ventilator.

38.116 The outcome in RDS is better if surfactant is given early in the course of the disease. However, there is an unresolved practical dilemma surrounding the early administration of surfactant in very preterm neonates who are at risk of RDS or who have only mild signs. These infants may not be intubated which means that if surfactant is used they have to be intubated specifically for that purpose. Intubation is not always well tolerated and it is sometimes the case that prompt intubation is not possible, thereby exposing the infant to additional complications. Although surfactant administration in ventilated neonates with RDS is routine practice in the UK, it is not standard practice to intubate infants specifically for surfactant administration with a view to extubating them within an hour or so. Some neonatal units extubate infants onto a less invasive form of respiratory support known as continuous positive airways pressure (CPAP) where breathing occurs spontaneously against a small positive pressure applied through nasal cannula.

Failure to transfer to a hospital with a designated neonatal intensive care unit

38.117 When things go wrong during the course of RDS it is sometimes alleged that the infant should have been transferred to a referral unit specialising in neonatal intensive care. Every maternity unit where a preterm birth may occur should have a written policy indicating the circumstances where transfer out might be a consideration. A note should be made in the medical records of the time that any request for transfer was made, the response, especially if the referral unit cannot accommodate the infant, and any advice that was given by telephone.

Failure to intervene by assisted ventilation

38.118 It may be alleged that cardio-respiratory collapse and subsequent ischaemic brain damage could and should have been avoided by earlier intervention with assisted ventilation. Signs of respiratory deterioration include an increase in the effort of breathing reflected in worsening recession of the thoracic cage on inspiration, and increasing tachypnoea. This is often referred to in the medical records as the neonate 'working hard'. Monitoring of oxygen saturation and blood gas levels are essential and deterioration is reflected by an increasing need for supplemental oxygen and a rising level of blood carbon dioxide (pCO_2).

38.119 Standard neonatal textbooks vary in their recommendations concerning the indications for mechanical ventilation, and it is a matter of clinical judgment taking the whole clinical picture into account rather than depending on a single blood gas result. As doctors and nurses on neonatal units become more experienced in mechanical ventilation, there is a trend towards earlier intervention. The downside is that if intubation proves difficult, perhaps because the neonate is struggling, hypoxaemia may be provoked which can be difficult to resolve even with supplemental oxygen.

38.120 Self-limiting apnoeic episodes during the evolution of RDS should be taken seriously as they may be followed by more serious episodes which may culminate in cardio-respiratory collapse. Recurrent apnoea in RDS is an absolute indication for assisted ventilation.

Failure to promptly recognise and treat endotracheal tube complications

38.121 Infants with RDS may deteriorate in spite of assisted ventilation, but this is not always due to the underlying RDS. If a misplaced or partially obstructed endotracheal tube is not promptly recognised, progressive deterioration may lead to cardio-respiratory collapse. Following intubation a chest X-ray should always be done to ensure that the tip of the endotracheal tube is in an appropriate position and care must be taken in securing the tube. In the context of a neonate deteriorating with RDS, if there is any doubt about the patency or position of an endotracheal tube it must be promptly removed and bag and mask ventilation given pending reintubation.

Pneumothorax

38.122 A pneumothorax is a collection of air outside the lungs and within the pleural space caused by leakage of air from lung tissue. A tension pneumothorax compresses the underlying lungs, interferes with respiratory function, and may impair venous return to the heart. It may develop insidiously with progressive deterioration in blood gases, especially a rising pCO_2 level, and increasing signs of respiratory distress, or it may present as acute cardio-respiratory collapse. The neonate with severe circulatory impairment is at risk of ischaemic brain injury. There is also an association between pneumothorax and intraventricular brain haemorrhage.

38.123 Pneumothorax must be borne in mind in any neonate with RDS who deteriorates, especially if this occurs suddenly. Auscultation may reveal diminished breath sounds on the affected side and displacement of the apex beat to the contralateral side. However, this cannot be relied upon and a chest X-ray is required for a definitive diagnosis. In urgent situations, and especially when a chest X-ray cannot be done promptly, the diagnosis can be suspected by transillumination of the chest. A small fibre-optic light is held against the chest wall on each side in turn. The presence of a pneumothorax may be revealed by a surrounding area of 'glow' on the affected side. It is not always easy to make the diagnosis in this way unless the pneumothorax is large. The room should be darkened or a black covering placed over the incubator to help in the interpretation of the findings. Oedema of the subcutaneous tissue, which is not uncommon in very preterm neonates, may produce excess glowing but this is normally symmetrical.

38.124 Another way of making the diagnosis in urgent situations is by 'needling the chest', although this must be done very carefully to avoid traumatising the lung and potentially making the air leak worse. Briefly, a small needle is attached to a length of plastic tubing which dips into a water-filled container (about 20 ml) and is inserted in the second intercostal space anteriorly. The presence of air in the pleural space is revealed by an immediate stream of bubbles appearing in the water container, followed by bubbling which is more marked on expiration. This should be followed by definitive drainage of a pneumothorax, which requires the insertion of a wider bore cannula which is connected to a drainage system. Following drainage, further chest X-rays are needed until it is clear that the pneumothorax has resolved and the radiological picture has stabilised.

Sepsis

38.125 Newborn babies, especially those who are very premature, are extremely vulnerable to infection. There is considerable variation in policy with respect to surveillance for sepsis in neonates with RDS. Most neonatal units rely on white cell counts done at least several times each week, supplemented by C-reactive protein levels which are raised in the presence of infection. Any suspicion should prompt a blood culture, and on some units blood cultures are done routinely once or twice at week.

38.126 The commonest infecting organisms are coagulase negative staphylococci (causing 90 per cent of infections), gram negative bacteria (such as E coli), group B streptococcus and fungi. Signs initially are usually non-specific, but the complication is potentially serious, but also treatable and therefore neonatal staff need to be aware and prepared to take appropriate action urgently, namely taking blood for microbiological culture and promptly instituting therapy with appropriate antibiotics.

Failure to recognise and manage over-ventilation

38.127 Ventilator settings are adjusted according to blood gas results. One effect of over-ventilation with too high a rate or pressure is to reduce the blood carbon dioxide (pCO_2) to abnormally low levels causing hypocapnia. There is a causal link between hypocapnia and periventricular leukomalacia (PVL) (see below). The risk of PVL seems to be related to a pCO_2 level of less than 3.5 kPa (<26 mm Hg) if sustained or if it occurs frequently over a period of some hours[1]. The ventilator settings should be appropriately reduced and blood gases checked 20–30 minutes later, with further adjustments to the settings if needed until the hypocapnia is resolved.

1 Giannakopoulou (et al) 'Significance of hypocarbia in the development of periventricular leukomalacia in preterm infants' (2004) 46(3) Pediatr Int 268–273.

Broncho-pulmonary dysplasia (BPD), chronic lung disease (CLD)

38.128 Around 25 per cent of neonates with RDS born below 30 weeks' gestation die before discharge home or develop chronic lung disease (CLD), also known as broncho-pulmonary dysplasia (BPD). CLD develops insidiously and is characterised by the appearance of chronic inflammatory or destructive changes on a chest X-ray associated with continuing oxygen dependency. A definition of CLD is continuing oxygen dependency until at least 36 weeks' post-conceptional age. Multiple factors are implicated in the development of CLD. These include extreme prematurity, inadvertent pulmonary trauma caused by mechanical ventilation, pulmonary infection, and a toxic effect of oxygen on lung tissue. In spite of efforts to prevent the disease by different styles of mechanical ventilation and by the postnatal use of steroids (glucocorticoids) it is still a prominent cause of morbidity and mortality.

38.129 Allegations that CLD was caused by a poor standard of care are uncommon. However, the longer a neonate requires neonatal intensive care the greater the risk of other complications that require prompt recognition and management. These include accidents relating to the use of intravenous catheters, sepsis, and laryngeal damage due to repeated intubations and local infection which can cause subglottic stenosis.

38.130 There is an emerging area of medico-legal interest regarding the use of steroids in the neonatal period for the prevention or treatment of CLD. The use of glucocorticoids, such as intramuscular dexamethasone in preterm neonates with RDS starting in the first two weeks of life with a gradual reduction in the dose over the ensuing 14 days is associated with a reduced incidence of CLD, less time spent on the ventilator, and improved survival at 28 days. However, there are complications, including gastrointestinal bleeding, intestinal perforation, a raised blood sugar, hypertension, cardiomyopathy, and infection. Furthermore there are reports of an increased incidence of developmental delay and cerebral palsy associated with postnatal steroids. It is possible that steroids may adversely affect the maturation of the white matter of the brain in preterm neonates. Following these reports, the use of postnatal steroids has diminished during the past five years or so and it is sensible to limit the treatment to high-risk neonates who cannot be weaned from mechanical ventilation, and to minimise the dose and duration of therapy. Parents should be informed of the possible side effects, risks and benefits. A note of the discussion should be made in the medical records, along with a careful description of the infant's condition making it clear why steroids were deemed appropriate.

Retinopathy of prematurity

Introduction

38.131 Retinopathy of prematurity (ROP) (formerly known as retrolental fibroplasia) is a disorder of prematurity in which there is abnormal vascularisation of the retina. It is potentially progressive and may culminate in detachment of the retina and blindness. However, at any stage in its evolution, arrest of the disorder can occur. In the early stages arrest often occurs spontaneously; in more advanced stages treatment may arrest progression.

38.132 Considering the retina to be a concave segment, vascularisation commences at the posterior pole around the fourth month of gestation, and advances forward with increasing gestational age such that by 36 weeks' gestation the retina is fully vascularised. Thus, prematurely born infants have an incompletely vascularised retina, and vascularisation has to occur in a very different environment from inside the womb. The hallmark of ROP is aberrant new vessels formation, retinal and vitreous haemorrhages, fibrous tissue formation and scarring, and retinal detachment.

38.133 Serial examination of the retina after birth reveals the progress of vascularisation and allows ROP to be classified according to its severity. The classification is complex but important because it is a guide to treatment and long-term prognosis. Briefly, the mildest form of the disorder is represented by a clear demarcation between the already vascularised and the avascular retina (stage 1) or by a slightly projecting ridge (stage 2). This mild form often does not progress and resolves spontaneously. In stage 3 fragile new vessels are seen sprouting from the ridge. The term 'plus disease' refers to the presence of dilated arterioles and veins. Stage 4 represents partial retinal detachment, and stage 5 total retinal detachment. The disease is also classified according to the extent of retinal involvement which may be confined centrally or extend to the periphery. Further classification is according to the number of 'clock-hours' affected. Using this classification, a picture of the progression of the disease is obtained and the need and timing of treatment is assessed. 'Pre-threshold ROP' is a severe form but not demanding treatment and 'threshold ROP' is the minimal severity which demands surgical intervention. The incidence of all forms of ROP, and severe ROP at different gestational ages is shown in Table 38.2 which illustrates the central role played by very preterm birth.

TABLE 38.2 INCIDENCE AND SEVERITY OF ROP IN VERY PRETERM INFANTS

	Gestational age [weeks]		
	≤ 27	28–31	≥ 32
All degrees of ROP	85–90 per cent	50 per cent	15 per cent
Severe ROP*	45 per cent	20 per cent	15 per cent

* Severe ROP is prethreshold disease or worse in one or both eyes.

38.134 The recognition of threshold disease is important because treatment at this stage has been shown in randomised controlled trials to be effective in halting the progression of the disorder. The basis of treatment is ablation of the avascular retina immediately anterior to the part affected by new and aberrant vessel formation. This was done by cryotherapy (freezing), and now more usually by laser. There are advantages and disadvantages with each method which are matters for the specialist ophthalmic surgeon. Crucial to timely treatment is the instigation of a screening programme for preterm neonates to identify those with ROP who may progress to threshold disease. A large scale screening programme in the United States as part of an early intervention study confirmed that severe but prethreshold disease was first recognised on average at a postnatal age of 10–11 weeks, and at the earliest seven weeks (Early Treatment for Retinopathy of Prematurity Cooperative Group 2005).

Screening for ROP and medico-legal implications

38.135 The screening programme that is current policy in the UK is based on the report of a Working Party of the Royal College of Ophthalmologists (RCO) and the British Association of Perinatal Medicine (BAPM) (1995). All infants less than 32 weeks' gestation, and those with birth weights ≤1500 g should have their retina examined for ROP by a skilled examiner at 6–7 weeks postnatal age. Subsequent examinations should be made at least every two weeks until vascularisation has progressed into the periphery.

38.136 Claims have been made where initial screening was not carried out, or subsequent screening examinations were curtailed because the infant was transferred from one hospital to another with no arrangements for follow-up. The neonatal unit staff must inform the receiving hospital that the screening process requires to be completed. Similarly if the infant is discharged home before screening is completed an appropriate follow up appointment must be made. At all stages the parents must be kept informed and details of treatment and prognosis should be discussed with an experienced ophthalmologist. There must be a record of the findings on ophthalmic examination.

38.137 In some regions there was a shortage of available ophthalmologists trained in screening for ROP and its treatment. It is, however, important for every neonatal unit caring for very preterm infants to establish appropriate lines of communications with ophthalmologists in the region so that the RCO/BAPM guidelines are followed.

38.138 The medical condition of infants requiring treatment for ROP may be unstable, especially those with chronic lung disease. It is common practice, although not universal, for operative treatment to be provided in a side room on the neonatal intensive care unit. Wherever treatment is given it is essential that staff trained in neonatal care are in attendance to manage any infant whose medical condition becomes compromised.

Risk factors in the development of ROP

38.139 The main risk factors for the development of ROP are prematurity and exposure to excessively high concentrations of oxygen for prolonged periods. Other risk factors include, intrauterine growth retardation[1], blood transfusion[2], the male gender, and possibly multiple pregnancy. The causal contribution of these risk factors are unclear.

1 Darlow, Hutchinson, Henderson-Smart, Donoghue, Simpson, Evans; Australian and New Zealand Neonatal Network 'Prenatal risk factors for severe retinopathy of prematurity among very preterm infants of the Australian and New Zealand Neonatal Network' (2005) 115(4) Pediatrics 990–996.
2 Dani, Reali, Bertini, Martelli, Pezzati, Rubaltelli 'The role of blood transfusions and iron intake on retinopathy of prematurity' (2001) 62(1) Early Hum Dev 57–63.

Oxygen and ROP

38.140 The normal vascularisation of the retina that occurs in utero is a carefully controlled process influenced by many factors including oxygen, a growth hormone known as IGF-1, and a protein (VEGF) that is induced by hypoxia and stimulates the normal proliferation of blood vessels. The details are not relevant here except to say that normal vascularisation occurs under relatively hypoxic conditions given that the fetal blood oxygen saturation in the womb is 70–80 per cent compared with >90 per cent after birth. A prematurely born infant is therefore exposed to relative hyperoxia, even when nursed in air. This causes temporary cessation of blood vessel production and vaso-obliteration. With maturation the metabolically active but avascular retina has increasing demands for oxygen which cannot be met and the avascular retina becomes hypoxic. Under these hypoxic conditions excess VEGF is produced which stimulates disorganised new vessels formation and the development of the condition known as ROP. This phase occurs at around 32–34 weeks' post-conceptional age. Thus, for an infant born at say 25 weeks' gestation, this phase would commence at around 7–9 weeks' postnatal age.

38.141 It has been known for over 50 years that the indiscriminate and uncontrolled use of supplementary oxygen for preterm neonates carries an increased risk of ROP. Early attempts to restrict inspired oxygen to an arbitrary level of around 40 per cent reduced the incidence of ROP but did not eradicate it. Furthermore, some preterm neonates who needed higher oxygen concentrations but were deprived of it suffered excess morbidity and mortality.

38.142 The critical factor is not the concentration of oxygen that a baby breathes but the level of oxygen in the blood. Some preterm infants with respiratory problems need a small amount such as 25 per cent (room air is 21 per cent oxygen, pure oxygen is 100 per cent), whereas others need more than 90 per cent. Coinciding with the development of improved methods of monitoring blood oxygen levels the survival rate of extremely preterm infants increased and so the population at risk for severe ROP increased. The term 'second epidemic' was applied to the increase in the incidence of ROP seen during the late 1970s and 1980s as a result of improved survival rates of extremely preterm infants.

38.143 There is no defined level of arterial oxygen above which severe ROP is inevitable. The duration of exposure to hyperoxaemia is almost certainly important, but again there is no reliable and consistent information relating duration of exposure to the development of severe ROP. There is some evidence to suggest that fluctuations in blood oxygen levels may play a role in the pathogenesis of ROP[1].

1 Cunningham, Fleck, Elton, McIntosh 'Transcutaneous oxygen levels in retinopathy of prematurity' (1995) 346(8988) Lancet 1464–1465.

38.144 This uncertainty and the existence of other risk factors for ROP should not be taken to imply that the control of oxygen therapy is unimportant. Neonatal staff must ensure that all preterm neonates who are receiving supplemental oxygen have their blood oxygen levels monitored. The aim is to achieve levels within a range that is currently considered acceptable, to document the levels in the medical records, and to try as far as possible to achieve stable levels, especially avoiding fluctuations between hypoxaemia and hyperoxaemia.

Monitoring oxygen therapy

38.145 Supplemental oxygen should be considered as a drug. The response to treatment is measured by the 'amount' of oxygen circulating in arterial blood, and in this way the dose is adjusted. There is no predictable relationship between the dose of oxygen and the arterial blood level; it varies according to the nature and severity of the underlying respiratory disorder.

38.146   A continuous measure of the oxygen in arterial blood was possible using a modified umbilical arterial catheter with an electrode at its tip, but this is now rarely used. In preterm neonates requiring supplemental oxygen an acceptable policy, where arterial oxygen (PaO2) is measured intermittently, is to aim to achieve a level within the range of 7.0 kPa–11.0 kPa (approximately 50–80 mm Hg). Intermittent sampling of arterial blood through an indwelling arterial catheter, most easily sited in the umbilical artery catheter or in a small peripheral artery, but access can be difficult in very small neonates and there are complications. Intermittent sampling by peripheral arterial puncture is generally unhelpful because it often causes crying which in itself may lower the PaO2.

38.147   Continuous non-invasive monitoring of arterial oxygen saturation saturation levels is now the most commonly used method, supplemented where possible by intermittent measurements of arterial oxygen tension PaO2 made 4–6 hourly. The oxygen saturation probe is attached to the infant's hand or foot. The definition of 'safe' oxygen saturation levels for neonates of different gestational ages is a subject of debate. However, it is an acceptable policy in preterm infants less than 32 weeks' gestation to maintain saturation levels between 85 per cent and 92 per cent.

Oxygen monitoring and litigation

38.148   Allegations that ROP was caused by the infant negligently receiving too much oxygen are likely to be based on some well-recognised pitfalls in management which are addressed below:

(1)   there are many different neonatal oxygen saturation monitors and staff should be trained so that they are familiar with the type in use on their unit. The relationship between oxygen saturation and PaO2 is not a straightforward one. If oxygen saturation is close to 100 per cent, the PaO2 may be extremely high (see Figure 38.8);

(2)   attention must be given to appropriately securing the probe so that it is protected from extraneous light sources which affect the saturation readings;

(3)   the 'high' and 'low' alarms on the monitor should be appropriately set, based on the desired oxygen saturation. All alarms must be responded to promptly and if the monitor alarms excessively the reason should be explored and on no account should the alarm be switched off;

(4)   if it is not possible to supplement saturation monitoring with intermittent PaO2 measurements then the reason should be stated in the medical records;

(5)   There should be documented evidence of adjustments made to inspired oxygen concentration in response to saturation or PaO2 levels that are outside the desirable range;

(6)   A false sense of security sometimes prevails when a preterm neonate requires only a small amount of oxygen which is sometimes given via

a nasal cannula. The concentration of inspired oxygen is unknown because it is variably diluted when the infant inspires. Such neonates may be nursed this way for many weeks and it is especially important for their oxygen saturation levels to be monitored.

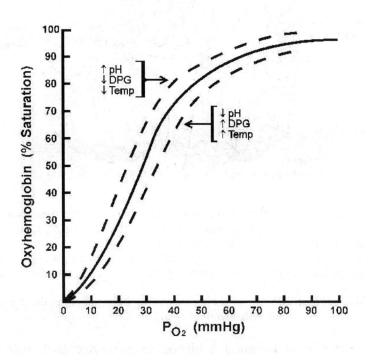

Oxygen dissociation curve showing the variable relationship between oxygen saturation and PaO2.

Cerebral complications in preterm neonates

Periventricular leukomalacia

38.149 Periventricular leukomalacia (PVL) is an uncommon but well-recognised form of brain injury that occurs almost exclusively in preterm infants born within a gestational age range of approximately 26–34 weeks. It is characterised by injury to the cerebral white matter regions of the brain adjacent to the lateral ventricles (the periventricular white matter). Extremely preterm infants born before 26 weeks rarely develop classical PVL but they often develop diffuse white matter injury and tissue loss.

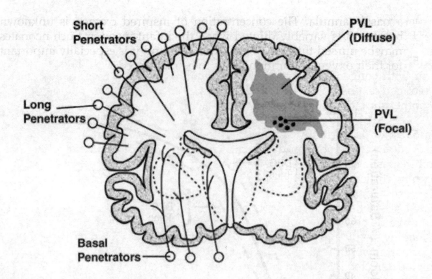

Short Penetrators

PVL (Diffuse)

Long Penetrators

PVL (Focal)

Basal Penetrators

Schematic of coronal section of cerebrum with focal and diffuse components of PVL shown in one hemisphere and the cerebral vascular supply shown in the other cerebral hemisphere. The focal necrotic component of PVL is depicted by black circles, and the diffuse component is indicated by grey shading. The long and short penetrating arteries supply the cerebral white matter as shown.

From: Volpe 'Neurobiology of periventricular leukomalacia in the premature infant' (2001) 50 Pediatric Research 553–562.

38.150 Scientific and clinical evidence has indicated that, within the gestational period of 26–34 weeks, the periventricular white matter regions are particularly vulnerable to permanent injury from a range of causal mechanisms. These include ascending infection before delivery (chorioamnionitis), placental abruption or other causes of severe disturbance to the fetal circulation, acute hypoxic ischaemia around the time of delivery, acute circulatory disturbance in the neonatal period, severe bacterial infections in the neonatal period and accidental hypocarbia (low arterial carbon dioxide tension) caused by inadvertent hyperventilation in the neonatal period. These causal factors have in common either the presence of bacterial infection which causes release of damaging chemical compounds called cytokines, or a severe and damaging reduction in the blood supply to the fetal or neonatal brain. However, in some cases of PVL in premature infants no cause is identified.

38.151 The association between PVL and hypocarbia due to inadvertent hyperventilation in preterm infants was first reported in 1987[1] and became generally accepted in the mid 1990s. It is not known how rapidly injury is sustained following exposure to hypocarbia. An attempt has been made to develop a cumulative index of exposure to hypocarbia from arterial carbon dioxide level over the first seven days of life, although the scientific basis for this approach is uncertain and open to question[2].

1 Calvert (et al) 'Etiological factors associated with the development of periventricular leukomalacia' (1987) 76(2) Acta Paediatrica Scand 254–259.

2 Shankaran (et al) 'Cumulative index of exposure to hypocarbia and hyperoxia as risk factors for periventricular leukomalacia in low birth weight infants' (2006) 118 Pediatrics 1654–1659.

38.152 Recent studies suggest PVL may also occur in infants born at term with congenital heart disease particularly following cardiac surgery. Prolonged exposure to cardiopulmonary bypass (with or without deep hypothermic circulatory arrest) is a risk factor.

38.153 PVL is normally symmetrical in distribution and it is particularly associated with cerebral palsy affecting both legs (spastic diplegia) or all four limbs (spastic quadriplegia). It is also associated with cognitive impairment, learning difficulties and visual processing abnormalities.

38.154 Established cystic PVL is usually visible by cranial ultrasound but obvious cysts may only become apparent two weeks or more after the damaging insult has occurred. Hence ultrasound may only give limited information about timing of the injury. More subtle white matter injury can only be detected by MRI in later infancy.

38.155 Establishing the causation of PVL frequently presents some difficulties. Preterm infants often undergo neonatal intensive care for many weeks and the white matter injury is commonly multifactorial in origin. It may be difficult if not impossible to establish the contribution of a single substandard period of care within a complex series of events and interventions. However guidelines for monitoring blood levels of carbon dioxide in preterm infants undergoing mechanical ventilation are well established, and prolonged periods of abnormally low CO_2 levels may be causally significant.

38.156 Although there is strong scientific evidence that maternal chorioamnionitis is causally associated with the development of PVL, to date there is no convincing evidence to show that once maternal chorioamnionitis has been diagnosed, early delivery of the fetus leads to a reduction in the incidence or severity of brain injury. It is likely that cytokines are released at an early stage of the maternal infection and although early delivery may remove the infant from the infected environment, brain injury due to cytokine activation may still occur. In addition early delivery will mean that the baby is delivered in a more premature condition and hence is at greater risk of brain injury from the complications of prematurity.

Periventricular haemorrhage

38.157 This form of brain injury (sometimes described as germinal matrix-intraventricular haemorrhage) is a relatively common occurrence in preterm infants born at less than 32 weeks. Haemorrhage commences in a central region of the brain known as the germinal matrix (or subependymal matrix) which is situated close to the lateral ventricles within the cerebral hemisphere. In preterm infants the germinal matrix is a relatively large structure with a rich blood supply. Bleeding commences within the germinal matrix around the time of birth or within the first 72 hours of life. The blood may then spread into the lateral ventricle and in the most severe cases haemorrhagic infarction occurs in a region of the brain tissue adjacent to the lateral ventricle, leading ultimately to focal loss of brain tissue (porencephaly or a porencephalic cyst). The presence of blood within the ventricular system may cause interference with the normal process of CSF absorption within the cranial cavity, leading to the subsequent development of hydrocephalus over the succeeding days and weeks.

38.158 Periventricular haemorrhage can be easily diagnosed by cranial ultrasound and the timing and progression of the haemorrhage can be monitored with sequential imaging. MRI in later infancy provides detailed information about the distribution of any permanent tissue injury.

38.159 Causal factors which are known to increase the risk of intraventricular haemorrhage include extreme prematurity, perinatal hypoxic ischaemia, respiratory illness in the neonatal period, mechanical ventilation, pneumothorax and blood clotting abnormalities. As with PVL it is often difficult to establish the causal contribution of a single substandard period of care within a complex series of events and interventions during a prolonged period of neonatal care.

38.160 Antenatal steroids have been demonstrated to be associated with a significant reduction in periventricular haemorrhage and adverse outcome in preterm infants below 34 weeks of gestation. The maximal effect is obtained 24-48 hours after the commencement of steroid administration

38.161 Follow up studies have indicated that haemorrhage which is limited to the germinal matrix or the lateral ventricles, and which is not associated with other complications such as hydrocephalus or haemorrhagic infarction, is not associated with a greatly increased risk of disability compared with infants in whom no haemorrhage is detected.

38.162 Porencephalic cystic development following periventricular haemorrhage is associated with cerebral palsy, usually in the form of hemiplegia. Hydrocephalus is not uncommon and may require the insertion of a surgical shunt, with risks of further complications due to shunt blockage or infection.

Meningitis

38.163 The meninges are the membranous coverings of the brain. Although infections which may be bacterial or viral can primarily affect the brain substance and are then most appropriately termed 'cerebritis', 'cerebral abscess' or 'encephalitis', it is more common for the primary site of the central nervous system to be within the meninges, hence 'meningitis'. Infection causes the meninges to be swollen and to impair their ability to contribute effectively to cerebrospinal fluid (CSF) and blood circulation within the nervous system. Brain function can also be compromised in meningitis by direct spread of the infection from the meninges.

38.164 In general, viral infections causing meningitis and encephalitis have less significance in both the short and long term than do bacterial ones. This is just as well, given the relative absence of useful anti-viral chemotherapeutic agents. The exception to this, however, is herpes simplex encephalitis. This has significant mortality and morbidity and it is now demonstrated that early treatment with the anti-viral agent acyclovir is likely to improve the prognosis. Acyclovir should be given early during the course of any non-specific encephalitic process in children if a herpes simplex viral infection cannot be excluded.

38.165 By contrast, bacterial meningitis is highly likely not only to cause children to be very seriously ill in the short term and to carry an appreciable risk of death, but also to cause brain damage and long-term neurological sequelae. It follows that its early identification and prompt and appropriate treatment are crucial. Even when these are ideal, however, the nature of the infection is such that there continues to be an appreciable morbidity. Medico-legal evaluation has to take this into account; death or neurological handicap does not necessarily equate with a child having received inappropriate standards of medical care.

From the clinical viewpoint it is helpful to pay specific attention to the age of the child and to the nature of the infecting micro-organisms.

Necrotising enterocolitis

38.166 Necrotising enterocolitis (NEC) is an inflammatory disorder of the bowel. It is a disease of prematurity and is more common in very preterm neonates. The ileum, colon, and jejunum are commonly affected. The disorder has a wide spectrum of severity and at worst it can have serious consequences including the need for extensive bowel resection, colostomy or ileostomy, and a prolonged need for parenteral nutrition with its associated complications. NEC has a multifactorial aetiology and the main components are thought to be infection – although not related to any specific organism – gut ischaemia, and impaired immune resistance of the bowel mucosa. Breast feeding and antenatal steroids afford some protection. The overall incidence is between 3 and 35 per 1,000 births, but in very premature infants of less than 32 weeks' gestation it is around 10 per cent. Mortality rates as high as 10–30 per cent have been reported, but the outcome depends on the severity of the disease.

38.167 In preterm infants the signs and symptoms generally present at around 7–20 days and the more premature the infant the later the presentation, so that babies born at the margins of viability may present with NEC even later than 20 days. The clinical features are often non-specific at first and include apnoeic attacks, lethargy, poor peripheral circulation, abdominal distension and erythema of the abdominal wall. Although an insidious course is common there may be cardio-respiratory collapse, shock, and a bleeding tendency and these signs may occasionally occur without warning.

38.168 NEC can also occur in term infants and tends to present earlier, usually in the first week of life, and often within the first few days. Affected infants may have predisposing factors that may cause gut ischaemia, such as severe fetal growth retardation, perinatal asphyxia, congenital heart disease, and metabolic abnormalities.

38.169   The most important diagnostic investigation is an abdominal X-ray. Typical findings include dilated loops of bowel with thickened walls and sometimes gas within the wall of the bowel which appears as thin translucent linear shadows rather like a tram line. Initial treatment is medical, which means discontinuing milk feeds and starting intravenous nutrition in order to rest the bowel, and a course of broad spectrum antibiotics. Some infants have a protracted medical course with attempts at re-introducing milk feeds leading to abdominal distension, resulting in prolonged reliance on parenteral nutrition with its complications.

38.170   X-rays may need to be repeated in order to recognise features that require a surgical opinion – bowel perforation, revealed as a collection of gas in the abdomen lying outside the bowel, and features of bowel obstruction due to strictures. Especially junior doctors may miss the presence of free gas on an abdominal X-ray, indicative of perforation. Bowel perforation is a most serious complication that requires an urgent surgical opinion. The decision whether to operate may be made more difficult by the baby's condition deteriorating rapidly. The use of an intra-abdominal drain is a temporary alternative to laparotomy in neonates who are critically ill.

38.171   Parents, having seen their extremely preterm infant making reasonably good progress, often taking some milk feeds, may have developed high expectations and then be extremely disappointed and concerned that the disease should have been picked up sooner or even prevented by different management, eg that milk feeds should have been introduced later.

THE INFANT AT, OR CLOSE TO, TERM

Neonatal encephalopathy

38.172   Term infants who have been exposed to an episode of brain damaging hypoxic ischaemia virtually always develop a characteristic neurological illness described as acute neonatal encephalopathy. The diagnosis is made on the presence of a constellation of signs. These comprise: (a) impaired conscious level; (b) impaired brainstem reflexes, especially the reflexes underlying feeding and airway protection; (c) abnormal muscle tone (either increased or decreased); and (d) seizures. The severity of the illness is classically divided into mild, moderate and severe, based on the clinical signs. This classification is helpful prognostically. Infants with mild encephalopathy generally have a good outcome; approximately one quarter of infants with moderate and nearly all infants with severe encephalopathy will have an adverse outcome (severe disability or death).

38.173   A critical diagnostic feature is that encephalopathy following injuring hypoxic ischaemia commences within approximately 24 hours of the damaging insult. The symptoms then frequently worsen with a maximum severity at 48–72 hours followed by gradual resolution. This characteristic temporal sequence parallels the development of impaired energy metabolism within the brain tissue.

38.174 The absence of encephalopathy in the first 24 hours of life makes it very unlikely that hypoxic-ischaemic brain injury was induced within a matter of hours prior to delivery. However it is important to recognise that the signs of mild encephalopathy may be missed in an infant who has received routine monitoring in a postnatal ward. The infant may simply be classified as a 'poor feeder' or 'sleepy'.

38.175 Conversely, the presence of the classical temporal pattern of encephalopathy commencing within 24 hours of delivery, strongly suggests that the damaging insult happened within 24 (or possibly up to 48) hours prior to delivery.

Long-term outcome

38.176 The classical teaching was that hypoxic-ischaemic brain damage in the term infant always resulted in some form of cerebral palsy (ie motor impairment), whether or not there was additional cognitive or sensory impairment. However long-term follow-up studies of infants who developed encephalopathy after birth have indicated that a significant number have mild to moderate cognitive problems causing educational difficulties without clear evidence of motor impairment or cerebral palsy. A specific form of memory impairment, episodic memory loss, that leads to pronounced amnesia for the episodes of everyday life, despite normal speech and language competence, has been associated with hippocampal injury in early life, and it is possible that this specific form of memory loss may be a consequence of the acute total pattern of asphyxial brain injury.

38.177 Isolated hearing loss may also rarely be seen following exposure to acute hypoxic ischaemia in the term infant. This is thought to be due to direct injury to the cochlea or to the thalamic nuclei within the auditory pathway.

Establishing causation

38.178 An international consensus statement providing criteria for defining a causal relation between acute intrapartum events and cerebral palsy was published in 1999[1]. These are as follows:

A   essential criteria (must meet all four):
  (i)   evidence of a metabolic acidosis in fetal umbilical cord arterial blood obtained at delivery (pH <7 and base deficit >=12 mmol/L);
  (ii)   early onset of severe or moderate neonatal encephalopathy in infants born at 34 or more weeks of gestation;
  (iii) cerebral palsy of the spastic quadriplegic or dyskinetic type;
  (iv)   exclusion of other identifiable aetiologies, such as trauma, coagulation disorders, infectious conditions, or genetic disorders;
B   criteria that collectively suggest an intrapartum timing (within close proximity to labour and delivery, eg 0–48 hours) but are nonspecific to asphyxial insults
  (i)   a sentinel (signal) hypoxic event occurring immediately before or during labour;
  (ii)   a sudden and sustained fetal bradycardia or the absence of fetal heart rate variability in the presence of persistent, late, or variable

decelerations, usually after a hypoxic sentinel event when the pattern was previously normal;

(iii) Apgar scores of 0–3 beyond 5 minutes;

(iv) onset of multisystem involvement within 72 hours of birth;

(v) early imaging study showing evidence of acute non-focal cerebral abnormality.

1 MacLennan 'A template for defining a causal relation between acute intrapartum events and cerebral palsy: international consensus statement' (1999) 319 BMJ 1054–1059.

38.179 If all these criteria are present they are sufficient to enable causation to be established. However it is highly questionable whether all these criteria are necessary for causation to be established and in clinical experience it is not uncommon for one or more of these criteria to be absent. For example, it is not unusual for there to be no recognisable 'sentinel event' during labour, the degree of cardiorespiratory depression (leading to very low Apgar scores) is variable and, as discussed previously, a severe metabolic acidosis may not always be documented at delivery. A revised consensus statement was published in 2014, reflecting the range of current opinion[1].

1 *Neonatal Encephalopathy and Neurologic Outcome* (2nd edn) 2014,

38.180 Cranial MRI is extremely valuable in establishing the regional pattern of injury. Early changes are seen within a week of delivery but imaging later in childhood provides more detailed assessment of the precise nature and severity of the injury, and gives valuable prognostic information.

Therapeutic hypothermia

38.181 There is strong evidence that moderate hypothermia commenced within six hours of delivery can be an effective treatment in term infants with encephalopathy and clinical evidence of acute intrapartum hypoxia. In several large randomised clinical trials, hypothermia treatment for a period of 72 hours was associated with a significant reduction in death and severe disability in surviving infants compared with controls. Hypothermia treatment has been recently adopted as a standard of care by NICE and several international bodies. In infants who have been resuscitated following evidence of acute intrapartum hypoxia and in whom encephalopathic signs are present, active rewarming should be avoided and immediate transfer arranged to a fully staffed neonatal intensive care unit capable of providing hypothermia treatment. In clinical trials the number of infants required to treat for significant improvement ranged between 1 in 5 and 1 in 9. At present hypothermia treatment has no proven value in infants born at less than 36 weeks gestational age.

SPECIFIC DISEASES AFFECTING ALL INFANTS

Superficial injury

Bruising

38.182 Superficial facial bruising is common, especially in association with forceps delivery. Marked bruising of the scrotum or labia can occur in breech deliveries and it may take several weeks before it fades. Following a traumatic breech delivery extravasation of blood may occur between the gluteal muscles, and its extent can be underestimated by the appearance of slight bruising on the surface of the buttocks. All bruising increases the risk of jaundice (see para **38.241**) due to the breakdown of red blood cells and haemoglobin in the bruised area.

38.183 It is important to distinguish bruising of the scrotal skin from a scrotal swelling, although co-existence is not rare. A scrotal haematoma may be associated with traumatic intra-abdominal bleeding or with a bleeding diathesis.

Caput succedaneum

38.184 This is a very common, benign localised swelling on the head due to tissue oedema. It is caused by pressure on the head as it descends through the dilating cervix at birth.

Cephalhaematoma

38.185 This localised swelling on the head is a collection of blood under the periosteal lining of the vault of the skull. As the periosteum is tightly bound down at the suture lines of the skull the swelling is characterised by not extending across the sutures. The incidence is about 1–2 per cent of live births, rising to 5–10 per cent in forceps deliveries. The swelling generally increases in size during the first week and may appear very unsightly. A skull X-ray reveals an underlying linear skull fracture in 10–25 per cent of cases. If the X-ray is done after discharge from the maternity hospital, the possibility of non-accidental injury as a cause for the fracture may be raised, and the subsequent investigation may be distressing.

38.186 Bilateral lesions can also occur. The edge of the swelling may feel very hard due to the periosteum being raised, and this may give the impression that the centre of the lesion is depressed, leading to an erroneous diagnosis of a depressed fracture.

38.187 Because the swelling is fluctuant, parents may be alarmed. It may take several months for the swelling to disappear and the larger masses may calcify and become less noticeable with growth and remodelling of the skull in the early years. There is no specific medical treatment.

Subaponeurotic (subgaleal) haemorrhage

38.188 This is the most important form of extracranial haemorrhagic head trauma because of its potential serious morbidity and mortality. Bleeding occurs between the inner layer of the scalp and the periosteum of the skull. This is an extensive space that consists of loose tissue transversed by small veins which drain into the scalp. When these rupture, blood accumulates and spreads within the subaponeurotic space. The space can potentially accommodate a very large amount of blood, around 250 ml, which is approaching the total blood volume of a term infant.

38.189 There is a strong causal association between subaponeurotic haemorrhages and instrumental delivery, especially vacuum extraction, but also the use of forceps. It is thought that the initiating factor is a shearing or traction force which separates the scalp from the underlying bone.

38.190 The presenting feature is a diffuse swelling over the head which has a boggy feel. Initially it may appear localised but it is not limited by the cranial sutures and expands as the bleeding progresses. It commonly involves the occipital region and back of the neck. There may be frontal swelling associated with peri-orbital bruising. The degree of haemorrhage and the rate of progression varies from case to case.

38.191 Because bleeding into the subaponeurotic space can be extensive, the baby may become seriously shocked because of anaemia and loss of circulating volume. It is important to suspect this lesion in any newborn baby with a diffuse swelling over the head, especially following instrumental delivery. An urgent blood transfusion, requiring the use of the emergency pack of O negative ('universal donor') blood that should be readily available on every maternity unit, and maintenance of blood pressure are the mainstays of treatment. Babies with extensive haemorrhage may develop secondary disseminated intravascular coagulopathy, which complicates management.

38.192 The mortality from subaponeurotic haemorrhage is high, between 20 and 25 per cent, with death being associated with haemorrhagic shock. Most infants who escape haemorrhagic shock survive and have a good long term neuro-developmental outcome. However, infants who have survived a period of severe hypotension may develop ischaemic brain damage and later disability.

Intracranial haemorrhage

Subdural haemorrhage

38.193 Although relatively uncommon, the importance of subdural haemorrhage in the newborn is that a small proportion of affected neonates deteriorate rapidly and for some there is a window of opportunity for surgery, which can be potentially lifesaving. The haemorrhage occurs from veins which drain from the cerebral and cerebellar hemispheres into venous sinuses which are channels within a membrane covering the brain and known as the dura. Rupture of the dura or tearing of the bridging veins that drain into the venous sinuses cause bleeding into the subdural space.

38.194 The causative trauma is from distorting forces acting on the head. Risk factors include babies who are large in relation to the size of the maternal pelvis, increased skull compliance in preterm babies, prolonged labour causing excessive moulding, a very brief labour with insufficient time for expansion of maternal pelvic structures, abnormal presentations, and instrumental delivery, although this is not a necessary factor.

Convexity subdural haemorrhage

38.195 This term describes a minor subdural haemorrhage over the surface (convexity) of one or both cerebral hemispheres. It is commonly seen as an incidental finding at post-mortem examination, especially in preterm infants. Significant convexity subdural bleeding is more common in term infants and presents on the second or third day of life with seizures, which are often focal. This contrasts with hypoxic-ischaemic encephalopathy which causes symptoms within 24 hours, often within 12 hours after birth. Other focal signs that may be observed in convexity subdural haemorrhage include deviation of the eyes to the opposite side of the haemorrhage, a poorly reactive and dilated pupil on the side of the lesion, and hemiparesis.

38.196 When a convexity subdural haemorrhage is clinically suspected, a CT brain scan should be done to confirm the diagnosis, which may be missed if reliance is placed on an ultrasound brain scan, which is poor at visualising lesions at the lateral edges of the brain. Lumbar puncture should not be performed because of the risk of herniation of the temporal lobe through the tentorial notch ('coning'), although a clinical judgment has to be made when meningitis is considered in the differential diagnosis.

38.197 Surgical evacuation of the haematoma is rarely required as most convexity haemorrhages resolve spontaneously. However, a neurosurgeon should be made aware of the situation when the diagnosis is confirmed to ensure that help is on hand should the infant's condition deteriorate. The need for surgery depends on the extent of the lesion on a brain scan, whether there are signs of raised intracranial pressure, and whether abnormal neurological signs are progressing.

38.198 The key to effective management is careful serial clinical observations, which should be documented in the medical records. These should comprise the infant's level of arousal, graded according to accepted definitions, muscle tone and its symmetry, the occurrence of seizures, anterior fontanelle tension, pupil size and reaction to light.

38.199 Although a CT scan is a reliable way of making a diagnosis it may mean transfer to an appropriate facility which is not desirable if the neonate is unstable. In these circumstances a subdural tap may be used to make the diagnosis but there are pitfalls. It needs to be done by a doctor who is experienced in the procedure because it is unhelpful when, due to poor technique, the result is reported as 'possibly a little blood'.

38.200 The outcome of convexity subdural haemorrhage is relatively good, with up to 90 per cent of infants having no significant impairments on follow up. The remainder often have signs of focal cerebral damage such as hemiplegia and focal epilepsy.

38.201 Rarely, a subdural haemorrhage may produce subtle signs in the first week that are not recognised, but over the ensuing months a chronic subdural effusion evolves. This may present as an enlarging head, which raises concerns about the possibility of evolving hydrocephaly. This is not generally associated with signs of raised intracranial pressure, but may alarm parents and other health care professionals. Brain imaging establishes the diagnosis. Fresh haemorrhage may occur in a chronic effusion and is said to be relatively easily provoked. This may cause considerable confusion in allegations of non-accidental injury in infancy.

Posterior fossa subdural haemorrhage

38.202 Posterior fossa haemorrhages associated with severe laceration of the tentorium, a horizontal shelf of dural membrane that separates the posterior part of the cerebral hemispheres from the cerebellum, is usually rapidly fatal. However, less severe tentorial lacerations or rupture of bridging veins draining from the cerebellum may cause a less severe clinical picture that may be delayed for 24–72 hours. The signs are usually those of raised intracranial pressure, such as a full or tense anterior fontanelle and an altered level of arousal, and are due to blockage of flow of cerebrospinal fluid in the posterior fossa. Brain stem signs may occur including deviation of the eyes, facial paralysis, and respiratory depression. Seizures do occur but they are probably related to associated haemorrhage over the surface of the brain rather than to the posterior fossa haemorrhage.

38.203 The diagnosis is made by a CT brain scan. Unless there are brain stem signs or evidence of clinical deterioration surgical evacuation of the clot is not indicated, which is why careful observation and collaboration with a neurosurgeon is important. The outcome in those infants who do not require surgery is good, with around 80–90 per cent having no major sequelae. The outcome in those receiving surgery is unclear at present as it is based on isolated case reports.

Fractures

Clavicular fracture

38.204 The clavicle is the most common bone to be fractured at delivery with a reported incidence of up to 4.5 per cent. In some case the diagnosis can be suspected soon after birth by swelling and crepitation at the site of the fracture and the diagnosis can be confirmed by X-ray. Fractures of the clavicle heal spontaneously and no treatment is required. Their importance rests with the fact that the presentation is often silent, with the diagnosis being made incidentally on a later chest X-ray, done perhaps because of a suspected chest infection. At this stage there is callus formation, reflecting healing. Although there are no adverse medical sequelae the revelation to parents that their baby suffered a broken bone at delivery and that it was not diagnosed may raise suspicions that other problems their baby might have may have been caused by inadequate care at birth.

38.205 Although instrumental delivery and shoulder dystocia are risk factors, clavicular fractures have also been observed following spontaneous vaginal delivery. Up to five per cent of cases are associated with brachial plexus injury (Erb's palsy) and this especially applies when shoulder dystocia has been the precipitating factor.

1344

Skull fracture

38.206 A linear non-depressed skull fracture, most commonly in the parietal region, may be associated with a cephalhaematoma (qv), and intracranial complications are rare. A depressed fracture of the skull refers to inward buckling of the bone, rather like a pressure on a ping-pong ball, with no loss of bone continuity. It is most commonly observed over the parietal region and is caused by compression forces, such as the use of forceps, although cases occurring in utero are reported, presumably due to compression of the head against the maternal pelvis, and such fractures may be caused by pressure from the hand of a birth attendant. Associated neurological signs are uncommon. Mild degrees of bony depression in otherwise well babies need not be treated. There is no consensus view about the treatment of deeper lesions[1] and even these can resolve spontaneously without complication. Surgical elevation may be necessary but this depends on the degree of bony depression and whether there is any underlying intracranial injury and should be discussed with a neurosurgeon.

1 Hung, Liao, Huang 'Rational management of simple depressed skull fractures in infants' (2005) J Neurosurg 103 (1 Suppl) 69–72.

Fractures of the humerus or femur

38.207 Mid-shaft fractures of the humerus or femur are usually recognised soon after birth and the obstetrician may well be aware of a limb fracture as it occurs. The neonatal features are impaired movement of the affected limb (pseudo-paralysis), and swelling and tenderness at the site of the fracture. The diagnosis is confirmed by X-ray, although epiphyseal separation without fracture may be less obvious to the untrained eye. As with all fractures in the newborn, parents may be distressed, and it is important that neonatal staff do not compound their suspicions of avoidable damage by giving inconsistent information about causation and the management of the fracture. The parents should meet with an experienced obstetrician who should discuss the injury in the context of the pregnancy, labour and delivery. An orthopaedic surgeon should be asked to review the infant as soon as possible as there are considerations about different methods of immobilising the limb and the potential harm of excess restriction of movement.

Brachial plexus injury

38.208 Damage to the brachial plexus occurs in 0.5–2.0 per 1,000 live births and mainly affects term infants. Although most recover spontaneously, severe lesions may result in considerable long-term disability due to contractures around the shoulder joint and elbow and impaired function of the arm and shoulder.

38.209 The brachial plexus is a leash of nerve fibres, which arises from the cervical region of the spinal cord and which control movements of the shoulder, arm, wrists and fingers. The most common site of damage is at the nerve roots as they emerge from the spinal cord. The nature of damage ranges from swelling around the roots to complete avulsion. The most common syndrome, known as Erb's palsy, is caused by damage to the upper roots of the plexus, mainly C5 and C6, with C7 making some contribution. Lesions at this level result in impaired movements or loss of movement of the arm affecting abduction of the shoulder, flexion and supination of the forearm and, to a variable extent, extension of the wrist and fingers. The position adopted by the arm at rest is due to the action of opposing muscle forces and is known as the 'waiter's tip' position with adduction of the shoulder, extension at the elbow joint, pronation of the forearm and some degree of flexion of the wrists and fingers. Lesions that also involve the lower roots of the plexus (C8 and T1) additionally impair movements of the fingers, typically causing an absent grasp reflex. Damage to certain nerve fibres at T1 may result in Horner's syndrome on the affected side, manifest as a droopy eyelid, and a constricted pupil.

38.210   The cause of brachial plexus injury is stretching of the plexus by traction on the head. This may occur in shoulder dystocia where traction has to be exerted on the head to deliver the shoulders, and in breech deliveries when traction is exerted on the shoulders to deliver the head. There is an association with generalised hypotonia due to fetal hypoxia during the delivery.

38.211   The diagnosis is made clinically and routine examination of the newborn should include observations for limb movements. When there are obstetric risk factors for birth trauma all forms of injury, including damage to the brachial plexus, should be considered by the examiner.

38.212   In most cases the clinical signs resolve spontaneously by three months and the outcome is good. Unfortunately this has led in some cases to over-optimistic counselling of parents and inadequate follow-up arrangements. Permanent disability, especially resulting from shoulder joint contracture, has been reported in up to 25 per cent of cases depending on the selection criteria.

38.213   Onset of recovery within 2–4 weeks is a favourable sign, and partial recovery can be expected if initial improvement takes 4–6 weeks. If there is no recovery by three months, permanent defects can be expected.

38.214   There needs to be an agreed management plan for all infants with brachial plexus injury. A physiotherapist with experience of this lesion should advise on physical treatment to prevent contractures and the avoidance of pain. This might entail temporary light splinting. A range of imaging investigations and neurophysiological tests are available for those neonates who are not showing any improvement, and these help to delineate the extent of the lesion. It is important to involve an orthopaedic surgeon, a plastic surgeon or a neurosurgeon early on, especially if the lesion is clinically severe. There are many different approaches to surgical management but there are few surgeons in the UK with experience in exploring congenital brachial plexus injuries in early infancy and whoever is involved should have appropriate expertise.

38.215   The medico-legal implications are two-fold. First, it may be alleged that the injury was caused by sub-standard obstetric care, and that excessive force was used to deliver the baby's shoulders; this is a matter for obstetric opinion. Second, a claim may centre on failure to make an early diagnosis and to offer appropriate follow-up care; this involves the paediatrician, paediatric neurologist, and possibly physiotherapist and specialist surgeon.

Spinal cord injury

38.216 Spinal cord injury at birth results from excessive cord traction or rotation. This may especially occur when a fetus is hypotonic as a result of hypoxia. The injury, which is uncommon, is associated with breech delivery and in vertex presentations where attempts at mid-cavity forceps delivery have been made.

38.217 In breech delivery the lesion tends to affect the lower cervical and upper thoracic region of the cord, whereas in cephalic births it involves the upper and mid-cervical region. The acute lesion consists of haemorrhage with varying degrees of stretching or disruption. Among survivors the healing process is characterised by fibrous adhesions and cystic cavity formation.

38.218 The neonatal syndrome consists of paucity of movement of the legs with absent tendon jerks, variable involvement of the upper limbs according to the level of the injury, diaphragmatic breathing due to loss of intercostal muscle function, a bulging abdomen due to lax musculature, an atonic anal sphincter, and a distended bladder that empties with pressure or as part of mass reflex activity stimulated by touch. A sensory level can usually be determined on testing for pain with a pin and observing for facial grimacing. There is respiratory failure with a continuing need for assisted ventilation when the injury affects the upper and mid-cervical region. The usual course in surviving neonates is the development of spasticity and flexion of the hips, knees and ankles, and persisting paralysis of bladder function. Spasticity of the arms occurs in higher lesions.

38.219 Difficult ethical issues arise when an infant requires continuing assisted ventilation for a seriously disabling but incurable disease. Claims of negligence tend to relate to sub-standard obstetric management rather than neonatal care.

Facial nerve injury

38.220 This is the most common peripheral nerve injury as a result of birth trauma and results in facial palsy. The incidence in term babies is probably in the order of 0.5–1.0 per cent when very minor degrees are included. Haemorrhage and swelling of the sheath of the facial nerve usually occurs close to where the nerve leaves the skull at the stylo-mastoid foramen. The most likely cause is compression of the nerve against the bony protuberance of the maternal sacral promontory as observed in the classical publication by Hepner[1] who showed that the affected side of the face normally corresponds with the obstetric presentation. There is also an association with forceps delivery, especially the use of mid-cavity forceps rather than outlet or low forceps[2], and other cases may be caused by extremes of fetal posture with the jaw pressed up against the shoulder.

1 Hepner 'Some observations on facial paresis in the newborn infant: etiology and incidence' (1951) 8(4) Pediatrics 494–497.
2 Hagadorn-Freathy et al.

38.221   Around 75 per cent of cases affect the left side of the face. If the signs are bilateral an alternative cause should be considered, including developmental abnormalities of cranial nerve nuclei and genetic muscle disorders. Normally the weakness affects the upper and lower parts of the face, and the classical signs at rest are flattening of the naso-labial fold, and a wider palpebral fissure on the affected side. The diagnosis usually becomes clear when facial movements are observed. Asymmetrical grimacing is associated with an inability to wrinkle the brow, close the eye, or effectively move the corner of the mouth. There may be drooling of saliva. Mild lesions can be missed in the maternity hospital when the neonate is examined at rest and is discharged home early. Facial asymmetry then becomes apparent to the parents at home when the infant cries.

38.222   The outcome of traumatic facial nerve palsy is normally excellent, with improvement in several weeks. In most cases complete recovery can be expected by several months. Because of inability to close the eyelid, lubricating eye drops need to be given to prevent the cornea becoming dry.

Intra-abdominal injury

38.223   These typically follow a complicated and difficult delivery of a large baby. The organs most likely to be injured are the liver, spleen and adrenal glands, resulting in bleeding. Although intra-abdominal birth trauma is uncommon its importance lies with the clinical presentation of abdominal distension, pallor, or unexplained anaemia, which can be due to a wide range of other conditions. When intra-abdominal haemorrhage is suspected it is important to investigate the infant's coagulation status.

38.224   The liver is the most common intra-abdominal organ to be injured at birth and injury characteristically results in a subcapsular haematoma. The haemorrhage may cease spontaneously at this stage and it is likely that small haematomas go unrecognised. If progressive enlargement of the haematoma occurs there is a risk of rupture with extensive peritoneal haemorrhage. Thus symptoms may range from a progressive unexplained anaemia and jaundice due to breakdown of haemoglobin, to a mass in the right upper area of the abdomen and hypovolaemic haemorrhagic shock.

38.225   The diagnosis is made by abdominal ultrasound or CT imaging. The mainstay of treatment is the maintenance of blood volume and correction of anaemia by blood transfusion. In most cases the haemorrhage resolves spontaneously unless there is an undiagnosed or uncorrected coagulation abnormality. Surgery which would entail partial liver resection is rarely performed unless medical measures fail and the baby's clinical state is deteriorating. In these cases the prognosis is extremely poor.

COMPLICATIONS ASSOCIATED WITH INTRAVASCULAR ACCESS

Introduction

38.226 The medico-legal issues that arise in connection with intravascular access are: (a) whether a drip was sited in a timely fashion; (b) the nature of the fluid infused; (c) whether the infusion became extravascular with consequent tissue damage; and (d) thrombosis and embolism.

38.227 All procedures aimed at gaining access to the circulation carry a risk of infection. In particular, bacteria and fungi on the skin may be introduced into the circulation and the ability of neonates to combat this varies according to their defence mechanisms which may be severely compromised in extremely preterm neonates and those debilitated by other disorders. Therefore preparation of the skin using an alcohol swab and allowing the skin to dry for 1–2 minutes is essential.

38.228 All types of access are more difficult to achieve in extremely small infants. Harm can be done when the first attempt fails and subsequent attempts are driven by personal challenge rather than by a proper appraisal of the situation. The considerations include the urgency of the situation and whether someone else with more experience is available to perform the procedure.

38.229 All procedures involving vascular access should be documented in the neonatal records with particular attention to the time it was carried out, the number of attempts made and an assessment of the ease or difficulty of the procedure. This may become critical if, many years later, the standard of neonatal care is questioned and it is alleged that a delay in carrying out a procedure contributed to damage.

Venous access

38.230 Peripheral intravenous infusions, requiring a cannula to be passed into a superficial vein, are the most common means of accessing the circulation for continuous periods of time. The choice of superficial vein depends on what is readily available and there may not be much choice in small neonates and in those whose veins have already been used and compromised by previous attempts. The most common complication is for the infusion to become extra-vascular ('tissued'). If this is not promptly recognised it may lead to considerable tissue swelling and may even compromise the arterial circulation to the affected part leading to subcutaneous and skin necrosis.

38.231 The intravenous site must be checked at regular intervals for swelling and this should form part of routine nursing observations and be recorded in the nursing records, normally on a chart along with other observations. Another implication of an infusion that has become extra-vascular is that drugs given through the cannula will not have their desired effect and this is of major importance in the management of symptomatic hypoglycaemia. The use of peripheral superficial veins for administering hyperosmolar solutions such as strong dextrose solutions (>10 per cent), calcium, and acidic solutions can readily cause damage to the wall of the vein, thrombosis, and subcutaneous necrosis.

38.232 An umbilical venous catheter is often inserted at or soon after birth as a convenient way of achieving immediate vascular access. The tip should be positioned in the inferior vena cava, about just above the diaphragm. If an X-ray shows that the catheter tip falls short of the desired position, it should not be advanced as this may increase the risk of introducing microorganisms from the umbilical site. Instead a new catheter should be inserted under sterile conditions. Complications apart from sepsis include air embolism if the proximal end of the catheter is left open, and thrombosis, liver damage and portal hypertension, particularly if hyperosmolar solutions are given through an umbilical venous catheter. This applies especially if the catheter tip failed to reach the inferior vena cava and is lodged instead in the liver. Umbilical venous catheters may remain in place for 7–14 days but there is an increasing risk of infection the longer they remain in position. If there is a predicted need for total parenteral nutrition for some weeks it is better to replace the catheter with a central venous catheter.

38.233 Central venous catheters, often referred to as 'long lines', are commonly inserted using a percutaneous technique as a means of providing total parenteral nutrition. After preparation of the skin, a needle is inserted into a suitable peripheral vein, commonly at the forearm or ankle, and a fine catheter on a mounting device is threaded through the needle until the tip of the catheter advances the required distance. The needle is then removed. Vigilance is required for sepsis. The catheter should be removed if there is any swelling or erythema at the site of entry or along the course of the catheterised vein, or if a blood culture proves positive.

38.234 The aim is to position the tip of the catheter in the superior or inferior vena cava a little way outside the heart. The position must be checked with an X-ray and on no account should the tip of the catheter lie within the right atrium of the heart. Catheters at this site can cause a collection of fluid within the pericardium, compressing the heart and impairing its function – a condition known as cardiac tamponade. As a result of four deaths due to cardiac tamponade in neonates who had central venous catheters within the right atrium the Chief Medical Officer of England additionally recommended that all central venous catheters inserted specifically for parenteral nutrition should be inserted using a full sterile technique by or under the direct supervision of a competent individual, and that assessment of the catheter position should routinely be by plain X-ray. If this is inadequate to identify the tip of the line, the use of contrast dye should be considered. A further recommendation was that records of insertion of all peripherally inserted central lines (including failed attempts) should be kept for future audit.

Arterial access

38.235 Access to arterial blood is needed for blood gas analysis, although over recent years it has become very common to employ non-invasive continuous measurements of oxygen saturation using a skin probe, supplemented by intermittent measurements of blood gases on arterial blood.

38.236 Umbilical arterial catheterisation is a common procedure on neonatal units and is often done soon after birth with simultaneous catheterisation of the umbilical vein. Either of the two umbilical arteries may be used and the route the catheter takes is downwards until the femoral artery is entered, and then the catheter curves upwards into the common iliac artery finishing in the descending aorta. One of the purposes of umbilical arterial catheterisation is to monitor arterial blood gasses. Errors have been made by inadvertent catheterisation of the umbilical vein and failure to recognise this on X-ray with serious consequences when the catheter was relied on for oxygen monitoring (*Wilsher v Essex Area Health Authority*[1]). Medical staff should be aware that on an abdominal X-ray the umbilical arterial catheter takes a downward dip prior to ascending in the aorta, whereas the venous catheter passes upwards from the point of insertion. If there is any doubt it can be resolved by a lateral X-ray which shows the arterial catheter is posterior, whereas a venous catheter is anterior.

1 [1988] AC 1074.

38.237 Thrombosis with blood clot in the area of the catheter tip and embolisation is a known complication and so the aim is to position the catheter away from the renal and mesenteric arteries. A favoured site for the tip of the catheter is at or just above the level of the diaphragm. In view of the risk of embolisation the toes and feet must be carefully examined at regular intervals for blue discolouration and this should be part of routine nursing observations and recorded in the nursing charts. The position of the umbilical arterial catheter should always be confirmed by an X-ray that includes the chest as well as the abdomen. As with umbilical venous catheters if the umbilical arterial catheter is positioned too high it may be pulled back, but if too low it should not be advanced, and instead a new catheter should be inserted under aseptic conditions.

38.238 Haemorrhage from the umbilical artery during insertion of the catheter is common and usually mild. However, if insertion proves difficult and the operator persists, the cumulative blood loss can be extensive. The attempt should be abandoned and firm pressure applied to the umbilical stump for at least five minutes. Insidious blood loss may also occur after the catheter has been inserted and this should be avoided by ensuring that appropriate measures are taken to secure the catheter.

38.239 Peripheral arterial catheterisation and sampling for the purpose of monitoring blood gasses is now best avoided because of the risk of serious thrombotic and embolic complications. Before the advent of non-invasive monitoring of oxygen saturation, when catheterisation of the radial or posterior tibial arteries was more common, there were occasional losses of fingers and toes as a result of gangrene, especially in very preterm neonates. The same considerations apply to intermittent peripheral arterial puncture to obtain blood for gas analysis. The information gained from intermittent arterial puncture may be unhelpful because it often induces crying and agitation which tend to lower both the oxygen level (PaO2) and the carbon dioxide ($PaCO_2$).

OTHER DISEASES AND CONDITIONS

Scrotal swelling

38.240 A scrotal swelling which easily trans-illuminates is normally a hydrocele which needs no treatment. If the swelling has a solid feel to it then a surgical opinion should be sought promptly, as it is important to distinguish prenatal torsion of the testis from a scrotal haematoma. Neither lesion will normally transilluminate and distinction may be impossible without operation.

Jaundice

38.241 When red blood cells have reached the end of their natural life span, or are destroyed as a result of haemolysis, the end product is unconjugated bilirubin, which is fat-soluble. It becomes bound to albumin in the blood stream and is transported to the liver where it undergoes conjugation with glucuronic acid and becomes water-soluble and is able to be excreted in the urine and the bowel. Conjugated bilirubin is excreted by the liver through the bile duct into the bowel where it is degraded by bacteria and excreted in the stool. If unconjugated bilirubin becomes unbound from albumin ('free bilirubin') and enters the brain it is neurotoxic because of its fat solubility.

38.242 In the first week of life around two-thirds of all newborn infants develop a mild degree of jaundice, which is physiological and harmless. In term infants this is characterised by a rise in unconjugated serum bilirubin reaching a peak of around 100 µmol/l at 48–72 hours with a decline to around 50 µmol/l by five days of life. In preterm infants, higher peak levels of around 200 µmol/l are reached on the fourth or fifth day and then gradually decline over the ensuing weeks. Note that bilirubin levels may also be expressed as 'mg per 100 ml' (mg per 100 ml × 17.1 = µmol/l).

38.243 The causes of pathological jaundice or hyperbilirubinaemia of the newborn include increased breakdown of red cells due to haemolytic disorders, defective uptake and conjugation of bilirubin by the liver due to enzyme defects, sepsis, and an insufficient intake of milk in breast-fed infants where various mechanisms operate. If the level of unconjugated bilirubin becomes very high and overwhelms the albumin binding capacity of the blood, free bilirubin entering the brain may cause irreversible damage, known as kernicterus, culminating in neurodevelopmental disability. This is characterised by bilirubin staining of certain groups of nuclei, especially the basal ganglia and brain stem nuclei. The mechanism of bilirubin brain damage is complex and is influenced by the amount of unconjugated bilirubin that enters the brain, the duration of exposure, the integrity of the blood-brain barrier, and neuronal susceptibility. Among preterm infants the presence of infection and acidaemia are additional risks for kernicterus in the presence of a raised serum bilirubin level.

38.244 The clinical presentation of kernicterus in the neonatal period is known as 'bilirubin encephalopathy'. It develops over the course of 1–2 weeks after birth, commencing with poor sucking, hypotonia, and impaired arousal, and evolving after a few days to hypertonia, neck and trunk retraction, fever, and sometimes a high pitched cry. Surviving infants develop athetoid (dystonic) cerebral palsy, hearing loss, paralysis of upward gaze and, less often, intellectual impairment. Dental dysplasia may be a feature in some children because the primary dentition is developing at the time that the baby is jaundiced.

38.245 The mainstay of clinical management is monitoring of serum bilirubin levels and intervention with phototherapy and in some cases exchange transfusion when certain levels are exceeded. There are transcutaneous devices which give a measure of total bilirubin based on spectral reflectance. They do not replace the need for blood sampling but they are a helpful adjunct in the management of jaundiced neonates, allowing progress to be monitored between blood sampling. There is no defined absolute serum bilirubin level above which kernicterus consistently occurs. It depends on the age of the infant, maturity, and the rate of rise, which can be very rapid in haemolytic disease, and the presence of associated illness in the neonate – especially sepsis. Therefore there is variation in practice concerning the levels of bilirubin at which phototherapy is started and the threshold at which exchange transfusion is carried out[1].

1 American Academy of Pediatrics 'Management of Hyperbilirubinemia in the Newborn Infant 35 or More Weeks of Gestation' Clinical Practice Guideline (2004) 114 Pediatrics 297–316; Bhutani, Johnson, Shapiro 'Kernicterus in sick and preterm infants (1999–2002): A need for an effective preventive approach' (2004) 28 Seminars in Perinatology 319–325.

38.246 Maternity units usually rely on graphs which apply to infants of different gestational ages and which show serum bilirubin levels plotted against postnatal age. Superimposed on these graphs are 'action lines' indicating recommended thresholds for starting phototherapy or exchange transfusion. For example, a very preterm infant might receive phototherapy in the first week of life at bilirubin levels of 100–140 µmol/l, whereas for a term infant the threshold would be in the region of 240 µmol/l. Similarly exchange transfusion would be a consideration in an ill very preterm neonate if the level arose above 200 µmol/l whereas in an otherwise healthy term infant the level might well be allowed to rise to 350 µmol/l.

38.247 Although kernicterus is uncommon, it is a potentially preventable disorder. In preterm infants the pitfalls include: (a) failure to recognise the importance of jaundice that is already established by 48 hours, especially when it may be masked by dark skin; (b) failure to recognise that early onset jaundice may progress rapidly; (c) failure to 'chase up' serum bilirubin results with the laboratory; (d) failure to appreciate that the signs of bilirubin encephalopathy may be subtle in very preterm neonates and may be masked by other disorders; and (e) failure to recognise that sepsis and acidaemia increase the risk of kernicterus.

38.248 Term and near-term jaundiced infants present special risks because of the trend towards early discharge home from the maternity unit before feeding has become established. Cases of kernicterus have been reported in near-term breast feeding infants who were not receiving adequate nutrition and hydration, although they appeared otherwise well. The pitfalls in term and near-term infants include:

(a)   failure to recognise that visual estimation of the degree of jaundice can lead to errors, particularly in infants with dark skin pigmentation;

(b)   failure to appreciate that bruising and a cephalhaematoma are potential sources of bilirubin;

(c)   failure to check the bilirubin level before discharge home in an infant noted to be jaundiced in the first 24 hours;

(d)   failure to appreciate that term and near-term infants, especially those who are breast fed, can quickly develop extremely high serum bilirubin levels and kernicterus;

(e)   failure to communicate effectively with the GP or domiciliary midwife when an infant is discharged home with mild jaundice, and to emphasise that close surveillance is required and that the serum bilirubin level needs to be monitored; and

(f)   failure on the part of community healthcare professionals to respond to parental concern regarding jaundice, poor feeding, or lethargy.

Hypoglycaemia

Introduction

38.249 An abnormally low blood glucose level occurring intermittently or sustained for a period of several hours can cause symptoms and may lead to permanent brain damage. However, there are uncertainties around the definition of hypoglycaemia and the context in which hypoglycaemic brain damage might occur. An adequate supply of glucose is needed for neurons and their supporting cells to function properly. Fetuses receive glucose from the maternal circulation, and this is normally sufficient. At birth, this supply is cut off and blood glucose levels fall reaching a nadir at about 1–2 hours, and increasing to a baseline level at around three hours. In preterm infants the fall is somewhat greater and it takes a little longer to reach a baseline level. During this transient reduction in the blood glucose level, and indeed at other times when there is relative glucose deficiency, the neonate is able to utilise other fuels for neural metabolism including ketones, lactate, and amino acids. The newborn baby's brain is therefore to some extent protected from hypoglycaemic injury.

Symptoms of hypoglycaemia

38.250 The signs and symptoms that have been observed in association with low blood glucose levels are non-specific and range from lethargy, poor feeding, apnoea and bradycardia episodes, cyanotic attacks to increased excitability with tachycardia, tremulous or jittery behaviour, and frank seizures. Low blood glucose levels often occur without symptoms. Therefore symptoms cannot be relied upon for the diagnosis of hypoglycaemia. Numerous attempts have been made to define the 'normal range' of blood glucose in the neonate but this is not a helpful concept when it comes to determining whether symptoms are due to hypoglycaemia.

The concept of an operational threshold

38.251 A useful concept is an 'operational threshold' and directing management to achieve levels above this threshold in a way which allows a margin of safety. Among neonates who are at risk for hypoglycaemia, a suggested blood glucose threshold is 2.0 mmol/l, whereas for those who have symptoms consistent with hypoglycaemia a threshold of 2.5 mmol/l is recommended[1]. (Blood glucose levels are sometimes expressed in units of 'mg per 100ml' (mg per 100ml ÷ 18 = mmol/l)).

1 Cornblath, Hawdon, Williams, Aynsley-Green Ward-Platt, Schwartz, Kalhan 'Controversies regarding definition of neonatal hypoglycaemia: Suggested operational thresholds' (2000) 105 Pediatrics 1141–1145.

38.252 The use of an operational threshold is helpful both from a clinical and medico-legal perspective. It sets a standard for the management of neonates who are at risk of hypoglycaemia, and separates this from the notion that there is a definable level of blood glucose that determines whether or not hypoglycaemic brain damage will occur.

Management of neonates at risk for hypoglycaemia

38.253 Babies who are born light because of intrauterine growth restriction are particularly vulnerable to hypoglycaemia. This is because glucose is stored as glycogen and such infants have low glycogen stores in the liver. This is well known and every maternity unit should have written guidelines on the management of growth restricted newborn babies. Neonatal and midwifery staff need to be aware of the risk factors for hypoglycaemia (Table 38.3). Healthy term infants who are not at risk do not need to have their blood glucose levels monitored. Infants identified as being at risk should have their blood glucose levels checked at intervals. Cot-side testing using a spot of capillary blood placed on a reagent strip which is then inserted into a small instrument known as a glucose reflectance meter is unreliable for monitoring hypoglycaemia in the newborn and is prone to produce misleading results[1].

TABLE 38.3 RISK FACTORS FOR NEONATAL HYPOGLYCAEMIA THAT INDICATE A NEED FOR BLOOD GLUCOSE MONITORING

Maternal diabetes or gestational diabetes
Maternal use of beta -blockers, or oral hypoglycemic drugs
Administration of glucose infusion during labour
Preterm birth (less than 37 weeks gestation)
Intrauterine growth impairment
Suspected birth asphyxia
Hypothermia
Infection
Infants receiving parenteral nutrition
Polycythaemia (raised red cell count)
Suspected endocrine disorders, inborn errors of metabolism, hydrops fetalis, and Beckwith-Weidemann syndrome (a syndrome with microcephaly, umbilical hernia, large tongue, and a tendency for hypoglycaemia).

1 Medical Devices Agency 'Extra-laboratory Use of Blood Glucose Meters and Test Strips: Contra-indications, Training and Advice to the Users' (1996) Safety Notice MDA SN 9616 June 1996.

38.254 A reasonable approach is to measure the blood glucose level 3–4 hours after birth, preferably before a feed. If it is above the threshold of 2.0 mmol/l and the infant is feeding normally then further tests can be done at approximately 12-hourly intervals until full oral milk feeds are established. If the result is ≤2.0 mmol/l then the approach depends on the clinical context. For those preterm neonates who are managing to suck and take milk feeds, all that is necessary is extra encouragement with feeds. If breast feeding is proving difficult it is better to give supplementary feeds of expressed breast milk or formula milk by bottle or by naso-gastric tube until the blood glucose level has stabilised. The notion of 'breast feeding at all costs' is potentially dangerous and has resulted in some cases in severe hypoglycaemia.

38.255 Preterm neonates below 32 weeks' gestation and infants who have illnesses that limit their ability to establish milk feeding should receive an intravenous infusion of 10 per cent glucose starting at around 90 ml/Kg/day and adjusted according to their blood glucose level, aiming to achieve a level >2.0 mmol/l. Most growth restricted neonates who are at term or approaching term are able to take their milk feeds, which should be introduced early after birth. If their blood glucose levels are sub-threshold in spite of an adequate milk intake then intravenous supplementation as for preterm infants should be provided to achieve a blood glucose level >2.0 mmol/l.

Infants of diabetic mothers

38.256 The main regulator of blood glucose levels is insulin, which is secreted by the pancreas. In maternal diabetes or gestational diabetes, the mother produces insufficient insulin, which causes high blood glucose levels in the mother. Glucose crosses the placenta and high levels cause overactivity of the fetal insulin-secreting cells in the fetal pancreas. After birth, when the maternal supply of glucose is cut off, this overactivity continues causing inappropriate insulin secretion in the newly born baby. This may cause asymptomatic hypoglycaemia in the first 6–12 hours, but sometimes extending to 48 hours. Most cases can be managed by the early introduction of milk feeds and monitoring of blood glucose levels until they stabilise to >2.0 mmol/l. As long as the infant has no symptoms, as is normally the case, intravenous glucose should be avoided as it may stimulate the over-receptive pancreas to further insulin production.

Treatment of hypoglycaemia

38.257 Neonates may be symptom-free, yet have very low blood glucose levels, that is <1.5 mmol/l. Some have risk factors which lead to their having their blood glucose level measured in the first place, and attempts to maintain their glucose levels above >2.0 mmol/l with milk feeds clearly failed. An infusion of 10 per cent dextrose should be commenced. This is intended to provide a margin of safety, given the current uncertainty about the relationship between blood glucose levels and brain damage. If there are also symptoms consistent with hypoglycaemia, particularly seizures, a depressed level of arousal, or hypotonia then the situation is more urgent and a rapid increase in the blood sugar level is needed. A bolus intravenous injection of 2 ml/Kg of 10 per cent dextrose is recommended followed immediately by a continuous infusion at 90 ml/Kg/day. However, repeated boluses should be avoided and the aim should be to adjust the rate of the infusion to achieve a blood glucose level >2.5 mmol/l.

38.258 Pitfalls in management include failure to ensure that the intravenous infusion is secure and has not leaked into the tissues, failure to check the blood glucose level within 1–2 hours of starting the infusion, and too rapid a reduction in the glucose infusion rate leading to rebound hypoglycaemia.

Hypoglycaemia and brain damage: issues of causation

38.259 Much of our information about the association of neonatal hypoglycaemia and brain damage derive from post-mortem accounts of brain pathology in neonates, descriptive accounts of neurodevelopmental impairment among survivors, and more recently brain scan appearances in surviving infants and children. Care needs to be applied to the interpretation of the documented blood glucose levels. It has always been recognised that the use of reagent strips for monitoring blood glucose levels in neonates is at best a crude screening test and that results should always be supplemented by laboratory measurements of blood glucose. Misleading results occur at extremes of haematocrit values, high bilirubin levels, and variations in blood oxygen tensions, and these are all situations that apply to neonates who may be at risk for hypoglycaemia. The problem for claimants is that in the absence of documented evidence of hypoglycaemia by laboratory methods – an omission that might indeed be negligent – it is difficult to show that hypoglycaemia was the cause of a child's later problems. However, recurrent non-reassuring results based on reagent strip measurements in the presence of symptoms consistent with hypoglycaemia and no other neonatal disorder may well suffice if supported by MRI brain scan evidence suggestive of hypoglycaemic damage; the occipital region at the back of the brain is particularly vulnerable to low blood glucose concentrations.

38.260 The duration of hypoglycaemia is also important when considering causation. A brief and transient episode of hypoglycaemia documented by a single blood glucose result is a most unlikely cause of brain damage. Reports describing the post-mortem appearances of hypoglycaemic damage and the more recent MRI brain scan observations in surviving neonates suggest that hypoglycaemic brain damage requires prolonged or intermittent hypoglycaemia for duration of many hours, rather than minutes.

38.261 Descriptions of poor outcomes following neonatal hypoglycaemia draw attention to symptoms occurring at the time of the hypoglycaemia. A need to show that restoration of normoglycaemia resulted in resolution of symptoms is often put forward as a necessary condition to show that long-term neuro-disability was caused by neonatal hypoglycaemia. However, it may not be all that helpful in a medico-legal context. In circumstances where hypoglycaemic symptoms have been reversed in this way it is almost implicit that the hypoglycaemia has in fact been recognised and treatment given. Furthermore, seizures may initially be due to untreated hypoglycaemia but subsequently be caused by secondary neural mechanisms which persist in spite of restoring normoglycaemia.

38.262 It is widely agreed that term infants with asymptomatic hypoglycaemia have a good prognosis. In a follow-up study of premature infants enrolled in a randomised controlled feeding trial it was shown that blood glucose levels of <2.6 mmol/l recorded over the course of many days were associated with lower developmental scores at 18 months[1]. However, these findings were not confirmed on longer follow-up. Additional studies are needed to clarify whether moderate hypoglycaemia in preterm infants causes developmental delay.

1 Lucas, Morley, Cole 'Adverse neurodevelopmental outcome of moderate neonatal hypoglycaemia' (1988) 297 British Medical Journal 1304–1308.

Brain scan appearances and neurological sequelae

38.263 Reports on the later MRI brain scan appearances of neonates who suffered severe hypoglycaemia are broadly consistent with pathological findings in the brain among those who died with hypoglycaemia. The main finding on later MR imaging is bilateral loss of cerebral cortical tissue especially in the occipital and posterior parietal lobes. White matter abnormalities in the periventricular areas of occipital and the parietal lobes have also been reported and may represent impaired or delayed myelination.

38.264 Alkalay[1] et al (2005) found involvement of the occipital lobes in 82 per cent of newly born babies who had profound hypoglycaemia. There was dilation of the ventricles secondary to white matter shrinkage in 41 per cent, parietal lobe involvement in 29 per cent and other areas of the brain affected in 12 per cent. Half of these infants had visual impairment. The median (range) postnatal age when hypoglycemia was first detected was 48 hours (1–72 hours), and the median (range) of plasma glucose values was 7 mg/dL (2–26 mg/dL). The appearances differ from the changes following hypoxic-ischaemic damage, although sometimes the two pathologies co-exist.

1 Alkalay, Sarnat, Flores-Sarnat, Simmons 'Neurologic aspects of neonatal hypoglycaemia' (2005) 7 Israel Medical Association Journal 188–192.

38.265 Later neurological sequelae for babies exposed to damaging hypoglycaemia are 65 per cent with motor or psycho-developmental delay, 41 per cent with visual impairment, and 35 per cent with microcephaly. It should also be noted that neonates with symptomatic hypoglycaemia may have transient abnormalities on scans which are no longer apparent at later imaging[1]. There is no evidence that such transient abnormalities are associated with long-term disability.

1 Kinnala, Rikalainen, Lapinleimu, Parkkola, Kormano, Kero 'Cerebral magnetic resonance imaging and ultrasonography findings after neonatal hypoglycemia' (1999) 103 Pediatrics 724–729.

CAUSATION

Hypoxia during labour and delivery

38.266 Hypoxia during labour and delivery can:

(1) be recognised by fetal symptoms, notably decreased fetal movements, heart rate abnormalities, meconium in the amniotic fluid and acidaemia;
(2) cause neonatal asphyxia recognised most easily by inadequate respiratory and circulatory function immediately after birth;
(3) cause neonatal neurological symptoms, termed hypoxic ischaemic encephalopathy associated with disturbance of function of other organs and systems;
(4) be responsible for the brain damage that causes cerebral palsy usually in association with other neuro-developmental problems.

38.267 Aetiological issues (ie causation), and the clinical features that are produced are usually complex. The nature of the insult to the nervous system, its timing in relation to the patient's age, the regions of the brain that are affected and the limiting effects of treatment on the symptoms all have to be borne in mind when patients present for diagnosis, or in clinical negligence litigation.

38.268 It is incumbent upon lawyers, therefore, to ensure that doctors clarify their degree of certainty when addressing these issues in individual cases. Against this background it is also incumbent upon both lawyers and medical experts to understand the reasons why parents become involved in litigation on behalf of their children. Very frequently this is so that they can ascertain if at all possible the cause of their child's disability rather than necessarily to obtain financial redress.

Prenatal issues

38.269 It does not follow that all children born with limb reduction deformities have been affected by thalidomide or any other drug. One sees in clinical practice one or two children each year born without one or more limbs or parts of limbs for which no cause can be found on full enquiry. Similarly, while it is a wise precaution in general for women to avoid medication in early pregnancy, the scientific evidence that some incriminated drugs actually cause fetal malformations is simply not available. An exception to this is a variety of anticonvulsant drugs used for the treatment of epilepsy in women who are pregnant. Sodium valproate (Epilim), carbamazepine (Tegretol) and phenytoin (Epanutin) all have associations with a variety of fetal malformations that cause both dysmorphic characteristics and developmental delay. What is hitherto unknown however is precisely when in gestation adverse effects are determined and also whether these are dose related. Moreover studies comparing the relative risk of untreated epilepsy on the one hand and maternal anticonvulsant therapy on the other have not hitherto been concluded. While it is accepted, therefore, that information that there is a potential risk of anticonvulsant therapy should always be offered to women with epilepsy, preferably prior to their becoming pregnant, successful claims against either pharmaceutical companies or clinicians have not hitherto been pursued through the courts.

38.270 Damage to the fetus in the second trimester of pregnancy following amniocentesis is a further recognised cause of prenatal brain damage. Consideration of appropriate amniocentesis practice and techniques is outside the remit of this chapter but the fetus can be injured during this procedure without necessarily then being aborted. After birth the demonstration of localised brain abnormalities both clinically and on magnetic resonance imaging, often together with finding a scar consistent with there having been a puncture site when amniocentesis has been performed, has led on a number of occasions to successful litigation being pursued[1].

1 Squier, Camberlain, Zaiwalla (et al) 'Five cases of brain injury following amniocentesis in mid-term pregnancy' (2000) 42 Developmental Medicine and Child Neurology 554–560.

38.271 It is generally held that trauma to the mother during pregnancy, if sufficiently severe, will produce abortion and death of the fetus rather than long-term neurological handicap. This subject has been well reviewed by Crosby as long ago as 1974[1]. Exceptions occur from time to time, however[2]. In such circumstances the trauma will normally produce some degree of placental separation or other damage. It is usual but not invariable in such circumstances for the mother to be symptomatic with abdominal bruising and tenderness and vaginal bleeding and possibly also to be hypotensive. Premature delivery often follows. Alternatively the infant may survive but fail to thrive in utero and, although apparently in good condition when eventually born, may subsequently show clinical and radiological features consistent with having sustained brain damage at the time of the original injury. Within this context appropriate radiological evidence supporting the time of the injury needs to be sought.

1 Crosby 'Trauma during Pregnancy: Maternal and Fetal Injury' (1974) 29 Obstetrical and Gynaecological Survey 10.
2 Hayes, Ryan, Stephenson, King 'Cerebral palsy after maternal trauma in pregnancy' (2007) Developmental Medicine and Child Neurology.

The perinatal period

The perinatal period

38.272 According to the World Health Organisation, the perinatal period commences at 22 completed weeks (154 days) of gestation and ends seven completed days after birth. Perinatal mortality refers to the number of stillbirths and deaths in the first week of life (early neonatal mortality) and is used as an index of national health and of the efficacy of local services. It is currently in the region of 10 per 1,000 births in the UK but with significant national and regional variations. Perinatal mortality is a very crude statistic and slightly more refined is perinatal morbidity, which includes children who have sustained brain damage. There has been much research and even more speculation on the numbers of children who acquire brain damage in the perinatal period, the mechanisms by which they do so, the clinical features that they demonstrate before and immediately after they are born and their long-term symptoms and outlook. All of these have to be seen against a background, first, that perinatal morbidity and mortality figures include far more children than those with neurological impairment, for example those with congenital heart disease, and second, that neurological abnormalities seen in the perinatal period or later by no means necessarily imply that the underlying brain damage was perinatally determined.

Deprivation of nutrients

38.273 This applies particularly during the last trimester of pregnancy. An unsuitable uterine environment due for example to pre-eclampsia (toxaemia of pregnancy) can cause failure of the baby to grow satisfactorily and to be light for gestational age (LGA). LGA infants are more likely to have a variety of neurological dysfunctions including cerebral palsy and mental retardation. The evaluation of the cause and possibly prevention of these features in individual cases requires careful consideration by obstetricians and neonatal paediatricians. In general, however, when failure to thrive in utero occurs due to inadequate placental function in the last weeks of pregnancy, brain development is largely spared, the evidence for this being preservation of a normal rate of head growth in utero. This is termed asymmetrical intrauterine growth retardation and can be contrasted with conditions where there is symmetrical intra-uterine growth retardation with restriction of both body and head growth, eg due to inherited conditions. From the medico-legal view point it is often difficult when there has been intra-uterine growth retardation of whatever degree leading to an infant who is LGA to establish that different obstetric and neonatal management would necessarily have led to a better outcome.

CONCLUSIONS

38.274 The policy of early discharge home from maternity units poses certain risks for the newborn which need to be recognised by both hospital and community staff. In particular, feeding may not have been established, jaundice often has not reached its peak, evolving sepsis may be missed, and congenital cardiac disease may be missed.

38.275   What is described as the new genetics involves the detailed mapping of genes on their particular chromosomes, and identification of the particular protein constituents of individual genes. It is adding an increased dimension to our understanding of genetic disorders and has implications for the advice and practice offered by specialist clinical genetic services. Referral of children with identified or unidentified syndromes that ultimately turn out to have genetic implications is increasingly regarded as an appropriate standard of practice.

38.276   Most disability in childhood is not acquired because of adverse perinatal events. But although modern genetics has shown previously undetected abnormalities, these may be compounded by adverse perinatal or neonatal events. Thus a child who has Down syndrome (trisomy 21) may be additionally damaged by hypoxic ischaemia.

38.277   If obstetric or neonatal complications arise, it is understandable that parents may be concerned about a causal link. However, in individual cases, establishing a causal relationship between the complications and brain damage is often complex.

38.278   Improved outcomes in preterm infants have led to high expectations among parents. The notion of unavoidable complications of prematurity, such as cerebral haemorrhage and ischaemia is increasingly being questioned as associations are found between clinical events and brain lesions.

38.279   In spite of better outcomes for most preterm babies, those born at the margins of viability (25 weeks gestation and less) have a very high risk of moderate and severe disabilities in childhood. Their initial management in the delivery room poses huge ethical and medical challenges and highlights the need for good communication with parents, and between obstetric and neonatal staff.

38.280   Severe birth trauma (injury) is now uncommon. However, any superficial trauma may be a pointer to other injuries that are not immediately obvious.

38.281   Neonatal intensive care exposes infants to a wide range of treatments and invasive procedures that carry risks which must be explained to parents.

38.282   Establishing causation and liability is complex and a combination of expertise is needed: an obstetrician and/or fetal medicine expert and midwife to consider events and care during the period from pre-conception to birth, a neonatal paediatrician and perhaps a neonatal nurse to consider events and care during the neonatal period, a paediatric neurologist and/ or developmental care specialist to consider the possibility of any other diagnosis and to establish condition and prognosis. Other specialties may also need to be involved depending on the details of the individual case, eg a physician specialising in diabetic care during pregnancy, a paediatric surgeon, cardiologist, endocrinologist, gastroenterologist and general practitioner.

CHAPTER 39

Imaging for perinatal and early childhood neurological problems

Dr Keiran Hogarth

INTRODUCTION; METHODS AND OBJECTIVES OF EXAMINATION

39.1   Most neuroradiologists in the UK are doctors who have undergone subspecialist or 'fellowship' training specifically in brain and spine imaging. They tend to work in regional neurosciences centres, which provide adult neurology and neurosurgery services. In addition, some centres also provide paediatric neurology and neurosurgery services. Brain imaging is also performed by radiologists, whose subspeciality training is in other disciplines such as paediatric radiology or oncological radiology.

39.2   The aims of neuroimaging include demonstration of structural brain abnormalities and diagnosis of the multifarious pathologies that affect the central nervous system. It primarily comprises so-called 'cross-sectional' imaging modalities, namely computed tomography (CT) and magnetic resonance (MR) imaging. In neonates (new-born infants), brain imaging is possible with ultrasound (US) scanning, using the gap between the calvarial bones (anterior fontanelle) as an 'acoustic window'. In pregnancy, ultrasound scanning is the primary investigation for evaluating the fetal brain and is generally performed at 10–14 weeks and 18–20 weeks. In recent years, MR imaging of the fetal brain has become more available to obstetricians as a second-line investigation (after fetal ultrasound scanning). This is primarily the result of the development of faster MR imaging sequences. As the fetus is often not static, faster sequences have meant that the problem of movement artefact has, to a reasonable extent, been overcome.

39.3   Routine fetal ultrasound scanning is generally performed by specialist-trained radiographers (ultrasonographers). In cases where an abnormality has been detected, an obstetric physician may also perform a fetal ultrasound scan prior to making a referral to neuroradiology for MR fetal brain imaging.

39.4   It is important to emphasise the point that the MR imaging appearances of the fetal brain change dramatically during normal development in early life. As a result of this, certain abnormalities may or may not be demonstrable on imaging at early stages (particularly in utero) and may only become detectable later. For example, subtle abnormalities of the cerebral cortex may not be amenable to diagnosis on fetal MR imaging but may become detectable once there has been sufficient maturation of the cerebral white matter (a process called myelination). In such cases, delayed imaging, usually after the age of two years, can be helpful to increase the sensitivity of the imaging investigation. This is particularly the case for subtle white matter damage, which is often undetectable until myelination has occurred. Sometimes, serial imaging can be helpful to assess the evolution in time of a pathological process, which may help to narrow the differential diagnosis.

39.5   CT scanning is the first-line imaging investigation for post-traumatic damage to the head and spine and for the early diagnosis of intracranial haemorrhage. Modern scanners are able to acquire image data extremely rapidly and therefore CT scans are generally far less prone to movement artefact than MRI. As CT scanning involves the use of X-ray radiation, its use has to be carefully considered, especially in young patients as they are more prone to the long-term risks of radiation exposure. It is important to point out that CT scans are of great utility in identifying bony abnormalities (such as skull fractures for example) whereas MR is less relied upon for this, in the context of neuroimaging at least.

39.6 In neuroradiology, imaging of the blood vessels can be obtained using CT angiography, MR angiography and invasive catheter digital subtraction angiography (DSA). All three methods require the use of an intravenous contrast agent to be injected into the patient. CT and MR angiography are generally performed in preference over DSA as the latter is an invasive procedure and as such has a greater risk burden than the non-invasive methods. Invasive catheter vascular imaging is now mainly performed when a treatment procedure is being undertaken, such as embolisation of a cerebral aneurysm or arteriovenous malformation.

39.7 Lastly, it must be recognised that MR imaging of infants usually requires general anaesthesia to ensure that the scan is unaffected by patient movement. In the hands of an experienced paediatric anaesthetist, the risk to the patient is minimal. In general anaesthesia, control of the airway is guaranteed and it is therefore safer than sedation, which produces less reliable results and has a more prolonged recovery.

PATHOPHYSIOLOGY IN RELATION TO HYPOXIC ISCHAEMIA AND TIMING OF DAMAGE

39.8 The relative vulnerability of cells in different regions of the brain varies with their state of development depending on the time of gestation at which an insult occurs. Therefore the appearance and distribution of end-stage brain damage may be used within limits to deduce the timing at which an insult occurred.

Malformations

39.9 Generally speaking, formation of the brain occurs during the first half of gestation and major malformations can be recognised by about 20 weeks on routine obstetric ultrasound studies. More detailed studies with ultrasound and/or magnetic resonance imaging are performed when malformations are suspected or are more likely because of a previous dysmorphic fetus or familial or genetic predisposition with a history of drug abuse in early pregnancy (alcohol, cocaine) or certain anticonvulsants for maternal epilepsy or from raised maternal serum alpha fetoprotein: spina bifida with myelomeningocele or lipomeningocele and Chiari II Type malformation, caudal regression, holoprosencephaly, hemimegalencephaly, callosal agenesis, primary microcephaly, schizencephaly may all be definitively diagnosed. Less specific enlargement of the ventricles due to hydrocephalus, congenital infection or malformation may be recognised. Normal and abnormal neuronal migration may be shown by fetal magnetic resonance imaging. The likely disability, which may be expected from detailed study of such abnormalities, will be the basis of discussion regarding therapeutic abortion and avoidance of birth of a malformed baby.

Germinal plexus and neuronal migration abnormalities

39.10 Neuronal proliferation and migration commences at around eight weeks of gestation and continues until around 23 weeks' gestation. The germinal plexuses continue to be active in producing glial cell precursors, gradually diminishing after 30 weeks' up to about 34 weeks' gestation. The germinal plexuses are supplied by a rich network of thin-walled vessels, which are prone to haemorrhage in premature infants, particularly if subjected to hypoxia during birth or in the early neonatal period or to rapid variations in venous pressure during ventilation necessary for pulmonary insufficiency.

Intraventricular haemorrhage

39.11 Haemorrhage distending the lateral ventricles tends to compress subependymal veins. Subsequent reduction in perfusion pressure may cause infarction of periventricular white matter and deep grey matter nuclei, which is usually haemorrhagic. It may be focal or multifocal, unilateral or bilateral but usually asymmetrical producing a typical appearance both during evolution (usually shown on ultrasound) and at end stage (best shown on MRI). The bleeding may also extend down through the ventricular system, causing obstructive or communicating hydrocephalus, which may be transient or progressive and requiring CSF diversion.

White matter injury of prematurity

39.12 The cerebral white matter is particularly vulnerable to insult between about the 26th and 34th weeks of gestation, when the majority of the developing oligodendroglia, the cells, which will later produce and maintain myelin, are at a critical stage of development. The resulting pathology mainly affects the cerebral hemispheric white matter around the lateral ventices and is often termed periventricular leukomalacia (PVL) but nowadays is increasingly referred to as white matter injury of prematurity. It can be visualised by imaging in the premature newborn, but will not be manifest clinically until several months after birth, when delay in motor function, which progresses to spastic diplegia, becomes apparent. The condition is not causally specific but it can be induced by perfusion failure associated with hypotension, hypoxia or hypocarbia, hence the relationship to ventilatory support. It can also be caused by toxins, especially by cytokines released from bacterial infections, usually from chorioamnionitis and hence the relationship to prolonged rupture of the fetal membranes. Blood breakdown products in the ventricular system following intraventricular haemorrhage may also be causative.

39.13 Marked prematurity alone does not cause brain damage, though statistics suggest it may be associated with slight reduction in the intelligence quotient.

39.14 Valuable information on the evolution of white matter injury of prematurity may be obtained from neonatal ultrasound studies. Reaction in the periventricular white matter may be visible as a flare within two to five days after an insult. Necrosis may occur with cystic change evidence between 10 and 21 days and ventricular dilatation may become apparent with collapse of the cysts between four and five weeks after an insult.

39.15 It is important to note that ultrasound, which is very accurate in the demonstration of intraventricular haemorrhage, is much less so in detection of periventricular leukomalacia. Autopsy studies and end stage computed imaging have shown that in many cases periventricular leukomalacia is not shown on early ultrasound studies, especially when cystic changes are inconspicuous or absent. End stage imaging shows dilatation of the lateral ventricles, which is usually bilateral and virtually symmetrical with irregular ventricular margins following absorption of cysts. Persistent cystic change may also be evident. There may be calcification in the damaged white matter and gliosis is usually apparent when the insult, or the reaction to it, is continuing after about the 28th week of gestation.

39.16 Similar damage to the cerebral white matter occurs much less commonly after the 34th week of gestation, even up to and past term. This is especially frequent in children suffering from cyanotic congenital heart disease, both before and after cardiac surgery. The effects of late onset periventricular white matter damage tend to be less severe, and necrosis with cystic change is infrequent.

39.17 The increase in high signal on T2-weighted sequences associated with gliosis after 28 weeks' gestation may be of help in the timing of white matter injury of prematurity and other pathologies.

Peripheral perfusion failure in the mature fetus

39.18 After 36 weeks gestational age the cerebral cortex becomes more vulnerable to ischaemia than the deep cerebral white matter. Vascular hypotension or peripheral perfusion failure occurs most commonly in labour following fetal hypoxia causing cardiac insufficiency, usually secondary to critical decrease in cardiac glycogen after increased cardiac activity. Less often it is caused by fetal circulatory volume loss. Circulatory volume loss may be caused at the time of twin-to-twin transfusion, by fetomaternal haemorrhage, by sequestration within the umbilical cord, by bleeding into the scalp or from blood loss into the gut or less commonly from other vessels.

39.19 The perfusion failure involves the borderzone regions between the cortical distributions of the main cerebral arteries, the width of the borderzone depending on the severity of the hypotension induced in the fetus or child. Motor defects may be very subtle and systemic sensory, visual and learning difficulties may predominate. In such circumstances neuroimaging by showing borderzone infarction may be crucial in confirming that peripheral perfusion failure is the underlying cause of the brain damage.

39.20 Autoregulation of brain vessels induces vasodilatation in response to gradually increasing hypotension. Compensation is considered to be effective in maintaining cerebral perfusion for at least about one hour after changes on a CTG suggest that a fetus is becoming hypoxic. It may continue for many hours or even indefinitely but once the borderzone becomes ischaemic neuronal damage will commence within 30 minutes. The typical result of such peripheral perfusion failure in the mature fetus is spastic quadriparesis in association with other neurological deficits. However, the typical imaging changes caused by peripheral perfusion failure may occur in the absence of spastic quadriparesis and it has similar medico-legal significance.

39.21 A high packed cell volume, whether it occurs spontaneously in polycythaemia or is induced iatrogenically during transfusion for sickle cell anaemia, may induce cellular aggregation in small peripheral cerebral vessels sufficient to cause cerebral infarction. When it is induced by over-transfusion it may be associated with vascular hypertension. This hyperviscosity syndrome may cause breakdown of the blood brain barrier with production of interstitial oedema within the brain substance, most frequently in the posterior parts of the cerebral hemispheres, but which may occur in other regions as an isolated phenomenon. Delay in treatment of the polycythaemia and the vascular hypertension may lead to assertions of negligence.

Profound circulatory insufficiency

39.22 In profound circulatory insufficiency or collapse of the circulation the whole of the brain is rendered ischaemic regardless of the cause of the collapse. It may be due to placental abruption, unrelieved umbilical cord compression, uterine rupture, cardiac arrest for any reason or acute fetal blood loss.

39.23 When the blood flow is insufficient to support aerobic metabolism, much less efficient anaerobic metabolism commences and damage, resulting in neuronal necrosis, begins in selected neuronal groups in proportion to the metabolic rate necessary to maintain cell wall function. Mammalian experiments and clinical experience suggests that such damage commences after about ten minutes of acute profound circulatory collapse in regions of high metabolism. Continuation of the collapse for more than 25 minutes may result in death or there may be survival with more extensive and severe brain damage affecting in addition the less metabolically active neurones and progressing to infarction.

39.24 In the fetus approaching maturity the most vulnerable structures include the putamina of the lentiform nuclei, the lateral nuclei of the thalami, the hippocampi and the pre and post central gyri and the superior vermis of the cerebellum. In the premature fetus, before the 34th week, the thalami and the cerebral white matter are most vulnerable.

Earlier still around the 25th to 30th week the globus pallidus and pontosubicular regions are vulnerable.

39.25 Development of the cerebellum may also be retarded in very premature fetuses, particularly if asphyxia is associated with bleeding around the cerebellum.

39.26   Beyond 40 weeks the optic radiation is more frequently involved and after about 42 weeks gestation the heads of the caudate nuclei.

39.27   Experiments on monkeys (Meyer) showed that involvement of the deep grey matter nuclei only occurred when profound asphyxia was preceded by a period of partial asphyxia. This appears to be the most usual case in the human situation.

39.28   The imaging in all cases of hypoxic-ischaemic brain damage reflects the effects of an event at a particular time of fetal maturity. The precise timing of that event requires detailed correlation with obstetric and paediatric expertise.

39.29   The most significant parameter in determining the degree of cerebral perfusion is mean arterial pressure. The usual parameter measured in the fetus is the heart rate. The precise heart rate level required to maintain an adequate blood pressure will vary with cardiac stroke volume so that extrapolation from pulse rate to mean blood pressure is inexact. For this reason it is often difficult to determine the time of onset of a critical profound perfusion failure. It may then be more appropriate in children born profoundly asphyxiated to calculate backwards the time, which is considered necessary to produce the imaging and clinical deficit backwards from the time at which an effective cerebral circulation is established after birth.

DIFFERENTIAL DIAGNOSIS OF HYPOXIC-ISCHAEMIC DAMAGE

39.30   When confronted with end-stage brain damage, apparently of ischaemic aetiology, it may be necessary to consider a differential diagnosis. The deep grey matter nuclei are damaged in inherited disorders of metabolism, particularly in mitochondrial enzyme defects. Though the damage varies in location, it usually involves the lentiform and often the caudate nuclei. It does not, however, involve the lateral nuclei of the thalami and is not restricted to the posterior halves of the putamina of the lentiform nuclei.

39.31   Damage to the cerebral white matter also can be produced by mitochondrial enzyme defects. This may be associated with damage in deep grey matter nuclei sometimes associated with calcification and with calcification in the peripheral cerebral white matter.

39.32   Damage to the cerebral white matter may also be caused by phenylketonuria. Particularly in tetramethylene dihydrofolate reductase deficiency this may be associated with calcification in the peripheral white matter best shown on computed tomography.

39.33   Diffuse white matter hypomyelination can occur in such rare cases as Pelizaeus-Merzbacher disease. In practice, the clinical picture and imaging appearances do not overlap with HIE sufficiently to cause any significant diagnostic confusion.

39.34   Very severe and diffuse and apparently disproportionate damage to the cerebral white matter following an insult should raise the question of the exceedingly rare entity of vanishing white matter disease, the onset of which may be precipitated by a traumatic incident. The progressive nature of this disease on serial brain imaging means that it is unlikely to be confused with HIE.

All these inherited disorders are of significance for genetic counselling.

Kernicterus

39.35   Hyperbilirubinaemia is an elevation of bilirubin in the blood which may lead to kernicterus in the neonate. Abnormally high levels of bilirubin may cause symmetrical damage in the globi pallidi and subthalamic nuclei as well as in the hippocampi. Such a distribution on MR of itself should suggest the diagnosis, which is then confirmed by the clinical history of hyperbilirubinaemia and hearing impairment.

Hypoglycaemia

39.36   It is generally considered that hypoglycaemia must be symptomatic to cause brain damage. In the children of insulin-dependent diabetic mothers and children who are small for dates, routine testing of neonatal blood sugar with measures to attain a blood glucose level greater than 2.6mmols/l is designed to prevent any question of damage being caused by prolonged asymptomatic hypoglycaemia. Symptomatic neonatal hypoglycaemia may produce diffuse brain damage, though it is generally considered that it must persist for several hours to do so. The diagnosis may be suggested or confirmed when the distribution of the damage is typical by being most severe in the parietooccipital regions where there is cerebral and cortical atrophy with or without signal change in the brain substance.

39.37   Hypoglycaemia occurring at the same time as peripheral perfusion failure has been shown experimentally to increase the degree and extent of the ischaemic brain damage.

Acquired microcephaly

39.38   Acquired microcephaly without signal change may follow neonatal hypoglycaemia. Other causes include congenital hypothyroidism. The condition may be genetically predetermined but often the cause is unknown.

FOCAL/MULTIFOCAL BRAIN DAMAGE

39.39   The aetiology of focal or multifocal brain damage may be apparent from the distribution.

Arterial distribution infarction

39.40   Damage in the distribution of a major cerebral artery or one of its branches is typical of an infarct produced by critical reduction in blood flow through that vessel. Occlusion of a normal artery may be due to thrombosis in situ or embolism, usually by blood clot, occasionally by air.

Thrombosis in situ is more frequent in arteries damaged by arteritis, which in children is usually in the context of septicaemia or meningitis either pyogenic or tuberculous.

39.41   In the context of birth asphyxia, an ischaemic stroke may occur if the asphyxia has caused hypoxia sufficient to result in peripheral perfusion failure, which has also caused borderzone infarction. Otherwise, in the absence of evidence of slowing of blood flow, the arterial occlusion is much more likely to be of embolic origin. Such emboli may occur at any time but are much more frequent during labour[1], when they presumably arise from the placenta and pass through the physiological right to left shunts present in the fetus.

1 Cowan et al.

39.42   Strokes are more frequent in the presence of inherited thrombophilia. They are also frequent in the neonatal period because of the normal thrombophilic tendency of the fetus and more so when the fetus is sick with disseminated intravascular coagulation or with polycythaemia.

39.43   The right to left shunts in cyanotic congenital heart disease are also associated with cerebral embolism, both sterile resulting in infarction and occasionally infected causing cerebral abscess.

39.44   Cardiac surgery for congenital heart defect may be associated with the generalised ischaemic damage, either profound affecting the deep grey matter, peripheral perfusion failure affecting the cerebral borderzones or damage to the cerebral white matter similar to periventricular leukomalacia.

39.45   Ischaemic strokes may also occur from air embolism, which may cause occlusion of major arterial branches or of multiple small arteries from emboli as small as 30microns. Both air and blood clot emboli from umbilical venous catheters may reach the brain and cause ischaemic stroke. Appropriately placed umbilical arterial catheters require monitoring for signs of limb ischaemia but are not a source of emboli to the cerebral circulation.

Venous distribution infarction

39.46   Venous occlusion in the mature fetus may also be related to genetic or acquired thrombophilia.

39.47   There is an epidemiological relationship to adverse events during labour.

Venous infarction may be ischaemic but it is commonly haemorrhagic. The haemorrhagic components may be increased where there is an acquired haemorrhagic tendency, as for example following omission of prophylactic Vitamin K or where extracorporeal membrane oxygenation (ECMO) is necessary for maintaining adequate oxygenation of the blood.

Timing of focal damage

39.48   The timing of focal brain damage from the end stage appearances on computed imaging assessed in isolation depends on the following features:

(1)   the presence of abnormally-sited grey matter in the margins of the damage suggests that it occurred in the second trimester before neuronal migration was complete;

(2)   the absence of marginal grey matter and of any sign of a gliotic response suggest that the damage occurred after neuronal migration was complete but before the end of the seventh month of gestation;

(3)   marginal high signal associated with a gliotic response is usual after the seventh month of gestation.

TRAUMA

39.49   Trauma may cause:

(1)   damage to neural tissues by penetration with disruption, direct impact with contusion, rapid deceleration with stretching and tearing;

(2)   disruption of larger blood vessels. The amount of bleeding is influenced by the efficiency of blood clotting. It may be markedly increased in haemorrhagic disease of the newborn due to deficiency of Vitamin K and in blood clotting disorders, such as haemophilia.

39.50   Haemorrhage may be sufficient to cause circulatory insufficiency and result in hypoxic ischaemic brain damage.

39.51   More commonly, the extravasated blood clots. The clot, which is of similar density on CT to brain substance, may be recognised from its mass effect. Contraction of the clot then occurs with extrusion of serum and increase in density typical of haematoma on computed X-ray tomography.

39.52   Bleeding may be extracranial, intracranial but outside brain substance, within the brain parenchyma or into the cerebrospinal fluid.

Birth trauma

39.53   Subgaleal haematoma spreads freely beneath the scalp and is thus distinguished from cephalhaematoma, which is limited by the margins of individual skull bones by attachment of the periosteum at the sutures.

39.54   Subgaleal haematoma may occur spontaneously during cephalic deliveries, but it is more frequent with ventouse assistance. The possibility of circulatory collapse requiring blood transfusion for prevention should be anticipated.

39.55 Cephalhaematoma is common with spontaneous cephalic deliveries, but more so in assisted deliveries. Fracture of the subadjacent bone is present in about one third. This is usually linear and not of clinical significance. There may, however, be underlying intracranial extracerebral haemorrhage, which may be significant if displacement is shown on ultrasound. Depressed fracture of the underlying bone may be associated with cerebral contusion and may require elevation.

39.56 Disruption of the underlying dura will allow local herniation of the brain adjacent to the tear and the normal pulsation of the brain substance may cause erosion of the margins of the fracture, a so-called 'growing fracture'. Cortical vessels may be compressed against the margins of the fracture, causing increasing brain damage unless the defect is repaired.

39.57 Small amounts of subdural and subarachnoid bleeding are common in normal deliveries and are usually absorbed without any permanent neurological disabilities.

39.58 The moulding deformity of the skull may cause stretching of superficial cerebral veins where they cross from the subarachnoid space to reach the major venous sinuses; this may be sufficient to cause tearing and result in significant subdural haematoma. Such haematomas are more common with assisted vertex deliveries along the cerebral convexities and adjacent to the falx and in assisted breach deliveries adjacent to the tentorium in the middle and posterior fossae. The haematomas may occlude veins by compression or cause herniation under the falx or through the tentorial hiatus causing further brain damage by occlusion of arteries adjacent to the edges of the membranes with infarction in the distal distribution of either the anterior or posterior cerebral arteries respectively.

39.59 Damage to the veins may also precipitate venous thrombosis and infarction.

39.60 Occipital osteodiastasis refers to intracranial displacement of the central part of the occipital bone causing an extracerebellar haematoma compressing and damaging the cerebellum. Occlusion of the fourth ventricle may cause hydrocephalus.

Prenatal trauma

39.61 Traumatic damage to the fetal brain in utero may be caused by penetrating or non-penetrating injury.

Amniocentesis

39.62 An important cause of penetrating injury is amniocentesis. Penetration of the brain by the amniocentesis needle may not be recognised by the operator, particularly if the procedure is performed without the benefit of ultrasound control.

39.63   Material obtained when aspiration is performed may be recognised as fetal, but frequently fetal tissue is not obtained at the time of the penetration.

39.64   If fetal penetration is suspected, an ultrasound study after the procedure may show intracranial haemorrhage. Ultrasound studies around the time of the amniocentesis may be valuable in showing normal intracranial anatomy.

39.65   If the possibility of injury is not recognised, the first diagnostic study may be postnatal magnetic resonance imaging showing the end-stage appearances of the damage.

39.66   Some or all of the following features may be recognised:

(1)   on physical examination, a scar in the skin;
(2)   an underlying small bone defect on CT scanning;
(3)   damage to the underlying brain. This may have been caused by trauma from the passage of the needle alone, by aspiration of neural tissue through the needle or by damage to blood vessels causing occlusion or bleeding. The most characteristic brain injury is damage involving regions in continuity but which are not in the distribution of a single artery or likely to have been caused by the focal mass of a single haematoma.

There may or may not be evidence of hemosiderin deposition.

39.67   The timing of the lesion will be suggested by retardation of normal maturation, by features of abnormal neuronal migration and by the inconspicuity of gliosis.

Blunt trauma

39.68   Blunt trauma may cause fetal head injury with contusion or haemorrhage or may cause damage indirectly by placental abruption or maternal hypotension resulting in ischaemic brain damage with features, which may be consistent with the gestational time at which the trauma occurred.

39.69   Around the time of the maternal trauma there may or may not be abdominal pain or uterine spasm or ultrasound or CTG evidence of placated disruption or fetal distress.

Postnatal trauma

39.70   Postnatal trauma in young infants associated with a history of significant head injury from a fall or motor vehicle accident show similar features on CT and MRI to those found in older children.

39.71 There may be similar difficulties with the clinical diagnosis of both sub and extradural haematomas and failure to recognise such extracerebral mass lesions may cause damage to the underlying brain or secondary effects due to coning, which should have been avoided.

39.72 Intracranial gas following injury is indicative of a compound fracture or a penetrating injury. A recent lumbar puncture at the source of air should be excluded by the history. The presence of fluid consistent with blood or cerebrospinal fluid in perinasal sinuses bordering on the skull base or in the middle ear or mastoid air cells also suggesting the possibility of a basal fracture may require further elucidation by thin section CT with bone window imaging, particularly if fluid leakage from the nose or an ear persists for more than a few days or recurs.

39.73 In the medico-legal context, end-stage appearances on MRI require detailed investigation for foci of gliosis using T2 weighted sequences and T2 weighted FLAIR as well as evidence of peripheral perfusion failure, and also gradient echo sequences for foci of hemosiderin deposition.

39.74 In the subacute phase, diffusion weighted imaging may be useful for showing diffuse axonal injury. When the main disabilities following a head injury concern emotional changes, lack of inhibitions and judgment problems, distinction from disabilities being entirely psychological in origin as distinct from end-stage brain damage is commonly based on the presence or absence of evidence of the latter on imaging. It should be clearly understood that even the most sophisticated imaging by comprehensive MRI is capable of showing only those lesions, which are either associated with persistent evidence of hemosiderin deposition, or with gliosis or with atrophy. Autopsy evidence invariably shows diffuse axonal injury to be more extensive than can be demonstrated by imaging.

39.75 Small non-specific foci of high signal commonly found incidentally in older patients do occur less frequently in children, only when associated with lesions in characteristic situations for diffuse axonal injury in the subcortical white matter particularly in the paracentral regions and in the posterior third of the corpus callosum can their presence be considered supportive. Some foci have been shown to be due to minor defects in neuronal migration and some may be small, post-inflammatory lesions and not of clinical significance.

39.76 In a child presenting with a history of impaired consciousness or with evidence of systemic trauma, superficial contusion, tearing of the frenulum or other mucosal injury or evidence of neglect without a history of trauma, non-accidental injury may be suspected. A skeletal survey, skull X-ray for the presence of fracture, multiple fractures, fractures with widely separated edges or splayed sutures in the absence of a history of severe head injury are suggestive of child abuse. A cranial CT should be performed to show intra or extracranial bleeding or ischaemic brain damage.

39.77 Important differential diagnoses include other causes of haemorrhagic brain damage, particularly herpes simplex encephalitis, in which subarachnoid extension from the haemorrhagic cortex may result in conspicuous subarachnoid haemorrhage, and haemopoietic disorders, including acute leukaemia, which are elucidated by haematological studies.

INFLAMMATION

Intrauterine infection

39.78 The reaction to intrauterine infections varies with the time in gestation at which the nervous system is involved.

39.79 Rubella acquired early in pregnancy damages the neuronal precursors in the germinal plexuses resulting in primary microcephaly.

39.80 Cytomegalic inclusion virus, if the infection is acquired during the first half of pregnancy, also affects the germinal plexuses and small blood vessels tending to cause multifocal brain damage and defects in neuronal migration involving the cerebrum and cerebellum. Later infection causes less severe multifocal brain damage without migrational abnormalities.

39.81 Both cytomegalovirus (CMV) and toxoplasma may cause obstructive hydrocephalus due to occlusion of the CSF pathways within the ventricular system.

39.82 Toxoplasma also causes multifocal brain damage, hydrocephalus and atrophy. It is not associated with neuronal migration abnormalities.

39.83 Herpes simplex, acquired in utero, causes devastating generalised brain damage.

39.84 In all inflammatory conditions, but particularly in CMV and toxoplasmosis, calcification is frequent in necrotic regions within parenchyma granulomas. Failure to diagnose and treat any of these conditions in the mother may lead to litigation.

Perinatal infection

39.85 Infection during passage down the birth canal is the usual source of neonatal herpes simplex Type II and of bacterial infections, most frequently by beta haemolytic streptococcus and coliform organisms.

39.86 If herpes simplex causes cutaneous or systemic infection, it may be recognised prior to involvement of the central nervous system.

39.87 Isolated herpes of the central nervous system occurring within a month of birth is a devastating generalised infection of the brain, which even with treatment tends to cause extensive neurological disability. Any suspicion of the possibility of herpes simplex should lead to Acyclovir treatment before positive laboratory or imaging evidence is acquired.

39.88   Streptococcal and coliform septicaemia may be diagnosed by routine blood cultures in a baby with a non-specific neonatal illness with or without pyrexia. The transition to meningitis may be heralded by an altered level of consciousness or convulsion without the signs of meningism more apparent in older children. Diagnosis is by lumbar puncture at an early stage of the septicaemic illness.

39.89   CT and MRI may show little in the early stages of an inflammatory process. This is particularly so in bacterial meningitis, which is a clinical diagnosis. Imaging is useful for detection of complications of meningitis, which include:

(1)   subdural effusions and empyema;
(2)   infarcts due to arterial or venous occlusion;
(3)   ependymitis;
(4)   hydrocephalus;
(5)   cerebral abscess.

Infantile infection

39.90   After the neonatal period meningococcus, pneumococcus and haemophilus influenzae are more frequent causes of bacterial infection. Again, early treatment in the septicaemic phase is important. Once meningitis has become established deafness and neurological deficit may be unavoidable though the damage may be limited by treatment before complications are evident on imaging.

39.91   Viral infections, which invade the nervous system, cause a wide variety of reactions, which in many cases, apart from the characteristic basal temporal and limbic involvement by herpes simplex, are non-specific but tend to be symmetrical. Specific diagnosis depends on laboratory investigations. Lymphocytic cerebrospinal fluid, particularly with relatively low glucose content occurs in tuberculous meningitis. Although uncommon, the condition does occur and clinical suspicion may be confirmed prior to identification of the bacillus by imaging. This may show meningeal abnormalities with enhancement after intravenous contrast medium and/or evidence of ischaemic damage due to occlusion of vessels in the subarachnoid space.

39.92   Viral meningoencephalitis, with or without febrile convulsions, may be associated later with bilateral hippocampal damage suggesting hippocampal sclerosis.

39.93   Febrile convulsions alone up to the age of six years may be associated with the development of hippocampal sclerosis and hippocampal sclerosis may complicate childhood epilepsy resulting from ante or perinatal brain damage.

39.94   Acute disseminated encephalomyelitis (ADEM) may follow a systemic infection (usually viral) or vaccination. Involvement of both white matter causing circumscribed foci of demyelination, which may enhance in the acute phase of the illness together with involvement of the deep grey matter nuclei, may suggest the diagnosis. A similar distribution of damage may occur in inherited disorders of metabolism, particular mitochondrial enzymes defects.

39.95 Inadequate systemic response by production of adrenal corticosteroids may predispose to circulatory collapse during stressful situations such as childhood illnesses. Underlying abnormalities of the pituitary as in septo-optic dysplasia and its variations and mitochondrial enzyme defects should be considered. Often other features of these conditions should have already been recognised and appropriate tests, including imaging, been performed.

39.96 Ataxia telangiectasia is usually apparent from the presence of the typical telangiectasia. Imaging may show cerebellar atrophy and evidence of previous multifocal bleeding.

Intracranial mass lesions

39.97 Cerebral abscess may also present as a primary intracranial mass, which is usually suspected in the clinical context. In atypical clinical cases it may simulate a tumour. It is uncommon to be able to diagnose the histology of an intrinsic mass from imaging and if a precise diagnosis is necessary, biopsy or aspiration is usual, occasionally a specific diagnosis is suggested by the referring clinician. When this assumed diagnosis is not the most likely one from the imaging appearances, then this should be clearly stated in a radiologist's report. This is particularly important when treatment of the tumour would be modified or if an inflammatory process cannot be excluded.

Hydrocephalus

39.98 Enlarged ventricles due to hydrocephalus are usually accompanied by cranial enlargement during the first two years after birth. Imaging, by showing the level at which dilatation of CSF pathways ceases, may suggest the site of blockage. It may also show the causative pathology.

39.99 Benign external hydrocephalus, thought to be caused by delayed development of arachnoid granulations causing some obstruction to the absorption of cerebrospinal fluid, usually presents in the first year of life with macrocephaly and imaging evidence of moderate ventricular dilatation and enlargement of the intracranial subarachnoid spaces in a child without evidence of neurological dysfunction. The condition is more frequent in boys and usually resolves spontaneously by the second year of life. Clinical observation with serial measurement of head circumference and neuroimaging may be indicated to exclude any progressive pathology.

39.100 In older children, when the sutures are no longer easily splayed, ventricular enlargement usually accompanies increasing intraventricular pressure, but it is important to note that this is not invariable, especially in association with dysfunction of ventricular shunts and in craniosynostosis. Failure of progressive ventricular dilatation does not override symptoms and clinical signs of raised intracranial pressure.

SPINAL IMAGING

39.101 The spinal ligaments and joint capsules in early childhood are sufficiently elastic to allow distraction and reducible dislocation without any residual evidence of damage to the spine on neuroimaging. Consequently damage to the spinal cord may occur resulting in distraction, contusion or myelomalacia in the absence of any evidence of damage to the spine itself. Such distraction may occur during birth and may be apparent on magnetic resonance imaging.

Birth trauma

39.102 Traction injuries may result during measures to overcome shoulder dystocia. These usually cause tearing of the brachial plexus, which may be peripheral but may be associated with a tearing of nerve roots from the spinal cord. These may be directly visualised or manifest as pseudomeningocele formation.

39.103 In breach deliveries the elasticity of the spinal ligaments may allow transient stretching of the spinal column without disruption. The spinal cord is much less elastic and may be damaged in the absence of any visible abnormality of the spinal column.

Childhood injury

39.104 The normal, relatively high elasticity of the spinal ligaments in childhood, combined with the more horizontal inclination of the cervical intervertebral apophyseal joints, is associated with a relatively higher degree of anterior translocation in the upper cervical region in children. This physiological translocation has been termed pseudosubluxation. In a child presenting with neck pain, especially if there is a history of trauma, it has been mistaken for subluxation, particularly when some spasm of the cervical muscles prevents extension of the spine. This may lead to unnecessary surgery. In circumstances where the spine is held in flexion, computed imaging showing anatomical continuity in any position which can be achieved in a normal child, without any direct evidence of damage to the bones, intervertebral discs or ligaments, should be interpreted as a normal variant and is a contraindication to surgery aimed at stabilisation.

Developmental abnormalities

39.105 Segmentation abnormalities of the spine are not usually associated with spinal cord abnormalities. Dysraphic abnormalities may be associated with obvious deformities due to meningocele, meningomyelocele, lipomeningocele, low extension of the spinal cord or tethering with or without diastematomyelia or the presence of a patch of hair or a dimple over the lower spine. All these conditions are easily diagnosed using MRI, which should include the whole spine and the craniocervical junction in order to show any associated Chiari II malformation or syrinx formation.

39.106 Imaging of the whole spinal neuraxis is indicated for elucidation of the cause or progressive idiopathic scoliosis. Progressive syringomyelia should be distinguished from the enlargement of the central canal of the spinal cord, which may be incidentally noted in the lower cervical and lumbosacral regions as a benign developmental variant.

39.107 Subluxation, particularly at atlantoaxial level, is a feature of certain inherited disorders including mucopolysaccharidosis and spondyloepiphyseal dysplasia. It may also occur in Down syndrome. Here the lax ligaments and/or abnormal cartilage allow abnormal increase in movement, particularly between the first and second cervical vertebrae. This prevents the normal development of the odontoid. Atlantoaxial subluxation may follow causing spinal cord compression, which may result in death or severe neurological disability. Failure to investigate for atlantoaxial abnormalities in these conditions may lead to litigation. Damage lower down the spine, especially near the thoracolumbar junction, may also occur in these conditions.

39.108 Achondroplasia and other conditions in which the sagittal diameter of the spinal canal may be critically reduced are at risk for spinal cord compression and should be investigated with magnetic resonance imaging if there are any symptoms or signs suggesting neurological disability.

39.109 Where focal or generalised enlargement of the spinal canal is suspected, corticated erosion of the margins of the canal should be sought. Even in equivocal cases magnetic resonance imaging is indicated, which will clearly demonstrate or exclude expansion of the spinal cord by tumour or syrinx or the presence of an extra-axial mass such as a neurofibroma displacing and compressing the spinal cord.

CHECKLIST

39.110

– Magnetic resonance imaging is the most sensitive modality for diagnosis of pathology related to the nervous system.
– Computed tomography is more freely available and more sensitive for diagnosis of acute haematoma and calcification.
– Reaction to damage varies with fetal maturity. The damage remains as a permanent indicator of timing of an insult.
– Reactive changes may become more evident as myelination progresses up to two years of age.
– Neuroimages reflect macroscopic neuropathy. The distribution may suggest the mechanism of damage.
– Serial neuroimaging may show the evolution of pathology.

CHAPTER 40

Sport and exercise medicine

Dr Simon Paul

BACKGROUND TO THE SPECIALITY OF SPORT AND EXERCISE MEDICINE

40.1   Sport and Exercise Medicine (SEM) was accepted as a discrete speciality of medicine in 2005, recognising the contribution that this discipline could make to the health of the nation. SEM doctors are trained in the accurate diagnosis, management and prevention of medical conditions and injury in those who participate in exercise and sporting activities. Whereas SEM doctors may treat elite sportspersons, SEM as a speciality enjoys much more far-reaching relevance in terms of promoting national health. SEM services can be delivered across primary, secondary, tertiary and intermediate/integrated care settings, as well as through public health, and it is clear to see why SEM practitioners should be at the front line of efforts to influence policy and encourage all people to become more physically active to improve their general health[1]. The role of SEM in improving the health of those with chronic disease is established, and in view of numerous clinical guidelines promoting physical activity as an important treatment, the potential indefensibility of practitioners who do not address their patients' physical inactivity has been highlighted[2].

1 Batt and Tanji 'The Future of Chronic Disease Management and the Role of Sport and Exercise Medicine Physicians' (2011) 21 Clin Jnl Sports Med 3–5.
2 NHS Sport and Exercise Medicine Services. NHS Northwest Sports and exercise medicine: A fresh approach' (2011).

SEM consultants

40.2   Speciality training covers three main elements:

(1)   exercise as a means of improving health;
(2)   exercise as treatment for illness; and
(3)   the management of injuries resulting from participation in sport.

To meet the wide demands of clinical practice, SEM consultants undergo six years of specialist training after foundation training. Qualified GPs may also enter the SEM speciality training programme. The SEM curriculum covers physical activity and chronic disease, exercise physiology, public health, primary care and musculoskeletal medicine. There are currently over 60 doctors on the GMC specialist register in SEM and approximately 14 full-time equivalent consultants working within the NHS, but it has been estimated that there is need for at least 300 SEM consultants across the UK[1].

1 Faculty of Sport and Exercise Medicine *A Fresh Approach in Practice: Sport and Exercise Medicine Services in the NHS* (2014) (available at from http://www.fsem.ac.uk/media/33484/a-fresh-approach-in-practice-full-pages.pdf). See also Williamson and Wilkes 'Sport and exercise medicine' (2013) (available from https://www.rcplondon.ac.uk/sites/default/files/sport_and_exercise_medicine.pdf).

40.3   SEM doctors are trained to diagnose and treat musculoskeletal conditions and sports injuries and effectively promote physical activity, through exercise prescription, rehabilitation, clinical exercise testing and risk assessment. Many also provide diagnostic musculoskeletal ultrasound and image-guided soft tissue and joint injections services.

40.4   SEM practitioners work in a variety of settings across primary (eg crowd doctor), and secondary and tertiary care (hospital-based SEM consultants). A number of models of delivery exist, and SEM is often practised using a multidisciplinary team approach with members of the treating team including physiotherapists, sports scientists, psychologists, podiatrists, GPs with a special interest, orthopaedic surgeons, rheumatologists, osteopaths and nurses[1].

1 Faculty of Sport and Exercise Medicine *A Fresh Approach in Practice: Sport and Exercise Medicine Services in the NHS* (2014).

The Faculty of Sport and Exercise Medicine

40.5   The Faculty of Sport and Exercise Medicine UK (FSEM) promotes the medical speciality of SEM and was launched in 2006[1]. It is an intercollegiate faculty of the Royal College of Physicians of London and the Royal College of Surgeons of Edinburgh. The FSEM oversees research, training, curriculum and assessment of SEM doctors and has over 500 Members and Fellows.

1 See the Faculty of Sport and Exercise Medicine website, www.fsem.ac.uk.

FSEM Code of Practice

40.6 It is axiomatic that practising doctors need to be familiar with the GMC guidance contained in *Good Medical Practice*, which describes the standards expected of doctors registered with the GMC[1].

1 General Medical Council *Good Medical Practice* (2013).

40.7 Operationally, it is clear that there are some areas that uniquely apply to the treatment of sportsmen and women, particularly elite athletes, including standards when accompanying teams overseas, dual responsibilities to sportspersons and clubs, anti-doping issues. Therefore, the FSEM Council agreed that a Professional Code was required to supplement the GMC guidance and the 2010 version remains extant, although it is in the process of being reviewed[1]. This Code does not enjoy statutory protection and does not replace the personal judgment of an SEM doctor, but helps guide practice. Its advice is broadly divided under the headings of consent, confidentiality and privacy, care and treatment, good clinical practice, rights and duties of practitioners, protection and promotion of the athlete's health, providing support for medical bodies, teaching, education and appraisals, relationships with patients and colleagues, probity and dealing with children. A few areas will be highlighted.

1 Faculty of Sport and Exercise Medicine *Professional Code* (2010).

40.8 In section 1.1, the duty of the practitioner to inform the sportsperson of potential risks of participation when injured or unwell is discussed, whilst the autonomy of the sportsperson to decide to participate is also highlighted. This section also includes the requirement to ensure adequate insurance or professional indemnity cover for any practice not covered by an employer's indemnity scheme.

40.9 When treating professional sportspersons, the practitioner needs to ensure sufficient indemnity to cover loss of future earnings if found liable for damages from a negligent act. West Bromwich Albion (WBA) Football Club player, Michael Appleton, suffered an injury to his right posterior cruciate ligament in 2001. His consultant surgeon, Mr El-Safty, advised that reconstructive surgery should be carried out. He performed the operation but it was unsuccessful; the player never fully recovered and he had to retire from professional football.

40.10 It was accepted that an initial conservative approach might have allowed a return to play within approximately four months. WBA claimed damages from the defendant surgeon for the losses it had allegedly suffered as a consequence of his negligence, the claimant's action being brought both in contract and in tort. The defendant denied that there was a contract with WBA and denied that he owed any duty to WBA in tort. The Court of Appeal held there was no contract between WBA and the Mr El-Safty nor any intention to create legal relations between WBA and the surgeon[1]. However, the general principles of damages for tort were seen to apply in the context of sport, and in this case quantum was high, reflecting the levels of remuneration in sport for future earnings, pain and suffering and loss of amenity[2].

1 *West Bromwich Albion Football Club Ltd v El-Safty* [2006] EWCA Civ 1299.
2 *Appleton v El-Safty* [2007] EWHC 631 (QB). See also Hassan 'Who is Michael Appleton?' (11 Nov 2011) BBC Sport Website (available at http://m.bbc.co.uk/sport/football/15673484. app).

40.11   FSEM Practice Code sections 1.1d, 3.2, 8.2, 16 make it clear that decisions on fitness of professional sportspersons must rest on their best medical interests, and should not be prejudiced by third parties such as family members, coaches, management or other individuals.

40.12   Section 3.6 offers guidance when seeking consent to collect biological material for drug testing, and emphasises the duty of the practitioner to ensure consent has been obtained correctly.

40.13   Section 4.3 discusses the conflict of interest that occurs when a doctor is both a primary GP to a club whilst also contracted to the club in an occupational health capacity. Information obtained in the former role must not be passed to the employer in the latter role without valid patient consent.

40.14   In section 8, concerning protection and promotion of the athlete's health, the FSEM highlight the need for practitioners to carefully consider their advice on nutritional supplements that may contain banned substances.

40.15   Sections 8.3 and 10 discuss care given at sporting events, whilst section 8.4 emphasises the need for careful consideration of the appropriateness of injections, where permitted within a sports regulatory framework.

40.16   Section 16 states that practitioners must resist any recommendation for children to engage in sports that are not appropriate to their developmental stage. The FSEM have produced guidance on the amount of physical activity appropriate for adolescents[1].

1 Faculty of Sport and Exercise Medicine *Physical Activity in Adolescence* (2014).

MEDICO-LEGAL ISSUES AFFECTING DOCTORS WHO PROVIDE MEDICAL SUPPORT AT SPORTING EVENTS

40.17   The 2012 London Olympic Games was acknowledged to have been a success. Vital to the operation of these Games was the contribution of 70,000 volunteers, which included 5,000 medical volunteers deployed across the competition venues. There was also medical support at the Central Polyclinic in the Olympic Village, whose facilities included a small accident and emergency department, primary care, sports and exercise medicine, physiotherapy, ophthalmology, dental services, imaging, podiatry and a pharmacy.

40.18 In the British Medical Association (BMA) Board of Science 2014 update, *An information resource for doctors providing medical care at sporting events,* the BMA encouraged doctors' participation in sporting events, through the acknowledgment that such assistance and provision of care is essential for the wellbeing and safety of participating sportspersons and spectators[1].

1 British Medical Association Board of Science *An information resource for doctors providing medical care at sporting events* (2014).

40.19 There are a number of roles that doctors and other healthcare professionals may undertake in terms of providing care for sportspersons and/or spectators at sporting events and fixtures. Such roles vary from a crowd doctor providing voluntary unpaid care on an ad hoc basis at one end, to a SEM specialist doctor who provides treatment on a regular basis to a Premier League football team both at national and international level. SEM specialists may cover such events as part of their full-time work in an occupational capacity. It is important that such doctors are aware that they need to be prepared to meet a variety of challenges and may find themselves providing assistance outside their normal role. If treatment results from inadequate level of provision or if foreseeable harm is suffered, they may face the threat of legal action.

40.20 Clearly, any doctor providing assistance to competitors at sporting events should ensure that they have knowledge of the sport, its rules, its risks and the potential injuries sustainable in that sport. In addition, doctors should have an understanding of pre-hospital management of sport-specific and general and foreseeable injuries, any specific guidance published by the sport's governing body, and any relevant anti-doping policies. In addition to ensuring that doctors have a GMC licence to practise, the BMA have identified a number of areas to help with risk reduction, including remaining up to date with all the necessary skills, experience and required qualifications[1]. SEM doctors who cover sporting events also complete approved courses in immediate care in sport and major incident management[2].

1 British Medical Association Board of Science *An information resource for doctors providing medical care at sporting events* (2014) p 5.
2 British Medical Association Board of Science *An information resource for doctors providing medical care at sporting events* (2014) pp 10, 11.

40.21 In addition to keeping accurate records and recognising influences such as the environment on a participant's ability to perform safely, the BMA publication has provided general principles for doctors providing medical care at sporting events and this guidance includes the following.

Indemnity arrangements

40.22 Clarifying the level of indemnity being offered by the sports club, professional body or organisers of the event, *before* the event takes place, is important. Should a doctor enter into a contract with a club, it may be a term that the club provides indemnity. If the organisation or body does not indemnify the work of its employees, then the doctor should contact their medical defence organisation (MDO) to discuss and arrange an appropriate level of professional indemnity cover. There are three main providers: the

Medical Defence Union; the Medical Protection Society; and the Medical and Dental Defence Union of Scotland.

An alternative is to obtain private cover from an insurance company. Indemnity will usually only cover claims made on behalf of patients, not their clubs, sponsors, agents or others. The BMA advises doctors to seek advice from their MDO as to the type and level of cover when looking after elite sportspeople[1]. Doctors working for Premier League football clubs are not generally covered by MDOs, which tend to provide discretionary indemnity[2]. Launched in 2010, Sempris provides indemnity cover for doctors whose practice includes the treatment of professional and elite sports people. It also provides cover for claims brought by certain third parties in relation to alleged negligent treatment of a player, as well as cover for pre-signing medical assessments undertaken for clubs, and worldwide indemnity when travelling overseas with teams[3]. There are other elite athletes who earn large sums (eg golfers, rugby players). Doctors who treat such athletes should contact their MDO to ensure their membership is appropriate to the work they are undertaking.

1 Medical Protection Society *Treating elite sportsmen and women* (2013).
2 British Medical Association Board of Science *An information resource for doctors providing medical care at sporting events* (2014) pp 48, 49.
3 SEMPRIS website, www.sempris.co.uk/index.php.

Importance of communication and planning

40.23 The BMA recommends early liaison with the sports club, sporting body or organiser to clarify responsibilities. Agreeing to offer assistance, at any level, carries legal implications and establishes a duty of care to the parties specified. Establishing at the planning stage, precisely for whom cover is being provided and the corporate/individual relationships and areas of responsibilities both vertically and horizontally, is vital. In addition, it is advised that the doctor consults in advance with the referee/official to clarify arrangements for stopping play if needed.

40.24 Advance liaison and planning with local emergency services, where appropriate, is very important, eg local ambulance services and accident and emergency department. The location of the doctor should be made known to relevant parties depending on their specific role.

Where possible, doctors must attempt to meet all their potential patients' communication needs (eg at international events such as the Olympic and Commonwealth Games).

Risk assessment and resource planning

40.25 Thoroughly assessing risk and the level of assistance required involves allowing for several factors, including the number of spectators, aid from other healthcare providers etc. Where crowds of over 2,000 people are expected, doctors should be aware of the statutorily required major incident management plan, any contingency plans, and their role within such plans. The organisers of the event may seek advice from the doctor on the level of risk and support required. Should the estimated level of provision subsequently be deemed inadequate and harm flows from this, then the doctor may be held liable for providing negligent advice[1].

1 British Medical Association Board of Science *An information resource for doctors providing medical care at sporting events* (2014) p 18

40.26 The practitioner must ensure that sufficient medical equipment and resources will be available (eg for cardiopulmonary resuscitation, spinal immobilisation), and that clinical protocols accord with the standards of the relevant professional and/or sporting body. If the resources do not meet standards, the practitioner should inform the organiser and request a postponement of the event until the deficiency has been rectified.

Acting as a 'Good Samaritan'

40.27 On 17 March 2012 a cardiologist, who happened to be in the crowd as a spectator during an FA Cup match, acted to save footballer Fabrice Muamba's life when the player suffered a cardiac arrest on the pitch[1]. This was an example of a Good Samaritan act that played out in very public view and attracted major media attention.

1 NHS Choices. The doctor who saved Fabrice Muamba's life (25 June 2013).

40.28 A Good Samaritan act occurs when medical assistance is provided in an emergency, without charge, by a doctor who is present in a personal rather than a professional capacity[1]. A doctor may be present at a sporting event as a spectator or a competitor and come across a person in need of medical assistance. A doctor acting as a Good Samaritan assumes a duty not to make the victim's condition worse, and notably in English law there is no legal duty to assist a stranger (excepting GPs, who have a duty of care within their practice area as set out in their contract)[2]. However, a doctor has a professional ethical responsibility to do what they reasonably can. Failure to act except in situations posing real personal danger could result in investigation by their medical council[3]. Guidance from the GMC states that:

'You must offer help if emergencies arise in clinical settings or in the community, taking account of your own safety, your competence and the availability of other options for care'[4].

1 Johnston and Bradbury '100 Cases in Clinical Ethics and Law' (2008) CRC Press p 182.
2 *Capital and Counties plc v Hampshire County Council* [1997] QB 1035B.
3 Brazier and Cave *Medicine, Patients and the Law* (5th Revised edn, 2011) p 178.
4 General Medical Council *Good Medical Practice* (2013) para 26.

40.29 Good Samaritan acts are usually included in MDO membership as long as they are ad hoc events with no evidence of any ongoing relationship with the club or patient. Doctors do not need to be trained in emergency care to act as Good Samaritans and the lack of a licence to practise does not prevent doctors from helping in emergencies since 'Any concerned citizen is able to perform such acts, with or without registration or a licence to practise'[1].

1 General Medical Council *Frequently asked questions about licensing*, available at http://www. gmc-uk.org/doctors/licensing/faq_licence_to_practise.asp (accessed December 2014).

40.30   Claims resulting from Good Samaritan incidents are extremely rare but in order to minimise potential legal risks, doctors should consider their position, especially if acting entails exceeding a doctor's competence and risks making the situation worse[1]. Just calling for help may be the most appropriate action in an emergency and merely arranging timely transfer of the patient to accident and emergency may provide an adequate defence[2]. In all situations, Good Samaritan acts can be seen as clinical interventions and it is sensible to make a record of the actions and situation to counter potential claims.

1 Williams K 'Doctors as Good Samaritans: Some Empirical Evidence Concerning Emergency Medical Treatment in Britain' (2003) Journal of Law and Society 30: 258–282.
2 Medical and Dental Defence Union of Scotland 'Summons Good Samaritan: Is there a doctor on board?' (2009) pp 9–10.

CONSENT

40.31   Common to other areas of medical care, SEM doctors need to obtain patient consent when performing examinations or providing treatment. Consent can be verbal, written or implied, and forms the willing agreement of an informed person and may be withdrawn. Obtaining consent should be considered a process, rather than an isolated event.

40.32   Clinical examination is an important part of sports injury work and management. Where valid consent has not been obtained, this exposes the practitioner to potential complaints, claims and criminal charges (eg for assault or battery), but fortunately such situations are rare. However, ignoring the GMC's advice on consent may also result in a professional misconduct allegation followed by investigation and sanction by the GMC[1].

1 Medical Protection Society, *Factsheets. Consent* (2013) (available at www.medicalprotection. org/uk/resources/factsheets/england/england-factsheets/uk-eng-consent-the-basics).

40.33   In some circumstances, patient consent cannot be obtained (eg during pitch-side cardiopulmonary resuscitation) and then a doctor may intervene in keeping with the Mental Capacity Act 2005, s 5. GMC guidance states:

'When an emergency arises in a clinical setting and it is not possible to find out a patient's wishes, you can treat them without their consent, provided the treatment is immediately necessary to save their life or to prevent a serious deterioration of their condition'[1].

1 General Medical Council *Consent guidance: patients and doctors making decisions together* (2008) para 79.

40.34   What about more routine situations eg a pre- or inter-employment medical examination? According to the FSEM Code of Practice, where a professional sportsperson is contractually obliged to undergo a medical examination in relation to their ability to undertake their sport, the examining doctor needs to obtain consent for the examination, consent for obtaining other health records and consent for medical reports to be passed to the sportsperson's management[1].

1 Faculty of Sport and Exercise Medicine *Professional Code* (2010) section 3.1.

40.35 For the collection and use of any biological samples, the practitioner should act within GMC guidelines to ensure that no testing occurs without obtaining valid consent. In some specific situations, the relevant testing authority will usually have notified the sportsperson of the requirements for drug testing. Nonetheless, the FSEM remains clear that it is the duty of the practitioner to ensure that valid consent has been obtained[1].

1 Faculty of Sport and Exercise Medicine *Professional Code* (2010) section 3.6.

CONFIDENTIALITY OF SPORTSPERSONS WHO ARE PATIENTS

40.36 A conflict may arise between a doctor's duty to protect patient confidentiality and their contractual obligations, eg to a sports club. Such arrangements may become even more complicated because of the many parties involved in looking after the sportsperson, eg physiotherapist, trainer, coach, dietician, psychologist, sports scientist, counsellor[1]. Consent to disclose to the necessary extent may also be required when transferring care to a medical colleague[2]. Coaches, managers, commercial sponsors, the media and others may exert pressure on doctors to supply confidential health information[3]. However, doctors must remain conscious of, and abide by the provisions of Data Protection Act 1998.

1 Kane, White 'Medical Malpractice and the Sports Medicine Clinician' (2009) 467 Clin Orthop Relat Res 412–419.
2 Faculty of Sport and Exercise Medicine *Professional Code* (2010) section 4.1.
3 Waddington, Roderick 'Management of medical confidentiality in English professional football clubs: some ethical problems and issues' (2002) 36 British Journal of Sports Medicine 118–123.

40.37 According to the FSEM Code of Practice:

'All information about a patient's health, diagnosis, prognosis, treatment, rehabilitation measures and all other personal information must be kept confidential at all times in accordance with the Data Protection Act 1998'[1].

1 Faculty of Sport and Exercise Medicine *Professional Code* (2010), section 4.

40.38 The British Olympic Association (BOA) published welcome guidance on athlete confidentiality in 2000, stating the importance of a professional's duty of care, including that of protecting confidentiality and was seen as a nod to the rights of the athlete[1]. The statement contained guidance on areas such as information disclosure, refusals to disclose and information pertaining to selection. The BOA made it clear that coaches who wish to be informed of an athlete's problems may only be given this information with the consent of the athlete, whilst recognising that owing to the nature of the athlete-coach relationship, the athlete can usually be reassured and convinced that the coach should be informed. The BOA commented that refusal by an athlete to consent to disclosure (even in the event of an athlete taking a prohibited substance) should be respected, except if the failure to disclose puts the athlete or a third party at risk of death or serious harm.

1 British Olympic Association. 'The British Olympic Association's position statement on athlete confidentiality' (2000) 34 British Journal of Sports Medicine 71–72. See also Macauley D, Bartlett R 'The British Olympic Association's position statement on athlete confidentiality' (2000) 34 British Journal of Sports Medicine 1–2.

40.39   The BOA statement acknowledged the potential for tension produced when medical staff who have signed a contract with a body are compelled to breach their duties of confidentiality and thereby fall foul of professional guidance. The BOA deemed it unreasonable to ask staff to sign such a contract. When a doctor is required by contract to release information which might put the patient at risk, the FSEM Code also endorses the stance of withholding the relevant information in the absence of consent, thereby upholding the supremacy of professional (GMC) guidance[1].

1 Faculty of Sport and Exercise Medicine Professional Code (2010) section 4.2

40.40   If the law requires disclosure (eg the notification of a communicable disease) or the court request information, then this may be disclosed in the absence of express consent.

PERFORMANCE-ENHANCING DRUGS

40.41   Doctors may find themselves in a situation of conflict between supporting a patient (while not excusing the doping behaviour) and maintaining patient confidentiality while working as a team or club doctor[1]. Practitioners must remember their primary duty is to promote the health of the sportsperson, but the patient should also be made aware of the doctor's role as the agent of the third party/club. Notably the FSEM advises that the practitioner should remind the sportsperson that periodic medical examinations, including drug testing, may affect the sportsperson's continued employment[2]. The BOA has recommended that a refusal to consent to disclose must be respected even in the event of an athlete taking a prohibited substance[3].

1 British Medical Association *Drugs in sport: the pressure to perform* (2002).
2 Faculty of Sport and Exercise Medicine *Professional Code* (2010) para 4.5
3 British Olympic Association. 'The British Olympic Association's position statement on athlete confidentiality' (2000) 34 Br J Sports Med 71–72.

40.42   Medical professional may also be approached to provide performance-enhancing drugs and banned substances. The GMC adopts an unequivocal stance on this issue:

'You must not prescribe or collude in the provision of medicines or treatment with the intention of improperly enhancing an individual's performance in sport. This does not preclude the provision of any care or treatment where your intention is to protect or improve the patient's health'[1].

1 General Medical Council *Good practice in prescribing and managing medicines and devices* (2013) para 75.

40.43   Athletes may suffer intercurrent illnesses or conditions that require medications. Practitioners must remember that certain drugs (eg the seemingly innocuous prescription of a beta agonist for the treatment of asthma) can result in an athlete contravening anti-doping regulations. Since 2004, the World Anti-Doping Agency (WADA) has published an annual List of Prohibited Substances and Methods as part of the World Anti-Doping Code[1]. This list identifies the substances and methods prohibited in- and out-of-competition season, and in particular sports[2]. UK Anti Doping (UKAD) was created in 2009 and follows the World Anti- Doping Code. It is the national organisation dedicated to protecting a culture of drug-free sport and is accountable to Parliament through the Department for Culture, Media and Sport.

1 *World Anti-Doping Code 2015* (available at https://www.wada-ama.org/en/resources/the-code/2015-world-anti-doping-code).
2 *The World Anti-Doping Code The 2015 Prohibited List* (September 2014).

40.44   If the medication an athlete needs to treat an illness falls under the WADA Prohibited List, a Therapeutic Use Exemption (TUE) may permit the athlete to take the medication. Strict guidelines govern the use of TUEs and doctors must remember their duty to promote their patient's best interests. For the majority of sports, international level athletes will be required to submit their TUE application to the International Federation of their sport. National level athletes generally submit their application to either their national governing body or to UKAD. An important consideration is that a TUE granted by the UK TUE Committee may not be accepted by the International Federation of that sport.

40.45   In the future, gene doping (the non-therapeutic use of cells, genes, genetic elements, or of the modulation of gene expression, having the capacity to improve athletic performance) could form a major challenge to athletes and those who care for and manage them, and those that regulate the sports they participate in. The ability to produce biologically active molecules that are potentially indistinguishable from endogenous proteins is clearly of interest to those seeking novel methods of delivering performance-enhancing substances in undetectable forms[1].

1 Gould 'Gene doping: gene delivery for Olympic victory' (2012) Br J Clin Pharmacol 22.

FITNESS TO PARTICIPATE AND PRESSURE ON ATHLETES TO RETURN TO SPORT

40.46   The doctor's prime responsibility is to the long-term health and wellbeing of the individual player or athlete. Injured sportspersons may find themselves pressurised to continue playing or to return early from an injury. An MDO has received concerns from its members about the extent of their liability when signing off athletes as fit for participation[1]. The BMA Board of Science recommends that doctors should not help the player continue playing (eg by providing pain killers), even if the player requests them, but should give information about the diagnosis and risks, thereby enabling the athlete to make an informed decision as to whether they should participate[2]. Any such discussions and advice given should be recorded.

1 Personal email communication from Medical Protection Society Medical Risk Manager (28 July 2014).
2 British Medical Association Board of Science *An information resource for doctors providing medical care at sporting events* (2014) p 22.

40.47   The FSEM too is clear about the primacy of duty to protect and promote the health of an athlete, and this duty may also include refusing to give treatments.

'The fundamental principle of the Practitioner is to protect the health of patients …
No intervention should be undertaken which is not medically indicated, even at the
request of the patient or other individual such as coach or manager'[1].

1 Faculty of Sport and Exercise Medicine *Professional Code* (2010) section 8.

40.48   Additionally, the FSEM code recommends 'A Practitioner should
discourage the use of therapies with unproven or potentially harmful
consequences …'[1].

1 Faculty of Sport and Exercise Medicine *Professional Code* (2010) section 8.

40.49   Doctors may want to resist pressure from team managers who want
them to perform an action that will not promote the health of a patient.
However, a doctor could find it too onerous to resist such pressure when
working under time stress, immersed in the intensive environment of
professional sport, where winning is hugely important not least in terms of
securing commercial sponsorship[1].

1 Anderson 'Bloodgate: were the punishments fair?' (2011) 45 British Journal of Sports Medicine
948–949.

40.50   The converse of pressure to return to sport was seen in a remarkable
case involving blatant cheating at high-level rugby, colloquially referred to as
Bloodgate. The series of unfortunate events started during a rugby union Cup
match in 2009 that led to a doctor being issued with a warning by the GMC
and a team physiotherapist initially being struck off.

40.51   Stephen Brennan was the Harlequins physiotherapist and was
instructed by the team's coach at that time, to bring a fake blood capsule onto
the pitch and give it to Harlequins player Tom Williams to enable him to fake
a blood injury, so he could be substituted by another player in an attempt to
win the fixture. It was heard later that the player, having realised the match
officials suspected that his injury was not real, asked a doctor to cut his lip to
cover up the deception.

Dr Wendy Chapman was the match doctor who was asked by Williams to
help simulate a blood injury and so cut Williams' lip. The player subsequently
decided to tell the truth.

40.52   In 2010, a GMC Fitness to Practise Panel heard that, not only did Dr
Chapman cut the player's lip, but also subsequently gave false evidence to
a European Rugby Cup Inquiry. The GMC panel accepted that Dr Chapman
had been placed under pressure from Williams to cut his mouth and
mitigation was served in her defence in the form of her severe depression and
undergoing investigation for breast cancer. Nonetheless, the GMC found that
Chapman's conduct warranted a warning finding it to have been dishonest
and a significant departure from *Good Medical Practice*[1]. Dr Chapman had
a duty of care but had not acted in her patient's best interests. The panel
stated that such misconduct would normally have resulted in a finding of
impaired fitness to practise. It has been commented that by not removing
herself when her own health concerns could affect her decision-making, Dr
Chapman showed poor judgment[2]. *Good Medical Practice* emphasises the

need to seek help to protect patients and colleagues from any risk posed by personal health concerns[3].

1 General Medical Council Fitness to Practise Panel 23rd August – 1 September 2010 (available at www.gmc-uk.org). See also *Doctors with Dual Obligations in Medical Ethics Today The BMA's Handbook of Ethics and Law* (3rd edn, 2012) p 682.
2 Anderson L 'Bloodgate: were the punishments fair?' (2011) 45 British Journal of Sports Medicine 948–949.
3 General Medical Council *Good Medical Practice* (2013) para 28.

40.53 The physiotherapist, Mr Brennan, accepted that he had given false evidence and that he had been involved in previous fake-blood injury incidents. As a result, he was banned from participating in rugby for two years, although the High Court quashed this decision finding that inadequate reasoning had been provided by the Health Professions Council, and remitted the decision to the same panel[1].

1 *Brennan v Health Professions Council* [2011] EWHC 41 (Admin).

DISCOURAGING PARTICIPATION ON HEALTH GROUNDS

40.54 Section 8.1 of the FSEM 2010 Code directs that when the patient's health is at risk by continuing, a practitioner must strongly discourage further training or competition and inform them of the risks of continuation.

A recent case[1] highlights the importance of good communication between health professionals when a risk is identified, and also the need to inform the sportsperson of the risk. Whilst playing for a Premier League football club youth team in 2006, the claimant tragically suffered a cardiac arrest, resulting in severe brain damage. The first defendant, a cardiologist, had earlier reviewed the player's cardiac screening tests for the club. It was claimed that the cardiac arrest and brain damage resulted from the negligence of the first defendant, and of the club through the third parties, who were both club sports physicians. Although the club was vicariously liable for its sports physicians' acts or omissions, the third parties agreed to indemnify the club in respect of any damages awarded.

Causation was not in issue, but liability was. The club accepted that it owed a duty of care, by virtue of both the doctor/patient relationship and the employer/employee relationship. The primary issue was whether the club had breached its duty of care to the claimant and, if so, how to apportion liability between the club and the first defendant. The main case against the club was its failure to arrange for the player to be clinically reviewed by the first defendant or another cardiologist after the player's ECG had shown an unequivocal abnormality. The court held that both defendants had been in breach of their respective duties to the claimant. One of the club sports physicians had been negligent in not appreciating that there was a risk to the young player of an adverse cardiac event by continuing to train and play football. A clinical review should have been arranged with a cardiologist (this would probably have been the first defendant) and the claimant would have ceased training and playing.

The apportionment as was divided as the first defendant 30% and the second defendant 70%. Quantum will be set at a future hearing and will probably be a multi-million pound figure. The court also commented on poor state of the claimant's medical records, as well as poor communication.

1 *Hamed v Mills* [2015] EWHC 298 (QB).

40.55   The Code advises that when there is a serious danger to a patient or risk of serious danger to a third party, a doctor must inform any relevant person/authority about their unfitness to participate in training or competition, even if so acting goes against the will of the patient.

40.56   Practitioners need to be familiar with sporting bodies' regulations regarding permission to return to competitive sport after injury, either on a temporary or permanent basis.

40.57   The FSEM has produced a specific position statement on the management of concussion in sport at all levels[1]. Concussion is generally considered part of the spectrum of traumatic brain injury. The Rugby Football Union advise that in the settings of professional clubs and rugby academies, who have a doctor with experience of concussion/traumatic brain injury management who can closely supervise the player, adult players with confirmed concussion may be able to return to play after a minimum of six days (longer for younger age groups and in other settings) and only then if the player is asymptomatic the day after the concussive event and progresses without incident through a graduated return to play programme[2].

1 Faculty of Sport and Exercise Medicine *Concussion Management Position Statement* (2013).
2 Rugby Football Union *Return to Play. Advice for Health Care Professionals.*

40.58   The FSEM has produced a guide for the immediate recognition and treatment of Exertional Heatstroke (EHS) for those engaged in sport and exercise[1]. EHS is a potentially fatal illness, defined as central neurological dysfunction associated with an elevated core temperature, above 40°C, during or after exercise. The number of cases of EHS appears to be on the rise. This may be due in part to increasing numbers of athletes participating in endurance events each year[2]. Practitioners need to be aware it can occur in cooler environments and that EHS may present with paradoxical signs of shivering and peripheral shutdown. Even when treated, there is a significant risk of short-term, but also delayed, complications after the first 24–48 hours, even in those who initially appear to have recovered rapidly. With regard to return to exercise, patients are advised to avoid all exercise until asymptomatic and laboratory tests have normalised. Any return to exercise should be gradual and under medical guidance.

1 Faculty of Sport and Exercise Medicine *Position Statement Exertional Heat Illness* (2014).
2 Walter, Venn, Stevenson 'Exertional heat stroke – the athlete's nemesis' (2012) 13(4) JICS 304–308.

INTRA-PROFESSIONAL RELATIONSHIPS

40.59   The FSEM Code recommends that medical and paramedical staff should inform the sportsperson's GP of any medical intervention but, save for emergency scenarios, a doctor should obtain the patient's consent before informing a patient's GP of any findings or treatment.

40.60 The FSEM Code echoes guidance found in *Good Medical Practice* on honesty in dealings with others:

'A doctor should not promote a particular medical option of care to a patient because of personal friendships or association and should not convey opinions on liability in accidents or injury without the consent of the parties involved'[1].

1 Faculty of Sport and Exercise Medicine *Professional Code* (2010) section 4.4

LOCAL ANAESTHETIC INJECTIONS

40.61 The use of local anaesthetic injections to reduce pain in order to enable a player to continue during a match has been carried out for many years[1]. The FSEM recommends that local anaesthetic injections (or other treatments producing analgesia) should only be administered with great caution when injected for the purpose of masking pain when directed so as to allow participation with an injury:

'The use of local anaesthetic injection or other treatments producing an analgesic effect, which allow a patient who is a sportsperson to practise a sport with an injury or illness, should be carried out only after careful consideration and consultation with the athlete and other health care providers. If there is a long-term risk to the health of a patient who is a sportsperson, such treatment should not be given'[2].

1 McCrory 'No pain, no gain. The dilemma of a team physician' (2001) 35 British Journal of Sports Medicine 141–141.
2 Faculty of Sport and Exercise Medicine *Professional Code* (2010) section 8.4.

40.62 Nonetheless, the prohibition on the use of local anaesthetic injections (apart from cocaine) was removed from WADA's list of prohibited substances in 2004. Clearly, pain-masking treatments may exacerbate an existing injury and such practice should be avoided, particularly if there is a longer-term risk to health. Even at international level, regular administration of pre-match corticosteroid and local and/or anaesthetic injections has been reported despite this practice being called into question on both scientific and ethical grounds[1].

1 *Sport and Exercise Medicine for Pharmacists* (2006) edited by Kayne, p 163. See also Tscholl and Dvorak 'Abuse of medication during international football competition in 2010 – lesson not learned' (2012) 46 British Journal of Sports Medicine 1140–1141.

BIBLIOGRAPHY

Anderson 'Bloodgate: were the punishments fair?' (2011) 45 Br J Sports M 948–949.
Appleton v El-Safty [2007] EWHC 631 (QB)
Batt, Tanji 'The Future of Chronic Disease Management and the Role of Sport and Exercise Medicine Physicians' (2011) 21 Clin J Sp Med 3–5
Brazier, Cave *Medicine, Patients and the Law* (5th edn, 2011) p 178
Brennan v Health Professions Council [2011] EWHC 41 (Admin)
British Medical Association *Drugs in sport: the pressure to perform* (2002)
British Medical Association *Doctors with Dual Obligations in Medical Ethics Today The BMA's Handbook of Ethics and Law* (3rd edn, 2012) p 682
British Medical Association Board of Science *An information resource for doctors providing medical care at sporting events* (2014)

British Olympic Association 'The British Olympic Association's position statement on athlete confidentiality' (2000) 34 Br J Sports Med 71–72

Capital and Counties plc v Hampshire County Council [1997] QB 1035B

Faculty of Sport and Exercise Medicine Website (available at www.fsem. ac.uk)

Faculty of Sport and Exercise Medicine *Professional Code* (2010)

Faculty of Sport and Exercise Medicine *Concussion Management Position Statement* (2013)

Faculty of Sport and Exercise Medicine *Physical Activity in Adolescence* (2014)

Faculty of Sport and Exercise Medicine *Position Statement Exertional Heat Illness* (2014)

Faculty of Sport and Exercise Medicine *A Fresh Approach in Practice: Sport and Exercise Medicine Services in the NHS* (2014)

General Medical Council *Consent guidance: patients and doctors making decisions together* (2008) para 79

General Medical Council Fitness to Practise Panel 23rd August – 1 September 2010

General Medical Council *Good Medical Practice* (2013)

General Medical Council *Good practice in prescribing and managing medicines and devices* (2013) para 75

General Medical Council *Frequently asked questions about licensing*

Gould 'Gene Doping: Gene delivery for Olympic victory' (2012) Br J Clin Pharmacol 22

Hamed v Mills [2015] EWHC 298 (QB)

Hassan 'Who is Michael Appleton?' (11 Nov 2011) BBC Sport Website

Johnston, Bradbury *100 Cases in Clinical Ethics and Law* (2008) p 182

Kane, White 'Medical Malpractice and the Sports Medicine Clinician' (2009) 467 Clin Orthop Relat Res 412–419

Kayne *Sport and Exercise Medicine for Pharmacists* (2006) p 163

Macauley, Bartlett 'The British Olympic Association's position statement on athlete confidentiality' (2000) 34 Br J Sports Med 1–2

McCrory 'No pain, no gain. The dilemma of a team physician' (2001) 35 Br J Sports Med 141–143

Medical and Dental Defence Union of Scotland *Summons Good Samaritan: Is there a doctor on board?* (2009) pp 9–10

Medical Protection Society *Treating elite sportsmen and women* (2013)

Medical Protection Society *Factsheets. Consent* (2013)

NHS Sport and Exercise Medicine Services 'NHS Northwest Sports and exercise medicine: A fresh approach' (2011)

NHS Choices. The doctor who saved Fabrice Muamba's life (25 June 2013)

Rugby Football Union. *Return to Play. Advice for Health Care Professionals*

SEMPRIS (www.sempris.co.uk/index.php)

Tscholl, Dvorak 'Abuse of medication during international football competition in 2010 – lesson not learned' (2012) 46 Br J Sports Med 1140–1141

West Bromwich Albion Football Club Ltd v El-Safty [2006] EWCA Civ 1299

Waddington, Roderick 'Management of medical confidentiality in English professional football clubs: some ethical problems and issues' (2002) 36 Br J Sports Med 118–123

Walter, Venn, Stevenson 'Exertional heat stroke – the athlete's nemesis' (2012) 13(4) JICS 304–308

Williams 'Doctors as Good Samaritans: Some Empirical Evidence Concerning Emergency Medical Treatment in Britain' (2003) 30 Journal of Law and Society 258–282

Williamson, Wilkes *Sport and exercise medicine* (2013) Royal College of Physicians

World Anti-Doping Agency. World Anti-Doping Code 2015 (2014)

World Anti-Doping Agency. The World Anti-Doping Code The 2015 Prohibited List (2014)

Index

[all references are to paragraph number]

A
Abdominal aortic aneurysms
elective treatment, 26.47–26.53
ruptured, 26.54–26.56
Abdominal pain
emergency medicine, and
ectopic pregnancy, 18.58–18.59
generally, 18.55–18.57
general surgery, and, 25.56–25.64
Abdominal surgery
urological surgery, and, 34.63–34.70
Abdominoplasty
plastic surgery, and, 33.49–33.53
Abortion
gynaecology, and, 36.199–36.200
Accessory nerve paralysis
otorhinolaryngology, and, 31.115–
31.117
Accident and emergency medicine
and see **Emergency medicine**
generally, 18.2
Accrual of cause of action
limitation of actions, and, 12.6–12.12
Acknowledgment of service
conduct of proceedings, and, 10.109
Acquired microcephaly
neuroimaging, and, 39.38
Acromegaly
endocrinology, and, 19.118–19.124
Acute abdomen
general surgery, and, 25.56–25.64
Acute appendicitis
paediatric surgery, and, 37.46–37.51
Acute coronary syndrome
emergency medicine, and,
18.38–18.43
Acute headaches
neurology, and, 20.32–20.34
Acute ischaemia
generally, 26.19–26.21
Acute pain
anaesthesia, and, 28.142–28.147
generally, 27.10
Acute subdural haematomas
elderly, in, 29.38–29.40
generally, 29.37
Addison's disease
endocrinology, and, 19.138–19.144

Adenotonsillectomy
otorhinolaryngology, and, 31.29–31.33
Adhesions
general surgery, and, 25.65–25.68
paediatric surgery, and, 37.52–37.53
Advance decisions/directives
consent to treatment, and,
11.48–11.52
Advanced endoscopic sinus surgery
otorhinolaryngology, and,
31.50–31.52
Advanced nurse practitioners (ANPs)
emergency medicine, and, 18.23
Adverse drug reaction reporting
'Black Triangle' scheme, 13.49
European requirements, 13.50–13.54
healthcare professionals, by, 13.45–
13.46
marketing authorisation holders, by,
13.47–13.48
Aesthetics
plastic surgery, and
abdominoplasty, 33.49–33.53
breast surgery, 33.28–33.43
introduction, 33.24–33.27
prominent ear correction, 33.54–
33.55
reconstruction, 33.9–33.10
rhinoplasty, 33.44–33.48
Aetiological fraction
calculation, 15.48
generally, 15.68–15.73
After the event insurance (ATE)
conduct of proceedings, and, 10.3
generally, 6.25–6.26
Ageing
plastic surgery, and
brow lift, 33.61–33.62
eyelid correction, 33.56–33.58
facelift, 33.58–33.60
labial surgery, 33.69–33.72
lasers, 33.68
liposuction, 33.63–33.67
vaginal surgery, 33.69–33.72
urological surgery, and, 34.15
Aggressive periodontitis
generally, 35.117–35.118
treatment, 35.125

Brain tumour
neurology, and, 20.36–20.38
Breach of duty of care
Bolam test
development, 1.64–1.72
generally, 1.59–1.63
Bolitho decision, 1.64–1.72
establishing
expert's role, 1.101–1.107
proof of negligence, 1.99–1.100
res ipsa loquitur, 1.108–1.114
expert's role, 1.101–1.107
generally, 1.56–1.57
precedent, practice and use of
literature, 1.115–1.116
proof of negligence, 1.99–1.100
res ipsa loquitur, 1.108–1.114
standard of care
alternative medical practitioner,
1.75
Bolam test, 1.59–1.72
disclosure of facts, 1.85–1.95
introduction, 1.58
lack of experience, 1.76–1.77
malcommunication, 1.96–1.98
particular aspects, 1.73–1.98
prevention of self-infliction of
harm, 1.78–1.84
specialists, 1.73–1.74
Breast surgery
adverse outcomes, 33.32–33.36
augmentation, 33.29–33.31
introduction, 33.28
mastopexy, 33.37–33.39
reduction, 33.40–33.43
Broncho-pulmonary dysplasia
neonatology, and, 38.128–38.130
Brow lift
plastic surgery, and, 33.61–33.62
Bruising
neonatology, and, 38.182–38.183
Buckle fracture
orthopaedics, and, 32.5
Bundles
conduct of proceedings, and, 10.272
Burden of proof
limitation of actions, and, 12.66
'But for' test
causation, and, 15.5–15.12

C
Calculation of time
conduct of proceedings, and, 10.83–
10.84
Cancer
causes, 21.5
chemotherapy, 21.30–21.32

Cancer – *contd*
clinical trials, 21.66–21.68
communication, 21.77
conclusion, 21.78–21.80
conformal radiotherapy, 21.54
consent, 21.28–21.29
decision making, 21.24–21.25
diagnosis, 21.14–21.23
end-of-life care, 21.73–21.76
environmental factors, 21.4
follow-up, 21.71–21.72
image guided, radiotherapy 21.56
intensity modulated radiotherapy,
21.55
introduction, 21.1–21.5
multi-disciplinary teams,
21.26–21.27
NHS Cancer Plan, 21.6
pain management, and, 27.15
palliative care, 21.73–21.76
pharmacological treatment
administration, 21.46–21.48
chemotherapy, 21.30–21.32
response assessment, 21.43–21.45
systemic anti-cancer treatment
delivery, 21.37–21.42
targeted therapy, 21.33–21.36
plastic surgery, and, 33.6
proton therapy, 21.58
radiotherapy
conformal, 21.54
image guided, 21.56
intensity modulated, 21.55
introduction, 21.49–21.53
patient pathway, 21.56–21.65
proton therapy, 21.58
stereotactic ablative, 21.57
screening, 21.11–21.13
services, 21.6–21.10
stereotactic ablative radiotherapy,
21.57
supportive care, 21.69–21.70
survival rates, 21.71–21.72
systemic anti-cancer treatment
delivery, 21.37–21.42
targeted therapy, 21.33–21.36
treatment
consent, 21.28–21.29
decision making, 21.24–21.25
modalities, 21.30–21.65
Candour
medical defence organisations, and,
3.67–3.73
negligence in general practice, and,
17.35–17.37
NHS complaints procedure, and,
2.93–2.109

F
Facelift
plastic surgery, and, 33.58–33.60
Facial dysmorphism
neonatology, and, 38.79
Facial nerve injury
neonatology, and, 38.220–38.222
Facial palsy
otorhinolaryngology, and, 31.84–31.87
Failure to provide sufficient information
consent to treatment, and, 11.11–11.15
Failure to diagnose
vascular surgery, and, 26.33–26.40
Failure to record decisions
vascular surgery, and, 26.41–26.42
Failure to warn
causation, and
generally, 15.77
hypothetical action of doctor, 15.78–15.79
subjective patient test, 15.80–15.83
consent to treatment, and, 11.16–11.17
Falls
neurology, and, 20.25–20.26
Fast track
generally, 10.141–10.147
interlocutory hearings, 10.210
pre-issue considerations, 10.38
Fatal accident claims
limitation of actions, and, 12.38
Feet
vascular surgery, and, 26.87–26.91
Femur fractures
neonatology, and, 38.207
Fetal abnormality
obstetrics, and, 36.48–36.60
Fetal 'autoresuscitation'
neonatology, and, 38.72–38.74
Fluid balance
general surgery, and, 25.31
Focal brain damage
arterial distribution infarction, 39.40–39.45
introduction, 39.39
timing, 39.48
venous distribution infarction, 39.46–39.47
Foetus
human rights, and, 4.12
Foreseeability
generally, 1.7
Fractures and dislocations
see also **Orthopaedics**
emergency medicine, and
cervical spine, 18.79–18.83
generally, 18.75–18.78

Fractures and dislocations – *contd*
emergency medicine, and – *contd*
lower limb sprains, 18.90–18.95
scaphoid injury, 18.89
shoulder dislocation, 18.84–18.88
fixation, 32.17–32.18
meaning, 32.2
neonatology, and
clavicular, 38.204–38.205
femur, 38.207
humerus, 38.207
skull, 38.206
Fraud
consent to treatment, and, 11.83
Functional endoscopic sinus surgery
otorhinolaryngology, and, 31.44–31.49
Funding claims
after the event insurance, 6.25–6.26
background, 6.3–6.14
before the event insurance
conduct of proceedings, and, 10.250–10.251
generally, 6.27
conclusion, 6.28
conditional fee agreements
conduct of proceedings, and, 10.248–10.249
generally, 6.20
Jackson report, 6.6, 6.9
conduct of proceedings, and
before the event insurance, 10.250–10.251
conditional fee agreements, 10.248–10.249
legal aid, 10.243–10.247
offers to settle, 10.260
pre-issue considerations, 10.15–10.35
private client, 10.252–10.253
schedule of loss, 10.254–10.259
costs follow the event, 6.12
damages based agreements, 6.21–6.22
introduction, 6.1–6.2
Jackson report, 6.5–6.8
legal aid
conduct of proceedings, and, 10.243–10.247
generally, 6.16–6.19
Jackson report, 6.8, 6.10
legislative framework
background, 6.3–6.14
generally, 6.15
introduction, 6.2
'loser pays' rule, 6.23
offers to settle, 10.260
pre-issue considerations, 10.15–10.35
private client, 10.252–10.253

NHS dentistry
  dental surgery, and, 35.16–35.24
NHS England
  generally, 1.10
NHS indemnity
  generally, 3.96
NHS Litigation Authority (NHS LA)
  aims, 3.100
  Clinical Negligence Scheme for
    Trusts, 3.98
  complaints procedure, and, 2.87–2.92
  conduct of litigation, 3.102–3.106
  costs rules
    developments, 3.111
    generally, 3.117–3.120
  establishment, 3.99
  Framework Document, 3.100–3.101
  function, 3.99
  introduction, 3.97
  National Clinical Assessment Service,
    3.109
  objectives, 3.100–3.101
  pre-action protocol, 3.105
  recent developments, 3.110–3.115
  Safety and Learning Service, 3.107–
    3.108
  statistics, 3.112–3.113
  status, 3.100
Nociceptive pain
  generally, 27.11–27.12
No-fault compensation
  ABI, from, 5.40
  clinical trials, 5.40
  Creutzfeld-Jakob disease, 5.41
  Finland, in, 5.32
  haemophiliacs, 5.41
  historical review, 5.29–5.37
  introduction, 5.23–5.28
  medical experiments in non-patient
    human volunteers, 5.40
  New Zealand, in, 5.31
  practice, in, 5.38–5. 42
  Sweden, in, 5.32
  vaccine damage, 5.39
  variant CJD, 5.41
Non-cancer pain
  generally, 27.15
'Non-pecuniary damage'
  human rights, and, 4.83–4.84
Non-steroidal anti-inflammatory
    drugs
  pain management, and, 27.41
'Nose payments'
  medical defence organisations, and,
    3.19
Null hypothesis
  causation, and, 15.45–15.46

Nurses
  emergency medicine, and, 18.22–18.23

O
Observation ward
  emergency medicine, and, 18.13–18.14
Observed associations
  epidemiology, and, 16.83
Obstetrics
  anoxia, 36.19
  ante-natal care
    booking visit, 36.43–36.47
    generally, 36.35–36.42
    Group B streprococcus, 36.98–
      36.106
    screening for fetal abnormality,
      36.48–36.60
    subsequent visits, 36.65–36.97
    ultrasound, 36.61–36.64
  brain damage, 36.16–36.18
  cardiotocograph interpretation, 36.16
  care after delivery, 36.164–36.169
  care of critically ill woman, 36.175–
    36.180
  cerebral palsy, 36.16–36.23
  changes in care, 36.5–36.10
  consent, 36.181–36.186
  delivery
    care after delivery, 36.164–36.169
    consent, 36.181–36.186
    generally, 36.150–36.163
    stillbirth, 36.170–36.174
  Down syndrome, 36.51–36.60
  eclampsia, 36.29
  fetal abnormality, 36.48–36.60
  generally, 36.16–36.34
  Group B streprococcus, 36.98–36.106
  hypoxia, 36.19–36.20
  induction of labour, 36.107–36.114
  inter-partum care, 36.115–36.149
  introduction, 36.1–36.15
  screening for abnormality
    Down syndrome, 36.51–36.60
    generally, 36.48–36.50
  stillbirth
    generally, 36.170–36.174
    introduction, 36.25
  streprococcus, 36.98–36.106
  ultrasound, 36.61–36.97
Occurrence-based indemnity
  medical defence organisations, and,
    3.18–3.20
Offers to settle
  generally, 10.260
  pre-issue considerations, 10.73–10.81
Oncology
  cancer services, 21.6–21.10